R. Gupta's®

Joint CSIR-UGC NET

Junior Research Fellowship & Eligibility for Lectureship

Mathematical Sciences

Practice Test Papers (Solved)

By

RPH Editorial Board

RAMESH PUBLISHING HOUSE, NEW DELHI

Published by

O.P. Gupta *for* Ramesh Publishing House

Admin. Office

12-H, New Daryaganj Road, Opp. Officers' Mess,
New Delhi-110002 ✆ 23261567, 23275224, 23275124

E-mail: info@rameshpublishinghouse.com
For Online Shopping: www.rameshpublishinghouse.com

Showroom

- Balaji Market, Nai Sarak, Delhi-6 ✆ 23253720, 23282525
- 4457, Nai Sarak, Delhi-6, ✆ 23918938

Book Code: R-1878

ISBN: 978-93-86298-36-2

Price: ₹ 460

Printed at: Deepak Offset, Delhi

CONTENTS

25 PRACTICE SETS (Solved)

PART–A

This common part pertaining to General Science, Quantitative Reasoning & Analysis and Research Aptitude.

SET (1 to 25) 1-120

PART–B

This part covering the topics given in the syllabus of Mathematical Sciences.

SET (1 to 25) 1-164

PART–C

This part designed to test a candidate's knowledge of scientific concepts and/ or application of the scientific concepts.

SET (1 to 25) 1-240

MATHEMATICAL SCIENCES

CSIR-UGC (NET) Exam for Award of Junior Research Fellowship and Eligibility for Lecturership shall be a Single Paper Test having Multiple Choice Questions (MCQs). The question paper shall be divided in three parts.

Part 'A': This part shall carry 20 questions pertaining to General Science, Quantitative Reasoning & Analysis and Research Aptitude. The candidates shall be required to answer any 15 questions. Each question shall be of two marks. The total marks allocated to this section shall be 30 out of 200.

Part 'B': This part shall contain 40 Multiple Choice Questions (MCQs) generally covering the topics given in the syllabus. A candidate shall be required to answer any 25 questions. Each question shall be of three marks. The total marks allocated to this section shall be 75 out of 200.

Part 'C': This part shall contain 60 questions that are designed to test a candidate's knowledge of scientific concepts and/or application of the scientific concepts. The questions shall be of analytical nature where a candidate is expected to apply the scientific knowledge to arrive at the solution to the given scientific problem. The questions in this part shall have multiple correct options. Credit in a question shall be given only on identification of ALL the correct options. No credit shall be allowed in a question if any incorrect option is marked as correct answer. No partial credit is allowed. A candidate shall be required to answer any 20 questions. Each question shall be of 4.75 marks. The total marks allocated to this section shall be 95 out of 200.

➤ For Part 'A' and 'B' there will be Negative marking @25% for each wrong answer. No Negative marking for Part 'C'.

CSIR-UGC (NET) JRF & LECTURESHIP EXAM

PART-A

25 Practice Sets

SET-1

CSIR-UGC (NET) JRF & LECTURESHIP EXAM

PART-A

1. A sphere of radius 4 cm is carved from a homogeneous sphere of radius 8 cm and mass 160 g. The mass of the smaller sphere is

(*a*) 80 g (*b*) 60 g
(*c*) 40 g (*d*) 20 g

2. Two boys A and B are at two diametrically opposite points on a circle. At one instant the two start running on the circle; A anticlockwise with constant speed v and B clockwise with constant speed $2v$. In 2 minutes, they pass each other for the first time. How much later will they pass each other for the second time?

(*a*) 1 minute (*b*) 2 minutes
(*c*) 3 minutes (*d*) 4 minutes

3. There are k baskets and n balls. The balls are put into the baskets randomly. If $k<n$,

(*a*) There is no empty basket
(*b*) There are exactly $(n - k)$ baskets with at least one ball
(*c*) There is at least one basket with two or more balls
(*d*) There are $(n - k)$ baskets with exactly two balls

4. An ant is crawling along the x-axis such that the graph of its position on the x-axis versus time is a semi-circle (see figure). The total distance covered in the 4 seconds is

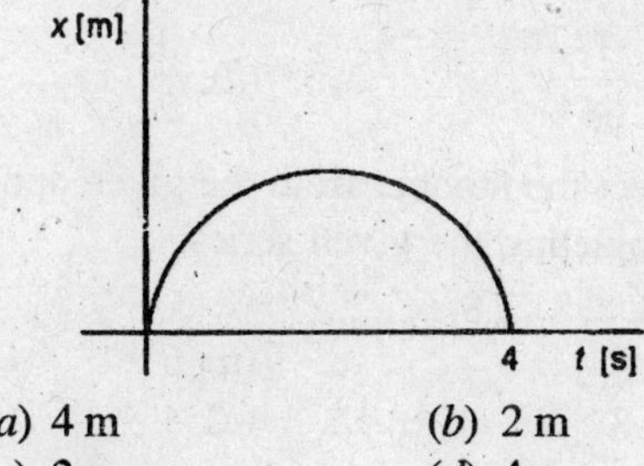

(*a*) 4 m (*b*) 2 m
(*c*) 2π m (*d*) 4π m

5. In a bag containing only blue, red and green marbles, all but 15 are blue, all but 13 are red and all but 12 are green. How many are red?

(*a*) 13 (*b*) 7
(*c*) 25 (*d*) 20

6. Find the missing numbers in the bottom middle circle. (Clue: left halves of the central circles relate to the left circles and the right halves to the right circles)

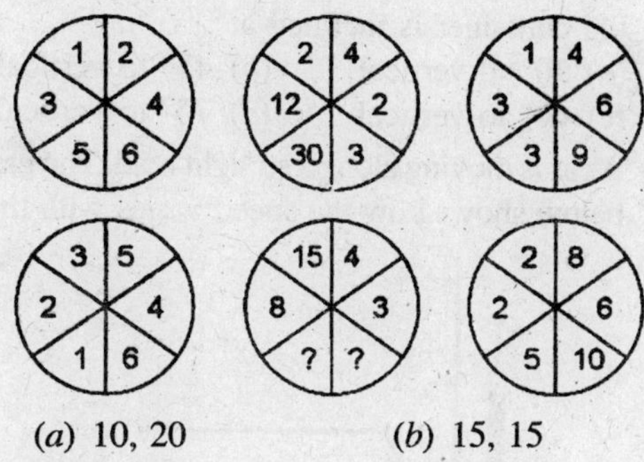

(*a*) 10, 20 (*b*) 15, 15
(*c*) 21, 2 (*d*) 6, 2

7. Identify the missing letter.

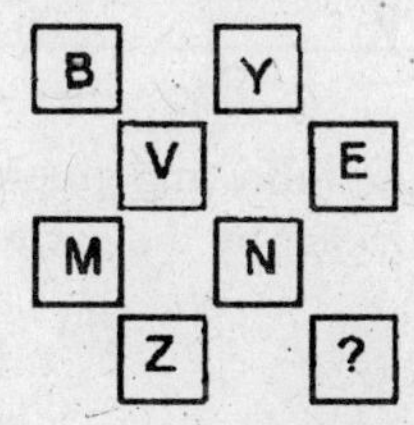

(*a*) W (*b*) A
(*c*) X (*d*) B

8. Identify the figure that comes next in the sequence.

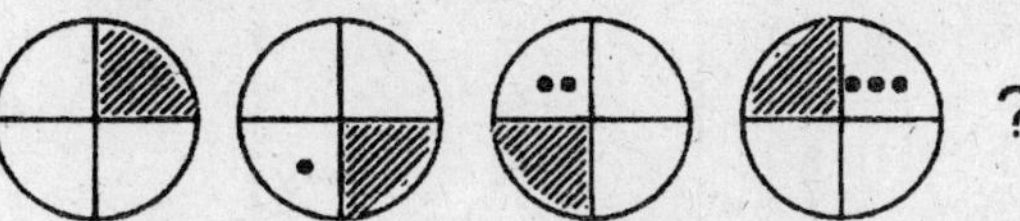

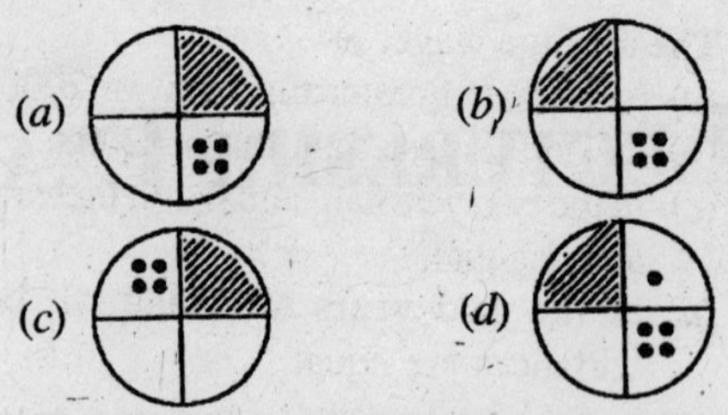

9. A person buys a shirt with marked price ₹ 300/- at 20% discount. In order to make a profit of 20% the person should sell the shirt for

(*a*) ₹ 288/- (*b*) ₹ 300/-
(*c*) ₹ 240/- (*d*) ₹ 360/-

10. A uniform cylindrical container is half filled with water. The height of the cylinder is twice its diameter. The cylinder is gradually tilted until the water touches the brim. At this instant, the container is inclined at

(*a*) 30° to vertical (*b*) 45° to vertical
(*c*) 60° to vertical (*d*) 75° to vertical

11. A car is moving along a straight road. The graph below shows how the speed varies with time.

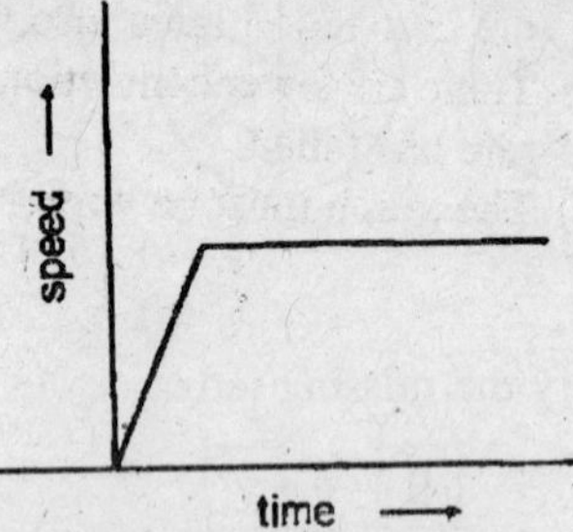

Which of the following graphs represents the distance covered by the car with time?

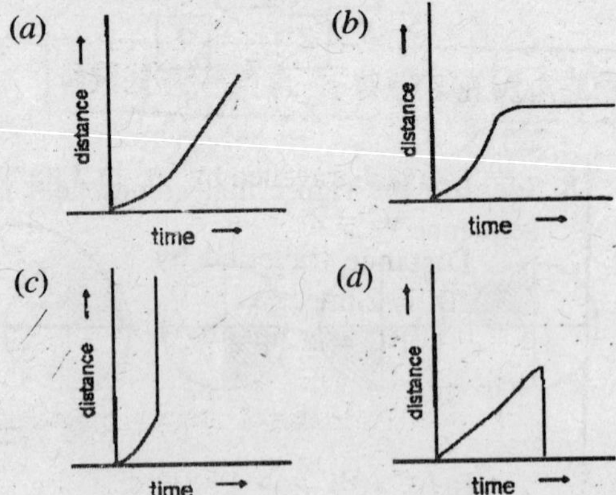

12. In triangle ABC, shown in the figure, AB is perpendicular to BC. Further, BD is perpendicular to AC. If AD = 9 cm and DC = 4 cm, the length BD is

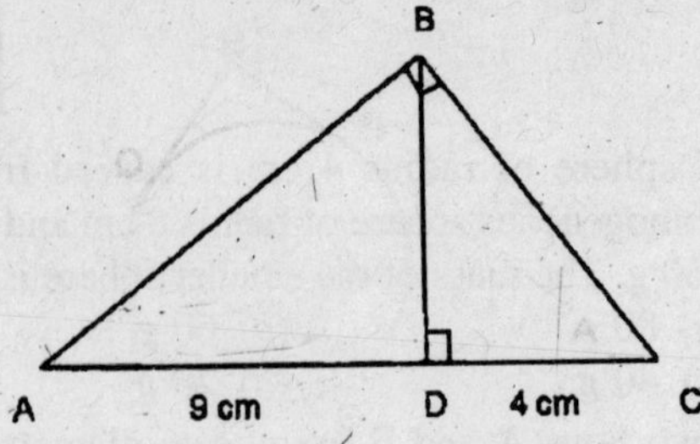

(*a*) 6 cm (*b*) 6.5 cm
(*c*) $\frac{36}{13}$ cm (*d*) $\frac{13}{36}$ cm

13. A box of sticks of equal lengths is provided. The minimum number of sticks needed to build a frame to enclose a 3-dimensional volume is

(*a*) 6 (*b*) 12
(*c*) 3 (*d*) 8

14. 5 kg of adulterated rice has 2% stones in it and the rest is rice. Half of the stone content was removed. Now the percentage of stone content in it is

(*a*) 0.99% (*b*) 1%
(*c*) 1.1% (*d*) 1.01%

15. A coin is tossed six times. The probability that head will occur at least once is

(*a*) $\frac{63}{64}$ (*b*) $\frac{1}{3}$
(*c*) $\frac{1}{64}$ (*d*) $\frac{3}{2}$

16. Select the number from the given options for completing the given series.

9, 8, 8, 8, 7, 8, 6, ...

(*a*) 5 (*b*) 6
(*c*) 8 (*d*) 4

17. Insert the missing number in 4 : 17 : : 17 : ?

(*a*) 48 (*b*) 50
(*c*) 49 (*d*) 51

18. Circle PQR is inscribed in a quadrilateral ABCD. The circle touches side AD at point S. AP = 8 cm, QC = 3 cm and DC = 6 cm. The length of side AD is

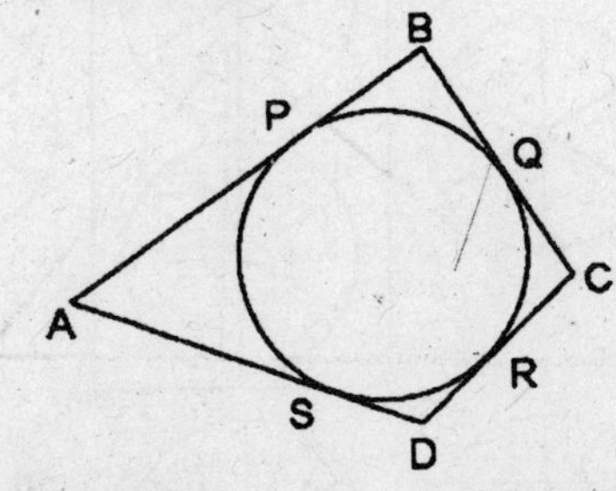

(*a*) 9 cm (*b*) 10 cm
(*c*) 11 cm (*d*) 12 cm

19. The distribution of wages in a population is shown below for 2 years.

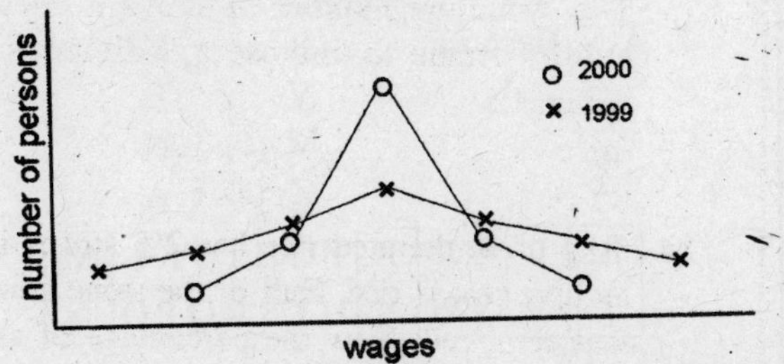

The average wage(s)
(*a*) in 1999 is greater than that in 2000.
(*b*) in 1999 is less than that in 2000.
(*c*) in the two years are equal, but the variances are unequal.
(*d*) in the two years are unequal, but the variances are equal.

20. The graph below shows crime rates and convictions for 5 years in a certain society.

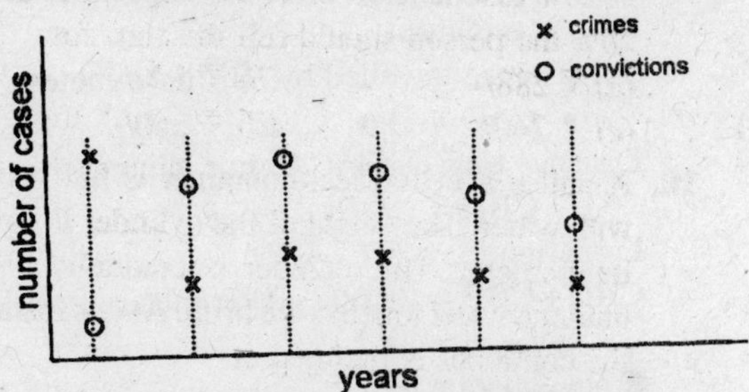

Which of the following is correct?
(*a*) The cause of convictions being on the rise is better law enforcement.
(*b*) Falling crime rates have slowly reduced the conviction rates also.
(*c*) There are fewer convictions because crime rate has fallen.
(*d*) The graph must be wrong.

ANSWERS

1	2	3	4	5	6	7	8	9	10
(*d*)	(*d*)	(*c*)	(*c*)	(*a*)	(*d*)	(*b*)	(*a*)	(*a*)	(*a*)
11	**12**	**13**	**14**	**15**	**16**	**17**	**18**	**19**	**20**
(*a*)	(*a*)	(*c*)	(*d*)	(*a*)	(*c*)	(*b*)	(*c*)	(*b*)	(*d*)

SOME SELECTED EXPLANATORY ANSWERS

1. $512\ \text{cm}^3 = 160$ g

$$64\ \text{cm}^3 = \frac{160}{512} \times 64 = 20\ \text{g}.$$

2. Let A and B meet at point 'C' after running 2 minutes.

So, distance ACB = $\frac{1}{2}$ × (Perimeter of circular path)

Distance travelled by 'A' in 2 minutes

AC = $2v$

Distance travelled by 'B' in 2 minutes

BC = $2(2v) = 4v$

$\frac{1}{2}$ × (Perimeter of circle)

$= AC + BC = 2v + 4v = 6v$

Perimeter of circle = $12v$
Now, from formula,
Perimeter of circle = $2\pi r$ {where r = radius}

$$2\pi r = 12v$$

$$r = \frac{6v}{\pi} \quad ...(i)$$

Again, let they meet 2nd time at point D after time 't' minutes.
So, distance travelled by 'B' in t minutes

$$CAD = 2vt$$

Distance travelled by 'A' in t minutes

$$CBD = v.t$$

From figure,

$$CAD + CBD = 2\pi.(r) \quad \text{\{Perimeter of circle\}}$$

$$2vt + vt = 2\pi.r$$

From equation (*i*),

$$r = \frac{6v}{\pi}$$

$$3vt = 2\pi \cdot \frac{6v}{\pi}$$

$$3vt = 12v$$

$$t = \frac{12v}{3v}$$

$$t = 4 \text{ minutes.}$$

3. As number of balls is greater than number of basket and if we put the ball into basket in sequence, then 'K' balls put into 'K' baskets. Then, remaining '$n - k$' balls must be placed into '$n - k$' baskets.
For $(n - k) < k$ at least '$n - k$' baskets have exactly 2 balls.
But, the given distribute of balls is randomly. So, it might be a case in which, all balls placed in one box.
So, correct answer = At least one basket with 2 or more balls.

4. Total distance covered in 4 seconds

$$= \frac{1}{2}[2\pi r]$$

$$= \frac{1}{2} \times 2 \times \frac{22}{7} \times 2 = 2\pi\text{m.}$$

6. 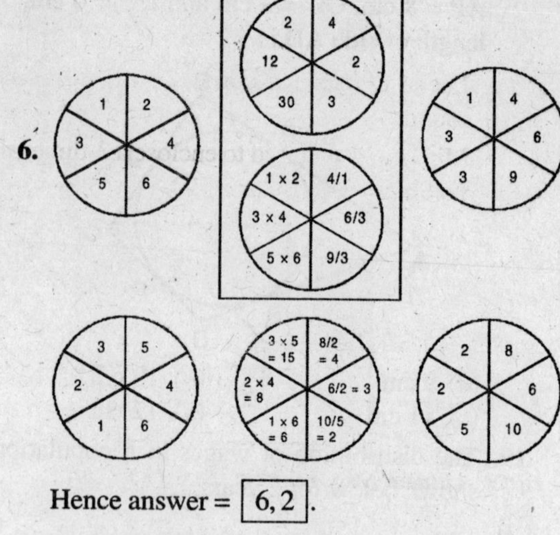

Hence answer = $\boxed{6, 2}$.

7. A Because

B	Y
V	E
M	N
Z	A

A	B	C D	E	F G H I J K L	M
Z	Y	X W	V	U T S R Q P O	N

8. (*a*) because number of dots is increasing and dot is ahead and net is at back.

9. $100 - 20 = 80$
When MP is 100 then CP = 80

When MP is 300 then CP = $\frac{80}{100} \times 300$ = ₹240

$100 + 20 = 120$
When CP 100 then SP = 120
When CP 240 then SP

$= \frac{120}{100} \times 240$ = ₹ 288.

11. Graph (*a*) represents the distance covered by the car with time.

12. In ΔBDC,

$$BD^2 = BC^2 - 16$$

$$BC^2 = 16 + BD^2$$

In ΔABC,

$$AB^2 = (13)^2 - BC^2 = 169 - 16 - BD^2$$

Again In ΔABD, $BD^2 = AB^2 - 81$

$$BD^2 = 169 - 16 - BD^2 - 81$$

$2BD^2 = 169 - 197 = 72$

$BD^2 = 36$

$\therefore \quad BD = 6$ cm.

13. Let us consider a corner of a 3-dimensional room.

Min. sticks required to enclose a 3-dimensional volume = AB, BC and BD

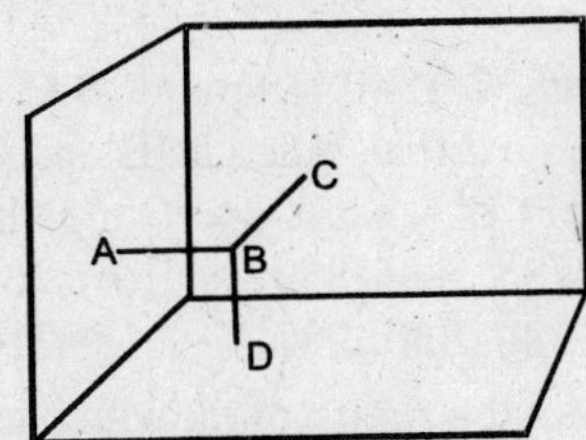

Hence, Min. number of sticks = 3.

14. 2% of 5 kg $= \frac{2}{100} \times 5000\text{g} = 100$ g

Amount of stone = 100 g

Amount of rice = 4900 g

Half of stone such that 50 gram stone removed.

Remaining amount of stone = 50 g.

Now, total amount of adulterated rice = 4950

% of stone content in it

$= \frac{50}{4950} \times 100 = \frac{100}{99} = 1.01\%.$

15. The probability that head occurs $= \frac{1}{2}$

Probability that head does not occur $= 1 - \frac{1}{2} = \frac{1}{2}$

The probability that head does not occur in any of the 6 trials $= \left(\frac{1}{2}\right)^6 = \frac{1}{64}$

So, the probability for head to occur at least once $= 1 - \frac{1}{64} = \frac{63}{64}$.

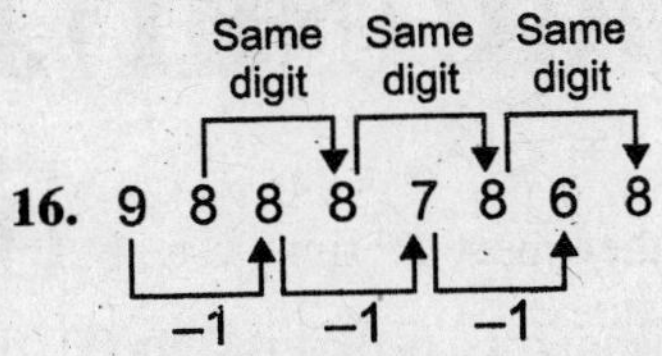

16. 9 8 8 8 7 8 6 8

–1 –1 –1

17. Since 4 → 17 ($4^2 + 1$)

Similarly, 7 → 50 ($7^2 + 1$)

18. $AP = AS$

So, $AS = 8$ cm

Again $CQ = CR \Rightarrow 3$ cm

Now, $CD = CR + DR$

$6 = 3 + DR$

$DR = 3$ cm

$SD = DR,$

$SD = 3$ cm.

$AD = AS + SD = 8 + 3 = 11$ cm.

19. From the graph, number of wages in 1999 is 7 whereas number of wages in 2000 is 5.

From the graph, we can estimate that average wages in 2000 is greater than 1999.

20. Here, no. of convictions is greater than number of crimes. This makes the graph wrong.

SET-2

CSIR-UGC (NET) JRF & LECTURESHIP EXAM

PART-A

1. The gross income of a person is ₹ 20000. 10% of his income is exempted from income tax and his net income is ₹ 19100. The rate of income tax is :
   (*a*) 3% (*b*) 2%
   (*c*) 4% (*d*) 5%

2. A man can row three quarters of a kilometer against the stream in 11¼ minutes and return in 7½ minutes. Find the speed of the man in still water.
   (*a*) 3 km/hr (*b*) 4 km/hr
   (*c*) 5 km/hr (*d*) 6 km/hr

3. Two dice are thrown simultaneously. The probability of obtaining a total score of 5 is :
   (*a*) 1/18 (*b*) 1/12
   (*c*) 1/9 (*d*) None of these

Directions (Q. 4) : *Refer to the graph below.*

Foren Farma Enterprises manufactures sprinklers. The company's sales data is given below.

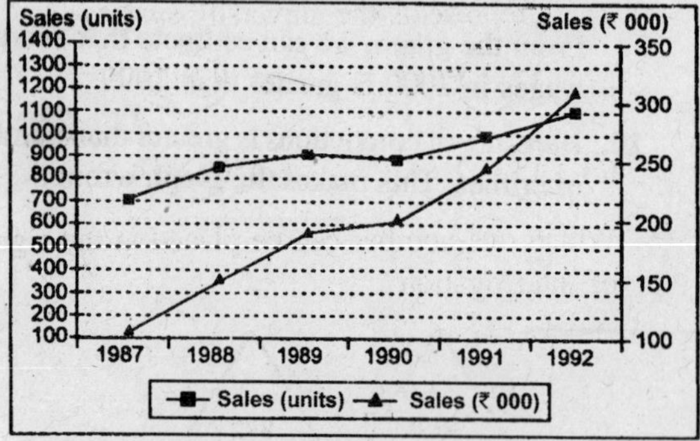

4. The maximum percentage price rise was displayed in the year :
   (*a*) 1987 (*b*) 1988
   (*c*) 1990 (*d*) 1991

5. Divide ₹ 1540 among A,B,C so that A shall receive 2/9 as much as B and C together, and B 3/11 of what A and C together do.
   (*a*) 285, 330, 830 (*b*) 280, 330, 930
   (*c*) 280, 330, 980 (*d*) 330, 380, 980

6. Select the right option which can be placed at the sign of interrogation?

4	8	20
9	3	15
6	6	?

   (*a*) 24 (*b*) 16
   (*c*) 20 (*d*) 18

7. If TOUR is written as 1234, CLEAR is written as 56784 and SPARE is written as 90847, find the code for CARE :
   (*a*) 1247 (*b*) 4847
   (*c*) 5247 (*d*) 5847

Directions (Q. 8) : *In the question that follows, problem figures have been given. Problem figures themselves are also the answer figures. Out of the four figures (a), (b), (c) and (d) three are similar in a certain way. One figure is not like the other three. Choose the figure which is different from the rest.*

8. 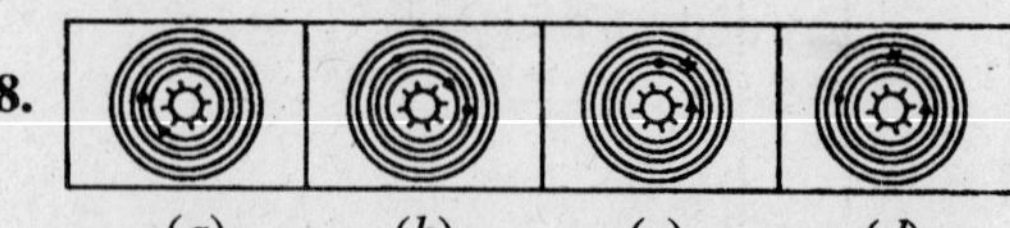

   (*a*) (*b*) (*c*) (*d*)

9. Two vessels A and B contain milk and water in the ratio 7 : 5 and 17 : 7 respectively. In what ratio mixtures from two vessels should be mixed to get a new mixture containing milk and water in the ratio 5 : 3?
   (*a*) 1 : 2 (*b*) 2 : 1
   (*c*) 2 : 3 (*d*) 3 : 2

10. A, B and C together start a business. The amounts invested by A and B are in the ratio of 4 : 3 whereas the ratio of investments of B and C is 2 : 3. If the total profit earned is ₹ 46000, what is C's share in the profit?

(*a*) ₹ 14000 (*b*) ₹ 15000

(*c*) ₹ 16000 (*d*) ₹ 18000

11. Given below are three graphs showing the consumption of electricity in three different households statement given in which of the following four alternatives is correct?

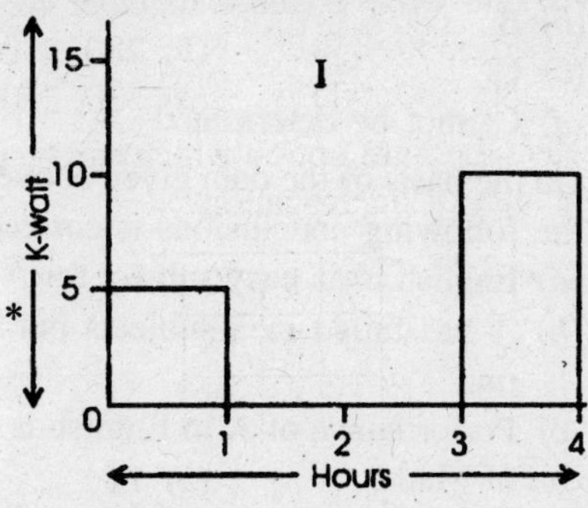

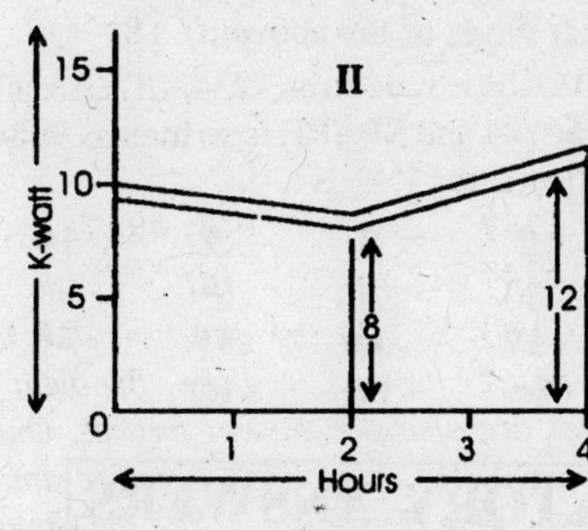

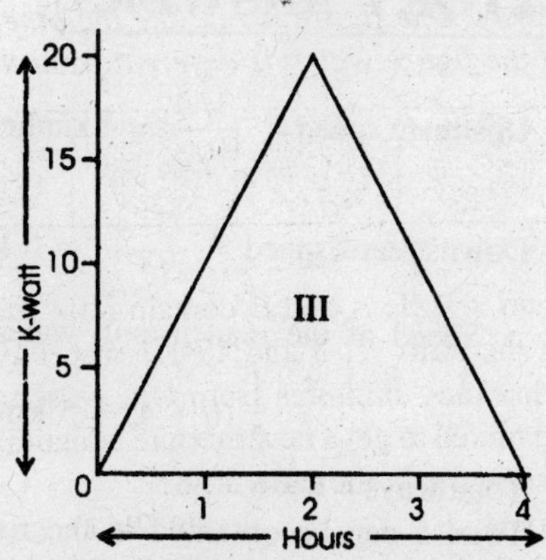

(*a*) Rates of electricity consumption in all the three households are identical

(*b*) Consumption of electricity in household-II is more than the other two houses

(*c*) Consumption in household-III is in between the consumptions of I & II

(*d*) Consumption of electricity in household I is minimum

12. A person standing on the bank of a river observes that the angle subtended by a tree on the opposite bank is 60°, when he retires 40 metres from the bank he finds the angle to be 30°. Then the breadth of the river is:

(*a*) 40 m (*b*) 60 m

(*c*) 20 m (*d*) 30 m

13. Find the number of different permutations of the letters of the word BANANA.

(*a*) 40 (*b*) 50

(*c*) 60 (*d*) 70

14. A bag contains 3 red, 4 white and 5 blue balls. All balls are different. Two balls are drawn at random. The probability that they are of different colours is :

(*a*) 47/66 (*b*) 10/33

(*c*) 5/22 (*d*) None of these

15. The following question is based on the diagram given below. If the two small circles represent formal class-room education and distance education, and the big circle stands for university system of education, which figure represents the university systems.

(*a*) (*b*)

(*c*) (*d*)

16. Which one number can be placed at the sign of interrogation?

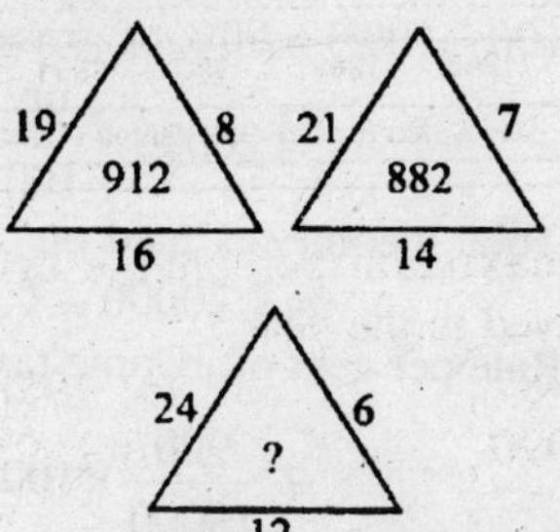

(a) 1356
(b) 862
(c) 1234
(d) 864

17. A six centimetre cube is painted green on all sides. It is cut into two centimetre cubes. How many cubes will be there with two sides painted?
(a) 12 (b) 8
(c) 24 (d) 4

18. The number of triangles in this figure are :

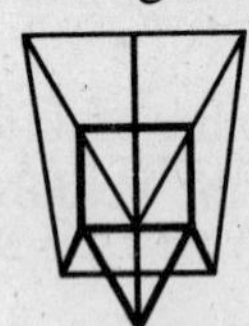

(a) 19 (b) 16
(c) 21 (d) 15

19. Study the following table and determine whose overall performance is best among the three.

Subject	A's Marks	B's Marks	C's Marks
Maths	30	40	35
English	60	50	45
Science	20	40	40
Soc. Sc.	40	55	40
G.K.	60	35	39
Hindi	30	20	41

(a) A
(b) B
(c) C
(d) Cannot be determined

20. On the basis of the data given above which of the following conclusions is correct?
(a) English is an easy subject for A
(b) A has failed in 3 subjects but B in only one
(c) Performance of A in English is twice that of Maths
(d) None of the above

ANSWERS

1	2	3	4	5	6	7	8	9	10
(d)	(c)	(c)	(b)	(c)	(d)	(d)	(d)	(b)	(d)
11	**12**	**13**	**14**	**15**	**16**	**17**	**18**	**19**	**20**
(d)	(c)	(c)	(a)	(b)	(d)	(a)	(b)	(c)	(d)

SOME SELECTED EXPLANATORY ANSWERS

1. Gross income = ₹ 20000
Income exempted from income tax = 10% of gross income
∴ Income on which income tax is chargeable = (100 – 10%) = 90% of gross income

$$= 20000 \times \frac{90}{100} = ₹\ 18000$$

∴ Total income tax paid on
= ₹ 20000 – ₹ 19100 = ₹ 900
∴ Rate per cent of income tax

$$= \frac{900}{18000} \times 100 = 5\%.$$

2. Upstream speed $= \dfrac{3/4}{45/_{4\times60}} = 4$ km/hr

Downstream speed $= \dfrac{3/4}{15/_{2\times60}} = 6$ km/hr

∴ Speed of the man in still water

$$= \frac{1}{2}(6 + 4) = 5 \text{ km/hr.}$$

3. Total ways = 6 × 6 = 36
Total 5 can be obtained in the following 4 ways : 1 + 4, 2 + 3, 3 + 2, 4 + 1
∴ Required probability = 4/36 = 1/9.

4. Calculate price for all the years. Price

$= \frac{\text{Sales (₹)}}{\text{Sales (Units)}}$

Year	Price	Per cent increase
1987	150	—
1988	180	20
1989	210	16.66
1990	230	9.5
1991	250	8.6
1992	280	12

Observe that in 1988, the per cent increase is the highest. (Note that $\frac{30}{150}$ is greater than $\frac{30}{250}$.) Hence, (*b*).

5. A's share : (B + C)'s share = 2 : 9 ...(1)
B's share (A + C)'s share = 3 : 11 ...(2)
Now dividing ₹ 1540 in the ratio of 2 : 9 and 3 : 11
A's share 2/11 of ₹ 1540 = ₹ 280
B's share = 3/14 of ₹ 1540 = ₹ 330
C's share = ₹ 1540 – (₹ 280 + ₹ 330) = ₹ 930.

6. $20 = 8 \times 2 + 4$, $15 = 3 \times 2 + 9$
$\therefore ? = 6 \times 2 + 6 = 18.$

7. R is in every group of letter and 4 is in every group of numbers so R = 4
C L E A R = 5 6 7 8 4 ...(*i*)
S P A R E = 9 0 8 4 7 ...(*ii*)
Here 847 are common
So CL = 56 and SP = 90
Thus C A R E = 5 8 4 7.

8. The cross and the circle are on the same orbit in figure (*d*).

9. First of all we write the fraction of milk present in three mixtures.

In A : $\frac{7}{12}$

In B : $\frac{17}{24}$

In combination of A and B : $\frac{5}{8}$

We now apply alligation rule on these fractions.

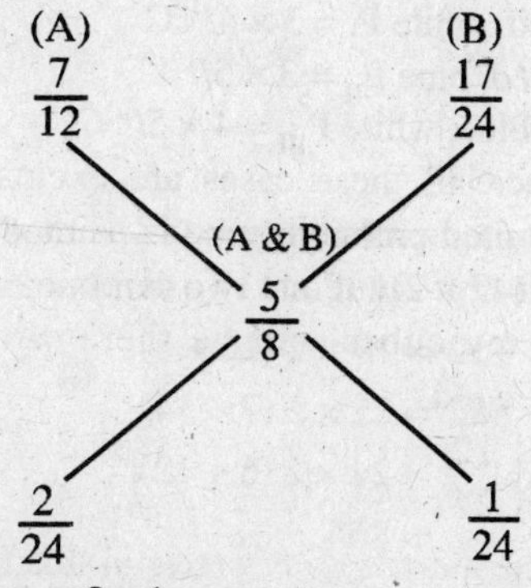

or, 2 : 1
So, ratio of A : B = 2 : 1.

10. A : B = 4 : 3 and B : C = 2 : 3, therefore, A : B : C = 8 : 6 : 9

Hence, C's profit = $\frac{9}{23} \times 46000$ = ₹ 18000.

11. It is clear from the positions of the cube that numbers adjacent to 3 are 1, 2, 4 and 5. So, the number on the opposite side to 3 will be 6.

12. Let A be the position of a person on the bank of a river and OP the tree on the opposite bank and ∠OAP = 60°. When the person retires to the position B, such that

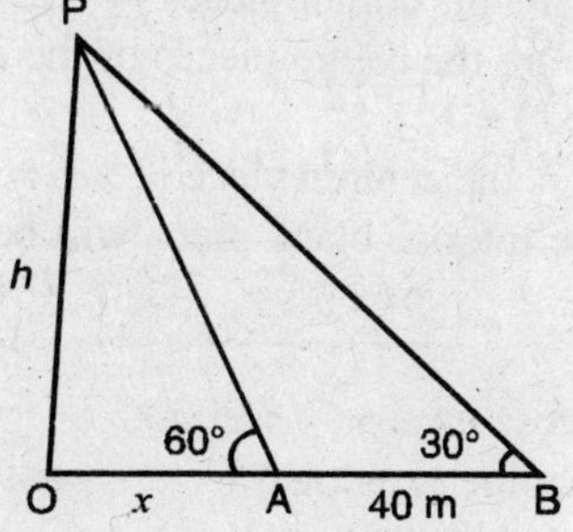

AB = 40 m then ∠ OBP = 30°
Let OA = x m and OP = h m
In Δ OAP, OP = OA tan 60° = $x\sqrt{3}$
and in Δ OBP, OP = OB tan 30° = $(x + 40)/\sqrt{3}$
$\therefore (x + 40)/\sqrt{3} = x\sqrt{3} \Rightarrow x = 20$ m.

13. BANANA
3A's, 2N's, B, *i.e.,* 6 letters, 3 alike of one type and 2 of another type. Number of words taken all at a time is $\frac{6!}{3!2!} = \frac{6 \times 5 \times 4}{2} = 60.$

14. We have the following pattern:
I red, white $P_I = 3 \times 4/{}^{12}C_2$
II red, blue $P_{II} = 3 \times 5/{}^{12}C_2$
III blue, white $P_{III} = 4 \times 5/{}^{12}C_2$
Since all these cases are exclusive, so the required probability = $(12 + 15 + 20)/{}^{12}C_2$
$= (47 \times 2)/(12 \times 11) = 47/66.$

16. $912 = 19 \times 2\,(16 + 8)$
$882 = 21 \times 2\,(7 + 14)$
and $? = 24 \times 2\,(6 + 12)$
$= 864.$

17. The smaller 27 pieces of the cube will be cut in the manner that :

1. 8 pieces will be painted on 3 sides,
2. 12 pieces on 2 sides,
3. 6 pieces on 1 side, and
4. 1 piece will not have paint at all.

Diagrammatically, the explanation taking one side of the cube will be :

a	b	a
b	c	b
a	b	a

1. 'a' are the corner pieces [4 × 2 = 8]
2. 'b' are the centre pieces of the cornered sides [4 × 3 = 12]
3. 'c' is the centred piece [1 × 6 = 6]
4. The interior blank piece will be only 1.

18.

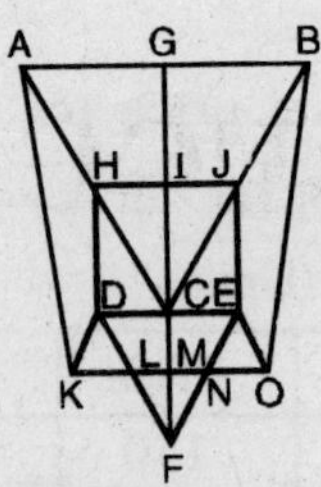

The main triangles are : ABC, DEF, LNF, and HJC *i.e.* 4 triangles
The simplest triangles are : HIC, IJC, HDC, JCE, DKL, LMF, MFN and NOE *i.e.* – 8 triangles
Other triangles are : AGC, GBC, DCF and CEF – *i.e.* 4 triangles
So, the total number of triangles is 4 + 8 + 4 = 16.

19. A, B and C's mean marks are equal but
A's range is 60 – 20 = 40
B's range is 55 – 20 = 35
C's range is 45 – 35 = 10
Standard deviation will be maximum in case of A then comes B and least SD will be there in case of C.

20. None of the conclusions is correct because
(*i*) Pass mark in each subject has not been given.
(*ii*) Each subject measures different types of abilities.
(*iii*) Scores in a particular subject depend not only on the nature of the subject but other variables like, interest, aptitude, method of teaching etc. also affect scores.

SET-3

CSIR-UGC (NET) JRF & LECTURESHIP EXAM

PART-A

1. Manoj walked from Mumbai to Thane on foot. Had he walked one mile/hr faster he would have reached $2\frac{1}{2}$ hrs earlier, and had he walked slower by one mile/hr, he would have taken 5 hrs. more. The distance between Mumbai and Thane is:
   (*a*) 20 miles (*b*) 30 miles
   (*c*) 40 miles (*d*) 60 miles

2. A can give B 50 m start and C 80 m start in the 1000 m race, how many metres start B give C in a 1000 m race?
   (*a*) 31 m (*b*) $31\frac{11}{19}$ m
   (*c*) $31\frac{2}{19}$ m (*d*) $30\frac{11}{19}$ m

3. One of the two exclusive events must occur, the chance of one is 2/3 of the other, then odds in favour of the other are :
   (*a*) 1 : 3 (*b*) 3 : 1
   (*c*) 2 : 3 (*d*) 3 : 2

4. The letters in the first set have a certain relationship. On the basis of this relationship mark the right choice for the second set :
   AST : BRU : : NQV : ?
   (*a*) ORW (*b*) MPU
   (*c*) MRW (*d*) OPW

5. Which one number can be placed at the sign of interrogation?

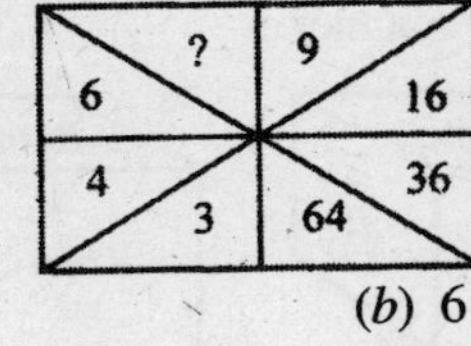

   (*a*) 12 (*b*) 6
   (*c*) 8 (*d*) 4

6. **Problem Figures**

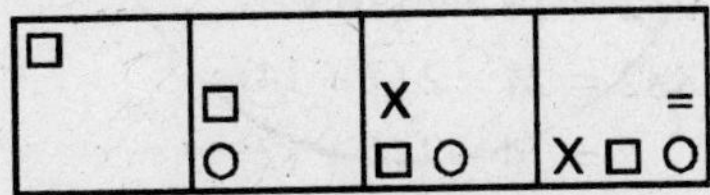

Answer Figures

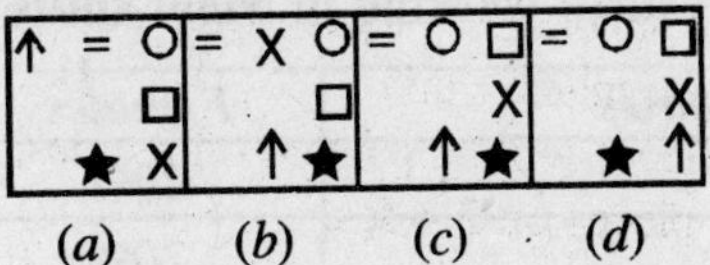

   (*a*) (*b*) (*c*) (*d*)

7. In a code language 35796 is written as 44887. Find the code for 46823.
   (*a*) 55914 (*b*) 57194
   (*c*) 55934 (*d*) 55745

8. Twelve coupons are numbered from 1 to 12. Six coupons are selected at random one at a time with replacement. The probability that the largest number appearing on a selected coupon is less than or equal to 8, is :
   (*a*) $(2/3)^6$ (*b*) $(7/12)^6$
   (*c*) 1/33 (*d*) None of these

9. A reduction of 20% in the price of coffee enables a purchaser to obtain 4 kg more for ₹ 80. The reduced price per kg of coffee is :
   (*a*) ₹ 5 (*b*) ₹ 6
   (*c*) ₹ 4 (*d*) ₹ 5.50

10. The sum of the length, breadth and depth of a cuboid is 19 cm and its diagonal is $5\sqrt{5}$ cm. Its surface area is :
   (*a*) 361 cm² (*b*) 125 cm²
   (*c*) 236 cm² (*d*) 486 cm²

Directions (Qs. 11 and 12): *Study the following Pie-chart carefully and answer the questions given below:*

Percentage of People in a City working in Night shifts from various Industries (Total number of people = 40250)

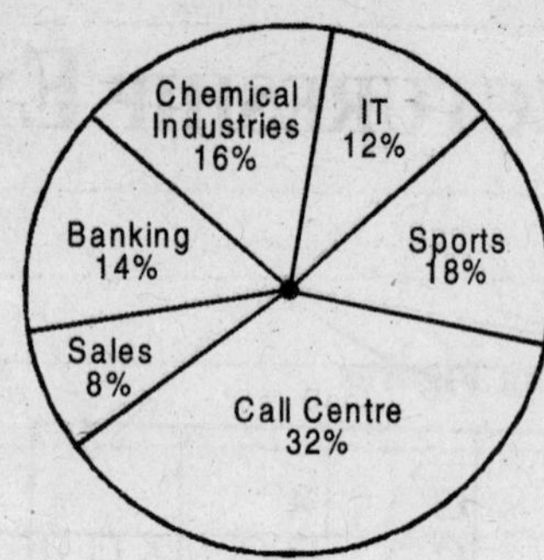

Percentage of Females from Various Industries working in Night shifts

Industries	*Females*
IT	*20%*
Sports	*20%*
Call Centre	*45%*
Sales	*60%*
Banking	*40%*
Chemical Industries	*15%*

11. What is the respective ratio of men to women working in night shifts from the Call Centre Industry?
(*a*) 9 : 11 (*b*) 11 : 9
(*c*) 8 : 13 (*d*) 13 : 8

12. The number of women from the sports industry are what per cent of the total number of people working in the night shifts from all the industries together?
(*a*) 3.2 (*b*) 3.6
(*c*) 4.4 (*d*) 5.6

13. 3 7 6 5 9 3 12 1 15 ....
(*a*) 18 (*b*) 13
(*c*) –1 (*d*) 3

14. A spherical iron shell with 21 cm external diameter weighs $22775\frac{5}{21}$ grams. Find the thickness of the shell if the metal weighs 10 gram per cu m.
(*a*) 0.5 cm
(*b*) 1.0 cm
(*c*) 2.0 cm
(*d*) 2.5 cm

15. A swimming pool 9 m wide and 12 m long is 1 m deep on the shallow side and 4 m deep on the deeper side. Find its volume.
(*a*) 270 m^3
(*b*) 300 m^3
(*c*) 360 m^3
(*d*) 420 m^3

16. A sum of money amounts to ₹ 1150 in 3 years and to ₹ 1250 in 5 years at a certain rate per cent p.a. simple interest. The rate per cent p.a. will be :
(*a*) 5% (*b*) 8%
(*c*) 7% (*d*) 6%

Directions (Q. 17) : *Study the diagram given below.*

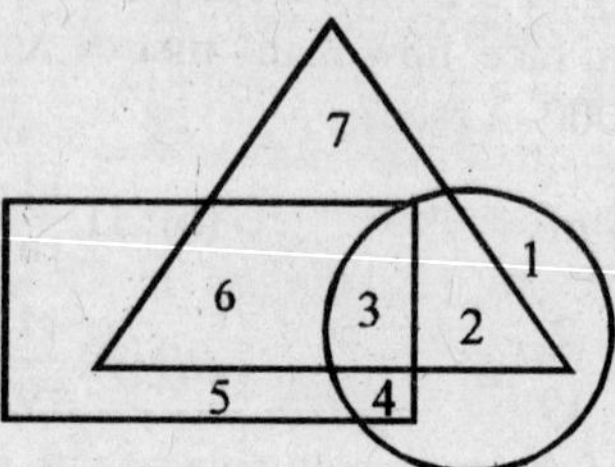

A college provides three different activities, students union represented by triangle, literary society represented by rectangle and social service league represented by circle.

17. Those who take part in both literary society and social service league but not in students union are represented by :
(*a*) 3 & 4 (*b*) 5 & 6
(*c*) 5 & 1 (*d*) 4

18. Six sides of the block are coloured Green, Blue, Red, Yellow, Orange, White in the following manner :

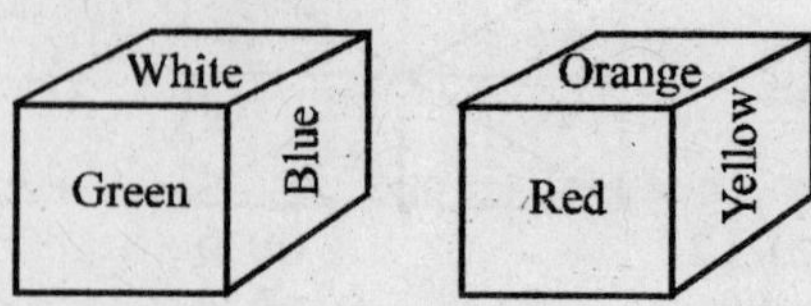

When Blue is on top, which colour will be at the bottom?

(*a*) Orange (*b*) Red
(*c*) White (*d*) Yellow

Direction (Q. 19) : *Study the graph and answer the question No. 19.*

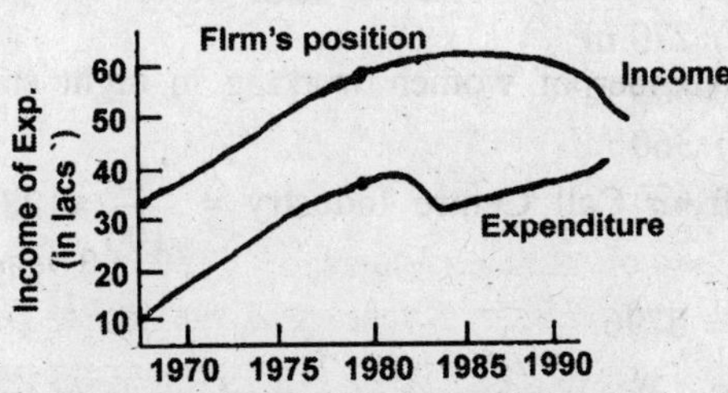

19. Which conclusion is not true?

(*a*) Profit of the firm was minimum in 1980 and maximum in 1985

(*b*) Rate of increase in income is less than that of increase in expenditure upto 1980

(*c*) There is a direct relation between income and expenditure after 1980

(*d*) All of the above

Directions (Q. 20): *Study the following Graph carefully and answer the question given below:*

Units of Raw Material Manufactured and Sold by a Company over the Years (Units in Crores)

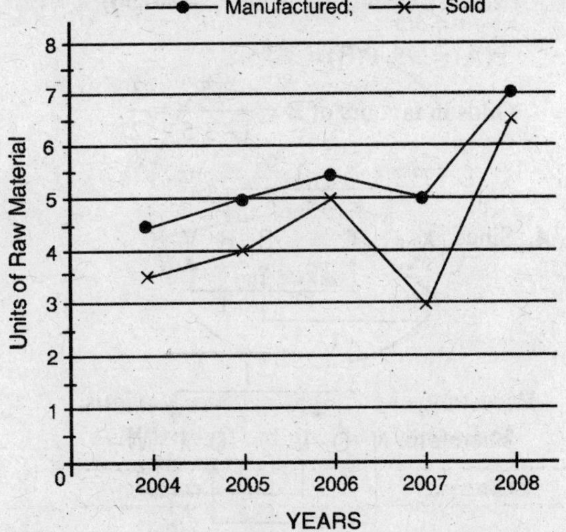

20. What is respective ratio of the difference between the number of units manufactured and sold in the year 2006 to the difference between the number of units manufactured and sold in the year 2007?

(*a*) 1 : 2 (*b*) 1 : 4
(*c*) 2 : 3 (*d*) 3 : 5

ANSWERS

1	2	3	4	5	6	7	8	9	10
(*b*)	(*b*)	(*d*)	(*d*)	(*c*)	(*a*)	(*a*)	(*a*)	(*c*)	(*c*)
11	**12**	**13**	**14**	**15**	**16**	**17**	**18**	**19**	**20**
(*b*)	(*b*)	(*c*)	(*c*)	(*a*)	(*a*)	(*d*)	(*d*)	(*c*)	(*b*)

SOME SELECTED EXPLANATORY ANSWERS

1. Let usual speed be x miles/hr and distance of the destination be d miles

Now, $\frac{d}{x} - \frac{d}{x+1} = \frac{5}{2} \Rightarrow d = \frac{5}{2}x(x+1)$ ...(i)

Again, $\frac{d}{x-1} - \frac{d}{x} = 5 \Rightarrow d = 5x(x-1)$ ...(ii)

From equations (i) and (ii)

$\frac{5}{2}x\ (x + 1) = 5x\ (x - 1) \Rightarrow x + 1 = 2x - 2$

$\therefore\ x = 3$ mile/hr

Now, from (*ii*), $d = 5 \times 3\ (3 - 1) = 30$ miles.

2. B runs 950 m while C 920 m

$\therefore$ B runs 1000 m while C

$\frac{920}{950} \times 1000 = \frac{18400}{19}$ m

Hence, in 1000 m race, B can give C

$\left(1000 - \frac{18400}{19}\right) = \frac{600}{19} = 31\frac{11}{19}$ m start.

3. Let P(B) = x, P(A) = $2x/3$

P(A) + P(B) = $x + 2x/3 = 1 \Rightarrow 5x/3 = 1$

$\Rightarrow x = 3/5$

P(A) = 2/5, P(B) = 3/5

Odds in favours of B = $\dfrac{3/5}{1-3/5} = \dfrac{3}{2}$.

4. Since,

Therefore, N O V O P W

−1

+1

+1

5. $9 = (3)^2$, $16 = (4)^2$, $36 = (6)^2$ and $64 = (8)^2$.

6. The elements are moved half step anticlockwise and a new element is added alternately in the front and back of the trail.

7. 3 + 1 = 4 of the code

5 − 1 = 4 of the code

7 + 1 = 8 of the code

9 − 1 = 8 of the code

6 + 1 = 7 of the code

as	3	5	7	9	6
	+1	−1	+1	−1	+1
	4	4	8	8	6
So	4	6	8	2	3
	+1	−1	+1	−1	+1
	5	5	9	1	4

8. Probability of a coupon selected with any number from 1 to 8 = 8/12.

In six trails: P (number from 1 to 8) = $(8/12)^6$

$P = (2/3)^6$.

9. Trick : Reduced price per kg.

$= \dfrac{80 \times 20}{100 \times 4} =$ ₹ 4 per kg.

10. $(l + b + h) = 19$ and $\sqrt{l^2 + b^2 + h^2} = 5\sqrt{5}$.

and so $(l^2 + b^2 + h^2) = 125$

Given $(l + b + h)^2 = 19^2$

Now $(l^2 + b^2 + h^2) + 2\,(lb + bh + lh) = 361$

$\Rightarrow 2\,(lb + bh + lh) = (361 - 125) = 236$

So, surface area = 236 cm^2.

11. Number of people working in night shifts from

Call Centre Industry = $\dfrac{32}{100} \times 40250 = 12880$

Number of women working in night shifts

from Call Centre Industry = $\dfrac{45}{100} \times 12880$

= 5796

So, the number of men working from same Industry = 12880 − 5796 = 7084

Hence, Required ratio = 7084 : 5796 = 11 : 9

12. Number of women from Sports Industry

$= \dfrac{20}{100} \times \dfrac{18}{100} \times 40250 = 1449$

Required percentage = $\dfrac{1449}{40250} \times 100 = 3.6\%$

13. There are two series, beginning respectively with 3 and 7. In one 3 is added and from other 2 is subtracted.

The next number is 1 − 2 = −1.

14. Let internal diameter be r cm.

Internal volume = $\dfrac{4}{3} \pi r^3$ cu. cm.

External radius = $\dfrac{21}{2}$ cm.

$\therefore$ External volume

$= \dfrac{4}{3} \times \dfrac{22}{7} \times \dfrac{21}{2} \times \dfrac{21}{2} \times \dfrac{21}{2} = 4851$ cm^3.

$\therefore$ Volume of the metal of the shell

$= \dfrac{478280}{21} \times \dfrac{1}{10} = \dfrac{47828}{21}$ cu. cm.

Internal volume of the metal of the shell

$= \left(4851 - \dfrac{47828}{21}\right) = \dfrac{54043}{21}$ cu. cm.

$\dfrac{4}{3} \pi r^3 = \dfrac{54043}{21}$

$$\frac{4}{3} \times \frac{22}{7} \times r^3 = \frac{54043}{21}$$

$\therefore\ r^3 = \dfrac{54043 \times 3 \times 7}{21 \times 4 \times 22}$ or $r^3 = 614.125$

or $r = 8.5$ cm.

$\therefore$ Thickness = (10.5 – 8.5) = 2 cm.

15. Volume of the swimming pool

$$= 12 \times 9 \times \left(\frac{4+1}{2}\right)$$

$$= 12 \times 9 \times \frac{5}{2} = 270 \text{ m}^3.$$

16. Here, simple interest for 2 years

= ₹ 1250 – ₹ 1150 = ₹ 100

$\therefore$ Simple interest for 3 years

$$= \frac{100 \times 3}{2} = ₹\ 150$$

Hence, P = ₹ 1150 – ₹ 150

= ₹ 1000

$$\therefore \quad \text{Rate} = \frac{50 \times 100}{1000 \times 1} = 5\%.$$

17.

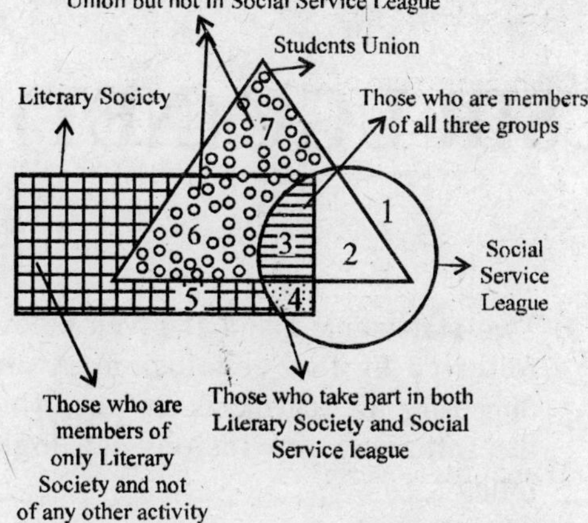

18. The coloured sides of the block which are clearly understood to be the opposites are: White – Orange, Blue – Yellow and Green – Red. So, when blue is on the top, yellow will be at the bottom.

19. Expenditure is highly fluctuating so relationship is not direct.

20. Required ratio = (5.5 – 5) : (5 – 3)

= 0.5 : 2 = 1 : 4

SET-4

CSIR-UGC (NET) JRF & LECTURESHIP EXAM

PART-A

1. Two statements I and II given below are followed by two conclusions A and B. Supposing the statements are true, which of the following conclusions can logically follow?

Statements :

I. Some flowers are red.

II. Some flowers are blue.

Conclusions :

A. Some flowers are neither red nor blue

B. Some flowers are both red and blue.

(*a*) Only A follows

(*b*) Only B follows

(*c*) Both A and B follows

(*d*) Neither A nor B follows

2. Three men Ram, Karan and Mohan run around an oval garden from a fixed post at the rates of 5, $5\frac{1}{7}$, $5\frac{1}{3}$ per hour. They come back to the fixed post in $3\frac{3}{4}$ hours. Find the greatest length, the race course can have.

(*a*) $\frac{28}{5}$ km (*b*) $\frac{5}{28}$ km

(*c*) $\frac{11}{28}$ km (*d*) $\frac{28}{11}$ km

3. A five digit number is formed by the digits 1, 2, 3, 4, 5, 6 and 8. The probability that the number has even digit at both ends is :

(*a*) 2/7 (*b*) 3/7

(*c*) 4/7 (*d*) None of these

Directions (Q. 4): *This question is based on the information given in the following graph.*

Rates of interest per cent per annum given by two companies 'A' and 'B' during the given years.

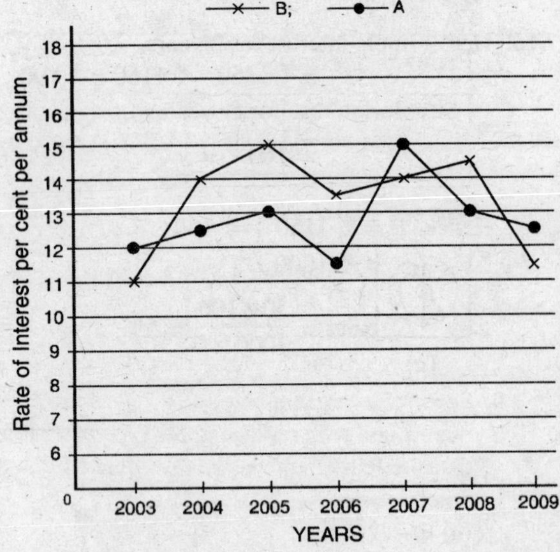

4. An amount of ₹ 20,000 was invested in Company 'B' in 2008 and after one year the entire amount alongwith interest will be reinvested in the Company A for one more year. What will be the total amount of interest accrued?

(*a*) ₹ 5199

(*b*) ₹ 5762.50

(*c*) ₹ 5533.75

(*d*) ₹ 54.25

5. If ÷ means ×, × means +, + means – and – means ÷. Find the value of 16 × 3 + 5 – 2 ÷ 4.

(*a*) 19 (*b*) 10

(*c*) 9 (*d*) None of these

6. Which one number can be placed at sign of interrogation?

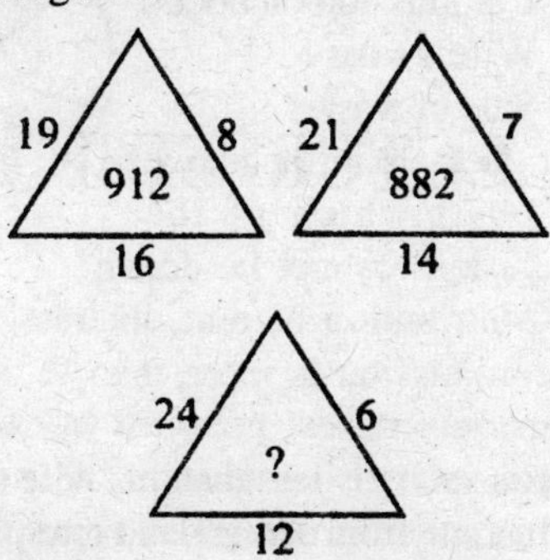

(*a*) 1356 (*b*) 862
(*c*) 1234 (*d*) 864

7. Problem Figures

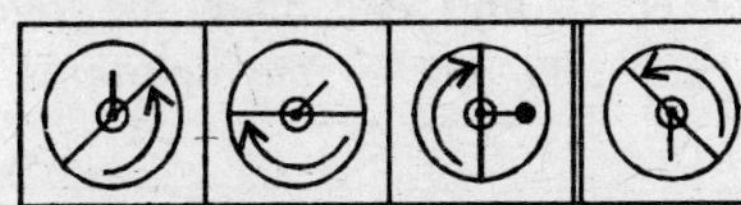

Answer Figures

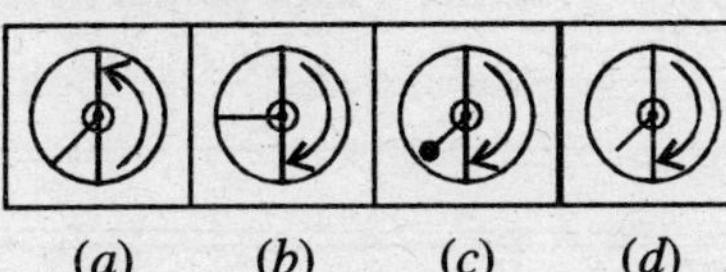

(*a*) (*b*) (*c*) (*d*)

8. Seven chits are numbered 1 to 7. Four are drawn one by one with replacements. The probability that the least number on any selected chits is 5 is :

(*a*) $1-(2/7)^4$ (*b*) $4.(2/7)^4$
(*c*) $(3/7)^4$ (*d*) None of these

Directions (Q. 9) : *The pie-chart, drawn here, shows the spending of a country on various sports during a particular year. Study the graph carefully and answer the question that follow:*

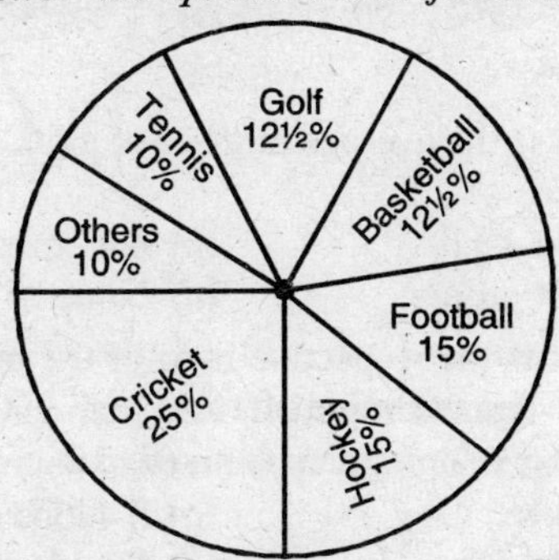

9. If the total amount spent on sports during the year was ₹ 30,00,000, the amount spent on cricket and hockey together was:

(*a*) ₹ 18,00,000
(*b*) ₹ 12,00,000
(*c*) ₹ 15,00,000
(*d*) ₹ 20,00,000

10. If the length of a rectangle is decreased by 40% and the breadth is increased by 30%, then what is increase or decrease per cent in the area of rectangle?

(*a*) 22% increase (*b*) 22% decrease
(*c*) 28% increase (*d*) 27% decrease

11. 2, 5, 10, 18, 26, 37, 50

(*a*) 2 (*b*) 5
(*c*) 37 (*d*) 18

Directions (Q. 12) : *The bar graph as shown below gives information about the sale and profit details of a departmental store during the years from 2001–2008. Study the graph carefully and answer the question asked here under.*

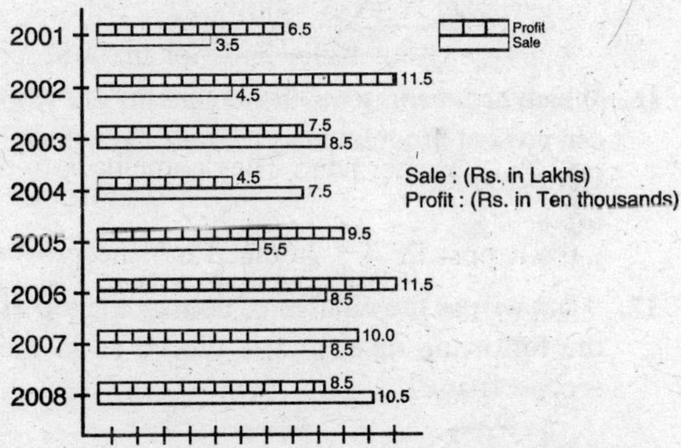

12. During which year between 2001 to 2006 profit made by the store as compared to the previous year was more than 100%?

(*a*) 2008 (*b*) 2007
(*c*) 2005 (*d*) 2003

13. Find the length of the longest rod that can be placed in a room 12 m long 9 m broad and 8 m high

(*a*) 16 m (*b*) 17 m
(*c*) 15 m (*d*) 12 m

14. Water flows through a cylindrical pipe of internal diameter 7 cm at 2 m/s. If the pipe is always half full, then find the volume of water discharged in 10 minutes.

(*a*) 1160 *l* (*b*) 2310 *l*
(*c*) 3850 *l* (*d*) 4620 *l*

15. If a certain sum of money at simple interest amounts to ₹ 1900 in 3 years and to ₹ 2050 in 5 years, the rate per cent per annum is :

(*a*) 4½% (*b*) 3½%
(*c*) 2½% (*d*) 5¼%

Directions (Q. 16) : *In the following diagram, rectangle represents Hindi Announcers, circle represents English Announcers, square represents French Announcers, and triangle represents German Announcers.*

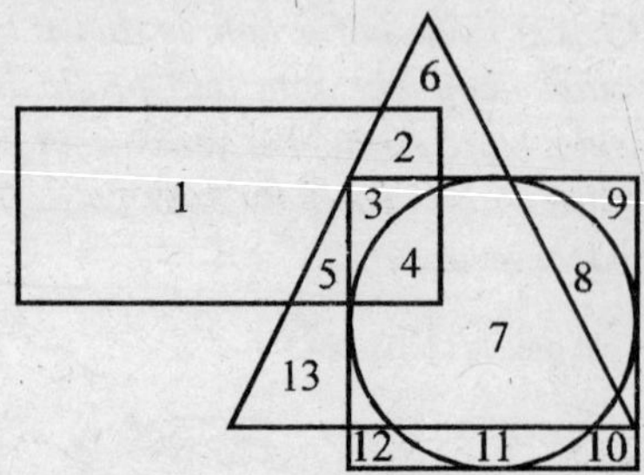

16. Which area represents those announcers who can present programmes in Hindi, French and German only?

(*a*) 1 (*b*) 2
(*c*) 3 (*d*) 4

17. What will be the number of dots on the top of the following dice, if it is placed as in the second figure?

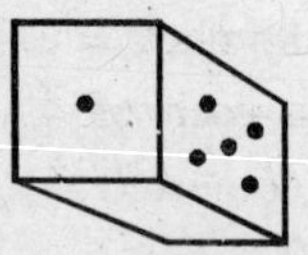
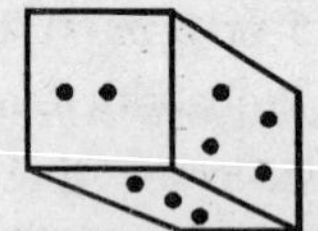

(*a*) 5 (*b*) 1
(*c*) 6 (*d*) Can't be said

18. Income of a person from different sources is expressed through the following pie chart. Study them and answer the following question.

1. Service
2. Rent
3. Bank interest
4. Company shares
5. Commission on books
6. Wife's salary
7. Sale of wastes

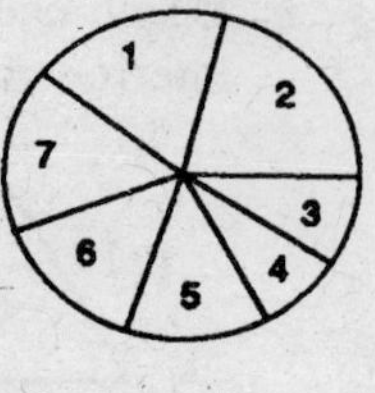

With the help of the above pie chart which of the conclusions cannot be drawn?

(*a*) Contribution of rent, interest, share and commission is more than ½ of the total income
(*b*) His salary is less than his wife salary
(*c*) Income from service and rent put together makes an obtuse angle in a pie chart
(*d*) His wife's salary is less than the income obtained from rent

Directions (Qs. 19 and 20): *Study the following graph carefully and answer the questions given below:*

Units of Raw Material Manufactured and Sold by a Company over the Years (Units in Crores)

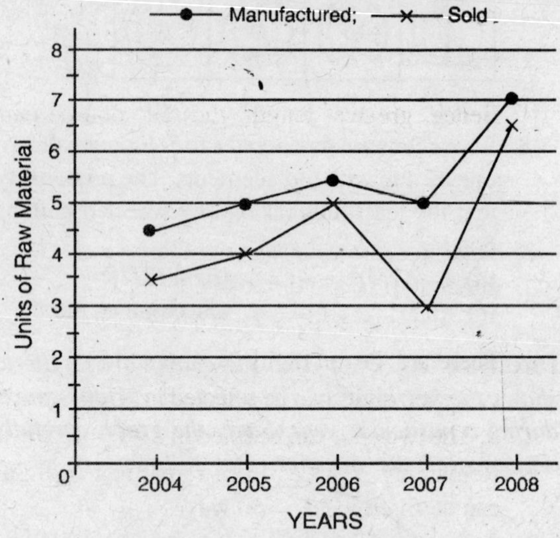

19. What is the average number of units sold over the years?

(*a*) 44 lakhs (*b*) 4.4 cores
(*c*) 44 crores (*d*) None of these

20. What is the respective ratio of the number of units manufactured in the year 2004 to the number of units manufactured in the year 2008?

(*a*) 7 : 9 (*b*) 7 : 11
(*c*) 9 : 11 (*d*) 9 : 14

ANSWERS

1	2	3	4	5	6	7	8	9	10
(a)	*(b)*	*(a)*	*(b)*	*(c)*	*(d)*	*(d)*	*(c)*	*(b)*	*(b)*
11	**12**	**13**	**14**	**15**	**16**	**17**	**18**	**19**	**20**
(d)	*(c)*	*(b)*	*(d)*	*(a)*	*(c)*	*(c)*	*(b)*	*(b)*	*(d)*

SOME SELECTED EXPLANATORY ANSWERS

2. Total number of rounds made by Ram in

$\frac{15}{4}$ hrs $= 5 \times \frac{15}{4} = \frac{75}{4}$

Total number of rounds made by Karan in

$\frac{15}{4}$ hrs $= \frac{36}{7} \times \frac{15}{4} = \frac{135}{7}$

Total number of rounds made by Mohan in

$\frac{15}{4}$ hrs $= \frac{16}{3} \times \frac{15}{4} = 20$

H.C.F. of $\frac{75}{4}$, $\frac{135}{7}$ and $20 = \frac{5}{28}$

Hence, greatest length, the race cource can have $\frac{5}{28}$ km.

3. Total number of 5 digit numbers obtained by the digits 1, 2, 3, 4, 5, 6 and 8.

$= {}^7P_5 = 7.6.5.4.3 = 2520$

There are 4 even digits (2, 4, 6 and 8).

$\therefore$ 2 even digits can be selected in ${}^4C_2 = 6$ ways

$\therefore$ The two ends can be filled in $2 \times 6 = 12$ ways

Remaining 3 places from remaining 5 digits can be filled in ${}^5P_3 = 60$ ways.

Hence, the required probability $= \frac{12 \times 60}{2520} = \frac{2}{7}$.

4. Interest received in 2009 from Company B

$= \frac{20000 \times 14.5 \times 1}{100} =$ ₹ 2900

Hence, their amount = 20000 + 2900 = ₹ 22900

Interest will be received in 2010 from Company A $= \frac{22900 \times 12.5 \times 1}{100} =$ ₹ 2862.50.

Hence, total amount of interests for both years = 2900 + 2862.50 = ₹ 5762.50.

5. $16 \times 3 + 5 - 2 \div 4$

In such type of questions apply the rule of BODMAS

B = Bracket O = of
D = Division M = Multiply
A = Adding S = Subtraction

$16 + 3 - 5 \div 2 \times 4$

$16 + 3 - 5 \times ½ \times 4$

$19 - 10 = 9.$

6. $912 = 19 \times 2\ (16+8)$

$882 = 21 \times 2\ (7 + 14)$

and $? = 24 \times 2\ (6 + 12) = 864.$

7. From figure one to figure two the diagonal with circle and dot bar are rotated 45° clockwise and the direction of the arrow is reversed. Same applies to figure three and figure four. Answer figure *(d)* coordinates with figure five.

8. P (5 or 6 or 7) in one draw = 3/7

$\therefore$ Probabilty that in each of 4 draws, the chits bear 5 or 6 or 7 $= (3/7)^4$.

9. 100% = ₹ 30,00,000

$\therefore$ Expenditure on the games of Cricket and Hockey = 25% + 15% = 40%

$\therefore$ Total expenditure on the games of Cricket and Hockey = 40% of 30,00,000

$= \frac{40 \times 30,00,000}{100} =$ ₹ 12,00,000.

10. Trick : Percentage increase or decrease

$= (30-40) - \frac{30\times40}{100}$

= –22 = 22% decrease.

Note : Negative sign shows decrease and positive sign shows increase.

11. 2 5 10 18 26 37 50

↓ ↓ ↓ ↓ ↓ ↓ ↓

1^2+1 2^2+1 3^2+1 4^2+1 5^2+1 6^2+1 7^2+1

Wrong no. = 18, Correct no. = 17.

12. Profit per cent during the year 2005 as compared to the previous year

$= \frac{(9.5-4.5)\times100}{4.5} = 111.11\%$

Hence, profit in the year 2005 was more than 100% as compared to the previous year.

13. The longest rod that can be placed in the room is equal to the length of its diagonal.

∴ length of longest rod

$= \sqrt{12^2+9^2+8^2} = \sqrt{144+81+64}$

$= \sqrt{289} = 17$m.

14. Length of water column in 10 minutes = 2 × 10 × 60 × 100 cm

Since, volume of water discharged in 10 minutes

$= \frac{22}{7}\times\frac{7}{2}\times\frac{7}{2}\times 2\times 10\times 60\times 100$ c.c.

= 4620 × 1000 c.c. = 4620 *l*

15. Simple interest for 2 years

= ₹ 2050 – ₹ 1900 = ₹ 150

∴ Simple interest for 1 year = ₹$\frac{150}{2}$ = ₹ 75

Since simple interest for 3 years

= ₹ 75 × 3 = ₹ 225

∴ Principal = ₹ 1900 – ₹ 225 = ₹ 1675

Hence, rate $= \frac{75\times100}{1675\times1} = 4\frac{1}{2}\%$.

16.

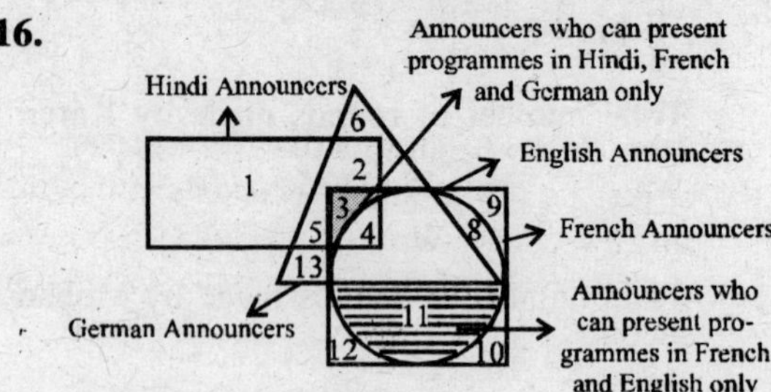

17. The numbers adjacent to 2 are 1, 5, 3 and 4. So, the number of dots opposite to the side with 2 dots will be 6.

18. Since the angle is not given here so nothing can be said so accurately.

19. Average number of units sold

$= \frac{3.5+4+5+3+6.5}{5} = \frac{22}{5} = 4.4$ crores.

20. Required ratio = 4.5 : 7 = 45 : 70 = 9 : 14.

SET-5

CSIR-UGC (NET) JRF & LECTURESHIP EXAM

PART-A

1. What is the smallest number of ducks that could swim in this formation — two ducks in front of a duck, two ducks behind a duck and a duck between two ducks?
   (*a*) 5 (*b*) 7
   (*c*) 4 (*d*) 3

2. Two clocks begin to strike 12 together. One strikes its strokes in 33 seconds and the other in 22 seconds. What is the interval between the 6th stroke of the first and 8th stroke of the second?
   (*a*) 3 seconds
   (*b*) 1 second
   (*c*) 11 seconds
   (*d*) strikes at the same time

3. Three cards are drawn successively with replacement. The probability of selecting 2 aces and one king is
   (*a*) $1/\{(13)^2 \times 17\}$
   (*b*) $1/(13)^3$
   (*c*) $3/(13)^3$
   (*d*) None of these

Directions (Q. 4): *Study the following graph carefully and answer the question given below.*

Number of Building constructed, demolished and redeveloped across various cities in a year

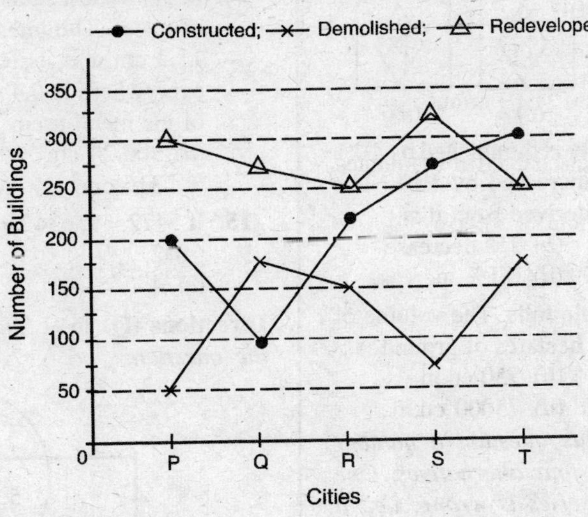

4. The total number of buildings constructed across the cities is approximately what per cent of the total number of buildings redeveloped across the cities?
   (*a*) 73 (*b*) 74
   (*c*) 79 (*d*) 89

5. If BOY is coded as ACNPXZ. What will be the code for LIFE?
   (*a*) KMHJEGDF (*b*) LMGHEGDF
   (*c*) LMHJGEFD (*d*) None of these

6. The probabilities of three mutually exclusive events A, B and C are given by 2/3, 1/4 and 1/6 respectively. The statement :

(*a*) is true

(*b*) is false

(*c*) Nothing can be said

(*d*) Could be either

7. Which one number can be placed at the sign of interrogation?

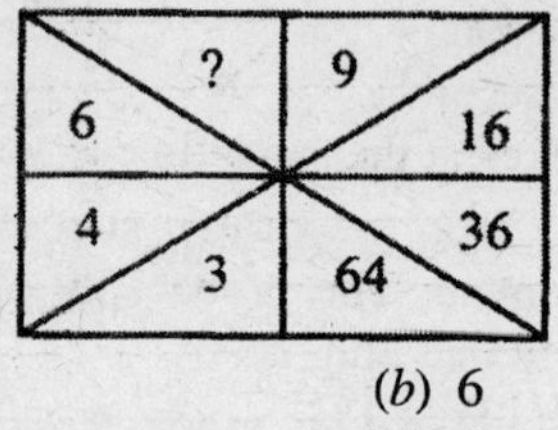

(*a*) 12 (*b*) 6

(*c*) 8 (*d*) 4

8. Problem Figures

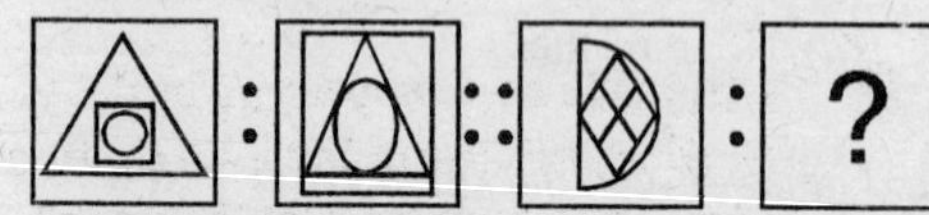

Answer Figures

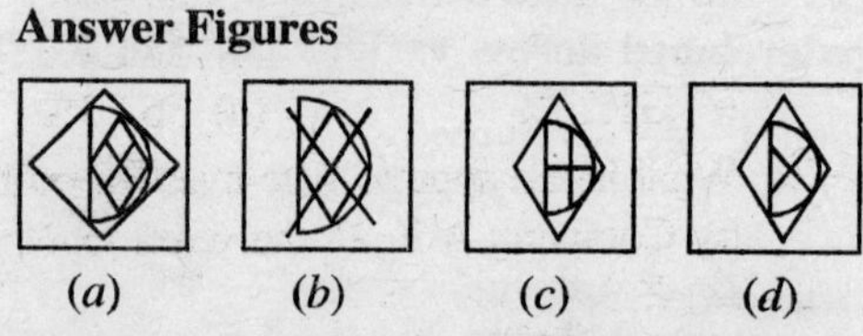

9. The tax on a commodity is diminished by 10% and its consumption increased by 10%. The effect on the revenue derived from it is :

(*a*) 0.1% decrease (*b*) 1% decrease

(*c*) 1% increase (*d*) 0.1% increase

10. In a shower 5 cm of rain falls. The volume of water that falls on 1.5 hectares of ground is :

(*a*) 75 cu.m. (*b*) 750 cu.m.

(*c*) 7500 cu.m. (*d*) 75000 cu.m.

Directions (Q. 11) : *In this question a number series is given followed by four alternatives. One term/element of the given series is wrong, i.e., it does not conform to the rule used in writing the series. This wrong term is depicted in the following alternatives. Spot out that wrong term/element and mark your answer.*

11. 508, 250, 124, 60, 28, 12, 4

(*a*) 28 (*b*) 124

(*c*) 60 (*d*) 250

Directions (Q. 12) : *The following bar graph shows the production of food grains in India during certain year. Study the graph carefully and answer the question given below:*

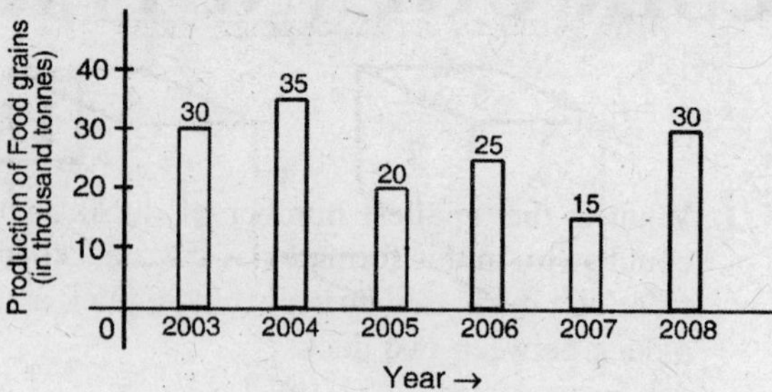

12. Percentage increase in the production of food-grains in the year 2008 over the year 2007 is:

(*a*) 15% (*b*) 30%

(*c*) 50% (*d*) 100%

13. Three cubes whose edges are 3 cm., 4 cm., and 5 cm. respectively are melted to form a single cube. The surface area of the new cube will be:

(*a*) 100 sq m (*b*) 216 sq m

(*c*) 200 sq m (*d*) 150 sq m

14. A cylindrical tube open at both ends is made of metal. The internal diameter of the tube is 11.2 cm and its length is 21 cm. The metal everywhere is 0.4 cm thick. Find the volume of the metal used.

(*a*) 306.24 cm^3 (*b*) 310.24 cm^3

(*c*) 316 cm^3 (*d*) 324.24 cm^3

15. If 5472 = 9, 6342 = 6, 7584 = 6, what is 9236?

(*a*) 2 (*b*) 3

(*c*) 4 (*d*) 5

Directions (Q. 16) : *Study the diagram to answer the question.*

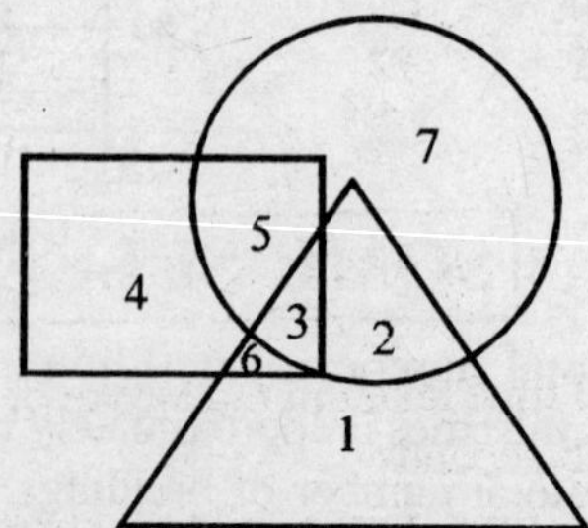

16. Number 6 is in :

(*a*) Rectangle and triangle

(*b*) Circle and triangle

(*c*) Rectangle and circle
(*d*) Rectangle only

17. Which of the following pairs of numbers of the dice given below does not correctly give the numbers on the opposite side?

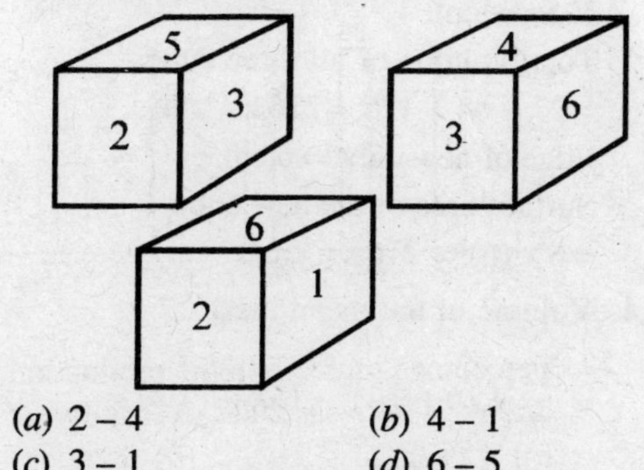

(*a*) 2 – 4 (*b*) 4 – 1
(*c*) 3 – 1 (*d*) 6 – 5

18. Which of the following figures does not represent a linear relationship between the variables X and Y ?

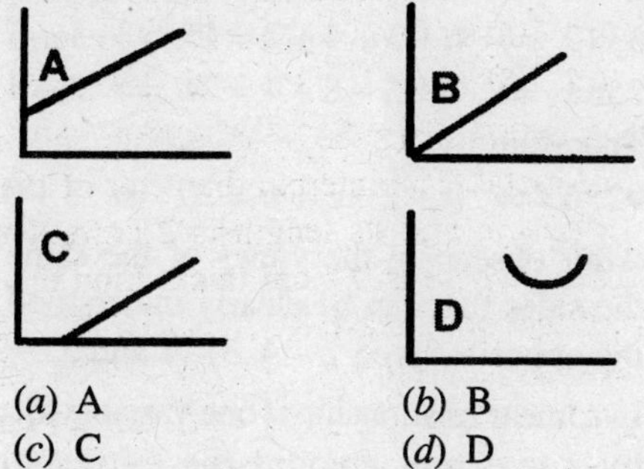

(*a*) A (*b*) B
(*c*) C (*d*) D

Directions (Qs. 19 and 20): *Study the graph carefully to answer the questions that follow.*

Profit (in lakhs) made by three companies over the years
Profit = Income – Expenditure

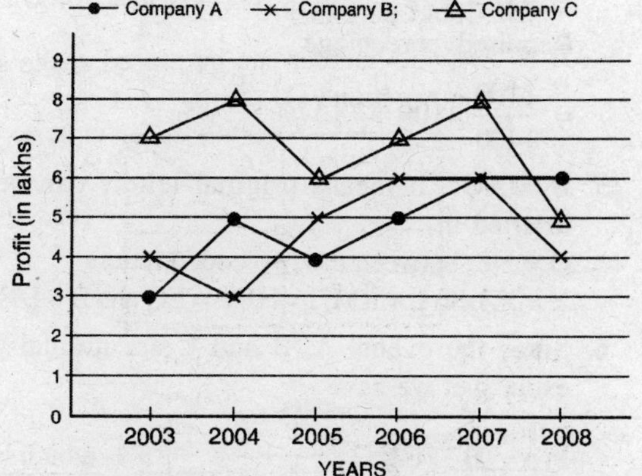

19. Profit made by Company A in the year 2004 was what per cent of the total profit made by all the three companies in that year?
(*a*) 21.43% (*b*) 28.24%
(*c*) 31.25% (*d*) 36.25%

20. What is the approximate average profit made by Company A in all the years together?
(*a*) ₹ 3,82,000
(*b*) ₹ 3,98,000
(*c*) ₹ 4,83,000
(*d*) ₹ 5,12,000

ANSWERS

1	2	3	4	5	6	7	8	9	10
(*a*)	(*c*)	(*c*)	(*c*)	(*a*)	(*b*)	(*c*)	(*d*)	(*b*)	(*b*)
11	**12**	**13**	**14**	**15**	**16**	**17**	**18**	**19**	**20**
(*d*)	(*d*)	(*b*)	(*a*)	(*a*)	(*a*)	(*b*)	(*d*)	(*c*)	(*c*)

SOME SELECTED EXPLANATORY ANSWERS

2. Total time taken in 6th stroke of first = 33 × 5 = 165 seconds

Total time taken in 8th stroke of second = 22 × 7 = 154 seconds.

Hence, required interval = 165 – 154 = 11 seconds.

3. $P(\text{ace}) = \frac{4}{52} = \frac{1}{13}$ $P(\text{king}) = \frac{4}{52} = \frac{1}{13}$

P (2 aces and one king)

$$= {}^3C_2 \cdot \left(\frac{1}{13}\right)^2 \left(\frac{1}{13}\right) = \frac{3}{(13)^3}.$$

4. Total number of buildings constructed across the cities

$= 200 + 100 + 225 + 275 + 300 = 1100$

Total number of buildings redeveloped across the cities

$= 300 + 275 + 250 + 325 + 250 = 1400$

Required percentage

$= \frac{1100}{1400} \times 100 = 78.57\% \approx 79\%.$

5. B = AC. It means original letters can be inserted in O = NP between the two coded letters Y = XZ. So L = KM, I = HJ, F = EG and E = DF.

6. Since the events A, B and C are mutually exclusive, we have

$P(A \cup B \cup C) = \frac{2}{3} + \frac{1}{4} + \frac{1}{6} = \frac{13}{12} > 1$, which is not possible.

Hence, the statement is false.

7. $9 = (3)^2$, $16 = (4)^2$, $36 = (6)^2$ and $64 = (8)^2$.

8. The middle and the inner most shapes are enlarged and the outermost shape is reduced and placed in the middle of the two enlarged shapes.

9. **Trick :** Effect = $(10^2/100)$ % = 1% decrease.

10. Area = (1.5 × 10000) sq . metres

= 15000 sq. metres.

Depth = 5/100 m = 1/20 m

So, Volume = (Area × Depth)

= (15000 × 1/20)= 750 cu. m.

11.

$0 \times 2 + 4 = 4$

$4 \times 2 + 4 = 12$

$12 \times 2 + 4 = 28$

$28 \times 2 + 4 = 60$

$60 \times 2 + 4 = 124$

$124 \times 2 + 4 = 252$ — $\boxed{250}$

$252 \times 2 + 4 = 508$

∴ 250 is wrong.

12. Percentage increase in foodgrain production

$= \frac{30-15}{15} \times 100 = 100\%.$

13. Volume of 1st, 2nd and 3rd cube is 27, 64 and 125 cu. cm.

Total volume of all three cubes

= 27 + 64 + 125 = 216 cu. cm.

Edge of new cube = 6 cm.

Surface area of the new cube

$= 6 \times (6)^2 = 216$ sq. cm.

14. Volume of the metal used

$= \frac{22}{7}\left[(5.6+0.4)^2 - (5.6)^2\right] \times 21$

$= 66 \times (6 + 5.6) \times (6 - 5.6)$

$= 66 \times 11.6 \times 0.4 = 306.24 \text{ cm}^3.$

15. Since,

$5472 \Rightarrow 5+4+7+2 = 18 \Rightarrow 1+8 = 9$

$6342 \Rightarrow 6+3+4+2 = 15 \Rightarrow 1+5 = 16$

$7584 \Rightarrow 7+5+8+4 = 24 \Rightarrow 2+4 = 6$

Therefore,

$9236 \Rightarrow 9+2+3+6 = 20 \Rightarrow 2+0 = 2$

17. After observing the views of the same dice, the sides that can be clearly understood to be the opposites are : 2 – 4, 3 – 1 and 5 – 6.

18. In a linear relationship if one variable increases by a constant amount the corresponding increase in the other variable is also constant.

19. Required percentage

$= \frac{5}{3+5+8} \times 100 = \frac{5}{16} \times 100 = 31.25\%.$

20. Average profit made by company A in all the years = ₹ $\frac{(3+5+4+5+6+6) \text{ lakhs}}{6}$

= ₹ $\frac{29 \text{ lakhs}}{6}$ ≈ ₹ 4.83 lakh = ₹ 4,83,000.

SET-6

CSIR-UGC (NET) JRF & LECTURESHIP EXAM

PART-A

1. There is a road beside a river. Two friends started from a place A, moved to a temple situated at another place B and then returned to A again. One of them moves on a cycle at a speed of 12 km/hr, while other sails on a boat at the speed of 10 km/hr. If the river flows at the speed of 4 km/hr, then which of the two friends will return to place A first?

(*a*) Cyclist
(*b*) Boat sailor
(*c*) Both in same time
(*d*) None of these

2. A shopkeeper has 50 kgs of rice. He sells a part of it at 20% profit and the rest at 40% profit. If he gains 25% on the whole, find the quantity of each part.

(*a*) 12.5 kgs and 37.5 kgs
(*b*) 37.5 kgs and 12.5 kgs
(*c*) 23.5 kgs and 21.5 kgs
(*d*) 21.5 kgs and 23.5 kgs

3. Three identical dice are rolled. The probability that the same number will appear on each of them is :

(*a*) 1/6 (*b*) 1/18
(*c*) 1/36 (*d*) None of these

Directions (Q. 4): *This question is based on the information given in the following graph.*

Rates of interest per cent per annum given by two companies 'A' and 'B' during the given years.

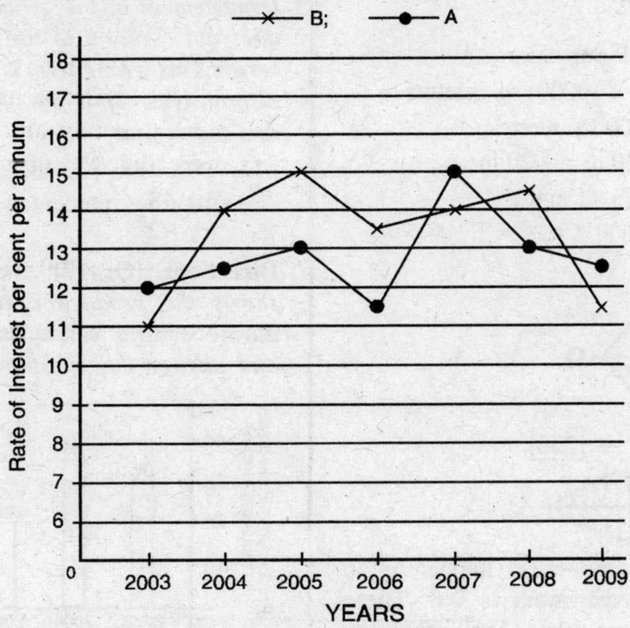

4. Samir invested ₹ 10,000 in the company 'A' for one year in 2006. He reinvested the total amount along with interest for next one year in 2007. If he had invested for both years in the Company 'B', what would have been the difference between the interests earned?

(*a*) ₹ 16.50 less (*b*) ₹ 116.50 more
(*c*) ₹ 128.50 less (*d*) ₹ 128.50 more

5. In a certain code language, CUL, WAP, DIR means red little box, SUT, MAD BIX, means well-arranged pile, BIX, FAC, DIR means pile of boxes. The code for 'of' here is?

(*a*) FAC (*b*) SUT
(*c*) DIR (*d*) BIX

6. A goat has been tied to two stakes at point P and Q. If length of each of the rope is 15 metres and P and Q points are 20 metres apart, then which of the following shaded portion will indicate the place of strolling of the goat?

(*a*) 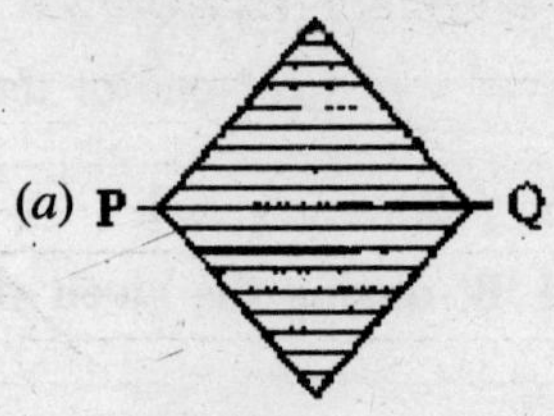

(*b*) 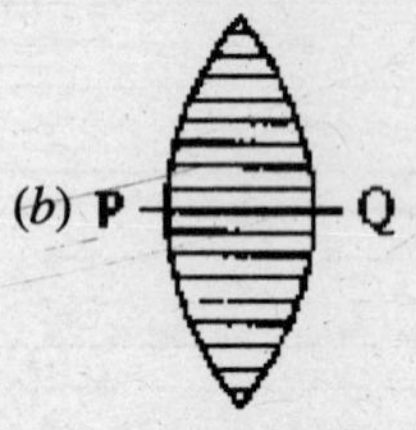

(*c*) 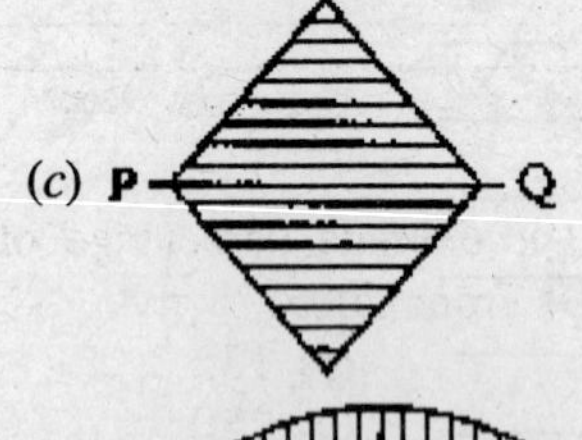

(*d*) 

7. The probability of an event happening in one trial of an experiment is 0.6. Three independent trials are made. The probability that the event happens at least once is

(*a*) 0.432 (*b*) 0.064
(*c*) 0.936 (*d*) 0.568

8. Problem Figures

Answer Figures

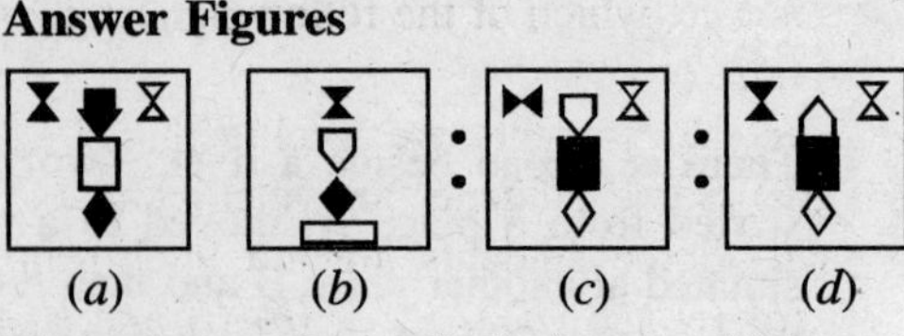

9. The volume of a wall, 5 times as high as it is broad and 9 times as long as it is high, is 12.8 cu. metres. The breadth of the wall is :

(*a*) 30 m (*b*) 40 m
(*c*) 22.5 m (*d*) 25 m

10. If the length of a rectangle is decreased by 40% and the breadth is increased by 30%, then what is increase or decrease per cent in the area of rectangle?

(*a*) 22% increase (*b*) 22% decrease
(*c*) 28% increase (*d*) 27% decrease

Directions (Q. 11): *In this question a number series is given, followed by four alternatives. One term/element of the given series is wrong, i.e., it does not conform to the rule used in writing the series. This wrong term is depicted in the following alternatives. Spot out that wrong term/element and mark your answer.*

11. 380, 188, 92, 48, 20, 8, 2

(*a*) 48 (*b*) 20
(*c*) 92 (*d*) 8

Directions (Q. 12): *The following bar graph shows the production of food grains in India during certain years. Study the graph carefully and answer the question given below:*

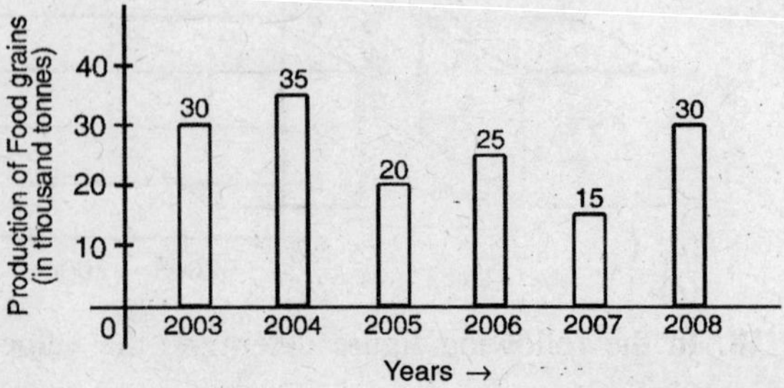

12. Rate of change in quantity of production in which of the following two consecutive years is at the minimum level?
(*a*) 2003 and 2004 (*b*) 2005 and 2006
(*c*) 2007 and 2008 (*d*) 2006 and 2007

13. If the statement 'all students are intelligent' is true, which of the following statements are false?
(*i*) No students are intelligent.
(*ii*) Some students are intelligent.
(*iii*) Some students are not intelligent.
(*a*) (*i*) and (*ii*) (*b*) (*i*) and (*iii*)
(*c*) (*ii*) and (*iii*) (*d*) (*i*) only

14. If a right circular cone of height 24 cm has a volume of 1232 cm^3, then find its curved surface area.
(*a*) 220 cm^2 (*b*) 330 cm^2
(*c*) 440 cm^2 (*d*) 550 cm^2

15. Monday falls in 20th March 1995. What was the day on 3rd November 1994?
(*a*) Thursday (*b*) Sunday
(*c*) Tuesday (*d*) Saturday

16. What is the number which is common to only two geometrical figures?

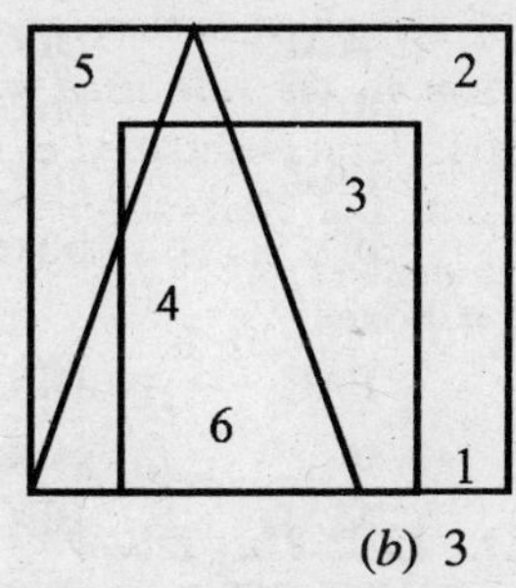

(*a*) 4 (*b*) 3
(*c*) 5 (*d*) 2

17. In the dice given below, which number will be on the top if 2 is at the bottom?

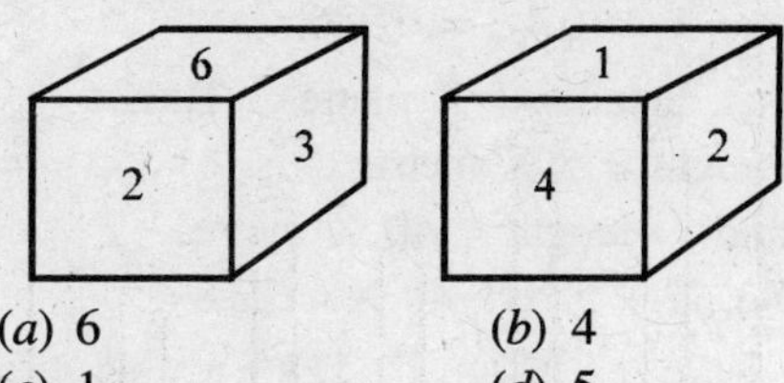

(*a*) 6 (*b*) 4
(*c*) 1 (*d*) 5

18. In the following figure determine the value of X

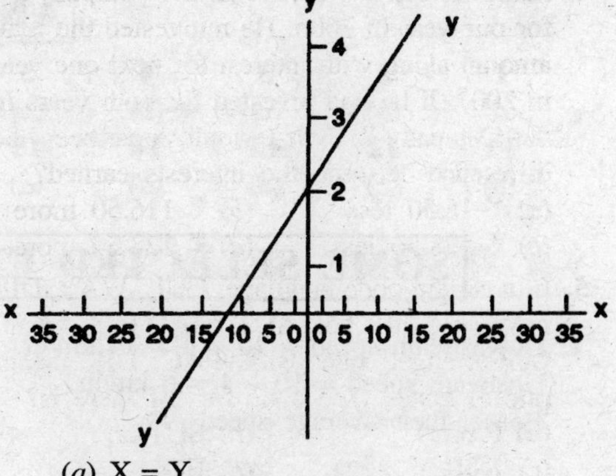

(*a*) X = Y
(*b*) X + Y = –2
(*c*) X – 2 = Y
(*d*) X = –Y + 2

Directions (Qs. 19 and 20): *Study the following graph to answer the given questions.*

Export over the years (in crore ₹)

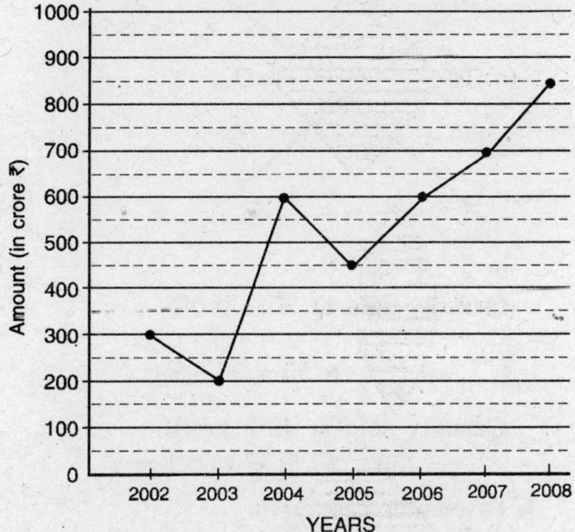

19. What is the approximate percentage of the export of 2004 from 2005?
(*a*) 120 (*b*) 135
(*c*) 145 (*d*) 150

20. What is the total export (in crore rupees) in the given years?
(*a*) 3700
(*b*) 3900
(*c*) 3950
(*d*) 4100

ANSWERS

1	2	3	4	5	6	7	8	9	10
(*a*)	(*b*)	(*c*)	(*b*)	(*a*)	(*d*)	(*c*)	(*c*)	(*b*)	(*b*)
11	**12**	**13**	**14**	**15**	**16**	**17**	**18**	**19**	**20**
(*a*)	(*c*)	(*d*)	(*d*)	(*a*)	(*b*)	(*d*)	(*a*)	(*b*)	(*a*)

SOME SELECTED EXPLANATORY ANSWERS

1. Downstream speed = 10 + 4 = 14 km/hr.
Upstream speed = 10 – 4 = 6 km/hr.
Hence, their average speed

$$= \frac{x+x}{\frac{x}{14}+\frac{x}{6}} = \frac{2x}{5x/21} = \frac{42}{5} = 8.4 \text{ km/hr.}$$

Since, average speed of cyclist (12 km/hr) > average speed of boat sailor (8.4 km/hr). Therefore, the cyclist will return to A first.

2.

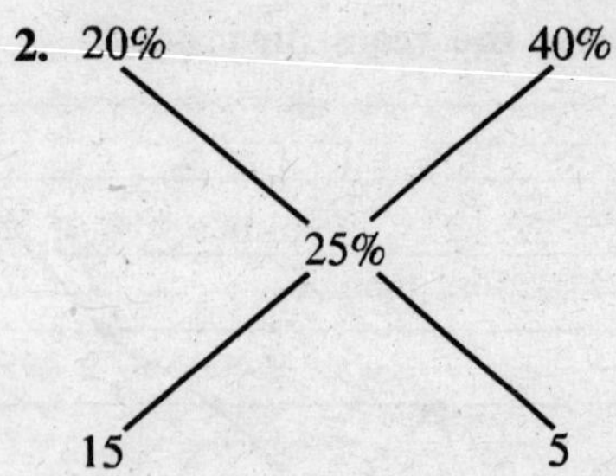

or 3 : 1

Quantity sold at 20% profit

$$= \frac{3}{3+1} \times 50 = 37.5 \text{ kgs.}$$

Quantity sold at 40% profit
= (50 – 37.5) = 12.5 kgs.

3. Favourable cases = 6
Total cases = 6^3= 216

$$\text{P(same number on three dice)} = \frac{6}{216} = \frac{1}{36}.$$

4. For Company A,
The amount received by Samir in 2008

$$= 10000\left(1+\frac{11.5}{100}\right)\left(1+\frac{15}{100}\right)$$

$$= 10{,}000 \times \frac{223}{200} \times \frac{23}{20} = ₹\ 12822.50$$

Hence, their interest = 12822.50 – 10000 = ₹ 2822.50

For Company B,
The amount received by Samir in 2008

$$= 10{,}000\left(1+\frac{13.5}{100}\right)\left(1+\frac{14}{100}\right)$$

$$= 10{,}000 \times \frac{227}{200} \times \frac{57}{50} = ₹\ 12939$$

Since, their interest = 12939 – 10000 = ₹ 2939
Hence, difference between the interests earned = 2939 – 2822.50 = ₹ 116.50
If Samir had invested the amount in company B for both years then he would get ₹ 116.50 more.

5.

CUR	WAP	DIR	.....(1)
red	little	boxes	
BIX	FAC	DIR	.....(2)
pile	of	boxes.	

So DIR = boxes

BIX	FAC	DIR	.....(2)
pile	of	boxes	
SUT	MAD	BIX	.....(3)
well	arrange	pile	

So BIX = pile
Thus of = FAC.

7. P = 1 – $(0.4)^3$ = 0.936.

9. Let, breadth = X metres . Then,
Height = 5 X metres
and length = 40 X metres
So, X + 5 X + 40 X = 12.8

$$\text{or} \quad X = \frac{12.8}{200} = \frac{128}{2000} = \frac{64}{1000}$$

So, X = 4 /10 m = (4/10 × 100) cm = 40 cm.

10. Trick : Percentage increase or decrease $= -30 \times 40 = -22 = 22\%$ decrease.

Note : Negative sign shows decrease and positive sign shows increase.

11. $2 \times 2 + 4 = 8$
$8 \times 2 + 4 = 20$
$20 \times 2 + 4 = 44$ — $\boxed{48}$
$44 \times 2 + 4 = 92$
$92 \times 2 + 4 = 188$
$188 \times 2 + 4 = 380$

12. Rate of change in the amount of production in the year 2004 over the year 2003

$$= \frac{35-30}{30} \times 100 = 16.67\%$$

Rate of change in the amount of production in the year 2006 over the year 2005

$$= \frac{(25-20)}{20} \times 100 = 25\%$$

Rate of change in the amount of production in the year 2008 over the year 2007

$$= \frac{(30-15)}{15} \times 100 = 100\%$$

Rate of change in the amount of production in the year 2007 over the year 2006

$$= \frac{(25-15)}{15} \times 100 = 66.67\%$$

Hence, it is clear that the rate of change in the amount of production during the consecutive years 2007 and 2008 is at the highest level.

14. Here, $\frac{1}{3}\pi r^2 \times 24 = 1232$

$$\Rightarrow r^2 = \frac{1232 \times 7}{22 \times 8} = 7 \times 7 \quad \therefore \quad r = 7 \text{ cm}$$

Hence, curved surface area of the cone

$$= \frac{22}{7} \times 7 \times \sqrt{7^2 + 24^2} = 22 \times 25 = 550 \text{ cm}^2.$$

16.

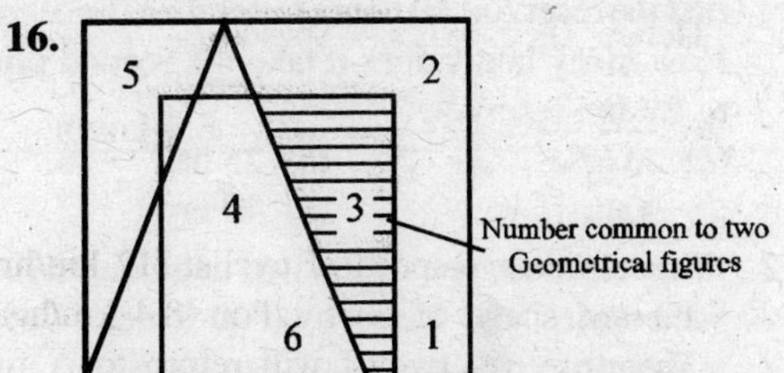

17. In the given dice, the numbers adjacent to 2 are 6, 3, 1 and 4. The only number that can be opposite to the side 2 is 5.

18. From O to the left is the minus sign of X and X is 2 point less than Y.

19. Required percentage $= \frac{600}{450} \times 100 = \frac{400}{3}$

$= 133.33\% \approx 135\%$.

20. Total export in given years = ₹ (300 + 200 + 600 + 450 + 600 + 700 + 850) crores = ₹ 3700 crores.

SET-7

CSIR-UGC (NET) JRF & LECTURESHIP EXAM

PART-A

1. If two pipes function simultaneously, the reservoir will be filled in 12 hours. One pipe fills the reservoir 10 hours faster than the other. How many hours does it take the second pipe to fill the reservoir?

(*a*) 20 hrs. (*b*) 25 hrs.
(*c*) 30 hrs. (*d*) 40 hrs.

2. In an election, one of the two candidates gets 40% votes and loses by 100 votes. Total number of votes is :

(*a*) 500 (*b*) 400
(*c*) 600 (*d*) 1000

Directions (Q. 3) : *The figure marked (X) is folded to produce different box patterns. Study the pattern to know if they can be produced from figure (X) and select the answer from the alternatives.*

3. (X)

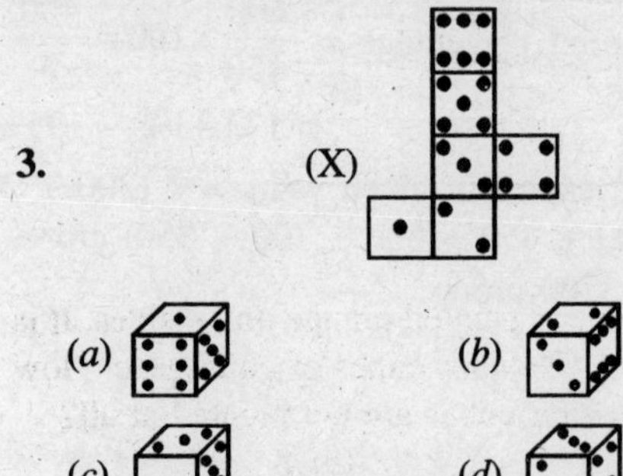

4. The odds in favour of A solving a problem are 3 to 4 and the odds against B solving the same problem are 5 to 7. If they both try the problem, the probability that the problem is solved is :

(*a*) 41/84 (*b*) 16/21
(*c*) 5/21 (*d*) 1/4

Directions (Q. 5) : *In the question given below, the question is followed by two statements.*

Mark (*a*) if statement I alone is sufficient but statement II alone is not sufficient.
Mark (*b*) if statement II alone is sufficient but statement I alone is not sufficient.
Mark (*c*) if both statement I and II together are sufficient but neither of them is not sufficient if considered alone.
Mark (*d*) if each statement, if considered alone, is sufficient.

5. In the figure alongside, QRS is a straight line and line TR bisects ∠PRS. Is TR parallel to PQ?

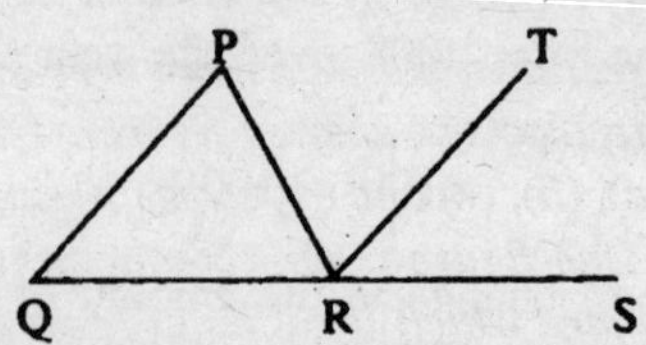

I. PQ = PR
II. QR = PR

6. A cricket team of 11 players is to be selected from 13 players; 4 of which are bowlers and 2 wicket keepers. The number of ways to select the team, consisting one wicket keeper and at least 3 bowlers, is:

(*a*) 8
(*b*) 22
(*c*) 112
(*d*) None of these

Directions (Q. 7) : *In the question given below, there are three rows of figures with one figure missing from the third row. Study the pattern of figures in the rows and columns and find out the missing figure from the alternative figures that shall complete the figure matrix.*

7.

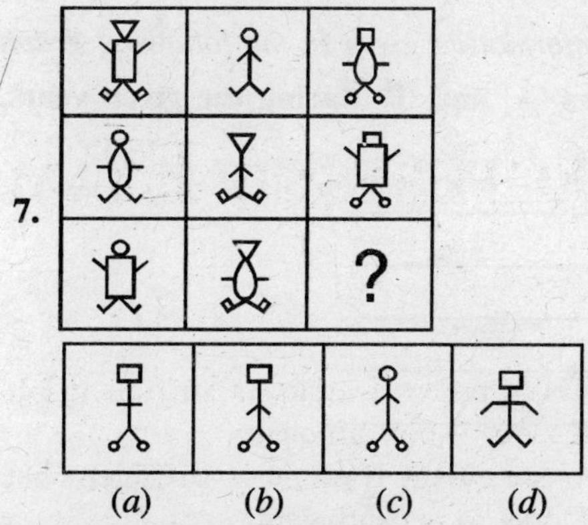

(*a*) (*b*) (*c*) (*d*)

Directions (Q. 8) : *Read the following statements and answer the question given below :*

Raghu and Gyan are good at cricket and hockey. Sohan and Gyan are good at hockey and chess. Raghu and Govind are good at swimming and cricket,

8. Who is good at swimming, hockey and cricket?

(*a*) Raghu (*b*) Sohan

(*c*) Govind (*d*) Gyan

Directions (Q. 9) : *In the question that follows, some problem figures have been given. Problem figures themselves are also the answer figures. Out of the four figures (a), (b), (c) and (d) three are similar in a certain way. One figure is not like the other three. Choose the figure which is different from the rest.*

9.

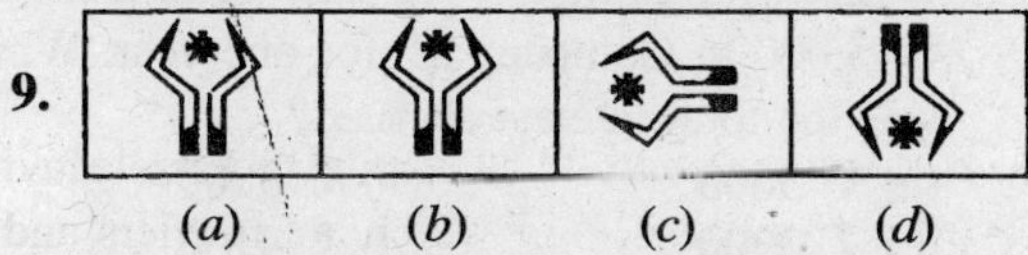

(*a*) (*b*) (*c*) (*d*)

10. Raju's average daily expenditure is ₹ 15 during September, ₹ 20 during October and ₹ 13 during November. What is the average daily expenditure for the three months?

(*a*) ₹ 16 approximately

(*b*) ₹ 18 approximately

(*c*) ₹ 19.50 approximately

(*d*) ₹ 17 approximately

Directions (Q. 11): *In this question a number series is given, followed by four alternatives. One term/element of the given series is wrong, i.e., it does not conform to the rule used in writing the series. This wrong term is depicted in the following alternatives. Spot out that wrong term/element and mark your answer.*

11. 3, 18, 38, 78, 123, 178, 24

(*a*) 3 (*b*) 18

(*c*) 123 (*d*) 178

12. The angle of elevation of the top of two vertical towers as seen from the middle point of the line joining the foot of the towers are 60° and 30° respectively. The ratio of the heights of the towers is:

(*a*) 2 : 1 (*b*) $\sqrt{3}$: 1

(*c*) 3 : 2 (*d*) 3 : 1

13. The number of rectangles in this figure are.

(*a*) 21

(*b*) 24

(*c*) 23

(*d*) 25

14. The difference between 89% of a number and 73% of the same number is 448. What is 49% of that number?

(*a*) 1124 (*b*) 1218

(*c*) 1372 (*d*) 1426

15. Three cards are drawn successively with replacement. The probability of selecting 2 aces and one king is :

(*a*) $1/\{(13)^2 \times 17\}$ (*b*) $1/(13)^3$

(*c*) $3/(13)^3$ (*d*) None of these

16.

14	12	7
8	?	16
11	12	10

(*a*) 6 (*b*) 12

(*c*) 9 (*d*) 10

17. A toy cube is painted orange on all sides. It is cut into 64 smaller cubes of equal size. How many smaller cubes are not painted at all?

(*a*) 4 (*b*) 8

(*c*) 16 (*d*) 20

18. Turkey carpet and oilcloth

In the centre of a room of 10 square metres, there is a square of turkey carpet, and the rest of the floor is covered with oilcloth. The carpet, and the oilcloth cost respectively ₹ 15 and ₹ 6.50 per square metre, and the total cost of the carpet and the oilcloth is ₹ 1338.50. Find the width of the oilcloth border.

(*a*) 2 dm (*b*) 3 dm

(*c*) 4 dm (*d*) 5 dm

Directions (Qs. 19 and 20): *These questions are based on the information given in the following graph.*

Rates of interest per cent per annum given by two companies 'A' and 'B' during the given years.

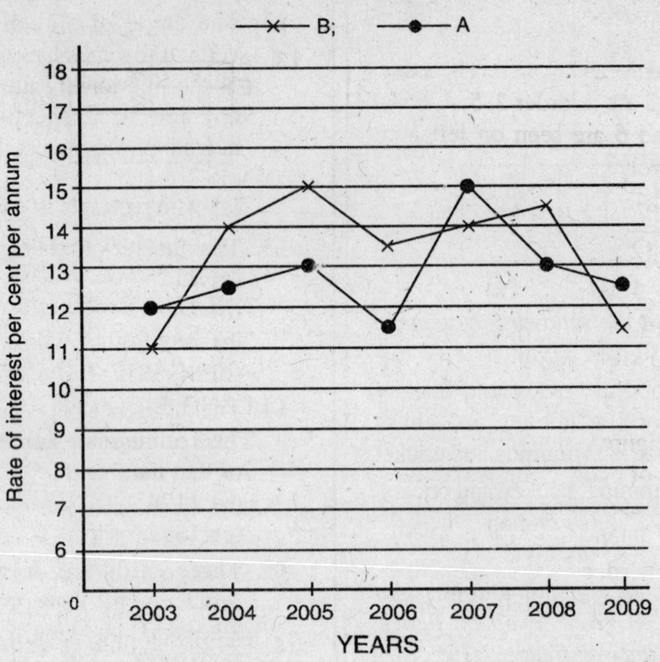

19. Samir invested ₹ 10,000 in the company 'A' for one year in 2006. He reinvested the total amount along with interest for next one year in 2007. If he had invested for both years in the Company 'B', what would have been the difference between the interests earned?

(*a*) ₹ 16.50 less (*b*) ₹ 116.50 more (*c*) ₹ 128.50 less (*d*) ₹ 128.50 more

20. In 2007, Saurabh invested an amount of ₹ 12000 in Company 'A' and an amount of ₹ 15,000 in Company 'B' for one year. What was the total interest accrued?

(*a*) ₹ 3600 (*b*) ₹ 3800 (*c*) ₹ 3900 (*d*) ₹ 4100

ANSWERS

1	2	3	4	5	6	7	8	9	10
(*c*)	(*a*)	(*d*)	(*b*)	(*b*)	(*b*)	(*b*)	(*a*)	(*a*)	(*a*)
11	**12**	**13**	**14**	**15**	**16**	**17**	**18**	**19**	**20**
(*d*)	(*d*)	(*c*)	(*c*)	(*c*)	(*c*)	(*b*)	(*d*)	(*b*)	(*c*)

SOME SELECTED EXPLANATORY ANSWERS

1. Let $(x - 10)$ and x hrs be the time taken by two pipes to fill the reservoir, then,

$$\frac{1}{x-10} + \frac{1}{x} = \frac{1}{12} \Rightarrow \frac{2x-10}{x^2-10x} = \frac{1}{12}$$

$$\Rightarrow x^2 - 34x + 120 = 0$$

$$\Rightarrow (x - 30)(x - 4) = 0$$

$\therefore$ $x = 30$ (Taking 30 only).

Hence, second pipe will fill the reservoir in 30 hours.

2. Out of 100, difference in votes = (60 – 40) = 20

20% of x = 100

$\therefore \quad x = \dfrac{100 \times 100}{20} = 500.$

3. The given figure is same as layout 4. The sides adjacent to top side 3 are in order 2, 5, 4, 6 — of these sides, 4 and 6 are seen on left and right sides respectively.

4. $P(A) = \dfrac{3}{7}, \quad P(B) = \dfrac{7}{12}$

$P(\overline{A}) = \dfrac{4}{7}, \quad P(\overline{B}) = \dfrac{5}{12}$

$\therefore P(A \cup B) = 1 - \dfrac{4}{7} \times \dfrac{5}{12} = \dfrac{16}{21}.$

7. Each row contains figures containing 3 forms of head and 3 forms of body, 3 forms of hands and 3 forms of legs used only once. In third row the forms left out for the third column figure are: a square head, a straight line body, lowered hands and circled legs. Option (*b*) fits the requirement.

10. Average daily expenditure

$= \dfrac{\text{The total expenditure}}{\text{Total days}}$

$= \dfrac{15 \times 30 + 20 \times 31 + 13 \times 30}{30 + 31 + 30}$

= ₹ 16 (approximately).

11. In the given sequence 3 is the only term which is a prime number. Therefore, alternative (*a*) consists of the wrong term.

12. Let AB and CD be two towers of heights h_1 and h_2 respectively and O the mid-point of the line joining the foots A and C of the towers.

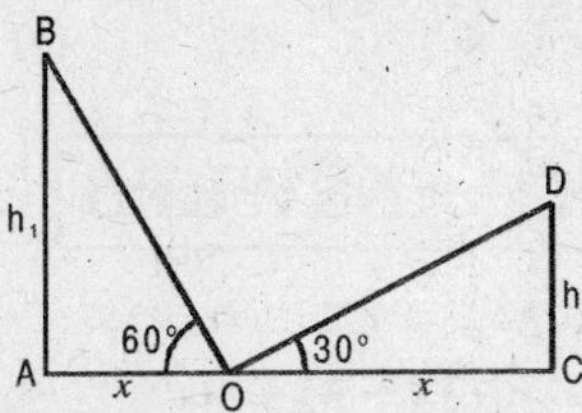

Let OA = OC = x

Then $h_1 = x \tan 60° = x\sqrt{3}$

and $h_2 = x \tan 30° = x/\sqrt{3}$

$\therefore \quad \dfrac{h_1}{h_2} = \dfrac{3}{1}$, Hence, $h_1 : h_2 = 3 : 1.$

13.

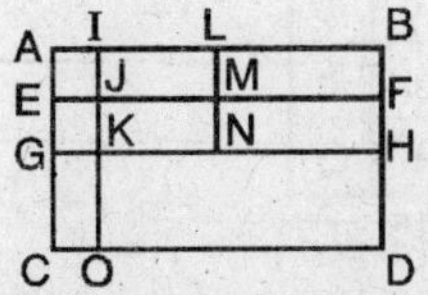

The main rectangle is ABCD *i.e.*, 1 rectangle.

The simplest rectangles are AIEJ, ILJM, LBMF, EJGK, JMKN, MFNH, GKCO and KHOD *i.e.* 8 rectangles.

The rectangles which have two parts are ALEM, IBJF, EMGN, JFKH, AIGK, IKLN, LBNH, EJCO and GHCD *i.e.* 9 rectangles.

The rectangles which have three parts are AICO, ABEF and EFGH *i.e.* 3 rectangles.

The rectangles which have four parts are ALGN and IBKH *i.e.* 2 rectangles.

So, the total number of rectangles

1 + 8 + 9 + 3 + 2 = 23.

14. Let the number be x; then

$(89 - 73) \times \dfrac{x}{100} = 448$

$\therefore \quad x = \dfrac{448 \times 100}{16} = 2800$

49% of 2800 = $\dfrac{49}{100} \times 2800 = 1372.$

15. $P(\text{ace}) = \dfrac{4}{52} = \dfrac{1}{13} \quad P(\text{king}) = \dfrac{4}{52} = \dfrac{1}{13}$

P (2 aces and one king)

$= {}^3C_2 \cdot \left(\dfrac{1}{13}\right)^2 \left(\dfrac{1}{13}\right) = \dfrac{3}{(13)^3}.$

16. Sum of the given numbers in row and in column is 33.

17. The smaller 64 pieces will be cut in the manner that :

1. 8 pieces will be painted on 3 sides,
2. 24 pieces on 2 sides.
3. 24 pieces on 1 side, and
4. 8 will not have paint at all.

Diagrammatically, the explanation taking one side of the cube will be :

a	b	b	a
b	c	c	b
b	c	c	b
a	b	b	a

1. 'a' are the corner pieces [$4 \times 2 = 8$]
2. 'b' are the centre pieces of the cornered sides [$8 \times 3 = 24$]
3. 'c' are the centre pieces [$4 \times 6 = 24$]
4. Remaining interior pieces
   $= 64 - (8 + 24 + 24)$
   $= 64 - 56 = 8.$

18. The area of the square room = 100 sq. metres

The mean cost per sq. metre = ₹ 1338.50
= ₹ 13.385

Carpet		Oilcloth
15		6.50
	13.385	
6.885		1.615

= 81 : 19

By the Allegation Rule, the area of the square is 81 sq. metres.

Therefore, the carpet is 9 metres both in length and breadth.

But the room is 10 metres in length and breadth.

Hence double the width of the border is (10 – 9) or 1 metre.

So, the width of the border = 1/2 metre = 5 dm.

19. For Company A,

The amount received by Samir in 2008

$$= 10000\left(1+\frac{11.5}{100}\right)\left(1+\frac{15}{100}\right)$$

$$= 10,000 \times \frac{223}{200} \times \frac{23}{20} = ₹\ 12822.50$$

Hence, their interest = 12822.50 – 10000 = ₹ 2822.50

For Company B,

The amount received by Samir in 2008

$$= 10,000\left(1+\frac{13.5}{100}\right)\left(1+\frac{14}{100}\right)$$

$$= 10,000 \times \frac{227}{200} \times \frac{57}{50} = ₹\ 12939$$

Since, their interest = 12939 – 10000 = ₹ 2939

Hence, difference between the interests earned = 2939 – 2822.50 = ₹ 116.50

If Samir had invested the amount in company B for both years then he would get ₹ 116.50 more.

20. Total interests accrued by Saurabh

$$= \frac{12000 \times 15 \times 1}{100} + \frac{15000 \times 14 \times 1}{100}$$

= 1800 + 2100 = ₹ 3900

SET-8

CSIR-UGC (NET) JRF & LECTURESHIP EXAM

PART-A

1. 400 persons working 9 hours a day complete $\frac{1}{4}$th of the work in 10 days. Find the number of additional persons, working 8 hours per day required to complete the remaining work in 20 days.

(*a*) 275 (*b*) 200
(*c*) 225 (*d*) 250

2. If the income tax is decreased by 26%, a man's net income increases by $\frac{2}{3}\%$. The rate of income tax is:

(*a*) $3\frac{1}{2}\%$ (*b*) $2\frac{1}{2}\%$
(*c*) $1\frac{1}{2}\%$ (*d*) 3%

3. The average of four consecutive even numbers is 27. The largest of these numbers is

(*a*) 36 (*b*) 32
(*c*) 30 (*d*) 28

4. Cards are drawn from a pack of 52 cards one by one. The probability that exactly 10 cards will be drawn before the first ace is :

(*a*) 241/1456 (*b*) 164/4165
(*c*) 451/884 (*d*) None of these

Directions (Q. 5) : *In the question given below, the question is followed by two statements.*

Mark (*a*) if statement I alone is sufficient but statement II alone is not sufficient.

Mark (*b*) if statement II alone is sufficient but statement I alone is not sufficient.

Mark (*c*) if both statement I and II together are sufficient but neither of them is not sufficient if considered alone.

Mark (*d*) if statement I and II together are not sufficient.

5. Is the radius of circle wiuh centre O a whole number?

I. The circumference of the circle is 12π.

II. The ratio of the circumference of the circle to the area of this circle is 1/4.

6. Jaya ranks 5th in a class of 53. What is her rank from the bottom in the class?

(*a*) 49th (*b*) 48th
(*c*) 47th (*d*) 50th

Directions (Q. 7) : *In the question given below, there are three rows of figures with one figure missing from the third row. Study the pattern of figures in the rows and columns and find out the missing figure from the alternative figures that shall complete the figure matrix.*

7.

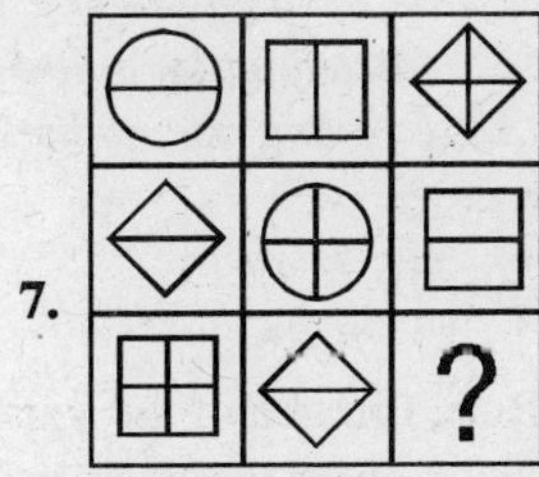

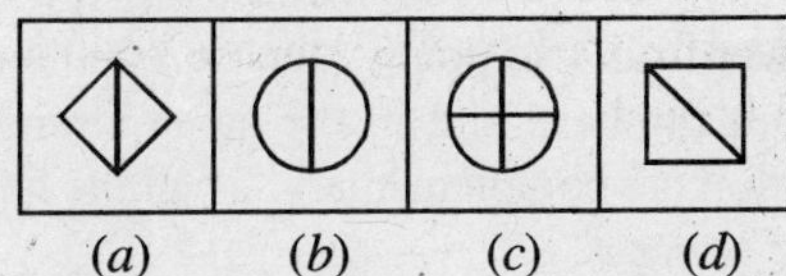

(*a*) (*b*) (*c*) (*d*)

Directions (Q. 8) : *Read the following directions and answer the question given below :*

There are five persons in a group. Out of these two are men. Only three persons know swimming, of which one is a man. There is a couple, of which the husband knows swimming. A is the younger sister of D and B is the husband of E. C is a swimming champion.

8. Who is the other man in the group?

(*a*) C (*b*) B

(*c*) A (*d*) D

Directions (Q. 9) : *In the question that follows, some problem figures have been given. Problem figures themselves are also the answer figures. Out of the four figures (a), (b), (c) and (d), three are similar in a certain way. One figure is not like the other three. Choose the figure which is different from the rest.*

9. 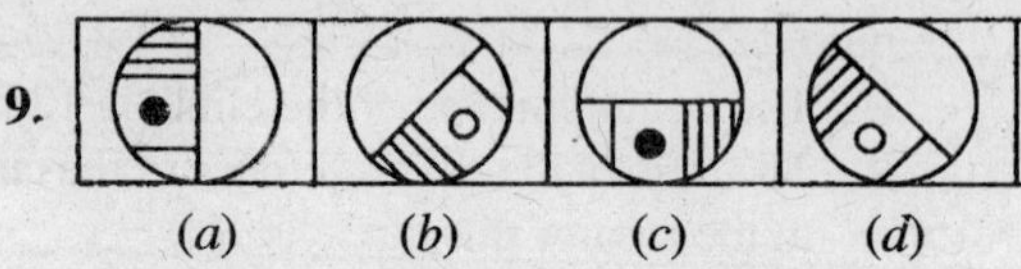

(*a*) (*b*) (*c*) (*d*)

10. If difference between the age of Ritu and Ram is 15 years and ratio of their ages is 3 : 2, then the age of Ram is :

(*a*) 25 years

(*b*) 20 years

(*c*) 28 years

(*d*) 30 years

Directions (Q. 11) : *In this question a number series is given, followed by four alternatives. One term/element of the given series is wrong, i.e., it does not conform to the rule used in writing the series. This wrong term is depicted in the following alternatives. Spot out that wrong term/element and mark your answer.*

11. 1, 6, 16, 26, 76, 156, 316

(*a*) 316 (*b*) 26

(*c*) 1 (*d*) 156

12. The angles of elevation of the top of a vertical tower from two points, distant *a* and *b* ($a > b$) from the base and in the same straight line with it are complementary. Then the height of the tower is:

(*a*) $\sqrt{(ab)}$ (*b*) $\sqrt{(a^2+b^2)}$

(*c*) $\sqrt{(a^2-b^2)}$ (*d*) $\sqrt{a(a-b)}$

13. How many triangles are there in this figure?

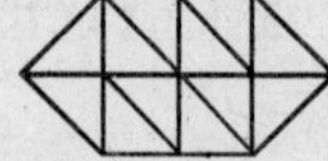

(*a*) 16 (*b*) 17

(*c*) 18 (*d*) 19

14. Nupur invests ₹ 89856, that is 26% of her annual income in mutual funds. What is her monthly income?

(*a*) ₹ 23980.50

(*b*) ₹ 28800

(*c*) ₹ 28990

(*d*) ₹ 33606.25

15. Three identical dice are rolled. The probability that the same number will appear on each of them is :

(*a*) 1/6

(*b*) 1/18

(*c*) 1/36

(*d*) None of these

16. Which one number can be placed at the sign (?) of interrogation?

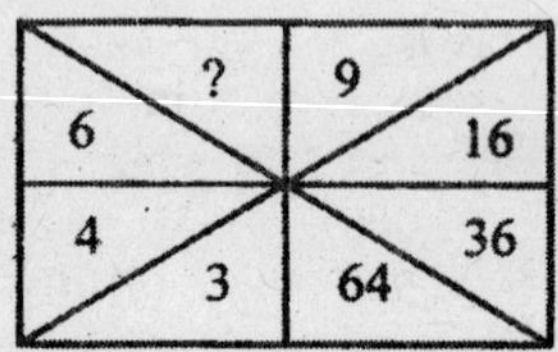

(*a*) 12 (*b*) 6

(*c*) 8 (*d*) 4

Directions (Q. 17) : *The question is based on the following statement :*

A cube is painted red on two adjacent faces, yellow on two opposite faces and green on the remaining faces. It is cut into 64 smaller cubes of equal size.

17. How many cubes are painted on two faces only and that too with the same colour?

(*a*) 0 (*b*) 4

(*c*) 8 (*d*) 16

18. A room 8 metres long, 6 metres broad and 3 metres high has two windows.

$1\frac{1}{2}$ m × 1 m and a door 2 m × $1\frac{1}{2}$ m

Find the cost of papering the walls with paper 50 cm wide at 25 p. per metre.

(*a*) ₹ 28 (*b*) ₹ 30

(*c*) ₹ 39 (*d*) ₹ 42

Directions (Qs. 19 and 20): *Study the following graph carefully and answer the questions given below it.*

Per cent profit earned by two Companies A and B over the years

Profit = Income – Expenditure

$$\text{Profit\%} = \frac{\text{Profit}}{\text{Expenditure}} \times 100$$

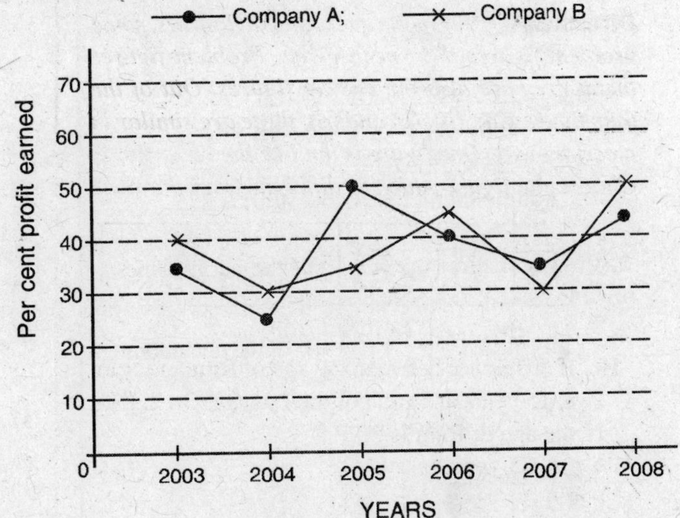

19. If the income of A in 2005 was ₹ 1,42,500, what was his expenditure in that year?

(*a*) ₹ 95,000 (*b*) ₹ 95,500

(*c*) ₹ 99,500 (*d*) ₹ 1,05,000

20. Expenditure of Company 'B' in 2006 was 90% of its expenditure in 2005. Income of Company 'B' in 2006 was what per cent of its income in 2005?

(*a*) $96\frac{2}{3}$ (*b*) $99\frac{1}{3}$

(*c*) 121.5 (*d*) 130.5

ANSWERS

1	**2**	**3**	**4**	**5**	**6**	**7**	**8**	**9**	**10**
(*a*)	(*b*)	(*c*)	(*b*)	(*d*)	(*a*)	(*b*)	(*d*)	(*a*)	(*d*)
11	**12**	**13**	**14**	**15**	**16**	**17**	**18**	**19**	**20**
(*b*)	(*a*)	(*a*)	(*b*)	(*c*)	(*c*)	(*b*)	(*c*)	(*a*)	(*a*)

SOME SELECTED EXPLANATORY ANSWERS

1. Here, work done $= \frac{1}{4}$th part

$\therefore$ Remaining work $= \left(1 - \frac{1}{4}\right) = \frac{3}{4}$

We have to find the number of additional men required, hence we shall compare each other item with the number of men.

Less hours per day, more men required (Indirect proportion)

More work, more men required (Direct proportion)

More days, less men required (Indirect proportion).

Work	Days	Hours/day	Men
$\frac{1}{4}$ ↓	10 ↑	9 ↑	400 ↓
$\frac{3}{4}$	20	8	x

Since, $\frac{x}{400} = \frac{3/4}{1/4} \times \frac{10}{20} \times \frac{9}{8} = \frac{27}{16}$

$\Rightarrow \quad x = 25 \times 27 = 675$

$\therefore$ Additional men = (675 – 400) = 275.

2. 26% of income tax = $\frac{2}{3}$% of the net income

$\therefore$ Income tax = $\left[\frac{2}{3} \times \frac{100}{26}\right]$% of the net income

$= \frac{100}{39}$% of the net income

Let net income = ₹ 3900

$\therefore$ Income tax $= 3900 \times \frac{100}{39 \times 100}$ = ₹ 100

$\Rightarrow$ Gross income = ₹ 3900 + ₹ 100 = ₹ 4000

$\therefore$ Rate % of income tax = $\left(\frac{100}{4000} \times 100\right)$%

$= 2\frac{1}{2}$%.

3. Let four consecutive even numbers are $x, x+2, x+4, x+6$

According to question,

$$\frac{x+x+2+x+4+x+6}{4} = 27$$

$$\Rightarrow \quad \frac{4x+12}{4} = 27$$

$$4x = 108 - 12$$

$$x = \frac{96}{4} = 24$$

Hence, the largest number $= x + 6 = 24 + 6 = 30$

4. P{(first 10 draws non-ace cards) (11th ace)}

$$= \frac{^{48}C_{10}}{^{52}C_{10}} \times \frac{4}{42} = \frac{164}{4165}.$$

7. Each row contains a circle, a square and a rhombus and either of the two are divided into two parts while the remaining one is divided into four equal parts.

10. Let Ritu's age = $3x$ years

Ram's age = $2x$ years

According to the question,

$$3x - 2x = 15$$

$$x = 15$$

$\therefore$ Ram's age = 2 × 15 = 30 years

11.

$1 \times 2 + 4 = 6$

$6 \times 2 + 4 = 16$

$16 \times 2 + 4 = 36$ — $\boxed{26}$

$36 \times 2 + 4 = 76$

$76 \times 2 + 4 = 156$

$156 \times 2 + 4 = 316$

12. Let CD = h unit be the height of the tower and A and B be the two points on the ground, such that DA = a; DB = b; $\angle$ DAC = α and $\angle$DBC = 90° – α

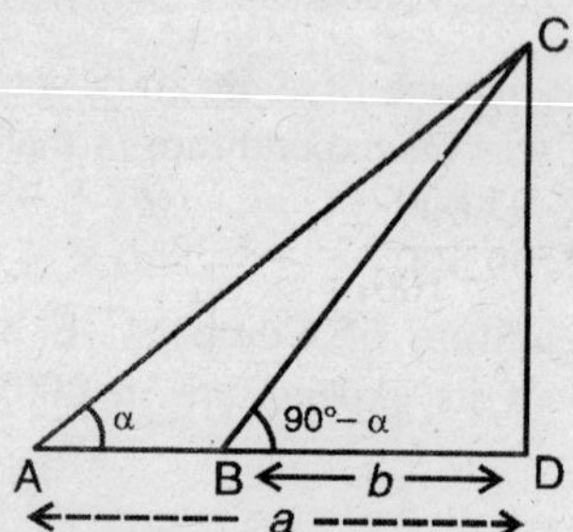

From right triangle ADC,

CD = $h = a \tan\alpha$ ...(*i*)

From right triangle BDC,

CD = $h = b \tan(90° - \alpha) = b \cot\alpha$ ...(*ii*)

Multiplying equations (*i*) and (*ii*), we get

$h^2 = a \tan\alpha \cdot b\cot\alpha$ Hence, $h = \sqrt{ab}$.

13.

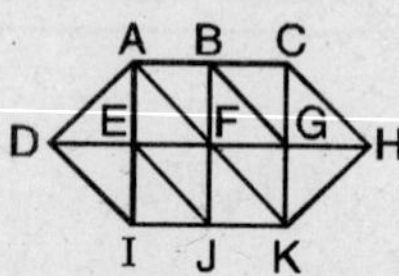

The simplest triangles are ADE, DEI, AEF, ABF, EIJ, EFJ, BFG, BCG, FJK, FGK, CGH and GHK – *i.e.,* – 12 triangles

The bisected triangles are ADI and CHK *i.e.* 2 triangles

Other triangles are AIK and ACK *i.e.*, 2 triangles

So, the total number of triangles is
$12+2+2=16.$

14. Let the Nupur's monthly income = ₹ x, then

$$\frac{26}{100}\times x=\frac{89856}{12}$$

$$\therefore\ x=\frac{7488\times 100}{26}=₹\,28800.$$

15. Favourable cases = 6
Total cases = $6^3 = 216$

$$P(\text{same number on three dice})=\frac{6}{216}=\frac{1}{36}.$$

16. $9=(3)^2$, $16=(4)^2$, $36=(6)^2$ and $64=(8)^2$.

18. Area of walls = 2(8 + 6) 3 = 84 sq.m
Area of two windows and door

$=2\times 1\frac{1}{2}\times 1+2\times 1\frac{1}{2}=6$ sq. m

Area to be covered = 84 – 6 = 78 sq.m

$$\text{So, length of paper}=\frac{78\times 100\text{ m}}{50}=156\text{ m}$$

$$\text{So, cost}=\frac{156\times 25}{100}=₹\,39.$$

19. Let expenditure of Company A in 2005 = ₹ x; then

$$x+\frac{50}{100}\times x=1\,42{,}500\ \Rightarrow\ \frac{3x}{2}=1{,}42{,}500$$

$$\therefore\ x=\frac{2\times 1{,}42{,}500}{3}=₹\,95000.$$

20. Let expenditure of Company B in 2005 = ₹ x; then

$$I_1\ (\text{Income})=x+\frac{35}{100}x=₹\frac{27x}{20}$$

Since, expenditure of Company B in 2006

$$=\frac{90}{100}\times ₹\,x=₹\,\frac{9x}{10},\ \text{then}$$

$$I_2\ (\text{Income})=\frac{9x}{10}+\frac{45}{100}\times\frac{9x}{10}=\frac{9x}{10}+\frac{81x}{200}$$

$$=₹\,\frac{261x}{200}$$

Hence, required percentage

$$=\frac{261x/200}{27x/20}\times 100=\frac{290}{3}=96\frac{2}{3}\%.$$

SET-9

CSIR-UGC (NET) JRF & LECTURESHIP EXAM

PART-A

1. The ratio of ages of Namrata and Divya is 4 : 3. The sum of their ages is 28 years. The ratio of their ages after 4 years will be:

(*a*) 3 : 4 (*b*) 5 : 4
(*c*) 5 : 6 (*d*) 6 : 5

2. If the price of a television set is increased by 25%, then by what percentage should the new price be reduced to bring the price back to original level?

(*a*) 15% (*b*) 20%
(*c*) 25% (*d*) 30%

Directions (Q. 3) : *The figure marked (X) is folded to produce different box patterns. Study the pattern to know if they can be produced from figure (X) and select the answer from the alternatives.*

3. (X)

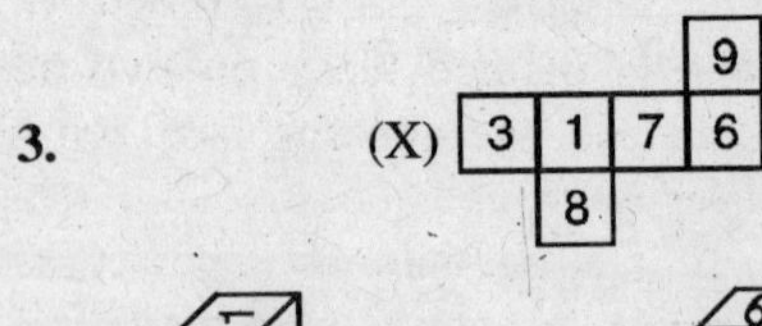

(*a*) (*b*)

(*c*) (*d*)

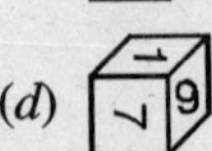

4. From eighty cards numbered 1 to 80, two cards are selected randomly. The probability that both the cards have the numbers divisible by 4 is given by :

(*a*) 21/316 (*b*) 19/316
(*c*) 1/4 (*d*) None of these

Directions (Q. 5) : *In the question given below, the question is followed by two statements.*

Mark (*a*) if statement I alone is sufficient but statement II alone is not sufficient.

Mark (*b*) if statement II alone is sufficient but statement I alone is not sufficient.

Mark (*c*) if both statement I and II together are sufficient but neither of them is not sufficient if considered alone.

Mark (*d*) if each statement, if considered alone, is sufficient.

5. If n and k are even integers, is $\frac{n}{3}+\frac{k}{2}$ an integer?

I. n is a multiple of 3.
II. k is a multiple of 4.

6. In a queue, Sadiq is 14th from the front and Joseph is 17th from the end, while Jane is in between Sadiq and Joseph. If Sadiq be ahead of Joseph and there be 48 persons in the queue, how many persons are there between Sadiq and Jane?

(*a*) 5 (*b*) 6
(*c*) 7 (*d*) 8

7. Which of the following conclusions is logically valid based on statement given below?

Statement : Most teachers are hard working.

Conclusion :

(*i*) Some teachers are hard working.
(*ii*) Some teachers are not hard working.

(*a*) Only (*i*) is implied
(*b*) Only (*ii*) is implied
(*c*) Both (*i*) and (*ii*) are implied
(*d*) Neither (*i*) nor (*ii*) is implied

8. A and D study in the same class. K and L study in the same class. In which class does D study? To answer the above question, which of the following informations given in the statements A and B is/are necessary?

(A) D studies one standard below L.

(B) A's elder brother studies with K.
(*a*) Both A and B together are not sufficient
(*b*) Only A is sufficient
(*c*) Only B is sufficient
(*d*) Either A or B is sufficient

Directions (Q. 9) : *In the question that follows, some problem figures have been given. Problem figures themselves are also the answer figures. Out of the four figures (a), (b), (c) and (d), three are similar in a certain way. One figure is not like the other three. Choose the figure which is different from the rest.*

9. 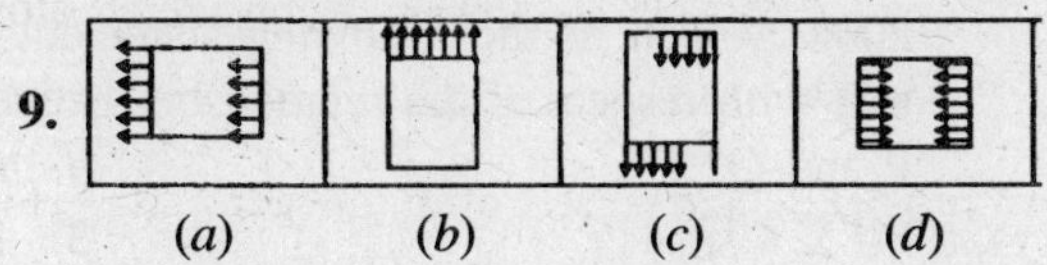

(*a*) (*b*) (*c*) (*d*)

10. The average score of a cricketer for 10 matches is 49.9 runs. If the average for the first six matches is 49, then what is average score for the last 4 matches?
(*a*) 48.7
(*b*) 49.8
(*c*) 46.4
(*d*) None of these

Directions (Q. 11): *In this question a number series is given, followed by four alternatives. One term/element of the given series is wrong, i.e., it does not conform to the rule used in writing the series. This wrong term is depicted in the following alternatives. Spot out that wrong term/element and mark your answer.*

11. 1, 4, 7, 11, 16, 22, 29
(*a*) 4 (*b*) 11
(*c*) 22 (*d*) 1

12. A vertical pole is 75 m high. Find the angle subtended by the pole at a point 75 m away from its base.
(*a*) 30° (*b*) 45°
(*c*) 60° (*d*) 90°

13. How many triangles are there in the figure given below?

(*a*) 24 (*b*) 27
(*c*) 25 (*d*) 26

14. 72% of the students of a certain class took Biology and 44% took Mathematics. If each student took at least one subject from Biology or Mathematics and 40 took both, then total number of students in the class is:
(*a*) 200 (*b*) 240
(*c*) 250 (*d*) 320

15. A five digit number is formed by the digits 1, 2, 3, 4, 5, 6 and 8. The probability that the number has even digits at both ends is :
(*a*) 2/7
(*b*) 3/7
(*c*) 4/7
(*d*) None of these

16. Select the right option which can be placed at the sign of interrogation?

4	8	20
9	3	15
6	6	?

(*a*) 24 (*b*) 16
(*c*) 20 (*d*) 18

17. A cube is painted black on two adjacent faces and on one opposite face, red on two opposite faces and green on the remaining face. If it is cut into 64 equal cubes, then how many cubes will have only one black coloured face?
(*a*) 32 (*b*) 16
(*c*) 12 (*d*) 8

18. A rectangular hall 12 m long and 10 m broad, is surrounded by a verandah 2 metres wide. Find the area of the verandah.

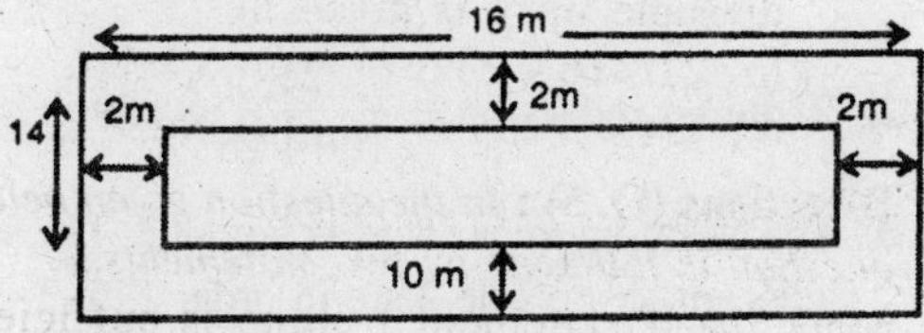

(*a*) 102 m^2
(*b*) 103 m^2
(*c*) 104 m^2
(*d*) 105 m^2

Directions (Qs. 19 and 20): *Study the following graph carefully and answer the questions given below it:*

Number of Tourist Hotels in a State

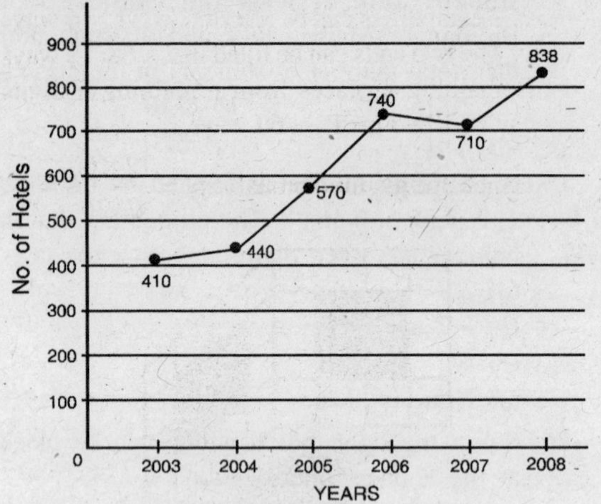

19. If in 2005 new hotels constructed were fewer by 10, what would have been the ratio between the new hotels constructed in 2004 and that constructed in 2005?

(*a*) 1 : 4
(*b*) 4 : 1
(*c*) 4 : 5
(*d*) 5 : 4

20. If P is the percentage increase in tourist hotels from 2005 to 2006 and Q is the percentage increase in the tourist hotels from 2006 to 2008. Which of the following statements is true with respect to the relationship between P and Q?

(*a*) P < Q
(*b*) P = Q
(*c*) P > Q
(*d*) None of these

ANSWERS

1	2	3	4	5	6	7	8	9	10
(*b*)	(*b*)	(*a*)	(*b*)	(*a*)	(*c*)	(*c*)	(*a*)	(*d*)	(*d*)
11	**12**	**13**	**14**	**15**	**16**	**17**	**18**	**19**	**20**
(*d*)	(*b*)	(*b*)	(*c*)	(*a*)	(*d*)	(*c*)	(*c*)	(*a*)	(*c*)

SOME SELECTED EXPLANATORY ANSWERS

1. Let the present ages of Namrata and Divya are $4x$ and $3x$ years respectively; then

$4x + 3x = 28 \quad \therefore \; x = 4$

Hence, their present ages are 16 and 12 years.

So, required ratio = (16 + 4) : (12 + 4)

= 20 : 16 = 5 : 4.

2. Required reduction = $\frac{25}{100+25} \times 100 = 20\%$.

3. The given figure is same as layout 3. The sides adjacent to top side 2 are in order 1, 5, 3, 6 — of these sides 1 and 5 are seen on left and right sides respectively.

4. Total ways = $^{80}C_2$

favourable ways = $^{20}C_2$

$$P = \frac{^{20}C_2}{^{80}C_2} = \frac{19}{316}.$$

8. There is no useful information in either of the two statements.

9. In all the figures except D the arrows point towards same direction.

10. Average Score = (10 × 49.9 – 6 × 49)/4 = 51.25 runs.

11. If first term of the series is replaced by 2 then difference between successive terms of the series will be in the order of 2, 3, 4, 5, 6, 7. Therefore, alternative (*d*) consists of the wrong term of the sequence.

12. Let AB = 75 m be the height of pole and C is a point on the ground such that BC = 75 m

Now, from right triangle ABC,

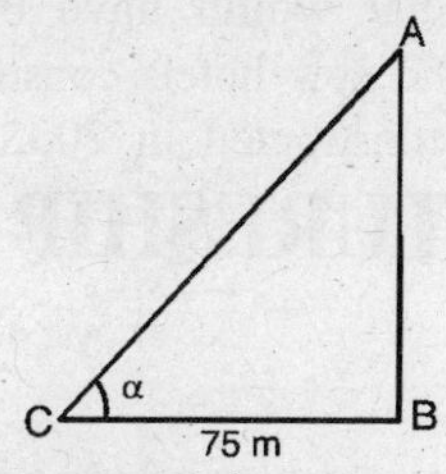

$$\tan\alpha = \frac{AB}{BC} = \frac{75}{75}$$

$\Rightarrow \quad \tan\alpha = 1 \quad \therefore \quad \alpha = 45°.$

13.

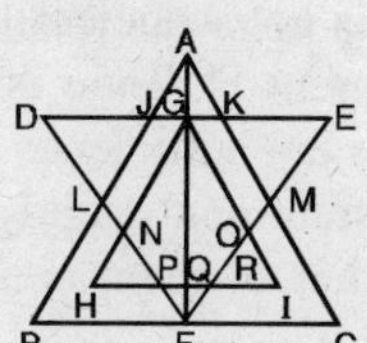

- The main triangles making the figure are ABC, DEF and GHI *i.e.,* 3 triangles
- The simplest triangles are AJG, AGK, KEM, DJL, NHP, PQF, QFR and ORI *i.e.,* 8 triangles
- The triangles formed by the bisecting line AF are ABF, AFC, GHQ, GQI, DGF and GFE *i.e.,* 6 triangles
- The triangles formed in-between the three triangles AJK, ALF, AMF, DGN, DGF, LBF, MFC, GEO, GNF and GOF *i.e.,* 10 triangles
- So, the total number of triangles is $3 + 8 + 6 + 10 = 27$.

14. Percentage of students who took both the subjects = (72 + 44) – 100 = 16%
Let total number of students = x
Now, 16% of $x = 40$

$$\therefore \quad x = \frac{40}{16} \times 100 = 250$$

15. Total number of 5 digit numbers obtained by the digits 1, 2, 3, 4, 5, 6 and 8.
$= {}^7P_5 = 7.6.5.4.3 = 2520$
There are 4 even digits (2, 4, 6 and 8).
$\therefore$ 2 even digits can be selected in ${}^4C_2 = 6$ ways
$\therefore$ The two ends can be filled in $2 \times 6 = 12$ ways
Remaining 3 places from remaining 5 digits can be filled in ${}^5P_3 = 60$ ways.

Hence, the required probability $= \dfrac{12 \times 60}{2520} = \dfrac{2}{7}$.

17.

Three faces of the cube are painted black and the rest are in different colours. If this cube is cut into 64 equal cubes, then only the 4 cubes in centre of one face will come out with only one black coloured face. So, the total number of one black coloured face small cubes will be $4 \times 3 = 12$.

18. Area of verandah = $16 \times 14 - 12 \times 10$
$= 204 - 120 = 104 \text{ m}^2$.

19. Required ratio = (440 – 410) : (570 – 10 – 440)
= 30 : 120 = 1 : 4.

20. Here, $P = \dfrac{740 - 570}{570} \times 100 = 29.8\%$

and also, $Q = \dfrac{838 - 740}{740} \times 100 = 13.2\%$

Hence, $P > Q$.

SET-10

CSIR-UGC (NET) JRF & LECTURESHIP EXAM

PART-A

1. The sum of digits of a three-digit number is 10 and the digit in the middle of this three digit number is equal to the sum of the remaining two digits. If the first and the third digits are interchanged, the value of this number increases by 99. Find the number.

(*a*) 385 (*b*) 253
(*c*) 154 (*d*) 374

2. If the rate of income tax is 5%, the net income of a person is ₹ 17100. If the rate of income tax is 6%, how much will be the net income?

(*a*) ₹ 15820 (*b*) ₹ 16920
(*c*) ₹ 17820 (*d*) ₹ 18920

Directions (Q. 3) : *The figure marked (X) is folded to produce different box patterns. Study the patterns to know if they can be produced from figure (X) and select the answer from the alternatives.*

3. (X) 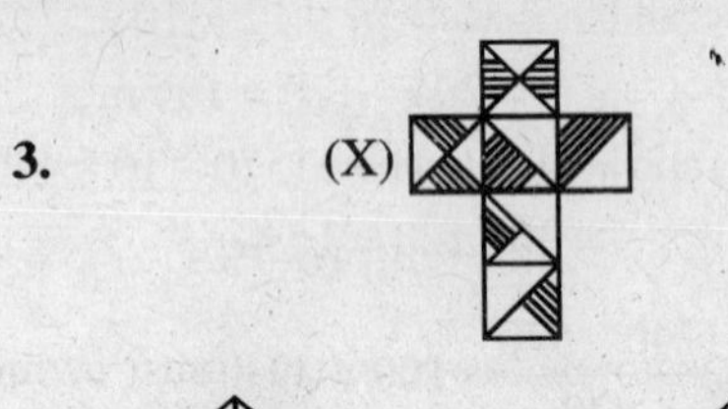

(*a*) 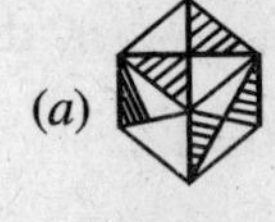 (*b*) 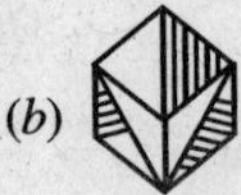

(*c*) 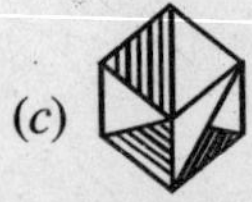 (*d*) 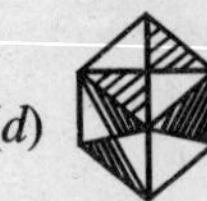

4. A cubical dice is thrown 6 times. The probability that 2 and 4 will turn up exactly 3 times each is given by :

(*a*) 5/11664 (*b*) 1/46656
(*c*) 1/5184 (*d*) None of these

Directions (Q. 5) : *In the question given below, the question is followed by two statements.*

Mark (*a*) if statement I alone is sufficient but statement II alone is not sufficient.

Mark (*b*) if statement II alone is sufficient but statement I alone is not sufficient.

Mark (*c*) if both statement I and II together are sufficient but neither of them is not sufficient if considered alone.

Mark (*d*) if each statement, if considered alone, is sufficient.

5. Are the triangle ABP and CBP congruent if P is the centre of the circle?

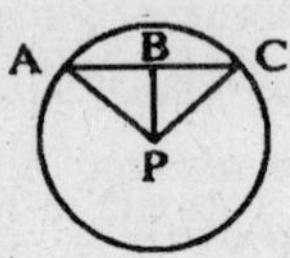

I. PB is perpendicular to AC

II. AB = CB

6. Rohan ranked eleventh from the top and twenty-seventh from the bottom among the students who passed the annual examination in a class. If the number of students who failed in the examination was 12, how many students appeared for the examination?

(*a*) 48
(*b*) 49
(*c*) 50
(*d*) Cannot be determined

Directions (Q. 7) : *In the question given below, there are three rows of figures with one figure missing from the third row. Study the pattern of figures in the rows and columns and find out the missing figure from the alternative figures that shall complete the figure matrix.*

7.

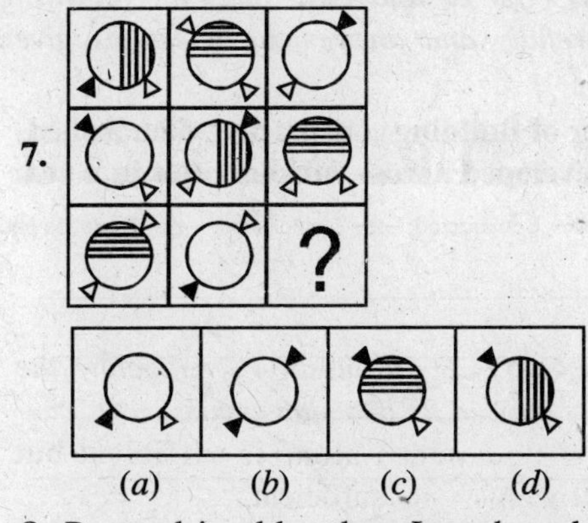

(*a*) (*b*) (*c*) (*d*)

8. Pramod is older than Jayesh and Sudhir. Vikas is younger than Anil. To find out who among them is the oldest, which of the following further information will be required, if any?

(*a*) Sudhir is older than Jayesh
(*b*) Anil is older than Jayesh
(*c*) Vikas is younger than Pramod'
(*d*) No further information is required

Directions (Q. 9) : *In the question that follows, some problem figures have been given. Problem figures themselves are also the answer figures. Out of the four figures (a), (b), (c) and (d), three are similar in a certain way. One figure is not like the other three. Choose the figure which is different from the rest.*

9.

(*a*) (*b*) (*c*) (*d*)

10. The present age difference between father and son is 14 years. The ratio of their age will be 4 : 3 after 11 years. How old is son now?

(*a*) 25 years (*b*) 31 years
(*c*) 30 years (*d*) 28 years

Directions (Q. 11): *In this question a number series is given, followed by four alternatives. One term/element of the given series is wrong, i.e., it does not conform to the rule used in writing the series. This wrong term is depicted in the following alternatives. Spot out that wrong term/element and mark your answer.*

11. 4, 6, 9, 18, 34, 59, 95

(*a*) 34 (*b*) 6
(*c*) 18 (*d*) 95

12. A person standing on the bank of river finds that the angle of elevation of the top of a tower on opposite side bank is 45°. Which of the following statement is correct?

(*a*) Breadth of the river is half of the height of the tower
(*b*) Breadth of the river and the height of the tower are equal
(*c*) Breadth of the river is twice the height of the tower
(*d*) None of these

13. How many parallelograms are there in this figure?

(*a*) 9 (*b*) 13
(*c*) 15 (*d*) 18

14. A fan is listed at ₹ 1400 and discount offered is 10%. What additional discount must be given to bring the net selling price to ₹ 1200?

(*a*) $4\frac{16}{21}\%$ (*b*) 5%
(*c*) 6% (*d*) $16\frac{2}{3}\%$

15. One of the two exclusive events must occur the chance of one is 2/3 of the other, then odds in favour of the other are :

(*a*) 1 : 3
(*b*) 3 : 1
(*c*) 2 : 3
(*d*) 3 : 2

16. If diameter of each of the following circles is 1 m, then area of the shaded part is:

(*a*) (1–π) square metre
(*b*) (4–π) square metre
(*c*) (π–1) square metre
(*d*) (1–π/4) square metre

17. Six sides of a cube are coloured in the following manner

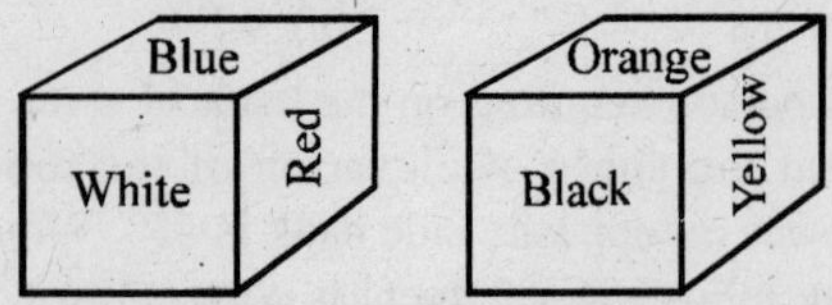

If blue and orange are opposite and red is on the top, which colour will be at the bottom?

(*a*) Orange

(*b*) Purple

(*c*) Black

(*d*) Yellow

18. An oblong piece of ground measures 19 m 2.5 dm by 12 metres 5 dm. From the centre of each side a path 2 m wide goes across to the centre of the opposite side. What is the area of the path? Find the cost of paving these paths at the rate of ₹ 1.32 per sq. metre.

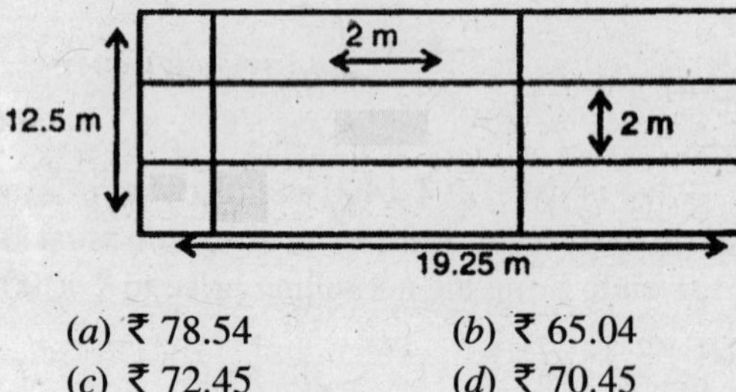

(*a*) ₹ 78.54 (*b*) ₹ 65.04

(*c*) ₹ 72.45 (*d*) ₹ 70.45

Directions (Qs. 19 and 20): *Study the following graph carefully and answer the questions given below.*

Number of Building constructed, demolished and redeveloped across various cities in a year

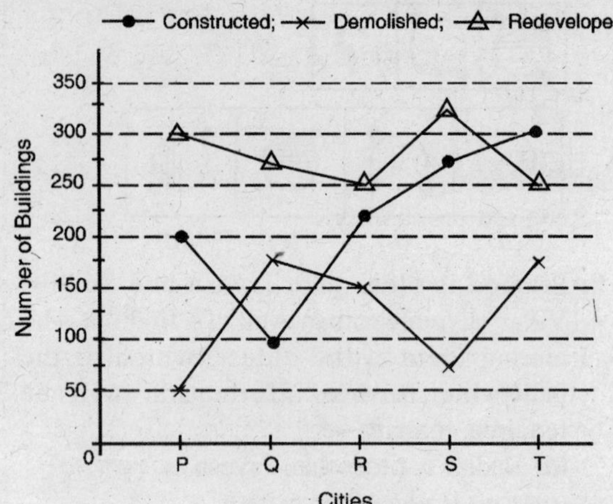

19. What is the average number of buildings demolished across the cities?

(*a*) 115 (*b*) 125

(*c*) 132 (*d*) 135

20. What is the respective ratio of the number of building demolished in city T to the number of buildings redeveloped in city P?

(*a*) 1 : 2 (*b*) 2 : 3

(*c*) 3 : 5 (*d*) 7 : 12

ANSWERS

1	2	3	4	5	6	7	8	9	10
(*b*)	(*b*)	(*c*)	(*a*)	(*d*)	(*b*)	(*d*)	(*c*)	(*b*)	(*b*)
11	**12**	**13**	**14**	**15**	**16**	**17**	**18**	**19**	**20**
(*b*)	(*b*)	(*d*)	(*a*)	(*d*)	(*d*)	(*d*)	(*a*)	(*b*)	(*d*)

SOME SELECTED EXPLANATORY ANSWERS

1. Let the three-digit number be $100x + 10y + z$, then

$$x + y + z = 10 \quad \text{...(i)}$$

$$x + z = y \quad \text{...(ii)}$$

From equations (i) & (ii) we get, $y = 5$ and

$$x + z = 5 \quad \text{...(iii)}$$

Again,

$$100z + 10y + x - (100x + 10y + z) = 99$$

$$\Rightarrow \quad 99z - 99x = 99$$

$$\therefore \quad z - x = 1 \quad \text{...(iv)}$$

Solving (iii) and (iv), we get $x = 2$, $z = 3$.

Hence, number $= 100 \times 2 + 10 \times 5 + 3 = 253$

2. Gross income = $\frac{100}{95} \times 17100$ = ₹ 18000

New net income = $\frac{94}{100} \times 18000$ = ₹ 16920

3. The given figure is same as layout 1. The sides adjacent to top side 6 are in order 1, 2, 3, 4 — of these sides 2 and 3 are seen on left and right sides respectively.

4. $P(2) = \frac{1}{6}$, $P(4) = \frac{1}{6}$

Required probability,

$$P = {}^6C_3 . \left(\frac{1}{6}\right)^3 . \left(\frac{1}{6}\right)^3 = \frac{1}{6^6} . \frac{6!}{3!3!} = \frac{5}{11664}.$$

7. In each row one figure is unshaded, one figure contains horizontal lines in top half part and one figure contains vertical lines in right half part. Also, two triangles in each row are shaded.

8. On the basis of age the descending order will be :

1. Pramod, Jayesh/Sudhir

and

2. Anil, Vikas.

Option (*c*) conects these two statements.

9. There are four letters in the bottom quadrant in figure (*b*).

10. The age of the son after 11 years
= 3 × 14 = 42 years
So, The present age of the son
= (42 – 11) years = 31 years.

11. If 6 is replaced by 5 then difference between successive terms will be in the order of 1, 4, 9, 16, 25, 36. Therefore, alternative (*b*) contains the wrong term.

12. Let AB = h m be the height of the tower; BC = x m be the breadth of the river and also $\angle ACB = 45°$

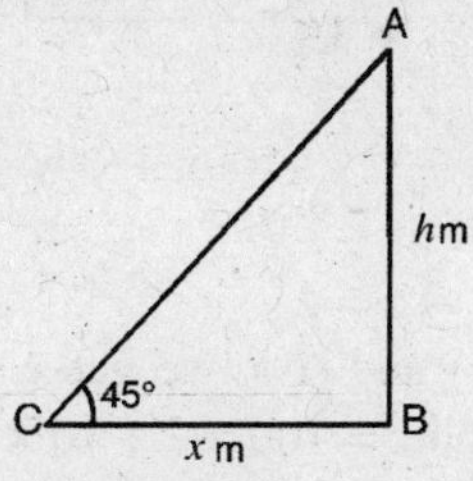

Now from right triangle ABC

$$\tan 45° = \frac{h}{x}$$

$$\Rightarrow \quad 1 = \frac{h}{x}$$

$$\therefore \quad x = h$$

Hence, breadth of the river = height of the tower

13.

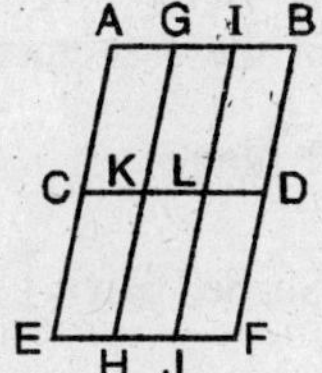

- The main parallelogram is ABEF *i.e.*, 1 parallelogram
- When divided into half by line CD the main figure has ABCD and CDEF *i.e.*, 2 parallelograms
- When further lines GH and IJ are drawn, the parallelograms are AGEH, GIJH and IBJF *i.e.*, 3 parallelograms
- The simplest parallelogram are AGCK, CKEH, GIKL, KLHJ, IBLD and LDJF *i.e.* 6 parallelograms

Other parallelograms are AICL, CLEJ, GBKD, KDHF, AIEJ and GBHF *i.e.*, 6 parallelograms

So, the total number of parallelograms is
1 + 2 + 3 + 6 + 6 = 18.

14. Price after 1st discount = $1400 - \frac{10}{100} \times 1400$

= ₹ 1260

Hence, additional discount

$$= \frac{1260 - 1200}{1260} \times 100 = \frac{60}{1260} \times 100 = 4\frac{16}{21}\%.$$

15. Let P(B) = x, P(A) = $2x/3$

P(A) + P(B) = $x + 2x/3 = 1 \Rightarrow 5x/3 = 1$

$\Rightarrow x = 3/5$

P(A) = 2/5, P(B) = 3/5

Odds in favours of B = $\frac{3/5}{1 - 3/5} = \frac{3}{2}$.

16.

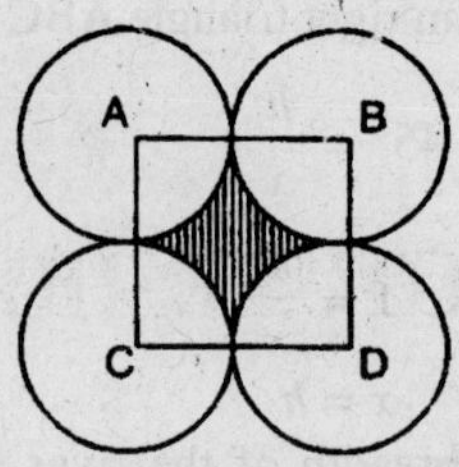

Area of square ABCD = 1^2 = 1 square metre

And Area of the 4 sectors = $4 \times \frac{1}{4}\pi\left(\frac{1}{2}\right)^2$

= $\pi/4$ square metre

$\therefore$ Area of the Shaded part = $\left(1-\frac{\pi}{4}\right)$ square metre

17.

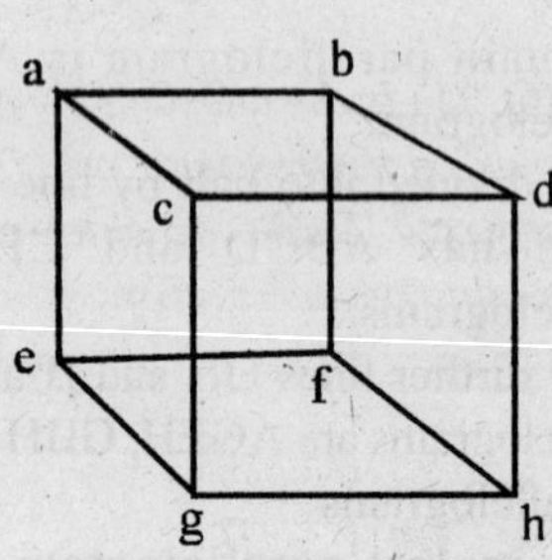

If side abcd is red; then abef will be white; and aceg will be blue. If side bdfh is orange (opposite to blue); then cdgh will be black; and efgh will be yellow (opposite to red and at the bottom).

18. In such problems, use the formula given below :

1. **Area of the path**
   = (width of path) (length + breadth of park – width of path)
2. **Area of the park minus the path**
   = (length of park – width of path) × (breadth of park – width of path)

   Now, for the given question,
   Area of path = 2 × (19.25 + 12.5 – 2)
   = 2 × 29.75 = 59.5 sq.m

   So, cost = rate × area
   = ₹ (59.5 × 1.32)
   = ₹ 78.54.

19. Average number of building demolished

$$= \frac{50+175+150+75+175}{5} = \frac{625}{5} = 125.$$

20. Required ratio = 175 : 300 = 7 : 12.

SET-11

CSIR-UGC (NET) JRF & LECTURESHIP EXAM

PART-A

1. Choose the number which is different from others in the group

(*a*) 4 (*b*) 63

(*c*) 77 (*d*) 81

2. One-eighth of a number is 17.25. What will 73% of the number be?

(*a*) 82.66 (*b*) 96.42

(*c*) 100.74 (*d*) 138.00

3. What will be the next letter in the following series :

DCXW, FEVU, HGTS, ...

(*a*) AKPO (*b*) JBYZ

(*c*) JIRQ (*d*) LMRS

4. There are 4 white and 4 black balls in a bag and 3 balls are drawn at random. If balls of same colour are identical, the probability that none of them is black, is :

(*a*) 1/4 (*b*) 1/14

(*c*) 1/2 (*d*) None of these

Directions (Q. 5) : *In the question given below, THE question is followed by two statements.*

Mark (*a*) if statement I alone is sufficient but statement II alone is not sufficient.

Mark (*b*) if statement II alone is sufficient but statement I alone is not sufficient.

Mark (*c*) if both statement I and II together are sufficient but neither of them is not sufficient if considered alone.

Mark (*d*) if statement I and II together are not sufficient.

5. In the figure, is $x \parallel y \parallel z$?

x, *y*, *z*, A, and B are straight lines.

I. CD = DE

II. PQ = DE

6. A box contains two white, three red and four black balls. If at least one red ball is to be included in the draw, the number of ways of drawing 3 balls is given by (all balls are considered to be different):

(*a*) 45 (*b*) 64

(*c*) 63 (*d*) 46

Directions (Q. 7) : *In the question given below, there are three rows of figures with one figure missing from the third row. Study the pattern of figures in the rows and columns and find out the missing figure from the alternative figures that shall complete the figure matrix.*

7.

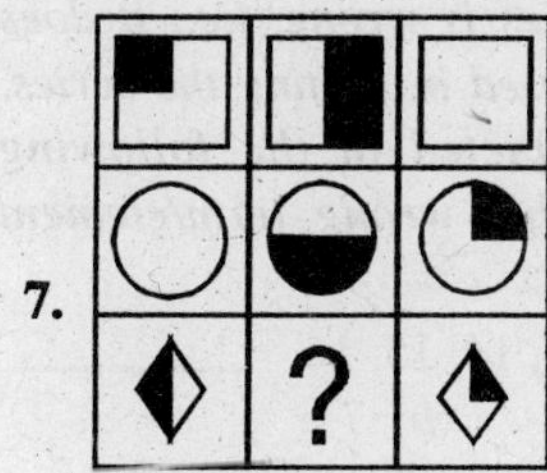

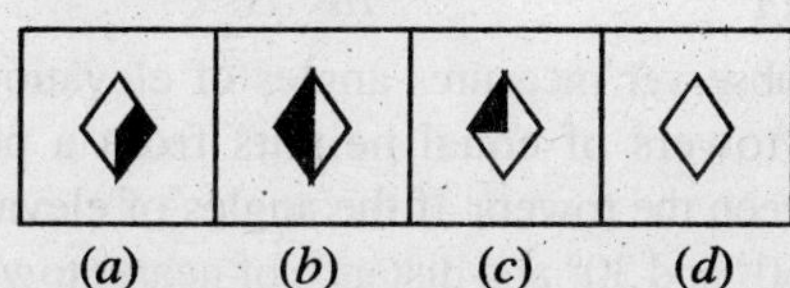

(*a*) (*b*) (*c*) (*d*)

Directions (Q. 8) : The following information is given about four persons P, Q, R and S who are mother, father, grandfather and grand-mother of U.

(*i*) P took birth before S.

(*ii*) R died before P.

(*iii*) Q died after P, R and S.

8. If Q took birth after the death of P, then which of the following statements can be correct?

(*a*) S was the guardian of P

(*b*) P was the guardian of R
(*c*) Q was the guardian of R
(*d*) Q is the life partner of P

Directions (Q. 9) : *In the question that follows, some problem figures have been given. Problem figures themselves are also the answer figures. Out of the four figures (a), (b), (c) and (d), three are similar in a certain way. One figure is not like the other three. Choose the figure which is different from the rest.*

9. 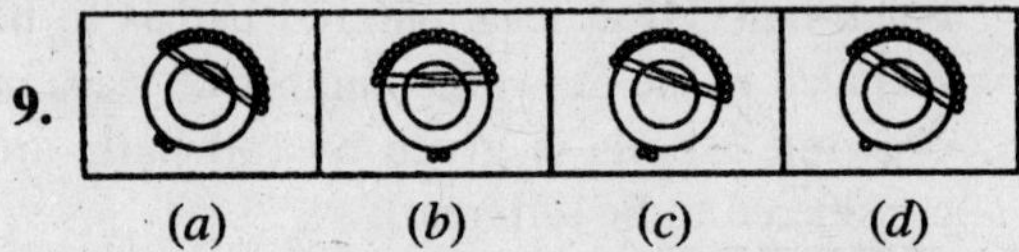

(*a*) (*b*) (*c*) (*d*)

10. A person reached Delhi from Jaipur by his car at a speed of 60 km per hour and returned to Agra along the same route at a speed of 40 km per hour. What is his average speed?
(*a*) 50 km per hour (*b*) 45 km per hour
(*c*) 48 km per hour (*d*) 55.5 km per hour

Directions (Q. 11): *In question a number series is given, followed by four alternatives. One term/ element of the given series is wrong, i.e., it does not conform to the rule used in writing the series. This wrong term is depicted in the following alternatives. Spot out that wrong term/element and mark your answer.*

11. 3, 5, 6, 7, 10, 11, 13, 14, 15, 16
(*a*) 10 (*b*) 7
(*c*) 11 (*d*) 16

12. An observer measures angles of elevation of two towers of equal heights from a point between the towers. If the angles of elevation are 60° and 30° and distance of nearer tower is 100 m, then the height of each tower and the distance between the towers, respectively are:
(*a*) $\frac{100}{\sqrt{3}}$ m and 300 m
(*b*) $\frac{100}{\sqrt{3}}$ m and 400 m
(*c*) $100\sqrt{3}$ m and 300 m
(*d*) $100\sqrt{3}$ m and 400 m

13. How many squares are hidden in this figure?
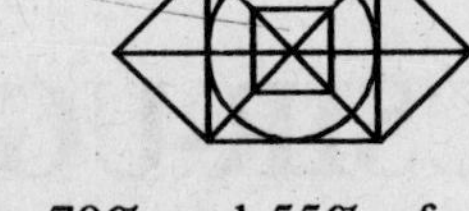
(*a*) 7
(*b*) 8
(*c*) 9
(*d*) 10

14. The difference between 70% and 55% of a number is 72. The number is:
(*a*) 370 (*b*) 460
(*c*) 480 (*d*) 520

15. If an integer p is chosen at random in the interval $0 \le p \le 5$, the probability that the roots of the equation $x^2 + px + p/4 + 1/2 = 0$ are real is :
(*a*) 4/5 (*b*) 2/3
(*c*) 3/5 (*d*) None of these

16. Drawn below is a circle of radius *r*. What is the area of shaded portion?
(*a*) $4/r$
(*b*) r^2
(*c*) $4/3r^2$
(*d*) $4r^2$

Directions (Q. 17) : *In the question given below, a dice has been marked with some letters or numerals and placed in three different positions. Answer the question that follows:*

17. Which letter is opposite to Q?

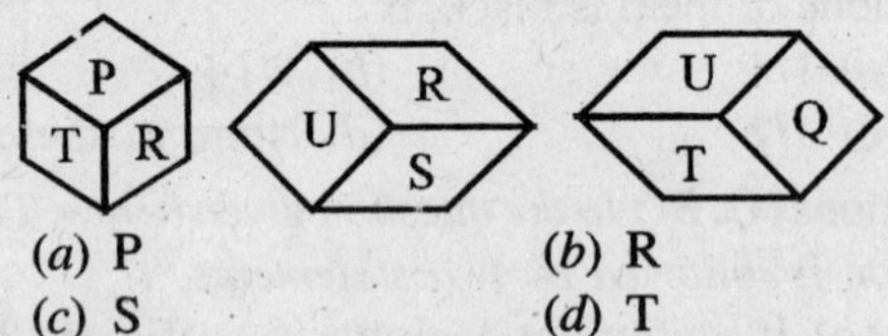

(*a*) P (*b*) R
(*c*) S (*d*) T

18. There is an equilateral triangle of which each side is 2 m. With all the three corners as centres circles are described each of radius 1 m. Find the area of the remaining portion of the triangle. (Take π = 3.1416)

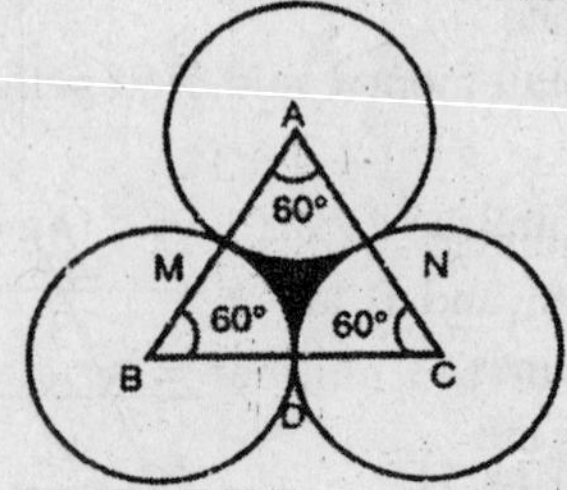

(*a*) 0.160 sq.m. (*b*) 0.161 sq.m.
(*c*) 0.162 sq.m. (*d*) 0.163 sq.m.

Directions (Qs. 19 and 20): *Study the following graph carefully and answer the questions given below.*

Number of Buildings constructed, demolished and redeveloped across various cities in a year

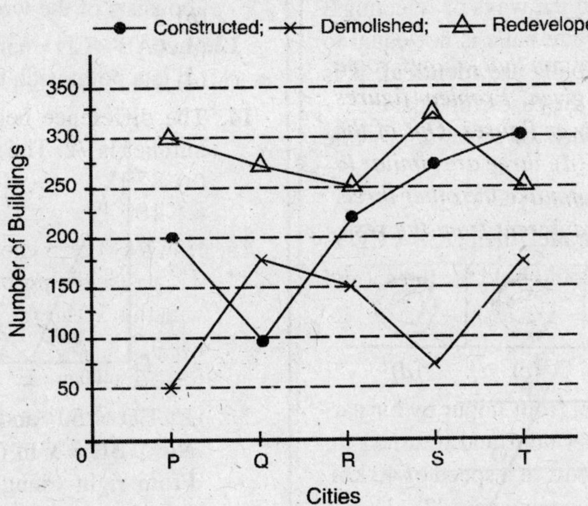

19. What is the difference between the total constructions (constructed, demolished and redeveloped) in city Q and city T?

(*a*) 125 (*b*) 175
(*c*) 180 (*d*) 200

20. The total number of buildings demolished across the cities is approximately what per cent of the total number of buildings redeveloped across the cities?

(*a*) 73 (*b*) 74
(*c*) 45 (*d*) 89

ANSWERS

1	**2**	**3**	**4**	**5**	**6**	**7**	**8**	**9**	**10**
(*c*)	(*c*)	(*c*)	(*a*)	(*d*)	(*b*)	(*d*)	(*a*)	(*d*)	(*c*)
11	**12**	**13**	**14**	**15**	**16**	**17**	**18**	**19**	**20**
(*d*)	(*d*)	(*d*)	(*c*)	(*b*)	(*b*)	(*b*)	(*b*)	(*b*)	(*c*)

SOME SELECTED EXPLANATORY ANSWERS

1. $40 \Rightarrow 4 + 0 = 4 = 2^2$

$63 \Rightarrow 6 + 3 = 9 = 3^2$

$77 \Rightarrow 7 + 7 = 14 = 1 + 4 = \boxed{5}$

$81 \Rightarrow 8 + 1 = 9 = 3^2$.

2. The number = 8 × 17.25 = 138.00

73% of the number $= \frac{73}{100} \times 138 = \frac{10074}{100}$

= 100.74.

3. Since

D C X W F E U V
(−1 −1 −1 −1)

H G T S ∴ J I P Q
(−1 −1 −1 −1)

4. There are 4 identical white and 4 identical black balls and we have to select 3, which can be selected in the following pattern:

white 3 2 1 –

black – 1 2 3
i.e., in all 4 ways.
It should be noted that the ways of selecting 3 white balls from 4 white balls is not equal to $^4C_3$ since the white balls are identical, it is equal to 1. Similar is the cases for 2, 1, etc.
Now the number of ways of selecting 3 white balls = 1.
Hence, required probability = 1/4.

5. If the lines must be parallel, then DCP = CDY.
A similar condition would hold for lines *y* and *z* to be parallel.

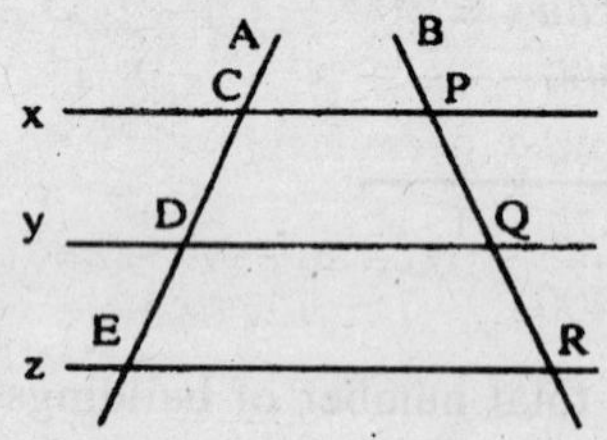

But from available information, we have only :
From statement I : CD = DE.
From statement II : PQ = DE.
But Z is not ∥ to *y*.
Therefore information is inadequate.
Therefore the answer is (*d*).

6.

Red balls (3)	**Others (6)**	**Ways**
1	2	$^3C_1 \times {}^6C_2 = 45$
2	1	$^3C_2 \times {}^6C_1 = 18$
3	×	$^3C_3 = 1$
		Total = 64

7. In each row one figure is unshaded, one is half shaded and one is one-fourth shaded.

8. If Q took birth after the death of P and given that P took birth before S, then S was the guardian of P.

9. There is only one small ring in the bottom of the circle (*d*).

10. Average speed $= \dfrac{2XY}{X+Y}$

$= \dfrac{2 \times 60 \times 40}{60+40} = 48$ kmph.

11. 16 is the only term in the series which is a perfect square. Therefore, alternative (*d*) consists of the wrong term.

12. Let AB = CD = *h* m be the heights of the towers. E is a point such that DE = 100m;

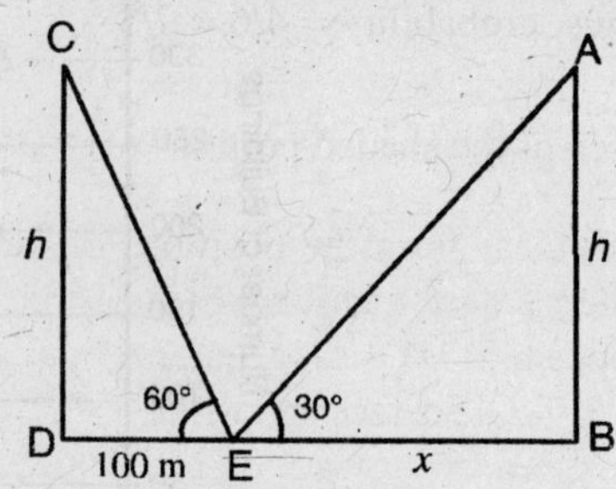

∠CED = 60° and ∠AEB = 30°
Now, BE = *x* m (say)
From right triangle CDE,
$h = 100 \tan 60° = 100\sqrt{3}$ m
From right triangle ABE,
$x = h \cot 30° = 100\sqrt{3} \times \sqrt{3} = 300$ m
Distance between the towers = DE + EB = 100 + 300 = 400 m
Height of the tower = $100\sqrt{3}$ m

13. 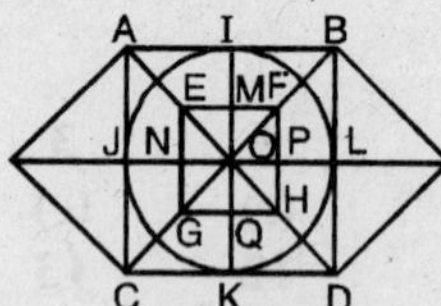

The main squares are ABCD and EFGH *i.e.*, 2 squares
The simplest outer squares are AIJO, IBOL, JOCK and OLKD *i.e.*, 4 squares
The simplest inner square are EMNO, NOGQ, MFOP and OPQH *i.e.*, 4 squares
There are no other squares formed in the figure
So, the total number of squares is
2 + 4 + 4 = 10.

14. Let the number be *x*; then

$(70-55) \times \dfrac{1}{100} \times x = 72$

$\therefore \quad x = \dfrac{100 \times 72}{15} = 480.$

15. Roots of the equation
$x^2 + px + p/4 + 1/2 = 0$ are real if $D = p^2 - 4(p/4 + 1/2) \geq 0$
i.e., $(p-2)(p+1) \geq 0$ *i.e.,* $p \leq -1$ or $p \geq 2$
In $0 \leq p \leq 5$, possible values of p are 2, 3, 4, 5
Thus, probability = 4/6 = 2/3.

16. Area of the shaded portion $= \frac{1}{2} \times 2r \times r = r^2$.

17. It is clear from the positions of the dice that letters adjacent to R are P, T, U and S. So, face opposite R is Q. Also, letters adjacent to U are R, S, T, Q. So, face opposite U is P. Now, clearly the opposite face are : R—Q, U—P and S—T.

18. Area of the shaded portion

$$= \frac{\sqrt{3}}{4}(2)^2 - 3 \times \frac{60}{360}\pi(1)^2$$

$$= \frac{\sqrt{3}}{4} \times 4 - \frac{\pi}{2} = \sqrt{3} - \frac{11}{7}$$

$= 1.732 - 1.571 = 0.161\ m^2$.

19. Total constructions in City
Q = 100 + 175 + 275 = 550
Total constructions in City
T = 175 + 250 + 300 = 725
Their difference = 725 − 550 = 175.

20. Total number of buildings demolished across the cities = 50 + 175 + 150 + 75 + 175 = 625
Total number of buildings redeveloped across the cities = 300 + 275 + 250 + 325 + 250 = 1400
Required percentage

$$= \frac{625}{1400} \times 100 = 44.64\% \approx 45\%.$$

SET-12

CSIR-UGC (NET) JRF & LECTURESHIP EXAM

PART-A

1. One-third of a certain journey was covered at the rate of 25 km per hour, one-fourth at the rate of 30 km per hour and the rest at 50 km per hour. What is the average speed per hour for the whole journey?

   (*a*) $33\frac{1}{3}$ kmph (*b*) $44\frac{1}{4}$ kmph

   (*c*) $22\frac{1}{2}$ kmph (*d*) 33 kmph

2. If 58% of 960 – *x*% of 635 = 277.4, find the value of *x*.

   (*a*) 24 (*b*) 36

   (*c*) 44 (*d*) 58

3. Determine the relationship between the pair of words ALWAYS : NEVER and then select from the following pair of words which have a similar relationship

   A. often : rarely

   B. frequently : occasionally

   C. constantly : frequently

   D. intermittently : casually

   (*a*) A and B (*b*) B and D

   (*c*) B and C (*d*) A and D

4. Two events A and B have probabilities 0.25 and 0.50 respectively. The probability that both A and B occur simultaneously is 0.12. Then the probability that neither A nor B occurs is :

   (*a*) 0.13 (*b*) 0.38

   (*c*) 0.63 (*d*) 0.37

5. There are five books A, B, C, D and E. The book C lies above D, the book E is below A and B is below E. Which is at the bottom?

   (*a*) E (*b*) B

   (*c*) A (*d*) C

6. There are five different houses, A to E, in a row. A is to the right of B and E is to the left of C and right of A, and B is to the right of D. Which of the houses is in the middle?

   (*a*) B (*b*) A

   (*c*) D (*d*) E

7. Veena ranks 73rd from the top in a class of 182. What is her rank from the bottom if 22 students have failed the examination?

   (*a*) 88 (*b*) 108

   (*c*) 110 (*d*) 90

Directions (Q. 8) : Four youngmen, Raj, Prem, Ved and Ashok are friendly with four girls Sushma, Kusum, Vimla and Poonam. Sushma and Vimla are friends. Ved's girlfriend does not like Sushma and Vimla. Kusum does not care for Ved. Prem's girlfriend is friendly with Sushma. Sushma does not like Raj.

8. With whom is Sushma friendly?

   (*a*) Kusum (*b*) Ashok

   (*c*) Raj (*d*) Prem

Directions (Q. 9) : *In the question that follows, some problem figures have been given. Problem figures themselves are also the answer figures. Out of the four figures (a), (b), (c) and (d), three are similar in a certain way. One figure is not like the other three. Choose the figure which is different from the rest.*

9. 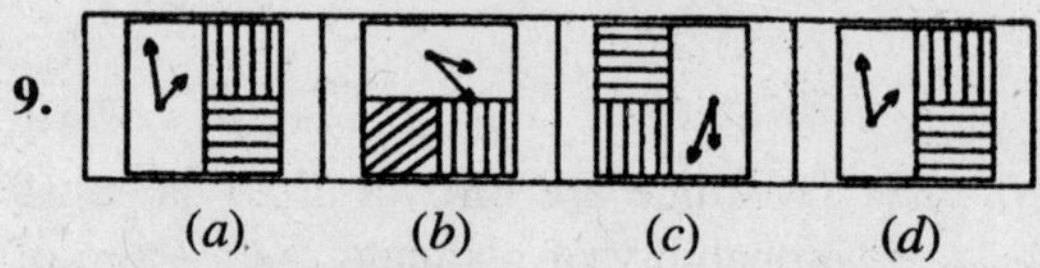

   (*a*) (*b*) (*c*) (*d*)

10. The average weight of 8 persons is increased by 2.5 kg. When one of them whose weight is 56 kg. is replaced by a new man. The weight of new man is :

    (*a*) 66 kg. (*b*) 75 kg.

    (*c*) 67.6 kg. (*d*) None of these

Directions (Q. 11): *In this question a number series is given, followed by four alternatives. One term/element of the given series is wrong, i.e., it does not conform to the rule used in writing the series. This wrong term is depicted in the following alternatives. Spot out that wrong term/element and mark your answer.*

11. 2, 3, 5, 8, 15, 21, 34, 55
(*a*) 5
(*b*) 8
(*c*) 3
(*d*) 15

12. On the ground level the angle of elevation of the top of a tower is 30°. On moving 20 m nearer the tower, the angle of elevation found to be 60°. The height of the tower is:
(*a*) 10 m (*b*) $10\sqrt{3}$ m
(*c*) 15 m (*d*) 20 m

13. How many squares are there in the figure given below?

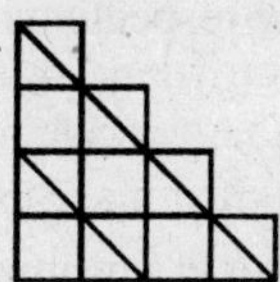

(*a*) 10 (*b*) 11
(*c*) 13 (*d*) 14

14. In the expression xy^2, the values of both variables x and y are decreased by 20%. By this, the value of the expression is decreased by
(*a*) 40%
(*b*) 48.8%
(*c*) 51.2%
(*d*) 80%

15. Two dice are thrown simultaneously. The probability of obtaining total score of seven is
(*a*) 5/6 (*b*) 1/6
(*c*) 1/7 (*d*) 7/6

16. If in the following figure, diameter of each of the bigger circle is D. What is the diameter of the smaller circle?

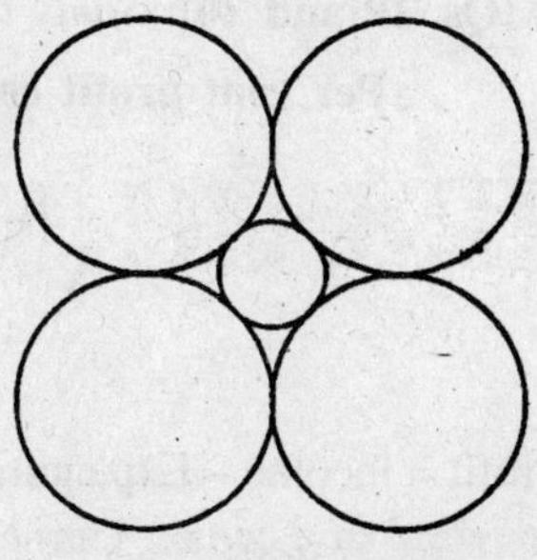

(*a*) D/4 (*b*) D
(*c*) D/2 (*d*) $\left(\sqrt{2}-1\right)$ D

Directions (Q. 17) : *In the question given below, a dice has been marked with some letters of numerals and placed in three different positions. Answer the question :*

17. If one of the 3 visible faces of the cube is hidden, which letter is opposite to O?

(*a*) L
(*b*) N
(*c*) P
(*d*) Q

18. The diameter of a coin is 1 cm. If four of these coins be placed on a table so that the rim of each touches that of the other two, find the area of the unoccupied space between them.
(Take π = 3.1416)

(*a*) 0.205 sq.cm.
(*b*) 0.215 sq.cm.
(*c*) 0.251 sq.cm.
(*d*) 0.262 sq.cm.

Directions (Qs. 19 and 20): *Study the following graph carefully and answer the questions given below it.*

Per cent profit earned by two Companies A and B over the years

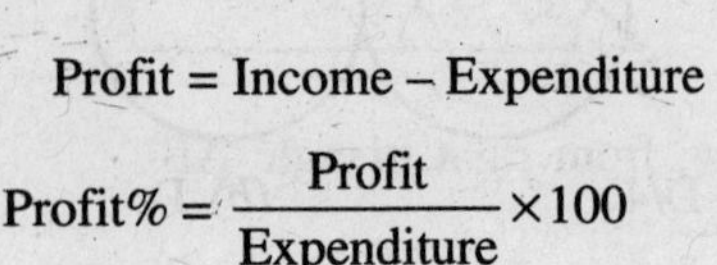

Profit = Income – Expenditure

$$\text{Profit\%} = \frac{\text{Profit}}{\text{Expenditure}} \times 100$$

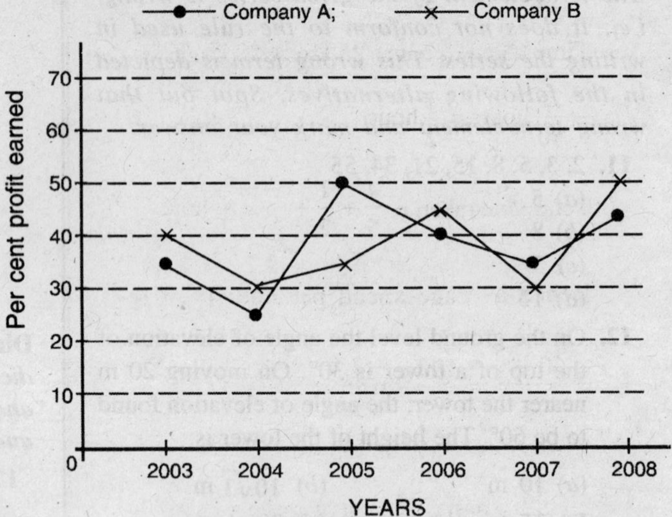

19. If the expenditure of Company 'A' in 2004 was ₹ 75 lakhs and income of Company A in 2004 was equal to its expenditure in 2005. What was the total income (in lakhs ₹) of the Company A in 2004 and 2005 together?

(*a*) 131.25 (*b*) 175

(*c*) 218.75 (*d*) 234.37

20. Expenditure of Company 'B' in years 2003 and 2004 were in the ratio of 5 : 7 respectively. What was the respective ratio of their incomes?

(*a*) 8 : 13

(*b*) 10 : 13

(*c*) 11 : 14

(*d*) 13 : 14

ANSWERS

1	2	3	4	5	6	7	8	9	10
(*a*)	(*c*)	(*a*)	(*d*)	(*b*)	(*b*)	(*a*)	(*b*)	(*d*)	(*d*)
11	**12**	**13**	**14**	**15**	**16**	**17**	**18**	**19**	**20**
(*d*)	(*b*)	(*c*)	(*b*)	(*b*)	(*d*)	(*a*)	(*b*)	(*d*)	(*b*)

SOME SELECTED EXPLANATORY ANSWERS

1. Let the total distance covered during journey = 60 km

$\frac{1}{3}$ of the distance covered during journey

$= 60 \times \frac{1}{3} = 20$ km

$\frac{1}{4}$ of the distance covered during journey

$= \frac{1}{4} \times 60 = 15$ km

∴ The distance covered during the rest of journey = 60 – (20 + 15) = 25 km

Time taken to cover 20 km at 25 km/h

$= \frac{20}{25}$ hours $= \frac{4}{5}$ hours

Time taken to cover 15 km at 30 km/h

$= \frac{15}{30}$ hours $= \frac{1}{2}$ hour

Time taken to cover 25 km at 50 km/h

$= \frac{25}{50}$ hours $= \frac{1}{2}$ hour

Total time taken $= \frac{4}{5} + \frac{1}{2} + \frac{1}{2} = \frac{9}{5}$ hours

Hence average speed per hour $= 60 \div \frac{9}{5}$

$= \frac{60 \times 5}{9} = \frac{100}{3}$ km / h $= 33\frac{1}{3}$ km / h .

2. 58% of 960 – x% of 635 = 277.4

$$\Rightarrow \frac{58}{100} \times 960 - \frac{x}{100} \times 635 = 277.4$$

$$\Rightarrow \frac{127x}{20} = 556.8 - 277.4$$

$$\therefore x = \frac{20 \times 279.4}{127} = 44.$$

4. $P(A \cup B) = P(A) + P(B) - P(A \cap B)$

$P(A \cup B) = 0.25 + 0.50 - 0.12 = 0.63$

$P\left(\overline{A \cup B}\right) = 1 - P(A \cup B) = 1 - 0.63 = 0.37.$

9. There are four lines in each of the two quadrants. Odd man (*d*) has four and three lines in its two quadrants.

10. Weight of the new man = 56 + 8 × 2.5 kg = (56 + 20) kg. = 76 kg.

11. If 15 is replaced by 13 then a particular order of terms in the series will be formed in which sum of two successive terms is equal to the next term. Therefore, alternative (*d*) consists of the wrong term.

12. Let AB = h m be the height of the tower; B and C are two points such that BC = 20 m;

∠ADB = 30°

and ∠ACB = 60°;

BC = x m (say)

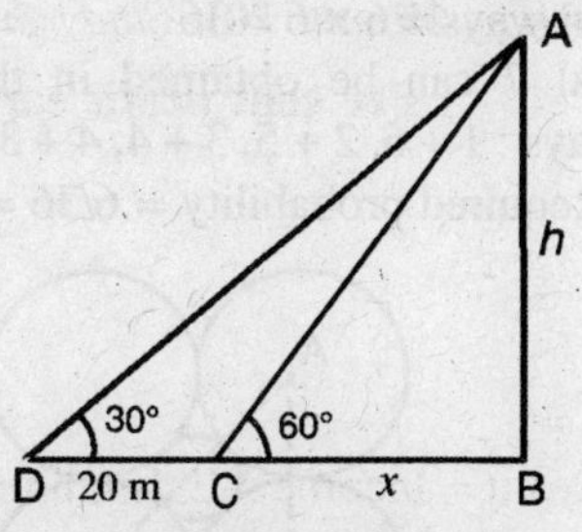

Now, from right triangle ABC,

$$x = h \cot 60° = \frac{h}{\sqrt{3}} \text{ m}$$

Again, from right triangle ABD,

$$h = (20 + x) \tan 30°$$

$$= \left(20 + \frac{h}{\sqrt{3}}\right) \times \frac{1}{\sqrt{3}} \qquad \left(\because x = \frac{h}{\sqrt{3}} \text{m}\right)$$

$$\Rightarrow h - \frac{h}{3} = \frac{20}{\sqrt{3}} \qquad \Rightarrow \frac{2h}{3} = \frac{20}{\sqrt{3}}$$

$$\therefore h = \frac{20 \times 3}{2\sqrt{3}} = 10\sqrt{3} \text{ m.}$$

13. 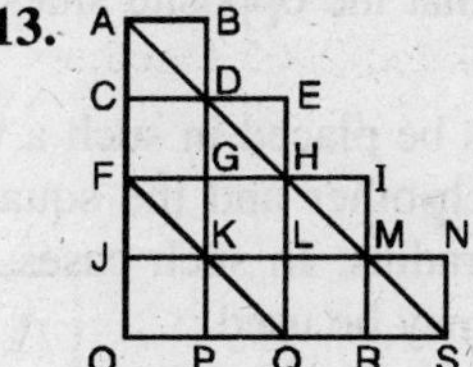

The simplest squares are : ABCD, CDFG, DEGH, FGJK, GHKL, HILM, JKOP, KLPQ, LMQR and MNRS *i.e.* 10 squares.

Other squares are : CEJL, FHOQ and GIPR *i.e.* 3 squares

So, the total number of squares is 10 + 3 = 13

14. Decrease in expression

$$= xy^2 - \frac{80}{100} \times x\left(\frac{80}{100}y\right)^2$$

$$= xy^2 - \frac{64}{125}xy^2 = \frac{61xy^2}{125}$$

Hence, decrease per cent

$$= \frac{61xy^2}{125 \times xy^2} \times 100 = 48.8\%.$$

15. Total ways = 6 × 6 = 36
Total 7 can be obtained in the following 6 ways : 1 + 6, 2 + 5, 3 + 4, 4 + 3, 5 + 2, 6 + 1
∴ Required probability = 6/36 = 1/6.

16.

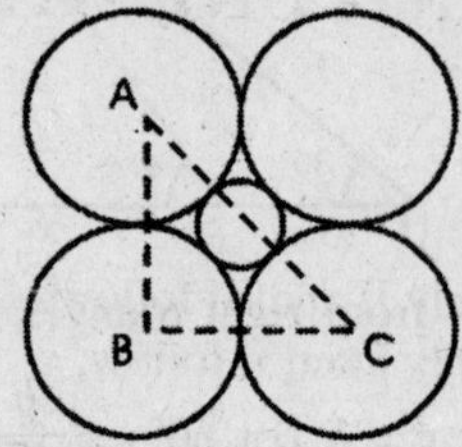

Suppose, diameter of the smaller circle = x

Therefore, $AC = x + \frac{D}{2} + \frac{D}{2}\ (x + D)$

And $AC^2 = AB^2 + BC^2$

$= D^2 + D^2 = 2D^2$

$(x + D)^2 = 2D^2$

or, $x + D = D\sqrt{2}$

or, $x = D\sqrt{2} - D = (\sqrt{2} - 1)D$

17. It is clear from the given positions of the dice that letters adjacent to L are P, N, M and Q. So, this clearly means that the opposite sides are O and L.

18. Again, if the circles be placed in such a way that they touch each other and the square's side is double the radius. In such cases, the following formula may be used :
Area of each sector = 1/4 × $(\text{radius})^2$
Area of remaining portion (shaded part)
$= (4 - \pi)(\text{radius})^2 = (0.86)(\text{radius})^2$
Now, in the given question,
Area of the unoccupied space = $(0.86)(\text{radius})^2$
$= (0.86)(1/2)^2 = 0.215$ sq.cm.

19. In 2004, expenditure of Company 'A' = ₹ 75 lakh
Since, income of the Company 'A' in 2004

$= 75 + \frac{25}{100} \times 75 =$ ₹ 93.75 lakhs

Now, expenditure of the company 'A' in 2005 = ₹ 93.75 lakhs

Since, their income $= 93.75 + \frac{50}{100} \times 93.75$
= ₹ 140.62 lakhs
Hence, total income for both the years
= 93.75 + 140.62 = ₹ 234.37 lakhs.

20. Let expenditures of Company B in 2003 and 2004 are ₹ $5x$ and ₹ $7x$ respectively; then

their income in 2003, $I_1 = 5x + \frac{40}{100} \times 5x =$ ₹ $7x$

Also their income in 2004,

$$I_2 = 7x + \frac{30}{100} \times 7x = ₹\ \frac{91x}{10}$$

Hence, the required ratio

$$= 7x : \frac{91x}{10} = 10 : 13.$$

SET-13

CSIR-UGC (NET) JRF & LECTURESHIP EXAM

PART-A

1. In how many years will a sum of ₹ 19200 placed at 10% per annum compound interest yield an interest of ₹ 4032?
(*a*) 1½ years (*b*) 2½ years
(*c*) 2 years (*d*) 3 years

2. Find the missing number for the question mark?
69, 55, 26, 13, ?
(*a*) 4 (*b*) 3
(*c*) 6.5 (*d*) 13

3. The owner of a cell phone shop charges his customer 32% more than the cost price. If a customer paid ₹ 6600 for the cell phone, then what was the cost price of the cell phone?
(*a*) ₹ 5000 (*b*) ₹ 5500
(*c*) ₹ 5800 (*d*) ₹ 6100

Directions (Q. 4) : *In this question below given is a statement followed by three courses of action numbered I, II and III. Assume everything in the statement to be true then dicide which of the given options suggests the logical answer.*

4. Statement :
In the city, over 75 per cent of the people are living in slums and sub-standard houses which is a reflection on the housing and urban development policies of the Government.

Courses of Action :
(*i*) There should be a separate department looking after housing and urban development.
(*ii*) The policies in regard to urban housing should be reviewed.
(*iii*) The policies regarding rural housing should also be reviewed so that such problems could be avoided in rural areas.
(*a*) Only I follows.
(*b*) Only II follows.
(*c*) Only II and III follow.
(*d*) Only I and II follow.

5. Divide ₹ 1540 among *A,B,C* so that *A* shall receive 2/9 as much as *B* and *C* together, and *B* 3/11 of what *A* and *C* together do.
(*a*) 285, 330, 830 (*b*) 280, 330, 930
(*c*) 280, 330, 980 (*d*) 330, 380, 980

Directions (Q. 6) : *In the question given below a figure is given. From the given alternatives select the one in which the given figure is embedded.*

6.

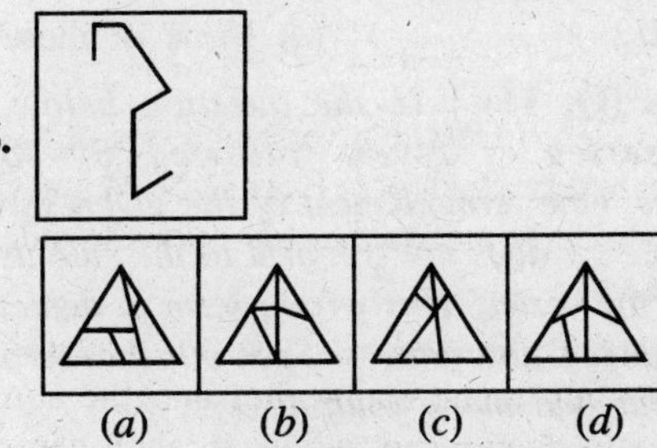

Directions (Q. 7) : *In the question given below, there are three rows of figures with one figure missing from the third row. Study the pattern of figures in the rows and columns and find out the missing figure from the alternative figures that shall complete the figure matrix.*

7.

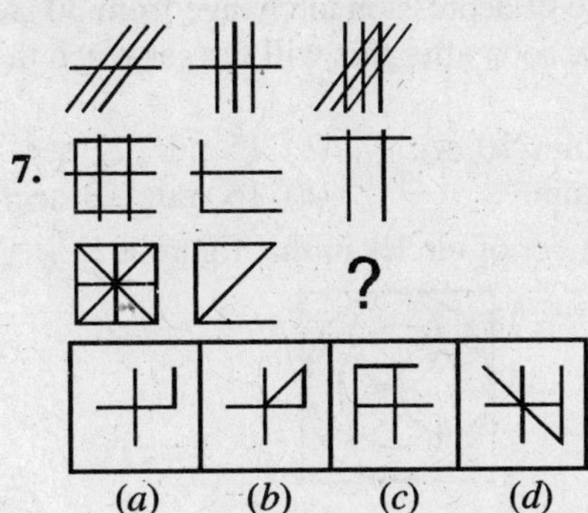

8. In a 1000 m race *A* can give *B* 100 m and *C* 280 m. In the same race, *B* can give *C* :

(*a*) 180 m (*b*) 200 m
(*c*) 270 m (*d*) 90 m

Directions (Q. 9) : *In the question that follows, some problem figures have been given. Problem figures themselves are also the answer figures. Out of the four figures (a), (b), (c) and (d), three are similar in a certain way. One figure is not like the other three. Choose the figure which is different from the rest.*

9. 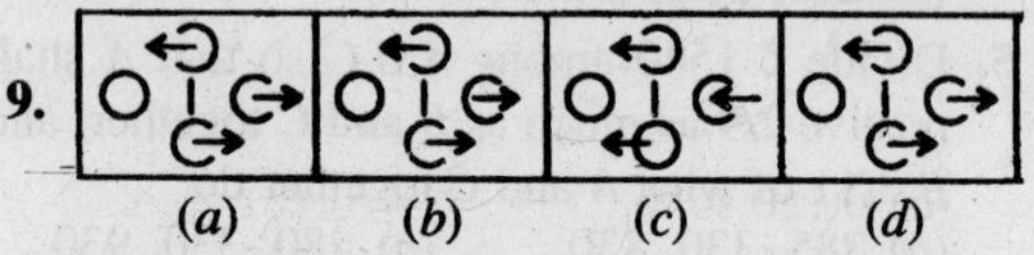

(*a*) (*b*) (*c*) (*d*)

10. The angles of a triangle are in A.P. and the radian measure of the smallest to the degree measure of the mean is π : 200. The greatest angle in radians is:

(*a*) $(11/30)\pi$ (*b*) $\pi/3$
(*c*) $\pi/2$ (*d*) None of these

Directions (Q. 11) : *In the question below, a number series is given followed by four alternatives. One term/element of the given series is wrong, i.e., it does not conform to the rule used in writing the series. This wrong term is depicted in the following alternatives. Spot out that wrong term/element and mark your answer.*

11. 12, 18, 27, 90, 270, 945, 3780

(*a*) 945 (*b*) 270
(*c*) 27 (*d*) 18

12. A man on the top of a vertical tower observes a car moving at a uniform speed coming directly towards it. If it takes 12 minutes for the angle of depression to change from 30° to 45°, how soon after this will the car reach the tower?

(*a*) 14 min 20 sec. (*b*) 15 min 22 sec.
(*c*) 16 min. (*d*) 16 min. 23 sec.

13. The number of circles in this figure is :

(*a*) 6 (*b*) 5
(*c*) 2 (*d*) 3

14. Probability of happening of at least one of the events is 0.6 and their simultaneous happening is 0.2. Then the value of [P(A) + P(B)] is :

(*a*) 0.8 (*b*) 0.6
(*c*) 0.2 (*d*) 0.4

Directions (Q. 15) : *A solid cube with each side 3 cm has been painted red, blue and green on pairs of opposite faces. It is then cut into small cubes with each side 1 cm. Answer the question that follows :*

15. How many cubes have one face painted red and one face painted green?

(*a*) 12 (*b*) 8
(*c*) 6 (*d*) 14

16. A and B jointly invest ₹ 2100 and ₹ 3100 respectively in a firm. A is an active partner and hence he gets 25% of the profit separately. If their business yields them total ₹ 1040 as profit, what will be the gain of each of them?

(*a*) ₹ 415, ₹ 625 (*b*) ₹ 575, ₹ 465
(*c*) ₹ 515, ₹ 525 (*d*) ₹ 560, ₹ 480

Directions (Qs. 17 and 18) : *Study carefully the graph given below and answer the questions that follow:*

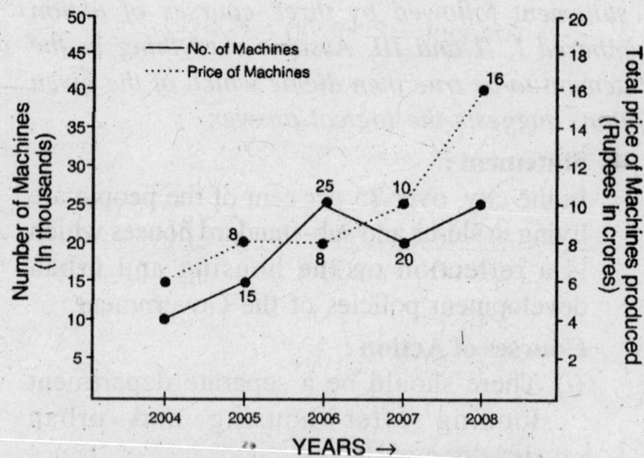

17. The percentage decrease in the production in 2007 over the previous year 2006 was:

(*a*) 5% (*b*) 20%
(*c*) 25% (*d*) 30%

18. Difference between the price of a machine in the year 2006 and that in the year 2007 was:

(*a*) ₹ 1500 (*b*) ₹ 2500
(*c*) ₹ 1800 (*d*) ₹ 3200

19. If all the faces of the figure given below is to be painted in such a manner that none of the two adjacent faces bear same colour, then how many different colours will be needed?

(*a*) 4 (*b*) 9
(*c*) 2 (*d*) 3

20. There is an equilateral triangle of which each side is 2 m. With all the three corners as centres, circles are described each of radius 1 m. Find the area of the remaining portion of the triangle. (Take π = 3.1416)

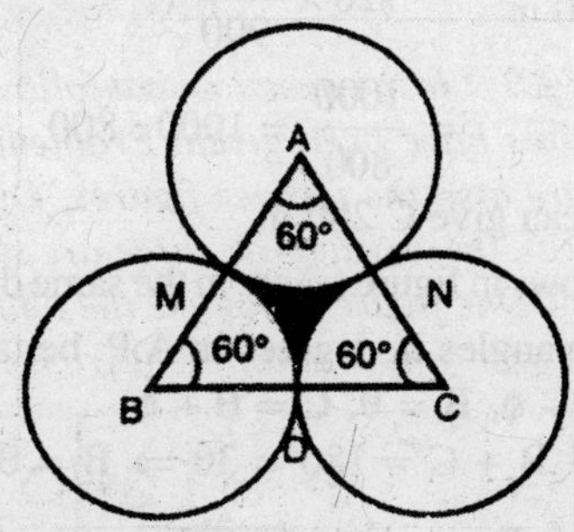

(*a*) 0.150 sq.m. (*b*) 0.181 sq.m.
(*c*) 0.162 sq.m. (*d*) 0.173 sq.m.

ANSWERS

1	2	3	4	5	6	7	8	9	10
(*c*)	(*a*)	(*a*)	(*d*)	(*b*)	(*a*)	(*d*)	(*b*)	(*c*)	(*a*)
11	**12**	**13**	**14**	**15**	**16**	**17**	**18**	**19**	**20**
(*c*)	(*d*)	(*a*)	(*a*)	(*a*)	(*b*)	(*b*)	(*c*)	(*d*)	(*c*)

SOME SELECTED EXPLANATORY ANSWERS

1. Amount = ₹ 19200 + ₹ 4032
= ₹ 23232

Now, $23232 = 19200\left(1+\frac{10}{100}\right)^n$

$\Rightarrow \frac{23232}{19200} = \left(\frac{11}{10}\right)^n \Rightarrow \frac{121}{100} = \left(\frac{11}{10}\right)^n$

$\Rightarrow \left(\frac{11}{10}\right)^2 = \left(\frac{11}{10}\right)^n$

$\therefore$ n = 2 years.

3. Let cost price of the cell phone be ₹ x; then

$x+\frac{32}{100}\times x = 6600 \Rightarrow \frac{132x}{100} = 6600$

$\therefore x = \frac{100\times 6600}{132}$ = ₹ 5000.

4. Considering the problem stated in the city, there is a need for reviewing the policies and a separate department can efficiently look after the housing and urban development. Rural housing problems are not mentioned in the statement. So, courses of action I and II follow.

5. A's share : (B + C)'s share = 2 : 9 ...(1)
B's share (A + C)'s share = 3 : 11 ...(2)
Now dividing ₹ 1540 in the ratio of 2 : 9 and 3 : 11
A's share 2/11 of ₹ 1540 = ₹ 280
B's share = 3/14 of ₹ 1540 = ₹ 330
C's share = ₹ 1540 – (₹ 280 + ₹ 330) = ₹ 930.

6. 

7. Duplicate lines of first two figures of each row are deleted in the third.

8. A : B : C = 100 : 900 : 720

So, $B : C = \frac{900}{720}$

$$= \frac{900 \times \frac{1000}{900}}{720 \times \frac{1000}{900}}$$

$$= \frac{1000}{800} = 1000 : 800$$

So, B can give C 200 m.

9. All arrows in figure (*c*) are in the same direction.

10. Let the angles in degrees in A.P. be taken as $A = \theta - \phi$, $B = \theta$, $C = \theta + \phi$

$\therefore A + B + C = 180° = 3\theta \Rightarrow B = \theta = 60°$

Now $\frac{\pi}{200} = \frac{\text{A in radian}}{\text{B in degrees}}$

$$= \frac{(60 - \phi)(\pi/180)}{60} \Rightarrow \phi = 6°$$

$\therefore$ Greatest angle $C = \theta + \phi = 66°$
$= 66 \times (\pi/180) = (11/30)\,\pi$ radians.

11. If 27 is replaced by 36, then a particular order is obtained in the series. That particular order is 12, 12 × 1.5 = 18, 18 × 2 = 36, 36 × 2.5 = 90, 90 × 3 = 270 and so on. Therefore, alternative (*c*) consists of the wrong term.

12. Let AB = *h* m be the height of the tower; B and C are two points such that $\angle ACB = 30°$; $\angle ADB = 45°$

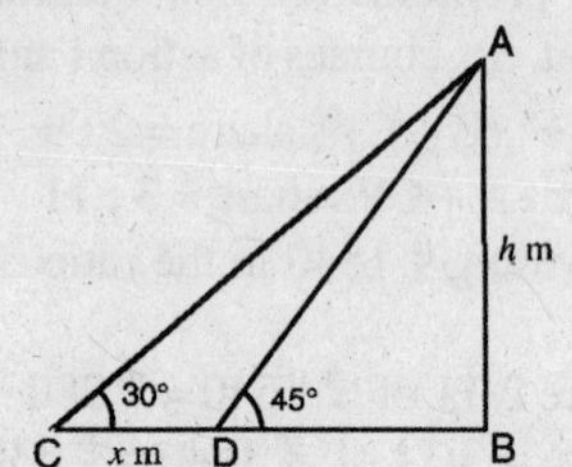

and CD = *x* m (say)

From right triangle ABD,

$$\tan 45° = \frac{h}{BD}$$

$\therefore$ BD = *h* m;

Again from right triangle ABC

$$\tan 30° = \frac{h}{h + x}$$

$\Rightarrow h + x = \sqrt{3}\,h$

$\therefore x = (1.73 - 1)h = 0.73h$

Now, 0.73h m covered in 12 min

Hence, *h* m covered in $\frac{12}{0.73} = \frac{1200}{73}$ min

$\simeq$ 16 min 23 sec.

13.

There are two main circles and four smaller circles intersecting each other.
So, the total number of circles is 2 + 4 = 6.

14. $P(A \cup B) = P(A) + P(B) - P(A \cap B)$
$\Rightarrow 0.6 = P(A) + P(B) - 0.2$
$\Rightarrow P(A) + P(B) = 0.8.$

16. Separate profit for A = $\frac{1040 \times 25}{100}$ = ₹ 260

Remaining profit = ₹ (1040 – 260) = ₹ 780

Ratio of capitals of A and B = 2100 : 3100 = 21 : 31

A's profit = $\frac{21}{52} \times 780$ = ₹ 315

B's profit = $\frac{31}{52} \times 780$ = ₹ 465

Total profit of A = ₹ (315 + 260) = ₹ 575

Therefore, A and B will make profit of ₹ 575 and ₹ 465 respectively.

17. Percentage decrease in production of machines during 2007 over the previous year 2006

$$= \frac{(25 - 20) \times 100}{25} = 20\%.$$

18. Price of 1 machine in 2006

$= \frac{80000000}{25000}$ = ₹ 3200

Price of 1 machine in 2007

$= \frac{100000000}{20000}$ = ₹ 5000

$\therefore$ Required difference
= ₹ (5000 – 3200) = ₹ 1800.

20. When the side of the equilateral triangle is double the radius of the circles, all circles touch each other and in such cases the following formula may be used :

Area of each sector = $1/6 \times \pi \times (\text{radius})^2$

Area of remaining portion = $(\sqrt{3} - \pi)(\text{radius})^2$

= $(0.162)(\text{radius})^2$

So, In this given question, the area common to all circles and triangle

= sum of the areas of three sectors *AMN, BML* and *CLN*

= $1/6\pi r^2 + 1/6\pi r^2 + 1/6\pi r^2 = 1/2\pi r^2$

= $1/2 \times 22/7 \times 1$

= 157 sq. m.

(*ii*) The area of the remaining portion of the triangle

= the area of the shaded portion

= $0.162 \times (1)^2 = 0.162$ sq.m.

SET-14

CSIR-UGC (NET) JRF & LECTURESHIP EXAM

PART-A

1. A and B jointly invest ₹ 2100 and ₹ 3100 respectively in a firm. A is an active partner and hence he gets 25% of the profit separately. If their business yields them total ₹ 1040 as profit, what will be the gain of each of them?

(*a*) ₹ 415, ₹ 625 (*b*) ₹ 575, ₹ 465
(*c*) ₹ 515, ₹ 525 (*d*) ₹ 560, ₹ 480

Directions (Q. 2) : *In the question given below, which one number when placed at the sign of interrogation shall complete the number matrix.*

2.

10	10	10	6
3	7	2	4
?	9	9	7
6	5	9	5

(*a*) 27 (*b*) 18
(*c*) 24 (*d*) 50

3. The price of rice is reduced by 2%. How many kilograms of rice can now be bought for the money which was sufficient to buy 49 kg of rice earlier?

(*a*) 51 kg (*b*) 50 kg
(*c*) 49 kg (*d*) 48 kg

Directions (Q. 4) : *In the following questions, select the set of conclusion which logically follows from the given statements.*

4. Statements :

I : All foxes are plates.
II : All plates are trees.

Conclusions :

I : All foxes are trees.
II : All trees are foxes.
III : Some trees are foxes.
IV : Some trees are plates.

(*a*) All conclusions are correct.
(*b*) Only conclusions I, III, and IV follow.
(*c*) Only conclusions II, III, and IV follow.
(*d*) Only conclusions I and IV follow.

5. The ratio between two numbers is 3 : 4. If each number be increased by 2, the ratio becomes 7 : 9. Find the numbers.

(*a*) 12, 16 (*b*) 16, 12
(*c*) 12, 15 (*d*) 13, 14

Directions (Q. 6) : *In the question given below, a figure is given. From the given alternatives select the one in which the given figure is embedded.*

6.

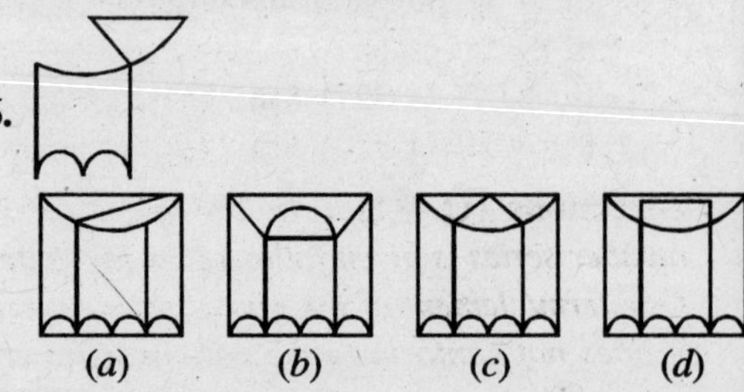

Directions (Q. 7) : *In the question given below, there are three rows of figures with one figure missing from the third row. Study the pattern of figures in the rows and columns and find out the missing figure from the alternative figures that shall complete the figure matrix.*

7.

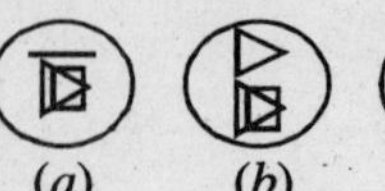

(*a*) (*b*) (*c*) (*d*)

8. *A* and *B* run a km and *A* wins by 1 minute. *A* and *C* run a km and *A* wins by 375 m. *B* and *C* run a km and *B* wins by 30 seconds. Find the time taken by each runner.
(*a*) 150, 210 sec (*b*) 200, 160 sec
(*c*) 300, 150 sec (*d*) 150, 200 sec

Directions (Q. 9) : *In the question that follows, some problem figures have been given. Problem figures themselves are also the answer figures. Out of the four figures (a), (b), (c) and (d), three are similar in a certain way. One figure is not like the other three. Choose the figure which is different from the rest.*

9. 
(*a*) (*b*) (*c*) (*d*)

10. The moon's distance from the earth is 3,50,000 kilometres and its diameter subtends an angle of 31' at the eye of the observer. The diameter of the moon is:
(*a*) 3157 (11/27) km (*b*) 315 (11/27) km
(*c*) 3050 (11/27) km (*d*) None of these

Directions (Q. 11) : *In the question below, a number series is given followed by four alternatives. One term/element of the given series is wrong, i.e., it does not conform to the rule used in writing the series. This wrong term is depicted in the following alternatives. Spot out that wrong term/element and mark your answer.*

11. 5, 11, 23, 47, 96, 191, 383
(*a*) 191 (*b*) 23
(*c*) 96 (*d*) 47

12. From a point P on a level ground, the angle of elevation of the top of a tower is 30°. If the tower is 100 m high, find the distance of point P from the foot of the tower.
(*a*) 100 m (*b*) 173 m
(*c*) 200 m (*d*) 273 m

13. How many triangles are there in the figure given below?
(*a*) 28
(*b*) 36
(*c*) 24
(*d*) 32

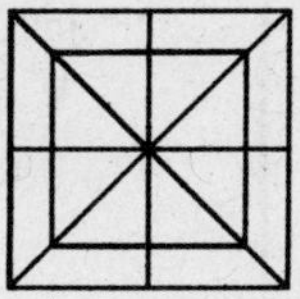

14. Let A and B be two events such that P(A) = 0.4, P(B) = 0.3 and P(A ∪ B) = 0.7. Then :
(*a*) A and B are independent
(*b*) A and B are exhaustive
(*c*) A and B are mutually exclusive
(*d*) None of these

Directions (Q. 15) : *Given below are the three positions of the same dice. Answer the question that follows :*

15. What is the number on the face opposite of face 2?
(*a*) 1
(*b*) 6
(*c*) 5
(*d*) Cannot be determined

16. Find the area of a rhombus one side of which measures 20 cm and one diagonal 24 cm.
(*a*) 384 cm²
(*b*) 374 cm²
(*c*) 382 cm²
(*d*) 380 cm²

Directions (Q. 17 and 18) : *Study the graph carefully to answer the questions that follow:*

Percentage Increase in profit of two companies over the years

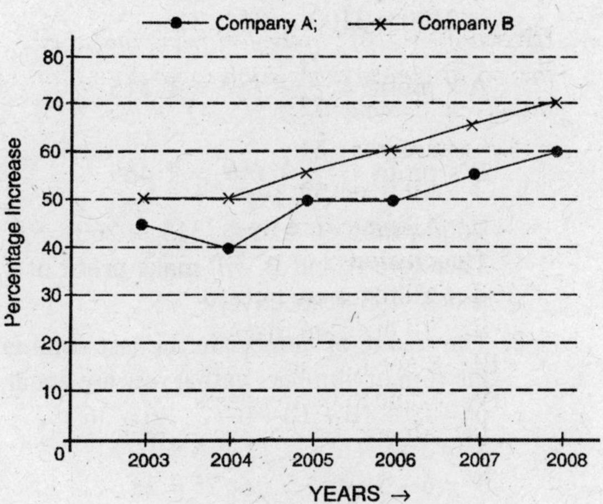

17. If the profit of Company B in the year 2003 was ₹ 6,79,995, what would its profit have been in the year 2002?
(*a*) ₹ 4,24,530 (*b*) ₹ 4,53,330
(*c*) ₹ 5,01,500 (*d*) ₹ 5,53,330

18. Based on the graph, which of the following statements is True?
(*a*) Company B has made the highest profit in the year 2008
(*b*) Company A has made the lowest profit in the year 2004
(*c*) Company B has made more amount of the profit than company A over the years
(*d*) There is no increase in the profit of company B in the year 2005 from the previous year

19. A started a business with an investment of ₹ 4000. B joined him after 4 months and C joined him after 5 months. At the end of year they get profit in the ratio of 3 : 4 : 7. Find the ratio of capitals invested in the business by B and C.
(*a*) 1 : 2 (*b*) 2 : 1
(*c*) 3 : 2 (*d*) 1 : 3

20. If all the faces of the figure given below is to be painted in such a manner that none of the two adjacent faces bear same colour, then how many different colours will be needed?
(*a*) 4
(*b*) 9
(*c*) 2
(*d*) 3

ANSWERS

1	2	3	4	5	6	7	8	9	10
(*b*)	(*c*)	(*b*)	(*b*)	(*a*)	(*c*)	(*b*)	(*a*)	(*b*)	(*a*)
11	**12**	**13**	**14**	**15**	**16**	**17**	**18**	**19**	**20**
(*c*)	(*b*)	(*d*)	(*c*)	(*b*)	(*a*)	(*b*)	(*a*)	(*a*)	(*d*)

SOME SELECTED EXPLANATORY ANSWERS

1. Separate profit for A = $\frac{1040 \times 25}{100}$ = ₹ 260
Remaining profit = ₹ (1040 – 260) = ₹ 780
Ratio of capitals of A and B
= 2100 : 3100 = 21 : 31

A's profit = $\frac{21}{52} \times 780$ = ₹ 315

B's profit = $\frac{31}{52} \times 780$ = ₹ 465

Total profit of A = ₹ (315 + 260) = ₹ 575
Therefore A and B will make profit of ₹ 575 and ₹ 465 respectively.

2. The square of number in the last column and the sum of numbers in that row are equal, *i.e.*,
$6^2 = 10 + 10 + 10 + 6$, *i.e.*, 36 = 36
$4^2 = 3 + 7 + 2 + 4$, *i.e.*, 16 = 16
$5^2 = 6 + 5 + 9 + 5$, *i.e.*, 25 = 25
$7^2 = 49$ and so, $49 - (9 + 9 + 7)$, *i.e.*, 24 in the first column completes the matrix.

3. Let original price of the rice = ₹ 100 per kg
Hence, reduced price of the rice = ₹ 98 per kg.
Let *x* kg of rice is now available for the same price, then
$x \times 98 = 100 \times 49$

$\therefore\ x = \frac{100 \times 49}{98} = 50$ kg.

4.

Trees
Plates
Foxes

When all foxes are plates and all plates are trees, then naturally all foxes will be trees and some trees will then have to be foxes. And when all plates are trees then some trees will have to be plates. Therefore, only conclusions I, III and IV are correct.

5. $\frac{3x+2}{4x+2} = \frac{7}{9}$

$\Rightarrow 28x + 14 = 27x + 18$

$x = 4$

numbers are $3 \times 4 = 12$ and $4 \times 4 = 16$

6. 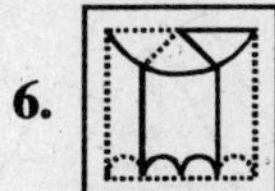

7. In each row the vertical object is moved 45° clockwise, then a further 45° clockwise and then doubled.

8. A beats B by 60 seconds, B beats C by 30 seconds

So, A beats C by 90 seconds or 375 m (given)

So, C covers 375 m in $\frac{90}{375} \times 1000$

$= 240$ second

Thus, time taken by A to cover 1 km

$= 240 - 90 = 150$ sec.

and time taken by B to cover 1 km

$= 240 - 30 = 210$ sec.

9. The thick curved arrow is in anti-clockwise direction in all the figures except (*b*). In figure (*b*) it is in clockwise direction.

10. Let l be the diameter of moon and a its distance from the earth. If the moon subtends an angle θ at the eye of the observer, then

$$l = a\theta = 350000 \times \left(\frac{31}{60} \times \frac{\pi}{180}\right)$$

$$= \frac{3500 \times 31}{6 \times 18} \times \frac{22}{7}$$

$$= 3157\frac{11}{27} \text{ km.}$$

11. $5 \times 2 + 1 = 11$

$11 \times 2 + 1 = 23$

$23 \times 2 + 1 = 47$

$47 \times 2 + 1 = 95$ — $\boxed{96}$

$95 \times 2 + 1 = 191$

$191 \times 2 + 1 = 383$

12. Let, AB = 100 m be the height of a tower, P is a point on the ground such that $\angle APB = 30°$ From right triangle ABP,

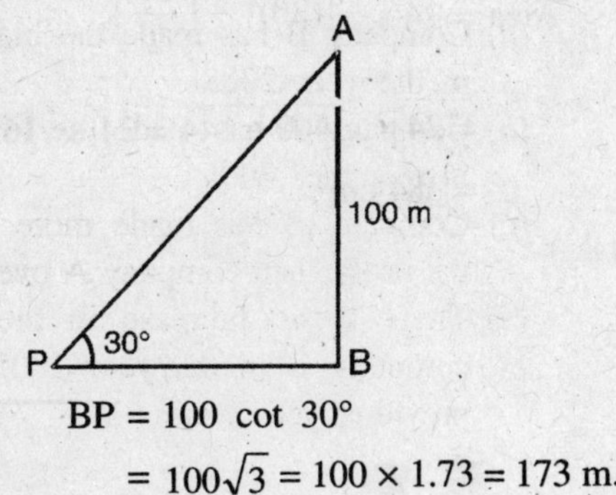

$BP = 100 \cot 30°$

$= 100\sqrt{3} = 100 \times 1.73 = 173$ m.

13. 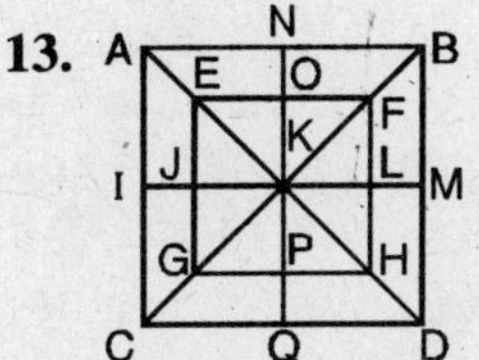

The larger triangles are : ABC, BCD, ABD and ACD *i.e.* 4 triangles.

The smaller triangles are : EFH, EGH, EFG and FGH *i.e.* 4 triangles.

The simplest triangles are : EJK, EOK, OFK, JKG, FKL, KLH, KGP and KPH *i.e.* 8 triangles.

The bisected triangles are: AKC, ABK, CKD, KBD, EKG, EKF, KHG, KHF, i.e., 8 triangles.

Other triangles are : ANK, NKB, KBM, KMD, KQD, KQC, KCI, IKA *i.e.* 8 triangles.

So, the total number of triangles is

$4 + 4 + 8 + 8 + 8 = 32$.

14. $P(A \cap B) = P(A) + P(B) - P(A \cup B)$

$= 0.4 + 0.3 - 0.7 = 0$

$\therefore P(A \cap B) \neq P(A)\,P(B)$ so A and B are not independent.

{Since $P(A \cap B) \neq 1$, A and B are not exhaustive.}

$P(A \cap B) = 0$ gives A and B are mutually exclusive.

16. Area of a rhombus

$$= \text{diagonal} \times \sqrt{(\text{side})^2 - \frac{(\text{diagonal})^2}{2}}$$

So, in the given question,

$$\text{Area} = 24 \times \sqrt{(20)^2 - \left(\frac{24}{2}\right)^2}$$

$$= 24 \times \sqrt{400 - 144} = 24 \times 16$$

$$= 384 \text{ cm}^2.$$

17. Required profit $= \frac{100}{150} \times 6{,}79{,}995 =$ ₹4,53,330.

18. It is clear from the graph that company B has made the highest profit in the year 2008, *i.e.,* 70%.

19. Let, B and C invest ₹ x and ₹ y respectively
∴ Ratio of their capitals = 48000 : $8x$: $7y$
But given ratio of the profits = 3 : 4 : 7

$$8x : 7y = 4 : 7 \quad \Rightarrow \quad \frac{x}{y} = \frac{1}{2}$$

Hence, $x : y = 1 : 2$.

SET-15

CSIR-UGC (NET) JRF & LECTURESHIP EXAM

PART-A

1. In a mixture of 60 litres, the ratio of milk and water is 2 : 1. If the ratio is to be 1 : 2, then the quantity of water to be further added is:
(*a*) 60 litres
(*b*) 40 litres
(*c*) 30 litres
(*d*) 20 litres

Directions (Q. 2) : *In the question given below which one number can be placed at the sign of interrogation?*

2. 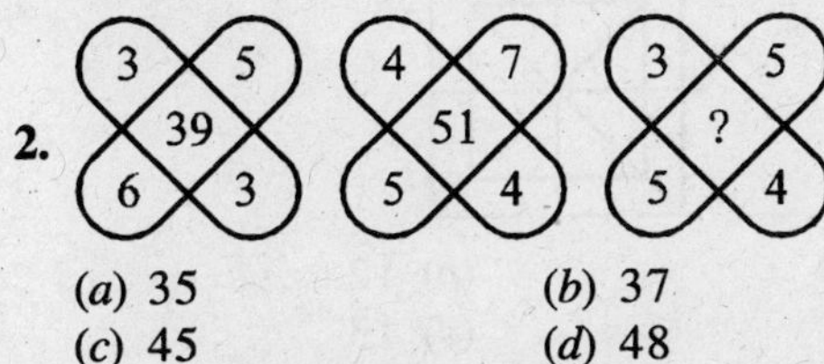

(*a*) 35 (*b*) 37
(*c*) 45 (*d*) 48

3. Three men Ram, Karan and Mohan run around an oval garden from a fixed post at the rates of 5, $5\frac{1}{7}$, $5\frac{1}{3}$ per hour. They come back to the fixed post in $3\frac{3}{4}$ hours. Find the greatest length, the race course can have.

(*a*) $\frac{28}{5}$ km (*b*) $\frac{5}{28}$ km
(*c*) $\frac{11}{28}$ km (*d*) $\frac{28}{11}$ km

Directions (Q. 4) : *The question given below consist of a question and two statements numbered I and II given below it. You have to decide whether data provided in the statements are sufficient to answer the question. Read both the statements and give answer :*

(*a*) if the data in statement I alone are sufficient to answer the question, while the data in statement II alone are not sufficient to answer the question.
(*b*) if the data in statement II alone are sufficient to answer the question, while the data in statement I alone are not sufficient to answer the question.
(*c*) if the data either in statement I or in statement II alone are sufficient to answer the question.
(*d*) If the data even in both statements I and II together are not sufficient to answer the question.

4. What is Shubha's date of birth?
I. On 21st September, 1994, Shubha completes 15 years, 3 months and 5 days.
II. Shubha's brother who is exactly two years younger to her, was born on June 16, 1981.

5. The G.C.M. of 9/45, 15/20, 16/20 and 15/25 is
(*a*) 1/20 (*b*) 1/40
(*c*) 1/60 (*d*) 1/15

Directions (Q. 6) : *In the question given below, a figure is given. From the given alternatives select the one in which the given figure is embedded.*

6. 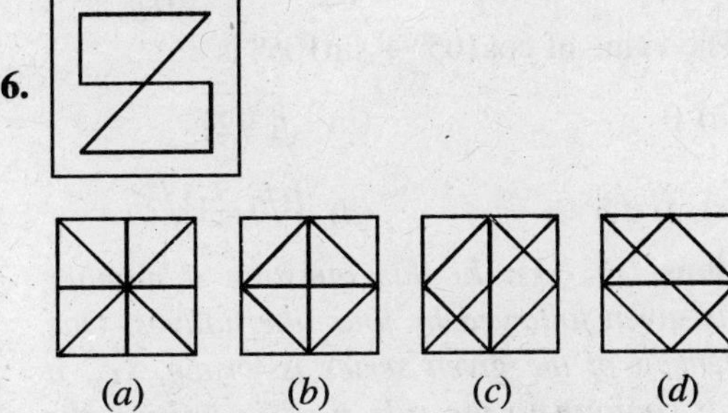

Directions (Q. 7) : *In the question given below, there are three rows of figures with one figure missing from the third row. Study the pattern of figures in the rows and columns and find out the missing figure from the alternative figures that shall complete the figure matrix.*

7. 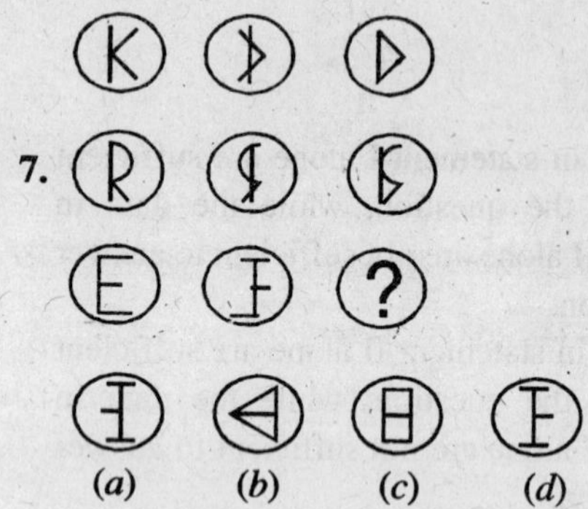

8. Two stations A and B are 110 km apart on some straight line. One train starts from *A* at 7 a.m. and travels towards B at 20 kmph. Another train starts from B at 8 a.m. and travels towards A at a speed of 25 kmph. At what time will they meet?
   (*a*) 9 a.m. (*b*) 10 a.m.
   (*c*) 11 a.m. (*d*) 10.30 a.m.

Directions (Q. 9) : *In the question that follows, some problem figures have been given. Problem figures themselves are also the answer figures. Out of the four figures (a), (b), (c) and (d), three are similar in a certain way. One figure is not like the other three. Choose the figure which is different from the rest.*

9. 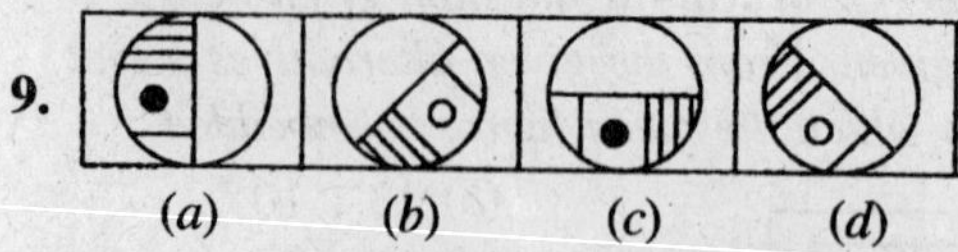

10. The value of $\cos 105° + \sin 105°$ is:
   (*a*) 0 (*b*) $\sqrt{(3/2)}$
   (*c*) $1/\sqrt{2}$ (*d*) $(\sqrt{3}+1)/2$

Directions (Q. 11): *In this question a number series is given followed by four alternatives. One term/element of the given series is wrong, i.e., it does not conform to the rule used in writing the series. This wrong term is depicted in the following alternatives. Spot out that wrong term/element and mark your answer.*

11. 112, 114, 120, 124, 132, 142, 154
   (*a*) 132 (*b*) 142
   (*c*) 124 (*d*) 120

12. A man is observing from the top of a tower a boat speeding away from the tower. The boat makes an angle of depression of 45° with the man's eye when at a distance of 60 m from the tower. After 5 seconds, the angle of depression becomes 30°. Find the speed of the boat, assuming that it is running in still water.
   (*a*) 30 km/hr. (*b*) 31.5 km/hr
   (*c*) 33 km/hr (*d*) 34 km/hr

13. How many straight lines are needed to draw the following figure?

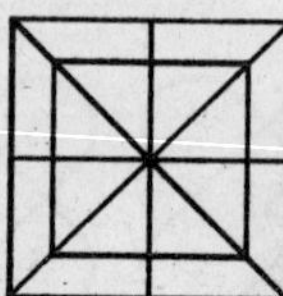

   (*a*) 10 (*b*) 12
   (*c*) 11 (*d*) 13

14. If the probabilities that A and B will die within a year are *p* and *q* respectively, then the probability that only one of them will be alive at the end of the year is :
   (*a*) $p + q$
   (*b*) $p + q - 2pq$
   (*c*) $p + q - pq$
   (*d*) $p + q + pq$

Directions (Q. 15) : *In the following question, a dice has been marked with some letters or numerals and placed in three different positions as shown in the figure.*

15. 

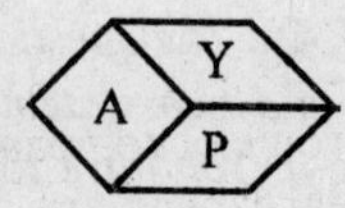

Which letter is opposite to L?
   (*a*) A (*b*) P
   (*c*) M (*d*) X

16. The base of a triangular field is 880 metres and its height 550 metres. Calculate the charges for supplying water to the field at the rate of ₹ 24.25 per sq. hectometer.

(*a*) ₹ 580.85 (*b*) ₹ 586.85
(*c*) ₹ 582.78 (*d*) ₹ 580.62

17. If in the following figure, area of the square ABCD is A then what is the area of the whole figure?

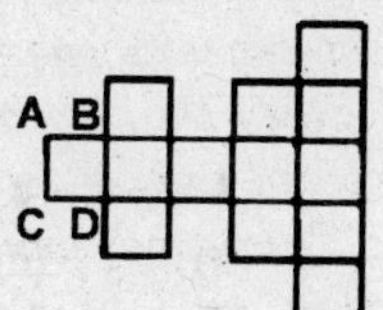

(*a*) 11A
(*b*) 13A
(*c*) $13A^2$
(*d*) $11A^2$

Directions (Qs. 18 and 19) : *Study the following graph carefully and answer the questions that follow:*

Percentage profit earned by two companies over the given years

$$\text{Profit\%} = \frac{\text{Income} - \text{Expenditure}}{\text{Expenditure}} \times 100$$

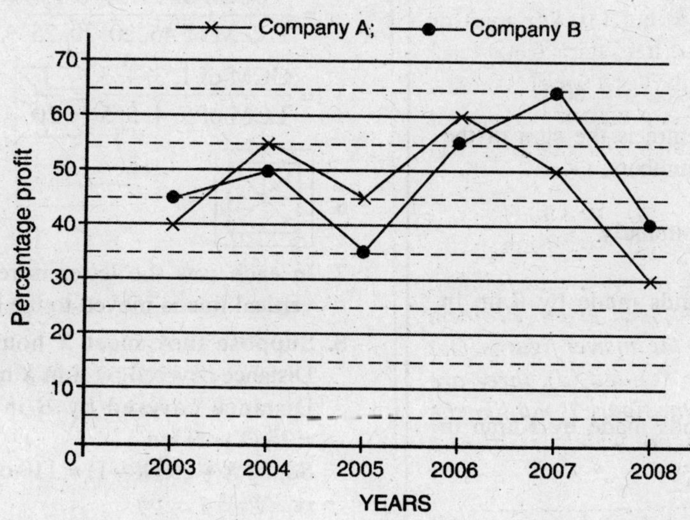

18. If the income of company A in 2005 was equal to its expenditue in 2007, what was the ratio between company's expenditure in the years 2005 and 2007 respectively?

(*a*) 19 : 20 (*b*) 20 : 19
(*c*) 20 : 29 (*d*) 29 : 20

19. If the income of company A in 2006 was equal to the total expenditure of company B in 2007, then what was the ratio of expenditure of company A in 2006 to the income of company B in 2007?

(*a*) 10 : 13 (*b*) 13 : 10
(*c*) 25 : 66 (*d*) 66 : 25

20. Mr. Jha invests a certain amount for 2 years at 6% p.a. to obtain a total amount of ₹ 33,384 at the end of 2 years. What was the amount invested by Mr. Jha?

(*a*) ₹ 24,560
(*b*) ₹ 29,712
(*c*) ₹ 30,000
(*d*) None of these

ANSWERS

1	2	3	4	5	6	7	8	9	10
(a)	(b)	(b)	(c)	(a)	(a)	(d)	(b)	(a)	(c)
11	**12**	**13**	**14**	**15**	**16**	**17**	**18**	**19**	**20**
(d)	(b)	(b)	(b)	(a)	(b)	(b)	(c)	(c)	(b)

SOME SELECTED EXPLANATORY ANSWERS

1. The amount of milk = $\frac{2}{3} \times 60 = 40\ l$

The amount of water = $\frac{1}{3} \times 60 = 20\ l$

Let the $x\ l$ water required for ratio 1 : 2.

Then, $\frac{40}{20+x} = \frac{1}{2}$

$\Rightarrow$ $20 + x = 80$ $\quad \therefore \quad x = 60\ l.$

2. The number in the centre is the sum of the products of diagonal numbers, *i.e.*,
$(3 \times 3) + (5 \times 6) = 39$
$(4 \times 4) + (7 \times 5) = 51$, similarly
$(3 \times 4) + (5 \times 5) = 37.$

3. Total number of rounds made by Ram in

$\frac{15}{4}$ hrs $= 5 \times \frac{15}{4} = \frac{75}{4}$

Total number of rounds made by Karan in

$\frac{15}{4}$ hrs $= \frac{36}{7} \times \frac{15}{4} = \frac{135}{7}$

Total number of rounds made by Mohan in

$\frac{15}{4}$ hrs $= \frac{16}{3} \times \frac{15}{4} = 20$

H.C.F. of $\frac{75}{4}$, $\frac{135}{7}$ and $20 = \frac{5}{28}$

Hence, greatest length, the race cource can have $\frac{5}{28}$ km.

4. According to statement I Shubha's date of birth is 21st September, 1994 less 15 years, 3 months and 5 days, *i.e.* 16th June 1979.

According to statement II Shubha's date of birth is June 16, 1981 less two years *i.e* June 16, 1979. So, either of the statements alone is sufficient to answer the question.

5. Trick :

G.C.M of the given fractions

$= \frac{\text{G.C.M of } 9, 15, 16, 15}{\text{L.C.M of } 45, 20, 20, 25}$

$= \frac{\text{GCM of } 1, 3, 4, 3}{\text{LCM of } 5, 4, 5, 5} = \frac{1}{20}.$

6. 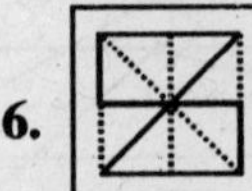

7. In each row the letter is reversed and the vertical line is moved to the left.

8. Suppose they meet X hours after 7 a.m.
Distance covered by A in X hours = $20\ X$ km.
Distance covered by B in $(X - 1)$ hours $= 25\ (X - 1)$ km
So, $20\ X + 25\ (X - 1) = 110$ or $45\ X = 135$
or $X = 3$
So, they meet at 10 a.m.

9. If the circle is shaded the single vertical line is at its left. If it is unshaded the line is at its right side. So odd man is figure (*a*).

10. $\cos 105° + \sin 105°$
$= \cos(60° + 45°) + \sin(60° + 45°)$
$= \cos60°\ \cos45° - \sin60°\ \sin45° + \sin60°\ \cos45° + \cos60°\ \sin45°$

$= \frac{1}{2}.\frac{1}{\sqrt{2}} - \frac{\sqrt{3}}{2}.\frac{1}{\sqrt{2}} + \frac{\sqrt{3}}{2}.\frac{1}{\sqrt{2}} + \frac{1}{2}.\frac{1}{\sqrt{2}}$

$= \frac{2}{2\sqrt{2}} = \frac{1}{\sqrt{2}}.$

11. A careful scrutiny of the number series reveals that if 120 is replaced by 118, then the difference between successive terms of the series will be in the order of 2, 4, 6, 8, 10, 12. Therefore, alternative (*d*) consists the wrong term of the series.

12. Let AB = *h* m be the height of the tower; C and D are the two points on the ground such that BC = 60 m; ∠ ACB = 45° and ∠ ADB = 30°

Now from right triangle ABC,

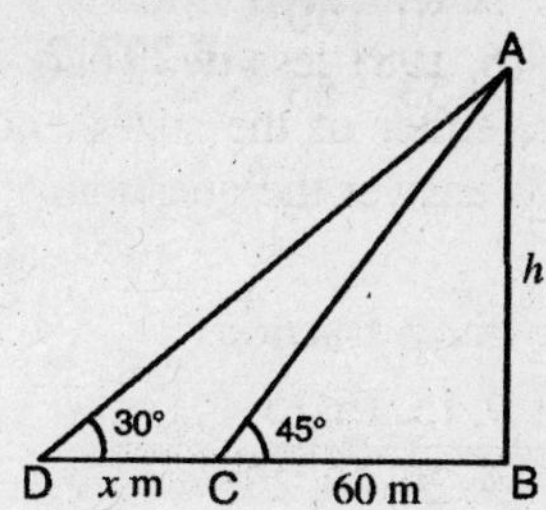

$$\tan 45° = \frac{h}{60}$$

$$\Rightarrow \quad 1 = \frac{h}{60} \qquad \therefore h = 60 \text{ m};$$

Again from right triangle ABD;

$$\tan 30° = \frac{h}{x+60}$$

$$\Rightarrow \frac{1}{\sqrt{3}} = \frac{60}{x+60}$$

$$\Rightarrow x + 60 = 60\sqrt{3}$$

$$\therefore x = 60\ (1.73 - 1) = 43.8\text{m}$$

Hence, speed of boat = $\frac{43.8}{5}$ m/s

$$= \frac{43.8}{5} \times \frac{18}{5} \simeq 31.5 \text{ km/hr.}$$

13.

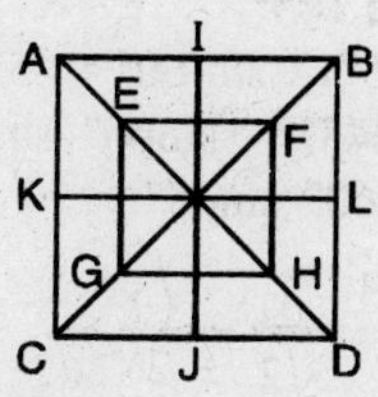

The horizontal lines are : AB, EF, KL, GH and CD *i.e.* – 5 lines.

The vertical lines are AC, EG, IJ, FH and BD *i.e.* – 5 lines.

The diagonal lines are : AD and BC *i.e.* 2 lines.

14. P (only one of A and B will die in a year)

$$= P(\bar{A}B) + P(A\bar{B})$$

$$= P(\bar{A})\,P(B) + P(A)\,P(\bar{B})$$

[Since A and B are independent]

$$= (1-p)q + p\,(1-q) = p + q - 2pq.$$

15. It is clear from the positions of the dice that letters adjacent to A are X, M, Y and P. So, the opposite letters are A and L.

16. Area of the field = $\frac{\text{Base} \times \text{Height}}{2}$

$= \frac{880 \times 550}{2}$ sq. metres = $\frac{440 \times 550}{100 \times 100}$ sq. hectometer = 24.20 sq. hectometres.

Cost of supplying water to 1 sq. hectometer = ₹ 24.25

So, cost of supplying water to the whole field = ₹ 24.20 × 24.25 = ₹ 586.85.

17. Complete figure is divided into 13 square of equal sizes. Therefore total area = 13A.

18. Let income of Company A in 2005 = Expenditure of Company A in 2007 = ₹ x and also expenditure of Company A in 2005 = ₹ x_1; then

For Company A in 2005,

$$\frac{x - x_1}{x_1} \times 100 = 45$$

$$\Rightarrow \quad 29x_1 = 20x$$

$$\therefore \quad x_1 = \frac{20x}{29}$$

Since, required ratio = $\frac{20x}{29} : x$ = 20 : 29.

19. Let income of company A in 2006 = Expenditure of company B in 2007 = ₹ x lakhs also ₹ x_1 lakhs, and ₹ x_2 lakhs be the expenditure of company A in 2006 and income of company B in 2007 respectively; then

For Company A in 2006,

$$\frac{x-x_1}{x_1}\times 100 = 60$$

$$\Rightarrow \quad 8x_1 = 5x$$

$$\therefore \quad x_1 = ₹\ \frac{5x}{8} \text{ lakhs}$$

For Company B in 2007,

$$\frac{x_2-x}{x}\times 100 = 65$$

$$\Rightarrow \quad 20x_2 = 33x.$$

$$\therefore \quad x_2 = ₹\ \frac{33x}{20} \text{ lakhs}$$

Since, required ratio

$$= \frac{5x}{8}:\frac{33x}{20} = \frac{5x}{8}\times 40 : \frac{33x}{20}\times 40 = 25 : 66.$$

20. Here, $P\left(1+\frac{6}{100}\right)^2 = 33{,}384$

$$\therefore \text{ P} = 33384 \times \frac{50}{53}\times\frac{50}{53} \approx ₹\ 29712.$$

SET-16

CSIR-UGC (NET) JRF & LECTURESHIP EXAM

PART-A

1. If $3a = 4b = 6c$ and $a + b + c = 27\sqrt{29}$, then $\sqrt{a^2 + b^2 + c^2}$ is:

(*a*) 89 (*b*) 87

(*c*) 81 (*d*) $3\sqrt{29}$

Directions (Q. 2) : *In the question given below which one number can be placed at the sign of interrogation?*

2.

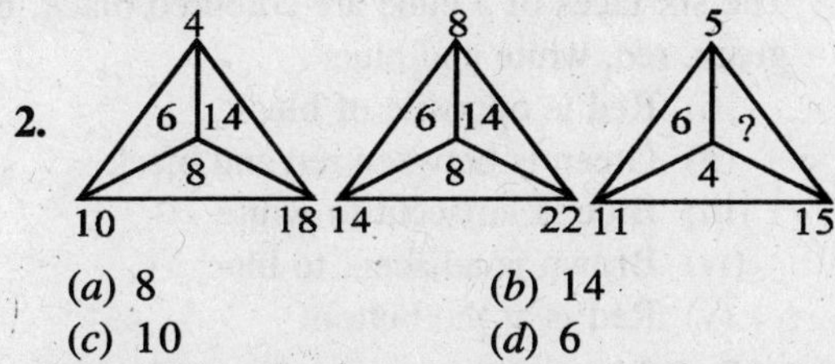

(*a*) 8 (*b*) 14

(*c*) 10 (*d*) 6

3. Two pipes can fill a cistern in 14 hours and 16 hours respectively. The pipes are opened simultaneously and it is found that due to leakage at the bottom, 32 minutes extra are taken for the cistern to be filled up. When the cistern is full, in what time will the leak empty it?

(*a*) 108 hours

(*b*) 112 hours

(*c*) 116 hours

(*d*) 120 hours

Directions (Q. 4) : *In the question below given is a statement followed by three courses of action numbered I, II and III. Assume everything in the statement to be true then decide which of the given options suggests the logical answer.*

4. *Statement :*

Over 27,000 bonded labourers indentified and freed are still awaiting rehabilitation.

Courses of Action :

(*i*) More cases of bonded labourers should be identified.

(*ii*) Till the proper rehabilitation facilities are available, the bonded labourers should not be freed.

(*iii*) The impediments in the way of speedy and proper rehabilitation of bonded labourers should be removed.

(*a*) Only I follows.

(*b*) Only II follows.

(*c*) Only III follows.

(*d*) Only II and III follow.

(*e*) None follows.

5. H.C.F. of 15, 45, 90 is

(*a*) 12 (*b*) 13

(*c*) 13 (*d*) 15

Directions (Q. 6) : *In the question given below, a figure is given. From the given alternatives select the one in which the given figure is embedded.*

6.

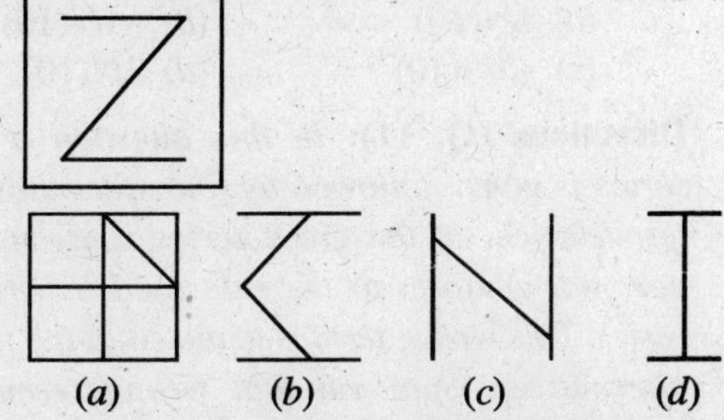

Directions (Q. 7) : *In the question given below, there are three rows of figures with one figure missing from the third row. Study the pattern of figures in the rows and columns and find out the missing figure from the alternative figures that shall complete the figure matrix.*

7. 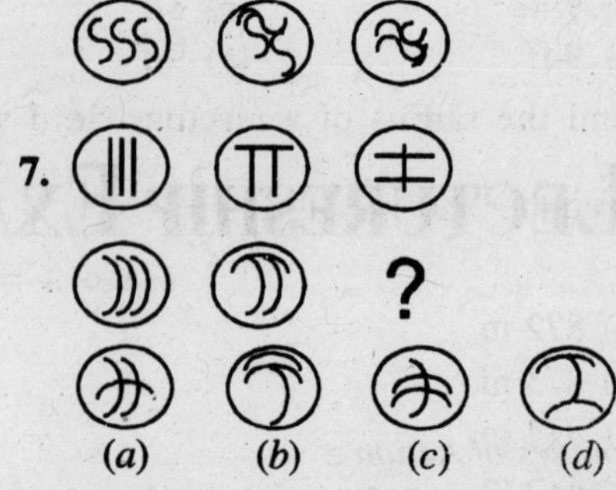

(a) (b) (c) (d)

8. A monkey tries to ascend a greased pole 14 metres high. He ascends 2 metres in first minute and slips down 1 metre in the alternate minute. If he continues to ascend in this fashion, how long does he take to reach the top?
(a) 26th min. (b) 28th min.
(c) 20th min. (d) 30th min.

Directions (Q. 9) : *In the question that follows, some problem figures have been given. Problem figures themselves are also the answer figures. Out of the four figures (a), (b), (c) and (d), three are similar in a certain way. One figure is not like the other three. Choose the figure which is different from the rest.*

9. 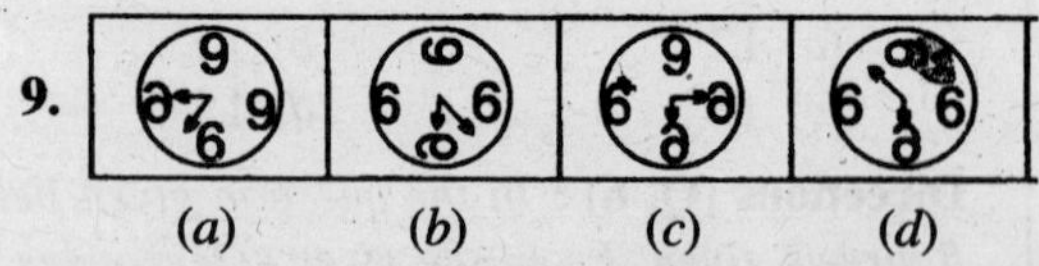

(a) (b) (c) (d)

10. If the angle θ is in the third quadrant and $\tan\theta = 3$, then the value of $\sin\theta$ is:
(a) $1/\sqrt{(10)}$ (b) $-1/\sqrt{(10)}$
(c) $-3/\sqrt{(10)}$ (d) $3/\sqrt{(10)}$

Directions (Q. 11): *In this question a number series is given, followed by four alternatives. One term/element of the given series is wrong, i.e., it does not conform to the rule used in writing the series. This wrong term is depicted in the following alternatives. Spot out that wrong term/element and mark your answer.*

11. 54, 43, 34, 26, 22, 19, 18
(a) 26 (b) 18
(c) 43 (d) 22

12. A tank is of the shape of a cuboid whose length is 7.2 m and breadth is 2.5 m. Water flows into it through a pipe whose cross-section is 5 cm × 3 cm at the rate of 10 m/s. Find the height to which water level will rise in the tank in 40 minutes.
(a) 1 m (b) 2 m
(c) 3 m (d) 4 m

13. How many squares are there in this figure?

(a) 15
(b) 11
(c) 8
(d) 3

14. A man is known to speak truth 3 out of 4 times. He throws a die and reports that it is a six, the probability that it is actually a six is :
(a) 3/8 (b) 1/5
(c) 3/5 (d) None of these

Directions (Q. 15) : *Study the information given below :*

The six faces of a cube are coloured black, brown, green, red, white and blue.
(i) Red is opposite of black
(ii) Green is between red and black
(iii) Blue is adjacent to white
(iv) Brown is adjacent to blue
(v) Red is at the bottom

15. Which colour is opposite of brown?
(a) White (b) Red
(c) Green (d) Blue

Directions (Q. 16 and 17) : *Study the following graph carefully to answer these questions:*

Quantity of Various items sold and price per kg

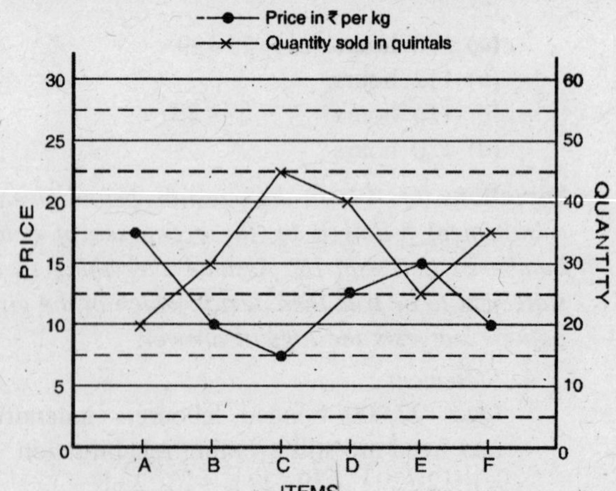

16. What is the ratio between the total values of quantity sold for items E and F respectively?

(*a*) 3 : 2 (*b*) 5 : 7
(*c*) 7 : 5 (*d*) 15 : 14

17. Total value of quantity sold for item C is what per cent of the total value of the quantity sold for item E?

(*a*) 85 (*b*) 87.5
(*c*) 90 (*d*) 111

18. In the following figure, diameter of each of the circles is 'd'. What is the area of the square ABCD?

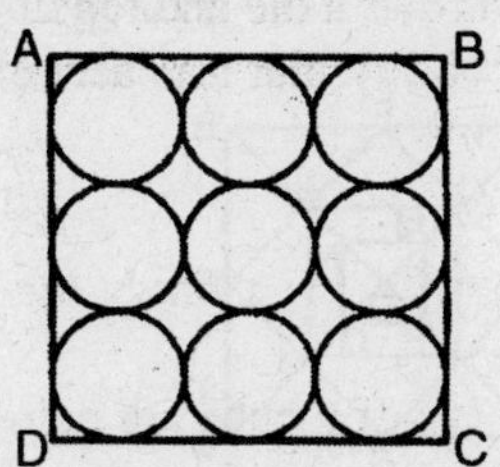

(*a*) $9/4d^2$ (*b*) $3d^2$
(*c*) $9d^2$ (*d*) $9d$

19. Find the radius of a circular field whose circumference measures $5\frac{1}{2}$ km.

(Take $\pi = 22/7$)

(*a*) 872 m
(*b*) 873 m
(*c*) 874 m
(*d*) 875 m

20. Samir invested ₹ 15000 at the rate of interest 10% p.a. for 1 year. If the interest compound every six months. What amount will Samir get at the end of the year?

(*a*) ₹ 16,500
(*b*) ₹ 16525.50
(*c*) ₹ 16537.50
(*d*) ₹ 18,150

ANSWERS

1	2	3	4	5	6	7	8	9	10
(*b*)	(*c*)	(*b*)	(*c*)	(*d*)	(*c*)	(*c*)	(*a*)	(*c*)	(*c*)
11	**12**	**13**	**14**	**15**	**16**	**17**	**18**	**19**	**20**
(*a*)	(*b*)	(*c*)	(*a*)	(*a*)	(*d*)	(*c*)	(*c*)	(*d*)	(*c*)

SOME SELECTED EXPLANATORY ANSWERS

1. Here, $3a = 4b = 6c$ $\therefore$ $a = 2c$ and $b = \frac{3}{2}c$

Now, $a + b + c = 27\sqrt{29}$

$\Rightarrow 2c + \frac{3}{2}c + c = 27\sqrt{29}$

$\Rightarrow \frac{9c}{2} = 27\sqrt{29}$ $\therefore$ $c = 6\sqrt{29}$

Again, $a = 2c = 2 \times 6\sqrt{29} = 12\sqrt{29}$

Now, $b = \frac{3}{2}c = \frac{3}{2} \times 6\sqrt{29} = 9\sqrt{29}$

Then,

$\sqrt{a^2 + b^2 + c^2}$

$= \sqrt{(12\sqrt{29})^2 + (9\sqrt{29})^2 + (6\sqrt{29})^2}$

$= \sqrt{144 \times 29 + 81 \times 29 + 36 \times 29}$

$= \sqrt{(144 + 81 + 36) \times 29} = \sqrt{261 \times 29}$

$= \sqrt{9 \times 29 \times 29} = 3 \times 29 = 87.$

2. The number inside each triangle is the difference of the numbers at its base *i.e.*

10 – 4 = 6, 18 – 4 = 14 and 18 – 10 = 8
14 – 8 = 6, 22 – 8 = 14 and 22 – 14 = 8,
Similarly
11 – 5 = 6, 15 – 5 = 10 and 15 – 11 = 4.

3. In 1 hour the part filled by both the pipes

$= \frac{1}{14} + \frac{1}{16} = \frac{15}{112}$

Hence, both the pipes will fill the cistern in $\frac{112}{15}$ min.

But due to leakage, the tank will be filled in

$$\frac{112}{15}+\frac{32}{60}=\frac{120}{15} = 8 \text{ hrs.}$$

Since, in 1 hr. the part emptied by the leakage

$$= \frac{15}{112}-\frac{1}{8}=\frac{1}{112}$$

Therefore, leakage will empty the tank in 112 hrs.

4. Bonded labour must be freed but when a large number of such freed labour is still awaiting rehabilitation, more cases can be identified later. The process of rehabilitation should be made easy. So, only course of action III follows.

5. **Trick :**

By Factorization Method

Factors of $15 = 3 \times 5$

Factors of $45 = 3^2 \times 5$

Factors of $90 = 3^2 \times 5 \times 2$

So, H.C.F. $= 3 \times 5 = 15$.

6. 

7. In each row one vertical line is moved to a horizontal position, then one more line is moved to a horizontal position.

8. In every 2 minutes, he is able to ascend $2 - 1 = 1$ metre. This way he ascends upto 12 metres because when he reaches at the top, he does not slip down. Thus, upto 12 metres he takes $12 \times 2 = 24$ minutes and for the last 2 metres he takes 1 minute. Therefore, he takes $24 + 1 = 25$ minutes to reach the top. That is, in 26th minute he reaches the top.

9. There are three sixes and one nine or three nines and one six in each figure. Odd man (*c*) has two of each.

10. $\because$ θ is in the third quadrant,

$\because$ $\sin\theta < 0$.

Thus $\sin\theta = -\tan\theta/\sqrt{(1+\tan^2\theta)} = -3/\sqrt{(10)}$.

11. If 26 is replaced by 27, then difference between successive terms of the series will be in the order of 11, 9, 7, 5, 3, 1. Therefore, alternative (*a*) consists the wrong term of the series.

12. Here, length of water column in 40 min $= 10 \times 40 \times 60$ m

Since, $7.2 \times 2.5 \times h$

$$= \frac{5}{100}\times\frac{3}{100}\times 10\times 40\times 60$$

$$\Rightarrow \quad h = \frac{36\times 100}{72\times 25} = 2 \text{ m.}$$

13. 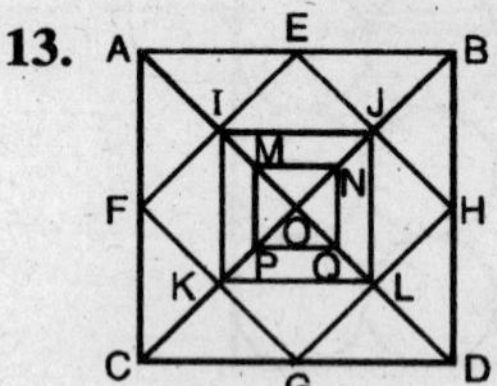

The main squares are : ABCD, IJKL, MNPQ and EFHG *i.e.* 4 squares.

Other squares are : EIJO, IFKO, JOLH and OKGL *i.e.* 4 squares

So, the total number of squares is $4 + 4 = 8$.

14. Let A denotes the event that a six occurs and B the event that the man reports that it is a six. Then the probability that it is actually a six is given by

$$P(A/B) = \frac{P(A\cap B)}{P(B)}$$

$$\text{Now } P(A\cap B) = \frac{1}{6}.\frac{3}{4}=\frac{3}{24}=\frac{1}{8}$$

$$P(B) = P(A\cap B) + P(\overline{A}\cap\overline{B})$$

$$= \frac{1}{6}.\frac{3}{4}+\frac{5}{6}.\frac{1}{4}=\frac{8}{24}=\frac{1}{3}$$

$$\text{Hence } P(A/B) = \frac{1/8}{1/3}=\frac{3}{8}.$$

16. Required ratio $= (25 \times 100 \times 15) : (35 \times 100 \times 10) = 15 : 14$.

17. Required percentage $= \frac{45\times 100\times 750}{25\times 100\times 15}\times 100$

$= 90\%$.

18. Length of each side of the square is $3d$

$\therefore$ Area of the square ABCD = $(3d)^2 = 9d^2$.

19. (*a*) $C = 2\pi r$

So, required circumference

$= 2 \times 22/7 \times 42$ metres = 264 metres

(*b*) $r = C/2\pi$

$$\text{So, required radius} = \frac{\frac{11}{2} \times 1000 \text{ m}}{2\pi}$$

$$= \frac{\frac{11}{2} \times 1000 \times 7}{2 \times 22} = 875 \text{ m.}$$

20. $A = 15000\left(1+\frac{5}{100}\right)^2 = 15000 \times \frac{441}{400}$

= ₹ 16537.50

SET-17

CSIR-UGC (NET) JRF & LECTURESHIP EXAM

PART-A

1. 10 men or 18 boys can do a piece of work in 15 days. In how many days would 25 men and 15 boys complete the same work working together?

(*a*) $5\frac{1}{2}$ days (*b*) $4\frac{1}{2}$ days

(*c*) $6\frac{2}{3}$ days (*d*) $2\frac{1}{3}$ days

Directions (Q. 2) : *In the following question, understand the arrangement pattern and then select the right answer from the given options.*

2. Mini is to the right of Rajni but to the left of Ananta. Saya is to the right of Mini but to the left of Jaya. Who is on the extreme left if all the girls are facing North?

(*a*) Jaya (*b*) Mini

(*c*) Rajni (*d*) Saya

3. Tarun bought a T.V. with 20% discount on the labelled price. Had he bought it with 25% discount, he would have saved ₹ 500. At what price did he buy the T.V.?

(*a*) ₹ 5000 (*b*) ₹ 8000

(*c*) ₹ 10000 (*d*) ₹ 12000

Directions (Q. 4) : *In the following question, select the set of conclusion which logically follows from the given statements.*

4. Statements :

I : All girls are pens.

II : Rahul is a boy.

Conclusions :

I : No boys are pens.

II : Rahul is not a pen.

III : Some pens are girls.

(a) Only conclusions II and III follow.

(b) Only conclusion I follows.

(c) All conclusions are correct.

(d) Only conclusions I and III follow.

5. What is the smallest number by which 3600 be multipled to make it a perfect cube?

(*a*) 9 (*b*) 50

(*c*) 300 (*d*) 60

Directions (Q. 6) : *In the question given below, a figure is given. From the given alternatives, select the one in which the given figure is embedded.*

6.

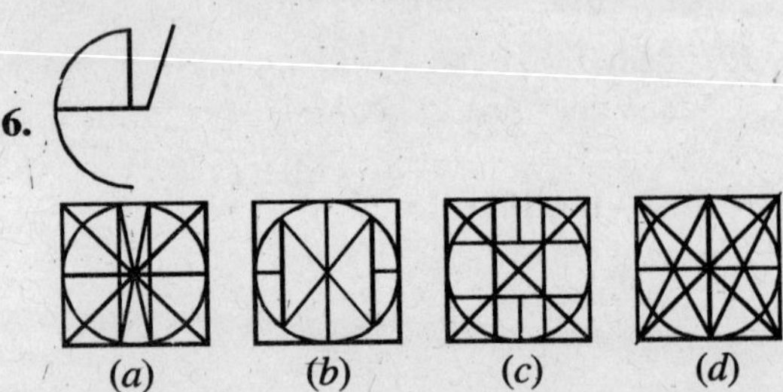

(*a*) (*b*) (*c*) (*d*)

Directions (Q. 7) : *In the question given below, there are three rows of figures with one figure missing from the third row. Study the pattern of figures in the rows and columns and find out the missing figure from the alternative figures that shall complete the figure matrix.*

7.

?

(*a*) (*b*) (*c*) (*d*)

8. Two stations A and B are 110 km apart on a straight line. One train starts from A at 7 a.m. and travels towards B at 20 km per hour speed. Another train starts from B at 8 a.m. and travels towards A at a speed of 25 km per hour. At what time will they meet ?

(*a*) 10 a.m.
(*b*) 11 a.m.
(*c*) 12 a.m.
(*d*) 13 a.m.

Directions (Q. 9) : *In the question that follows, some problem figures have been given. Problem figures themselves are also the answer figures. Out of the four figures (a), (b), (c) and (d), three are similar in a certain way. One figure is not like the other three. Choose the figure which is different from the rest.*

9.

(*a*) (*b*) (*c*) (*d*)

10. If sin θ = – 3/5 and θ lies in the third quadrant, then the value of cos (θ/2) is:

(*a*) 1/5
(*b*) $-1/\sqrt{(10)}$
(*c*) –1/5
(*d*) $1/\sqrt{(10)}$

Directions (Q. 11): *In this question a number series is given, followed by four alternatives. One term/element of the given series is wrong, i.e., it does not conform to the rule used in writing the series. This wrong term is depicted in the following alternatives. Spot out that wrong term/element and mark your answer.*

11. 15, 45, 90, 360, 1080, 2160, 6480

(*a*) 6480 (*b*) 1080
(*c*) 360 (*d*) 2160

12. The diameters of the ends of a dustbin 24 cm high, which is in the shape of a frustum of a cone are 30 cm and 10 cm. Determine its capacity and surface area. $\left(\text{Use } \pi = \dfrac{22}{7}\right)$

(*a*) 8000 cm^3; 2000 cm^2
(*b*) 81100 cm^3; 2200 cm^2
(*c*) 81100 cm^3; 2400 cm^2
(*d*) 8171.43 cm^3; 2420 cm^2

13. The number of squares in the figure below is :

(*a*) 6 (*b*) 10
(*c*) 8 (*d*) 12

14. The probability that an event A happens in one trial of an experiment is 0.7. Three independent trials of the experiment are performed. The probability that the event A happens atleast once is

(*a*) 0.657
(*b*) 0.973
(*c*) 0.189
(*d*) None of these

15. Which one number can be placed at the sign (?) of interrogation?

$$3 \times 6 = 18$$
$$4 \times 7 = 22$$
$$9 \times 1 = 20$$
$$5 \times 2 = ?$$

(*a*) 3 (*b*) 50
(*c*) 14 (*d*) 7

Directions (Q. 16) : *In the figure given below there are 27 cubes. Answer the question that follows :*

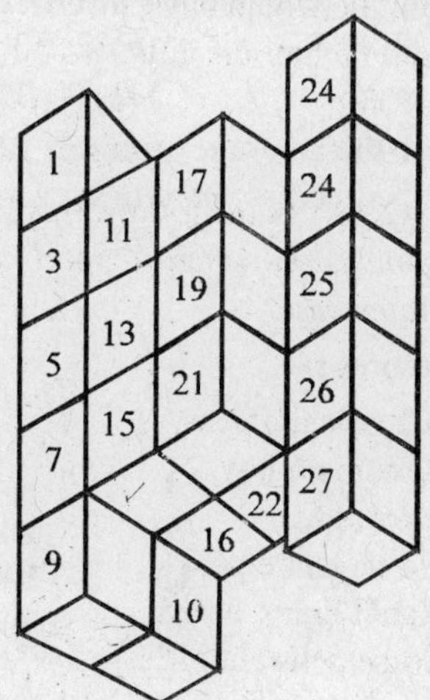

16. Number of cubes which have minimum number of faces touching the other cubes is :
(*a*) 1 (*b*) 2
(*c*) 4 (*d*) 6

17. A closed box measures externally 9 dm long, 6 dm broad, $4\frac{1}{2}$ dm high, and is made of wood $2\frac{1}{2}$ cm thick. Find the cost of lining it on the inside with metal at 6 P per sq. m.
(*a*) ₹ 12.30
(*b*) ₹ 10.32
(*c*) ₹ 12.33
(*d*) ₹ 10.33

Directions (Qs. 18 and 19): *Study the following graph carefully and answer the questions given below.*

Number of Building constructed, demolished and redeveloped across various cities in a year

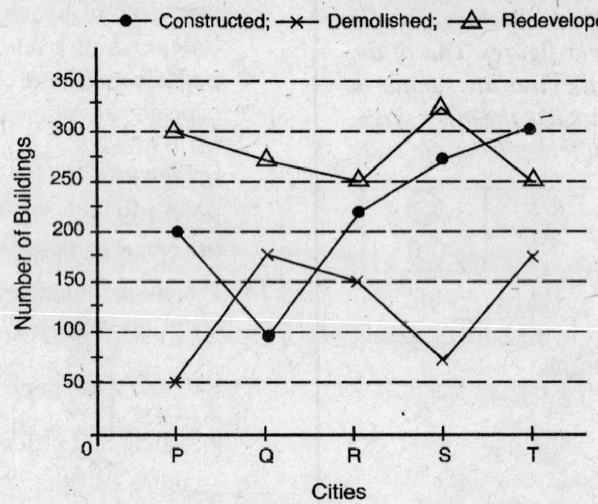

18. What is the respective ratio of the number of building demolished in city T to the number of buildings redeveloped in city P?
(*a*) 1 : 2 (*b*) 2 : 3
(*c*) 3 : 5 (*d*) 7 : 12

19. What is the average number of buildings demolished across the cities?
(*a*) 115 (*b*) 125
(*c*) 132 (*d*) 135

20. What will be the cost of tiling the floor @ ₹ 38/- per m^2, if the hall is of a square shape and has perimeter of 400 m?
(*a*) ₹ 3,20,000
(*b*) ₹ 3,40,000
(*c*) ₹ 3,60,000
(*d*) ₹ 3,80,000

ANSWERS

1	2	3	4	5	6	7	8	9	10
(*b*)	(*c*)	(*b*)	(*a*)	(*d*)	(*a*)	(*c*)	(*a*)	(*d*)	(*b*)
11	**12**	**13**	**14**	**15**	**16**	**17**	**18**	**19**	**20**
(*a*)	(*d*)	(*c*)	(*b*)	(*c*)	(*b*)	(*c*)	(*d*)	(*b*)	(*d*)

SOME SELECTED EXPLANATORY ANSWERS

1. 10 men ≡ 18 boys

25 men ≡ $\frac{18}{10}\times 25 = 45$ boys

Hence, 25 men + 15 boys = 45 + 15 = 60 boys
Now, 18 boys can do a piece of work in 15 days.
Hence, 60 boys will do a piece of work in

$\frac{15\times 18}{60} = \frac{9}{2}$ days = $4\frac{1}{2}$ days.

2. The order in which the girls are positioned is :
Rajni, Mini, Ananta, Saya, Jaya.
or
Saya, Jaya, Ananta
or
Saya, Ananta, Jaya

3. Here, 5% = 500

$\therefore$ 100% = $\frac{500}{5}\times 100$ = ₹ 10,000

Hence, labelled price = ₹ 10,000

$\therefore$ S.P. = $\frac{80}{100}$ × ₹ 10,000 = ₹ 8000.

4. When all girls are pens then,
(*i*) some pens must be girls and also
(*ii*) when Rahul is a boy, he cannot be a pen.

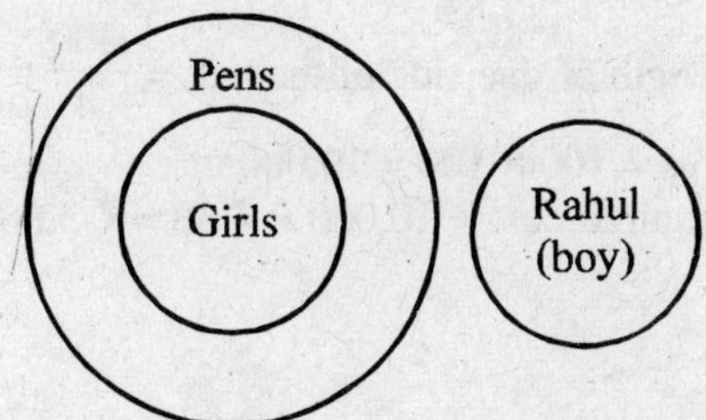

5. 3600 = 2 × 2 × 2 × 2 × 3 × 3 × 5 × 5.
To make it a perfect cube, we should multiply it by 2 × 2 × 3 × 5 = 60.

6. 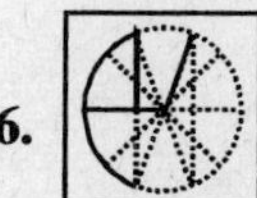

7. In each row the horizontal object is moved down and the small shape is moved down and then up again.

8. Till 8 a.m., the train from *A* covers a distance of 20 km.
Now, the remaining distance 110–20 = 90 km is covered by the trains with relative speed = 20 + 25 = 45 km/hr.

So, they meet after = $\frac{90}{45}$ = 2 hrs

That is , at 8 + 2 = 10 a.m.

Quicker Maths (Direct formula) :
They will meet at

$$8\text{ a.m.} + \frac{110-(8\text{ a.m.}-7\text{ a.m.})\,20}{20+25}$$

= 8 a.m. + 2 hr = 10 a.m.

9. In all the figures except (*d*) the circle and the pentagon have a hexagon inside them. In (*d*) the circle and pentagon have a pentagon.

10. $\because$ θ lies in the third quadrant
$\because$ cos θ is –ve
$\because$ sin θ = – 3/5
$\Rightarrow$ cosθ = – √(1 – sin² θ) = – 4/5

Now, $\cos^2\frac{1}{2}\theta = \frac{1}{2}(1+\cos\theta)$

$= \frac{1}{2}(1-4/5) = 1/10$

$\Rightarrow \cos\frac{1}{2}\theta = \pm 1/\sqrt{(10)}$

But given that, 180° < θ < 270°
⇒ 90° < θ/2 < 135°
i.e., θ/2 lies in the second quadrant

$\Rightarrow \cos\frac{1}{2}\theta$ is –ve

Hence, $\cos\frac{1}{2}\theta = -1/\sqrt{10}$.

11. A quick scrutiny of the series reveals that second term is three times the first, third term is two times the second and fourth term is four times the third. The same pattern is being followed by the remaining terms of the series. Therefore, 6480 should be replaced by 2160 × 4 = 8640. Hence, alternative (*a*) contains the wrong term.

12. Slant height, $l=\sqrt{h^2+(R-r)^2}$

$=\sqrt{(24)^2+(15-5)^2}=\sqrt{676}=26$ cm

Now, capacity of the dustbin

$=\frac{\pi h}{3}\left(R^2+r^2+Rr\right)$

$=\frac{22\times 24}{7\times 3}(15^2+5^2+15\times 5)$

$=\frac{22\times 8}{7}(225+25+75)=\frac{22\times 8}{7}\times 325$

$=\frac{57200}{7}=8171.43\text{ cm}^3$

Surface area of the dustbin

$=\pi\left[\left(R^2+r^2\right)+l(R+r)\right]$

$=\frac{22}{7}\left[(15)^2+(5)^2+26(15+5)\right]$

$=\frac{22}{7}[225+25+520]=\frac{22}{7}\times 770=2420\text{ cm}^2.$

13. 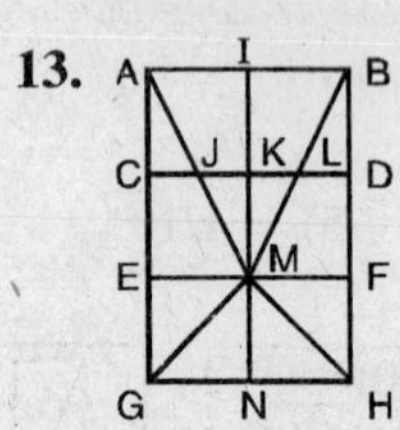

The simplest squares are : AICK, CKEM, EMGN, IBKD, KDMF and MFNH *i.e.* 6 squares. Other squares are ABEF and CDGH *i.e.* 2 squares.

So, the total number of squares is 6 + 2 = 8.

14. $P(A)=0.7\ \therefore\ P(\overline{A})=0.3$

P(at least once) = 1 – P (no occurrence)
$= 1-(0.3)^3 = 0.973.$

17. The internal dimensions are

$8\frac{1}{2}$ dm, $5\frac{1}{2}$ dm, 4 dm.

Area of the 4 sides $2\left(8\frac{1}{2}+5\frac{1}{2}\right)\times 4$ sq. dm

= 112 sq. dm

Area of bottom and top $=2\times 8\frac{1}{2}\times 5\frac{1}{2}$ sq. dm

$=\frac{187}{2}$ sq. dm

Total area to be lined $=\left(112+\frac{187}{2}\right)^2$ sq. dm

So, cost $=41\frac{1}{2}\times 6\text{P}=$ ₹ 12.33.

18. Required ratio = 175 : 300 = 7 : 12.

19. Average number of buildings demolished

$=\frac{50+175+150+75+175}{5}=\frac{625}{5}=125.$

20. Length of one side of the hall $=\frac{400}{4}=100$ m

Area = 100 × 100 = 10,000 m²

Required cost = 10,000 × ₹ 38 = ₹ 3,80,000.

SET-18

CSIR-UGC (NET) JRF & LECTURESHIP EXAM

PART-A

1. A monkey wants to climb up a glazed pole. He climbs 12 metres in 1 minute and then he slips back 3 metres in the next minute. If the pole is 63 metre high, how long does he take to climb at the top of the pole?

(*a*) $11\frac{1}{4}$ min (*b*) $12\frac{1}{2}$ min

(*c*) $12\frac{3}{4}$ min (*d*) $14\frac{3}{4}$ min

Directions (Q. 2) : *Read the following statements and answer the question given below :*

Rajat, Sushil and Nagesh play football, hockey and cricket. Rajat, Ramu and Nagesh play hockey, cricket and basketball. Rajat, Sushil, Mayank and Nagesh play football and cricket.

2. Which of the following two boys play all the games?

(*a*) Nagesh, Rajat (*b*) Mayank, Ramu

(*c*) Ramu, Nagesh (*d*) Sushil, Mayank

3. A owns a house worth ₹ 10000. He sells it to B at a profit of 10% based on the worth of the house. B sells the house back to A at a loss of 10%. In this transaction A gets:

(*a*) no profit no loss (*b*) profit of ₹ 1000

(*c*) profit of ₹ 1100 (*d*) profit of ₹ 1200

Directions (Q. 4) : *The question given below consists of a question and two statements numbered I and II given below it. You have to decide whether data provided in the statements are sufficient to answer the question. Read both the statements and give answer—*

(*a*) if the data in statement I alone are sufficient to answer the question, while the data in statement II alone are not sufficient to answer the question.

(*b*) if the data in statement II alone are sufficient to answer the question, while the data in statement I alone are not sufficient to answer the question.

(*c*) if the data either in statement I or in statement II alone are sufficient to answer the question.

(*d*) if the data even in both statements I and II together are not sufficient to answer the question.

4. Rajiv's rank is 17th in his class. What is his rank from the last?

I. There are 70 students in his class.

II. Abhijit who ranks 20th in Rajiv's class is 51st from the last.

5. The sum of two numbers is 528, and their H.C.F. is 33. How many pairs of such numbers can be formed?

(*a*) 4 (*b*) 5

(*c*) 6 (*d*) 7

Directions (Q. 6) : *In the question given below, a figure is given. From the given alternatives select the one in which the given figure is embedded.*

6.

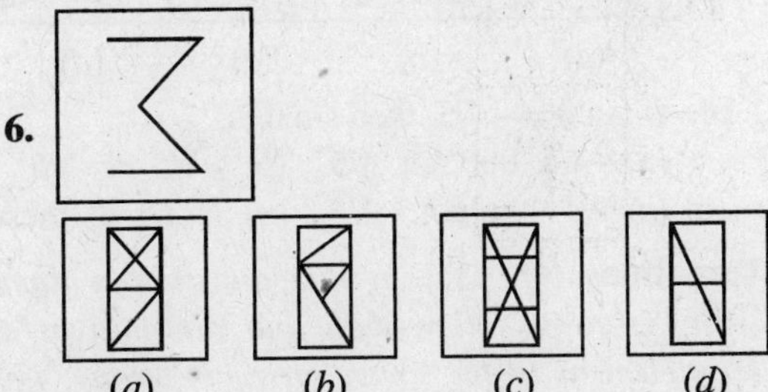

Directions (Q. 7) : *In the question given below, there are three rows of figures with one figure missing from the third row. Study the pattern of figures in the rows and columns and find out the missing figure from the alternative figures that shall complete the figure matrix.*

7. 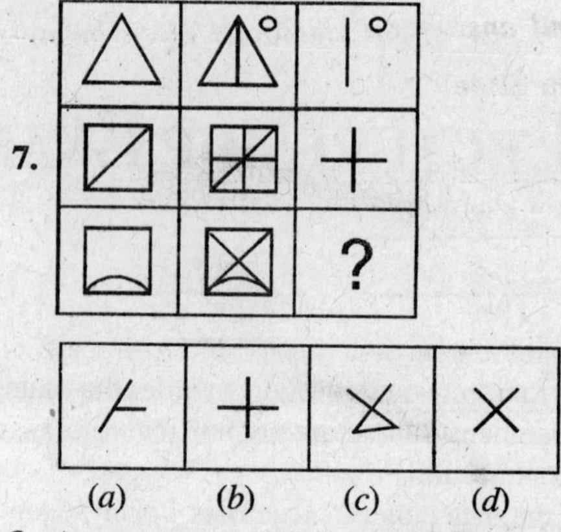

(a) (b) (c) (d)

8. A man travels 360 km in 4 hrs, partly by air and partly by train. If he had travelled all the way by air, he would have saved 4/5 of the time he was in train and would have arrived at his destination 2 hours early. Find the distance he travelled by air and train.

(a) 80 km (b) 90 km
(c) 70 km (d) 95 km

Directions (Q. 9) : *In the question that follows, some problem figures have been given. Problem figures themselves are also the answer figures. Out of the four figures (a), (b), (c) and (d), three are similar in a certain way. One figure is not like the other three. Choose the figure which is different from the rest.*

9. 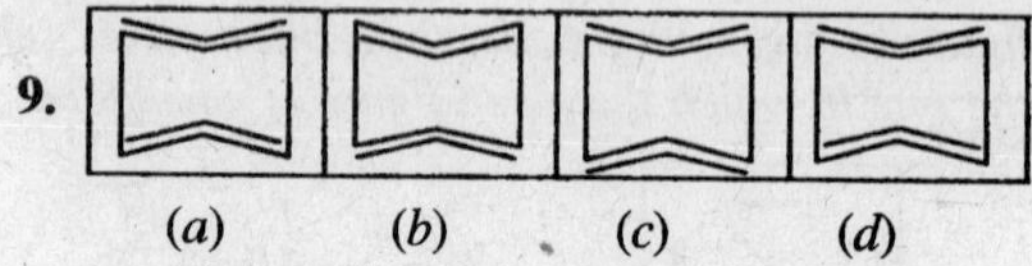

(a) (b) (c) (d)

10. If tan θ = – 4/3, then sin θ is:

(a) –4/5 but not 4/5 (b) –4/5 or 4/5
(c) 4/5 but not –4/5 (d) None of these

Directions (Q. 11): *In this question a number series is given, followed by four alternatives. One term/element of the given series is wrong, i.e., it does not conform to the rule used in writing the series. This wrong term is depicted in the following alternatives. Spot out that wrong term/element and mark your answer.*

11. 2, 9, 17, 65, 126, 217, 344

(a) 17 (b) 126
(c) 217 (d) 344

12. The surface area of a cuboid is 22 cm^2 and sum of the lengths of all its edges is 24 cm. Find the length of a diagonal of the cuboid.

(a) 2.74 cm (b) 3 cm
(c) 3.74 cm (d) 4 cm

13. How many hexagons are there in the figure given below?

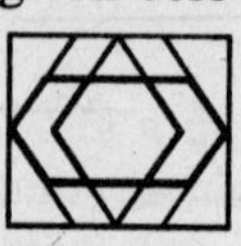

(a) 1 (b) 2
(c) 4 (d) 5

14. The probability of a problem being solved by two students are 1/2, 1/3. The probability of the problem being solved is :

(a) 2/3 (b) 4/3
(c) 1/3 (d) 1

Directions (Q. 15) : *In the question given below, a dice has been marked with some letters of numerals and placed in three different positions. Answer the questions that follow :*

15. Which letter/numeral is opposite to 3?

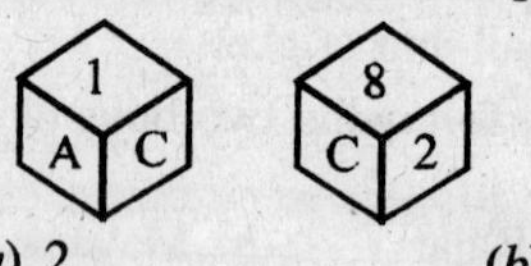

(a) 2 (b) A
(c) B (d) C

16. If '$\sqcap$' means '+'; $\sqsubset$ means '–'; $\sqsupset$ means '×'; $\sqcup$ means '+'; $||$ means '='; '→' means '>' and '←' means '<', then which of the following expressions is correct?

(a) (12 $\sqsubset$ 4) $\sqsupset$ (5 $\sqsupset$ 1) ← (10 $\sqcap$ 20)
(b) (20 $\sqsubset$ 8) $\sqcup$ (4 $\sqsubset$ 1) $||$ (4 $\sqcap$ 1)
(c) (10 $\sqcap$ 2) $\sqsubset$ (2 $\sqcup$ 2) → (10 $\sqcup$ 2)
(d) (18 $\sqcup$ 3) $\sqsupset$ (3 $\sqcap$ 1) $\sqcap$ (5 $||$ 120)

17. A room 8 metres long, 6 metres broad and 3 metres high has two windows of size $1\frac{1}{2}$ m × 1 m and a door 2 m × $1\frac{1}{2}$ m. Find the cost of papering the walls with paper 50 cm wide at 25 p. per metre.

(a) ₹ 39 (b) ₹ 30
(c) ₹ 36 (d) ₹ 42

Directions (Qs. 18-19): *Study the following graph carefully and answer the questions given below it:*

Number of Tourist Hotels in a State

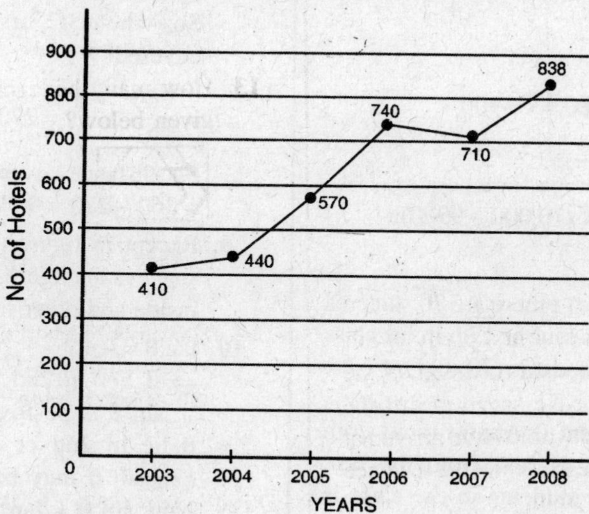

18. During which of the given years increase in number of hotels over the previous year was the highest?
(*a*) 2004 (*b*) 2006
(*c*) 2005 (*d*) 2008

19. What is the approximate percentage increase in tourist hotels in 2008 over that in 2003?
(*a*) 75 (*b*) 100
(*c*) 125 (*d*) 150

20. If the length and breadth of a rectangular field are increased, the area increases by 50%. If the increase in length was 20%, by what percentage was the breadth increased?
(*a*) 20% (*b*) 25%
(*c*) 30% (*d*) 40%

ANSWERS

1	2	3	4	5	6	7	8	9	10
(*c*)	(*a*)	(*c*)	(*c*)	(*a*)	(*b*)	(*d*)	(*b*)	(*c*)	(*b*)
11	**12**	**13**	**14**	**15**	**16**	**17**	**18**	**19**	**20**
(*a*)	(*c*)	(*c*)	(*a*)	(*d*)	(*d*)	(*a*)	(*b*)	(*b*)	(*b*)

SOME SELECTED EXPLANATORY ANSWERS

1. The monkey climbs 12 metres in 1 minute and then he slips back 3 metres in the next minute
∴ The monkey climbs in the first 2 minutes $= 12 - 3 = 9$ metres
∴ In the first 12 minutes the monkey climbs $= 9 \times 6 = 54$ metres
Remaining height of the pole to be covered by the monkey $= 63 - 54 = 9$ metres
∴ The monkey will climb the height of 9 metres in the 13th minute
∵ The monkey climbs 12 metres in 1 minute
∴ The monkey will climb 9 metres in $\frac{1}{12} \times 9$

$= \frac{3}{4}$ minute

$\therefore$ Time spent in climbing at the top of the pole $= \left(12+\frac{3}{4}\right)$ minutes $= 12\frac{3}{4}$ minutes.

3. Final C.P. for A

$= \frac{110}{100} \times \frac{90}{100} \times ₹\ 10000 = ₹\ 9900$

Hence, profit for A

$= \frac{10}{100} \times ₹\ 10{,}000 + ₹\ (10{,}000 - 9900)$

$= ₹\ 1100.$

4. According to statement I there are 70 students in the class. If Rajiv's rank is 17th in his class then his rank from the last is (70 – 17) + 1 *i.e.* 54th.

According to statement II Abhijit ranks 20th in Rajiv's class and is 51st from the last. The total number of students in the class is (20 + 51) – 1 *i.e.* 70. Now, Rajiv's rank from last will be (70 – 17) + 1 *i.e.* 54th.

So, either of the statements alone is sufficient to answer the question.

5. Trick :

Let the numbers be 33 a and 33 b

Now, 33 a + 33b = 528

or, 33 (a + b) = 528

So, $a + b = 16$

The possible values of a and b are (1, 15); (2, 14); (3, 13); (4, 12); (5, 11); (6, 10); (7, 9) and (8, 8)

Of these, the pairs of numbers that are prime to each other are (1, 15); (3, 13) ; (5, 11) ; and (7, 9)

So, the possible pairs of numbers are (33, 495); (99, 429); (165, 363); (231, 297).

6. 

7. In each row the components of the figure in first column removed from the figure in the second column gives the components in the third column.

8. 4/5 of total time in train = 2 hours.

So, total time in train $= 2 \times \frac{5}{4} = 5/2$ hrs

So, total time spent in air = 4 – 5/2 = 3/2 hrs.

By the given hypothesis, if 360 km is covered by air, then time taken is 4 – 2 = 2 hrs.

So, when 3/2 hrs is spent in air, distance covered

$= \frac{360}{2} \times \frac{3}{2} = 270$ km

So, distance covered by train

= 360 – 270 = 90 km.

9. Except in figure (c), the defined part of the shape in the figures is double-walled; one from inside and other from outside.

10. $\tan\theta = -4/3$

$\Rightarrow$ θ lies in 2nd or 4th quadrant.

$\therefore$ $\sin\theta$ is positive or negative according as θ lie in 2nd or 4th quadrant respectively, *i.e.*, $\sin\theta$ may be positive or negative.

Now $\sin\theta = \tan\theta/\sqrt{(1 + \tan^2\theta)} = 4/5$

Hence $\sin\theta = -\ 4/5$ or $4/5$.

11. If 17 is replaced by 28, then terms of the series will be in the order of $1^3 + 1$, $2^3 + 1$, $3^3 + 1$, $4^3 + 1$, $5^3 + 1$, $6^3 + 1$ and $7^3 + 1$. Therefore, alternative (a) consists the wrong term.

12. Here, $2(lb + bh + hl) = 22$ cm and

also, $4(l + b + h) = 24$ cm

$\Rightarrow$ $(l + b + h) = 6$ cm

Now,

$l^2 + b^2 + h^2 = (l + b + h)^2 - 2(lb + bh + hl)$

$= (6)^2 - 22 = 14$

Since, diagonal,

$d = \sqrt{l^2 + b^2 + h^2} = \sqrt{14} = 3.74$ cm.

13. 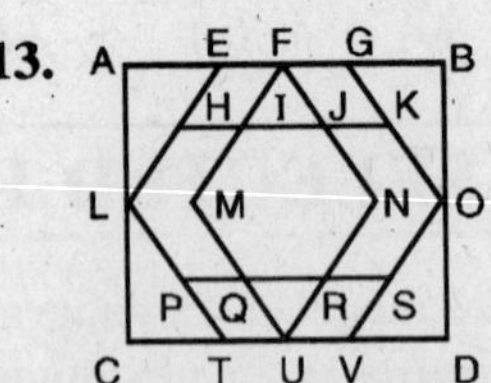

The larger hexagon is : EG – GO – GV – VT – TL – LE *i.e.* – 1 hexagon.

The smaller hexagons are : IJ – JN – NR – RQ – QM – MT, HJ – JN – NR – RP – PL – LH and IK – KO – OS – SQ – QM – MI, *i.e.*, –3,

hexagons. So, the total number of hexagons is $1 + 3 = 4$
(Hexagon is a figure having six sides of equal length.)

14. The probability that the problem is not being solved by any of the two students
$= (1 - 1/2)(1 - 1/3) = 1/3$
$\therefore$ Probability that the problem is solved
$= 1 - 1/3 = 2/3.$

15. After observing the views of the same dice the sides that can be clearly understood to be the opposites are : 1—8, A—2 and C—3.

17. Area of walls = 2(8 + 6) 3 = 84 sq.m
Area of two windows and door
$= 2 \times 1\frac{1}{2} \times 1 + 2 \times 1\frac{1}{2} = 6$ sq. m
Area to be covered = 84 – 6 = 78 sq.m
So, length of paper $= \dfrac{78 \times 100 \text{ m}}{50} = 156$ m
So, cost $= \dfrac{156 \times 25}{100} =$ ₹ 39.

18. Increase in number of hotels over previous years are as follows:
In 2004, 440 – 410 = 30
In 2005, 570 – 440 = 130
In 2006, 740 – 570 = 170
In 2008, 838 – 710 = 128
Hence, in 2006, increase in number of hotels over 2005 was the highest.

19. Required percentage of increase
$= \dfrac{838 - 410}{410} \times 100 = \dfrac{428}{410} \times 100$
$= 104.4\% \approx 100\%.$

20. Here, $20 + x + \dfrac{20 \times x}{100} = 50$
$\Rightarrow x + \dfrac{x}{5} = 30$
$\Rightarrow \dfrac{6x}{5} = 30 \qquad \therefore\ x = \dfrac{5 \times 30}{6} = 25$
Hence, breadth was increased by 25%.

SET-19

CSIR-UGC (NET) JRF & LECTURESHIP EXAM

PART-A

1. Perimeter of a rectangular field is 760 m and its length and breadth are in the ratio 11 : 8. Area of this rectangular field is

(*a*) 35200 sq. m. (*b*) 34700 sq. m.
(*c*) 35600 sq. m. (*d*) 45200 sq. m.

2. If → stands for subtract, ← stands for add, ↑↑ stands for multiply, ↓↓ stands for divide, ↔ for greater than, ←┬→ stands for equal to, then which of the following alternatives is true?

(*a*) 4 ← 6 ↑↑ 2 ←→ 3 → 12 ← 12
(*b*) 10 ↓↓ 5 ↑↑ 5 ←→ 9 → 3 ← 4
(*c*) 15 ↑↑ 2 → 5 ←→ 12 ↓↓ 4 ← 3
(*d*) 13 ↓↓ 13 ← 1 ↔ 20 → 5 ↑↑ 2

3. Given that 5th July 1981 was Sunday, what was the day on 5th April of the same year?

(*a*) Friday (*b*) Monday
(*c*) Saturday (*d*) Sunday

Directions (Qs. 4 and 5): *Study the following Pie-chart carefully and answer the questions given below:*

Percentage of People in a City working in Night shifts from various Industries (Total number of people = 40250)

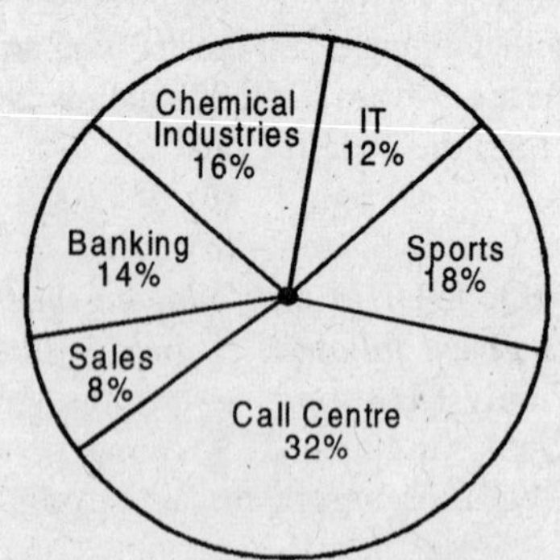

Percentage of Females from Various Industries working in Night shifts

Industries	*Females*
IT	20%
Sports	20%
Call Centre	45%
Sales	60%
Banking	40%
Chemical Industries	15%

4. What is the respective ratio of men to women working in night shifts from the Call centre Industry?

(*a*) 9 : 11
(*b*) 11 : 9
(*c*) 8 : 13
(*d*) 13 : 8

5. What is the difference between the total number of men and the total number of women working in night shifts from all the industries together?

(*a*) 13254 (*b*) 13363
(*c*) 13524 (*d*) 13542

Directions (Q. 6) : *In the question given below, which one would be the mirror image of the given figure when the mirror is placed along the line shown in the figure.*

6. Problem Figure

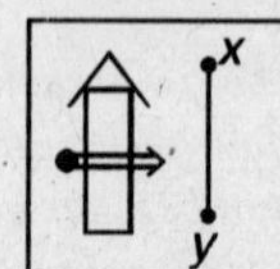

Answer Figures

   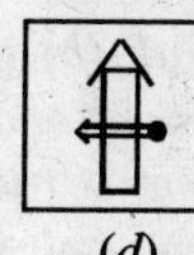

(*a*) (*b*) (*c*) (*d*)

7. A five digit number divisible by 3 is to be formed using the numbers 0, 1, 2, 3, 4 and 5 without repetitions. The total number of ways this can be done is:

(*a*) 216 (*b*) 600
(*c*) 240 (*d*) 3125

Directions (Q. 8) : *In the question given below a figure is given. From the given alternatives select the one in which the given figure is embeded.*

8. 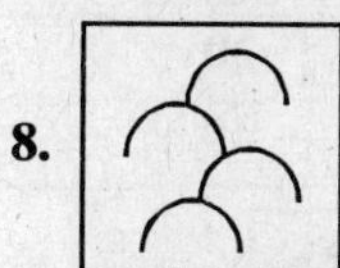

 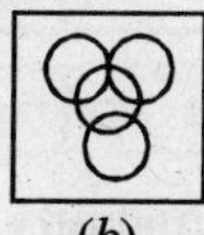 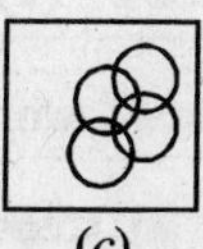 

(*a*) (*b*) (*c*) (*d*)

9. How many rectangles are there in the figure given below?

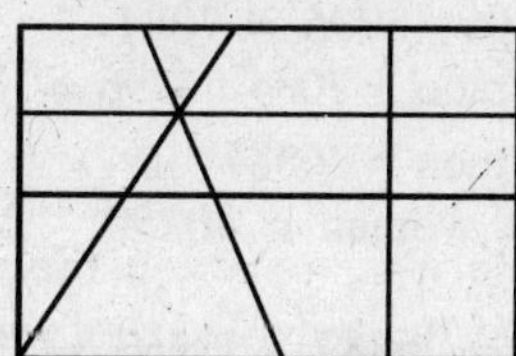

(*a*) 16 (*b*) 18
(*c*) 17 (*d*) 19

10. Vipul is taller than Hans. Hans is taller than Anand. Alok is taller than Ashok. Ashok is taller than Hans. Who among them is the tallest?

(*a*) Vipul
(*b*) Alok
(*c*) Ashok
(*d*) Cannot be determined

Directions (Q. 11): *In the question below, a number series has been given, followed by four alternatives. One term/element of the given number series is wrong. Find out that wrong term and spot out a number from the alternatives which will replace the wrong term of the series.*

11. 0, 9, 64, 169, 576, 1225

(*a*) 225 (*b*) 360
(*c*) 444 (*d*) 556

12. $\log_{10} \tan 1° + \log_{10} \tan 2° + ... + \log_{10} \tan 89° = ?$

(*a*) 0 (*b*) 1
(*c*) 2 (*d*) 3

13. The number of parallelograms in this figure is :

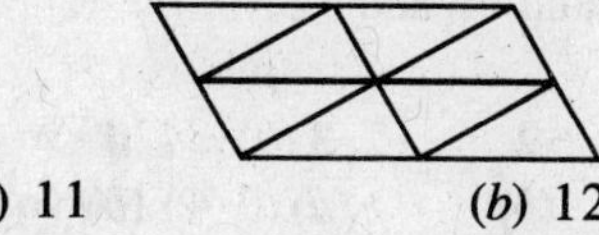

(*a*) 11 (*b*) 12
(*c*) 9 (*d*) 10

14. A dice is thrown. Consider two events A = {1, 2, 3, 4}, B = {4, 5, 6}. Then the events A and B are :

(*a*) independent (*b*) dependent
(*c*) mutually exclusive (*d*) exhaustive

15. What angle will the two hands of a clock make at 6.20 a.m.?

(*a*) 60° (*b*) 70°
(*c*) 75° (*d*) 45°

16. A, B, C, D and E are in a row. B is between A and C, D is between C and E. Who is in the middle?

(*a*) B (*b*) D
(*c*) A (*d*) C

17. Some persons can do a piece of work in 12 days. Two times the number of such persons will do half of that work in:

(*a*) 12 days (*b*) 3 days
(*c*) 6 days (*d*) 4 days

18. In a code language 256 means 'you are good', 637 means 'we are bad', 358 means 'good and bad'. Find the code for 'and'.

(*a*) 2 (*b*) 5
(*c*) 8 (*d*) 3

Directions (Q. 19) : *In the following question, a statement is given, followed by two Arguments.*
Mark (*a*) if only I is strong.
Mark (*b*) if only argument II is strong.
Mark (*c*) if both the arguments are strong, and
Mark (*d*) if neither I nor II is strong.

19. Statement: Computer based technology is very fruitful for industrial development in India.

Arg. I: Yes, accuracy, fast production and fineness are possible through computer technology.

Arg. II: No, it will increase unemployment in the country.

Directions (Q. 20) : *There are two statements P and Q each followed by an inference. Now determine which of the statements supports its inference. Mark (a) if only statement P is true, Mark (b) if only statement Q is true, mark (c) if both P and Q are true and mark (d) if neither of them is true in accordance with logic.*

20. (P) Water boils at 100ºC. This liquid boils at 100ºC. Therefore, this liquid is water.

(Q) Every bottle with a green label contains apple juice. Apple juice is safe to drink. Therefore, it is harmless to drink from every bottle with green label.

ANSWERS

1	2	3	4	5	6	7	8	9	10
(*a*)	(*b*)	(*d*)	(*b*)	(*c*)	(*d*)	(*a*)	(*c*)	(*b*)	(*d*)
11	**12**	**13**	**14**	**15**	**16**	**17**	**18**	**19**	**20**
(*a*)	(*a*)	(*a*)	(*d*)	(*b*)	(*d*)	(*b*)	(*c*)	(*c*)	(*b*)

SOME SELECTED EXPLANATORY ANSWERS

1. Suppose length and breadth of the rectangular field are $11x$ m and $8x$ m.

$\therefore$ Perimeter of the field $= 2(11x + 8x)$
$= 2 \times 19x = 38x$ m.

Now, $38x = 760 \Rightarrow x = \frac{760}{38} = 20$

$\therefore$ Length of the field $= 11 \times 20 = 220$ m

Breadth of the field $= 8 \times 20 = 160$ m

$\therefore$ Area of the field $= 220 \times 160 = 35200$ sq. m.

2. (*a*) $4 + 6 \times 2 = 3 - 12 + 12$
$16 = 3$

(*b*) $10 \div 5 \times 5 = 9 - 3 + 4$
$10 = 10$

(*c*) $15 \times 2 - 5 = 12 \div 4 + 3$
$25 = 6$

(*d*) $13 \div 13 + 1 > 20 - 5 \times 2$
$2 > 10$

3. Number of days between 5th April, 1981 and 5th July, 1981 = 25 + 31 + 30 + 5 = 91 days

Hence, if 5th July, 1981 was Sunday, then 5th April, 1981 was also Sunday.

4. Number of people working in night shifts from Call Centre Industry $= \frac{32}{100} \times 40250 = 12880$

Number of women working in night shifts from Call Centre Industry $= \frac{45}{100} \times 12880$
$= 5796$

So, the number of men working from same Industry = 12880 – 5796 = 7084

Hence, Required ratio = 7084 : 5796 = 11 : 9.

5. Total number of men = 26887

Total number of women = 40250 – 26887 = 13363

Their difference = 26887 – 13363 = 13524.

7. The number is divisible by 3 if the sum of all its digits is divisible by 3.

Here sum of all six digits is 15. The sum of five digits will also be divisible by 3 if we leave either 0 or 3 from the six digits.

Leaving 3, total no. of numbers = 5! – 4!.

(Since the number having 0 as first place are of four digits like 01245).

And leaving 0, total no. of number = 5!.

Hence, the required number = (5! – 4!) + 5! = 216.

8. 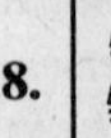 

9. 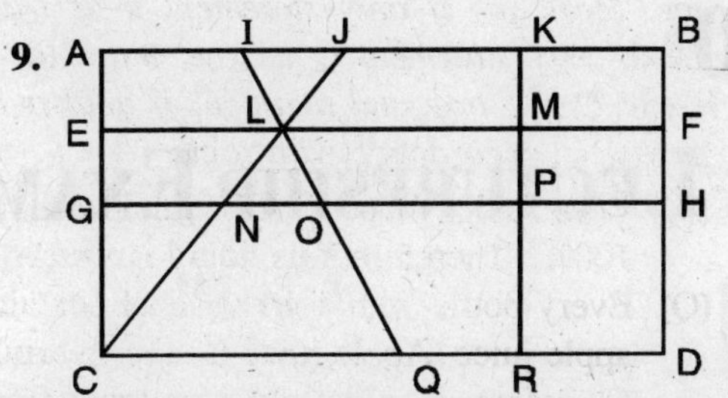

The main rectangle is ABCD *i.e.* 1 rectangle
The simplest rectangles are AKEM, KBMF, EMGP, MFPH, GPCR and PHRD *i.e.* 6 rectangles
The rectangles divided into two parts are KBPH and MFRD *i.e.* 2 rectangles
Other rectangles are ABEF, ABGH, AKGP, AKCR, EFGH, EFCD, EMCR, GHCD and KBRD *i.e.* 9 rectangles
So, the total number of rectangles is
$1 + 6 + 2 + 9 = 18$.

10. On the basis of height, the descending order will be Vipul/Alok, Ashok, Hans, Anand. Either Vipul or Alok is the tallest.

11. If 169 is replaced by 225, then the terms will get arranged in a particular series, *i.e.*, $(1^2 - 1)^2$, $(2^2 - 1)^2$, $(3^2 - 1)^2$, $(4^2 - 1)^2$, $(5^2 - 1)^2$ and $(6^2 - 1)^2$. Therefore, (*a*) is the correct alternative.

12. $\log \tan 89° = \log \cot 1°$
$= -\log \tan 1°$. etc.
$\therefore$ Given expression
$= \log \tan 1° + \log \tan 2° + \ldots + \log \tan 44° + \log \tan 45° - \log \tan 44° - \ldots - \log \tan 2° - \log \tan 1°$
$= \log \tan 45° = \log 1 = 0$.

13. 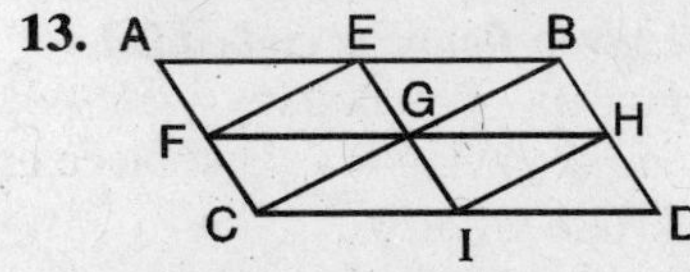

The main parallelogram in ABCD *i.e.* 1 parallelogram
The simplest parallelograms are : AEFG, FGCI, EBGH, GHID, FECG and GBIH *i.e.* 6 parallelograms
Other parallelograms are : ABFH, FHCD, AECI and EBID *i.e.* 4 parallelograms
So, the total number of parallelograms is
$1 + 6 + 4 = 11$.

14. P(A) = 4/6 = 2/3, P(B) = 3/6 = 1/2
P(AB) = 1/6
P(A).P(B) = 1/3
As $P(AB) \neq P(A).P(B)$
$\therefore$ A and B are not independent. Occurrence of one does not effect the occurrence of other,
$P(A \cap B) \neq$ null set
$\therefore$ Events are not mutually exclusive.
All the possible outcomes are existing, *i.e.*, $A \cup B$ is equal to sample space {1, 2, 3, 4, 5, 6}, therefore, events A and B are exhaustive.

15. 30 + 30 + 1/3 of 30 angles will be made by two hands of the clock.

17.

Work	Persons	Days
1 ↓	x ↑	12 ↓
$\frac{1}{2}$	$2x$	a

$$\Rightarrow \frac{a}{12} = \frac{x}{2x} \times \frac{1}{2}$$

$$\therefore \quad a = \frac{1}{4} \times 12 = 3 \text{ days.}$$

18. You are good = 256 ....(1)
We are bad = 637 ....(2)
Are = 6
We are bad = 637 ....(2)
Good and bad = 358 ....(3)
bad = 3
you are good = 256
good and bad = 358
good = 5 so and = 8.

19. There is no doubt at all about the first argument, and argument II is also strong because India is a populous country where labour intensive technique is more suitable than capital intensive technique.

20. No conclusion can be drawn from two "I" premises so statement P is wrong. Statement Q is correctly based on valid syllogism because of the word "every bottle" used in the statement provided we assume "safe" and "harmless" as synonymous.

SET-20

CSIR-UGC (NET) JRF & LECTURESHIP EXAM

PART-A

1. If perimeter of a right angled triangle is six times its smallest side, then the three sides of this triangle are in the ratio of :

(*a*) 13 : 5 : 12 (*b*) 13 : 12 : 5
(*c*) 12 : 5 : 13 (*d*) 13 : 5 : 10

2. If Δ denotes =; + denotes >, – denotes <, □ denotes ≠, × denotes > and ÷ denotes < then a + b – c denotes :

(*a*) b Δ c □ a (*b*) b □ a ÷ c
(*c*) a ÷ b × c (*d*) b – a + c

3. In a race of 300 metres A beats B by 15 metres or 5 seconds. How much time does A take to complete the race?

(*a*) 105 seconds (*b*) 100 seconds
(*c*) 95 seconds (*d*) 90 seconds

Directions (Qs. 4 and 5): *Study the following pie-chart carefully and answer the following questions.*

Pie-chart given below shows the expenditure incurred in bringing out the steel production

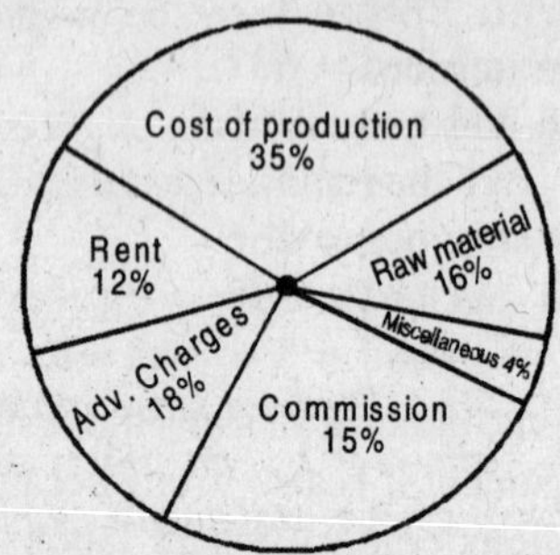

4. What should be the central angle of the sector for the cost of the raw material?

(*a*) 16° (*b*) 22.5°
(*c*) 54.8° (*d*) 57.6°

5. Commission on the steel is less than the advertisement charges by

(*a*) 8% (*b*) $12\frac{2}{3}\%$
(*c*) $16\frac{2}{3}\%$ (*d*) 18%

Directions (Q. 6) : *In the question given below, which one would be the mirror image of the given figure when the mirror is placed along the line shown in the figure.*

6. Problem Figure

Answer Figures

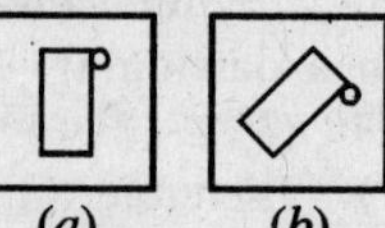
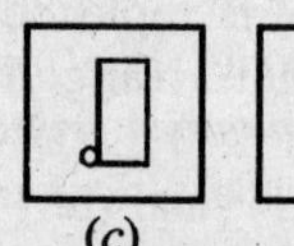
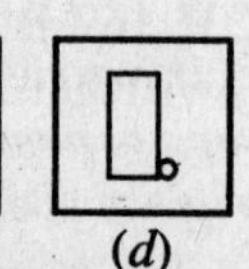

(*a*) (*b*) (*c*) (*d*)

7. Everybody in a room shakes hands with everybody else. The total number of hand shakes is 66. The total number of persons in the room is:

(*a*) 11 (*b*) 12
(*c*) 8 (*d*) 14

Directions (Q. 8) : *In the question given below, a figure is given. From the given alternatives select the one in which the given figure is embedded.*

8.

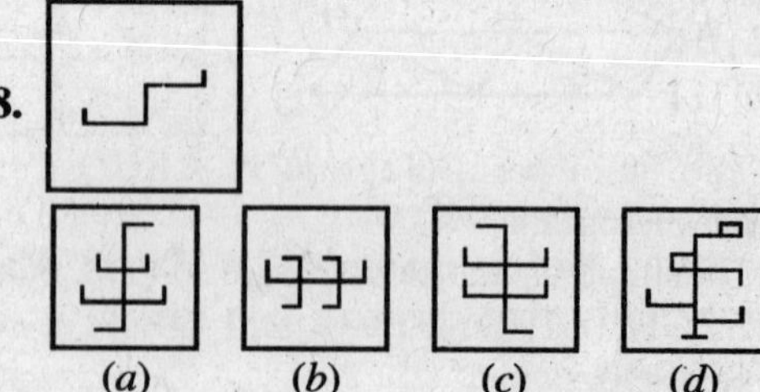

(*a*) (*b*) (*c*) (*d*)

9. How many sets of parallel lines are there in the following figure?

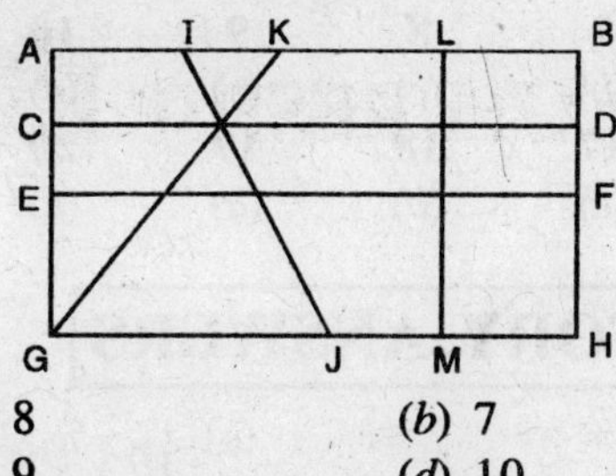

(*a*) 8 (*b*) 7
(*c*) 9 (*d*) 10

10. Sushma is richer than Rashmi whereas Anand is richer than Priya. Arun is as rich as Rashmi. Shoba is richer than Sushma.

Which of the following statements is correct according to the above propositions?

(*a*) Rashmi is poorer than Priya
(*b*) Priya is richer than Arun
(*c*) Arun is poorer than Sushma
(*d*) Anand is richer than Rashmi

Directions (Q. 11): *In the question below, a number series has been given, followed by four alternatives. One term/element of the given number series is wrong. Find out that wrong term and spot out a number from the alternatives which will replace the wrong term of the series.*

11. 5, 10, 17, 26, 39, 50, 65

(*a*) 39 (*b*) 36
(*c*) 37 (*d*) 42

12. $\log_{10}^{5} + \log_{10}^{(5x+1)} = \log_{10}^{(x+5)} + 1$, where value of x is:

(*a*) –8 (*b*) 3
(*c*) 6 (*d*) 10

13. The number of squares in the figure given below is

(*a*) 8
(*b*) 10
(*c*) 11
(*d*) 12

14. Host, his wife and 8 guests are to be seated on a round dining table at random. The probability that the host and his wife sit together is :

(*a*) 1/9 (*b*) 2/9
(*c*) 1/5 (*d*) 1/10

15. How many times the hands of a clock will be in vertically opposite directions from 10 a.m. to 10 p.m.?

(*a*) 12 times (*b*) 25 times
(*c*) 48 times (*d*) 36 times

16. A is the father of B, C is the brother of A, F is the sister of B. If M is the father of A, then establish relationship between F and C?

(*a*) Daughter and Father
(*b*) Husband and Wife
(*c*) Brother and Sister
(*d*) Niece and Uncle

17. 2 men and 7 boys can do a piece of work in 14 days; 3 men and 8 boys can do the same work in 11 days. Then 8 men and 6 boys can do three times of this work in

(*a*) 30 days (*b*) 4 days
(*c*) 21 days (*d*) 18 days

18. If TOM = 48 and DICK = 27. Find the value of CATTLE ?

(*a*) 93 (*b*) 61
(*c*) 91 (*d*) 65

Directions (Q. 19) : *In the following question a statement is given followed by two Arguments.*
Mark (*a*) if only I is strong.
Mark (*b*) if only argument II is strong.
Mark (*c*) if both the arguments are strong, and
Mark (*d*) if neither I nor II is strong.

19. Statement: Should there be women chief ministers in states?

Arg. I: Yes, only then the plight of women will be removed and their condition will improve.

Arg. II: No, a woman is not capable of ruling a state.

Directions (Q. 20) : *There are two statements P and Q, each followed by an inference. Now determine which of the statements supports its inference. Mark (a) if only statement P is true, Mark (b) if only statement Q is true, mark (c) if both P and Q are true and mark (d) if neither of them is true in accordance with logic.*

20. (P) All, that twinkles, are stars. Moon does not twinkle. Therefore moon is not a star.

(Q) All the metals are not in solid forms. Mercury is in a liquid form. Therefore, mercury is also a metal.

ANSWERS

1	2	3	4	5	6	7	8	9	10
(b)	(d)	(c)	(d)	(c)	(c)	(b)	(c)	(c)	(c)
11	**12**	**13**	**14**	**15**	**16**	**17**	**18**	**19**	**20**
(c)	(b)	(c)	(b)	(a)	(d)	(c)	(b)	(d)	(d)

SOME SELECTED EXPLANATORY ANSWERS

1. Suppose, the three sides of the triangle are *a, b* and *c* and *a* is the largest while *c* is the smallest side of the triangle.

Now, $(a + b + c) = c \times 6$

$\Rightarrow \quad a + b = 5c$

Again, $a^2 - b^2 = c^2$

$\Rightarrow \quad (a + b)(a - b) = c^2$

$\Rightarrow \quad 5c(a - b) = c^2$

$\Rightarrow \quad a - b = \frac{c}{5}$ [$\because a + b = 5c$]

Now, $a + b = 5c, a - b = \frac{c}{5}$

Since, $a = \frac{1}{2}\left(5c + \frac{c}{5}\right) = \frac{13c}{5}$

and $b = \frac{1}{2}\left(5c - \frac{c}{5}\right) = \frac{12c}{5}$

Hence, $a : b : c = \frac{13c}{5} : \frac{12c}{5} : c = 13 : 12 : 5.$

2. What is given is a > b < c

The equations are :

(*a*) b = c ≠ a which is wrong

(*b*) b ≠ a < c which is wrong

(*c*) a < b > c which is wrong

(*d*) b < a > c which is correct

Therefore, '*d*' is the answer.

3. From the question it is clear that speed of B

$= \frac{15}{5} = 3$ m/s

The time taken by B to cover 300 m $= \frac{300}{3}$

= 100 sec.

Hence, time taken by A to complete the race = 100 – 5 = 95 sec.

4. Required central angle $= \frac{16}{100} \times 360° = 57.6°.$

5. Required percentage $= \frac{18-15}{18} \times 100$

$= \frac{3}{18} \times 100 = 16\frac{2}{3}\%.$

7. Let there be *n* persons in a room.

$\therefore$ Total no. of shakehands $= {}^nC_2 = 66$

$\Rightarrow \frac{1}{2}n(n-1) = 66 \Rightarrow n^2 - n - 132 = 0$

$\Rightarrow (n + 11)(n - 12) = 0$

$\therefore \quad n = 12 \quad (\because n \neq -11)$

8. 

9. 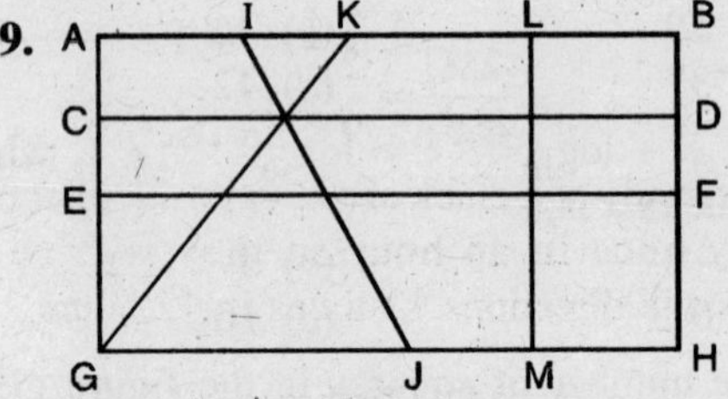

The horizontal lines are AB, CD, EF and GH *i.e.* 4 lines

The vertical lines are AG, LM and BH *i.e.* 3 lines

So, the total number of lines used to draw this figure is 4 + 3 + 2 = 9

10. On the basis of wealth, the descending order will be :

1. Shobha, Sushma, Rashmi/Arun
2. Anand, and Priya

(The two statements are not inter-related.)

11. If 39 is replaced by 37, then the terms of the series will be in a particular order of $2^2 + 1$, $3^2 + 1$, $4^2 + 1$, ... *etc*. Therefore, alternative (*c*) is the correct alternative.

12. $\log_{10}^{5} + \log_{10}^{(5x+1)} = \log_{10}^{(x+5)} + 1$

$\Rightarrow \log_{10}^{5} + \log_{10}^{(5x+1)} = \log_{10}^{(x+5)} + \log_{10}^{10}$

$\Rightarrow \log_{10}^{5(5x+1)} = \log_{10}^{10(x+5)} + \log_{10}^{10}$

$\Rightarrow \log_{10}^{5(5x+1)} = \log_{10}^{10(x+5)}$

$\Rightarrow 5(5x + 1) = 10(x + 5)$

$\Rightarrow 5x + 1 = 2x + 10 \quad \Rightarrow 3x = 9 \quad \therefore x = 3.$

13. 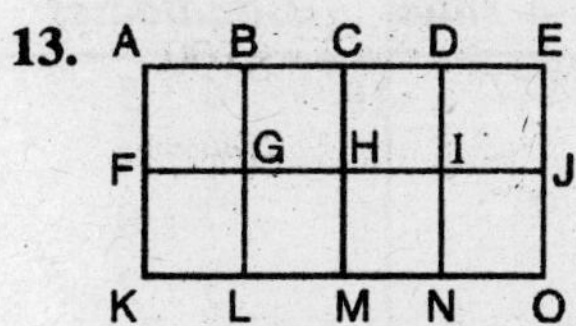

The simplest squares are ABFG, FGKL, BCGH, GHLM, CDHI, HIMN, DEIJ and IJNO *i.e.* 8 squares.

Other squares are ACKM, BDLN and CEMO *i.e.*, 3 squares.

So, the total number of squares is 8 + 3 = 11 squares.

14. Favourable ways = 2!.8!.

Total ways of arrangement of 10 persons = (10 – 1)! = 9!

$\therefore \quad P = \frac{2!8!}{9!} = \frac{2}{9}.$

15. The hands of a clock are in opposite direction only once in an hour so they will be in opposite directions 12 times in 12 hours.

16.

```
            M — Father
            |
(Brother) C — A — Father
              |
(Sister)    F — B
```

Here M is the father of A and A is the father of B.

17. Here, 14×2 men + 14×7 boys ≡ 11×3 men + 11×8 boys

⇒ 28 men + 98 boys ≡ 33 men + 88 boys

⇒ 5 men = 10 boys $\quad \therefore$ 1 man = 2 boys

Then, 2 men and 7 boys ≡ 4 boys + 7 boys = 11 boys

and also, 8 men and 6 boys ≡ 16 boys + 6 boys = 22 boys

Work	Persons	Days
1 ↓	11 ↑	14 ↓
3	22	x

$\Rightarrow \quad \frac{x}{14} = \frac{11}{22} \times \frac{3}{1}$

$\therefore \quad x = \frac{1}{2} \times 3 \times 14 = 21 \text{ days.}$

18. TOM $\qquad$ DICK

20 + 15 + 13 = 48 $\qquad$ 4 + 9 + 3 + 11 = 27

CATTLE

3 + 1 + 20 + 20 + 12 + 5 = 61.

19. The history illustrates that sufferings of women were stopped by men and so is the case even today. So argument I is weak and argument II is also weak because many of the women happened to be the rulers of states and nations and they are ruling well even today.

20. 'All that' twinkles are stars means some stars twinkle. So moon may or may not be a star. See the figure below:

```
M ——— P
S ——— M
S ——— P
```

Here the syllogism is AOO which is not valid according to figure number I. So P is not true.

In the statement Q, there are four terms (*i*) all the metals (*ii*) solid form (*iii*) mercury and (*iv*) liquid form. So no conclusion can be drawn.

SET-21

CSIR-UGC (NET) JRF & LECTURESHIP EXAM

PART-A

1. A horse and a cow were sold for ₹ 12000 each. The horse was sold at a loss of 20% and the cow at a gain of 20%. The entire transaction resulted in :

(*a*) no loss no gain
(*b*) loss of ₹ 1000
(*c*) gain of ₹ 1000
(*d*) loss of ₹ 2000

2. Which set of numbers has the same property as the following numbers?
21, 38, 55

(*a*) 47, 64, 80 (*b*) 19, 36, 55
(*c*) 23, 40, 57 (*d*) 35, 62, 79

3. When 60% of a number A is added to another number B, B becomes 175% of its previous value. Which one of the following is correct?

(*a*) A > B (*b*) B > A
(*c*) A = B (*d*) Data inadequate

Directions (Qs. 4 and 5): *Study the following pie-chart and table carefully and answer the questions given below it:*

Distribution of Candidates appeared in a competitive examination from seven states Total Candidates appeared = 3 lakh

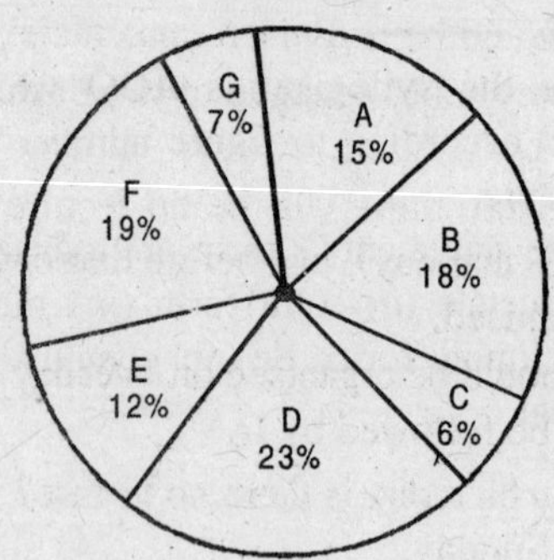

State-wise percentage and ratio of male and female qualified candidates

State	*% Qualified over appeared from a state*	*Ratio of qualified Candidates*
A	49	4 : 5
B	61	6 : 4
C	54	7 : 8
D	45	3 : 2
E	65	7 : 6
F	57	11 : 8
G	48	9 : 1

4. What is the number of male candidates qualified from state 'G'?

(*a*) 4536 (*b*) 4568
(*c*) 5454 (*d*) 5544

5. What is the total number of candidates qualified from states 'E' and D together?

(*a*) 45540 (*b*) 54410
(*c*) 54450 (*d*) 54540

Directions (Q. 6) : *In the question given below, which one would be the mirror image of the given figure when the mirror is placed along the line shown in the figure.*

6. Problem Figure

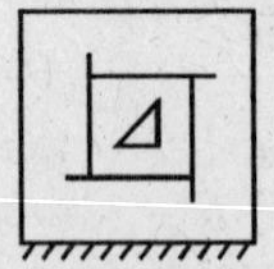

Answer Figures

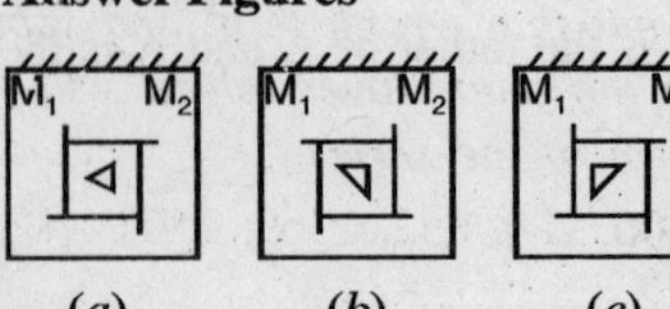

(*a*) (*b*) (*c*) (*d*)

7. A polygon has 44 diagonals, then the number of its side are:

(*a*) 11
(*b*) 7
(*c*) 8
(*d*) None of these

Directions (Qs. 8) : *In the question given below find the figure form which is embedded in the given pattern.*

8.

(*a*) (*b*) (*c*) (*d*)

9. The number of squares in the figure below is :

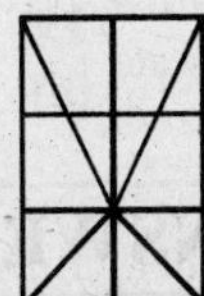

(*a*) 6 (*b*) 10
(*c*) 8 (*d*) 12

Directions (Q. 10) : *A. Gopal is shorter than Ashok but taller than Kuhav; B. Navin is shorter than Kuhav; C. Jayesh is taller than Navin; D. Ashok is taller than Jayesh.*

10. Who among them is the tallest?

(*a*) Gopal (*b*) Ashok
(*c*) Jayesh (*d*) Navin

Directions (Q. 11): *In the question below, a number series has been given, followed by four alternatives. One term/element of the given number series is wrong. Find out that wrong term and spot out a number from the alternatives which will replace the wrong term of the series.*

11. 4, 25, 100, 289, 652, 1369, 2500

(*a*) 2022
(*b*) 342
(*c*) 676
(*d*) 978

12. If N = *m*! (*m* is a fixed positive integer > 2), then

$$\frac{1}{\log_2 N}+\frac{1}{\log_3 N}+\ldots\ldots\ldots+\frac{1}{\log_m N}$$ is equal to:

(*a*) – 1 (*b*) 0
(*c*) 1 (*d*) 2

13. How many circles are there in the figure given below?

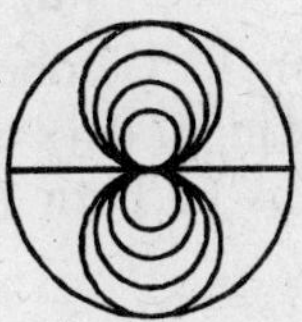

(*a*) 5 (*b*) 6
(*c*) 8 (*d*) 9

14. In order to get at least once a head with probability ≥ 0.9, the number of times a coin needs to be tossed is :

(*a*) 3
(*b*) 4
(*c*) 5
(*d*) None of these

Directions (Qs. 15 and 16) : *Read the following information to answer the given questions :*

Six lectures A, B, C, D, E and F are to be organised in a span of seven days — from Sunday to Saturday, only one lecture on each day in accordance with the following :

(*i*) A should not be organised on Thursday.
(*ii*) C should be organised immediately after F.
(*iii*) There should be a gap of two days between E and D.
(*iv*) One day there will be no lecture (Friday is NOT that day), just before that day D will be organised.
(*v*) B should be organised on Tuesday and should not be followed by D.

15. On which day is there no lecture?

(*a*) Sunday
(*b*) Friday
(*c*) Monday
(*d*) Can't be determined

16. Which of the informations is NOT required in finding the complete sequence of organisation of lectures?
(*a*) (*i*) only (*b*) (*ii*) only
(*c*) (*v*) only (*d*) All are required

17. The ratio between Sumit's and Prakash's age at present is 2 : 3. Sumit is 6 years younger than Prakash. The ratio of Sumit's age to Prakash's age after 6 years will be:
(*a*) 1 : 2 (*b*) 2 : 3
(*c*) 3 : 4 (*d*) 3 : 8

18. I was born on 12 October, 1965 and my brother is 2 years 27 days older than me. On which day was he born if I was born on Monday?
(*a*) Monday (*b*) Tuesday
(*c*) Sunday (*d*) Saturday

19. At 10.30 p.m. the hour hand will point in which direction.
(*a*) North-East
(*b*) South-West
(*c*) East
(*d*) North-West

20. If 15 apples and 20 oranges cost as much as 20 apples and 15 oranges which of the following conclusions is correct?
(*a*) Orange and apple have identical prices
(*b*) Orange's price is double that of apple
(*c*) No conclusion can be drawn
(*d*) Apple is cheaper than orange

ANSWERS

1	2	3	4	5	6	7	8	9	10
(*b*)	(*c*)	(*a*)	(*a*)	(*c*)	(*b*)	(*a*)	(*a*)	(*c*)	(*b*)
11	**12**	**13**	**14**	**15**	**16**	**17**	**18**	**19**	**20**
(*c*)	(*c*)	(*d*)	(*b*)	(*c*)	(*d*)	(*c*)	(*c*)	(*d*)	(*a*)

SOME SELECTED EXPLANATORY ANSWERS

1. $$\text{Loss \%} = \left(\frac{20}{10}\right)^2 = (2)^2 = 4\%$$

Total S.P. = ₹ 24000

and Total C.P. = Rs. $\left(\frac{100}{96} \times 24000\right)$ = ₹ 25000

∴ Loss = ₹ (25000 – 24000) = ₹ 1000.

2. The difference between the numbers is 17, *i.e.*, 21 + 17 = 38; 38 + 17 = 55. Similarly, 23 + 17 = 40; 40 + 17 = 57.

3. Here, $\frac{60}{100} A + B = \frac{175}{100} \times B$

$$\Rightarrow \frac{3}{5} A + B = \frac{7}{4} B$$

$$\Rightarrow \frac{3}{5} A = \frac{3}{4} B$$

$$\therefore \frac{A}{B} = \frac{5}{4}$$ Hence, A > B.

4. Number of candidates qualified from State G

$$= \frac{48}{100} \times \frac{7}{100} \times 3{,}00{,}000 = 10080$$

Number of male candidates qualified from State G

$$= \frac{9}{9+11} \times 10080 = \frac{9}{20} \times 10080 = 4536.$$

5. Required number of candidates

$$= \frac{65}{100} \times \frac{12}{100} \times 300000 + \frac{45}{100} \times \frac{23}{100} \times 300000$$

= 23400 + 31050 = 54450.

7. If n is the number of sides, then the no. of diagonals = ${}^nC_2 - n = 44$

$$\Rightarrow \frac{1}{2} n(n-1) - n = 44$$

$$\Rightarrow (n-11)(n+8) = 0$$

$\therefore n = 11.$ $(\because n \neq -8)$

8. 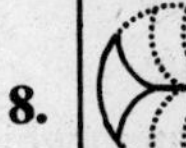

9. The simplest squares are : AICK, CKEM, EMGN, IBKD, KDMF ad MFNH *i.e.* 6 squares Other squares are ABEF and CDGH *i.e.* 2 squares. So, the total number of squares is 6 + 2 = 8.

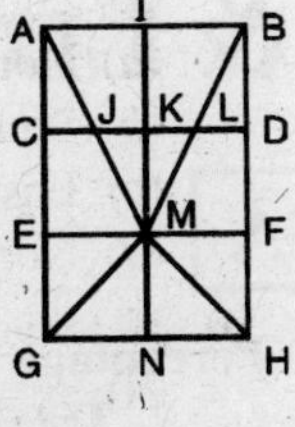

10. On the basis of height, the descending order will be :

Ashok, Gopal/Jayesh, Kuhav, Navin

or

Ashok, Gopal, Kuhav/Jayesh, Navin.

11. If 652 is replaced by 676, then terms of the series get arranged in a particular order, *i.e.*, $(1^2+1)^2, (2^2+1)^2, (3^2+1)^2, (4^2+1)^2, (5^2+1)^2, (6^2+1)^2$ and $(7^2+1)^2$. Therefore, alternative (*c*) is the correct answer.

12. Given expression

$$= \log_N 2 + \log_N 3 + ... + \log_N m$$
$$= \log_N (2.3. ... m) = \log_N m!$$
$$= \log_{m!} m! = 1.$$

13. 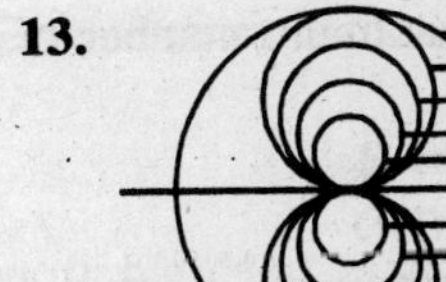

There is 1 main circle, 4 circles on the top of the horizontal lines and 4 circles below it. So, the total number of circles is 1 + 4 + 4 = 9.

14. Probability of getting at least one head in *n* tosses = $1 - (½)^n \geq 0.9$

$\Rightarrow \quad (½)^n \leq 0.1$

$\Rightarrow \quad 2^n \geq 10$

$\Rightarrow \quad n \geq 3$

Hence, least value of *n* = 4.

17. Let their ages be $2x$ and $3x$ years.

$\Rightarrow \quad 3x - 2x = 6$

$\Rightarrow \quad x = 6$

Sumit's age = 12 years

Prakash's age = 18 years

After 6 years, Sumit's age = 18 years and Prakash's age = 24 years

$\therefore$ Ratio of their ages = 18 : 24 = 3 : 4.

18. 2 years 27 days = 2 × 365 + 27 = 757 days.

757 ÷ 7 = 108 weeks and one day. Thus my brother was born on Sunday.

19. 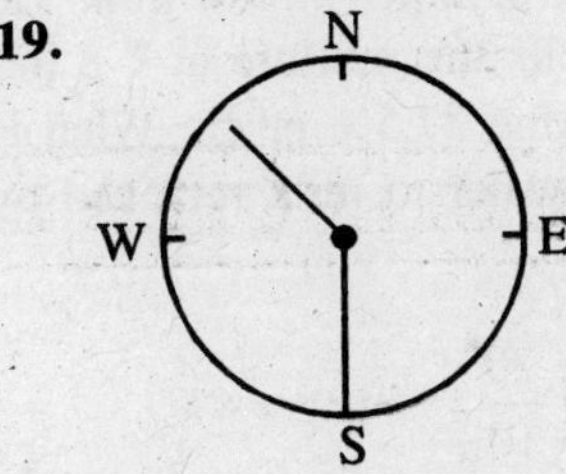

20. 15 apples + 20 Oranges = 20 apples + 15 oranges

20 O – 15 O = 20 A – 15 A

5 O = 5 A, So oranges = Apple.

SET-22

CSIR-UGC (NET) JRF & LECTURESHIP EXAM

PART-A

1. A student who secures 20% marks in an examination fails by 30 marks. Another student who secures 32% gets 42 marks more than those required to pass. The percentage of marks required to pass is:

(*a*) 20 (*b*) 25
(*c*) 28 (*d*) 30

2. Which one number is like the given number set : (363, 489, 579)?

(*a*) 281 (*b*) 382
(*c*) 471 (*d*) 562

3. A dairyman pays ₹ 6.40 per litre of milk. He adds water and sells the mixture at ₹ 8 per litre, there by making 37.5% profit. What is the proportion of water to milk received by the customers?

(*a*) 1 : 15
(*b*) 1 : 10
(*c*) 1 : 7
(*d*) 1 : 5

Directions (Qs. 4 and 5) : *Study the pie-charts carefully to answer the questions that follow.*

Percentage of Students in Six different Colleges
Total number of Students = 3500

A 21%
B 9%
C 33%
D 18%
E 7%
F 12%

Percentage of Girls in each of the Colleges
Total number of Girls = 1800

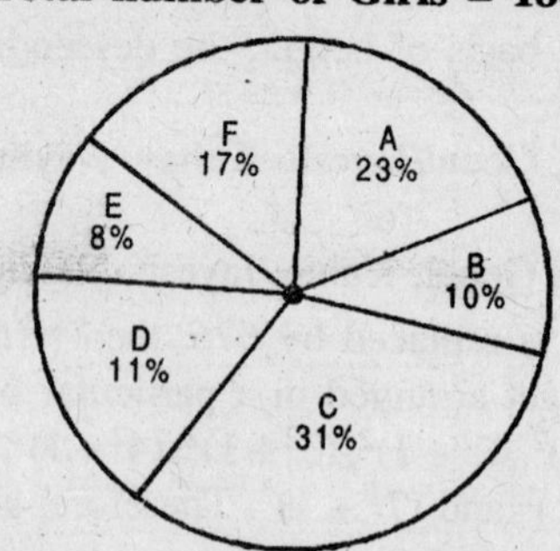

4. The number of boys from College A form what per cent of total number of students from that college?

(*a*) 22.83 (*b*) 38.41
(*c*) 43.67 (*d*) 56.29

5. Which college has the maximum number of boys?

(*a*) A (*b*) B
(*c*) C (*d*) D

Directions (Q. 6) : *In the question given below, which one would be the mirror image of the given figure when the mirror is placed along the line shown in the figure.*

6. Problem Figure

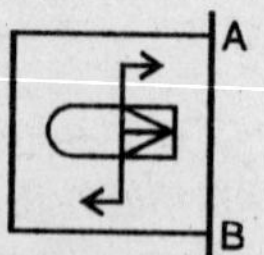

Answer Figures

(*a*)

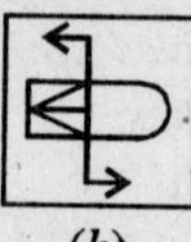
(*b*)

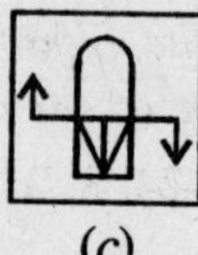
(*c*)

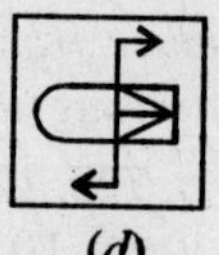
(*d*)

7. A cricket team of 11 players is to be selected from 13 players; 4 of which are bowlers and 2 wicket keepers. The number of ways to select the team, consisting one wicket keeper and at least 3 bowlers, is:

(*a*) 8 (*b*) 22
(*c*) 112 (*d*) None of these

Directions (Q. 8) : *In the question given below find the figure form which is embedded in the given pattern.*

8. 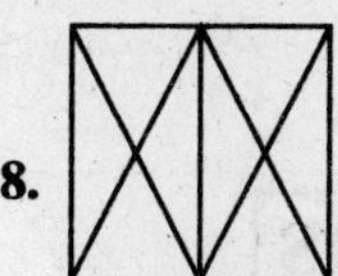

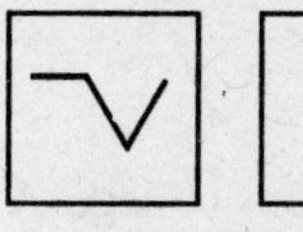   

(*a*) (*b*) (*c*) (*d*)

9. How many triangles are there in the figure given below?

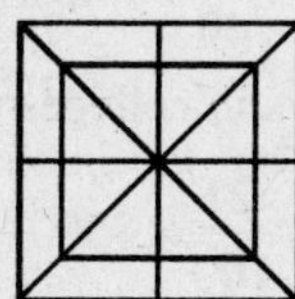

(*a*) 28 (*b*) 36
(*c*) 24 (*d*) 32

10. If $\frac{\log_8 17}{\log_9 23} - \frac{\log_{2\sqrt{2}} 17}{\log_3 23} = ?$

(*a*) 0 (*b*) 1
(*c*) 17/8 (*d*) 23/17

Directions (Q. 11): *In the question below, a number series has been given, followed by four alternatives. One term/element of the given number series is wrong. Find out that wrong term and spot out a number from the alternatives which will replace the wrong term of the series.*

11. 720, 120, 24, 8, 2, 1, 1

(*a*) 10 (*b*) 6
(*c*) 110 (*d*) 640

12. A bag contains 25 paise, 10 paise and 5 paise coins in the ratio 1 : 2 : 3. If their total value is ₹ 30, the number of 5 paise coin is:

(*a*) 50 (*b*) 100
(*c*) 150 (*d*) 200

13. How many triangles are there in the figure?

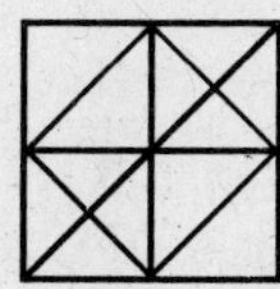

(*a*) 26 (*b*) 25
(*c*) 28 (*d*) 27

14. From a pack of cards, 2 are drawn at random one by one with replacement. The probability that first is heart and 2nd is king is :

(*a*) 1/26 (*b*) 1/52
(*c*) 1/13 (*d*) None of these

Directions (Qs. 15 and 16) : *Four youngmen, Raj, Prem, Ved and Ashok are friendly with four girls Sushma, Kusum, Vimla and Poonam. Sushma and Vimla are friends. Ved's girlfriend does not like Sushma and Vimla. Kusum does not care for Ved. Prem's girlfriend is friendly with Sushma. Sushma does not like Raj.*

15. Who is Poonam's boy friend?

(*a*) Raj (*b*) Ashok
(*c*) Prem (*d*) Ved

16. Who is Raj's girl friend?

(*a*) Poonam (*b*) Vimla
(*c*) Sushma (*d*) Kusum

17. If 3rd of the month is Friday what day will be on the 4th day after the 21st of the month?

(*a*) Monday (*b*) Tuesday
(*c*) Saturday (*d*) Sunday

18. At 2 p.m. the minute hand will point toward :

(*a*) North (*b*) North-West
(*c*) South (*d*) West

19. A garden has as many flower bearing trees as fruit bearing trees. 3/4 trees are old and ½ are grafted. Which of the following interferences are definitely true?

(*a*) All flower bearing trees are grafted

(*b*) Only fruit bearing trees are grafted
(*c*) At least one half of the flower bearing trees are old
(*d*) All of these

20. If Δ means square the first number and then multiply it by the next number and ▭ means multiply with the second number and subtract the second number from the product of the two numbers then find the value of 5 ▭ 3 ▭ 2 Δ 2 ?
(*a*) 484 (*b*) 441
(*c*) 968 (*d*) None of these

ANSWERS

1	2	3	4	5	6	7	8	9	10
(*b*)	(*c*)	(*b*)	(*c*)	(*c*)	(*b*)	(*b*)	(*a*)	(*d*)	(*a*)
11	**12**	**13**	**14**	**15**	**16**	**17**	**18**	**19**	**20**
(*b*)	(*c*)	(*a*)	(*b*)	(*d*)	(*d*)	(*c*)	(*a*)	(*c*)	(*c*)

SOME SELECTED EXPLANATORY ANSWERS

1. 20% of x + 30 = 32% of x – 42

$\Rightarrow$ 12% of x = 72

$\Rightarrow x = \frac{72 \times 100}{12} = 600$

Pass Mark = 20% of 600 + 30 = 150

Pass percentage = $\left(\frac{150}{600} \times 100\right)\% = 25\%$.

2. The numbers are divisible by 3.

3. C.P. of 1 kg mixture = $\frac{100}{137.5} \times 8 = ₹\ \frac{64}{11}$

Now applying rule of alligation,

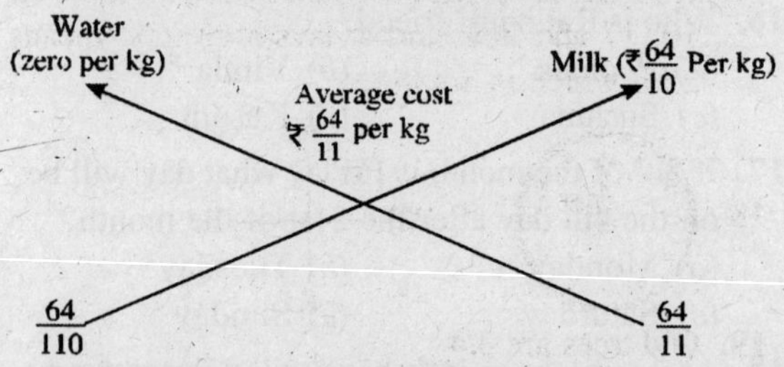

Hence, ratio of water to milk

$= \frac{64}{110} : \frac{64}{11} = 1 : 10.$

4. Number of students from College A

$= \frac{21}{100} \times 3500 = 735$

Number of girls from College A

$= \frac{23}{100} \times 1800 = 414$

Since, number of boys from college A = 725 – 414 = 321

Required percentage

$= \frac{321}{735} \times 100 = \frac{2140}{49} = 43.67\%.$

5. Number of boys in college A

$= \frac{21}{100} \times 3500 - \frac{23}{100} \times 1800$

$= 735 - 414 = 321$

Number of boys in college B

$= \frac{9}{100} \times 3500 - \frac{10}{100} \times 1800$

$= 315 - 180 = 135$

Number of boys in college C

$= \frac{33}{100} \times 3500 - \frac{31}{100} \times 1800$

$= 1155 - 558 = 597$

Number of boys in college D

$= \frac{18}{100} \times 3500 - \frac{11}{100} \times 1800$

$= 630 - 198 = 432$

Hence, number of boys in college C is the maximum.

7. There are two cases:

Case I. 3 bowlers : In this case, we have

W. Keeper		Bowlers		Others
1 from 2		3 from 4		7 from remaining 7
$^2C_1$	×	$^4C_3$	×	$^7C_7 = 8$ ..... (1)

Case II. 4 bowlers : In this case, we have

W. Keeper		Bowlers		Others
1 from 2		4 from 4		6 from 7
$^2C_1$	×	$^4C_4$	×	$^7C_6 = 14$ ..... (2)

Adding (1) and (2), we get the required number of selections = 8 + 14 = 22

8.

9. The larger triangles are : ABC, BCD, ABD and ACD *i.e.* 4 triangles.

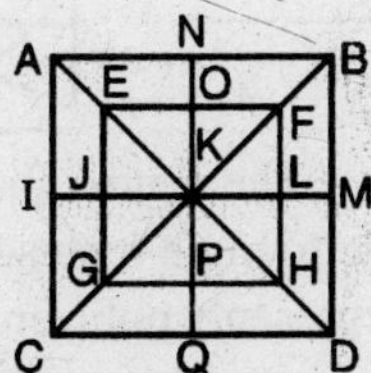

The smaller triangles are : EFH, EGH, EFG and FGH *i.e.* 4 triangles.
The simplest triangles are : EJK, EOK, OFK, JKG, FKL, KLH, KGP and KPH *i.e.* 8 triangles.
The bisected triangles are: AKC, ABK, CKD, KBD, EKG, EKF, KHG, KHF, *i.e.,* 8 triangles.
Other triangles are : ANK, NKB, KBM, KMD, KQD, KQC, KCI, IKA *i.e.* 8 triangles.
So, the total number of triangles is
4 + 4 + 8 + 8 + 8 = 32.

10. Given expression $= \dfrac{\log_{2^3} 17}{\log_{3^2} 23} - \dfrac{\log_{2^{3/2}} 17}{\log_3 23}$

$$= \frac{\frac{1}{3}\log_2 17}{\frac{1}{2}\log_3 23} - \frac{\frac{2}{3}\log_2 17}{\log_3 23} = 0.$$

12. Ratio of their values $= \dfrac{1}{4} : \dfrac{2}{10} : \dfrac{3}{20} = 5 : 4 : 3$

$\therefore$ Value of 5 paise coins $= ₹\left(30 \times \dfrac{3}{12}\right) = ₹\,7.50$

$\therefore$ Number of 5 paise coins $= \dfrac{750}{5} = 150.$

13. The larger triangles are : ABC and BCD *i.e.,* 2 triangles.

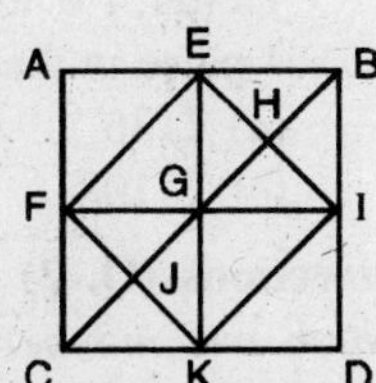

The simplest triangles are : AEF, EFG, EGH, EHB, HBI, HGI, FCJ, FGJ, GJK, JCK, GIK and IKD *i.e.* 12 triangles.
The bisected triangles are : FCK, FGC, FGK, GCK, EGI, EGB, EBI, BGI *i.e.* 8 triangles.
Other triangles are : EFI, EFK, EKI, FIK *i.e.* 4 triangles
So, the total number of triangles is
2 + 12 + 8 + 4 = 26.

14. Probability of getting heart $= (13/52) = \dfrac{1}{4}$

Probability of getting king $= 4/52 = \dfrac{1}{13}$

$\therefore$ Probability that first is heart and 2nd is king is $1/4 \times 1/13 = 1/52$.

17. If Friday is on 3rd then next Fridays will be on 10, 17 and 24th and 4 days after 21st means 25th which is Saturday.

18.  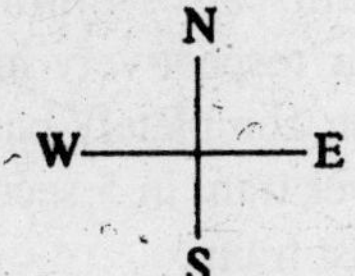

19. Old trees are 3/4
1/2 of the flower bearing trees = 1/4 = old
3/4 − 1/4 = 1/2 remain left
Fruit bearing trees are 1/2 of the total. If all of them are old, it means 1/2 = 1/2 are old.
1/4 + 1/2 = 3/4 are old in total.

20. 5 ▭ 3 ▭ 2 Δ 2 = (5 × 3 − 3 ▭ 2 Δ 2
= (12 × 2 − 2) Δ 2
= (22 × 22) × 2 = 484 × 2 = 968.

SET-23

CSIR-UGC (NET) JRF & LECTURESHIP EXAM

PART-A

1. What is the market price of a 3% stock if it yields 4% after paying an income tax of 4 paise in the rupee?
(*a*) ₹ 36 (*b*) ₹ 72
(*c*) ₹ 108 (*d*) ₹ 144

Directions (Q. 2) : *In the question given below, which one number can be placed at the sign of interrogation?*

2.

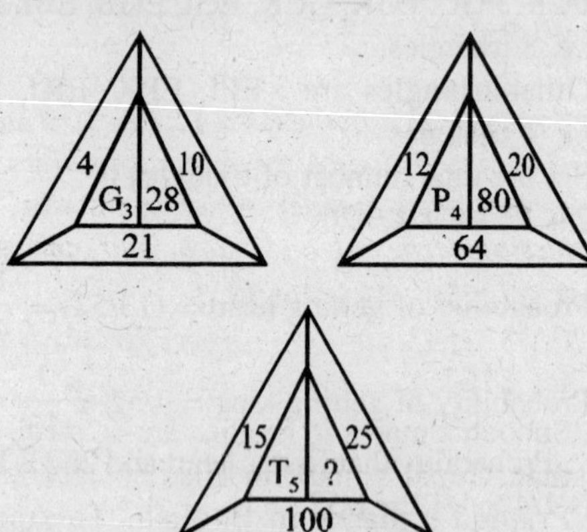

(*a*) 64 (*b*) 92
(*c*) 120 (*d*) 146

3. Two trains are running at 40 km/hr and 20 km/hr respectively in the same direction. Fast train completely passes a man sitting in the slower train in 5 seconds. Find the length of the fast train.

(*a*) $27\frac{7}{9}$ m (*b*) 27 m

(*c*) $23\frac{2}{9}$ m (*d*) 23 m

Directions (Q. 4) : *The question below is based on this figure.*

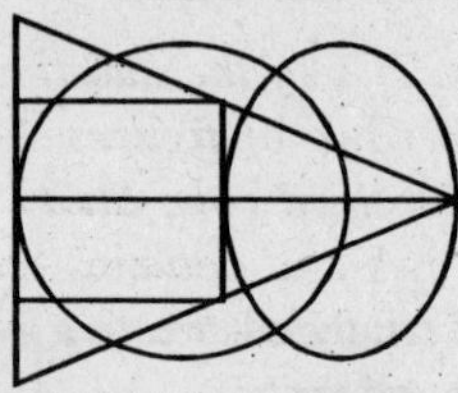

The figure above represents a set of persons : the triangle represents educated persons, the square represents policemen, the circle represents road tax payers and the ellipse represents shopkeepers.

4. According to the given figure we can say that :
(*a*) Some of the road tax payee policemen are shopkeepers too.
(*b*) Some of the educated shopkeepers pay road tax.
(*c*) Some of the road tax payee shopkeepers are policemen too.
(*d*) Some of the uneducated policemen pay road tax.

Directions (Qs. 5 and 6): *Study the following pie-chart and answer the questions given below:*

Sales of car in U.K. according to their colour

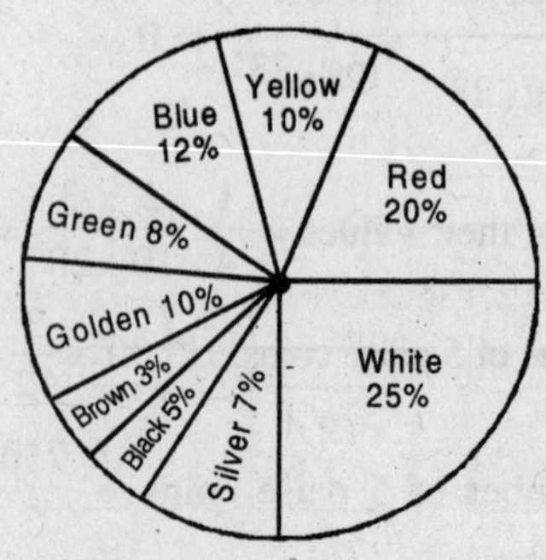

5. 3% increase in the production of Cars of which colour along with red cars will make them 35% of the total cars?

(*a*) Black (*b*) Blue
(*c*) Silver (*d*) Yellow

6. The Cars of which colours together make them 50%?

(*a*) Blue, Black, Red
(*b*) White, Black, Red
(*c*) White, Blue, Green
(*d*) White, Silver, Blue

Directions (Qs. 7) : *In the question given below, there are three rows of figures with one figure missing from the third row. Study the pattern of figures in the rows and columns and find out the missing figure from the alternative figures that shall complete the figure matrix.*

7.

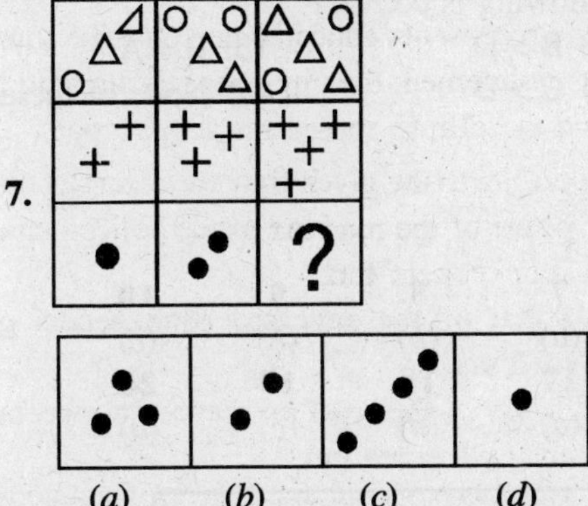

(*a*) (*b*) (*c*) (*d*)

Directions (Q. 8) : *In the question given below, which one would be the mirror image of the given figure when the mirror is placed along the line shown in the figure.*

8. Problem Figure

Answer Figures

(*a*) (*b*) (*c*) (*d*)

9. A box contains two white, three red and four black balls. If at least one red ball is to be included in the draw, the number of ways of drawing 3 balls is given by (all balls are considered to be different):

(*a*) 45 (*b*) 64
(*c*) 63 (*d*) 46

Directions (Q. 10) : *In the question given below, which one number when placed at the sign of interrogation shall complete the number matrix.*

10.

2	?	6	7
5	8	2	4
8	6	4	1
5	9	2	3

(*a*) 6 (*b*) 2
(*c*) 4 (*d*) 7

Directions (Q. 11): *In the question below, a number series is given followed by four alternatives. One term of the given number series is missing. Find that missing term out and mark your answer.*

11. 4, 27, 256, 3125, 46656, ?

(*a*) 823543 (*b*) 576811
(*c*) 676801 (*d*) 567801

12. Subodh's marks in English are as much more than Gopal's mark in History as less than Pramod's marks in English. To find out Subodh's marks in English, which of the following informations given in the statements (A) and (B) is/are sufficient?

(A) Gopal's marks in Histroy.
(B) Pramod's marks in History.

(*a*) Both A and B together are needed
(*b*) Only B is sufficient
(*c*) Either A or B is sufficient
(*d*) Both A and B together are not sufficient

13. How many straight lines are used to make this figure?

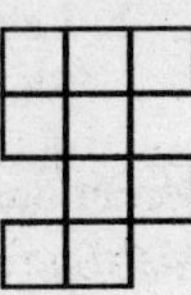

(*a*) 7
(*b*) 11
(*c*) 8
(*d*) 10

14. The letters of the word ALLAHABAD are arranged at random. The probability that in the word so formed, all similar letters are found together, is :

(*a*) 16/21 (*b*) 16/17
(*c*) 5!/9! (*d*) None of these

15. The number $\log_2 7$ is:

(*a*) an integer
(*b*) a rational number
(*c*) an irrational number
(*d*) a prime number

16. The sum of the ages of Ram, Shyam and Mohan is 93 years. Ten years ago, the ratio of their ages was 2 : 3 : 4. The present age of Mohan is:

(*a*) 38 years (*b*) 34 years
(*c*) 32 years (*d*) 24 years

17. Which of the following months will have the same day on the last day of the months?

(*a*) January-October (*b*) April-June
(*c*) February-October (*d*) (*a*) and (*c*)

18. Two trains of 200 metre long, each travelling in opposite directions with equal speed cross each other in 10 seconds. Find the speed of the trains?

(*a*) 18 Km/hr (*b*) 100 Km/hr.
(*c*) 72 Km/hr. (*d*) 36 Km/hr.

19. In a certain code Language
134 means good and tasty
478 means see good picture
729 means picture are faint
Which number has been used here for faint?

(*a*) 9
(*b*) 2
(*c*) data are inadequate
(*d*) 7

20. If q means >, ▭ means < and Δ means = and if A ▭ B BqC and D Δ A, then which of the following is correct?

(*a*) B > D (*b*) B = A
(*c*) C > D (*d*) None of these

ANSWERS

1	2	3	4	5	6	7	8	9	10
(*b*)	(*c*)	(*a*)	(*b*)	(*b*)	(*b*)	(*a*)	(*b*)	(*b*)	(*c*)
11	**12**	**13**	**14**	**15**	**16**	**17**	**18**	**19**	**20**
(*a*)	(*d*)	(*b*)	(*a*)	(*c*)	(*a*)	(*d*)	(*d*)	(*c*)	(*a*)

SOME SELECTED EXPLANATORY ANSWERS

1. Income tax on ₹ 3 = 3 × 0.04 = ₹ 0.12

Net income on ₹ 100 stock = ₹ 3 – 0.12 = ₹ 2.88

Now, ₹ 4 = Interest on ₹ 100

$$₹\ 2.88 = \text{Interest on } ₹\ \frac{100}{4} \times 2.88$$

= Interest on ₹ 72

∴ The market price of the stock is ₹ 72.

2. Letter G is 7th in order of alphabetical series. Starting from left section of the big triangle the order is G – 3, *i.e.*, 7 – 3 = 4; G + 3, *i.e.*, 7 + 3 = 10 and G × 3, *i.e.*, 7 × 3 = 21. The number in the right section of inner triangle is the sum of outer numbers minus G, *i.e.*, (4 + 10 + 21) – 7 = 35 – 7 = 28

Letter P is 16th in order so

16 – 4 = 12; 16 + 4 = 20; 16 × 4 = 64; further

(12 + 20 + 64) – 16 = 96 – 16 = 80;

Similarly,

letter T is 20th in order so

20 – 5 = 15; 20 + 5 = 25; 20 × 5 = 100 further

(15 + 25 + 100) – 20 = 140 – 20 = 120.

3. Their relative speed = (40 – 20) km/hr

$$= 20 \times \frac{5}{18} = \frac{50}{9} \text{ m/s}$$

Length of the fast train

$= \frac{50}{9} \times 5 = \frac{250}{9}$ m $= 27\frac{7}{9}$ m.

5. If 3% increase in the production of Blue cars, then percentage of Blue cars = 12 + 3 = 15
Hence, percentage of (Blue + Red) cars = 15 + 20 = 35

6. The percentage of White, Black and Red Cars = 25 + 20 + 5 = 50%.

7. In each row one element is increased at each step.

9.

Red balls (3)	Others (6)	Ways
1	2	$^3C_1 \times {^6C_2} = 45$
2	1	$^3C_2 \times {^6C_1} = 18$
3	×	$^3C_3 = 1$
		Total = 64

10. The sum of numbers in each row is 19,

i.e., 5 + 8 + 2 + 4 = 19
8 + 6 + 4 + 1 = 19
5 + 9 + 2 + 3 = 19

So, 19 – (2 + 6 + 7), *i.e.,* 4 in the second column completes the matrix.

11. In this series, terms of the series follow n^n rule where n = 2, 3, 4, 5 .... *etc*. Therefore, alternative (*a*) is the correct answer.

12. Comparison in marks do not clarify Subodh's marks in a subject.

13.

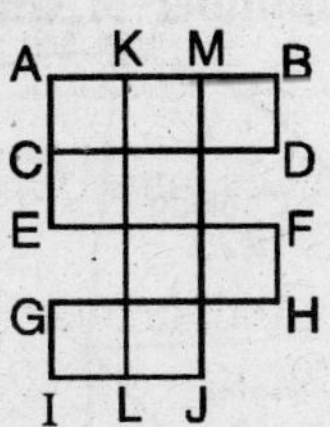

The horizontal lines are AB, CD, EF, GH and IJ *i.e.* 5 lines
The vertical lines are AC, KL MJ, BD, FH and GI *i.e.* 6 lines
So, the total number of lines used to draw this figure is 5 + 6 = 11.

14. Total ways of arranging letters of words

$\text{ALLAHABAD} = \frac{9!}{4!2!}$

Favourable ways = 4!.2!.5!

$\therefore \quad p = \frac{4!2!5!4!2!}{9!} = \frac{16}{21}.$

15. Suppose that $\log_2 7$ is rational number.
$\therefore$ Let $\log_2 7 = p/q$, where $p, q \in$ N.
$\Rightarrow 7 = 2^{p/q} \Rightarrow 7^q = 2^p$.
Obviously (1) is false, as the L.H.S. is odd while the R.H.S. is even and the two cannot be equal. Thus, $\log_2 7$ is not a rational number. Also $\log_2 7$ is not an integer and so it cannot be a prime number.
Hence, $\log_2 7$ is an irrational number.

16. Let 10 years ago, ages of Ram, Shyam and Mohan were $2x$, $3x$ and $4x$ years respectively; then
$2x + 10 + 3x + 10 = 93$
$\Rightarrow 9x = 63 \quad \therefore \; x = 7$
Hence, present age of Mohan = $4x + 10$ = 4 × 7 + 10 = 38 years.

17. Add 28 + 31 + 30 + 31 + 30 + 31 + 31 + 30 + 31 = 273 ÷ 7 = 39
It is divisible by seven and add 31 + 30 + 31 + 30 + 31 + 31 + 30 + 31 = 245 which is also divisible by seven. In such cases, two months will have the same day on the first or last day of the month.

18. For crossing the train, it will have to move only 100 metres.

$\text{Speed} = \frac{3600 \times 100}{1000 \times 10} = 36$ Km/h.

19. 4 = good, 7 = Picture and 2 and 9 = are and faint respectively.

20.

A < B ...(1)
B > C ...(2)
D = A ...(3)
B > C, B > A = D

SET-24

CSIR-UGC (NET) JRF & LECTURESHIP EXAM

PART-A

1. The interest on a certain sum of money is ₹ 67.20 and the discount on the same sum of money for the same time and at the same rate is ₹ 60. What is the sum?

(*a*) ₹ 560 (*b*) ₹ 500
(*c*) ₹ 460 (*d*) ₹ 400

Directions (Q. 2) : *In each question given below, which one number can be placed at the sign of interrogation?*

2.

9
2 [19] M
5

11
9 [4] B
2

3
? [6] E
7

(*a*) 1 (*b*) 3
(*c*) 9 (*d*) 13

3. Two goods trains each 500 m long are running in opposite directions on parallel tracks. Their speeds are 45 km/hr and 30 km/hr respectively. What is the time taken by the slower train to pass the driver of the faster one?

(*a*) 60 sec. (*b*) 48 sec.
(*c*) 24 sec. (*d*) 12 sec.

Directions (Q. 4) : *The question below consists of a question and two statements numbered I and II given below it. You have to decide whether data provided in the statements are sufficient to answer the question. Read both the statements and give answer—*

(*a*) if the data in statement I alone are sufficient to answer the question, while the data in statement II alone are not sufficient to answer the question.

(*b*) if the data in statement II alone are sufficient to answer the question, while the data in statement I alone are not sufficient to answer the question.

(*c*) if the data either in statement I or in statement II alone are sufficient to answer the question.

(*d*) If the data even in both statements I and II together are not sufficient to answer the question and

(*e*) if the data in both statements I and II together are necessary to answer the question.

4. In a certain code '1 3' means 'stop smoking' and '5 9' means 'injurious habit'. What is the meaning of '9' and '5' respectively in that code?

I. '1 5 7' means 'stop bad habit'.

II. '8 3 9' means 'smoking is injurious'.

Directions (Qs. 5 and 6): *Study the pie-chart carefully to answer the questions that follow:*

Percentage of students enrolled in different Hobby classes in a school
Total number of students = 3600

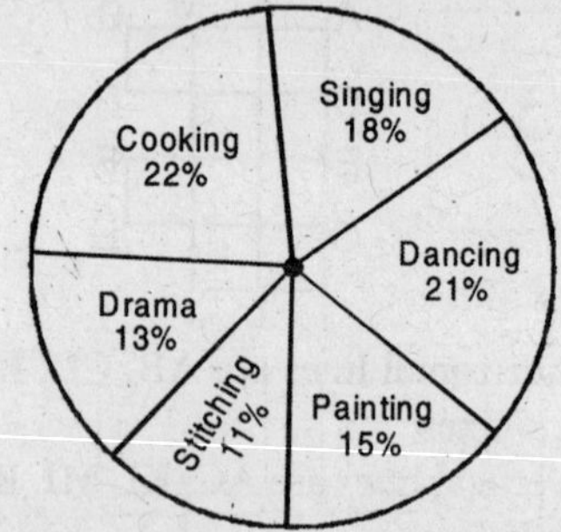

5. The number of students enrolled in Cooking classes is what per cent of those enrolled in Dancing classes?

(*a*) 101.45 (*b*) 104.76
(*c*) 110.28 (*d*) 113.84

6. What is the ratio of number of students enrolled in Singing and Dancing Classes together to those enrolled in Drama Classes respectively?

(*a*) 3 : 1 (*b*) 3 : 5
(*c*) 4 : 7 (*d*) 7 : 5

Directions (Q. 7) : *In the question given below, there are three rows of figures with one figure missing from the third row. Study the pattern of figures in the rows and columns and find out the missing figure from the alternative figures that shall complete the figure matrix.*

7.

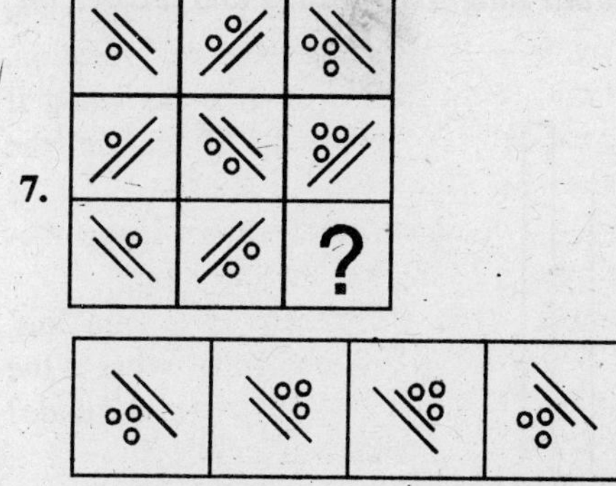

(*a*) (*b*) (*c*) (*d*)

Directions (Q. 8) : *In the question given below, which one would be the mirror image of the given figure when the mirror is placed along the line shown in the figure.*

8. Problem Figure

Answer Figures

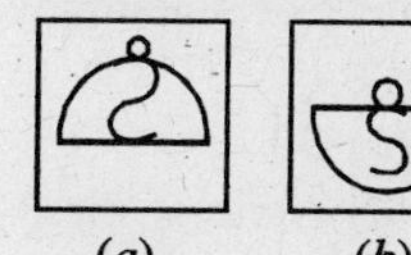

(*a*) (*b*) (*c*) (*d*)

9. The sides AB, BC, CA of a triangle ABC have 3, 5 and 6 interior points respectively on them. The number of triangles that can be constructed using these points as vertices is given by:

(*a*) 364 (*b*) 333
(*c*) 240 (*d*) None of these

Directions (Q. 10) : *In the question given below, which one number when placed at the sign of interrogation shall complete the number matrix.*

10.

10	10	10	6
3	7	2	4
?	9	9	7
6	5	9	5

(*a*) 27 (*b*) 18
(*c*) 24 (*d*) 50

Directions (Q. 11): *In the question below, a number series is given, followed by four alternatives. One term of the given number series is missing. Find that missing term out and mark your answer.*

11. 512, 128, 32, 8, 2, ?

(*a*) $\frac{1}{4}$ (*b*) $\frac{1}{2}$
(*c*) $\frac{1}{8}$ (*d*) $\frac{1}{16}$

12. Ashok is younger than Prabir and Gopal. Sohan is younger than Prabir but older than Gopal. Which of the following statements is definitely true?

(*a*) Ashok is older than Sohan
(*b*) Sohan is the oldest among them
(*c*) Gopal is younger than Ashok
(*d*) Gopal is next to the youngest among them

13. The number of triangles in this figure is :

(*a*) 20 (*b*) 22
(*c*) 26 (*d*) 28

14. If A and B are two events such that

$P(A \cup B) = 5/6$, $P(\overline{A}) = 1/4$, $P(B) = 1/3$, then A and B are :

(*a*) mutually exclusive (*b*) dependent
(*c*) independent (*d*) None of these

15. If $\log_8 m + \log_8{}^{1/6} = \frac{2}{3}$; then m is equal to:

(*a*) 4 (*b*) 12
(*c*) 18 (*d*) 24

16. Three years ago, the average age of a family of five members was 17 years. A baby having been born, the average age of the family is the same as what was three years ago. The present age of the baby is:

(*a*) 6 months (*b*) 9 months
(*c*) 1 year (*d*) 2 years

17. A is 300 days older than B, and C is 50 weeks older than A. If C was born on Tuesday, on which day was B born?

(*a*) Tuesday (*b*) Thursday
(*c*) Wednesday (*d*) Monday

18. In a certain language if A is written as 2, B as 4 and C as 6 what do the figure 12, 10, 10, 8 stand for?

(*a*) DEEP (*b*) DOOR
(*c*) DEER (*d*) FEED

Directions (Q. 19) : *Population growth in India is shown through a bar diagram. Study it and answer the question.*

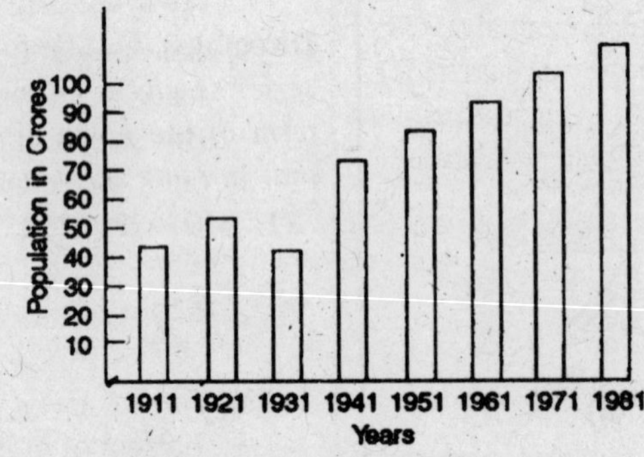

19. Which of the following conclusions is not true?

(*a*) Average annual increase of India's population is about one crore
(*b*) Population of India in 1990 is expected to rise by 10% or more
(*c*) Population in India in 1901 must have been less than 25 crores
(*d*) Growth rate of population from 1951 to 1961 is maximum

20. According to the survey of 2000 educated unemployed persons in which 1200 were men and 800 were women, the following data were collected:

Qualification	*Unemployed Men*	*Unemployed Women*
Doctors	12.5%	15%
Engineers	20%	7.5%
Trained Teachers	15%	22.5%
Postgraduates	22.5%	25%
Graduates	30%	30%

On the basis of the above table, what is the difference in the number of unemployed men and women doctors?

(*a*) 20 (*b*) 30
(*c*) 40 (*d*) None of these

ANSWERS

1	2	3	4	5	6	7	8	9	10
(*a*)	(*b*)	(*b*)	(*c*)	(*b*)	(*a*)	(*b*)	(*c*)	(*b*)	(*c*)
11	**12**	**13**	**14**	**15**	**16**	**17**	**18**	**19**	**20**
(*b*)	(*d*)	(*d*)	(*c*)	(*d*)	(*d*)	(*d*)	(*d*)	(*b*)	(*b*)

SOME SELECTED EXPLANATORY ANSWERS

1. $\because$ Interest on Sum – T.D. = Interest on T.D.

$\therefore$ ₹ 67.20 – ₹ 60 = Interest on ₹ 60

Now, ₹$7\frac{1}{5}$ = Interest on ₹ 60

$\therefore$ ₹$67\frac{1}{5}$ = Interest on $\frac{60}{7\frac{1}{5}} \times 67\frac{1}{5}$

Hence, the required sum = $\frac{60 \times 5}{36} \times \frac{336}{5}$

= ₹ 560

2. Letter M is 13th in order of alphabetical series. So 13 (= M) × 2 (number on the opposite side) = 9 × 5 (product of numbers above and below the square) – 19 (number inside the square) *i.e.*,

$13 \times 2 = (9 \times 5) - 19$
$26 = (45 - 19)$
$26 = 26$

Letter B is 2nd in order, so

$2 \times 9 = (11 \times 2) - 4$
$18 = 22 - 4$
$18 = 18$

Similarly, letter E is 5th in order

$5 \times ? = (3 \times 7) - 6$
$5 \times ? = 21 - 6$
$5 \times ? = 15$
$? = 15 \div 5 = 3.$

3. Their relative speed = (45 + 30) km/hr

$= 75 \times \frac{5}{18}$ m/s $= \frac{125}{6}$ m/s

Required time = $\frac{500 + 500}{125/6}$

$= \frac{1000 \times 6}{125} = 48$ sec.

4. According to statement I '1 5 7' means 'stop bad habit'. Code '5 9' means 'injurious habit'. Here code '5' and 'habit' are common and then '9' is the code for 'injurious'. According to statement II '8 3 9' means 'smoking is injurious'. Code '5 9' means 'injurious habit'. Here code '9' and 'injurious' are common and then '5' is the code for 'habit'. So, either of the statements alone is sufficient to answer the question.

5. Required percentage = $\frac{22}{21} \times 100 = 104.76.$

6. Required ratio $= (18 + 21) : 13 = 39 : 13 = 3 : 1.$

7. In each row the position and placement of lines is same in first and third column. The number of circles is increased at each step and they are always facing the longer line.

9. Selection of 3 points from given 14 pts can be made in ${}^{14}C_3 = 364$ ways.
But selection of 3 points from the points on one line cannot give any triangle. Such selections are
${}^3C_3 + {}^5C_3 + {}^6C_3 = 1 + 10 + 20 = 31$
Hence total number of triangles that can be formed = 364 – 31 = 333.

10. The square of number in the last column and the sum of numbers in that row are equal,

i.e., $6^2 = 10 + 10 + 10 + 6$, *i.e.*, $36 = 36$
$4^2 = 3 + 7 + 2 + 4$, *i.e.*, $16 = 16$
$5^2 = 6 + 5 + 9 + 5$, *i.e.*, $25 = 25$
$7^2 = 49$ and so, $49 - (9 + 9 + 7)$, *i.e.*,

24 in the first column completes the matrix.

11. Terms of the series are obtained on dividing each previous term by 4. Therefore, alternative (*b*) is the correct term to replace the question mark.

12. On the basis of age, the descending order will be : Prabir, Sohan, Gopal, Ashok.

13.

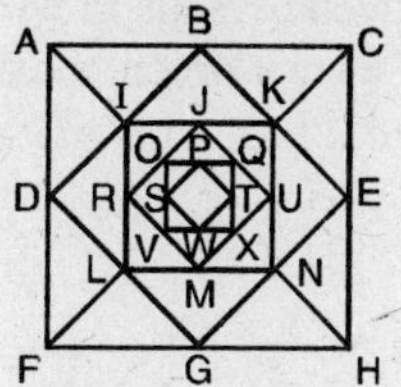

The simple outer triangles are : AID, AIB, BIK, BCK, CKE, KEN, ENH, NGH, NGL LFG, DLF and DLI *i.e.*, 12 triangles

The simple middle triangles are : IJR ORV, RLM, VXM, UMN, QUX, KJU and JOQ *i.e.,* 8 triangles
The simple innermost triangles are : OSP, PQT, SVW and TWX *i.e.* – 4 triangles. The bisected triangles are : ABD, BCE, DFG and EGH *i.e.* 4 triangles
So, the total number of triangles is 12 + 8 + 4 + 4 = 28.

14. $P(A \cup B) = P(A) + P(B) - P(A \cap B)$
$\therefore$ $P(A \cap B) = 1/3 + 3/4 - 5/6 = 3/12 = 1/4$
$P(A)\,P(B) = 1/3.3/4 = 1/4$
As $P(A)\,P(B) = P(A \cap B)$
$\therefore$ A and B are independent.
Also $P(A \cap B) \neq 0$
$\therefore$ A and B are not exclusive.

15. $\log_8{}^m + \log_8{}^{1/6} = \frac{2}{3} \quad \Rightarrow \quad \log_8{}^{\left(m \times \frac{1}{6}\right)} = \frac{2}{3}$

$\Rightarrow m \times \frac{1}{6} = 8^{2/3} \quad \Rightarrow \quad \frac{m}{6} = \left(2^3\right)^{2/3}$

$\Rightarrow \frac{m}{6} = 4 \quad \therefore \quad m = 24.$

16. The present age of baby = 17 × 6 – 20 × 5 = 2 years

17. C is older than B by 50 × 7 + 300 = 650 days. Divide it by 7 and you will get remainder 6. It means B was born 6 days after Tuesday.

18.

12	10	10	8
F	E	E	D

19. Only estimation is possible and nothing can be definitely said about future.

20. (12.5 × 1200)/100 = 150 men
(15 × 800)/ 100 = 120 women
Difference = 150 – 120 = 30.

SET-25

CSIR-UGC (NET) JRF & LECTURESHIP EXAM

PART-A

1. The ages of Samir and Saurabh are in the ratio of 8 : 15 respectively. After 9 years the ratio of their ages will be 11 : 18. What is the difference between their ages in years?
(*a*) 20 years
(*b*) 21 years
(*c*) 22 years
(*d*) 24 years

2. How many 4's are there in the following series which are preceded by 7, but are not preceded by 8?
3 4 5 7 4 3 7 4 8 5 4 3 7 4 9 8 4 7 2 7 4 1 3 6
(*a*) 1 (*b*) 2
(*c*) 3 (*d*) 4

3. A farmer took a loan at 12 per cent per annum at simple interest. After 4 years he settled the loan by paying ₹ 2442. What was the principal amount?
(*a*) ₹ 1542 (*b*) ₹ 1550
(*c*) ₹ 1600 (*d*) ₹ 1650

Directions (Qs. 4 and 5) : *The pie-chart, drawn here, shows the spending of a country on various sports during a particular year. Study the graph carefully and answer the questions that follow:*

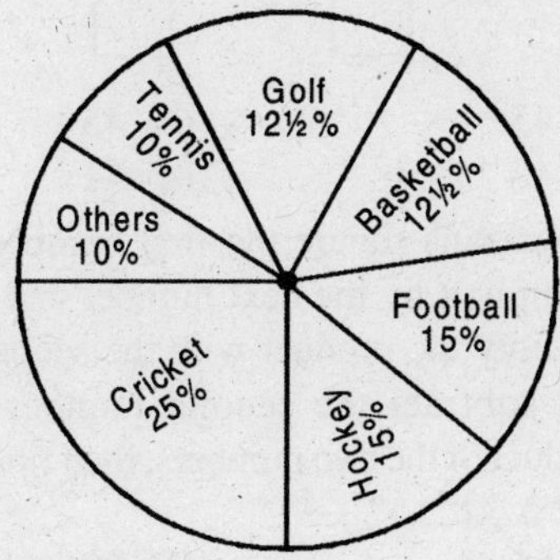

4. If the total amount spent on sports during the year was ₹ 1,20,00,000, how much was spent on basketball?
(*a*) ₹ 16,00,000
(*b*) ₹ 18,00,000
(*c*) ₹ 3,00,000
(*d*) ₹ 15,00,000

5. If the total amount spent on sports during the year was ₹ 30,00,000, the amount spent on cricket and hockey together was:
(*a*) ₹ 18,00,000 (*b*) ₹ 12,00,000
(*c*) ₹ 15,00,000 (*d*) ₹ 20,00,000

Directions (Q. 6) : *In the question given below, which one would be the mirror image of the given figure when the mirror is placed along the line shown in the figure.*

6. Problem Figure

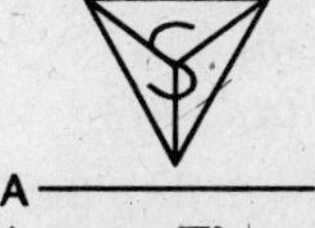

Answer Figures

(*a*)

(*b*)

(*c*)

(*d*)

7. Out of 18 points in a plane, no three are in the same straight line except five points which are collinear. The number of straight lines that can be formed joining them is:
(*a*) 143 (*b*) 144
(*c*) 153 (*d*) None of these

Directions (Q. 8) : *In the question given below, find the figure form which is embedded in the given pattern.*

8. 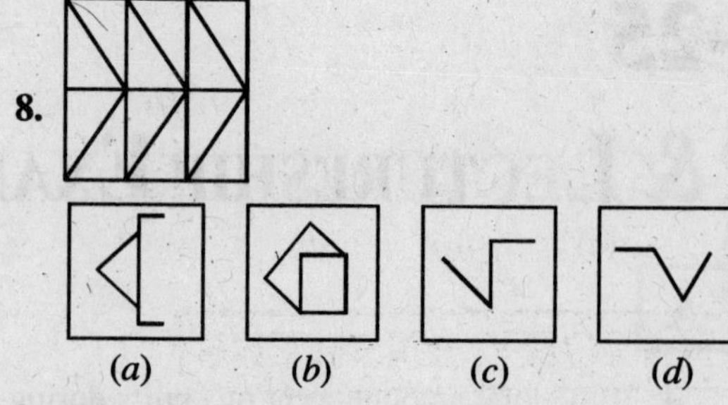

9. How many triangles are there in the figure given below?

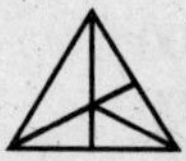

(*a*) 11 (*b*) 12
(*c*) 9 (*d*) 10

10. In a certain code language, HOTEL has been coded as 55. How will you code BORE in the same code language?

(*a*) 56 (*b*) 30
(*c*) 36 (*d*) 46

Directions (Q. 11): *In the question below a number series is given, followed by four alternatives. One term of the given number series is missing. Find that missing term out and mark your answer.*

11. 1432, 4321, 3214, ?

(*a*) 2140 (*b*) 1143
(*c*) 2143 (*d*) 1743

12. If $\log_{10}(x + 5) + \log_{10}{}^{10} = 4$, then the value of x is:

(*a*) 795 (*b*) 890
(*c*) 995 (*d*) 1000

13. How many squares are there in the figure given below?

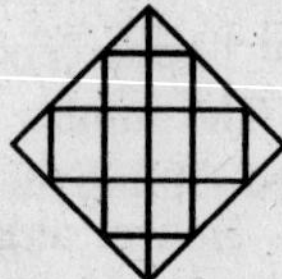

(*a*) 9 (*b*) 10
(*c*) 11 (*d*) 12

14. An urn contains 8 blue and 4 green balls. Two balls are drawn at random. The probability that both balls are of the same colour is :

(*a*) 17/33 (*b*) 1/33
(*c*) 14/33 (*d*) 1/11

15. A can do a work in 30 days, B in 15 days and C in 10 days. If all three work together, how long will they take to do the same work?

(*a*) 5 days (*b*) 4 days
(*c*) 3 days (*d*) 2 days

16. What will be the angle between two hands of a clock at 8:30?

(*a*) 60° (*b*) 45°
(*c*) 75° (*d*) 35°

17. Rahim went 30 km to the North, then turning to East he went 40 km, then turning to right he went 20 km and then he turns to right again and went 40 km. How far was he from his starting point?

(*a*) 10 km (*b*) 20 km
(*c*) 5 km (*d*) 1 km

18. ₹ 675 was divided among 75 boys and girls. Each boy gets ₹ 20 whereas a girl gets ₹ 5. Find the number of boys and girls.

(*a*) 20, 55 (*b*) 15, 60
(*c*) 25, 50 (*d*) 30, 45

19. If the area of a given square ABCD is 3, find the total area of the entire figure?

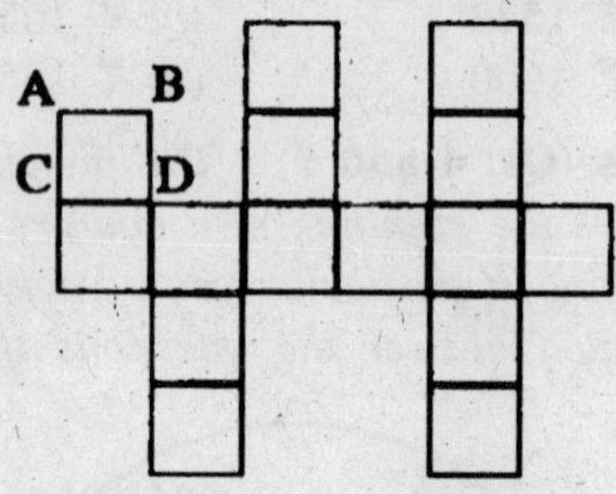

(*a*) 45^2 (*b*) 45
(*c*) 48 (*d*) 31

20. If Δ means square the first number and then multiply it by the next number and ▭ means multiply the product with the second number and subtract the second number from the product of the two numbers, then find the value of 2 Δ 3 ▭ 5?

(*a*) 55 (*b*) 60
(*c*) 7 (*d*) 24

ANSWERS

1	2	3	4	5	6	7	8	9	10
(*b*)	(*d*)	(*d*)	(*d*)	(*b*)	(*a*)	(*b*)	(*c*)	(*b*)	(*c*)
11	**12**	**13**	**14**	**15**	**16**	**17**	**18**	**19**	**20**
(*c*)	(*c*)	(*c*)	(*a*)	(*a*)	(*c*)	(*a*)	(*a*)	(*b*)	(*a*)

SOME SELECTED EXPLANATORY ANSWERS

1. Let the present ages of Samir and Saurabh are $8x$ and $15x$ years respectively; then

$$\frac{8x+9}{15x+9} = \frac{11}{18}$$

$\Rightarrow 144x + 162 = 165x + 99$

$\Rightarrow 21x = 63 \quad \therefore \quad x = 3$

Hence, difference of their ages

$= 15x - 8x = 7x = 7 \times 3 = 21$ years.

2. 3 4 5 <u>7 4</u> 3 <u>7 4</u> 8 5 4 3 <u>7 4</u> 9 8 4 7 2 <u>7 4</u> 1 3 6
(1, 2, 3, 4)

3. Let principal = ₹ x, then

$$x + \frac{x \times 12 \times 4}{100} = 2442$$

$$\Rightarrow \frac{37x}{25} = 2442$$

$$\therefore \quad x = \frac{2442 \times 25}{37} = ₹\ 1650.$$

4. 100% = ₹ 1,20,00,000

$\therefore$ Expenditure on the game of Basketball = 12½% of 1,20,00,000

$$= \frac{25 \times 1{,}20{,}00{,}000}{100} = ₹\ 15{,}00{,}000.$$

5. 100% = ₹ 30,00,000

$\therefore$ Expenditure on the games of Cricket and Hockey = 25% + 15% = 40%

$\therefore$ Total expenditure on the games of Cricket and Hockey = 20% of 30,00,000

$$= \frac{40 \times 30{,}00{,}000}{100} = ₹\ 12{,}00{,}000.$$

7. The number of st. lines = ${}^{18}C_2 - ({}^{5}C_2 - 1) = 144$.

8. 

9. The main triangle is : ABC *i.e.* 1 triangle the simplest triangles are : ABE, AED, EBF, EDC and EFC *i.e.* 5 triangles

The triangles divided into two parts are : ABF, ABD, AEC and EBC *i.e.* 4 triangles

Other triangles are : AFC and DBC *i.e.* 2 triangles

So, the total number of triangles is 1 + 5 + 4 + 2 = 12.

10.

H		O		T		E		L		
8	+	15	+	20	+	5	+	12	=	60

No. of letters in HOTEL = 5.

So, code = 60 – 5 = 55

Clearly, forward coding sequence has been used (A = 1, B = 2 ......).

Similarly,

B		O		R		E		
2	+	15	+	18	+	5	=	40

No. of letters in BORE = 4

So, code = 40 – 4 = 36.

11. Order of digits has been depicted in this number series. Hence, alternative (*c*) is the correct alternative to replace the question mark.

12. $\log_{10}^{(x+5)} + \log_{10}^{10} = 4$

$\Rightarrow \log_{10}^{(x+5)} + 1 = 4$

$\Rightarrow \log_{10}^{(x+5)} = 3$

$\Rightarrow x + 5 = 10^3$

$\therefore \quad x = 1000 - 5 = 995.$

13. The main square is ABCD *i.e.* 1 square

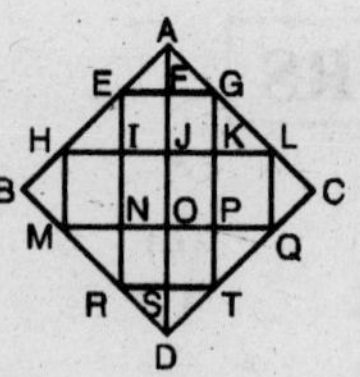

The simplest squares are : EFIJ, FGJK, HIMN, IJNO, JKOP, KLPQ, NORS and OPST *i.e.* 8 squares

Other squares are : EGNP and IKRT *i.e.* 2 squares

So, the total number of squares is 1 + 8 + 2 = 11

14. Required probability $= \frac{{}^8C_2 + {}^4C_2}{{}^{12}C_2} = \frac{17}{33}$.

15. (A + B + C)'s 1 day's work

$= \frac{1}{30} + \frac{1}{15} + \frac{1}{10} = \frac{12}{60} = \frac{1}{5}$

Hence, (A + B + C) will do the work in 5 days.

16. Angle will be 30 + 30 + 15 = 75° at 8 : 30.

17.

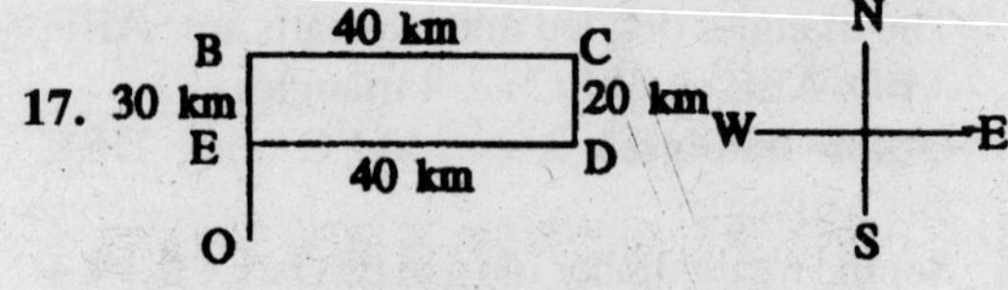

18. Average money per head (boy or girl) $= ₹\ \frac{675}{75}$

$= ₹\ 9$

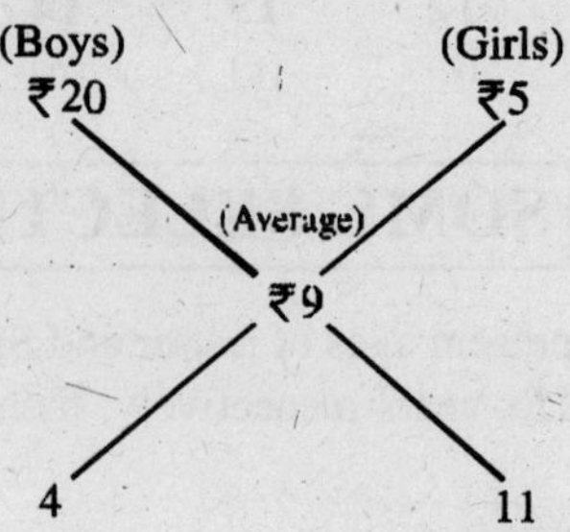

Number of boys $= \frac{4}{4+11} \times 75 = 20$

Number of girls $= \frac{11}{4+11} \times 75 = 55.$

19. Count the number of squares in the figure and multiply it by 3.

20. 2 Δ 3 ▭ 5

2 × 2 × 3 ▭ 5

12 ▭ 5 = 12 × 5 − 5 = 55.

CSIR-UGC (NET) JRF & LECTURESHIP EXAM

(PART-B)

MATHEMATICAL SCIENCES

25 PRACTICE SETS

SET–1

CSIR–UGC (NET) MATHEMATICAL SCIENCES

PART-B

1. Solving by variation of parameter for the equation $y''+y = \sec x$, the value of Wronskion is –

A. 1
B. 2
C. 3
D. 4

2. $\frac{\partial^2 z}{\partial x^2}+2\frac{\partial^2 z}{\partial x \partial y}+\frac{\partial^2 z}{\partial y^2}+2\left(\frac{\partial z}{\partial x}+\frac{\partial z}{\partial y}\right)+z = 0$

A. $z = 2e^{-x} f_1(y+x)$
B. $z = e^{-x} f_1(y-x) + xe^{-x} f_2(y-x)$
C. $z = f_1(y-x) + x f_2(y-x)$
D. None of these

3. For a given probability distribution

$f(x) = \frac{1}{8}\binom{3}{x}$, $x = 0, 1, 2, 3$

for a random variable x, the moment– generating function of this is

A. $\frac{1}{8}\left(1+e^t\right)^3$
B. $\frac{1}{4}e^t$
C. $\left(1+e^t\right)^2$
D. e^t

4. Which of the following functions can be represented as the probability distribution of a random variable with the given range for $x = 1,2,3,4$?

A. $f(x) = \frac{x-2}{5}$
B. $f(x) = \frac{x^2}{30}$
C. $f(x) = \frac{1}{5}$
D. None of these

5. Let X be a random variable, denotes the number of points rolled with a balanced die. The expected value of $g(X) = 2X^2 + 1$ is

A. $\frac{94}{4}$
B. $\frac{94}{3}$
C. $\frac{94}{2}$
D. 94

6. Let X_1 and X_2 be two independent variables and $y = a_1 X_1 + a_2 X_2$ then var (y) is

A. $a_1\, var\,(X_1) + a_2\, var\,(X_2)$
B. $a_1 X_1 + a_2 X_2$
C. $a_1^2\, var\,(X_1) + a_2^2\, var\,(X_2)$
D. None of these

7. The centre of convergence for the power series $\sum_{n=1}^{\infty} n\left(z+i\sqrt{2}\right)^n$ is

A. $-i\sqrt{2}$
B. $-i$
C. $\sqrt{2}$
D. None of these

8. Let V be an inner product space and $\alpha, \beta \in V$ then α and β are orthogonal to each other if

A. $(\alpha/\beta) > 0$
B. $(\alpha/\beta) < 0$
C. $(\alpha/\beta) = 0$
D. None of these

9. If $\bar{x}_B$ and $\overset{\Delta}{x}_B$ are two basic feasible solution to linear programming problem max, $z = \bar{c}\,\bar{x}$ subject to $\bar{A}\,\bar{x} = \bar{b}$, $\bar{x} \geq 0$, and $\bar{c}_B$ and $\overset{\Delta}{c}_B$ are respected cost associated vector to $\bar{x}_B$ and $\overset{\Delta}{x}_B$. Then $\overset{\Delta}{x}_B$ is improved basic feasible solution, then $\bar{x}_B$ if

A. $\overset{\Delta}{x}_B\, \overset{\Delta}{c}_B \leq \bar{c}_B \bar{x}_B$
B. $\overset{\Delta}{c}_B\, \overset{\Delta}{x}_B \geq \bar{c}_B \bar{x}_B$
C. $\bar{c}_B\, \bar{x}_B < \overset{\Delta}{c}_B\, \overset{\Delta}{x}_B$
D. $\bar{c}_B\, \bar{x}_B > \overset{\Delta}{c}_B\, \overset{\Delta}{x}_B$

10. The equation of line passing through points $\bar{x}_1$ and $\bar{x}_2$ $(\bar{x}_1 \neq \bar{x}_2)$ in E^n is

A. $\lambda\, \bar{x}_2 + (1-\lambda)\, \bar{x}_1 = \bar{x} \in E^n$, λ any real number
B. $\lambda\, \bar{x}_2 + (1-\lambda)\, \bar{x}_1 = \bar{x} \in E^n, \lambda < 0$
C. $\lambda\, \bar{x}_2 + (1-\lambda)\, \bar{x}_1 = \bar{x} \in E^n, 1 < x < 0$
D. None of these

11. A : If linear programming problem have feasible solution then it also has a basic feasible solution.

B : There exist only finite number of feasible solutions.

A. A and B both false
B. A is true only
C. B is true only
D. A and B both true

12. P : Every solution satisfies non-negativity restriction in *l*.p.p.

Q : Every feasible solution satifies non-negativity restriction.

A. P and Q both true
B. P is true
C. Q is true
D. Both P and Q false

Directions (Q 13 to 16) : The cost of parameter and other factors for a production inventory system of automobile pistons are given below :

Demand per year = 6,000 unit
Unit cost = Rs. 40
Setup cost = Rs. 500
Production rate per year = 36,000 unit
Holding cost per year = Rs. 8
Shortage cost per unit per year = Rs. 20

13. The optimal lot size is

A. No unit B. 2,000 unit
C. 500 unit D. 1,123 unit

14. The number of shortages is

A. 567 unit B. 157 unit
C. 267 unit D. None of these

15. The manufacturing time is

A. 2 days B. App. 12 days
C. App. 20 days D. App. 50 days

16. The set up time is

A. $2\frac{1}{4}$ months B. 5 months
C. 8 months D. None of these

17. A function $f(x)$ has the continuity at $x = a$ if

A. $f(a+) = f(a-) = f(a)$
B. $f(a+) = f(a-) \neq f(a)$
C. $f(a+) \neq f(a-)$
D. $f(a+) \neq f(a)$

18. If f is increasing function on $E \subset D$, then for $x, y, \in E$

A. $x < y \Rightarrow f(x) \leq f(y)$
B. $x < y \Rightarrow f(x) \geq f(y)$
C. $x < y \Rightarrow f(x) > f(y)$
D. None of these

19. The union of any finite collection of non-empty closed set is

A. Open set B. Closed set
C. Null set D. None of these

20. $\phi = \{F_1 ...., F_n\}$ is a countable collection of sets then ϕ has finite intersection property of

A. $\bigcap_{i=1}^{n} F_i = \phi$ B. $\bigcap_{i=1}^{n} F_i \neq \phi$
C. $\bigcup_{i=1}^{n} F_i = \phi$ D. None of these

21. The function $P : X \to D$ is called Pseudo matrix if

A. $P(x, y) = 0$, iff $x = y$
B. $P(x, y) = 0$ for some $x \neq y$
C. $P(x, y) \neq 0$ for $x = y$
D. None of these

22. A real valued function f has discontinuity of second kind at $x = a$ if

A. Neither $f(a+)$ nor $f(a-)$ exist
B. $f(a+)$ exist only
C. $f(a-)$ exist only
D. $f(a+)$ and $f(a-)$ both exist

23. The total variation of F on $[a, b]$, $V_f(a, b) = 0$, then

A. $a = b$
B. F is constant on $[a, b]$
C. F is monotonic on $[a, b]$
D. None of these

24. If polynomial is said to be integer monic if

A. Its coefficients are integers and highest coefficient is 1.
B. Its coefficients are real numbers.
C. Its coefficients are real numbers and highest coefficient is 0.
D. Its coefficients are integers and highest coefficient is 2.

25. Given a polynomial $f(x) = a_0 + a_1 x + ... + a_n x^n$, where as are integers, then content of $f(x)$ is

A. g.c.d. of integers $a_0, ..., a_n$
B. Mean of integers $a_0, ..., a_n$
C. Mode of integers $a_0, ..., a_n$
D. None of these

26. If $f, g : D \to R$ are differentiable at x_0, then (f/g) is differentible at x_0, if

A. $g(x_0) \neq 0$ B. $g(x_0) = 0$
C. $g(x_0) = \infty$ D. None of these

27. The series $1 + \frac{x}{1^2} + \frac{x^2}{2^2} + \frac{x^3}{3^2} + ...$

A. Diverges for $|x| > 1$
B. Converges for $|x| < 1$
C. Diverges for $|x| = 1$
D. None of these

28. The reciprocal $a+ib$ is equal to

A. $\frac{1}{a^2+b^2} - ib$ B. $\frac{ib}{a+ib} - a$
C. $\frac{a^2}{a^2+b^2} - \frac{b^2 i}{a^2+b^2}$ D. $\frac{a}{a^2+b^2} - \frac{bi}{a^2+b^2}$

29. If (z_1, z_2, z_3) is an orientiation of Γ, then right side of Γ with respect to (z_1, z_2, z_3) is

A. $\{Z : \text{Im}(z, z_1, z_2, z_3) < 0\}$
B. $\{Z : \text{Im}(z, z_1, z_2, z_3) > 0\}$
C. $\{Z : \text{Re}(z, z_1, z_2, z_3) < 0\}$
D. None of these

30. If $y : [0, 1] \to C$ is closed rectifiable curve and $a \notin \{y\}$, then $\frac{1}{2\pi} \int_y \frac{dz}{z-a}$ is

A. An integer B. Rational number
C. Real number D. Complex number

31. The real part of the complex number $(1+i)^n$ is

A. $2^{n/2} \cos \frac{n\pi}{4}$ B. $2^n \cos \frac{n\pi}{2}$
C. $2^{-n/2} \cos n\pi$ D. $2^{-n} \cos \frac{n\pi}{2}$

32. If in a simplex table the relative cost $Z_j - C_j$ is zero for a nonbasic variable, then there exists an alternate optimal solution, provided

A. It is starting simplex table
B. It can be any simplex table
C. It is optimal simplex table
D. None of these

33. If in using VAM or any other method to obtain a starting solution the allocation made in a cell is not maximum possible, then the resulting solution is

A. A basic feasible solution
B. A basic solution but not basic feasible solution
C. Not a basic feasible solution
D. None of these

34. Let x_1, be a feasible solution to Min $\phi(x) = c^T x$ subject to $Ax \geq b$, $x \geq 0$ and y_1 be a feasible solution to Max $\psi(y) = b^T y$. subject to $A^T y \leq c$, $y \geq 0$, then

A. $\phi(x_1) \geq \psi(y_1)$ B. $\phi(x_1) \leq \psi(y_1)$
C. $\phi(x_1) = \psi(y_1)$ D. None of these

35. If the value of the objective function is unbounded in primal, then the dual of the problem have

A. Infeasible solution B. Feasible solution
C. Bonded solution D. Unbounded solution

36. The dual of a dual linear programming problem is:

A. Primal B. Dual
C. Dual of a dual D. None of these

37. Find the optimum integer solution to the following L.P.P.:

Maximise $Z = x_1 + 4x_2$ subject to the constraints: $2x_1 + 4x_2 \leq 7$, $5x_1 + 3x_2 \leq 15$; $x_1, x_2 \geq 0$ and are integers.

A. $-1, 4$ Max. $Z = 15$ B. $2, 3$ Max. $Z = 14$
C. $1, 1$, max. $Z = 5$ D. $0, -3$, Max. $Z = -12$

38. A person numbered as 2 tosses a die marked as 112233 twice. The probability that, he gets his number at least once (assume all cases are equally likely) is:

A. $\frac{9}{5}$ B. $\frac{5}{9}$
C. $\frac{3}{5}$ D. $\frac{5}{3}$

39. The residue of $\frac{\phi(z)}{(z-a)^n}$ at $z = a$ is:

A. $\phi^n(a)$ B. $\frac{\phi^n(a)}{n!}$
C. $\frac{\phi^n(a)}{n}$ D. $\frac{\phi^n(a)}{(n-1)!}$

40. For $a, x \in G$, the ranks of a and $x^{-1}ax$ are:

A. Unequal B. Equal
C. Same D. None is correct

ANSWERS

1	2	3	4	5	6	7	8	9	10
A	B	A	B	B	C	A	C	C	A
11	12	13	14	15	16	17	18	19	20
D	C	D	C	B	A	A	A	B	B
21	22	23	24	25	26	27	28	29	30
B	A	B	A	A	A	A	D	B	A
31	32	33	34	35	36	37	38	39	40
A	C	C	A	A	C	C	B	D	C

Some Selected Explanatory Answers

1. The solution of corresponding homogeneous equation is
$y = C_1 \cos x + C_2 \sin x$

$$\therefore W(y_1, y_2) = \begin{vmatrix} \cos x & \sin x \\ -\sin x & \cos x \end{vmatrix} = 1$$

2. $(D^2 + 2DD' + D'^2 + 2D + 2D' + 1)z = 0$
$\Rightarrow (D + D' + 1)^2 z = 0$
$Z = e^{-x} f_1(y - x) + x e^{-x} f_2(y - x)$

3. $M_x(t)\, E(e^{tx}) = \frac{1}{8}\sum_{x=1}^{3} e^{tx}\binom{3}{x} + \frac{1}{8}$

$= \frac{1}{8}(1 + e^t)^3$

4. For $f(x) = \frac{x^2}{30}$

$\sum_x f(x) = 1$

5. For balanced die $f(x) = \frac{1}{6}$, $x = 1, 2, \ldots\ldots 6$

$= E[g(x)] = \sum_X g(x) f(x)$

$= \sum_{x=1}^{6} (2x^2 + 1)\frac{1}{6}$

$= \frac{94}{3}$

Q. 13 to 16

From data of the problem : D = 6,000 units/years;
C_o = Rs. 500; C_n = Rs. 8; C_b = Rs. 20;
C = Rs. 40, P = 36000 units/year

13. EOQ, Q*

$$= \sqrt{\frac{2DC_0}{C}\left(\frac{P}{P-d}\right)\left(\frac{C_n + C_b}{C_b}\right)}$$

$$= \sqrt{\frac{2 \times 6{,}000 \times 500}{8}\left(\frac{36{,}000}{36{,}000 - 6{,}000}\right)\left(\frac{8 + 20}{20}\right)}$$

$= \sqrt{12{,}60{,}000} = 1{,}123$ unit

14. $S^* = Q^*\left(\frac{C_n}{C_n + C_b}\right)\left(\frac{P-d}{P}\right)$

$= 1{,}123\left(\frac{8}{8+20}\right)\left(\frac{36{,}000 - 6{,}000}{36{,}000}\right)$

$= 267$ Unit

15. $t_1^* = \frac{Q^*}{P} = \frac{1{,}123}{36{,}000} = 0.031$ year = 12 days

16. $t^* = \frac{Q^*}{D} = \frac{1{,}123}{6{,}000} = 0.19$ year = 2.28 months

20. $\therefore F = \{F_1, F_2, \ldots\ldots\ldots F_n, \ldots\ldots\ldots\}$ is a countable collection of sets then F has finite intersection property if $\bigcap_{i=1}^{n} F_i \neq \phi$

21. $P : x \to D$ is called Pseudo matrix if $P(x, y) = 0$ for some $x \neq y$

22. According to second kind discontinuity. Neither $f(a+)$ nor $f(a-)$ exist

31. $Z = (1 + i)^n$

$\text{Re}(z) = 2^{n/2} \cos \frac{n\pi}{4}$

SET–2

CSIR–UGC (NET) MATHEMATICAL SCIENCES

PART-B

1. If I is an identity transformation on finite dimensional vector space V then

A. Nullity T > dim V B. Nullity T < dimV

C. Nullity T = dim V D. None of these

2. If V is of finite dimension, dim V = n, S ⊂ V is any subset with m (< n) elements then

A. Subset S can span V

B. Subset S can not span V

C. Subset S is equal to V

D. None of these

3. Given $\sum a_{ij}\ x_j \geq b_i$, to convert it into equality we introduce

A. Slack variable

B. Surplus variable

C. Unrestricted variable

D. None of these

4. The hyperplane in E^n passing through the origin for given z is

A. $[x \mid Cx = z))$ B. $(x \mid Cx = 0)$

C. $(x \mid Cx > z)$ D. None of these

5. Let X be set in E^n and any x_1, $x_2 \in X$ set X is convex if

A. Line segment joining x_1 and x_2 belongs to X

B. Line segment joining x_1 and x_2 belongs to x_2

C. Line segment joining x and x_2 belongs to x_1

D. None of these

6. Statement P : All cyclic groups are abelian

Statement Q : The order of cyclic group is same as the order of generator

A. P and Q are false

B. P is true, Q is false

C. Q is true, P is false

D. P and Q are true

7. A integral domain D is of finite characteristic if ∀a ∈ D, there exist m, a positive integer such that

A. $ma = 1$ B. $ma = 0$

C. $ma = a$ D. None of these

8. In a group G for each element a ∈ G there is

A. No inverse

B. A unique inverse $a^{-1} = G$

C. More than one inverse

D. None of these

9. A ring (R,+, .) is said to be a ring without zero divisor if

A. $a, b \in R, a.b = 0 \Rightarrow a \neq 0$ or, $b \neq 0$

B. $a, b \in R, a.b = 0 \Rightarrow a \neq 0$ and $b \neq 0$

C. $a, b \in R, a.b = 0 \Rightarrow a = 0$ or $b = 0$ or, both are zero

D. $a, b \in R, a.b = 0 \Rightarrow a = 0$ and $b \neq 0$

10. Statement P : f is continuous

Statement Q : f is differentiable

A. If P is true, then Q is true

B. If P is false, then Q is false

C. If Q is true, then P is true

D. If Q is true, then P is false

11. If $(b_n)_{n=1}^{\infty}$ is an decreasing and bounded, then $(b_n)_{n=1}^{\infty}$ is

A. Convergent sequence

B. Divergent sequence

C. Non-Cauchy sequence

D. None of these

12. The series $\sum_{n=1}^{\infty} \frac{1}{n^n}$ is

A. Convergent B. Divergent

C. Oscillatory D. None of these

13. Let $f : [a, b] \to R$ be continuous on $[a, b]$ and f is differential on (a, b) if $f(a) = f(b) = 0$ there exists C such that $f'(c) = 0$, then

A. $C \notin [a, b]$ B. $C \in [a, b]$

C. $C \notin (a, b)$ D. $C \in (a, b)$

14. If $Z = a$ is an isolated singularity of f and $f(z) = \sum_{-\infty}^{\infty} a_n (z-a)^n$ is its Laurent expansion in ann(a:0. R) then if $a_n = 0$ for $n \leq -1$, $z = a$ is

A. A pole of order m

B. An essential singularity

C. A removable singularity

D. None of these

15. If $2\cos\alpha_1 = a + \frac{1}{a}$, $2\cos\alpha_2 = b + \frac{1}{b}$ etc........, then $abc...... + \frac{1}{abc....}$ will be given by

A. $\cos(2\alpha_1 + 2\alpha_2 + ...)$

B. $2\cos(\alpha_1 + \alpha_2 + ...)$

C. $2\sin(\alpha_1 + \alpha_2 + ...)$

D. $\sin(2\alpha_1 + 2\alpha_2 + ...)$

16. If m and n are integers, then the value of the complex number $\log_i i$ is given by

A. $\frac{4m+1}{4n+1}$ B. $e^{\frac{4m+1}{4n+1}}$

C. $\text{Log}\frac{4m+1}{4n+1}$ D. 1

17. Suppose a, a', b and b' are real numbers, then $\frac{(a+ib)}{(a'+ib')}$ will also be real number if

A. $ab - a'b' = 0$ B. $ab' + a'b = 0$

C. $aa' - bb' = 0$ D. $ab' - a'b = 0$

Directions (Q 18 to 19) : Given Min $-3x_1 - 2x_2$

Subject to $x_1 - x_2 \geq 1$, y_1

$-3x_1 + 2x_2 \geq -2$, y_2

$x_1 \geq 0$, x_2 unrestricted to sign

18. The min $-3x_1 - 2x_2$ is

A. 12 B. 20

C. 2 D. 5

19. The dual variable are

A. Positive B. Negative

C. Non – negative D. Non – positive

20. If X is non-empty set $p: X \to D(X_1 p)$ is Pseudo – metric then $\forall x, y \in X$

A. $x = y \Rightarrow p(x_1 y) = 0$

B. $x \neq y \Rightarrow p(x_1 y) = 0$

C. $p(x, y) = 0$ for some $x \neq y$

D. None of these

21. The function $f(x) = \begin{cases} \frac{\sin x}{x} & x \neq 0 \\ 0 & x = 0 \end{cases}$ has

A. Discontinuity of first kind at $x = 0$

B. Discontinuity of second kind at $x = 0$

C. Continuity at $x = 0$

D. None of these

22. Given probability density function of random variable x

$$f(x) = \begin{cases} \frac{4}{\pi(1+x^2)} & 0 < x < 1 \\ 0 & \text{otherwise} \end{cases}$$

the second moment about the origin of a random variable x is

A. $\frac{4}{\pi}$ B. $\frac{4}{\pi} - 1$

C. 4π D. $\frac{\pi}{4} - 1$

23. Let x_1 and x_2 be two independent random variables then moment generating fucntion of $M_{(x_1+x_2)}(t)$ is

A. $M_{x_1}(t)$ B. $M_{x_2}(t)$

C. $M_{x_1}(t) M_{x_2}(t)$ D. $\frac{M_{x_1}(t)}{M_{x_2}(t)}$

24. The random variable x takes the value 1, 2..... with probability function $\frac{\lambda^r}{\lfloor r}$, r = 1, 2, 3........∞ the value of λ is

A. $\log e^2$ B. $\log e^1$

C. $\log e^5$ D. None of these

25. A manufacturer of still blade found 5% of its blade defective. He sales blades in packets, each contaning five blades. The probability that a packet contains are defective blade is

A. $0.25e^{-0.25}$ B. 0.5

C. $e^{-0.25}$ D. 0.25

26. What is the order and degree of a differential equation

$$\frac{d^2y}{dx^2}+\sqrt{1+\left(\frac{dy}{dx}\right)^3}=0$$

A. First order, second degree
B. First order, First degree
C. Second order, First degree
D. Second order, second degree

27. $4\frac{\partial^2 z}{\partial x^2}-4\frac{\partial^2 z}{\partial x\partial y}+\frac{\partial^2 z}{\partial y^2}=16\log(x+2y)$ has the solution

A. $z=f_1(2y+x)+xf_2(2y+x)+2x^2\log(x+2y)$
B. $z=2x^2\log(x+2y)$
C. $z=2f_1(2y+x)+2x^2\log(x+2y)$
D. None of these

28. General solution of $\frac{dy}{dx}+2xy=2e^{-x^2}$ is

A. $y=(2x+c)\,e^{-x^2}$ B. $y=2xe^{-x}$
C. $y=e^{-x}$ D. None of these

29. If $q=X^T AX$, q is positive definite, then

A. $|A|<0$ B. $|A|>0$
C. $|A|=0$ D. None of these

30. Let $A=[a_{ij}]_{m\times n}$, and $\bar{A}=[a_{ij}, b_i]_{m\times(n+1)}$ for $Ax=\bar{b}$, then

A. A is coefficient matrix and $\bar{A}$ the augmented matrix
B. $\bar{A}$ is coefficient matrix and A is augmented matrix
C. A, $\bar{A}$ are coefficient matrix
D. None of these

31. If $A=\begin{bmatrix}3 & 2\\1 & 4\end{bmatrix}$, then A (*adj* A) is

A. $\begin{bmatrix}10 & 0\\0 & 10\end{bmatrix}$ B. $\begin{bmatrix}0 & 10\\10 & 0\end{bmatrix}$

C. $\begin{bmatrix}1 & 3\\-2 & 1\end{bmatrix}$ D. $\begin{bmatrix}3 & -14\\4 & -2\end{bmatrix}$

32. If $A=\text{diag}(a_{11}\ldots\ldots\ldots a_{nn})$, then A^{-1} is

A. $\text{diag}(a_{11}\ldots\ldots\ldots a_{nn})$
B. diag (1, 11..................1)
C. $\text{diag}\left(\frac{1}{a_{11}}\ldots\ldots\frac{1}{a_{nn}}\right)$
D. diag (0, 0....................0)

33. The series $\left\{\frac{n\pi i}{n+i}\right\}_{n=1}^{\infty}$ is

A. Unbounded B. Divergent
C. Convergent D. None of these

34. Let $f(z)=\sum_{n=0}^{\infty}a_nZ^n$ and $f'(z)=\sum_{n=0}^{\infty}na_nZ^{n-1}$ have the radius of convergence L and L' respectively, then

A. L=L' B. L>L'
C. L<L' D. None of these

35. If $f(z)$ is analytic in a simple connected domain D, then for every simple closed path C in D is

A. $\oint_c f(z)\,dz=0$ B. $\oint_c f(z)\,dz>0$
C. $\oint_c f(z)\,dz<0$ D. none of these

36. The function $f(z)=|z|^2$ is

A. Every where analytic
B. Nowhere analytic
C. Analytic at $z=0$
D. None of these

37. Five dice were thrown 96 times and the numbers 4, 5 and 6 were thrown as given below:

No. of dice throwing 4, 5 or 6 :	5	4	3	2	1	0
Frequency :	7	19	35	24	8	3

The value of χ^2 is:

A. 3.7 B. 5.3
C. 8.3 D. 9.7

38. The origin and the points representing the roots of the equation $z^2+pz+q=0$ form an equilateral triangle if

A. $p=3q$ B. $p=3q^2$
C. $p^2=3q^2$ D. $p^2=3q$

39. If ΣS_n converges to S and Σt_n converges to T, then $\Sigma(S_n+t_n)$ converges to:

A. S + T B. S − T
C. S/T D. ST

40. If $a=(135)(12)$ and $b=(1579)$, then $a^{-1}ba$ equals:

A. (5 3 2 1) B. (3 7 9 5)
C. (1 2 5 3) D. (5 7 9 2)

ANSWERS

1	2	3	4	5	6	7	8	9	10
B	B	B	B	A	D	B	B	C	C
11	12	13	14	15	16	17	18	19	20
A	A	B	C	B	D	D	C	C	C
21	22	23	24	25	26	27	28	29	30
B	B	C	A	A	C	A	A	B	A
31	32	33	34	35	36	37	38	39	40
A	C	C	A	A	B	C	D	A	B

Some Selected Explanatory Answers

1. $\because$ Nullity I + rank I = dim V
$\Rightarrow$ Nullity I < dimV

2. dim V = n, S $\subset$ V
Subset S can not span V

3. Surplus variable as we have to remove $\geq$ sign (greater than equal to sign) otherwise slak variable i.e remove $\leq$ sign

4. Hyperplane in E^n passing through origin is $(x : cx = 0)$

5. Set X is convex if line segment joining x_1 and x_2 is in X

7. D is of finite characteristic if $\forall a \in$ D $\exists$ in m, positive integer such that $ma = 0$

8. In a group G there exist inverse of each element i.e. for $a \in G \ni a^{-1} \in G$

9. A ring (R,+,.) is without zero divisor if $a, b \in$ R, $a.b = 0 \Rightarrow a = 0 \Rightarrow$ or $b = 0$ or both are zero

10. If Q is true then P is true since every differential function is continuous

11. $\{b_n\}_{n=1}^{\infty}$ a convergent sequence
$\because \exists$ limit for $\{b_n\}_{n=1}^{\infty}$

12. The series $\sum \frac{1}{n^p}$ is convergent iff $p > 1$

13. According to continuity
C$\in [a, b]$

14. $\because z = a$ is a removable singularity as $f(z) = \sum_{-\infty}^{\infty} a_n(z-a)^n$ is a Laurent's expansion of at $z = a$ (which is isolated singularity)

15. $2\cos\alpha_1 = a + \frac{1}{a}$

$$\Rightarrow a^2 - 2a\cos\alpha_1 + 1 = 0$$

$$\Rightarrow a = \frac{2\cos\alpha_1 \pm \sqrt{4\cos^2\alpha_1 - 4}}{2}$$

$$= \cos\alpha_1 \pm i\sin\alpha_1$$

Similarly from $2\cos\alpha_2 = b + \frac{1}{b}$

$b = \cos\alpha_2 \pm i\sin\alpha_2$ etc.

$$abc\ldots\ldots\ldots\ldots + \frac{1}{abc\ldots\ldots}$$

$$= (\cos\alpha_1 + i\sin\alpha_1)(\cos\alpha_2 + i\sin\alpha_2)\ldots..$$

$$+ \frac{1}{(\cos\alpha_1 + i\sin\alpha_1)(\cos\alpha_2 + i\sin\alpha_2)\ldots..}$$

$$= \{\cos(\alpha_1 + \alpha_2 + \ldots.) + i\sin(\alpha_1 + \alpha_2 + \ldots.)\}$$

$$+ \frac{1}{\cos(\alpha_1 + \alpha_2 + \ldots.) + i\sin(\alpha_1 + \alpha_2 + \ldots.)}$$

$$= \{\cos(\alpha_1 + \alpha_2 + \ldots.) + i\sin(\alpha_1 + \alpha_2 + \ldots.)\}$$

$$+ \{\cos(\alpha_1 + \alpha_2 + \ldots.) - i(\sin\alpha_1 + \alpha_2 + \ldots.)\}$$

$$= 2\cos(\alpha_1 + \alpha_2 + \ldots\ldots..)$$

16. We know that
$\log_a a = 1$
$\log_i i = 1$

17. $\frac{a+ib}{a'+ib'} = \frac{a+ib}{a'+ib'} \times \frac{a'-ib'}{a'-ib'}$

$= \frac{(aa'+bb') + i\,(a'b - ab')}{(a')^2 + (b')^2}$ This number will be real if its imaginary part is zero

$\because a'b - ab' = 0$

18. The min $-3x_1 - 2x_2$ is '2' as per the solution $x_1 = 0, x_2 = -1$

$-3 \times 0 - 2(-1) = 2$

19. Dual variable is Non-negative as it is negative in primal

20. If X is non-empty set $p : X \to 0\ (X, p)$ is Pseudo–metrix then $\forall\ x, y \in X - p(x, y) = 0$ for some $x \neq y$

21. $F(0+) = \lim_{x\to 0+} \frac{\sin x}{x} = \lim_{h\to 0} \frac{\sin(h+0)}{0+h}$

= Undefined

$f(0-) = \lim_{x\to 0-} \frac{\sin x}{x} = \lim_{h\to 0} \frac{\sin(0-h)}{0-h}$

= Undefined

and $f(0) = 0$

$\because f(0+)$ and $f(0^-)$ are undefined. Discontinuous at $x = 0$ and this discontinuity is of second kind.

22. $\Rightarrow \mu'_r = E(x^r)$

$$= \int_{-\infty}^{\infty} x^r f(x)\,dx$$

$$\Rightarrow \mu'_2 = \frac{4}{\pi}\int_0^1 \frac{x^2}{1+x^2}\,dx$$

$$= \frac{4}{\pi} - 1$$

23. $M_{(x_1+x_2)}(t) = [e^{t(x_1+x_2)}]$

$= E(e^{tx_1} . e^{tx_2})$

$= E(e^{tx_1})\,E(e^{tx_2})$

($\because x_1$ and x_2 are independent)

$= Mx_1(t)\,Mx_2(t)$

24. $\because \sum f(x) = 1$

$$\Rightarrow \sum_{r=0}^{\infty} \frac{\lambda^r}{\lfloor r} = \frac{\lambda}{\lfloor 1} + \frac{\lambda^2}{\lfloor 2} + \frac{\lambda^3}{\lfloor 3} + \ldots\ldots\ldots = 1$$

$\Rightarrow e^{\lambda} - 1 = 1$

$$\left(\because e^{\lambda} = 1 + \lambda + \frac{\lambda^2}{\lfloor 2} + \frac{\lambda^3}{\lfloor 3} + \ldots\ldots\ldots\right)$$

$\Rightarrow e^{\lambda} = 2$

$\Rightarrow \lambda \log e_e = \log_e^2$

$\Rightarrow \lambda = \log_e^2$

25. Here $P = 5\% = 0.05$

$n = 5$

$\lambda = np$

$0.05 \times 5 = 0.25$

let x = number of defective blades, Poisson law

$p(X = x)$

$= e^{-\lambda}\frac{\lambda^x}{\lfloor x}$

$P(x = 1) = 0.25e^{-0.25}$

26. $\frac{d^2y}{dx^2} + \sqrt{1 + \left(\frac{dy}{dx}\right)^3} = 0$

order is 2 it is the order of highest order derivative and degree one accordingly

27. $(4D^2 - 4DD^1 + D'^2)\,z = 16\log(x + 2y)$

Alternate equation

$4m^2 - 4m + 1 = 0 \Rightarrow (2m-1)^2 = 0$

$z_h = f_1(2y + x) + xf_2(2y + x)$

$$z_p = \frac{1}{4D^2 - DD' + D'^2}16\log(x+2y)$$

$$= \frac{1}{(2D^2 - D')^2}16\log(x+2y)$$

$$= \frac{x^2}{2^2 2!}16\log(x+2y)$$

$= 2x^2 \log(x + 2y)$

$z = z_h + z_p$

28. Here $p = 2x$, $9.F = e^{\int p dx} = e^{x^2}$

$\therefore e^{x^2}\frac{dy}{dx} = 2xe^{x^2}\,y = 2$

$\Rightarrow \frac{dy}{dx}(ye^{x^2}) = 2$

$\Rightarrow ye^{x^2} = 2x + c$

$\Rightarrow y = e^{-x^2}(2x + c)$

29. $|A| > 0$ then only $q = X^TAX$. where q is +ve definite

30. A is coefficient matrix and $\bar{A}$ is the augmented matrix for $A \times \bar{b}$

31. $A = \begin{bmatrix} 3 & 2 \\ 1 & 4 \end{bmatrix}$ multiplying A by its adjoint we have

$$A\,(\text{adj } A) = \begin{bmatrix} 10 & 0 \\ 0 & 10 \end{bmatrix}$$

33. $\left\{\dfrac{n\pi i}{n+i}\right\}_{n=1}^{\infty}$ is convergent as it converges to 1 by definition

34. $f(z) = \sum_{n=0}^{\infty} a_n z^n$ and $f'(z) = \sum_{n=0}^{\infty} n a_n z^{n-1}$ then radius of convergence of f |z| = radius of convergance of $f'(z)$

i.e. $L = L^1$

35. $\oint_c f(z)\,dz = 0$ (property of analytic function)

36. $f(z) = |z|^2$ is nowhere analytic (according to definition)

37. $P = \dfrac{3}{6} = \dfrac{1}{2}$ and $q = 1 - p = \dfrac{1}{2}$

The theorical frequencies of getting 5, 4, 3, 2, 1, 0 successes are respectively the successive terms of $96\left(\dfrac{1}{2}+\dfrac{1}{2}\right)^5$ viz 3, 15, 30, 30, 15, 3.

Since no frequency should be less than 10, so on regrouping

	5 or 4	3	2	1 or 0
Oi :	26	35	24	11
Fi :	18	30	30	18

$$\chi^2 = \frac{(26-18)^2}{18} + \frac{(35-30)^2}{30} + \frac{(24-30)^2}{30} + \frac{(11-18)^2}{18}$$

$= 8.3$

40. $a = (135)\,(12) = (1\ 2\ 3\ 5)$

$a^{-1}\,ba = (5\ \ 3\ \ 2\ \ 1)\ (1\ \ 5\ \ 7\ \ 9)\ (1\ \ 2\ \ 3\ \ 5)$

$= (3\ \ 7\ \ 5\ \ 9)$

SET–3

CSIR–UGC (NET) MATHEMATICAL SCIENCES

PART-B

1. The integration factor for the Leibnitz linear equation, $\frac{dy}{dx} + Py = Q$ is

A. $\int Pdx$ B. $\int Qdx$

C. $\exp\left(\int Qdx\right)$ D. $\exp\left(\int Pdx\right)$

2. The particular solution of $\frac{d^3y}{dx^3} + y = \cos(2x-1)$ is

A. $\frac{1}{65}[\cos(2x-1) - 8]$

B. $\frac{1}{65}[\cos(2x-1) - 8\sin(2x-1)]$

C. $\frac{1}{65}[\cos(2x+1) + 8]$

D. None of these

3. In a sample survey, the chances of young professionals courses MBA degree, MCA degree or both are 0.86, 0.35 and 0.29 respectviely. What is the probability of owing either or both degrees?

A. 0. 82 B. 0. 92

C. 0. 08 D. 0. 18

4. If x_1 has the mean 4 and x_2 has the mean 2 and x_1 and x_2 are independent random variables then $E(2x_1 + x_2 - 5)$ is

A. 1 B. 2

C. 3 D. 4

5. The series $\left\{\frac{e^{\frac{n\pi}{4}}}{n}\right\}_{n=1}^{\infty}$ is

A. Unbounded B. Bounded

C. Divergent D. None of these

6. If $f(z)$ is analytic and has a pole at $z = z_0$ then

A. $|f(z)| = c$, a constant as $z \to z_0$

B. $|f(z)| \to 0$, as $z \to z_0$

C. $|f(z)| = \infty$ as $z \to z_0$

D. None of these

7. A function $f(z) = \frac{1}{z^2}$ has real and imaginary parts as

A. $\text{Re}(f(z)) = x^2$, $\text{Im}(f(z)) = y^2$

B. $\text{Re}(f(z)) = x^2 - y^2$, $\text{Im}(f(z)) = 2xy$

C. $\text{Re}(f(z)) = \frac{1}{x^2 - y^2}$, $\text{Im}(f(z)) = \frac{-1}{2xy}$

D. $\text{Re}(f(z)) = \frac{x^2 - y^2}{(x^2+y^2)^2}$, $\text{Im}(f(z)) = \frac{-2xy}{(x^2+y^2)^2}$

8. The characteristic equation for the unitary matrix of matrix $A = \begin{bmatrix} 3+4i & -5i \\ -7 & 6-2i \end{bmatrix}$, is

A. $\lambda^2 - i\lambda - 1 = 0$ B. $\lambda^2 + i\lambda = 0$

C. $\lambda^2 + i\lambda + 1 = 0$ D. None of these

9. If $A = \begin{bmatrix} 5 & 0 & 0 \\ 0 & 5 & 0 \\ 0 & 0 & 5 \end{bmatrix}$, then det A is

A. 125 B. 15

C. 0 D. None of these

10. The rank of the matrix $A = \begin{bmatrix} 1 & 2 & 3 \\ 4 & 5 & 6 \\ 2 & 1 & 2 \end{bmatrix}$ is

A. 1 B. 2

C. 3 D. 4

11. If A is a square matrix of order n, then A^{-1} exits if

A. Rank A= 0 B. Rank A= n

C. Rank A < n D. None of these

12. If A is matrix then

A. Row Rank (A) = column rank (A)

B. Row Rank (A) ≠ column rank (A)

C. Row Rank (A) > column rank (A)

D. None of these

13. If T is a linear operator on vector space U and W is a subspace of U. Then W is invariant under T if

A. $\forall \alpha \in W \Rightarrow T\alpha \in W$
B. $\forall \alpha \in T(W) \Rightarrow \alpha \in W$
C. $W = T(W)$
D. None of these

14. If w_1 and w_2 are subspaces of vector space and w_1 is the subspace spanned by vectors $\alpha_1.....\alpha_n$, then if $\alpha_1.....\alpha_n \in W_2$

A. $w_1 = w_2$ B. $w_1 \subset w_2$
C. $w_1 \supset w_2$ D. $w_1 \cap w_2 = \phi$

15. Let E^n be an Euclidean space, a hypersphere in E^n with centre at $\bar{a}$ and radius $\in > 0$ is a set of points

A. $\{ \bar{x} \,||\, \bar{x} - \bar{a} | > \in \}$ B. $\{ \bar{x} \,||\, \bar{x} - \bar{a} | < \in \}$
C. $\{ \bar{x} \,||\, \bar{x} - \bar{a} | = \in \}$ D. None of these

16. A Point of $\bar{x} \in X$ is an extreme point of convex set X iff there donot exist points $\bar{x}_1, \bar{x}_2$ ($\bar{x}_1 \neq \bar{x}_2$) in X such that

A. $\bar{x} = (1-\lambda)\bar{x}_1 + \lambda\bar{x}_2, 0 < \lambda < 1$
B. $\bar{x} = (1-\lambda)\bar{x}_1 + \lambda\bar{x}_2, 0 \le \lambda \le 1$
C. $\bar{x} = (1-\lambda)\bar{x}_1 + \lambda\bar{x}_2$, λ real
D. None of these

17. If linear programming problem have basic feasible solution if we drop one basic vector and introduce a non basic vector in basis, then new solution obtained is

A. A basic feasible solution
B. A non basic feasible solution
C. Non solution exist
D. None of these

18. All x_js equal to zero, in l.p.p are

A. Solution to l.p.p.
B. Feasible solution to l.p.p.
C. Optimal solution to l.p.p.
D. No solution to l.p.p.

19. The EOQ model is of particular importance because

A. It is fairly simple and easy to understand
B. It is the most realistic model which can be formulated
C. There are only a few assumption to satisfy and the needed information is always easy to obtain
D. No other model can be applied if it can not be used

20. Let P_n be the probability that n service occured out of N in (Pure death model) time t with inter-departure time exponentialy distributed with mean μ, then

A. $P_n = \dfrac{(\mu t)^{N-n}\, e^{-\mu t}}{\underline{|N-n}}, 0 < n < N$

B. $P_n = \dfrac{(\mu t)^{N} e^{-\mu t}}{\underline{|n}}$

C. $P_n = \dfrac{(\mu t)^{n}\, e^{-\mu t}}{\underline{|n}}$

D. None of these

21. If arrival is 20 customers/week and service rate is 50 customers/week, then the expected number of busy servers for M|M|1 queueing system are

A. 2/5 B. 5/2
C. 5 D. None of these

22. The function $f(x) = \dfrac{1}{x-a} \sin \dfrac{1}{x-a}$ has

A. Discountinuity of first kind at $x = a$
B. Discountinuity of second kind at $x = a$
C. Continuity at $x = a$
D. None of these

23. If f is decreasing function on $E \subset D$, then for $x, y \in E$ we have

A. $x < y \Rightarrow f(x) \le f(y)$
B. $x < y \Rightarrow f(x) \ge f(y)$
C. $x < y \Rightarrow f(x) < f(y)$
D. None of these

24. A function f of metric space $\langle X, P_1 \rangle$ on to $\langle Y, P_2 \rangle$ is homomorphism if

A. $f(X) = Y$ B. $f(X) \subset Y$
C. $f(X) \neq Y$ D. None of these

25. If f is constant function on $[a, b]$, then total variation of f on $[a, b]$

A. $V_f(a, b) = 0$ B. $V_f(a, b) \ge 0$
C. $V_f(a, b) \le 0$ D. None of these

26. If f is of bounded variation on $[a, b]$ and $c \in [a, b]$ then
A. f is of bounded variation on $[a, b]$ and on $[c, b]$
B. f is not of bounded variation on $[a, c]$ and on $[c, b]$
C. f is constant on $[a, c]$ and on $[c, b]$
D. None of these

27. If a, b, $\in$, D, where D is an ordered set, then which of the following is false
A. $a < b \Rightarrow -a > -b$ B. $|ab| = |a|\,|b|$
C. $-|a| \leq a \leq |a|$ D. $|a + b| \geq |a| + |b|$

28. I is an ordered integral domain and a, b$\in$, I, if $a > b$ then
A. $a + c \geq b + c, \forall c \in I$
B. $a + c \leq b + c, \forall c \in I$
C. $a + c < b + c, \forall c \in I$
D. $a + c > b + c, \forall c \in I$

29. The series $1 + x + x^2 ...... + x^n + ...$
A. Converges for $|x| < 1$
B. Diverges for $|x| > 1$
C. Converges for $|x| = 1$
D. None of these

30. If $z = a$ is an isolated singularity of f and $f(z) = \sum_{-\infty}^{\infty} a_n (z-a)^n$ is its Laurent expansion in $ann\,(a, o, R)$. Also if $a_n \neq 0$ for infinitely many negative integers n, then
A. $z = a$ is a removable singularity
B. $z = a$ is a pole of order in
C. $z = a$ is an essential singularity
D. None of these

31. Let z_1 and z_2 are two complex numbers with α and β as their principle arguments such that $\alpha + \beta > \pi$ then Arg $(z_1 . z_2)$ is given by
A. $\alpha + \beta$ B. $\alpha + \beta - \pi$
C. $\alpha + \beta + \pi$ D. $\alpha + \beta - 2\pi$

32. If Υ is a closed rectifiable curve in C, then for a $a \notin \{\Upsilon\}$, the index of Υ with respect to point a is
A. $n(\Upsilon; a) = = \frac{1}{2\pi i}\int_y z\,dz$
B. $n(\Upsilon; a) = = \frac{1}{2\pi i}\int_y (z-a)^{-1} dz$
C. $(\Upsilon; a) = = \frac{1}{2\pi i}\int_y a\,dz$
D. None of these

33. If in the primal the number of constraints are m and in dual the number of variable are n then
A. $m \geq n$ B. $m \leq n$
C. $m = n$ D. None of these

34. In a transportation problem (TP) the dual variables μ_1 and v_j are unrestricted in sign because
A. The TP is a minimization problem
B. The TP is with all equality constraints
C. In TP all decision variables are ≥ 0
D. None of these

35. The optimal basis of primal consists of variables x_1 and x_2. The cost of these are 3 and 0 and the corresponding columns all $(3, 2)^T$ and $(0, -1)^T$. The optimal solution (y_1, y_2) of dual is
A. (3,0) B. (1,0)
C. (1,2) D. (0,0)

36. The drawback to use the transportation problem programming in solving an assignment problem is
A. The assignment problem can't be formulated as transportation problem
B. The assignment problem is an unbalanced transportation problem
C. Degeneracy results from every improvement in the total cost
D. None of these

37. If θ is the acute angle between the two regression lines, then:
A. $\sin\theta \leq 1 - r^2$ B. $\sin\theta \geq 1 - r^2$
C. $\sin\theta \leq 1 + r^2$ D. $\sin\theta \geq 1 + r^2$

38. The residue of $f(z) = \cot z$ at any of its poles is
A. 0 B. $\sqrt{5}$
C. $\sqrt{3}$ D. 1

39. Which one is not an ordered field?
A. $(q, +, \cdot)$ B. $(C, +, \cdot)$
C. $(IR, +, \cdot)$ D. $(I, +, \cdot)$

40. If $f: R \to R$ is a differentiable function and $f(1) = 4$, then the value of
$$\lim_{x \to 1}\left[\int_4^{f(x)} \left\{\frac{2t}{x-1}\right\} dt\right]$$ is given by
A. $\frac{f'(1)}{4}$ B. $2f'(1)$
C. $4f'(1)$ D. $8f'(1)$

ANSWERS

1	2	3	4	5	6	7	8	9	10
D	B	B	A	B	C	D	A	A	C
11	12	13	14	15	16	17	18	19	20
B	A	A	B	C	A	A	B	C	A
21	22	23	24	25	26	27	28	29	30
A	B	B	A	A	A	D	D	A	C
31	32	33	34	35	36	37	38	39	40
D	B	C	B	B	C	A	D	B	D

Some Selected Explanatory Answers

2. $y_p = \frac{1}{D^3+1}\cos(2x-1)$

(Put $D^2 = -2^2 = -4$)

$= \frac{1}{D(-4)+1}\cos(2x-1)$

$= \frac{1+4D}{1-16D^2}\cos(2x-1)$

(Put $D^2 = -2^2 = -4$)

$= \frac{1}{65}[\cos(2x-1) + 4D\cos(2x-1)]$

$= \frac{1}{65}[\cos(2x-1) - 8\sin(2x-1)]$

4. $E(2x_1 + x_2 - 5) = E(2x_1 + x_2) - 5$

$= 2E(x_1) + E(x_2) - 5$

$= 2\mu_1 + \mu_2 - 5$

$= 2\times 4 + (-2) - 5$

$= 1$

5. Bounded

$\therefore \exists$ lower and upper bounds of the series i.e. series is bounded above as well as bounded below

10. $|a_{11}| = 1 \neq 0$

$$\begin{vmatrix} 1 & 2 \\ 4 & 5 \end{vmatrix} = -3 \neq 0$$

$$\begin{vmatrix} 1 & 2 & 3 \\ 4 & 5 & 6 \\ 2 & 1 & 2 \end{vmatrix} \neq 0$$

$\therefore$ Rank A = 3

12. By property of rank of matrix

Row Rank (A) = column rank (A)

13. T is a linear operator on vector space V and W is a subspace of V. Then W is a invariant under T if $T\alpha \in W \; \forall \; \alpha \in W$

22. $f(0+) = \lim_{x\to 0+} f(x) = \lim_{h\to 0} f(a+h)$

$= \lim_{h\to 0} \frac{1}{a+h-a}\sin\frac{1}{a+h-a}$

= Undefinied = ∞

$f(0-)$ = Undefined

and $f(a)$ = Undefined = ∞

37. The angle θ between the two regression lines is

$$\tan\theta = \frac{1-r^2}{r}\cdot\frac{\sigma_x\sigma_y}{\sigma_x^2+\sigma_y^2} \quad ...(i)$$

Since A.M. $\geq$ G.M.

$\therefore \frac{1}{2}(\sigma_x^2+\sigma_y^2) > \sqrt{\sigma_x^2\cdot\sigma_y^2} = \sigma_x\sigma_y$

$\Rightarrow \sigma_x^2+\sigma_y^2 \geq 2\sigma_x\sigma_y$

$$\Rightarrow \frac{\sigma_x+\sigma_y}{\sigma_x^2+\sigma_y^2} \leq \frac{1}{2} \quad ...(ii)$$

From (i) and (ii), $\tan\theta \leq \frac{1-r^2}{2r}$

$\Rightarrow \sin\theta \leq \frac{1-r^2}{1+r^2}$ $\qquad \Rightarrow \sin\theta \leq 1-r^2$

$$\left[\because \; 1+r^2 \geq 1 \Rightarrow \frac{1}{1+r^2} \leq 1\right]$$

38. Singularities of $f(z)$ are $z = n\pi$, $n = 0, \pm 1, \pm 2, ...$

$f(z)$ has a simple pole.

Residue $f(z) = \lim_{z\to n\pi}(z-n\pi)\frac{\cos z}{\sin z} = \frac{(-1)^n}{(-1)^n} = 1$

SET–4

CSIR–UGC (NET) MATHEMATICAL SCIENCES

PART-B

1. Let f, g be bounded functions defined on $[a, b]$ and let P be any partition of $[a, b]$, then which of the following is true

A. $L(p, f+g) \le L(p, f) + L(p, g)$

B. $L(p, f+g) \ge L(p, f) + L(p, g)$

C. $L(p, f+g) = L(p, f) + L(p, g)$

D. None of the above

2. The function $f(x) = \begin{Bmatrix} 2x+1, & x \le 1 \\ \alpha x^2 + \beta x, & x < 1 \end{Bmatrix}$ is differentiable for every x, then the value of α and β are given by

A. $\alpha = 0$, $\beta = 2$ B. $\alpha = 3$, $\beta = 0$

C. $\alpha = 4$, $\beta = -1$ D. $\alpha = -1$, $\beta = 4$

3. For the function $f(x) = |x|$, Lagrange's M.V.T. does not hold in the interval

A. $[-1, 0]$ B. $[0, 1/2]$

C. $[0, 1]$ D. $[-1, -1]$

4. The characteristic vectors $x_1 .... x_n$ are said to be linearly independent if for any scalars $\alpha_1 ...., \alpha_n$ which condition is hold good.

A. $\alpha_1 x_1 + ... + \alpha_n x_n = 0 \Rightarrow \alpha_1 = \alpha_2 .... = \alpha_n = 0$

B. $\alpha_1 x_1 + ... + \alpha_n x_n \ne 0 \Rightarrow \alpha_1 = \alpha_2 = ... = \alpha_n = 0$

C. $\alpha_1 x_1 + ... + \alpha_n x_n = 0 \Rightarrow \alpha_1 \ne \alpha_2 \ne ... \ne \alpha_n \ne 0$

D. None of the above

5. The characteristic roots of the matrix $A = \begin{bmatrix} 1 & 4 \\ 2 & 3 \end{bmatrix}$ are

A. 2 and 3 B. 5 and 1

C. 5 and -1 D. -5 and 1

6. The solution of L. P. P

$\max z = 6x_1 + 11x_2$

s.t $2x_1 + x_2 \le 104$

$x_1 + 2x_2 \le 76$; $x_1, x_2 \ge 0$ is

A. $x_1 = 8, x_2 = 16$ and $\max z = 104$,

B. $x_1 = 10, x_2 = 12$ and $\max z = 404$

C. $x_1 = 9, x_2 = 20$ and $\max z = 430$

D. $x_1 = 44, x_2 = 16$ and $\max z = 440$

7. The function $f(x) = x^2$ is uniformly continuous in

A. $]-1, 1[$ B. $(-1, 1)$

C. $]-2, 2[$ D. $[-2, 2]$

8. If $f(z) = \dfrac{1}{(z+5)^3 (z-4)^2}$ then $z = -5$ is a pole of order

A. 5 B. 4

C. 3 D. 2

9. The value of $\displaystyle\int_0^a \frac{dx}{(1+x^2)^2}$ is

A. $\dfrac{\pi}{8}$ B. $\dfrac{\pi}{4}$

C. $\dfrac{\pi}{2}$ D. π

10. The polynomial $f(z) = 2z + 6z^3$ has a

A. Pole of fifth order at ∞

B. Pole of third order at ∞

C. Pole of second order at ∞

D. None of the above

11. The power series $\displaystyle\sum_{n=0}^{\infty} \frac{z^n}{n!} = 1 + z + \frac{z^2}{2!} + \frac{z^3}{3!} + ...$

A. Converges

B. Diverges

C. Oscillates

D. None of the above

12. The imaginary part of $\dfrac{2z+1}{iz+1}$ is -2, the locus of the point representing z in the complex plane is

A. A parabola B. A circle

C. A straight line D. None of the above

13. The functoin $f(z) = x^2 y + iy^2$ is

A. An analytic

B. Not an analytic function

C. Neither analytic nor continuous

D. None of these

14. If $f(z)$ is analytic within a circle c, given by $|z-a| = R$ and if $|f(z)| \leq M$ on c, then $|f^n(a)|$

A. $\geq \frac{Mn!}{R^n}$ B. $\leq \frac{Mn!}{R^n}$

C. $< \frac{n!}{R^n}$ D. None of these

15. If $F(z) = \frac{z^2}{(z^2+a^2)^3}$ then it has the poles of order

A. 1 B. 2

C. 3 D. 4

16. A polynomial of nth degree has

A. n zeros

B. More than n zeros

C. Less than n zeros

D. $(n-1)$ zeros

17. Any function of x, y which possesses continuous partial derivatives of the first and second orders and satisfies Laplace's equation is called

A. An identity

B. An entire function

C. A harmonic function

D. None of these

18. Choose Laplace's equation

A. $\frac{\partial^2 v}{\partial x^2} + \frac{\partial^2 v}{\partial y^2} = 0$ B. $\frac{\partial^2 v}{\partial x^2} - \frac{\partial^2 v}{\partial y^2} = 1$

C. $\frac{\partial^2 v}{\partial x^2} - \frac{\partial v}{\partial y} = 3$ D. $\frac{\partial v}{\partial x} + \frac{\partial v}{\partial y} = 0$

19. $v = y^3 - 3x^2 y$ is a

A. Harmonic function

B. Entire function

C. Neither harmonic nor identity function

D. None of the above

20. If $f(x) = 3x^7 + 2x + 3$, $g(x) = 5x^3 + 2x + 6$ be two polynomials over the field $z_7 = (\{0, 1, 2, 3, 4, 5, 6,\} +_7, X_7)$ then the values of $\frac{d}{dx} f(x)$ is

A. 1 B. 2

C. 3 D. 4

21. The value of x in the equation $3x = 2$ is the field $(z_7, +_7, X_7)$ is

A. 5 B. 3

C. 2 D. 1

22. In residue class–field (mod 17), $\frac{5}{7} = x$ then the value of x is

A. 2 B. 4

C. 8 D. 16

23. Which of the following rings is not an integral domain

A. (I, + , .) Where I is the set of integers

B. (M, +, .) Where M is the set of 2×2 matrices

C. (R, +, .) Where R is the set of real numbers

D. (C,+, .) Where C is the set of complex number

24. Let R be any ring. The union of an increasing chain of ideals $I_1 \subset I_2 \subset$..........., is

A. Not an ideal B. An ideal

C. A field D. A ring

25. Let A *be* an m×n matrix with real entries. A = 0 (null matrix) iff trace (A' A) is equal to

A. 0 B. 1

C. 2 D. 3

26. Suppose T :V → V is linear and suppose that $f(t)$ is any polynomial. Then the kernal of $f(t)$ is

A. Invariant under T

B. Not invariant under T

C. Invariant under f

D. None of the above

27. Let $\{w_i\}$ be a collection of T invariant subspaces of a vector space V then the intersection $w = \text{ι } w_i$ is also

A. Vector spaces B. Subspaces

C. Invariant D. None of the above

28. Let T : V → V be linear. Let for v∈ V, $T^K(v) = 0$ but $T^{K-1}(v) \neq 0$ then the subspace W generated by $\{V, T(V), T^2(V), \ldots, T^{K-1}(V)\}$ is

A. T– invariant B. K–invariant

C. F– invariant D. None of these

29. Which of the following statements is/are true, if F: V → U be a linear mapping

A. Rank (F) + nullity (F) = dim V

B. Rank (V) + nullity (F) = dim U

C. Rank (V) – nullity (F) = dim V

D. None of the above

30. Let T be a linear operation on V. Suppose A is a matrix of T relative to basis B and C is the matrix of T relative to basis B$'$. If P is the transition matrix from the basis B to the basis 'B$'$ then which of the following result is correct

A. $C = P^{-1} AP$ B. $C = A^{-1} PA^{-1}$
C. $A = (P^{-1} A)^2$ D. $C = (P^{-1} AP)^2$

31. Let A and B be the two square matrices of order *n* over *a* field F and $\lambda \in F$. If tr. denots trace, then which of the following is true.

A. $tr.(\lambda.A) = tr.(\lambda^2.A)$
B. $tr.(\lambda.A) = tr.(\lambda.A^2)$
C. $tr.(\lambda.A) = tr.\ \lambda + tr.A$
D. $tr.(\lambda.A) = \lambda.tr.A$

32. Let V be the vector space of polynomials in t over R. Let $I : V \rightarrow R$ be the integral operator defined by $I(P(t)) = \int_0^1 P(t)dt$. I is linear and hence it is a

A. Linear functional on V
B. Functional on V
C. Functional in V
D. None of these

33. The mapping $T : V_2(R) \rightarrow V_3(R)$ defined as $T(a,b) = (a + b, a - b, b)$ is a linear transformation from V_2 (R) into V_3 (R). Then rank and nullity of T are

A. 2, 0 B. 1, 1
C. 3, 2 D. 5, 5

34. Let $T : R^3 \rightarrow R^3$ the linear transformation defined by $T(x, y, z) = (x + 2y - z, y + z, x + y - 2z)$ then the basis of R (T) is

A. {(1, 2, 1), (2, 4, 4), (–1, 1, –2)}
B. {(1, 3, 1), (2, 9, 4), (–1, 1, –2)}
C. {(1, 0, 1), (2, 1, 1), (–1, 1, –2)}
D. None of the above

35. The equation $x^3p^2 + x^2\ yp + 1 = 0$ has a discriminant relation

A. $y(x-y) = 2$
B. $x(xy-2) = 0$
C. $x^3(xy^2-4) = 0$
D. None of the above

36. The equation $(D^2 - 3D + 2)\,y = e^x$ has a particular integral

A. $-xe^x$ B. xe^x
C. $x^2\ e^{2x}$ D. None of the above

37. Suppose there are two market products of brands A and B respectively. Let each of these two brands have exactly 50% of the total market in same period and let the market be of a fixed size. The transition matrix is given below

$$\text{From}\ \begin{array}{c} \\ A \\ B \end{array}\!\!\begin{array}{c} \text{To} \\ \begin{array}{cc} A & B \end{array} \\ \begin{bmatrix} .9 & .1 \\ .5 & .5 \end{bmatrix} \end{array}$$

If the initial market share break down is 50% for each brand then their market shares in steady state are

A. for A is 5/7 and for B is 4/6
B. for A is 6/5 and for B is 6/4
C. for A is 5/3 and for B is 2/3
D. for A is 5/6 and for B is 1/6

38. The probability for the realisation of any combination $j (= 1, 2, 3, 4)$ of 4 events A_1, A_2, A_3, A_4 is then $1/4^j$. The probability for the relation of at least one of these four events is:

A. $1 - \left(\frac{3}{4}\right)^4$ B. $1 + \left(\frac{3}{4}\right)^4$

C. $1 + \left(\frac{1}{4}\right)^3$ D. $1 - \left(\frac{1}{4}\right)^3$

39. If $x > -1$ and $x \neq 0$ then $(1 + x^n)$ for $n = 2, 3, ...$ is:

A. $1 + nx$ B. $< (1 + nx)$
C. $> (1 + nx)$ D. None of these

40. In the Laurent Series expansion of $f(z) = \frac{1}{z-1} - \frac{1}{z-2}$ valid in the region $|z| > 2$, the coefficient of $\frac{1}{z^2}$ is:

A. –1 B. 0
C. 1 D. 3

ANSWERS

1	2	3	4	5	6	7	8	9	10
B	D	D	A	C	D	D	C	B	B
11	**12**	**13**	**14**	**15**	**16**	**17**	**18**	**19**	**20**
A	C	B	B	C	A	C	A	A	B
21	**22**	**23**	**24**	**25**	**26**	**27**	**28**	**29**	**30**
B	C	C	B	A	A	C	A	A	A
31	**32**	**33**	**34**	**35**	**36**	**37**	**38**	**39**	**40**
D	A	A	C	C	A	B	A	A	A

Some Selected Explanatory Answers

2. The given function is

$$f(x) = \begin{cases} 2x+1 \quad , & x \le 1 \\ \alpha x^2 + \beta x \, , & x > 1 \end{cases}$$

$$Lf'(1) = \lim_{h\to 0} \frac{f(1-h) - f(1)}{-h}$$

$$= \lim_{h\to 0} \frac{[2(1-h)+1]-3}{-h} = 2$$

$$Rf'(1) = \lim_{h\to 0} \frac{f(1+h) - f(1)}{h}$$

$$= \lim_{h\to 0} \frac{\left[\alpha(1+h)^2 + \beta(1+h)\right] - 3}{h}$$

$$= \lim_{h\to 0} \frac{(\alpha+\beta-3)+(2\alpha+\beta)h+\alpha h^2}{h}$$

$Rf'(1)$ will be exist if

$\alpha+\beta-3=0$

$Rf'(1) = \lim_{h\to 0} (2\alpha+\beta)+\alpha h = 2\alpha+\beta$

$f(x)$ will be diff. if

$Rf'(1) = Lf'(1)$

$\Rightarrow 2\alpha+\beta = 2$

$\alpha = -1, \beta = 4$

5. The characteristic equation of the matrix A is

$|A - \lambda I| = 0$

$$\text{or} \begin{vmatrix} 1-\lambda & 4 \\ 2 & 3-\lambda \end{vmatrix} = 0$$

or $(1-\lambda)(3-\lambda)-8=0$

$\Rightarrow \lambda = 5, -1$

and these are the characteristic roots of A.

6. We consider the constraints as equalities

$$2x_1 + x_2 = 104$$
$$x_1 + 2x_2 = 76$$

We draw lines in 2D plane

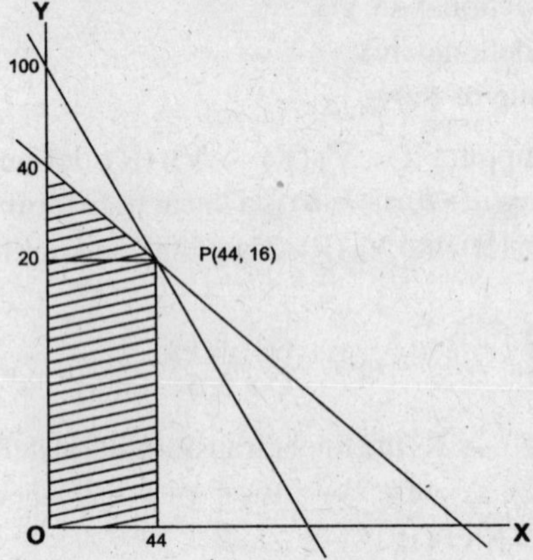

The shaded region in the fig. is the permissible region for the values of the variables x_1 and x_2 max z, is obtained at the point $P(44, 16)$

Which is the point of intersection of lines

$$2x_1 + x_2 = 104$$
$$x + 2x_2 = 76$$

$\max z = 6\times 44 + 11\times 16 = 440$

8. $f(z) = \dfrac{1}{(z+5)^3(z-4)^2}$ then $z = -5$ is a pole of order '3'

9. Suppose $f(z) = \frac{1}{(1+z^2)^2}$ consider the integral

$\int_C f(z)dz$ where C is closed contour

$f(z)$ has only on a pole of order two at $z = i$ within C.

$$F(z) = \frac{\phi(z)}{(z-i)^2} \text{ where } \phi(z) = \frac{1}{(z+i)^2}$$

$$\phi'(z) = \frac{-2}{(z+i)^3}$$

$$\therefore \phi^1(i) = \frac{-2}{-8i}$$

$$\text{Re } (z = i) = \frac{1}{(n-1)!} \phi^{(n-1)}(i) = \frac{\phi^1(i)}{1!} = \frac{1}{4i}$$

$$\int_0 f(z)dz = 2\pi i \text{ (sum of residues within C)}$$

$$= \frac{2\pi i}{4i} = \frac{\pi}{2}$$

$$\int_0 f(z)dz + \int_{-R}^{R} f(x)dx = \frac{\pi}{2}$$

$$\lim_{R\to\infty} z f(z) = \lim_{|z|\to\infty} \frac{z}{(1+z^2)^2} = 0$$

$$\lim_{R\to\infty} \int_0 f(z)dz = i(\pi - 0)(0) = 0$$

$$\int_{-\infty}^{\infty} f(x)dx = 2\int_0^{\infty} \frac{dx}{(1+x^2)} = \frac{\pi}{2}$$

$$\Rightarrow \int_0^{\infty} \frac{dx}{(1+x^2)} = \frac{\pi}{4}$$

13. Solution, $f(z) = x^2 y + iy^2$

Here $u = x^2y$ and $v = y^2$

$$\therefore \frac{\partial u}{\partial x} = 2xy; \qquad \frac{\partial v}{\partial x} = 0$$

$$\frac{\partial u}{\partial y} = x^2, \qquad \frac{\partial v}{\partial y} = 2y$$

Thus we find that

$$\frac{\partial u}{\partial x} \neq \frac{\partial v}{\partial y} \text{ and } \frac{\partial u}{\partial y} \neq \frac{\partial v}{\partial x}$$

i.e. Cauchy – Riemann equations are not satisfied so the given function $f(z) = x^2y + iy^2$ is not an analytic function.

14. Solution, we know that

$$F^n(a) = \frac{n!}{2\pi i}\int_c \frac{F(z)dz}{(z-a)^{n+1}}$$

$$\therefore \left|f^n(a)\right| = \left|\frac{n!}{2\pi i}\int_c \frac{f(z)dz}{(z-G)^{n+1}}\right| \leq \frac{n!}{|2\pi i|}\int \frac{|f(z)||dz|}{|(z-a)|^{n+1}}$$

$$\leq \frac{n!}{2\pi}.\frac{M}{R^{n+1}}\int_0^{2\pi} Rd\theta$$

$$\leq \frac{n!}{2\pi}.\frac{M}{R^{n+1}}.2\pi R$$

$$\leq \frac{M.n!}{R^n} \left[\begin{array}{l} \because z = R.e^{i\theta} \\ \because dz = iR.e^{i\theta}d\theta \\ \because |dz| = |iR.e^{i\theta}d\theta| \\ \quad = R.d\theta \end{array}\right]$$

20. $f(x) = 3x^7 + 2x + 3$

and $g(x) = 5x^3 + 2x + 6.$

$$\frac{d}{dx}f(x) = 21x + 2$$

over field $c_7 = (\{0, 1, 2, 3, 4, 5, 6\} +_7, x_7)$

$$\frac{d}{dx}f(x) = 2$$

24. Let I denotes the union of the chain. If x, y are in I, then they are in I_n for some n.

Then $x + y$ and $r x$ are also in I_n.

They are in I.

26. Suppose that $V \in \ker f(t)$

To show that $F(T)(T(V)) = 0$

$$F(t)\, t = t.F(t)$$
$$F(T)\, T = T.\, F(T)$$
$$F(T)\, T(V) = T.F(T)(V)$$
$$= T(0) = 0$$

27. Let $V \in w$

$V \in w$ for each i

w_1 is T – invariant,

$T(V) \in w$, for every i.

$\therefore$ $T(V) \in w = \bigcap_i w_i$

$\therefore$ which is T – invariant

28. Suppose that $V \in w$

$V = bv + b_1 T(v) + b_2 T^2(v) + ... + b_{K-1} T^{K-1}(v)$

$T(v) = bT(v) + ... + b_{K-2} T^{K-1}(v) \in w$

which is T-invariant

31. Suppose $A = [a_{ij}]_{n \times n}$ & $B = [b_{ij}]_{n \times n}$

$$\lambda.A = [\lambda.a_{ij}]_{n \times n}$$

$$tr(\lambda A) = \sum_{i=1}^{n} \lambda.a_n$$

$$= \lambda \sum_{i=1}^{n} a_{ii}$$

$$= \lambda.tr.A$$

33. Suppose that $\alpha = (a_1, b_1)$

$\beta = (a_2, b_2) \in V_2(R)$

$\therefore$ $T(\alpha) = T(a_1, b_1)$

$= (a_1 + b_1, a_1 - b_1, b_1)$

$T(\beta) = (a_2 + b_2, a_2 - b_2, b_2)$

$T(a\alpha + b\beta) = T[a(a_1, b_1) + b(a_2, b_2)]$

$= T(aa_1 + ba_2, ab_1 + bb_2)$

$= aT(\alpha) + bT(\beta)$

$\therefore$ T is a linear transformation from v_2 (R) is v_3 (R)

The vectors (1, 1, 0), (1, –1, 1) form a basis to range of T.

$\therefore$ rank of T = dim of range of T = 2

Nullity of T = dimension of v_2 (R) – Rank (T) $= 2 - 2 = 0$

34. $T : R^3 \to R^3$ is a Linear transformation defined by $T(x, y, z) = (x + 2y - z, y + z, x + y - 2z)$

Now basis of R(T) is {(1,0,1), (2,1,1), (–1,1,–1)}.

38. For combinaton of 1 event each

$$P(A_1) = P(A_2) = P(A_3) = P(A_4) = \frac{1}{4}$$

For combination of 2 events,

$$P(A_1 \cap A_2) = P(A_2 \cap A_3) = P(A_3 \cap A_4)$$

$$= P(A_4 \cap A_1) = P(A_3 \cap A_1) = P(A_2 \cap A_4)$$

$$= \frac{1}{4^2}$$

For combination of 3 events,

$$P(A_1 \cap A_2 \cap A_3) = P(A_2 \cap A_3 \cap A_4)$$

$$= P(A_3 \cap A_4 \cap A_1) = P(A_1 \cap A_2 \cap A_4) = \frac{1}{4^3}$$

For combination of 4 events,

$$P(A_1 \cap A_2 \cap A_3 \cap A_4) = \frac{1}{4^4}$$

$$\therefore \text{ P (atleast one)} = \frac{4}{4} - \frac{6}{4^2} + \frac{4}{4^3} - \frac{1}{4^4}$$

$$= 1 - \left(1 - \frac{4}{4} + \frac{6}{4^2} - \frac{4}{4^3} + \frac{1}{4^4}\right)$$

$$= 1 - (1 - 1/4)^4 = 1 - \left(\frac{3}{4}\right)^4$$

Set–5

CSIR–UGC (NET) Mathematical Sciences

PART-B

1. $\frac{d^3y}{dx^3}+\frac{d^2y}{dx^2}+4\frac{dy}{dx}+4=0$, has the solution
   A. $y=c_1e^{-x}+xc_2e^{-x}+x^2c_3e^{-x}$
   B. $y=c_1\cos 2x+c_2\sin 2x$
   C. $y=c_1e^{-x}+c_2\cos 2x+c_3\sin 2x$
   D. None of these

2. The partial differential equation formed by eliminating arbitrary functions from the relation $z=f(x+at)+g(x-at)$ is
   A. $\frac{\partial^2 z}{\partial t^2}-a^2\frac{\partial^2 z}{\partial x^2}=0$ B. $a^2\frac{\partial z}{\partial t}+\frac{\partial z}{\partial x}=0$
   C. $a\frac{\partial^2 z}{\partial t^2}+\frac{\partial^2 z}{\partial x^2}=0$ D. None of these

3. The partial differential equation
   $y^2z\frac{\partial z}{\partial x}+zx^2\frac{\partial z}{\partial y}=xy^2$ has the general solution
   A. $f(x^3+y^3, x^2+y^2)=0$
   B. $f(x^3-y^3, x^2-y^2)=0$
   C. $f(x^2+y, x-y)=0$
   D. None of these

4. Solution of $p^2+px+py+xy=0, \left(P=\frac{dy}{dx}\right)$ is
   A. $(2y+x^2+c_1)(x+\log y)=0$
   B. $(2y+x^2-c_1)(x+\log y-c_2)=0$
   C. $(2y+x^2+c_1)=0$
   D. None of these

5. Let x have the probability density function
   $$f(x)=\begin{cases}0.75(1-x^2) & x\in[-1,1]\\ 0 & \text{otherwise.}\end{cases}$$
   The probability distribution function F(x) is given by
   A. $F(x)=0.5+0.75x-0.25x^3, x\in(-1,1)$
   B. $F(x)=0.75x-0.25x^3, x\in(-1,1)$
   C. $F(x)=0.5-0.25x^2, x\in(-1,1)$
   D. $F(x)=0.5x^2-0.2x^2, x\in(-1,1)$

6. For given constants a and b, $E(ax+b)$ is equal to
   A. $a\,E(x)+b$ B. $a\,E(x)+E(b)$
   C. $a\,E(x)$ D. $a+b$

7. For the function $f(z)=z^2$ the value of derivative at $z=4$ is
   A. 2 B. 5
   C. 8 D. 6

8. The value of $\oint_c \frac{z^3-6}{2z-i}dz$ is
   A. $\pi/8$ B. $6\pi i$
   C. $(\pi/8)-6\pi i$ D. $-6\pi i-(\pi/8)$

9. The centre of convergence of the power series $\sum_{n=0}^{\infty}(n+2i)^n z^n$ is
   A. 0 B. 1
   C. 2 D. 3

10. Which of the following statements is true
    A. $(A^T)^{-1}=(A^{-1})^T$ B. $(A^T)^{-1}=(A^T)$
    C. $(A^T)^{-1}=A^{-1}$ D. None of these

11. A square matrix Q is orthogonal, if
    A. $p^{-1}=p^T$ B. $p=p^T$
    C. $p^{-1}=p$ D. None of these

12. If $|A|\neq 0$, then
    A. $|adj\,A|=|A|^{n-1}$ B. $|adj\,A|=|A|^n$
    C. $|adj\,A|=0$ D. None of these

13. If w_1 and w_2 are the subspaces of a vector space V and $w_1\cup w_2$ is also a subspace of V, then
    A. Either $w_1\subset w_2$ or $w_2\subset w_1$
    B. $w_1\cap w_2=\phi$
    C. $w_1=w_2$
    D. None of these

14. If V is an inner product space, then for $\alpha,\beta\in V$
    A. $|(\alpha/\beta)|=\|\alpha\|\,\|\beta\|$
    B. $|(\alpha/\beta)|\geq\|\alpha\|\,\|\beta\|$
    C. $|(\alpha/\beta)|\leq\|\alpha\|\,\|\beta\|$
    D. None of these

15. The dimension of the vector space is
A. Number of elements in vector space
B. Number of elements in basis of the vector space
C. Subspace of vector space
D. None of these

16. If V is finite dimensional vector space with dim V = m and w_1 and w_2 are two subspaces of V_1 with dim $w_1 = n_1$ and dim $w_2 = n_2$ then
A. $n_1 + n_2 = m$ B. $n_1 + n_2 \leq m$
C. $n_1 + n_2 \geq m$ D. None of these

17. Let $\bar{c} \neq 0$ be a n–component vector, and z be given scalar, then the equation of a hyperplane in E^n is a set of points
A. $\{\bar{x} \mid \bar{c}\,\bar{x} > z\}$ B. $\{\bar{x} \mid \bar{c}\,\bar{x} > z\}$
C. $\{\bar{x} \mid \bar{c}\,\bar{x} = z\}$ D. None of these

18. Let
A : the number of units in the system
B : the number of units waiting for **service**
C : the number of services
The following relation holds
A. C = A – B B. C = A + B
C. C = A/B D. None of these

19. For M|M|1 model the expected number of busy servers are equal to
A. Traffic intensity p B. Arrival rate λ
C. Service rate μ D. None of these

20. If D = 2000, Q* = 115, S* = 29, C_0 = 25, C_n = 10, C_b = 30 then what is the total annual inventory cost?
A. Rs. 560 B. Rs. 986
C. Rs. 867 D. Rs. 800

21. The function $f(x) = \begin{cases} \sin 1/x, & x \neq 0 \\ 1, & x = 0 \end{cases}$ has –
A. Removable discontinuity at $x = 0$
B. Non-removable discontinuity at $x = 0$
C. Mixed discontinuity at $x = 0$
D. Continuity at $x = 0$

22. A continuous image of compact set is
A. Compact B. Non-compact
C. Unbounded D. None of these

23. The union of two non–empty closed sets of metric space is
A. Open set B. Closed set
C. Null set D. None of these

24. The set of real number in the closed interval [0,1] is
A. Countable set B. Uncountable set
C. Finite set C. None of these

25. If f is continuous on $[a, b]$ then f is bounded variation on $[a, b]$ iff
A. f is the difference of two monotone continuous functions on $[a, b]$
B. f is the product of two monotone continuous function $[a, b]$
C. f is the quotient of two monotone continuous functions on $[a, b]$
D. None of these

26. The homomorphism ϕ of rings R into R$'$ is an isomorphism iff the kernel I (ϕ) is
A. $I(\phi) = (0)$ B. $I(\phi) = R$
C. $I(\phi) = R'$ D. None of these

27. If (G, *) is *a* group of $\forall a, b, \in G$
$b^{-1} * a^{-1} * b * a = e$, then G is
A. Abelian group B. Non–Abelian
C. Ring D. Field

28. The series $\sum_{n=1}^{\infty} (-1)^n$ is
A. Divergent B. Convergent
C. Unbounded D. None of these

29. The sequence $\left\{\frac{n}{n+1}\right\}$ is
A. Decreasing sequence
B. Bounded
C. Unbounded
D. None of these

30. The radius of convergence of the series
$\frac{x+2}{1} + \frac{(x+2)^2}{2} + ... + \frac{(x+2)^n}{n} + ...$
A. 1 B. ∞
C. zero D. None of these

31. The series $1.x + 1.2.x^2 + 1.2.3.x^3 ... + \lfloor n \, x^n + ...$ is
A. Divergent every where except $x = 0$
B. Convergent every where except $x = 0$
C. Divergent for $x = 0$
D. None of these

32. If γ and σ are closed rectifiable curves having same initial point then for every, $a \notin \{\gamma\}$

A. $n(\gamma ; a) = -n(\gamma ; a)$

B. $n(\gamma ; a) = n(-\gamma ; a)$

C. $n(\gamma ; a) = -n(-\gamma ; a)$

D. None of these

33. If f has pole of order m at $z = a$ and $g(z) = (z-a)^m f(z)$, then

A. $\text{Res}(f; a) = \frac{1}{\lfloor m-1} g^{(m-1)}(a)$

B. $\text{Res}(f; a) = g^{(m-1)}(a)$

C. $\text{Res}(f; a) = \frac{1}{\lfloor m-1} g(a)$

D. None of these

34. The locus of the complex number satisfying $\arg \frac{z-1}{z+1} = \frac{\pi}{3}$ is a

A. Straight line B. Circle

C. Parabola D. Hyperbola

35. In a maximization linear programming problem the variable corresponding to minimum ratio on which solution column leaves the basis. This ensures

A. That next solution will be a basic feasible solution

B. The next solution will not be a basic feasible solution

C. This solution is feasible

D. None of these

36. If the dual of the problem has infeasible solution, then the value of objective function is

A. Unbounded B. Bounded

C. No solution D. None of these

37. The system of equations

$2x + 2y - 3z - 1 = 0$

$4x + 4y + z - 2 = 0$

$6x + 6y - z - 3 = 0$, has

A. A unique solution

B. Infinite solutions

C. No solution

D. Two solutions

38. Let X_0 be a feasible solution to the primal problem Maximize $f(x) = cx$ subject to : $Ax \leq b,\ x \geq 0$ where x^T and $c \in R^n$, $b^T \in R^m$, and A is an m × n real matrix. If w_0 be a feasible solution to the dual of the primal, namely

Minimize $g(w) = b^T w$ subject to : $A^T w > C^T,\ w \geq 0$ where $w^T \in R^m$, then $cx_0 < b^T w_0$.

This represents:

A. Weak duality theorem

B. Basic duality theorem

C. Conditions of optimality

D. Complementary slackness theorem

39. If X ~ bin (n, p), then $P(X \leq 2) = P(X \geq n-2)$ if and only if:

A. $p = \frac{1}{4}$ B. $p = \frac{1}{3}$

C. $p = \frac{1}{2}$ D. $p = 1$

40. If $x = \{8^n - 7n - 1 : n \in N\}$ and $y = \{49(n-1) : (n \in N\}$ then

A. $x = y$ B. $x \subseteq y$

C. $y \subseteq x$ D. $x < y$

ANSWERS

1	2	3	4	5	6	7	8	9	10
C	A	B	B	A	A	C	C	A	A
11	**12**	**13**	**14**	**15**	**16**	**17**	**18**	**19**	**20**
A	A	A	C	B	B	C	A	A	C
21	**22**	**23**	**24**	**25**	**26**	**27**	**28**	**29**	**30**
B	A	B	B	A	A	A	A	B	A
31	**32**	**33**	**34**	**35**	**36**	**37**	**38**	**39**	**40**
A	C	A	B	A	A	B	A	C	A

Some Selected Explanatory Answers

1. Characteristic equation

$m^3+m^2+4m+4=0$

$\Rightarrow (m^2+4)(m+1)=0, m=-1, \pm 2i$

$\therefore\ y=c_1e^{-x}+c_2\cos 2x+c_3\sin 2x$

2. $z=f(x+at)+g(x-at)$

Differentiating partially twice with respect to x and t.

3. Lagrange's subsidiary equations are

$$\frac{\partial x}{y^2z}=\frac{\partial y}{zx^2}=\frac{\partial z}{xy^2}$$

First and second, $x^3-y^3=c_1$

First and third, $x^2-y^2=c_2$

4. $p=-x$

and $p=-y$

$\Rightarrow\quad 2y=-x^2+c_1$

and $x=-\log y+c_2$

$\Rightarrow (2y+x^2-c_1)(x+\log y-c_2)=0$

5. $F(x)=\int_{-\infty}^{x} f(t)dt$

$=0.75\int_{-1}^{x}(1-t^2)dt$

$=0.5+0.75x-0.25x^3$

for $x\in(-1, 1)$]

and $f(x)=0$ if $x\le 1$

$f(x)=1$ if $x>1$

10. $AA^{-1}=A^{-1}A=1$

$\Rightarrow (AA^{-1})^T=(A^{-1}A)^T=I^T$

$\Rightarrow (A^{-1})^TA^T=(A)^T(A^{-1})^T=I$

$\Rightarrow (A^{-1})^T$ is the inverse of A^T

$\Rightarrow (A^{-1})^T=(A^T)^{-1}$

11. Any square matrix Q is said to be orthogonal if $Q^{-1}=Q^T$

12. $A(adj\, A)=|A|I$

$$A(A\,adj)=\begin{bmatrix}|A| & 0 & 0 & 0 & 0\\ 0 & |A| & 0 & 0 & 0\\ \vdots & \vdots & & & \vdots\\ 0 & \cdots & \cdots & \cdots & |A|\end{bmatrix}$$

$$\Rightarrow \det A|adj A|=\det\begin{bmatrix}|A| & 0 & \cdots & 0\\ 0 & |A| & \cdots & 0\\ \vdots & \vdots & & \vdots\\ \vdots & \cdots & \cdots & |A|\end{bmatrix}=|A|^n$$

$\Rightarrow |adj\ A|=|A|^{n-1}$

13. According to the property of subspaces either $w_1\subset w_2$ or $w_2\subset w_1$

15. The dimensions of a vector space is number of elements in basis of a vector space

18. The number of services =

The number of units in the system

– The number of units waiting for the service

19. Expected number of busy servers = traffic intensity

20. Total annual inventory cost TC(Q*) is given by

$$TC(Q^*)=\frac{D}{Q^*}C_0+\frac{(Q^*-S^*)^2}{2Q^*}C_n+\frac{S^{*2}}{2Q^*}\times C_b$$

$$=\frac{2{,}000}{115}\times 25+\frac{(86)^2}{2(115)}\times 10+\frac{(29)^2}{2(115)}\times 30$$

$=435+321.6+109.7$

$=$ Rs. 866.3

21. $F(0+)=\lim_{x\to 0+}F(x)=\lim_{h\to 0}F(0+h)$

$=\lim_{h\to 0}\sin\frac{1}{0+h}=\infty=$ Not a finite number

$F(0-)=\infty$, not a finite number

$\therefore$ F (0 +) and F(0 –) do not exist

$\therefore$ F (x) has non-removable discontinuity at $x=0$

22. Compact (property of compactness)

23. Union of two non empty closed set is always a closed set.

24. Uncountable. As its not having one to one correspondence with N.

27. We have

$a^*b=a^*b^*e$

$=a^*b^*(b^{-1*}a^{-1*}b^*a)$

$\because (b^{-1*}a^{-1*}b^*a=e)$

$= a^*(b^*b^{-1})^*a^{-1*}b^*a$
$= a^*e^*a^{-1*}b^*a$
$= (a^*a^{-1})^*b^*a$
$= e^*b^*a$
$= b^*a$

28. $S_n = \sum_{n=1}^{n}(-1)^k = 1$ or 0, as n is odd or even

$\Rightarrow \{S_n\}=\{1, 0, 1, 0,.........\}$ it is divergent sequence

$\Rightarrow \sum_{n=1}^{\infty}(-1)^n$ is divergent

29. $x_n = \dfrac{n}{n+1} = \dfrac{1}{1+\frac{1}{n}}$

$\forall n \in \mathbb{N}, 1 \geq x_n$ (bounded above) and

$\forall n \in \mathbb{N}, \frac{1}{2} \leq x_n$ (bounded below)

$\therefore \{x_n\}$ is bounded

30. Here $x_0 = -2$ and $a_n = \dfrac{1}{n}$

$$\left|\frac{a_n+1}{a_n}\right| = \frac{1}{n+1}.\frac{n}{1} = \frac{n}{n+1} = \frac{1}{1+\frac{1}{n}}$$

$$\Rightarrow L = \lim_{n\to\infty}\frac{1}{1+\frac{1}{n}} = 1$$

and the radius of convergence $R = \dfrac{1}{L} = 1$

31. Here $a_n = \lfloor n$

and $\left|\dfrac{a_{n+1}}{a_n}\right| = \dfrac{\lfloor n+1}{\lfloor n} = n+1$

$$\Rightarrow L = \lim_{n\to\infty}\left|\frac{a_{n+1}}{a_n}\right| = \infty$$

The radius of convergence R = 0

$\therefore$ The series converges only at $x = 0$

34. Let $z = x + iy$

$$\therefore \frac{z-1}{z+1} = \frac{(x-1)+iy}{(x+1)+iy}$$

$$= \frac{(x-1)+iy}{(x+1)+iy}\times\frac{(x+1)-iy}{(x+1)-iy} = \frac{(x^2+y^2-1)+2iy}{(x+1)^2+y^2}$$

$$\because \text{Arg}\left(\frac{z-1}{z+1}\right) = \frac{\pi}{3}$$

$$\Rightarrow \tan^{-1}\frac{2y}{x^2+y^2-1} = \frac{\pi}{3}$$

$$\Rightarrow \frac{2y}{x^2+y^2-1} = \tan\frac{\pi}{3} = \sqrt{3}$$

$$\Rightarrow x^2+y^2-\frac{2}{\sqrt{3}}y-1 = 0$$

which is a circle.

36. In such case the value of objective function is unbounded.

37. The system of equations has infinite solutions

$\therefore |A| = 0$

39. $P(0) = P(1) + P(2) = P(n-2) + P(n-1) + P(n)$

$\Rightarrow q^n + npq^{n-1} + \frac{1}{2}n(n-1)p^2q^{n-2} = \frac{1}{2}n(n-1)$

$p^{n-2}q^2 + np^{n-1}q + p^n$

$\Rightarrow (q^n - p^n) + npq(q^{n-2} - p^{n-2}) + \frac{1}{2}n(n-1)$

$p^2q^2(q^{n-4} - p^{n-4}) = 0$

$\Rightarrow q-p = 0$, since $(q-p)$ is a factor of the above expression.

$\Rightarrow q = p = \frac{1}{2}$

SET–6

CSIR–UGC (NET) MATHEMATICAL SCIENCES

PART-B

1. The series $\sum_{n=1}^{\infty} \frac{1}{\left(1+\frac{1}{n}\right)^{n^2}}$ is

A. convergent B. divergent
C. oscillatory D. none of these

2. If $\frac{4+3i}{3-4i} = x + iy$, then $\frac{x}{y}$ is equal to

A. 0 B. 1
C. $\frac{4}{3}$ D. $\frac{4}{5}$

3. Let $A=\begin{vmatrix} 3 & 1 & -1 \\ 2 & 2 & -1 \\ 2 & 2 & 0 \end{vmatrix}$ then the characteristic polynomial for A is

A. x^2+5x^2+8x+4 B. x^2+5x
C. x^3-5x^2+8x-4 D. None of these

4. If $G=\{(0,1,2,3,4), V_5\}$, the order of 2 is

A. One B. Two
C. Four D. Five

5. If G is a group of even order, $\forall a \notin e$ if $a^2 = e$ then G is

A. Abelian group B. Sub-group
C. Normal group D. None of these

6. The permutation $\begin{pmatrix} 1 & 2 & 5 & 3 & 4 \\ 3 & 4 & 1 & 5 & 2 \end{pmatrix}$ is equal to

A. (1 5) (1 3) (2 4) B. (1) (2) (3)
C. (1 3 5) (5 6) D. (1 4 2) (5 3)

7. The equation $x = A\cos(pt-\alpha)$ can be expressed as

A. $\frac{d^2x}{dt^2}=x$ B. $\frac{d^2x}{dt^2}=-p^2x$
C. $\frac{d^2x}{dt^2}=0$ D. None of these

8. Elimation of a function f from $z=f\left(\frac{y}{x}\right)$ gives a partial diffrential equation

A. $x\frac{dz}{dx}+y\frac{dz}{dy}=0$ B. $\frac{dz}{dx}+\frac{dz}{dy}=0$
C. $x+y=0$ D. $x-y=0$

9. For M|M|1|N the identity holds

A. $\sum_{n=0}^{N} P_n = 1$ B. $\sum_{n=0}^{N} P_n > 1$
C. $\sum_{n=0}^{N} P_n < 1$ D. None of these

10. If I is an unit matrix of order n, then

A. Rank (I) $= n$ B. Rank (I) $\leq n$
C. Rank (I) $\leq n$ D. None of these

11. If random variable x has the probability function $f(x)=\frac{k}{x!}(x = 0, 1, 2..........)$ the value of k is

A. $\frac{1}{e}$ B. e
C. $1-\frac{1}{e}$ D. None of these

12. If two vectors $\bar{a}_1$ and $\bar{a}_2$ are linearly dependent, then

A. $\bar{a}_1 = c\bar{a}_2$, for some c
B. $\bar{a}_1 \neq c\bar{a}_2$, for some c
C. $\bar{a}_1 > c\bar{a}_2$, for some c
D. None of these

13. If I is an identity transformation of finite vector space V. The nullity of I is

A. dim V B. Zero
C. 1 D. None of these

14. For the power series $\sum \frac{n!}{n^{n}} z^n$ the radius of convergence is

A. e B. 1
C. ∞ D. zero

15. $f(z)=\frac{\sin z}{(z-\pi)^2}$ have the pole of order

A. 1 B. 2
C. 3 D. 0

16. The sequence $\{1, 0, 1, 0, ...\}$ is

A. Increasing B. Decreasing
C. Bounded D. None of these

17. If a ring $R \neq \{0\}$ has the multiplicative identity 1 then

A. $1>0$ B. $1=0$
C. $1\neq 0$ D. None of these

18. The function $f(x)=x\ \sin\left(\frac{1}{x}\right)$ if $x\neq 0$ and $f(0) = 1$ has discontinuity, at

A. 0 B. 1
C. 2 D. None of these

19. If $f(z)=\dfrac{1-e^z}{1+e^z}$ then at $z=\infty$, $f(z)$ have

A. Pole
B. Removable singularity
C. Isolated singularity
D. None – isolated singularity

20. The complex numbers $z_1 = 1 + 2i$, $z_2 = 4 - 2i$ and $z_3 = 1 - 6i$ from the vertices of a

A. Right angled triangle
B. Isosceles triangle
C. Equilateral triangle
D. Scalene triangle

21. The product of (1 2 4 5) (3 2 1 5 4) is

A. (2 3) B. (1 5)
C. (3 4 1) D. (1 5 3 1)

Directions (Q.22 to 25): *Suppose that xyz has a product for which the assumption of the inventory model with planned shortages are valid. The following data is given for the company.*

Annual demand = 2,000 units per year
Cost of an item = Rs. 50 per unit
Ordering cost = Rs. 25 per order
Inventory carrying cost = 20%
Back order cost = Rs. 30 per year

22. What is the minimum cost order quantity?

A. 100 units B. 115 units
C. 130 units D. 60 units

23. What are the maximum number of back order units?

A. 29 units B. 50 units
C. 46 units D. 55 units

24. What is the maximum inventory level?

A. 86 units B. 50 units
C. 36 units D. 46 units

25. What is the time between orders?

A. 30 days B. 21 days
C. 60 days D. 5 days

26. Let V be finite dimentional vector space. If V* is the dual of V, then

A. dim V = dim V* B. dimV > dim V*
C. dimV < dim V* D. None of these

27. The following vectors $\left(\frac{1}{4},0-\frac{1}{4}\right),\left(\frac{1}{3},-\frac{1}{3},0\right)$ and $\left(0,\frac{1}{2},-\frac{1}{2}\right)$ are

A. Linearly independent
B. Linearly dependent
C. Constant
D. None of these

28. If I is an identity matrix, then

A. $I^n = I$ B. $I^n = 0$
C. $I^n = 1/I$ D. None of these

29. Let x has the probability density function $f(x)=\begin{cases}0.75(1-x^2) & x\in[-1,1]\\ 0 & \text{otherwise}\end{cases}$ what is probability $P\left(-\frac{1}{2}\leq x\leq\frac{1}{2}\right)$?

A. 0.68 B. 0.60
C. 0.65 D. None of these

30. For $\frac{d^2y}{dx^2}+4y=\tan 2x$, solving by variation of parameters. The value of Wronskion W is

A. 1 B. 2
C. 3 D. 4

31. Given, $P(A_i)=\left(\frac{1}{2}\right)^i$ and $\bigcup_{i=1}^{\infty} A_i = s$, the sample space where A_i are mutually exclusive events, then $p(s)$ is

A. 0 B. 1
C. ∞ D. None of these

32. The random variable X takes the value 0, 1, 2, and 3 with probabilities $\frac{1}{125}, \frac{123}{125}, \frac{48}{125}$ and $\frac{64}{125}$

the value of E (X) is

A. $\frac{12}{4}$ B. $\frac{12}{7}$

C. $\frac{12}{5}$ D. None of these

33. Let A be the matrix of order $m \times n$, then the determinants of A exist iff

A. $m>n$ B. $m<n$

C. $m \neq n$ D. $m=n$

34. Let V be a vector space, and (1) be an inner product on V. If $(\alpha/\beta)=0$ for all $\beta \in$ V, then

A. $\alpha \neq 0$ B. $\alpha = 0$

C. $\alpha > 0$ D. $\alpha < 0$

35. M|G|2, queue description, the departure arrival distribu'ion respectively are

A. General and Markovian

B. Markovian and general

C. Markoven

D. None of these

36. Let C be the expected number of servers in the system. $\bar{c}$ the expected number of servers not busy and C the expected number of servers busy, then

A. $\bar{c} = C - c$ B. $\bar{c} = c - C$

C. $C = \bar{c}/c$ D. $C = c/\bar{c}$

37. If the ring R has unities e_1 and e_2 then

A. $e_1 = e_2$ B. $e_1 = me_2$

C. $e_1 \neq e_2$ D. None of these

38. If $f = (2, 3)$ and $g = (4, 5)$ are two permutation on five symbols 1, 2, 3, 4, 5 then gf is

A. $\begin{pmatrix} 1 & 2 & 3 & 4 & 5 \\ 1 & 3 & 5 & 4 & 2 \end{pmatrix}$ B. $\begin{pmatrix} 1 & 2 & 3 & 5 & 6 \\ 1 & 4 & 6 & 5 & 4 \end{pmatrix}$

C. $\begin{pmatrix} 1 & 2 & 3 & 5 & 7 \\ 1 & 4 & 6 & 4 & 1 \end{pmatrix}$ D. $\begin{pmatrix} 1 & 2 & 3 & 4 & 5 \\ 1 & 3 & 2 & 5 & 4 \end{pmatrix}$

39. A shopkeeper has a uniform demand on an item at the rate of 50 items per month, he buys from a supplier at a cost of Rs. 6 per item and the cost of ordering is Rs. 10 each time. If the stock holding costs are 20% per year of stock value. How frequently should he replenish his stocks?

A. 2 months B. 7 months

C. 9 months D. 11 months

40. $\frac{1}{2\pi i}\oint_c \frac{e^z}{z-2} dz$ if C $|z|=3$ and $|z|=1$

A. $e, 1$ B. o, e^z

C. e^z, o D. $e^2, 1$

ANSWERS

1	2	3	4	5	6	7	8	9	10
A	A	C	D	A	A	B	A	A	A
11	**12**	**13**	**14**	**15**	**16**	**17**	**18**	**19**	**20**
A	A	B	A	B	C	C	A	A	B
21	**22**	**23**	**24**	**25**	**26**	**27**	**28**	**29**	**30**
A	B	A	A	B	A	A	A	A	B
31	**32**	**33**	**34**	**35**	**36**	**37**	**38**	**39**	**40**
B	C	D	B	A	A	A	D	A	C

Some Selected Explanatory Answers

1. Here $a_n = \frac{1}{\left(1+\frac{1}{n}\right)^{n^2}}$ By Cauchy Root test

$$\lim_{n\to\infty} \sqrt[n]{a_n} = \lim_{n\to\infty} \frac{1}{\left(1+\frac{1}{n}\right)^n} = \frac{1}{e} < 1$$

$\therefore$ The series is convergent

2. $\frac{4+3i}{3-4i} = x+iy$

$\therefore$ $4+3i = 3x+4y+(3y-4x)\,i$

$\therefore$ $3x+4y=4$ ...(*i*)

and $3y-4x=3$ ...(*ii*)

Solving (*i*) and (*ii*), we get

$x=0, y=1$

3. $F(x) = |xI - A|$

$$= \begin{vmatrix} x-3 & -1 & 1 \\ -2 & x-2 & 1 \\ -2 & -2 & x \end{vmatrix}$$

$$= x-3\begin{vmatrix} x-2 & 1 \\ -2 & x \end{vmatrix} + \begin{vmatrix} -2 & 1 \\ -2 & x \end{vmatrix} - \begin{vmatrix} -2 & x-2 \\ -2 & -2 \end{vmatrix}$$

$= x^3 - 5x^2 + 8x - 4$

5. $a, b \in G \Rightarrow ab \in G, \forall, a, b \in G$

$\Rightarrow (ab)^2 = e$

$\Rightarrow (ab)(ab) = e$

$\Rightarrow (ab)^{-1} = ab$ ...(*i*)

$\Rightarrow b^{-1}a^{-1} = ab$

But $a^2 = e \Rightarrow a.a = e$

$\Rightarrow a^{-1} = a$ ...(*ii*)

and $b^2 = e$

$\Rightarrow b^{-1} = b$ ...(*iii*)

$\therefore$ By (*ii*), (*iii*) and (*i*) we have

$ab = ba$

$\therefore$ G is Abelian group

6. $$\begin{pmatrix} 1 & 2 & 5 & 3 & 4 \\ 3 & 4 & 1 & 5 & 2 \end{pmatrix} = \begin{pmatrix} 1 & 3 & 5 & 2 & 4 \\ 3 & 5 & 1 & 4 & 2 \end{pmatrix}$$

$= (1\ 3\ 5)\ (2\ 4)$

$= (1\ 5)\ (1\ 3)(2\ 4)$

7. $$\frac{dx}{dt} = -pA\sin(pt - \alpha)$$

$$\frac{d^2x}{dt^2} = -p^2A\cos(pt - \alpha)$$

$= -p^2 x$

8. $$z = f\left(\frac{y}{x}\right)$$

$$\frac{dz}{dx} = -\frac{y}{x^2} f'\left(\frac{y}{x}\right)$$

and $$\frac{dz}{dy} = \frac{1}{x} f'\left(\frac{y}{x}\right)$$

$$\Rightarrow x\frac{dz}{dx} + y\frac{dz}{dy} = 0$$

9. For M|M|1|N for $n \geq N$, $P_n = 0$

$$\therefore \sum_{n=0}^{\infty} P_n = 1 \Rightarrow \sum_{n=0}^{N} P_n + \sum_{n=N+1}^{\infty} P_n = 1$$

$$\Rightarrow \sum_{n=0}^{N} P_n = 1$$

10. $|1| = 1 \neq 0$

$$\begin{vmatrix} 1 & 0 \\ 0 & 1 \end{vmatrix} = 1 \neq 0$$

$$\begin{vmatrix} 1 & 0 & 0 \\ 0 & 1 & 0 \\ 0 & 0 & 1 \end{vmatrix} = 1 \neq 0$$

$\therefore$ Rank of $I_n = n$

11. $$\sum_x f(x) = 1$$

$$\Rightarrow k\sum_x \frac{1}{x!} = 1$$

$\Rightarrow ke = 1$

$$\Rightarrow k = \frac{1}{e}$$

12. $\bar{a}_1$ and $\bar{a}_2$ are linearly dependent if

$\alpha, \beta \neq 0$

$\alpha\bar{a}_1 + \beta\bar{a}_2 = 0$

$$\Rightarrow \bar{a}_1 + \frac{\beta}{\alpha}\bar{a}_2 = 0$$

$$\Rightarrow \bar{a}_1 = \left(-\frac{\beta}{\alpha}\right)\bar{a}_2$$

$\bar{a}_1 = c\bar{a}_2$

13. Nullity (I) = dim (null space of I)

= dim {0}

= 0

14. We have an $a_n = \dfrac{n!}{n^n}$ $a_{n+1} = \dfrac{(n+1)!}{(n+1)^{n+1}}$

$$R = \lim_{n\to\infty} \frac{a_n}{a_{n+1}} = \lim_{n\to\infty} \frac{n!}{n^n} \cdot \frac{(n+1)^{n+1}}{(n+1)!}$$

$$= \lim_{n\to\infty}\left(1 + \frac{1}{n}\right)^n = e$$

15. Let $f(z)=\dfrac{\sin z}{(z-\pi)^2}$

Then singularities of $f(z)$ are given by

$(z-\pi)^2=0$

$\Rightarrow z=\pi$ is a pole of order two of $f(z)$

16. $\forall n\in \text{N}, 0\le x_n$

$\forall n\in \text{N}, 1\ge x_n$

$\therefore \{1, 0, 1, 0.........\}$ is bounded

17. If $1\in \text{R}$ is an multiplicative identity then $1.a=a$, and $1=0\Rightarrow a.1=0$, which is the contradiction

$\therefore 1\neq 0$

18. At $x=0$,

$f(0+)=\lim_{x\to 0+} f(x)=\lim_{h\to 0} f(0+h)$

$=\lim_{h\to 0} f(0+h)\sin\left(\dfrac{1}{0+h}\right)$

$=0$, finite number $=0$

$f(0-)=\lim_{x\to 0} f(x)=\lim_{h\to 0} f(0-h)$

$=\lim_{h\to 0} f(0-h)\sin\left(\dfrac{1}{0-h}\right)$

$=0$, finite number $=0$

and $f(0)=1$

$\therefore f(0+)=f(0-)\neq f(0)$

$\therefore f$ is discontinuous at $x=0$

19. Here $f(z)=\dfrac{1-e^z}{1+e^z}$

Poles of $f(z)$ are obtained by equating to zero the denominator of $f(z)$, i.e.,

$1+e^z=0\Rightarrow e^z=-1=e^{2n\pi i+\pi i}$

$z=(2n+1)\pi i$ where n is any integer

Hence $z=(2n+1)\pi i$ ($n\in$ I) are the simple poles of $f(z)$. Obviously $z=\infty$ is a limit point of these poles, therefore, $z=\infty$ is a non– isolated essential singularity

20. $z_1=(1, 2)$, $z_2=(4, -2)$, $z_3=(1, -6)$ Here distance between z_1 and z_2.

= distance between z_2 and z_3 = 5

But distance between z_1 and z_3 = 8

Hence, z_1, z_2 and z_3 form an isosceles triangle

21. $(1\,2\,4\,5)(3\,2\,1\,5\,4)=\begin{pmatrix}1\,2\,3\,4\,5\\2\,4\,3\,5\,1\end{pmatrix}\begin{pmatrix}1\,2\,3\,4\,5\\5\,1\,2\,3\,4\end{pmatrix}$

$=\begin{pmatrix}1\,2\,3\,4\,5\\1\,3\,2\,4\,5\end{pmatrix}=(2\,3)$

Q. 22 to 25

From the given data of the problem, in usual notation

Annual demand, D = 2,000 units

Cost of an item, C = Rs. 50

Ordering cost, C_o = Rs. 25

Inventory carrying cost, C_h = 20% of Rs. 50 = Rs. 10

Back order cost, C_b = Rs. 10

22. Minimum cost order quantity or EOQ is given by

$Q^*=\sqrt{\dfrac{2DC_0}{C_h}\left(\dfrac{C_h+C_b}{C_b}\right)}$

$=\sqrt{\dfrac{2\times 2000\times 25}{10}\left(\dfrac{10+30}{30}\right)}=115$ units

23. Maximum number of back – order units is given by

$S^*=Q^*\left(\dfrac{C_h}{C_h+C_b}\right)$

$=115\left(\dfrac{10}{10+30}\right)=29$ units

24. Maximum inventory level is

$I_{max}=Q^*-S^*=115-29=86$ unit

25. Time between orders

$=\dfrac{Q^*}{D}=\dfrac{115}{2{,}000}\times 365$

= 21 days

26. V* is a dual of V i.e. V* = L(V,F)

By the statement, If V is n dimentional and W is m dimensional vector space then dim L (V,W) = mn

$\Rightarrow$ dimV* = dim L (V, F) = dim V,

dim F = dim V(क्यो dim F = 1)

28. I in an identity matrix $\Rightarrow I^2=I$

$I^3=I^2.I=I.I=I$

$I^{n-1}=I$

$I^n=I^{n-1}.I=I.I=I$

29. $P(a \le x \le b) = F(b) - F(a)$

$$= \int_a^b f(t)dt$$

$$\Rightarrow P\left(-\frac{1}{2} \le x \le \frac{1}{2}\right) = F\left(\frac{1}{2}\right) - F\left(-\frac{1}{2}\right)$$

$$= 0.75 \int_{-\frac{1}{2}}^{\frac{1}{2}} \left(1 - t^2\right) dt$$

$$= 0.68$$

30. $\frac{d^2y}{dx^2} + 4y = \tan 2x$

corresponding homogeneous equation

$$\frac{d^2y}{dx^2} + 4y = 0$$

$$\Rightarrow m^2 + 4 = 0$$

$$m = \pm 2i$$

31. $P(S) = p(\cup Ai) = p(A_1) + p(A_2) + \dots\dots\dots$

$$= \frac{1}{2} + \left(\frac{1}{2}\right)^2 + \left(\frac{1}{2}\right)^3 + \dots\dots\dots$$

$$= \frac{\frac{1}{2}}{1 - \frac{1}{2}} = 1$$

32. $E(x) = \sum_x xf(x)$

$$= 0.\frac{1}{125} + 1.\frac{12}{125} + 2.\frac{48}{125} + 3.\frac{64}{125}$$

$$= \frac{12}{5}$$

33. The determinant exists only for square matrix

$\therefore m = n$

34. $(\alpha + \beta) = (\alpha/\beta) + (\beta/\beta)$

$(\alpha/\beta) = 0$

$\Rightarrow (\alpha + \beta/\beta) = (\beta/\beta)$

$\Rightarrow \alpha + \beta = \beta$

$\Rightarrow \alpha = 0$

35. $a|b|c$

$a \equiv$ Arrival distribution

$b \equiv$ Departure distribution

here arrival is Markovian and departure is general.

36. Expected number of servers busy + Expected number of servers idle = Expected number of servers.

37. $e_1 \in R$ is unity then

$e_1.a = a.e_1 = a, \ \forall a \in R$

$e_2 \in R$ is unity then

$e_2.a = a.e_2 = a, \forall a \in R$

$\Rightarrow e_1.a = e_2\ a$

$e_1 = e_2$

38. If $= \begin{pmatrix} 1 & 2 & 3 & 4 & 5 \\ 1 & 2 & 3 & 5 & 4 \end{pmatrix}\begin{pmatrix} 1 & 2 & 3 & 4 & 5 \\ 1 & 3 & 2 & 4 & 5 \end{pmatrix}$

$$= \begin{pmatrix} 1 & 2 & 3 & 4 & 5 \\ 1 & 2 & 3 & 5 & 4 \end{pmatrix}\begin{pmatrix} 1 & 2 & 3 & 5 & 4 \\ 1 & 3 & 2 & 5 & 4 \end{pmatrix}$$

$$= \begin{pmatrix} 1 & 2 & 3 & 4 & 5 \\ 1 & 3 & 2 & 5 & 4 \end{pmatrix}$$

39. Uniform demand of an item at the rate r

$\lambda = 50$ items/month $= 600$ items/year

$P = 6$ Rs./item

$I = 20\%$ per year

C_3 (cost of ordering) $= 10$

$$\therefore q' = \sqrt{\frac{2 \times 10 \times 600 \times 100}{20 \times 6}} = 100$$

Lot size 100 items after every 2 months,

$$t' = \frac{q'}{r} = \frac{100}{600} y = 2 \text{ months}$$

SET–7

CSIR–UGC (NET) MATHEMATICAL SCIENCES

PART-B

1. The solution of the given partial differential equation $\frac{d^2z}{dx^2} - a^2\frac{d^2z}{dy^2} = 0$ is

A. $z = f_1(y+ax) + f_2(y-ax)$
B. $z = 2f_1(y+ax)$
C. $z = f_1(y+ax) + f_2(y)$
D. None of these

2. The value of Wronskion W (x, x^2, x^3) is

A. $2x^4$ B. $2x^2$
C. $2x^3$ D. None of these

3. The equation $ydx - xdy = 0$ is

A. Exact differential equation
B. Non-exact differential equation
C. Partial differential equation
D. None of these

4. The expected value of the random variable x whose probability density is given by

$$f(x) = \begin{cases} \frac{x+1}{8} & 2 < x < 4 \\ 0 & \text{otherwise} \end{cases}$$

A. $\frac{37}{6}$ B. $\frac{37}{12}$
C. $\frac{37}{18}$ D. $\frac{37}{24}$

5. For any random variable x for which E(x) exist. The zeroth moment about the mean, μ_0 is

A. Zero B. One
C. Mean itself D. None of these

6. What is the probability of getting seven heads in 12 flips of a balanced coin?

A. 0.90 B. 0.19
C. 0.39 D. 0.49

7. A function $f(z) = \cos z$, have real and imaginary parts as

A. $Re(f(z)) = -\cos x \cosh y, Im(f(z)) = +\sin x \sin hy$
B. $Re(f(z)) = \cos x \cosh y, Im(f(z)) = -\sin x \sin hy$
C. $Re(f(z)) = \cos x, Im(f(z)) = -\sin x$
D. $Re(f(z)) = \cos hy, Im(f(z)) = -\sin hy$

8. The function $f(z) = \begin{cases} (\text{Re}\, z^2)/|z| & z \neq 0 \\ 0 & z = 0 \end{cases}$ i continuous at $z = 0$

A. No B. Can not define
C. Yes D. None of these

9. $\sum_{n=0}^{\infty} (-1)^n \frac{Z^{2n}}{\lfloor 2n}$ is equal to

A. $\sin z$ B. $\cos z$
C. $\tan z$ D. None of these

10. The complement of the unit disc $|z| \leq 1$ is

A. $|z| > 1$ B. $|z| < 1$
C. $|z| = 1$ D. None of these

11. The eigen values of the matrix $\begin{vmatrix} 1 & 1 & 3 \\ 1 & 5 & 1 \\ 3 & 1 & 1 \end{vmatrix}$ is

A. +2, 3, 6 B. 2, 6, 7
C. −2, 3, 6 D. None of these

12. The following vectors (0, 5, −1), (−3, 8, 16) anc (9, 56, −64) are

A. Linearly independent
B. Linearly dependent
C. Constant
D. None of these

13. If A is a $(n \times 1)$ non–zero matrix and B is $(1 \times n)$ non-zero matrix, then

A. Rank (AB) = 1 B. Rank (AB) = n
C. Rank (AB) = 0 D. None of these

14. A square matrix A is orthogonal if

A. $AA^T \neq 1$ B. $AA^T = A^T A = 1$
C. $AA^T = 0$ D. None of these

15. If v and w are finite dimensional and v and w are isomorphic iff

A. $\dim v > \dim w$ B. $\dim v < \dim w$
C. $\dim w = \dim v$ D. None of these

16. If T is a linear transformation from vector space V to w. Let dim $v = m$, dim $w = n$ then rank of T is

A. m B. n

C. $m-n$ D. $m+n$

17. Let X be a set in E^n and $\bar{x}_1, \bar{x}_2 \in X$. The set x is connected, if

A. Line segment joining $\bar{x}_1$ and $\bar{x}_2$ belongs to x

B. Line segment joining $\bar{x}_1$ and $\bar{x}_2$ does not belongs to x

C. Polygonal path joining $\bar{x}_1$ and $\bar{x}_2$ belongs to x

D. Polygonal path joining $\bar{x}_1$ and $\bar{x}_2$ does not belong to x

18. If $\bar{x}_1, \bar{x}_2, \ldots\ldots \bar{x}_k$ are different optimal solutions to linear programming problem, then any convex combination of $\bar{x}_1, \bar{x}_2, \ldots\ldots \bar{x}_k$ is

A. Not an optimal solution

B. An optimal solution

C. None feasible solution

D. None of these

19. P : Every optimal solution is feasible solution in l.p.p

Q: Every feasible solution is optimal solution in l.p.p

A. P and Q both true B. P is true

C. Q is true D. Both P and Q false

20. Let $\bar{a} \in E^n$ is a boundry point of set $A \subset E$ and N_ϵ is the ϵ –neighburhood of $\bar{a}$, then

A. $N_\epsilon = \{x \mid x \in A \text{ or } x \in A^c\}$

B. $N_\epsilon = \{x \mid x \in A, x \notin A^c\}$

C. $N_\epsilon = \{x \mid x \notin A, x \in A^c\}$

D. None of these

21. Let W_s and W_q be the expected waiting time in system and queue, and L_s and L_q be the expected number of customers in system and queue then

A. $\frac{L_s}{W_s} < \frac{L_q}{W_q}$ B. $\frac{L_s}{W_s} > \frac{L_q}{W_q}$

C. $\frac{L_s}{W_s} = \frac{L_q}{W_q}$ D. None of these

22. The arrival of customers (with no departure) in system, in queuing theory can be stated as

A. The pure birth process

B. The pure death process

C. The birth process

D. None of these

23. "Every non-empty set s of real numbers which is bounded above has supremum" is

A. Field axiom

B. Ordered axiom

C. Completeness axiom

D. None of these

24. If f is one-to-one and continuous on $[a,b]$, then

A. f is strictly monotonic

B. f is monotonic

C. f is constant

D. None of these

25. In a maximization lpp, if a variable corresponding to positive $Z_j - C_j$ is entered, the leaving variable rule is followed (and solutions space is not unbounded), then

A. The next basic solution will not be basic feasible solution

B. The value of the objective function will decrease

C. The value of the objective function will increase

D. The value of the objective function remains constant

26. The dual of maximize $3x_1 + 5x_2$ subject to

$2x_1 - 3x_2 = 8$

$4x_1 + x_2 \geq 3$

$x \leq 1$

and $x_1, x_2 \geq 0$

A. Min $8\mu_1 - 3\mu_2 + \mu_3$

Subject to

$2\mu_1 - 4\mu_2 \geq -3$

$-3\mu_1 - \mu_2 + \mu_3 \geq -5$

μ_1, unrestricted

$\mu_2, \mu_3 \geq 0$

B. Min $3x_1 + 5x_3$

Subject to

$2x_1 - 3x_2 \leq 8$

$4x_1 + x_2 \leq 3$

$x_2 \geq 1$

$x_1, x_2 \leq 0$

C. (A) and (B) both true

D. None of these

27. In the optimal table of a transportation problem a zero in the south – west corner rule shows that
A. An alternate optimal solution exists
B. The optimal solution is degenerated
C. (A) and (B) both are true
D. None of these

28. In an assignment problem with m–jobs and m–persons the number of basic variable at zero level in a basic feasible solution is
A. m B. $m+1$
C. $m-1$ D. None of these

29. The necessary condition that the points A, B, C representing number z_1, z_2, z_3 respectively on the Argand plane be the vertices of an equilateral triangle is that

A. $\frac{1}{z_1 - z_2} = \frac{1}{z_3 - z_1} + \frac{1}{z_2 - z_3}$

B. $\frac{1}{z_1 - z_2} = \frac{1}{z_1 - z_3} + \frac{1}{z_2 - z_3}$

C. $\frac{1}{z_1 - z_2} = \frac{1}{z_1 - z_3} + \frac{1}{z_3 - z_2}$

D. None of these

30. If f is a analytic function in some domain, then in that domain
A. f is continuous only
B. f is differentiable only
C. f is continuous and differentiable both
D. None of these

31. An analytic function is
A. Infinitely differentiable
B. Finitely differentiable
C. Not differentiable
D. None of these

32. $\text{Arg}\left(-1+\sqrt{3}i\right)$ equals
A. $\pi/3$ B. $\pi/6$
C. $2\pi/3$ D. $5\pi/6$

33. Given a function $f(x) = |x|$ for all $x \in$ R. The function f is
A. Differentiable at zero
B. Continuous at zero
C. (A) is true (B) is false
D. (A) and (B) are both false

34. If f is Riemann integrable on $[a, b]$. Then
A. $\int_{-a}^{b} f dx \geq \int_{a}^{-b} f dx$ B. $\int_{-a}^{b} f dx = \int_{a}^{-b} f dx$
C. $\int_{-a}^{b} f dx \leq \int_{a}^{-b} f dx$ D. None of these

35. $f: [a, b] \rightarrow R$, P and Q are partitions of $[a, b]$ such $P \subset Q$, then
A. $L(P, f) \leq L(Q, f)$
B. $L(P, f) \geq L(Q, f)$
C. (A) is true (B) is false
D. (B) is true (A) is false

36. Let sequence $\{a_n\}_{n=1}^{\infty}$ converges to A and sequence $\{b_n\}_{n=1}^{\infty}$ converges to B, with $a_n \leq b_n$ for all n, then
A. $A \leq B$ B. $A = B$
C. $A \geq B$ D. None of these

37. Let (D, +, .) b an integral domain, D is a field if
A. For, $\forall a \in D$ there exist $a^{-1} \in D : a\,a^{-1} = 1$
B. For, $\forall a \in D$ there exist $a^{-1} \in D : a + a^{-1} = 0$
C. For, $\forall a \in D$ there exist $b \in D : ab = 0$
D. None of these

38. The generators of the group $G = \{a, a^2, a^3, a^4 = e\}$ are –
A. a only B. a and a^2
C. a and a^3 D. a and a^4

39. Let X_1 and X_2 be two independent random variables having variances k and 2 respectively. If the variance of $Y = 3X_2 - X_1$ is 25, then:
A. $k=3$ B. $k=5$
C. $k=7$ D. $k=9$

40. The value of integral $\int_c \frac{3z^{99}+1}{z^2-1} dz$ where c is the ellipse $x^2 + 2y^2 = 8$ described in the positive sense is:
A. $6\pi i$ B. $4\pi i$
C. $2\pi i$ D. 0

ANSWERS

1	2	3	4	5	6	7	8	9	10
A	C	A	B	B	B	B	A	B	A
11	**12**	**13**	**14**	**15**	**16**	**17**	**18**	**19**	**20**
C	B	A	B	C	A	C	B	B	A
21	**22**	**23**	**24**	**25**	**26**	**27**	**28**	**29**	**30**
C	A	C	A	B	A	B	C	C	C
31	**32**	**33**	**34**	**35**	**36**	**37**	**38**	**39**	**40**
A	C	B	B	A	A	A	C	C	C

Some Selected Explanatory Answers

1. $(D^2 - a^2 D^2)\, z = 0$

Alternate equation

$m^2 - a^2 = 0$

$\Rightarrow m = \pm a$

$\therefore$ Solution $z = f_1(y + ax) + f_2(y - ax)$

2. $W(x, x^2, x^3) = \begin{vmatrix} x & x^2 & x^3 \\ 1 & 2x & 3x^2 \\ 0 & 2 & 6x \end{vmatrix} = 2x^3$

3. $ydx - x\,dy = 0$

$ydx = xdy$

$\frac{dx}{x} = \frac{dy}{y}$

$\therefore$ it is an exact differential equation.

4. $f(x) = \begin{Bmatrix} x + 1/8 & 2 < x < 4 \\ 0 & \text{otherwise} \end{Bmatrix}$

$\therefore \int_2^4 xf(x)dx = E(x)$

$\Rightarrow$ The expected value is 37/12

5. $\mu_r = E\left[x - \mu)^r\right]$

$= \sum_x (x - \mu)^r f(x)$

$\Rightarrow \mu_0 = \sum_x (x - \mu)^0 f(x)$

$= \sum_x f(x) = 1$

6. $x = 7, n = 12, P = \frac{1}{2}$

By Binomial distribution, the probability of getting 7 heads in 12 flips is

$b(x; n, p) = \binom{12}{7}\left(\frac{1}{2}\right)^7 \left(1 - \frac{1}{2}\right)^5$

$= 0.19$

7. $f(z) = \cos z$

$\text{Re} f(z) = \cos x \cos hy$

$\text{Im} f(z) = -\sin x \sin hy$

8. $f(z) = \begin{Bmatrix} \text{Re}\, z^2 / |z| & z \neq 0 \\ 0 & z = 0 \end{Bmatrix}$

by using continuity definition we find it is not continuous at $z = 0$

10. $|z| \leq 1$ is the equation of unit disc and the complement is given by $|z| > 1$

11. $|A - \lambda I| = 0$

$\Leftrightarrow \begin{vmatrix} 1-\lambda & 1 & 3 \\ 1 & 5-\lambda & 1 \\ 3 & 1 & 1-\lambda \end{vmatrix}$

$= (1-\lambda)\begin{vmatrix} 5-\lambda & 1 \\ 1 & 1-\lambda \end{vmatrix} - 1\begin{vmatrix} 1 & 1 \\ 3 & 1-\lambda \end{vmatrix} + 3\begin{vmatrix} 1 & 5-\lambda \\ 3 & 1 \end{vmatrix}$

$\Rightarrow (\lambda + 2)(\lambda - 3)(\lambda - 6) = 0$

$\lambda = -2, 3, 6$

13. Rank (AB) = 1

because A is of size $(n \times 1)$ and B is of $(1 \times n)$ hence by using property of rank of matrix

14. Orthogonal matrix : $A^T = A^{-1} \Rightarrow AA^T = 1$

16. $\therefore \dim v = m, \dim w = n$

then rank of T is m

$\because$ T is a linear transform from vector space W

18. $\bar{x}_1, \bar{x}_2, \ldots\ldots\ldots, \bar{x}_K$ are different optimal solutions then by definition of convex combination of $\bar{x}_1, \bar{x}_2, \ldots\ldots\ldots, \bar{x}_K$ is an optimal solution

21. Littles formula

$L_S = \lambda W_S$ and $L_q = \lambda W_q$

$\Rightarrow \frac{L_S}{W_S} = \frac{L_q}{W_q}$

22. Under pure birth process only arrival occurs.

24. If f is one to one and continuous then by property it is strictly monotonic.

26. Given maximize $3x_1 + 5x_2$

Subject to

$$2x_1 - 3x_2 = 8$$
$$4x_1 + x_2 \geq 3$$
$$x_2 \leq 1$$

Writing this in standard form leaving the equation in the constraints as it is, the primal is maximize $-3x_1 - 5x_2$

Subject to

$$2x_1 - 3x_2 = 8$$
$$4x_1 - x_2 \leq -3$$
$$x_2 \leq 1$$
$$x_1 \geq 0$$
$$x_2 \geq 0$$

Now the dual is,

Minimize $8\mu_1 - 3\mu_2 + \mu_3$

Subject to

$2\mu_1 - 4\mu_2 \geq -3$

$3\mu_1 - \mu_2 + \mu_3 \geq -5$

$\mu_2 \geq 0, \mu_3 \geq 0$

and μ_1 is restricted in sign

29. $\alpha = z_2 - z_3$

$\beta = z_3 - z_1$

$\gamma = z_1 - z_2$

Then, $\alpha + \beta + \gamma = 0$

Since ABC is an equilateral triangle

$\therefore$ AB = BC = CA

$\Rightarrow |z_2 - z_3|^2 = |z_3 - z_1|^2 = |z_1 - z_2|^2$

$\Rightarrow \alpha\bar{\alpha} = \beta\bar{\beta} = \gamma\bar{\gamma} = K$

$[\because |z|^2 = z\bar{z}]$

From (i)

$\bar{\alpha} + \bar{\beta} + \bar{\gamma} = 0$

$$\frac{K}{\alpha} + \frac{K}{\beta} + \frac{K}{\gamma} = 0$$

or, $\frac{1}{z_2 - z_3} + \frac{1}{z_3 - z_1} + \frac{1}{z_1 - z_2} = 0$

or, $\frac{1}{z_1 - z_2} = \frac{1}{z_1 - z_3} + \frac{1}{z_3 - z_2}$

30. f is continuous and differentiable both as any analytic function in its domain is differentiable and continuous.

31. By definition analytic function is infinitely differentiable.

32. Arg $(-1 + \sqrt{3}\,i)$ equals $\frac{2\pi}{3}$

As, Arg $= \tan^{-1}\left(\frac{\sqrt{3}}{-1}\right) = \tan^{-1}\left(-\sqrt{3}\right)$

$= \frac{2\pi}{3}$

33. $f(x) = |x|\ \forall x \in \mathbb{R}$

$\Rightarrow$ It is continuous but not differentiable at $x = 0$ (According to definition of differentiability)

34. $\int_{-a}^{b} f dx = \int_{a}^{-b} f dx$

36. Since $\{a_n\}_{n=1}^{\infty} \to A$

and $\{b_n\}_{n=1}^{\infty} \to B$

then for $a_n \leq b_n$

$A \leq B$ (property of convergence)

37. For (D, +, .) is an integral domain

then D will be a field iff

for $\forall a \in D\ \exists a^{-1} \in D$ such that $aa^{-1} = 1$

38. a is one of the generator

a^p is generator of G of order n iff $(n, p) = 1$

$1 < p < n$

Here $n = 4$

and $(4, 3) = 1$

$\therefore a^3$ is also a generator of G

39. Var (Y) = Var $(3X_2 - X_1) = 9$ Var (X_2) + Var (X_1), Since X_1 and X_2 are independent random variables.

$$25 = 9 \times 2 + k$$
$$\Rightarrow k = 25 - 18 = 7$$

SET–8

CSIR–UGC (NET) MATHEMATICAL SCIENCES

PART-B

1. The degree of the equation $y\frac{dy}{dx} = x\left(\frac{dy}{dx}\right)^2 + x$ is

A. Zero B. One
C. Two D. Three

2. The solution of $\frac{\partial^2 z}{\partial x^2} + \frac{\partial^2 z}{\partial y^2} = \frac{z}{a}$ is

A. $Z = e^{y/a} f(x - y)$
B. $Z = e^{y/a} f(x)$
C. $Z = e^{y} f(y)$
D. $Z = e^{a} f(x + y)$

3. $\left(\frac{\partial z}{\partial x}\right)^2 - \frac{\partial^2 z}{\partial x^2} + \frac{\partial z}{\partial x} = 1$ has the solution

A. $z = f_1(y) + e^{-x} f_2(y + x) + x$
B. $z = f_1(y) + e^{-x} f_2(y + x)$
C. $z = x$
D. None of these

4. The differential equation $\frac{\partial^2 y}{\partial x^2} + 6\frac{\partial y}{\partial x} + 9y = 50e^{2x}$ has particular integral

A. $\frac{2e^{2x}}{3}$ B. $2e^{2x}$
C. e^{2x} D. None of these

The p – discriminant of equation $4xp^2 = (3x - a)^2$ is

A. $x = 0$ B. $3x = b^2$
C. $(3x - a)^2 = 0$ D. None of these

For any random variable, for which mean μ exist, the first moment about the mean is equal to

A. Zero B. One
C. Mean itself D. None of these

Which of the following can serve as probability distribution?

A. $f(x) = \frac{x-2}{2}$ $x = 1, 2, 3, 4$

B. $h(x) = \frac{x^2}{25}$ $x = 1, 2, 3, 4$

C. $f(x) = \frac{x-2}{5}$ $x = 1, 2, 3, 4$

D. $g(x) = \frac{1}{4}$ $x = 1, 2, 3, 4$

8. The series $\sum_{n=0}^{\infty} \frac{z^n}{|\underline{n}}$ converges at

A. $z = 0$ B. $z = 1$
C. $z = 2$ D. None of these

9. The characteristic roots of skew–symmetric matrix are

A. Zero
B. Zero or pure imaginary
C. Complex number
D. None of these

10. If $q = X^T A X$ is positive definite, if

A. A is singular matrix
B. A is non – singular matrix
C. $|A| < 0$
D. None of these

11. The rank of the matrix $\Lambda = \begin{bmatrix} 0 & i & -i \\ -i & 0 & i \\ 1 & -i & 0 \end{bmatrix}$ is

A. 1 B. 2
C. 3 D. 4

12. If V is a finite dimensional vector space, then if w is a subspace of V then

A. w is a finite dimensional
B. w is infinite dimensional
C. The dimension of w is greater than V
D. None of these

13. If w_1 and w_2 are subspaces of finite dimensional vector space then

A. $(w_1 + w_2)^\circ = w_1^\circ \cap w_2^\circ$
B. $(w_1 + w_2)^\circ \geq w_1^\circ + w_2^\circ$
C. $(w_1 + w_2)^\circ \leq w_1^\circ + w_2^\circ$
D. None of these

14. Let V be a vector space and $(\,/\,)$ an inner product on V then $(0/\beta)$ is equal to, for all $\beta \in V$

A. Zero

B. Greater than zero

C. Less than zero

D. None of these

15. The inside of the sphere in E^3, with centre $\bar{a}$ and radius $\in > 0$ is the set of points

A. $\{x \mid |\bar{x}-\bar{a}| < \in\}$ B. $\{x \mid |\bar{x}-\bar{a}| > \in\}$

C. $\{x \mid |\bar{x}-\bar{a}| = \in\}$ D. None of these

16. Given $\bar{c}\;\bar{x} = z$ an hyper plane in D^n, then the following sets define open half space

A. $\{\bar{x}/\bar{c}\;\bar{x} \le z\}$ and $\{\bar{x}/\bar{c}\;\bar{x} \ge z\}$

B. $\{\bar{x}/\bar{c}\;\bar{x} < z\}$ and $\{\bar{x}/\bar{c}\;\bar{x} > z\}$

C. $\{\bar{c}/\bar{x} \ge z\}$ and $\{\bar{c}/\bar{x} \le z\}$

D. None of these

17. Set of feasible solution to $\bar{A}\,\bar{x} = \bar{b}$ is

A. Convex set

B. Non-convex set

C. Disconnected set

D. None of these

18. Let λ be an arrival rate of customer in a system, μ be an service rate of the system then the expected number of busy servers are

A. λ/μ B. $\lambda+\mu$

C. $\lambda\mu$ D. None of these

19. In a pure birth model if λ is an arrival rate, $P_0(t)$ the probability of 0 arrivals, then

A. $P'_0(t) = -\lambda/P_0(t)$

B. $P'_0(t) = \lambda P_0(t)$

C. $P'_0(t) = P_0(t)$

D. None of these

20. If arrival rate is 3 customers/day and service rate is 5 customer/day for |M|N|I queueing system the expected number of customers in the system at certain day is

A. 1.5 B. 2

C. 3 D. 5

21. If $C = \{x+iy : x,\ y \in D,\ i = \sqrt{-1}\ \}$ is a field with respect to ordinary addition and multiplication, then the multiplicative inverse of non-zero element of $a+ib \in C$ is

A. $a+b$

B. $\left(\dfrac{a}{a^2+b^2}\right)+i\left(\dfrac{-b}{a^2+b^2}\right)$

C. $\dfrac{a+ib}{a^2+b^2}$

D. None of these

22. If U is an ideal of ring R, then

A. U/R is a ring B. R/U is a ring

C. RU is a ring D. None of these

23. Field having no proper subfield is

A. Prime field B. Division field

C. Integral field D. None of these

24. If F is a subfield of L, and K is a subfield of L which contains F, then

A. $[K:F] \mid [L:F]$ B. $[K:F]\times[L:F]$

C. $[F:K] \mid [F:L]$ D. $[F:K]\times[F:L]$

25. If N is a set of natural numbers then under binary operation $ab = a - b$, (N, .) is

A. Quasi group B. Semi-group

C. Monoid D. Group

26. If a sequence $\{a_n\}_{n=1}^{\infty}$ converges to a real number A, then $\{a_n\}_{n=1}^{\infty}$ is

A. Unbounded sequence

B. Bounded sequence

C. Divergent sequence

D. None of these

27. The sequence $\left\{(-1)^n\right\}_{n=1}^{\infty}$ is

A. Bounded and convergent

B. Convergent and unbounded

C. Bounded and divergent

D. Divergent and unbounded

28. The sequence $\left\{\dfrac{n+1}{n}\right\}$ is

A. Increasing sequence

B. Decreasing sequence

C. Unbounded

D. None of these

29. If 1, ω, ω^2 are the cube roots of unity, then the roots of $(x-1)^3+8=0$ are

A. $-1, -1, -1$ B. $-1, 1+2\omega, 1+2\omega^2$

C. $1, \omega, 2\omega$ D. $-1, 1-2\omega, 1-2\omega^2$

30. If $\phi:[a,b]\times[c,d]\to C$ is a continuous function and $g:[c,d]\to C$ is such that

$$g(t)=\int_a^b \phi(s,t)ds$$

A. g is not a continuous function
B. g is a continuous function
C. g is increasing function
D. g is a decreasing function

31. The mobius transform takes
A. Circle into line B. Circle into circle
C. Circle into square D. None of these

32. If $(1,0,\infty)$ is the orientiation of D : then the cross into
A. $(z,1,0,\infty)=1$ B. $(z,1,0,\infty)=0$
C. $(z,1,0,\infty)=0$ D. $(z,1,0,\infty)=z$

33. If $\gamma:[a,b]\to C$ and γ is bounded variation then total variation $V(\gamma)$ is

A. $V(\gamma)\le\int_b^i|\gamma'(t)|\,dt$

B. $V(\gamma)\ge\int_b^i|\gamma'(t)|\,dt$

C. $V(\gamma)=\int_b^i|\gamma'(t)|\,dt$

D. None of these

34. Let B $=(A_1, A_4, A_6)$ constitute a basis for linear programming problem. Let $A_2=aA_1+bA_4+cA_6$. Let in B the column A_4 be replaced by A_2. Then new B will be again a basis provided
A. a, b, c all are positive
B. $b=0$
C. $b\neq 0$
D. None of these

35. An integer n is a prime number if
A. $n>1$ and n is divisible by itself
B. $n<1$ and n is divisible by itself
C. $n=1$
D. $n=1$ and n/n

36. If $x\in S$ a set of real numbers, then
A. Sup $(-x)=-\text{In} f(x)$
B. Sup $(-x)=\text{In} f(-x)$
C. Sup $(-x)=-\text{In} f(-x)$
D. Sup $x=\text{In} f x$

37. If f' exist and is monotonic on $[a, b]$, then
A. f' is continuous on $[a, b]$
B. f' is discontinuous on $[a,b]$
C. f' is constant
D. None of these

38. Two fair dice are tossed. The probability that the sum will be equal to 7 is:
A. $\frac{1}{6}$ B. $\frac{5}{6}$
C. $\frac{7}{6}$ D. $\frac{13}{6}$

39. If $z=\lambda+3+i\sqrt{5-\lambda^2}$, then the locus of z is:
A. an ellipse B. a parabola
C. a circle D. a straight line

40. If F is a homomorphism of a group G into a group G' with Kernel k then:
A. k is a subgroup of G but not a normal subgroup of G
B. k is a normal subgroup of G
C. k is a complex of G
D. None of the above is correct

ANSWERS

1	2	3	4	5	6	7	8	9	10
C	A	A	B	C	A	D	A	B	B
11	12	13	14	15	16	17	18	19	20
B	A	A	A	A	A	A	A	A	A
21	22	23	24	25	26	27	28	29	30
B	A	A	A	A	B	C	B	D	B
31	32	33	34	35	36	37	38	39	40
B	D	C	C	A	A	A	A	C	B

Some Selected Explanatory Answers

1. $y\frac{dy}{dx}=x\left(\frac{dy}{dx}\right)^2+x$

Degree of the equation is '2' because degree of highest order of derivatives is '2'

2. Lagrange's subsidiary equation

$$\frac{\partial x}{1}=\frac{\partial y}{1}=\frac{\partial z}{z/a}$$

$\Rightarrow \quad x-y=c_1$

and $\quad z=c_2\,e^{y/a}$

$z=e^{y/a}f(x-y)$

3. $(D^2-DD^1+D)z=1$

$\Rightarrow D(D-D^1+1)z=1$

$Z_h=e^{0.x}f_1(y)+e^{-x}f_2(y+x)$

$=f_1(y)+e^{-x}f_2(y+x)$

$$Z_p=\frac{1}{D(D-D^1+1)}.1$$

$$=\frac{1}{D}(1+D-D')^{-1}.1=\frac{1}{D}.1=x$$

$Z=Z_h+Z_p$

4. P.I is $\frac{1}{(D+3)^2}50e^{2x}=\frac{50e^{2x}}{(2+3)^2}=2e^{2x}$

5. $4xp^2=(3x-a)^2$

Obiviously p. discrimination is $(3x-a)^2=0$

6. $\mu_r=E[(x-\mu)^r]$

$$=\sum_x(x-\mu)^r f(x)$$

$$\Rightarrow \mu_1=\sum_x xf(x)-\mu\sum_x f(x)$$

$$=\mu-\mu.1\left(\because \sum_x f(x)=1\right)$$

$=0$

7. (a) $f(1)=-\frac{1}{2}$ negative

(b) $\sum_x f(x)=\frac{6}{5}\neq 1$

(c) $F(1)=\frac{-1}{5}$ negative

(d) $\sum_x g(x)=1$

8. $\sum_{n=0}^{\infty}\frac{z^n}{n!}$

we have it as $\left\{\frac{1}{1},\frac{z}{1},..........\right\}$

converges to zero. As $\lim_{n\to\infty}\frac{z^n}{n!}=0$

10. $|A|\neq 0$ i.e. if A is non-singular

11. $|A|=0$

and $\begin{bmatrix}0 & i\\ -i & 0\end{bmatrix}\neq 0$

$\therefore$ Rank $A=2$

14. $(0+\beta/\beta)=(0/\beta)+(\beta/\beta)$

$\Rightarrow(\beta/\beta)=(0/\beta)+(\beta/\beta)$

$\Rightarrow(0/\beta)=0$

15. Set of points can be given by $\{x:|\bar{x}-\bar{a}|<\epsilon\}$

17. Always a convex set (According to definition)

18. Traffic intensity $=\frac{\lambda}{\mu}$

19. $P_0(t+\Delta t)=P_0(t)(1-\lambda\Delta t)$

$$\Rightarrow \lim_{\Delta t\to 0}\frac{P_0(t+\Delta t)-P_0(t)}{\Delta t}=-\lambda P_0(t)$$

$\Rightarrow P_0^1(t)=-\lambda P_0(t)$

20. $\lambda=3,\mu=5$

$\Rightarrow P=\frac{3}{5}$

$$L_s=\frac{P}{1-P}=\frac{3/5}{1-(3/5)}=\frac{3}{2}=1.5$$

21. $C=\{x+iy:x,y\in D, i=\sqrt{-1}\}$

The non zero element is $a+ib\in C$. Then its multiplicative inverse will be given by

$(a+ib)^{-1}=1/(a+ib)$

$$=\frac{(a-ib)}{(a+ib)\times(a-ib)}$$

$$= \frac{a-ib}{a^2-(ib)^2} = \frac{a-ib}{a^2-i^2b^2}$$

$$= \frac{a-ib}{a^2+b^2} = \left(\frac{a}{a^2+b^2}\right) - i\left(\frac{b}{a^2+b^2}\right)$$

22. $\because$ U is an ideal ring of R therefore by property of rings U/R is a ring.

23. Field having no proper subfield is known as a prime field.

24. [K : F]/[L : F] (using property of subfield)

25. Quasi group [by applying postulates property]

26. $\{a_n\}_{n=1}^{\infty}$ Converges to a real number A. Then

$\{a_n\}_{n=1}^{\infty}$ is a Bounded sequence as it is bounded above as well as bounded below.

27. $x_n = (-1)^n \forall n \in N$

$\forall n \in N, -1 \le x_n$

and $\forall n \in N, 1 \ge x_n$

$\Rightarrow \{(-1)^n\}$ is bounded

For even number, $\lim_{n\to\infty} (-1)^n = 1$

For odd number, $\lim_{n\to\infty} (-1)^n = -1$

$\therefore$ Sequence is divergent

8. $x_n = \frac{n+1}{n} = 1 + \frac{1}{n}$

$$x_{n+1} = \frac{(n+1)+1}{(n+1)} = 1 + \frac{1}{n+1}$$

$$x_{n+1} - x_n = \frac{1}{n+1} - \frac{1}{n} = \frac{-1}{n(n+1)}$$

$\Rightarrow x_{n+1} - x_n < 0$

$\Rightarrow x_{n+1} < x_n$

$\Rightarrow \{x_n\}$ is decreasing sequence.

29. $(x-1)^3 + 8 = 0$

$\Rightarrow (x-1)^3 = -8$

$\therefore\ x - 1 = (-8)^{1/3}$

$= -2, -2\omega, -2\omega^2$

Hence $x = -1, 1-2\omega, 1-2\omega^2$

30. g is continuous (using the definition of continuity)

33. for $v : [a,b] \to C$ then

$$v(\gamma) = \int_b^i |v'(t)|\, dt$$

35. For any integer 'n' to be a prime number if $n > 1$ and divisible by itself (by using definition of prime).

36. Sub $(-x) = -inf\ (x)$ by using definition of supremum and infimum.

38. The no. on the first die are 1, 2, 3, 4, 5, 6 and the same is on second die.

Total no. of ways $= 6 \times 6 = 36$, i.e. $n(s) = 36$

No. of favourable cases for the event (E), consider the following table:

No. on first die	1 2 3 4 5 6
No. on second die	6 5 4 3 2 1
Sum	= 7 7 7 7 7 7

$\therefore$ No. of favourable cases, $n(E) = 6$

$$\therefore\ P(E) = \frac{n(E)}{n(S)} = \frac{6}{36} = \frac{1}{6}$$

SET–9

CSIR–UGC (NET) MATHEMATICAL SCIENCES

PART-B

1. The partial differential equation formed by eliminating arbitrary functions from the equation $Z= f(x^2-y^2)$ is

A. $xp + yq = 0$ B. $xq + yp = 0$

C. $\frac{x}{y} = P$ D. $\frac{x}{y} = q$

2. The solution of differential equation

$$\frac{dy}{dx} = \frac{3x^2y^4 + 2xy}{x^2 - 2x^3y^3}$$

A. $x^3y^2 + \frac{x^2}{y} = \frac{x}{y}$ B. $x^3y^2 + \frac{x^2}{y^2} = x$

C. $x^3y^2 + \frac{x^2}{y} = c$ D. None of these

3. The P–discriminant of equation $y^2p^2 + y^2 - r^2 = 0$ is

A. $y^2 = 0$ B. $y^2 = r^2$

C. $y^2(y^2 - r^2) = 0$ D. $y^2 = 0$

4. We have a biased die such that, each even number is twice likely to occur for odd number. What is the probability of getting a numbers greater than 3, in a single roll of die ?

A. $\frac{4}{9}$ B. $\frac{5}{9}$

C. $\frac{3}{9}$ D. $\frac{1}{9}$

5. $E[(ax + b)^n]$ is equal to

A. $\sum_{i=0}^{n} \binom{n}{i} a^{n-i} b^i \, E(x^{n-i})$

B. $a\,E(x) + b^n$

C. $E(a^n x) + b^n$

D. $\sum_{i=0}^{n} \binom{n}{i} a^{n-i} b^{n-i} \, E(x^{n-i})$

6. What is the probability that 3 out of 10 student will pass the exam, given that any one of that can pass it with probability 0.80?

A. 0.30 B. 0.10

C. 0.20 D. None of these

7. Let the probability density function be $f(x) = \begin{cases} kx^2, & 0 \le x \le 2 \\ 0 & \text{otherwise} \end{cases}$ .The value of k is given by

A. $\frac{1}{8}$ B. $\frac{3}{8}$

C. $\frac{2}{5}$ D. None of these

8. Two complex number $z_1 = x + iy$ and $z_2 = a + ib$ are equal iff

A. $x = a, y = b$ B. $x = b, y = a$

C. $x = i, y = a$ D. $x = b, y = i$

9. Let $z_1 = -2 + 2i$ and $z_2 = 2i$, then $z_1 z_2$ is equal to

A. $+6(1 + i)$ B. $-6(1+i)$

C. $6 + i$ D. none of these

10. The radius of convergence of the power series $\sum_{n=0}^{\infty} \frac{n+5i}{\lfloor 2n}(z-i)^n$ is

A. 0 B. ∞

C. One D. None of these

11. The solution of

$$3x + 7y + 8z = -13$$
$$2x + 9z = -5$$
$$-4x + y - 26z = 2 \text{ is}$$

A. $x = -7, y = 0, z = 2$

B. $x = 0, y = 0, z = 3$

C. $x = -7, y = 0, z = 1$

D. None of these

12. If I_n is an identity matrix of order n, and k any scalar
A. $adj\,(k\,I_n) = k\,I_n$
B. $adj\,(k\,I_n) = k^n\,I_n$
C. $adj\,(k\,I_n) = k^{n-1}\,I_n$
D. None of these

13. If S is a linearly independent set and $W \subset S$, then
A. W is linearly dependent
B. W = S
C. W is linearly independent
D. None of these

14. If a system contains a single non- zero vector, it is always
A. Linearly independent
B. Linearly dependent
C. Subspace
D. None of these

15. Empty set is
A. Linearly dependent
B. Linearly indpendent
C. Does not span {0}
D. None of these

16. A holded disk is
A. Convex set B. Connected set
C. Disconnected set D. None of these

17. If there is an optimal basic feasible solution to a linear programming problem, and for some $\overline{a}_j$ not in the basis, $z_j - c_j = 0$, $Y_{ij} \leq 0$ for all i, then
A. Non-basic optima will exist
B. Non-basic optima will not exist
C. Sometimes optima will exist
D. None is true

18. Let E^3 be a Euclidean space, an equation of sphere with centre $\overline{a}$ and radius $\in$ is
A. $|\overline{x} - \overline{a}| < \in$
B. $|\overline{x} - \overline{a}| > \in$
C. $|\overline{x} - \overline{a}| = \in$
D. None of these

19. The convex combination of two points $\overline{x}_1, \overline{x}_2 \in X$ is reffered as
A. $(1-\lambda)\overline{x}_1 + \lambda\overline{x}_2, 0 \leq \lambda \leq 1$
B. $(1-\lambda)\overline{x}_1 + \lambda\overline{x}_2, \lambda$ any real number
C. $\lambda\overline{x}_1 + \lambda\overline{x}_2, 0 \leq \lambda \leq 1$
D. $\lambda\overline{x}_1 + \lambda\overline{x}_2, \lambda$ any real number

20. Under exponential assumptions P{more than one service is completion in $\Delta t = 0$ per more than one unit in system}is
A. Zero B. Positive
C. Negative D. None of these

21. In the EOQ model with back logging the optimal number of order to back log is
A. Directly proportional to inventory
B. Directly proportional to the square root of inventory
C. Not dependent on inventory
D. Directly proportional to the reciprocal of inventory

22. If L_s be the expected length of customers in the system and W_s be the expected waiting time in the system, by Little's formula for arrival rate λ in the system
A. $L_s = \lambda w_s$ B. $L_s w_s = \lambda$
C. $w_s = \lambda L_s$ D. None of these

23. In queueing description M|M|I the arrival and departure distribution are
A. Both Markovian B. Binomial
C. General D. None of these

24. If the interarrival time is exponential with mean $1/\lambda$ then the number of arrivals in $(0, t)$ is
A. Poisson distributed
B. Binomial distributed
C. Exponential distributed
D. None of these

25. A function $f(x)$ has no jump discontinuity at $x = a$ if
A. $f(a+) = f(a-) = f(a)$
B. $f(a+) \neq f(a-)$
C. $f(a+) \neq f(a)$
D. $f(a+) = f(a-) \neq f(a)$

26. If R is a set of real numbers then $x, y \in R$, then
A. $x > 0$ and $y > 0 \Rightarrow xy > 0$
B. $x > 0$ and $y > 0 \Rightarrow xy < 0$
C. $x > 0$ and $y > 0 \Rightarrow xy = 0$
D. $x > 0$ and $y > 0 \Rightarrow xy = 1$

Directions (Q.27 to 30) : *A marketing manager has 5 salesman and 5 districts, considering the capabilities of the salesman and the nature of districts, the marketing manager estimates that sales* *per month (in hundred rupees) for each salesman in each district would be follows :*

Jobs	Machine				
	A	B	C	D	E
1	32	38	40	28	40
2	40	24	28	21	36
3	41	27	33	30	37
4	22	38	41	36	36
5	29	33	40	35	39

27. The optimal assignment is

A. $4 \to B, 5 \to A$ B. $4 \to C, 5 \to D$
C. $4 \to E, 5 \to D$ D. $4 \to A, 5 \to B$

28. The optimal assignment is

A. $4 \to B, ? \to$ A or E
B. $4 \to C, 2 \to$ A or E
C. $4 \to D, 2 \to$ A or E
D. $4 \to E, 2 \to A$

29. The optimal assignment is

A. $1 \to A$ and $2 \to B$
B. $1 \to B$ and $2 \to$ E or A
C. $1 \to C$ and $2 \to D$
D. $1 \to D$ and $2 \to B$

30. The maximum profit is

A. Rs. 600 B. Rs. 591
C. Rs. 191 D. Rs. 91

31. The primal LPP is

$max\ z = y_1 - 2y_2$

subject to $y_1 - 3y_2 \le -3$

$-y_1 + 2y_2 = -2$

$y_1, y_2 \ge 0$

Then $C_B^T B^{-1}$ of optimal table of above is (0,1). Then the optimal solution (x_1, x_2) of dual is

A. (0, 1) B. (0, –1)
C. (0, 0) D. None of these

32. If $\left|\dfrac{z-5i}{z+5i}\right| = 1$, then $z = x + iy$ lie on

A. The real axis
B. The straight line $x = 5$
C. The straight line $y = 5$
D. A circle passing through origin

33. A sequence $\{a_n\}_{n=1}^{\infty}$ is bounded from above if for real number R

A. $a_n \ge R$ for all n B. $a_n \le R$ for all n
C. $a_n = R$ for all n D. None of these

34. The nth term of the sequence $\left\{1, \frac{5}{2}, \frac{5}{3}, \frac{9}{4}, \frac{9}{5}, \ldots\right\}$ is

A. $\dfrac{2n+(-1)^n}{2n}$ B. $\dfrac{2n+(-1)^n}{n}$
C. $\dfrac{2n+(1)^n}{n}$ D. None of these

35. If F is a field then its only ideals are A : F a field itself, B : (0)

A. A and B are true
B. A is true, B is false
C. A is false, B is true
D. A and B false

36. The product of permutation (1 2 3).(2 4 3).(1 3 4) is equal to

A. 1 B. $\begin{pmatrix}1 & 2 & 3 & 4\\ 5 & 6 & 2 & 1\end{pmatrix}$
C. $\begin{pmatrix}1 & 2 & 5 & 1\\ 1 & 6 & 5 & 1\end{pmatrix}$ D. $\begin{pmatrix}1 & 2 & 5 & 3\\ 1 & 2 & 3 & 4\end{pmatrix}$

37. If in a ring R with unity, $(xy)^2 = x^2y^2, \forall x, y \in R$, then

A. R is a commutative ring
B. R is an integral domain
C. R is field
D. None of these

38. A company uses annually 12,000 units of a raw material costing Rs. 1.25 per unit. Placing each other costs Rs. 0.45 and the carrying costs are 15% per year per unit of the average inventory. The Economic Order Quantity is:

A. 120 units B. 160 units
C. 240 units D. 320 units

39. The generator of the cyclic group of nth roots of unity is:

A. $e^{2\pi i/n}$ B. $e^{4\pi i/n}$
C. $e^{5\pi i/n}$ D. $e^{7\pi i/n}$

40. If $y_1(x)$ and $y_2(x)$ are the solutions of $y'' + x^2y' + (1-x)y = 0$, such that $y_1(0) = 0$, $y_1'(0) = 1$, $y_2'(0) = 1$, $y_2(0) = 1$, then the Wronskian $W(y_1, y_2)$ on R:

A. –1 B. 0
C. 1 D. 2

ANSWERS

1	2	3	4	5	6	7	8	9	10
B	C	C	B	A	C	B	A	D	B
11	**12**	**13**	**14**	**15**	**16**	**17**	**18**	**19**	**20**
C	C	C	A	B	B	A	C	A	A
21	**22**	**23**	**24**	**25**	**26**	**27**	**28**	**29**	**30**
D	A	A	A	A	A	B	B	B	C
31	**32**	**33**	**34**	**35**	**36**	**37**	**38**	**39**	**40**
B	A	B	B	A	A	B	C	A	A

Some Selected Explanatory Answers

1. $z = f(x^2 - y^2)$

$p = f^1(x^2 - y^2)2x$

$q = f^1(x^2 - y^2)(-2y)$

$$\Rightarrow \frac{p}{q} = -\frac{x}{y}$$

i.e., $xq + yp = 0$

2. The given equation can be rewritten as

$$(3x^2y^4 + 2xy) + (2x^3y^3 - x^2)\frac{dy}{dx} = 0$$

Dividing by y^2, we get

$$\left(3x^2y^2 + \frac{2x}{y}\right)dx + \left(2x^3y - \frac{x^2}{y^2}\right)dy = 0$$

$$\Rightarrow d\left(x^3y^2 + \frac{x^2}{y}\right) - 0$$

$$\Rightarrow x^3y^2 + \frac{x^2}{y} = \text{constant}$$

4. $S = \{1, 2, 3, 4, 5, 6\}$

If w is the probability of occurence of odd number then $2w$ is of even number and $w + 2w + w + 2w + w + 2w = 1$

$$\Rightarrow w = \frac{1}{9}$$

$$P\{\text{a number greater than } 3\} = \frac{2}{9} + \frac{1}{9} + \frac{2}{9}$$

$$= \frac{5}{9}$$

5. By Binomial theorem

$$(ax + b)^n = \sum_{i=0}^{n}\binom{n}{i}(ax)^{n-i}b^i$$

$$\Rightarrow E\big[(ax+b)\big] = E\left[\sum_{i=0}^{n}\binom{n}{i}a^{n-i}b^i x^{n-i}\right]$$

$$= \sum_{i=0}^{n}\binom{n}{i}(a^{n-i})b^i E(x^{n-i})$$

6. $x = 3, n = 10, p = 0.80$

$$b(x; n, p) = \binom{10}{3}(0.80)^3(1 - 0.80)^{10-7}$$

$= 0.20$

7. $$\int_{-\infty}^{\infty} f(x)dx = 1$$

$$\Rightarrow \int_0^2 f(x)dx = \int_0^2 kx^2dx$$

$$= k\int_0^2 x^2dx$$

$$= k\left(\frac{x^3}{3}\right)_0^2 = 1 \Rightarrow k\left(\frac{8}{3} - 0\right) = 1$$

$$\Rightarrow k = \frac{3}{8}$$

8. Two complex numbers

$z_1 = x + iy$

$z_2 = a + ib$ are equal iff

$x = a, y = b$

9. $z_1 = -2 + 2i$ and $z_2 = 2i$

$$z_1 . z_2 = (-2+2i).(2i) = -4i + 4i^2 = -4 - 4i = -4[1+i]$$

11. $$\begin{bmatrix} 3 & 7 & 8 \\ 2 & 0 & 9 \\ -4 & 1 & -26 \end{bmatrix}\begin{bmatrix} x \\ y \\ z \end{bmatrix} = \begin{bmatrix} -13 \\ -5 \\ 2 \end{bmatrix}$$

By Cramer's rule

$$\frac{x}{\begin{vmatrix} -13 & -5 & 2 \\ 2 & 0 & 9 \\ -4 & 1 & -26 \end{vmatrix}} = \frac{y}{\begin{vmatrix} 3 & 7 & 8 \\ -13 & -5 & 2 \\ -4 & 1 & -26 \end{vmatrix}}$$

$$= \frac{z}{\begin{vmatrix} 3 & 7 & 8 \\ 2 & 0 & 9 \\ -13 & -5 & 2 \end{vmatrix}}$$

$$= \frac{1}{\begin{vmatrix} 3 & 7 & 8 \\ 2 & 0 & 9 \\ -4 & 1 & -26 \end{vmatrix}}$$

$x = -7, y = 0, z = 1$

12. $(k I_n)\, adj\, (k I_n) = |k I_n| I_n$

$\Rightarrow (k I_n)\, adj\, (k I_n) = k^n I_n$

$\Rightarrow adj\, (k I_n) = k^{n-1} I_n$

15. Empty set is linearly independent.

∵ It contains no element.

20. Under exponential assumption $\Delta t = 0$, at most one service can occur.

21. Directly proportional to the reciprocal of inventory.

22. Little's formula states that

$L_s = \lambda W_s$

23. M represents Markovian (exponential/poisson)distribution for arrival (departure)

24. If the number of arrivals in $(0, t)$ is poisson with mean λ then the interval time is exponential with mean $1/\lambda$

Direction: For 27 to 30

	A	B	C	D	E
1	32	38	40	28	40
2	40	24	28	21	36
3	41	27	33	30	37
4	22	38	41	36	36
5	29	33	40	35	39

This is maximization problem. First convert it into min. problem by subtracting max. C_{ij} from all elements.

	A	B	C	D	E
1	9	3	1	13	1
2	1	17	13	20	5
3	0	14	8	11	4
4	19	3	0	5	5
5	12	8	1	6	2

→ Row reduction matrix

	A	B	C	D	E
1	8	2	0	12	0
2	0	16	12	19	4
3	0	14	8	11	4
4	19	3	0	5	5
5	11	7	0	5	1

→ Column reduction matrix

	A	B	C	D	E
1	8	[0]	~~0~~	7	~~0~~
2	[0]	14	12	14	4
3	~~0~~	12	8	6	4
4	19	1	0	0	5
5	11	5	0	0	1

→

	A	B	C	D	E
1	9	0	1	8	0
2	[0]	13	12	14	3
3	~~0~~	11	8	6	3
4	19	0	0	0	4
5	11	4	0	0	0

→

	A	B	C	D	E
1	12	[0]	1	8	✗
2	[0]	10	9	11	✗
3	✗	8	5	3	[0]
4	22	✗	[0]	✗	4
5	14	4	✗	[0]	✗

$1 \to B$

$2 \to A$ (or E)

$3 \to E$ (or A)

$4 \to C$

$5 \to D$

Maz. Prof. is,

$38+40+37+41+35=191$

32. $\left|\frac{z-5i}{z+5i}\right|=1$

$\Rightarrow |z-5i|=|z+5i|$

$\Rightarrow |x+(y-5)i|=|x+(y+5)i|$

$\Rightarrow x^2+(y-5)^2=x^2+(y+5)^2$

$\Rightarrow y=0$

33. $\{a_n\}_{n=1}^{\infty}$ is bounded above if for real no R $a_n \le R$

$\forall\, n$ by definition of upper bound of a sequence

34. $a_1 = 1 = 2-1$

$$a_2 = \frac{5}{2} = \frac{4+1}{2}$$

$$a_3 = \frac{5}{3} = \frac{6-1}{3}$$

⋮

$$a_n = \frac{2n+(-1)^n}{n}$$

36. $(1\,2\,3).(2\,4\,3).(1\,3\,4)$

$$= \begin{pmatrix}1&2&3&4\\2&3&1&4\end{pmatrix}\begin{pmatrix}1&2&4&3\\1&4&3&2\end{pmatrix}\begin{pmatrix}1&2&3&4\\3&2&4&1\end{pmatrix}$$

$$= \begin{pmatrix}1&2&3&4\\2&3&1&4\end{pmatrix}\begin{pmatrix}2&3&1&4\\4&2&1&3\end{pmatrix}\begin{pmatrix}1&2&3&4\\3&2&4&1\end{pmatrix}$$

$$= \begin{pmatrix}1&2&3&4\\4&2&1&3\end{pmatrix}\begin{pmatrix}4&2&1&3\\1&2&3&4\end{pmatrix}$$

$$= \begin{pmatrix}1&2&3&4\\1&2&3&4\end{pmatrix}$$

37. $xy \in R$

$\Rightarrow (xy)(xy) = xy\,xy$

$= xy\,xy$ (if R is commutative)

$= x^2y^2$

38. $R = 12{,}000$, $P =$ Rs. 1.25, $C_3 = 0.45$

I = 15% per year/unit of average inventory

$$q' = \sqrt{\frac{2\times0.45\times12000\times100}{15\times1.25}} = 240 \text{ units.}$$

40. $W(y_1, y_2) = \begin{vmatrix} y_1(0) & y_2(0) \\ y_1'(0) & y_2'(0)\end{vmatrix} = \begin{vmatrix}0 & -1\\ -1 & 1\end{vmatrix}$

$= -1 \neq 0$

and y_1, y_2 are solutions,

$\Rightarrow W(y_1, y_2)(x) \neq 0 \quad \forall \quad x \in R$

Set–10
CSIR–UGC (NET) Mathematical Sciences

PART-B

1. The dual of the L.P.P

Minimize $z = 4x_1 + 6x_2 + 18x_3$

$s.t\ x_1+3x_2 \geq 3, x_2+ 2x_3 \geq 5, x_1 \geq 0$ is

A. Maximize $Z^* = 3w_1 + 5w_2$

$s.t\ w_1 \leq 4, 3w_1 + w_2 \leq 6, 2w_2 \leq 18, w_1, w_2 \geq 0$

B. Maximize $Z^* = 3w_1 + 5w_2$

$s.t\ w_1 \geq 4, 3w_1 + w_2 \geq 6, 2w_2 \geq 18, w_1, w_2 \geq 0$

C. Minimize $Z^* = 3w_1 + 5w_2$

$s.t\ w_1 \geq 4, 3w_1 + w_2 \geq 6, 2w_2 \geq 18, w_1, w_2 \geq 0$

D. None of the above

2. Let primal LPP be

max $f(x) = c^T x$, $Ax \leq b, x \geq 0$ and dual be

min $g(y) = b^T y$, $A^T y \geq c, y \geq 0$. Let x^* and y^* be feasible solution of primal and dual, then

A. $f(x^*) \leq g(y^*)$ B. $f(x^*) \geq g(y^*)$

C. $f(x^*) = g(y^*)$ D. None of these

3. If $P_o(t)$ states the probability that no event occurs in $(0, t)$ then under exponential assumptions

A. $P_o(t) = e^{-N}, t > 0$ B. $P_o(t) = 1$

C. $P_o(t) = \dfrac{e^{-N}}{t}, t > 0$ D. None of these

4. A first order differential equation

$M(x,y)\, dx + N(x, y)\, dy = 0$ is exact if

A. $\dfrac{dM}{dx} = \dfrac{dN}{dy}$ B. $\dfrac{dM}{dx} \neq \dfrac{dN}{dy}$

C. $\dfrac{dM}{dy} = \pm\dfrac{dM}{dx}$ D. $\dfrac{dM}{dy} = \dfrac{dN}{dx}$

5. Replacement problem is associated with

A. Setup cost

B. Maintenance cost

C. Value of the equipment

D. None of these

6. If V and W are finite dimensional vector spaces over the same field, then V and W are isomorphic if

A. dim V > dim W B. dim V = dim W

C. dim V < dim W D. None of these

7. The norm of α with respect to inner product (α/α) is

A. $\| \alpha \| = (\alpha / \alpha)$

B. $\| \alpha \|^2 = (\alpha / \alpha)$

C. $\| \alpha \| = (\alpha / \alpha)^2$

D. None of these

8. General solution of $2\dfrac{d^2y}{dx^2} + 5\dfrac{dy}{dx} + 2y = 0$ is

A. $y = Ae^{-2x}$ B. $y = Be^{\frac{1}{2}x}$

C. $y = Ae^{-2x} + Be^{-\frac{1}{2}x}$ D. None of these

9. Elimination of a and b from $z = ae^{bt} \sin bx$ gives the partial differential equation

A. $\dfrac{d^2z}{dx^2} + \dfrac{d^2z}{dt^2} = 0$ B. $\dfrac{dz}{dx} + \dfrac{dz}{dt} = 0$

C. $\dfrac{dz}{dx} + z = 0$ D. None of these

10. A general solution of linear differential equation with constant coefficient is

A. Sum of particular solution and complementary function

B. Product of particular solution and complementary function

C. Quotient of particular solution and complementary function

D. None of these

11. If two vectors α and β are linearly dependent then some scalar 'c'

A. $\alpha = c\beta$ B. $\alpha = c + \beta$

C. $\alpha = c - \beta$ D. None of these

12. If f and g are linear functionals on a vector space V then g is a scalar multiple of f if

A. $f(\alpha) = 0 \Rightarrow g(\alpha) = 0$

B. $g(\alpha) = 0 \Rightarrow f(\alpha) = 0$

C. $f(\alpha) = 0 \Rightarrow g(\alpha) = \text{Constant}$

D. $g(\alpha) = 0 \Rightarrow f(\alpha) = \text{Constant}$

13. If G = (1, –1, i, –i) is a multiplicative group then order of –i is

A. One B. Two

C. Three D. Four

14. In real part of $exp\ i\theta$ is

A. $e^{\cos\theta}$ B. $e^{\cos\theta}\sin(\sin\theta)$

C. $e^{\cos\theta}\cos(\sin\theta)$ D. $e^{\cos\theta}\cos(\cos\theta)$

15. For complex number z, $|z+5|^2 + |z-5|^2 = 75$ represents

A. A circle B. An ellipse

C. A triangle D. A straight line

16. If γ is a rectifiable curve and f is continuous function on (γ) then if $c\in C$

A. $\int_{\gamma} f(z)dz = \int_{\gamma+c} f(z-c)dz$

B. $\int_{\gamma} f(z)dz = \int_{\gamma} f(z-c)dz$

C. $\int_{\gamma} f(z)dz = \int_{\gamma} f(c)dz$

D. None of these

17. If K is an extension of field F and $a\in$ K is algebraic of degree n over F then

A. $(F(a):F)=n$ B. $(F(a):K)=n$

C. $(K:K(a))=n$ D. $(F:F(a))=n$

18. $A=\begin{bmatrix}1 & 1\\ 1 & 1\end{bmatrix}$ and $B=\begin{bmatrix}1 & 0\\ -1 & 0\end{bmatrix}$ are

A. Zero divisors

B. None zero divisors

C. A = 0 or B = 0

D. AB ≠ 0

19. If a_1^{-1} are a_2^{-1} are two multiplicative inverses of non-zero elements $a\in f$, a field then

A. $a_1^{-1}\neq a_2^{-1}$ B. $a_1^{-1}=a_2^{-1}$

C. $a_1^{-1}<a_2^{-1}$ D. None of these

20. If f : G → c is analytic and R=d (a, ∂G) then for $a\in$ G and $|z-a|$ < R

A. $f(z) = a_n (z-a)^n$

B. $f(z)=\sum_{n=0}^{\infty} a_n(z-a)^n$

C. $f(z)=\sum (z-a)^n$

D. None of these

21. Γ is a circle through points z_2, z_3, z_4 the points z_1 $z^*\in C_\infty$ are symmetric with respect of Γ if

A. $(z^*, z_2, z_3, z_4)\neq(z_1, z_2, z_3, z_4)$

B. $(z^*, z_2, z_3, z_4)=(z_1, z_2, z_3, z_4)$

C. $z^*, z_2 = z_1\, z_2$

D. None of these

22. If G is a regeion and f : G → C is continuous function such that $\int_{\gamma} f=0$ for every closed path γ in G, then

A. f is analytic in G

B. f is continuous in G

C. f is non – analytic in G

D. f is discontinuous in G

23. $f(x)=\begin{cases}\cos x & ; x\geq 0\\ -\cos x & ; x<0\end{cases}$ then, function f

A. is continuous at 0

B. has removable discontinuity at 0

C. has irremovable discontinuity at 0

D. None of these

24. If S is set of real numbers and C_1 & C_2 are least upper bounds of S then

A. $C_1=C_2$ B. $C_1>C_2$

C. $C_1<C_2$ D. $C_1\neq C_2$

25. If $\text{Lim}\, x_n = l$ exist, then

A. $\underline{\text{Lim}}\, x_n = \overline{\text{Lim}}\, x_n = l$

B. $\underline{\text{Lim}}\, x_n \neq \overline{\text{Lim}}\, x_n = l$

C. $l = \underline{\text{Lim}}\, x_n \neq \overline{\text{Lim}}\, x_n$

D. $\underline{\text{Lim}}\, x_n \leq \overline{\text{Lim}}\, x_n \leq l$

26. Let $F_n = \left[-\frac{1}{n}, \frac{1}{n}\right]$ be given interval, then $\bigcap_{n=1}^{\infty} F_n$ is

A. A closed set B. Open set

C. Null set D. None of these

27. If X and Y are metric spaces and for every open set O ⊂ Y, f^{-1} (0) ⊂ X is open then,

A. f is continuous function

B. f is constant function

C. f is increasing function

D. f is decreasing function

28. The following $f(x)=\begin{cases} e^{\frac{1}{x}} & x\neq 0 \\ 0 & x=0 \end{cases}$ has

A. Removable discontinuity at $x=0$
B. Irremoveable discontinuity at $x=0$
C. Continuity at $x=0$
D. None of these

29. If x and y are independent then their covariance $E((x_1-\mu_x),(y-\mu_y))$ is equal to

A. Zero B. One
C. Two D. Three

30. For many real numbers a and b, $a\leq b$ the probability density function of a continuous random variable x is given by

A. $P(a\leq x\leq b)=\int_a^b f(x)dx$

B. $P(a\leq x\leq b)=-\int_a^b f(x)dx$

C. $P(a\leq x\leq b)=1-\int_a^b f(x)dx$

D. $P(a\leq x\leq b)=\int_a^b f(x)dx-1$

31. A card is drawn at random from the pack of playing cards. The probability of getting a face card is

A. 4/13 B. 13
C. 3/13 D. None of these

32. The relationship between mean μ, variance σ^2 and second moments about the origin μ_2^1 is

A. $\sigma^2=\mu_2^1-\mu^2$ B. $\sigma^2=\mu-\mu_2^1$
C. $\sigma^2=\mu_2^1+\mu$ D. None of these

33. A basic solution to the system $\bar{A}\,\bar{x}=\bar{b}$ is non degenerated if

A. No basic variable is equal to zero
B. No basic variable is negative
C. No basic variable is positive
D. None of these

34. The basic to $\begin{pmatrix}1 & 2 & 3\\ 2 & 1 & 5\end{pmatrix}\begin{pmatrix}x_1\\ x_2\\ x_3\end{pmatrix}=\begin{pmatrix}4\\ 5\end{pmatrix}$ is

A. $\begin{pmatrix}1 & 2\\ 2 & 1\end{pmatrix}$ B. $\begin{pmatrix}1 & 2\\ 1 & 2\end{pmatrix}$

C. $\begin{pmatrix}1 & 3 & 1\\ 5 & 6 & 2\end{pmatrix}$ D. $\begin{pmatrix}1 & 2 & 3\\ 2 & 1 & 5\end{pmatrix}$

35. The following have the solution $\begin{bmatrix}2 & 3\\ 4 & 6\end{bmatrix}\begin{bmatrix}x\\ y\end{bmatrix}=\begin{bmatrix}8\\ 16\end{bmatrix}$

A. $x=1, y=2$ B. $x=y=1$
C. $x=y=0$ D. None of these

36. A real quadratic form $X^T A X$ is positive definite if

A. All eigen values of $A>0$
B. All eigen values of $A<0$
C. All eigen values of $A=0$
D. None of these

37. A sequence $(a_n)_{n=1}^{\infty}$ is bounded if there is a real number S such that

A. $|a_n|\leq S$ for all n
B. $|a_n|\geq S$ for all n
C. $|a_n|=S$ for all n
D. None of these

38. The probability of a 4 turning up at least once in two tosses of a fair die is:

A. $\frac{1}{36}$ B. $\frac{7}{36}$
C. $\frac{13}{36}$ D. $\frac{11}{36}$

39. The standard deviation of the sum obtained in tossing a pair of fair dice is:

A. $\sqrt{\frac{31}{6}}$ B. $\sqrt{\frac{35}{6}}$
C. $\sqrt{\frac{37}{6}}$ D. $\sqrt{\frac{41}{6}}$

40. In a central grain store, it takes about 15 days to get the stock after placing the order and daily 500 tons are despatched to neighbouring markets. On an adhoc basis safety stock is assumed to be 10 days stock. The re-order point P is:

A. 12500 tons B. 14700 tons
C. 15100 tons D. 16000 tons

ANSWERS

1	2	3	4	5	6	7	8	9	10
A	A	A	D	B	B	B	C	A	A
11	**12**	**13**	**14**	**15**	**16**	**17**	**18**	**19**	**20**
A	A	D	C	A	A	A	A	B	B
21	**22**	**23**	**24**	**25**	**26**	**27**	**28**	**29**	**30**
B	A	C	A	A	A	A	A	A	A
31	**32**	**33**	**34**	**35**	**36**	**37**	**38**	**39**	**40**
C	A	A	A	D	A	A	D	B	A

Some Selected Explanatory Answers

1. Standard primal, using and introducing surplus variables $x_4 \geq 0$ and $x_5 \geq 0$ the standard form of the linear programming problem is minimize

$z = 4x_1 + 6x_2 + 18x_3 + 0S_1 + 0S_2$

$s.t.\ x_1 + 3x_2 - x_4 = 3$

$0x_1 + x_2 + 2x_1 - x_5 = 5$

$x_j \geq 0\ (j = 1, 2, ...5)$

Dual, If w_1, w_2 be the dual variable corresponding to each primal constraint– the dual problem is maximize $z^* = 3w_1 + 5w_2$ subject to the constraint

$w_1 + 0w_2 \leq 4$

$3w_1 + w_2 \leq 6$

$0w_1 + 2w_2 \leq 18$

$-w_1 + 0w_2 \leq 0$ and $0w_1 - w_2 \leq 0$

w_1 and w_2 unrestricted

2. $f(x^*) \leq g(y^*)$

i.e. solution to a L.P.P is equal to or less than the solution to its dual.

4. $M(x, y)\, dx + N(x, y)\, dy = 0$

$\Rightarrow M(x, y)\, dx = -N(x, y)\, dy$

$$\Rightarrow \frac{dx}{N(x, y)} = -\frac{dy}{M(x, y)}$$

$$\Rightarrow \frac{dM}{dy} = -\frac{dN}{dx}$$

$$\Rightarrow \frac{dx}{N(x, y)} + \frac{dy}{M(x, y)} = 0$$

Hence $M(x, y)\, dx + N(x, y)\, dy$ is exact only when $\frac{dM}{dy} = \frac{dN}{dx}$

7. Norm of α will be defined as

$\|\alpha\|^2 = (\alpha/\alpha)$

8. A. E–is $2m^2 + 5m + 2 = 0$

$\Rightarrow m = -2, -1/2$

$\therefore$ General solution is

$y = Ae^{-2x} + Be^{-\frac{1}{2}x}$

9. $$\frac{\partial z}{\partial x} = abe^{bt} \cos bx$$

$$\frac{\partial^2 z}{\partial x^2} = -ab^2 e^{bt} \sin bx$$

and $$\frac{\partial z}{\partial t} = abe^{bt} \sin bx$$

$$\frac{\partial^2 z}{\partial t^2} = ab^2\, e^{bt} \sin bx$$

$$\Rightarrow \frac{\partial^2 z}{\partial x^2} = -\frac{\partial^2 z}{\partial t^2}$$

10. General solution of a linear differential equation with constant co-efficient is = particular solution + C. F.

11. α and β are linearly dependent

$\Rightarrow C.\alpha + C'\beta = 0,\ C \neq 0$

$$\Rightarrow \alpha = \left(\frac{-C}{C}\right)\beta$$

$$\Rightarrow \alpha = c\,\beta,\ c = \frac{-C'}{C}$$

12. When f and g are two linear functionals on a vector space V then $f(\alpha)=0 \Rightarrow g(\alpha)=0$ states that g is a scalar multiple of f.

13. Here I is an identity as $(-i)^4=1$
$\Rightarrow O(-i)=4$
$\Rightarrow O(a)=P$
$\Rightarrow$ P is the least positive integer $\therefore a^P=c$ identity

14. $exp\,(expi\,\theta)=e^{e^{i\theta}}=e^{\cos\theta+i\sin\theta}$
$=e^{\cos\theta}\;e^{i\sin\theta}$
$=e^{\cos\theta}\;(\cos(\sin\theta))+i\sin(\sin\theta)$
$\therefore$ Real $(exp\,(expi\,\theta))=e^{\cos\theta}\cos(\sin\theta)$

15. $|z+5|^2+|z-5|^2=75$
$\Rightarrow |(x+5)+iy|^2+|(x-5)+iy|^2=75$
$\Rightarrow 2x^2+2y^2=25$
which is a circle.

16. y to be a rectifiable curve and z is a continuous function on y for z
$\int y\, f(z)dz$
and for $c\in$ C
$\int y\, f(z)dz=\int_{y+c} f(z-c)dz$

17. $\because a\in$ K is an alegebraic structure of degree n over F
where F is a field then
$\{F(a):F\}=n$
i.e. of order n

18. A and B are zero divisors if $AB=0 \Rightarrow A\neq 0$ and $B\neq 0$
Here $\begin{vmatrix}1 & 1\\1 & 1\end{vmatrix}\begin{vmatrix}1 & 0\\-1 & 0\end{vmatrix}=\begin{vmatrix}0 & 0\\0 & 0\end{vmatrix}$

19. Let 1 be the unity of the field F
$a.\,a_1^{-1}=1$ and $a.\,a_2^{-1}=1$
$\Rightarrow a.\,a_1^{-1}=a.\,a_2^{-1}$
$\Rightarrow a_1^{-1}=a_2^{-1}$

20. If f is a mapping from G to C, which is analytic and $R=d\,(a,\partial G)$
then for $a\in G$ and $|z-a|<R$

$$f(z)=\sum_{n=0}^{\infty}a_n(z-a)^n \text{ (by property of analyticity)}$$

23. $f(0+)=\lim_{x\to 0+}f(x)=\lim_{h\to 0}\cos(0+h)=1$
$f(0-)=\lim_{x\to 0-}f(x)=\lim_{h\to 0}-\cos(0-h)=-1$
$f(0+)\neq f(0-)$
Irremoveal discontinuity

24. Least upper bound mean supremum and by the property of supremum, supremum of a subset of real numbers is unique hence,
$C_1=C_2$.

25. If $\exists$ limit of a squence then LHL = RHL = $l(say)$
$\therefore \underline{\text{Lim}}\, \overline{x}_n=\overline{\text{Lim}}\, \overline{x}_n=l$

26. $F_n=\left[-\frac{1}{n},\frac{1}{n}\right]$ then $\tau_{n=1}^{\infty} F_n$ is a closed set, since there exist lower as well as upper bound for the interval

28. $f(0+)=\lim_{x\to 0+}e^{1/x}=\lim_{h\to 0}e^{(1/0+h)}$
$f(0-)=\lim_{x\to 0-}e^{1/x}=\lim_{h\to 0}e^{(1/0-h)}$
$f(0)=0$
$\therefore f(0+)=f(0-)\neq f(0)$
Removeable discontinuity

31. N(s) = 52, E = event getting face card
N(E) = 12
$\therefore P(E)=\frac{12}{52}=\frac{3}{13}$

32. $O^2=E((x-\mu)^2)=E((x^2-2\mu x+\mu^2))$
$=E(x^2)-2\mu E(x)+E(\mu^2)$
$=\mu_2^1-2\mu E(x)+E(\mu^2)$
$=\mu_2^1-\mu^2$

33. None of the basic variables is zero i.e. linearly independent

35. $\begin{bmatrix}2 & 3\\4 & 6\end{bmatrix}\begin{bmatrix}x\\y\end{bmatrix}=\begin{bmatrix}8\\16\end{bmatrix}$

Here $A = \begin{bmatrix} 2 & 3 \\ 4 & 6 \end{bmatrix}, X = \begin{bmatrix} x \\ y \end{bmatrix}, B = \begin{bmatrix} 8 \\ 16 \end{bmatrix}$

$\Rightarrow$ A X = B, rank (A) = rank (A/B),

= 1, infinitely many solution

36. $Q(x) = x^T Ax$ is positive definite

$\Leftrightarrow Q(x) > 0, x \neq 0$

$\Leftrightarrow$ All eigien values of A are > 0

37. Any sequence is bounded if $u \leq a_n \leq S \ \forall n$ i.e. sequence is both bounded above as well as bounded below

or $\langle a_n \rangle$ said to be bounded if $\exists$ a real no. S. s.t

$| a_n | \leq S, \forall n$

38. Events A_1 and A_2 are not mutually exclusive, but they are independent

$$\begin{bmatrix} \textit{Here}, A_1 = \text{event '4 on first toss'} \\ A_2 = \text{event '4 on second toss'} \\ A_1 \cup A_2 = \text{event 'atleast one 4 turns up} \end{bmatrix}$$

$$\begin{aligned} P(A_1 \cup A_2) &= P(A_1) + P(A_2) - P(A_1 \cap A_2) \\ &= P(A_1) + P(A_2) - P(A_1) P(A_2) \\ &= \frac{1}{6} + \frac{1}{6} - \frac{1}{6} \times \frac{1}{6} \\ &= \frac{11}{36} \end{aligned}$$

39. Suppose X and Y be points on two dice, any one of the values 1, 2, 3, 4, 5, 6 each with equal probability $\frac{1}{6}$.

$$E(x) = E(y) = \frac{1}{6}(1+2+3+4+5+6) = \frac{21}{6} = \frac{7}{2}$$

$$E(X+Y) = E(X) + E(Y) = \frac{7}{2} + \frac{7}{2} = 7$$

$$E(x^2) = E(y^2) = \frac{1}{6}(1^2+2^2+3^2+4^2+5^2+6^2) = \frac{91}{6}$$

$$\text{Var}(X) = \text{Var}(Y) = \frac{91}{6} - \left(\frac{7}{2}\right)^2 = \frac{35}{12}$$

$$\text{Standard deviation} = \sqrt{Var(X+Y)} = \sqrt{Var(X) + Var(Y)}$$

$$= \sqrt{\frac{35}{12} + \frac{35}{12}} = \sqrt{\frac{35}{6}}$$

40. Here safety stock B = 10 days stock = 10×500 = 5000 tons

L = 15 days & r = 500 tons

Re-order point P = B + Lr

= $5000 + 15 \times 500$

= 5000×7500 = 12500 tons

SET–11

CSIR–UGC (NET) MATHEMATICAL SCIENCES

PART-B

1. A function F from the set of natural numbers to integers defined by

$$f(n)=\begin{cases}\frac{n-1}{2}, \text{ when n is odd}\\ -\frac{n}{2}, \text{ when n is even}\end{cases}$$

A. One – one but not onto
B. Onto but not one – one
C. One – one and onto both
D. Neither one – one nor onto

2. Let z_1 and z_2 be two roots of the equation $z^2+ax+b=0$, z being complex. Further, assume that the origin, z_1 and z_2 from an equilateral triangle. Then

A. $a^2=b$
B. $a^2=2b$
C. $a^2=3b$
D. $a^2=4b$

3. If the system of linear equation

$x+2ay+az=0$
$x+2by+bz=0$
$x+4cy+cz=0$

has a non-zero solution, then a, b, c

A. are in A.P
B. are in G.P
C. are in H.P
D. satisfy $a+2b+3c=0$

4. The value of 'a' for which one root of the quadratic equation $(a^2-5a+3)x^2+(3a-1)x+2=0$, is twice the other root, is

A. $\frac{2}{3}$
B. $\frac{-2}{3}$
C. $\frac{1}{3}$
D. $\frac{1}{2}$

5. If $A=\begin{bmatrix} a & b \\ b & a\end{bmatrix}$ and $A^2=\begin{bmatrix}\alpha & \beta \\ \beta & \alpha\end{bmatrix}$, then

A. $\alpha=a^2+b^2,\ \beta=ab$
B. $\alpha=a^2+b^2,\ \beta=2ab$
C. $\alpha=a^2+b^2, \beta=a^2-b^2$
D. $\alpha=2ab,\ \beta=-a^2+b^2$

6. A student is to answer 10 out of 13 questions in an examination such that he must choose at least 4 from the first five questions. The number of choices available to him is

A. 140
B. 196
C. 280
D. 346

7. The sum of the series $\frac{1}{1.2}-\frac{1}{2.3}+\frac{1}{3.4}-\ldots\ldots\ldots$ upto ∞ is equal to

A. $2\log_e^2$
B. $\log_e^2-1$
C. $\log_e^2$
D. $\log_e\left(\frac{4}{e}\right)$

8. Let $f(x)=ax^2+bx+c$ be a polynomial function of second degree, if $f(1)=f(-1)$ and a, b, c are in AP, then $f^1(a), f^1(b)$ and $f^1(c)$ are in

A. AP
B. GP
C. HP
D. Arithmetico – Geometric progression

9. The sum of the radii of inscribed and circumscribed circles for an n sided regular polygon of side a, is

A. $a\cot\left(\frac{\pi}{n}\right)$
B. $\frac{a}{2}\cot\left(\frac{\pi}{2n}\right)$
C. $a\cot\left(\frac{\pi}{2n}\right)$
D. $\frac{a}{4}\cot\left(\frac{\pi}{2n}\right)$

10. The trignometric equation $\sin^{-1}x=2\sin^{-1}a$ has a solution for

A. $\frac{1}{2}<|a|<\frac{1}{2}$

B. all real values of a

C. $|a| < \frac{1}{2}$

D. None of these

11. If $F: R \to R$ satisfies $f(x+y) = f(x) + f(y)$, for all x, $y \in R$ and $f(1) = 7$, then $\sum_{r=1}^{n} f(r)$ is

A. $\frac{7n}{2}$ B. $\frac{7(n+1)}{2}$

C. $7n(n+1)$ D. $\frac{7n(n+1)}{2}$

12. If $f(x) = x^n$, then the value of $f(1) - \frac{f'(1)}{1!} + \frac{f''(1)}{2!} - \frac{f'''(1)}{3!} + \text{---} + \frac{(-1)^n f^n(1)}{n!}$ is

A. 2^n B. 2^{n-1}

C. 0 D. 1

13. Domain of the definition of the function $F(x) = \frac{3}{4-x^2} + \log_{10}(x^3 - x)$ is

A. $(1, 2)$

B. $(-1, 0) \cup (1, 2)$

C. $(1, 2) \cup (2, \infty)$

D. $(-1, 0) \cup (1, 2) \cup (2, \infty)$

14. $\lim_{x \to \frac{\pi}{2}} \frac{\left[1 - \tan\left(\frac{x}{2}\right)\right][1 - \sin x]}{\left[1 + \tan\left(\frac{x}{2}\right)\right][\pi - 2x]^3}$

A. $\frac{1}{8}$ B. 0

C. $\frac{1}{32}$ D. ∞

15. If $\lim_{x \to 0} \frac{\log(3+x) - \log(3-x)}{x} = k$, the value of k is

A. 0 B. $-\frac{1}{3}$

C. $\frac{2}{3}$ D. $-\frac{2}{3}$

16. Let $f(a) = g(a) = k$ and their n^{th} derivatives $f^n(a)$, $g^n(a)$ exist and are not equal for some n. Further if $\lim_{x \to \frac{\pi}{2}} \frac{f(a)g(x) - f(a) - g(a)f(x) + g(a)}{g(x) - f(x)} = 4$ then the value of k is

A. 4 B. 2

C. 1 D. 0

17. If the function $f(x) = 2x^3 - 9ax^2 + 12a^2x + 1$, where $a > 0$, attain its maximum and minimum at p and q respectively such that $p^2 = q$, then a equals

A. 3 B. 1

C. 2 D. $\frac{1}{2}$

18. If $f(y) = e^y$, $g(y) = y$, $y > 0$ and $f(t) = \int_0^t f(t-y)\, g(y) dy$, then

A. $f(t) = 1 - e^{-t}(1+t)$

B. $f(t) = e^t - (1+t)$

C. $f(t) = te^t$

D. $f(t) = te^{-t}$

19. If $f(a+b-x) = f(x)$, then $\int_a^b x f(x)\, dx$ is equal to

A. $\frac{a+b}{2} \int_a^b f(b-x) dx$

B. $\frac{a+b}{2} \int_a^b f(x) dx$

C. $\frac{b-a}{2} \int_a^b f(x) dx$

D. $\frac{a+b}{2} \int_a^b f(a+b-c) dx$

20. The value of $\lim_{x \to 0} \frac{\int_0^{x^2} \sec^2 t\, dt}{x \sin x}$ is

A. 3 B. 2

C. 1 D. –1

21. $\lim_{n\to\infty} \frac{1+2^4+3^4+.....+n^4}{n^5} - \lim_{x\to\infty} \frac{1+2^3+3^3+.....+n^3}{n^5}$ is

A. $\frac{1}{30}$ B. zero

C. $\frac{1}{4}$ D. $\frac{1}{5}$

22. Let $\frac{d}{dx}F(x) = \left(\frac{e^{\sin x}}{x}\right)$, $x>0$. If $\int_1^4 \frac{3}{x} e^{\sin x^3} dx = f(K) - f(1)$, then one of the possible values of K, is

A. 15 B. 16

C. 63 D. 64

23. The area of the region bounded by the curves $y = |x-1|$ and $y = 3 - |x|$ is

A. 2 sq. units B. 3 sq. units

C. 4 sq. units D. 6 sq. units

24. Let $f(x)$ be a function satisfying $f^1(x) = f(x)$ with $f(0) = 1$ and $g(x)$ be a function that satisfies $f(x) + g(x) = x^2$, then the value of the integral $\int_0^1 f(x).g(x)\,dx$, is

A. $e - \frac{e^2}{2} - \frac{5}{2}$ B. $e + \frac{e^2}{2} - \frac{3}{2}$

C. $e - \frac{e^2}{2} - \frac{3}{2}$ D. $e + \frac{e^2}{2} + \frac{5}{2}$

25. The solution of the differential equation,

$(1+y^2)+(x-e^{\tan^{-1}y})\frac{dy}{dx} = 0$, is

A. $(x-2) = Ke^{-\tan^{-1}y}$

B. $2xe^{-\tan^{-1}y} = e^{-2\tan^{-1}y} + k$

C. $xe^{-\tan^{-1}y} = \tan^{-1}y + k$

D. $2xe^{\tan^{-1}y} = e^{2\tan^{-1}y} + k$

26. Locus of centroid of the triangle whose vertices are $(a \cos t, a \sin t)$, $(b \sin t, -b \cos t)$ and $(1, 0)$, where t is a parameter, is

A. $(3x-1)^2 + (3y)^2 = a^2 - b^2$

B. $(3x-1)^2 + (3y)^2 = a^2 + b^2$

C. $(3x+1)^2 + (3y)^2 = a^2+b^2$

D. $(3x+1)^2 + (3y)^2 = a^2-b^2$

27. Two system of rectangular axes have the same origin. If a plane cuts them at distance a, b, c and a', b', c' from the origin, then

A. $\frac{1}{a^2}+\frac{1}{b^2}+\frac{1}{c^2}+\frac{1}{a'^2}+\frac{1}{b'^2}+\frac{1}{c'^2}=0$

B. $\frac{1}{a^2}+\frac{1}{b^2}-\frac{1}{c^2}+\frac{1}{a'^2}+\frac{1}{b'^2}-\frac{1}{c'^2}=0$

C. $\frac{1}{a^2}-\frac{1}{b^2}-\frac{1}{c^2}+\frac{1}{a'^2}+\frac{1}{b'^2}-\frac{1}{c'^2}=0$

D. $\frac{1}{a^2}+\frac{1}{b^2}+\frac{1}{c^2}-\frac{1}{a'^2}-\frac{1}{b'^2}-\frac{1}{c'^2}=0$

28. $\vec{a}, \vec{b}, \vec{c}$ are 3 vectors such that $\vec{a}+\vec{b}+\vec{c} = 0, |\vec{b}| = 2, |\vec{c}| = 3$, then $\vec{a}.\vec{b}+\vec{b}.\vec{c}+\vec{c}.\vec{a}$ is equals to

A. 0 B. –7

C. 7 D. 1

29. A particle acted on by constant forces $4\hat{i}+\hat{j}-3\hat{k}$ to $3\hat{i}+\hat{j}-\hat{k}$ displaced from the point $5\hat{i}+4\hat{j}+\hat{k}$. The total work done by the forces is

A. 20 units B. 30 units

C. 40 units D. 50 units

30. The median of a set of 9 distinct observations is 20.5. If each of the largest 4 observations of the set is increased by 2, then the median of the new set

A. Is increased by 2

B. Is decreased by 2

C. Is two times the original median

D. Remains the same as that of the original set

31. In an experiment with 15 observations on x, the following results were available $\sum x^2 = 2830$, $\sum x = 170$ one observation that was 20 was found to be wrong and was replaced by the correct value 30. Then the corrected variance is

A. 78.00 B. 188.66

C. 177.33 D. 8.33

32. Five hours are in race, Mr. A selects two of the horses at random and bets on them. The probability that Mr. A selected the winning horse is

A. $\frac{4}{5}$ B. $\frac{3}{5}$

C. $\frac{1}{5}$ D. $\frac{2}{5}$

33. Events A, B, C are mutually exclusive events such that $P(A) = \frac{3x+1}{3}$, $P(B) = \frac{1-x}{4}$ and $P(C) = \frac{1-2x}{2}$. The set of possible value of x are in the interval

A. $\left[\frac{1}{3}, \frac{1}{2}\right]$ B. $\left[\frac{1}{3}, \frac{2}{3}\right]$

C. $\left[\frac{1}{3}, \frac{13}{3}\right]$ D. $[0, 1]$

34. The mean and variance of a random variable x having binomial distribution are 4 and 2 respectively, then p (x = 1) is

A. $\frac{1}{32}$ B. $\frac{1}{16}$

C. $\frac{1}{8}$ D. $\frac{1}{4}$

35. The resultant of forces $\overline{P}$ and $\overline{Q}$ is $\overline{R}$. If $\overline{Q}$ is doubled then $\overline{R}$ is doubled. If the direction of $\overline{Q}$ is reversed, then $\overline{R}$ is again doubled, then $P^2 : Q^2 : R^2$ is

A. 3 : 1 : 1 B. 2 : 3 : 2

C. 1 : 2 : 3 D. 2 : 3 : 1

36. These refer to decision situations wherein the decision-maker chooses from among several possible outcomes where possibilities of occurrence can be stated (or determined) objectively from the past data.

A. Decisions under certainity

B. Decisions under uncertainty

C. Decision under risk

D. Decisions under conflict

37. The characteristic function of the random variable X having density function $F(x) = Ce^{-a|x|}, -\infty < x < \infty$, where $a > 0$ and C is a suitable constant is:

A. $\frac{a^2}{a^2+\omega^2}$ B. $\frac{a^2}{a^2-\omega^2}$

C. $\frac{a^2+\omega^2}{a^2}$ D. $\frac{a^2-\omega^2}{a^2}$

38. The generators of $\{1, \omega, \omega^2\}$ are:

A. 1 B. ω

C. ω^2 D. ω and ω^2

39. If $a \in R^+$ then there is precisely one positive real number b such that b^2 equals:

A. $-a$ B. a

C. $-a^2$ D. a^2

40. The integral $\int_{|z|=2} \frac{\cos z}{z^3} dz$ equals:

A. $-2\pi i$ B. $-\pi i$

C. $2\pi i$ D. πi

ANSWERS

1	2	3	4	5	6	7	8	9	10
C	C	C	A	B	B	D	A	B	D
11	**12**	**13**	**14**	**15**	**16**	**17**	**18**	**19**	**20**
D	C	D	C	C	A	C	B	B	C
21	**22**	**23**	**24**	**25**	**26**	**27**	**28**	**29**	**30**
D	D	C	C	D	B	D	B	C	D
31	**32**	**33**	**34**	**35**	**36**	**37**	**38**	**39**	**40**
A	D	A	A	B	C	A	D	B	B

Some Selected Explanatory Answer

1. $f(n) = \begin{cases} \frac{n-1}{2}, \text{when n is odd} \\ -\frac{n}{2}, \text{when n is even} \end{cases}$

and $f : N \to I$ Where N is the set of natural numbers and I is the set of integers

Let $x, y, \in N$ and both are even

then $f(x) = f(y)$

$$-\frac{x}{2} = -\frac{y}{2} \Rightarrow x = y$$

Again $x, y \in N$ and both are odd then $f(x) = f(y)$

$\frac{x-1}{2} = \frac{y-1}{2} \Rightarrow x = y$

i.e. mapping is one–one

Since each negative integer is an image of even natural number and positive integer is an image of odd natural number. So mapping is onto. Hence, mapping is one – one, onto.

2. If z_1, z_2, and z_3 are the vertices of a equilateal triangle then

$z_1^2 + z_2^2 + z_3^2 = z_1 z_2 + z_2 z_3 + z_3 z_1$

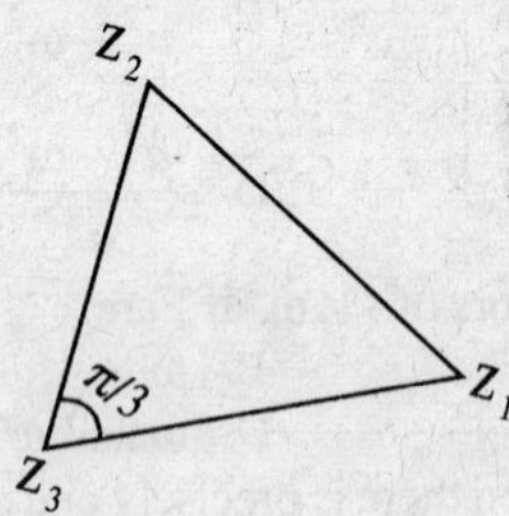

but $z_3 = 0$

$\Rightarrow z_1^2 + z_2^2 = z_1 z_2 \Rightarrow (z_1 + z_2)^2 = 3 z_1 z_2$ ...(*i*)

Again z_1, z_2 are the roots of

$z^2 + az + b = 0$

then $z_1 + z_2 = -a$

and $z_1 z_2 = b$

Putting in (*i*), we have

$(-a)^2 = 3b.$

$\Rightarrow \quad a^2 = 3b$

3. The system of linear equation has a non-zero solution then

$$\begin{vmatrix} 1 & 2a & a \\ 1 & 3b & b \\ 1 & 4c & c \end{vmatrix} = 0$$

$R_2 \to R_2 - R_1, R_3 \to R_3 - R_1$

$$\begin{vmatrix} 1 & 2a & a \\ 0 & 3b-2a & b-a \\ 0 & 4c-2a & c-a \end{vmatrix} = 0$$

$\Rightarrow (3b-2a)\ (c-a) - (4c-2a)\ (b-a) = 0$

$\Rightarrow 3bc - 3ba - 2ac + 2a^2 = 4bc - 2ab - 4ac + 2a^2$

$\Rightarrow 4ac - 2ac = 4bc - 2ab - 3bc + 3ab$

$\Rightarrow 2ac = bc + ab$

Dividing by *abc*, we get

$\frac{2}{b} = \frac{1}{a} + \frac{1}{c}$

i.e. *a*,*b*,*c* are in HP

4. $(a^2 - 5a + 3)\,x^2 + (3a-1)\,x + 2 = 0$

Let α and 2 α are the roots of this equation then

$$\alpha + 2\alpha = -\frac{3a-1}{(a^2-5a+3)}$$

$$\Rightarrow 3\alpha = -\frac{(3a-1)}{(a^2-5a+3)}$$

$$\text{and } \alpha.2\alpha = \frac{2}{(a^2-5a+3)}$$

$$\Rightarrow 2\alpha^2 = \frac{2}{(a^2-5a+3)}$$

$$\Rightarrow 2\left[\frac{-(3a-1)}{3(a^2-5a+3)}\right]^2 = \frac{2}{(a^2-5a+3)}$$

$$\Rightarrow \frac{(3a-1)^2}{9(a^2-5a+3)^2} = \frac{1}{(a^2-5a+3)}$$

$\Rightarrow (3a-1)^2 = 9(a^2 - 5a + 3)$

$\Rightarrow 9a^2 + 1 - 6a = 9a^2 - 45a + 27$

$\Rightarrow 45a - 6a = 27 - 1$

$\Rightarrow 39a = 26$

$\Rightarrow a = \frac{2}{3}$

5. $A = \begin{bmatrix} a & b \\ b & a \end{bmatrix}, A^2 = \begin{bmatrix} \alpha & \beta \\ \beta & \alpha \end{bmatrix}$

$$A^2 = A.A = \begin{bmatrix} a & b \\ b & a \end{bmatrix}\begin{bmatrix} a & b \\ b & a \end{bmatrix}$$

$$A^2 = \begin{bmatrix} a^2+b^2 & ab+ba \\ ba+ab & b^2+a^2 \end{bmatrix}$$

$$= \begin{bmatrix} a^2+b^2 & 2ab \\ 2ab & a^2+b^2 \end{bmatrix}$$

$$\Rightarrow \begin{bmatrix} \alpha & \beta \\ \beta & \alpha \end{bmatrix} = \begin{bmatrix} a^2+b^2 & 2ab \\ 2ab & a^2+b^2 \end{bmatrix}$$

$\Rightarrow \alpha = a^2 + b^2, \beta = 2ab$

6. The number of choices available to him is

$= {}^5C_4 \times {}^8C_6 + {}^5C_5 \times {}^8C_5$

$= \frac{5!}{4!1!} \times \frac{8!}{6!\times 2!} + \frac{5!}{5!0!} \times \frac{8!}{5!3!}$

$= 5 \times \frac{8\times 7}{2} + 1 \times \frac{8\times 7\times 6}{3\times 2}$

$= 5\times 4\times 7 + 8\times 7$

$= 140 + 56 = 196$

7. $\frac{1}{1.2} - \frac{1}{2.3} + \frac{1}{3.4}$..............

$= \left(1-\frac{1}{2}\right) - \left(\frac{1}{2}-\frac{1}{3}\right) + \left(\frac{1}{3}-\frac{1}{4}\right)$..........

$= 1 - 2.\frac{1}{2} + 2.\frac{1}{3} - 2.\frac{1}{4} + ...$

$= 2\left[1 - \frac{1}{2} + \frac{1}{3} - \frac{1}{4} ....\right] - 1$

$= 2\log(1+1) - 1$

$= 2\log 2 - \log e$

$= \log 4 - \log e$

$= \log\frac{4}{e}$

8. Let $f(x) = ax^2 + bx + c$

$f(1) = a+b+c$

$f(-1) = a-b+c$

$\Rightarrow f(1) = f(-1)$

$\Rightarrow a+b+c = a-b+c$

$\Rightarrow 2b = 0$

$\Rightarrow b = 0$

i.e., $f(x) = ax^2 + c$

$f^1(x) = 2ax$

$f^1(a) = 2a^2, f^1(b) = 2ab, f^1(c) = 2ac$

Now $2f^1(b) = f^1(a) + f^1(c)$

$2.\ 2ab = 2a^2 + 2ac$

$2b = a + b$

$\Rightarrow$ *a, b, c* are in AP

$\Rightarrow f^1(a), f^1(b), f^1(c)$ are in AP

9. $AB = a$

$ON \perp AB$ and $AN = BN$

In Δ AON

$\tan\frac{\pi}{n} = \frac{AN}{ON}$

$ON = AN\cot\frac{\pi}{n}$

$= \frac{a}{2}\cot\frac{\pi}{n}$

and $\sin\frac{\pi}{n} = \frac{AN}{OA}$

$OA = AN\ \text{cosec}\frac{\pi}{n} = \frac{a}{2}\ \text{cosec}\frac{\pi}{n}$

Sum of the radii $= ON + OA$

$= \frac{a}{2}\cot\frac{\pi}{n} + \frac{a}{2}\ \text{cosec}\frac{\pi}{n}$

$= \frac{a}{2}\left[\frac{\cos\frac{\pi}{n}}{\sin\frac{\pi}{n}}\right] + \frac{a}{2}.\frac{1}{\sin\pi/n}$

$= \frac{a}{2}.\frac{1}{\sin\pi/n}\left(\cos\pi/n + 1\right)$

$= \frac{a}{2} \times \frac{1}{2\sin\pi/2n\cos\pi/2n} \times 2\cos^2\pi/2n$

$= \frac{a}{2}\cot\frac{\pi}{2n}$

10. $\sin^{-1}x = 2\sin^{-1}a$

$\Rightarrow -\frac{\pi}{2} \le \sin^{-1}x \le \frac{\pi}{2}$

$\Rightarrow -\frac{\pi}{2} \le 2\sin^{-1}a \le \frac{\pi}{2}$

$\Rightarrow -\frac{\pi}{4} \le \sin^{-1}a \le \frac{\pi}{4}$

$\Rightarrow \sin\left(-\frac{\pi}{4}\right) \le a \le \sin\frac{\pi}{4}$

$\Rightarrow -\frac{1}{\sqrt{2}} \le a \le \frac{1}{\sqrt{2}}$

$\Rightarrow |a| \le \frac{1}{\sqrt{2}}$

No option is correct

11. $\sum_{r=1}^{n} f(r) = f(1) + f(2) + f(3) + ... + f(n)$

$= f(1) + 2f(1) + 3f(1) .... + nf(1)$

[since $f(x+y) = f(x) + f(y)$]

$= (1+2+3+........+n)f(1)$

$= \frac{n(n+1)}{2}.7 = \frac{7n(n+1)}{2}$

12. $f(x)=x^n \Rightarrow f(1)=1$

$f'(x)=n\,x^{n-1} \Rightarrow f'(1)=n$

$f''(x)=n(n-1)\,x^{n-2} \Rightarrow f''(1)=n(n-1)$

$f^n(x)=n(n-1)(n-2)............2.1$

$f^n(1)=n(n-1)(n-2)............2.1$

We have

$$f(1)-\frac{f'(1)}{1!}+\frac{f''(1)}{2!}-\frac{f'''(1)}{3!}+..................+\frac{(-1)^n f^{\,n}(1)}{n\,!}$$

$$=1-\frac{n}{1!}+\frac{n(n-1)}{2!}-\frac{n(n-1)(n-2)}{3!}+........+\frac{(-1)^n n(n-1)(n-2)..........2!}{n!}$$

$=(1-1)^n=0$

13. $f(x)=\dfrac{3}{4-x^2}+\log_{10}(x^3-x)$

For domain of $f(x)$

$\log_{10}(x^3-x)>0$

$\Rightarrow x^3-x>0$

$\Rightarrow x(x-1)(x+1)>0$

$-\;+\;-\;+$

$-1\quad 0\quad 1$

Region is $(-1,0)\cup(1,\infty)$

common region is $(-1,0)\cup(1,2)\cup(2,\infty)$

14. $$\lim_{x\to\frac{\pi}{2}}\frac{\left[1-\tan\frac{x}{2}\right][1-\sin x]}{\left[1+\tan\frac{x}{2}\right][\pi-2x]^3}$$

Let $x=\dfrac{\pi}{2}-h$ as $x\to\dfrac{\pi}{2}, h\to 0$

$$\therefore \lim_{h\to 0}\frac{1-\tan\left(\frac{\pi}{4}-\frac{h}{2}\right)}{1+\tan\left(\frac{\pi}{4}+\frac{h}{2}\right)}\cdot\frac{(1-\cos h)}{(2h)^3}$$

$$\Rightarrow \lim_{h\to 0}\frac{1}{4}\cdot\frac{\tan\frac{h}{2}}{\frac{h}{2}\times 2}\times\left(\frac{\sin\frac{h}{2}}{\frac{h}{2}}\right)^2\times\frac{1}{4}$$

$$\Rightarrow \lim_{h\to 0}\frac{1}{32}\cdot\frac{\tan\frac{h}{2}}{\frac{h}{2}}\times\left(\frac{\sin\frac{h}{2}}{\frac{h}{2}}\right)^2=\frac{1}{32}$$

15. $$\lim_{x\to 0}\frac{\log(3+x)-\log(3-x)}{x}=k$$

Applying L' Hospital rule

$$\Rightarrow \lim_{x\to 0}\frac{\left[\frac{1}{3+x}+\frac{1}{3-x}\right]}{1}=k$$

$\Rightarrow \dfrac{1}{3}+\dfrac{1}{3}=\text{k}$

$\Rightarrow \text{k}=\dfrac{2}{3}$

16. $$\lim_{x\to a}\frac{f(a)\,g(x)-f(a)-g(a)\,f(x)+g(a)}{g(x)-f(x)}=4$$

Applying L' Hospital rule

$$\Rightarrow \lim_{x\to a}\frac{f(a)\,g'(x)-g(a)\,f'(x)}{g'(x)-f'(x)}=4$$

$$\Rightarrow \lim_{x\to a}\frac{kg'(x)-k\,f'(x)}{g'(x)-f'(x)}=4$$

$$\Rightarrow \lim_{x\to a}\frac{k\left[g'(x)-f'(x)\right]}{g'(x)-f'(x)}=4$$

$\Rightarrow k=4$

17. $f(x)=2x^3-9ax^2+12a^2x+1$

$\Rightarrow f'(x)=6x^2-18ax+12a^2=0$

$\Rightarrow 6[x^2-3ax+2a^2]=0$

$\Rightarrow x^2-2ax-ax+2a^2=0$

$\Rightarrow x(x-2a)-a(x-2a)=0$

$\Rightarrow (x-a)(x-2a)=0$

$\Rightarrow x=a,\qquad x=2a$

$f''(x)=12x-18a$

at $x=a$

$f(x)$ will be maximum

i.e., $p=a$

at $x=2$ a

$f''(x)=24a-18a=6a$

$f(x)$ will be minimum

i.e., $q=2a$

Given $p^2=q$

$a^2=2a$

$\Rightarrow a=2$

18. $f(t)=\int_0^t f(t-y)\,g(y)\,dy$

$=\int_o^t e^{t-y}.y dy = e^t\int_o^t e^{-y} y dy$

$=e^t\left[\left(-ye^{-y}\right)_o^t-\int_0^t 1(-e^{-y})dy\right]$

$=e^t\left[\left(-te^{-t}-0\right)-(e^{-y})_0^t\right]$

$=e^t\left[-te^{-t}-(e^{-t}-1)\right]$

$=\left[1-e^{-t}(1+t)\right]e^t$

$=e^t-(1+t)$

19. $\text{I}=\int_a^b x f(x)dx$

$\text{I}=\int_a^b (a+b-x)f(a+b-x)dx$

$=\int_a^b (a+b-x)f(x)dx \quad [\because f(a+b-x)=f(x)]$

$=(a+b)\int_a^b f(x)\,dx-\text{I}$

$\Rightarrow \text{I}=\frac{a+b}{2}\int_a^b f(x)\,dx$

20. $\lim_{x\to 0}\frac{\int_0^{x^2}\sec^2 t dt}{x\sin x},\ \left(\frac{0}{0}\text{form}\right)$

Applying L' Hospital rule

$=\lim_{x\to 0}\frac{\sec^2 x^2.2x}{x\cos x+\sin x}$

Again applying L'Hospital rule

$=\lim_{x\to 0}\frac{2\times 2\sec^2 x^2.\tan x^2.2x+2\sec^2 x^2}{-x\sin x+\cos x+\cos x}$

$=\frac{0+2\sec^2 0}{0+2\cos 0}=1$

21. $\lim_{n\to\infty}\frac{1+2^4+3^4+........+n^4}{n^5}$

$-\lim_{n\to\infty}\frac{1+2^4+3^4+........+n^4}{n^5}$

$=\lim_{n\to\infty}\frac{1}{n}\sum_{r=1}^{n}\left(\frac{r}{n}\right)^4-\lim_{n\to\infty}\frac{1}{n}\times\lim_{n\to\infty}\frac{1}{n}\sum_{r=1}^{n}\left(\frac{r}{n}\right)^3$

$=\int_0^1 x^4\,dx-\lim_{n\to\infty}.\frac{1}{n}\int_0^1 x^3 dx$

$=\left[\frac{x^5}{5}\right]_0^1-0=\frac{1}{5}$

22. $\frac{d}{dx}\text{F}.(x)=\frac{e^{\sin x}}{x},\ x>0$

Integrating

$\text{F}(x)=\int\frac{e^{\sin x}}{x}dx \qquad ...(i)$

Also $\int_1^4\frac{3}{x}\ e^{\sin x}dx=\int_1^4\frac{3x^2}{x^3}.\ e^{\sin x^3}dx$

$=\text{F}(\text{k})-\text{F}(1)$

Let $x^3=z\Rightarrow 3x^2dx=dz$

$\Rightarrow\int_1^{64}\frac{e^{\sin z}}{z}\ dz=\text{F}(\text{k})-\text{F}(1)$

Using eq. (i)

$\left[\text{F}(z)\right]_1^{64}=\text{F}(k)-\text{F}(1)$

$\text{F}(64)-\text{F}(1)=\text{F}(k)-\text{F}(1)$

$\Rightarrow k=64$

23. $y=|x-1|$

$y=x-1$ and $y=-(x-1)$

$y=x-1$ and $y=-x+1$

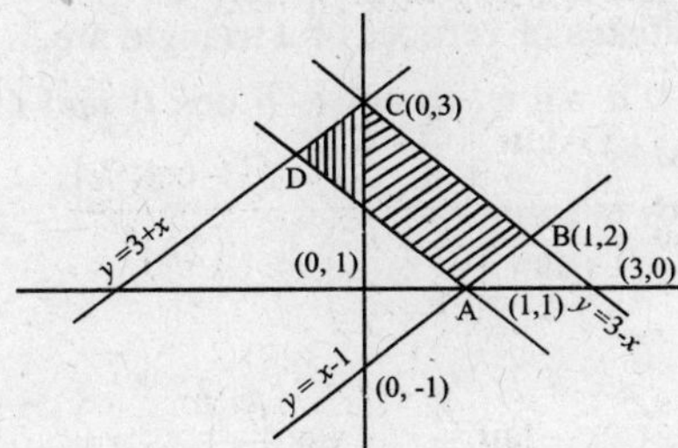

Also $y=3-|x|$

$y=3-x$ and $y=3+x$

Solving $y=x-1$ and $y=3-x$

$\Rightarrow x-1=3-x$
$2x=4 \Rightarrow x=2$
and $y=3-2$
$y=1$
$AB^2=(2-1)^2+(1-0)^2=1+1=2$
$AB=\sqrt{2}$
$BC^2=(2-0)^2+(1-3)^2$
$=4+4=2\sqrt{2}$
Area of rectangle ABCD = AB × BC
$\sqrt{2}\times 2\sqrt{2}=4$ sq. units.

24. Given $f'(x)=f(x)$ and $f(0)=1$
then let $f(x)=e^x$
Also $f(x)+g(x)=x^2$
$g(x)=x^2-e^x$
Again

$$\int_0^1 f(x)\,g(x)\,dx=\int_0^1 e^x(x^2-e^x)dx$$
$$=\int_0^1(x^2e^x-e^{2x})\,dx$$
$$=\int_0^1 x^2e^x dx-\int_0^1 e^{2x}dx$$
$$=\left[x^2e^x-\int 2xe^x dx\right]_0^1-\frac{1}{2}\left[e^{2x}\right]_0^1$$
$$=\left[x^2\,e^x-2\right]\left(xe^x-e^x\right)_0^1-\frac{1}{2}\left(e^2-e^0\right)$$
$$=\left[x^2\,e^x-x\,e^x+e\right]_0^1-\frac{1}{2}\;e^2+\frac{1}{2}$$
$$=\left[(1-2+2)e^1-(0-0+2)e^0\right]-\frac{1}{2}e^2+\frac{1}{2}$$
$$=[e-2]-\frac{1}{2}e^2+\frac{1}{2}$$
$$=e-\frac{1}{2}e^2-\frac{3}{2}$$

26. Co-ordinates of vertices of a triangle are (a cos t, a sin t), (b sin t,–b cos t) and (1, 0) centroid is

$$x=\frac{a\cos t+b\,\text{sint}\,t+1}{3}$$

$\Rightarrow 3x-1=a\cos t+b\sin t$ ...(*i*)

and $y=\dfrac{a\sin t-b\cos t}{3}$

$\Rightarrow 3y=a\sin t-b\,\text{cost}\,t$ ... (*ii*)

Squaring and adding (*i*) and (*ii*), we get

$(3x-1)^2+(3y)^2=(a\cos t+b\sin t)^2$
$+(a\sin t-b\,\text{cost}\,t)^2$

$(3x-1)^2+(3y)^2=a^2+b^2$

37. Since $F(x)$ is density function $\int_{-\infty}^{\infty}F(x)dx=1$

$$C\int_{-\infty}^{\infty}e^{-a|x|}dx=C\left[\int_{-\infty}^{0}e^{-a(x)}dx+\int_{0}^{\infty}e^{-a(x)}dx\right]$$
$$=C\left[\frac{e^{ax}}{a}\right]_{-\infty}^{0}+C\left[\frac{e^{-ax}}{-a}\right]_{0}^{\infty}=\frac{2C}{a}=1$$
$$\Rightarrow C=\frac{a}{2}$$

The characteristic function

$$E(e^{i\omega x})=\int_{-\infty}^{\infty}e^{i\omega x}F(x)dx$$
$$=\frac{a}{2}\left[\int_{-\infty}^{0}e^{i\omega x}e^{-a(-x)}dx+\int_{0}^{\infty}e^{i\omega x}e^{-ax}dx\right]$$
$$=\frac{a}{2}\left[\int_{-\infty}^{0}e^{(a+i\omega)x}dx+\int_{0}^{\infty}e^{-(a-i\omega)x}dx\right]$$
$$=\frac{a}{2}\left|\frac{e^{(a+i\omega)x}}{(a+i\omega)}\right|_{-\infty}^{0}+a\left|\frac{e^{-(a-i\omega)x}}{-(a-i\omega)}\right|_{0}^{\infty}$$
$$=\frac{a}{2(a+i\omega)}+\frac{a}{2(a-i\omega)}$$
$$=\frac{a^2}{a^2+\omega^2}$$

SET–12

CSIR–UGC (NET) MATHEMATICAL SCIENCES

PART-B

1. Let $\{a_n\}_{n=1}^{\infty}$ be a sequence converges to 0 and $\{b_n\}_{n=1}^{\infty}$ b∈ a sequence that is bounded, then $\{a_n b_n\}_{n=1}^{\infty}$ is a sequence that

A. Converges to one
B. Converges to zero
C. In divergent sequence
D. None of these

2. P: Every bounded sequence is convergent
Q: Every convergent sequence is bounded

A. P and Q are true
B. P is true, Q is false
C. Q is true, P is false
D. P and Q are false

3. If f is Riemann integrable with respect to x on $[a, b]$ then

A. f is increasing and x is bounded function
B. f is bounded and x is decreasing function
C. f and x are both bounded
D. f and x are both increasing

4. Let R be a commutative ring with unit element whose only ideals are (o) and R itself then

A. R is finite integral domain
B. R is integral domain
C. Division ring
D. None of these

5. Let G be a group of square matrices of same order with respect to matrix multiplication then it is not a

A. Quasi group B. Abelian group
C. Semi group D. None of these

6. If given permutations are $A = \begin{pmatrix} 1 & 2 & 3 & 4 & 5 \\ 2 & 3 & 1 & 5 & 4 \end{pmatrix}$ $B = \begin{pmatrix} 1 & 2 & 3 & 4 & 5 \\ 1 & 3 & 4 & 5 & 2 \end{pmatrix}$ find BA

A. $\begin{pmatrix} 1 & 2 & 3 & 4 & 5 \\ 2 & 1 & 5 & 4 & 3 \end{pmatrix}$ B. $\begin{pmatrix} 2 & 1 & 5 & 3 & 5 \\ 1 & 6 & 4 & 2 & 1 \end{pmatrix}$

C. $\begin{pmatrix} 1 & 2 & 3 & 4 & 5 \\ 1 & 2 & 5 & 4 & 1 \end{pmatrix}$ D. $\begin{pmatrix} 1 & 2 & 3 & 4 & 5 \\ 1 & 2 & 3 & 4 & 5 \end{pmatrix}$

7. If L_S be the number of customer in the system, L_q be the number of customer in the queue, in the system then

A. $L_S \geq L_q$ always B. $L_S < L_q$ always
C. $L_S \neq L_q$ always D. $L_S < L_S$ never

8. For M|M|1|N system, the expected waiting time in the system for $p = 1$ is

A. $w_s = \dfrac{N}{2\lambda}$ B. $w_s = \dfrac{N}{2}$

C. $w_s = \dfrac{1}{\lambda}$ D. None of these

9. Under exponential assumptions, P,{more than one arrivals occurs in $\Delta t = 0$ }is

A. Zero B. Positive
C. Negative D. None of these

10. The hyperplanes $\bar{c}_1\bar{x} = z_1$ are $\bar{c}_2\bar{x} = z_2$ are parallel, if

A. $C_1 = \lambda c_2, \lambda \neq 0$ B. $Z_1 = \lambda c_2, \lambda \neq 0$
C. $\lambda c_1 = z_1$ D. $\lambda c_2 = z_2$

11. Given $\begin{pmatrix} 2 & 1 & -1 \\ 3 & 2 & 1 \end{pmatrix}\begin{pmatrix} x_1 \\ x_2 \\ x_3 \end{pmatrix} = \begin{pmatrix} 2 \\ 3 \end{pmatrix}$ the one of the basis is

A. $\begin{pmatrix} 2 & 1 \\ 3 & 2 \end{pmatrix}$ B. $\begin{pmatrix} 2 & 1 & -1 \\ 3 & 2 & 1 \end{pmatrix}$

C. $\begin{pmatrix} 2 & 3 \\ 2 & 2 \end{pmatrix}$ D. $\begin{pmatrix} 1 & 6 \\ 3 & 4 \end{pmatrix}$

12. P : The intersection of any number of subspaces of a vector space V(f) is a subspace of V(f)

Q : The union of any number of subspaces of a vector space V(f) is a subspace of V(f)

A. P is false
B. P is true, Q is false
C. P and Q both true
D. P and Q both false

13. Let V be finite dimensional vector space, T is a zero transformation on V, then null space of T is
A. V B. {0}
C. ϕ D. None of these

14. A linear transformation T from V on to W, is non-singular if
A. $T\alpha = 0 \Rightarrow \alpha = 0$
B. $T\alpha = 0 \Rightarrow \alpha \neq 0$
C. $T\alpha = C \Rightarrow \alpha = 0$
D. None of these

15. If W is a subspace of, V and $\alpha, \beta \in W$, then for any scalar c
A. $c\alpha + \beta \in W$ B. $c\alpha + \beta \in V$
C. $c\alpha + \beta \notin V$ D. $c\alpha + \beta \notin W$

16. If $T_1(z) = \dfrac{z+2}{z+3}$ and $T_2(z) = \dfrac{z}{z+1}$, then $T_2^{-1}T_1(z)$ is
A. $z+3$ B. $z+2$
C. $z+4$ D. $z-3$

17. The amplitude of the complex number $\left(\dfrac{1}{1-2i}+\dfrac{3}{1+i}\right)\left(\dfrac{3+4i}{2-4i}\right)$ is given by
A. $\tan^{-1} 6$ B. $\tan^{-1} 9$
C. $\tan^{-1} 3$ D. $\tan^{-1}\dfrac{3}{2}$

18. If G is a open connected set in C and $f: G \to C$ is a continuous function, then f is a branch of logarithm if for $z \in G$
A. $z = \sin f(z)$ B. $z = \cos f(z)$
C. $z = \exp f(z)$ D. $z = f(z)$

19. If Υ is a rectifiable curve and f is continuous function on $\{\Upsilon\}$, then
A. $\int_{\Upsilon} f = -\int_{\Upsilon} f$ B. $\int_{\Upsilon} f\,dt = -\int_{-\upsilon} f\,dt$
C. $\int_{\Upsilon} f\,dt = -\int_{\Upsilon} f\,dt$ D. $\int_{\Upsilon} f\,dt = \int_{-\Upsilon} f\,dt$

20. $\dfrac{\partial^2 z}{\partial x^2} - \dfrac{\partial^2 z}{\partial y^2} + \dfrac{\partial z}{\partial x} - \dfrac{\partial z}{\partial y} = 0$ has the solution
A. $z = f_1(y-x) + e^x f_2(y-x)$
B. $z = f_1(y+x) + f_2(y-x)$
C. $z = e^{-x} f(y-x)$
D. $z = f_1(y+x) + e^{-x} f_2(y-x)$

21. If y_1 and y_2 are two solution of $y'' + p(x)y' + q(x)y = 0$ then for general solution of this general equation y_1 and y_2 are
A. Linearly dependent
B. Linearly independent
C. Proprotional
D. None of these

22. What is the order and degree of a differential equation $\left[1+(y')^2\right]^{3/2} - py'' = 0$?
A. First order, second degree
B. Second order, first degree
C. Second order, second degree
D. Third order, second degree

23. The general integral of the partial differential equation $p_2 + p_3 = 1 + p_1$
A. $f(x_1 + z_1 x_1 + x_2) = 0$
B. $f(x_1 + x_2, x_1 + x_3) = 0$
C. $f(x_1 + z_1 x_1 + x_2, x_1 + x_3) = 0$
D. None of these

24. P : Cauchy sequence is convergent
Q : Cauchy sequence is bounded
A. P and Q both true B. P is false
C. Q is false D. P and Q both true

25. Suppose that E (x, y) is a function of two variables (vectors) $x \in E^n$ and $y \in E^m$ both max. min. E(x, y) and mini.max. E(x, y) exist. Then necessary and sufficient condition for E(x, y) to posses a saddle point (x^*, y^*) is that
A. $\max_x \min_y E(x, y) = (x^*, y^*) = \min_y \max_x E(x, y)$
B. $\max_x \min_y E(x, y) \leq \max_x \min_y E(x, y)$
C. $\min_y E(x, y) \leq \max_x E(x, y)$
D. None of these

26. If x_0 is an optimal solution to the primal then an optimal solution to the dual is
A. $w_0 = C_B^{-1} B$
B. $w_0 = B^{-1} C_B$ where B is the primal optimal basic

C. $w_0 = BC_B$

D. None of these

27. The value of the game

	I	II	III
AI	6	8	6
II	4	12	2

A. 6 for A and – 6 for B

B. – 6 for A and 2 for B

C. 3 for A and 12 for B

D. None of these

28. Let $f(z) = \sum_{n=0}^{\infty} \frac{a_n}{n+1} z^n$ and $f'(z) = \sum_{n=0}^{\infty} a_n z^n$ have the radius of converges L and L' respectively, then

A. L>L'

B. L<L'

C. L=L'

D. None of these

29. The sequence $\left\{(-1)^n + 100i\right\}_{n=1}^{\infty}$ is

A. Unbounded

B. Bounded

C. Convergent

D. None of these

30. The average incoming call rate is 4 per minute. The probability that there are not more than 3 calls is

A. $\frac{71}{3}e^{-4}$

B. e^{-6}

C. $-\frac{71}{3}$

D. e^{-4}

31. Given a probability density function

$$f(x) = \begin{cases} e^{-x} & x \geq 0 \\ 0 & x < 0 \end{cases}$$

find the probability $p\ (1 \leq x \leq 2)$

A. $e^{-1} + e^{-2}$

B. e^{-2}

C. e^{-1}

D. $e^{-1} - e^{-2}$

32. The random variable x has the probability density function $f(x) = \begin{cases} ke^{-3x} & x > 0 \\ 0 & \text{otherwise} \end{cases}$ the value of k is

A. 1

B. 2

C. 3

D. 4

33. If $\lambda_1 \ldots\ldots \lambda_n$ are eigen values of matrix A, then trace of A is

A. $\lambda_1\lambda_2\lambda_3 \ldots\ldots\ldots \lambda_n$

B. $\lambda_1 + \lambda_2 + \lambda_3 + \ldots\ldots\ldots + \lambda_n$

C. $\frac{1}{\lambda_1\lambda_2\lambda_3 \ldots\ldots\ldots \lambda_n}$

D. $\frac{1}{\lambda_1 + \lambda_2 + \lambda_3 + \ldots\ldots\ldots + \lambda_n}$

34. The rank of the matrix $\begin{bmatrix} 0 & 2 & -3 \\ 2 & 0 & 5 \\ -3 & 5 & 0 \end{bmatrix}$ is

A. 4

B. 3

C. 2

D. 1

35. In two person zero sum game if one player gains amount A

A. Opponent player also gains amount A

B. Opponent player losses amount A

C. Opponent player neither losses nor gains

D. None of these

36. In simplex method, the variable x_j leave the basis in some iteration. Then

A. s_j can enter the basis in the next iteration

B. x_j does not enter the basis in next iteration

C. (A) and (B) both true

D. None of these

37. In simplex table of a maximization lpp the column corresponding to a variable x_j is $(2; -1, 0, -3)^T$. The $z_j - c_j = 2$ is not most negative. Then

A. the solution is unbounded

B. the solution is bounded

C. the solution may be bounded or unbounded

D. none of these

38. If X and Y are r.v. having finite means, then:

A. E [Min (X, Y)] ≥ Min [E(X), E(Y)]

B. E [Min (X, Y)] ≤ Min E(X), E(Y)]

C. E (Min (X, Y) = Min [E (X), E (Y)]

D. None of these

39. In the context of inventory management, the following need to be addresed:

A. When do order

B. How much to order

C. How much safety to keep

D. Maximum of the total inventory cost

40. The function sin z is analytic in:

A. C

B. C – {0}

C. C ∪ {∞}

D. except on negative real *axis*

ANSWERS

1	2	3	4	5	6	7	8	9	10
B	C	B	A	B	A	A	A	A	A
11	**12**	**13**	**14**	**15**	**16**	**17**	**18**	**19**	**20**
A	B	A	A	A	B	B	C	B	D
21	**22**	**23**	**24**	**25**	**26**	**27**	**28**	**29**	**30**
B	B	C	A	A	B	A	C	B	A
31	**32**	**33**	**34**	**35**	**36**	**37**	**38**	**39**	**40**
D	C	B	B	B	B	A	B	A	B

Some Selected Explanatory Answers

1. $\because \{a_n\}_{n=1}^{\infty}$ converges to 0 and $\{b_n\}_{n=1}^{\infty}$ is a bounded sequence then $\{a_n b_n\}_{n=1}^{\infty}$ converges to zero by property of convergence

2. Every bounded sequence need not be convergent, some can be non convergent but every convergent sequence is bounded

If $<a_n>$ is convergent

$\Rightarrow \lim\limits_{x\to\infty} a_n = l$

Let $\in = 1$. then $\exists$ *a* +ve integer *m* such that

$|a_n - l| < 1 \forall n \geq m$

$\Rightarrow l-1 < a_n < l+1 \forall n \geq m$ ...(*i*)

Let $K = \max\{a_1, a_2, \ldots\ldots\ldots, a_{m-1}, l+1\}$ ...(*ii*)

$k = \min\{a_1, a_2, \ldots\ldots\ldots, a_{m-1}, l-1\}$ ...(*iii*)

from (*i*), (*ii*) and (*iii*)

$k \leq a_n \leq K \forall n$

$\Rightarrow <a_n>$ is bounded

for example $<(-1)^n> = <-1, 1\ldots\ldots\ldots>$ is bounded but not convergent.

5. Abelian group because commutative property is not satisfied i.e. If A and B are two square matrices $\Rightarrow AB \neq BA$

6. $$BA = \begin{pmatrix} 1 & 2 & 3 & 4 & 5 \\ 1 & 3 & 4 & 5 & 2 \end{pmatrix}\begin{pmatrix} 1 & 2 & 3 & 4 & 5 \\ 2 & 3 & 1 & 5 & 4 \end{pmatrix}$$

$$= \begin{pmatrix} 1 & 2 & 3 & 4 & 5 \\ 1 & 3 & 4 & 5 & 2 \end{pmatrix}\begin{pmatrix} 1 & 3 & 4 & 5 & 2 \\ 2 & 1 & 5 & 4 & 3 \end{pmatrix}$$

$$= \begin{pmatrix} 1 & 2 & 3 & 4 & 5 \\ 2 & 1 & 5 & 4 & 3 \end{pmatrix}$$

7. $L_s = L_q + c$

$\Rightarrow L_s \geq L_q$

8. $W_s = \dfrac{L_s}{\lambda} = \dfrac{N}{2} \times \dfrac{1}{\lambda}$ for $p = 1$

11. $\begin{pmatrix} 2 & 1 & -1 \\ 3 & 2 & 1 \end{pmatrix}\begin{pmatrix} x_1 \\ x_2 \\ x_3 \end{pmatrix} = \begin{pmatrix} 2 \\ 3 \end{pmatrix}$ basis is $\begin{pmatrix} 2 & 1 \\ 3 & 2 \end{pmatrix}$ for two values on RHS.

12. $\bigcap\limits_{n=1}^{\infty} A_n$ is a subspace of V(F) where A_n are subspaces of V(F).

$\bigcap\limits_{n=1}^{\infty} A_n$ is not a subspace of V(F) where A_n are subspaces of V(F)

16. $$T_2^{-1} T_1(z) = T_2^{-1}\left(\frac{z+2}{z+3}\right)$$

$$= \frac{\frac{z+2}{z+3}}{1 - \frac{z+2}{z+3}} = z+2$$

17. $$z = \left(\frac{1}{1-2i} + \frac{3}{1+i}\right)\left(\frac{3+4i}{2-4i}\right)$$

$$= \frac{4-5i}{(1-2i)(1+i)} \times \left(\frac{3+4i}{2-4i}\right)$$

$$= \frac{32+i}{2(1-7i)}$$

$$= \frac{32+i}{2(1-7i)} \times \left(\frac{1+7i}{1+7i}\right)$$

$= \frac{25+225i}{100} = \frac{1}{4} + \frac{9}{4}i$

$\therefore$ Amp z $= \tan^{-1}\frac{9/4}{1/4} = \tan^{-1} 9$

18. $\because$ G is a open and connected in C and f is a function from G to C (Continuous) then for $z \in$ G $z = e^{f(z)}$

20. $(D^2 - D'^2 + D - D')z = 0$

$\Rightarrow (D - D')(D + D' + 1) = 0$

$z = f_1(y + x) + e^{-x} f_2(y - x)$

21. $y'' + p(x)y' + q(x)y = 0$ is a general equation

$\frac{\partial^2 y}{\partial x^2} + P(x)\frac{\partial y}{\partial x} + q(x)y = 0$ has its solutions as linearly independent

22. $[1 + (y)'2]^{3/2} - py'' = 0$

$\Rightarrow \left[1 + \left(\frac{\partial y}{\partial x}\right)^2\right]^{3/2} - P\frac{\partial^2 y}{\partial x^2} = 0$ is of second order, first degree

23. $-P_1 + P_2 + P_3 = 1$

The Lagrange's subsidiary equations are

$\frac{\partial x_1}{-1} = \frac{\partial x_2}{1} = \frac{\partial x_3}{1} = \frac{\partial z}{1}$

First and fourth, $x_1 + z = c_1$

First and second, $x_1 + x_2 = c_2$

First and third, $x_1 + x_3 = c_3$

$f(x_1 + z,\ x_1 + x_2, x_1 + x_3) = 0$

27. Value of game

		I	II	III
A	I	6	8	6
	II	4	12	2

using the rule of dominance the above matrix reduces to

		I	II	III
A	I	6	8	
	II	4	12	

also $x_{11} = 6, x_{12} = 8$

$x_{21} = 4\ x_{22} = 12$

value of game can be find by formula

$V = \frac{x_{11}x_{22} - x_{12}x_{21}}{(x_{11} + x_{22}) - (x_{12} + x_{21})}$ therefore V = 6 for A and –6 for B

28. $\because\ f(z) = \sum_{n=0}^{\infty} \frac{a_n}{n+1} z^n$ Convergence radius = l

and $f'(z) = \sum_{n=0}^{\infty} a_n z^n$

$\therefore\ l = l^1$

29. Let $a_n = \{(-1)^n + 100\,i\}_{n=1}^{\infty}$

$\Rightarrow a_n = \{(-1+100\,i), (1+100\,i), \ldots\ldots\}$

$\Rightarrow a_n = -1+100i$ when n is odd

& $a_n = 1+100i$ when n is even

$\Rightarrow |a_n| = \sqrt{1+100^2}, \forall n$

$\Rightarrow \{a_n\}$ is bounded.

30. X = Number of calls per minute

$P(x = x) = e^{-\lambda}\frac{\lambda^x}{\lfloor x}$

$P(x > 3) = P(x \le 3)$

$= \sum_{x=0}^{3} e^{-\lambda}\frac{\lambda^x}{\lfloor x}\Big|_{\lambda=4}$

$= e^{-4}\left[1 + \frac{4}{1} + \frac{4^2}{2!} + \frac{4^3}{3!}\right]$

$= \frac{71}{3}e^{-4}$

31. $P(1 \le x \le 2) = \int_1^2 f(x)dx$

$= \int_1^2 e^{-x}dx$

$= e^{-1} - e^{-2}$

32. $\int_{-\infty}^{\infty} f(x)dx = 1$

$$\Rightarrow \int_0^{\infty} ke^{-3x} dx = k\int_0^{\infty} e^{-3x} dx = 1$$

$$\Rightarrow \frac{k}{3} = 1$$

$$\Rightarrow k = 3$$

36. $\Delta = \begin{vmatrix} 0 & 2 & -3 \\ 2 & 0 & 5 \\ -3 & 5 & 0 \end{vmatrix}$

$$= 0\begin{vmatrix} 0 & 5 \\ 5 & 0 \end{vmatrix} - 2\begin{vmatrix} 2 & 5 \\ -3 & 0 \end{vmatrix} - 3\begin{vmatrix} 2 & 0 \\ -3 & 5 \end{vmatrix}$$

$$= 0 - 2(15) - 3(10)$$

$$= -30 - 30$$

$$= -60 \neq 0$$

$\therefore$ Rank is three

37. Opponent players losses equal ammount gained by A because two players have conflicting objectives.

38. $E[\text{Min}(X, Y)] = \frac{1}{2}\ E(X+Y) - E|X-Y|$

$\because E(X+Y) = E(X) + E(Y)$

$|E(X-Y)| \leq E|(X-Y)| \geq -|E(X-Y)| \geq -E|X-Y|$

$-E|X-Y| \leq -|E(X-Y)| - |E(X) - E(Y)|$

$\therefore E[\text{Min}(X, Y)] \leq \frac{1}{2}\ [E(X) + E(Y)] - |E(X) - E(Y)| \leq \text{Min}\{E(X), E(Y)\}$

SET–13

CSIR–UGC (NET) MATHEMATICAL SCIENCES

PART-B

1. The general solution of the equation $ydx - xdy = 0$ is

A. $\frac{x}{y} = c$ B. $x + y = c$

C. $xy = c$ D. $x - y = c$

2. The solution $\frac{\partial^2 z}{\partial x^2} - 5\frac{\partial^2 z}{\partial x \partial y} + 4\frac{\partial^2 z}{\partial y^2} = \sin(4x+y)$ is

A. $z = \frac{1}{3}x\cos(4x+y)$

B. $z = f_1(y+x) + f_2(y+4x)$

C. $z = f(y+x) - \frac{1}{3}x\cos(4x+y)$

D. $z = f_1(y+x) + f_2(y+4x) - \frac{1}{3}x\cos(4x+y)$

3. The equation $y = Ae^{3x} + Be^{5x}$ can be represented as

A. $y'' - 8y' + 15y = 0$ B. $y'' + 8y' = 0$

C. $y' - 8y' = 0$ D. $y'' + 8y' + 15y = 0$

4. If, $P(B/A) = P(B)$, $P(B) \neq 0$, then

A. $P(A/B) = P(A)$

B. $P(A/B) = P(A).P(B)$

C. $P(A/B) = P(A)/P(B)$

D. $P(A/B) = P(B)$

5. For real constants a and b with $a \leq b$ and $f(x)$ the probability distribution function of random variable x the following is true

A. $P(a \leq x \leq b) = F(b) - F(a)$

B. $P(a \leq x \leq b) = F(a) - F(b)$

C. $P(a \leq x \leq b) = F(b)$

D. $P(a \leq x \leq b) = F(a)$

6. For the given exponential distribution $f(x) = \frac{1}{c}e^{-x/c}, c > 0$. The first mean about the origin is

A. c^4 B. c^3

C. c^2 D. c

7. Let the probability distributions functions be $f(x) = \begin{cases} 0 & x < 0 \\ 1 - e^{-x}, & x > 0 \end{cases}$ find the probability density function?

A. $f(x) = \begin{cases} 0 & x < 0 \\ e^{-x} & x > 0 \end{cases}$

B. $f(x) = 1 - e^{-x}$

C. $f(x) = \begin{cases} 0 & x < 0 \\ e^{x} & x > 0 \end{cases}$

D. None of these

8. If $f(z)$ is analytic in a domain D, then

A. $f^{(n)}(z)$ exists in D

B. $f^{(n)}(z)$ does not exist in D

C. $f^{(n)}(z)$ exists for all n in D

D. None of these

9. The poles of first order are known as

A. Complex set B. Simple pole

C. Singularities D. None of these

10. The characteristic equation and eigen value for matrix $A = \begin{vmatrix} 3-4i & -7 \\ 5i & 6+2i \end{vmatrix}$ are

A. $\lambda^2 - 11\lambda + 18 = 0, 9, 2$

B. $\lambda^2 - 2i\lambda + 8 = 0, 3, 4$

C. $\lambda^2 + 6\lambda + 2 = 0, 1, 3$

D. None of these

11. If $\lambda_1, \lambda_2, \ldots\ldots\lambda_n$ are the characteristic roots of matrix A, then the A^{-1} have the roots

A. $\frac{1}{\lambda_1}, \frac{1}{\lambda_2}, \ldots\ldots \frac{1}{\lambda_n}$ B. $\lambda_1, \lambda_2 \ldots\ldots\ldots\lambda_n$

C. Zero D. None of these

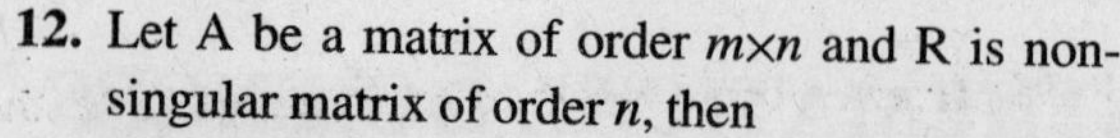

12. Let A be a matrix of order $m \times n$ and R is non-singular matrix of order n, then
    A. Rank (RA) $\neq$ Rank A.
    B. Rank (RA) $\geq$ Rank A.
    C. Rank (RA) $\leq$ Rank A.
    D. Rank (RA) = Rank A.
13. If w_1 and w_2 are subspaces of a finite dimensional vector space then $w_1 = w_2$ iff
    A. $w_1^0 = w_2^0$ B. $w_1^0 - w_2^0 = \{0\}$
    C. $w_1^0 \neq w_2^0$ D. None of these
14. If N is the hyper space of vector space V and W is any subspace of V that contains N then
    A. W = N or W = V B. W = N only
    C. W = V only D. None of these
15. In linear programming problem
    A. Objective function, constaints and variable are all linear
    B. Only objective function to be linear
    C. Only constraints are to be linear
    D. Only variables are to be linear
16. If $\bar{c}\,\bar{x}, = z (z \neq 0)$ is a hyperplane and $\bar{x}_1$ are $\bar{x}_2$ are two points on this hyperplane, then
    A. $\bar{c}\,\bar{x}_1 \neq \bar{c}\,\bar{x}_2$ B. $\bar{c}\,\bar{x}_1 > \bar{c}\,\bar{x}_2$
    C. $\bar{c}\,\bar{x}_1 = \bar{c}\,\bar{x}_2$ D. None of these
17. When p = 1for M|M|1|N queueing system expected number of customer in the system are
    A. N/2 B. N/6
    C. N D. None of these
18. Little formula state the relationship between
    A. W_s, W_q and λ B. L_s, L_q and λ
    C. W_s, L_s and λ D. None of these
19. Under exponential assumption, let μ be the service rate then P_r\{service completion on $\Delta t \approx 0$ system not empty\}is
    A. $\mu\,\Delta t + 0(t)$ B. $\mu\,\Delta t$
    C. $0\,(t)$ D. None of these
20. M|M|3| N, Queue description states the number of servers and buffer capacity as
    A. 3 and M B. M and 3
    C. 3 and N D. None of these
21. If the ring R has left identity e_1 and right identiry e_2 then
    A. $e_1 = e_2$ B. $e_1 \neq e_2$
    C. $e_1 = me_2$ D. None of these
22. The element $a \neq 0 \in$ R, the commutative ring is an integral domain if
    A. $ab = 0$, $b \in$ R and $b = 0$
    B. $ab = 0$, $b \in$ R and $b \neq 0$
    C. $ab \neq 0$, $b \in$ R and $b = 0$
    D. $ab = 0$, $b \in$ R and $b = 0$
23. If L is a finite extension of F and K is a subfield of L which contains F, then
    A. $[L:F] \mid [K:F]$ B. $[K:F] \mid [L:F]$
    C. $[K:F] \mid [F:L]$ D. $[F:K] \mid [L:F]$
24. If G = \{1, – 1\}is a group with ordinary multiplication the order of –1 is
    A. One B. Two
    C. Zero D. None of these
25. If the ring R is such that $(ab)^2 = a^2b^2$, $ab \in$ R, then
    A. R is commutative
    B. R is non–commutative
    C. R is zero ring
    D. None of these
26. If U is an ideal of ring R and I $\in$ U, then
    A. U is a proper subset of R
    B. U is equal to R
    C. U is superset of R
    D. U = ϕ
27. If C = (1, 2, 3, 4) then C^2 is
    A. (1 3) (2 4) B. (1 3)
    C. (2 4) D. (2 3) (3 4)
28. f: E $\rightarrow$ Q and g : E $\rightarrow$ R and both are continuous at x_0, then
    A. f/g is continuous at x_0
    B. f/g is discontinuous at x_0
    C. f/g is continuous at x_0 if $g(x_0) \neq 0$
    D. None of these
29. If sequence $\{a_n\}_{n=1}^{\infty}$ and $\{b_n\}_{n=1}^{\infty}$ are divergent sequences, then
    A. $\{a_n + b_n\}_{n=1}^{\infty}$ is always divergent
    B. $\{a_n + b_n\}_{n=1}^{\infty}$ is always convergent
    C. $\{a_n + b_n\}_{n=1}^{\infty}$ sometimes convergent
    D. None of these

30. If ϒ is a piecewise smooth and $f : [a, b] \to C$ is continuous, then

A. $\int_0^b f dy = \int_a^b f(t) y'(t) dt$

B. $\int_a^b f dy = \int_a^b f(t) y(t) dt$

C. $\int_a^b f dy = \int_a^b f'(t) y(t) dt$

D. None of these

31. What is the radius of convergence for power series $f(z) = \sum \frac{1}{n^p} z^n$?

A. 1 B. 2
C. 0 D. ∞

32. If cube roots of $a + ib$ is $x + iy$, then $4(x^2 - y^2)$ is equal to

A. $\frac{a}{x} + \frac{b}{y}$ B. $\frac{x}{a} + \frac{y}{b}$
C. $ax + by$ D. $ax - by$

33. In a linear programming problem in standard form there are six variables and four constraints. Then number of basic feasible solution are

A. 15 B. Less than 15
C. More than 15 D. None of these

34. Assignment problem is a

A. Integer programming problem
B. Non-integer programming problem
C. Non-linear programming problem
D. None of these

35. If x_j is a basic variables in a simplex table, then the relative cost

A. $Z_j - C_j < 0$ B. $Z_j - C_j > 0$
C. $Z_j - C_j = 0$ D. None of these

36. If S is a non-empty of S has no upper bound then

A. Sup S = ∞ B. Inf S = ∞
C. Sup S = $-\infty$ D. Inf S = $-\infty$

37. For open interval (a, b), where $a < b$, $x \in (a,b)$ we have

A. $a \le x \le b$ B. $a < x < b$
C. $a \le x < b$ D. $a < x \le b$

38. A symmetric die is thrown 600 times. The lower bound for the probability of getting 80 to 120 sixes is

A. $\frac{9}{24}$ B. $\frac{13}{24}$
C. $\frac{17}{24}$ D. $\frac{19}{24}$

39. A set with a pre-metric can be made into a metric space by identifying any two elements x, $\bar{x}$ such that

A. $d(x) = 0$ B. $d(\bar{x}) = 0$
C. $d(x, \bar{x}) = 0$ D. None of these

40. If $G = \{1, -1, i, -i\}$ is a group with multiplication operation then:

A. $\{1, -1\}$ is a subgroup of G
B. $\{1, -1, i\}$ is a subgroup
C. $\{i, i, -i\}$ is a subgroup
D. $\{i, -i\}$ is a subgroup

ANSWERS

1	2	3	4	5	6	7	8	9	10
A	D	A	A	B	D	A	C	B	A
11	12	13	14	15	16	17	18	19	20
A	D	A	A	A	C	A	C	A	C
21	22	23	24	25	26	27	28	29	30
A	A	B	B	A	A	A	C	C	A
31	32	33	34	35	36	37	38	39	40
A	A	B	A	C	A	B	D	C	A

Some Selected Explanatory Answers

1. $ydx - xdy = 0$ has a general solution as

$$\frac{dx}{x} = \frac{dy}{y}$$

$$\Rightarrow \log x = \log y + \log c$$

$$\frac{x}{y} = c$$

2. $(D^2-5DD_1+4D_1^2)z=\sin(4x+y)$

Alternate equation

$m^2-5m+4=0$

$\Rightarrow (m-1)(m-4)=0$

$\Rightarrow m=1,4$

$z_n=f_1(y+x)+f_2(y+4x)$

$$z_p=\frac{1}{D^2-5DD'+4D'^2}\sin(4x+y)$$

$$=\frac{1}{(D-4D')(D-D')}\sin(4x+y)$$

$$=\frac{1}{(D-4D')}\frac{1}{(4-1)}\{-\cos(4x+y)\}$$

$$=\frac{1}{(D-4D')}\left\{-\frac{1}{3}\cos(4x+y)\right\}$$

$$=-\frac{x}{3}\cos(4x+y)$$

$z=z_n+z_p$

3. $y=Ae^{3x}+Be^{5x}$

$$\frac{dy}{dx}=3Ae^{3x}+5Be^{5x}$$

$$=3y+2Be^{5x}$$

$$\Rightarrow \frac{d^2y}{dx^2}=3\frac{dy}{dx}+10Be^{5x}$$

$$=3\frac{dy}{dx}+5\left(\frac{dy}{dx}-3y\right)=3\frac{dy}{dx}+5\frac{dy}{dx}-15y$$

$$y''=8\frac{dy}{dx}-15y$$

$$y''-8\frac{dy}{dx}+15y=0$$

$y''-8y'-15y=0$

4. $$P(A/B)=\frac{P(A\cap B)}{P(B)}$$

$$=\frac{P(A)P(B/A)}{P(B)}$$

$$=\frac{P(A)P(B)}{P(B)}=P(A)$$

6. $$M_0(t)=\int_0^{\infty}e^{tx}f(x)dx$$

$$=\int_0^{\infty}e^{tx}\frac{1}{c}e^{-4c}dx$$

$$=\frac{1}{c}\int_0^{\infty}e^{\left(t-\frac{1}{c}\right)x}dx$$

$$=\frac{1}{c}\frac{1}{\left(t-\frac{1}{c}\right)}.e^{\left(t-\frac{1}{c}\right)x}\Bigg|_0^{\infty}$$

$=(1-ct)^{-1}$

$=1+ct+c^2t^2+.........$

$$\text{then } \mu_1=\frac{\partial}{\partial t}M_0(t)|_{t=0}$$

$=(c+2c^2t+3c^3t^2+.....)_{t=0}$

$=c$

7. $$f(x)=\begin{Bmatrix}0 & x\le 0\\ e^{-x} & x>0\end{Bmatrix}\because \text{P.D.F.}=\int_{-\infty}^{\infty}f(x)dx=1$$

10. $|A-\lambda I|=0$

$$\Rightarrow\begin{vmatrix}3+4i-\lambda & -5i\\ -7 & 6-2i-\lambda\end{vmatrix}=0$$

$\Rightarrow (3+4i-\lambda)(6-2i-\lambda)-(5i)(7)=0$

$\Rightarrow \lambda^2-11\lambda+18=0$

$\Rightarrow (\lambda-9)(\lambda-2)=0$

11. $\frac{1}{\lambda_1},\frac{1}{\lambda_2}............\frac{1}{\lambda_n}$ by the property of inverse

12. By the property of rank of a matrix Rank (R A) = Rank (A)

17. $$L_s=\sum_{n=0}^{N}n_{p_n}=\frac{1}{N+1}\left(\sum_{n=0}^{N}n\right)$$

$$=\frac{1}{N+1}\frac{(n+1)N}{2}=\frac{N}{2}$$

$$\because \sum_{n=0}^{N}n=\frac{(n+1)N}{2}$$

and $P_n=\frac{1}{n+1}$ *for* $P=1$

18. According to Little's formula

$L=\lambda W$

or $L_Q=\lambda W_Q$

or $w = W_Q + 1/m$

|L – is length of system
|w – weighting time in a system
|λ – arrival rate

20. $a|b|c|d$
c = Number of servers, here $c = 3$
d = System capacity, here d = N

21. By the property of identity of ring
left identity = Right identity

22. $\forall a, b \in R$ If $ab = 0$, and $a \neq 0 \Rightarrow b = 0$
The commulative ring is an integral domain by definition

23. $\because k$ is a subfield of $L \supset F$ then
[K : F]/[L : F]

24. Here 1is an identity element
also $(-1)^2 = 1$
$\therefore 0(-1) = 2$
$\because 0(a) = P$
$\Rightarrow$ P is the least positive integer: $a^P = e$, an identity.

25. R is commutative
$(ab)^2 = ab.ab$
$= aa.bb$
$= a^2b^2$

26. For a proper subset of R unity element must be in subset
$\therefore$ for $\cup$ to be a proper subset of R $I \in \cup$. or vice–versa

27. $C^2 = C.C$

$$= \begin{pmatrix} 1 & 2 & 3 & 4 \\ 2 & 3 & 4 & 1 \end{pmatrix} \begin{pmatrix} 1 & 2 & 3 & 4 \\ 2 & 3 & 4 & 1 \end{pmatrix}$$

$$= \begin{pmatrix} 1 & 2 & 3 & 4 \\ 2 & 3 & 4 & 1 \end{pmatrix} \begin{pmatrix} 2 & 3 & 4 & 1 \\ 3 & 4 & 1 & 2 \end{pmatrix}$$

$$= \begin{pmatrix} 1 & 2 & 3 & 4 \\ 3 & 4 & 1 & 2 \end{pmatrix}$$

= (1 3) (2 4)

28. f/g is continuous at x_0 if $g(x_0) \neq 0$
i.e. if g after maps x_0 and image of $x_0 \neq 0$

29. By the property of divergent sequence $\{a_n + b_n\}_{n=1}^{\infty}$ some times convergent for $\{a_n\}_{n=1}^{\infty}$ and $\{b_n\}_{n=1}^{\infty}$ to be continuous

32. Given by

$$(a+ib)^{\frac{1}{3}} = x + iy$$

$$\Rightarrow (a+ib) = (x+iy)^3$$

$$\therefore a + ib = (x^3 - 3xy^2) + i\,(3x^2y - y^3)$$

Comparing real and imaginary parts, we get
$\therefore x^3 - 3xy^2 = a,\ 3x^2y - y^3 = b$
or, $x(x^2 - 3y^2) = a,\ y\,(3x^2 - y^2) = b$

or, $x^2 - 3y^2 = \dfrac{a}{x}$

$3x^2 - y^2 = \dfrac{b}{y}$

or, $(x^2 - 3y^2) + (3x^2 - y^2) = \dfrac{a}{x} + \dfrac{b}{y}$

or, $4(x^2 - y^2) = \dfrac{a}{x} + \dfrac{b}{y}$

34. Assignment problem is a special case of a linear programming problem of integer programming problem.

38. Let S be total no. of successes, then

$$E(S) = np = 600 \times \frac{1}{6} = 100$$

$$V(S) = npq = 600 \times \frac{1}{6} \times \frac{5}{6} = \frac{500}{6}$$

Using Chebychev's inequality,

$$P\{|S - E(S)| < k\sigma\} \geq 1 - \frac{1}{k^2}$$

$$\Rightarrow P\{|S - 100| < k\sqrt{500/6}\} \geq 1 - \frac{1}{k^2}$$

$$\Rightarrow P\{100 - k\sqrt{500/6} < S < 100 + k\sqrt{500/6}\} \geq 1 - \frac{1}{k^2}$$

Taking $k = \dfrac{20}{\sqrt{500/6}}$

$$\Rightarrow P(80 \leq S \leq 120) \geq 1 - \frac{1}{400 \times 6/500} = \frac{19}{24}$$

SET–14

CSIR–UGC (NET) MATHEMATICAL SCIENCES

PART-B

1. Let R_1 and R_2 respectively by the maximum ranges up and down an inclined plane and R be the maximum range on the horizontal plane. Then R_1, R, R_2 are in
   A. Arithmetic – Geometric Progression (AGP)
   B. Arithmatic Progression
   C. Geometric Progression
   D. Harmonic Progression

2. A couple is of moment $\vec{G}$ and the force forming the couple is $\vec{P}$. If $\vec{P}$ is turned through a right angle, the moment of the couple thus formed is $\vec{H}$. If instead the force $\vec{P}$ is turned through an angle a, then the moment of couple becomes
   A. $\vec{G}\sin a - \vec{H}\cos a$ B. $\vec{H}\cos a + \vec{G}\sin a$
   C. $\vec{G}\cos a + \vec{H}\sin a$ D. $\vec{H}\sin a - \vec{G}\cos a$

3. Two particles start simultaneousily from the same point and move along two straight lines one with uniform velocity $\overline{u}$ and the other from rest with uniform acceleration f. Let a be the angle between their direction of motion. The relative velocity of second particle with respect to the first is least after a time
   A. $\dfrac{u\sin a}{f}$ B. $\dfrac{f\cos a}{u}$
   C. $u\sin a$ D. $\dfrac{u\cos a}{f}$

4. Two stones are projected from the top of a cliff h metres high, with the same speed u, so as to hit the ground at the same spot. If one of the stones is projected horizontally and the other is projected at an angle θ to the horizontal then $\tan\theta$ equals
   A. $\sqrt{\dfrac{2u}{gh}}$ B. $2g\dfrac{u}{h}$
   C. $2h\sqrt{\dfrac{u}{g}}$ D. $u\sqrt{\dfrac{2}{gh}}$

5. A body travels a distance S in t seconds. It starts from rest and ends at rest. In the first part of the journey, it moves with constant acceleration f and in the second part with constant retardation r the value of t is given by
   A. $2S\left(\dfrac{1}{f}+\dfrac{1}{r}\right)$ B. $\dfrac{2S}{\dfrac{1}{f}+\dfrac{1}{r}}$
   C. $\sqrt{2S(f+r)}$ D. $\sqrt{2S\left(\dfrac{1}{f}+\dfrac{1}{r}\right)}$

6. $\sum_{n=0}^{\infty}\dfrac{(\log_e^{X})^n}{n!}$ is equal to
   A. log e X B. X
   C. log Xe D. None of these

7. $\text{Exp}.\left[(x-1)-\frac{1}{2}(x-1)^2+\frac{(x-1)^3}{3}-\frac{(x-1)^4}{4}+\ldots..\right]$ equal to
   A. Log $(x-1)$ B. Log x
   C. x D. None of these

8. The number of real roots of $3^2x^2-7x+7=9$ is
   A. zero B. 2
   C. 1 D. 4

9. If e and e' be the eccentricities, of a hyperbola and its conjugate, then $\dfrac{1}{e'}+\dfrac{1}{e'^2}$ is equal to
   A. 0 B. 1
   C. 2 D. None of these

10. The minimum value of the expression $\sin\alpha+\sin\beta+\sin\gamma$ where a,β,γ are real numbers satisfying $a+\beta+\gamma = \pi$ is
    A. Positive B. Zero
    C. Negative D. -3

11. The directions of three forces 1N, 2N and 3N acting at a point are parallel to the sides of equilateral triangle taken in order. The magnitude of their resultant is

A. Zero B. $\sqrt{\frac{3}{2}}$N

C. $\frac{3}{2}$N D. $\sqrt{3}$N

12. A point D divides the line joining the point B to the point C in the ratio 1:3, A particle moves along BC with uniform speed of 10 *m/sec* from B to D, then moves with uniform speed of 20*m/sec* from D to C. If V is the avarage speed of the paricle from B to C, then the following is true

A. V = 8 *m/sec* B. V = 15 *m/sec*

C. V = 16 *m*/sec D. V = 17 · 5 *m/sec*

13. The maximum value of (cos a_1) (cos a_2)....... (cosa_n) under the restriction $0 \le a_1 a_2 ....a_n \le \frac{\pi}{2}$ and $(\cot a_1)(\cot a_2)....(\cot a_n) = 1$ is

A. $\frac{1}{2^{n/2}}$ B. $\frac{1}{2^n}$

C. $-\frac{1}{2^n}$ D. 1

14. Probable error of *r* is

A. $0.6754\left(\frac{1+r^2}{\sqrt{n}}\right)$ B. $0.6745\left(\frac{1-r^2}{\sqrt{n}}\right)$

C. $0.6547\left(\frac{1-r^2}{n}\right)$ D. $0.6754\left(\frac{1-r^2}{n}\right)$

15. If *x* and *y* are two uncorrelated, variables and if $u = x + y$ and $v = xy$, then *r* (*u*, *v*) is equal to

A. $\frac{\sigma_x^2 - \sigma_y^2}{\sigma_x^2 + \sigma_y^2}$ B. $\frac{\sigma_x^2 + \sigma_y^2}{\sigma_x^2 - \sigma_y^2}$

C. $\sigma_x^2 + \sigma_y^2$ D. None of these

16. If the two lines of regression are $x + 4y = 3$ and $3x + y = 15$ then value of *x* for $y = 3$ is

A. 4 B. 9

C. −4 D. None of these

17. If $f(x) = \log|x|, x \ne 0$ then $f'(x)$ equals

A. $\frac{1}{|x|}$ B. $\frac{-1}{x}$

C. $\frac{1}{x}$ D. None of these

18. If a parallelopiped has sides $\vec{a}$, $\vec{b}$ and $\vec{c}$ such that $\vec{a} . \vec{b} = \vec{b} . \vec{c} = \vec{c} . \vec{a} = 0$ then the shape of parallelopiped is

A. Cuboid B. Rectangular

C. Both D. None of these

19. In a right angle ΔABC, $\angle A = 90°$ and sides *a*, *b*, *c* are respectively, 5*cm*, 4*cm* and 3*cm*. If a force $\vec{F}$ has moment 0, 9 and 16 *in* N*cm* units respectively about vertices A, B and C, then magnitude of $\vec{F}$ is

A. 3 B. 4

C. 5 D. 9

20. The weighted arithmetic mean of first *n* natural numbers whose weights are equal to the corresponding numbers themselves is equal to

A. $\frac{(n+1)(2n+1)}{6}$ B. $\frac{(2n+1)}{3}$

C. $\frac{n(n+1)(2n+1)}{6}$ D. $\left(\frac{2n+1}{6}\right)$

21. The rank of the matrix $A = \begin{bmatrix} 2 & 3 & 1 & 4 \\ 0 & 1 & 2 & -1 \\ 0 & -2 & -4 & 2 \end{bmatrix}$ is

A. 2

B. 3

C. 1

D. Can not be determined

22. For positive numbers *x*, *y*, *z* the numerical value of $\begin{vmatrix} 1 & \frac{\log y}{\log x} & \frac{\log z}{\log x} \\ \frac{\log x}{\log y} & 1 & \frac{\log z}{\log y} \\ \frac{\log x}{\log z} & \frac{\log y}{\log z} & 1 \end{vmatrix}$ is

A. 0 B. 1

C. $\log x + \log y + \log z$ D. $\log(x + y + z)$

23. If $f(t) = \frac{t}{e^t - 1} + \frac{t}{2}$ then

A. $f(t) = -f(t)$ B. $f(t) = f(-t)$

C. $f(t).f(-t) = 0$ D. None of these

24. The differential equation of all simple harmonic motions $x = a\cos(nt + b)$ and given period $\frac{2\pi}{n}$ *is*

A. $\frac{d^2x}{dt^2} - n^2x = 0$ B. $\frac{d^2x}{dt^2} + n^2x = 0$

C. $\frac{d^2x}{dt^2} - nx = 0$ D. $\frac{d^2x}{dt^2} + \frac{1}{n^2}x = 0$

25. The elimination of constant A, B and C from $Y = A + Bx - Ci^{-x}$ leads the differential equation

A. $y'' + y' = 0$ B. $y'' - y' = 0$

C. $y' + e^x = 0$ D. $y'' + e^x = 0$

26. $\int \frac{a^{\sqrt{x}}}{\sqrt{x}} dx$ is equal to

A. $\frac{a^{\sqrt{x}}}{\log a} + c$ B. $\frac{2a^{\sqrt{x}}}{\log a} + c$

C. $2a^{\sqrt{x}} \log a + c$ D. None of these

27. N cadet have to stand in a row if all possible permutations are equally likely, the probability of two particular cadets standing side by side is

A. $\frac{4}{N}$ B. $\frac{3}{N^2}$

C. $\frac{1}{2N}$ D. $\frac{2}{N}$

28. In a simultaneous throw of 2 coins the probability of having 2 heads is

A. $\frac{1}{4}$ B. $\frac{1}{2}$

C. $\frac{1}{8}$ D. $\frac{1}{6}$

29. The probability of getting more than 7 when a pair of dice are thrown

A. $\frac{7}{36}$ B. $\frac{5}{12}$

C. $\frac{7}{12}$ D. None of these

30. If sets A and B are defind as A=$\{(x,y)/\ y = e^x, x \in R\}$B=$(x, y) \mid y = x,\ x \in R\ \}$ then

A. $B \subset A$ B. $A \subset B$

C. $A \cap B = \phi$ D. $A \cup B = A$

31. Let A=$\{X : X$ is a multiple of $3\}$ and B = $\{X : X$ is a multiple of $5\}$ then $A \cap B$ is given by

A. $\{15, 30, 45..........\}$ B. $\{3, 6, 9...........\}$

C. $\{15, 10, 15, 20....\}$ D. $\{5, 10, 20........\}$

32. If A = $\begin{vmatrix} 3 & -3 & 4 \\ 2 & -3 & 4 \\ 0 & -1 & 1 \end{vmatrix}$, then A^{-1} equal to

A. A B. A^2

C. A^3 D. A^4

33. A speaks truth in 75% and B in 80% of the cases. In what percentage of cases are they likely to contradict each other narrarting the same incident

A. 35% B. 45%

C. 15% D. 5%

34. If $y = e^{ax} \cos bx$, then $\frac{dy}{dx}$ equals

A. $e^{ax}(a \cos bx + b \sin bx)$

B. $e^{ax}(a \cos bx - b \sin bx)$

C. $e^{ax}(a \sin bx + b \sin bx)$

D. $e^{ax}(b \sin ax - a \cos bx)$

35. The solution of $\frac{dy}{dx} = \frac{ax + h}{by + k}$ represents a parabola when

A. $a = 1, b = 2$ B. $a = 0, b = 0$

C. $a = 0, b \neq 0$ D. $a = 2, b = 1$

36. The mean of the Beta distribution $\mu = E(X) = \frac{r(\alpha+\beta)}{r(\alpha)r(\beta)} \int_0^1 x\left[x^{\alpha-1}(1-x)^{\beta-1}\right] dx$ is:

A. $\frac{\alpha}{\alpha+\beta}$ B. $\frac{\beta}{\alpha+\beta}$

C. $\frac{\alpha}{\alpha-\beta}$ D. $\frac{\beta}{\alpha-\beta}$

37. Utilization of M/M/1 system is:

A. $\lambda\mu$ B. λ/μ

C. μ/λ D. $1/\lambda\mu$

38. If H and K are the subgroups of order 3 and 5 respectively. If O (G) = 4, then

A. $H \cap K \neq \{e\}$

B. $H \cap K = \{e\}$

C. $H \cup K = \{e\}$

D. None of these

39. The residue of $\sin^2 z/z^8$ at $z = 0$ is:

A. $-\frac{1}{7!}$ B. $-\frac{1}{8!}$

C. 0 D. $\frac{1}{7!}$

40. The differential equation y" – y = 0 has solution:

A. e^x

B. e^{2x}

C. $e^x + c$

D. None of these

ANSWERS

1	2	3	4	5	6	7	8	9	10
D	C	D	D	D	B	C	B	B	C
11	**12**	**13**	**14**	**15**	**16**	**17**	**18**	**19**	**20**
D	C	A	B	A	A	C	B	C	B
21	**22**	**23**	**24**	**25**	**26**	**27**	**28**	**29**	**30**
A	A	D	B	B	B	D	A	B	C
31	**32**	**33**	**34**	**35**	**36**	**37**	**38**	**39**	**40**
A	C	A	B	C	A	B	A	C	D

Some Selected Explanatory Answers

1. We have $R_1 = \frac{u^2}{g(1+\sin\beta)}$

$R_2 = \frac{u^2}{g(1-\sin\beta)}$, $R = \frac{u^2}{g}$

Now, $\frac{1}{R_1} + \frac{1}{R_2} = \frac{g(1-\sin\beta)}{u^2} + \frac{g(1-\sin\beta)}{u^2}$

$= \frac{g(1+\sin\beta + 1 - \sin\beta)}{u^2}$

$= \frac{2g}{u^2} = \frac{2}{R}$, *i.e.* $\frac{1}{R_1} + \frac{1}{R_2} = \frac{2}{R}$

$\Rightarrow \frac{1}{R_1}, \frac{1}{R}$ and $\frac{1}{R_2}$ are in AP

$\Rightarrow R_1, R, R_2$ in HP

2. Let AB = d, AM is the perpendicular distance from A to $\overrightarrow{P}$

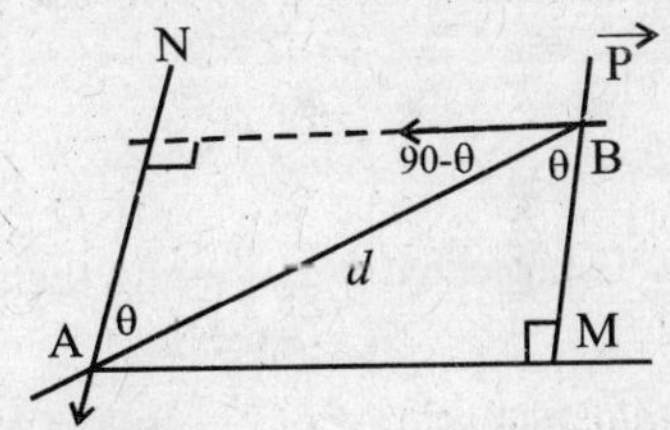

In Δ ABM

$\sin\theta = \frac{AM}{AB}$

AM = d sin θ

Moment of couple $\overrightarrow{G} = \overrightarrow{P}AM = P.d \sin\theta$ ...(*i*)

When $\overrightarrow{P}$ is turned through a right angle then Moment of couple

$\overrightarrow{H} = \overrightarrow{P} d \sin(90° + \theta) = \overrightarrow{P} d \cos\theta$ ...(*ii*)

When $\overrightarrow{P}$ is turned through an angle a then moment of couple

$= \overrightarrow{P} d \sin(a + \theta)$

$= \vec{P} d\,[\sin a \cos\theta + \cos a \sin\theta]$
$(\vec{P}.d \cos\theta)\,\sin a + (\vec{P}.d \sin\theta) \cos a$
$= \vec{G} \cos a + \vec{H} \sin a$
[using (*i*) and (*ii*)]

3. We have $R^2 = u^2 + f^2t^2 + 2uft \cos(180° - a)$

$R^2 = u^2 + f^2t^2 - 2uft \cos a$

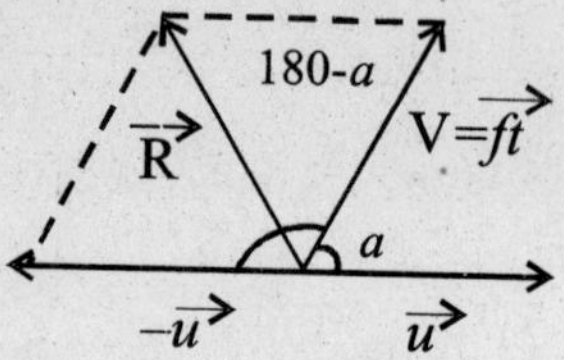

Let $V = u^2 + f^2t^2 - 2uft \cos a$

$$\frac{dv}{dt} = 0 + 2f^2t - 2uf \cos a$$

$$\frac{d^2v}{dt^2} = 2f^2 = +\text{Ve}$$

i.e. velocity will be least after a time

$$\frac{dv}{dt} = 0 = 2f^2t - 2uf \cos a$$

$$2f^2t = 2uf \cos a$$

$$t = \frac{2uf \cos a}{2f^2}$$

$$t = \frac{u \cos a}{f}$$

4. When stone is projected horizontally then

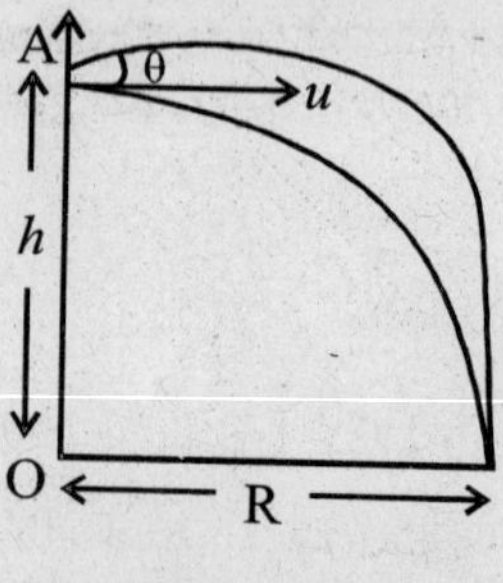

$R = u \cos\theta \times t$

$h = u \sin\theta \times t + \frac{1}{2} gt^2$

$R = ut$ and $h = \frac{1}{2} gt^2$

$R = ut$ and $t = \sqrt{\frac{2h}{g}}$

$$\Rightarrow R = u\sqrt{\frac{2h}{g}} \quad ...(i)$$

When stone is projected at an angle of θ to the horizontal then

$$R = u \cos\theta \times t \quad ...(ii)$$

and $h = -u \sin\theta \times t + \frac{1}{2} gt^2$ ...(*iii*)

using (*i*) in (*ii*) we get

$$u\sqrt{\frac{2h}{g}} = u \cos\theta \times t$$

$$\Rightarrow t = \frac{1}{\cos\theta}\sqrt{\frac{2h}{g}} \quad ...(iv)$$

using (*iv*) in (*iii*) we get

$$h = \frac{-u\sin\theta}{\cos\theta}\sqrt{\frac{2h}{g}} + \frac{1}{2} g \frac{1}{\cos^2\theta}\left(\frac{2h}{g}\right),$$

$$h = -u \tan\theta\sqrt{\frac{2h}{g}} + \frac{h}{\cos^2\theta}$$

$$\Rightarrow h\left[1 - \frac{1}{\cos^2\theta}\right] = -u \tan\theta\sqrt{\frac{2h}{g}}$$

$$\Rightarrow h(-\tan^2\theta) = -u \tan\theta\sqrt{\frac{2h}{g}}$$

$$\Rightarrow \tan\theta = u\sqrt{\frac{2}{gh}}$$

5. Here $x_1 + x_2 = S$

$t_1 + t_2 = t$

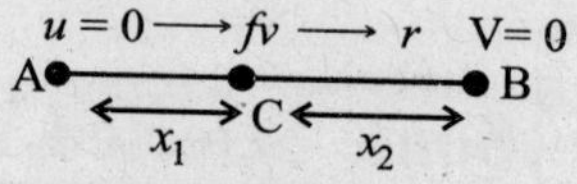

we have from A to C

$v^2 = u^2 + 2fx_1$

$v^2 = 0 + 2fx_1$

$$\Rightarrow x_1 = \frac{v^2}{2f} \quad ...(i)$$

and $v = u + ft$

$v = 0 + ft_1$

$$\Rightarrow t_1 = \frac{v}{f} \quad ...(ii)$$

from C to B $v^2 = u^2 + 2fs$

$v^2 = u^2 - 2rx_2$

$0 = v^2 - 2rx_2$

$$\Rightarrow x_2 = \frac{v^2}{2r} \quad ...(iii)$$

and $v = v - rt_2$

$0 = v - rt_2$

$$\Rightarrow t_2 = \frac{v}{r} \quad ...(iv)$$

Adding (*i*) and (*iii*)

$$x_1 + x_2 = \frac{v^2}{2}\left(\frac{1}{f} + \frac{1}{r}\right)$$

$$2S = v^2\left(\frac{1}{f}+\frac{1}{r}\right) \quad ...(v)$$

Adding (*ii*) and (*iv*)

$$t_1 + t_2 = v\left(\frac{1}{f}+\frac{1}{r}\right)$$

$$t = v\left(\frac{1}{f}+\frac{1}{r}\right)$$

$$t^2 = v^2\left(\frac{1}{f}+\frac{1}{r}\right)^2 \quad ...(vi)$$

Dividing (*vi*) by (*v*)

$$\frac{t^2}{2S} = \frac{v^2\left(\frac{1}{f}+\frac{1}{r}\right)^2}{v^2\left(\frac{1}{f}+\frac{1}{r}\right)} = \left(\frac{1}{f}+\frac{1}{r}\right)$$

$$t = \sqrt{2S\left(\frac{1}{f}+\frac{1}{r}\right)}$$

6. $\sum_{n=0}^{\infty}\frac{(\log x)^n}{n!} = e\log e^x = x$

7. We have $\exp.\left[(x-1)-\frac{1}{2}(x-1)^2+\frac{1}{3}(x-1)^3....\right]$

$= \exp.[\log(1+x-1)] = x$

8. We have $3^2x^2 - 7x + 7 = 9$

$\Rightarrow 9x^2 - 7x - 2 = 0$

$D = b^2 - 4ac$

$= 49 + 72$

$= 121$

The discriminant of this equation is positive, hence, it has two real roots

10. Given $\alpha + \beta + \gamma = \pi$

Taking $\alpha = -\frac{\pi}{2}, \beta = -\frac{\pi}{2}$ and $\gamma = 2\pi$ (Note)

$\therefore \sin\alpha + \sin\beta + \sin\gamma = -1 - 1 + 0 = -2$

But, $\sin\alpha + \sin\beta + \sin y \le 3$ for any α, β, γ. Hence minimum value of $\sin\alpha + \sin\beta + \sin\gamma$ is negative.

12. Total time taken

$\left(\frac{K}{10}+\frac{3K}{20}\right)\sec = \frac{K}{4}\sec$

Total distance = 4K

$\therefore$ Average speed$= \frac{4K}{K/4} = 16$ m/sec

13. Given $(\cot a_1)(\cot a_2).......(\cot a_n) = 1$

$$\Rightarrow \prod_{i=1}^{n}\cos a_i = \prod_{i=1}^{n}\sin a_i$$

$$\Rightarrow \prod_{i=1}^{n}\cos^2 a_i = \prod_{i=1}^{n}\sin a_i \cos a_i$$

$$= \prod_{i=1}^{n}\frac{\sin 2ai}{2}, \quad \le \frac{1}{2^n}$$

$$\Rightarrow \prod_{i=1}^{n}\cos ai \le \frac{1}{2^{n/2}}$$

Hence, maximum value of $\prod_{i=1}^{n}\cos ai$ is $\frac{1}{2^{n/2}}$

15. Putting $a = b = 1$ and $a = 1, b = -1$

We get $\sigma_{x+y}^2 = \sigma_x^2 + \sigma_y^2$

And $\sigma_{x-y}^2 = \sigma_x^2 + \sigma_y^2 \quad ...(i)$

we have $\text{cor}(u,v) = \sigma_x^2 - \sigma_y^2$

$r(u,v) = \frac{\text{cor}(u.\,v)}{\sigma_u^2}$ from (*i*)

$= \frac{\sigma_x^2 - \sigma_y^2}{\sigma_x^2 - \sigma_y^2}$

16. We have $x + 4y = 3$ and $3x + y = 15$ as the lines of regression of y on x and x on y respectively. Thus for given value of y, x is obtained from the line of regression of x on y i.e. on $3x + y = 15$, we get $x = 4$

17. $f(x) = \log|x| = \begin{cases}\log x, & x > 0\\ \log(-x), & x < 0\end{cases}$

$\therefore f'(x) = \begin{cases}1/x, & x > 0\\ \frac{1}{-x}\times(-1) = \frac{1}{x}, & x < 0\end{cases}$

$\Rightarrow f'(x) = \frac{1}{x}$ for all $x \ne 0$.

18. Since $(\vec{a}\times\vec{b}).\vec{c}$ is the volume with adjacent sides $\vec{a}, \vec{b}$ and $\vec{c}$ if $|(\vec{a}\times\vec{b})\vec{c}| = |\vec{a}|.|\vec{b}|.|\vec{c}|$ then the parallelopiped is a rectangular *i.e* edges are at right angle to one another

$\therefore \vec{a}.\vec{b}=0,\ \vec{b}.\vec{c}=0,\ \vec{c}.\vec{a}=0$

19. Moment of force F about A = 0

$\therefore$ Line of action of force F passes through A

Let angle between $\overrightarrow{AB}$ and $\vec{F}$ be θ

$\therefore$ Moment of force F about B

$= F.\,3\sin\theta = 9$ ...(*i*)

And moment of force F about C

$F.4\cos\theta = 16$ ...(*ii*)

From (*i*) and (*ii*) $f = 5$N

20. Weighted arithmetic mean

$$=\frac{1\times1+2\times2+3\times3+\ldots\ldots\ldots\ldots+n\times n}{1+2+3+\ldots\ldots\ldots+n}$$

$$=\frac{(1^2+2^2+3^2+\ldots\ldots\ldots+n^2}{\frac{1}{2}n(n+1)}$$

$$=\frac{n(n+1)(2n+1)}{6}\times\frac{2}{n(n+1)}$$

$$=\frac{2n+1}{3}$$

21. $$A\sim\begin{bmatrix}2&3&1&4\\0&1&2&-1\\0&0&0&0\end{bmatrix}(R_3\to R_3+2R_2)$$

So, rank (A) = 2

22. $$\Delta=\begin{vmatrix}1&\frac{\log y}{\log x}&\frac{\log z}{\log x}\\\frac{\log x}{\log y}&1&\frac{\log z}{\log y}\\\frac{\log x}{\log z}&\frac{\log y}{\log z}&1\end{vmatrix}$$

$[R_1\to(\log x)R_1, R_2\to(\log y)R_2$ and $R_3\to(\log z)R_3]$

$$\Rightarrow\frac{1}{\log x.\log y.\log z}=\begin{vmatrix}\log x&\log y&\log z\\\log x&\log y&\log z\\\log x&\log y&\log z\end{vmatrix}=0$$

24. The displacement x for all SHM is given by $x = a\cos(nt+b)$

$$\therefore\frac{dx}{dt}=-na\sin(nt+b)$$

$$\Rightarrow\frac{d^2x}{dt^2}=-n^2a\cos(nt+b)$$

$$\Rightarrow\frac{d^2x}{dt^2}=-n^2x$$

$$\text{or }\frac{d^2x}{dt^2}+n^2x=0$$

26. (b) Putting $\sqrt{x}=t$ and $\frac{1}{2\sqrt{x}}dx=dt,$

we get $\int\frac{a^{\sqrt{x}}}{\sqrt{x}}dx=2\int a^t\,dt$

$$=\frac{2a^t}{\log a}+c=\frac{2a^{\sqrt{x}}}{\log a}+c$$

27. $n(s)$ = number of ways of arranging N persons in a row.

$={}^NP_N=N!$

Consider two particular cadets as one. The, (N – 1) persons can be arranged (N – 1)! ways and these two cadets can be arranged amongest them selves in 2! ways.

$\therefore n(E)=(N-1)!\times2!$

Hence required probability.

$$=\frac{(N-1)!\times2!}{N!}=\frac{2}{N}$$

29. Clearly $n(s) = (6\times6) = 36$

Let E = event of getting the sum 7 or less than,

E = {(1, 1) (1, 2) (2, 1) (1, 3) (3, 1) (2, 2) (1, 4) (4, 1) (2, 3) (3, 2) (1, 5) (2, 4) (3, 3) (5, 1)(4, 2) (1, 6) (2, 5) (3, 4) (6, 1) (5, 2) (4, 3)}

$$\therefore P(E)=\frac{21}{36}=\frac{7}{12}$$

Required probability

$$=P(\bar{E})=1-P(E)=\left(1-\frac{7}{12}\right)=\frac{5}{12}$$

30. The set A is the set of all points on the curve $y=e^x$ and the set B is the set of all points on the line $y=x$, passing through the origin and making 45° angle with x– axis. These two curves do not intersect therefore $A\cap B=\phi$.

31. Since $x \in A \cap B \Rightarrow x \in A$ and $x \in B \Rightarrow x$ is a multiple of 3 and x is a multiple of 5 $\Rightarrow x$ is multiple of 15. Hence $A \cap B = \{x \mid x \text{ is a multiple of } 15\}$

32. By direct multiplication, we find that $A^4 = I$
Hence $A \cdot A^3 = I$
$A^{-1} = A^3$

33. Let E = event that A speaks the truth
F = event that B speaks the truth then,

$$P(E) = \frac{75}{100} = \frac{3}{4}, P(F) = \frac{80}{100} = \frac{4}{5}$$

$$P(\bar{E}) = \left(1 - \frac{3}{4}\right) = \frac{1}{4},\ P(\bar{F}) = \left(1 - \frac{4}{5}\right) = \frac{1}{5}$$

P(A and B condradict each other)
= P [A Speaks truth and B tells a lie)
or (A tells a lie and B speaks the truth)]

$$= P(E \text{ and } \bar{F}) + P(\bar{E} \text{ and } F)$$

$$= P(E).P(\bar{F}) + P(\bar{E}).P(F)$$

$$= \frac{3}{4} \times \frac{1}{5} + \frac{1}{4} \times \frac{4}{5} = \frac{3}{20} + \frac{1}{5} = \frac{7}{20}$$

$$= \left(\frac{7}{20} \times 100\right)\% = 35\%$$

35. $\dfrac{dy}{dx} = \dfrac{ax+h}{by+k}$

$$\Rightarrow (by + k)\, dy = (ax + h)\, dx$$

$$\Rightarrow \frac{b}{2} y^2 + ky = \frac{a}{2} x^2 + hx + c$$

For this to represent a parabola one of the two terms x^2 or y^2 is zero. Therefore,
either $a = 0, b \neq 0$ or $a \neq 0, b = 0$

36. $\dfrac{r(\alpha+\beta)}{r(\alpha)r(\beta)} \displaystyle\int_0^1 x^{\alpha}(1-x)^{\beta-1}\, dx$

$$= \frac{r(\alpha+\beta)}{r(\alpha) \cdot r(\beta)} \cdot \frac{r(\alpha+1)r(\beta)}{r(\alpha+1+\beta)}$$

$$= \frac{r(\alpha+\beta)\alpha r(\alpha)r(\beta)}{r(\alpha) \cdot r(\beta)(\alpha+\beta)r(\alpha+\beta)}$$

$$= \frac{\alpha}{\alpha+\beta}$$

SET–15

CSIR–UGC (NET) MATHEMATICAL SCIENCES

PART-B

1. If $A=\begin{bmatrix}\cos x & \sin x\\ -\sin x & \cos x\end{bmatrix}$ and A *adj* (A) $= k\begin{bmatrix}1 & 0\\ 0 & 1\end{bmatrix}$ then the value of k is

A. $\sin x \cos x$ B. 1

C. 2 D. 3

2. If $A=\begin{bmatrix}a & b\\ b & a\end{bmatrix}$ and $A^2=\begin{bmatrix}\alpha & \beta\\ \beta & \alpha\end{bmatrix}$ then

A. $\alpha = a^2+b^2,\ \beta = ab$

B. $\alpha = a^2+b^2,\ \beta = 2ab$

C. $\alpha = a^2+b^2,\ \beta = a^2-b^2$

D. $\alpha = 2ab,\ \beta = a^2+b^2$

3. The minimum value $px + qy$ when $xy = r^2$ is

A. $2r\sqrt{pq}$ B. $2pr\sqrt{r}$

C. $-2r\sqrt{pq}$ D. None of these

4. The general solution of the trigonometrical equation $\sin x + \cos x = 1$, for $n = 0, \pm 1$....... given by

A. $x = 2n\pi$

B. $x = 2n\pi + \pi/2$

C. $x = n\pi + (-1)^2\pi/4 - \pi/4$

D. None of these

5. $\lim_{x\to 0}\dfrac{\int_0^{x^2}\sin\sqrt{t}\,dt}{x^3}$ is equal to

A. 1/3 B. 1

C. 2/3 D. None of these

6. If $f(x) = \begin{cases} mx+1, x\le \pi/2\\ \sin x + n, x > \pi/2\end{cases}$ is continuous at $x = \pi/2$ then

A. $m=1, n=0$ B. $m=\dfrac{n\pi}{2}+1$

C. $n=\dfrac{m\pi}{2}$ D. $m=\dfrac{n\pi}{2}$

7. The function f defined by $f(x) = (x+2)\,e^{-x}$ is

A. Decreasing for all x

B. Decreasing in $(-\infty, -1)$ and increasing in $(-1, \infty)$

C. Increasing for all x

D. Decreasing in $(-1, \infty)$ and increasing in $(-\infty, -1)$

8. Domain of $f(x) = \dfrac{\sqrt{x^2-4}}{\cos^{-1}(2-x)} =$

A. $[-2, 3]$ B. $[1, 2]$

C. $[2, 3]$ D. $[-2, 2]$

9. If $f(x) = x + 2$, then $f^1\{f(x)\}$ at $x = 4$ is

A. 8 B. 1

C. 4 D. 5

10. The domain of definition of the function $y(x)$ given by equation $2x + 2y = 2$ is

A. $0 < x \le 1$ B. $0 \le x \le 1$

C. $-x < x \le 0$ D. $-x < x < 1$

11. The angle of intersection of the curves $y = x^2$, $6y = 7 - x^3$ at (1, 1) is

A. $\pi/4$ B. $\pi/3$

C. $\pi/2$ D. None of these

12. The area between the curve $y = 2x^4 - x^2$, the x-axis and the coordinate of two minima of the curve is

A. $\dfrac{7}{120}$ B. $\dfrac{9}{120}$

C. $\dfrac{11}{120}$ D. None of these

13. The set of all values of a for which the function $f(x) = \left(\dfrac{\sqrt{a+y}}{1-a} - 1\right)x^5 - 3x + \log 5$ decrease for all real x is

A. $(-a, a)$

B. $(1,a)$

C. $\left(-3,\dfrac{5-\sqrt{27}}{2}\right) \cup (2,a)$

D. $\left(-4,\dfrac{3-\sqrt{21}}{2}\right) \cup (1,a)$

14. The area of the figure bounded by the lines $x = 0$, $x = \pi/2$ and $f(x) = \sin x$, $g(x) = \cos x$, is

A. $2\left(\sqrt{2}+1\right)$ B. $\sqrt{3}-1$

C. $2\left(\sqrt{3}-1\right)$ D. $2\left(\sqrt{2}-1\right)$

15. $\displaystyle\int_{\pi/6}^{\pi/3} \frac{dx}{1+\sqrt{\cot x}}$ is

A. $\pi/3$ B. $\pi/6$

C. $\pi/12$ D. $\pi/2$

16. $\displaystyle\int \frac{dx}{1+3\sin^2 x}$ is equal to

A. $\frac{1}{3}\tan^{-1}(3\tan^2 x)$ B. $\frac{1}{2}\tan^{-1}(2\tan x)$

C. $\tan^{-1}(\tan x)$ D. None of these

17. If $g(x) = \displaystyle\int_0^x \cos^4 t\,dt$ then $g(x+\pi)$ equals

A. $g(x) + g(\pi)$ B. $g(x) - g(\pi)$

C. $g(x)\,g(\pi)$ D. $\dfrac{g(x)}{g(\pi)}$

18. The function $L(x) = \displaystyle\int_1^x \frac{dt}{t}$ satisfies the equation

A. $L(x+y) = L(x) + L(y)$

B. $L\left(\dfrac{x}{y}\right) = L(x) + L(y)$

C. $L(xy) = L(x) + L(y)$

D. None of these

19. Area of the region bounded by the curve $y = \tan x$, tangent, drawn to the curve at $x = \dfrac{\pi}{4}$ and the x-axis is

A. $\log\sqrt{2}$ B. $\log\sqrt{2}+\frac{1}{4}$

C. $\log\sqrt{2}-\frac{1}{4}$ D. $\frac{1}{4}$

20. $\displaystyle\int_1^2 e^{-1/x}\frac{dx}{x^2}$ is equal to

A. $\dfrac{1}{\sqrt{e}}+\dfrac{1}{e}$ B. $\dfrac{1}{\sqrt{e}}-\dfrac{1}{e}$

C. $\dfrac{1}{e}-\dfrac{1}{\sqrt{e}}$ D. None of these

21. The solution of $\dfrac{dy}{dx}+2y\tan x = \sin x$ is

A. $y\sec^3 x = \sec^2 x + c$

B. $y\sec^2 x = \sec x + c$

C. $y\sin x = \tan x + c$

D. None of these

22. If $x = a(\cos\theta + \theta\sin\theta)$, $y = a(\sin\theta - \theta\cos\theta)$, $\dfrac{dy}{dx}$ is equal to

A. $\cos\theta$ B. $\tan\theta$

C. $\sec\theta$ D. $\operatorname{cosec}\theta$

23. The solution of $\dfrac{dy}{dx}+\sqrt{\left[\dfrac{1-y^2}{1-x^2}\right]} = 0$ is

A. $\tan^{-1}x + \cot^{-1}x = c$

B. $\sin^{-1}x + \sin^{-1}y = c$

C. $\sec^{-1}x + \operatorname{cosec}^{-1}x = c$

D. None of these

24. The solution of $\cos(x+y)\,dy = dx$ is

A. $y = \tan\left(\dfrac{x+y}{2}\right)+c$

B. $y = \cos^{-1}\left(\dfrac{y}{x}\right)+c$

C. $y = x\sec\left(\dfrac{y}{x}\right)+c$

D. None of these

25. If $y^2 = ax^2 + bx + c$, then $y^3\dfrac{d^2y}{dx^2}$ is

A. A constant

B. A function of x only

C. A function of y only

D. A function of x and y

26. The differential equation of all 'simple harmonic motions' of given period $\dfrac{2\pi}{n}$ is

A. $\frac{d^2x}{dt^2}+nx=0$ B. $\frac{d^2x}{dt^2}+n^2x=0$

C. $\frac{d^2x}{dt^2}-n^2x=0$ D. $\frac{d^2x}{dt^2}+\frac{1}{n^2}x=0$

27. If A and B are such events that P(A) > 0 and P (B) ≠ 1 then $P(\overline{A/B})$ is equal to

A. $1-P(A/B)$ B. $1-P(\overline{A}/B)$

C. $\frac{1-P(A \cup B)}{P(\overline{B})}$ D. $\frac{P(\overline{A})}{P(\overline{B})}$

28. An unbiased die with faces marked 1, 2, 3, 4, 5 and 6 is rolled four times out of four face values obtained, the probability that the minimum face value is not less than 2 and the maximum face value is not greater than 5 is then

A. 16/81 B. 1/81

C. 80/81 D. 65/81

29. The probability of event A occuring is 0.5 and B occuring is 0.3, if A and B are mutually exclusive events, then the probability of neither A nor B occuring is

A. 0.6 B. 0.5

C. 0.7 D. None of these

30. A coin is tossed 3 times by 2 persons. What is the probability that both get equals numbers of heads?

A. $\frac{3}{8}$ B. $\frac{1}{9}$

C. $\frac{5}{16}$ D. None of these

31. A person writes 4 letters and addresses 4 envelopes, if the letters are placed in the envelopes at random. What is the probability that all letters are not placed in the right envelopes?

A. $\frac{1}{4}$ B. $\frac{11}{24}$

C. $\frac{15}{24}$ D. $\frac{23}{24}$

32. Four persons are selected at random from a group of 3 men, 2 women and 4 children. What is the chance that exactly 2 of them are children?

A. $\frac{9}{21}$ B. $\frac{10}{23}$

C. $\frac{11}{24}$ D. $\frac{10}{21}$

33. Taking n = 4, by trapezoidal rule the value of $\int_0^2 \frac{dx}{1+x}$ is

A. 1.1167 B. 1.1176

C. 1.118 D. None of these

34. The rational number which is equal to the number 2.375 with recurring decimal is

A. $\frac{2355}{1001}$ B. $\frac{2370}{997}$

C. $\frac{2355}{999}$ D. None of these

35. Simpson's one third rule for evalution $\int_a^b f(x)dx$ requires the interval [a, b] to be divided into

A. An even number of sub = intervals of equal width

B. Any number of sub = intervals

C. Any number of sub = intervals of equal width

D. An odd number of sub = interval of equals width

36. When a number is rounded to n decimal digit then the magnitude of the relative error can not exceed

A. 10^n B. 10^{n+1}

C. $0.5\times10^{n+1}$ D. None of these

37. Seven non-defective radio tubes are mixed up with 3 defective radio tubes. Find the probability that 5 or more trials are needed to detect all defective radio tubes:

A. $\frac{29}{30}$ B. $\frac{27}{29}$

C. $\frac{29}{27}$ D. $\frac{22}{30}$

38. The blocking probability of M/M/1/N queueing system is

A. $\frac{\rho}{1-\rho^N}$ B. $\frac{1-\rho}{1-\rho^{N+1}}$

C. $(1-\rho)\rho^N$ D. $\frac{(1-\rho)}{1-\rho^{N+1}}\rho^N$

39. If A = {ϕ, {ϕ}} then the power set of A is:

A. ϕ

B. A

C. {ϕ, {ϕ}, {{ϕ}}, A}

D. None of these

40. "Let $f(z)$ and $g(z)$ be analytic inside and on a simple closed curve C and let $|g(z)| < |f(z)|$ on C. Then $f(z)$ and $f(z) + g(z)$ have the same number of zeroes inside C." This statement is known as:

A. Luca's Theorem

B. Rouche's Theorem

C. Morera's Theorem

D. Lioville's Theorem

ANSWERS

1	2	3	4	5	6	7	8	9	10
B	B	D	C	C	C	D	C	B	D
11	**12**	**13**	**14**	**15**	**16**	**17**	**18**	**19**	**20**
C	A	D	D	C	B	A	C	A	B
21	**22**	**23**	**24**	**25**	**26**	**27**	**28**	**29**	**30**
B	B	B	A	A	B	C	A	D	C
31	**32**	**33**	**34**	**35**	**36**	**37**	**38**	**39**	**40**
D	D	A	C	A	C	A	D	C	B

Some Selected Explanatory Answers

1. A *adj* (A)

$$= \begin{bmatrix} \cos x & \sin x \\ -\sin x & \cos x \end{bmatrix} \begin{bmatrix} \cos x & \sin x \\ \sin x & \cos x \end{bmatrix}$$

$$= \begin{bmatrix} 1 & 0 \\ 0 & 1 \end{bmatrix} \therefore \text{k}=1$$

2. $A \times \Lambda = \begin{bmatrix} a^2+b^2 & 2ab \\ 2ab & a^2+b^2 \end{bmatrix}$

$\therefore \alpha = a^2+b^2,\ \beta = 2ab$

3. $xy = r^2 \Rightarrow x = \frac{r^2}{y}$

$\therefore z = px + qy = \frac{\text{P}r^2}{y} + qy$

or $qy^2 - zy + pr^2 = 0$

For $y \in \text{R}$, $z^2 \ge 4qpr^2$

$\Rightarrow \left(z+2r\sqrt{pq}\right)\left(z-2r\sqrt{pq}\right) \ge 0$

$\therefore \min z = -\infty$

4. $\sin x + \cos x = 1$

$\Rightarrow \sin(x+\pi/4) = 1/\sqrt{2} = \sin\pi/4$

$\Rightarrow x+\pi/4 = n\pi + (-1)^n \pi/4$

$\Rightarrow x = n\pi + (-1)^n \frac{\pi}{4} - \frac{\pi}{4}$

5. Using L–H rule

$$\lim_{x\to 0} \frac{\int_0^{x^2} \sin\sqrt{t}\, dt}{x^3}$$

$$= \lim_{x\to 0} \frac{2x \sin x}{3x^2} = \frac{2}{3}$$

6. R.H.L $= f(\pi/2)$

$\Rightarrow 1 + n = \frac{m\pi}{2} + 1 \Rightarrow \text{n} = \frac{m\pi}{2}$

7. $f(x) = e^{-x} - e^{-x}(x+2)$

$= e^{-x}(-1-x)$

$= -e^{-x}(1+x)$

$\therefore$ decreasing in $(-1, \infty)$ and increasing in $(-\infty - 1)$

8. Domain of $\sqrt{x^2-4}$

$\Rightarrow x \le -2$ or $x \ge 2$

domain of $\cos^{-1}(2-x)$

$\Rightarrow -1 \le 2-x < 1$

$\Rightarrow x > 1$ and $x \le 3$

$\therefore$ domain = [2, 3]

9. Since $f(x) = x+2$

$= f\{f(x)\} = f(x+2)$

$= x+2+2 = x+4$

$\therefore f\{f(x)\} = x+4 \Rightarrow f'(f(x)) = 1$

$\Rightarrow f'(f(x))$ at 4 is 1

10. For choice A and B, $2^x, 2^y \geq 2$. There fore A and B are not true and for C, $2x+2y \leq 2$, therefore C is also not possible. Thus only D is the possible option

11. The two curves are $y = x^2$ and $6y = 7 - x^3$

Differentiating $y = x^2$ w. r. t x we get

$$\frac{dy}{dx} = 2x$$

$$\therefore m_1 = \left(\frac{dy}{dx}\right)_{(1,1)} = 2$$

Differentiating $6y = 7 - x^3$ w. r. t. x,

we get $\frac{dy}{dx} = -x^2/2$

$$\therefore m_2 = \left(\frac{dy}{dx}\right)_{(1,1)} = -\frac{1}{2}$$

$\therefore m_1 m_2 = -1$ .Hence, the angle of intersection of two curves is $\pi/2$

12. We have $y = 2x^4 - x^2$

$$\therefore \frac{dy}{dx} = 8x^3 - 2x$$

Putting $\frac{dy}{dx} = 0$, we get $x = 0$

$$x = \pm\frac{1}{2}$$

Now $\frac{d^2y}{dx^2} = 24x^2 - 2$ it can be easily seen that y is minimum for $x = \pm\frac{1}{2}$, then the required area

$$= \left|\int_{-1/2}^{1/2} y dx\right| = \left|\int_{-1/2}^{1/2} (2 \times x^4 - x^2) dx\right|$$

$$= \left|2\int_0^{1/2} 2x^4 - x^2) dx\right|$$

$$= \left|2\left[\frac{2x^5}{5} - \frac{x^3}{3}\right]_0^{1/2}\right|$$

$$= \left|2\left[\frac{1}{80} - \frac{1}{24}\right]\right| = \frac{7}{120}$$

15. $$I = \int_{\pi/6}^{\pi/3} \frac{dx}{1+\sqrt{\cot x}}$$

$$= \int_{\pi/6}^{\pi/3} \frac{\sqrt{\sin x}}{\sqrt{\sin x} + \sqrt{\cos x}} dx$$

$$= \frac{1}{2}\left(\frac{\pi}{3} - \frac{\pi}{6}\right) = \frac{\pi}{12}$$

16. $$I = \int \frac{dx}{1+3\sin^2 x}$$

$$= \int \frac{dx}{\cos^2 x + 4\sin^2 x}$$

$$= \int \frac{\sec^2 x}{1+4\tan^2 x} dx$$

Let $\tan x = z$

$\Rightarrow \sec^2 x dx = dz$

$$\therefore \int \frac{dz}{1+4z^2} = \frac{1}{4}\int \frac{dz}{z^2 + \left(\frac{1}{2}\right)^2}$$

$$= \frac{1}{4}\frac{1}{1/2}\tan^{-1}\frac{z}{1/2}$$

$$= \frac{1}{2}\tan^{-1}(2\tan x)$$

17. $$g(x+\pi) = \int_0^{x+\pi} \cos^4 .t\, dt$$

$$= \int_0^{\pi} \cos^4 t dt + \int_{\pi}^{x+\pi} \cos^4 t dt$$

$$= g(\pi) + \int_{\pi}^{x+\pi} \cos^4 t\, dt$$

Putting $t = z + \pi \therefore dt = dz$

when $t = \pi \Rightarrow z = 0$

when $t = x + \pi \Rightarrow z = x$

$$\therefore g(x+\pi) = g(\pi) + \int_0^x \cos^4(\pi + z)dz$$

$$= g(\pi) + \int_0^x \cos^4 zdz$$

$$= g(\pi) + \int_0^x \cos^4 tdt$$

$$= g(\pi) + g(x)$$

18. $L(x) = \int_1^x \frac{dt}{t} = \log x$

$\therefore$ $L(xy) = \log(xy) = \log(x) + \log(y)$
$= L(x) + L(y)$

20. $\int_1^2 e^{1/x} \frac{dx}{x^2} = \left|e^{-1/x}\right|_1^2$

$= e^{-1/2} - e^{-1}$

$= \frac{1}{\sqrt{e}} - \frac{1}{e}$

21. $\frac{dy}{dx} + 2y \tan x = \sin x$ is a linear differential equation of the form

$\frac{dy}{dx} + y.f(x) = g(x)$, Hence integration factor (I.F.) is

$\text{I.F.} = \exp \int f(x)dx = \exp \int 2\tan x dx$

$= e^{2\log(\sec x)}$

$= e^{\log \sec^2 x} = \sec^2 x$

Hence, the solution is

$y \times \text{I.F.} = \int g(x).\text{I.F.}dx + c$

$y(\sec^2 x) = \int \sin x \sec^2 x\, dx. + c$

$y(\sec^2 x) = \int \sec x \tan x\, dx + c$

$y(\sec^2 x) = \sec x + c$

22. $\frac{dy}{dx} = \frac{dy/d\theta}{dx/d\theta}$

$$= \frac{a[\cos\theta - \theta(-\sin\theta) - (\cos\theta)]}{a[-\sin\theta + \theta\cos\theta + \sin\theta]}$$

$$= \frac{\theta \sin\theta}{\theta\cos\theta} = \tan\theta$$

23. Given equation is

$$\int \frac{dy}{\sqrt{1-y^2}} + \int \frac{dx}{\sqrt{1-x^2}} = 0$$

Intergating we get $\sin^{-1} y + \sin^{-1} x = c$

24. $\cos(x+y)\, dy = dx$ ...(*i*)

Put $x + y = v$, Differentiating

$$1 + \frac{dy}{dx} = \frac{dv}{dx}$$

Put these value in (*i*)

$$\cos v.\left(\frac{dv}{dx} - 1\right) = 1$$

$$\Rightarrow \cos v \frac{dv}{dx} = 1 + \cos v$$

$$\Rightarrow \frac{\cos v}{1+\cos v} dv = dx$$

$$\Rightarrow \left[\frac{2\cos^2(v/2) - 1}{2\cos^2(v/2)}\right] dv = dx$$

$$\Rightarrow \left[1 - \frac{1}{2}\sec^2(v/2)\right] dv = dx$$

integrate $\Rightarrow$

$v - \tan(v/2) = x + c$

$$x + y - \tan\left(\frac{x+y}{2}\right) = x + c$$

$$y = \tan\left(\frac{x+y}{2}\right) + c$$

25. $y^2 = ax^2 + bx + c$

$$\Rightarrow 2y \frac{dy}{dx} = 2ax + b$$

$$\Rightarrow 2\left(\frac{dy}{dx}\right)^2 + 2y.\frac{d^2y}{dx^2} = 2a$$

$$\Rightarrow y.\frac{d^2y}{dx^2} = a - \left(\frac{dy}{dx}\right)^2$$

$$\Rightarrow y.\frac{d^2y}{dx^2} = a - \left(\frac{2ax+b}{2y}\right)^2$$

$$\Rightarrow y.\frac{d^2y}{dx^2} = \frac{4ay^2-(2ax+b)^2}{4y^2}$$

$$\Rightarrow 4y^3\frac{d^2y}{dx^2} = 4a(ax^2+bx+c) - (4a^2x^2+4abx+b^2)$$

$$\Rightarrow 4y^3.\frac{d^2y}{dx^2} = 4ac-b^2$$

$$\Rightarrow y^3.\frac{d^2y}{dx^2} = \frac{4ac-b^2}{4} = \text{a constant}$$

26. The displacement x for all SHM is given by

$x = a\cos(nt+b)$ $\therefore \frac{dx}{dt} = -na\sin(nt+b)$

$$\Rightarrow \frac{d^2x}{dt^2} = -n^2a\cos(nt+b)$$

$$\Rightarrow \frac{d^2x}{dt^2} = -n^2x \text{ or } \frac{d^2x}{dt^2} + n^2x = 0$$

27. $P(\bar{A}/\bar{B}) = \frac{P(\bar{A}\cap\bar{B})}{P(\bar{B})}$

$$= \frac{P(\overline{A\cap B})}{P(\bar{B})} = \frac{1-P(A\cup B)}{P(\bar{B})}$$

28. In a single throw, favourable points are 2, 3, 4 and 5. There number is 4. All possible outcomes are 6

$$P = \frac{4}{6} = \frac{2}{3}$$

Since the die is rolled four times and all results are independent

$\therefore$ Required probability $= \left(\frac{2}{3}\right)^4 = \frac{16}{81}$

29. $P(\bar{A}\cap\bar{B}) = P(\overline{A\cup B})$

$= 1-P(A\cup B)$

$= 1-[P(A)+P(B)]$

$= 1-0.5-0.3$

$= 0.2$

$\therefore$ Events A, B are mutually exclusive we have

$P(A\cap B) = P(A)+P(B)$

30. The condition will be satisfied if both get 0, 1, 2 or 3 heads either [0 head by A and 0 head by B] or 1 head by A and 1 head by B or 2 head by A and 2 head by B or 3 heads by A and 3 head by B

$\therefore$ Required probability

$$= \left[\frac{1}{8}\times\frac{1}{8}+\frac{3}{8}\times\frac{3}{8}+\frac{3}{8}\times\frac{3}{8}+\frac{1}{8}\times\frac{1}{8}\right]$$

$$= \frac{5}{16}$$

31. The total number of ways in which 4 letters can be placed in 4 envelopes = 4!

Now, all the letters can be placed in their corresponding envelopes correctly in only 1 way

Hence, the number of ways that all the letters are not placed in their corresponding envelopes correctly = (4!–1)

$\therefore$ Required probability $= \frac{4!-1}{4!} = \frac{23}{24}$

32. Total number of persons = 2 + 3 + 4 = 9

$\therefore$ Total no. of ways in which 2 persons can be selected $= {}^9C_4$

Total no. of ways in which 2 persons can be selected out of (2 men and 3 women = 5 persons and 2 out of 4 children)

$= {}^5C_2 \times {}^4C_2$

$\therefore$ Required probability $= \frac{{}^5C_2\times{}^4C_2}{{}^9C_4}$

$$\frac{\frac{5\times4}{2\times1}\times\frac{4\times3}{2\times1}}{\frac{9\times8\times7\times6}{4\times3\times2\times1}} = \frac{10\times6}{126}$$

$$= \frac{10}{21}$$

33. Here $y=\frac{1}{1+x}$, $n=4$

So, $h=2/4=0.5$

S.No.	x	y
1	0	1
2	.5	.667
3	1	.5
4	1.5	.4
5	2	.333

By trapezoidal rule

$$\int_0^2 \frac{1}{1+x}dx=\frac{h}{2}\left[(y_1+y_5)+2(y_2+y_3+y_4)\right]$$

$$=\frac{1}{4}\left[(1+.333)+2(.667+.5+4)\right]$$

$$=\frac{1}{4}\times 4.467=1.1167$$

34. Let $x = 2.357357$ ...(*i*)

Multiply with 1000

$1000x=2357.357357$ ...(*ii*)

Subtract (*ii*) and (*i*)

$1000x-x=2355$

$999x=2355$

$$x=\frac{2355}{999}$$

36. If a number is rounded off to n, decimal digits then $|E_R|<0.5\times 10^{n+1}$

i.e. Max^m error due to rounding off $=0.5\times 10^{n+1}$

37. If random variable X is defined as the no. of trials needed to get all defective radio tubes,

$$f(x)=\binom{7}{x-3}\frac{\binom{3}{2}}{\binom{10}{x-1}}\cdot\frac{1}{10-x+1}\quad \text{for } x\geq 3$$

$$=\sum_{x=5}^{10}\frac{\binom{3}{2}\binom{7}{x-3}}{\binom{10}{x-1}(10-x+1)}=\frac{29}{30}$$

SET–16
CSIR–UGC (NET) MATHEMATICAL SCIENCES

PART-B

1. If α, β and ϒ are the roots of $x^3 + qx + r = 0$ then $\sum \frac{\alpha}{\beta + \gamma}$ is

A. 3 B. $q + r$
C. q/r D. -3

2. For $1 \le r \le n$, the value of ${}^nC_r + {}^{n-1}C_r + {}^{n-2}C_r + \ldots\ldots + {}^rC_r$

A. ${}^nC_{r+1}$ B. ${}^{n+1}C_r$
C. ${}^{n+1}C_{r+1}$ D. None of these

3. If α and β are the roots of the equation $x^2 - p(x+1) - q = 0$ then the value of $\frac{\alpha^2+2\alpha+1}{\alpha^2+2\alpha+9} + \frac{\beta^2+2\beta+1}{\beta^2+2\beta+9}$ is

A. 2 B. 1
C. 0 D. None of these

4. The inequality $|2x - 3| < 1$ is valued when x lies in the interval :

A. (3, 4) B. (1, 2)
C. (–1, 2) D. None of these

5. Sum of the series $\log_e 2 + \frac{(\log_e 2)^2}{2!} + \frac{(\log_e 2)^3}{3!} + \ldots$ is equal to

A. 3 B. 2
C. 1 D. 0

6. If Z_1, Z_2, Z_3, Z_4 are four complex numbers, represented by the vertices of a quadrilateral taken in this order such that $Z_1 - Z_4 = Z_2 - Z_3$ and amp. $\frac{Z_4 - Z_1}{Z_2 - Z_1} = \frac{\pi}{2}$ then the quadrilateral is:

A. Square
B. Rectangle
C. Rhombus
D. A cyclic quadrilateral

7. The determinant $\begin{vmatrix} \cos C & \tan A & 0 \\ \sin B & 0 & -\tan A \\ 0 & \sin B & \cos C \end{vmatrix}$

A. $\pi/3$ B. $\pi/2$
C. $2\pi/3$ D. 0

8. If a, b, c, are linearly independent vectors and $\Delta = \begin{vmatrix} a & b & c \\ aa & a.b & a.c \\ ac & bc & cc \end{vmatrix}$ then

A. $\Delta = 0$
B. $\Delta = 1$
C. Δ any non zero value
D. None of these

9. Let pair of vectors $\vec{a}, \vec{b}$ and $\vec{c}, \vec{d}$ each determine a plane. Then the planes are parallel if

A. $(\vec{a} \times \vec{c}) \times (\vec{b} \times \vec{d}) = 0$
B. $(\vec{a} \times \vec{c}) . (\vec{b} \times \vec{d}) = 0$
C. $(\vec{a} \times \vec{b}) \times (\vec{c} \times \vec{d}) = 0$
D. $(\vec{a} \times \vec{b}) \cdot (\vec{c} \times \vec{d}) = 0$

10. Volumes of the parallelopiped whose sides $\overrightarrow{OA} = 2\hat{i} - 3\hat{j}$, $\overrightarrow{OB} = \hat{i} + \hat{j} - \hat{k}$; $\overrightarrow{OC} = 3i - \hat{k}$ is

A. $4/13$ B. 4
C. $2/7$ D. $3/7$

11. $\sqrt{\sin x} + \sqrt{16 - x^2}$ is defined on

A. $(\pi, 4)$ B. $[-4, -\pi]$
C. $[-\pi, 4]$ D. $[-4, \pi]$

12. Find the value of x for which $f(x) = \frac{(x-1)(x-2)}{(x-3)} \ge 0$

A. $(-\infty\ 1) \cup (2,3)$ B. $[-\infty\ 1]\quad (2,3)$
C. $(1,2) \cup (3, \infty)$ D. $[1,2] \cup (3, \infty)$

13. Period of the function $\left|\sin^3 \frac{x}{2}\right| + \left|\cos^5 \frac{x}{5}\right|$ is

A. 2π B. 10π
C. 8π D. 5π

14. $\lim_{x\to 0}\left(\frac{1+5x^2}{1+3x^2}\right)^{1/x^2}$ is equal to

A. e B. e^2
C. $\sqrt{e}$ D. $1/\sqrt{e}$

15. If $\lim_{x\to 0}\frac{(1+a\cos x)-b\sin x}{x^3}=1$, then a, b are

A. $\frac{1}{2}, -\frac{3}{2}$ B. $\frac{5}{2}, -\frac{3}{2}$
C. $-\frac{5}{2}, -\frac{3}{2}$ D. None of these

16. The greatest value of $f(x)=(x+1)^{1/3}-(x-1)^{1/3}$ on [0, 1] is

A. 1 B. 2
C. 3 D. $2^{1/3}$

17. If $g(x)$is a function defined on [–1, 1] and the area of the equilateral triangle with two of its vertices at (0,0) and $\{x, g(x)\}$ is $\frac{\sqrt{3}}{4}$ then the function is

A. $g(x)=\pm\sqrt{1-x^2}$
B. $g(x)=\sqrt{1-x^2}$
C. $g(x)=\sqrt{x^2-1}$
D. $g(x)=\sqrt{x^2+1}$

18. If the normal to the curve $y = f(x)$ at the point (3,4) makes an angle $\frac{3\pi}{4}$ with the positive axis, then $f'(3)$ is equal to

A. –1 B. –3/4
C. 4/3 D. 1

19. What is the area bounded by the curves $x^2 + y^2 = 9$ and $y^2 = 8x$

A. 0
B. $2\sqrt{2}+\frac{9\pi}{2}-9\sin^{-1}\left(\frac{1}{3}\right)$
C. 16π
D. None of these.

20. What are the minimum and maximum values of the function $x^5-5x^4+5x^3-10$

A. –37,–9
B. –10, 0
C. It has 2 minimum and 1 maximum values
D. It has 2 maximum and 1 minimum values

21. The value of the integral $\int_0^1 \cot^{-1}(1-x+x^2)\,dx$ is

A. $\pi-\log 2$ B. $\frac{\pi}{2}-\log 2$
C. $\pi+\log 2$ D. $\frac{\pi}{2}+\log 2$

22. The area bounded by the Y-axis, $y = \cos x$ and $y = \sin x, 0 \le x \le \pi/2$ is

A. $2(\sqrt{2}-1)$ B. $\sqrt{2}-1$
C. $\sqrt{2}+1$ D. $\sqrt{2}$

23. If $\int(a+b-x)=f(x)$, then $\int_a^b xf(x)\,dx$ is equal to

A. $\frac{a+b}{2}\int_a^b f(b-x)\,dx$

B. $\frac{a+b}{2}\int_a^b f(x)\,dx$

C. $\frac{b-a}{2}\int_a^b f(x)\,dx$

D. None of these.

24. $\int_0^{\pi/2}\frac{dx}{1+\tan^3 x}$ is

A. $\pi/2$ B. $\pi/4$
C. π D. 0

25. The integral $\int_0^{1.5}\left[x^2\right]dx$ where $[x]$ denotes the greatest integer less than or equal to x equals

A. $2+\sqrt{2}$ B. $2-\sqrt{2}$
C. 1.5 D. None of these.

26. If $f: R\to R$ and $g: R \to R$ are one to one real valued functions, then the value of the integral $\int_{-\pi}^{\pi}\left[f(x)+f(-x)\right][g(x)-g(-x)]dx$ is

A. 0 B. π
C. 1 D. None of these

27. If $y=\{f(x)\}^{\phi(x)}$ then $\frac{dy}{dx}$ is

A. $e^{\phi \log f}\left[\frac{\phi}{f}\frac{df}{dx}+\log f\frac{d\phi}{dx}\right]$

B. $\frac{\phi}{f}\left(\frac{df}{dx}\right)+\log f\left(\frac{d\phi}{dx}\right)$

C. $e(\phi)\log f\left[\phi\frac{f}{f}+\phi^1 \log f^1\right]$

D. None of these

28. The solution of the differential equation $2x+\frac{dy}{dx}-y=3$, given that $y(0)=-1$ represents a/an

A. Straight line B. Circle
C. Parabola D. Ellipse

29. A coin is tossed $2n$ times. The chance that number of times one gets head is not equal to the number of times one gets tail is

A. $\frac{(2n!)}{n!}\left(\frac{1}{2}\right)^{2n}$ B. $\frac{(2n!)}{(n!)^2}$

C. $1-\frac{(2n!)}{n!}\cdot\frac{1}{4^n}$ D. None of these

30. The probability that at least one of the events A and B occurs is 3/5. If A and B occur simultaneously with probability 1/5 then $P(A^1)+P(B')$ is

A. $\frac{2}{5}$ B. $\frac{4}{5}$
C. $\frac{6}{5}$ D. $\frac{7}{5}$

31. The probability that at least one of the events A and B occurs is 0.6. If A and B occurs simultaneously with probability 0.2 then $P(\overline{A})+P(\overline{B})$ is

A. 0.4 B. 0.8
C. 1.2 D. 1.4

32. Three of six vertices of a rectangular hexagon, are chosen at random. The possibility that the triangle with three vertices is equilateral, equals

A. $\frac{1}{2}$ B. $\frac{1}{5}$
C. $\frac{1}{10}$ D. $\frac{1}{20}$

33. If a balanced coin is flipped twice, what is the probability of getting at least one head?

A. $\frac{3}{4}$ B. $\frac{1}{2}$
C. $\frac{1}{4}$ D. $\frac{2}{3}$

34. Let $f(0)=1$, $f(1)=2.72$ then the trapezoid rule gives approximate value of $\int_0^1 f(x)dx$

A. 3.73 B. 1.86
C. 1.72 D. 0.86

35. By Simpson rule taking $n = 4$, the value of the integral $\int_0^1 \frac{1}{1+x^2}dx$ is equal to

A. 0.785 B. 0.788
C. 0.781 D. None of these

36. An algorithm must terminate in

A. One iteration
B. One step
C. Finite number of steps
D. Finite number of steps but sometimes infinite number of steps

37. A point $Z_o=0$ is called Zero of $f(z)$, if

A. $f(z_o)$ is constant B. $f(z_o)=0$
C. $f(z_o)\geq 0$ D. None of these

38. A game is a fair game if:

A. $\underline{v}=0$ B. $\overline{v}=0$
C. $\underline{v}=\overline{v}=0$ D. $\overline{v}=\underline{v}=v$

39. The complex analytic function $f(z)$ with the imaginary part $e^x(y\cos y+x\sin y)$ is:

A. ze^z B. ze^{iz}
C. e^z/z D. ize^z

40. Partial differential equation of second order in canonical forms $Rr+Ss+Tt+f(x,y,z,p,q)=0$, then $S^2-4RT>0$ represents:

A. Parabolic B. Hyperbolic
C. Elliptic D. Straight line

ANSWERS

1	2	3	4	5	6	7	8	9	10
D	B	B	B	C	B	D	C	C	B
11	**12**	**13**	**14**	**15**	**16**	**17**	**18**	**19**	**20**
B	D	D	B	C	B	A	D	B	A
21	**22**	**23**	**24**	**25**	**26**	**27**	**28**	**29**	**30**
B	B	B	B	B	A	A	A	C	C
31	**32**	**33**	**34**	**35**	**36**	**37**	**38**	**39**	**40**
C	C	A	B	A	C	B	D	A	B

Some Selected Explanatory Answers

1. $\alpha+\beta+\gamma=0$ ...(i)

$$\sum\frac{\alpha}{\beta+\gamma}=\sum\frac{\alpha+\beta+\gamma}{\beta+\gamma}-1=-3$$

2. $S={}^{n}C_r+{}^{n+1}C_r+\ldots\ldots\ldots$

$$+{}^{r+2}C_r+{}^{r+1}C_r+{}^{r}C_r$$

$S={}^{n}C_r+{}^{n-1}C_r+\ldots\ldots\ldots\ldots$

$$+{}^{r+2}C_2+{}^{r+1}C_1+{}^{r+1}C_0$$

$S={}^{n}C_r+{}^{n-1}C_r+\ldots\ldots\ldots\ldots$

$$+{}^{r+2}C_2+{}^{r+1}C_1$$

Similarly, $S={}^{n+2}C_r$

3. $$\frac{(\alpha+1)^2}{(\alpha+1)^2-(1-9)}+\frac{(\beta+1)^2}{(\beta+1)^2-(1-9)}$$

$$=\frac{(\alpha+1)^2}{(\alpha+1)^2-(\alpha+1)(\beta+1)}+\frac{(\beta+1)^2}{(\beta+1)^2-(\alpha+1)(\beta+1)}$$

$$=\frac{\alpha+1}{\alpha-\beta}+\frac{\beta+1}{\beta-\alpha}=1$$

4. $|2x-3|<1$

$\Rightarrow -1<(2x-3)<1$

$\Rightarrow x\in(1,2)$

5. $e^{\log 2}-1=2-1=1$

6.

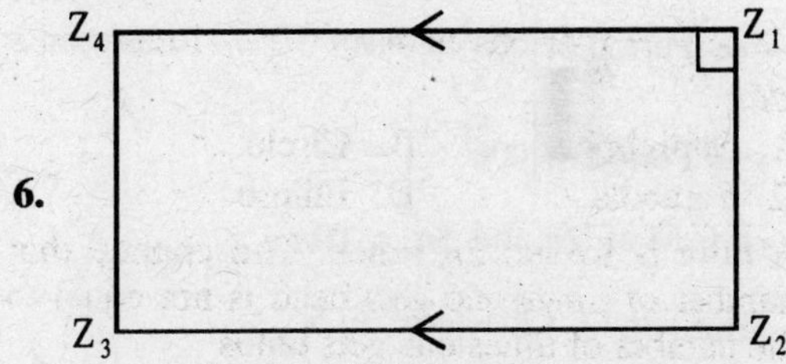

$\therefore$ Two sides are parallel and equal and angle between adjacent sides is $90°$. Z_1, Z_2, Z_3, Z_4 form a rectangle.

7. $\Delta=\tan A\sin B\cos C-\tan A\sin B\cos C=0$

8. If a, b, c are coplanar then, $\begin{vmatrix} a & b & c \\ a.a & a.b & a.c \\ a.c & b.c & c.c\end{vmatrix}=0$

when a, b, c are linerarly independent then it will have any non–zero value.

9. Planes are parallel, if their perpendiculars are parallel

$\therefore\ (\vec{a}\times\vec{b})\times(\vec{c}\times\vec{d})=0$

10. Since, the determinant of integers will be an integer, therefore, only B is the possible option.

11. Domain of $\sqrt{16-x^2}=[-4,4]$

Domain of $\sqrt{\sin x}=[0,\pi]=[-2\pi,-\pi]$

12. $\dfrac{(x-1)(2-x)}{(x-3)} \le 0$

$x \in [1, 2] \cup [3, \infty]$

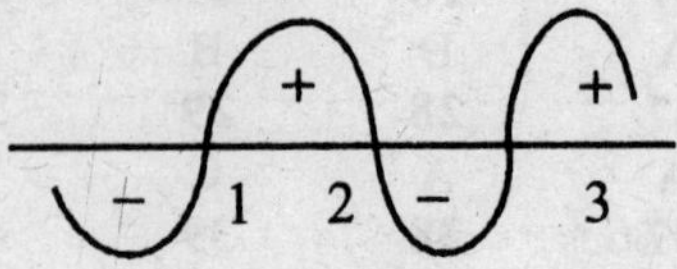

13. Period of $\sin^3 x = 2\pi$

$\Rightarrow$ Period of $|\sin^3 x| = \pi$

$\Rightarrow$ Period of $\left|\sin^3 \dfrac{x}{2}\right| = 2\pi$

Period of $\cos^5 x = 2\pi$

$\Rightarrow$ Period of $|\cos^5 x| = \pi$

$\Rightarrow$ Period of $\left|\cos^5 \dfrac{x}{5}\right| = 5\pi$

L C M of 2π and $5\pi = 10\pi$

But $|\sin^3 x/2| + |\cos^5 x/5|$

is an even function,

$\therefore$ Period $= 10\pi/2 = 5\pi$

15. By using the expansion of $\sin x$, $\cos x$, we get

$1 + a - b = 0$ and $\dfrac{b}{6} - \dfrac{a}{2} = 1$

$\therefore b = -\dfrac{3}{2},\ a = -\dfrac{5}{2}$

16.

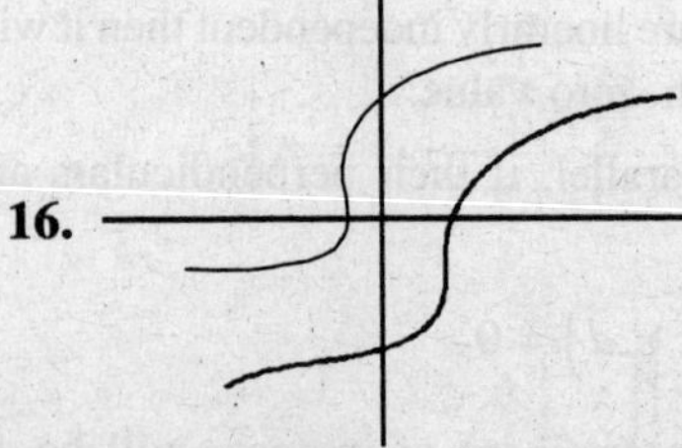

$\therefore (x+1)^{1/3} - (x-1)^{1/3}$ is a decreasing function in [0.1]

$\therefore$ it will have greatest at $x = 0$

$\therefore f(0) = 2$

17. Area $= \dfrac{\sqrt{3}}{4} a^2 = \dfrac{\sqrt{3}}{4}$

or, $a^2 = 1 \Rightarrow a = 1$

Now, $\dfrac{1}{\sqrt{[g(x)]^2 + x^2}} = 1$

$\Rightarrow [g(x)]^2 = 1 - x^2$

$\therefore g(x) = \pm\sqrt{1 - x^2}$

18. Slope of the normal

$= \dfrac{-1}{dy/dx} = \tan \dfrac{3\pi}{4}$

$= -1$ at $x = 3$

$\therefore \dfrac{dy}{dx} = 1$ at $x = 3$

$\therefore f'(3) = 1$

19. Solving the two equations,

we get $x^2 + y^2 = 9$ ...(*i*)

$y^2 = 8x$ ...(*ii*)

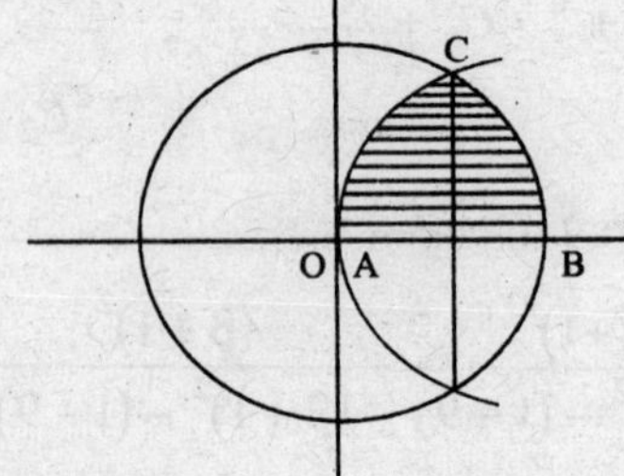

Put (*ii*) in (*i*)

$x^2 + 8x - 9 = 0$

$(x+9)(x-1) = 0$

i.e. $x = -9$ or 1

$x = -9$ gives imaginary value of y for equation (*ii*) hence neglected

$\therefore$ A : (1,0) and B : (3, 0)

$\therefore$ Required area = 2 times the hatched areas

$= 2\left[\int_0^1 y \cdot dx \text{ for } (ii) + \int_1^3 y \cdot dx \text{ for} (i)\right]$

$$=2\left[2\sqrt{2}+\left(\frac{x^{3/2}}{3/2}\right)_0^1+\left(\frac{x\sqrt{9-x^2}}{2}+\frac{9}{2}\sin^{-1}\left(\frac{x}{3}\right)^3\right]_1^3\right.$$

$$=2\left[2\sqrt{2}+\frac{9}{2}\times\frac{\pi}{2}-\frac{\sqrt{8}}{2}-\frac{9}{2}\sin^{-1}\left(\frac{1}{3}\right)\right]$$

$$=2\sqrt{2}+\frac{9\pi}{2}-9\sin^{-1}\left(\frac{1}{3}\right)$$

20. $y=x^5-5x^4+5x^3-10$

$$\therefore \frac{dy}{dx}=5x^4-20x^3+15x^2$$

$$=5x^2\left(x^2-4x+3\right)$$

$$=5x^2(x-3)(x-1)$$

$\frac{dy}{dx}=0$ gives $x=0, 1, 3$ ...(*i*)

Now, $\frac{d^2y}{dx^2}=20x^3-60x^2+30x$

$=10x(2x^2-6x+3)$

$$\frac{d^3y}{dx^3}=10\left(6x^2-12x+3\right)$$

For $x=0$

$$\frac{dy}{dx}=0,\ \frac{d^2y}{dx^2}=0,\ \frac{d^3y}{dx^3}\neq 0$$

$\therefore$ Neither min. nor max.

for $x=1$, $\frac{d^2y}{dx^2}=-10=$ negative

$\therefore$ max. and x max. $=-9$

for $x=3$, $\frac{d^2y}{dx^2}=90=$ positive

$\therefore$ min, and x min $=-37$

21. $\int_0^1 \tan^{-1}\left(\frac{1}{1-x+x^2}\right)dx$

$$=\int_0^1 \tan^{-1}\left(\frac{x-(x-1)}{1+x(x-1)}\right)dx$$

$$=\int_0^1 \tan^{-1} x.1\,dx$$

$$=2\left(x\tan^{-1}x\right)_0^1-\int_0^1\frac{x}{1+x^2}dx$$

$$=\frac{\pi}{2}-\log 2$$

22.

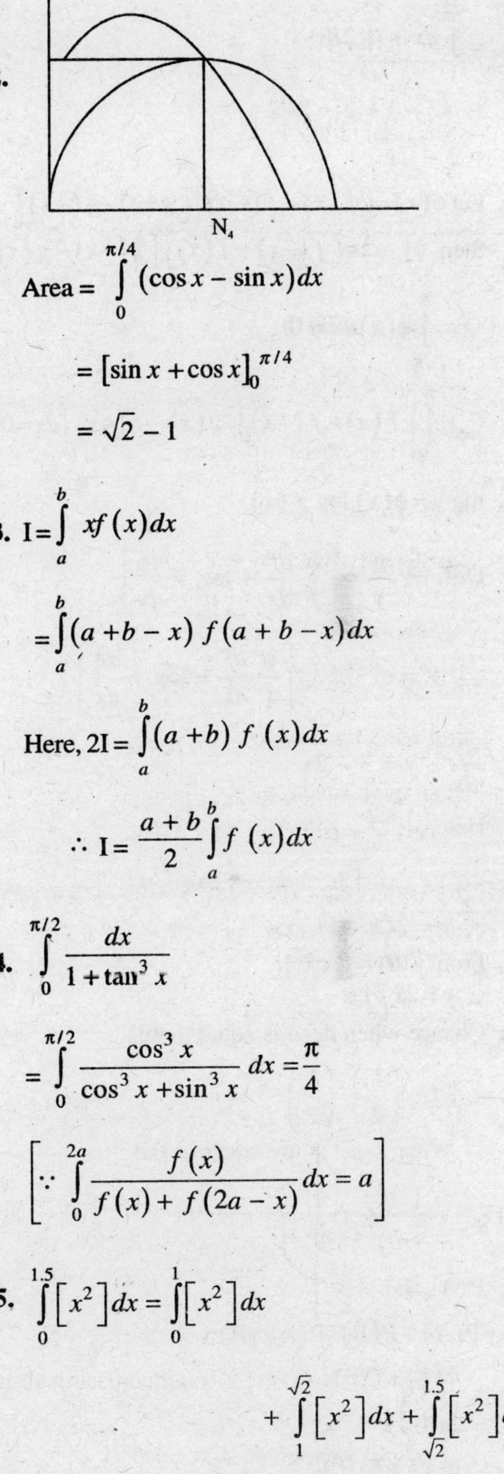

$$\text{Area}=\int_0^{\pi/4}(\cos x-\sin x)dx$$

$$=[\sin x+\cos x]_0^{\pi/4}$$

$$=\sqrt{2}-1$$

23. $I=\int_a^b xf(x)dx$

$$=\int_a^b (a+b-x)\,f(a+b-x)dx$$

$$\text{Here, } 2I=\int_a^b (a+b)\,f(x)dx$$

$$\therefore I=\frac{a+b}{2}\int_a^b f(x)dx$$

24. $\int_0^{\pi/2}\frac{dx}{1+\tan^3 x}$

$$=\int_0^{\pi/2}\frac{\cos^3 x}{\cos^3 x+\sin^3 x}dx=\frac{\pi}{4}$$

$$\left[\because \int_0^{2a}\frac{f(x)}{f(x)+f(2a-x)}dx=a\right]$$

25. $\int_0^{1.5}\left[x^2\right]dx=\int_0^1\left[x^2\right]dx$

$$+\int_1^{\sqrt{2}}\left[x^2\right]dx+\int_{\sqrt{2}}^{1.5}\left[x^2\right]dx$$

$$= \int_1^{\sqrt{2}} dx + \int_{\sqrt{2}}^{1.5} 2dx$$

$$= \sqrt{2} - 1 + 3 - 2\sqrt{2}$$

$$= 2 - \sqrt{2}$$

26. Let $\phi(x) = [f(x) + f(-x)][g(x) - g(-x)]$

then $\phi(-x) = [f(-x) + f(x)][g(-x) - g(x)]$

$$\therefore \int_{-\pi}^{\pi} \phi(x) dx = 0$$

$$\Rightarrow \int_{-\pi}^{\pi} [f(x) + f(-x)][g(x) - g(-x)] dx = 0$$

27. $\log y = \phi(x) \log f(x)$

Diff. $\Rightarrow \frac{y'}{y} = \left[\frac{\phi}{f}\frac{df}{dx} + \log f \frac{d\phi}{dx}\right]$

$$\Rightarrow y' = e^{\phi(x)\log f(x)}\left[\frac{\phi}{f}\frac{df}{dx} + \log f \frac{d\phi}{dx}\right]$$

28. $\frac{dy}{dx} - y = 3 - 2x$

Here, $e^{\int -1.dx} = e^{-x}$

$\therefore ye^{-x} = \int 3e^{-x} dx - \int 2xe^{-x} dx$

$\therefore y = 2(x-1) + c$

From $y(0) = 1, c = 1$

$\therefore y = 2x - 1$

29. Chance when head is equal to tail

$$= {}^{2n}C_n \left(\frac{1}{2}\right)^n \left(\frac{1}{2}\right)^n$$

$\therefore$ When head is not equal to tail

$$= 1 - \frac{(2n!)}{(n!)^2} \times \frac{1}{4^n}$$

30. $P(A \cup B)$

$P(A) + P(B) - P(A \cap B)$

$\therefore P(A) + P(B)$

$= 3/5 + 1/5 = 4/5$

$\therefore P(A') + P(B')$

$= 2 - 4/5 = 6/5$

31. $P(A \cup B) = 0.6$ and $P(A \cap B) = 0.2$

$P(A) + P(B) - P(A \cap B) = 0.6$

$P(A) + P(B) = 0.8$

Now $P(\overline{A}) + P(\overline{B}) = 1 - P(\overline{A}) + 1 - P(\overline{B})$

$= 2 - 0.8$

$= 1.2$

32. Total number of triangles that can be formed $= {}^6C_3 = 20$,

Out of these only 2 are equilateral triangles

$\therefore$ Required Probability $= \frac{2}{20} = \frac{1}{10}$

34. By Trapezoidal rule

$$\int_0^1 f(x) dx = \frac{h}{2}\left[(y_o + y_n) + 2(y_1 + y_2 + y_{n-1})\right]$$

$$= \frac{1}{2}[f(0) + f(1)]$$

$$= \frac{1}{2}[1 + 2.72] = 1.86$$

35. Here $h = \frac{1}{4} = 0.25$, $y = \frac{1}{1+x^2}$

	x	y
1	0	1
2	.25	.941
3	.5	.8
4	.75	.64
5	1	.5

By Simpson rule

$$\int_0^1 \frac{dx}{1+x^2}$$

$$= \frac{1}{4\times 3}[(1+.5) + 4(.941 + .64) + 2(.8)]$$

$$= \frac{1}{12}[1.5 + 4\times 1.581 + 1.6]$$

$$= \frac{1}{12}[1.5 + 6.324 + 1.6]$$

$$= \frac{1}{12}\times 9.424$$

$= 0.785$

SET–17

CSIR–UGC (NET) MATHEMATICAL SCIENCES

PART-B

1. If $z = xiy$ and $\omega = \dfrac{1-iz}{z-i}$ then $|\omega| = 1$, implies that in the complex plane:

A. z lies on the imaginary axis
B. z lies on the real axis
C. z lies on the unit circle
D. None of these

2. At what value of x, will $\begin{vmatrix} x+\omega^2 & 1 & \omega \\ \omega & \omega^2 & 1+x \\ 1 & x+\omega & \omega^2 \end{vmatrix} = 0$

A. $x=0$ B. $x=1$
C. $x=-1$ D. None of these

3. If $\cos 20° = k$ and $\cos x = 2k^2 - 1$, then the possible values of x between 0° to 360° are :

A. 140° B. 40° and 140°
C. 40° and 320° D. 50° and 130°

4. The real part of $\dfrac{1}{1-\cos\theta + i\sin\theta}$ is

A. $\dfrac{1}{1-\cos\theta}$ B. $\dfrac{1}{2}$
C. $\dfrac{\tan\theta}{2}$ D. 2

5. If $\bar{d}$ makes an acute angle with $\bar{b}$ and $\bar{r} \times \bar{b} = \bar{c} \times \bar{b}$ and $\bar{r}\,\bar{a} = 0$ then $\bar{r}$ is equal to

A. $\bar{a} \times \bar{c} - \bar{b}$ B. $\bar{c} \times \bar{a}$
C. $\bar{c} - \dfrac{\bar{c}\cdot\bar{a}}{\bar{b}\cdot\bar{a}}\bar{b}$ D. $\bar{c} + \dfrac{\bar{c}\cdot\bar{a}}{\bar{b}\cdot\bar{a}}\bar{b}$

6. $\hat{a}, \hat{b}, \hat{c}$ are three unit vectors. $\hat{a}$ and $\hat{b}$ are perpendicular to each other and vector $\hat{c}$ is equally inclined to both $\hat{a}$ and $\hat{b}$ at an angle θ. If $\hat{c} = \alpha\hat{a} + \beta\hat{b} + \gamma(\hat{a} \times \hat{b})$ where α, β, γ are constants, then

A. $\alpha=\beta=-\cos\theta, \gamma^2=\cos 2\theta$
B. $\alpha=\beta=\cos\theta, \gamma^2=\cos 2\theta$
C. $\alpha=\beta=\cos\theta, \gamma^2=-\cos 2\theta$
D. $\alpha=\beta=-\cos\theta, \gamma^2=-\cos 2\theta$

7. Karl Perason's coefficient of skewness of a distribution is 0.32 its S.D is 6.5 and mean is 39.6. The median of the distribution is given by

A. 28.61 B. 38.91
C. 29.13 D. 28.31

8. It the two lines of regression are $x - y = 3$ and $3x + y = 15$ then value of x for $y = 3$ is

A. 4 B. -9
C. -4 D. None of these

9. Angle between two lines of regression is given by

A. $\tan^{-1}\left[\dfrac{b_{yx} - \dfrac{1}{b_{xy}}}{1 + \dfrac{b_{xy}}{b_{yx}}}\right]$

B. $\tan^{-1}\left[\dfrac{b_{yx}.b_{xy} - 1}{b_{yx}, + b_{xy}}\right]$

C. $\tan^{-1}\left[\dfrac{b_{yx} + \dfrac{1}{b_{xy}}}{1 - \dfrac{b_{xy}}{b_{yx}}}\right]$

D. $\tan^{-1}\left[\dfrac{b_{yx} - b_{xy}}{1 + b_{yx} \cdot b_{xy}}\right]$

10. Consider any set of observations $x_1, x_2 \ldots\ldots x_{101}$, it is given that $x_1 < x_2 < x_3 < \ldots\ldots <_{100} < x_{101}$. Then the mean deviation of this set of observations about a point k is minimum when k equals

A. x_1 B. x_{51}
C. $\dfrac{x_1 + x_2 + \ldots + x_{101}}{101}$ D. x_{50}

11. The mean of a binomial distribution of 10 and its standard deviation is 2. What is the value of q

A. 1 B. 0.8
C. 0.6 D. 0.4

12. If $y = \sec^{-1}\left[\frac{x+1}{x-1}\right] + \sin^{-1}\left[\frac{x-1}{x+1}\right]$, then $\frac{dy}{dx}$ is

A. 1 B. $\frac{x-1}{x+1}$
C. 0 D. $\frac{x+1}{x-1}$

13. The differential coefficient of $f(\log x)$ w.r.t.x where $f(x) = \log x$ is

A. $x/\log x$ B. $(\log x)/x$
C. $(x\log x)^{-1}$ D. None of these

14. If $y = x^y$, then $(1 - y\log x)\frac{dy}{dx}$ is

A. x^2/y B. y^2/x
C. xy^2 D. None of these

15. The domain of the function $f(x) = \frac{1}{\log_{10}(1-x)} + \sqrt{x+2}$ is

A. $]-3,-2.5[\,\cup\,]-2.5,-2[$
B. $[-2,0)\cup(0,1)$
C. $]0,1[$
D. None of these

16. If $f(x) = \begin{cases} x & : x < 0 \\ 1 & : x = 0 \\ x^2 & : x > 0 \end{cases}$

Then, $\lim_{x\to 0}(x) = x^2 : x > 0$

A. 0 B. 1
C. 2 D. Does not exist

17. If $\int_0^{\pi/2} \frac{dx}{1+\tan x} = ?$

A. 0 B. $\frac{\pi}{4}$
C. $\frac{\pi}{2}$ D. $\frac{3\pi}{2}$

18. $\int_{-1}^{2} |x|\,dx = ?$

A. 5/2 B. 2
C. 3/2 D. 1

19. $\int 5^{5^{5^x}} \cdot 5^{5^x} \cdot 5^x\,dx$ is equal to

A. $\frac{5^{5^{5^x}}}{(\log 5)^3} + c$

B. $5^{5^{5^x}}(\log 5)^3 + c$

C. $\frac{5^{5^{5^x}}}{(\log 5)^3 + c}$

D. None of these

20. $\int_0^{\pi/4} \frac{\sin x + \cos x}{3 + \sin 2x}\,dx$ equal to

A. $\frac{-1}{4}\log 3$ B. $\frac{1}{4}\log 3$
C. $\frac{-1}{3}\log 4$ D. None of these

21. The value of integral $\int_0^{\pi} x f(\sin x)\,dx$ is

A. 0 B. $\pi\int_0^{\pi} f(\sin x)\,dx$
C. $\frac{\pi}{2}\int_0^{\pi} f(\sin x)\,dx$ D. None of these

22. The integral $\int_{-1}^{1} \frac{|x+2|}{x+2}\,dx$ is equal to

A. 1 B. 2
C. 0 D. –1

23. Solution of the equation $(1+y^2)\,dx + (x - e^{-\tan^{-1}x})dy = 0$ is

A. $ye^{\tan^{-1}x} = \tan^{-1}x + c$

B. $xe^{\tan^{-1}y} = \tan^{-1}y + c$

C. $y = \tan^{-1}xe^{\tan^{-1}x} + c$

D. $y = xe^{-\tan^{-1}x} + c$

24. The solution of differential equation $\frac{dy}{dx}=\left(x^2+xy+y^2\right)/x^2$ is

A. $\tan^{-1}\left(\frac{x}{y}\right)=\log y+c$

B. $\tan^{-1}\left(\frac{y}{x}\right)=\log x+c$

C. $\tan^{-1}\left(\frac{x}{y}\right)=\log x+c$

D. $\tan^{-1}\left(\frac{y}{x}\right)=\log y+c$

25. If p and q are the order and degree of the differential equation $y\frac{dy}{dx}+x^3\left(\frac{d^2y}{dx^2}\right)^3+xy=\cos x$ then

A. $p<q$ B. $p=q$

C. $p>q$ D. None of these

26. For a unbiased die, the probabilities for the different faces to form up are

Fase	1	2	3	4	5	6
P	0.1	0.32	0.21	0.15	0.05	0.17

This die is tossed and you are told that either face 1or face 2 has turned up, then the probability that it is face1is

A. 16/21 B. 1/10

C. 5/16 D. 5/21

27. α and β are any two events. The probability that exactly one of them occurs is equal to

A. $p(\alpha)-p(\beta)-2p(\alpha\cap\beta)$

B. $p(\alpha)+p(\beta)$

C. $p(\alpha)-p(\beta)-p(\alpha\cap\beta)$

D.None of these

28. Let A and B be two events such that, $p(A)=7/20$, $p(B)=9/20$, $p(A\cup B)=11/20$, $p(A\cap\bar{A})=1$, then the value of $p\left(\bar{A}\cap\bar{B}\right)$ is equal to

A. 1/4 B. 1/5

C. 1/10 D. None of these

29. A bag A contains 2 white and 2 red balls and another bag B contains 4 white and 5 red balls. A ball is drawn and is found to be red. The probability that it was drawn from the bag B is

A. 25/52 B. 1/2

C. 10/19 D. 5/19

30. Given a throw of three unbiased dice shows different faces, the probability that at least one face shows 6 is

A. 5/6 B. 5/18

C. 1/2 D. 13/18

31. The probability that any one of the men A_1, A_2, A_3, A_4 is alive after 95 years of age is 1/2. The probability that A_1 will die at the age of 95 and will be the first to die is

A. 15/16 B. 15/64

C. 1/4 D. 8/15

32. Using successive bisection method a root of equation $x^3-4x+1=0$ lies between 1 and 2. At the end of first iteration it lies between:

A. 1.62 and 1.75 B. 1.5 and 1.75

C. 1.75 and 1.87 D. None of these

33. By Trapezoid rule, the value of $\int_1^2\frac{dx}{x}$ is

A. 0.216 B. 0.813

C. 0.921 D. None of these

34. In how many intervals the interval (a, b) be sub divided to calculate the integral $\int_a^b f(x)dx$ by trapezoidal rule?

A. $3n$ intervals

B. $(n+1)$ intervals

C. $2n$ intervals

D. Any number of intervals.

35. If the relation $w=\frac{5-4z}{4z-2}$ transform at the circle $|z|=1$ into a circle of radius unity in the w-plane then the centre of the circle is

A. $(0,1)$ B. $(2,3)$

C. $\left(\frac{1}{2},0\right)$ D. None of these

36. For what values of z does the series $\sum_{n=1}^{\infty} \frac{1}{(z^2+1)^n}$ converge?

A. $|z| > 1$ B. $|z^2+1| > 1$

C. $|z^2-5| < 1$ D. $|z| = 2$

37. The ring $R^{n \times n}$ of all $n \times n$ matrices with real entries is a

A. Commutative ring

B. Not a commutative ring

C. Subring

D. None of these

38. The m.g.f. of the r.v. whose moments are : $\mu'r = (r+1)!\, 2^r$, is:

A. $(1-t)^{-2}$ B. $(1-2t)^{-2}$

C. $(1+t)^{-2}$ D. $(1+2t)^{-2}$

39. For a game $\begin{pmatrix} u & -v \\ -w & x \end{pmatrix}$ value of the game:

A. $\frac{uv+wx}{u+v+w+x}$ B. $\frac{ux-vw}{u+v-w-x}$

C. $\frac{ux-vw}{u+v+w+x}$ D. $\frac{-ux+vw}{-u-v+w+x}$

40. If $\sum_{n=1}^{\infty} a_n$, $a_n > 0$ is convergent then

A. $\sum_{n=1}^{\infty} a_n^2$ is convergent

B. $\sum_{n=1}^{\infty} a_n^2$ is divergent to $-\infty$

C. $\sum_{n=1}^{\infty} a_n^2$ is divergent to $+\infty$

D. $\sum_{n=1}^{\infty} a_n^2$ is oscillates infinitely.

ANSWERS

1	2	3	4	5	6	7	8	9	10
B	A	C	B	C	C	B	A	B	B
11	12	13	14	15	16	17	18	19	20
D	C	C	B	B	D	B	A	C	B
21	22	23	24	25	26	27	28	29	30
C	B	B	B	A	D	D	A	B	C
31	32	33	34	35	36	37	38	39	40
C	D	B	D	C	B	C	B	C	A

Some Selected Explanatory Answers

1. $W = \frac{1-iz}{z-i} \Rightarrow |W| = \left|\frac{1-iz}{z-i}\right|$

$\Rightarrow 1 = \left|\frac{1-iz}{z-i}\right| \Rightarrow \left|\frac{1-iz}{z-i}\right| = 1$

$\Rightarrow$ locus of z is real axis

3. We have, $\cos 20° = k$ and $\cos x = 2k^2 - 1$

$\therefore \cos x = 2\cos^2 20° - 1$

$\Rightarrow \cos x = \cos 40°$ or $\cos x = \cos 2\pi/9$

$\Rightarrow x = 2n\pi \pm \frac{2\pi}{9}, n \in z$

$\Rightarrow x = 40°$ and $320°$

7. We have

$$\text{Sk} = \frac{3(\text{mean} - \text{median})}{\text{SD}}$$

$\therefore 0.32 = (39.6 - \text{median})/6.5$

$\Rightarrow 0.32 \times 6.5 = 3(39.6) - 3(\text{Median})$

$\therefore \text{Median} = \frac{1}{3}[3(39.6) - 0.32 \times 6.5]$

$= 38.91$

8. We have $x - y = 3$ and $3x + y = 15$ as the lines of regression of y on x and x on y respectively. Thus

for given value of y, x is obtained from the line of regression of x on y i.e. $3x + y = 15$
we get $x = 4$

9. The slopes of the lines of regression of y on x and x on y are $m_1 = b_{yx}$ and $m_2 = \frac{1}{b_{xy}}$ respectively

$\therefore$ The angle between them is given by

$$\tan\theta = \frac{m_1 - m_2}{1 + m_1 m_2} = \frac{b_{yx} - \frac{1}{b_{xy}}}{1 + \frac{b_{yx}}{b_{xy}}}$$

$$= \frac{b_{yx} \cdot b_{xy} - 1}{b_{yx} + b_{xy}}$$

$$\therefore \theta = \tan^{-1}\left(\frac{b_{yx} \cdot b_{xy} - 1}{b_{yx} + b_{xy}}\right)$$

12. $y = \sec^{-1}\left(\frac{x+1}{x-1}\right) + \sin^{-1}\left(\frac{x-1}{x+1}\right)$

Put, $\left(\frac{x-1}{x+1}\right) = Z \Rightarrow \left(\frac{x+1}{x-1}\right) = \frac{1}{z}$

Substituting, $y = \sec^{-1}\left(\frac{1}{z}\right) + \sin^{-1} z$

$$= \cos^{-1} z + \sin^{-1} z$$

$$\therefore y = \frac{\pi}{2}$$

$$\left[\because \cos^{-1} z + \sin^{-1} z = \frac{\pi}{2}\right]$$

$$\Rightarrow \frac{dy}{dx} = 0$$

13. $y = f(\log x) = \log(\log x)$

$$\therefore \frac{dy}{dx} = \frac{1}{x \log x}$$

$$= (x \log x)^{-1}$$

14. Let $y = x^y \therefore \log y = y \log x$

Differentiating

$$x(1 - y\log x)\frac{dy}{dx} = y^2$$

$$\Rightarrow (1 - y\log x)\frac{dy}{dx} = \frac{y^2}{x}$$

15. $(x+2) \geq 0$, *i. e.* $x \geq -2$ *or* $-2 < x$ also

$\log_{10}(1-x) \neq 0$

$\therefore x \neq 0$

Again $1 - x > 0$

or $x < 1$

All these can be combined as $[-2, 0) \cup (0, 1)$

16. L.H.L = 0 and R.H.L cannot be found as the function is not defined for $x > 0$.

17. $I = \int_0^{\pi/2} \frac{\cos x\, dx}{\sin x + \cos x}$ ...(*i*)

change x into $\left(\frac{\pi}{2} - x\right)$

$I = \int_0^{\pi/2} \frac{\sin x\, dx}{\sin x + \cos x}$ ...(*ii*)

Add (*i*) and (*ii*)

$$2\text{I} = \int_0^{\pi/2} \frac{\sin x + \cos x}{\sin x + \cos x} dx$$

$$= \int_0^{\pi/2} dx = \frac{\pi}{2}$$

$$\therefore \text{I} = \frac{\pi}{4}$$

18. $\int_{-1}^{2} [x] dx = \int_{-1}^{0} (-x) dx + \int_0^2 x dx$

$$= \left[\frac{-x^2}{2}\right]_{-1}^{0} + \left[\frac{x^2}{2}\right]_0^2$$

$$= \left[0 + \frac{1}{2}\right] + [2 - 0] = \frac{5}{2}$$

19. Putting $5^{5^{5^x}} = t$

and $5^{5^{5^x}} . 5^{5^x} . 5^x (\log 5)^3\, dx = dt$

we get $\int 5^{5^{5^x}} . 5^{5^x} . 5^x\, dx = \frac{1}{(\log 5)^3} \int 1.dt$

$$= \frac{t}{(\log 5)^3} + c = \frac{5^{5^{5^x}}}{(\log 5)^3} + c$$

20. Putting $\sin x - \cos x = t$ and $(\sin x + \cos x)\, dx = dt$

$$\int_0^{\pi/4} \frac{\sin x + \cos x}{3 + 1 - t^2} dx$$

$$= \int_{-1}^{0} \left| \frac{dt}{3 + 1 - t^2} = \int_{-1}^{0} \right| \frac{dt}{2^2 - t^2}$$

$$= \frac{1}{4}\left(\log\left(\frac{2 + t}{2 - t} \right) \right)_{-1}^{0}$$

$$= -\frac{1}{4} \log \frac{1}{3} = \frac{1}{4} \log 3$$

21. $I = \int_0^{\pi} xf(\sin x) dx$

$I = \int_0^{\pi} (\pi - x) f \sin(\pi - x) dx$

$\Rightarrow \left(\text{Using} \int_0^a f(x) dx = \int_0^a f(a - x) dx \right)$

$\Rightarrow I = \pi \int_0^{\pi} f(\sin x) dx - \int_0^{\pi} xf(\sin x) dx$

$\Rightarrow 2I = \pi \int_0^{\pi} f(\sin x) dx$

22. We have

$$\int_{-1}^{1} \frac{|x + 2|}{x + 2} dx = \int_{-1}^{1} \frac{x + 2}{x + 2} dx = \int_{-1}^{1} 1.\, dx = 2$$

$(\therefore x + 2 \geq 0 \text{ for } -1 \leq x \leq 1)$

$\therefore |x + 2| = x + 2$

35. The given transformation is

$$\omega = \frac{2z + 3}{z - 4}$$

or $\omega z - 4\omega = 2z + 3$ or $(\omega - 2)z = 4\omega + 3$

or $z = \dfrac{4\omega + 3}{\omega - 2}$ $\therefore \bar{z} = \dfrac{4\bar{\omega} + 3}{\omega - 2}$

where $\omega = u + iv$

The circle is $x^2 + y^2 - 4x = 0$

or $(x + iy)(x - iy) - 4x = 0$

or $z\bar{z} - 2(z + \bar{z}) = 0$

$\left| \therefore z = x + iy \right|$

$\left| \therefore z + \bar{z} = 2x \right|$

36. Here $u_n = \dfrac{1}{(z^2 + 1)^n}$

$$\therefore u_{n+1} = \frac{1}{(z^2 + 1)^{n+1}}$$

$$\frac{u_{n+1}}{u_n} = \frac{(z^2 + 1)^n}{(z^2 + 1)^{n+1}} = \frac{(z^2 + 1)^n}{(z^2 + 1)^n (z^2 + 1)}$$

$$= \frac{1}{z^2 + 1} \therefore \lim_{n \to \infty} \left| \frac{U_{n+1}}{u_n} \right| = \left| \frac{1}{z^2 + 1} \right|$$

Hences the series converges for $|z^2 + 1| > 1$

38. Moment generating function of $X = M_x(t) = \sum_{r=0}^{\infty} \frac{t^r}{r!} \mu'_r$

$$= \sum_{r=0}^{\infty} \frac{t^r}{r!} (r + 1)!\, 2^r = \sum_{r=0}^{\infty} (r + 1)(2t)^r$$

$$= 1 + 2(2t) + 3(2t)^2 + 4(2t)^3 + \ldots\ldots = (1 - 2t)^{-2}$$

SET–18

CSIR–UGC (NET) MATHEMATICAL SCIENCES

PART-B

1. The number of real roots of the equation $|x|^2 - 3|x| + 2 = 0$ is

A. 4 B. 3
C. 2 D. 1

2. A polygon has 44 diagonals, then the number of its sides are

A. 11 B. 7
C. 8 D. None of these

3. $\begin{vmatrix} x+1 & \omega & \omega^2 \\ x+\omega & \omega^2 & 1 \\ x+\omega^2 & 1 & \omega \end{vmatrix} = 3$ in an equation in x, where ω, ω^2, ω are the complex cube roots of unity, what is the value of x ?

A. 0 B. 1
C. –1 D. 2

4. If the imaginary part of $\frac{2z+1}{iz+1}$ is –2, then the locus of the point represented by z is a

A. Circle B. Straight line
C. Parabola D. None of these

5. If the perimeter of a triangle is 6 times the arithemetic mean of the sines of its angles and the side a is 1, then angle A is equal to

A. 30° B. 45°
C. 60° D. 120°

6. The three lines

$ax + by + c = 0$, $bx + cy + a = 0$
$cx + ay + b = 0$
are concurrent only when

A. $a + b + c = 0$

B. $a^2 + b^2 + c^2 = ab + bc + ca$

C. $a^3 + b^3 + c^3 = 3abc$

D. All of the above

7. The equation $\frac{x^2}{1-r} - \frac{y^2}{1-r} = 1$, $r > 1$ represents

A. A hyperbola B. An ellipse
C. A circle D. None of these

8. The volume of a tetrahedron, the position vectors of whose vertices are
$5i - j + k$, $7i - 3j + 7k$
$i - 6j + 10k$ and $-i - 3k + 7j$ is

A. 15 B. 3
C. 11 D. 7

9. If the points $P(\vec{a}+\vec{b}+c), Q(\overrightarrow{2a}+\overrightarrow{3b}), R(\vec{b}+\vec{tc})$ are collinear, where $\vec{a}, \vec{b}, \vec{c}$ are three coplanar vectors, the value of t is

A. –2 B. –1/2
C. 1/2 D. 2

10. If $\vec{a}+\vec{b}+\vec{c} = \alpha\vec{d}, \vec{b}+\vec{c}+\vec{d} = \beta\vec{a}$ and $\vec{a}, \vec{b}, \vec{c}$ are non-coplanar then the sum $\vec{a} + \vec{b} + \vec{c} + \vec{d}$ equals

A. $\vec{0}$ B. $(\beta - 1)\vec{d}$
C. $(\alpha - 1)\vec{a}$ D. None of these

11. If $f(a) = 2$, $f'(a) = 1$, $g(a) = -1$, $g'(a) = 2$ then value of $\lim_{x \to a} \frac{g(x)f(a) - f(x)g(a)}{x-8}$

A. 0 B. 1
C. 5 D. 3

12. $\lim_{x \to 0} \frac{(1+x)^{1/x} - e + \frac{ex}{2}}{x^2}$ is equal to

A. $\frac{11e}{24}$ B. $\frac{-11e}{24}$
C. $\frac{e}{24}$ D. None of these

13. The number of values where the function $f(x) = \cos x + \cos(\sqrt{2x})$ attains its maximum is

A. 0 B. 1
C. 2 D. Infinite

14. $f(x)=\begin{vmatrix} x^3 & x^4 & 3x^2 \\ 1 & -6 & 4 \\ p & p^2 & p^3 \end{vmatrix}$ then $\frac{d^3 f(x)}{dx^3}$ is

A. Proportional to x^2

B. Proportional to x

C. Proportional to x^3

D. A constant

15. If the function $f(x) = x^3 + \alpha^2 + \beta + 1$ has maximum value at $x = 0$ and minimum at $x = 1$, then

A. $\alpha = 2/3, \beta = 0$

B. $\alpha = \frac{-3}{2}, \beta = 0$

C. $\alpha = 0, \beta = \frac{3}{2}$

D. None of these

16. $x(x-2)(x-4), 1 \le x \le 4$ will satisfy mean value theorem at x

A. 1 B. 2

C. 3 D. 4

17. A spherical balloon is being inflated so that its volume increases uniformly at the rate of 40cm^3/min. How much the radius will increase during the next 1/2 minute?

A. 0.015cm B. 0.005cm

C. 0.025cm D. 0.035cm

18. If $f(x) = 2x^3 + mx^2 - 13x + n$ and 2, 3 are roots of the equation $f(x) = 0$, the values of m and n are

A. $5, -30$ B. $-5, 30$

C. $5, 30$ D. None of these

19. $\int_0^{\pi/2} \frac{1}{1+\cot^3 x} dx$ is equal to

A. 0 B. 1

C. $\pi/2$ D. $\pi/4$

20. $\int_0^{1.5} [x^2] dx$ is

A. $4 + 2\sqrt{2}$ B. $2 + \sqrt{2}$

C. $2 - \sqrt{2}$ D. None of these

21. If $f: R \to R$, $g: R \to R$ are continuous functions

The value of integral

$\int_0^{\pi/2} [f(x)+f(-x)][g(x)-g(-x)] dx$ is

A. π B. 1

C. -1 D. 0

22. What is the value of the integral $I = \int \frac{dx}{(1+e^x)(1+e^{-x})}$

A. $\frac{-1}{1+e^x}$ B. $\frac{e^x}{1+e^x}$

C. $\frac{1}{1+e^x}$ D. None of these

23. $\int_1^x \frac{\log(x^2)}{x} dx$ is equal to

A. $(\log x)^2$ B. $\frac{1}{2}(\log x)^2$

C. $\frac{\log x^2}{2}$ D. None of these

24. The differential equation of all parabola whose axes are parallel to Y-axis is

A. $\frac{d^3 y}{dx^3} = 0$ B. $\frac{d^2 x}{dy^2} = 0$

C. $\frac{d^3 y}{dx^3} + \frac{d^2 x}{dy^2} = 0$ D. $\frac{d^2 y}{dx^2} + 2\frac{dy}{dx} = 0$

25. The solution of the differential equation $(x^2+1)dy/dx + y^2 + 1 = 0$ is

A. $y = 2 + x^2$

B. $(1 + x)/(1 - x)$

C. $y = x(x - 1)$

D. $y = (1 - x)/(1 + x)$

26. The solution of the differential equation $dy/dx - ky = 0, y(0) = 1$ approaches zero when $x \to \infty$ if

A. $k = 0$ B. $k > 0$

C. $k < 0$ D. None of these

27. The probability that a student is not a swimmer is $\frac{1}{5}$, what is the probability that out of 5 student 4 are swimmers

A. ${}^5C_4 \left(\frac{4}{5}\right)^4 \frac{1}{5}$ B. $\left(\frac{4}{5}\right)^4 \frac{1}{5}$

C. ${}^5C_1 \frac{1}{5}\left(\frac{4}{5}\right)^4 \times {}^5C_4$ D. None of these

28. Out of 21 tickets marked with numbers from 1 to 21, three are drawn at random. What is that chance the numbers of them are in A.P

A. 10/133 B. 9/15

C. 13/261 D. None of these

29. In shuffling a pack of playing cards, four are accidently dropped. The probability that the missing card should be one from each suit is

A. $\frac{1}{256}$ B. $\frac{1}{270725}$

C. $\frac{2197}{20825}$ D. None of these

30. A six faced die is so biased that it is twice to show an even number as an odd number when thrown. If it is thrown twice the probability that the sum of two numbers thrown is even is

A. 4/9 B. 5/9

C. 1/9 D. None of these

31. The Newton–Rapshon method converges fast if $f^1(\alpha)$ is (α is the exact value of root)

A. small B. large

C. 0 D. None of these

32. Two random variables have as least square regression lines $3x+2y=26$ and $6x+y=31$, then coefficient of correlation between x and y is

A. −0.5 B. 0.5

C. 0.25 D. None of these

33. If the angle between the two lines of regression is 90° then it represents

A. Perfect correlation

B. Perfect negative correlation

C. No linear correlation

D. None of these

34. If a, b, h, k are constants, while u and v are, $u=\frac{x-a}{h}$, $v=\frac{y-b}{k}$ then

A. $\text{cov}(x\cdot y)=\text{cov}(u\cdot v)$

B. $\text{cov}(x\cdot y)=hk\ \text{cov}(u\cdot v)$

C. $\text{cov}(x\cdot y)=ab\ \text{cov}(u\cdot v)$

D. $\text{cov}(u\cdot v)=hk\ \text{cov}(x\cdot y)$

35. The two regression lines are $2x-9y+6=0$ and $x-2y+1=0$. What is the correlation coefficient between x and y?

A. $\frac{-2}{3}$ B. $\frac{2}{3}$

C. 4/9 D. None of these

36. The mean of item is $\overline{x}$, if the first term is increased by 1 second by 2 and so on then the new mean is

A. $\overline{x}+n$ B. $\overline{x}+\frac{n}{2}$

C. $\overline{x}+\frac{n+1}{2}$ D. None of these

37. For given constants a and b, $E(ax+b)$ is equal to

A. $a\,E(x)+b$

B. $a\,E(x)+E(b)$

C. $a\,E(x)$

D. $a+b$

38. The general linear programming problem is in standard from, if:

A. The constraints are strict equations.

B. The constraints are inequalities of '≤' type.

C. The constraints are inequalities of '≥' type

D. The decision variables are unrestricted in sign.

39. $\lim_{n\to\infty}\sum_{k=1}^{n}\frac{1}{3n+k}$ is

A. $\log\frac{3}{2}$ B. $\log\frac{5}{4}$

C. $\log\frac{3}{4}$ D. $\log\frac{4}{3}$

40. The differential equation whose general solution is $y=C_1+C_2x+C_3x^2$, is given by:

A. $y'''=0$

B. $y^2+x^2=4x$

C. $y^3=x^2+x$

D. $y^3=2x+x^2$

ANSWERS

1	2	3	4	5	6	7	8	9	10
A	A	B	B	A	D	D	C	D	A
11	**12**	**13**	**14**	**15**	**16**	**17**	**18**	**19**	**20**
C	A	B	D	B	B	C	B	D	C
21	**22**	**23**	**24**	**25**	**26**	**27**	**28**	**29**	**30**
D	A	A	A	D	C	A	A	C	B
31	**32**	**33**	**34**	**35**	**36**	**37**	**38**	**39**	**40**
B	A	C	B	B	C	A	A	D	A

Some Selected Explanatory Answers

1. For $x>0$

$x^2-3x+2=0$

$\Rightarrow (x-1)(x-2)=0 \Rightarrow x=1,2$

For $x<0$,

$x^2+3x+2=0$

$\Rightarrow (x+1)(x+2)=0$

$\Rightarrow x=-1,-2$

$\therefore$ 4 roots

2. ${}^{n}C_2-n=44$

$\Rightarrow n^2-3n-88=0$

$\therefore n=11,-8 \;\therefore\; n=11$

3. $$\begin{vmatrix} x+1 & \omega & \omega^2 \\ x+\omega & \omega^2 & 1 \\ x+\omega^2 & 1 & \omega \end{vmatrix}=3$$

$R_1 \to R_1+R_2+R_3$

$$\begin{vmatrix} 3x & 0 & 0 \\ x+\omega & \omega & 1 \\ x+\omega^2 & 1 & \omega \end{vmatrix}$$

$\Rightarrow 3x=3 \Rightarrow x=\frac{3}{3}=1$

4. Let $z=x+iy$, then $Ip\left(\frac{2z+1}{iz+1}\right)=-2$

$\Rightarrow Ip\left[\frac{(2x+1)+2iy}{(1-y)+ix}\right]=-2$

$\Rightarrow 2y(1-y)-x(2x+1)=-2\left[x^2+(1-y)^2\right]$

$\Rightarrow 2y-2y^2-2x^2-x=-2x^2-2y^2+4y$

$\Rightarrow 2y+x=0$, which is a straight line

5. $\sum a=6\sum\frac{\sin A}{3}=2\sum\sin A$

$\Rightarrow k\sum\sin A=2\sum\sin A$

$\therefore\; k=2$ or $\frac{a}{\sin A}=k=2$

or $\sin A=\frac{1}{2}(a=1)$

$\therefore$ A=30°

6. Three lines are concurrent if,

$$\begin{vmatrix} a & b & c \\ b & c & a \\ c & a & b \end{vmatrix}=0$$

or, $3abc-a^3-b^3-c^3=0$

$\therefore\; a^3+b^3+c^3=3abc$ which is C

Also $a^3+b^3+c^3-3abc=0$

$\Rightarrow (a+b+c)\left(a^2+b^2+c^2-ab-bc-ca\right)=0$

$\Rightarrow a+b+c=0$ which is A

or, $a^2+b^2+c^2=ab+bc+ca$ which is B

$\therefore$ Answers are A, B, C

11. $\lim\limits_{x\to 0}\frac{g(x)f(a)-f(x)g(a)}{x-a}$

$=f(a)g'(a)-g(a)f'(a)$

$=4+1=5$

12. $\lim_{x\to 0}\dfrac{(1+x)^{1/x}-e+\dfrac{e}{2}x}{x^2}=\dfrac{11}{24}e$

13. Period of $y=\cos(\sqrt{2}x)$ is $\dfrac{2\pi}{\sqrt{2}}=\sqrt{2}\pi$ and for that of $y=\cos x$ is 2π. Graph will be as shown below. So, the function $\cos x+\cos(\sqrt{2}x)$ attains max. value at $x=0$ (i.e. $x=0,\ y=2$) only once

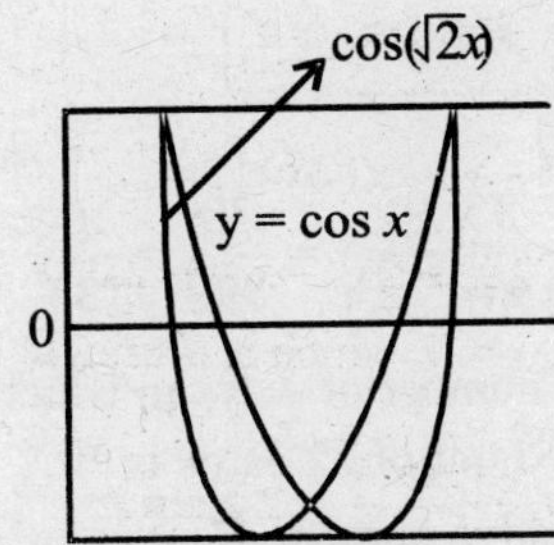

14. $f(x)=\begin{vmatrix} x^3 & x^2 & 3x^2 \\ 1 & -6 & 4 \\ p & p^2 & p^3 \end{vmatrix}$

$f(x)=x^3(-6p^3-4p^2)-x^2(p^3-4p)+3x^2(p^2+6p)$

$=-6p^3x^3-4p^2x^3-x^2p^3+4px^2+3p^2x^2+18px^2\ \dfrac{d}{dx}f(x)$

$=-36p^3x-24p^2x-2p^3+8p+6p^2+36p\dfrac{d^3f(x)}{dx^3}=36p^3-24p^2$

= a constant

19. $I=\int_0^{\pi/2}\dfrac{dx}{1+\cot^3 x}$

$=\int_0^{\pi/2}\dfrac{dx}{1+\dfrac{\cos^3 x}{\sin^3 x}}$

$=\int_0^{\pi/2}\dfrac{\sin^3 x}{\sin^3 x+\cos^3 x}dx$ ...(i)

$I=\int_0^{\pi/2}\dfrac{\sin^3(\pi/2-x)}{\sin^3(\pi/2-x)+\cos^3(\pi/2-x)}dx$

$=\int_0^{\pi/2}\dfrac{\cos^3 x}{\sin^3 x+\cos^3 x}dx$ ...(ii)

Adding (i) and (ii)

$2I=\int_0^{\pi/2}\dfrac{\sin^3 x+\cos^3 x}{\sin^3 x+\cos^3 x}dx$

$=\int_0^{\pi/2}1.dx=[x]_0^{\pi/2}=\pi/2$

$\therefore I=\dfrac{\pi}{4}$

20. If we plot $y=[x]^2$ which is greatest integer function, we get the graph for $x=0$ to 1.5 as follows :

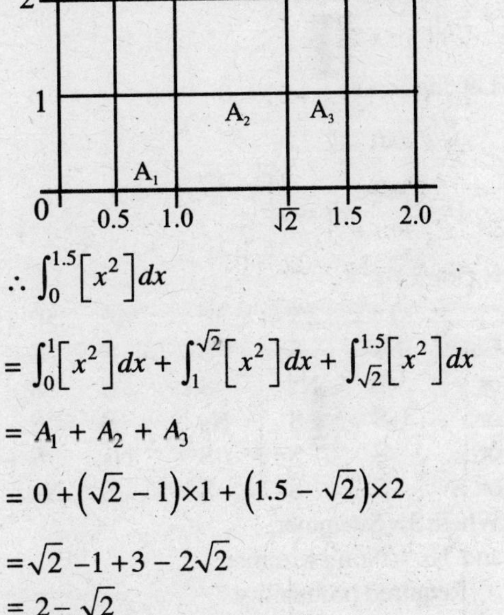

$\therefore \int_0^{1.5}[x^2]dx$

$=\int_0^1[x^2]dx+\int_1^{\sqrt{2}}[x^2]dx+\int_{\sqrt{2}}^{1.5}[x^2]dx$

$=A_1+A_2+A_3$

$=0+(\sqrt{2}-1)\times 1+(1.5-\sqrt{2})\times 2$

$=\sqrt{2}-1+3-2\sqrt{2}$

$=2-\sqrt{2}$

21. Here integral

$F(x)=[f(x)+f(-x)][g(x)-g(-x)]$

$\therefore F(-x)=[f(-x)+f\{-(-x)\}][g(-x)-g\{-(-x)\}]$

$=[f(-x)+f(-x)][g(-x)-g(x)]$

$-[f(x)+f(-x)][g(x)-g(-x)]$

$=-F(x)$

$\therefore$ By property, given integral = 0

22. $I = \int \frac{dx}{(1+e^x)\left(1+\frac{1}{e^x}\right)}$

$= \int \frac{e^x}{(1+e^x)^2} dx$

Let $1 + e^x = t$

$\therefore e^x.dx = dt$

$\therefore I = \int \frac{dt}{t^2} = \int t^{-2} dt$

$= \frac{t^{-1}}{-1} = \frac{(1+e^x)^{-1}}{-1}$

$= \frac{-1}{1+e^x}$

23. $I = \int_1^x \frac{2\log x}{x} dx$

Let $\log x = t$

$\therefore \frac{dx}{x} = dt$

$\therefore$ I$= 2\int_0^{\log x} t dt = 2\left[\frac{t^2}{2}\right]_0^{\log x}$

$= (\log x)^2$

27.

	1st	2nd	3rd	4th	5th
Either	Ns	S	S	S	S
or	S	Ns	S	S	S
or	S	S	Ns	S	S
or	S	S	S	Ns	S
or	S	S	S	S	Ns

Where S = Swimmer

and Ns = Non-swimmer

$\therefore$ Required probability

$= \frac{1}{5}\times\frac{4}{5}\times\frac{4}{5}\times\frac{4}{5}\times\frac{4}{5}+\frac{4}{5}\times\frac{1}{5}\times\frac{4}{5}\times\frac{4}{5}\times\frac{4}{5}+$

$\frac{4}{5}\times\frac{4}{5}\times\frac{1}{5}\times\frac{4}{5}\times\frac{4}{5}+\frac{4}{5}\times\frac{4}{5}\times\frac{4}{5}\times\frac{1}{5}\times\frac{4}{5}$

$+\frac{4}{5}\times\frac{4}{5}\times\frac{4}{5}\times\frac{4}{5}\times\frac{1}{5}$

$= {}^5C_4\left(\frac{4}{5}\right)^4 \frac{1}{5}$

Note: It can be done summarily as follows. 4 swimmers out of 5 can be selected in ${}^5C_4$ ways with the prob. that 4 are swimmers and 1is non–swimmer

$\left[\left(\frac{4}{5}\right)^4 \times \frac{1}{5}\right]$ $\therefore$ Required probability is

${}^5C_4\left(\frac{4}{5}\right)^4 \frac{1}{5}$

28. If $(2n+1)$ tickets are so numbered, then required probability

$= \frac{3n}{4n^2-1}$

$\therefore$ Here, $\frac{3\times 10}{4(10)^2-1} = \frac{30}{399} = \frac{10}{133}$

29. The total number of ways in which 4 cards can be selected out of 52 cards is ${}^{52}C_4$

$\therefore$ Exhaustive number of cases = ${}^{52}C_4$

There are four suits and each suit contains 13 cards. Therefore, the number of ways of selecting one card from each suit is ${}^{13}C_1$

$\therefore \frac{({}^{13}C_1)^4}{{}^{52}C_4} = \frac{2197}{20825}$

30. Let 'P' be the probability of getting an even number and q that of an odd number. Then

$p = 2q$ and $p+q=1 \Rightarrow p = \frac{2}{3}$ and $q = \frac{1}{3}$. Required

Probability = Prob. that an odd number appears both times + prob. that an even number appears both times.

$= 2C_0\left(\frac{2}{3}\right)^2 + 2C_2\left(\frac{1}{3}\right)^2 = \frac{4}{9}+\frac{1}{9}=\frac{5}{9}$

31. The rate of convergence of Newton–Raphson method is $\frac{1}{2}\frac{F''(a)}{F'(a)}$ which will be small if $F^1(\alpha)$ is large.

32. Equations of regression lines are

$3x + 2y = 26$ ...(*i*)

and $6x + y = 31$ ...(*ii*)

(*i*) can be rewritten as $x = \frac{-2}{3}y + \frac{26}{3}$

or $y = \frac{-3}{2}x + 13$ and (*ii*) can be rewritten as

$x = -(1/6)y + 31/6,$

or $y = -6x + 31$

Since $b_{xy} . b_{yx} \le 1,$

$b_{yx} = -3/2$ and $b_{xy} = -1/6$

$\therefore r^2 = (-3/2)(-1/6) = 1/4$

Since $b_{xy} < 0, r < 0$

So, $r = -1/2 = -0.5$

34. Covariance is independent of the shift of origin, hence *a* and *b* will not matter

Hence *x* becomes *h* times *u i* and I becomes *k* times *v*. Hence *cov.* $(x,y) = hk$ *cov* (u,v)

35. Regression line (*y* on *x*) is $2x - 9y + 6 = 0$

or $y = \frac{2}{9}x + \frac{2}{3}$

$\therefore b_{yx} = \frac{2}{9}$ ...(*i*)

Similarly, Regression line (*x* only) is $x = 2y - 1$

$\therefore r^2 = b_{yx} \times b_{xy}$

$= \frac{2}{9} \times 2 = \frac{4}{9}$

$\therefore r = \pm \frac{2}{3}$

Now, b_{yx} and b_{xy} both have same sign.

$\therefore r = \frac{2}{3}$

36. Let $x_1, x_2 .... x_n$ be *n* items.

Then $\bar{x} = \frac{1}{n}\sum x_i$ *Let* $y_1 = x_1 + 1,\ y_2 = x_2 + 2,\ y_3 = x_3 + 3.....y_n = y_n + n$

Then the mean of the new $\frac{1}{n}\sum y_i = \frac{1}{n}, \sum (x_i + i)$

$= \frac{1}{n}\sum x_i + \frac{1}{n}(1 + 2 + 3 + ...n)$

$= \bar{x} + \frac{1}{n}\frac{n(n+1)}{2} = \bar{x} + \frac{n+1}{2}$

39. $\lim_{n \to \infty} \sum_{k=1}^{n} \frac{1}{3n+k} = \lim_{n \to \infty} \frac{1}{n} \sum_{k=1}^{n} \frac{1}{3 + k/n}$

$= \int_0^1 \frac{dx}{3+x} = \left|\log(3+x)\right|_0^1 = \log\frac{4}{3}$

SET–19

CSIR–UGC (NET) MATHEMATICAL SCIENCES

PART-B

1. Let $R = \{(1, 2), (2,4)\ (2, 3)\ (3, 1)\}$ be a relation on the set $A = \{1, 2, 3, 4\}$. The relation R is

A. A function B. Transitive

C. Not symmetric D. Reflexive

2. The range of the function $f(x) = {}^{7-x}P_{x-3}$ is

A. $\{1, 3\}$

B. $\{1, 2, 3, 4, 5, 6\}$

C. $\{1, 2, 3, 4\}$

D. $\{1, 2, 3, 4, 5\}$

3. Let z, ω be complex numbers such that $\overline{z}+i\overline{\omega}=0$ and $\arg(z\omega)=\pi$ Then $arg\ z$ equals

A. $\pi/4$ B. $\pi/2$

B. $3\pi/4$ D. $5\pi/4$

4. if $z = x - i\ y$ and $z^{1/3} = p + iq$ then $\dfrac{\frac{x}{p}+\frac{y}{q}}{p^2+q^2}$ is equal to

A. 1 B. –1

C. –2 D. 2

5. $\left|z^2-1\right| = |z|^2 + 1$ then z lies on

A. The real axis

B. The imaginary axis

C. A circle

D. An ellipse

6. Let $A = \begin{pmatrix} 0 & 0 & -1 \\ 0 & -1 & 0 \\ -1 & 0 & 0 \end{pmatrix}$, the only correct Statement about the matrix A is

A. A is zero matrix

B. $A = (-1)I$

C. A^{-1} does not exist

D. $A^2 = I$ is the unit matrix

7. Let $A = \begin{pmatrix} 1 & -1 & 1 \\ 2 & 1 & -3 \\ 1 & 1 & 1 \end{pmatrix}$ and $10\ B = \begin{pmatrix} 4 & 2 & 2 \\ -5 & 0 & a \\ 1 & -2 & 3 \end{pmatrix}$ if B is the inverse of matrix A then a is

A. – 2 B. – 1

C. 2 D. 5

8. If $a_1, a_2, a_3 \ldots\ldots\ldots a_n$ are in G.P then the value of the determinant

$$\begin{vmatrix} \log a_n & \log a_{n+1} & \log a_{n+2} \\ \log a_{n+3} & \log a_{n+4} & \log a_{n+5} \\ \log a_{n+6} & \log a_{n+7} & \log a_{n+8} \end{vmatrix}$$ is

A. 0 B. 1

C. 2 D. –2

9. Let S (k) = 1 + 3 + 5 + ...+ (2k–1) = 3 + k² Then which of the following is true?

A. $S(1)$ is correct

B. $S(k) \Rightarrow S(k+1)$

C. $S(k) \not\Rightarrow S(k+1)$

D. Principle of mathematical induction can be used to prove the formula

10. How many ways are there to arrange the letters in the word GARDEN with the vowels in alphabetical order?

A. 120 B. 240

C. 360 D. 480

11. The number of ways of distributing 8 identical balls in 3 distinct boxes so that none of boxes is empty is

A. 5 B. 21

C. 3^8 D. ${}^8C_3$

12. The coefficient of the middle term in the binomial expansion in powers of a of $(1+ax)^4$ and of $(1-ax)^6$ is the same if a equals

A. – 5/3 B. 10/3

C. – 3/10 D. 3/5

13. The coefficient of x^n in expansion of $(1+x)(1-x)^n$ is

A. $(n-1)$ B. $(-1)^n(1-n)$

C. $(-1)^n(n-1)^2$ D. $(-1)^{n-1}.n$

14. If $S_n = \sum_{r=0}^{n} \frac{1}{^nC_r}$ *and* $t_n = \sum_{r=0}^{n} \frac{r}{^nC_r}$, then $\frac{t_n}{S_n}$ is equal to

A. $\frac{1}{2}n$ B. $\frac{1}{2}n-1$

C. $n-1$ D. $\frac{2n-1}{2}$

15. The sum of the first n term of the series $1^2+2.2^2+3^2+2.4^2+5^2+2.6^2+$.....is $\frac{n(n+1)^2}{2}$ when n is even. When n is odd the sum is

A. $\frac{3n(n+1)}{2}$ B. $\frac{n^2(n+1)}{2}$

C. $\frac{n(n+1)^2}{2}$ D. $\left[\frac{n(n+1)}{2}\right]^2$

16. The sum of series $\frac{1}{2!}+\frac{1}{4!}+\frac{1}{6!}+$......is

A. $\frac{(e^2-1)}{2}$ B. $\frac{(e-1)^2}{2e}$

C. $\frac{(e^2-1)}{2e}$ D. $\frac{(e^2-2)}{e}$

17. If $f:R\to S$ defined by $f(x)=\sin x-\sqrt{3}\cos x+1$ is onto, then the interval of S is

A. $[0,3]$ B. $[-1,1]$

C. $[0,1]$ D. $[-1,3]$

18. The domain of the function $f(x)=\frac{\sin^{-1}(x-3)}{\sqrt{9-x^2}}$ is

A. $[2, 3]$ B. $[2, 3)$

C. $[1, 2]$ D. $[1, 2)$

19. If $\lim_{x\to\infty}\left(1+\frac{a}{x}+\frac{b}{x^2}\right)^{2x}=e^2$, then the value of a and b are

A. $a\in R$ $b\in R$

B. $a=1$, $b\in R$

C. $a\in R$, $b=2$

D. $a=1$ and $b=2$

20. $f(x)=\lim_{x\to\pi/4}\frac{1-\tan x}{4x-\pi}, x\neq\frac{\pi}{4} x\in[0,\pi/2]=f\left(\frac{\pi}{4}\right)=-\frac{1}{2}$

if $f(x)$ is continuous in $\left[0,\frac{\pi}{2}\right]$ then $f\left(\frac{\pi}{2}\right)$ is

A. 1 B. $1/2$

C. $-1/2$ D. -1

21. If $x=e^y+$........to ∞, then $\frac{dy}{dx}$ is

A. $\frac{x}{1+x}$ B. $\frac{1}{x}$

C. $\frac{1-x}{x}$ D. $\frac{1+x}{x}$

22. $\lim_{n\to\infty}\sum_{r=1}^{n}\frac{1}{n}e^{r/n}$ is

A. e B. $e-1$

C. $1-e$ D. $e+1$

23. If $\int\frac{\sin x}{\sin(x-\alpha)}dx = Ax+B\log\sin(x-\alpha)+C$ then value of (A,B) is

A. $\sin\alpha, \cos\alpha$ B. $\cos\alpha, \sin\alpha$

C. $-\sin\alpha, \cos\alpha$ D. $-\cos\alpha, \sin\alpha$

24. The value of $\int_{-2}^{3}\left|1-x^2\right|dx$ is

A. $\frac{28}{3}$ B. $\frac{14}{3}$

C. $\frac{7}{3}$ D. $\frac{1}{3}$

25. The value of $\int_0^{\pi/2}\frac{(\sin x+\cos x)^2}{\sqrt{1+\sin^2 x}}dx$ is

A. 0 B. 1

C. 2 D. 3

26. If $\int_0^{\pi} xf(\sin x)dx = A\int_0^{\pi/2} f(\sin x)dx$, then A is

A. 0 B. π

C. $\pi/4$ D. 2π

27. If $f(x)=\dfrac{e^x}{1+e^x}, I_1=\int_{f(-a)}^{f(a)} xg\{x(1-x)\}dx$ and $I_2=\int_{f(-a)}^{f(a)} g\{x(1-x)\}dx$ then the value of $\dfrac{I_2}{I_1}$ is

A. 2 C. -3

C. −4 D. 1

28. The differential equation for the family if curves $x^2+y^2-2ay=0$ where a is an arbitrary constant is

A. $2(x^2-y^2)y'=xy$

B. $2(x^2-y^2)y'=xy$

C. $(x^2-y^2)y'=2xy$

D. $(x^2+y^2)y'=xy$

29. The solution of the differential equation $ydx+(x+x^2y)dy=0$ is

A. $-\dfrac{1}{xy}=C$

B. $-\dfrac{1}{xy}+\log y=C$

C. $\dfrac{1}{xy}+\log y=C$

D. $\log y=Cx$

30. If the straight lines $x=1+s, y=-3-\lambda s, z=1+\lambda s$ and $x=\dfrac{t}{2}, y=1+t, z=2-t$, with parameters s and t respectively, are coplanar then λ equals

A. −2 B. −1

C. −1/2 D. 0

31. A Particle is acted upon by constant forces $4\hat{i}+\hat{j}-3\hat{k}$ and $3\hat{i}+\hat{j}-\hat{k}$ which displace it from a point $\hat{i}+2\hat{j}+3\hat{k}$ to the point $5\hat{i}+4\hat{j}+\hat{k}$. The work done in standard units by the forces is given by

A. 40 B. 30

C. 25 D. 15

32. Consider the following statements

A. Mode can be computed from histogram

B. Median is not independent of change of scale

C. Variance is independent of changes of origin and scale. Which of these is/are correct?

A. Only A. B. Only B.

C. Only A and B. D. A. B. and C.

33. In a series of $2n$ observations half of them equal a and remaining equal $-a$. If the standard deviation of the observation is 2 then a equals

A. $1/n$ B. $\sqrt{2}$

C. 2 D. $\dfrac{\sqrt{2}}{n}$

34. The probability that A speaks a truth is $\frac{4}{5}$ while this probability for B is $\frac{3}{4}$. The probability that they contradict each other when asked to speak on a fact is

A. 3/20 B. 1/5

C. 7/20 D. 4/5

35. A random variable x has the probability distribution

x:	1	2	3	4
$p(x)$	0.15	0.23	0.12	0.10
x:	5	6	7	8
$p(x)$	0.20	0.08	0.07	0.05

For the events $E=\{x \text{ is Prime number}\}$ and $F=\{x<4\}$, the probability $P(E\cup F)$ is

A. 0.87 B. 0.77

C. 0.35 D. .50

36. The mean and the variance of a binomial distribution are 4 and 2 respectivily. Then the probability of 2 successes is

A. 37/256 B. 219/256

C. 128/256 D. 28/256

37. The scientific method in Operation Research consists of:

A. action phase B. research phase

C. judgement phase D. formulation phase

38. The generators of {1, −1, i, −i) are:

A. −1, −i B. 1, −1

C. 1, i D. i, −i

39. "If all the zeros of a polynomial $P_n(z)$ lie in a half plane, then all the zeros of the derivative $P_n'(z)$ lie in the same half plane". This statement is known as:
A. Luca's theorem
B. Milni-Thomson's Method
C. Cauchy Gourgat theorem
D. Cauchy's Fundamental theorem

40. Let $f(x) = 1$, if x is rational in [0, 1]
$= -1$, if x is irrational in [0, 1]
then in [0, 1]:
A. $f(x)$ is continuous only at the irrationals
B. $f(x)$ is continuous everywhere
C. $f(x)$ is Riemann integrable
D. $f(x)$ is not Riemann integrable

ANSWERS

1	2	3	4	5	6	7	8	9	10
C	A	B	C	B	D	D	A	B	C
11	12	13	14	15	16	17	18	19	20
B	C	B	A	B	B	D	B	B	C
21	22	23	24	25	26	27	28	29	30
C	B	B	A	C	B	A	C	B	A
31	32	33	34	35	36	37	38	39	40
A	C	C	C	B	D	D	D	A	D

Some Selected Explanatory Answers

1. The given relation is (1) not a function as both (2, 4) (2, 3) $\in R$ (2) not a transitive relation as (2, 3) and (3, 1) $\in R$ but (2, 1)$\notin R$ (3) not a symmetric relation as (2, 3) $\in R$ but (3, 2) (4) not a reflexive relation as (1,1) or (2, 2) or (3, 3) $\notin R$

2. For domain $7-x>0 \Rightarrow x<7, x-3 \geq 0 \Rightarrow x \geq 3$ and $7-x \geq x-3$
$\Rightarrow 2x \leq 10$
$\Rightarrow x \leq 5$
$\therefore 3 \leq x \leq 5$
$\therefore x$ may be 3,4 or 5

When $x = 3$, $f(3) = {}^4P_0 = \frac{4!}{4!} = 1$

$x = 4$, $f(4) = {}^3P_1 = \frac{3!}{2!} = 3$

$x = 5, f(5) = {}^2P_2 = 1$

$\therefore$ Range $= \{1, 3\}$

3. $\bar{z} + i\bar{\omega} = 0$ and $\text{Arg}(z\omega) = \pi$

$\Rightarrow \bar{z} = -i\bar{\omega}$ and $\text{Arg}(z) + \text{Arg}(\omega) = \pi$ ....(i)

$\Rightarrow \bar{z} = i\bar{\omega} \Rightarrow \text{Arg}(z) = \frac{\pi}{2} + \text{Arg}(\omega)$ ...(ii)

from (i) and (ii)

$\text{Arg}(z) = \frac{3\pi}{4}$

4. Let $x = r\cos\theta$
$y = r\sin\theta$
$\therefore z = r(\cos\theta - i\sin\theta)$

$= re^{-i(\theta + 2n\pi)}, n \in 1$

$z^{1/3} = r^{1/3} e^{-i\left(\frac{\theta + 2n\pi}{3}\right)}$

$= r^{1/3} = \left[\cos\left(\frac{\theta + 2n\pi}{3}\right) - i\sin\left(\frac{\theta + 2n\pi}{3}\right)\right]$

$\therefore p = r^{1/3}\cos\left(\frac{\theta + 2n\pi}{3}\right)$ and

$q = r^{1/3}\cos\left(\frac{\theta + 2n\pi}{3}\right)$

$$\therefore \frac{\frac{x}{p} + \frac{y}{q}}{p^2 + q^2} = \frac{\cos\theta}{\cos\left(\frac{\theta + 2n\pi}{3}\right)} - \frac{\sin\theta}{\sin\left(\frac{\theta + 2n\pi}{3}\right)}$$

$$= \frac{\sin\left(\frac{\theta + 2n\pi}{3} - \theta\right)}{\cos\left(\frac{\theta + 2n\pi}{3}\right)\sin\left(\frac{\theta + 2n\pi}{3}\right)}$$

$$= \frac{2\sin\left(\frac{2n\pi - 2\theta}{3}\right)}{\sin\left(\frac{2\theta + 4n\pi}{3}\right)} = -2\frac{\sin\left(\frac{2n\pi - 2\theta}{3}\right)}{\sin\left(\frac{2\theta + 2n\pi}{3}\right)}$$

$= -2$

5. As we know $\left|z^2 - 1\right| \le \left|z\right|^2 + 1$ equality holds iff z^2 and (-1) are in the same direction.

$\therefore$ Arg $\left(z^2\right) = \pi$

$\Rightarrow Arg(z) = \pi/2 \; or - \pi/2$

$\therefore$ z lies on imaginary axis

6. $A^2 = \begin{pmatrix} 0 & 0 & -1 \\ 0 & -1 & 0 \\ -1 & 0 & 0 \end{pmatrix} \times \begin{pmatrix} 0 & 0 & -1 \\ 0 & -1 & 0 \\ -1 & 0 & 0 \end{pmatrix}$

$= \begin{pmatrix} 1 & 0 & 0 \\ 0 & 1 & 0 \\ 1 & 0 & 0 \end{pmatrix} = 1$

7. If $B = A^{-1}$

$\therefore AB = I = \begin{pmatrix} 1 & 0 & 0 \\ 0 & 1 & 0 \\ 0 & 0 & 1 \end{pmatrix}$

$A(10.B) = \begin{pmatrix} 10 & 0 & 0 \\ 0 & 10 & 0 \\ 0 & 0 & 10 \end{pmatrix}$

$\Rightarrow \begin{pmatrix} 1 & -1 & 1 \\ 2 & 1 & -3 \\ 1 & 1 & 1 \end{pmatrix} \times \begin{pmatrix} 4 & 2 & 2 \\ -5 & 0 & a \\ 1 & -2 & 3 \end{pmatrix}$

$= \begin{pmatrix} 10 & 0 & 0 \\ 0 & 10 & 0 \\ 0 & 0 & 10 \end{pmatrix} \Rightarrow 1.2 + 1.a + 1.3 = 10$

$\Rightarrow a = 5$

9. $S(k) = 1 + 3 + 5 + ... + (2k - 1) = 3 + k^2$

$S(k+1) = 1+3+5+....+(2k-1)+(2k+1)$

$= 3 + k^2 + (2k + 1) = 3 + (k + 1)^2$

$\therefore S(k) \Rightarrow S(k + 1)$

10. Total ways is which the letters of the word GARDEN may be arranged = 6!. Out of these exactly in half of the words A appears before E and an exactly half of the word E appears before A

$\therefore$ The required number of ways $= \frac{6!}{2} = 360$

12. Middle term in $(1 + ax)^4 = {}^4C_2 \; a^2x^2$

and middle term in $(1 - ax)^6 = -{}^6C_3a^3x^3$

As coefficient are equal

$\Rightarrow {}^4C_2a^2 = -{}^6C_3a^3$

$\Rightarrow 6a^2 = -20a^3 \Rightarrow 20a^3 + 6a^2 = 0$

$\Rightarrow 2a^2(10a+3) = 0 \Rightarrow a = -3/10 \; as \, a \ne 0$

14. $t_n = \sum_{r=0}^{n} \frac{r}{{}^nC_r}$

$t_n = \sum_{r=0}^{n} \frac{n-r}{{}^nC_r}$

$= \sum_{r=0}^{n} \frac{n}{{}^nC_r} - \sum_{r=0} \frac{r}{{}^nC_r}$

$= n \times s_n - t_n$

$\Rightarrow 2t_n = n.S_n \Rightarrow \frac{t_n}{s_n} = \frac{n}{2}$

16. $e^x = 1 + \frac{x}{1!} + \frac{x^2}{2!} + \frac{x^3}{3!} + \frac{x^4}{4!} + .. + \infty$ put $x = 1$

$e^1 = 1 + \frac{1}{1!} + \frac{1}{2!} + \frac{1}{3!} + \frac{1}{4!} + .. + \infty$

$e^1 + e^{-1} = 2\left(1 + \frac{1}{2!} + \frac{1}{4!} + \frac{1}{6!} + .. + \infty\right)$

$\therefore \frac{(e-1)^2}{2e} = \left(\frac{1}{2!} + \frac{1}{4!} + \frac{1}{6!} + .. + \infty\right)$

17. As $f(x)$ is on to

$\therefore$ S = Range

Minimum value of

$f(x) = -\sqrt{1 + \left(-\sqrt{3}\right)^2} + 1 = -1$

And maximum value of

$f(x) = +\sqrt{1 + \left(-\sqrt{3}\right)^2} + 1 = 3$

$\Rightarrow S = [-1.3]$

18. Domain of $f(x)=\dfrac{\sin^{-1}(x-3)}{\sqrt{9-x^2}}$

Here $-1\le(x-3)\le 1$ and $9-x^2>0$
$\Rightarrow\ 2\le x\le 4$ and $-3<x<3$
So, $2\le x<3$

19. $\lim\limits_{x\to\infty}\left(1+\dfrac{a}{x}+\dfrac{b}{x}\right)^{2x}=e^2$

$\Rightarrow\ \lim\limits_{e^x\to\infty}\left(\dfrac{a}{x}+\dfrac{b}{x^2}\right)2x=e^2$

$\Rightarrow\ e^{2a}=e^2\Rightarrow a=1$ and $b\in R$

20. Since $f(x)$ is continuous $\left[0,\dfrac{\pi}{2}\right]$

$\Rightarrow\ \lim\limits_{x\to\pi/4}\dfrac{1-\tan x}{4x-\pi}=f\left(\dfrac{\pi}{4}\right)$

$\Rightarrow\ f\left(\dfrac{\pi}{4}\right)=-\dfrac{1}{2}$

21. Here $x=e^{y+x}$
$x+y=\log x$

$1+\dfrac{dy}{dx}=\dfrac{1}{x}\Rightarrow\dfrac{dy}{dx}=\dfrac{1-x}{x}$

22. $\lim\limits_{n\to\infty}\sum\limits_{r=1}^{n}\dfrac{1}{n}e^{r/n}=\int_0^1 e^x dx=e-1$

24. $I=\int_{-2}^{-1}\left(x^2-1\right)dx+\int_{-1}^{1}\left(1-x^2\right)dx+\int_{1}^{3}\left(x^2-1\right)dx$

$=\dfrac{28}{3}$

25. $I=\int_0^{\pi/2}\dfrac{(\sin x+\cos x)^2}{\sqrt{1+\sin 2x}}dx$

$I=\int_0^{\pi/2}(\sin x+\cos x)dx=2$

26. $I=\int_0^{\pi}xf(\sin x)dx$ ...(*i*)

$I=\int_0^{\pi}(\pi-x)f(\sin x)dx$ ...(*ii*)

$\Rightarrow\ 2I=\pi\int_0^{\pi}f(\sin x)dx=2\pi\int_0^{\pi/2}f(\sin x)dx$
$\Rightarrow\ A=\pi$

27. Here $f(a)+f(-a)=1$

$I_1=\int_{f(-a)}^{f(a)}xg\{x(1-x)\}dx$

$=\int_{f(-a)}^{f(a)}(1-x)g\{x(1-x)\}dx$

$=I_2-I_1\Rightarrow\dfrac{I_2}{I_1}=2$

28. $x^2+y^2-2ay=0$ ...(*i*)
On differentiating $2x+2yy'-2ay'=0$ ...(*ii*)
Eliminating a from (*i*) and (*ii*)
$(x^2-y^2)\,y'=2xy$

29. $ydx+xdy=-x^2ydy$

$\int\dfrac{d(xy)}{x^2.y^2}=\int-\dfrac{1}{y}dx$

30. $x=1+s, y=-3-\lambda s, z=1+\lambda s......(L_1)$

$x=\dfrac{t}{2};\ y=1+t;\ z=1-t.........(L_2)$

Two lines are coplanar if (1) either they intersect And (2) parallel to each other L_1 is parallel to $\left(i-\lambda j+\lambda\hat{k}\right)=\overrightarrow{b_1}$ (say)

And L_2 is parallel to $\dfrac{1}{2}\left(\hat{i}+\hat{j}-\hat{k}\right)=\overrightarrow{b_2}$ (say)

$\therefore$ if $\lambda=-2$
$\overrightarrow{b_1}=\hat{i}+2\hat{j}$ and $\overrightarrow{b_2}=\dfrac{1}{2}\hat{i}+\hat{j}+\hat{k}$

as $\overrightarrow{b_1}=2\overrightarrow{b_2}$. Then L_1 parallel to L_2 then L_1 and L_2 will be coplanar
if L_1 and L_2 intersect then

$1+s=\dfrac{t}{2}$ ...(*i*)
$-3-\lambda s=1+t$ ...(*ii*)
$1+\lambda s=1-t$ ...(*iii*)
Form (*ii*) and (*iii*) it can be seen that L_1 and L_2 cannot intersect
$\therefore\ \lambda=-2$ is the only answer

33. $2 = \sqrt{\frac{\Sigma(x_1 - \bar{x})^2}{N}}$

$\Rightarrow\ 2 = \sqrt{\frac{\Sigma(x_1)^2}{N}}$

as $\bar{x} = 0$

$2 = \sqrt{\frac{a^2 2n}{2n}}$

$\Rightarrow\ |a| = 2$

35. $P(E) = P(2) + P(3) + P(5) + P(7)$

$= 0.23 + 0.12 + 0.20 + 0.07 = 0.62$

$P(F) = P(1) + P(2) + P(3) = 0.50$

$\therefore\ P(EUF) = 0.62 + 0.5 - 0.35 = 0.77$

36. If n is number of trials and P be probability of success.

Then mean $np = 4$

and variance $npq = 2$(Q = probability of failure)

$\therefore\ Q = \frac{1}{2}$ and $P = \frac{1}{2}$

$\therefore$ Probability of 2 successes ${}^8C_2\left(\frac{1}{8}\right)^2 = \frac{28}{256}$

40. $\int_a^{\bar{b}} f dx = b - a$

$\int_{\underline{a}}^{b} f dx = -(b-a)\ \Rightarrow f$ is not integrable

Set–20

CSIR–UGC (NET) Mathematical Sciences

PART-B

1. If $y=\left(x+\sqrt{1+x^2}\right)^n$ then $\left(1+x^2\right)\dfrac{d^2y}{dx^2}+x\dfrac{dy}{dx}$

A. n^2y B. $-n^2y$

C. $-y$ D. $2x^2y$

2. A problem in mathematics is given to three students A, B, C and their respective probability of solving the problem is $\frac{1}{2},\frac{1}{3}$ and $\frac{1}{4}$. Probability that the problem is solved is

A. $\frac{3}{4}$ B. $\frac{1}{2}$

C. $\frac{2}{3}$ D. $\frac{1}{2}$

3. *l, m, n,* are the pth, q^{th} and r^{th} terms of a G. P., all positive, then $\begin{vmatrix} \log l & p & 1 \\ \log m & q & 1 \\ \log n & r & 1 \end{vmatrix}$ equals

A. 3 B. 2

C. 1 D. Zero

4. $\lim\limits_{x\to 0}\sqrt{\dfrac{1-\cos 2x}{2x^2}}$ is

A. x B. -1

C. Zero D. Does not exist

5. In a class of 100 students there are 70 boys whose average marks in a subject are 75 if the average marks of the complete class is 72, then what is the average of the girls?

A. 73 B. 65

C. 68 D. 74

6. The order and degree of the differential equation $\left(1+3\dfrac{dy}{dx}\right)^{2/3}=4\dfrac{d^3y}{dx^3}$ are

A. $1,\frac{2}{3}$ B. (3, 1)

C. (3, 3) D. (1, 2)

7. The solution of the equation $\dfrac{d^2y}{dx^2}=e^{-2x}$

A. $\dfrac{e^{-2x}}{4}$ B. $\dfrac{e^{-2x}}{4}+cx+d$

C. $\frac{1}{4}e^{-2x}+cx^2+d$ D. $\frac{1}{4}e^{-2x}+c+d$

8. $\lim\limits_{x\to\infty}\left(\dfrac{x^2+5x+3}{x^2+x+2}\right)^x$

A. e^4 B. e^3

C. e^2 D. e

9. The domain of $\sin^{-1}\left[\log^3(x-3)\right]$ is

A. $[1, 9]$ B. $[-1, 9]$

C. $[-9, 1]$ D. $[-9, -1]$

10. $\int_0^{10\pi}|\sin x|\,dx$

A. 20 B. 8

C. 10 D. 18

11. $I_n=\int_0^{\pi/4}\tan^n x.dx$ then $\lim\limits_{n\to\infty} n\left[l_n+l_{n+2}\right]$ equal

A. $\frac{1}{2}$ B. 1

C. ∞ D. Zero

12. $\int_0^2\left[x^2\right]dx$ is

A. $2-\sqrt{2}$ B. $2+\sqrt{2}$

C. $\sqrt{2}-1$ D. None of these

13. $\int_0^{\pi} \frac{2\times(1+\sin x)}{1+\cos^2 x} dx$ is

A. $\frac{\pi^2}{4}$ B. π^2

C. Zero D. $\frac{\pi}{2}$

14. The period of the function

$f(x) = \sin^4 x + \cos^4 x$ is

A. π B. $\frac{\pi}{2}$

C. 2π D. None of these

15. The domain of the function

$f(x) = \sqrt{\log_{10}\left(\frac{5x - x^2}{4}\right)}$ is

A. $[1,4]$ B. $[1,0]$

C. $[0,5]$ D. $[5,0]$

16. If $\sin y = a\sin(x+y)$, then $\frac{dy}{dx}$ is

A. $\frac{\sin a}{\sin^2(a+y)}$ B. $\frac{\sin^2(a+y)}{\sin a}$

C. $\sin a \sin^2(a+y)$ D. $\frac{\sin^2(a-y)}{\sin a}$

17. If $x^y = e^{x-y}$ then $\frac{dy}{dx}$ is

A. $\frac{1+x}{1+\log x}$ B. $\frac{1-\log x}{1+\log x}$

C. Not defined D. $\frac{\log x}{(1+\log x)^2}$

18. The greatest value of $f(x) = (x+1)^{1/3} - (x-1)^{1/3}$ on [0, 1] is

A. 1 B. 2

C. 3 D. 1/3

19. The function $f(x) = \cot^{-1} x + x$ increases in the interval

A. $(1, \infty)$ B. $(-1, \infty)$

C. $(-\infty, \infty)$ D. $(0, \infty)$

20. Evaluate $\int_0^{\pi/2} \frac{\sin x}{\sqrt{\sin x} + \sqrt{\cos x}} dx$

A. $\frac{\pi}{4}$ B. $\frac{\pi}{2}$

C. Zero D. 1

21. $\int \frac{dx}{x(x^n+1)} dx$ equal to

A. $\frac{1}{n}\log\left(\frac{x^n}{x^n+1}\right)+c$

B. $\frac{1}{n}\log\left(\frac{x^n+1}{x^n}\right)+c$

C. $\log\left(\frac{x^n}{x^n+1}\right)+c$

D. None of these

22. The area bounded by the curve $y = 2x - x^2$ and the straight line $y = -x$ is given by

A. $\frac{9}{2}$ B. $\frac{43}{6}$

C. $\frac{35}{6}$ D. None of these

23. The differential equation of all non vertical lines in a plane is

A. $\frac{d^2y}{dx^2} = 0$ B. $\frac{d^2y}{dy^2} = 0$

C. $\frac{dy}{dt} = 0$ D. $\frac{dx}{dy} = 0$

24. A and B play a game where each is asked to select a number from 1to 25, if the two number match both of them win a prize. The probability that they will not win prize in a single trial is

A. $\frac{1}{25}$ B. $\frac{24}{25}$

C. $\frac{2}{25}$ D. None of these

25. If A and B are two mutually exclusive events then

A. $P(A) < P(\bar{B})$ B. $P(A) > P(\bar{B})$

C. $P(A) < P(B)$ D. None of these

26. Let T_n denote the number of triangles which can be formed using the vertices of a regular polygon of n sides if $T_{n+1} - T_n = 21$, then n equals

A. 5 B. 7
C. 6 D. 4

27. For $x \in R$ $\lim_{x\to\infty}\left(\frac{x-3}{x+2}\right)^x$

A. e B. e^{-1}
C. e^{-5} D. e^5

28. If ω is an imaginary cube root of unity then $(1+\omega-\omega^2)^7$ equals

A. $128\,\omega$ B. $-128\,\omega$
C. $128\,\omega^2$ D. $-128\,\omega^2$

29. If $\begin{vmatrix} 6! & -3! & 1 \\ 4 & 3! & -1 \\ 20 & 3 & 1 \end{vmatrix} = x + iy$ then

A. $x = 3,\ y = 1$ B. $x = 1,\ y = 3$
C. $x = 0,\ y = 3$ D. $x = 0,\ y = 0$

30. The probability of India winning a test match against West Indies is $\frac{1}{2}$. Assuming independence from match to match the probability that in a test series India's second win occurs at the third test is

A. $\frac{1}{8}$ B. $\frac{1}{4}$
C. $\frac{1}{2}$ D. $\frac{2}{3}$

31. If $(\omega \neq 1)$ is a cubic root of unity, then

$$\begin{vmatrix} 1 & 1+i+\omega^2 & \omega^2 \\ 1+i & -1 & \omega^2 - 1 \\ -i & -1+\omega-i & -1 \end{vmatrix}$$ equals

A. Zero B. 1
C. i D. ω

32. A baised coin with probability P, $0 < P < 1$ of heads, is tossed until a head appears for the first time. If the probability that, the number of tosses required is even is $\frac{2}{5}$, then p equals

A. $\frac{1}{3}$ B. $\frac{2}{3}$
C. $\frac{2}{5}$ D. $\frac{3}{5}$

33. A fair die is tossed eight times. The probability that a third six is observed on the eight throw is

A. $\frac{{}^7C_2 \times 5^5}{6^6}$ B. $\frac{{}^7C_2 \times 5^5}{6^8}$
C. $\frac{{}^7C_2 \times 5^5}{6^6}$ D. None of these

34. Let $f(2) = 4$ and $f'(2) = 4$

Then $\lim_{x\to 2}\frac{xf(2) - 2f(x)}{x-2}$ is given by

A. 2 B. −2
C. −4 D. 3

35. The equation $a\sin x + b\cos x = c$ where $|c| > \sqrt{a^2+b^2}$ has

A. a unique solution
B. infinite no. of solutions
C. no solutions
D. None of these

36. Which of the following property of regression is incorrect?

A. $b_{yx} \,.\, b_{xy} \le 1$
B. G.M. of coefficients is r
C. A.M. of coefficients $> |r|$
D. None of these

37. A two person game is said to be zero sum, if:

A. gain of one player is exactly matched by a loss to the other so that their sum is equal to zero.

B. gain of one player does not match the loss to the other.

C. diagonal entries of the pay off matrix are zero.

D. both the players must have an equal member of strategies.

38. Real part of a^i is:

A. $\cos a$

B. $e^{-in\pi}(\log_e a)$

C. $e^{-2n\pi}\cos(\log_e a)$

D. $e^{n\pi}\cos(\log_e a)$

39. The equation $e^x - 4x^2 = 0$ has a root between 4 and 5. Fixed point iteration with iteration function $\frac{1}{2}e^{x/2}$:

A. Converges

B. Diverges

C. Converges monotonically

D. Oscillates

40. If $T:V \to v$ be linear then Kernel of T is given by:

A. variant under T

B. invariant under T

C. an operator on R^2

D. None of these

ANSWERS

1	2	3	4	5	6	7	8	9	10
A	A	D	D	B	B	B	A	A	A
11	12	13	14	15	16	17	18	19	20
B	D	B	B	A	B	D	B	C	A
21	22	23	24	25	26	27	28	29	30
A	A	A	B	A	B	C	D	D	B
31	32	33	34	35	36	37	38	39	40
A	A	B	C	C	D	A	C	B	B

Some Selected Explanatory Answers

1. We have $y = \left(x + \sqrt{1+x^2}\right)^2$ ...(*i*)

Let, $\dfrac{d^2y}{dx^2} = y_2$

$\dfrac{dy}{dx} = y_1$ So, differentiating

Eq. (*i*) we get,

$$\frac{dy}{dx} = n\left[x + \sqrt{1+x^2}\right]^{n-1}\left(1 + \frac{x}{\sqrt{x^2+1}}\right)$$

$$= \frac{n\left[x+\sqrt{1+x^2}\right]^n}{\sqrt{1+x^2}}$$

or $\dfrac{dy}{dx} = \dfrac{ny}{\sqrt{1+x^2}}$

$$y_1^2\left(1+x^2\right) = n^2y^2$$

Again differentiating we get

$$2y_1y_2\left(1+x^2\right) + 2xy_1^2 = 2n^2yy_1$$

Dividing by $2y_1$

$$y_2(1+x^2) + xy_1 = n^2y$$

or $\dfrac{d^2y}{dx^2}(1+x^2) + \dfrac{xdy}{dx} = n^2y$

2. $P(E_1) = \dfrac{1}{2},\ P(E_2) = \dfrac{1}{3}$ *and* $P(E_3) = \dfrac{1}{4}$

$$P(E_1 \cup E_2 \cup E_3) = 1 - P(\overline{E_1})P(\overline{E_2})P(\overline{E_3})$$

$$= 1 - \left(1-\frac{1}{2}\right)\left(1-\frac{1}{3}\right)\left(1-\frac{1}{4}\right)$$

$$= 1 - \frac{1}{2}\times\frac{2}{3}\times\frac{3}{4} = \frac{3}{4}$$

3. $l = AR^{P-1} \Rightarrow \log l = \log A + (P-1)\log R$

$m = AR^{q-1} \Rightarrow \log m = \log A + (q-1)\log R$

$n = Ar^{r-1} \Rightarrow \log n = \log A + (r-1)\log R$

Now

$$R = \begin{vmatrix} \log l & p & 1 \\ \log m & q & 1 \\ \log n & r & 1 \end{vmatrix}$$

$$= \begin{vmatrix} \log A + (p-1)\log R & p & 1 \\ \log A + (q-1)\log R & q & 1 \\ \log A + (r-1)\log R & r & 1 \end{vmatrix} = 0$$

4. $\lim_{x\to 0} \frac{\sqrt{2\sin^2 x}}{\sqrt{2x^2}} \Rightarrow \lim_{x\to 0} \frac{|\sin x|}{x}$

$\lim_{x\to 0} \frac{\sqrt{1-\cos^2 x}}{x} \Rightarrow \lim_{x\to 0} \frac{|\sin x|}{x}$

So, $f(x) = \frac{|\sin x|}{x}$

Now, $f(0+0) = \lim_{h\to 0} \frac{|(\sin(0+h))|}{h}$

$= \lim_{h\to 0} \frac{\sinh}{h} = 1$

$f(0-0) = \lim_{h\to 0} \frac{|\sin(0-h)|}{-h}$

$\lim_{h\to 0} \frac{\sin h}{-h} = -1$

फ $f(0+0) \neq f(0-0)$

$\therefore$ The limit does not exit

5. Total student = 100
Average marks = 72
Total average marks = 72 × 100 = 7200
Average in respect to boys = 70 ×75 = 5250
So, 7200 – 5250 = 1950
Average of girls $\frac{1950}{30} = 65$

7. $\frac{d^2y}{dx^2} = e^{-2x}$

$\frac{dy}{dx} = \frac{e^{-2x}}{-2} + c$

$y = \frac{e^{-2x}}{4} + cx + d$

8. $\lim_{x\to\infty} \left[1 + \frac{4x+1}{x^2+x+2}\right]^x$

$= \lim_{x\to\infty} \left[(1+a)^{1/a}\right]^{ax}$

where $a = \frac{4x+1}{x^2+x+2}$

$= \frac{4+\frac{1}{x}}{1+\frac{1}{x}+\frac{2}{x^2}}$

and $\frac{4+\frac{1}{x}}{1+\frac{1}{x}+\frac{2}{x^2}} \to 4 \; as \; x \to \infty$

$\Rightarrow$ Given limit = e^4

9. $f(x) = \sin^{-1}(\log)\left(\frac{x}{3}\right)$ exists if

$-1 \le \log_3\left(\frac{x}{3}\right) \le 1 \Leftrightarrow 3^{-1} \le \frac{x}{3} \le 3^1$

$\Rightarrow -1 \le x \le 9 \Rightarrow [1,9]$

10. $\int_0^{10\pi} |\sin x| dx$

$= 10\left[\int_0^{\pi/2} \sin x dx + \int_{\pi/2}^{\pi} \sin x dx\right]$

$= 10\left[[-\cos x]_0^{\pi/2} + [-\cos x]_{\pi/2}^{\pi}\right]$

$= 10[1+1] = 10 \times 2 = 20$

11. $I_n + I_{n+2} = \int_0^{\pi/4} \tan^n x(1+\tan^2 x)dx$

$= \int_0^{\pi/4} \tan^n x \sec^2 x dx$

$= \int_0^{\pi/4} t^n \, dt$ where $t = \tan x$

$l_n + l_{n+2} = \frac{1}{n+1}$

$$\Rightarrow \lim_{n\to\infty} n\left[I_n + I_{n+2}\right]$$

$$\Rightarrow \lim_{n\to\infty} n\frac{1}{n+1} = \lim_{x\to\infty}\frac{n}{n+1}$$

$$= \lim_{n\to\infty}\frac{n}{n\left(1+\frac{1}{n}\right)} = 1$$

12. $\int_0^1\left[x^2\right]dx + \int_1^{\sqrt{2}}\left[x^2\right]dx + \int_{\sqrt{2}}^{\sqrt{3}}\left[x^2\right]dx$

$$+ \int_{\sqrt{3}}^{2}\left[x^2\right]dx$$

$$= \int_0^1 0\,dx + \int_1^{\sqrt{2}} 1\cdot dx + \int_{\sqrt{2}}^{\sqrt{3}} 2\,dx + \int_{\sqrt{3}}^{2} 3\,dx$$

$$= 0 + 1\left(\sqrt{2}-1\right) + 2\left(\sqrt{3}-\sqrt{2}\right) + \left(2-\sqrt{3}\right)$$

$$= 1 + \sqrt{3} - \sqrt{2}$$

13. $\int_0^{\pi}\frac{2x\,(1+\sin x)}{1+\cos^2 x}dx$

$$= \int_0^{\pi}\frac{2x}{1+\cos^2 x}dx + 2\int_0^{\pi}\frac{x\sin x}{1+\cos^2 x}dx$$

$$I = 0 + 4\int_0^{\pi}\frac{(\pi - x)\sin(\pi - x)}{1+\cos^2(\pi - x)}dx$$

$$I = 4\int_0^{\pi}\frac{(\pi - x)\sin x}{1+\cos^2 x}dx$$

$$I = 4\pi\int_0^{\pi}\frac{\sin x}{1+\cos^2 x}dx - 4\int_0^{\pi}\frac{x\sin x}{1+\cos^2 x}dx$$

$$2I = 4\pi\int_0^{\pi}\frac{\sin x}{1+\cos^2 x}dx$$

Put $\cos x = t$

$\Rightarrow -\sin x dx = dt \Rightarrow \sin x dx = -\,dt$

$$I = 2\pi\int_1^{-1}\frac{-\,dt}{1+t^2} = 2\pi\int_{-1}^{1}\frac{dt}{1+t^2}$$

$$= 2\pi\left[\tan^{-1} t\right]_{-1}^{1}$$

$$= 2\pi\left[\tan^{-1}(1) - \tan^{-1}(-1)\right]$$

$$= 2\pi\left[\frac{\pi}{4}+\frac{\pi}{4}\right] = 2\pi\times\frac{\pi}{2} = \pi^2$$

14. $f(x) = \sin^4 x + \cos^4 x$

$$= \left(\sin^2 x + \cos^2 x\right)^2 - 2\sin^2 x\cos^2 x$$

$$= 1 - \frac{1}{2}(\sin 2x)^2 = 1 - \frac{1}{2}\left[\frac{1-\cos 4x}{2}\right]$$

$$= \frac{3}{4} + \frac{1}{4}\cos 4x$$

Since $\cos x$ is periodic with period 2π

$$= \frac{2\pi}{4} = \frac{\pi}{2}$$

15. The function $f(x) = \sqrt{\log_{10}\left(\frac{5x - x^2}{4}\right)}$

exists for

$$\frac{5x - x^2}{4} \geq 1$$

$$\Rightarrow 5x - x^2 - 4 \geq 0$$

$$\Rightarrow x \in [1, 4]$$

16. $\sin y = x\sin(a + y)$

$$x = \frac{\sin y}{\sin(a+y)}$$

$$\Rightarrow \frac{dx}{dy} = \frac{\sin(a+y)\cos y - \sin y\cos(a+y)}{\sin^2(a+y)}$$

$$\frac{dx}{dy} = \frac{\sin(a+y-y)}{\sin^2(a+y)}$$

$$\frac{dy}{dx} = \frac{\sin^2(a+y)}{\sin a}$$

17. $x^y = e^{x-y}$

Taking the log of both sides

$y\log x = x - y$

$$\Rightarrow y = \frac{x}{1+\log x}$$

$$\frac{dy}{dx} = \frac{(1+\log x) - x\times\frac{1}{x}}{(1+\log x)^2} = \frac{\log x}{(1+\log x)^2}$$

18. We have $f(x) = (x+1)^{1/3} - (x-1)^{1/3}$

$$\therefore f'(x) = \frac{1}{3}\left[\frac{1}{(x+1)^{2/3}} - \frac{1}{(x-1)^{2/3}}\right]$$

$$= \frac{(x-1)^{2/3} - (x+1)^{2/3}}{3(x^2-1)^{2/3}}$$

Clearly $f'(x) \neq 0$ for any other value of $x \in [0, 1]$. The value of $f(x)$ at $x = 0$ is 2. Hence the greatest value of $f(x)$ is 2

19. $f(x) = \cot^{-1} x + x$

$$\Rightarrow f'(x) = -\frac{1}{1+x^2} + 1$$

$= \frac{x^2}{1+x^2}$, Clearly, $f'(x) > 0$ for all x

So, $f(x)$ increases in (∞, ∞)

20. $I = \int_0^{\pi/2} \frac{\sqrt{\sin x}\, dx}{\sqrt{\cos x} + \sqrt{\sin x}}$ ...(*i*)

$$I = \int_0^{\pi/2} \frac{\sqrt{\sin(\pi/2 - x)}}{\sqrt{\cos(\pi/2 - x)} + \sqrt{\sin(\pi/2 - x)}} dx$$

$$I = \int_0^{\pi/2} \frac{\sqrt{\cos x}}{\sqrt{\sin x} + \sqrt{\cos x}} dx$$

Adding eqs. (*i*) and (*ii*)

$$2I = \int_0^{\pi/2} dx \Rightarrow I = \frac{\pi}{4}$$

21. $\int \frac{dx}{x(x^n + 1)}$

Putting $x^n + 1 = t$, $nx^{n-1} dx = dt$

$$= \frac{1}{n}\int \frac{dt}{t(t-1)} = \frac{1}{n}\int\left(\frac{1}{t-1} - \frac{1}{t}\right)dt$$

$$= \frac{1}{n}\log\left(\frac{t-1}{t}\right) + c = \frac{1}{n}\log\left(\frac{x^n}{x^n+1}\right) + c$$

22. Required area $= \int_0^3 (y_1 - y_2)dx$

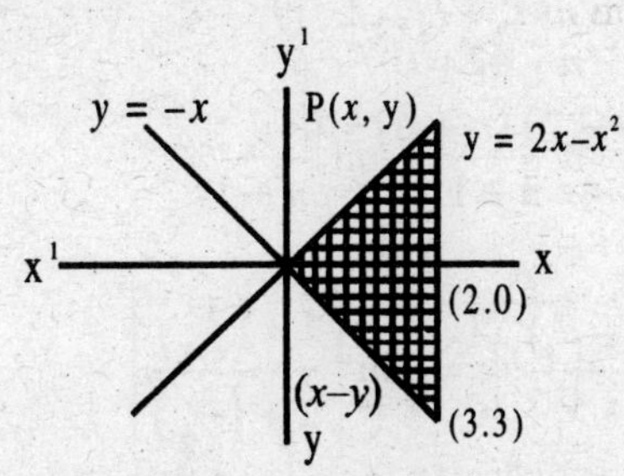

$$\int_0^3 \left[(2x - x^2) - (-x)\right]dx = \int_0^3 (3x - x^2)dx$$

$$= \left[\frac{3x^2}{2} - \frac{x^3}{3}\right]_0^3 = \frac{27}{2} - 9 = \frac{9}{2}$$

23. The general equation of all non – vertical lines is plane is $ax + hy = 1$, where $h \neq o$

$$\Rightarrow a + h\frac{dy}{dx} = 0$$

$$\Rightarrow hx\frac{d^2y}{dx^2} = 0$$

$$\Rightarrow \frac{d^2y}{dx^2} = 0$$

24. The number of ways in which either player can choose a number from 1 to 25 is 25. So, the total number of ways a choosing numbers is $25 \times 25 = 625$. So the probability that they will not win a prize in a single trial $= 1 - \frac{1}{25} = \frac{24}{25}$

25. Since A and B mutually exclusive events therefore.

$A \cap B = \phi$

$\Rightarrow A \subseteq \bar{B}$

and $B \subseteq \bar{A}$

$\Rightarrow P(\bar{A}) \leq P(\bar{B})$

and $P(B) \leq P(A)$

26. $\Rightarrow T_n = {}^nC_3 \Rightarrow T_{n+1} - T_n = 21$

$\Rightarrow {}^{n+1}C_3 - {}^nC_3 = 21$

$\Rightarrow {}^nC_2 + {}^nC_3 - {}^nC_3 = 21$

$\Rightarrow {}^nC_2 = 21$

${}^nC_2 = 21$

$$\Rightarrow \frac{n(n-1)}{2} = 21$$
$$\Rightarrow n^2 - n - 42 = 0$$
$$\Rightarrow (n-7)(n+6) = 0$$
$n = 7$ As $n \geq 1$

27. $$\lim_{x\to\infty}\left(\frac{x-3}{x+2}\right)^x = \lim_{x\to\infty}\left[\frac{1-\left(3/x\right)}{2+\left(2/x\right)}\right]^x$$

$$= \lim_{x\to\infty}\frac{\left(1-\frac{3}{x}\right)^x}{\left(1+\frac{2}{x}\right)^x}$$
$$\Rightarrow \frac{e^{-3}}{e^2} = e^{-5}$$

28. We have $\left(1+\omega-\omega^2\right)^7 = \left(-\omega^2-\omega^2\right)^7$
$=(-2)^7\left(\omega^2\right)^7$
$=-128\omega^2$

29. $$x+iy = \begin{vmatrix} 6i & -3i & 1 \\ 4 & 3i & -1 \\ 20 & 3 & i \end{vmatrix}$$
$$= -3i\begin{vmatrix} 6i & 1 & 1 \\ 4 & -1 & -1 \\ 20 & i & i \end{vmatrix} = 0$$
$$\Rightarrow x+iy = 0$$
$$\Rightarrow x = 0,\ y = 0$$

30. Required probability,
$P(A_1, A_2, A_3) + P(A_1, A_2, A_3)$
$= P(A_1).P(A_2)\,P(A_3) + P(A_1)$
$P(A_2)P(A_3)$
$$= \left(\frac{1}{2}\right)^3 + \left(\frac{1}{2}\right)^3$$
$$= \frac{1}{8} + \frac{1}{8} = \frac{2}{8} = \frac{1}{4}$$

31. Applying $R_1 \to R_1 + R_3$, we obtain
$$\begin{vmatrix} 1-i & \omega^2+\omega & \omega^2-1 \\ 1-i & -1 & \omega^2-1 \\ -i & -1+\omega-i & -1 \end{vmatrix} = 0$$
$\therefore\ \omega^2+\omega = -1$, for which R_1 and R_2 become indentical

32. Let $q = 1-p$. Since head appears first time in an even throw 2 or 4 or 6
$$\therefore \frac{2}{5} = qp + q^3p + q^5 . p + ...$$
$$\therefore \frac{2}{5} = \frac{qp}{1-p^2} \Rightarrow \frac{2}{5} = \frac{(1-p)p}{1-(1-p)^2}$$
$$= \frac{1-p}{2-p}$$
$$\frac{2}{5} = \frac{1-p}{2-p}$$
$$\Rightarrow 4-2p = 5-5p$$
$$3p = 1$$
$$\Rightarrow p = \frac{1}{3}$$

33. Required probability
$$= {}^7C_2\left(\frac{1}{6}\right)^2\left(\frac{5}{6}\right)^5 \times \frac{1}{6}$$
$$= \frac{{}^7c_2 \times 5^5}{6^8}$$

34. $$\lim_{x\to 2}\frac{xf(2)-2f(x)}{x-2}$$
$$= \lim_{x\to 2}\frac{xf(2)-2f(x)+2f(2)-2f(2)}{x-2}$$
$$= \lim_{x\to 2}\frac{(x-2)f(2)}{x-2} - 2\lim_{x\to 2}\frac{f(x)-f(2)}{x-2}$$
$$= f(2) - 2f'(2)$$
$$= 4 - 2\times 4$$
$$= -4$$

38. $$a^i = e^{i\log_e a} = e^{i(2\pi i+\log_e a)}$$
$$= e^{-2n\pi}\cdot e^{i\log_e a}$$
$$= e^{-2n\pi}\left[\cos(\log_e a) + i\sin(\log_e a)\right]$$
$$\text{Re}\left(a^i\right) = e^{-2n\pi}\left[\cos(\log_e a)\right]$$

Set–21
CSIR–UGC (NET) Mathematical Sciences
PART-B

1. $\int_{-\frac{\pi}{2}}^{\pi} \sin^2 x \cos^2 x(\sin x + \cos x)dx$

A. $2/15$ B. $4/15$

C. $\frac{e}{2} - 1$ D. $\frac{e-3}{2}$

2. $2\left\{\frac{m-n}{m+n} + \frac{1}{3}\left(\frac{m-n}{m+n}\right)^3 + \frac{1}{5}\left(\frac{m-n}{m+n}\right)^5 + ...\right\}$

A. $\log_e \frac{(m-1)}{m+1}$ B. $\log_e m - \log_e^n$

C. $\log_e m + \log_e^n$ D. $\log_e \frac{(m+n)}{m-n}$

3. The value of θ lying between θ = 0 and $\theta = \pi/2$ satisfying the equation

$$\begin{vmatrix} 1+\sin^2\theta & \cos^2\theta & 4\sin 4\theta \\ \sin^2\theta & 1+\cos^2\theta & 4\sin 4\theta \\ \sin^2\theta & \cos^2\theta & 1+\sin 4\theta \end{vmatrix} = 0$$ are

A. $7\pi/24$ B. $5\pi/24$

C. $10\pi/24$ D. $\pi/24$

4. $f(x) = \cos(\ln(x))$, then $f(x)f(y) - \frac{1}{2}\left[f\left(\frac{y}{x}\right) + f(x-y)\right]$ has the value

A. –1 B. $1/2$

C. –2 D. None of these

5. For a real no. y let $[y]$ denote the greatest integer less than or equal to y. Then the function $f(x) = \frac{\tan(\pi[x-\pi])}{1+[x]^2}$ is

A. Discontinuous at some x

B. Continuous at all x but the second derivative of $f(x)$ does not exist for some x

C. $f(x)$ exists for all x but the derivative $f'(x)$ does not exist for some x

D. $f(x)$ exists for all x

6. The function $f(x) = \begin{cases} x, \text{ when } x \text{ is rational} \\ -x, \text{ when } x \text{ is irrational} \end{cases}$

A. $f(x)$ is continuous for all values of x

B. $f(x)$ is discontinuous for all values of x except at $x = 0$

C. The derivative of $f(x)$ is positive for all

D. None of the above

7. $\int_{-1}^{\frac{3}{2}} |x \sin \pi x| dx = ?$

A. $\left(3 + \frac{1}{\pi}\right)$ B. $\left(3 - \frac{1}{\pi}\right)$

C. $\frac{1}{\pi}\left(3 + \frac{1}{\pi}\right)$ D. $\frac{1}{2\pi}\left(3 + \frac{1}{\pi}\right)$

8. Seven chits are numbered 1 to 7, four are drawn one by one with replacements. The probability that the least number appearing on any selected coupon 5 is

A. $\left(5/7\right)^4$ B. $\left(6/7^3\right)$

C. $\frac{5.4.3}{7^3}$ D. $\left(3/7\right)^4$

9. Each of the four inequalities given below defines a region in the x y plane. One of these regions does not have the following property for any two points (x_1, y_1) and (x_2, y_2) in the region given below the points $\left\{\frac{x_1 + x_1}{2}, \frac{y_1 + y_2}{2}\right\}$ is also in the region. The inequality defining this region is

A. $x^2 + 2y^2 \leq 1$ B. $Max\{|x|, |y|\} \leq 1$

C. $x^2 - y^2 \leq 1$ D. $y^2 \leq x$

10. The point (4, 1) undergoes the following three transformation successively

I. Reflexion about the line $y = x$

II. Transformation through a distance 2 units along the positive direction of X axis

III. Rotation through an angle 45° in the anti clockwise direction. The final position of the points is given by coordinates

A. $\left(1/\sqrt{2}, 7/\sqrt{2}\right)$ B. $\left(-\sqrt{2}, 7\sqrt{2}\right)$

C. $\left(\frac{-1}{\sqrt{2}}, \frac{7}{\sqrt{2}}\right)$ D. $\left(\sqrt{2}, 7\sqrt{2}\right)$

11. If $xy + yz + zx = 1$, $\frac{x}{1-x^2} + \frac{y}{1-y^2} + \frac{z}{1-z^2} = ?$

A. $\frac{x}{(1-x^2)(1-y^2)(1-z^2)}$

B. $\frac{4xy}{(1-x^2)(1-y^2)(1-z^2)}$

C. $\frac{4xyz}{(1-x^2)(1-y^2)(1-z^2)}$

D. $\frac{4xyz}{(1-x^2)(1-y^2)}$

12. $A = \left\{x : \frac{\pi}{6} \le x \le \frac{\pi}{3}\right\}$ and $f(x) = \cos x - x(1+x)$ then $f(A) = ?$

A. $f(A) = \left\{y : \frac{1}{2} - \frac{\pi}{3}\left(1 + \frac{\pi}{3}\right) \le y \le \sqrt{\frac{3}{2}} - \frac{\pi}{6}\left(1 + \frac{\pi}{6}\right)\right\}$

B. $f(A) = \left\{y : 1 - \frac{\pi}{3}\left(1 + \frac{\pi}{3}\right) \le y \le \sqrt{3} - \frac{\pi}{3}\left(1 + \frac{\pi}{3}\right)\right\}$

C. $f(A) = \{y : -1 \le y \le 1\}$

D. $f(A) = \{y : -0 \le y < 1\}$

13. $\lim_{x\to\infty} \frac{2x^2 + 2x - \sin^2 x}{3x^2 - 4x + \cos^2 x}$

A. $\frac{1}{3}$ B. $\frac{1}{6}$

C. $\frac{2}{3}$ D. 1

14. If g is the inverse of f and $f(x) = \frac{1}{1+x^3}$, $g'(x) = ?$

A. $1 + \{g(x)\}^2$ B. $1 + \{g(x)\}^3$

C. $\{1 + g(x)\}^2$ D. $\{1 + g(x)\}^3$

15. If $1, a_1, a_2 \ldots a_{n-1}$ are the n roots of unity then $(1-a_1)(1-a_2)\ldots\ldots\ldots(1-a_n) = ?$

A. 1 B. n

C. n^2 D. None of these

16. If $ax^2 + \frac{b}{x} \ge c$ for all the x where $a > 0$ and $b > 0$, then $27\,ab^2$

A. $\ge 4c^3$ B. $< 4c^2$

C. None of these D. $= 1$

17. $\int x \frac{(\sec 2x - 1)}{(\sec 2x + 1)} dx = ?$

A. $x \tan x + \log(\cos x) - \frac{x^2}{2} + c$

B. $x \tan x - \frac{x^2}{2} + c$

C. $x \cot x + \log(\cos x) - \frac{x^2}{2} + c$

D. $x \tan x - \log(\cos x) + \frac{x^2}{2} + c$

18. $I = \int \frac{\sqrt{1 + \sqrt[3]{x}}}{\sqrt[3]{x^2}} dx = ?$

A. $2\left(1 + x^{2/3}\right)^{1/3}$ B. $2\left(1 + x^2\right)^{1/3}$

C. $2\left(1 + x^{1/3}\right)^{3/2}$ D. $2\left(1 + x^{1/3}\right)^{1/3}$

19. $\lim_{n\to\infty}\left[\frac{1}{n+1}+\frac{1}{n+2}+.....+\frac{1}{n+n}\right]=?$

A. $ln2$ B. $ln3$
C. 0 D. $2ln2$

20. $\lim_{n\to\infty}\left(\lim_{x\to\infty}\left(\cos^{2m}(n\pi x)\right)\right)$ is equal to

A. 0 for all x
B. 1 for all x
C. 0 or 1 according as x rational or irrational
D. 1 or 0 according as x rational or irrational

21. A function f is such that $f(x)=2x\sin\frac{1}{x}-\cos\frac{1}{x}$, $x\neq 0$, $f(0)=f\left(\frac{1}{\pi}\right)=0$

A. f is differentiable at 0
B. f is not differentiable but is continuous at 0
C. f is not continuous also
D. None of these

22. The transverse axis of a hyperbola is $2a$ its vertex bisects the distance between centre and focus, its equation is

A. $y^2-3x^2=3a^2$ B. $3x^2-y^2=3a^2$
C. $y^2-3x^2=6a^2$ D. $3x^2-y^2=6a^2$

23. For a real number x, $[x]$ denotes the integral part of x the value of $\left[\frac{1}{2}\right]+\left[\frac{1}{2}+\frac{1}{100}\right]+\left[\frac{1}{2}+\frac{2}{100}\right]+........+\left[\frac{1}{2}+\frac{99}{100}\right]$

A. 49 B. 50
C. 51 D. 48

24. The value of $\lim_{n\to\infty}\frac{1}{n}\sum_{r=1}^{3n}\frac{r}{n+r}$ is

A. $ln\,4-3$ B. $2-ln3$
C. $3-ln\,4$ D. None of these

25. How many solutions in positive integers are there for the equation $x_1+x_2+x_3+x_4=16$

A. ${}^{16}C_3$ B. ${}^{15}C_3$
C. ${}^{17}C_4$ D. None of these

26. If $a_1, a_2, a_3\,(a_1>0)$ be three successive terms of a G.P with common ratio r, the value of r for which inequality $b_3>4b_2-3b_1$ holds is, given by

A. $r=5$ B. $r>3$
C. $r<2$ D. None of these

27. If 1, ω, ω² are the cube roots of unity then the roots of $(x-1)^3+8=0$ are

A. $-1,-1,1$
B. $1, 1+2\omega, 1+2\omega^2$
C. $1, \omega, 2\omega$
D. $-1, 1-2\omega, 1-2\omega^2$

28. Let R be the set of real numbers if $f:R\to R$ is defined by $f(x)=e^x$ then f is

A. Surjective but not injective
B. Injective but not surjective
C. Bijective
D. Surjective but not bijective

29. The greatest and least value of $f(x)=x^4-8x^3+22x^2-24x+1$ in $[0, 2]$ are

A. 0, 8 B. 0, −8
C. 1, 8 D. 1, −8

30. The value of integral $\int_a^b\frac{\log x}{x}dx$ is

A. $\frac{1}{2}\log\left(\frac{b}{a}\right)\log\left(\frac{a}{b}\right)$

B. $\frac{1}{2}\log\left(\frac{a}{b}\right)\log(ab)$

C. $\frac{1}{2}\log\left(\frac{b}{a}\right)\log(ab)$

D. None of these

31. $\int\frac{xe^n}{(x+1)^2}$ is equal to

A. $\frac{e^x+1}{x+1}$ B. $\frac{e^x-1}{x+1}$
C. $\frac{e^x}{x+1}$ D. $\frac{e^x}{x-1}$

32. $\sin x dx+y dy=0$, $y(0)=-2$ then the value of $y(\pi)$ is

A. 2 B. $\sqrt{2}$
C. 0 D. −2

33. Polar representation of $1+i$ is

A. $\sqrt{2}\cos\frac{\pi}{4}$ B. $\sqrt{2}\sin\frac{\pi}{4}$

C. $\frac{1}{\sqrt{2}}\left[\cos\frac{\pi}{4}+i\sin\frac{\pi}{4}\right]$ D. $\sqrt{2}\left[\cos\frac{\pi}{4}+i\sin\frac{\pi}{4}\right]$

34. If $\vec{e}_1$, $\vec{e}_2$ are two unit vectors and Q is the angle between them, then $\cos\frac{Q}{2}$ is

A. $\frac{1}{2}|\vec{e}_1+\vec{e}_2|$ B. $|\vec{e}_1-\vec{e}_2|$

C. $\left|\frac{\vec{e}_1\cdot\vec{e}_2}{2}\right|$ D. $\frac{|\vec{e}_1\cdot\vec{e}_2|}{2|\vec{e}_1||\vec{e}_2|}$

35. Of sigarette smoking population 70% are men and 30% are women, 10% of these men and 20% of women smoke wills. Probability that a person seen smoking a wills to be male is

A. $1/5$ B. $7/13$

C. $5/13$ D. $7/10$

36. Let $f: R \to R$ be differentiable function and $f(1)=8$ then the value of $\lim_{x\to 1}\int_4^{f(x)}\frac{2t}{x-1}dt$

A. $8f(1)$ B. $4f(1)$

C. $16f(1)$ D. None of these

37. If $f(x)=\frac{\sin[x]}{[x]}, [x]\neq 0$ where [x] denotes to 0 when [x] = 0 the greatest integer less than or equal to x, then $\lim_{x-0} f[x]$ equals

A. 1 B. 0

C. $1/2$ D. None of these

38. The system of equations $kx+2y-z=1$, $(k-1)y-2z=z$ and $(k+2)z=3$ have a unique solution if K equals

A. –2 B. –1

C. c D. 1

39. A series represents a continuous function $f(x)$ within the interval of convergence of the series is called:

A. Power Series B. Laurent's Series

C. Maclaurin's Series D. Taylor's Series

40. If $(q_{-1}, 0)^*$ is a group with $a \circ b = a+b+ab$, then for $a \in q_{-1}$, a^{-1} is:

A. $-a$ B. $-a-1$

C. $-a+1$ D. $-\frac{a}{(a+1)}$

ANSWERS

1	2	3	4	5	6	7	8	9	10
B	B	A	D	D	B	C	D	C	C
11	12	13	14	15	16	17	18	19	20
C	A	C	D	B	A	A	C	C	D
21	22	23	24	25	26	27	28	29	30
A	B	B	C	B	B	D	B	D	C
31	32	33	34	35	36	37	38	39	40
C	C	D	A	B	D	D	B	A	D

Some Selected Explanatory Answers

3. Determinant we get, $1+\sin^2\theta+\cos^2\theta+4\sin 4\theta=0$

4. Put value of f in given experssion

5. $\tan(\pi[x-\pi])=0$ as $[x-\pi]$ is always an integer while the denominator is not zero

8. Probability $=\frac{3}{7}\times\frac{3}{7}\times\frac{3}{7}\times\frac{3}{7}$

10. Step 1: Reflexing of (4,1) through $y=x$ is (1,4)

Step 2: $x \to x+2$

$\to$ coordinate = (3;4)

Step 3: rotation though 45° in anticlock direction

$x \to x\cos(360°-45°)+y\sin(360°-\theta)$

$\rightarrow \frac{3}{\sqrt{2}} - \frac{4}{\sqrt{2}} = \frac{-1}{\sqrt{2}}$

$y \rightarrow x\cos(360° - 45°) - y\sin(360° - \theta)$

$\rightarrow \frac{3}{\sqrt{2}} + \frac{4}{\sqrt{2}} = \frac{7}{\sqrt{2}}$

Point $\left(-\frac{1}{\sqrt{2}}, \frac{7}{\sqrt{2}}\right)$

12. $f(x)$ is continuous, so it takes each and every real value between its maximum (*l*: U.*b*) and minimum (*g.l.b*) where (*l.u.b* = least upper bound and g.l.b = greatest lower bound, Here $\cos x$ is a decreasing function and $x(1+x)$ is an increasing function.

Hence at $\pi/3$ it has minimum value and a $\pi/6$ it has maximum value

$$f(A)=\left\{f:\frac{1}{2}-\frac{\pi}{3}\left(1+\frac{\pi}{3}\right)\leq y\leq\frac{\sqrt{3}}{6}-\frac{\pi}{6}\left(1+\frac{\pi}{6}\right)\right\}$$

3. $$\lim\frac{2+\frac{2}{x}-\frac{\sin^2 x}{x^2}}{3-\frac{4}{x}+\frac{\cos^2 x}{x^2}}$$

$= 2/3$ As $x \rightarrow \infty$, $1/x \rightarrow 0$

$-1 \leq \sin x \leq 1$:

$-1 \leq \cos x \leq 1$:

$\therefore \lim\frac{\sin x}{x}=0, \lim\frac{\cos x}{x}=0$

4. $g(x) = f^{-1}(x)$

$\Rightarrow f(g(x)) = x$

$f'(g(x))g'(x) = 1$

$$g'(x) = \frac{1}{f'(g(x))}$$

$\Rightarrow g'(x)=1+(g(x))^3$

15. 1, $a_1 \ldots a_{n-1}$ are roots of $x^n = 1$ i.e, $x^n - 1 = 0$

$(x-1)x^{n-1}+x^{n-2}+x^{n-3}+---x+1)=0$

$\Rightarrow a_1, a_2 \ldots a_{n-1}$ are $n-1$ roots of the equation

$x^{n-1}+x^{n-2}+x+1=0$

$\therefore (x-a_1)(x-a_2)\ldots\ldots(x-a_{n-1})$

$=x^{n-1}+x^{n-2}+\ldots\ldots\ldots(x+1)$

Put $x = 1$

$\therefore (1-a_1)(1-a_2)\ldots\ldots(1-a_{n-1})=1+1+\ldots n$ terms

$= n$

16. $f(x)=ax^2+\frac{b}{x}-c \Rightarrow f'(x)=2ax+\left(\frac{-b}{x^2}\right)=2ax-\frac{b}{x^2}$

$f''(x) = 2a + \frac{2b}{x^3} \geq 0$

$\therefore f'(x) = 0 \Rightarrow x = \left(\frac{b}{2a}\right)^{1/3} \geq 0$

$f''(x)+ve \Rightarrow f(x)$ has minimum at $x=\left(\frac{b}{2a}\right)^{1/3}$

and $f\left[\left(\frac{b}{2a}\right)^{1/3}\right]\left(\left(\frac{2a}{b}\right)^{1/3}\left(\frac{3b}{2}\right)-6\right)\geq 0$

$\Rightarrow 27ab^2 \geq 4c^3$

17. $$I=\int x\left(\frac{\frac{1}{\cos 2x}-1}{\frac{1}{\cos 2x}+1}\right)dx$$

$= x\frac{2\sin^2 x}{2\cos^2 x}dx = \int x\tan^2 x\,dx$

$I = \int\left(x\sec^2 x - x\right)dx$

$= x\tan x + \log(\cos x) - \frac{x^2}{2} + c$

18. $I = \int x^{-2/3}\left(1+x^{1/3}\right)^{1/2} dx$

Here $m = -2/3$, $n = 1/3$, $p = 1/2$

$\frac{m+1}{n} = 1$ i.e. a integer

$1 + x^{1/3} = t^2$

$\therefore \frac{1}{3} x^{2/3} dx = 2tdt$

$I = 2\left(1 + x^{1/3}\right)^{3/2} + c$

19. $\frac{1}{n+1} + \frac{1}{n+2} + -- \frac{1}{n+n} = \frac{n}{2} \frac{1}{n+r}$

$r = 1,\ z = \frac{1}{n} \frac{1}{\left(1 + r/n\right)}$

$\lim \frac{n}{2} \frac{1}{n} \frac{1}{\left(1 + r/n\right)} = \int 1 \frac{dn}{1+n} = ln2$

$n \to \infty$

20. When x is rational i.e. equal to p/q then $\angle n\pi x$ is an integral multiple of π for all $x > 9$. Therefore $\cos(n\pi x) = \pm 1$ and $\cos^{2m}(n\pi x) = 1$ for all x rational $n \to \infty, m \to \infty$
when x is irrational $(n\pi x)$ is not an integral multiple of π and $|\cos(n\pi x)| < 1$
$\therefore \lim \cos^{2m}(n\pi x) = 0$

21. For $x \neq 0$, we have $f(x) = \int f(x) dx$

$f(x) = \int 2x \sin \frac{1}{x} dx - \int \cos \frac{1}{x} dx$

$f(0) = \lim \frac{f(x) - f(0)}{x} = 0$

22. Distance from centre Q to focus S is ae and distance from centre O to vertex A is $\frac{1}{2} 2a = a$

$\therefore$ A bisects OS $\Rightarrow \therefore OA = \frac{1}{2} OS$

$a = \frac{1}{2} ae \Rightarrow e = 2$

$b^2 = a^2 (4 - 1) = 3a^2$

Equation of hyperbola

$3x^2 - y^2 = 3a^2$

23. $\left[\frac{1}{2}\right] + \left[\frac{1}{2} + \frac{1}{100}\right] + \left[\frac{1}{2} + \frac{2}{100}\right] + \ldots.. + \left[\frac{1}{2} + \frac{99}{100}\right]$

$= \left[\frac{1}{2} + \frac{50}{100}\right] + \left[\frac{1}{2} + \frac{51}{100}\right] + \ldots.. + \left[\frac{1}{2} + \frac{99}{100}\right] = 50$

24. $\text{Lim} \frac{1}{n} \sum_{r=1}^{3n} \frac{r}{n+r}$ put $m = 3n$

$n \to \infty, m \to \infty$ it becomes

$\lim \frac{3}{m} \sum_{r=1}^{m} \frac{3n}{3n+1}$

$n \to \infty$

$= 3\int_0^1 \frac{3xdx}{3x+1}$

25. No. of positive solutions of $(x_1 + x_2 + x_3 + x_4 = 16)$

$=$ coeffi of $x^{16} in \left(x + x^2 + x^3 + \ldots\ldots\right)^4$

$=$ coeffi of $x^{16} in\, x^4 (1 - x)^{-4}$

$=$ coeffi of $x^{12} in\ 1 + {}^4C_1 x + {}^5C_2 x^2$

$= {}^{15}C_{12}\ x^{12}$

$= {}^{15}C_{12} \Rightarrow {}^{15}C_3$

26. $b_3 > 4b_2 - 3b_1$

$\Rightarrow b_1 r^2 > 4b_1 r - 3b_1$

$\Rightarrow r^2 > 4r - 3$

$\Rightarrow (r-3)(r-1) > 0$

$r > 3$

27. $(x-1)^3 + 8 = 0$

$(x-1) = (-8)^{1/3}$

$= -2, -2w, -2w^2$

$x = -1, 1-2w, 1-2w^2$

28. $x_1 - x_2 \in R$ and $x_1 \neq x_2$

$\Rightarrow e^{x_1} \neq e^{x_2}$

$\Rightarrow f(x_1) \neq f(x_2)$

f is not surjective

Since $e_x > o$ for all real x and so, no negative real number can be the image of any real number. So f is injective.

29. $f(x) = 4x^3 - 24x^2 + 44x - 24$, for maximum and minimum, $f'(x) = 0$

$x = 1, 2, 3$

$x = 3 \notin [0, 2]$

Now $f(0) = 1$

$f(2) = -7$

$f''(1) = 0$

at $x = 1, f(x)$ is minimum

$f(1) = -8$

Greatest of (x) = largest of $\{1, -7 - 8\} = 1$

Least of $f(x)$ = Smallest of $\{1, -7 - 8\} = -8$

30. Put, $\log x = t \Rightarrow \frac{1}{x}dx = dt$, $\int_a^b \frac{\log x}{x}dx =$

$$\left[\frac{-t^2}{2}\right]_a^b = \frac{1}{2}\log\left(b/a\right)\log(ab)$$

31. $\int \frac{xe^x}{(x+1)^2}dx = x\,e^x \frac{(x+1)^{-2+1}}{-2+1}$

$$-\int\left(xe^x + e^x\right)\frac{(x+1)^{-2+1}}{-2+1}$$

$$= \frac{-xe^x}{x+1} + \int e^x(x+1)\frac{1}{x+1}dx$$

$$= \frac{e^x}{x+1}$$

32. $-\cos x + \frac{1}{2}y^2 = c$

Given that $y(0) = -2$

$\therefore -\cos 0 + \frac{1}{2}(-2)^2 = c$

$\Rightarrow c = 1$

$\frac{y^2}{2} - \cos x = 1$

Put $x = \pi$

$y = 0$

33. $Z = 1 + i = |Z| \Rightarrow \sqrt{1^2 + 1^2} = \sqrt{2}$

& argument (z) = $\tan^{-1} 1 = \frac{\pi}{4}$

$$\therefore Z = \sqrt{2}\left[\cos\frac{\pi}{4} + i\sin\frac{\pi}{4}\right]$$

34. $\left(\vec{e_1} + \vec{e_2}\right)^2 = \vec{e_1}\ \vec{e_1} + 2\vec{e_1}\ \vec{e_2} + \vec{e_2}\ \vec{e_2}$

$= \left|\vec{e_1}\right|^2 + 2\left|\vec{e_1}\right|\ \left|\vec{e_2}\right| \cos\theta + e_2^2$

$= 1 + 2\cos\theta + 1$

$\left|\vec{e_1} + \vec{e_2}\right|^2 = 2 + 2\cos\theta$

$\left|\vec{e_1} + \vec{e_2}\right|^2 = 4\cos^2 \theta/2$

$\cos \theta/2 = \frac{1}{2}\left|\vec{e_1} + \vec{e_2}\right|$

35. Let the number is 100 then person smoking wills

$$= \frac{70\times10}{100} + \frac{30\times20}{100} = 13$$

Now male smoking wills $= \frac{70\times10}{100} = 7$

Required Prob $= 7/13$

36. $\lim_{x\to1} \int_4^{f(x)} f(x)\frac{2t}{x-1}dt = \lim_{x\to1}\frac{1}{x-1}\left(t^2\right)_4^{f(x)}$

$$= \lim_{x\to1} \frac{[f(x)]^2 - 16}{x-1} = \frac{64-16}{0} = \infty$$

37. $[x] = 0$ when $0 \le x < 1$, $= 1$ when $-1 \le x < 0$

$f(x) = \frac{\text{Sin }(-1)}{1} = \sin 1, 1 \le x < 0$

$f(x) = 0$ when $0 \le x \le 1$

LHL = Sin 1

RHL = 0

So limit does not exist.

SET–22

CSIR–UGC (NET) MATHEMATICAL SCIENCES

PART-B

1. If the area of the triangle on the complex plane formed by the points z, $z+iz$ and iz is 50. Then $|z|$ is

A. 1 B. 5

C. 10 D. $5\sqrt{2}$

2. Sum to n terms of the series

$\frac{1}{2}+\frac{3}{4}+\frac{7}{8}+\frac{15}{16}+$..........is,

A. $2^{-n}+n-1$ B. $1-2^{n}$

C. $2^{n}+n-1$ D. $2^{n}-1$

3. The value of $\int_0^1 \frac{dx}{\left(x^2-2x\cos a+1\right)}$ for $0<a<\pi$ is

A. $\sin a$ B. $\tan^{-1}\sin a$

C. $a\sin a$ D. $\frac{a}{2}(\sin a)^{-1}$

4. The value of $\int_0^{\pi}\sqrt{\frac{1+\cos 2x}{2}}\,dx$ is

A. -2 B. 2

C. 0 D. -3

5. The value of $\int_0^{\infty}\frac{x\log x}{\left(1+x^2\right)^2}\,dx$

A. 0 B. log 7

C. 5 log 13 D. None of these

6. The number of unit vectors perpendicular to the vector $a=(1,1,0)$ and $b=(0,1,1)$ is,

A. One B. Two

C. Three D. None of these

7. The degree of the differential equation

$$\frac{d^2y}{dx^2}+3\left(\frac{dy}{dx}\right)^2=x\log\frac{d^2y}{dx^2}$$ is

A. 1 B. 2

C. 3 D. None of these

8. If $y=a\log|x|+bx^2+x$ has its extremum values at $x=-1$ and $x=2$ then

A. $a=2, b=-1$ B. $a=2, b=\frac{-1}{2}$

C. $a=-2, b=\frac{1}{2}$ D. None of these

9. If $f(2)=4$ and $f'(2)=1$, then

$\lim_{x\to 2}\frac{xf(2)-2f(x)}{x-2}$ is

A. 2 B. -2

C. 1 D. 3

10. If the function

$$f(x)=\begin{cases}\dfrac{x^2-(A+2)x+A}{x-2}, & \text{for } x\neq 2 \text{ is}\\ 2, & \text{for } x=2\end{cases}$$

A. $A=0$ B. $A=1$

C. $A=-1$ D. None of these

11. The values of $\lim_{x\to -2}\frac{\left(x^2-x-6\right)^2}{(x+2)^2}$ is

A. 6 B. 25

C. 9 D. 16

12. The domain of the function $f(x)=\sqrt{x-1}+\sqrt{6-x}$ is

A. $(1,\infty)$ B. $(-\infty,6)$

C. $[1,6]$ D. None of these

13. If for positive integers $r>1$, $n>2$ the coefficient of the$(3r)^{th}$ and $(r+2)^{th}$ powers of x in the expansion of $(1+x)^{2n}$ are equal then

A. $n=2r$ B. $n=3r$

C. $n=2r+1$ D. None of these

14. $\lim_{x\to 0}\frac{1-\cos^3 x}{x\sin x\cos x}$ is equal to

A. $\frac{2}{5}$ B. $\frac{3}{5}$

C. $\frac{3}{2}$ D. $\frac{3}{4}$

15. $\int \frac{dx}{a^2\cos^2 x + b^2\sin^2 x}$ is equal to

A. $\tan^{-1}\left(\frac{a}{b}\tan x\right)+c$

B. $\frac{1}{ab}\tan^{-1}\left(\frac{b}{a}\cot x\right)+c$

C. $\frac{1}{ab}\tan^{-1}\left(\frac{b}{a}\tan x\right)+c$

D. $\tan^{-1}\left(\frac{b}{a}\tan x\right)+c$

16. If $\int \frac{\cos 4x+1}{\cot x-\tan x}dx = k\cos 4x + c$ then

A. $k=-\frac{1}{2}$ B. $k=-\frac{1}{8}$

C. $k=-\frac{1}{4}$ D. None of these

17. $\int \frac{e^x(1+\sin x)}{1+\cos x}dx$ is equal to

A. $\log|\tan x|+c$ B. $e^x\tan\frac{x}{2}+c$

C. $\sin\log x+c$ D. $e^x\cot x+c$

18. There are M persons sitting in a row. Two of them are selected at random. The probability that the two selected persons are not together is

A. $\frac{2}{M}$ B. $1-\frac{2}{M}$

C. $\frac{M(M-1)}{(M+1)(M+2)}$ D. None of these

19. If f and g are two functions satisfying the following conditions

$g(0)=0, f(0)=1, f(x)=g(x), g(x)=f(x)$

find the value of $f(1)$ correct to three decimal places

A. 1.511 B. 1.543

C. 1.501 D. 1.591

20. Given that the cubic curve vanishes at $x=-2$ and relative max/min at $x=-1$ and $x=1/3$. Also given area of the curve between $x=-1$ and $x=+1$ is 14/3. Find the equation of the curve

A. $(x-2)(x^2-x+1)$

B. $(x+2)(x^2+2x+2)$

C. $(x+2)(x^2-1x+1)$

D. $(x-4)(x^2+x-1)$

21. Area bounded by $x=1, x=3, y=\log e^x$ and $y=2^x$

A. $(6/\log 2-3\log 3+2)$ sq. units

B. $(6/\log 2-3+2\log 9)$ sq. units

C. 27.59 units

D. $(2\log 3+5)$ sq. units

22. $f(x)=ae^{2x}+be^x+cx, f(0)=-1, f(ln2)=31$ and $\int_0^{ln4}[f(x)-cx]dx=19.5$. Find the value of a, b and c

A. $a=5, b=2$

B. $a=5, b=-6, c=3$

C. $a=-5, b=0, c=3$

D. $a=6, b=-7, c=13$

23. The solution of equation $x^{x+y}=y^n$ and $y^{x+y}=x^{2n}y^n$ is

A. $x=\left(-1+\sqrt{1+7x^2}\right)/16, y=1$

B. $x=\left(\pm\sqrt{1+8x}\right)/2, y=\left(4x+1-\sqrt{1+8x}\right)/2$

C. $x=0, y=\left(4x+1-\sqrt{1+8x}\right)/2$

D. $x=\left(-1+\sqrt{1+8x}\right)/4, y=0$

24. A man aims to shoot a bird at a distance r, shooting chance $=x^2/r^2$ if he missses and reloads the gun then he next shoots at $r=2x$, $r=3x$ and so on. The probability that he misses n^{th} time i.e. at nx distance is

A. $(n+1)/2n$ B. $1/n$

C. $n+2/n$ D. $n/n+1$

25. A bag contains 4 balls : 2 black, 2 white. We have to draw 3rd ball as black. Given that if ball is white it is not replaced into bag otherwise it is replaced along with another ball of the same colour. The probability of 3rd ball being black is

A. 23/30 B. 24/31

C. 21/37 D. 1/19

26. For real value of x the permissible values of the expression $(x^2+34x-71)/(x^2+2x-7)$ are

A. $x \geq 9, x \leq 5$

B. $x \geq 9, x \leq 6$

C. $x \geq 12, x{=}9, x{=}5.9$

D. $x \leq -5, x = 12, x = 9$

27. The value of $\lim_{x \to 0}\left[\tan\left(\frac{\pi}{4}+x\right)\right]^{1/x}$ is

A. e B. e^2

C. $2e$ D. 1

28. The value of $\lim_{x \to 0} \frac{100x - 25x - 4x + 1}{\sqrt{2}\sqrt{1+\cos x}}$

A. $4\sqrt{2}\,(ln\ 4)(ln\ 25)$

B. $-4(ln\ 4)^2$

C. $(ln\ 5)^8\,(ln\ 4)$

D. 15

29. The shape of a curved mirror such that light from source at origin will be reflected in a beam parallel to the X-axis is given by the equation.

A. $y^2 = 2\,c\,x \pm c^2$

B. $y^2 = \pm 2\,c\,x + c^2$

C. $y^2 = x \pm c$

D. $y^2 = -x + 2c$

30. The solution of the differential equation $\sqrt{(1-x^2)}\,dy + \sqrt{(1-y^2)}dx = 0$ is

A. $\sin^{-1} y + \sin^{-1} x = c, \sin^{-1} y + \sin^{-1} x = \pi/3$
$x^2 + 2xy\cos c + y^2 = \sin^2 c$

B. $\sin^{-1} y + \sin^{-1} x = \pi/3\ \sin^{-1}$
$x + \sin^{-1} y = \pi/2,\ \sin^{-1} y + \cos^{-1} x = 1$

C. $\sin^{-1} y + \cos^{-1} x = \cos y,\ \sin^{-1} y + \sin^{-1} x = e$

D. $x^2 + 2xy\cos c + y^2 = \sin^2 c, \sin^{-4} y +$
$\sin^{-1} x = 2\pi/3$

31. The solution for the differential equation $(-x+2y-7)\,dy - (2x+2y-4)\,dx = 0$ is

A. $(2y + x - 5)\,(y - 2x - 5)^2 = cy + x = 5,$
$4 + 2x = 5$

B. $(2y + x - 5)^2\,(y - 2x - 5)^3 = c, x + 2y - 5 = 0,$
$y - 2x - 5 = 0$

C. $2y + x - 5 = 0, (2y + x + 5)\,(y - 2x - 5)^2 = 0$
$2y + x = 0$

D. $y - 2x - 5 = 0, (2y + x - 5)\,(y + 2x + 5)^2 = 0$
$x - y = 5$

32. The value of $\int \frac{1}{x^2\left(x^4+1\right)^{3/4}}$ is

A. $\frac{\left(x^4+1\right)^{1/4}}{x} + c$

B. $-\left(1+1/x^4\right) + c$

C. $2/3x^{3/2}\,(\log x)^2 - 8/9x^{3/2}\log x + 16/27x^{3/2} + c$

D. None of these

33. Let $f(x)$ be a second degree ploynomial in x such that $f(0){=}f(1){=}3f(2){=}{-3}$, Then $\int \frac{f(x)}{x^3-1}$ is

A. $-\log(x-1) - \log\left(x^2+x+1\right)$
$+ (2/3)\tan^{-1}(2x+1)/\sqrt{3} + c$

B. $-\log(x-1) - \log\left(x^2+x+1\right)$
$+ \frac{2}{3}\sin^{-1}\frac{2x+1}{\sqrt{3}} + c$

C. $-\log(x-1) - \log(x^2 + x + 1)^2 + c$

D. $\frac{2}{3}\tan^{-1}\frac{2x+1}{\sqrt{3}} + c$

34. What is the value of μ for $(p,q,r) \neq (0,0,0)$ and $(i + j + 3k)\,p + (3i - 3j + k)\,q + (-4i + 5j)\,r = \mu\,(pi + qj + rk)$

A. –1, 1 B. 1, 0
C. 0, –1 D. 0

35. The values of *a, b, c* for, which the function

$$f(x) = \frac{\sin(a+3)x + \sin x}{x}, x < 0$$

$$= c, x = 0$$

$$= \left((x+b_x^2)^{\frac{1}{2}} - x^{\frac{1}{2}}\right) \Big/ 2bx^{3/2}, x > 0$$

is continuous at $x = 0$ are

A. $a = -3/2, b = 1, 2, c = 1/2$
B. $a = -3/2, b = 0, 1, c = 1/2$
C. $a = -3/2, b = 2, 2, c = -1/2$
D. $a = -3/2$ $b = 2, 1, c = 1/2$

36. Let X be a binomial variate with parametes *n* and *p*. Then:

A. Cov $(X, n - X) = np$
B. Cov $(X, n - X) = npq$
C. Cov $(X, n - X) = -np$
D. Cov $(X, n - X) = -npq$

37. A simplex is an n-dimensional convex Polyhedron having exactly:

A. *n* vertices B. $(n + 1)$ vertices
C. $n(n + 1)$ vertices D. $(n + 1)^2$ vertices

38. The value of sin (log i^i) is:

A. 1 B. π
C. –1 D. $-\pi$

39. Every matrix is similar to a matrix in:

A. Rational canonical form
B. Jordan canonical form
C. Canonical form
D. None of these

40. Let (C, +) be a group, F : C → C, defined by F(*z*) $= \bar{z}$, $\bar{z} \in c$, $\bar{z}$ being conjugate of *z*, then F is

A. Isomorphism B. Automorphism
C. Endomorphism D. None of these

ANSWERS

1	2	3	4	5	6	7	8	9	10
C	A	D	B	A	B	D	B	A	A
11	**12**	**13**	**14**	**15**	**16**	**17**	**18**	**19**	**20**
B	C	C	C	C	B	B	B	B	C
21	**22**	**23**	**24**	**25**	**26**	**27**	**28**	**29**	**30**
A	B	B	A	A	A	B	A	B	A
31	**32**	**33**	**34**	**35**	**36**	**37**	**38**	**39**	**40**
B	A	C	C	B	D	A	C	B	B

Some Selected Explanatory Answers

1. Let $z = x + iy$, then

$z + iz = (x - y) + i(x + y)$

and $iz = -y + ix$

The area of the triangle formed by these points is

$$A = \frac{1}{2}\begin{vmatrix} x & y & 1 \\ x-y & x+y & 1 \\ -y & x & 1 \end{vmatrix}$$

Applying $R_2 \to R_2 - R_1 - R_3$

We get $A = \frac{1}{2}\begin{vmatrix} x & y & 1 \\ 0 & 0 & -1 \\ -y & x & 1 \end{vmatrix}$

$$= \frac{1}{2}\left(x^2 + y^2\right)$$

$$= \frac{1}{2}|z|^2 \text{ or } |z|^2 = 100$$

or $|z| = 10$

2. Let t_r denote the rth term of the series. Then

$$t_r = 1 - \frac{1}{2^r}$$

we have

$$\frac{1}{2} + \frac{3}{4} + \frac{7}{8} + \ldots = \left(1 - \frac{1}{2}\right)\left(1 - \frac{1}{4}\right) + \left(1 - \frac{1}{2^3}\right) + \ldots$$

$$= n-\left(\frac{1}{2}+\frac{1}{2^2}+\frac{1}{2^3}+\frac{1}{2^4}..........+\frac{1}{2^n}\right)$$

$$= n-\frac{\frac{1}{2}\left[1-\left(\frac{1}{2}\right)^n\right]}{\left(1-\frac{1}{2}\right)}$$

$$= n - 1 + 2^{-n}$$

3. $\int_0^1 \frac{dx}{x^2+2x\cos a+1}$

$$= \int_0^1 \frac{dx}{(x+\cos a)^2+1-\cos^2 a}$$

$$= \int_0^1 \frac{dx}{(x+\cos a)^2+\sin^2 a}$$

$$= \left[\frac{1}{\sin a}\tan^{-1}\frac{x+\cos a}{\sin a}\right]_0^1$$

$$= \frac{1}{\sin a}\left(\tan^{-1}\cot\frac{a}{2}-\tan^{-1}\cot a\right)$$

$$= \frac{1}{\sin a}\left(\frac{\pi}{2}-\frac{a}{2}-\frac{\pi}{2}+a\right)$$

$$= \frac{a}{2}(\sin a)^{-1}$$

4. $\sqrt{\frac{1+\cos 2x}{2}} = \sqrt{\frac{2\cos^2 x}{2}}$

$$\therefore \int_0^{\pi}\sqrt{\frac{1+\cos 2x}{2}}dx$$

$$= \int_0^{\frac{\pi}{2}}\cos x\,dx+\int_{\frac{\pi}{2}}^{\pi}-\cos x\,dx$$

$$= \sin x\Big|_0^{\frac{\pi}{2}} + (\sin x)\Big|_{\frac{\pi}{2}}^{\pi}$$

$$= 2$$

5. $\int_0^{\infty}\frac{x\log x}{(1+x^2)^2}dx$

$$= \int_0^1 \frac{x\log x}{(1+x^2)^2}dx+\int_1^{\infty}\frac{x\log x}{(1+x^2)^2}dx$$

$x = \frac{1}{y}$ in second integral, so that,

$dx = -\frac{1}{y^2}dy$ if $x \to \infty, y \to 0$

and if $x = 1, y = 1$

$$\therefore \int_1^{\infty}\frac{x\log x}{(1+x^2)^2}dx$$

$$= \int_1^0 \frac{1\log y^{-1}}{y\left(1+\frac{1}{y^2}\right)^2}\left(\frac{-1}{y^2}\right)dy$$

$$= \int_1^0 \frac{y^4\log y}{y^3(1+y^2)^2}dy$$

$$= \int_0^1 \frac{y\log y}{(1+y^2)^2}dy$$

$$\Rightarrow \int_0^{\infty}\frac{x\log x}{(1+x^2)^2}dx$$

$$= \int_0^1 \frac{x\log x}{(1+x^2)^2}dx-\int_0^1\frac{x\log x}{(1+x^2)^2}dx$$

$$= 0$$

6. The vector perpendicular to a and b is

$$a\times b = \begin{vmatrix} i & j & k \\ 1 & 1 & 0 \\ 0 & 1 & 1 \end{vmatrix} = i-j+k$$

Since the length of this vector is $\sqrt{3}$. The unit vector perpendicular to a and b, is

$$\pm\frac{a+b}{|a\times b|} = \pm(i-j+k)$$

Hence these two are such vectors

7. Since the equation is not a polynomial in all the differential coefficients. So the degree of the equation is not defined.

8. We have y = $\frac{a}{x}+2bx+1$

and $y(-1)=0$ and $y(2)=0$

$\therefore -a-2b+1=0$ and $\frac{a}{2}+4b+1=0$

$\Rightarrow \frac{a}{2}-2a+2+1=0$

Hence $a=2$ and $b=-\frac{1}{2}$

9. $\lim_{x\to 2}\frac{xf(2)-2f(x)}{x-2}$

$=\lim_{x\to 2}\frac{xf(2)-2f(2)+2f(2)-2f(x)}{x-2}$

$=\lim_{x\to 2}\frac{(x-2)f(2)}{x-2}-2\lim_{x\to 2}\frac{f(x)-f(2)}{x-2}$

$=f(2)-2f(2)$

$=4-2\times 1=2$

10. Since f is continuous at $x=2$, the only possibility is that

$x-2$ is a factor of $x^2-(A+2)x+A$

$\therefore 4-2(A+2)+A=0$

$\Rightarrow -A=0 \Rightarrow A=0$

11. $\lim_{x\to -2}\frac{(x^2-x-6)^2}{(x+2)^2}=\lim_{x\to -2}\frac{[(x+2)(x-3)]^2}{(x+2)^2}$

$=\lim_{x\to -2}(x-3)^2$

$=(-5)^2=25$

12. $\sqrt{x-1}$ Is meaningful if $x\geq 1$ and $\sqrt{6-x}$ is meaningful if $x\leq 6$

Hence domain of given functions is [1,6]

13. The cooefficient of x^m in $(1+x)^{2n}$ is ${}^{2n}C_m$

According to the given condition

${}^{2n}C_{3r}={}^{2n}C_{r+2}$

Hence either, $3r=r+2$ or $2n=3r+r+2$

That is $r=1$

or $n=2r+1$

Since $r>1$ we get $n=2r+1$

14. $\lim_{x\to 0}\frac{1-\cos^3 x}{x\sin x\cos x}$

$=\lim_{x\to 0}\frac{(1-\cos x)(1+\cos^2 x+\cos x)}{x\sin x\cos x}$

$=\lim_{x\to 0}\frac{2\sin^2\frac{x}{2}(1+\cos^2 x+\cos x)}{2x\sin x/2\cdot\cos x/2\cdot\cos x}$

$=\lim_{x\to 0}\frac{1}{2}\frac{\sin x/2}{x/2}\cdot\frac{1+\cos^2 x+\cos x}{\cos x/2\cos x}$

$=\frac{1}{2}1.3=\frac{3}{2}$

15. Putting, $\tan x=t$, we get

$\int\frac{dx}{a^2\cos^2 x+b^2\sin^2 x}$

$=\int\frac{\sec^2 x}{a^2+b^2\tan^2 x}dx$

$=\int\frac{dt}{a^2+b^2t^2}$

$=\frac{1}{b^2}\int\frac{dt}{t^2+\frac{a^2}{b^2}}$

$=\frac{1}{b^2}\frac{b}{a}\tan^{-1}\left(\frac{b}{a}t\right)+c$

$=\frac{1}{ab}\tan^{-1}\left(\frac{b}{a}\tan x\right)+c$

16. $\int\frac{\cos 4x+1}{\cot x-\tan x}dx$

$=\int\cos 2x\,\sin 2x\,dx$

$= \frac{1}{2}\int \sin 4x\, dx$

$= -\frac{1}{8}\cos 4x + c$

Hence $k = -\frac{1}{8}$

17. $\int \frac{e^x(1+\sin x)}{1+\cos x}dx$

$= \int \frac{e^x\left[1+2\sin\left(x/2\right)\cos\left(x/2\right)\right]}{2\cos^2\left(x/2\right)}dx$

$= \int e^x\left(\frac{1}{2}\sec^2 x/2 + \tan x/2\right)dx$

$= \frac{1}{2}\int e^x \sec^2 x/2\, dx + \int e^x \tan x/2\, dx$

$= \frac{1}{2}\int e^x \sec^2 \frac{x}{2} dx + e^x \tan\frac{x}{2} - \frac{1}{2}$

$= \frac{1}{2}\int e^x \sec^2 x/2 + c$

[Integrating by Parts]

$= e^x \tan x/2 + c$

18. The total number of ways of selecting two persons out of M is

$^{M}C_2 = \frac{M\ (M-1)}{2}$

The number of ways in which the two selected persons are together is (M–1), therefore the number of ways in which the two selected persons are not together is,

$^{M}C_2 - (M-1) = \left(\frac{(M-1)(M-2)}{2}\right)$

Thus the probability of the required event is

$\frac{\frac{(M-1)(M-2)}{2}}{\frac{M\ (M-1)}{2}} = \frac{M-2}{M} = 1 - \frac{2}{M}$

20. Cubic equation vanishes at $x = -2$

$\Rightarrow f(x) = (x+2)\,(ax^2 + bx + c),$

$f^1(x) = (x+2\,)\,2ax + b\,(ax^2+bx+c)$ for max./min

$f^1(x) = 0$ at $x = -1, x = 1/3$

$a + c = 0$

$a + b = 0$

solving $c = 0, b = -a$

$f(x) = a\,(x+2)\,(x^2 - x + 1)$

$\int_{-1}^{1} f(x)d(x) = \int_{-1}^{1} a(x+2)(x^2 - x + 1)dx = 14/3$

$\Rightarrow a\cdot 14/3 = 14/3$

$\Rightarrow a = 1, b = -1, c = 0$

$f(x) = (x+2)\,(\,x^2 - x + 1)$

21. $f(x) = ae^2x + be^{\,x} + cx$

$f(0) = -1$

$a + b = -1$ ...(*i*)

$f^1(x) = 2\,ae^{2x} + be^x + c$

$f^1(ln2) = 31$

$\Rightarrow 2\,ae^2\,ln2 + be\,ln2 + c = 31$

i.e. $8a + 2b + c = 31$ ...(*ii*)

$\int_0^{ln4} [f(x) - cx]dx = 19.5$

$\int_0^{ln4} \left[ae^2 x + be^x\right]dx = 19.5$

$\Rightarrow \left(ae^2\, x/2 + be^x\right)_0^{ln4} = 19.5$

$7.5a + 3b = 19.5$ ...(*iii*)

solving $a = 5, b = -6, c = 39$

23. $x^{\,x+4} = y^{\,n}$ ...(*i*)

$y^{\,x+4} = x^{2n}y^{\,n}$ ...(*ii*)

Multiplying $(xy)^{x+4} = (xy)^{2n}$

$x + y = 2n$ ... (*iii*)

from (*i*), $x^{\,2n} = \Rightarrow x^2 = y^2$

Putting in (*iii*)

$x^2 + x - 2x = 0$

$x = \frac{-1 \pm \sqrt{1+8x}}{2}$

+*ve* solution $x = \dfrac{-1 \pm \sqrt{1+8x}}{2}$

$y = (4x+1) - \dfrac{\sqrt{1+8x}}{2}$

24. Chance of missing at *k* distance

$= 1 - \dfrac{x^2}{k^2 x^2} = 1 - \dfrac{1}{k^2}$

$k = 2, 3, 4 \ldots\ldots n$

$\therefore$ Probability of missing *n*th target

$$P = \left(1 - \frac{1}{2^2}\right)\left(1 - \frac{1}{3^2}\right) \ldots\ldots \left(1 - \frac{1}{n^2}\right)$$

$$\Rightarrow \left[\left(1 - \frac{1}{2}\right)\left(1 - \frac{1}{3}\right) \ldots\ldots \left(1 - \frac{1}{n}\right)\right]$$

$$\left[\left(1 + \frac{1}{2}\right)\left(1 + \frac{1}{3}\right) \ldots\ldots \left(1 + \frac{1}{n}\right)\right]$$

$$\Rightarrow \left[\frac{1}{2} \cdot \frac{2}{3} \cdot \frac{3}{4} \ldots\ldots \frac{n-1}{n}\right)\left(\frac{3}{2} \cdot \frac{4}{3} \cdot \frac{5}{4} \ldots\ldots \frac{n+1}{n}\right]$$

$$= \frac{n+1}{2n}$$

25. There are four possible ways of drawing first ball

1. I^{st} = white, IInd = white
2. I^{st} = white, IInd = black
3. I^{st} = black, IInd = white
4. I^{st} = black, IInd = black

$$P(E_1) = \frac{2}{4} \times \frac{1}{3} = \frac{1}{6}, P\left(\frac{E}{E_1}\right) = \frac{2}{2} = 1$$

$$P(E_2) = \frac{2}{4} \times \frac{2}{3} = \frac{1}{3}, P\left(\frac{E}{E_2}\right) = \frac{3}{4}$$

$$P(E_3) = \frac{2}{4} \times \frac{2}{5} = \frac{1}{5}, P\left(\frac{E}{E_3}\right) = \frac{3}{4}$$

$$P(E_4) = \frac{2}{4} \times \frac{3}{5} = \frac{3}{10}, P\left(\frac{E}{E_4}\right) = \frac{2}{3}$$

$$P(E) = P(E_1)P\left(\frac{E}{E_1}\right) + P\ (E_2).P\left(\frac{E}{E_2}\right) +$$

$$P\ (E_3)P\left(\frac{E}{E_3}\right) + P(E_4)P\left(\frac{E}{E_4}\right)$$

$$\Rightarrow \frac{1}{6} \times 1 + \frac{1}{3} \times \frac{3}{4} + \frac{1}{5} \times \frac{3}{4} + \frac{3}{10} \times \frac{2}{3} = \frac{23}{30}$$

26. Let $y = \dfrac{x^2 + 34x - 71}{x^2 + 2x - 7}$

$\Rightarrow x^2 + 34x - 71 = y(x^2 + 2x - 7)$

$x^2(1-y) + 2(17-y)x - (71-7y) = 0$

For real value of x, $b^2 - 4ac \geq 0$

$\Rightarrow 4(17-y^2) + 4(1-y)(71-7y) \geq 0$

$\Rightarrow 8y^2 - 112y + 360 \geq 0$

$\Rightarrow y^2 - 14y + 45 \geq 0$

$\Rightarrow (y-5)(y-9) \geq 0$

For x to be real $y \leq 5$ or $y \geq 9$, not between 5 and 9

29.

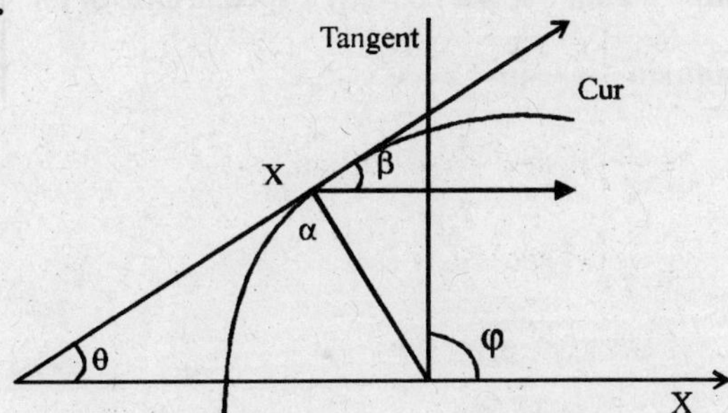

By symmetry the mirror has a shape of surface of revolution obtained by revolving a curve about x-axis. Let (x, y) be any point on the curve in the x–y plane

Law of reflection $\alpha = \beta = \theta$

Since the interior angles of A add upto 180^0

$\psi = \alpha + \theta = 2\theta$

$y' = \tan\theta$ and $y/x = \tan\psi$

$$\Rightarrow \frac{y}{x} = \tan\psi = \tan 2\theta = \frac{2\tan\theta}{1 - \tan^2\theta}$$

$$\frac{y'}{1-(y')^2} = y(y)^2 + xy^1 - y = 0$$

$$\Rightarrow y' = \frac{-x \pm \sqrt{(x^2+y^2)}}{y}$$

$$\Rightarrow xdx+ydy = \pm\sqrt{(x^2+y^2)} = dx$$

using. $\sqrt{(x^2+y^2)} = x\,dx + \frac{ydx}{\sqrt{x^2+y^2}}$

$$\Rightarrow \sqrt{(x^2+y^2)} = \pm x + c$$

or $y^2 = \pm 2cx + c^2$

30. Equation is $\sqrt{(1-x^2)}dy + \sqrt{(1-y^2)}dx = 0$

Separating the variables, we get

$\frac{dy}{c} + dx = 0 \Rightarrow \sin^{-1} y + \sin^{-1} x, \sqrt{(1-y^2)}\sqrt{(1-x^2)}$

$\sin^{-1} y + \sin^{-1} x = \pi/3$ (only a special case of C)

from $\sin^{-1} y + \sin^{-1} x = C$

$$\cos\left[\sin^{-1} y + \sin^{-1} x\right] = \cos C$$

$$x^2 + 2xy \cos C + y^2 = \sin 2C$$

34. Since $(i + j + 3k)\,p + (3i - 3j + k)\,q$
$+ (-4i + 5j)\,r = \mu\,(pi + 9j + rk)$

$\therefore (p + 3q - 4r - \mu p)\,i + (p - 3q + 3r - \mu q)$
$jk\,(3p + q - \mu r)\,k = 0$

since i, j, k are coplanar

$\therefore (1-\mu)p + 3q - 4r = 0$

$p - (3+\mu)\,q + 5r = 0$

and $3p + q - \mu r = 0$

Eliminating $p.\ q\ r$

$$\begin{vmatrix} 1-\mu & 3 & -4 \\ 1 & -(3+\mu) & 5 \\ 3 & 1 & -\mu \end{vmatrix} = 0$$

Expanding above and solving we get $\mu = 0$ and -1

36. $\text{Cov}\,(aX + b, (Y + d) = ac\,\text{Cov}\,(X, Y)$

$\Rightarrow \text{Cov}\,(X, n-X) = -\text{Cov}\,(X, X) = -\text{Var}\,(X) = -npq$

SET–23

CSIR–UGC (NET) MATHEMATICAL SCIENCES

PART-B

1. Let z and w be two complex number such that $|z + iw| = 2 = |z-iw|$ then z equals

A. 1 or i B. i or $-i$
C. 1 or -1 D. i or -1

2. If $\omega(\neq 1)$ is a cube root of unity and $(1+\omega)^7 = A + B\omega$ than A and B are respectively the number

A. 0, 1 B. 1, 1
C. 1, 0 D. −1, 1

3. The value of the sum $\sum_{n=1}^{13}\left(i^n + i^{n+1}\right)$, where $i=\sqrt{-1}$, equals

A. i B. $i-1$
C. $-i$ D. 0

4. If the system of equations $x + 2y - z = 1$ $(\lambda+3)z = 3$, $(2\lambda+1)x + z = 0$ is inconsistent then the value of λ is equal to

A. $-\frac{1}{2}$ B. −3
C. 2 D. 0

5. If the system of equations $x+2y-3z = 1$ $(k+z)z = 3$, $(2k+1)y + z = 2$ is inconsistent then the value of k is

A. 2 B. 0
C. $-\frac{1}{2}$ D. −2

6. The value of the determinant

$$\begin{vmatrix} x & x+a & x+2a \\ x+1 & x+2a & x+4a \\ x+2 & x+3a & x+6a \end{vmatrix} \text{ is}$$

A. 0 B. $(x-a^2)^3$
C. x^3-a^2 D. $a^3 - x^3$

7. If $b > a$, then the equation $(x-a)(x-b) - 1 = 0$, has:

A. both roots in (a, b)
B. both roots in $(-\alpha, a)$
C. both roots in $(b, +\alpha)$
D. one root in $(-\alpha, a)$ and other in $(b, +\alpha)$

8. If the roots of the equation $x^2 - 2ax + a^2 + a - 3 = 0$ are real, less than 3, then

A. $a < 2$ B. $2 \le a \le 3$
C. $3 < a \le 4$ D. $a > 2$

9. How many different nine digit numbers can be formed from the number 223355888 by rearranging its digits so that the odd digits occupy even positions?

A. 16 B. 36
C. 60 D. 60

10. The number of numbers that can be formed by the digits 1,2,3,4, 3,2,1 with odd digits at odd places is given by

A. 430 B. 36
C. 18 D. None of these.

11. The expression

$$\left\{x + (x^3-1)^{1/2}\right\}\left\{x - \left(x^3-1\right)^{1/2}\right\}^5$$

Is a polynomial of degree

A. 5 B. 6
C. 7 D. 8

12. If P is nearly equal to q and $n > 1$, such that $\frac{(n+1)^p + (n-1)^q}{(n-1)^p + (n+1)^q} = \left(\frac{p}{q}\right)^x$ then the value of x is

A. $\frac{1}{n+1}$ B. $\frac{1}{n}$
C. $n+1$ D. n

13. Let n (>1) be a positive integer then the largest integer m, such that (n^m+1) divides $(1+n+n^2+\ldots\ldots+n^{127})$ is

A. 127 B. 63
C. 64 D. 32

14. Let $f : R \to R$ be any function. Define $g : R \to R$ $g(x) = |f(x)|$ for all x. Then g is

A. Onto if f is onto

B. One-one if, f is one-one continuous
C. Continuous if, f is continuous
D. Differentiable if, f is differentiable

15. The domain of definition of the function $f(x)$ given by the equation $2^x + 2^y = 2$ is

A. $0 < x \le 1$ B. $0 \le x \le 1$
C. $-\infty < x \le 0$ D. $-\infty < x < 1$

16. For $x \in R, \lim_{x \to \infty}\left(\frac{x-3}{x+2}\right)^x =$

A. e B. e^{-1}
C. e^{-5} D. e^5

17. Let $f(x) = \int e^x(x-1)(x-2)dx$ then f decreases in the interval

A. $(-\infty, -2)$ B. $(-2, -1)$
C. $(1, 2)$ D. $(2, \infty)$

18. For all $x \in (0,1)$

A. $e^x < 1 + x$ B. $\log_e(1+x) < x$
C. $\sin x > x$ D. $\log e^x > x$

19. Let $f(x) = \begin{cases} |x|, \text{for } 0 < |x| \le 2 \\ 1, \text{for } x = 0 \end{cases}$ Then at $x = 0$, f has

A. a local maximum
B. no local maximum
C. a local minimum
D. no exteremum

20. Consider the following statements S and R: S: both $\sin x$ and $\cos x$ are decreasing functions in the interval $(\pi/2, \pi)$ R:if a differentiable function decreases in an interval (a, b) then its derivative also decreases in(a, b)

Which of the following is true?
A. Both S and R are wrong.
B. Both S and R are correct,but R, is not the correct explanation for S
C. S is correct and R is the correct explanation for S.
D. S is correct and R is wrong

21. If the normal to the curve $y = f(x)$ at the point (3,4) markes an angle $\frac{3\pi}{4}$ with the positive, x-axis then $f(3)$ is

A. –1 B. $-\frac{3}{4}$
C. $\frac{4}{3}$ D. 1

22. Let $f(x) = (x+1)^2 - 1, (x > -1)$, then the set $S = \{x : f(x) = f^{-1}(x)\}$ is

A. $\left\{0, \frac{-3+1\sqrt{3}}{2}, \frac{-3-1\sqrt{3}}{2}\right\}$
B. $\{0, 1, -1\}$
C. $\{0, -1\}$
D. empty

23. The function $f(x) = [x]\cos\left(\frac{2x-1}{2}\right)\pi$ where [ ] denotes the greatest integer function is discontinuous at

A. all x
B. all integer points
C. no x
D. x which is not an integer

24. Let $f(x)$ be defined for all $x > 0$ and be continuous. Let $f(x)$ satisfy $f\left(\frac{x}{y}\right) = f(x) - f(y)$ all x, y and $f(e) = 1$, then

A. $f(x)$ is bounded
B. $f\left(\frac{1}{x}\right) \to 0, as\ x \to \infty$
C. $f\left(\frac{1}{x}\right) \to 1, as\ x - \infty$
D. $f(x) = \log x$

25. The function $f(x) = \frac{ln(\pi + x)}{ln(e + x)}$ is

A. increasing on $[0, \infty]$
B. decreasing on $[0, \infty]$
C. increasing on $\left[0, \frac{\pi}{e}\right)$ and decreasing on $\left[\frac{\pi}{e}, \infty\right)$
D. decreasing on $\left[0, \frac{\pi}{e}\right)$ and increasing on $\left[\frac{\pi}{e}, \infty\right)$

26. If $f(x)=A\sin\left(\frac{\pi x}{2}\right)+B f\left(\frac{1}{2}\right)\sqrt{2}$ and $\int_0^1 f(x)dx=\frac{2A}{\pi}$, then constants A and B are respectively

A. $\frac{\pi}{2}$ and $\frac{\pi}{2}$ B. $\frac{2}{\pi}$ and $\frac{3}{\pi}$

C. 0 and $\frac{-\pi}{4}$ D. $\frac{4}{\pi}$ and 0

27. $\int_{\pi/4}^{3\pi/4} \frac{dx}{1+\cos x}$ is equal to

A. 2 B. –2

C. $\frac{1}{2}$ D. $-\frac{1}{2}$

28. If for a real numbers y, $[y]$ is the greatest integers less than or equal to y then the value of the integral $\int_{\pi/2}^{3\pi/2} [2\sin x]dx$ is

A. $-\pi$ B. 0

C. $\frac{-\pi}{2}$ D. $\frac{\pi}{2}$

29. If $\int_0^x f(t)dt = x+\int_x^1 tf(t)dt$ then the value of $f(1)$ is

A. $\frac{1}{2}$ B. 0

C. 1 D. $-\frac{1}{2}$

30. Let $f(x)=x-[x]$ for every real number x, where $[x]$ is the integral part of x, then $\int_{-1}^{1} f(x)dx$ is

A. 1 B. 2

C. 0 D. $\frac{1}{2}$

31. Let f be a positive function Let $I_1=\int_{1-k}^{k} xf|x(1-x)|\,dx$ and $\int_{1-k}^{k} f|x(1-x)|\,dx$ where $2k-1>0$, the $\frac{I_1}{I_2}$ is

A. 2 B. k

C. $\frac{1}{2}$ D. I

32. If $g(x)=\int_0^x \cos^4 t\, dt$, then $g(x+\pi)$ equals

A. $g(x)+g(\pi)$ B. $g(x)-g(\pi)$

C. $g(x)\,g(\pi)$ D. $\frac{g(x)}{g(\pi)}$

33. The differential equation $\frac{d^2y}{dx^2}+x\frac{dy}{dx}+\sin y+x^2=0$

A. Linear B. Homogeneous

C. Order two D. Order one

34. The differential equation $(4x-3y)dx+(y-x)dy=0$ is of the following type

A. non – linear

B. homogeneous of degree two

C. homogeneous of degree one

D. None of them

35. The differential equation $x\frac{dy}{dx}=k\,(y\log x-y\log y)$ is

A. Linear but not homogeneous

B. Homogeneous but not linear

C. Both homogeneous and linear

D. Neither homogeneous nor linear

36. The algebraic sum of deviation of 10 observations measured from 15 is 7. Then the mean of the observation is

A. 150 B. 70

C. 15.7 D. None of these

37. The probability of India wining a test match against West-Indies is $\frac{1}{2}$. Assuming independence from match to match the probability that in a 5 match series India's second win occurs at the third test is

A. $\frac{1}{8}$ B. $\frac{1}{4}$

C. $\frac{1}{2}$ D. $\frac{2}{3}$

38. For two random variables x and y with the same mean, the two regression equations are $y=ax+b$, $x=\alpha y+\beta$. Then:

A. $\frac{b}{\beta}=\frac{1-a}{1-\alpha}$ B. $\frac{a}{\alpha}=\frac{b}{\beta+1}$

C. $\frac{\alpha}{a}=\frac{\beta-1}{b}$ D. $\frac{\beta}{b}=\frac{1+\alpha}{1+a}$

39. Order of i in $(\{1,-1,i,-i\},\cdot)$ is:

A. 0 B. 2

C. 3 D. 4

40. The series:

$$\left(\frac{2^2}{1^2}-\frac{2}{1}\right)^{-1}+\left(\frac{3^3}{2^3}-\frac{3}{2}\right)^{-2}+\left(\frac{4^4}{3^4}-\frac{4}{3}\right)^{-3}+\ldots \text{ is:}$$

A. convergent

B. divergent

C. oscillating infinitely

D. oscillating finitely

ANSWERS

1	2	3	4	5	6	7	8	9	10
C	B	B	B	D	A	D	A	C	C
11	**12**	**13**	**14**	**15**	**16**	**17**	**18**	**19**	**20**
C	B	C	C	D	C	C	B	A	D
21	**22**	**23**	**24**	**25**	**26**	**27**	**28**	**29**	**30**
D	C	C	D	B	D	A	C	A	A
31	**32**	**33**	**34**	**35**	**36**	**37**	**38**	**39**	**40**
C	A	C	C	B	C	B	A	D	A

Some Selected Explanatory Answers

1. We have $4=|z+iw|^2=(z+iw)\ (z-i\overline{w})$
$\Rightarrow 4=zz+iwz-iwz+ww$, Also $4=z-iw^2=(z-iw)\ (z+iw)\Rightarrow 4=z\,z-iwz+iwz+ww$

Subtracting (2) from (1), we get, $iwz-iwz+iwz-iwz=0\Rightarrow ww\,(z-w)+w\,(z-z)=0\Rightarrow w=-w$ or $z=z$, if $w=w$, then Re $w=0$ and also $|w|=1$
$\therefore w=\pm 1$

Thus $4=z-1^2=(z-1)\,(z-1)$
$\Rightarrow 4=|z|-1^2=(z-1)\,(z-1)$
$\Rightarrow 4=|z|^2=-z+1$
$\Rightarrow (z+z)=-2$
$\Rightarrow$ Re $(z)=-1\Rightarrow Im(z)=0$, since $|z|=1$ $\therefore$ $z=1$

Again if $z=z$, then $1=|z|^2=z.z$
$=z^2$, Hence, $z=1$ or -1

2. Given $(1+\omega)^7=A+B\,\omega$
$\Rightarrow A+B\,\omega=(1+\omega)^7=(-\omega^2)^7$, as $1+\omega+\omega^2=0$
$=-\omega^{14}=-(\omega^3)^4.\omega^2=-\omega^2$, as $\omega^3=1$
$=1+\omega$

Hence A = 1, B = 1

3. We have

$$\sum_{n=1}^{13}\left(i^n+i^{n+1}\right)=\sum_{n=1}^{13}(1+i)i^n$$

$=(1+i)\,[i+i^2+i^3+\ldots\ldots\ldots\ldots\ldots+i^{13}]$

$$=(1+i)\left[\frac{i(1-i^{13})}{1-i}\right]$$

$$=(1+i)\left[\frac{i(1-i)}{1-i}\right]$$

$$\left[\text{as } i^{13}=\left(i^4\right)^3.i=1.\ i=i\right]$$

$=i(1+i)=i-1$

4. Here coefficient matrix $\begin{vmatrix}1 & 2 & -3\\ 0 & 0 & \lambda+3\\ 2\lambda+1 & +1 & 1\end{vmatrix}$

and augmented matrix

$$[AB]=\begin{bmatrix}1 & 2 & -3:1\\ 0 & 0 & \lambda+3:3\\ 2\lambda+1 & 1 & 1:0\end{bmatrix}$$

$$\Rightarrow [AB]=\begin{bmatrix}1, & 2 & -3:1\\ -2\lambda+1, & 0 & 1:0\\ 0 & 0 & \lambda+3:3\end{bmatrix}$$

If $\lambda + 3 = 0$, then

$$[AB] \sim \begin{bmatrix} 1, & 2, & -3:1 \\ -2\lambda+1, & 0, & 1:0 \\ 0 & 0 & 0:3 \end{bmatrix} \quad ...(i)$$

Clearly rank ([AB]) = 3

$$\text{By}(i) A \sim \begin{bmatrix} 1 & 2 & -3 \\ 2\lambda+1 & 0 & 1 \\ 0 & 0 & 1 \end{bmatrix}$$

rank (A) = 2

rank (A) $\neq$ rank ([AB])

Hence, the system of equation is inconsistent if $\lambda = -3$

5. Here, augmented matix

$$= \begin{bmatrix} 1 & 2 & -3:1 \\ 0 & 0 & k+2:3 \\ 0 & 2k+1 & 1:2 \end{bmatrix}$$

$$=0\begin{bmatrix} 1 & 2 & -3:1 \\ 0 & 2k+1 & 1:2 \\ 0 & 0k+2 & 2:3 \end{bmatrix}$$

Interchanging R_2 and R_1

This shows that the system of equations will be inconsistent if K+2 = 0 *i.e.* k = –2

6. Applying $R_3 - R_2$ and $R_2 - R_1$ we get

$$\begin{vmatrix} x & x+a & x+2a \\ x+1 & x+2a & x+4a \\ x+2 & x+3a & x+6a \end{vmatrix}$$

$$= \begin{vmatrix} x & x+a & x+2a \\ 1 & a & 2a \\ 1 & a & 2a \end{vmatrix}$$

= 0, Since, R_2 and R_3 are identical.

7. If $b > a$ and equation is

$(x-a)(x-b) - 1 = 0$

Let $y = (x-a)(x-b) - 1$

$= x^2 - (a+b)x + ab - 1$

$$= \left(x - \frac{a+b}{2}\right)^2 - \left(\frac{b-a}{2}\right)^2 - 1$$

$$= \left(x - \frac{a+b}{2}\right)^2 = y + 1 + \left(\frac{b-a}{2}\right)^2$$

which is a parabola with vertex

$$\left[\frac{a+b}{2} - \left\{1 + \frac{(b-a)^2}{2}\right\}\right]$$

$\therefore$ At $x = a, y = -1$

It is clear that parabola

cuts X–axis at $x = \alpha > a$ and $x = \beta > b$

Hence, $d \in (-\alpha, a)$, $b \in (b, -\alpha)$

8. The given equation can be written as

$(x-a)^2 = 3 - a$

$\Rightarrow a \leq 3$ and $x = a \pm \sqrt{(3-a)}$

Since both the roots of the given equation are less than 3, so the largest of the two roots is less than 3.

$\therefore a + \sqrt{(3-a)} < 3$

$\Rightarrow \sqrt{(3-a)} - (3-a) < 0$

$\Rightarrow \sqrt{(3-a)} - (1 - \sqrt{3-a}) < 0$

$\Rightarrow a < 3$ and $1 - \sqrt{3-a} < 0$

$\therefore \sqrt{(3-a)} > 1 \Rightarrow 3 - a > 1$ or $a > 2$

$\therefore a < 2$ and $a < 3 \Rightarrow a < 2$

9. The four digits 3, 3, 5, 5 can be arranged at four even places in $\frac{4!}{2!2!} = 6$ ways

The remaining digits 2,2,8,8,8 can be arranged at five odd places in $\frac{5!}{2!3!} = 10$ ways

$\therefore$ The number of possible arrangements $= 6 \times 10 = 60$

10. The number formed by using all digits 1, 2, 3, 4, 2, 1 will be 7 digit numbers. Therefore in each number there are four odd places and 3 even places therefore, odd places are to be filled up by four odd digits 1, 3, 3, 1, (2 are alike of one kind *i.e.* 1, 1 and 2 are alike of another kind *i.e.* 3, 3) we can arrange these four odd digits at four places in $\frac{4!}{2!2!} = 6$ ways

Again there are 3 even places namely 2nd, 4th and 6th at which 3 even numbers 2,4,2 (two are alike i.e. 2,2) are to arranged. These can be arrranged in $\frac{3!}{2!} = \frac{3\times2}{1\times2} = 3$ ways

Hence, by fundamental theorem of association the total number of numbers thus formed = 6×3 = 18

11. Let $\left(x^3-1\right)^{\frac{1}{2}}=4$, then given expression

$= (x+y)^5 + (x-y)^5$

$$=2\left[{}^5C_0x^5+{}^5C_2x^3y^2+{}^5C_4x^4\right]$$

$$=2\left[{}^5C_0x^5+{}^5C_2x^3\left(x^3-1\right)+{}^5C_4x\left(x^3-1\right)^2\right]$$

$$=2\left[{}^5C_0x^5+{}^5C_2x^3\left(x^6-x^3\right)+{}^5C_4\left(x^3-1\right)^2\right]$$

$$=2\left[{}^5C_0x^5+{}^5C_2\left(x^6-x^3\right)+{}^5C_4\left(x^7-2x^4+x\right)\right]$$

which is polynomial of degree 7

12. Given $\dfrac{(n+1)p+(n-1)q}{(n-1)p+(n+1)q}=\left(\dfrac{p}{q}\right)^x$

or $\dfrac{n(p+q)+(p-q)}{n(p+q)-(p-q)}=\left(\dfrac{p}{q}\right)^x$

$$\Rightarrow \frac{1+\frac{1}{n}\left(\frac{p-q}{p+q}\right)}{1-\frac{1}{n}\left(\frac{p-q}{p+q}\right)}=\left(\frac{p}{q}\right)^x$$

$$\frac{\left(1+\frac{p-q}{p+q}\right)^{\frac{1}{n}}}{\left(1-\frac{p-q}{p+q}\right)^{\frac{1}{n}}}=\left(\frac{p}{q}\right)^x$$ Using binomial

theorem as p is very close to q so higher power of $\dfrac{p-q}{p+q}$ can be neglected

or, $\dfrac{(2p)^{\frac{1}{n}}}{(2q)^{\frac{1}{n}}}=\left(\dfrac{p}{q}\right)^x$.

$$\left(\frac{p}{q}\right)^{\frac{1}{n}}=\left(\frac{p}{q}\right)^x$$

Thus $x=\dfrac{1}{n}$

13. We have

$1+n+n^2+\dots\dots\dots\dots+n^{127}$

$$\frac{n^{128}-1}{n-1}=\frac{\left(n^{64}-1\right)\left(n^{64}+1\right)}{n-1}$$

$=(1+n+n^2+\dots\dots\dots\dots+n^{63})\,(n^{64}+1)$

Hence the largest integer m such that (n^m+1) divides $(1+n+n^2+\dots\dots\dots+n^{127})$ is 64.

13. Since x, y, z are in G.P. then

$y^2=xz$

$\Rightarrow 2\ln y=\ln x+\ln z$

$\Rightarrow \ln x$, $\ln y$, $\ln z$ are in A.P.

$\Rightarrow 1+\ln x$, $1+\ln y$, $1+\ln z$ are in A.P.

$\Rightarrow \dfrac{1}{1+\ln x},\dfrac{1}{1+\ln y},\dfrac{1}{1+\ln z}$ are in H.P.

14. Let $a\in R$ it is continuous then, $f(a-0)$
$=f(a+a)=f(a)$ Now $g(x)=|f(x)|$

$\therefore$ get $(a-0)=\lim\limits_{h\to 0} g.(a-h)$

$\lim\limits_{h\to 0}|f(a-h)|=|f(a)|$

Similarly

$g(a+0)=\lim\limits_{h\to 0} g\,(a+h)$

$=\lim\limits_{h\to 0}|f(a+h)|=|f(a)|$

$\therefore\ g(a-0)=g\,(a+0)$

$=|f(a)|=g\,(a)$

Hence, g is continuous. Thus g is continuous if f is continuous.

15. $\therefore\ 2^x+2^y=2$

$\because\ 2^y=2-2^x$

$\Rightarrow y=\log e^{(2-2x)}$

$\Rightarrow y$ is real if $2-2^x>0$

or $2>2^x$

$\therefore\ x\in(-\infty,1)$

Hence $-\infty<x<1$

16. $$\lim_{x\to\infty}\left(\frac{x-3}{x+2}\right)^x=\lim_{x\to\infty}\frac{\left(1-\frac{3}{x}\right)^x}{\left(1+\frac{2}{x}\right)^x}$$

$$=\frac{\lim\limits_{x\to\infty}\left[\left(1-\frac{3}{x}\right)^{-\frac{x}{3}}\right]^{-3}}{\lim\limits_{x\to\infty}\left[\left(1+\frac{2}{x}\right)^{\frac{x}{2}}\right]^{2}}=\frac{e^{-3}}{e^2}=e^{-5}$$

17. $f(x)=\int e^x(x-1)(x-2)dx$

$\therefore f(x)=e^x(x-1)(x-2)$

If f decreases $f(x)<0$

$\therefore e^x(x-1)(x-2)<0$

But $e^x>0$

$\therefore (x-1)(x-2)<0$

$\Rightarrow 1<x<2$

Hence $x\in(1,2)$

18. Here $x\in(0,1)$

Let $g(x)=e^x-1-x$, then

$g(x)=e^x-1>0$ or $x(0,1)$

$\therefore g(x)$ increases on $(0,1)$

$\Rightarrow g(x)>g(0)$, for $0<x<1$

$\Rightarrow .e^x-1-x>0$, or $e^x>1+x$, for $0<x<1$

Thus (A) does not hold

Next Let $f(x)=\log(1+x)-x$, then

$f(x)=\dfrac{1}{1+x}-1,$

$=\dfrac{1-1-x}{1+x}=\dfrac{-x}{1+x}$

$<0, for\ x\in(0,1)$

$\because f(0)=0$

$\therefore f$ is decreasing function

$\because f(x)<f(0)$

$\Rightarrow f(x)<0$

$\therefore \log(1+x)-x<0$

$\Rightarrow \log(1+x)<x\forall x\in(0,1)$

Similarly, it can be checked that (C) and (D) do not hold

19. $f(x)=\begin{cases}|x|, for\ 0<|x|\le 2\\ 1, for\ x=0\end{cases}$

The graph of the function in the interval [–2, 2] is given by, $y=-x$ for $-2\le x<0$

$y=1$, for $x=0$

$y=x$ for $0<x\le 2$

The function is discontinuous at $x=0$. In the neighbourhood of $x=0$ the value of y is less than 1. Hence the function has a local maximum at $x=0$

20. From the figure, it is clear that both sin x and cos x decreases in $\left(\dfrac{\pi}{2},\pi\right)$

$\therefore$ S is correct

Now, it a differentiable

Function decreases

then its derivative is negative it may increase or decrease therefore R is not correct.

21. Given That

$\tan\left(\dfrac{3\pi}{4}\right)$ = gradient of normat (3,4)

$\therefore -\dfrac{1}{\dfrac{dy}{dx}}=\tan\left(\dfrac{3\pi}{4}\right)$

$=\tan\left(\pi-\dfrac{\pi}{4}\right)$

$\therefore=-\tan\dfrac{\pi}{4}=-1$

or $f(3)=1$

22. Let $y=f(x)=(x+1)^2-1$

$\Rightarrow y+1=(x+1)^2\Rightarrow x=\sqrt{y+1}-1$

$\Rightarrow f^{-1}(y)=\sqrt{y+1}-1$

Thus $f^{-1}(x)=\sqrt{x-1}-1$

$\therefore S=\{x:f(x)=f^{-1}(x)\}$

$=\{x:(x+1)^2-1=\sqrt{x+1}-1\}$

$=\{x:(x+1)^2=\sqrt{x+1}\}$

$=\{0,-1\}$

23. For $x\in 1$

$\lim\limits_{x\to n} f(x)=\lim\limits_{x\to n}\left[x^+\right]\cos\left(\dfrac{2x-1}{2}\right)\pi$

$=n\cos\left(\dfrac{2x-1}{1}\right)\pi$

$=0$

$\lim\limits_{x\to^+ n} f(x)=\lim\limits_{x\to n^+}[x]\cos\left(\dfrac{2x-1}{2}\right)\pi$

$(n-1)\cos\left(\dfrac{2x-1}{2}\right)\pi$

$=0$

$\therefore f$ is continuous for $x=n\in 1$

But the function $f(x)=[x]$ and $f(x)=\cos\left(\dfrac{2x-1}{2}\right)\pi$ are continuous on $x\in R-1$. Hence $f(x)$ is continuous everywhere *i.e.* discontinuous nowhere

24. Taking $f(x) = \log x$ it is clear that

$$f\left(\frac{x}{y}\right) = f(x) - f(y)$$

as, $\log\left(\frac{x}{y}\right) = \log x - \log y$

and $f(e) = 1$ as $\log e = 1$

Also $f(x)$ is not bounded and $f\left(\frac{1}{x}\right)$

$= \log x \to \infty$ as $x \to 0$ Again $x\, f(x) = x \log x \to 0$, as $x \to 0$

25. Since,

$$f(x) = \frac{\log(\pi + x)}{\log(e + x)}$$

$$\therefore f'(x) = \frac{\frac{\log(e+x)}{\pi + x} - \frac{\log(\pi + x)}{e + x}}{\{\log(e+x)\}^2}$$

$$= \frac{(e+x)\log(e+x) - (\pi + x)\log(\pi + x)}{(\pi + x)(e+x)\{\log(e+x)\}^2}$$

we know that $\log x$ increases for $x > 1$

$\therefore (e+x)\log(e+x) < (\pi + x)\log(\pi + x)$

for $x \geq 0$, Thus $f(x) < 0$, for $x \geq 0$

Hence if (x) decreases on $[0, \infty)$

26. Since, $f(x) = A \sin\left(\frac{\pi x}{2}\right) + B$ ...(*i*)

$$\therefore f'(x) = A\frac{\pi}{2}\cos\left(\frac{\pi x}{2}\right)$$

$$\sqrt{2} = \left(f^{\frac{1}{2}}\right) = A.\ \frac{\pi}{2}.\frac{1}{\sqrt{2}}$$

$\Rightarrow A = \frac{4}{\pi}$ ...(*ii*)

$$\text{Now} \int_0^1 \sin\left(\frac{\pi x}{2}\right)dx + \int_0^1 B\,dx = \frac{8}{\pi^2}$$

by (*i*) and (*ii*)

$$\Rightarrow \frac{4}{\pi}\left[-\frac{2}{\pi}\cos\left(\frac{\pi x}{2}\right)\right]_0^1 + B\ [x]_0^1 = \frac{8}{\pi^2}$$

$$\Rightarrow \frac{8}{\pi^2}[0+1] + B[1-0] = \frac{8}{\pi^2}$$

$\Rightarrow B = 0$

Thus $A = \frac{4}{\pi}$ and $B = 0$

27. We know that

$$\Rightarrow \int_a^b f(x)dx = \int_a^b f(a+b-x)dx$$

$$\therefore I = \int_{\pi/4}^{3\pi/4} \frac{dx}{1+\cos x}$$

$$= \int_{\pi/4}^{3\pi/4} \frac{dx}{1+\cos(\pi - x)}$$

$$= \int_{\pi/4}^{3\pi/4} \frac{dx}{1-\cos x}$$

$$\text{Thus } 21 = \int_{\pi/4}^{3\pi/4}\left[\frac{1}{1+\cos x} + \frac{1}{1-\cos x}\right]$$

$$= \int_{\pi/4}^{3\pi/4} \frac{2}{1-\cos^2 x}dx$$

$$= 2\int_{\pi/4}^{3\pi/4} \text{cosec}^2 x\, dx$$

$$I = [-\cot x]_{\pi/4}^{3\pi/4} = -\cot\frac{3\pi}{4} + \cot\frac{\pi}{4}$$

$= -(-1) + 1 = 2$

29. Given, $\int_0^x f(t)dt = x + \int_x^1 tf(t)dt$ ...(*i*)

Differentiating to the sides of (*i*) *w.r.* to x we get $f(x) = 1 + (-xf(x))$

$\Rightarrow (1+x)f(x) = 1$ or $f(x) = \frac{1}{1+x}$

Thus $f(1) = \frac{1}{2}$

30. Let $t = \int_{-1}^1 f(x)dx = \int_{-1}^1 (x = [x])dx$

$$= \int_{-1}^1 x\,dx - \int_{-1}^1 (x = [x])dx$$

$$= \int_{-1}^{1} [x]\,dx, [\text{since } x \text{ is an odd function}]$$

But $[x]\begin{cases} -1, \text{if } -1 \le x < 0 \\ 0, \text{if } 0 \le x < 1 \\ 1, \text{if } x = 1 \end{cases}$

Thus $1 = -\int_{-1}^{0} [x]\,dx - \int_{0}^{1} [x]dx$

$$= -\int_{-1}^{0} (-1)dx - \int_{0}^{1} (0)dx$$

$$= [x]_1^0 = 0 + 1 = 1$$

31. We know that

$$\int_a^b f(x)dx = \int_a^b f[a+b) - x]dx$$

$$\therefore I_1 = \int_{1-k}^{k} x\sqrt{[x(1-x)]}dx$$

$$= \int_{1-k}^{k} (1-x)f[(1-x)\{1-(1-x)\}]dx$$

$$= \int_{1-k}^{k} f[(1-x)x]dx$$

$$= \int_{1-k}^{k} xf[(1-x)x]dx$$

$$= I_2 - I_1$$

$$\Rightarrow 2I_1 = I_2 \text{ or } \frac{I_1}{I_2} = \frac{1}{2}$$

32. Here

$$g(x) = \int_0^k \cos^4 t dt$$

$$\therefore g(x+\pi) = \int_0^{k+x} \cos^4 t dt$$

$$= \int_0^{\pi} \cos^4 t dt + \int_{\pi}^{k+x} \cos^4 t dt$$

$$= g(\pi) + I \qquad ...(i)$$

Where $I_1 = \int_{\pi}^{\pi+x} \cos^4 t dt \qquad ...(ii)$

Put $t = \pi + z$, so $dt = dz$ in (2), we get

$$I_1 = \int_0^x \cos^4(\pi + z)dz$$

$$= \int_0^k (-\cos z)^4 dz$$

$$= \int_0^k \cos^4 z dz \qquad ...(iii)$$

By (*i*) and (*iii*), we have $g(x+\pi) = g(\pi) + g(x)$

34. $(4x-3y)\,dx + (y-x)\,dy = 0$

$\Rightarrow \frac{dy}{dx} = \frac{4x-3y}{x-y}$, which is linear and homogeneous equation of degree one.

35. $x\frac{dy}{dx} = k(y\log x - y\log y)$

$$\Rightarrow \frac{dy}{dx} = k\frac{y}{x}\log\left(\frac{x}{y}\right)$$

Which is clearly homogeneous but not linear differential equation.

36. Given that Mean $\sum(x-15) = 7$

$$\Rightarrow \sum x - \sum 15 = 7$$

$$\Rightarrow \sum x - 10 \times 15 = 7$$

$$\Rightarrow \sum x = i57$$

$$\therefore \text{Mean } \bar{x} = \frac{\sum x}{N} = \frac{157}{10} = 15.7$$

37. Let A*i* denote the event that India wins *i*th match

Required probability

$= P(A_1 A_2 A_3) + P(A_1 A_2 A_3)$

$= P(A_1)P(A_2)P(A_3) + P(A_1)P(A_2)P(A_3) = \left(\frac{1}{2}\right)^3 + \left(\frac{1}{2}\right)^3$

$= \frac{1}{4}$

38. Let $\bar{x} = \bar{y} = m$, since the regression lines pass through the point $(\bar{x}, \bar{y}) = (m, m)$, therefore, $m = am + b$ and $m = \alpha m + \beta$

$$\Rightarrow m = \frac{b}{1-a} = \frac{\beta}{1-\alpha}$$

$$\Rightarrow \frac{b}{\beta} = \frac{1-a}{1-\alpha}$$

SET–24

CSIR–UGC (NET) MATHEMATICAL SCIENCES

PART-B

1. Set A has 3 elements and B has 4 elements. The number of injections that can be defined from A and B is

A. 144 B. 12
C. 24 D. 64

2. If ω is an imaginary cube root of unity then $\left(1+\omega-\omega^2\right)^7$ equals

A. 128ω B. -128ω
C. $128\omega^2$ D. $-128\omega^2$

3. If $\begin{vmatrix} 6i & -3i & 1 \\ 4 & 3i & -1 \\ 20 & 3 & i \end{vmatrix} = x+iy$, then

A. $x=5, y=1$ B. $x=1, y=3$
C. $x=0, y=3$ D. $x=0, y=0$

4. For positive integers the value of the expression $(1+i)^{n_1}+\left(1+i^3\right)^{n_1}+\left(1+i^5\right)^{n_2}+\left(1+i^7\right)^{n_2}$
Where $i=\sqrt{-1}$ is a real number if and only if

A. $n_1=n_2+1$ B. $n_1=n_2-1$
C. $n_1=n_2$ D. $n_1>0, n_2>0$

5. If ω is complex root of the equation $z^3=1$ then $\omega+\omega^{\left(\frac{1}{2}+\frac{3}{8}+\frac{9}{23}+\frac{27}{128}+.....\right)}$ is

A. 0 B. 1
C. -2 D. -1

6. If $\Delta = \begin{vmatrix} -1 & 1 & 1 \\ 1 & -1 & 1 \\ 1 & 1 & -1 \end{vmatrix}$ then Δ is

A. -4 B. 0
C. 2 D. 4

7. A root of the equation $\begin{vmatrix} 3-x & -6 & 3 \\ -6 & 3-x & 3 \\ 3 & 3 & -6-x \end{vmatrix} = 0$ is

A. 6 B. 2
C. 0 D. None of these

8. Three linear equation will have consistent solution, if

A. $\begin{vmatrix} a_1 & b_1 & c_1 \\ a_2 & b_2 & c_2 \\ a_3 & b_3 & c_3 \end{vmatrix} \neq 0$

B. $\begin{vmatrix} a_1 & b_1 & c_1 \\ a_2 & b_2 & c_2 \\ a_3 & b_3 & c_3 \end{vmatrix} = 0$

C. $a_1b_1+a_2b_2+a_3b_3=0$

D. None of these

9. An n–digit number is a positive number with exactly n digits. Nine hundred distinct n digit numbers are to be formed using only the three digits 2,5 and 7. The smallest value of n for which this is possible is

A. 6 B. 7
C. 8 D. 9

10. A five digit number divisible by 3 is to be formed using the numerals 0,1, 2, 3, 4 and 5 without repetition. The total number of ways in which this can be done is

A. 216 B. 240
C. 600 D. 3125

11. The sum of the series

$1+\frac{1}{5}+\frac{1.3}{5.10}+\frac{1.3.5}{5.10.15}+.........$ is

A. $\sqrt{3}$ B. $\sqrt{5}$
C. $\sqrt{\frac{5}{3}}$ D. $\sqrt{\frac{3}{5}}$

12. The product of n positive numbers is unity then their sum is

A. a positive integer B. divisible by n
C. equal to $n+\frac{1}{n}$ D. never less than n

13. On the interval [0,1] the function $x^{25}(1-x)^{35}$ takes its maximum value at the point

A. 0 B. $\frac{1}{4}$

C. $\frac{1}{2}$ D. $\frac{1}{3}$

14. The function $f(x)=|px-q|+r|x|, x\in(-\infty,\infty)$ where $p>0$, $q>0$, $r>0$ assumes its minimum value only at one point if

A. $p\neq q$ B. $r\neq q$

C. $r\neq p$ D. $p=q=r$

15. If the function $f:|1,\infty)\to|1,\infty)$ is defined by $f(x)=2^{x(x-1)}$ then $f^{-1}(x)$ is

A. $\left(\frac{1}{2}\right)^{x(x-1)}$

B. $\frac{1}{2}\left(1+\sqrt{1+4\log_2 x}\right)$

C. $\frac{1}{2}\left(1-\sqrt{1+4\log_2 x}\right)$

D. Not defined

16. $\lim\limits_{x\to 0}\frac{x\tan 2x-2x\tan x}{(1-\cos 2x)^2}$ is

A. 2 B. −2

C. $\frac{1}{2}$ D. $-\frac{1}{2}$

17. The function $f(x)=[x]^2-[x^2]$, (where $[y]$ is the greatest integer less than or equal to y) is discontinuous at:

A. all integers

B. all integers except 0 and 1

C. all integers except 0

D. all intergers except 1

18. The function $f(x)=(x^2-1)|x^2-3x+2|+\cos|x|$ is not differentiable at

A. −1 B. 0

C. 1 D. 2

19. The function, $f(x)=\sin^4 x+\cos^4 x$ increases if

A. $0<x<\frac{\pi}{8}$ B. $\frac{\pi}{4}<x<\frac{3\pi}{8}$

C. $\frac{3\pi}{8}<x<\frac{5\pi}{8}$ D. $\frac{5\pi}{8}<x<\frac{3\pi}{8}$

20. If $f(x)=3x-5$, then $f^{-1}(x)$

A. is given by $\frac{1}{3x-5}$

B. is given by $\frac{x+5}{3}$

C. does not exist because f is not in to

D. does not exist because f is not on to

21. $\lim\limits_{x\to 1}\sqrt{\frac{1-\cos 2(x-1)}{x-1}}$

A. exists and it equals $\sqrt{2}$

B. exists and it equals $-\sqrt{2}$

C. does not exist because $x-1\to 0$

D. does not exist because the left hand limit is not equal to the right hand limit

22. If $f(x)=\frac{x^2-1}{x^2+1}$ for every real number x then the minimum value of f

A. does not exist because f is unbounded

B. is not attained even through is bounded

C. is equal to 1

D. is equal to −1

23. The number of values of x where the function $f(x)=\cos x+\cos(\sqrt{2}x)$ attains its maximum is

A. 0 B. 1

C. 2 D. Infinite

24. $f(x)=\frac{x}{\sin x}$ and $g(x)=\frac{x}{\tan x}$, where $0<x\leq 1$ then in this interval

A. both $f(x)$ and $g(x)$are increasing functions

B. both $f(x)$and $g(x)$ are decreasing functions

C. $f(x)$ is an increasing function

D. $g(x)$ is an increasing funtion

25. The value of $I=\int_0^{\frac{\pi}{2}}\frac{dx}{1+\tan^3 x}$ is

A. 0 B. 1

C. $\frac{\pi}{2}$ D. $\frac{\pi}{4}$

26. Let $f:R\to R$ and $g:R\to R$ be continuous function then the value of the integral

$\int_{-\pi/2}^{\pi/2}|f(x)+f(-x)|[g(x)-g(-x)dx$ is

A. π B. 1

C. −1 D. 0

27. If $[x]$denotes the greatest intger less than or equal to x, then the value of $\int_1^5 [|x-3|]\,dx$ is

A. 1 B. 2
C. 4 D. 8

28. $\int_0^{2\pi} |\sin^3 x|\,dx$ is equal to

A. 0 B. π
C. $\frac{8}{3}$ D. $\frac{3}{8}$

29. $\int_{-n}^{n} (1+x^3)^{-1}\,dx$

A. $2\int_0^a (1+x^3)^{-1}\,dx$
B. $2\int_0^a (1-x^6)^{-1}\,dx$
C. 0
D. $2\int_0^a 1+(a-x^3)^{-1}\,dx$

30. $\int_{-1}^{1} \frac{\sin x + x^2}{3-|x|}\,dx$ is equal to

A. $2\int_0^1 \frac{\sin x + x^2}{3-|x|}\,dx$ B. 0
C. $2\int_0^1 \frac{x^2}{3-|x|}$ D. $2\int_0^1 \frac{\sin x^2}{3-|x|}dx$

31. Solution of the equation $\int_3^x \sqrt{x+1}\,dx = 0$ is

A. 0 B. 1
C. 2 D. 3

32. The differential equation $(x + y)\,dx + dy = 0$ is

A. homogeneous but not linear
B. linear but not homogeneous
C. both homogeneous and linear
D. neither homogeneous nor liner.

33. If $\frac{dy}{dx} + 2xy = y$ then y is

A. $2e^{x-x^2}$ B. $e^{-x^{2+x}}$
C. e^{-2x} D. e^{-x^2}

34. If $\frac{dy}{dx} = k\,y$ then y is

A. ce^{-kx} B. ce^{kx}
C. $\frac{kxy^2}{2}$ D. e^{-kc+c}

35. The mean wages of 100 workers on a factory running two shifts of 60 and 40 workers is 38. The mean wags of 60 workers in the morning shift in Rs 40, then the mean wages of 40 workers in the evening shift is

A. Rs 37 B. Rs 36
C. Rs 35 D. Rs 40

36. Average rainfall of city from monday to saturday is 0.3 inch. Due to heavy rainfall on sunday, the average rainfall increased to 0.5 inches. What was the rainfall on sunday?

A. 1.7 inches B. 1.8 inches
C. 0.8 inch D. 3.5 inches

37. A committee consists of a experts taken from three institutions A, B and C of which 2 are from A, 3 from B and 4 from C if three experts resign, then the probability that they belong to different institutions is

A. $\frac{2}{7}$ B. $\frac{1}{729}$
C. $\frac{1}{21}$ D. $\frac{1}{24}$

38. If the minimax value is equal to maximini value, then corresponding pure strategies are called optimal strategies and the game is said to have:

A. Critical point B. Constant point
C. Saddle point D. None of these

39. Which one is monoid?

A. $(I, \cdot)$ B. $(I^+, +)$
C. $(I, +)$ D. $(I, -)$

40. Let $f(z)$ be an analytic function in a simply connected domain D enclosed by a rectifiable Jordan curve C and let $f(z)$ be continuous on C,

then $f(z_0) = \frac{1}{2\pi i}\int \frac{f(z)}{z-z_0}dz$ where z_0 is any point of D.

This statement is known as

A. Cauchy Gourgat theorem
B. Cauchy's Integral Formula
C. Taylor's theorem
D. Laurants' series

ANSWERS

1	2	3	4	5	6	7	8	9	10
C	D	D	D	D	D	C	A	B	A
11	**12**	**13**	**14**	**15**	**16**	**17**	**18**	**19**	**20**
C	D	B	C	B	C	D	D	B	B
21	**22**	**23**	**24**	**25**	**26**	**27**	**28**	**29**	**30**
D	D	B	C	D	D	C	C	B	C
31	**32**	**33**	**34**	**35**	**36**	**37**	**38**	**39**	**40**
D	C	A	B	C	A	A	C	A	B

Some Selected Explanatory Answers

1. Since O (A) = 3, O (B) = 4 the number of injection (one-one mapping) given by ${}^4p_3 = 4.3.2 = 24$

2. We have

$\left(1+\omega-\omega^2\right)^7 = \left(-\omega^2-\omega^2\right)^7$, as, $1+\omega+\omega^2=0$

$=(-2)^7\left(\omega^2\right)^7 = -128\omega^{14}$

$= -128\omega^2$

as $\omega^{14} = \left(\omega^3\right)^4\omega^2 = (1)^4\omega^2 = \omega^2$

3. We have

$$x+iy = \begin{vmatrix} 6i & -3i & 1 \\ 4 & 3i & -1 \\ 20 & 3 & i \end{vmatrix}$$

$$x+iy = (-3i)\begin{vmatrix} 6i & 1 & 1 \\ 4 & -1 & -1 \\ 20 & 1 & i \end{vmatrix}$$

Taking $(-3i)$ common out form C_2

$\Rightarrow x+iy = 0$ [$\because c_2$ and c_3 are same]

$\Rightarrow x = 0, y = 0$

4. Since $i^3 = -i$, $i^5 = i$ and $i^7 = -i$

$\therefore (1+i)^{n_1} + \left(1+i^3\right)^{n_1} + \left(1+i^5\right)^{n_2} + \left(1+i^7\right)^{n_2}$

$= \left[(1+i)^{n_1} + (1-i)^{n_1}\right] + \left[(1+i)^{n_2} + (1-i)^{n_2}\right]$

$= 2\left[{}^{n_1}C_0 + {}^{n_1}C_2 i^2 + {}^{n_1}C_4 i^4 + \ldots\ldots.\right]$

$\quad + 2\left[{}^{n_2}C_0 + {}^{n_2}C_2 i^2 + {}^{n_2}C_4 i^4 + \ldots\ldots\ldots\right]$

$= 2\left[{}^{n_1}C_0 - {}^{n_1}C_2 i^2 + {}^{n_1}C_4 \ldots\ldots\ldots\right]$

$\quad + 2\left[{}^{n_2}C_0 - {}^{n_2}C_2 i^2 + {}^{n_2}C_4 \ldots\ldots\ldots\right]$

Which is a real number irrespective of the values of n_1 and n_2

5. Let $S = \frac{1}{2} + \frac{3}{8} + \frac{9}{32} + \frac{27}{128} + \ldots\ldots\ldots$

$\Rightarrow S = \frac{1}{2} + \frac{3}{4}\left(\frac{1}{2} + \frac{3}{8} + \frac{9}{32} + \ldots\ldots\ldots\right)$

$\Rightarrow S = \frac{1}{2} + \frac{3}{4}(S)$

$\Rightarrow \left(1 - \frac{3}{4}\right)S = \frac{1}{2} \Rightarrow S = 2$

$\therefore \omega + \omega^{\left(\frac{1}{2}+\frac{3}{8}+\frac{9}{32}+\frac{27}{128}+\ldots\ldots\right)}$

$= \omega + \omega^2$

$= -1$

as $1 + \omega + \omega^2 = 0$

6. Operating $C_2 \to C_2 + C_1$ and $C_3 \to C_3 + C_1$

$$\text{we get} \begin{vmatrix} -1 & 0 & 0 \\ 1 & 0 & 2 \\ 1 & 2 & 0 \end{vmatrix}$$

$= -(0-4) = 4$

7. Operating $R_1 \to R_1 + R_2 + R_3$ we get

$$\begin{vmatrix} -x & -x & -x \\ -6 & 3-x & 3 \\ 3 & 3 & -6-x \end{vmatrix} = 0$$

$$\Rightarrow \begin{vmatrix} -x & 0 & 0 \\ -6 & 9-x & 9 \\ 3 & 0 & -9-x \end{vmatrix} = 0$$

$C_2 \to C_2 - C_1$ and $C_3 \to C_3 - C_1$

$$-x\{-(9-x)(9+x)-0\}=0$$

$$x(9-x^2)=0$$

$x=0, x=\pm 3$

from the given choices, we have

$x=0$

8. There linear equations will have consistent solution if determinant of the their coefficient matrix is non zero *i.e.*

$$\begin{vmatrix} a_1 & b_1 & c_1 \\ a_2 & b_2 & c_2 \\ a_3 & b_3 & c_3 \end{vmatrix} \neq 0$$

9. Distinct n digit numbers which can be formed using digits 2, 5 and 7

$3\times 3\times 3$................ upon n times

$=3^n$

We have to find n so that $3^n \geq 900$

$\Rightarrow 3^n \geq 3^2 \times 100$

$\Rightarrow 3^{n-2} \geq 100$

$\Rightarrow n-2 \geq 5$

$\Rightarrow n \geq 7$

$\therefore$ The smallest value of n is 7

10. Sum of 0, 1, 2, 3, 4, 5 is 15. If a five digit number is to be divisible by 3 then out of the six digits we shall have to leave either 0 or 3. If we leave 0, then remaining digits can be arranged in ${}^5P_5 - {}^4P_4 = (5!-4!)$ ways. Hence the total number of such 5 digits numbers is

$=5!+5!-4!$

$=120+120-24=216$

11. We have

$$1+\frac{1}{5}+\frac{1.3}{5.10}+\frac{1.3.5}{5.10.15}+\ldots\ldots\ldots\ldots\ldots$$

$$\Rightarrow 1+\left(-\frac{1}{2}\right)\left(-\frac{2}{5}\right)+\frac{\left(-\frac{1}{2}\right)\left(-\frac{3}{2}\right)}{2!}\left(-\frac{2}{5}\right)^2$$

$$+\frac{\left(-\frac{1}{2}\right)\left(-\frac{3}{2}\right)\left(-\frac{5}{2}\right)}{3!}\left(-\frac{2}{5}\right)^3+\ldots\ldots\ldots\ldots\ldots$$

$$=\left(1-\frac{2}{5}\right)^{-\frac{1}{2}}=\left(\frac{3}{5}\right)^{-\frac{1}{2}}=\sqrt{\frac{5}{3}}$$

12. Given $a_1 \cdot a_2 \ldots\ldots\ldots\ldots\ldots a_n = 1$

when $a_1 \cdot a_2 \ldots\ldots\ldots\ldots\ldots a_n$ an are n positive real number since A.M. $\geq$ G.M

$$\Rightarrow \frac{a_1+a_2\ldots\ldots+a_n}{n} \geq (a_1, a_2\ldots\ldots\ldots a_n)^{1/n}=1$$

$$\Rightarrow a_1+a_2\ldots\ldots\ldots+a_n \geq n$$

13. Let $f(x)=x^{25}(1-x)^{75}$

$$\therefore f'(x)=25x^{24}(1-x)^{75}-75x^{25}(1-x)^{74}$$

$$\Rightarrow f'(x)=25x^{24}(1-x)^{74}(1-4x)$$

$$\Rightarrow f'(x)=0, \text{ for } x=0,1,\frac{1}{4}$$

Now $f(0)=0, f(1)=0$ and $f\left(\frac{1}{4}\right)=\left(\frac{1}{4}\right)^{25}\left(\frac{3}{4}\right)^{75}$

Hence $f(x)$ has maximum value at $x=\frac{1}{4}$

14. The given function can be written as

$$\begin{cases} px-q-rx, & x\leq 0 \\ -px+q+rx, & 0<x\leq\frac{q}{p} \\ px=q+rx, & x>\frac{q}{p} \end{cases}$$

If $r \neq p$, f has infinite points of minimum

If $r \neq p$, then $x=\frac{q}{p}$ is the point of minimum if $r<p$ and $x=0$ is the point of minimum if $r>p$

15. Let $f(x)=2^{x(x-1)}$ where $y\geq 1$ as $x\geq 1$

$\therefore \log_2 y = x(x-1)$

$\Rightarrow x^2-x-\log_2 y=0$

$$\Rightarrow x=\frac{1\pm\sqrt{1+4\log_2 y}}{2}$$

for $y\geq 1, 1-\sqrt{1+4\log_2 y}\leq 0$

As $x\geq 1$ we take

$$x = \frac{1}{2}\left(1 + \sqrt{1 + 4\log_2 y}\right)$$

Hence $f^{-1}(x) = \frac{1}{2}\left(1 + \sqrt{1 + 4\log_2 x}\right)$

16. We have, given limit

$$= \lim_{x\to 0} \frac{x\tan 2x - 2x\tan x}{4\sin^4 x}$$

$$= \lim_{x\to 0} \frac{2x\tan x}{4\sin^4 x}\left[\frac{2\tan x}{1 - \tan^2 x} - 2\tan x\right]$$

$$= \lim_{x\to 0} \frac{2x\tan x}{4\sin^4 x}\left[\frac{1 - 1 + \tan^2 x}{1 - \tan^2 x}\right]$$

$$= \frac{1}{2}\lim_{x\to 0} \frac{x\tan^3 x}{\sin^4 x\left(1 - \tan^2 x\right)}$$

$$= \frac{1}{2}\lim_{x\to 0}\left(\frac{x}{\sin x}\right)\frac{1}{\cos^3 x}\left(\frac{1}{1 - \tan^2 x}\right)$$

$$= \frac{1}{2}\lim_{x\to 0}(1)\frac{1}{(1)^3}\left(\frac{1}{1-0}\right) = \frac{1}{2}$$

17. $\because f(x) = [x]^2 - \left[x^2\right]$

$\therefore$ It is clear that $f(x) = 0$ for each integral value of x

Also if $0 < x < 1 \Rightarrow 0 < x^2 < 1$

$\therefore [x] = 0$ and $[x^2] = 0$

So $f(x) = 0$ for $0 < x < 1$

Again if $1 < x < \sqrt{2}$, than $1 < x^2 < 2$

$\therefore [x] = 1$ and $[x]^2 = 1$

Thus, $f(x) = [x]^2 - \left[x^2\right]$

$= 1 - 1 = 0$ *for* $1 < x < \sqrt{2}$

It follows that $f(x) = 0$ for $0 \le x < \sqrt{2}$

Thus $f(x)$ is continuous at $x = 1$

But at point x other than integers and not lying between $\left(0, \sqrt{2}\right)$, $f(x) \ne 0$

Hence $f(x)$ is discontinuous at all integers except 1

18. Since

$$|x| = \begin{cases} -x, & \text{if } x < 0 \\ x, & \text{if } x \ge 0 \end{cases}$$

and $x^2 - 3x - 2 = |(x-1)(x-2)|$

$$\begin{cases} (1-x)(2-x), & \text{if } x \le 1 \\ (x-1)(2-x), & \text{if } x \le 2 \\ (x-1)(x-2), & \text{if } x > 1 \end{cases}$$

Also $\cos(-\theta) = \cos\theta$, then we get $\cos(|x|) - \cos x \forall x$

$\therefore f(x) = \left(x^2 - 1\right)\left|x^2 - 3x + 2\right| + \cos(|x|)$

$$\therefore \begin{cases} \left(x^2-1\right)(x-1)(x-2) + \cos x \text{ if } x \le 1 \\ -\left(x^2-1\right)(x-1)(x-2) + \cos x \text{ if } 1 < x \le 2 \\ \left(x^2-1\right)(x-1)(x-2) + \cos x \text{ if } x > 2 \end{cases}$$

It is clear that f is differentiable at all points except possibly at $x = 1$ and $x = 2$. Now

$$Lf(1) = \lim_{x\to 1^-} \frac{f(x) - f(1)}{x - 1}$$

$$= \lim_{x\to 1^-}\left[\left(x^2 - 1\right)(x - 2) + \frac{\cos x - \cos 1}{x - 1}\right]$$

$= 0 - \sin 1 = -\sin 1$

and $Rf(1) = \lim_{x\to 1^+} \dfrac{f(x) - f(1)}{x - 1}$

$$\lim_{x\to 1^+}\left[-\left(x^2 \quad 1\right)(x - 2) + \frac{\cos x - \cos 1}{x - 1}\right]$$

$\therefore 0 - \sin 1 = -\sin 1$

$\therefore Lf(i) = Rf(ii) \Rightarrow f$ is differentiable at $x = 1$, Again $Lf(2)$

$$= \lim_{x\to 2^-} \frac{f(x) - f(2)}{x - 2}$$

$$= \lim_{x\to 2^-}\left[-\left(x^2-1\right)(x-1) + \frac{\cos x - \cos 2}{x-2}\right]$$

$= -(4-1)(2-1) - \sin 2 = -3 - \sin 2$

and $Rf(2) = \lim_{x\to 2^+} \dfrac{f(x) - f(2)}{x - 2}$

$$= \lim_{x\to 2^+}\left[\left(x^2 - 1\right)(x - 1) + \frac{\cos x - \cos 2}{x - 2}\right]$$

$= (4-1)(2-1) - \sin 2 = 3 - \sin 2$

$\therefore Lf(2) \neq Rf(2) \Rightarrow$ is not differentiable at $x = 2$

19. Here $f(x) = \sin^4 x + \cos^4 x$

$f'(x) = 4\sin^3 x \cos x - 4\cos^3 x \sin x$

$= 4\sin x \cos x\left(\sin^2 x - \cos^2 x\right)$

$= 2\sin 2x(-\cos 2x) = -\sin 4x$

$f(x) > 0, 4x < 0$, *i.e.* if $4x$ lies in the third quadrant, or if $4x < \frac{3\pi}{2}$ or if $\frac{\pi}{4} < x < \frac{3\pi}{8}$

21. $1 - \cos 2(x-1) = 2\sin^2(x-1)$

$\Rightarrow$ Now $\lim_{x \to 1^-} \sqrt{\frac{1-\cos 2(x-1)}{x-1}}$

$= \lim_{x \to 1^-} \frac{\sqrt{2}|\sin(x-1)|}{x-1}$

$= \lim_{h \to 0^+} \frac{\sqrt{2}|\sin(1-h-1)|}{1-h-1}$

$= \sqrt{2} \lim_{h \to 0^+} \frac{|\sin h|}{h}$

$= \sqrt{2} \lim_{h \to 0^+} \frac{\sin h}{h}$

$= \sqrt{2}(1) = \sqrt{2}$ $\therefore$ Left hand limit $\neq$ right hand limit. Hence, given limit does not exist

22. Given $f(x) = \frac{x^2-1}{x^2+1} = 1 - \frac{2}{x^2+1}$ ...(*i*)

From (*i*) it is clear that $f(x)$ will attain its minimum value when $\frac{2}{x^2+1}$ is maximum, when x^2+1 is minimum *i.e.* at $x = 0$. Hence, Minimum value of $f(x) = f(0) = -1$

23. The Maximum value of

$f(x) = \cos x + \cos\left(\sqrt{2}x\right)$

is 2 which occurs at $x = 0$, Also there is no other value of x for which this value will be attend again.

Hence, numbers of values of x where f is maximum is one.

24. Here, $f(x) = \frac{x}{\sin x}, g(x) = \frac{x}{\tan x}$, where $0 < x \leq 1$

Since $\sin x < x \Rightarrow \frac{x}{\sin x} > 1$, Hence, the function ($f$) is increasing. Again $\tan x > x \Rightarrow \frac{x}{\tan x} < 1$,

$\therefore$ The function $g(x)$ is decreasing.

25. Let

$I = \int_0^{\pi/2} \frac{dx}{1+\tan^3 x}$

$I = \int_0^{\pi/2} \frac{\cos^3 x}{\cos^3 x + \sin^3 x} dx$ ...(*i*)

$\Rightarrow I = \int_0^{\pi/2} \frac{\cos^3\left(\frac{\pi}{2}-x\right)}{\cos^3\left(\frac{\pi}{2}-x\right)+\sin^3\left(\frac{\pi}{2}-x\right)} dx$

[By property of Definite integrals]

$I = \int_0^{\pi/2} \frac{\sin^3 x}{\sin^3 x + \cos^3 x} dx$ ...(*ii*)

$= 2I = \int_0^{\pi/2}\left(\frac{\sin^3 x}{\sin^3 x+\cos^3 x} + \frac{\cos^3 x}{\sin^3 x+\cos^3 x}\right)dx$

$= \int_0^{\pi/2}(1)dx = [x]_0^{\pi/2} = \frac{\pi}{2}$

Hence $I = \frac{\pi}{4}$

26. Since $f(x) + f(-x)$ is an even function and $g(x) - g(-x)$ is an odd function.

$\therefore [f(x)+f(-x)][g(x)-g(-x)]$ is an odd function.

Hence, by property of Definite Integrals

$\int_{-\pi/2}^{\pi/2}[f(x)+f(-x)][g(x)-g(-x)]dx = 0$

27. $\int_1^5 [|x-3|]dx = \int_1^3 [|x-3|]dx + \int_3^5 [|x-3|]dx$

$= \int_1^3 [3-x]dx + \int_3^5 [x-3]\,dx = \left[3x - \frac{x^2}{2}\right]_{x=1}^3$

$\left[\frac{x^2}{2} - 3x\right]_{x=3}^5 = \left[9 - \frac{9}{2}\right] - \left[3 - \frac{1}{2}\right] + \left[\frac{25}{2} - 15\right] - \left[\frac{9}{2} - 9\right]$

$= \left[\frac{9}{2}\right] - \left[\frac{5}{2}\right] + \left[-\frac{5}{2}\right] - \left[-\frac{9}{2}\right]$

$= \frac{9-5-5+9}{2} = \frac{8}{2} = 4$

28. Let $I = \int_0^{2\pi} |\sin^3 x| dx$

$I = \int_0^{\pi} |\sin^3 x| dx + \int_{\pi}^{2\pi} |\sin^3 x| dx$

$= \int_0^{\pi} \sin^3 x dx + \int_{\pi}^{2\pi} (-\sin^3 x) dx$

Put $x = \pi + \theta$; So, $dx = d\theta$ in the second integral

we get, $I = \int_0^{\pi} \sin^3 x dx + \int_0^{\pi} \sin^3 (\pi + \theta) d\theta$

$= \int_0^{\pi} \sin^3 x dx + \int_0^{\pi} \sin^3 \theta \, d\theta$

$= 2\int_0^{\pi/2} \sin^3 x dx + 2\int_0^{\pi/2} \sin^3 \theta \, d\theta$

$= 2\times\frac{2}{3} + 2\times\frac{3}{3} = \frac{8}{3}$

29. $\int_{-a}^{a} (1+x^3)^{-1} dx = \int_{-a}^{a} \frac{1}{1+x^3} dx$

$= \int_{-a}^{a} \frac{1-x^3}{(1+x^3)(1-x^3)} dx$

$= \int_{-a}^{a} \frac{1}{1-x^6} dx - \int_{-a}^{a} \frac{x^3}{1-x^6} dx$

By Property of definite integrals $= 2\int_0^{a} (1-x^6)^{-1} dx$

30. Let $I = \int_{-1}^{1} \frac{\sin x + x^2}{3-|x|} dx$

$I = \int_{-1}^{1} \frac{\sin x}{3-|x|} dx + \int_{-1}^{1} \frac{x^2}{3-|x|} dx$ ...(*i*)

By property of definite integrals

$= \int_{-a}^{a} f(x) dx = 2\int_0^{a} f(x) dx$

If (x) is an even function

$= 0$; if $f(x)$ is an odd function

Then, $f(x) = \frac{\sin x}{3-|-x|} = \frac{\sin x}{3-|x|}$; as

i.e. $f(-x) = -(x), |-x| = |x| = f(x)$

31. Here $\int_3^{x} \sqrt{x+1} \, dx = 0$

or $\int_3^{x} (x+1)^{\frac{1}{2}} dx = 0$

$\Rightarrow \left[\frac{2}{3}(x+1)^{\frac{3}{2}}\right]_3^x = 0$

$\Rightarrow \left[(x+1)^{\frac{3}{2}} - (3+1)^{\frac{3}{2}}\right] = 0$

$\Rightarrow (x+1)^{3/2} = 4^{3/2}$

$\Rightarrow x+1 = 4$ or $x = 3$

32. $(x+y)\, dx + x\, dy = 0$ ...(*i*)

$\Rightarrow \frac{dy}{dx} = -\frac{x+y}{x}$, which is homogenous. Also (1) can be written as; $\frac{dy}{dx} + \frac{1}{x} = -1$ which is linear differential equation. Thus equation (1) is both homogenous and linear.

33. $\frac{dy}{dx} + 2xy = y$

$\Rightarrow \frac{dy}{dx} = (1-2x)y$

$\Rightarrow \log y = x - x^2 + \log c$, where c is arbitrary constant.

$\Rightarrow y = ce^{x-x^2}$

Taking $c = 2$ than

$y = 2e^{x-x^2}$

34. $\frac{dy}{dx} = ky \Rightarrow \frac{dy}{y} = k dx$

$\Rightarrow \log y = kx + \log c$, where c is arbitrary constant

$\Rightarrow y = ce^{kx}$

35. Here $N_1 = 60$, $N_2 = 40$, $\bar{X}_1 = 40$, $\bar{X}_2 = ?$ and $\bar{X}_{12} = 38$. Using formulae for combined mean.

$\bar{X}_{12} = \frac{N_1\bar{X}_1 + N_2\bar{X}_2}{N_1 + N_2}$

$\Rightarrow 38 = \frac{60\times 40 + 40\,\bar{X}_2}{60\times 40}$

$\bar{X}_2 = \frac{1400}{40} = 35$ Rs.

37. The required probability

$P = \frac{n(E)}{n(s)} = \frac{2c_1 \times {}^3c_1 \times {}^4c_1}{{}^9c_3}$

$= \frac{2\times 3\times 4}{\left(\frac{9\times 8\times 7}{3\times 2\times 1}\right)} = \frac{2\times 3\times 4}{3\times 4\times 7} = \frac{2}{7}$

SET–25

CSIR–UGC (NET) MATHEMATICAL SCIENCES

PART-B

1. For the sequence $<x_n>$ where $x_n = (-1)^n \left(1+\frac{1}{n}\right)$ $\lim_{n\to\infty} x_n$ is equal to

A. $-\infty$ B. -1

C. ∞ D. 1

2. $x, y, z \in D$ *and* $x < y$ then

A. $xz > yz, z < 0$

B. $xz > yz, z > 0$

C. $xz > yz, z = 0$

D. $xz > y^2$, $\bar{z}$ is positive, negative or zero

3. A real valued function $f(x)$ has discontinuity of first kind at $x = a$ if

A. $f(a+)$ and $f(a-)$ does not exist

B. $f(a+) = f(a-)$

C. $f(a+) \neq f(a-)$

D. $f(a+) = f(a-) \neq f(a)$

4. If D* is an extended real number system then the least upper bound of D* is

A. ∞

B. $-\infty$

C. 0

D. No least upper bound

5. If f is continuous on $[a,b]$ and f^1 exist at each $x \in (a,b)$ then If $f > 0$ in (a, b) then

A. f is strictly increasing

B. f is strictly decreasing

C. f is constant

D. None of these

6. If E is a non-empty closed set of metric space then the closure $\bar{E}$ of E in

A. $\bar{E}cE$ B. $Ec\bar{E}$

C. $\bar{E} = \phi$ D. None of these

7. The moment generating function of the random variable x, whose moment are $\mu_r = (r+1)2$ is

A. $(1-2t)^{-1}$ B. $(1-2t)$

C. 2t D. $\frac{1}{2t}$

8. 6 coins are tossed 6,400 times what is the probability of getting 6 holds x times?

A. $e^{-100}x$ B. $\frac{1}{\lfloor x}e^{-100}x$

C. $e^{-100}\frac{100x}{\lfloor x}$ D. None of these

9. If x has the probability density $f(x)$ $\begin{cases} e^x & x > 0 \\ 0 & \text{otherewise} \end{cases}$ and $g(x) = e^{3x/4}$ then what is the expected value of $g(x)$?

A. 4 B. 3

C. 2 D. 1

10. What is the probability of getting doubles when two dice are thrown simultaneously?

A. $\frac{1}{2}$ B. $\frac{1}{3}$

C. $\frac{1}{6}$ D. $\frac{2}{3}$

11. A square matrix of order n. $\hat{A}$ is similar to square matrix of order n A, then for same non-singular n-order square matrix

A. $\hat{A} \neq p^{-1}AP$ B. $\hat{A} = p^{-1}AP$

C. $\hat{A} = p^{-1}A$ D. $\hat{A} = P\,P^{-1}A$

12. If rank of matrix A is 5 and nullity of A is 3 then the order of the matrix is

A. 5 B. 3

C. 8 D. 0

13. If $\{z_n\}_{n=1}^{\infty}$ converges to 1 and $\{z'_n\}_{n=1}^{\infty}$ converges to 1 then $\{z_n + z'_n\}$ converges to

A. $1+L_1$ B. $1-L_1$

C. $1/L_1$ D. 1L

14. The function $f(z)=\begin{cases}\dfrac{\text{Im } z}{|z|}, \\ 0 \quad z=0\end{cases}$ is continuous then $z=0$

A. No B. Yes

C. can defined D. None of these

15. A game for which maxi min for A = mini max for B called

A. A game with no saddle point

B. A game with saddle point

C. A game

D. None of these

16. The number of basic variables of the general transportation problem at any stage of feasible solution must be equal to

A. m B. $m+n$

C. $m+n+1$ D. $m+n-1$

17. If x and w feasible solution to the primal and dual problems respectively then will be optimall iff

A. $w_1\left(b_1-\sum_{t=1}^{n} a_n x_1^0\right)=0$

and $x_1^0\left(\sum_{t=1}^{m} a_n w_1^0 - c_1\right)=0$

B. $w_1\left(b_1+\sum_{i=t}^{n} a_n x_t\right)=0$

and $x_1\left(\sum_{i=1}^{m} a_n x_i - c_1\right)=0$

C. $w_1\left(b_1 \pm \sum_{i=t}^{n} a_n x_t\right)=0$

and $x_1\left(\sum_{i=t}^{n} a_{ij} + w_t + c_1\right)=0$

D. None of these

Directions –(Q. 18 to 20): *Answer the following questions on the basis of given passage:*

Ashok Prakashan used 10,000, envelopes per year. Each envelopes costs Rs.32. The production department estimates setup cost as Rs. 55 and accounting department estimates the holding cost as 12.5% of the value of inventory. Replenishment rate is uniform 120 envelops per day. Assuming 250 working days.

18. What is the optimal order quantity?

A. Rs. 703 B. Rs. 600

C. Rs. 643 D. Rs. 896

19. What is the total inventory cost on the basis of optimal policy?

A. Rs. 2644 B. Rs. 1564

C. Rs. 1714 D. Rs. 1800

20. What are the optimal number of setups.

A. 5 setups B. 8 setups

C. 10 setups D. 16 setups

21. The different equation, derived from $y = Ae^{2x} + Be^{-2x}$ have the order where A, B, are constants

A. 3 B. 2

C. 1 D. None of these

22. If y_1 and y_2 are two solutions's of initial value, problem $y''+p(x)y'+q(x)y=0, y(x_0)=y_0$ $y'(x_0)=y_0$ and the Wornskion $w(y_1, y_2)=0$ then y_1 and y_2 are

A. Linearly dependent

B. Linearly independent

C. Proportional

D. None of these

23. The solution of $\dfrac{dy}{dx}+\dfrac{y\cos x+\sin y+y}{\sin x+x\cos y+x}=0$ is

A. $y\sin x+(\sin y+y)x=c$

B. $y\sin x+(\sin x+x)=c$

C. $y=\sin x+y\sin y+c$

D. None of these

24. If number of left cosets of H in G are n and the number of right cosets of H in G are m then

A. $m=n$ B. $m \geq n$

C. $m \leq n$ D. None of these

25. **Statement A :** Every isomorphic image to a cyclic group is cyclic

Statement B: Every homomorphic image of a cyclic group is cyclic

A. Both A and B are true

B. Both A and B are false

C. A is true only

D. B is true only

26. The ring of complex number $c=\{x+iy \mid x, y$ are real number $\hat{i}=\sqrt{-1}\}$ is

A. Not an integral domain
B. An integral domain
C. Ordered set
D. None of these

27. If $T_1(z)=\dfrac{z+2}{z+3}$ and $T_2(z)=\dfrac{z}{z+1}$ $T_1T_2(z)$ is...

A. $z+2$ B. $\dfrac{2}{2z+5}$
C. $\dfrac{z+2}{2z+5}$ D. None of these

28. If $a<0<b$, then $\int_a^b \frac{|x|}{x}dx=?$

A. $(a-b)$ B. $(a+b)$
C. $(b-a)$ D. $-(a+b)$

29. If $\{0\}$ is a zero subspace of inner product space v then $\{0\}'$ is equal to

A. $\{0\}$ B. v
C. ϕ D. None of these

30. A linear transfrom T from V into W is non singular if

A. Null space of T is $\{0\}$
B. Null space of T = $\{a\} a \neq 0$
C. Null space of T is not $\{0\}$
D. None of these.

31. If w_1 and w_2 are subspaces of finite dimensional space then $w_1 = w_2$ if

A. $w_1 = w_2$ B. $w_1 \neq w_2$
C. $w_1 \subset w_2$ D. $w_1 \supset w_2$

32. For given $x_1+2x_2+x_3=4$ and $2x_1+x_2+5x_3=5$ one basic solution is

A. (2, 1) B. (5, 6)
C. (2, 2) D. None of these

33. Set $A \subset E^n$ is strictly bounded if for $r>0$, every $\bar{a} \in A-$

A. $|\bar{a}| \leq r$ B. $|\bar{a}| \geq r$
C. $|\bar{a}| = r$ D. $|\bar{a}| < r$

34. For given $\bar{c}=(6,7,8), z=9$ the negative closed half plane is the set

A. $6x_1 + 7x_2 + 8x_3 \geq 9$
B. $6x_1 + 7x_2 + 8x_3 \leq 9$
C. $6x_1 + 7x_2 + 8x_3 = 9$
D. None of these

35. Given the hyperplane $\bar{c}\,\bar{x}=z$ in E^n $(c_2 \neq 0)$ then

A. Vector $\bar{c}$ is normal to the hyperplane
B. Vector $\bar{c}$ is not normal to the hyperplane
C. Vector $\bar{c}$ is unit vector
D. None of these

36. Given $\begin{pmatrix}1 & 2 & 1\\ 2 & 1 & 5\end{pmatrix}\begin{pmatrix}x_1\\ x_2\\ x_3\end{pmatrix}=\begin{pmatrix}4\\ 5\end{pmatrix}$ the maximum possible basic solution is

A. 3 B. 4
C. 2 D. 6

37. A function F is Riemann integrable on L if

A. Only $\int_a^{-b} fdx$ exist
B. Only $\int_{-a}^{b} fdx$
C. $\int_a^{-b} fdx \neq \int_a^b fdx$
D. $\int_a^{-b} fdx = \int_a^b fdx$

38. If f differentiable on $[a,b]$ and $f'(x) \neq 0$ for all $x \in (a,b)$. Then for all $x \in (a,b)$ $f(x)$ is

A. Either increasing or decreasing function
B. Neither increasing nor decreasing
C. A constant function
D. None of these

39. If X_1 and X_2 are two independent Poisson variates with means 1 and 2 respectively. Then the probability that $X_1+X_2 \geq 4$ is:

A. $1-13e^{-3}$ B. $1-e^{-3}$
C. $13e^{-3}$ D. e^{-3}

40. If $G=\{1, \omega, \omega^2\}$, then there may be

A. 2 subgroups
B. 3 subgroups
C. Infinite subgroups
D. No subgroup

ANSWERS

1	2	3	4	5	6	7	8	9	10
B	A	B	A	A	A	A	C	A	C
11	12	13	14	15	16	17	18	19	20
B	C	A	A	B	D	A	C	C	D
21	22	23	24	25	26	27	28	29	30
B	B	A	A	A	B	C	B	A	B
31	32	33	34	35	36	37	38	39	40
A	A	D	B	A	A	D	A	A	A

Some Selected Explanatory Answers

7. Here $M_x(x) = 1 + \mu_1^1\, t + \mu_2^1\, \frac{t^2}{2!} + ...$

$= 1 + 2t + 2!\ 2^2 \frac{t^2}{2!}$

$= 3!\, 2^3 \frac{t^3}{3!} + ...$

$1 + 2t + (2t)^2 + (2t)^3 + ...$

$= (1 - 2t)^{-1}$

8. Here $\lambda = np$

$= 6400 \times \left(\frac{1}{4}\right)^3$

$p(x = x) = e^{-\lambda} \frac{\lambda x}{\lfloor x} = e^{-100} \frac{100x}{\lfloor x}$

9. $E[gx] = \int_0^\infty g(x) f(x) dx$

$= \int_0^\infty e^{3\times 14} e^{\sigma x} dx$

$= \int_0^\infty e^{-x/4} dx = 4$

10. $N(S) = 6 \times 6 = 36$

E = Double is

$\{(x, x) : x = 1.....6\}$

N (E) = 6

$P(E) = \frac{6}{36} = \frac{1}{6}$

17. $x°$ and $w°$ will be optimal if and only if w^{o^T} $(b - Ax_o) = 0$ and $x_0^1 \left(c^T - A^T w_o\right) = 0$ Since each term in the summation.

$w_o^T (b - Ax_0)$ is positive then

$w_1^o \left(bi - \sum_{t=1}^{n} a_{ij}\, x_1^{\ 0} \right) = 0$

$y = 1, 2 .... m.$

Similary

$x_1^o \left(bi - \sum_{t=1}^{m} a_n\, w_t - c_1 \right) = 0$

$j = 1, 2 ....n$

18. $EOQ = \sqrt{\frac{2DC_o}{ch}\left(\frac{p}{p-q}\right)}$

$= \sqrt{\frac{2 \times 10{,}000 \times 55}{4}\left(\frac{120}{120 - 40}\right)}$

$= 642.26$ value

19. Optimal total annual stocking cost is

$TC(Q) = \frac{Q}{2}\left(\frac{p-q}{p}\right)ch + \left(\frac{D}{Q}\right)C_o$

$= \frac{642.26}{2}\left(\frac{120 - 40}{120}\right)4 + \left(\frac{10{,}00}{642.26}\right)55$

= Rs. 856.8 + 856.35

= Rs. 1713.15 per year

27. $T_2\, T_1(z) = T_2\left(\frac{z+2}{z+3}\right)$

$= \frac{z+2}{z+3}$

$= \frac{2z+5}{z+3}$

$= \frac{z+2}{z+3} + 1$

39. $X_1 + X_2$ is a Poisson variate with mean $\lambda = 1 + 2 = 3$

$P(X < 4) = P(0) + P(1) + P(2) + P(3)$

$= e^{-\lambda}\left(1 + \lambda + \frac{\lambda^2}{2!} + \frac{\lambda^3}{3!}\right) = 13e^{-3}$

$\Rightarrow P(X \geq 4) = 1 - P(X < 4)$

$= 1 - 13e^{-3}$

CSIR-UGC (NET) JRF & LECTURESHIP EXAM

(PART-C)

MATHEMATICAL SCIENCES

25 PRACTICE SETS

SET–1

CSIR–UGC (NET) MATHEMATICAL SCIENCES

PART-C

1. Let T be the linear operator on C^3 defined by $T(x, y, z) = (2x + iy, y - 5iz, x + (1 - i) y + 3z)$, then $T^*(x, y, z)$ is given by

A. $(2x - z, ix - y + (1 + i)z, 5(iy + 3z)$

B. $(2x + z, ix + y + (1 - i)z, 5iy, + 3z)$

C. $(2x + z, -ix + y + (1 + i)z, 5iy + 3z)$

D. $(2x + z, x + iy + (1 + i)z, 5y + 3iz)$

2. Consider the matrix $M = \begin{bmatrix} a^2 & ab & ac \\ ab & b^2 & bc \\ ac & bc & c^2 \end{bmatrix}$, where a, b and c are non-zero real numbers. Then the matrix has

A. three non-zero real eigen values.

B. complex eigen values.

C. two non-zero eigen values.

D. only one non-zero eigen values.

3. Let M be the real 5×5 matrix having all of its entries equal to 1. Then

A. M is not diagonalizable

B. M is idempotent

C. M is nilpotent

D. the minimal polynomial and the characteristic polynomial of M are not equal

4. Let $M = \begin{bmatrix} 1 & 1 & 2 \\ 0 & 1 & 1 \\ 0 & 1 & 1 \end{bmatrix}$ and $\mathbf{U} = \{Mx^t : x \in R^3\}$.

Then orthonormal basis for V is

A. $\left\{(1,0,0)^t, \left(0, \frac{2}{\sqrt{5}}, \frac{1}{\sqrt{5}}\right)^t, \left(\frac{2}{\sqrt{6}}, \frac{1}{\sqrt{6}}, \frac{1}{\sqrt{6}}\right)^t\right\}$

B. $\left\{(1,0,0)^t, \left(0, \frac{1}{\sqrt{2}}, \frac{1}{\sqrt{2}}\right)^t\right\}$

C. $\left\{(1,0,0)^t, \left(\frac{1}{\sqrt{3}}, \frac{1}{\sqrt{3}}, \frac{1}{\sqrt{3}}\right)^t, \left(\frac{2}{\sqrt{6}}, \frac{1}{\sqrt{6}}, \frac{1}{\sqrt{6}}\right)^t\right\}$

D. $\{(1,0,0)^t, (0,0,1)^t\}$

5. If A and B are symmetric matrices of the same order, then which one of the following is **not** correct?

A. A + B is a symmetric matrix.

B. AB – BA is a symmetric matrix.

C. AB + BA is a symmetric matrix.

D. $A + A^T$ and $B + B^T$ are symmetric matrix.

6. Let S $\{(1, i, 0), (2i, 1, 1), (0, 1 + i, 1 - i)\}$ be a subset of the complex vector space $\mathbf{C}^3$ and $T = \{(1, 1, 1), (1, 1, 0), (1, 0, 0)\}$ be a subset of the real vector space $\mathbf{R}^3$. Which one of the following statement is correct?

A. S and T are both basis.

B. S a basis but T is not a basis.

C. S is not a basis but T is a basis.

D. Neither S nor T is a basis.

7. Let $P_2[x]$ be the vector space of all polynomials over **R** of degree less than or equal to 2. Let D be the differential operator on $P_2[x]$. Then matrix of D relative to the basis $\{x^2, 1, x\}$ is equal to

A. $\begin{bmatrix} 0 & 0 & 0 \\ 0 & 0 & 1 \\ 2 & 0 & 0 \end{bmatrix}$ B. $\begin{bmatrix} 0 & 0 & 0 \\ 2 & 0 & 0 \\ 0 & 0 & 1 \end{bmatrix}$

C. $\begin{bmatrix} 0 & 0 & 2 \\ 0 & 0 & 0 \\ 0 & 1 & 0 \end{bmatrix}$ D. $\begin{bmatrix} 0 & 0 & 0 \\ 0 & 0 & 2 \\ 0 & 1 & 0 \end{bmatrix}$

8. Consider the following assertions :

1. Rank (ST) = Rank S = Rank T
2. Rank (ST) = Rank S, if T is non-singular

3. Rank (ST) = Rank T, if T is non-singular where S, T : V → V are linear transformations of a finite dimensional vector space V. Which of these is/are correct?

A. only 1 B. only 2
C. 1 and 2 D. 2 and 3

9. The determinant of the matrix A =

$$\begin{bmatrix} r & q & s & t \\ -q & r & -t & s \\ -s & t & r & -q \\ -t & -s & q & r \end{bmatrix}$$ is equal to

A. $r^2 + q^2 + s^2 + t^2$
B. $(r^2 + q^2 + s^2 + t^2)^4$
C. $(r^2 + q^2 + s^2 + t^2)^2$
D. 0

10. The dimension of the vector space of all 3 × 3 real symmetric matrices is

A. 3 B. 9
C. 6 D. 4

11. Let M = $\begin{bmatrix} 1 & 3 & 3 \\ 0 & 4 & 5 \\ 0 & 0 & 9 \end{bmatrix}$. Then

A. M is diagonalizable but not M^2.
B. M^2 is diagonalizable but not M.
C. both M and M^2 are diagonalizable.
D. neither M nor M^2 is diagonalizable.

12. The minimal polynomial of the matrix

$$\begin{bmatrix} 3 & 3 & 0 \\ 3 & 3 & 0 \\ 0 & 0 & 6 \end{bmatrix}$$ is

A. $x(x - 1)(x - 6)$
B. $x(x - 3)$
C. $(x - 3)(x - 6)$
D. $x(x - 6)$

13. Let M be a $m \times n$ $(m < n)$ matrix with rank m. Then

A. For every b in R^m, MX = b has unique solution.
B. For every b in R^m, MX = b has a solution but it is not unique.
C. There exists $b \in R^m$ for which M$x = b$ has no solution.
D. None of the above.

14. Let M = $\begin{bmatrix} 1 & 1 & 0 \\ -1 & 1 & 2 \\ 2 & 2 & 0 \\ -1 & 0 & 1 \end{bmatrix}$. Then the rank of M is equal to

A. 3 B. 4
C. 2 D. 1

15. Let I = $\int \frac{f(z)}{(z-1)(z-2)} dz$, where $f(z) = \sin\frac{\pi z}{2} + \cos\frac{\pi z}{2}$ and c is the curve $|z| = 3$ oriented anticlockwise. Then the value of I is

A. $4\pi i$ B. 0
C. $-2\pi i$ D. $-4\pi i$

16. Which of the following is not the real part of an analytic function?

A. $x^2 - y^2$ B. $\frac{1}{1+x^2+y^2}$
C. $\cos x \cosh y$ D. $x+\frac{x}{x^2+y^2}$

17. The harmonic conjugate of $u(x, y) = x^2 - y^2 + xy$ is

A. $x^2 - y^2 - xy$ B. $x^2 + y^2 - xy$
C. $2xy+\frac{1}{2}(y^2-x^2)$ D. $\frac{1}{2}xy+2(y^2-x^2)$

18. The value of the integral $\frac{1}{2\pi i}\int \frac{ze^z}{(z-a)^3} dz$ over contour $|z - a| = r$ is

A. $e^a\left(1+\frac{a}{2}\right)$ B. $\frac{e^a}{2}(1+a)$
C. 0 D. ae^a

19. If $f(z) = u + iv$ and $u - v = e^x(\cos y - \sin y)$, then the value of $f(z)$ in terms of z is given by.

A. $e^z + c$ B. $ze^z + c$
C. $\frac{e^z}{z}+c$ D. $z^2e^z + c$

20. If $u = e^{-2xy} \sin(x^2 - y^2)$ is harmonic function, then its conjugate harmonic function v is
A. $e^{2xy} \cos(x^2 - y^2) + c$
B. $e^{-2xy} \cos(x^2 - y^2) + c$
C. $e^{-2xy} \cos(x^2 + y^2) + c$
D. $e^{2xy} \cos(x^2 + y^2) + c$

21. The function $f(z) = z^2$ maps the first quadrant onto
A. itself B. upper half plane
C. third quadrant D. right half plane

22. The sum of the all the residues of the function

$$\frac{z^3}{(z-1)(z-2)(z-3)}$$ is equal to

A. 6 B. –6
C. ∞ D. 0

23. Find the complex number z such that $|z| + z^2 = 0$
A. $z = 0, \pm i$ B. $z = \pm i$
C. $0, i$ D. $0, -i$

24. The greatest lower bound and least upper bound of $\left\{\frac{1}{2}, \frac{3}{4}, \ldots\ldots, \frac{2^n - 1}{2^n}, \ldots\ldots\right\}$ are

A. $\frac{1}{2}, \infty$ B. $0, \frac{1}{2}$

C. $\frac{1}{2}, 1$ D. $0, 1$

25. $S = \{a \in R$: 'a' is a recurring decimal no$\}$
$T = \{b \in R : b = \sqrt{p/q}$ for some distinct prime p and $q\}$ then
A. S is countable but T is not
B. T is countable but S is not
C. S and T both are countable set
D. S and T are u_n uncountable set

26. Let $f(x) = x - [x]$, $x > 0$ where $[x]$ denotes the integral part of x.
1. $f(x)$ is continuous for all integral values of x.
2. $f(x)$ is not differentiable for positive integral values of x.
3. $\lim_{x \to 2} f(x)$ does not exist.

Which of the above statements are correct?
A. 1 and 2 only B. 2 and 3 only
C. 1 and 3 only D. 1, 2 and 3

27. The maximum magnitude of the directional derivative for the surface $x^2 + xy + yz = 9$ at the point (1, 2, 3) is along the direction
A. $\hat{i} + \hat{j} + \hat{k}$ B. $2\hat{i} + 2\hat{j} + \hat{k}$
C. $\hat{i} + 2\hat{j} + 3\hat{k}$ D. $\hat{i} - 2\hat{j} + 3\hat{k}$

28. For the given sequence $\left\{(-1)^n\left(1 + \frac{1}{n}\right)\right\}$

Which one of the following statement is correct?
A. Limit superior = limit inferior
B. Neither limit superior nor limit inferior exist
C. Limit superior = 1 and limit inferior = –1
D. Limit superior = 1 and limit inferior = 0

29. Consider a mapping f from the set of natural numbers N to the set of integers z defined by

$$f(n) = \begin{cases} \frac{n-1}{2}, & \text{when } n \text{ is odd} \\ \frac{-n}{2}, & \text{when } n \text{ is even} \end{cases}$$

The $f : N \rightarrow Z$ is
A. one-one but not onto
B. onto but not one-one
C. both one-one and onto
D. neither one-one nor onto

30. Let $\langle u_n \rangle = \frac{u_{n+1} + v_{n-1}}{2}$ and $\langle v_n \rangle = \frac{u_{n-1} + 2v_{n-1}}{3}$ also $u_0 < v_0$ then select the correct statement
A. $\langle u_n \rangle$ is convergent if $\langle v_n \rangle$ is convergent and if $\langle u_n \rangle$ is convergent then $\langle v_n \rangle$ may or maynot be
B. $\langle u_n \rangle$ and $\langle v_n \rangle$ both are convergent and convergent to same limit
C. $\langle u_n \rangle$ and $\langle v_n \rangle$ both are convergent but convergent to different limit
D. $\langle u_n \rangle$ and $\langle v_n \rangle$ both are divergent

31. Consider the following statements:

1. A differentiable function is continuous
2. A continuous function is differentiable
3. A continuous function on a closed interval $[a, b]$ of finite length is uniformly continuous on $[a, b]$

Which of these statements are correct?

A. 1, 2 and 3 B. 2 and 3
C. 1 and 3 D. 1 and 2

32. The value of $\int_0^{\pi}\int_x^{\pi}\int_0^{2}\frac{\sin y}{y}\,dzdydx$ is

A. –2 B. 2
C. –4 D. 4

33. The directional derivative of $f(x, y, z) = x^2yz + 4xz^2$ at the point (1, –2, –1) in the direction of the vector $2i - j - 2k$

A. $\frac{13}{3}$ B. $\frac{27}{3}$
C. $\frac{37}{3}$ D. $\frac{47}{3}$

34. The set of limit points of the set $A = \left\{\frac{1}{p}+\frac{1}{q}; p,q \in N\right\}$ is

A. N
B. R
C. $\{0\}$ 0 $\left\{\frac{1}{q}: q \in N\right\}$
D. $\left\{\frac{1}{q}: q \in N\right\}$

35. If $f(x)$ is a real valued function such that $2f(x) + 3f(-x) = 15 - 4x$ for every $x \in R$, then $f(2)$ is

A. –15 B. 22
C. 11 D. None of these

36. Consider the following differential equations

1. $x^2\left(\frac{d^2y}{dx^2}\right)^6 + y^{-2/3}\sqrt{1+\left(\frac{d^3y}{dx^3}\right)^5} + \frac{d^2}{dx^2}\left\{\left(\frac{d^2y}{dx^2}\right)^{-2/3}\right\} = 0$

2. $\frac{dy}{dx} - 6x = \left(ay + bx\frac{dy}{dx}\right)^{-3/2}, \quad b \neq 0$

The sum of the order of the 1st differential equation and the degree of the second differential equation is

A. 6 B. 7
C. 8 D. 9

37. The largest Picard's interval in which solution of the Initial Value Problem $\frac{dy}{dx} = x^2 + y^2$, $y(0) = 0$ exists uniquely is

A. $|x| \le \frac{1}{\sqrt{2}}$ B. $|x| \le \frac{1}{\sqrt{3}}$
C. $|x| \le 5$ D. $|x| \le \frac{1}{\sqrt{7}}$

38. The general solution of the system of differential equations

$$y + \frac{dz}{dx} = 0, \quad \frac{dy}{dx} - z = 0 \text{ is given by}$$

A. $y = \alpha e^x + \beta e^{-x}$, $z = \alpha e^x - \beta e^{-x}$
B. $y = \alpha\cos x + \beta\sin x$, $z = \alpha\sin x - \beta\cos x$
C. $y = \alpha\sin x - \beta\cos x$, $z = \alpha\cos\alpha + \beta\sin x$
D. $y = \alpha e^x - \beta e^{-x}$, $z = \alpha e^x + \beta e^{-x}$.

39. The solution of the differential equation $(D^2 - 1)y = x^2\cos x$ is

A. $y = c_1e^x + c_2e^{-x} + \left(\frac{1}{2}\right)(1 - x^2)\cos x + x\sin x.$

B. $y = c_1e^x + c_2e^{-x} - \frac{1}{2}(x^2 - 1)\sin x + x^2\cos x.$

C. $y = c_1e^x + c_2e^{-x} + \left(\frac{1}{2}\right)(x^2 - 1)\cos x + x\sin x.$

D. $y = c_1e^x + c_2e^{-x} - \left(\frac{1}{2}\right)(1 - x^2)\sin x + x\cos x.$

40. Two linearly independent solutions of the differential equation $4\left(\frac{d^2y}{dx^2}\right) + 4\left(\frac{dy}{dx}\right) + 5y = 0$ are

A. $e^{-x/2}\cos x$ and $e^{-x/2}\sin x$.
B. $e^{x/2}\cos x$ and $e^{x/2}\sin x$.
C. $e^{x/2}\cos x$ and $e^{-x/2}\sin x$.
D. $e^{-x/2}\cos x$ and $e^{x/2}\sin x$.

41. Let $y = \psi(x)$ be a bounded solution of the equation $(1 - x^2) y'' - 2xy' + 30y = 0$. Then

A. $\int_{-1}^{1} x^3\psi(x)dx \neq 0$

B. $\int_{-1}^{1} (1+x^3+x^4)\psi(x)dx \neq 0$

C. $\int_{-1}^{1} x^5\psi(x)dx = 0$

D. $\int_{-1}^{1} x^{2m}\psi(x)dx = 0$ for all $n \in N$

42. Consider the following system of differential equations in $x(t)$, $y(t)$ and $z(t)$

$$\begin{bmatrix} x^1 \\ y^1 \\ z^1 \end{bmatrix} = \begin{bmatrix} 0 & 1 & 0 \\ 1 & 0 & 0 \\ 1 & 1 & 1 \end{bmatrix} \begin{bmatrix} x \\ y \\ z \end{bmatrix}.$$

Then there exists a choice of 3 linearly independent vectors u, v, w in R^3 such that vectors, forming a fundamental set of solutions of the above system are given by

A. $e^{-t}u$, $e^t v$, $te^t w$

B. $e^t u$, $te^t v$, $t^2e^t w$

C. $e^{-t}u$, $te^{-t}v$, $e^t w$

D. u, tv, $e^t w$

43. A particular integral of the differential equation $\frac{d^2 y}{dx^2} + a^2 y = \sin ax$ is

A. $\frac{1}{2a}\cos ax$ B. $-\frac{1}{2a}x\cos ax$

C. $\frac{1}{2a}x\cos 2ax$ D. $-\frac{1}{2a}x\cos 2ax.$

44. Consider the following statements:

The differential equation $\frac{2x}{y^3}dx + \frac{y^2 - 3x^2}{y^4}dy = 0$ is

1. Exact 2. Homogeneous 3. Linear

of these statements.

A. 1 and 2 are correct

B. 1 and 3 are correct

C. 2 and 3 are correct

D. All of the above less

45. The family of straight lines passing through the origin is represented by the differential equation

A. $ydx + xdy = 0$ B. $xdx + ydy = 0$

C. $xdy - ydx = 0$ D. $ydy - xdx = 0$

46. The differential equation of a family of circles having the radius r and centre on the x-axis is

A. $y^2\left[1+\left(\frac{dy}{dx}\right)^2\right] = r^2$

B. $x^2\left[1+\left(\frac{dy}{dx}\right)^2\right] = r^2$

C. $(x^2+y^2)\left[1+\left(\frac{dy}{dx}\right)^2\right] = r^2$

D. $r^2\left[1+\left(\frac{dy}{dx}\right)^2\right] = x^2$

47. The primitive of the differential equation $(D^2 - 2D + 5)^2 y = 0$, $\left(\text{where } D \equiv \frac{d}{dx}\right)$ is

A. $e^x\{(c_1 + c_2x)\cos 2x + (c_3 + c_4x)\sin 2x\}$

B. $e^{2x}\{(c_1 + c_2x)\cos x + (c_3 + c_4x)\sin x\}$

C. $(c_1e^x + c_2e^{2x})\cos x + (c_3e^x + c_4e^{2x})\sin x$

D. $e^x\{c_1\cos x + c_2\cos 2x + c_3\sin x + c_4\sin 2x\}$

48. Let $y_1(x)$ and $y_2(x)$ be solutions of $y''x^2 + y' + (\sin x)y = 0$, which satisfy the boundary conditions $y_1(0) = 0$, $y_1'(1) = 1$ and $y_2(0) = 1$, $y_2'(1) = 0$ respectively. Then

A. y_1 and y_2 do not have common zeros.

B. y_1 and y_2 have common zeros.

C. either y_1 or y_2 has a zero of order 2.

D. both y_1 and y_2 have zeros of order 2.

49. The differential equation $\frac{dy}{dx} + x\sin 2y = x^3\cos^2 y$ is reduced to linear form $\frac{dv}{dx} + Pv = Q$, where P and Q are function of x alone, by changing the variable as

A. $\sin y = v$ B. $\cos y = v$

C. $\tan y = v$ D. $\sin 2y = v$

50. The general solution of $\frac{d^4y}{dx^4}+y=0$ is

A. $y=\exp\left(\frac{x}{\sqrt{2}}\right)\left[c_1\cos\frac{x}{\sqrt{2}}+c_2\sin\frac{x}{\sqrt{2}}\right]$
$+\exp\left(-\frac{x}{\sqrt{2}}\right)\left[c_3\cos\frac{x}{\sqrt{2}}+c_4\sin\frac{x}{\sqrt{2}}\right]$

B. $y = c_1\sin x + c_2\cos x + c_3\sin hx + c_4\cos hx$

C. $y = c_1e^x + c_2e^{-x} + c_3e^{-2x} + c_4e^{2x}$

D. $y = c_1\sin 2x + c_2\cos 2x + c_3\sin h2x + c_4\cos h2x$

51. A particular integral of
$\frac{d^2y}{dx^2}-(a+b)\frac{dy}{dx}+aby=Q(x)$ is

A. $e^{ax}\int\left[e^{(a-b)x}\left(\int Qe^{bx}dx\right)\right]dx$

B. $e^{ax}\int\left[e^{(b-a)x}\left(\int Qe^{-bx}dx\right)\right]dx$

C. $e^{-ax}\int\left[e^{(b-a)x}\left(\int Qe^{bx}dx\right)dx\right]$

D. $e^{-ax}\int\left[e^{(b-a)x}\left(\int Qe^{-bx}dx\right)\right]dx$

52. What is the solution of differential equation
$\frac{dy}{dx}=\frac{y}{x}+\frac{\phi(y/x)}{\phi'(y/x)}$?

A. $\phi\left(\frac{y}{x}\right)=kx$ B. $\phi\left(\frac{y}{x}\right)=ky$

C. $x\phi\left(\frac{y}{x}\right)=k$ D. $y\phi\left(\frac{y}{x}\right)=k$

for some constant k.

53. If $m = 2$ is a double root and $m = -1$ is another root of the auxiliary equation of a homogeneous differential equation with constant coefficients. What is the differential equation?

A. $(D^3 + 3D^2 + 4)y = 0$

B. $(D^3 + 3D^2 - 4)y = 0$

C. $(D^3 - 3D^2 + 4)y = 0$

D. $(D^3 - 3D^2 - 4)y = 0$

54. The equation whose solution family is self orthogonal is

A. $p-\frac{1}{p}=p^2,\ p=\frac{dy}{dx}$

B. $(px-y)(yp+x)-\lambda p=0,\ p=\frac{dy}{dx}$

C. $(px-y)(x+yp)-\lambda p=0,\ p=\frac{dy}{dx}$

D. $(px+y)(x-yp)-\lambda p=0,\ p=\frac{dy}{dx}$

55. The general solution of differential equation $\frac{d^2y}{dx^2}+9y=\sin^3 x$, is

A. $y=A\cos(3x+B)+\frac{1}{24}\sin x-\sin 3x.$

B. $y=Ae^{3x}+Be^{-3x}+\frac{1}{32}\sin x+\frac{1}{2}\cos 3x.$

C. $y=A+Bxe^{3x}+2\sin x-\frac{5}{13}\sin 3x.$

D. $y=A\sin(3x+B)+\frac{3}{32}\sin x+\frac{x}{24}\cos 3x.$

56. For any two real number $a, b \in R$ defined a map $f_{ab} : R \to R$ such that $f_{ab}(x) = ax + b\ \forall\ x \in R$.

Then $G = \{f_{ab} : a \neq 0\}$ form a group under composition of map. Then the inverse of any element $f_{ab} \in G$ is

A. $f_{\frac{1}{a}\frac{b}{a}}$ B. $f_{\frac{1}{a}\frac{-b}{a}}$

C. $f_{\frac{1}{a}\frac{1}{b}}$ D. None of these

57. Let $K[x]$ be a polynomial ring over field K and $A=\langle x^2+1\rangle$ is an ideal of $K[x]$. Then consider the following statements :

1. A is maximal ideal of $K = Z_m$, where m is prime.
2. A is prime ideal of $K = Z_m$, where m is prime.

Codes :

A. Both 1 and 2 are correct

B. Neither 1 nor 2 correct

C. 1 is correct, 2 incorrect

D. 2 is correct, 1 incorrect

58. Consider the following statements:

I. A ring without unity can have maximal ideal which is not prime.

II. The number of maximal ideal in a commutative ring with unity always less than or equal to number of prime ideal.

Then

A. I is correct, II incorrect

B. II is correct, I incorrect

C. Both I and II are correct

D. Both I and II are incorrect

59. Suppose that $O(x) = 24$, then find a generator for $\langle x^{21} \rangle \ n \ \langle x^{10} \rangle$.

A. x^6, x^{18} B. x^5, x^7

C. x^3, x^2 D. x^9, x^{15}

60. Let G be a cyclic group of order 60. Then the number of subgroups of G is

A. 1 B. 2

C. 9 D. 12

ANSWERS

1	2	3	4	5	6	7	8	9	10
C	A	D	B	B	A	A	D	C	C
11	**12**	**13**	**14**	**15**	**16**	**17**	**18**	**19**	**20**
C	D	C	C	D	B	C	A	A	B
21	**22**	**23**	**24**	**25**	**26**	**27**	**28**	**29**	**30**
B	D	A	C	C	B	B	A	C	B
31	**32**	**33**	**34**	**35**	**36**	**37**	**38**	**39**	**40**
C	D	C	C	C	C	A	A	A	A
41	**42**	**43**	**44**	**45**	**46**	**47**	**48**	**49**	**50**
B	A	B	A	C	B	A	B	C	A
51	**52**	**53**	**54**	**55**	**56**	**57**	**58**	**59**	**60**
B	A	C	C	D	C	D	C	A	D

SOME SELECTED EXPLANATORY ANSWERS

1. The standard basis of C^3 are $\{e_1 = (1, 0, 0), e_2 = (0, 1, 0), e_3 = (0, 0, 1)\}$

Then $T(e_1) = (2, 0, 1)$;

$T(e_2) = (i, 1, (1 - i)$

$T(e_3) = (0, -5i, 3)$

Then $[T] = \begin{bmatrix} 2 & i & 0 \\ 0 & 1 & -5i \\ 1 & 1-i & 3 \end{bmatrix}$

As the standard basis are orthonormal. Hence the matrix of T* is the conjugate transpose of T.

i.e. $[T^*] = \begin{bmatrix} 2 & 0 & 1 \\ -i & 1 & 1+i \\ 0 & 5i & 3 \end{bmatrix}$

Accordingly, $T^*(x, y, z) = (2x + z, -ix + y + (1 + i)z, 5iy + 3z)$.

2. Given $M = \begin{bmatrix} a^2 & ab & ac \\ ab & b^2 & bc \\ ac & bc & c^2 \end{bmatrix}$

$\therefore |M| = \begin{vmatrix} a^2 & ab & ac \\ ab & b^2 & bc \\ ac & bc & c^2 \end{vmatrix} = abc \begin{vmatrix} a & b & c \\ a & b & c \\ a & b & c \end{vmatrix} = 0$

3. Given $M = \begin{bmatrix} 1 & 1 & 1 & 1 & 1 \\ 1 & 1 & 1 & 1 & 1 \\ 1 & 1 & 1 & 1 & 1 \\ 1 & 1 & 1 & 1 & 1 \\ 1 & 1 & 1 & 1 & 1 \end{bmatrix}$

the characteristic polynomial is $|M - \lambda I| = 0$

$$\text{i.e.}\quad \begin{vmatrix} 1-\lambda & 1 & 1 & 1 & 1 \\ 1 & 1-\lambda & 1 & 1 & 1 \\ 1 & 1 & 1-\lambda & 1 & 1 \\ 1 & 1 & 1 & 1-\lambda & 1 \\ 1 & 1 & 1 & 1 & 1-\lambda \end{vmatrix} = 0.$$

Apply $R_1 \to R_1 + R_2 + R_3 + R_4 + R_5$, we get

$$\begin{vmatrix} 5-\lambda & 5-\lambda & 5-\lambda & 5-\lambda & 5-\lambda \\ 1 & 1-\lambda & 1 & 1 & 1 \\ 1 & 1 & 1-\lambda & 1 & 1 \\ 1 & 1 & 1 & 1-\lambda & 1 \\ 1 & 1 & 1 & 1 & 1-\lambda \end{vmatrix} = 0$$

$$\text{or } (5-\lambda) \begin{vmatrix} 1 & 1 & 1 & 1 & 1 \\ 1 & 1-\lambda & 1 & 1 & 1 \\ 1 & 1 & 1-\lambda & 1 & 1 \\ 1 & 1 & 1 & 1-\lambda & 1 \\ 1 & 1 & 1 & 1 & 1-\lambda \end{vmatrix} = 0$$

Apply $R_2 \to R_2 - R_1$, $R_3 \to R_3 - R_1$, $R_4 \to R_4 - R_1$, $R_5 \to R_5 - R_1$, we get

$$(5-\lambda) \begin{vmatrix} 1 & 1 & 1 & 1 & 1 \\ 0 & -\lambda & 0 & 0 & 0 \\ 0 & 0 & -\lambda & 0 & 0 \\ 0 & 0 & 0 & -\lambda & 0 \\ 0 & 0 & 0 & 0 & -\lambda \end{vmatrix} = 0.$$

i.e. Characteristic polynomial is $(5 - \lambda)\lambda^4 = 0$.

For minimum polynomial we check

$$M(5-M) = \begin{bmatrix} 1 & 1 & 1 & 1 & 1 \\ 1 & 1 & 1 & 1 & 1 \\ 1 & 1 & 1 & 1 & 1 \\ 1 & 1 & 1 & 1 & 1 \\ 1 & 1 & 1 & 1 & 1 \end{bmatrix} \times$$

$$\begin{bmatrix} -4 & 1 & 1 & 1 & 1 \\ 1 & -4 & 1 & 1 & 1 \\ 1 & 1 & -4 & 1 & 1 \\ 1 & 1 & 1 & -4 & 1 \\ 1 & 1 & 1 & 1 & -4 \end{bmatrix} = \begin{bmatrix} 0 & 0 & 0 & 0 & 0 \\ 0 & 0 & 0 & 0 & 0 \\ 0 & 0 & 0 & 0 & 0 \\ 0 & 0 & 0 & 0 & 0 \\ 0 & 0 & 0 & 0 & 0 \end{bmatrix}$$

i.e. Minimum polynomial is $(5 - \lambda)\lambda$.

i.e. Minimum polynomial and characteristic polynomial of M are not equal.

4. The usual basis of $\mathbf{R}^3$ are $e_1 = (1, 0, 0)$, $e_2 = (0, 1, 0)$, $e_3 = (0, 0, 1)$.

$$\text{Hence } \mathbf{U} = \begin{bmatrix} 1 & 1 & 2 \\ 0 & 1 & 1 \\ 0 & 1 & 1 \end{bmatrix} \begin{bmatrix} 1 \\ 0 \\ 0 \end{bmatrix} = \begin{bmatrix} 1 \\ 0 \\ 0 \end{bmatrix} = v_1 \text{ (say)}$$

$$\begin{bmatrix} 1 & 1 & 2 \\ 0 & 1 & 1 \\ 0 & 1 & 1 \end{bmatrix} \begin{bmatrix} 0 \\ 1 \\ 0 \end{bmatrix} = \begin{bmatrix} 1 \\ 1 \\ 1 \end{bmatrix} = v_2 \text{ (say)}$$

$$\& \quad \begin{bmatrix} 1 & 1 & 2 \\ 0 & 1 & 1 \\ 0 & 1 & 1 \end{bmatrix} \begin{bmatrix} 0 \\ 0 \\ 1 \end{bmatrix} = \begin{bmatrix} 2 \\ 1 \\ 1 \end{bmatrix} = v_3 \text{ (say)}.$$

Now we find the orthonormal set u_1, u_2, u_3 with the set $\{v_1, v_2, v_3\}$.

Now let define $u_1 = \dfrac{v_1}{\|v_1\|} = (1, 0, 0)^t$

$$w_2 = v_2 - \langle v_2, u_1 \rangle u_1$$
$$= (1, 1, 1) - 1(1, 0, 0) = (0, 1, 1).$$

Now we normalize w_2 by defining

$$u_2 = \frac{w_2}{\|w_2\|} = \frac{(0,1,1)}{\sqrt{2}} = \left(0, \frac{1}{\sqrt{2}}, \frac{1}{\sqrt{2}}\right)$$

Now $\quad w_3 = v_3 - \langle v_3, u_2 \rangle u_2 - \langle v_3, u_1 \rangle u_1$

$$= (2,1,1> - \sqrt{2} \cdot \frac{1}{\sqrt{2}}(0,1,1) - 2(1,0,0)$$
$$= (2, 1, 1) - (0, 1, 1) - (2, 0, 0)$$
$$= (0, 0, 0)$$

i.e. the required orthonormal set are

$$\left\{(1,0,0)^t, \left(0, \frac{1}{\sqrt{2}}, \frac{1}{\sqrt{2}}\right)^t\right\}.$$

7. $D\{x^2\} = 2x = 0.x^2 + 0.1 + 2.x$

$D\{1\} = 0 = 0.x^2 + 0.1 + 0.x$

$D\{x\} = 1 = 0.x^2 + 1.1 + 0.x.$

Hence, matrix of T relative to $\{x^2, 1, x\}$ is

$$\begin{bmatrix} 0 & 0 & 0 \\ 0 & 0 & 1 \\ 2 & 0 & 0 \end{bmatrix}.$$

9. Since $A = \begin{bmatrix} r & q & s & t \\ -q & r & -t & s \\ -s & t & r & -q \\ -t & -s & q & r \end{bmatrix}$

hence

$$|A.A| = \begin{vmatrix} r & q & s & t \\ -q & r & -t & s \\ -s & t & r & -q \\ -t & -s & q & r \end{vmatrix} . \begin{vmatrix} r & q & s & t \\ -q & r & -t & s \\ -s & t & r & -q \\ -t & -s & q & r \end{vmatrix}$$

$$\Rightarrow |A|^2 = \begin{vmatrix} r^2+q^2+s^2+t^2 & 0 & 0 & 0 \\ 0 & r^2+s^2+q^2+t^2 & 0 & 0 \\ 0 & 0 & r^2+s^2+q^2+t^2 & 0 \\ 0 & 0 & 0 & r^2+s^2+q^2+t^2 \end{vmatrix}$$

$$= (r^2 + q^2 + s^2 + t^2)^4$$

$$\Rightarrow \quad |A| = (r^2 + q^2 + s^2 + t^2)^2.$$

10. As the basis of a 3 × 3 real symmetric matrices are

$$\left\{ \begin{pmatrix} 1 & 0 & 0 \\ 0 & 0 & 0 \\ 0 & 0 & 0 \end{pmatrix}, \begin{pmatrix} 0 & 0 & 0 \\ 0 & 1 & 0 \\ 0 & 0 & 0 \end{pmatrix}, \begin{pmatrix} 0 & 0 & 0 \\ 0 & 0 & 0 \\ 0 & 0 & 1 \end{pmatrix}, \right.$$

$$\left. \begin{pmatrix} 0 & 1 & 0 \\ 1 & 0 & 0 \\ 0 & 0 & 0 \end{pmatrix}, \begin{pmatrix} 0 & 0 & 0 \\ 0 & 0 & 1 \\ 0 & 1 & 0 \end{pmatrix}, \begin{pmatrix} 0 & 0 & 1 \\ 0 & 0 & 0 \\ 1 & 0 & 0 \end{pmatrix} \right\}$$

Which are six independent member and hence dimension of 3 × 3 real symmetric matrices is 6.

12. The given matrix is $\begin{bmatrix} 3 & 3 & 0 \\ 3 & 3 & 0 \\ 0 & 0 & 6 \end{bmatrix}$ = A (say)

the characteristic equation is

$$|A - xI| = 0 \quad \begin{vmatrix} 3-x & 3 & 0 \\ 3 & 3-x & 0 \\ 0 & 0 & 6-x \end{vmatrix} = 0$$

or, $(3 - x)^2 (6 - x) - 9(6 - x) = 0$

or, $(6 - x) (x^2 - 6x + 9 - 9) = 0$

or, $(6 - x) (x^2 - 6x) = -x(x - 6)^2$

i.e. minimal polynomial of A will either be $x(x - 6)$ or $x(x - 6)^2$.

Now if $f(x) = x(x - 6)$

$$\text{then} \quad f(A) = \begin{bmatrix} 3 & 3 & 0 \\ 3 & 3 & 0 \\ 0 & 0 & 6 \end{bmatrix} \begin{bmatrix} -3 & 3 & 0 \\ 3 & -3 & 0 \\ 0 & 0 & 0 \end{bmatrix}$$

$$= \begin{bmatrix} 0 & 0 & 0 \\ 0 & 0 & 0 \\ 0 & 0 & 0 \end{bmatrix}$$

i.e. $f(x) = x(x - 6)$ is the minimal polynomial.

14. The given matrix M is $M = \begin{bmatrix} 1 & 1 & 0 \\ -1 & 1 & 2 \\ 2 & 2 & 0 \\ -1 & 0 & 1 \end{bmatrix}$

Apply $R_2 \to R_2 + R_1$, $R_3 \to R_3 - 2R_1$ and $R_4 \to R_4 + R_1$ we get

$$\begin{bmatrix} 1 & 1 & 0 \\ 0 & 2 & 2 \\ 0 & 0 & 0 \\ 0 & 1 & 1 \end{bmatrix} \sim \begin{bmatrix} 1 & 1 & 0 \\ 0 & 2 & 2 \\ 0 & 0 & 0 \\ 0 & 0 & 0 \end{bmatrix}$$

i.e. rank (M) = 2.

$$R_4 \to R_4 - \frac{1}{2} R_2.$$

15. Given, $I = \int \frac{f(z)}{(z-1)(z-2)} dz$

$$= \int \frac{f(z)}{(z-2)} dz - \int \frac{f(z)}{(z-1)} dz$$

using Cauchy integral formula,
we get $I = 2\pi i\, f(2) - 2\pi i\, f(1)$

$$= 2\pi i \left[\sin \pi + \cos \pi - \sin \frac{\pi}{2} - \cos \frac{\pi}{2} \right]$$

$$= -4\pi i.$$

16. From the given choice

if $u = x^2 - y^2$ then $\nabla^2 u = 2 - 2 = 0$

i.e. u satisfies Laplace equation.

i.e. u is harmonic hence u is real part of an analytic function.

If $u = \frac{1}{1+x^2+y^2}$ then $\frac{\partial u}{\partial x} = \frac{-2x}{\left(1+x^2+y^2\right)^2}$

and $\frac{\partial^2 u}{\partial x^2} = -2\left[\frac{1}{\left(1+x^2+y^2\right)^2} + \frac{-4x^2}{\left(1+x^2+y^2\right)^3}\right]$

$$= -2\frac{\left(1+y^2-3x^2\right)}{\left(1+x^2+y^2\right)^3}$$

Similarly, $\frac{\partial^2 u}{\partial y^2} = -2\frac{\left(1+x^2-3y^2\right)}{\left(1+x^2+y^2\right)^3}$

Clearly $\frac{\partial^2 u}{\partial x^2} + \frac{\partial^2 u}{\partial y^2} \neq 0$ *i.e.* correct choice is (B).

17. $u(x, y) = x^2 - y^2 + xy,$

let, v be the harmonic conjugate of u.

Then, $dv = v_x dx + v_y dy$

$$= -u_y dx + u_x dy$$

$$= (2y - x)dx + (2x + y)dy$$

$$= 2xy + \frac{1}{2}\left(y^2 - x^2\right).$$

18. The given integral $I = \frac{1}{2\pi i}\int_{|z-a|=r} \frac{ze^z}{(z-a)^3}dz$

Using Cauchy integral formula

$$I = \frac{1}{2\pi i}\cdot\frac{2\pi i}{2!}f''(z)\Big|_{z=a}$$

where $f(z) = ze^z$

$$= \frac{1}{2}\left[(2+z)e^z\right]_{z=a}$$

$$= \left(\frac{a}{2}+1\right)e^a$$

19. We have $u - v = e^x(\cos y - \sin y)$

then, $\frac{\partial u}{\partial x} - \frac{\partial v}{\partial x} = e^x(\cos y - \sin y)$ ...(1)

and $\frac{\partial u}{\partial y} - \frac{\partial v}{\partial y} = e^x(-\sin y - \cos y)$

$$= -e^x(\sin y + \cos y)$$

or, $-\frac{\partial v}{\partial x} - \frac{\partial u}{\partial x} = -e^x(\sin y + \cos y)$

by Cauchy-Riemann equation

or, $\frac{\partial v}{\partial x} + \frac{\partial u}{\partial x} = e^x(\sin y + \cos y)$ ...(2)

from eqn. (1) and (2), we get

$$\frac{\partial u}{\partial x} = e^x \cos y = \phi_1(x, y)$$

and $\frac{\partial v}{\partial x} = e^x \sin y = \phi_2(x, y)$

Now, $f'(z) = \frac{\partial u}{\partial x} + \frac{i\partial v}{\partial x} = \phi_1(z,0) + i\phi_2(z,0)$

$\therefore$ $f(z) =$

$$\int\left[\phi_1(z,0) + i\phi_2(z,0)\right]dz + c$$

$$= \int\left(e^z\cos 0 + ie^z\sin 0\right)dz$$

$$= \int e^z dz + c = e^z + c.$$

27. The maximum magnitude of the directional derivative is along the direction of del operator.

Now the given function is

$$f = x^2 + xy + yz - 9$$

$$\nabla f = (2x+y)\hat{i} + (x+z)\hat{j} + 9\hat{k}.$$

Now, $\nabla f|_{(1,2,3)} = 4\hat{i} + 4\hat{j} + 2\hat{k}$

$$= 2(2\hat{i} + 2\hat{j} + \hat{k}).$$

32. The given integral is $\int_0^\pi\int_x^\pi\int_0^2 \frac{\sin y}{y}dz\,dy\,dx$

changing the order of integral for x and y, we get

$$\int_{z=0}^{2} dz \int_{y=0}^{\pi}\int_{x=0}^{y} \frac{\sin y}{y}dx\,dy = \int_{z=0}^{2} dz \int_{y=0}^{\pi} \frac{\sin y}{y}x\Big|_0^y dy$$

$$= \int_{z=0}^{2} dz \int_{y=0}^{\pi} \frac{\sin y}{y}(y-0)dy = 2\int_{y=0}^{\pi}\sin y\,dy$$

$$= 2[-\cos y]_0^\pi = 2(1 + 1) = 4.$$

33. The given scalar function is
$f(x, y, z) = x^2yz + 4xz^2$.

Hence $\nabla f = (2xyz + 4z^2)\hat{i} + (xz^2)\hat{j} + (x^2y + 8xz)\hat{k}$

i.e. $\nabla f|_{(1,-2,-1)} = (2.1.2 + 4)\hat{i} + (1.1)\hat{j} + (-2 - 8)\hat{k}$
$= 8\hat{i} + \hat{j} - 10\hat{k}.$

Hence, also unit vector along the prescribed direction

$$\hat{n} = \frac{2\hat{i} - \hat{j} - 2\hat{k}}{\sqrt{4+1+4}} = \frac{2\hat{i} - \hat{j} - 2\hat{k}}{3}.$$

Hence, directional derivative along the required direction

$$\nabla f \cdot \hat{n}|_{(1,-2,-1)} = (8\hat{i} + \hat{j} - 10\hat{k}) \cdot \frac{(2\hat{i} - \hat{j} - 2\hat{k})}{3}$$

$$= \frac{16+1+20}{3} = \frac{37}{3}.$$

35. The given functional relation is
$2f(x) + 3f(-x) = 15 - 4x$ ...(1)
put $x = -x$ in the above relation, we get
$2f(-x) + 3f(x) = 15 + 4x$ ...(2)
Apply (1) × 2 – (2) × 3, we get
$4f(x) - 9f(x) = 30 - 8x - 45 - 12x$
i.e. $f(x) = 4x + 3$
hence $f(2) = 4.2 + 3 = 8 + 3 = 11.$

39. The given differential equation is
$(D^2 - 1) = x^2 \cos x.$
The auxiliary equation is $D^2 - 1 = 0$
or $D = \pm 1.$
Hence the complementary function is given by
$y = c_1e^x + c_2e^{-x}.$
The particular integral is given by,

$$y = \frac{1}{(D^2-1)}(x^2\cos x) = \frac{1}{D^2-1}\text{Re}\{x^2e^{ix}\}$$

$$= \text{Re}\left\{e^{ix} \cdot \frac{1}{(D+i)^2-1}x^2\right\}$$

$$= \text{Re}\left\{e^{ix}\frac{1}{(D^2+2iD-2)}x^2\right\}$$

$$= \text{Re}\left\{e^{ix}\frac{1}{-2\left[1-\frac{(D^2+2iD)}{2}\right]}x^2\right\}$$

$$= \text{Re}\left\{\frac{-e^{ix}}{2}\left(1-\frac{(D^2+2iD)}{2}\right)^{-1}x^2\right\}$$

$$= \text{Re}\left\{\frac{-e^{ix}}{2}\left(1+\frac{(D^2+2iD)}{2}-D^2\right)x^2\right\}$$

$$= \text{Re}\left\{\frac{-e^{ix}}{2}\left[x^2-1+2ix\right]\right\}$$

$$= \frac{1}{2}(1-x^2)\cos x + x\sin x.$$

40. The given differential equation is

$$4\left(\frac{d^2y}{dx^2}\right)+4\frac{dy}{dx}+5y = 0.$$

The auxiliary equation is given by,
$4m^2 + 4m + 5 = 0$

$$\Rightarrow \quad m = \frac{-4\pm\sqrt{16-80}}{8}$$

$$= \frac{-4\pm 8i}{8} = \frac{-1}{2}\pm i.$$

Hence, the required solution is given by,
$y = c_1e^{-x/2}\cos x + c_2e^{-x/2}\sin x.$

55. The given differential equation is

$$\frac{d^2y}{dx^2}+9y = \sin^3 x.$$

The complementary function is given by
$y = C_1 \cos 3x + C_2 \sin 3x$
& the particular integral

$$y = \frac{1}{D^2+9}\sin^3 x = \frac{1}{D^2+9}\frac{(3\sin x-\sin 3x)}{4}$$

$$= \frac{3}{4}\cdot\frac{1}{(D^2+9)}\sin x - \frac{1}{4}\cdot\frac{\sin 3x}{D^2+9}$$

$$= \frac{3}{4}\cdot\frac{\sin x}{8}+\frac{x\cos 3x}{4.6}$$

$$= \frac{3}{32}\sin x+\frac{x}{24}\cos 3x$$

i.e. $y = C_1\cos 3x + C_2\sin 3x + \frac{3}{32}\sin x + \frac{x}{24}\cos 3x$

$= A\sin(3x + B) + \frac{3}{32}\sin x + \frac{x}{24}\cos 3x.$

SET–2

CSIR–UGC (NET) MATHEMATICAL SCIENCES

PART-C

1. The Lagrangian L of a simple pendulum of string length l which is deflected through an angle θ from rest position is given by

A. $L = \frac{1}{2}ml^2\dot{\theta}^2 - mgl(1-\cos\theta)$

B. $L = \frac{1}{2}ml^2\dot{\theta}^2 + mgl(1-\cos\theta)$

C. $L = ml^2\dot{\theta}^2 + mgl(1+\cos\theta)$

D. $L = \frac{1}{2}ml^2\dot{\theta}^2 - mgl(1-\sin\theta)$

2. The middle points of the opposite sides of a jointed quadrilateral are connected by light rods of length l, l'. If T, T′ be the tensions in these rods, then which of the following relation is true?

A. $Tl + T'l' = 0$

B. $\frac{T}{l'} + \frac{T'}{l} = 0$

C. $\frac{T}{l} + \frac{T'}{l'} = 0$

D. None of these

3. Introducing the new co-ordinate $Q = q\sin wt$ in the Lagrangian.

$$L = \frac{m}{2}(\dot{q}^2\sin^2 wt + \dot{q}qw\sin 2wt + q^2w^2)$$

the Hamiltonian H equals. (p is the conjugate momentum)

A. $\frac{m}{2}\left(\frac{p^2}{m^2} - Q^2w^2\right)$

B. $\frac{m}{2}\left(\frac{p^2}{m^2} + Q^2w^2\right)$

C. $\frac{m}{2}\left(\frac{p^2}{m^2} - Q^2w^2 + 2w^2Q\,\text{cosec}\,wt\right)$

D. $\frac{m}{2}\left(\frac{p^2}{m^2} + Q^2w^2 - 2w^2Q\,\text{cosec}\,wt\right)$

4. Let $q_1, q_2, \ldots\ldots, q_n$ be the generalized co-ordinates and $\dot{q}_1, \dot{q}_2, \ldots\ldots, \dot{q}_n$ be the generalized velocities in a conservative force field. If under a transformation ϕ, the new co-ordinate system has the generalized co-ordinates $Q_1, Q_2, \ldots\ldots, Q_n$ and velocities $\dot{Q}_1, \dot{Q}_2, \ldots\ldots, \dot{Q}_n$. Then the equation $\frac{\partial L}{\partial q_K} = \frac{d}{dt}\left(\frac{\partial L}{\partial \dot{Q}_K}\right)$ takes the form.

A. $\frac{\partial L}{\partial Q_K} = \phi\frac{d}{dt}\left(\frac{\partial L}{\partial \dot{Q}_K}\right)$

B. $\phi\frac{\partial L}{\partial Q_K} = \frac{d}{dt}\left(\frac{\partial L}{\partial \dot{Q}_K}\right)$

C. $\frac{\partial L}{\partial Q_K} = -\phi\frac{d}{dt}\left(\frac{\partial L}{\partial \dot{Q}_K}\right)$

D. $\frac{\partial L}{\partial Q_K} = \frac{d}{dt}\left(\frac{\partial L}{\partial \dot{Q}_K}\right)$

5. Consider a planet of mass m orbiting around the sun under the inverse square law of attraction $\frac{\mu m}{r^2}, \mu>0$. If the position of the planet at time t is given by the polar co-ordinates (r, θ), then the Lagrangian L of the system is given by

A. $\frac{1}{2}m(\dot{r}^2 + r^2\dot{\theta}^2) - \frac{\mu m}{r}$

B. $\frac{1}{2}m(\dot{r}^2 + r^2\dot{\theta}^2) + \frac{\mu m}{r}$

C. $\frac{1}{2}m(\dot{r}^2 + \dot{\theta}^2) + \frac{\mu m}{r}$

D. $\frac{1}{2}m(\dot{r}^2 + \dot{\theta}^2) - \frac{\mu m}{r}$

6. Let Q = {(x, y) in $\mathbf{R}^2$ | $x \geq 0, y \geq 0$} be the first quadrant in R^2 with usual topology. Then Q is closed because

A. It is compact
B. It does not contain all its limit points
C. Its complement is open
D. It is connected

7. Let norms $||x||_1 = \sum_{i=1}^{n} |\xi_i|$ and $||x||_2 = \left(\sum_{i=1}^{n} |\xi_i|^2\right)^{1/2}$ induce topologies τ_1 and τ_2 and R^n, the n-dimensional Euclidean space, then

A. τ_1 is weaker than τ_2
B. τ_1 is stronger than τ_2
C. τ_1 is equivalent to τ_2
D. τ_1 and τ_2 are incomparable

8. Three houses are available in a locality. Three persons apply for the houses. Each applies for one house without consulting others. The probability that all the three apply for the same house is

A. $\frac{2}{9}$ B. $\frac{1}{9}$
C. $\frac{8}{9}$ D. $\frac{7}{9}$

9. The event A, B, C are mutually exclusive events such that $P(A) = \frac{3x+1}{3}$ $P(B) = \frac{1-x}{4}$ and $P(C) = \frac{1-2x}{2}$, the set of possible values of x are in the interval

A. $\left[\frac{1}{3}, \frac{1}{2}\right]$ B. $\left[\frac{1}{3}, \frac{2}{3}\right]$
C. $\left[\frac{1}{3}, \frac{13}{3}\right]$ D. [0, 1]

10. The probabilities that a student passes in Mathematics, Physics and Chemistry are m, p and c respectively. Of these subjects, the student has a 75% chance of passing in at least one, a 50% chance of passing in at least two and 40% chance of passing in exactly two. Which of the following relations are true?

A. $p + m + c = \frac{19}{20}$ B. $p + m + c = \frac{27}{20}$
C. $pmc = \frac{1}{10}$ D. $pmc = \frac{1}{4}$

11. If for the three events A, B and C, P(exactly one of the events A or B occurs) = P(exactly one of the events B or C occurs) = P(exactly one of the events C or A occurs) = p and P(all the three events occur simultaneously) = p^2, where, $0 < p < \frac{1}{2}$, then the probability of at least one of the three events A, B and C occurring is

A. $\frac{3p+2p^2}{2}$ B. $\frac{p+p^2}{4}$
C. $\frac{p+p^2}{2}$ D. $\frac{3p+2p^2}{4}$

12. The probability that at least one of the events A and B occur is 0.6. If A and B occur simultaneously with probability 0.2, then $P(\bar{A})+P(\bar{B})$ is

A. 0.4 B. 0.8
C. 1.2 D. 1.4

13. A Barber shop has space to accomodate only 5 customers. He can serve only one person at a time. If a customer comes to his shop and find it full. He goes to the next shop. Customers arrive in poisson fashion with rate 10 per hour and the barber service time is negative exponential with an average of 3 minutes per customer, the probability that the space of barber shop is full is

A. $\frac{1}{63}$ B. $\frac{32}{63}$
C. $\frac{11}{31}$ D. None of these

14. Let, X_1 and X_2 be independent random variables with respective moment generating functions

$M_1(t) = \left(\frac{3}{4}+\frac{1}{4}e^t\right)^3$ and $M_2(t) = \left(e^{2(e^t-1)}\right)$

$-\infty < t < \infty$.

Then the values of $P(X_1 + X_2 = 1)$ is

A. $\frac{81}{64}e^{-2}$ B. $\frac{27}{64}e^{-2}$

C. $\frac{11}{64}e^{-2}$ D. $\frac{27}{64}e^{-2}$

15. Let, X_1, X_2, ... X_6 be independent random variable such that $P(X_i = -1) = P(X_i = 1) = \frac{1}{2}$, $i = 1, 2, ... 6$.

Then, $P\left[\sum_{i=1}^{6} X_i = 4\right]$ is

A. $\frac{3}{32}$ B. $\frac{3}{4}$

C. $\frac{3}{64}$ D. $\frac{3}{16}$

16. If $f(x, y, z) = 8(1-x)(1-y)(1-z)$ where $0 < x, y, z < 1$ is the joint probability distribution function of X, Y, Z then

$\frac{P(X>Y)}{P(X>Y>Z)}$ is equal to

A. 1 B. 2

C. 3 D. 4

17. What is the probability that both people in a couple will have the SAME blood type if matings are random with respect to blood type, *i.e.* one partner blood type does not influence the blood type of other partner.

A. about 0.21 B. about 0.16

C. about 0.002 D. about 0.38

18. Choose the statement that is not correct

A. If primal problem have m constraints in n variables, then its dual will have n constraints in m variables.

B. In order that dual to an LPP may be written, it is necessary that it has at least as many constraints as the number of variables.

C. The optimal values of dual variables are obtained from $z_j - c_j$ values (index number) from slack/surplus variables, in the optimum solution table of the primal.

D. If the optimal solution to an LPP exists then the objective function values of both the primal and its dual must be equal consider the LPP.

19. Consider the LPP

Min $z = 3x_1 - 2x_2$

subject to $2x_1 - 3x_2 \geq 6$; $3x_1 + 2x_2 \geq 6$

$x_1, x_2 \geq 0$

then the LPP has

A. Unique optimal solution but unbounded feasible region

B. Unbounded optimal solution as well as unbounded feasible region

C. Alternative optimal solution with bounded feasible region

D. None of the above

20. Using the Hungarian method, the optimal value of the assignment problem whose cost matrix is given by

5	23	14	8
10	25	1	23
35	16	15	12
16	23	11	7

is

A. 29 B. 52

C. 26 D. 44

21. Which of the following is a correct statement?

A. If the primal problem is in its standard form, dual variables will be non-negatives.

B. Dual simplex method always leads to generate basic feasible solution.

C. Dual simplex method is applicable to an LPP, if initial basic feasible solution is not optimum.

D. If the number of primal variables is very small and the number of constraints is very large, then it is more efficient to solve the dual rather than the primal problem.

22. The number of basic feasible solution of the LPP.

$$2x_1 + 3x_2 - x_3 + 4x_4 = 8,$$
$$x_1 - 2x_2 + 6x_3 - 7x_4 = -3,$$
$$x_1, x_2, x_3, x_4 \geq 0$$

with respect to objective function

Max $z = 2x_1 + 3x_2 + 4x_3 + 7x_4$

A. 2 B. 3

C. 4 D. 6

23. In the above problem, the value of z for the optimal solution

A. 25.4 B. 27.2

C. 28.9 D. 30.4

24. In which situation the variational problem $\int_{t_1}^{t_2} F(t, y, y')\,dt$, $y(t_1) = y_1$, $y(t_2) = y_2$ becomes meaning less.

A. When $F(t, y, y') = M(t, y)\,dt + N(t, y)\,dy$.

B. When Euler's equation reduces into identity.

C. When $y(t)$ exists but it not satisfies the given boundary conditions.

D. All of the above

25. The Euler's equation to find the extremal of the functional $\int_D (y'^2 + z''^2)\,dx$

A. $\frac{\partial F}{\partial y} - \frac{d}{dx}\left(\frac{\partial F}{\partial y'}\right) = 0$; $\frac{\partial F}{\partial z} - \frac{d}{dx}\left(\frac{\partial F}{\partial z'}\right) = 0$

B. $\frac{\partial F}{\partial y} - \frac{d}{dz}\left(\frac{\partial F}{\partial y'}\right) = 0$

C. $\frac{\partial F}{\partial y} - \frac{d}{dz}\left(\frac{\partial F}{\partial y'}\right) + \frac{d^2}{dx^2}\left(\frac{\partial F}{\partial y''}\right) = 0$;

$\frac{\partial F}{\partial z} - \frac{d}{dx}\left(\frac{\partial F}{\partial z'}\right) + \frac{d^2}{dx^2}\left(\frac{\partial F}{\partial z''}\right) = 0$

D. $\frac{\partial F}{\partial z} - \frac{d}{dx}\left(\frac{\partial F}{\partial z'}\right) + \frac{d^2}{dx^2}\left(\frac{\partial F}{\partial z''}\right) = 0$

26. The total number of *injective functions* from a set having m elements to a set having n elements where $m > n$, is equal to

A. 0 B. $\frac{n!}{n-m!}$

C. $\frac{m!}{m-n!}$ D. n^m

27. The exact nbd of $a + b$, $a - b$, ab is $|x-a| < \frac{1}{2}$, $|y-b| < \frac{1}{3}$ and $a = 2$, $b = 3$ is given by

A. $2 < xy - ab < \frac{7}{3}$

B. $-2 < xy - ab < \frac{7}{3}$

C. $3 < xy - ab < \frac{7}{3}$

D. None of these

28. If the sequence $< a_n >$ and $< b_n >$ tend to a and b respectively the sequence $< c_n >$, when $c_n = \frac{1}{n}(a_1 b_n + a_2 b_{n-1} + a_3 b_{n-2} + \ldots + a_n b_1)$ tends to

A. a B. b

C. $\frac{a}{b}$ D. ab

29. A simplex in n-dimension is a convex polyhedron having exactly

A. $(n - 1)$ vertices B. n vertices

C. $(n + 1)$ vertices D. n sides

30. Let **U** be the vector space of all 2 × 2 matrices over the field **R** of real number and B = $\begin{bmatrix} 1 & 2 \\ 0 & 3 \end{bmatrix}$. If T : V → V is a linear transformation defined by T(A) = AB – BA, then what is the dimension of the Kernel of T?

A. 1 B. 2

C. 3 D. 4

31. Let $\sum_{-\infty}^{\infty} a_n z^n$ be the Laurent series expansion of the function $f(z) = \frac{1}{(z+1)(z+2)}$, $1 < |z| < 3$, then which one of the following is correct?

A. $b_{-2} = \frac{1}{2}, b_0 = \frac{1}{6}, b_2 = \frac{1}{54}$

B. $b_{-2} = -\frac{1}{2}, b_0 = -\frac{1}{6}, b_2 = -\frac{1}{54}$

C. $b_{-2} = \frac{-1}{2}, b_0 = \frac{1}{6}, b_2 = \frac{1}{54}$

D. $b_{-2} = \frac{1}{2}, b_0 = \frac{1}{6}, b_2 = -\frac{1}{54}$

32. The equation $\tan z = z$ has
A. only real roots
B. purely imaginary roots
C. complex roots with non-zero real part
D. No roots

33. The orthogonal trajectories of the parabolas $y^2 = 4a(x + a)$, a being the parameter, are the curves given by
A. $y^2 = 4b(x + b)$, b being a parameter
B. $y = 4b(x + b)$, b being a parameter
C. $y^2 = 4bx$, b being a parameter
D. $x^2 = 4by$, b being a parameter

34. $\lim_{n\to\infty}\left[(n+1)\int_0^1 x^n \log(1+x)dx\right]$
A. 0 B. log 2
C. log 3 D. ∞

35. Consider the following permutations on {1, 2, 3, 4, 5, 6};

$$\sigma = \begin{pmatrix} 1 & 2 & 3 & 4 & 5 & 6 \\ 3 & 1 & 4 & 5 & 6 & 2 \end{pmatrix}$$

$$\tau = \begin{pmatrix} 1 & 2 & 3 & 4 & 5 & 6 \\ 2 & 4 & 1 & 3 & 6 & 5 \end{pmatrix}$$

$$\mu = \begin{pmatrix} 1 & 2 & 3 & 4 & 5 & 6 \\ 5 & 2 & 4 & 3 & 1 & 6 \end{pmatrix}$$

which of the above is/are correct?
1. $\sigma^6 = \tau^3$ 2. $\mu^2 = \sigma^6$

Select the correct answer using the code given below:
A. 1 only B. 2 only
C. Both 1 and 2 D. Neither 1 nor 2

36. $f(x) = x^2 \sin\frac{1}{x}$ if $x > 0$
$= 0$ if $x < 0$
then is [0, 1]
A. $f(x)$ is of bounded variation and $f'(x)$ exists
B. $f(x)$ is of bounded variation anf $f'\left(\frac{1}{2}\right)$ does not exists
C. $f(x)$ is not of bounded variation and $f(x)$ is continuous
D. $f(x)$ is discontinuous at $x = \frac{2}{\pi}$

37. With the help of two basic feasible solution of an L.P.P. we can generate how many non basic feasible solutions?
A. Finite B. Infinite
C. Exactly one D. Zero

38. Given a non-trivial normed linear space, the nontriviality of tis dual space is assured by
A. the Hahn-Banach Theorem
B. the Principle of Uniform Boundedness
C. the Open Mapping Theorem
D. the Closed Graph Theorem

39. The harmonic conjugate of $u(x, y) = y^3 - 3x^2y$ is
A. $-y^3 + 3x^2y + c$ B. $y^3 - 3xy^2 + c$
C. $x^3 - 3x^2y + c$ D. $x^3 - 3xy^2 + c$

40. The minimum value of $\frac{(x+1)(x+4)}{(x-1)(x-4)}$ is
A. $-\frac{1}{3}$ B. $-\frac{1}{6}$
C. $-\frac{1}{9}$ D. $-\frac{1}{12}$

41. PDE of second order in canonical forms $Rr + Ss + Tt + f(x, y, z, p, q) = 0$ then $S^2 - 4RT > 0$ represent
A. Hyperbolic B. Parabolic
C. Elliptic D. Straight line

42. If the minimax value is equal to maximini value, then corresponding pure strategies are called optimal strategies and the game is said to have
A. Critical point B. Constant point
C. Saddle point D. None

43. Consider the basis $S = \{v_1, v_2, v_3\}$ for $\mathbf{R}^3$ where $v_1 = (1, 1, 1)$, $v_2 = (1, 1, 0)$, $v_3 = (1, 0, 0)$ and let $T : R^3 \to R^2$ be a linear transformation such that $T(v_1) = (1, 0)$, $T(v_2) = (2, -1)$, $T(v_3) = (4, 3)$. Then $T(2, -3, 5)$ is
A. (–1, 5) B. (3, 4)
C. (0, 0) D. (9, 23)

44. If $f(x)$ is real valued function defined on $[0, \infty]$ such that $f(0) = 0$ and $f''(x) > 0$ for all x, then the function $h(x) = \frac{f(x)}{x}$ is

A. increasing in [0, ∞]
B. decreasing in [0, 1]
C. increasing in [0, 1 and decreasing in [1, ∞]
D. decreasing in [0, 1] and increasing in [1, ∞]

45. Let u be a harmonic function in the interior of a rectangle $0 \le x \le a$, $0 \le y \le b$ in the xy plane, satisfying Laplace equation $\frac{\partial^2 u}{\partial x^2}+\frac{\partial^2 u}{\partial y^2}=0$ with $u(0, y) = 0$, $u(a, y)$, $u(x, b) = 0$ and $u(x, 0) = f(x)$. Then u can be written as $u(x, y) = \Sigma u_n(x, y)$ where $u_n(x, y)$ is

A. $F_n \cos\left(\frac{n\pi x}{a}\right)\cos h\left\{\frac{n\pi(b-y)}{a}\right\}$

B. $F\cos\left(\frac{n\pi y}{b}\right)\sin\left\{\frac{n\pi(b-x)}{a}\right\}$

C. $F_n \sin\left(\frac{n\pi x}{b}\right)\sin h\left\{\frac{n\pi(b-y)}{a}\right\}$

D. $F\sin\left(\frac{n\pi x}{a}\right)\cos h\left\{\frac{n\pi(b-y)}{a}\right\}$

46. Let $f(z)$ be an analytic function with a simple pole at $z = 1$ and a double pole at $z = 2$ with residue 1 and –2 respectively. Further if $f(0) = 0$, $f(3)=\frac{3}{4}$ and f is bounded as $z \to \infty$, then $f(z)$ must be

A. $z(z-3)-\frac{1}{4}+\frac{1}{z-1}-\frac{2}{z-1}+\frac{1}{(z-2)^2}$

B. $-\frac{1}{4}+\frac{1}{z-1}-\frac{2}{z-2}+\frac{1}{(z-2)^2}$

C. $\frac{1}{z-1}-\frac{2}{z-2}+\frac{5}{(z-2)^2}$

D. $\frac{15}{4}+\frac{1}{z-1}+\frac{2}{z-2}-\frac{7}{(z-2)^2}$

47. Let X be the space of polynomials in one variable

For $p \in X$, $p(t) = a_0 + a_1 t + \ldots\ldots + a_n t^n$, let

$\|p\| = \text{sub}\ \{1p(t) : 0 \le t \le 1\}$,

$\|p\|_1 = |a_0| + |a_1| + \ldots\ldots + |a_n|$.

Then

A. X is complete with $\|\cdot\|$
B. X is complete with $\|\cdot\|$, .
C. X cannot be normal so as to make it complete
D. None of the above

48. The characteristic of the equation

$$x^2\left(\frac{\partial^2 z}{\partial x^2}\right)-y^2\left(\frac{\partial^2 z}{\partial y^2}\right)=0 \text{ are}$$

A. $xy, \frac{x}{y}$ B. $x + y, x - y$
C. $\frac{x}{y}, \frac{y}{x}$ D. $xy, x^2 y^2$

49. What is the limit of the sequence $\{a_n\}_{n\ge1}$ where $a_n=\frac{n!}{n^n}$?

A. 0 B. 1
C. ∞ D. $\frac{1}{\ln 2}$

50. General solution of homogeneous part of

$$x\frac{dy}{dx}-y=(x-1)\left\{\frac{d^2y}{dx^2}-x+1\right\}$$

A. $c_1x + c_2x^2$ B. $c_1x + c_2e^x$
C. $c_1e^x + c_2x^2$ D. $c_1x + c_2e^{-x}$

51. Which one is a group? If V is a set of all vectors.

A. (V, +)
B. (V – {0}, +) where + stands for vector addition operation
C. (V, ×) where × stands for vector cross product
D. (V, ×) where '×' stands for scalar product

52. Sequencing probability may be complicated by the following given conditions in number

A. 5 B. 9
C. 7 D. 10

53. Let S and T be two linear operators on $\mathbf{R}^3$ defined by

$S(x, y, z) = (x, x + y, x - y - z)$

$T(x, y, z) = (x + 2z, y - z, x + y + z)$.

Then

A. S is invertible but not T
B. T is invertible but not S
C. both S and T are invertible
D. neither S nor T is invertible

54. What is the value of $\lim_{x\to\infty} xe^{-x^2} \cdot \int_0^x e^{t^2}\, dt$?

A. 0 B. $\frac{1}{2}$

C. $\frac{1}{e+1}$ D. ∞

55. Let $f_n(x) = \frac{x^n}{1+x}$ and $g_n(x) = \frac{x^n}{1+nx}$ for $x \in [0, 1]$ and $x \in N$. Then on the interval [0, 1]

A. both $\{f_n\}$ and $\{g_n\}$ converge uniformly
B. neither $\{f_n\}$ nor $\{g_n\}$ converge uniformly
C. $\{f_n\}$ converges uniformly but $\{g_n\}$ does not converge uniformly
D. $\{g_n\}$ converges uniformly but $\{f_n\}$ does not converge uniformly

56. In Inventory which of the following is correct?

A. With increases in the carrying cost, the optimum order quantity also increases.
B. Total ordering cost = total holding cost.
C. An increase is the set up cost per production run leads to a decrease in the economic lot size.
D. For economic log size, the total set-up cost need not be equal to the total holding cost.

57. Which statement is true

A. $P(A) = 0 \Rightarrow A = \phi$
B. $P(A \cap B) = P(A)\ P(B) \Rightarrow A$ and B are independent
C. $P(A) + P(B) \leq P(A \cup B) \geq P(A \cap B)$
D. If A and B are mutually exclusive then $P\left(\frac{A}{B}\right) = \frac{P(A)}{1-P(B)}$

58. Let M be $m \times n$ $(m < n)$ matrix with rank m, then

A. for every b in R^m, $M_x = b$ has unique solution
B. for every b is R^m, $M_n = b$ has solution but it is not unique.
C. there exists $b \in R^m$ for which $M_n = b$ has no solution.
D. None of the above

59. Let $f(x, y) = \frac{x^3 - y^3}{x^2 + y^2}$ when (x, y) ¹ $(0, 0)$

$= 0$ when $(x, y) = (0, 0)$

Then the function is

A. continuous at the origin
B. discontinuous at the origin
C. continuous but not differentiable at (0, 0)
D. None of these

60. Which one of the following statements is correct?

A. There is no vector space of dimension 1.
B. Any three vectors of a vector space of dimension 3 are linearly independent.
C. There is one and only one basis of a vector space of finite dimension.
D. If a non-zero vector space V is generated by a finite set S, then V can be generated by a linearly independent subset of S.

ANSWERS

1	2	3	4	5	6	7	8	9	10
A	C	A	D	B	A	C	B	A	B
11	12	13	14	15	16	17	18	19	20
A	C	A	A	A	C	D	B	C	A
21	22	23	24	25	26	27	28	29	30
D	C	C	D	C	A	B	D	C	B

31	32	33	34	35	36	37	38	39	40
C	A	B	B	B	A	A	A	D	A
41	**42**	**43**	**44**	**45**	**46**	**47**	**48**	**49**	**50**
A	C	D	A	C	B	B	A	A	B
51	**52**	**53**	**54**	**55**	**56**	**57**	**58**	**59**	**60**
A	C	A	B	A	B	D	B	C	D

SOME SELECTED EXPLANATORY ANSWERS

1. With reference to figure 2, the angle θ between rest position and deflected position is chosen as generalized co-ordinate.

If the string is of length l, then kinetic energy is

$$T = \frac{1}{2}mv^2 = \frac{1}{2}m(l\dot{\theta})^2$$
$$= \frac{1}{2}ml^2\dot{\theta}^2$$

O, θ, l, C, B, A

where m is the mass of the bob.

In coming from position B to A, the mass has fallen freely through a vertical distance CA. Thus potential energy is

$$V = mg(OA - OC) = mg(1 - l\cos\theta)$$
$$= mgl\ (1 - \cos\theta)$$

where the reference level or zero level of potential energy has been taken at a distance l below the point of suspension.

Thus Lagrangian is L = T – V

$$= \frac{1}{2}ml^2\dot{\theta}^2 - mgl(1-\cos\theta).$$

3. $L = \frac{m}{2}(\dot{q}^2\sin^2 wt + \dot{q}qw\sin 2wt + q^2w^2)$

$$Q = q\ \sin wt$$

$$\therefore \quad \dot{Q} = \dot{q}\sin wt + qw\cos wt$$

Substituting for q and $\dot{q}$ in terms of Q and $\dot{Q}$, we get

$$L = \frac{m}{2}\left[\dot{Q}^2 - w^2Q^2\right]$$

But $\quad H = \frac{\partial L}{\partial \dot{Q}}\dot{Q} - L = \frac{m}{2}\left[\dot{Q}^2 - w^2Q^2\right]$

Further $\quad P = \frac{\partial L}{\partial \dot{Q}} = m\dot{Q}$

$$\therefore \quad H = \frac{m}{2}\left[\frac{P^2}{m^2} - w^2Q^2\right].$$

20. The given assignment cost matrix is

5	23	14	8
10	25	1	23
35	16	15	12
16	23	11	7

Apply the Hungarian method (*i.e.* substracting the minimum cost of each row to the other element of the same row)

then

0	18	9	3
9	24	0	22
23	4	3	0
9	16	4	0

As the second column does not any zero, apply the Hungarian rule for second column, we get

~~0~~	14	9	3
9	20	~~0~~	22
23	~~0~~	3	0
9	12	4	~~0~~

i.e. Hence the optimal cost

= 5 + 1 + 16 + 7 = 29.

30. Let $\quad A = \begin{bmatrix} x & y \\ z & t \end{bmatrix}$ where $x, y, z, t \in R$.

then $T(A) = \begin{bmatrix} x & y \\ z & t \end{bmatrix}\begin{bmatrix} 1 & 2 \\ 0 & 3 \end{bmatrix} - \begin{bmatrix} 1 & 2 \\ 0 & 3 \end{bmatrix}\begin{bmatrix} x & y \\ z & t \end{bmatrix}$

$$= \begin{bmatrix} x & 2x+3y \\ z & 2z+3t \end{bmatrix} - \begin{bmatrix} x+2z & y+2t \\ 3z & 3t \end{bmatrix}$$

$$= \begin{bmatrix} -2z & 2x+2y-2t \\ -2z & -2z \end{bmatrix}$$

Now if $A \in \ker(T)$ then $\begin{bmatrix} -2z & 2x+2y-2t \\ -2z & -2z \end{bmatrix}$

$$= \begin{bmatrix} 0 & 0 \\ 0 & 0 \end{bmatrix}$$

hence $z = 0$ and $x + y - t = 0.$

i.e. dim of kernel of T = 2.

31. We have, $f(z) = \dfrac{1}{(z+1)(z+3)}$

Resolving into partial fractions, we get

$$f(z) = \frac{1}{2(z+1)} - \frac{1}{2(z+3)}.$$

Now, as the given region is $1 < |z| < 3$.

Then we have $\dfrac{1}{|z|} < 1$ and $\dfrac{|z|}{3} < 1$.

Now, $\dfrac{1}{2(z+1)} = \dfrac{1}{2z\left(1+\frac{1}{z}\right)} = \dfrac{1}{2z}\left(1+\dfrac{1}{z}\right)^{-1}$

$$= \frac{1}{2z}\left(1 - \frac{1}{z} + \frac{1}{z^2} - \frac{1}{z^3} + \ldots\right)$$

$$= \frac{1}{2z} - \frac{1}{2z^2} + \frac{1}{2z^3} - \ldots.$$

and $\dfrac{1}{2(z+3)} = \dfrac{1}{6\left(1+\frac{z}{3}\right)} = \dfrac{1}{6}\left(1+\dfrac{z}{3}\right)^{-1}$

$$= \frac{1}{6}\left(1 - \frac{z}{3} + \frac{z^2}{9} - \frac{z^3}{27} + \ldots.\right)$$

$$= \frac{1}{6} - \frac{1}{18}z + \frac{1}{54}z^2 - \frac{1}{162}z^3 + \ldots$$

Thus, the Laurent's series valid for the region $1 < |z| < 3$ is

$$f(z) = \ldots. + \frac{1}{2z^3} - \frac{1}{2z^2} + \frac{1}{2z} + \frac{1}{6} - \frac{1}{18}z + \frac{1}{54}z^2 - \frac{1}{162}z^3 + \ldots.$$

$$\Rightarrow \quad b_{-2} = -\frac{1}{2},\ b_0 = \frac{1}{6},\ b_2 = \frac{1}{54}.$$

35. The given permutation can be written as

$\sigma = (134562);\ \tau = (1243)\ (56);$

$\mu = (15)\ (34)$

then $\sigma^6 = (1)$ and $\mu^2 = (1)$ however

$\tau^2 = (1243)\ (56) \Rightarrow \tau^2 = (14)\ (23)$

also $\tau^3 = (14)\ (23)\ (1243)\ (56)$

$= (1342)\ (56)$

Clearly $\mu^2 = \sigma^6$.

Hence, B is correct answer.

36. $f(x) = x^2 \sin\dfrac{1}{x}$ if $x \neq 0, f(0) = 0$

Clearly, f is continuous on [0, 1] and

$$f'(x) = 2x\sin\left(\frac{1}{x}\right) - \cos\left(\frac{1}{x}\right), \text{ if } x \neq 0$$

$$f'(0) = \lim_{x\to 0} \frac{x^2\sin(1/x) - 0}{x} = 0$$

Also

$|f'(x)| \leq 3$, for all $x \in [0, 1]$

Thus f' exists and bounded on [0, 1] the function f is of bounded variation on [0, 1]

40. The given expression is

$$\frac{(x+1)(x+4)}{(x-1)(x-4)} = y \text{ (let)}$$

Then $x^2 + 5x + 4 = y(x^2 - 5x + 4)$

or, $(y - 1)x^2 - 5x(y + 1) + 4(y - 1) = 0$

Now for real x discriminant of above equation should be greater than zero

i.e. $25(y + 1)^2 - 16(y - 1)^2 \geq 0$

$\Rightarrow \quad (9y + 1)\ (y + 9) \geq 0$

$\Rightarrow \quad y \leq -9$

or $\quad y \geq \dfrac{-1}{9}$

i.e. minimum value of the expression $y = \dfrac{-1}{9}$.

41. $S^2 - 4RT > 0$ (Hyperbolic)
$S^2 - 4RT = 0$ (Parabolic)
$S^2 - 4RT < 0$ (Elliptic)

43. Let $(2, -3, 5) = av_1 + bv_2 + cv_3$

or, $(2, -3, 5) = a(1, 1, 1) + b(1, 1, 0) + c(1, 0, 0)$

or $(2, -3, 5) = (a + b + c, a + b, a)$

or $a = 5, \quad a + b = -3$

$\Rightarrow$ $b = -8.$

$a + b + c = 2$

$\Rightarrow$ $c = 5.$

i.e. $(2, -3, 5) = 5.v_1 - 8.v_2 + 5.v_3$

hence $\tau(2, -3, 5) = 5T(v_1) - 8T(v_2) + 5T(v_3)$
$= 5(1, 0) - 8(2, -1) + 5(4, 3)$
$= (5, 0) - (16, -8) + (20, 15)$
$= (9, 23).$

44. $h(x) = \dfrac{f(x)}{x}, x > 0$

$h'(x) = \dfrac{x f'(x) - F(x)}{x^2}$

$h'(x) > 0$
$g(x) = x f'(x) - f(x)$
$g(0) = 0$
$\Rightarrow$ g is strictly increasing
$\Rightarrow$ $g(x) >> 0$
$\therefore$ $h'(x) >> 0$
$\Rightarrow$ h is strictly increasing in $(0, \infty)$

45. Using separation of variable method $u(x, y) = X(x).Y(y)$. *i.e.* $X''Y + Y''X = 0$ or $-\dfrac{X''}{X} = \dfrac{Y''}{Y}$

As x and y are independent, each side of above equation must be equal to same constant (say μ). Then it can also be shown that for non-trivial solution $\mu < 0$ *i.e.* $\mu = -\lambda^2$ (say).

Now $\dfrac{X''}{X} = -\lambda^2 \Rightarrow X(x) = A\cos\lambda x + B\sin\lambda x.$

Using boundary conditions, we get $A = 0$

and $\sin\lambda a = 0 \Rightarrow \lambda = \dfrac{n\pi}{a}.$

i.e. $X_n(x) = B_n \sin\left(\dfrac{n\pi_x}{a}\right)$

Also $-\dfrac{Y''}{Y} = -\lambda^2 \Rightarrow Y'' - \left(\dfrac{n^2\pi^2}{a^2}\right)Y = 0.$

$\Rightarrow$ $Y_n(y) = C_n e^{\frac{n\pi}{a}.y} + D_n e^{-\frac{n\pi}{a}.y}$

Using boundary condition $Y(b) = 0$

$\Rightarrow C_n e^{\frac{n\pi b}{a}} + D_n e^{-\frac{n\pi b}{a}} = 0$

$\Rightarrow$ $C_n = -D_n \dfrac{e^{-n\pi b/a}}{e^{n\pi b/a}}.$

Putting this value in $Y_n(y)$, we get

$$Y_n(y) = D_n \frac{\left\{e^{\frac{n\pi y}{a}}.e^{\frac{n\pi b}{a}} - e^{\frac{n\pi y}{a}}.e^{-\frac{n\pi b}{a}}\right\}}{e^{\frac{n\pi b}{a}}}$$

$$= D_n \frac{\left\{e^{\frac{n\pi(b-y)}{a}} e^{-\frac{n\pi(b-y)}{a}}\right\}}{e^{\frac{n\pi b}{a}}}$$

or $Y_n(y) = 2D_n e^{\frac{n\pi b}{a}} \sin h\left(\dfrac{n\pi(b-y)}{a}\right\}$

$\therefore$ $u_n(x, y) = X_n(x).Y_n(y)$

$= F_n \sin\left(\dfrac{n\pi x}{a}\right).\sin h\left(\dfrac{n\pi(b-y)}{a}\right).$

46. As $f(z)$ has a simple pole at $z = 1$ with residue 1. Therefore the principal part of $f(z)$ must contain term $\dfrac{1}{z-1}$.

Again $z = 2$ is a double pole with residue -2, so that the principal part of $f(z)$ must contain the term $-\dfrac{2}{z-2} + \dfrac{b}{(z-2)^2}$.

Hence, $f(z) + a_0 + a_1 z + a_2 z + a_2 z^2 + \ldots$

$$+ \frac{1}{z-1} - \frac{2}{z-2} + \frac{b}{(z-2)^2} \quad \ldots(i)$$

Given $z \to \infty$, $f(z)$ is bounded so that there are no singularities at $z \to \infty$. It means that $f\left(\frac{1}{t}\right)$ has no singularity at $t = 0$.

Hence, principal part of $f\left(\frac{1}{t}\right)$ should not contain any term.

$$f\left(\frac{1}{t}\right) = a_0 + \frac{a_1}{t} + \frac{a_2}{t^2} + \ldots \frac{t}{1-t} + \frac{(-2t)}{1-2t} + \frac{bt^2}{(1-t)^2}.$$

The principal part of $f\left(\frac{1}{t}\right)$ is $\frac{a_1}{t} + \frac{a_2}{t^2} + \ldots$

The above can be zero if $a_1 = 0$, $a_2 = 0$ ......

$$\therefore \quad f(z) = a_0 + \frac{1}{z-1} - \frac{2}{z-2} + \frac{b}{(z-2)^2} \quad \ldots(ii)$$

$$f(0) = a_0 - 1 + 1 + \frac{b}{4} = a_0 + \frac{b}{4} = 0 \quad \ldots(iii)$$

and $\quad f(3) = a_0 + \frac{1}{2} - 2 + b = a_0 + b - \frac{3}{2} = -\frac{3}{4}$

$$\Rightarrow \quad a_0 + b = \frac{3}{4} \quad \ldots(iv)$$

from (iii) & (iv), we get $a_0 = -\frac{1}{4}$, $b = 1$

$$\therefore \quad f(z) = -\frac{1}{4} + \frac{1}{z-1} - \frac{2}{z-2} + \frac{1}{(z-2)^2}.$$

50. The given differential equation is

$$x\frac{dy}{dx} - y = (x-1)\left\{\frac{d^2y}{dx^2} - x + 1\right\}$$

or, $$\frac{x}{x-1}\frac{dy}{dx} - \frac{y}{x-1} = \frac{d^2y}{dx^2} - (x-1)$$

or, $$\frac{d^2y}{dx^2} - \frac{x}{x-1}\frac{dy}{dx} + \frac{y}{x-1} = (x-1)$$

for homogeneous part, the right hand side should be equal to zero.

i.e. $$\frac{d^2y}{dx^2} - \frac{x}{x-1} + \frac{y}{x-1} = 0$$

clearly $\quad P = -\frac{x}{x-1}$, $\quad Q = \frac{1}{x-1}$

on comparison with standard equation $y_2 + Py_1 + Q = 0$.

Clearly $1 + P + Q = 1 - \frac{x}{x-1} + \frac{1}{x-1} = 0.$

& $\quad P + Qx = 0$

hence x and e^x are the complementary function.

i.e. $\quad y = C_1x + C_2e^x.$

53. For invertible, it should be one-to-one.

i.e. Kernel of such mapping only contains (0, 0, 0).

Now $\quad S(x, y, z) = (x, x + y, x - y - z)$

Now $\quad S(x, y, z) = (0, 0, 0)$

$\Rightarrow \quad (x, x + y, x - y - z) = (0, 0, 0)$

$\Rightarrow \quad x = 0, y = 0, z = 0$

i.e. S is one-one and hence invertible.

Again, $\quad T(x, y, z) = (x + 2z, y - z, x + y + z)$

Now $\quad T(x, y, z) = (0, 0, 0)$

$\Rightarrow \quad (x + 2z, y - z, x + y + z) = (0, 0, 0)$

$\Rightarrow \quad y = z, \; x = -2z$

i.e. $(-2, 1, 1) \in \text{Ker}(T)$ *i.e.* It is not invertible.

54. $$\lim_{x\to\infty} xe^{-x^2}\int_0^x e^{t^2}dt = \lim_{x\to\infty} \frac{\int_0^x e^{t^2}dt}{\frac{e^{x^2}}{x}} \left(\frac{\infty}{\infty}\text{case}\right)$$

Applying L' Hospital's rule.

$$= \frac{e^{x^2}}{\frac{xe^{x^2}(2x) - e^{x^2}}{x^2}} = \frac{1}{\frac{2x^2-1}{x^2}} = \frac{1}{2}.$$

58. $M_x = b$ where M be $m \times n$ order matrix rank $r = m$

$\therefore$ Rank, M = Rank [M, b] = m hence equations are consistent.

$(n - r)$ *i.e,* $(n - m) \Rightarrow$ Numher of linearly independent solution.

Now any linear combination of $(n - m)$ independent solution will also be a solution. Hence other are infinite number of solutions.

SET–3

CSIR–UGC (NET) MATHEMATICAL SCIENCES

PART-C

1. For a positive real number p, let $\{f_n : n = 1, 2, ...\}$ be a sequence of functions defined on $[0, 1]$ by

$$f_n(x) = \begin{cases} n^{p+1}x, & \text{if } 0 \le x \le \frac{1}{n} \\ \frac{1}{x^p}, & \text{if } \frac{1}{n} < x \le 1 \end{cases}$$

Let $f(x) = \lim_{n\to\infty} f_n(x)$, $x \in [0, 1]$. Then on $[0, 1]$,

A. f is Riemann integrable

B. The improper integral $\int_0^1 f(x)dx$ converges for $p \ge 1$

C. The improper integral $\int_0^1 f(x)dx$ converges for $p < 1$

D. f_n converges uniformly

2. Consider $Z[x]$, the set of polynomials with integer coefficients and $Q[\sqrt{2}]$, the set of all real numbers of the form $p+q\sqrt{2}$ with p, q rational numbers. Which of the following is correct about $Z[x]$ and $Q[\sqrt{2}]$?

A. Both are rings, but only one has unity.

B. Both are commutative rings, but only one is an integral domain.

C. Both are integral domains, but only one is a field.

D. Both are field.

3. The value of the integral $\oint \frac{\sin \pi z^2 + \cos \pi z^2}{(z-4)(z-2)} dz$ where c is the circle $|z| = 3$ traced anticlockwise is

A. $-2i\pi$ B. $i\pi$

C. $-i\pi$ D. $2i\pi$

4. If f be a homomorphism from $(Z, +)$ to $(R, \times)$, if $f(2) = \frac{1}{3}$ then value of $f(8)$ is

A. $\frac{1}{27}$ B. 27

C. 81 D. $\frac{1}{81}$

5. Let $(C, *)$ denote the multiplicative group of non-zero complex numbers. Let G_1 be the cyclic subgroup generated by $1 + i$ and G_2 be the cyclic subgroup generated by $(1+i)/\sqrt{2}$. Which one of the following is correct?

A. Both G_1 and G_2 are infinite group.

B. G_1 is finite, but G_2 is infinite group.

C. G_2 is finite, but G_1 is infinite group.

D. Both G_1 and G_2 are finite groups.

6. Let V be the space of 2×2 matrices over **R**, and let $M = \begin{pmatrix} 1 & 2 \\ 3 & 4 \end{pmatrix}$. Let T be the linear operator on V defined by T(A) = MA. Then the trace of T is equation.

A. 5 B. 10

C. 15 D. 20

7. All norms on a normed vector space X are equivalent provided

A. X is reflexive

B. X is complete

C. X is finite dimensional

D. X is an inner product space

8. Which of the following statement is TRUE in respect of the converges of the Newton-Raphson procedure?

A. It converges always under all circumstances.
B. It does not converge to a root where the second differential co-efficient changes sign.
C. It does not converge to a root where the second differential coefficient vanishes.
D. None of these

9. Let $f_n(x) = \dfrac{\sin x}{\sqrt{n}}$, $n = 1, 2, \ldots$ and $x \in [-1, 1]$ then as $n \to \infty$

A. $\{f_n(x)\}_{n=1}^{\infty}$ does not converge uniformly in [– 1, 1]

B. $\lim_{n\to\infty} \int_{-1}^{1} F_n(x)dx$ 1 0

C. $\{f_n^1(x)\}$ does not converge uniformly in [–1, 1]

D. $f_n(x)$, $n = 1, 2$, is not uniformly continuous in [–1, 1]

10. Which of the following is not true?

A. In the generalized queuing model, an arrival can be considered as births where as a departure can be looked upon as a death.
B. When the service rate increases with increase in queue length, the queueing situation is known as queueing problem with infinite number of service facilities.
C. The distribution of waiting time is not related to queue discipline used in selecting the waiting customers for service.
D. The probability of n customers arriving during a time interval t, according to Poisson law, is given by $P(n) = e^{-\lambda t}(\lambda t)^n/n!$

11. Let y_1 and y_2 be any two solution of a second-order linear non-homogeneous ordinary differential equation and c be an arbitrary constant. Then in general.

A. $y_1 + y_2$ is its solution, but cy_1 is not
B. cy_1 is its solution, but $y_1 + y_2$ is not
C. both $y_1 + y_2$ and cy_1 are its solution
D. neither $y_1 + y_2$ nor cy_1 is its solution

12. The characteristic curve of $2yu_x + (2x + y^2)u_y = 0$ passing through (0, 0) is

A. $y^2 = 2(e^x + x - 1)$
B. $y^2 = 2(e^x - x + 1)$
C. $y^2 = 2(e^x - x - 1)$
D. $y^2 = (e^x + x + 1)$

13. Consider the equation AX = B, where

$A = \begin{bmatrix} -1 & 2 \\ 2 & -1 \end{bmatrix}$, $B = \begin{bmatrix} 3 \\ 1 \end{bmatrix}$, then

A. the equation has no solution.
B. $\begin{pmatrix} 0 \\ 0 \end{pmatrix}$ is a solution of the equation.
C. there exists a non-zero unique solution.
D. the equation has infinitely many solutions.

14. Expression of the function $x^3 + x^2 - 5x + 2$ in factorial notation is

A. $x^{(3)} + 4x^{(2)} - 3x^{(1)} + 2$
B. $x^{(3)} - 4x^{(2)} - 3x^{(1)} + 2$
C. $x^{(3)} - 4x^{(2)} + 3x^{(1)} + 2$
D. $x^{(3)} + 4x^{(2)} - 3x^{(1)} - 2$

15. The Lagrangian L of a linear harmonic oscillator of natural length l and the spring constant K is defined as

A. $L = mx^2 + Kx^2$
B. $L = \frac{1}{2}mx^2 + \frac{1}{2}Kx^2$
C. $L = \frac{1}{2}mx^2 - \frac{1}{2}Kx^2$
D. None of these

16. Let $I = \dfrac{1}{2\pi i}\oint_c \dfrac{e^{zt}}{z^2(z^2+2z+2)}dz$ around the circle C|z| = 3. Then the value of I is

A. $\frac{t+1}{2} - \frac{1}{2}e^{-t}\cos t$
B. $\frac{t-1}{2} + \frac{1}{2}e^{t}\cos t$
C. $\frac{t-1}{2} + \frac{1}{2}e^{t}\sin t$
D. $\frac{t-1}{2} + \frac{1}{2}e^{-t}\cos t$

17. Let, $S = \{x\sqrt{2} : x \in Q\}$ then the derived set of S is

A. Empty set

B. Singleton set
C. Equivalent to the set of natural numbers
D. Uncountable set

18. The probability of a student getting 1st, 2nd and 3rd division in an examination are respectively $\frac{1}{10}$, $\frac{3}{5}$ and $\frac{1}{4}$. The probability, that a student fails in the examination is

A. $\frac{197}{200}$ B. $\frac{27}{100}$
C. $\frac{83}{100}$ D. $\frac{33}{200}$

19. If q_1 stands for the set of rational numbers except 1 and operation $*$ is defined as $a * b = a + b - ab$, then $(q_1, *)$ is a group verify it. Now for $a \in q_1$, a^{-1} is

A. $a - 1$ B. $a + 1$
C. $\frac{a}{a-1}$ D. $\frac{a}{a+1}$

20. A random variate X takes the value -1, 1, 3 and 5 with associated probabilities $\frac{1}{6}$, $\frac{1}{6}$, $\frac{1}{6}$ and $\frac{1}{2}$. Then $P(|X - 3| \geq 1)$ is less than

A. $\frac{8}{3}$ B. $\frac{4}{3}$
C. $\frac{13}{6}$ D. $\frac{16}{3}$

21. If the integrating factor of $(x^7y^2 + 3y)dx + (3x^8y - x)dy = 0$ is x^my^n, then

A. $m = -7, n = 1$ B. $m = 1, n = -7$
C. $m = n = 0$ D. $m = n = 1$

22. The following functions u are harmonic. Find the conjuate harmonic function v.
$u = e^{-2xy} \sin (x^2 - y^2)$

A. $v = -e^{-2xy} \cos (x^2 - y^2) + C$
B. $v = e^{-2xy} \cos (x^2 - y^2) + C$
C. $v = e^{+2xy} \cos (x^2 - y^2) + C$
D. $v = -e^{-2xy} \sin (x^2 - y^2) + C$

23. For $0 < \theta < \pi$, the matrix $\begin{bmatrix} \cos\theta & -\sin\theta \\ \sin\theta & \cos\theta \end{bmatrix}$

A. has no real eigenvalue
B. is orthogonal
C. is symmetric
D. is skew-symmetric

24. The first three terms in the power series for log $(1 + \sin x)$ are:

A. $x - \frac{1}{2}x^3 + \frac{1}{4}x^5$ B. $x - \frac{1}{2}x^2 + \frac{1}{3}x^4$
C. $-x + \frac{x^2}{2} - \frac{1}{6}x^3$ D. $x - \frac{x^2}{2} + \frac{1}{6}x^3$

25. The solution of $\frac{dy}{dx} + \frac{1}{x}\sin 2y = x^2 \cos^2 y$ is given by

A. $\tan y = \frac{x^3}{5}$ B. $\tan y = \frac{x^4}{5}$
C. $\tan y = x^3$ D. $\tan y = x^4$

26. The complete integral of the equation $p.q = 1$ is

A. $z = ax - \frac{y}{a} + b$ B. $z = ax + \frac{y}{a} + b$
C. $z = -ax + \frac{y}{a} + b$ D. None of these.

27. The greatest common divisor (*g.c.d.*) of $10 + 11i$ and $8 + i$ in $Z[i]$ is.

A. $8 + i$ B. $5 + i$
C. $3 + 2i$ D. $2 + i$

28. Let the linear transformations S and T : $R^3 \to R^3$ be defined by
$S(x, y, z) = (2x, 4x - y, 2x + 3y - z)$
$T(x, y, z) = (x \cos\theta - y \sin\theta, \sin\theta + y \cos\theta, z)$
where $0 < \theta < \frac{\pi}{2}$. Then

A. S is one-to-one but not T.
B. T is one-to-one but not S.
C. both S and T are one-to-one.
D. neither S nor T is one-to-one.

29. As a subset of [0, 1] equipped with the usual topology, the cantor set is

A. closed but not compact, nowhere dense and uncountable
B. not closed, dense and countable

C. closed, dense and uncountable

D. compact, nowhere dense and uncountable

30. Let X be the space of polynomials in one variable For P ∈ X, $P(t) = a_0 + a_1 t + ... a_n t^n$ let

$||P|| = \text{Sup}\{|P(t)| : 0 \le t \le 1\}$

$||P||_1 = |a_0| + |a_1| + ... + |a_n|$

then

A. X is complete with $||.||$

B. X is comlete with $||.||_1$

C. X connot be normed so as to make it complete.

D. None of the above

31. Which of the following is efficient tool for smooth functioning of O.R. problems

A. Calculator

B. Analog computer

C. Digital coumputer

D. Super computer

32. Consider the power series $\sum_{n=1}^{\infty} \frac{x^n}{\sqrt{n}}$ and $\sum_{n=1}^{\infty} \frac{x^n}{n}$.

Then

A. both converge on (–1, 1]

B. both converge on [–1, 1)

C. exactly one of them converges on (–1, 1]

D. none of them converges on [–1, 1]

33. Let I = $\int_c \frac{\cot(\pi z)}{(z-i)^2} dz$, where c is the contour $4x^2 + y^2 = 2$ (counter clockwise). Then I is equal to

A. 0

B. $-2pi$

C. $2\pi i\left[\frac{\pi}{\sin h^2\pi} - \frac{1}{\pi}\right]$

D. $-\frac{2\pi i^2}{\sin h^2\pi}$

34. Which one of the following statements is correct where $R[x]$ denotes the polynomial ring in one variable x over a ring R:

A. If R is a field then $R[x]$ is a field.

B. If R is an integral domain, then $R[x]$ is a field.

C. If R is a field, then $R[x]$ is an integral domain.

D. Every integral domain is a field.

35. If Mdx + Ndy = 0 is a differential equation and is $\frac{1}{M}\left(\frac{\partial N}{\partial x} - \frac{\partial M}{\partial y}\right)$ is a function of y alone, say $f(y)$ then integrating factor is

A. e^x

B. e^{x+y}

C. $e^{\int f(y)dy}$

D. None of the above

36. Let the optimal of an L.P.P. occur at two vertices x_1 and x_2, then it also occurs at $x = (1 - \lambda) x_1 + \lambda x_2$, $0 < \lambda < 1$ and

A. x is B.S.

B. x is a B.F.S.

C. x is not a B.S.

D. None of the above

37. What is the dimension of the subspace generated by the vectors (2, 1, 4, 3), (2, 1, 2, 0), (0, 0, 2, 3) and (4, 2, 6, 3) in V = $\mathbf{R}^4$?

A. 1

B. 2

C. 3

D. 4

38. The general solution of the differential equation

$$\frac{d^4y}{dx^4} + 2\frac{d^2y}{dx^2} + y = 0 \text{ is}$$

A. $y = (c_1 + c_2x) \sin x + (c_3 + c_4x) \cos x$

B. $y = c_1\sin x + c_2\cos x + x\sin x + x\cos x$

C. $y = c_1\sin x + c_2\cos x + c_3\tan x + c_4\cot x$

D. $y = c_1\sin x + c_2\cos x + c_3x + c_4$.

39. Which one of the following test does not give absolute convergence of a series?

A. Root test

B. Comparison test

C. Ratio test

D. Leibnitz test

40. Which of following iteration formula have the slowest rate of convergence?

A. Bisection method

B. Regula-Falsi method

C. Newton-Raphson method

D. Secant method

41. Which one is correct definition of ring.

A. (R, +, .) is a ring if (R_1) (R, +) is an abelian ring (R_2) (R, .) is groupoid (R_3) ∵ distributive over 't'.

B. (R, +, .) is a ring if (R_1) (R, +) is an abelian ring (R_2) (R, .) is semi group (R_3) '.' is left distributive but not right distributive over '+'.

C. (R_2, +, .) is a ring if (R_1) (R, +) is an abelian ring (R_2) (R, .) is semi group (R_3) '.' is distributive (left and right both).

D. None of these

42. If the integers m and n are chosen at random between 1 and 100, then the probability that the number of the form $7^m + 7^n$ is divisible by 5 equals

A. $\frac{1}{4}$ B. $\frac{1}{7}$

C. $\frac{1}{8}$ D. $\frac{1}{49}$

43. The work done in moving a particle in the force field $\bar{F} = 5x^2\hat{i}+(xz-y)\hat{j}+3z\hat{k}$ along the straight line joining (0, 0, 0) to (1, 1, 1) is

A. 0 B. 1

C. 2 D. 3

44. The number of solutions of the equation $z^2 = \bar{z}$ are

A. four B. three

C. two D. one

45. Let X and Y be normal linear spaces. Every linear map T : X → Y is continuous if

A. dim (X) < ∞ B. dim (Y) < ∞

C. dim (Y) = l D. X = l^2

46. Which statement is exact about the polynomial P(z), if all zeros of P(z) lie in a half plane then

A. zeros of the derivative also lie in the same half plane.

B. at least one zero lies in the same half plane.

C. at the most one zero lies in the same half plane

D. no zero lies in the same half-plane.

47. Three men are assigned to do three different jobs. From past records, the time each man take to do each job is known and is given below.

Men	Jobs		
	1	2	3
1	3	10	3
2	7	9	8
3	5	7	6

Assume each one is assigned to only one job and each job is assigned to only one man. Then the minimum time taken to complete the three jobs by three men is equal to :

A. 20 B. 16

C. 18 D. 17

48. The given Linear Programming Problem is

Min: $z = 5x_1 + 8x_2$

such that $x_1 + x_2 = 5$, $0 \le x_1 \le 4$, $0 \le x_2 > 2$

then its dual has.

A. No feasible solution

B. Unbounded solution

C. Unique optimal solution

D. Either A or B

49. The solution of the differential equation

$$y'' + (3i - 1)y' - 3iy = 0 \text{ is}$$

A. $y = c_1e^x + c_2e^{3ix}$ B. $y = c_1e^{-x} + c_2e^{3ix}$

C. $y = c_1e^{-x} + c_2e^{-3ix}$ D. $y = c_1e^{-x} + e^{-3ix}$

50. There are 8 players from which four teams each of two players are formed. What is the probability that two specific players are in one team?

A. $\frac{1}{4}$ B. $\frac{15}{28}$

C. $\frac{1}{8}$ D. $\frac{1}{7}$

51. Let H = $Z_2 \times Z_6$ and K = $Z_2 \times Z_4$, then

A. H is isomorphic to K since both are cyclic

B. H is isomorphic to K since 2 divides 6 and $g.c.d$ (3, 4) = 1

C. H is not isomorphic to K since K is cyclic whereas H is number.

D. H is not isomorphic to K since there is no homomorphism from H to K

52. The solution of the equation

$\frac{d^2y}{dx^2}+\frac{dy}{dx}-2y=0$ with $y(0) = 0$, $y'(0) = 3$ is

A. $e^x + e^{-2x}$ B. $e^x - e^{-2x}$

C. $e^x - e^{2x}$ D. $e^x + e^{2x}$

53. The complete integral of the partial differential equation $x^2p^2 + y^2q^2 = z^2$ where $p = \partial z/\partial x$ and $q = \partial z/\partial y$.

A. $z = cx^a y^b$
B. $z = c[ax + by]$
C. $z = \left[\dfrac{x^a}{y^b}\right] + xy$
D. $z = cxy$

54. Which of the following statements approves that (2z, +, ·) is not a PID.

1. 4z is a maximal ideal of 2z but not a prime ideal
2. 2z is without unity.
3. 2z has ideals which are not principal.

Codes :

A. 1 and 2
B. 1 and 3
C. 2 and 3
D. All of these

55. The singular solution of the differential equation $xyp^2 - (x^2 + y^2 + 1)p + xy = 0$, where $p \equiv \dfrac{dy}{dx}$.

A. $y = 0$
B. $y^2 = (x - 1)^2$
C. does not exist
D. None of these

56. The solution of integral equation

$$u(x) = \frac{5x}{6} + \frac{1}{2}\int_0^1 xt\,u(t)\,dt$$

by using initial approximation $u_0(x) = 0$ is

A. x^2
B. x
C. $\dfrac{5}{2}x$
D. $x + 2$

57. If $E(\theta) = \begin{bmatrix} \cos^2\theta & \cos\theta\sin\theta \\ \cos\theta\sin\theta & \sin^2\theta \end{bmatrix}$, θ and ϕ differ by an odd multiple of $\dfrac{\pi}{2}$, then E(θ) E(ϕ) is a

A. null matrix
B. unit matrix
C. diagonal matrix
D. None of these

58. $\lim_{x\to\pi/2} (1+\cos x)^{\tan x}$

A. e^{-1}
B. 0
C. 2
D. e

59. Z is a complex no. $\left|z + \dfrac{1}{z}\right| = a$. What is the greatest value of ½z½

A. $\left\{a + \sqrt{a^2 + 4}\right\}/2$
B. $\left\{a - \sqrt{a^2 + 4}\right\}/2$
C. $\left\{2a + \sqrt{a^2 + 4}\right\}/2$
D. $\left\{(a^2 + 4)/2\right\}$

60. Which one of the following statements is correct?

A. Abelian groups may have non-abelian subgroups.
B. Non-abelian groups may have abelian subgroups.
C. Cyclic groups may have non-cyclic subgroups.
D. Non-cyclic groups cannot have cyclic subgroups.

ANSWERS

1	2	3	4	5	6	7	8	9	10
C	C	C	D	C	B	D	B	C	D
11	12	13	14	15	16	17	18	19	20
A	C	C	A	C	D	D	B	C	D
21	22	23	24	25	26	27	28	29	30
A	A	B	D	C	B	C	A	C	B
31	32	33	34	35	36	37	38	39	40
B	A	C	C	C	B	B	A	D	A
41	42	43	44	45	46	47	48	49	50
C	A	D	B	B	A	D	C	D	D
51	52	53	54	55	56	57	58	59	60
C	B	A	A	B	A	A	A	A	B

SOME SELECTED EXPLANATORY ANSWERS

2. The ring of Polynomial is an integral domain but not a field.

3. $\oint_c \frac{\sin \pi z^2 + \cos \pi z^2}{(z-4)(z-2)} dz = \frac{1}{2}\int_c \frac{f(z)}{z-4}dz - \frac{1}{2}\int \frac{f(z)}{z-2}dz$

where $f(z) = \sin\pi z^2 + \cos\pi z^2$

1st integral is zero as it is analytic inside on c: $|z| = 3$.

$$\therefore \oint \frac{f(z)}{(z-4)(z-2)} dz = -\frac{1}{2}.2\pi i\, f(z)$$

$$= -\frac{1}{2}.2\pi i[\sin 4\pi + \cos 4\pi]$$

$$= -\pi i.$$

4. $\because f(2) = \frac{1}{3}$

$\therefore f(8) = f(2 + 2 + 2 + 2) = f(2) \cdot f(2) \cdot f(2) \cdot f(2)$

$$= \frac{1}{81}.$$

6. First we find the matrix representation of T. We choose the usual basis of V:

$$\left\{E_1 = \begin{pmatrix} 1 & 0 \\ 0 & 0 \end{pmatrix}, E_2 = \begin{pmatrix} 0 & 1 \\ 0 & 0 \end{pmatrix}, E_3 = \begin{pmatrix} 0 & 0 \\ 1 & 0 \end{pmatrix}, E_4 = \begin{pmatrix} 0 & 0 \\ 0 & 1 \end{pmatrix}\right\}$$

Then

$$T(E_1) = ME_1 = \begin{pmatrix} 1 & 2 \\ 3 & 4 \end{pmatrix}\begin{pmatrix} 1 & 0 \\ 0 & 0 \end{pmatrix} = \begin{pmatrix} 1 & 0 \\ 3 & 0 \end{pmatrix}$$

$$= 1.E_1 + 0.E_2 + 3.E_3 + 0.E_4$$

$$T(E_2) = ME_2 = \begin{pmatrix} 1 & 2 \\ 3 & 4 \end{pmatrix}\begin{pmatrix} 0 & 1 \\ 0 & 0 \end{pmatrix} = \begin{pmatrix} 0 & 1 \\ 0 & 3 \end{pmatrix}$$

$$= 0.E_1 + 1.E_2 + 0.E_3 + 3.E_4$$

$$T(E_3) = ME_3 = \begin{pmatrix} 1 & 2 \\ 3 & 4 \end{pmatrix}\begin{pmatrix} 0 & 0 \\ 1 & 0 \end{pmatrix} = \begin{pmatrix} 2 & 0 \\ 4 & 0 \end{pmatrix}$$

$$= 2.E_1 + 0.E_2 + 4.E_3 + 0.E_4$$

$$T(E_4) = ME_4 = \begin{pmatrix} 1 & 2 \\ 3 & 4 \end{pmatrix}\begin{pmatrix} 0 & 0 \\ 0 & 1 \end{pmatrix} = \begin{pmatrix} 0 & 2 \\ 0 & 4 \end{pmatrix}$$

$$= 0.E_1 + 2.E_2 + 0.E_3 + 4.E_4$$

Hence $[T]_E = \begin{bmatrix} 1 & 0 & 2 & 0 \\ 0 & 1 & 0 & 2 \\ 3 & 0 & 4 & 0 \\ 0 & 3 & 0 & 4 \end{bmatrix}$ hence, $tr(T)$

$$= 1 + 1 + 4 + 4 = 10.$$

13. The matrix A has a non-zero determinant.

14. Let $x^3 + x^2 - 5x + 2$

$= Ax^{(3)} + Bx^{(2)} + Cx^{(1)} + D$

$= Ax(x-1)(x-2) + Bx(x-1) + Cx + D$ ...*(i)*

Putting $x = 0$ on both sides of *(i)*, we get D = 2.

Again putting $x = 1$, we get C + D = 1, which gives C = – 3.

Next putting $x = 2$ on both sides of *(i)* we get 2B + 2C + D = 4, giving B = 4.

Again equating the coefficient of x^3, we get A = 1.

Hence

$x^3 + x^2 - 5x + 2 = x^{(3)} + 4x^{(2)} - 3x^{(1)} + 2.$

15. Lagrange's equation of motion for one dimensional motion (say in x direction) can be written as :

$$\frac{d}{dt}\left(\frac{\partial L}{\partial \dot{x}}\right) - \frac{\partial L}{\partial x} = 0$$

K

m

The kinetic energy of this system is

$$T = \frac{1}{2}m\dot{x}^2$$

and the potential energy is $V = -\int \overline{F} \cdot d\overline{x} =$

$$-\int -Kx dx = \frac{1}{2}Kx^2 + C$$

where C is constant of integration and K is spring constant.

If we choose the horizontal plane passing through the position of equilibrium as the reference level, then V = 0 at $x = 0$ so that C = 0. Thus the Lagrangian is

$$L = \frac{1}{2}m\dot{x}^2 - \frac{1}{2}Kx^2.$$

16. The integrand $\dfrac{e^{zt}}{z^2(z^2+2z+2)}$ has a double pole at $z = 0$ and two simple poles at $z = -1 \pm i$. All these poles are inside c.

Residue at $z = 0$ is

$$\lim_{z\to 0}\frac{1}{1!}\frac{d}{dz}\left\{z^2.\frac{e^{zt}}{z^2(z^2+2z+2)}\right\}$$

$$= \lim_{z\to 0}\frac{(z^2+2z+2).(te^{zt}) - e^{zt}(2z+2)}{(z^2+2z+2)^2}$$

$$= \frac{t-1}{2}.$$

Residue at $z = -1+i$ is

$$\lim_{z\to -1+i}\left\{z-(-1+i)\frac{e^{zt}}{z^2(z^2+2z+2)}\right\}$$

$$= \lim_{z\to -1+i}\left(\frac{e^{zt}}{z^2}\right)\lim_{z\to -1+i}\left\{\frac{z+1-i}{z^2+2z+2}\right\} = \frac{e^{(-1+i)t}}{4}$$

Residue at $z = -1-i$ is

$$\lim_{z\to -1-i}\left\{z-(-1-i)\frac{e^{zt}}{z^2(z^2+2z+2)}\right\} = \frac{e^{(-1-i)t}}{4}$$

∴ Then by the residue theorem

$$\int\frac{e^{zt}}{z^2(z^2+2z+2)}dz = 2\pi i \text{ (sum of residues)}$$

$$= 2\pi i\left[\frac{t-1}{2} + \frac{e(-1+i)t}{4} + \frac{e^{(-1-i)t}}{4}\right]$$

$$= 2\pi i\left[\frac{t-1}{2} + \frac{1}{2}e^{-t}\cos t\right].$$

23. Let

$$A = \begin{bmatrix}\cos\theta & -\sin\theta\\ \sin\theta & \cos\theta\end{bmatrix}$$

then

$$A' = \begin{bmatrix}\cos\theta & \sin\theta\\ -\sin\theta & \cos\theta\end{bmatrix}$$

then $AA' =$

$$\begin{bmatrix}\cos^2\theta+\sin^2\theta & \cos\theta\sin\theta-\cos\theta\sin\theta\\ \sin\theta\cdot\cos\theta-\cos\theta\sin\theta & \sin^2\theta+\cos^2\theta\end{bmatrix}$$

$$= \begin{bmatrix}1 & 0\\ 0 & 1\end{bmatrix}.$$

i.e. A is orthogonal.

24. $\log(1+\sin x) = \sin x - \dfrac{\sin^2 x}{2} + \dfrac{\sin^3 x}{3} - \dfrac{\sin^4 x}{4} + \ldots\ldots$

$$= \left(x - \frac{x^3}{3!} + \frac{x^5}{5!}\ldots\ldots\right) - \frac{1}{2}\left(x - \frac{x^3}{3!} + \frac{x^5}{5!}\ldots\ldots\right)^2 + \frac{1}{3}\left(x - \frac{x^3}{3!} + \ldots\ldots\right)^3$$

$$= x - \frac{x^2}{2} + x^3\left(\frac{1}{3} - \frac{1}{6}\right) + \ldots\ldots = x - \frac{x^2}{2} + \frac{x^3}{6}.$$

25. The given differential equation is

$$\frac{dy}{dx} + \frac{1}{x}\cdot\sin 2y = x^2\cos^2 y$$

or, $\sec^2 y\dfrac{dy}{dx} + \dfrac{1}{x}2\tan y = x^2$

let $v = \tan y$, then $\dfrac{dv}{dx} = \sec^2 y\dfrac{dy}{dx}$

or, $\dfrac{dv}{dx} + \dfrac{2}{x}\cdot v = x^2.$

Hence, the integrating factor is $= e^{\int\frac{2}{x}dx} = x^2$

$\Rightarrow \quad v.x^2 = \dfrac{x^5}{5}$

or, $\tan y = \dfrac{x^3}{5}.$

27. We have

$$\frac{10+11i}{8+i} = \frac{(10+11i)(8-i)}{(8+i)(8-i)}$$

$$= \frac{91+78i}{65} = \frac{7}{5} + \frac{6}{5}i$$

or $$\frac{10+11i}{8+i} = (1+i)+\left(\frac{2}{5}+\frac{1}{5}i\right)$$

or $$(10 + 11i) = (1 + i)(8 + i) + \left(\frac{2}{5}+\frac{1}{5}i\right)(8 + i)$$

or, $$10 + 11i = (1 + i)(8 + i) + (3 + 2i)$$

Now we consider

$$\frac{(8+i)}{(3+2i)} = \frac{(8+i)(3-2i)}{(3+2i)(3-2i)} = \frac{26-13i}{13} = 2-i$$

or $$(8 + i) = (2 - i)(3 + 2i)$$

i.e. $(3 + 2i)$ is the *g.c.d.* of $10 + 11i$ and $8 + i$.

28. Given linear transformation is

$$S(x, y, z) = (2x, 4x - y, 2x + 3y - z)$$

Now $S(x, y, z) = (0, 0, 0)$

$\Rightarrow (2x, 4x - y, 2x + 3y - z) = (0, 0, 0)$

$\Rightarrow \quad 2x = 0,\ 4x - y = 0\ \ 2x + 3y - z = 0$

$\Rightarrow \quad x = y = z = 0$

i.e. S is one-to-one.

Now $T(x, y, z) = (x\cos\theta - y\sin\theta, \sin\theta + y\cos\theta, z)$

Now $T(x, y, z) = (0, 0, 0)$

$\Rightarrow (x\cos\theta - y\sin\theta, \sin\theta + y\cos\theta, z) = (0, 0, 0)$

$\Rightarrow z = 0\ \ \&\ \ x\cos\theta - y\sin\theta = 0$

$\sin\theta + y\cos\theta = 0$ or $y = -\tan\theta$

& $$x\cos\theta = \frac{\sin^2\theta}{\cos\theta}$$

or $$x = \tan^2\theta.$$

i.e. $(\tan^2\theta, -\tan\theta, 0) \in \text{Ker}(T)$

Hence, T is not one-to-one.

37. The dimension of the subspace is equal to number of independent rows in the matrix (formed by given vectors) in echelon form.

$$\begin{bmatrix} 2 & 1 & 4 & 3 \\ 2 & 1 & 2 & 0 \\ 0 & 0 & 2 & 3 \\ 4 & 2 & 6 & 3 \end{bmatrix} \sim \begin{bmatrix} 1 & 1/2 & 2 & 3/2 \\ 2 & 1 & 2 & 0 \\ 0 & 0 & 2 & 3 \\ 4 & 2 & 6 & 3 \end{bmatrix} \sim$$

$$\begin{bmatrix} 1 & 1/2 & 2 & 3/2 \\ 0 & 0 & -2 & -3 \\ 0 & 0 & 2 & 3 \\ 0 & 0 & -2 & -3 \end{bmatrix} \sim \begin{bmatrix} 1 & 1/2 & 2 & 3/2 \\ 0 & 0 & -2 & -3 \\ 0 & 0 & 0 & 0 \\ 0 & 0 & 0 & 0 \end{bmatrix}$$

i.e. dimension of subspace = 2.

38. The given differential equation is

$$\frac{d^4y}{dx^4}+2\frac{d^2y}{dx^2}+y = 0 \quad ...(1)$$

The auxiliary equation is given by

$$(m^4 + 2m^2 + 1) = 0$$

$\Rightarrow \quad (m^2 + 1)^2 = 0$

$\Rightarrow \quad m = \pm\, i$ (two times)

hence the general solution of above differential equation is given by

$$y = (c_1 + c_2x)\sin x + (c_3 + c_4\, x)\cos x.$$

43. The work done,

$$\int_C \bar{F}\cdot d\bar{r} = \int 5x^2dx+(xz-y)dy+3zdz.$$

The parametric form,

$$x(t) = t,\ y(t) = t, \text{ and } z(t) = t.$$

$$\therefore \quad \int_C \bar{F}\cdot d\bar{r} = \int_0^1 5t^2dt+\int_0^1 (t^2-t)dt+3\int_0^1 tdt$$

$$= \frac{5t^3}{3}\bigg|_0^1 + \left[\frac{t^3}{3}-\frac{t^2}{2}\right]_0^1 + \frac{3t^2}{2}\bigg|_0^1$$

$$= \frac{5}{3}+\left(\frac{1}{3}-\frac{1}{2}\right)+\frac{3}{2} = 3.$$

55. The given differential equation is

$$xyp^2 - (x^2 + y^2 + 1)p + xy = 0$$

The *p*-discriminant of the above equation is given by

$$(x^2 + y^2 + 1)^2 - 4.xy.xy = 0$$

or, $$(x^2 + y^2 + 1)^2 - (2xy)^2 = 0$$

or, $$(x^2 + y^2 + 1 + 2xy)(x^2 + y^2 + 1 - 2xy) = 0$$

or, $$[(x + y)^2 + 1][(x - y)^2 + 1] = 0$$

57. From question $\theta - \phi = (2n+1)\frac{\pi}{2}$

or, $\theta = (2n+1)\frac{\pi}{2} + \phi$

$\because$ $E(\theta) = \begin{bmatrix} \cos^2\theta & \cos\theta\sin\theta \\ \cos\theta\sin\theta & \sin^2\theta \end{bmatrix}$

$\Rightarrow$ $E(\theta) = \begin{bmatrix} \sin^2\phi & -\cos\phi\sin\phi \\ -\cos\phi\sin\phi & \cos^2\phi \end{bmatrix}$

$$\therefore E(\theta)E(\phi) = \begin{bmatrix} \sin^2\phi & -\cos\phi\sin\phi \\ -\cos\phi\sin\phi & \cos^2\phi \end{bmatrix}\begin{bmatrix} \cos^2\phi & \cos\phi\sin\phi \\ \cos\phi\sin\phi & \sin^2\phi \end{bmatrix}$$

$$= \begin{bmatrix} \cos^2\phi\sin^2\phi - \cos^2\phi\sin^2\phi & \cos\phi\sin^3\phi - \cos\phi\sin^3\phi \\ -\cos^3\phi\sin\phi + \cos^3\phi\sin\phi & -\cos^2\phi\sin^2\phi + \cos^2\phi\sin^2\phi \end{bmatrix}$$

$$= \begin{bmatrix} 0 & 0 \\ 0 & 0 \end{bmatrix}.$$

58. $\log y = \log(1 + \cos x)^{\tan x}$

$$y = e^{\tan x \log\left(1+2\cos^2 x/2-1\right)}$$

$$= e^{\tan.\left(\log 2 + 2\cos\frac{x}{2}\right)}$$

$$= e^{\frac{0+2.\cos\frac{x}{2}\sin\frac{x}{2}}{2\cos^2\frac{x}{2}\left(-\operatorname{cosec}^2 x\right)}}$$

$$= e^{-\frac{\sin x}{2\cos^2\frac{x}{2}\operatorname{cosec}^2 x}}$$

$$\lim_{y\to\frac{\pi}{2}} y = \lim_{y\to\frac{\pi}{2}} e^{-\frac{\sin x}{2\cos^2\frac{x}{2}\cos^2 x}}$$

$$= e^{-1}$$

59. $|z|$ Assumes the maximum possible value $\left|\frac{1}{z}\right| = \frac{1}{|z|}$ assumes the minimum value.

$\therefore$ $|z| \geq \left|\frac{1}{z}\right|$, let $z = r(\cos\theta + i\sin\theta)$

Since $\left|z + \frac{1}{z}\right| = a$

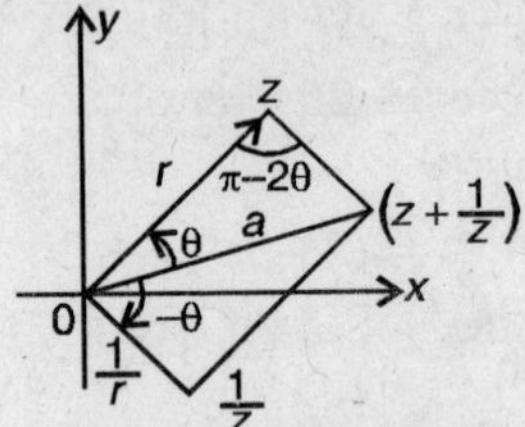

$$\left(r\cos\theta + \frac{1}{r}\cos\theta\right)^2 + \left(r\sin\theta + \frac{1}{r}\sin\theta\right)^2 = a^2$$

$$a^2 = r^2 + \frac{1}{r^2} + 2\cos 2\theta$$

$$\left(r - \frac{1}{r}\right)^2 = a^2 - 4\cos^2\theta$$

As r increases then $\left(r - \frac{1}{r}\right)$ increases

$$\therefore \left(r - \frac{1}{r}\right)^2 = a^2 - 4\cos^2\theta \leq a^2$$

when $\theta = \frac{\pi}{2}$; $\left(r - \frac{1}{r}\right)^2 = a^2$

$$\Rightarrow | \; r = \left\{a + \sqrt{(a^2+4)}\right\}/2$$

The greatest value of $|z| = \left\{a + \sqrt{(a^2+4)}\right\}/2$

The smallest value of $|z| = -ri$

$$= -i\left\{\sqrt{(a^2+4)} - a\right\}/2$$

SET–4

CSIR–UGC (NET) MATHEMATICAL SCIENCES

PART-C

1. Let $f_n(x) = \dfrac{x}{1+nx^2}$, $x \in R$ and $n \in N$

Now define $g_n(x) = f'_n(x)$ then

A. $f'(x) = g(x)\ \forall\ x \in R - \{0\}$

B. $f'(x) \neq g(x)$ for any value of x

C. $f'(x) = g(x) = 0$

D. None of these

2. Let $v_1 = (1, 2, 0, 3, 0)$, $v_2 = (1, 2, -1, -1, 0)$, $v_3 = (0, 0, 1, 4, 0)$, $v_4 = (2, 4, 1, 10, 1)$, and $v_5 = (0, 0, 0, 0, 1)$. Then, the dimension of the linear span of $\{v_1, v_2, v_3, v_4, v_5\}$ is

A. 2 B. 3

C. 4 D. 5

3. Let R_1 and R_2 be two integral domain. Let $R_1 \times R_2 = \{(a, b) \mid a \in R_1, b \in R_2\}$ and $(a, b) + (c, d) = (a + c, b + d)$, $(a, b)\cdot(c, d) = (ac, bd)$ which one of the following is correct?

A. $R_1 \times R_2$ is also an integral domain, but not necessarily a field.

B. $R_1 \times R_2$ need not be an integral domain.

C. $R_1 \times R_2$ is not a ring.

D. $R_1 \times R_2$ is a field.

4. An inventory prop exists if the amount of the resources is subject to control and if there is atleast one cost that decreases.

A. As inventory decreases

B. As inventory increases

C. As inventory remains constant

D. None of the above.

5. If $I = \displaystyle\int_{-\infty}^{\infty} \frac{x^2 dx}{(x^2+1)(x^2+4)}$ then the value of integral is equal to

A. $\dfrac{\pi}{6}$ B. $\dfrac{\pi}{3}$

C. $\dfrac{\pi}{2}$ D. π

6. The solution of $p^2 - px = q$ is given by

A. $z = axe^{-y}$

B. $z = aye^{-x}$

C. $z = axe^{-y} - \frac{1}{2}a^2e^{-2x} + b$

D. $z = aye^{-x} + \frac{1}{2}a^2e^{-2x} + b$

7. Let

$$f(x) = \begin{cases} x & \text{when } 0 \le x < \frac{1}{2} \\ 1 & \text{when } x = \frac{1}{2} \\ 1 - x & \text{when } \frac{1}{2} < x < 1 \end{cases}$$

then $f(x)$ is

A. continuous at $x = \frac{1}{2}$

B. not defined at $x = \frac{1}{2}$

C. discontinuous at $x = \frac{1}{2}$

D. continuous for all x, 0 £ $x < 1$

8. Which one of the following differential equations has the same order and degree?

A. $\dfrac{d^4y}{dx^4} + 8\left(\dfrac{dy}{dx}\right)^4 + 5y = e^x.$

B. $5\left(\dfrac{d^3y}{dx^3}\right)^4 + 8\left(\dfrac{dy}{dx}+1\right)^2 + 5y = x^3.$

C. $\left[1+\left(\dfrac{dy}{dx}\right)^3\right]^{2/3} = 4\left(\dfrac{d^3y}{dx^3}\right).$

D. $y = x^2\left(\dfrac{dy}{dx}\right) + \sqrt{\left(\dfrac{dy}{dx}\right)^2 + 1}.$

9. Let (X, d) be a complete metric space and f : X $\to$ X satisfies $d(f(x), f(y)) \leq \alpha(x, y)$ for some α, $0 \leq \alpha \leq 1$ for all $x, y \in$ X. Then

A. f is bounded function on X.

B. f need not be continuous on X.

C. $f(p) = p$ for some $p \in$ X.

D. $\{f(X_n)\}_{n=1}^{\infty}$ may not be Cauchy sequence even though $\{(X_n)\}_{n=1}^{\infty}$ is a Cauchy sequence in X.

10. Consider the following basis of Euclidean space $\mathbf{R}^3$:
$\{v_1 = (1, 1, 1), v_2 = (0, 1, 1), v_3 = (0, 0, 1)\}$, then using the Gram-Schmidt orthogonalization process, the orthonormal basis $\{u_i\}$ can be represented by following set

A. $\left\{u_1 = \left(\frac{1}{\sqrt{3}}, \frac{-1}{\sqrt{3}}, \frac{1}{\sqrt{3}}\right), u_2 = \left(\frac{2}{\sqrt{6}}, \frac{-1}{\sqrt{6}}, \frac{-1}{\sqrt{6}}\right), u_3 = \left(0, \frac{-1}{\sqrt{2}}, \frac{1}{\sqrt{2}}\right)\right\}$

B. $\left\{u_1 = \left(\frac{1}{\sqrt{3}}, \frac{1}{\sqrt{3}}, \frac{1}{\sqrt{3}}\right), u_2 = \left(\frac{-2}{\sqrt{6}}, \frac{1}{\sqrt{6}}, \frac{1}{\sqrt{6}}\right), u_3 = \left(0, \frac{-1}{\sqrt{2}}, \frac{1}{\sqrt{2}}\right)\right\}$

C. $\left\{u_1 = \left(\frac{1}{\sqrt{3}}, \frac{1}{\sqrt{3}}, \frac{1}{\sqrt{3}}\right), u_2 = \left(\frac{2}{\sqrt{6}}, \frac{-1}{\sqrt{6}}, \frac{-1}{\sqrt{6}}\right), u_3 = \left(0, \frac{1}{\sqrt{2}}, \frac{1}{\sqrt{2}}\right)\right\}$

D. $\left\{u_1 = \left(\frac{1}{\sqrt{3}}, \frac{1}{\sqrt{3}}, \frac{1}{\sqrt{3}}\right), u_2 = \left(\frac{2}{\sqrt{6}}, \frac{1}{\sqrt{6}}, \frac{1}{\sqrt{6}}\right), u_3 = \left(0, \frac{1}{\sqrt{2}}, \frac{1}{\sqrt{2}}\right)\right\}$

11. Read the following statements :

1. There exists two non-isomorphic infinite cyclic groups.
2. There exists two non-isomorphic abelian group of order pq wher p and q are distinct prime.

A. 1 and 2 are incorrect

B. 1 and 2 both are correct

C. 1 is correct but 2 is not

D. 2 is correct but 1 is not

12. Pick out the largest of the sets given below on which the sequence of functions $\left\{e^{-n\cos^2 x}\right\}_{n=1}^{\infty}$ converges uniformly

A. $\left[0, \frac{9\pi}{20}\right) \cup \left(\frac{11\pi}{20}, \pi\right]$

B. $\left[0, \frac{\pi}{2}\right) \cup \left(\frac{\pi}{2}, \pi\right]$

C. $\left[0, \frac{\pi}{2} - \delta\right) \cup \left(\frac{\pi}{2} + \delta, \pi\right], 0 < \delta < \frac{\pi}{100}$

D. $(0 \ \pi]$

13. An integrating factor for $ydx - xdy = 0$

A. $\frac{x}{y}$

B. $\frac{y}{x}$

C. $\frac{1}{x^2 + y^2}$

D. $\frac{1}{x^2 + y}$

14. The set of four rotations of a square in its plane about a normal passing through the centre of the plane form *a*.

A. Group which is not abelian

B. Abelian group but not cyclic

C. Cyclic group

D. Symmetric group

15. There are four machines and it is known that exactly two of them are faulty. They are tested one by one, in a random order till both the faulty machines are identified. Then the probability that only two tests are needed is

A. $\frac{1}{3}$

B. $\frac{1}{6}$

C. $\frac{1}{2}$

D. $\frac{1}{4}$

16. Area of the triangle whose vertices are the points z_1, z_2, z_3 on the argand diagram is

A. $\Sigma\{(z_2 - z_3)|z_1|^2/4iz_1\}$

B. $\Sigma\{(z_2 - z_1)|z_1|^2/4iz_2\}$

C. $\Sigma\{(z_1 - z_3)|z_1|^2/4iz_3\}$

D. $\Sigma\{(z_1 - z_2)|z_2|^2/4iz_3\}$

17. The singular solution of the differential equation $y = xp + a\sqrt{1+p^2}$ is a

A. parabola
B. hyperbola
C. circle
D. straight line

18. Let Γ be any circle enclosing the origin and oriented counter-clockwise. Then the value of the integral $\int_\Gamma \frac{\cos z}{z^2} dz$ is

A. $2\pi i$
B. 0
C. $-2\pi i$
D. undefined

19. A rigid body which is capable of oscillating in a vertical plane above a fixed horizontal axis passing through point O. If m be the mass of the pendulum moment of inertia about axis of rotation I and distance between the centre of mass and point o is l then the Lagrangian (L) and the time period (T) of oscillation is given by

A. $L = \frac{1}{2}I\dot{\theta}^2 - mgl\cos\theta$, $T = 2\pi\sqrt{\frac{mgl}{I}}$

B. $L = \frac{1}{2}I\dot{\theta}^2 + mgl\sin\theta$, $T = 2\pi\sqrt{\frac{I}{mgl}}$

C. $L = \frac{1}{2}I\dot{\theta}^2 + mgl\cos\theta$, $T = 2\pi\sqrt{\frac{l}{g}}$

D. $L = \frac{1}{2}I\dot{\theta}^2 + mgl\cos\theta$, $T = 2\pi\sqrt{\frac{I}{mgl}}$

20. Consider the following statements:

1. {[1], [3], [5]} is a subgroup of {[1], [2], [3], [4], [5], [6]} under modulo 7.
2. If G is a group of order 5, it has no proper subgroup.

Which of the statements given above is/are correct?

A. 1 only
B. 2 only
C. Both 1 and 2
D. Neither 1 nor 2

21. A natural number is selected from the first 20 natural numbers. The probability that $\frac{x^2 - 15x + 50}{x - 15} < 0$

A. $\frac{1}{5}$
B. $\frac{2}{5}$
C. $\frac{3}{5}$
D. $\frac{4}{5}$

22. Which one is not a group.

A. {0, 1, 2, 3}, under operation addition modulo 4.
B. {0, 1, 2, 3}, under operation multiplication modulo 4.
C. {[0], [1], [2], [3], [4]}, composition addition of congruence classes modulo 5.
D. {1, 2, 3} composition multiplication modulo 4.

23. The general solution of $\frac{\partial^2 u}{\partial x^2} + \frac{\partial^2 u}{\partial y^2} = 0$ is of the form

A. $u = f(x + iy) + g(x - iy)$
B. $u = f(x + y) + g(x - y)$
C. $u = cf(x - iy)$
D. $u = g(x + y)$

24. If $A = \begin{pmatrix} 1 & 1 & 2 \\ 2 & 1 & 0 \end{pmatrix}$ and $B = \begin{pmatrix} 1 & 2 \\ 2 & 0 \\ -1 & 1 \end{pmatrix}$, then (AB)′ (AB)′ denotes the transpose of (AB) is

A. $\begin{pmatrix} 1 & 4 \\ 4 & 4 \end{pmatrix}$
B. $\begin{pmatrix} 1 & 4 \\ 1 & 4 \end{pmatrix}$
C. $\begin{pmatrix} 1 & 4 \\ 4 & 1 \end{pmatrix}$
D. $\begin{pmatrix} 1 & 1 \\ 4 & 4 \end{pmatrix}$

25. Let X = [0, 1] ∪ [2, 3] with the subspace topology induced by the usual topology on R, and let f : X → R be defined by

$$f(x) = x \quad \text{if} \quad 0 \le x < 1$$
$$= 2 \quad \text{if} \quad 2 \le x \le 3$$

Then

A. f(G) is open in R for every open set G in X.
B. f(H) is closed in R for every closed set H in X.
C. f is a continuous function.
D. f is a discontinuous function.

26. The maximum ratio criterion is the simplex method ensures that :

A. There is a maximum possible improvement in the objective function

B. The next iterative solution obtained is basic

C. The next iterative solution obtained is feasible

D. The column introduced is independent of the columns constituting the present basis

27. Under the influence of a force field $\vec{F}$, a particle of mass '*m*' moves along the ellipse $r = a \cos wt\, \hat{i} + b \sin wt\, \hat{j}$. Then $\bar{r} \times \bar{F}$ is

A. 0

B. $mw^2(a^2\cos^2 wt + b^2 \sin^2 wt)\, \hat{k}$

C. $mw^2(a^2 + b^2) \cos wt + \sin wt\, \hat{k}$

D. $ma^2w^2\, \hat{k}$

28. Let $G \neq \{e\}$ be a group with no subgroup other than $\{e\}$ and G. Then which one of the following is correct?

A. G is an infinite cyclic group.

B. G is a finite cyclic group.

C. G is an abelian non-cyclic group.

D. G is neither abelian nor cyclic.

29. Name the singularities in the finite z plane if

$$f(z) = \frac{\cos z}{(z+i)^3}$$

A. $z = -i$ pole of order 3

B. $z = +i$ pole of order 3

C. $z = 1$ pole of order 2

D. $z = -1$ pole of order 1

30. Consider the vector space V over the field of real numbers spanned by the set

S = {(0, 1, 0, 0), (1, 1, 0, 0), (1, 0, 1, 0), (0, 0, 1, 0), (1, 1, 1, 0), (1, 0, 0, 0)}

What is the dimension of V?

A. 1 B. 2

C. 3 D. 4

31. The value of $\int_0^\infty \int_{1/y}^\infty x^4 e^{-x^3 y}\, dx\, dy$ equals

A. $\frac{1}{4}$ B. $\frac{1}{3}$

C. $\frac{1}{2}$ D. 1

32. If y_1 and y_2 are the solution of $y'' + x^2y' + (1 - x)y = 0$ on $[-1, 1]$ such that $y_1(0) = 0$, $y_2(0) = -1$, $y_1'(0) = -1$, $y_2'(0) = 1$ then

A. y_1, y_2 are linear independent on $[-1, 1]$

B. y_1, y_2 are linear dependent on $[-1, 1]$

C. y_1, y_2 are linear dependent on $[0, 1]$

D. y_1, y_2 are linear dependent on $[-1, 0]$

33. A matrix M has eigen values 1 and 4 with corresponding eigen vectors

$X_1 = \begin{bmatrix} 1 \\ -1 \end{bmatrix}$ and $X_2 = \begin{bmatrix} 2 \\ 1 \end{bmatrix}$ respectively then M is

A. $\begin{pmatrix} -4 & -8 \\ 5 & 9 \end{pmatrix}$ B. $\begin{pmatrix} 9 & -8 \\ 5 & -4 \end{pmatrix}$

C. $\begin{pmatrix} 2 & 2 \\ 1 & 3 \end{pmatrix}$ D. $\begin{pmatrix} 3 & 2 \\ 1 & 2 \end{pmatrix}$

34. The standard form of an L.P. P will have its objective function of

A. Maximization type

B. Minimization type

C. Both Max or Min. types

D. None of these

35. Which one of the following differential equations represents the orthogonal trajectories of the family of curves $xy = k^2$?

A. $xdy - ydx = 0$ B. $xdy + ydx = 0$

C. $xdx - ydy = 0$ D. $xdx + ydy = 0$

36. The accuracy of Simpson's rule quadrature for a step size 'h' is

A. $0(h^2)$ B. $0(h^4)$

C. $0(h^3)$ D. $0(h^5)$

37. Which of the following relation is false?

A. $E = 1 + \Delta$

B. $E^{-1} = 1 - \nabla$

C. $\nabla.\nabla = 1 - 2E^{-1} + E^{-2}$

D. None of these

38. Let $I = \frac{1}{2\pi i} \oint_c \frac{e^{zt}}{(z^2+1)^2} dz$, (if $t > 0$) and c is the circle $|z| = 3$, then I is equal to

A. $(\sin t + t\cos t)$ B. $\frac{1}{2}(\sin t - t\cos t)$

C. $\frac{1}{2}(\sin t + t\cos t)$ D. $\frac{1}{2}(\cos t - t\sin t)$

39. The pay of martix of A in a two person zero–sum game is given below. Determine the value of the game.

		B		
		I	II	III
A	I	–1	2	1
	II	1	–2	2
	III	3	4	–3

A. 0 B. 10/23
C. 15/23 D. 21/27

40. The value of $\lim_{x\to 0} \frac{x \cdot e^{x^2}}{\int_0^x e^{t^2}\,dt}$

A. is 0 B. is 1
C. does not exist D. is –1

41. The following table is given:

x:	0	1	2	5
$f(x)$:	2	3	12	147

then using Lagrange interpolation formula, the polynomial $f(x)$ is given by

A. $x^3 + x^2 + x + 2$ B. $x^2 - x^2 - x + 2$
C. $x^3 + x^2 - x + 2$ D. None of these

42. An isomorphism of F of a group G onto G′ has the following properties :

A. F is operation preserving and onto
B. F is operation preserving and one–one
C. F is only operation preserving
D. F is operation preserving one–one and onto

43. The singular solution of partial differential equation $z = px + qy + pq$ is

A. $z = -2xy$ B. $z = 2xy$
C. $z = -xy$ D. $z = xy$

44. Let T : $\mathbf{R}^3 \to \mathbf{R}^3$ be a linear transformation given by $T(x, y, z) = (2x, 4x - y, 2x + 3y - z)$ for all $(x, y, z) \in R^3$. Which one of the following is correct?

A. T is onto, but not one-one.
B. T is one-one, but not onto.
C. T is onto and one-one.
D. T is neither one-one nor onto.

45. If the set Z of integers is a group under the binary operation $*$ defined as $m*n = m + n + 1$, $m, n \in Z$ then the inverse of the element 5 is

A. 5 B. –5
C. –6 D. –7

46. The mean and variance of a random variable X having a binomial distribution are 4 and 2 respectively. Then, $P(X = 1)$ is

A. $\frac{1}{32}$ B. $\frac{1}{16}$
C. $\frac{1}{8}$ D. $\frac{1}{4}$

47. The function $f(z) = \frac{(z+2)}{z(z^2+1)}$ has singular points at

A. 0, 1 B. 0, i
C. 0, $\pm i$ D. 0, 1, i, $-i$, 2

48. The extremal of the function

$$I[u(x)] = \int_{-1}^{0} 480\left[u(x) - \left(\frac{d^3u}{dx^3}\right)^2\right]dx;$$

$u(0) = u'(0) = u''(0) = 0$ is

A. $y = -\left(\frac{x^3}{3}\right) + Ax^4 + Bx^5 + Cx^2$

B. $y = -\left(\frac{x^3}{3}\right) + Ax^4 + Bx^3 + Cx^2$

C. $y = -\left(\frac{x^6}{3}\right) + Ax^4 + Bx^5 + Cx^3$

D. None of these

49. $\frac{1}{2\pi i}\oint_C \frac{e^z}{z-2}dz$ if C is $|z| = 3$ and $|z| = 1$

A. e^2, 1 B. e^2, 0
C. e, 1 D. 0, e^2

50. The *g.c.d.* of 2 and $3 + 5i$ in $Z[i]$

A. i B. $1 + i$
C. $2 + i$ D. None of these

51. The solution of

$$\frac{dy}{dx}+\frac{\sqrt{1-y^2}}{1-x^2}=0 \text{ is given by}$$

A. $x\left(y^2-1\right)/y = \log y+\frac{1}{2}x^2+c$

B. $y\left(x^2-1\right)/x = \log x+\frac{1}{2}x^2+c$

C. $2y(y^2-1) = \log x-\frac{1}{2}x^2+C$

D. None of the above.

52. The equation $y - 2x = c$ represents the orthogonal trajectories of the family

A. $y = ce^{-2x}$ B. $x^2 + 2y^2 = c$

C. $xy = c$ D. $x + 2y = c$

53. Which of the following series is divergent?

A. $\sum_{n=1}^{\infty}\sqrt{n}\sin\frac{1}{n}$

B. $\sum_{n=1}^{\infty}\sqrt{n}\sin^{-1}\left(\frac{1}{n^2}\right)$

C. $\sum_{n=1}^{\infty}n\tan\left(\frac{1}{n^3}\right)$

D. $\sum_{n=1}^{\infty}\tan^{-1}\left(\frac{1}{n^2}\right)$

54. The LPP

Max $z = 2x_1 + 3x_2 + x_3$

subject to $-2x_1 + 3x_2 + 5x_3 \geq 5$

$-x_1 + 2x_2 + 3x_3 \leq 4$

$x_1, x_2, x_3 \geq 0$ has

A. Optimal solution

B. Unbounded solution

C. No feasible solution

D. No solution

55. Let ξ_1, ξ_2 and ξ_3 be vectors of a vector space $\mho$ over the field F. If r and s are arbitrary elements of F and the set $(\xi_1, \xi_2, r\xi_1 + s\xi_2 + \xi_3)$ is linear dependent, then (ξ_1, ξ_2, ξ_3) is

A. linearly dependent set

B. a null set

C. linearly independent set

D. None of the above

56. If G is a group and H is a subgroup of G, then which statement is not equivalent to other statment.

A. H is normal subgroup of G

B. H is a subgroup of G

C. H is the kernal of homomorphism of G

D. Every left coset of H in G is right coset of H in G

57. Consider the following statements regarding the differential equation.

$$\left|\frac{dy}{dx}\right|+|y|=0,\ 0<x<1.$$

Satisfying $y(0) = 1$.

1. It is a linear differential equation.
2. It has an unique solution.

Which of the statements given above is/are correct?

A. 1 only

B. 2 only

C. Both 1 and 2

D. Neither 1 nor 2

58. Which of the following set is/are convex sets

A. $\{(x, y) : x^2 + y^2 \geq 1\}$

B. $\{(x, y) : y^2 \geq x\}$

C. $\{(x, y) : 3x^2 + 3y^2 \geq 5\}$

D. $\{(x, y) : y \geq 2, y \leq 4\}$

59. If a square matrix of order 10 has exactly 4 distinct eigenvalues, then the degree of its minimal polynomial is

A. at least 4

B. at most 4

C. at least 6

D. at most 6

60. Principal value of log i is.

A. $\frac{i\pi}{2}$ B. $-\frac{i\pi}{2}$

C. $\frac{\pi}{2}$ D. $\frac{i}{2}$

ANSWERS

1	2	3	4	5	6	7	8	9	10
A	B	B	C	B	C	B	C	C	B
11	**12**	**13**	**14**	**15**	**16**	**17**	**18**	**19**	**20**
C	A	C	C	B	A	C	B	D	B
21	**22**	**23**	**24**	**25**	**26**	**27**	**28**	**29**	**30**
B	B	A	A	C	A	A	A	A	C
31	**32**	**33**	**34**	**35**	**36**	**37**	**38**	**39**	**40**
C	A	D	C	C	C	C	B	C	B
41	**42**	**43**	**44**	**45**	**46**	**47**	**48**	**49**	**50**
C	D	C	C	D	A	C	D	B	B
51	**52**	**53**	**54**	**55**	**56**	**57**	**58**	**59**	**60**
B	D	A	A	A	A	D	D	D	A

SOME SELECTED EXPLANATORY ANSWERS

2. The dimension of the linear span of $\{v_1, v_2, v_3, v_4, v_5\}$ is equal to the number of independent rows in the echelon form of v_1, v_2, v_3, v_4, v_5.

$$i.e.\quad \begin{bmatrix} 1 & 2 & 0 & 3 & 0 \\ 1 & 2 & -1 & -1 & 0 \\ 0 & 0 & 1 & 4 & 0 \\ 2 & 4 & 1 & 10 & 1 \\ 0 & 0 & 0 & 0 & 1 \end{bmatrix} \sim$$

$$\begin{bmatrix} 1 & 2 & 0 & 3 & 0 \\ 0 & 0 & -1 & -4 & 0 \\ 0 & 0 & 1 & 4 & 0 \\ 0 & 0 & 1 & 4 & 1 \\ 0 & 0 & 0 & 0 & 1 \end{bmatrix} \sim \begin{bmatrix} 1 & 2 & 0 & 3 & 0 \\ 0 & 0 & -1 & -4 & 0 \\ 0 & 0 & 0 & 0 & 0 \\ 0 & 0 & 0 & 0 & 0 \\ 0 & 0 & 0 & 0 & 1 \end{bmatrix}$$

i.e. dimension = 3.

3. The binary composition is given as

$(a, b) + (c, d) = (a + c, b + d)$

& $(a, b)(c, d) = (ac, bd)$

let $(a, b) = (1, 0)$

and $(c, d) = (0, 1)$

then $(1, 0)(0, 1) = (1.0, 0.1) = (0, 0)$

i.e., $R_1 \times R_2$ has zero divisors.

Hence, $R_1 \times R_2$ is not an integral domain.

5. Consider $\int_C f(z)dz = \int_c \frac{z^2 dz}{(z^2+1)(z^2+4)}$

where C is the contour consisting of a large semi-circle Γ of radius R together with real axis from –R to R.

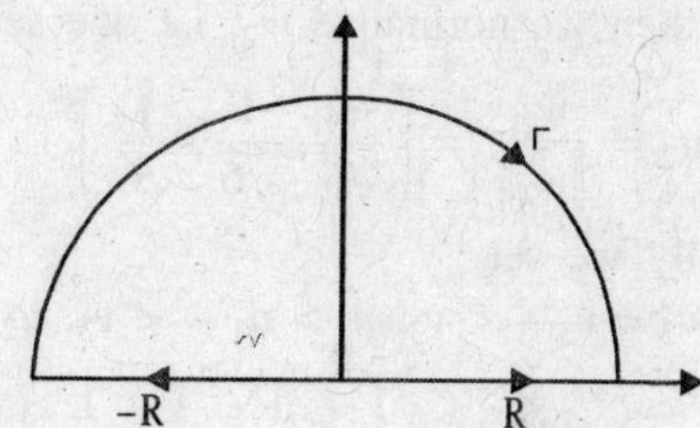

Now, by Cauchy's integral formula

$$\int_c f(z)dz = \int_{-R}^{R} \frac{x^2}{(x^2+1)(x^2+4)}dx + \int_\Gamma \frac{z^2}{(z^2+1)(z^2+4)}dz = 2\pi i \Sigma R^+$$

as $\lim_{R\to\infty} zf(z) = \lim_{z\to\infty} z.\frac{z^2}{(z^2+1)(z^2+4)} = 0$

$$\therefore \lim_{R\to\infty} \int_\Gamma \frac{z^2}{(z^2+1)(z^2+4)}dz = 0.$$

Also, $z = \pm i, \pm 2i$ are the simple poles of $f(z)$. Out of these $z = i, 2i$ lie inside c.

Residue at $z = i$ is

$$\lim_{z\to i}(z-i)f(z) = \lim_{z\to i} \frac{z^2}{(z^2+i)(z^2+4)} = \frac{-1}{6i}$$

residue at $z = zi$ is $\lim\limits_{z \to 2i} (z - 2i) f(z)$

$$= \lim_{z \to 2i} \frac{z^2}{(z^2+1)(z+2i)} = \frac{1}{3i}$$

$\therefore$ Sum of the residues inside $c = -\frac{1}{6i} + \frac{1}{3i} = \frac{1}{6i}$

$$\therefore \int_{-\infty}^{\infty} \frac{x^2}{(x^2+1)(x^2+4)} dx = 2\pi i . \frac{1}{6i} = \frac{\pi}{3}.$$

10. First we normalize v_1, *i.e.* we get

$$u_1 = \frac{v_1}{\|v_1\|} = \frac{(1,1,1)}{\sqrt{3}} = \left(\frac{1}{\sqrt{3}}, \frac{1}{\sqrt{3}}, \frac{1}{\sqrt{3}}\right).$$

Next we set

$$w_2 = v_2 - < v_2, u_1 > u_1$$

$$= (0,1,1) - \frac{2}{\sqrt{3}}\left(\frac{1}{\sqrt{3}}, \frac{1}{\sqrt{3}}, \frac{1}{\sqrt{3}}\right)$$

$$= \left(\frac{-2}{3}, \frac{1}{3}, \frac{1}{3}\right)$$

and then we normalize w_2, *i.e.* we set

$$u_2 = \frac{w_2}{\|w_2\|} = \left(\frac{-2}{\sqrt{6}}, \frac{1}{\sqrt{6}}, \frac{1}{\sqrt{6}}\right)$$

Finally we set

$$w_3 = v_3 - < v_3, u_1 > u_1 - < v_3, u_2 > u_2$$

$$= (0,0,1) - \frac{1}{\sqrt{3}}\left(\frac{1}{\sqrt{3}}, \frac{1}{\sqrt{3}}, \frac{1}{\sqrt{3}}\right) - \frac{1}{\sqrt{6}}$$

$$\left(\frac{-2}{\sqrt{6}}, \frac{1}{\sqrt{6}}, \frac{1}{\sqrt{6}}\right) = \left(0, \frac{-1}{2}, \frac{1}{2}\right)$$

and then we normalize w_3,

$$u_3 = \frac{w_3}{\|w_3\|} = \left(0, \frac{-1}{\sqrt{2}}, \frac{1}{\sqrt{2}}\right).$$

i.e. The required orthonormal basis of $\mathbf{R}^3$ is

$$\left\{u_1 = \left(\frac{1}{\sqrt{3}}, \frac{1}{\sqrt{3}}, \frac{1}{\sqrt{3}}\right), u_2 = \left(\frac{-2}{\sqrt{6}}, \frac{1}{\sqrt{6}}, \frac{1}{\sqrt{6}}\right),\right.$$

$$\left. u_3 = \left(0, \frac{-1}{\sqrt{2}}, \frac{1}{\sqrt{2}}\right)\right\}$$

17. The given differential equation is

$$y = xp + a\sqrt{1+p^2}$$

or, $(y - xp)^2 = a^2(1 + p^2)$

or, $y^2 + x^2p^2 - 2xyp = a^2(1 + p^2)$

or, $p^2(x^2 - a^2) - 2xyp + (y^2 - a^2) = 0$

p-discriminant of the above equation is given by,

$$(2x - y)^2 - 4.(x^2 - a^2)(y^2 - a^2) = 0$$

or, $4x^2y^2 - 4(x^2y^2 - a^2y^2 - a^2x^2 + a^4) = 0$

or, $x^2 + y^2 = a^2$

which represents a circle.

18. $\displaystyle\int_{|z|=r} \frac{\cos z}{z^2} dz$

using Cauchy intergral formula, above integral is equal to $2\pi i f'(0)$ where $f(z) = \cos z$

$\Rightarrow \qquad 2\pi i.0 = 0.$

19. A rigid body capable of oscillating in vertical plane above a fixed horizontal axis is called a compound pendulum. Let the vertical plane of oscillation be XY, O the point through which axis of rotation passes, C is the centre of mass.

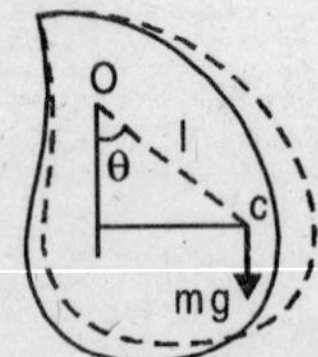

Let mass of pendulum be m, moment of inertia about axis of rotation I and distance OC = l.

If θ is the angle through which the body is deflected, then kinetic energy is

$$T = \frac{1}{2} I\dot{\theta}^2$$

The potential energy relative to a horizontal plane through O is

$$V = -mgl \cos \theta.$$

The Lagrangian is

$$L = T - V = \frac{1}{2} I\dot{\theta}^2 + mgl\cos\theta.$$

24. $A = \begin{pmatrix} 1 & 1 & 2 \\ 2 & 1 & 0 \end{pmatrix}$, $B = \begin{pmatrix} 1 & 2 \\ 2 & 0 \\ -1 & 1 \end{pmatrix}$

hence $\quad AB = \begin{pmatrix} 1 & 4 \\ 4 & 4 \end{pmatrix}$

hence $(AB)^1 = \begin{pmatrix} 1 & 4 \\ 4 & 4 \end{pmatrix}.$

30. The dimension of V is equal to the number of independent rows which written as a row vectors.

i.e. $\begin{bmatrix} 0 & 1 & 0 & 0 \\ 1 & 1 & 0 & 0 \\ 1 & 0 & 1 & 0 \\ 0 & 0 & 1 & 0 \\ 1 & 1 & 1 & 0 \\ 1 & 0 & 0 & 0 \end{bmatrix} \sim \begin{bmatrix} 0 & 1 & 0 & 0 \\ 1 & 0 & 0 & 0 \\ 1 & 0 & 1 & 0 \\ 0 & 0 & 1 & 0 \\ 1 & 1 & 1 & 0 \\ 1 & 0 & 0 & 0 \end{bmatrix} \sim \begin{bmatrix} 0 & 1 & 0 & 0 \\ 0 & 0 & 0 & 0 \\ 1 & 0 & 0 & 0 \\ 0 & 0 & 1 & 0 \\ 0 & 0 & 0 & 0 \\ 0 & 0 & 0 & 0 \end{bmatrix}$

i.e. dim $(s) = 3$

31. The given integral is

$$I = \int_0^\infty \int_{1/y}^\infty x^4 e^{-x^3 y} dx\, dy.$$

By change of the order of integration, we get

$$I = \int_0^\infty \int_0^{1/x} x^4 e^{-x^3 y} dy\, dx.$$

$$\Rightarrow \quad I = \int_0^\infty x^4 \left. \frac{e^{-x^3 y}}{-x^3} \right|_0^{1/x} dx = \int_0^\infty -xe^{-x^2} dx$$

$$= -\frac{1}{2}\left[-xe^{-x^2}\right]_0^\infty = -\frac{1}{2}(0-1) = \frac{1}{2}.$$

33. Let $\begin{pmatrix} a_{11} & a_{12} \\ a_{21} & a_{22} \end{pmatrix} = M$, $MX = \lambda IX$

Corresponding to 1

$$\Rightarrow \begin{pmatrix} a_{11} & a_{12} \\ a_{21} & a_{22} \end{pmatrix}\begin{pmatrix} 1 \\ -1 \end{pmatrix} = \begin{pmatrix} 1 \\ -1 \end{pmatrix} \quad \text{... (A)}$$

Corresponding to 4

$$\Rightarrow \begin{pmatrix} a_{11} & a_{12} \\ a_{21} & a_{22} \end{pmatrix}\begin{pmatrix} 2 \\ 1 \end{pmatrix} = \begin{pmatrix} 8 \\ 4 \end{pmatrix} \quad \text{... (B)}$$

$\therefore \quad a_{11} = 3,\ a_{12} = 2$
$\quad\ \ a_{21} = 1,\ a_{22} = 2$

$\therefore$ Matrix $M = \begin{pmatrix} 3 & 2 \\ 1 & 2 \end{pmatrix}$

38. Given, $I = \dfrac{1}{2\pi i}\displaystyle\int \frac{e^{zt}}{(z^2+1)^2} dz$

The pole of $\dfrac{e^{zt}}{(z^2+1)^2} = \dfrac{e^{zt}}{(z^2+i)^2 (z-i)^2}$

are at $z = \pm\, i$ inside c ($|z| = 3$) and are both of order two.

Residue at $z = i$ is

$$\lim_{z\to i} \frac{1}{1!}\frac{d}{dz}\left\{(z-i)^2 \frac{e^{zt}}{(z-i)^2 (z+i)^2}\right\}$$

$$= \lim_{z\to i} \frac{(z+i)te^{zt} - 2e^{zt}}{(z+i)^3}$$

$$= \frac{2i\,te^{it} - 2e^{it}}{8i^3}$$

Similarly at $\quad z = -i = -\dfrac{2i\,te^{-it} - 2e^{-it}}{-8i^3}$

$\therefore$ By Residue theorem

$$I = \frac{2\pi i}{2\pi i}\left[\frac{2i}{8i^3}.t\left(e^{it} + e^{-it}\right) + \frac{1}{4i}\left(e^{it} - e^{-it}\right)\right]$$

$$= \frac{1}{2}(\sin t - t\cos t).$$

40. The given limit function is $\lim\limits_{x\to 0} \dfrac{xe^{x^2}}{\int_0^x e^{t^2} dt}$

Apply L'Hospital Rule, we get

$$\lim_{x\to 0} \frac{e^{x^2} + 2x^2 e^{x^2}}{e^{x^2}} = \lim_{x\to 0} \frac{e^{x^2}(1+2x^2)}{e^{x^2}}$$

$$= (1 + 2x^2) = 1.$$

41. Here, $x_0 = 0$, $x_1 = 1$, $x_2 = 2$ and $x_3 = 5$.

By Lagrange's formula, we have

$$f(x) = \frac{(x-1)(x-2)(x-5)}{(0-1)(0-2)(0-5)} \times 2$$

$$+ \frac{(x-0)(x-2)(x-5)}{(1-0)(1-2)(1-5)} \times 3$$

$$+ \frac{(x-0)(x-1)(x-5)}{(2-0)(2-1)(2-5)} \times 12$$

$$+\frac{(x-0)(x-1)(x-2)}{(5-0)(5-1)(5-2)}\times 147$$

or $f(x) = -\frac{1}{5}(x-1)(x-2)(x-5)+\frac{3}{4}$
$x(x-2)(x-5)-2x(x-1)(x-5)$

$+\frac{49}{20}x(x-1)(x-2) = x^3 + x^2 - x + 2.$

44. The given linear transformation T : $R^3 \to R^3$ is

$$T(x, y, z) = (2x, 4x - y, 2x + 3y - z)$$

Now $T(x, y, z) = (0, 0, 0)$

$\Rightarrow (2x, 4x - y, 2x + 3y - 2) = (0, 0, 0)$

$\Rightarrow \quad 2x = 0 \quad \Rightarrow \quad x = 0$

$4x - y = 0 \quad \Rightarrow \quad y = 4x = 0$

& $2x + 3y - z = 0 \quad \Rightarrow \quad z = 2x + 3y = 0.$

i.e. $(0, 0, 0) \in \text{Ker (T)}$

i.e. T is non-singular

hence T should be one-one and onto.

45. The given binary composition is

$$m * n = m + n + 1$$

then if e is identity of m then

$$m * e = m + e + 1 \Rightarrow e = -1$$

i.e., if m' is inverse of m then

$$m * m' = -1$$

$\Rightarrow m + m' + 1 = -1$

$\Rightarrow \quad m' = -2 - m$

i.e., inverse of $5 = -2 - 5 = -7$.

50. $\frac{3+5i}{2} = \frac{3}{2}+\frac{5i}{2} = (1+2i)+\left(\frac{1}{2}+\frac{1}{2}i\right)$

or $(3 + 5i) = (1 + 2i)\cdot 2 + (1 + i)$

where $d(1 + i) < d(2)$

Now $\frac{2}{1+i} = \frac{2(1-i)}{(1+i)(1-i)}$

$= \frac{2-2i}{2} = 1 - i$

i.e. $2 = (1 + i)(1 - i)$

i.e. $1 + i$ is the *g.c.d.* of 2 and $3 + 5i$.

59. As the matrix M is real symmetric matrix. It will have only real eigenvalues, *i.e.* both positive and negative real eigenvalues.

SET–5

CSIR–UGC (NET) MATHEMATICAL SCIENCES

PART-C

1. Let $M = \begin{bmatrix} 0 & 0 & -1 & 0 \\ 2 & 0 & 0 & 0 \\ 0 & 0 & 0 & 3 \\ 0 & -4 & 0 & 0 \end{bmatrix}$. Then

A. $MM^T = I$ where M^T is the transpose of M and I is the identity matrix.
B. Column vectors of M form an orthogonal system of vectors.
C. Column vectors of M form an orthonormal system of vectors.
D. $(MX, MY) = (X, Y)$ for all X, Y in $\mathbf{R}^4$ where (,) is the standard inner product on $\mathbf{R}^4$.

2. Let $\sum_{n=0}^{\infty} a_n z^{2n+1}$ be the Taylor series expansion of $f(z) = \tan z$, $|z| < \frac{\pi}{2}$ then which one of the following is correct?

A. $a_0 = 1, a_1 = \frac{4}{3}, a_2 = \frac{2}{15}$

B. $a_0 = 1, a_1 = \frac{2}{3}, a_2 = \frac{1}{15}$

C. $a_0 = 1, a_1 = \frac{1}{3}, a_2 = \frac{2}{15}$

D. $a_0 = 2, a_1 = \frac{2}{3}, a_2 = \frac{4}{15}$

3. The solution of the differential equation

$$e^y \frac{dy}{dt} - \left[-t + \frac{t^3}{3!5!} - \frac{t^5}{} + \ldots\right] = 0$$

which satisfies $y(0) = 0$ $t \in \left(-\frac{\pi}{2}, \frac{\pi}{2}\right)$ is

A. Periodic and bounded
B. Periodic and unbounded
C. Non-Periodic and bounded
D. Non-Periodic and unbounded

4. The solution of the Cauchy problem $u_{yy} - u_{xx} = 0$, $u(x, 0) = 0$, $u_y(x, 0) = x$ is $u =$

A. $\frac{x}{y}$ B. xy

C. $xy + \frac{x}{y}$ D. 0.

5. Consider the

set $S_1 = \left\{\begin{pmatrix} a & 0 \\ b & 0 \end{pmatrix} : a, b \text{ are integers}\right\}$ and

set $S_2 = \left\{\begin{pmatrix} a & b \\ 0 & 0 \end{pmatrix} : a, b \text{ are integers}\right\}$

over the ring of 2 × 2 matrices over integers then choose the correct alternative.

A. S_1 is left ideal and S_2 is right ideal
B. S_1 is right ideal and S_2 is left ideal
C. Both S_1 and S_2 are left ideal
D. Neither S_1 nor S_2 are right ideal

6. The solution of the partial differential equation $(x^2D^2 + 2xy\,DD' + y^2D'^2)z = x^2y^2$ is

A. $z = \phi\left(\frac{x}{y}\right) + x\psi\left(\frac{y}{x}\right) + \frac{1}{12}x^2y^2$

B. $z = \phi\left(\frac{y}{x}\right) + x\psi\left(\frac{y}{x}\right) + \frac{1}{12}x^2y^2$

C. $z = \phi(yx) + x\psi\left(\frac{x}{y}\right) - \frac{1}{12}x^2y^2$

D. $z = \phi(xy) + x\psi\left(\frac{x}{y}\right) + x^2y^2$

7. The order of each element of a finite group
A. is less than or equal to the order of the group
B. is greater than or equal to the order of the group
C. is equal to the order of the group
D. none is correct

8. The general solution of the differential equation

$$\frac{d^4y}{dx^4}-6\frac{d^3y}{dx_3}+12\frac{d^2y}{dx^2}-8\frac{dy}{dx}=0 \text{ is}$$

A. $y = c_1 + [c_2 + c_3x + c_4x^2]e^{2x}$
B. $y = [c_1 + c_2x + c_3x^2]e^{2x}$
C. $y = c_1 + c_2x + c_3x^2 + c_4x^3$
D. $y = c_1 + c_2x + c_3x^2 + c_4e^{2x}$.

9. The set $U = \{(x, y) \in \mathbf{R}^2 : xy \geq 0\}$ is
A. a vector subspace of $\mathbf{R}^2$.
B. not a vector subspace of $\mathbf{R}^2$ since every element does not have an inverse in V.
C. not a vector subspace of $\mathbf{R}^2$ since it is not closed under scalar multiplication.
D. not a vector subspace of $\mathbf{R}^2$ since it is not closed under vector addition.

10. If $\alpha = (13)(27)(456)(8)$ and $\beta = (1237)(648)(5)$, then what is the value of $\alpha\beta$?
A. (1372) (84) (56)   B. (1237) (4856)
C. (1732) (48) (56)   D. (1732) (45) (86)

11. Let $f : \mathbb{R}^2 \to \mathbb{R}$ be a smooth function with positive definite. *Hessian* at every point. Let $(a, b) \in \mathbb{R}^2$ be a p critical point of f. then.
A. f has a global minimum at (a, b)
B. f has a local, but not a global maximum at (a, b).
C. f has a local, but not a global maximum at (a, b)
D. f has a global maximum at (a, b)

12. Let $f(x, y) = \dfrac{xy}{(x^2+y^2)^{5/2}}[1-\cos(x^2+y^2)]$,

$(x, y) \neq (0, 0) = K, (x, y) = (0, 0)$

Then the value of K for which $f(x, y)$ is continuous at (0, 0) is

A. 0   B. $\frac{1}{2}$
C. 1   D. $\frac{3}{2}$

13. Value of the game whose pay-off matrix is—

		B			
		I	II	III	IV
A x_1	I	1	3	−3	7
A x_2	II	2	5	4	−6

A. 0   B. 1
C. 2   D. 1/2

14. Two uniform rods AB and AC smoothly jointed at A are in equilibrium in a vertical plane, B and C rest on a smooth horizontal plane and the middle points of AB and AC are connected by a string then the tension of the string is

A. $T = \dfrac{W}{\cot B+\cot C}$

B. $T = \dfrac{W}{\tan A-\tan B}$

C. $T = \dfrac{W}{\tan B+\tan C}$

D. None of these

15. A function $f(t) = \dfrac{d}{dt}\left\{\dfrac{dx}{1-\cos t\cos x}\right\}$ satisfies the differential equation

A. $\dfrac{df}{dt}+2f(t)\cos t = 0$

B. $\dfrac{df}{dt}-2f(t)\cos t = 0$

C. $\dfrac{df}{dt}+2f(t)\sin t$

D. $\dfrac{df}{dt}.2f(t)\sin t = 0$

16. The series $\sum\dfrac{(-1)^{n-1}}{n^p}, p>0$ is
A. convergent
B. divergent

C. oscillates finitely
D. oscillates infinitely

17. Let the sequence $\{e_n\}$ be a complete orthonormal set in a Hilbert space H. Then

A. For all bounded linear operators T on H, the sequence $\{Te_n\}$ is convergent in H.

B. For the identity operator I on H the sequence $\{Ie_n\}$ is convergent in H.

C. For all bounded linear functional f on H the sequence $\{fe_n\}$ is convergent in R.

D. None of the above

18. A biased coin is tested 4 times or until a head turns up whichever occurs earlier. The distribution of the number of fails turning up is

A. Binomial
B. Geometric
C. Negative Binomial
D. None of these

19. Real part of the principal value of $e^{\log(1+i)}$ is

A. $e^{-\pi^2/8}\cos\left(\frac{\pi}{4}\log 2\right)$

B. $e^{\pi/8}\log 2$

C. $e^{\pi/8}\cos\frac{\pi}{4}\log 2$

D. $e^{\pi/8}$

20. The solution of equation $\frac{dy}{dx}=\cos(x-y)$ is

A. $y+\cot\left(\frac{x-y}{2}\right)=c$

B. $x+\cot\left(\frac{x-y}{2}\right)=c$

C. $x+\tan\left(\frac{x-y}{2}\right)=c$

D. None of these.

21. The fixed points of $f(z) = \frac{2iz+5}{z-2i}$ are

A. $1 \pm i$ B. $1 \pm 2i$
C. $2i \pm 1$ D. $1 \pm i$

22. In an abelian group, the order of an element a is 4 and the order of an element b is 3, then $(ab)^{14}$ is equal to

A. a^2b^{-1} B. $(ab)^{-2}$
C. a^2 D. b

23. A particle of mass 4 units moves along x-axis attracted towards the origin by a force whose magnitude is $8x$. If it is initially at rest at $x = 10$, then the frequency of the particle is

A. $10\sqrt{2}\pi$ B. π

C. $\frac{\pi}{10\sqrt{2}}$ D. $\frac{1}{\sqrt{2}\pi}$

24. Let $\Sigma S_n = S_1 + S_2 + S_3 + ... + S_n ...$ be a given positive series, and let $\Sigma t_n = (S_1 + S_2) + S_3 + (S_4 + S_5) + S_6 + ...$ be obtained from it by the insertion of parentheses according to the pattern 2, 1, 2, 1, 2, 1 then Σt_n.

A. Converges
B. Conditionally converges
C. Diverges
D. Oscillates

25. The value of α for which the system of equations

$x + y + z = 0$
$y + 2z = 0$
$\alpha x + z = 0$ has more than one solution is

A. -1 B. 0

C. $\frac{1}{2}$ D. 1

26. The following table gives the times (In hours) required for processing different jobs on two machines A and B in that order.

Job	a	b	c	d	e	f
A	8	6	3	9	7	5
B	4	12	7	1	6	2

The sequence which minimises the makespan is

A. $c\ f\ b\ e\ a\ d$ B. $d\ f\ a\ e\ c\ b$
C. $c\ b\ e\ a\ f\ d$ D. $d\ f\ a\ e\ b\ c$

27. Let T : $\mathbf{R}^3 \to \mathbf{R}^3$ be defined by T$(x, y, z) = (x, y, 0)$ and S : $\mathbf{R}^2 \to \mathbf{R}^2$ be defined by S$(x, y) = (2x, 3y)$, be linear transformations on the real vectors spaces $\mathbf{R}^3$ and $\mathbf{R}^2$ respectively. Then which one of the following is correct?

A. T and S are both singular.
B. T and S are both non-singular.
C. T is singular and S is non-singular.
D. S is singular and T is non-singular.

28. In the group $(G, +_6)$ where $G = \{0, 1, 2, 3, 4, 5\}$ and $+_6$ is addition modulo 6, what is the inverse of $(2 +_6 3^{-1} +_6 4)$?

A. 0 B. 2
C. 3 D. 5

29. The solution of the differential equation

$$x\left\{y\frac{d^2y}{dx^2}+\left(\frac{dy}{dx}\right)^2\right\}=y\frac{dy}{dx} \text{ is}$$

A. $ax + by = c$ B. $ax^2 + by = 0$
C. $ax^2 + by^2 = 1$ D. $ax + by^2 = 0$

30. The statement "The dual space of a non-empty normed linear space is non-empty" follows from

A. Uniform Boundedness Principle
B. Mahn-Banach theorem
C. Riesez representation theorem
D. Closed graph theorem

31. If the primal problem is given by

Min $z = 2x_2 + 5x_3$

subject to $x_1 + x_2 \geq 2$

$2x_1 + x_2 + 6x_3 \leq 6$

$x_1 - x_2 + 3x_3 = 4$

$x_1, x_2, x_3 \geq 0$

then its dual is

A. Max $z' = 2w_1 + 6w_2 - 4w_3$
subject to $w_1 + 2w_2 - w_3 \leq 0$
$w_1 + w_2 + w_3 \leq 2$
$-6w_2 - 3w_3 \leq 5$
$w_1, w_2 \geq 0$ and w_3 unrestricted

B. Max $z' = 2w_1 - 6w_2 + 4w_3$
subject to $w_1 - 2w_2 + w_3 \leq 0$
$w_1 - w_2 - w_3 \leq 2$
$-6w_2 + 3w_3 \leq 5$
$w_1, w_2 \geq 0$ and w_3 unrestricted

C. Max $z' = 2w_1 - 6w_2 - 4w_3$
subject to $w_1 - 2w_2 - w_3 \leq 0$
$w_1 - w_2 + w_3 \leq 2$
$-6w_2 - 3w_3 \leq 5$
$w_1, w_2, w_3 \geq 0$

D. None of these

32. Let $A \in C_{m \times n}$ and A' A^* denote the transpose and conjugate transpose of A respectively, then

A. rank (AA^*A) = rank (A)
B. rank (A) = rank (A^2)
C. rank (A) = rank $(A'A)$
D. rank (A^2) – rank (A) = rank (A^3) – rank (A^2)

33. Most of inventory theory has been concerned with only the first two types

A. Uncontrolled variables
B. Controlled variables
C. Both A and B
D. None

34. The boundary value problem $y'' + ky = 0$, $y'(0) = 0$, $y'(\pi) = 0$ has non-trivial solution for

A. All negative values of k
B. All values of k
C. $k = 0$
D. $k = \pm n$, $n = 1, 2, ...$

35. The extremal of $\int_0^1 yy'^3 dx;\ y(0) = 0,\ y(1) = 1.$

A. $y = x^{3/4}$ B. $y = \frac{4}{3}x$
C. $y^{4/3} = x^{1/3}$ D. $y = x^{-3/4}$

36. If $I = \int_0^\infty \frac{dx}{x^4+1}$, then the value of integral I is equal to

A. $\frac{\pi}{4}$ B. $\frac{\pi}{2\sqrt{2}}$
C. $\frac{\pi}{2}$ D. $\frac{\pi}{\sqrt{2}}$

37. Let G be an infinite cyclic group and H is its subgroup. Which one of the following is correct?

A. H is not necessarily cyclic
B. H is finite
C. H is infinite
D. H is not necessarily abelian

38. The inverse of $A = \begin{pmatrix} 1 & 2 & 3 & 4 & 5 & 6 \\ 3 & 4 & 5 & 6 & 2 & 1 \end{pmatrix}$ is

A. $\begin{pmatrix} 1 & 2 & 3 & 4 & 5 & 6 \\ 6 & 5 & 1 & 2 & 3 & 4 \end{pmatrix}$

B. $\begin{pmatrix} 3 & 4 & 5 & 1 & 2 & 6 \\ 1 & 2 & 3 & 4 & 5 & 6 \end{pmatrix}$

C. $\begin{pmatrix} 1 & 2 & 3 & 4 & 5 & 6 \\ 1 & 2 & 6 & 5 & 4 & 3 \end{pmatrix}$

D. $\begin{pmatrix} 1 & 2 & 3 & 4 & 5 & 6 \\ 1 & 2 & 4 & 3 & 6 & 5 \end{pmatrix}$

39. If $z_1 = r_1(\cos\theta_1 + i\sin\theta_1)$ and $z_2 = r_2(\cos\theta_2 + i\sin\theta_2)$ then, which of the following is true.

A. $|z_1 + z_2|^2 + |z_1 - z_2|^2 = 2(|z_1|^2 + |z_2|^2)$
B. $|z_1 + z_2|^2 + |z_1 - z_2|^2 \geq 2(|z_1|^2 + |z_2|^2)$
C. $|z_1 + z_2|^2 + |z_1 - z_2|^2 \leq 2(|z_1|^2 + |z_2|^2)$
D. $|z_1 + z_2|^2 - |z_1 - z_2|^2 = 2(|z_1|^2 + |z_2|^2)$

40. The function $f(z) = \log(z + 2)$ has a branch point at

A. $z = -2$ B. $z = \pm 2$
C. $z = 0$ D. $z = \infty$

41. What is the solution of the differential equation

$$\frac{dy}{dx} = \frac{x(2\log x + 1)}{\sin y + y\cos y}$$

A. $y\sin y = x^2\log x + c$
B. $(1 + y^2)\cos y = x^2\log x + x + c$
C. $y\sin y + \cos y = x^2 + \log x + c$
D. None of these

42. If $\bar{E}$ and $\bar{F}$ are complementary events of the events E and F respectively and if $0 < P(F) < 1$, then

A. $P(E/F) + P(\bar{E}/F) = 1$
B. $P(E/F) + P(E/\bar{F}) = 1$
C. $P(\bar{E}/F) + P(E/\bar{F}) = 1$
D. $P(E/\bar{F}) + P(\bar{E}/\bar{F}) = 1$

43. If X and Y are independent variate with parameters $B\left(5, \frac{1}{2}\right)$ and $B\left(7, \frac{1}{2}\right)$ then $P(X + Y = 3)$

A. $\frac{55}{1024}$ B. $\frac{90}{1024}$
C. $\frac{45}{1024}$ D. $\frac{124}{1024}$

44. Given an L.P.P. to maximize
$z = -5x_2$
Subject to
$x_1 + x_2 \leq 1$
$0.5x_1 + 5x_2 \geq 0$
and $x_1 \geq 0$, $x_2 \geq 0$
using graphical method we have.

A. No feasible solution
B. Unbounded solution
C. Unique optimum solution
D. Muttiple optimum solutions

45. Let **U** be the vector space of all real polynomials. Consider the subspace W spanned by $t^2 + t + 2$, $t^2 + 2t + 5$, $5t^2 + 3t + 4$ and $2t^2 + 2t + 4$.

Then, the dimension of W is

A. 4 B. 3
C. 2 D. 1

46. Which one is not right statement.

A. Let $(G, \cdot)$ be group, $F : G \to G$ is such that $F(x) = e\ \forall\ x \in G$ is homomorphism.
B. Group $(R, +)$ and $(R_0, \cdot)$ are given, A mapping $F : R \to R_0$ is defined as $F(n) = 2^x$ is homomorphism.
C. Group $(I, +)$ is given $F : I \to I$ given by $F(x) = 2^x$, $\forall\ x \in I$, F is homomorphism.
D. $F : R \to R$ is given by $F(x) = 3x^2\ \forall\ x \in R$ $(R, +)$ is a group, F is homomorphism.

47. In which of the following methods proper choice of initial value is very important?

A. False position
B. Bisection method
C. Bairsto method
D. Newton-Raphson

48. If the set A and B are defined as
$A = \{(x, y) : y = e^x, x \in R\}$ and
$B = \{(x, y) : y = x, x \in R\}$ then

A. $B \subseteq A$ B. $A \subseteq B$
C. $A \cap B = \phi$ D. $A \cup B = A$

49. The value of E^2x^2, when the value of x vary by a constant increment of 2 is

A. $x^2 + 4x + 4$ B. $x^2 + 2$
C. $x^2 + 8x + 16$ D. None of these

50. If for a matrix A, $A^2 + I = 0$, where I is the identity matrix, then A is equal to which one of the following?

A. $\begin{bmatrix} 1 & 0 \\ 0 & 1 \end{bmatrix}$ B. $\begin{bmatrix} -i & 0 \\ 0 & -i \end{bmatrix}$

C. $\begin{bmatrix} 1 & 2 \\ -1 & 1 \end{bmatrix}$ D. $\begin{bmatrix} -1 & 0 \\ 0 & -1 \end{bmatrix}$

51. The function f be defined for all x and suppose the $|f(x) - f(y)| \le (x - y)^2$ for all real x and y. Then
A. f is strictly increasing
B. f is strictly decreasing
C. f is constant
D. f is strictly increasing for $x > 0$

52. If $f(x) = x^2$ if x is rational
$= -x^2$ if x is irrational

Then
A. $f(x)$ is nowhere continuous
B. $f(x)$ is nowhere differentiable
C. $f(x)$ has only one point of differentiability but $f''(x)$ doesn't exist there it
D. $f(x)$ has only one point of continuity but $f'(x)$ does not exist there at

53. Let X = R with co-finite topology. Then X is a
A. first countable space
B. T_1-space
C. Regular space
D. normal space

54. Let z denote the set of integers. Let p be a prime number and let z_1 {0, 1}
Let $f : z \to z$ and $g : z \to z_1$,
be defined as follows:
$f(n) = p_n$ for any $n \in z$
$g(n) = 1$, if n is a perfect square
$= 0$ otherwise
If we consider the composite function gof, then
A. gof is onto but f is not onto
B. gof is one-to-one but g is not one-to-one
C. gof is invertible but g is not invertible
D. f and g both are one-to-one

55. Five horses are in a race. Mr. A selects two of the horses at random and bets on them. The probability that Mr. A selected the winning horse is

A. $\frac{4}{5}$ B. $\frac{3}{5}$

C. $\frac{1}{5}$ D. $\frac{2}{5}$

56. If $y_1(x)$ and $y_2(x)$ are solution of
$y'' + x^2y' + (1 - x)y = 0$
such that
$y_1(0) = 0$, $y_1{}^1(0) = 1$
$y_2{}^1(0) = 1$, $y_2(0) = 1$
then the wronskian $W(y_1\ y_2)$ on R
A. 0 B. 1
C. – 1 D. 2

57. What is the solution of the differential equation $\sin px.\cos y = \cos px.\sin y + p$?
A. $y = cx^2 - \sin^{-1}c$
B. $y = cx - \sin^{-1}c$
C. $x = cy - \sin^{-1}c$
D. $x = cy^2 - \sin^{-1}c$.

58. Find the derivatives of the following at the indicated points. $(z + 2i)(i - z)/(2z - 1)$ at $z = i$

A. $-\frac{6+3i}{5}$ B. $\frac{6+3i}{5}$

C. $\frac{6-3i}{5}$ D. $-\frac{3}{5}(2+i)$

59. Consider the following linear transformation from the vector space $\mathbf{R}^2$ into the vector space $\mathbf{R}^3$:

$$T(x, y) = (-x - y, 3x + 8y, 9x - 11y)$$

Then the rank and nullity of T are respectively.
A. 2 and 0 B. 1 and 3
C. 2 and 1 D. 2 and 3

60. Let D be an integral domain with unity and I be an ideal of D then
A. If I is maximal then I is prime
B. If I is prime then I is maximal
C. $\langle 0 \rangle$ is maximal ideal of PD
D. If I is prime then D/I is field

ANSWERS

1	2	3	4	5	6	7	8	9	10
B	C	A	B	A	B	A	A	D	C
11	12	13	14	15	16	17	18	19	20
C	A	D	C	A	A	B	B	A	B
21	22	23	24	25	26	27	28	29	30
C	A	D	C	A	C	C	C	C	B
31	32	33	34	35	36	37	38	39	40
B	C	C	D	A	B	C	A	A	A
41	42	43	44	45	46	47	48	49	50
A	B	A	A	C	D	D	C	C	B
51	52	53	54	55	56	57	58	59	60
C	A	B	A	D	C	B	A	A	A

SOME SELECTED EXPLANATORY ANSWERS

2. Maclaurian series of tan$z$ is given by

$$\tan z = f(0)+\frac{z}{1!}f'(0)+\frac{z^2}{2!}f''(0)+\frac{z^3}{3!}f'''(0)$$

$$+\frac{z^4}{4!}-f^{iv}(0)+\frac{z^5}{5!}f^{v}(0)+....$$

Now, $f(0) = 0$

$f'(z) = \sec^2 z \Rightarrow f'(0) = 1$

$f''(z) = 2\sec^2 z \tan z \Rightarrow f''(0) = 0$

$f'''(z) = 2[\sec^4 z + 2\sec^2 z \tan^2 z]$

$\Rightarrow f'''(0) = 2$

$f^{iv}(z) = 2[4\sec^4 z \tan z + 4\sec^4 z \tan z + 2\tan^2 z.2\sec^2 z \tan z]$

$f^{iv}(z) = 2[8\sec^4 z \tan z + 4\tan^3 z \sec^2 z]$

$\Rightarrow f^{iv}(0) = 0$

$f^{v}(z) = 8[2\sec^6 z + 2.4\sec^4 z \tan^2 z + 3\tan^2 z \sec^4 z + \tan^3 z.2\sec^2 z \tan z]$

$\Rightarrow f^{v}(0) = 16.$

$$\therefore \quad \tan z = 0+z+0+\frac{z^3}{3!}.2+0+\frac{z^5}{120}\times 16+...$$

$$\Rightarrow \quad a_1 = 1,\ a_2 = \frac{1}{3},\ a_3 = \frac{2}{15}.$$

5. Clearly both S_1 and S_2 are closed under addition.

Let $A = \begin{pmatrix} p & q \\ r & s \end{pmatrix} \in M_{2\times 2}(R)$

then for $X_2 = \begin{pmatrix} a & b \\ 0 & 0 \end{pmatrix} \in S_2$

$$X_2A = \begin{pmatrix} a & b \\ 0 & 0 \end{pmatrix}\begin{pmatrix} p & q \\ r & s \end{pmatrix}$$

$$= \begin{pmatrix} ap+br & aq+bs \\ 0 & 0 \end{pmatrix} \in S_2$$

$\Rightarrow S_2$ is right ideal.

Similarly for $X_1 = \begin{pmatrix} a & 0 \\ b & 0 \end{pmatrix} \in S_1$

$$AX_1 = \begin{pmatrix} p & q \\ r & s \end{pmatrix}\begin{pmatrix} a & 0 \\ b & 0 \end{pmatrix}$$

$$= \begin{pmatrix} ap+br & 0 \\ aq+bs & 0 \end{pmatrix} \in S_1$$

Hence, S_1 is left ideal.

10. Given α = (13) (27) (456) (8) and β = (1237) (648) (5).

The computation of $\alpha\beta$ is done by expressing a permutation in a disjoint cycle form (*i.e.,* the various cycles have no number in common). Keeping this, the function composition is done from right to left and that each cycle that does not contain a symbol fixes the symbol, we observe that: (5) fixes 1; (648) fixes 1; (1237)

sends 1 to 2; 8 fixes 2; (456) fixes 2; (27) sends 2 to 7; and (13) fixes 7. So the net effect to $\alpha\beta$ is to send 1 to 7. Thus we begin $\alpha\beta$ = (17......). Now, repeating the entire process beginning with 7, we have cycle by cycle, right to left, $7 \to 7 \to 7 \to 1 \to 1 \to 1 \to 3$ so that $\alpha\beta$ = (173......) .... Ultimately, we have $\alpha\beta$ = (1732) (48) (56).

14. AB and AC are the two uniform rods smoothly jointed at A. They rest in a vertical plane with the ends B and C placed on a smooth horizontal plane.

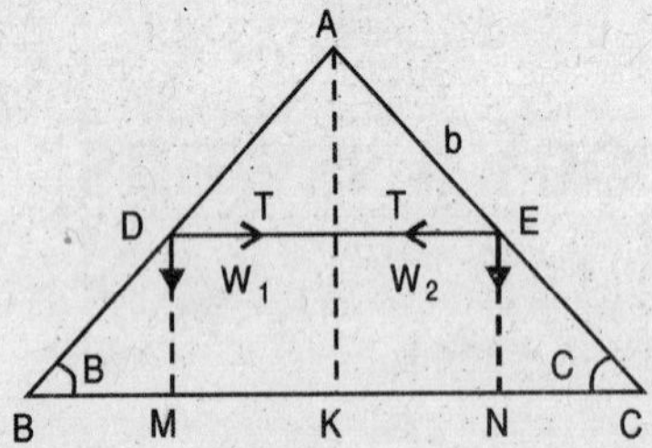

Let T be the system in the string connecting the middle points D and E of AB and AC respectively.

Let AB = $2a$ and AC = $2b$.

The weight W_1 of the rod AB acts at its middle point D and the weight W_2 of the rod AC acts at its middle point E.

Therefore total weight W = $W_1 + W_2$ of the two rods AB and AC acts at some point of the line DE which is parallel to BC.

Give the system a small displacement in which the angle B changes to B + δB and C changes to C + δC. The level of the line BC lying on the horizontal plane remain fixed and the points B and C move on this line.

The lengths of the rods AB and AC do not change, the length DE changes and the points D and E move.

We have

$$DE = DH + HE = a \cos B + b \cos C$$

the height of any point of the line DE above BC

$$= DM = a \sin B.$$

The equation of virtual work is

$$-T\delta(a \cos B + b \cos C) - W\delta(a \sin B) = 0$$

or $aT\sin B\delta B + bT\sin C\delta C - aW\cos B\delta B = 0$

or $a(W\cos B - T\sin B)\delta B = bT\sin C\delta C$ ...(1)

From the figure,

$$DM = a \sin B \text{ and } EN = b \sin C$$

Since DM = EN,

therefore $a \sin B = b \sin C$

$\therefore$ $\delta(a \sin B) = \delta(b \sin C)$

or $a \cos B\ \delta B = b \cos C\ \delta C$ ...(2)

dividing (1) by (2), we get

$$\frac{W\cos B - T\sin B}{\cos B} = \frac{T\sin C}{\cos C}$$

$$W - T\tan B = T\tan C$$

or $$T = \frac{W}{\tan B + \tan C}.$$

16. The series $\sum \frac{(-1)^{n-1}}{n^p}$, $p > 0$.

The above series is an alternating series.

Also for above series $u_n > u_{n+1}$ and $\lim_{n\to\infty} u_n \to 0$.

Hence by Leibnitz test, the above series is convergent.

19. $i^{\log(1+i)} = e^{\log_e(1+i).\log i}$

$$= e^{\left[\log\sqrt{1^2+1^2} + i\tan^{-1}1\right], \frac{1}{2}\pi i}$$

$$= e^{\left(\frac{1}{2}\log_e 2 + \frac{1}{4}\pi i\right)\left(\frac{\pi i}{2}\right)}$$

$$= e^{-\frac{\pi^2}{8}}.e^{i\left(\frac{\pi}{4}\log_e 2\right)}$$

$$= e^{-\frac{\pi^2}{8}}\left[\cos\left(\frac{\pi}{4}\log 2\right) + i\sin\left(\frac{\pi}{4}\log 2\right)\right]$$

$$\text{Real part} = e^{-\frac{\pi^2}{8}}\cos\left(\frac{\pi}{4}\log_e 2\right)$$

21. At fixed point $w = z$

$$\Rightarrow \quad z = \frac{2iz+5}{z-2i} \Rightarrow z^2 - 2iz = 2iz + 5$$

or $z^2 - 4iz - 5 = 0$

$\therefore \quad z = \dfrac{4i \pm \sqrt{-16+20}}{2} = \dfrac{4i \pm 2}{2}$

$= 2i \pm 1.$

23. $4\ddot{x} = -8x$

i.e. $w^2 = 2.$

Hence frequency $f = \dfrac{w}{2\pi} = \dfrac{\sqrt{2}}{2\pi} = \dfrac{1}{\sqrt{2}\pi}.$

27. T : $\mathbf{R}^3 \to \mathbf{R}^3$ be defined as $T(x, y, z) = (x, y, 0)$ The standard basis of $\mathbf{R}^3$ are {(1, 0, 0), (0, 1, 0), (0, 0, 1)}

Then T(1, 0, 0) = (1, 0, 0)
T(0, 1, 0) = (0, 1, 0)
T(0, 0, 1) = (0, 0, 0)

Clearly dim T = 2 < dim $\mathbf{R}^3$

i.e. T is singular

However $S(x, y) = (2x, 3y) = (0, 0)$

$\Rightarrow \quad x = 0, y = 0.$

i.e. Kernel(S) = (0, 0)

$\Rightarrow$ S is non-singular.

28. The given group is

$G = \{0, 1, 2, 3, 4, 5\}$

$(2 +_6 3^{-1} +_6 4) =_6 (2 + 3 + 4) =_6 9 = 3$

Also inverse of 3 = 3.

41. The given differential equation is

$$\frac{dy}{dx} = \frac{x(2\log x + 1)}{\sin y + y\cos y}$$

or, $(\sin y + y\cos y)dy = x(2\log x + 1)dx$

integrating we get

$y\sin y = x^2 \log x + c.$

45. The coordinate vectors of members of W with respect to basis $\{t^2, t, 1\}$ is (1, 1, 2), (1, 2, 5), (5, 3, 4), (2, 2, 4).

Now dimension of W is equal to number of independent rows in echelon form of co-ordinate vectors.

$$\text{i.e.} \begin{bmatrix} 1 & 1 & 2 \\ 1 & 2 & 5 \\ 5 & 3 & 4 \\ 2 & 2 & 4 \end{bmatrix} \sim \begin{bmatrix} 1 & 1 & 2 \\ 0 & 1 & 3 \\ 0 & -2 & -6 \\ 0 & 0 & 0 \end{bmatrix} \sim \begin{bmatrix} 1 & 1 & 2 \\ 0 & 1 & 3 \\ 0 & 0 & 0 \\ 0 & 0 & 0 \end{bmatrix}$$

i.e. dim (W) = 2.

49. Here

$E^2x^2 = E(Ex^2) = E(x + 2)^2$

$= (x + 2 + 2)^2 = (x + 4)^2 = x^2 + 8x + 16.$

56. $W(y_1, y_2)(0) = \begin{vmatrix} y_1(0) & y_2(0) \\ y_1^1(0) & y_2^1(0) \end{vmatrix}$

$= \begin{vmatrix} 0 & -1 \\ -1 & 1 \end{vmatrix} = -1 \neq 0$

and y_1, y_2 are solutions

$\Rightarrow W(y_1, y_2)(x) \neq 0 \qquad \forall x \in R$

59. The standard basis of $\mathbf{R}^2$ are $e_1 = (1, 0)$ and $e_2 = (0, 1)$.

Hence $T(e_1) = (-1, 3, 9)$

and $T(e_2) = (-1, 8, -11)$

Clearly (1, 3, 9) and (–1, 8, –11) are linear independent

hence dim (range T) = 2.

Also dim [range (T)] + dim(Ker T) = dim U where U = domain

$\Rightarrow$ dim (Ker T) = 2 – 2 = 0.

Set–6

CSIR–UGC (NET) Mathematical Sciences

PART-C

1. Let $f(z) = u + iv$ is an analytic function whose real part u is given as $e^{-x}(x\sin y - y\cos y)$ then the value of v is given by

A. $e^{-x}(y\cos y + x\sin y) + c$
B. $e^{-x}(y\sin y - x\cos y) + c$
C. $e^{-x}(y + x)\cos y + c$
D. $e^{-x}(y\sin y + x\cos y) + c$

2. If Σu_n is a series of positive terms, then

A. convergence of $\Sigma(-1)^n u_n$ implies the convergence of Σu_n
B. convergence of Σu_n implies the convergence of $\Sigma(-1)^n u_n$
C. convergence of $\Sigma(-1)^n u_n$ implies the divergence of Σu_n
D. divergence of Σu_n implies the divergence of $\Sigma(-1)^n u_n$

3. Let $f : \mathbf{R}^4 \to \mathrm{R}$ be a linear functional defined by $f(x_1, x_2, x_3, x_4) = -x_2$.

If $< . , . >$ denotes the standard inner product on $\mathbf{R}^4$, then the unique vector $v \in \mathrm{R}^4$ such that $f(w) = (v, w)$ for all $w \in \mathbf{R}^4$, is

A. $(0, -1, 0, 0)$ B. $(-1, 0, -1, 1)$
C. $(0, 1, 0, 0)$ D. $(1, 0, 1, -1)$

4. Let G be a group of order 45. Let H be a 3-Sylow subgroup of G and K be a 5-Sylow subgroup of G. Then

A. both H and K are normal in G.
B. H is normal in G but K is not normal in G.
C. H is not normal in G, but K is normal in G.
D. Both H and K are not normal in G.

5. The Newton-Raphson iteration $x_{n+1} = \dfrac{x_n}{2} + \dfrac{3}{2x_n}$ can be used to solve the equation

A. $x^3 = 2$ B. $x^2 = 2$
C. $x^3 = 3$ D. $x^2 = 3$

6. The General integral of equation $(y+zx)\dfrac{\partial z}{\partial x} - (x+yz)\dfrac{\partial z}{\partial y} + y^2 - x^2 = 0$ is given by $F(u, v) = 0$ where $u(x, y, z) = c_1$, $v(x, y, z) = c_2$ are given by one of the following

A. $u = x^2 + y^2 - z^2$, $v = xy + z$
B. $u = x^2 + y^2 + z^2$, $v = xz + y$
C. $u = x^2 + y^2 - z^2, \; v = \dfrac{x}{y} - z$
D. $u = x^2 + y^2 + z^2, \; v = \dfrac{x}{y} + z$

7. The general solution of $\dfrac{d^2y}{dx^2} - y = \sin x$ is $Ae^x + Be^x - \dfrac{1}{2}\sin x$, (A, B are constant). Which part of this solution is a particular integral

A. Ae^x B. Be^{-x}
C. $Ae^x + Be^{-x}$ D. $-\dfrac{1}{2}\sin x$

8. The integrating factor of the differential equation $[y + x \{x^2 + y^2) + \log(x^2 + y^2) + \tan(x^2 + y^2)\}]dx + [y(x^2 + y^2) - x]dy$ is

A. $\dfrac{1}{x^2 + y^2}$ B. $\dfrac{1}{xy}$
C. xy D. x^2y^2

9. The complete integral of the Partial Differential Equation is

$6zpq = 3p^2(3p^3 + 2xq) + 2q^2(2q^2 + 3yp)$ is

A. $z = 2ax + 3by + \dfrac{4a^4}{b} + \dfrac{4b^4}{a}$

B. $z = ax + by + \dfrac{4b^4}{a} + \dfrac{9a^4}{b}$

C. $z = ax + by + \frac{3a^4}{2b} + \frac{2b^4}{3a}$

D. $z = \frac{2}{3}ax + \frac{1}{3}by + \frac{3a^4}{2b} + \frac{2b^4}{3a}$

10. If C is a non-singular matrix and B $= C\begin{bmatrix} 0 & x & y \\ 0 & 0 & z \\ 0 & 0 & 0 \end{bmatrix}C^{-1}$, then

A. $B^2 = I$ B. $B^2 = 0$
C. $B^3 = I$ D. $B^3 = 0$

11. Four uniform rods are freely jointed at their extremities and form a parallelogram ABCD, which is suspended by the joint A, and is kept in shape by a string AC. Then the relation between tension of the string, and weight of all the four rods is given by

A. $T = \frac{1}{4}W$ B. $T = \frac{1}{2}W$
C. $T = W$ D. $T = 2W$

12. Let $\sigma = C_1 \cdot C_2$ where C_1 and C_2 both are disjoint cycles of S_n then which is incorrect?
A. σ has even order
B. σ is even permutation
C. If $\tau = T_1 \cdot T_2$ where T_1 and T_2 both are disjoint k-cycles then τ and σ are conjugate
D. None of these

13. If $\Sigma C_i X^i$ converges to the function $f(x)$ as an interval I, and if a and b are within the interval, then $\int_a^b f(x)\,dx$ is equal to

A. $\sum_{i=0}^{\infty} \int_a^b C_i X^i \, dx$

B. $-\int_a^b C_i X^i \, dx$

C. $\sum C_i X_i$

D. None of the above

14. Two linearly independent solutions of the differential equation $4\frac{d^2y}{dx^2} + 4\frac{dy}{dx} + 5y = 0$ are

A. $e^{-x/2}\cos x$ and $e^{-x/2}\sin x$
B. $e^{x/2}\cos x$ and $e^{x/2}\sin x$
C. $e^{x/2}\cos x$ and $e^{-x/2}\sin x$
D. $e^{-x/2}\cos x$ and $e^{x/2}\sin x$

15. The function $f(z)$ has a double pole at $z = 0$ with residue 2, a simple pole at $z = 1$ with residue 2, is analytic at all other finite points of the plane and is bounded as $|z| \to \infty$. If $f(z) = 5$ and $f(-1) = 2$ then $f(z)$.

A. $1 - \frac{2}{z-1} + \frac{2}{z} + \frac{4}{z^2}$ B. $1 + \frac{2}{z-1} + \frac{3}{z} + \frac{4}{z^2}$

C. $1 + \frac{2}{z-1} + \frac{2}{z} + \frac{4}{z^2}$ D. None of these

16. What is the solution of the differential equation $\frac{d^2y}{dx^2} - 2\frac{dy}{dx} + 2y = 0$, with the given conditions $y(0) = 0$ and $y'(0) = 1$?
A. $y = e^{-x}\cos x$
B. $y = e^{-x}\sin x$
C. $y = (\cos x + \sin x)e^{-x}$
D. $y = \sin x$

17. Three of the six vertices of a regular hexagon are chosen at random. The probability that the triangle with these three vertices is equilateral equals.

A. $\frac{1}{2}$ B. $\frac{1}{5}$

C. $\frac{1}{10}$ D. $\frac{1}{20}$

18. Consider the ring $\mathbb{Z}_n = \{\bar{0}, \bar{1}, \bar{2}, ..., \bar{n}\}$ of congruent modulo n classes. Under addition and multiplication modulo n, consider the following statements:
1. In $\mathbb{Z}_6$, $\bar{4}$ divides $\bar{2}$.
2. In $\mathbb{Z}_8$, $\bar{3}$ divides $\bar{7}$.
3. In $\mathbb{Z}_{15}$, $\bar{9}$ divides $\overline{12}$.

Which of the statements given above are correct?
A. 1 and 2 only B. 2 and 3 only
C. 1 and 3 only D. All of these

19. The solution of integral equation with the aid of resolved kernel $\phi(x) = \sin x + 2\int_0^x e^{x-t}\phi(t)\,dt$ will satisfy.

A. $\phi(0)+\phi\left(\frac{\pi}{2}\right)-\phi(\pi) = \frac{1}{5}e^{3\pi}(e^{\pi}-1)+\frac{2}{5}$

B. $\phi\left(\frac{\pi}{2}\right)-\phi(\pi) = \frac{1}{5}e^{\pi}\left(e^{\frac{3\pi}{2}}-1\right)+\frac{2}{5}$

C. $\phi(0)+\phi\left(\frac{\pi}{2}\right) = \frac{2}{5}$

D. $\phi\left(\frac{\pi}{2}\right)+\phi(\pi) = \frac{1}{5}e^{3\pi/2}+\frac{2}{5}$

20. Let G be a group then F : G → G defined by $F(a) = a^{-1}$ is automorphism if and only if

A. G is abelian B. G is non-abelian
C. G si complex D. None of these

21. If R_1 and R_2 be the ring with unity and $R = R_1 \times R_2$. Then

A. R is commutative iff R_1 and R_2 commutative
B. R is commutative even if both R_1 and R_2 are not
C. R is commutative then R_1 and R_2 commutative but need not be conversely
D. None of these

22. For the differential equation $xy' - y = 0$ which of the following function is not in integrating factor.

A. $\frac{1}{x^2}$ B. $\frac{1}{y^2}$
C. $\frac{1}{xy}$ D. $\frac{1}{x+y}$

23. Characteristic curves of $x^2r + 2xys + y^2t = 0$ are

A. family of circles with centre at origin.
B. family of straight lines passing through origin.
C. family of rectangular hyperbola.
D. family of helix.

24. The primal LPP is
Max $z = 7x_1 - 3x_2$
subject to $x_1 + x_2 \geq 3$, $8x_1 + 4x_2 \leq 16$, $5x_1 + 3x_2 \geq 15$, $x_1, x_2 \geq 0$
Then dual of this problem has

A. Unique feasible and optimal solution
B. No feasible solution
C. Infinite number of feasible solution but not any optimal solution
D. Degenerate optimal solution

25. The degree of the differential equation $\left(\frac{d^2y}{dx^2}\right)^{3/2} - \left(\frac{dy}{dx}\right)^{1/2} - 4 = 0$ is given

A. 2 B. 3
C. 4 D. 6

26. The topology D τ on the real line R generated by the class $\mathfrak{I}$ of all closed intervals $[d, d + l]$ with length l is

A. increase
B. discrete
C. standard topology
D. neither discrete nor Housdorff

27. The L.P.P. max
$z = 3x_1 - 4x_2$
subject to
$x_1 - x_2 \geq 0$
$x_1 \leq 6$, $x_1, x_2 \geq 0$ has

A. No solution
B. Multiple optimal solution
C. Unique optimal solution
D. Unbounded solution

28. Let T be the linear operator on C^3 defined by $T(x, y, z) = (2x + (1 - i)y, (3 + 2i)x - 4iz, 2ix + (4 - 3i)y - 3z)$, then $T^*(x, y, z)$ is given by

A. $(2x + (3 + 2i)y + 2iz, (1 - i)x + (4 - 3i)z, 4iy - 3z)$
B. $(2x + (3 - 2i)y - 2iz, (1 + i)x + (4 + 3i)z, 4iy - 3z)$
C. $(2x + (3 - 2i)y + 2iz, (1 + i)x + (4 - 3i)z, 4iy + 3z)$
D. None of the above

29. Let $A \in R^{n\times n}$, $B \leftarrow R^n$, consider the two system of linear equations
(A) $Ax = b$
(B) $A'Az = A'n$

then

A. Both (A) and (B) have the same sol.

B. (A) has more solutions than (B)

C. Both (A) and (B) may not have any solution

D. (A) may not have any solution but (B) always has atleast one solution

30. Degree and order of differential equation of all parabolas whole axis is x axis are

A. 2, 1 B. 3, 2

C. 1, 2 D. None of these

31. The optimal value z^* of the objective function of the L.P.P.

min $z = 3x_1 + 5x_2 + 7x_3$

subject to $5x_1 + 15x_2 + 10x_3 = 150$

$x_1, x_2, x_3 \geq 0$ is

A. $10 < z^* < 20$ B. $25 \leq z^*$ £ 40

C. $z^* > 60$ D. $40 < z^* < 60$

32. If z is a complex number satisfying $\left|z+\frac{1}{z}\right| = a.$

Then the greatest value of $|z|$ is

A. $\frac{\left\{a+\sqrt{a^2+4}\right\}}{2}$ B. $\frac{\left\{a-\sqrt{a^2+4}\right\}}{2}$

C. $\frac{\left\{2a+\sqrt{a^2+4}\right\}}{2}$ D. $\left\{\frac{\left(a^2+4\right)}{2}\right\}$

33. The set $X = \mathbb{R}$ with metric $d(x, y) = \frac{|x-y|}{1+|x-y|}$

is

A. bounded but not compact

B. bounded but not complete

C. complete but not bounded

D. compact but not complete

34. If $i^{i^i} = \cos\theta + i\sin\theta$, value of θ

A. $\left(2m+\frac{1}{2}\right)\pi.e^{-\left(2n+\frac{1}{2}\right)\pi}$

B. $\left(2m-\frac{1}{2}\right)\pi e^{-\left(2n+\frac{1}{2}\right)\pi}$

C. $\left(2m+\frac{1}{2}\right)\pi.e^{-\left(2n-\frac{1}{2}\right)\pi}$

D. $\left(2m+\frac{1}{2}\right)\pi e^{+\left(2n-\frac{1}{2}\right)\pi}$

35. The function f defined by

$$f(x) = \frac{x^2}{a} - a, \qquad (0 < x < a)$$

$$= a - \frac{a^3}{x^2} \qquad x \geq a$$

A. is not continuous on $(0, \infty)$

B. is not differentiable on $(0, \infty)$

C. is differentiable on $(0, \infty)$

D. is differentiable on $(0, \infty)$ except at $x = a$

36. Find the smallest subgroup of Z containing 8 and 13 the notation for this $\langle 8, 13\rangle$.

A. $8Z$ B. Z

C. $13Z$ D. $104Z$

37. The differential equation $(y - 2x^3)dx - x(1 - xy)dy = 0$ becomes exact on multiplication with which one of the following?

A. x B. x^2

C. $1/x^2$ D. $1/x$

38. If $y = f(x)$ satisfies the differential equation $y(0) = 0$ then

A. $|f(x)| \leq x^2$ B. $|f(x)| \leq |x|$

C. $|f(x)| \leq |\sin x|$ D. $|f(x)| \leq |\cos x|$

39. In the motion of a two particle system, if two particles are connected by a rigid weightless rod of constant length, then the number of degrees of freedom of the system is

A. 2 B. 3

C. 5 D. 6

40. If $f(x) = \sum_{n=1}^{\infty}\frac{\sin nx}{n^3}$ then $\int_0^{\pi} f(x)dx$ be

A. $2\sum_{n=1}^{\infty}\frac{1}{(n-1)^4}$ B. $2\sum_{n=1}^{\infty}\frac{1}{(2n-1)^4}$

C. $4\sum_{n=1}^{\infty}\frac{1}{n^4}$ D. $6\sum_{n=1}^{\infty}\frac{1}{(2n+1)^4}$

41. The fixed or invariant points of the transformation $w = \frac{2z-5}{z+4}$ is given by

A. $2 \pm i$ B. $-2 \pm i$

C. $1 \pm 2i$ D. $-1 \pm 2i$

42. If A = $\begin{bmatrix} 0 & \alpha \\ \beta & 0 \end{bmatrix}$ then when is $A^3 + A = 0$?

A. If $\alpha\beta = 0$ B. If $\alpha\beta = \frac{1}{2}$

C. If $\alpha\beta = 1$ D. If $\alpha\beta = -1$

43. The solution of the differential equation $xdy - ydx = \sqrt{x^2 - y^2}\,dx$ is

A. $y = x\sin(c + \log y)$

B. $y = x^2\sin(c + \log x)$

C. $y = x\sin(cx + \log x)$

D. None of these

44. A random variable X has the following probability distribution

X:	1	2	3	4	5	6	7	8
$P(x)$	0.15	0.23	0.12	0.10	0.20	0.08	0.007	0.05

For the events E {X is a prime number} and F = {$X < 4$}, the probability $P(E \cup F)$ is

A. 0.87 B. 0.77

C. 0.35 D. 0.50

45. The equation $az^n = e^z$, if $a > e$, inside $|z| = 1$ has

A. n roots B. $(n - 1)$ roots

C. no roots D. only one root

46. $z_1 = x_1 + iy_1$ and $z_2 = x_2 + iy_2$, value of $z_1 \times z_2$ is

A. $\frac{1}{2i}\{\bar{z}_1 z_2 - z_1\bar{z}_2\}$ B. $-\frac{1}{2i}\{\bar{z}_1 z_2 - z_1\bar{z}_2\}$

C. $\frac{1}{2}\{\bar{z}_1 z_2 - z_1\bar{z}_2\}$ D. $\frac{1}{i}\{\bar{z}_1 z_2 + z_1\bar{z}_2\}$

47. If $A = \{(x, y) : y = e^x, x \in R\}$ and $B = \{(x, y) : y = e^{-x}, x \in R\}$ then

A. $A \cap B = \phi$ B. $A \cup B \neq \phi$

C. $A \cap B = R^2$ D. None of these

48. Consider the set S for all real numbers except -1 and the binary operation $*$ on S defined by $a*b = a + b + ab$.

Consider the equation $2 * x * 2 * 2 = 2$ in S. Which one of the following is correct?

A. The equation has no solution in S.

B. The equation has a solution which is a positive integer.

C. The solution is a positive rational number.

D. The equation has a negative solution.

49. Let $f(z) = |z|\mathrm{Re}(z)$ or 0 according as Re $(z) \neq 0$ or Re $(z) = 0$, then at $z = 0$, the function $f(z)$ is:

A. having nozero limit

B. differentiable

C. continuous but not differentiable

D. neither continuous nor differentiable

50. For a game $\begin{pmatrix} a & -b \\ -c & d \end{pmatrix}$ value of the game

A. $ab + cd/a + b + c + d$

B. $ad - bc/a + b - c - d$

C. $ad - bc/a + b + c + d$

D. $-ad + bc/-a - b + c + d$

51. The density function of random variable X is given by

$$f(x) = \begin{cases} a + bx^2, & 0 \le x \le 1 \\ 0 & \text{otherwise} \end{cases}.$$

If the expected value of X equals $\frac{2}{3}$, then

A. $a = 3, b = \frac{1}{2}$ B. $a = 0, b = 3$

C. $a = \frac{1}{3}, b = 2$ D. $a = 2, b = \frac{1}{3}$

52. The selection of an appropriate order in which to service waiting customers is called

A. Queueing probability

B sequencing

C. Pert path

D. None

53. The value of $\frac{\Delta^2}{E}\sin x$ is

A. 2 sin x (sinh + 1)

B. 2 sin x (sinh − 1)

C. 2 sin x (cosh + 1)

D. 2 sin x (cosh − 1)

54. If n is a positive integer and A = $\begin{bmatrix} \cos\theta & \sin\theta \\ -\sin\theta & \cos\theta \end{bmatrix}$, then what is A^n equal to

A. $\begin{bmatrix} \cos n\theta & -\sin n\theta \\ \sin n\theta & \cos n\theta \end{bmatrix}$

B. $\begin{bmatrix} -\cos n\theta & \sin n\theta \\ \sin n\theta & \cos n\theta \end{bmatrix}$

C. $\begin{bmatrix} \cos n\theta & \sin n\theta \\ \sin n\theta & -\cos n\theta \end{bmatrix}$

D. $\begin{bmatrix} \cos n\theta & \sin n\theta \\ -\sin n\theta & \cos n\theta \end{bmatrix}$

55. Let B a Banach space (not finite dimensional) and T : B → B be a continuous operator such that the range of T is B and $T(x) = 0 \Rightarrow x = 0$. Then

A. T maps bounded sets to compact sets
B. T^{-1} maps bounded sets to compact sets
C. T^{-1} maps bounded sets to bounded sets
D. T maps compact sets to open set

56. If $5f(x) + 3f\left(\frac{1}{x}\right) = x + 2$ and $y = xf(x)$, then $\left(\frac{dy}{dx}\right)_{x=1}$ is equal to

A. 14 B. $\frac{7}{8}$
C. 1 D. $\frac{8}{7}$

57. A ring (R, +, .) is called commutative ring if for a, b, ∈ R.

A. $(ab)\,c = a\,(bc)$ B. $ab = ba$
C. $a + b = b + a$ D. None of these

58. Let A = $\begin{pmatrix} \lambda & a \\ 0 & \lambda \end{pmatrix}$ where $a \neq 0$. If $m(x)$ and $\xi(x)$ are the minimum and the characteristic polynomial respectively of A, then

A. $m(x) \neq \xi(x)$
B. the degree of the minimum polynomial is I
C. $m(x) = \xi(x)$
D. A has two distinct characteristic roots

59. If A = $\begin{bmatrix} 3 & 8 \\ 2 & 1 \end{bmatrix}$, then A^{-1} is

A. $\frac{1}{13}\begin{bmatrix} 3 & 2 \\ 8 & 1 \end{bmatrix}$ B. $-\frac{1}{13}\begin{bmatrix} 1 & -8 \\ -2 & 3 \end{bmatrix}$

C. $\frac{1}{-13}\begin{bmatrix} 3 & 2 \\ 8 & 1 \end{bmatrix}$ D. $\frac{1}{13}\begin{bmatrix} 1 & -8 \\ -2 & 8 \end{bmatrix}$

60. Let M = $\begin{bmatrix} 1 & a & b \\ 0 & 2 & c \\ 0 & 0 & 1 \end{bmatrix}$, $a, b, c \in$ R.

Then, M is diagonalizable, if and only if

A. $a = bc$ B. $b = ac$
C. $c = ab$ D. $a = b = c$

ANSWERS

1	2	3	4	5	6	7	8	9	10
B	B	A	A	D	A	D	A	C	D
11	12	13	14	15	16	17	18	19	20
B	C	A	A	C	B	C	D	A	B
21	22	23	24	25	26	27	28	29	30
A	D	C	B	C	B	D	B	C	D
31	32	33	34	35	36	37	38	39	40
C	A	B	A	D	B	C	C	D	B
41	42	43	44	45	46	47	48	49	50
D	D	D	B	A	A	B	D	D	C
51	52	53	54	55	56	57	58	59	60
C	B	D	D	C	B	B	C	B	B

SOME SELECTED EXPLANATORY ANSWERS

1. Given, $u = e^{-x}(x\sin y - y\cos y)$

then, $u_x = e^{-x}(-x\sin y + y\cos y + \sin y)$

$u_y = e^{-x}(x\cos y - \cos y + y\sin y)$

$\therefore \quad dv = v_x dx + u_y dy$

$= u_{ydx} + u_x \, dy$

$= e^{-x}(\cos y - x\cos y - y\sin y)dx$
$+ e^{-x}(-x\sin y + y\cos y + \sin y)dy$

on integrating, we get

$e^{-x}(y\sin y - x\cos y) + c.$

10. Given $B = C\begin{bmatrix}0 & x & y\\ 0 & 0 & z\\ 0 & 0 & 0\end{bmatrix}C^{-1}$

hence

$$B^2 = C\begin{bmatrix}0 & x & y\\ 0 & 0 & z\\ 0 & 0 & 0\end{bmatrix}C^{-1}, C\begin{bmatrix}0 & x & y\\ 0 & 0 & z\\ 0 & 0 & 0\end{bmatrix}C^{-1}$$

$$= C\begin{bmatrix}0 & x & y\\ 0 & 0 & z\\ 0 & 0 & 0\end{bmatrix}\begin{bmatrix}0 & x & y\\ 0 & 0 & z\\ 0 & 0 & 0\end{bmatrix}C^{-1}$$

$$= C\begin{bmatrix}0 & 0 & xz\\ 0 & 0 & 0\\ 0 & 0 & 0\end{bmatrix}C^{-1}$$

hence

$$B^3 = C\begin{bmatrix}0 & 0 & xz\\ 0 & 0 & 0\\ 0 & 0 & 0\end{bmatrix}C^{-1}\cdot C\begin{bmatrix}0 & x & y\\ 0 & 0 & z\\ 0 & 0 & 0\end{bmatrix}C^{-1}$$

$$= C^{-1}\begin{bmatrix}0 & 0 & xz\\ 0 & 0 & 0\\ 0 & 0 & 0\end{bmatrix}\begin{bmatrix}0 & x & y\\ 0 & 0 & z\\ 0 & 0 & 0\end{bmatrix}C^{-1}$$

$$= C^{-1}\begin{bmatrix}0 & 0 & 0\\ 0 & 0 & 0\\ 0 & 0 & 0\end{bmatrix}C = 0.$$

11. ABCD is a framework in the shape of a parallelogram formed of four uniform rods. It is suspended from the point A and is kept in shape by a string AC.

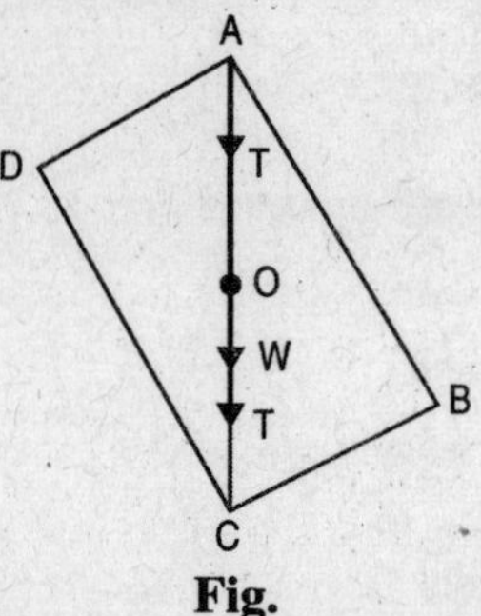

Fig.

Let T be the tension in the string AC.

The total weight W of all the four rods AB, BC, CD and DA can be taken as acting at O, the middle point of AC.

Since the force of reaction at the point of suspension A balances the weight W at O, therefore, the line AO must be vertical,

let $AC = 2x$.

Give the system a small displacement in which x changes to $x + \delta x$ and AC remains vertical.

The point A remains fixed, the point O changes and the length AC changes.

We have, $AO = x$.

By the principle of virtual work, we have

$$-T\delta(AC) + W\delta(AO) = 0$$

or $$-T\delta(2x) + W\delta(x) = 0$$

or $$-2T\delta x + W\delta x = 0$$

or $$-2T + W = 0$$

or $$T = \frac{1}{2}W.$$

15. The function $f(z)$ is given to have a pole of order one at $z = 1$ with residue 2 and a double pole at $z = 0$ with residue 2 so the principal part of $f(z)$ is of the from $\dfrac{2}{z-1}+\dfrac{2}{z}+\dfrac{b}{z^2}$.

The Laurent's expansion of $f(z)$ will be of the form

$$f(z) = \sum_{n=0}^{\infty} a_n z^n + \frac{2}{z-1} + \frac{2}{z} + \frac{b}{z^2} \quad ...(1)$$

As $f(z)$ is bounded when $|z| \to \infty$ therefore there exist a positive constant M such that $|f(z)| \leq M$ for all z. It means $f(z)$ has no singularity at $z = \infty$. Consequently, $f\left(\frac{1}{w}\right)$ has no singularity at $w = 0$.

Therefore, the principal part of $f\left(\frac{1}{w}\right)$ contains no term.

We have, $f\left(\frac{1}{w}\right) = a_0 + \sum \frac{a_n}{w^n} + \frac{2w}{1-w} + 2w + bw^2.$

As principal part of $f\left(\frac{1}{w}\right)$ contain no term if

$$a_1 = a_2 = a_3 = ...0.$$

Hence, (1) becomes

$$f(z) = a_0 + \frac{2}{z-1} + \frac{2}{z} + \frac{b}{z^2} \quad ...(2)$$

From question, $f(2) = 5$, $f(-1) = 2$.

Substituting these, we get $a_0 = 1$, $b = 4$.

$$\therefore \quad f(z) = 1 + \frac{2}{z-1} + \frac{2}{z^2} + \frac{4}{z^2}.$$

18. $\overline{4} \cdot \overline{5} = \overline{2}$ in z_6.

$\overline{3} \cdot \overline{5} = \overline{7}$ in z_8.

$\overline{9}\ \overline{3} = \overline{12}$ in z_{12}.

i.e., all are true.

24. The given primal LPP is

$$\max Z = 7x_1 - 3x_2$$

subject to

$x_1 + x_2 \geq 3$, $8x_1 + 4x_2 \leq 16$, $5x_1 + 3x_2 \geq 15$

as primal LPP is of maximization type, converting all the inequalities into ($\leq$) type. We get

$$\max Z = 7x_1 - 3x_2$$

subject to
$$-x_1 - x_2 \leq -3$$
$$8x_1 + 4x_2 \leq 16$$
$$-5x_1 - 3x_2 \leq -15.$$

Now by the duality principle, we get

$$\text{Min } Z' = -3y_1 + 16y_2 - 15y_3$$

subject
$$-y_1 + 8y_2 - 5y_3 \geq 7$$
$$-y_2 + 4y_2 - 3y_3 \geq -3$$

for determining the basic solution, we make any one out of three equal to zero, case by case.

Case I: When $y_1 = 0$

then
$$8y_2 - 5y_3 = 7$$
$$4y_2 - 3y_3 = -3$$
$$\Rightarrow \quad -5y_3 + 6y_3 = 13$$
$$\Rightarrow \quad y_3 = 13$$
$$\Rightarrow \quad 8y_2 = 7 + 65 = 72$$
$$y_2 = \frac{72}{8} = 9.$$

i.e. $y_1 = 0$, $y_2 = 9$, $y_3 = 13$.

Case II: When $y_2 = 0$

then
$$-y_1 - 5y_3 = 7$$
$$-y_1 - 3y_3 = -3$$
$$\Rightarrow \quad -2y_3 = 10 \quad y_3 = -5 \text{ (not basic)}$$

Case III: When $y_3 = 0$

$$-y_1 + 8y_2 = 7$$
$$-y_1 + 4y_2 = -3$$
$$\Rightarrow \quad 4y_2 = 10$$
$$y_2 = \frac{5}{2}$$
$$-y_1 + 10 = -3$$
$$\Rightarrow \quad y_1 = 13.$$

28. The matrix A representing T in the usual basis of C^3

$$A = \begin{bmatrix} 2 & 1-i & 0 \\ 3+2i & 0 & -4i \\ 2i & 4-3i & -3 \end{bmatrix}$$

Hence the conjugate transpose A* of A is given by

$$A^* = \begin{bmatrix} 2 & 3-2i & -2i \\ 1+i & 0 & 4+3i \\ 0 & 4i & -3 \end{bmatrix}$$

Thus T*(x, y, z) = {2x + (3 – 2i)y – 2iz, (1 + i)x + (4 + 3i)z, 4iy – 3z}.

36. Also (8, 13) = 1 both 8Z, and 13Z will be completely contained in Z only.

40. $\left|\dfrac{\sin nx}{n^3}\right| \le \dfrac{1}{n^3} \quad \forall x$

By weierstrass's M-test, the given series is uniformly convergent for all x, particular $0 \le x \le \pi$ and can be integrated term by term.

$$\int_0^{\pi} f(x)dx = \int_0^{\pi}\left(\sum_{n=1}^{\infty}\frac{\sin nx}{n^3}\right)dx$$

$$= \sum_{n=1}^{\infty}\int_0^{\pi}\frac{\sin nx}{n^3}dx = \sum_{n=1}^{\infty}\left(\frac{1-\cos n\pi}{n^4}\right)$$

$$= 2\left(\frac{1}{1^4}+\frac{1}{3^4}+\frac{1}{5^4}+...\right) = 2\sum_{n=1}^{\infty}\frac{1}{(2n-1)^4}$$

41. The fixed points are solutions to

$$z = \frac{2z-5}{z+4}$$

or, $z^2 + 2z + 5 = 0$

i.e. $z = -1 \pm 2i$.

42. If $A = \begin{bmatrix} 0 & \alpha \\ \beta & 0 \end{bmatrix}$

then $A^2 = \begin{bmatrix} 0 & \alpha \\ \beta & 0 \end{bmatrix}\begin{bmatrix} 0 & \alpha \\ \beta & 0 \end{bmatrix} = \begin{bmatrix} \alpha\beta & 0 \\ 0 & \alpha\beta \end{bmatrix}$

and $A^3 =$

$$\begin{bmatrix} \alpha\beta & 0 \\ 0 & \alpha\beta \end{bmatrix}\begin{bmatrix} 0 & \alpha \\ \beta & 0 \end{bmatrix} = \begin{bmatrix} 0 & \alpha^2\beta \\ \alpha\beta^2 & 0 \end{bmatrix}$$

Now $A^3 + A = \begin{bmatrix} 0 & \alpha^2\beta \\ \alpha\beta^2 & 0 \end{bmatrix} + \begin{bmatrix} 0 & \alpha \\ \beta & 0 \end{bmatrix}$

$$= \begin{bmatrix} 0 & \alpha(1+\alpha\beta) \\ \beta(1+\alpha\beta) & 0 \end{bmatrix} = \begin{bmatrix} 0 & 0 \\ 0 & 0 \end{bmatrix}$$

$\Rightarrow \alpha(1 + \alpha\beta) = 0$ & $\beta(1 + \alpha\beta) = 0$

both of above equation will satisfy for $\alpha\beta = -1$.

43. The given differential equation is

$$xdy - ydx = \sqrt{x^2 - y^2}\,dx$$

or, $x\dfrac{dy}{dx} - y = \sqrt{x^2 - y^2}$

or, $\dfrac{dy}{dx} - \dfrac{y}{x} = \sqrt{1 - \dfrac{y^2}{x^2}}$

let $y = vx$ then $\dfrac{dy}{dx} = v + x\dfrac{dv}{dx}$

$\Rightarrow \quad v + x\dfrac{dv}{dx} - v = \sqrt{1 - v^2}$

or, $\dfrac{dv}{\sqrt{1-v^2}} = \dfrac{dx}{x}$

integrating both the sides, we get

$$\sin^{-1}v = \log x + C$$

or, $v = \sin(C + \log x)$

i.e. $\dfrac{y}{x} = \sin(C + \log x)$

or, $y = x\sin(C + \log x)$.

46. $z_1 = x_1 + iy_1$; $z_2 = x_2 + iy_2$ complex vectors

$\bar{z}_1 z_2 = (x_1 - iy_1)(x_2 + iy_2)$

$= (x_1x_2 + y_1y_2) + i(x_1y_2 - x_2y_1)$

$= \quad z_1 . z_2 \quad + i \quad z_1 \times z_2$

Dot product   Vector product

$\because \quad z_1.z_2 = |z_1||z_2|\cos\theta = x_1x_2 + y_1y_2$

$$= \text{Re}(\bar{z}_1 z_2) = \frac{1}{2}(\bar{z}_1 z_2 + z_1\bar{z}_2)$$

$\because \quad z_1 \times z_2 = |z_1||z_2|\sin\theta\, i = (x_1y_2 - y_1x_2)i$

$$= I_m(\bar{z}_1 z_2) = \frac{1}{2i}(\bar{z}_1 z_2 - z_1\bar{z}_2)$$

48. The given equation is

$$2*x*2*2 = 2$$

$\Rightarrow \quad 2*x(2 + 2 + 2.2) = 2$

$\Rightarrow \quad 2*(x*8) = 2$

$\Rightarrow \quad 2 * (x + 8 + x.8) = 2$

$\Rightarrow \quad 2 * (9x + 8) = 2$

$\Rightarrow \quad 2 + 9x + 8 + 2(9x + 8) = 2$

$\Rightarrow \quad 27x + 26 = 2$

$\Rightarrow \quad x = -\dfrac{8}{9} \in R.$

53. $\dfrac{\Delta^2}{E}$ (sin x) (E – 2 + E^{-1}) (sin x)

= sin ($x + h$) – 2 sin x + sin ($x - h$)

$= \sin(x+h) + \sin(x-h) - 2\sin x$

$$= 2\sin\frac{(x+h)+(x-h)}{2}\cos\frac{(x+h)-(x-h)}{2} - 2\sin x$$

$= 2\sin x.\cos h - 2\sin x = 2\sin x(\cosh - 1)$.

54. Since $A = \begin{bmatrix}\cos\theta & \sin\theta\\ -\sin\theta & \cos\theta\end{bmatrix}$

$$A^2 = \begin{bmatrix}\cos\theta & \sin\theta\\ -\sin\theta & \cos\theta\end{bmatrix}\begin{bmatrix}\cos\theta & \sin\theta\\ -\sin\theta & \cos\theta\end{bmatrix}$$

$$= \begin{bmatrix}\cos^2\theta - \sin^2\theta & 2\cos\theta\sin\theta\\ -2\sin\theta\cdot\cos\theta & -\sin^2\theta+\cos^2\theta\end{bmatrix}$$

$$= \begin{bmatrix}\cos 2\theta & \sin 2\theta\\ -\sin 2\theta & \cos 2\theta\end{bmatrix}$$

Also $A^3 = \begin{bmatrix}\cos 2\theta & \sin 2\theta\\ -\sin 2\theta & \cos 2\theta\end{bmatrix}\begin{bmatrix}\cos\theta & \sin\theta\\ -\sin\theta & \cos\theta\end{bmatrix}$

$$= \begin{bmatrix}\cos 2\theta\cdot\cos\theta - \sin 2\theta\cdot\sin\theta & \cos 2\theta\cdot\sin\theta + \sin 2\theta\cdot\sin\theta\\ -\sin 2\theta\cdot\cos\theta - \cos 2\theta\cdot\sin\theta & -\sin 2\theta\cdot\sin\theta + \cos 2\theta\cdot\cos\theta\end{bmatrix}$$

$$= \begin{bmatrix}\cos 3\theta & \sin 3\theta\\ -\sin 3\theta & \cos 3\theta\end{bmatrix}$$

Similarly,

$$A^n = \begin{bmatrix}\cos n\theta & \sin n\theta\\ -\sin n\theta & \cos n\theta\end{bmatrix}$$

56. The given functional relation is

$$5f(x) + 3f\left(\frac{1}{x}\right) = x + 2 \qquad ...(1)$$

putting $\frac{1}{x}$ in place of x, we get

$$5f\left(\frac{1}{x}\right) + 3f(x) = \frac{1}{x} + 2 \qquad ...(2)$$

Apply $5 \times (1) - 3 \times (2)$, we get

$$(25-9)f(x) = 5(x+2) - 3\left(\frac{1}{x}+2\right)$$

$$= \left(5x - \frac{3}{x} + 4\right)$$

$$\Rightarrow \quad f(x) = \frac{1}{16}\left[5x - \frac{3}{x} + 4\right]$$

Now $\quad y = xf(x)$

$$\Rightarrow \quad \frac{dy}{dx} = f(x) + xf'(x)$$

Hence $\quad \left.\frac{dy}{dx}\right|_{x=1} = f(1) + f'(1)$

Now $\quad f(x) = \frac{1}{16}\left[5x - \frac{3}{x} + 4\right]$

$$\Rightarrow \quad f(1) = \frac{1}{16}[5-3+4] = \frac{6}{16} = \frac{3}{8}$$

$$f'(x) = \frac{1}{16}\left[5 + \frac{3}{x^2}\right]$$

$$= \frac{1}{16}[5+3] = \frac{8}{16} = \frac{1}{2}.$$

Hence $\quad \left.\frac{dy}{dx}\right|_{x=1} = \frac{3}{8} + \frac{1}{2} = \frac{3+4}{8} = \frac{7}{8}.$

59. The given matrix A is

$$A = \begin{bmatrix}3 & 8\\ 2 & 1\end{bmatrix} \quad |A| = 3 - 16 = -13.$$

$$\text{Adj } A = \begin{bmatrix}1 & -8\\ -2 & 3\end{bmatrix}$$

$$\Rightarrow \quad A^{-1} = \frac{\text{Adj } A}{|A|} = -\frac{1}{13}\begin{bmatrix}1 & -8\\ -2 & 3\end{bmatrix}.$$

60. Any matrix is diagonalizable if algebraic multiplicity of its each eigenvalue should be equal to corresponding geometric multiplicity.

Now the given matrix $M = \begin{bmatrix}1 & a & b\\ 0 & 2 & c\\ 0 & 0 & 1\end{bmatrix}$ the characteristic equation is $|M - \lambda I| = 0$

$$\text{or} \quad \begin{bmatrix}1-\lambda & a & b\\ 0 & 2-\lambda & c\\ 0 & 0 & 1-\lambda\end{bmatrix} = 0$$

or $(1-\lambda)^2(2-\lambda) = 0$

or $\lambda = 1, 1, 2$.

Now for $\lambda = 1$, $|M - \lambda I| = 0$

$$\Rightarrow \begin{vmatrix}0 & a & b\\ 0 & 1 & c\\ 0 & 0 & 0\end{vmatrix} = 0.$$

However, above determinant must have rank = 1, so that it shall have two eigenvectors. for this to happen, $ac - b = 0$, *i.e.* $b = ac$.

SET–7
CSIR–UGC (NET) MATHEMATICAL SCIENCES
PART-C

1. Let $\{v_1, v_2, ..., v_{16}\}$ be an ordered basis for V $= C^{16}$. If T is a linear transformation on V defined by $T(v_i) = v_i + 1$ for $1 \le i \le 15$ and $T(v_{16}) = -(v_1 + v_2 + ... + v_{16})$. Then

A. T is singular with rational eigenvalues.

B. T is singular but has no rational eigenvalues.

C. T is regular (invertible) with rational eigenvalues.

D. T is regular but has no rational eigenvalues.

2. If $f(z)=\dfrac{1}{z(e^z-1)}$ is expanded by Laurent series in form of $\sum_{n=-\infty}^{\infty} a_n z^n$ then the value of a_2 is

A. $-\dfrac{1}{12}$ B. $-\dfrac{1}{120}$

C. $-\dfrac{1}{720}$ D. $-\dfrac{1}{7200}$

3. The value of $\iint_S (\bar{\nabla}\times\bar{A})\cdot\hat{n}\,ds$ where $A = (x - z)\hat{i} + (x^2 + yz)\hat{j} - 3xy^2\hat{k}$ and S is the surface of the cone $z = 2-\sqrt{x^2+y^2}$ above xy plane

A. 4π B. 8π

C. 12π D. 16π

4. Let $T : R^3 \to R^2$ be the linear transformation given by $T(x, y, z) = (x, y)\ \forall\ (x, y, z) \in R^3$ with respect to standard basis of $\mathbf{R}^3$ and the basis of $\{(1, 0), (1, 1)\}$ of $\mathbf{R}^2$, what is the matrix representation of T?

A. $\begin{bmatrix} 1 & 0 \\ -1 & 1 \\ 0 & 0 \end{bmatrix}$ B. $\begin{bmatrix} 0 & 1 & 1 \\ 0 & 0 & 1 \end{bmatrix}$

C. $\begin{bmatrix} 1 & -1 & 0 \\ 0 & 1 & 0 \end{bmatrix}$ D. $\begin{bmatrix} 0 & 0 \\ 1 & 0 \\ 1 & 1 \end{bmatrix}$

5. In the interval $[-1, 1]$ the series $\sum_{n=1}^{\infty}(-1)^{n-1}\dfrac{x^2+n^2}{n^3}$ is

A. uniformly and absolutely convergent

B. absolutely convergent but not uniformly convergent

C. neither uniformly nor absolutely convergent

D. uniformly convergent but not absolutely convergent

6. The differential equation of family of curves of tangent form an angle of $\dfrac{\pi}{4}$ with the hyperbola $xy = c$ is

A. $\dfrac{dy}{dx}=\dfrac{x^2-c}{x^2+c}$ B. $\dfrac{dy}{dx}=xy$

C. $\dfrac{dy}{dx}=\dfrac{x^2+c}{x^2-c}$ D. $\dfrac{dy}{dx}=\dfrac{x+c}{x-c}$

7. The Hamiltonian equation of motion for a simple pendulum of string length l which is deflected through an angle θ from its rest position is given by

A. $\dot{\theta} = \dfrac{p\theta}{ml^2},\ \ p\dot{\theta} = mgl\sin\theta$

B. $\dot{\theta} = \dfrac{p\theta}{ml^2},\ \ p\dot{\theta} = mgl\cos\theta$

C. $\dot{\theta} = \frac{p\theta}{ml^2}$, $p\dot{\theta} = -mgl \sin\theta$
D. None of these

8. $f(x) = e^{-1/x^2} \sin\frac{1}{x}$ when $x \neq 0$
$= 0$ when $x = 0$
then,
A. f is differentable at $x = 0$
B. f is not differentable at $x = 0$
C. f is differentiable at $x \neq 0$
D. f is not differentiable at $x \neq 0$

9. The characteristic curves of $y^2r - x^2t = 0$ are
A. $x^2 + y^2 = c_1$, $x^2 - y^2 = c_2$
B. $x^2 + y^2 = c_1$, $x^3 - y^3 = c_2$
C. $x^2 + y^2 = c_1$, $-x^2 + y^2 - y = c_2$
D. None of the above

10. The limit of a convergent sequence of rational numbers
A. need not exist at all
B. exist and is always rational
C. exist and is always irrational
D. exists but it may be rational or irrational

11. Let X = (0, 1) ∪ (2, 3) be an open set in R. Let f be a continuous function on X such that the derivative $f'(x) = 0$ for all x. Then the range of f has
A. uncountable number of points
B. countably infinite number of points
C. at most 2 points
D. at most 1 point

12. A monoid is a semi group G if
A. G has identity element
B. Every element of G has its inverse
C. G is commutative semi-group
D. None of these

13. The complete integral of non-linear P.D.E. $y(1 + x^2)p^2 - 9x^2 = 0$ is
A. $z = \pm a.\sqrt{1+x^2} + \frac{a^2y^2}{2} + c$
B. $z = \pm\frac{a}{\sqrt{1+x^2}} + a^2y^2 + c$
C. $z = \pm\frac{2}{3}a\left(1+x^2\right)^{3/2} + \frac{a^2y^2}{2} + c$
D. $z = \pm a\sqrt{1+x^2} + a^2y^2 + c$

14. The bilinear transformation which maps points $z = 0, -i, 1$ into $w = i, 1, 0$ is
A. $w = i\left(\frac{z-1}{z+1}\right)$
B. $\frac{1}{i}\left(\frac{z-1}{z+1}\right)$
C. $\frac{1}{i}\left(\frac{z+1}{z-1}\right)$
D. $-\frac{1}{i}\left(\frac{z+1}{z-1}\right)$

15. Let $R[x]$ be a set of polynomial over R (ring of integer) then the set $A = (2, x)$ is then choose the correct statement out of the following :
1. A is a maximal ideal
2. A is a prime ideal
A. 1 only
B. 2 only
C. Both of them
D. None of them

16. $\oint_C (8\bar{z} + 3z)dz$ around the hypocycloid $x^{2/3}+y^{2/3} = a^{2/3}$.
A. $\frac{6\pi i a^2}{8}$
B. $6\pi i a^2$
C. $\frac{4}{6}\pi i a^2$
D. 0

17. Let, E and F be two mutually disjoint events. Further, let E and F be independent of G. If $p = P(E) + P(F)$ and $q = P(G)$, then $P(E \cup F \cup G)$ is
A. $1 - pq$
B. $q + p^2$
C. $p + q^2$
D. $p + q - pq$

18. The series $1+\frac{2}{6}+\frac{2.5}{6.12}+\frac{2.5.8}{6.12.18}+......$ is
A. divergent
B. convergent
C. oscillate finitely
D. oscillates infinitely

19. The ring $Z\left[\sqrt{-11}\right]$ is
A. an Euclidean domain.
B. a Principal Ideal Domain, but not a Euclidean Domain.
C. an Unique Factorization Domain, but not a Principal Ideal Domain.
D. not an Unique Factorization Domain

20. Let P be a matrix of order $m \times n$ and Q be a matrix of order $n \times p$, $n \neq p$. If rank (P) = n and rank (Q) = p, then the rank (PQ) is

A. n B. p
C. np D. $n + p$

21. Consider the vector space **C** over R and let $T : \mathbf{C} \to \mathbf{C}$ be a linear transformation given by $T(z) = \bar{z}$. Then which one of the following is correct?

A. T is one-one, but not onto.
B. T is onto, but not one-one.
C. T is one-one as well as onto.
D. T is neither one-one nor onto.

22. The probability of India winning a test match against West Indies is $\frac{1}{2}$. Assuming independence from match to match, the probability that is a 5 match India's second win occurs at the third test is

A. $\frac{1}{8}$ B. $\frac{1}{4}$
C. $\frac{1}{2}$ D. $\frac{2}{3}$

23. The primitive of differential equation $(2xy^4e^y + 2xy^3 + y)dx + (x^2y^4e^y - x^2y^2 - 3x)dy = 0$ is

A. $x^2e^y + \frac{x^2}{y} + \frac{x}{y^2} = c$

B. $x^2e^y - \frac{x^2}{y} + \frac{x}{y^3} = c$

C. $x^2e^y + \frac{x^2}{y} + \frac{x}{y^3} = c$

D. $x^2e^y - \frac{x^2}{y} - \frac{x}{y^3} = c$

24. The solution $y = A\cos(x + B)$ is equivalent to $\alpha \sin x + \beta \cos x$ where

A. $\alpha = A \sin B$ and $\alpha = A \cos B$
B. $\alpha = B \sin B$ and $\alpha = B \cos B$
C. $\alpha = -A \sin B$ and $\alpha = A \cos B$
D. None of the above

25. What is the approximate value of the root of the equation $x^2 - 3x + 1 = 0$. When the iterative method is applied on the interval [3, 5] with the transformation $x = \frac{x^2+1}{3}$ and the initial guess $x_0 = 3$?

A. 3.333 B. 4.037
C. 5.766 D. 6.845

26. If h is the interval of differencing, then $(\Delta - \nabla)\, x^2$ equals

A. $2h$ B. $2h^2$
C. $2h^3$ D. None of these

27. The extremum of the functional $I[y(x)] = \int_b^a y'^3 dx$, $y(0) = 0$, $y(a) = b$; $a > 0$, $b > 0$ attains

A. Strong maxima B. Weak maxima
C. Strong minima D. Weak minima

28. The system of equations

$$x - y + 3z = 0$$
$$x + z = 0$$
$$x + y - z = 0$$

has

A. a unique solution
B. finitely many solutions
C. infinitely many solutions
D. no solution

29. $\oint_c \frac{(x+1)dy - ydx}{(x+1)^2 + y^2}$ be

A. 0 B. π
C. 2π D. $n\pi$

30. Let $A : H \to H$ be any bounded linear operators on a complex Hilbert space H such that $\|Ax\| = \|A^* x\|$ for all x in H, where A* is the adjoint of A. If there is a non-zero x in H such that

$$A^*(x) = (2 + 3i)x, \text{ then A is}$$

A. a unitary operator on H.
B. a self-adjoint operator on H but not unitary.
C. a self-adjoint operator on H but not normal.
D. a normal operator.

31. Consider the second order ordinary differential equation $y'' + 3y' + 2y = 0$. Then $\lim_{n\to\infty} y(t)$ is

A. a non-zero finite number
B. 0
C. $-\infty$
D. ∞

32. The cross ratio of the four points (z_1, z_2, z_3, z_4) is real if and only if the four points lie on a
A. circle
B. straight line
C. circle and on a straight line
D. circle or on a straight line.

33. Which one is correct.
A. Let (I, +) be addition group of integers and let H = {δn/n ∈ I}, then H is a subgroup of I.
B. A non empty subset H of a group G which is closed under binary operation is a subgroup of G.
C. If G is a group and H is a non-empty subset of G such that $H^2 = H$, then H is a subgroup of G.
D. None of these

34. If the primal problem is unsymmetric its dual problem will have its variables.
A. Unrestricted in sign
B. Strictly greater than zero
C. ≥ 0
D. $= 0$ or ≤ 0 according to the situation

35. Let A be an $n \times n$ complex matrix whose characteristic polynomial is given by $f(t) = t^n + C_{n-1}t^{n-1} + \dots\dots\dots + C_1 t + C_0$.
Then
A. det (A) = C_{n-1}
B. det (A) = C_0
C. det (A) = $(-1)^n C_{n-1}$
D. det (A) = $(-1)^n C_0$

36. Let R be a finite ring with unity 1. Let m be the least positive integer such that $ma = 0$ for all $a \in R$ and let n be the least positive integer such that $n.1 = 0$. Which one of the following is correct?
A. m and n may not exist
B. m and n exist, but $m < n$
C. m and n exist, but $n < m$
D. m and n exist and $m = n$

37. The particular integral of

$$\frac{d^2y}{dx^2}+\frac{dy}{dx}=x^2+2x+4$$

A. $\frac{x^3}{3}+4x$ B. $\frac{x^3}{3}-4x$
C. $\frac{x^3}{3}+4$ D. $\frac{x^3}{3}+4x^2$

38. For the function $f(z)=\frac{z-\sin z}{z^3}$, at the point $z = 0$ is
A. a pole of order 3
B. a pole of order 2
C. an essential singularity
D. a removable singularity

39. For the function $f(z)=\frac{z-\sin z}{z^3}$, the point $z = 0$ is
A. a pole of order 3
B. a pole of order 2.
C. an essential singularity
D. a removable singularity

40. Which of the following is not correct?
A. An infeasible solution exists, when there is no feasible solution.
B. Iso–profit lines an a graph of an L.P.P. would always be parallel to each other.
C. An iso–cost line cannot be parallel to the line of any constraint.
D. Every L.P.P has an uniqude optimum solution

41. The equation $x^2(y-1)z_{xx} - x(y^2-1)z_{xy} + y(y^2-1)z_{yy} + z_x = 0$ is hyperbolic in the entire xy-plane except along
A. x-axis
B. a line parallel to y-axis
C. y-axis
D. y-axis and the line parallel to x-axis

42. Let $f(z) = u + iv$ be an analytic function, whose real part is $u(x, y) = 2xy + \cosh x \sin y$, with the condition $f(0) = 0$ then $f(z)$ is given by
A. $z^2 + \sin hz$ B. $z^2 + \cosh z$
C. $z^2 - i\sin hz$ D. $(z + \cosh z)^2$

43. What is the solution of the differential equation

$$\left(1+e^{x/y}\right)dx+e^{x/y}\left(1-\frac{x}{y}\right)dy=0?$$

A. $x + ye^{x/y} = c$

B. $y + xe^{x/y} = c$
C. $x - ye^{x/y} = c$
D. None of the above

44. Consider the Linear Programming Problem
Maximize $z = 3x + 9y$
subject to $x + 4y \leq 8$
$x + 2y \leq 4,\ x, y \geq 0$
The maximum value of z is

A. 6 B. 15
C. 18 D. 21

45. Which statement is not true
A. Every group of order 2 is cyclic
B. Every group of order 3 is cyclic
C. Every group of order 4 is cyclic
D. None of these

46. The mean and variance of a random variable X having a binomial distribution are 4 and 2 respectively. Then $P(X = 1)$ is

A. $\frac{37}{256}$ B. $\frac{219}{256}$
C. $\frac{128}{256}$ D. $\frac{28}{256}$

47. Let $M_{2\times2}(R)$ be the vector space of all 2 × 2 matrices over **R** and let

$$W_1 = \left\{\begin{bmatrix} x & y \\ 0 & x \end{bmatrix} : x, y \in \mathbf{R}\right\}$$

and $$W_2 = \left\{\begin{bmatrix} x & y \\ z & 0 \end{bmatrix} : x, y, z \in \mathrm{R}\right\},$$ then

dim $(W_1 \cap W_2)$ is equal to

A. 0 B. 1
C. 2 D. 3

48. In a group that contains elements x and y such that $O(x) = O(y) = 2$ and $O(xy) = 3$ is
A. Abelian but not cyclic
B. Cyclic
C. Not abelian
D. None of these

49. If there exist feasible solution to both the primal and its dual. Then
A. The primal may have an unbounded solution while the dual a bounded solution
B. The primal may have a bounded solution while the dual an unbounded solution
C. Both the primal and the dual, may have unbounded solutions
D. Both the primal and the dual, must have bounded optimal solutions

50. Which of the following is not true.
In the context of inventory management, the following need to be addressed :
A. How much to order
B. When to order
C. How much safety to keep
D. Maximum of the total inventory cost

51. Consider the L.P.P.
max $z = 2x_1 - 4x_2$
s.t. $x_1 + 2x_2 \leq 3$
$3x_1 + 4x_2 \leq 5$
$x_1, x_2 \geq 0$, the total number of basic solution is

A. 2 B. 6
C. 4 D. Infeasible

52. If G is a group of all 2 × 2 matrices $\begin{pmatrix} a & b \\ c & d \end{pmatrix}$ where $(ad - bc) \neq 0$ and a, b, c, d are integers modulo 3, relative to matrix multiplication, then what is the number of elements in G?

A. 8 B. 16
C. 48 D. 81

53. If $A = \begin{pmatrix} 1 & 2 & 3 & 4 & 5 \\ 1 & 3 & 4 & 5 & 2 \end{pmatrix}$ and

$B = \begin{pmatrix} 1 & 2 & 3 & 4 & 5 \\ 5 & 4 & 3 & 2 & 1 \end{pmatrix}$, then which one is true.

A. $\begin{pmatrix} 1 & 2 & 3 & 4 & 5 \\ 5 & 4 & 3 & 2 & 1 \end{pmatrix}$
B. $\begin{pmatrix} 1 & 2 & 3 & 4 & 5 \\ 4 & 3 & 5 & 1 & 2 \end{pmatrix}$
C. $\begin{pmatrix} 1 & 2 & 3 & 4 & 5 \\ 5 & 3 & 2 & 1 & 4 \end{pmatrix}$
D. $\begin{pmatrix} 1 & 2 & 3 & 4 & 5 \\ 3 & 4 & 5 & 2 & 1 \end{pmatrix}$

54. Match the following, they represent the loci.

(a)	$\lvert z-4i\rvert^2 + \lvert z+4i\rvert^2 = 10$	1.	Ellipse
(b)	$\lvert z-4i\rvert^2 + \lvert z+4i\rvert^2 = 10^2$	2.	Straight line
(c)	$\lvert z-4i\rvert^2 - \lvert z+4i\rvert^2 = 10$	3.	Circle
(d)	$\lvert z-4i\rvert + \lvert z+4i\rvert = 10$	4.	None

	(a)	(b)	(c)	(d)
A.	4	3	2	1
B.	4	3	1	2
C.	1	2	3	4
D.	1	2	4	3

55. Choose which are correct
1. Binomial : Variance < Mean
2. Poisson : Variance = Mean
3. Negative Binomial : Variance > Mean

A. 1 and 2 correct
B. 2 and 3 correct
C. 1 and 3 correct
D. 1, 2 and 3 correct

56. Consider the system of linear equations $x + y + z = 3$, $x - y - z = 4$, $x - 5y + kz = 6$. Then the value of k for which this system has an infinite number of solutions is

A. $k = -5$ B. $k = 0$
C. $k = 1$ D. $k = 3$

57. Curves passing through the point (0, 1) and satisfying the equation $\sin\left(\frac{dy}{dx}\right) = c$ are given by

A. $\cos\left(\frac{y+1}{x}\right) = c$ B. $\cos\left(\frac{x}{y+1}\right) = c$
C. $\sin\left(\frac{y-1}{x}\right) = c$ D. $\sin\left(\frac{x}{y+1}\right) = c$

58. The value of the wronskian of the function x^2, $3x + 2$, $2x + 3$.

A. 0 B. $2 + x$
C. $10 + x^2$ D. -10

59. Let G be cyclic group of order 20 and A be group of automorphism on G then no element of order 2 in A

A. 2 B. 3
C. 4 D. 5

60. Let $M = \begin{bmatrix} 0 & 0 & -1 & 0 \\ 2 & 0 & 0 & 0 \\ 0 & 0 & 0 & 3 \\ 4 & -4 & 0 & 0 \end{bmatrix}$. then

A. $MM^T = I$ where M^T is the transpose of M and I is the identity matrix
B. Column vectors of M from an orthogonal system of vectors.
C. Column vectors of M^T from an orthogonal system of vectors
D. (MX, MY) = (X, Y) for all X, Y in R^4 where (,) is the standard inner product of R^4.

ANSWERS

1	2	3	4	5	6	7	8	9	10
D	C	C	C	D	C	C	A	A	D
11	**12**	**13**	**14**	**15**	**16**	**17**	**18**	**19**	**20**
D	A	B	C	B	B	D	B	D	B
21	**22**	**23**	**24**	**25**	**26**	**27**	**28**	**29**	**30**
C	B	C	C	A	B	D	C	C	A
31	**32**	**33**	**34**	**35**	**36**	**37**	**38**	**39**	**40**
B	D	A	A	D	D	A	D	B	C
41	**42**	**43**	**44**	**45**	**46**	**47**	**48**	**49**	**50**
C	C	A	C	C	D	B	C	D	B
51	**52**	**53**	**54**	**55**	**56**	**57**	**58**	**59**	**60**
B	C	C	A	D	A	C	D	B	B

SOME SELECTED EXPLANATORY ANSWERS

2. As $f(z) = \dfrac{1}{z\left(e^z-1\right)}$

$$= \frac{1}{z\left(1+z+\frac{z^2}{2!}+\frac{z^3}{3!}+\ldots-1\right)}$$

$$= \frac{1}{z^2}\left(1+\frac{z}{2}+\frac{z^2}{6}+\frac{z^3}{24}+\ldots.\right)^{-1}$$

$$= \frac{1}{z^2}\left[1-\left(\frac{z}{2}+\frac{z^2}{6}+\frac{z^3}{24}+\ldots.\right)\right.$$

$$\left.+\left(\frac{z}{2}+\frac{z^2}{6}+\frac{z^3}{24}+\ldots.\right)^2-\ldots.\right]$$

$$= \frac{1}{z^2}\left[1-\frac{z}{2}+\left(-\frac{1}{6}+\frac{1}{4}\right)z^2+\left(-\frac{1}{24}+\frac{1}{6}-\frac{1}{8}\right)z^3\right.$$

$$\left.+\left(-\frac{1}{120}+\frac{1}{36}+\frac{1}{24}-\frac{1}{8}+\frac{1}{16}\right)z^4+\ldots.\right]$$

$$= \frac{1}{z^2}\left[1-\frac{z}{2}+\frac{z^2}{12}-\frac{z^4}{120}+\ldots.\right]$$

$$= \frac{1}{z^2}-\frac{1}{2z}+\frac{1}{12}-\frac{1}{720}z^2$$

$$\Rightarrow\ a_2 = -\frac{1}{720}.$$

4. The standard basis of $\mathbf{R}^3$ are {(1, 0, 0), (0, 1, 0), (0, 0, 1)}

hence T(1, 0, 0) = (1, 0) = 1.(1, 0) + 0.(1, 1)

T(0, 1, 0) = (0, 1) = –1(1, 0) + 1.(1,1)

T(0, 0, 1) = (0, 0) = 0.(1, 0) + 0.(1, 1)

hence the matrix representation of T with respect to given basis are $\begin{bmatrix}1 & -1 & 0\\ 0 & 1 & 0\end{bmatrix}$.

6. Let the given family of curves is

$$y = f(x) \quad i.e.\quad \frac{dy}{dx} = f'(x)$$

from question $\tan\dfrac{\pi}{4} = \dfrac{\dfrac{dy}{dx}-\dfrac{c}{x^2}}{1+\dfrac{dy}{dx}\cdot\dfrac{c}{x^2}}$

or $1 = \dfrac{\dfrac{dy}{dx}-\dfrac{c}{x^2}}{1+\dfrac{dy}{dx}\cdot\dfrac{c}{x^2}}$

or $1+\dfrac{dy}{dx}\cdot\dfrac{c}{x^2} = \dfrac{dy}{dx}-\dfrac{c}{x^2}$

or $\dfrac{dy}{dx}\left(1-\dfrac{c}{x^2}\right) = 1+\dfrac{c}{x^2}$

$\Rightarrow$ $\dfrac{dy}{dx} = \dfrac{x^2+c}{x^2-c}.$

7. Refer to fig.

T (Kinetic energy of the bob is) $= \frac{1}{2}ml^2\dot{\theta}^2$

and potential energy is V $= mgl(1 - \cos\theta)$

so the Lagrangian is L = T – V

$$= \frac{1}{2}ml^2\dot{\theta}^2 - mgl(1-\cos\theta)$$

giving $p\theta = \dfrac{\partial L}{\partial\dot{\theta}} = ml^2\dot{\theta}$.

The Hamiltonian H is

$$H = \Sigma p_j\dot{q}_j - L = p_\theta\dot{\theta} - L$$

$$= ml^2\dot{\theta}^2 - \left\{\frac{1}{2}ml^2\dot{\theta}^2 - mgl(1-\cos\theta)\right\}$$

$$= \frac{1}{2}ml^2\dot{\theta}^2 + mgl\,(1-\cos\theta)$$

$$= T + V.$$

Also $p\theta = ml^2\dot{\theta} \Rightarrow \dot{\theta} = \dfrac{p\theta}{ml^2}$

hence $H = \dfrac{1}{2}ml^2\left(\dfrac{p\theta}{ml^2}\right)^2 + mgl(1-\cos\theta)$

giving $\dfrac{\partial H}{\partial p\theta} = \dfrac{p\theta}{ml^2}$, $\dfrac{\partial H}{\partial\theta} = mgl\sin\theta.$

Thus Hamilton's equation of motion for this system is

$$\dot{\theta} = \frac{\partial H}{\partial p\theta} = \frac{p\theta}{ml}$$

$$p\dot{\theta} = \frac{-\partial H}{\partial \theta} = -mgl \cos\theta.$$

i.e. $ml^2\dot{\theta} = -mgl \sin\theta$

or, $\ddot{\theta}+\frac{g}{l}\theta = 0$

which represents the equation of motion of a simple pendulum with period $2\pi\sqrt{\frac{l}{g}}$ as obtained.

8. $$Rf'(0) = \lim_{h\to 0}\frac{f(0+h)-F(0)}{h}$$

$$= \lim_{h\to 0}\frac{e^{-\frac{1}{h^2}}\sin\frac{1}{h}}{h}$$

$$= \lim_{h\to 0}\frac{\sin\frac{1}{h}}{h\left[1+\frac{1}{h^2}+\frac{1}{2!h^4}+...\right]}$$

$$= \lim_{h\to 0}\frac{\sin\frac{1}{h}}{h+\frac{1}{h}+\frac{1}{2h^3}+...}$$

$$= \frac{\text{finite quantity}}{\infty} = 0$$

$Lf'(0) = 0$ Thus $Lf'(0) = Rf'(0)$
so that f is differential at $x = 0$

14. Let, $$w = \frac{\alpha z+\beta}{rz+\delta},$$

$\because$ $w(0) = i \Rightarrow i = \frac{\beta}{\delta}$ ...(*i*)

$w(-i) = 1 \Rightarrow 1 = \frac{\alpha(-i)+\beta}{r(-i)+\delta}$ ...(*ii*)

$w(-1) = 0 \Rightarrow 0 = \frac{\alpha(-1)+\beta}{r(-1)+\delta} \Rightarrow \alpha = \beta.$

Now, from (*i*) $\delta = \frac{\beta}{i} = -i\alpha$

from (*ii*),

$$\alpha(-i) + \beta = r(-i) + \delta$$

or, $\alpha(-i) + \beta = -ir - i\alpha \Rightarrow \beta = -ir$

$\Rightarrow$ $r = i\beta = i\alpha.$

Now, $$w = \frac{\alpha z+\beta}{rz+\delta}$$

$\Rightarrow$ $$\frac{\alpha z+\alpha}{i\alpha z-i\alpha} = \frac{1}{i}\left(\frac{z+1}{z-1}\right) = -i\left(\frac{z+1}{z-1}\right)$$

or, $$w = -i\left(\frac{z+1}{z-1}\right).$$

18. The given series is

$$\Sigma u_n = 1+\frac{2}{6}+\frac{2.5}{6.12}+\frac{2.5.8}{6.12.18}+......$$

omitting the first term, the *n*th term of the series is given by

$$u_n = \frac{2.5.8.......(3n-1)}{6.12......6n}$$

and $$u_{n+1} = \frac{2.5.8.......(3n-1)(3n+2)}{6.12.18......6n.6(n+1)}$$

Then $$\frac{u_n}{u_{n+1}} = \frac{2.5.8.......(3n-1)}{6.12.18......6n}\cdot\frac{6.12.......6n.6(n+1)}{2.5.8......(3n-1)(3n+2)}$$

$\Rightarrow$ $$\frac{u_n}{u_{n+1}} = \frac{6(n+1)}{3n+2}$$

$\Rightarrow$ $$\lim_{n\to\infty}\frac{u_n}{u_{n+1}} = \lim_{n\to\infty}\frac{6n+6}{3n+2} = \frac{6}{3} = 2.$$

Hence, the given series Σu_n is convergent.

19. The element of $Z\left[\sqrt{-11}\right]$ is written as $a + b\sqrt{11}i$ where $a, b \in z$

then $(1+\sqrt{11}i)(1-\sqrt{11}i) = 1 + 11 = 12 = 2.6.$

i.e. $(1+\sqrt{11}i)(1-\sqrt{11}i) = 2.6.$

Then by the properties of U.F.D.

2 and 6 are must be associates of $(1+\sqrt{11}i)$ or $(1-\sqrt{11}i)$.

However that is not the case.

Hence, $Z\sqrt{-11}$ is not a U.F.D.

20. $P_{m\times n} \cdot Q_{n\times p} = (PQ)_{m\times p}$

rank $n \quad p \qquad p$

26. Here $(\Delta - \nabla)x^2 = \Delta x^2 - \nabla x^2$

$= (x + h)^2 - x^2 - x^2 + (x - h)^2$

$= x^2 + 2xh + h^2 - 2x^2 + x^2 - 2xh + h^2$

$= 2h^2.$

28. This determinant of co-efficient matrix is

$$|A| = \begin{vmatrix} 1 & -1 & 3 \\ 1 & 0 & 1 \\ 1 & 1 & -1 \end{vmatrix}$$

$$= 1(0 - 1) + 1(-1 - 1) + 3(1 - 0)$$

$$= -1 - 2 + 3 = 0.$$

i.e. The system of equations will have infinitely many solutions.

37. The given differential equation is

$$\frac{d^2y}{dx^2} + \frac{dy}{dx} = x^2 + 2x + 4.$$

The particular integral is given by,

$$y = \frac{1}{(D^2 + D)}(x^2 + 2x + 4)$$

$$= \frac{1}{D(1+D)}(x^2 + 2x + 4)$$

$$= \frac{1}{D}(1+D)^{-1}(x^2 + 2x + 4)$$

$$= \frac{1}{D}[1 - D + D^2 - D^3 + ...](x^2 + 2x + 4)$$

$$= \frac{1}{D}[x^2 + 2x + 4 - 2x - 2 + 2]$$

$$= \frac{x^3}{3} + 4x.$$

42. $\because$ $u = 2xy + \cosh x \sin y$

$u_x = 2x + \sinh x \sin y = \phi_1(x, y)$ (say)

$u_y = 2y + \cosh x \cos y = \phi_2(x, y)$ (say)

then by Milne's Thompson formula

$$f(z) = \int \phi_1(z,0)dz - i\int \phi_2(z,0)dz$$

$$= \int 2z dz - i\int \cosh hz\, dz + c$$

$$f(z) = z^2 - i\sin hz + c.$$

$f(0) = 0 \Rightarrow c = 0$

$\therefore \quad f(z) = z^2 - i \sinh z.$

44. The given LPP is

$$\max Z = 3x + 9y$$

subject to $x + 4y \le 8$

$x + 2y \le 4$

$x, y \ge 0$

Solution space is shown in the given by the shaded region of the plotted graph.

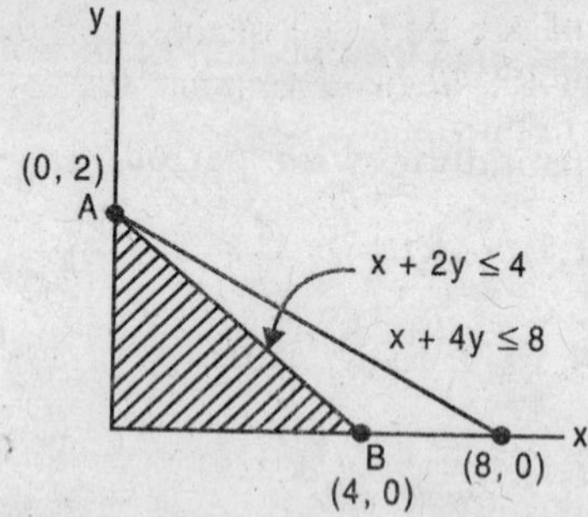

The optimum value of the objective function is obtained at the boundary of the region *i.e.* either at A(0, 2) or at B(4, 0).

Now at $Z(A) = 3.0 + 9.2 = 18$

and $Z(B) = 3.4 + 9.0 = 12.$

Hence the maximum value of Z is at the point A.

i.e. $Z_{max} = 18.$

56. The augment matrix of given system of linear equation is

$$\left[\begin{array}{ccc|c} 1 & 1 & 1 & 3 \\ 1 & -1 & -1 & 4 \\ 1 & -5 & K & 6 \end{array}\right] \sim \left[\begin{array}{ccc|c} 1 & 1 & 1 & 3 \\ 0 & -2 & -2 & 1 \\ 0 & -6 & K-1 & 3 \end{array}\right] \sim$$

$$\left[\begin{array}{ccc|c} 1 & 1 & 1 & 3 \\ 0 & -2 & -2 & 1 \\ 0 & 0 & K+5 & 0 \end{array}\right]$$

Now for infinite number of solution $K + 5 = 0$ $\Rightarrow K = -5.$

58. Wronskian $(x^2, 3x + 2, 2x + 3)$

$$= \begin{vmatrix} x^2 & 3x+2 & 2x+3 \\ 2x & 3 & 2 \\ 2 & 0 & 0 \end{vmatrix} = 2(6x + 4 - 6x - 9)$$

$$= 2(-5) = -10$$

SET–8

CSIR–UGC (NET) MATHEMATICAL SCIENCES

PART-C

1. Consider $\mathbf{R}^3$ with the standard inner product. Let S = {(1, 1, 1), (2, –1, 2), (1, –2, 1)}. For a subset W of $\mathbf{R}^3$, let L(W) denote the linear span of W of R^3. Then an orthonormal set T with L(S) = L(T) is

A. $\left\{\frac{1}{\sqrt{3}}(1,1,1), \frac{1}{\sqrt{6}}(1,-2,1)\right\}$.

B. {(1, 0, 0), (0, 1, 0), (0, 0, 1)}

C. $\left\{\frac{1}{\sqrt{3}}(1,1,1), \frac{1}{\sqrt{2}}(1,-1,0)\right\}$

D. $\left\{\frac{1}{\sqrt{3}}(1,1,1), \frac{1}{\sqrt{2}}(0,1,-1)\right\}$

2. The function $f(z) = |z|^2$ is

A. differentiable everywhere

B. differentiable only at the origin

C. not differentiable anywhere

D. differentiable on real x-axis

3. The particular solution of $\frac{d^2y}{dx^2} + y = \operatorname{cosec} x$ is given by

A. $\sin x \log(\sin x) - x\cos x$

B. $\sin x \log(\sin x) + x\cos x$

C. $(\sin x)(\log x) - x\sin x$

D. $\sin x \log(\cos x) + x\sin x$

4. Consider the following statements:

I. A commutative ring with unity is simple if and only if it is field.

II. If M be an ideal of ring R and N be an ideal of M then N is ideal of R.

A. I is correct, II incorrect

B. II is correct, I incorrect

C. Both I and II are correct

D. Neither I nor II is correct

5. $P(A/A \cup B) = ?$ A, B being mutually exclusive event, and $P(A \cup B) \neq 0$.

A. $\frac{P(A)}{P(A)+P(B)}$ B. $\frac{P(A)}{P(A)-P(B)}$

C. $\frac{P(B)}{P(A \cap B)}$ D. $\frac{P(B)}{1-P(A \cap B)}$

6. The value of $\iint_S (ax^2 + by^2 + (z^2)ds$ over the sphere $x^2 + y^2 + z^2 = 1$ using divergence theorem is

A. $(a + b + c)\,\pi$ B. $(abc)\,\pi$

C. $(a+b+c)\frac{4}{3}\pi$ D. $(abc)\frac{4\pi}{3}$

7. If the general solution of $(mz - ny)p + (nx - lz)q = ly - mx$ is given by $\phi(u, v) = 0$ then u and v be given by

A. $u = x + y + z,\ v = x^2 + y^2 + z^2$

B. $u = \frac{x}{l} + \frac{y}{m} + \frac{z}{n},\ v = lx^2 my^2 + nz^2$

C. $u = lx + my + nz,\ v = x^2 + y^2 + z^2$

D. None of these

8. Which one is right statement.

A. They may be non-abelian subgroup of an abelian group.

B. A non-abelian group has abelian subgroup.

C. A non-abelian group has abelian subgroup.

D. None of these

9. Let A_t be the stock at time t, B–the quantity added to the inventory in the interval t to t', and D the demand. Then the physical stock at time t' is given by

A. $A_{t'} = A_t - B - D$ B. $A_{t'} = A_t + B + D$

C. $A_{t'} = A_t + B - D$ D. $A_{t'} = A_t - B + D$

10. The group $Z_2 \oplus D_3$ is isomorphic to which one of the following is correct?

A. Z_{12}

B. $Z_2 \oplus Z_2 \oplus Z_3$

C. A_4

D. D_6

11. Let $f(x) = \begin{cases} |x| & \text{if } x \in Q^C \text{ or } x = 0 \\ \dfrac{qx}{q+1} & \text{if } x = \dfrac{p}{q} p \in Z, q \in N \end{cases}$

p, q are co-prime

then select the correct options.

A. f is continuous only $x = 0$

B. f is continuous at all irrationals

C. f is Riemann integrable on [0, 1]

D. None of these

12. If $P = \dfrac{dy}{dx}$, then solution of differential equation $P^2 - 5P + 6 = 0$ are

A. $(y - 4x - c)(y - 3x - c) = 0$

B. $(y - 2x - c)(y - 3x - c) = 0$

C. $(y - x - c)(y - 5x - c) = 0$

D. None of the above

13. Consider the Banach space $C[0, \pi]$ with supremum norm. The norm of the linear functional $l : C[0, \pi] \to R$, given by $l(f)$

$= \int_0^{\pi} f(x) \sin^2 x \, dx$, is

A. 1 B. $\frac{\pi}{2}$

C. π D. 2π

14. If $0 < P(A) < 1$, $0 < P(B) < 1$ and $P(A \cup B) = P(A) + P(B) - P(A) P(B)$, then

A. $P(B/A) = P(B) - P(A)$

B. $P(A' \cup B') = P(A') + P(B')$

C. $P(A \cup B') = P(A') P(B')$

D. $P(A/B) = P(A)$

15. If $f(x) = \tan^{-1}x$. $x > 0$ then by Lagrang's MVT.

A. $\dfrac{x}{1+x^2} < \tan^{-1} x < x$

B. $\dfrac{x}{1+x^2} > \tan^{-1} x > x$

C. $\dfrac{x}{1+x^2} > \tan^{-1} x < x$

D. $\dfrac{x}{1+x^2} < \tan^{-1} x > x$

16. Which one of the following is NOT a solution of the differential equation $\left(\dfrac{dy}{dx}\right)^2 + x\dfrac{dy}{dx} - y = 0$?

A. $x^2 + 4y = 0$ B. $y = x + 1$

C. $y + x = 1$ D. $y^2 - 4x = 0$

17. A particle of mass m is projected with initial velocity u at an angle α with the horizontal. Then the Lagrangian function (L) is given by

A. $L = m(\dot{x}^2 + y^2) - mgy$

B. $L = \frac{1}{2}m(\dot{x}^2 + y^2) - mgx$

C. $L = \frac{1}{2}m(\dot{x}^2 + y^2) + mgy$

D. None of these

18. Let $A = \begin{bmatrix} 1 & 1 & 1 \\ 2 & 2 & 3 \\ x & y & z \end{bmatrix}$ and let $V = \{(x, y, z) \in R^3 : \det(A) = 0\}$. Then the dimension of V equals

A. 0 B. 1

C. 2 D. 3

19. Which of the following statement is not correct?

A. The set of rationals is a field.

B. Z_{31}, the ring of integers modulo 31 is a field.

C. $R[x]$, the set of polynomials over the set of real numbers is an integral domain but not a field.

D. $R[x]$ is not an integral domain.

20. A metric space is always

A. first countable

B. second countable

C. Lindelof

D. separable

21. z_1 and z_2 are two complex no. then the magnitude of the projection of z_1 on z_2 is

A. $|z_1 . z_2|/|z_2|$ B. $|z_1|^2/|z_2|$

C. $|z_2|^2/|z_1|$ D. $|z_1 z_2|/|z_1|^2$

22. Consider the following transportation problem

	A	B	C	D	**Demand**
I	21	16	25	13	11
II	17	18	14	23	13
III	32	27	18	41	19
Requirement	6	10	12	15	43

Then the optimal cost of the above problem is

A. 796 B. 804

C. 812 D. 820

23. Let $f(z) = \dfrac{z^2 - 2z}{(z+1)^2 (z^2+4)}$ then the value of residue of $f(z)$ at $z = -1$ is given by

A. $\dfrac{3}{7}$ B. $\dfrac{9}{16}$

C. $-\dfrac{14}{25}$ D. $\dfrac{8}{15}$

24. The general solution $u(x, y)$ of partial differential equation $\dfrac{\partial u}{\partial x} + \dfrac{\partial u}{\partial y} = u$ passing through the curves $x = t$, $y = 2t$ and $u = 1$ then $u(5, 7)$ is

A. e^3 B. e^2

C. $1/e$ D. $1/e^2$

25. Let $a_n = \sum_{k=1}^{n} \dfrac{n}{n^2 + k}$, for $n \in \mathbb{N}$. Then the sequence $\{a_n\}$ is

A. Convergent

B. Bounded but not convergent

C. Diverges to ∞

D. Neither bounded nor diverges to ∞

26. Let A be any $n \times n$ non-singular complex matrix and let B = $(\bar{A})^t A$, where $(\bar{A})^t$ is the conjugate transpose of A. If λ is an eigenvalue of B, then

A. λ is real and $\lambda < 0$

B. λ is real and $\lambda \leq 0$

C. λ is real and $\lambda \geq 0$

D. λ is real and $\lambda > 0$

27. A basic feasible solution of $m \times n$ transportation table contains atmost how many independent allocations

A. $m + n - 1$ B. $m + n$

C. $mn - 1$ D. mn

28. Match the power series with the respective radius of convergence

(a) $\sum_{n=0}^{\infty} (3+4i)^n z^n$ 1. 0

(b) $\sum_{n=1}^{\infty} (-1)^n n^{-1} (z-2i)^n$ 2. 1

(c) $\sum_{n=1}^{\infty} \dfrac{1}{n^p} z^n$ 3. $\dfrac{1}{5}$

(d) $\sum (\log n)^n z^n$ 4. 1

	(a)	(b)	(c)	(d)
A.	1	2	3	4
B.	3	2	4	1
C.	3	2	1	4
D.	1	4	3	2

29. If $2\begin{bmatrix} x & y \\ z & p \end{bmatrix} + 9\begin{bmatrix} -2 & 2 \\ 1 & 0 \end{bmatrix}$ = 18 I, where I is the identity matrix, then the values of x and y are

A. $x = 0, y = -9$ B. $x = 9, y = 0$

C. $x = 18, y = 2$ D. $x = 18, y = -9$

30. In an non-abelian group the element x has order 108. Then the order of x^{42} is

A. 54 B. 27

C. 18 D. 9

31. Let W be the space spanped by $f = \sin x$ and $g = \cos x$. Then for any real value of θ, $f_1 = \sin(x + \theta)$ and $g_1 = \cos(x + \theta)$.

A. Are vectors in W

B. Are linearly independent

C. do not form a basis for W

D. Form a basis for W.

32. Let $B = \{(x, y, z) | x, y, z \in R$ and $x^2 + y^2 + z^2 \leq 4\}$. Let $v(x, y, z) = x\hat{i} - y\hat{j} + z\hat{k}$ be a vector-valued function defined on B.

If $r^2 = x^2 + y^2 + z^2$, the value of the integral $\iiint_B \bar{\nabla}\cdot(r^2 v(x,y,z)dV$ is

A. 16π B. 32π
C. 64π D. 128π

33. Probability that A speaks truth is $\frac{4}{5}$, while this probability for B is $\frac{3}{4}$. The probability that they contradict each other when asked to speak on a fact is

A. $\frac{3}{20}$ B. $\frac{1}{5}$
C. $\frac{7}{20}$ D. $\frac{4}{5}$

34. The value of the integral $\int \frac{dz}{z^2-1}, c:|z|=3$ is equal to

A. πi B. 0
C. $-\pi i$ D. $2\pi i$

35. The differential of the differential equation $(3a^2x^2 + by\cos x)dx + (2\sin x - 4ay)dy$ is exact for

A. $a = 3, b = 2$ B. $a = 2, b = 3$
C. $a = 3, b = 4$ D. $a = 2, b = 5$

36. Which one of the following ideals of the ring $Z[i]$ of Gaussian integer is NOT maximal?

A. $\langle 1+i \rangle$ B. $\langle 1-i \rangle$
C. $\langle 2+i \rangle$ D. $\langle 3+i \rangle$

37. If $f(z) = z^3$, then it

A. has an essential singularity at $z = \infty$
B. has a pole of order 3 at $z = \infty$
C. has a pole of order 3 at $z = 0$
D. is analytic at $z = \infty$

38. An archer makes 10 independent attempts at a target and his probability of hitting the target at each attempt is $\frac{5}{6}$. Then the conditional probability that his last two attempts are successful given that he has a total of 7 successful attempts is

A. $\frac{1}{55}$ B. $\frac{7}{15}$
C. $\frac{25}{36}$ D. $\frac{8!}{3!5!}\left(\frac{5}{6}\right)^7\left(\frac{1}{6}\right)^3$

39. If $T : \mathbf{R}^2 \to R^3$ is a linear transformation such that $T(1, 0) = (2, 3, 1)$ and $T(1, 1) = (3, 0, 2)$, then which of the following statements is correct?

A. $T(x, y) = (x + y, 2x + y, 3x - 3y)\ \forall\ (x, y) \in \mathbf{R}^2$
B. $T(x, y) = (2x + y, 3x - 3y, x + y)\ \forall\ (x, y) \in \mathbf{R}^2$
C. $T(x, y) = (2x - y, 3x + 3y, x - y)\ \forall\ (x, y) \in \mathbf{R}^2$
D. $T(x, y) = (x - y, 2x - y, 3x + 3y)\ \forall\ (x, y) \in \mathbf{R}^2$

40. Let α be a root of the equation $x^2 + x - 2 = 0$. Which of the following statement is/are true?

I. $\alpha \in [0, 1]$
II. $\alpha \in [2, 3]$
III. The bisection algorithm is applicable to $[1, 2]$ to approximate α.

A. I only B. II only
C. III only D. I and III only

41. If $A = \{x : f(x) = 0\}$ and $B = \{x : g(x) = 0\}$ then $A \cap B$ is equal to

A. $\frac{f(x)}{g(x)}$
B. $f(x)\ g(x) = 1$
C. $\frac{g(x)}{f(x)}$
D. $\{f(x)\}^2 + \{g(x)\}^2 = 0$

42. If R is a ring and S is additive subgroup of R, then

A. S is a subring of R
B. S is not necessarily a subring of R
C. S is an abelian ring
D. None of these

43. For the set N of natural numbers, consider the following operations:

$m \times n$ = *l.c.m.* of m and n.

$m + n$ = *g.c.d.* of m and n.

which one of the following is correct?

A. (ℕ, ⊗) is a group, but (ℕ, ⊕) is not a group.

B. (ℕ, ⊕) is a group, but (ℕ, ⊗) is not a group.

C. Both (ℕ, ⊗) and (ℕ, ⊕) are groups.

D. Neither (ℕ, ⊗) nor (ℕ, ⊕) is a group.

44. The LPP

Min $z = x_1 - 2x_2 + 3x_3 + 4x_4$

subject to $\frac{x_1}{2} - x_2 + \frac{3x_3}{2} + 2x_4 \geq 8$

$x_1, x_2, x_3, x_4 \geq 0$

A. no feasible solution

B. an unbounded solution

C. unique optimal solution

D. None of these

45. The value of $\lim_{n\to\infty} \sum_{k=1}^{n} \frac{1}{\sqrt{n^2 + kn}}$ is

A. $2\left(\sqrt{2}-1\right)$ B. $2\sqrt{2}-1$

C. $2-\sqrt{2}$ D. $\frac{1}{2}\left(\sqrt{2}-1\right)$

46. $\oint_C \bar{z}dz$ around *(i)* $|z-2| = 3$ *(ii)* the squares with vertices at $z = 0, 2, 2i$ and $2 + 2i$ *(iii)* $|z-3|+|z+3| = 10$

	(i)	*(ii)*	*(iii)*
A.	$18\pi i$	$8i$	$40\pi i$
B.	$9\pi i$	$8i$	$20\pi i$
C.	$10\pi i$	$10i$	$10\pi i$
D.	0	1	πi

47. The integrating factor of the differential equation $(2xy^4e^4 + 2xy^3 + y)dx + (x^2y^4e^4 - x^2y^2 - 3x)dy = 0$

A. $\frac{1}{x^4}$ B. $\frac{y^2}{x^4}$

C. $\frac{1}{y^4}$ D. None of these

48. Which of the following is not an integrating factor of

$xdy - ydx = 0$

A. $\frac{1}{x^2}$ B. $\frac{1}{x^2 + y^2}$

C. $\frac{1}{xy}$ D. $\frac{x}{y}$

49. The solution $y(x)$ of the differential equation $\frac{d^2y}{dx^2} + 4\frac{dy}{dx} + 4y = 0$ satisfying the conditions $y(0) = 4, \frac{dy}{dx}(0) = 8$ is

A. $4e^{2x}$ B. $(16x + 4)e^{-2x}$

C. $4e^{-2x} + 16x$ D. $4e^{-2x} + 16xe^{2x}$

50. The root of $x^3 - 2x - 5 = 0$, correct to three decimal places by using Newton-Raphson method is

A. 0.7011 B. 1.7321

C. 1.0404 D. 2.0946

51. If there exist feasible solutions to both the primal and its dual then

A. The primal may have an unbounded solution while the dual a bounded solution.

B. The primal may have a bounded solution while the dual an unbounded solution.

C. Both, the primal and the dual, may have unbounded solutions.

D. Both, the primal and the dual must have bounded optimal solutions.

52. If T is a linear transformation from a real vector space $\mathbf{R}^2$ to a real vector space $\mathbf{R}^3$ such that $T(x, y) = (x - y, y - x, -x)$, then what is the nullity of T?

A. 0 B. 1

C. 2 D. 3

53. Let $\vec{F} = ay\hat{i} + z\hat{j} + x\hat{k}$ and C be the positively oriented closed curve given by $x^2 + y^2 = 1$, $z = 0$. If $\oint_C \vec{F}.\overrightarrow{dr} = \pi$, then the value of a is

A. −1 B. 0

C. $\frac{1}{2}$ D. 1

54. If $y = a2^x + bx\ 2^x$ and $h = 1$, then $\left(\Delta^2 - 2\Delta + 1\right)y$ equals

A. 0 B. 1

C. 2 D. None of these

55. The angular momentum of the system about the origin at $t = 1/2$ is given by

A. zero vector B. $4(-4\hat{j}+\pi\hat{k})$

C. $4(-4\hat{j}+\pi\hat{k})$ D. None of these

56. Consider R^2 with the usual metric and the functions

$f: [0, (2\pi) \to R^2$ and $g : [0, 2\pi] \to R^2$ defined by

$f(t) = (\cos t, \sin t)$, $0 \leq t < 2\pi$ and $g(t) = (\cos t, \sin t)$, $0 \leq t \leq 2\pi$

Then on the respective domain

A. f is uniformly continuous but not g

B. g is uniformly continuous but not t

C. both f and g are uniformly continuous

D. Neither f nor g is uniformly continuous

57. Consider the system $x' = -y$, $y' = x$ with $x(0) = 1$, $y(0) = 1$. Then

<where y', x' represent first differential of y and x>

A. $y = \sin t + \cos t$

B. $y = -\sin t + \cos t$

C. $y = te^t + e^t$

D. y is not any of the above

58. If the cumulative function of a continuous *r.v.* X is F(x) then the cumulative distribution function of Y = aX.

A. F (x/a) if $a > 0$
1 – F (x/a) if $a < 0$

B. F (x/a) if $a < 0$
F (ax) if $a > 0$

C. F (x/a) if $a > 0$
1 – F (x/a) if $a > 0$

D. F (x/a) if $a > 0$
F (ax) if $a < 0$

59. The complete integral of PDE $4xyz = pq + 2px^2y + 2qxy^2$, where $p=\frac{\partial z}{\partial x}, q=\frac{\partial z}{\partial y}$ is

A. $z=ax^3+by^3+\frac{1}{ab}$ B. $z=\frac{x}{a}+\frac{y}{b}+\frac{1}{ab}$

C. $z=\frac{x^2}{a}+\frac{y^2}{b}+\frac{1}{ab}$ D. None of these

60. The general linear programming problem is in standard form, if

A. The constraints are strict equations.

B. The constraints are inequalities of '≤' type.

C. The constraints are inequalities of '≥' type.

D. The decision variables are unrestricted in sign.

ANSWERS

1	2	3	4	5	6	7	8	9	10
A	A	A	C	A	C	C	C	C	D
11	12	13	14	15	16	17	18	19	20
C	B	A	C	A	D	C	C	D	A
21	22	23	24	25	26	27	28	29	30
A	A	C	A	B	D	A	B	D	C
31	32	33	34	35	36	37	38	39	40
D	B	C	B	B	D	D	D	B	D
41	42	43	44	45	46	47	48	49	50
D	B	D	D	A	A	C	D	B	D
51	52	53	54	55	56	57	58	59	60
D	A	A	A	D	B	A	A	B	A

SOME SELECTED EXPLANATORY ANSWERS

1. The given subset of $\mathbf{R}^3$ have members

$$S = \{1, 1, 1), (2, -1, 2), (1, -2, 1\}$$

Clearly, $(2, -1, 2) = (1, 1, 1) + (1, -2, 1)$

hence S is linear dependent set *i.e.* dim(S) = 2.

Now L(T) = L(W).

Then the orthonormal set of T can be obtained by Gram-Schmidt orthogonalization process.

Let $u_1 = \frac{(1,1,1)}{\|(1,1,1)\|} = \frac{1}{\sqrt{3}}(1,1,1)$

$= \left(\frac{1}{\sqrt{3}}, \frac{1}{\sqrt{3}}, \frac{1}{\sqrt{3}}\right).$

Now let $w_2 = v_2 - < u_1, v_2 > u_1$

$= (1, -2, 1) - 0.$

Now we normalise $w_2 = \frac{w_2}{\|w_2\|} = \frac{(1,-2,1)}{\sqrt{6}}$

$= \frac{1}{\sqrt{6}}(1,-2,1)$

Hence, the orthonormal set is

$$\left\{\frac{1}{\sqrt{3}}(1,1,1), \frac{1}{\sqrt{6}}(1,-2,1)\right\}.$$

3. The given differential equation is

$$\frac{d^2y}{dx^2} + y = \operatorname{cosec} x.$$

The particular integral is $= \frac{1}{D^2+1}\operatorname{cosec} x$

$= \frac{1}{(D+i)(D-i)}\operatorname{cosec} x$

$= \frac{1}{2i}\left[\frac{1}{D-i} - \frac{1}{D+i}\right]\operatorname{cosec} x$

$= \frac{1}{2i}\left[e^{ix}\int e^{-ix}\operatorname{cosec} x\,dx - e^{-ix}\int e^{ix}\operatorname{cosec} x\,dx\right]$

$= \frac{1}{2i}\Big[e^{ix}\int(\cos x.\operatorname{cosec} x - i)\,dx$

$\qquad -e^{-ix}\int(\operatorname{cosec} x\cdot\cos x + i)\,dx\Big]$

$= \frac{1}{2i}\left[\left(e^{ix} - e^{-ix}\right)\log\sin x - i\left(e^{ix} + e^{-ix}\right)x\right]$

$= \frac{1}{2i}[2i\sin x\log\sin x - i\,2\cos x\cdot x]$

$= \sin x \log x - x \cos x.$

5. $P(A/A\cup B) = \frac{P\{A\cap(A\cup B)\}}{P(A\cup B)}$

$= \frac{P\{(A\cap A)\cup(A\cap B)\}}{P(A)+P(B)} = \frac{P(A)}{P(A)+P(B)}.$

6. The given surface integral is $\iint_S (ax^2 + by^2 + cz^2)ds$ and the given surface (sphere) is $= x^2 + y^2 + z^2 = 1$.

Now the unit outward normal at any point P is given by

$$\hat{n} = \frac{\nabla(x^2+y^2+z^2-1)}{|\nabla(x^2+y^2+z^2-1)|} = \frac{2x\hat{i}+2y\hat{j}+2z\hat{k}}{\sqrt{4x^2+4y^2+4z^2}}$$

$= x\hat{i} + y\hat{j} + z\hat{k}.$

Now $\iint_S (ax^2+by^2+cz^2)\,ds$

$= \iint_S \left(ax\hat{i}+by\hat{j}+cz\hat{k}\right)\cdot\left(x\hat{i}+y\hat{j}+z\hat{k}\right)ds.$

Hence by Gauss's Divergence Theorem.

$\iint_S \left(ax\hat{i}+by\hat{j}+cz\hat{k}\right)\cdot\left(x\hat{i}+y\hat{j}+z\hat{k}\right)ds$

$= \iiint \nabla\cdot(ax\hat{i}+by\hat{j}+cz\hat{k})\,dV$

$= (a+b+c)\iiint_{x^2+y^2+1\le 1} dV$

$= (a+b+c)\frac{4}{3}\pi = \frac{4}{3}\pi(a+b+c).$

7. The Lagrange's auxiliary equations of given equation are

$$\frac{dx}{mz-ny} = \frac{dy}{nx-lz} = \frac{dz}{ly-mx} \quad \text{...(1)}$$

Choosing x, y, z as multipliers, each fraction of (1).

$= \frac{xdx+ydy+zdz}{x(mz-ny)+y(nx-lz)+z(ly-mx)}$

$= \frac{xdx+ydy+zdz}{0}$

$\therefore\ xdx + ydy + zdz = 0$

or $\quad x^2 + y^2 + z^2 = c_1 \quad$ ...(2)

Again, choosing l, m, n as multipliers, each fraction of (1).

$= \frac{ldx+mdy+ndz}{l(mx-ny)+m(nx-lz)+n(ly-mx)}$

$= \frac{ldx+mdy+ndz}{0}$

$\therefore\ ldx + mdy + ndz = 0$ so that

$$lx + my + nz = c_2$$

$\Rightarrow$ (C) is the correct choice.

15. $f(x) = \tan^{-1}x$ $\qquad x > 0$

Applying first MVT on[0, x]

$$\frac{f(x)-f(0)}{x-0} = f'(x) \qquad c\ \hat{I}\ (0, x)$$

$$\frac{\tan^{-1}x - \tan^{-1}0}{x-0} = \frac{1}{1+c^2}$$

$$\tan^{-1}x = \frac{x}{1+c^2},\ 0 < c < x$$

$$x > c > 0$$

$$x > \frac{x}{1+c^2} > \frac{x}{1+x^2}$$

$$\text{or, } \frac{x}{1+x^2} < \frac{x}{1+c^2} < x$$

$$\therefore\ \frac{x}{1+x^2} < \tan^{-1}x < x$$

17. Let P(x, y) be the position of the particle at any instant t in XY plane with x-axis as horizontal.

The kinetic energy of the particle will be

$$T = \frac{1}{2}m\left(\dot{x}^2 + \dot{y}^2\right)$$

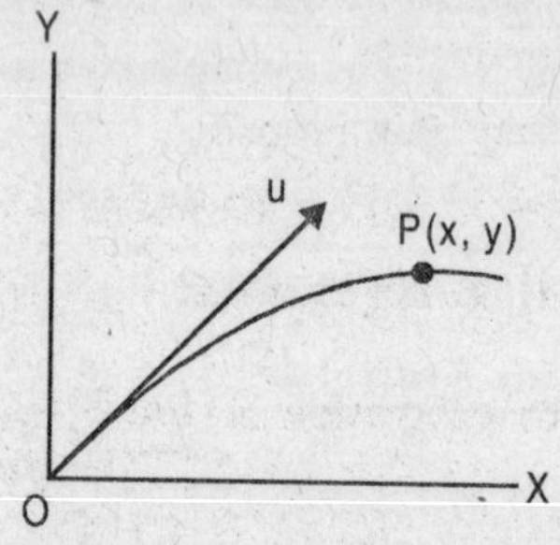

and the potential energy, taking x-axis as the reference level, will be

$$V = mgy.$$

The Lagrangian is then

$$L = \frac{1}{2}m\left(x^2 + y^2\right) - mgy.$$

18. Given $A = \begin{bmatrix} 1 & 1 & 1 \\ 2 & 2 & 3 \\ x & y & z \end{bmatrix}$ hence det(A) =

$$\begin{vmatrix} 1 & 1 & 1 \\ 2 & 2 & 3 \\ x & y & z \end{vmatrix} = \begin{vmatrix} 1 & 0 & 0 \\ 2 & 0 & 1 \\ x & y-x & z-x \end{vmatrix} = 0.$$

$$\Rightarrow \qquad y = x.$$

Hence basis of **U** are {(1, 1, 0), (0, 0, 1)}

i.e. dimension of V = 2.

26.

	A	B	C	D	Demand
I	21	16	25	13	11
II	17	18	14	23	13
III	32	27	18	41	19
	6	10	12	15	43

Apply the Vogel's Approximation method, for the initial basic feasible solution.

			(11)		
21	16	25	13	11	[3]
17	18	14	23	13	[3]
32	27	18	41	19	[9]
6	10	12	15	43	
[4]	[2]	[4]	[10]		

(6)					
17	18	14	23	13	[3]
32	27	18	41	19	[9]
6	10	12	4	32	
[15]	[9]	[4]	[18]		

		(4)		
18	14	23	7	[4]
27	18	41	19	[9]
10	12	4		
[9]	[4]	[18]		

(3)			
18	14	3	[4]
27	18	19	[9]
10	12		
[9]	[4]		

(7)	(12)	
27	18	19
7	12	

Hence, the initial basic solution is given as

			(11)	
21	16	25	13	11
(6)	(3)		(4)	
17	18	14	23	13
	(7)	(12)		
32	27	18	41	19
6	10	12	15	

the optimal cost = 11 × 13 + 17 × 6 + 18 × 3 + 23 × 4 +27 × 7 + 12 × 18 = 796.

23. Residue at $z = -1$ is given by

$$= \lim_{z\to-1}\frac{d}{dz}\left(\frac{z^2-2z}{z^2+4}\right)$$

$$\lim_{z\to-1}\frac{(z^2+4)(2z-2)-(z^2-2z).2z}{(z^2+4)^2}$$

$$= -\frac{14}{25}.$$

25. Clearly $a_n = \frac{n}{n^2+1}+\frac{n}{n^2+2}+\ldots\ \frac{n}{n^2+n}$

$< \frac{n}{n^2}+\frac{n}{n^2}+\ldots\frac{n}{n^2}=\frac{n.n}{n^2}\ \forall\ n \in \mathrm{N}$

$\Rightarrow a_n < 1$ for $n \in \mathrm{N}$

i.e. the sequence is bounded

However $a_n \to 1$ as $n \to \infty$. It is not convergent.

32. The given integral is

$$\iiint_B \overline{\nabla}\cdot(r^2 v(x,y,z))\,dV$$

Now, $\nabla\cdot(r^2\, V\,(x, y, z))$

$= \nabla\cdot\left[(x^2+y^2+z^2)(x\hat{i}+y\hat{j}+z\hat{k})\right]$

$= [3x^2 + y^2 + z^2 + x^2 + 3y^2 + z^2 + x^2 + y^2 + 3z^2]$
$= 5(x^2 + y^2 + z^2)$

i.e. $\iiint_B 5(x^2+y^2+z^2)\,dV$

$(x^2 + y^2 + z^2 \le 4)$

Changing it into polar co-ordinates, we get

$$5\iiint r^2\cdot r^2\sin\theta\, dr\, d\theta\, d\phi$$

$$= 5\int_{\phi=0}^{2\pi}\int_{\theta=0}^{\pi}\int_0^2 r^4\sin\theta\, dr\, d\theta\, d\phi$$

$$= 5\cdot\frac{2^5}{5}\cdot(2\pi)(1+1) = 128\pi.$$

35. The given differential equation is
$(3a^2x^2 + by\cos x)dx + (2\sin x - 4ay)dy$ ...(1)

Comparing with $\mathrm{M}dx + \mathrm{N}dy = 0$,
we get $\mathrm{M} = 3a^2x^2 + by\cos x$,
$\mathrm{N} = 2\sin x - 4ay$.

Now for (1) to be exact

$$\frac{\partial \mathrm{M}}{\partial y} = \frac{\partial \mathrm{N}}{\partial x}.$$

Now $\frac{\partial \mathrm{M}}{\partial y} = b\cos x$

& $\frac{\partial \mathrm{N}}{\partial x} = 2\cos x.$

$\Rightarrow$ $b = 2$. (for exact)

36. Using the standard result in $Z[i]$. (a Euclidean domain) under the non-negative function $d(a + ib) = a^2 + b^2$, then $a + ib$ is irreducible iff is $a^2 + b^2$ is prime.

Also we know any ideal in $Z[i]$ is maximal iff if it is irreducible.

Hence using this property

$d(3 + i) = 3^2 + 1^2 = 10$ which is not prime.

i.e. $\langle 3+i\rangle$ is not maximal.

45. The given expression is $\lim_{n\to\infty}\sum_{k=1}^{n}\frac{1}{\sqrt{n^2+kn}}$

$$= \lim_{n\to\infty}\sum_{k=1}^{n}\frac{1}{\sqrt{1+\frac{k}{n}}}\times\frac{1}{n}$$

By limit definition of integration, above expression equal to

$$\int_0^1\frac{1}{\sqrt{1+x}}\,dx = 2\sqrt{1+x}\Big|_0^1$$

$$2\sqrt{2}-2 = 2\left(\sqrt{2}-1\right).$$

47. The given differential equation is
$(2xy^4e^y + 2xy^3 + y)dx + (x^2y^4e^y - x^2y^2 - 3x)dy = 0.$

Comparing with the general equation

$$Mdx + Ndy = 0$$

we get $M = 2xy^4e^y + 2xy^3 + y$

& $N = x^2y^4e^y - x^2y^2 - 3x$

$$\frac{\partial M}{\partial y} = 2xy^4e^y + 8xy^3e^y + 6xy^2 + 1$$

$$\frac{\partial N}{\partial x} = 2xy^4e^y - 2xy^2 - 3$$

then $\frac{\partial N}{\partial x} - \frac{\partial M}{\partial y} = 2xy^4e^y - 2xy^2 - 3 - 2xy^4e^y - 8xy^3e^y - 6xy^2 - 1$

$$= -8xy^3e^y - 8xy^2 - 4$$

i.e. $\frac{1}{M}\left(\frac{\partial N}{\partial x} - \frac{\partial M}{\partial y}\right) = -\frac{4(2xy^3e^y + 2xy^2 + 1)}{y(2xy^3e^y + 2xy^2 + 1)}$

$$= -\frac{4}{y} \text{ (a function of } y \text{ only)}$$

hence the I.F. $= e^{-\int \frac{4}{y} dy} = e^{-4\log y} = \frac{1}{y^4}$.

49. The given ODE is $\frac{d^2y}{dx^2} + \frac{4dy}{dx} + 4y = 0$

Its general solution is given by $(C_1 + C_2x)e^{-2x}$.

$\therefore$ $y(0) = 4 \Rightarrow C_1 = 4$

$y'(0) = 8 \Rightarrow (4 + C_2x)(-2) + C_2 = 8$

$C_2 - 8 = 8 \Rightarrow C_2 = 16$

Its required solution is $(16x + 4)e^{-2x}$.

52. Given linear transformation is $T(x, y) = (x - y, y - x, -x)$

Now $T(x, y) = (0, 0)$

$\Rightarrow (x - y, y - x, -x) = (0, 0, 0)$

$\Rightarrow -x = 0 \Rightarrow x = 0$ & $y - x = 0$

$\Rightarrow y = x \Rightarrow y = 0$

i.e. $(0, 0) \in$ Null(T)

i.e. nullity (dimension of Kernel of T) = 0.

53. $\oint_C \vec{F}.\vec{dr} = \int_C aydx$ in the given closed curve

$$= \int_{\theta=0}^{2\pi} a.\sin\theta(-\sin\theta d\theta) = -a\int_{\theta=0}^{2\pi} \sin^2\theta d\theta$$

$$= -4a\frac{1}{2}\frac{\pi}{2} = \pi$$

(from question)

$\Rightarrow -a\pi = \pi \Rightarrow a = -1.$

54. We have $\Delta^2 - 2\Delta + 1 = (\Delta - 1)^2$

$= (E - 2)^2$ [$\because E = +\Delta$]

$= E^2 - 4E + 4$

$\therefore (\Delta^2 - 2\Delta + 1)y$

$= (E^2 - 4E + 4)(a\,2^x + bx\,2^x)$

$= E^2(a\,2^x + bx\,2^x) - 4E(a\,2^x + bx\,2^x) + 4(a\,2^x + bx\,2^x)$

$= a\,2^{x+2} + b(x+2)\,2^{x+2} - 4\,[a2^{x+1} + b(x+1)\,2^{x+1}] + 4(a\,2^x + bx\,2^x)$

$= a\,2^{x+2} + 2bx\,2^{x+1} + 4b\,2^{x+1} - 2a\,2^{x+2} - 4bx\,2^{x+1} - 4b\,2^{x+1} + a\,2^{x+2} + 2bx\,2^{x+1}$

$= 0.$

58. $G(n) = P(aX \leq x) = P(X \leq \frac{x}{a}) = F(x/a)$ if $a > 0$

$G(n) = P(X \geq x/a) = 1 - P(P \leq x/a) = 1 - F(x/a)$ if $a < 0$.

SET–9

CSIR–UGC (NET) MATHEMATICAL SCIENCES

PART-C

1. Let T : $R^3 \to R^3$ be a linear transformation defined by

$T(x, y, z) = (x + y - z, x + y + z, y - z)$

Then the matrix of the linear transformation T with respect to the ordered basis B = {(0, 1, 0), (0, 0, 1), (1, 0, 0)} of R^3 is

A. $\begin{bmatrix} 1 & 1 & -1 \\ 1 & 1 & 1 \\ 0 & 1 & -1 \end{bmatrix}$ B. $\begin{bmatrix} 1 & 1 & 0 \\ 1 & 1 & 1 \\ 1 & 0 & -1 \end{bmatrix}$

C. $\begin{bmatrix} 1 & 1 & 1 \\ 1 & -1 & 0 \\ 1 & -1 & 1 \end{bmatrix}$ D. $\begin{bmatrix} 1 & -1 & 1 \\ 1 & 1 & 1 \\ 1 & -1 & 0 \end{bmatrix}$

2. If $S = \left\{\frac{1}{2m} + \frac{1}{3n}; m, n \in N\right\}$ then the derived set S' and S'' has the property

A. S' and S'' both are finite

B. S' is finite and S'' is empty

C. S' is infinite and S'' is singleton

D. S' and S'' both are infinite

3. What is the equation of the curve whose tangent at any point (x, y) makes an angle $\tan^{-1}(2x + 3y)$ with x-axis and which passes through (1, 2)?

A. $4 + 8x + 10y = 32e^{2(x-1)}$

B. $2 + 6x + 9y = 26e^{3(x-1)}$

C. $2x + 3y = 8e^{3(x-1)}$

D. None of the above

4. If the general solution of $y^2p - xyq = x(z - 2y)$ is given $\phi(u, v) = 0$ then u and v can be given as

A. $u = x^2 - y^2, v = zy + y^2$

B. $u = x^2 - y^2, v = zy - y^2$

C. $u = x^2 + y^2, v = zy - y^2$

D. $u = x^2 + y^2, v = zy + y^2$

5. Let $f(z) = \frac{z^8 + z^4 + 2}{(z-1)^3(3z+2)^2}$ then which of the following is *not* true about the $f(z)$?

A. $f(z)$ is analytic everywhere except at point $z = 1$ and $z = -\frac{2}{3}$.

B. $f(z)$ has a pole of order 3 at $z = \infty$.

C. Order of pole at $z = 1$ is order is equal to order of pole at $z = -\frac{2}{3}$.

D. The $f(z)$ has three singularities.

6. A bead slides on a wire in the shape of a cycloid described by equations $x = a(\theta - \sin\theta)$, $y = a(1 + \cos\theta)$ where $0 \le \theta \le 2\pi$ then the Lagrangian function (1) is given by

A. $L = ma^2\dot{\theta}^2(1-\cos\theta) - mga(1-\sin\theta)$

B. $L = ma^2\dot{\theta}^2(1-\sin\theta) - mga(1+\sin\theta)$

C. $L = ma^2\dot{\theta}^2(1-\cos\theta) - mga(1+\cos\theta)$

D. None of these

7. If A = {1, 2, 3, 4} then which of the following are functions from A to itself

A. $f_1 = \{(x, y) : x - y = 5\}$

B. $f_2 = \{(x, y) : x - y = 6\}$

C. $f_3 = \{(x, y) : x + y = 5\}$

D. $f_4 = \{(x, y) : x + y > 4\}$

8. **Assertion** A. **:** There is at least one cyclic group of order 100 which has only 5 subgroups.

Reason (R) : A finite cyclic group of order m has a unique subgroup of order n, where n is a divisor of m.

A. Both (A) and (R) are individually true and (R) is the correct explanation of (A).

B. Both (A) and (R) individually true but (R) is not the correct explanation of (A).
C. (A) is true but (R) is false
D. (A) is false but (R) is true

9. A cube of unit mass is suspended vertically from one of its edges. If the length of its edge is $\sqrt{2}$, then the length of the equivalent simple pendulum is

A. $\frac{4}{3}$ B. $\frac{2}{3}$

C. $\frac{2\sqrt{2}}{3}$ D. $2\sqrt{2}$

10. Δ^2 cos $2x$ with h interval is equal to
A. cos 2 $(x + h)$
B. 2 $\sin^2 h$ cos 2 $(x + h)$
C. sin $2h$ cos 2 $(x + h)$
D. None of these

11. Which is the false among these statements
A. Dual simplex method can't give unbounded solution.
B. In simplex method, we always get an optimal solution in finite number of iterations.
C. Always choosing the variable corresponding which $z_j - c_j$ is most negative, as entering variable is not the best strategy. In dual simplex method it is possible to get no feasible solution.
D. In dual simplex method, it is possible to get no feasible solution.

12. The eigenvalues of a 3 × 3 real matrix P are 1, –2, 3. Then

A. $P^{-1} = \frac{1}{6}(5I + 2P - P^2)$

B. $P^{-1} = \frac{1}{6}(5I - 2P + P^2)$

C. $P^{-1} = \frac{1}{6}(5I - 2P - P^2)$

D. $P^{-1} = \frac{1}{6}(5I + 2P + P^2)$

13. Newton-Raphson iteration formula for finding $\sqrt[3]{C}$, where $C > 0$, is

A. $x_{n+1} = \frac{2x_n^3 + \sqrt[3]{C}}{3x_n^2}$ B. $x_{n+1} = \frac{2x_n^2 - C}{3x_n^2}$

C. $x_{n+1} = \frac{2x_n^3 - \sqrt[3]{C}}{3x_n^2}$ D. $x_{n+1} = \frac{2x_n^2 + C}{3x_n^2}$

14. Which statement is true.
A. There are exactly two improper subgroups
B. Every non-empty subset of a group is a complex
C. Every subset of a group is a complex
D. Every complex of a group is a subgroup.

15. $P(A/B) + P(A/B^C)$ is
A. $P(A)$ B. 1
C. greater than $P(A)$ D. None of these

16. Let $I = \int_c \bar{z}\, dz$ from $z = 0$ to $z = 4 + 2i$ and c is the curve defined $z = t^2 + it$ then I equals

A. $10 + \frac{8i}{3}$ B. $10 - \frac{8i}{3}$

C. $\frac{1}{3}(10 + 8i)$ D. $\frac{1}{3}(10 - 8i)$

17. Let X be the indiscrete space and Y a to space. If f : X → Y is continuous, then
A. X must be a one-point space
B. Y must be discrete
C. f must be a constant
D. Y must be a one-point space

18. Let $f(z)$ be analytic for $|z| \le R$, $f(0) = 0$ and $|f(z)| \le M$, then

A. $|f(z)| \le \frac{Mz}{R}$ B. $\left|\frac{f(z)}{z}\right| \le \frac{M}{R}$

C. $\left|\frac{f(z)}{z}\right| > \frac{M}{R}$ D. $\left|\frac{f(z)}{z}\right| \ge \frac{M}{R}$

19. The partial differential equation of $\phi(x^2 + y^2 + z^2, z^2 - 2xy) = 0$ is $\left[p = \frac{\partial z}{\partial x}, q = \frac{\partial z}{\partial y}\right]$

A. $(p - q)z = y - x$ B. $(p + q)z = y - x$
C. $(p - q)z = y + x$ D. $(p + q)z = y + x$

20. Let G be a group of order 144. For any $a \in G$, $O(a) = 36$ then $O(a^6)$ is equal to

A. 4 B. 6
C. 12 D. 24

21. Let $M = \begin{bmatrix} 1 & 1+i & 2i & 9 \\ 1-i & 3 & 4 & 7-i \\ -2i & 4 & 5 & i \\ 9 & 7+i & -i & 7 \end{bmatrix}$ then

A. M has purely imaginary eigen values
B. M is not diagonalizable
C. M has eigen values which are neither real nor purely imginarly
D. M has only real eigen values.

22. Consider the subspace W = $\{[a_{ij}] : a_{ij} = 0$ if i is even$\}$ of all 10×10 real matrices. Then the dimension of W is

A. 25 B. 50
C. 75 D. 100

23. Let V be the region bounded by the planes $x = 0$, $x = 2$, $y = 0$, $z = 0$ and $y + z = 1$. Then the value of the integral $\iiint_V y\, dx\, dy\, dz$ is

A. $\frac{1}{2}$ B. $\frac{4}{3}$
C. 1 D. $\frac{1}{3}$

24. The principal value of $(i)^{-2i}$ is

A. $e^{-\pi}$ B. e^{π}
C. $e^{-\frac{\pi}{2}}$ D. $e^{-2\pi}$

25. The family of curves $\frac{x^2}{a^2+\lambda} + \frac{y^2}{b^2+\lambda} = 1$ (where λ is the only parameter) is

A. self orthogonal
B. has circles as their orthogonal trajectory
C. has parabolas as their orthogonal trajectory
D. None of the above

26. The general sol of the differential equation

$$\frac{d^3y}{dx^3} - \frac{2d^2y}{dx^2} - \frac{dy}{dx} + 2y = 0$$

A. $(c_1e^x + c_2e^{2x} + c_3e^{3x})$
B. $(c_1e^{-x} + c_2e^x + c_3e^{2x})$
C. $(c_1 + c_2x)e^x + c_3e^{2x}$
D. None of the above

27. In M/M/m system probability of n customers in the system ($n \geq m$) is

A. $\frac{1}{m!\,m^{n-m}}\left(\frac{\lambda}{\mu}\right)^n \rho_0$ B. $\frac{1}{m!}\left(\frac{\lambda}{\mu}\right)^n \rho_0$

C. $\left(\frac{\lambda}{\mu}\right)^n \rho_0$ D. $\left(\frac{\lambda}{\mu}\right)^n$

28. Which one of the following is a cyclic group?

A. Set of non-zero square matrices of order 2×2 over R under matrix multiplication.
B. The group of roots (real or complex) of the equation $x^n - 1 = 0$ where n is a natural number.
C. The group $Q - \{0\}$ of non-zero rationals under multiplication.
D. The group Q of rationals under addition.

29. The extremal of functional

$$\iint\left[\left(\frac{\partial z}{\partial x}\right)^2 + \left(\frac{\partial z}{\partial y}\right)^2 + 2z\,f(x, y)\right] dx\,dy.$$

A. Harmonic function
B. Laplace equation
C. Poisson's equation
D. None of these

30. The system of equations $kx + y + z = 1$, $x + ky + z = k$ and $x + y + kz = k^3$ does **not** have a solution if k is equal to

A. 0 B. 1
C. −1 D. −2

31. Which of the following conditions does **not** ensure the convergence of a real sequence $(a_n\}$?

A. $|a_n - a_{n+1}| \to 0$ as $n \to \infty$
B. $\sum_{n=1}^{\infty} |a_n - a_{n+1}|$ is convergent
C. $\sum_{n=1}^{\infty} na_n$ is convergent
D. The sequences (a_{2n+1}), (a_{2n+1}) and (a_{3n}) are convergent

32. Find the mean, mode and median for the distribution $df = \frac{1}{2}\sin x\,dx$, $0 \le x \le \pi$

A. $\frac{\pi}{2}, \frac{\pi}{2}, \frac{\pi}{2}$ B. $\frac{\pi}{2}, \frac{3\pi}{2}, \frac{3\pi}{4}$

C. 0, 1, 2 D. $1, \frac{4}{3}, \frac{5}{3}$

33. Which of the following is not an assumption underlying fundamental problem of EOQ?

A. Demand is known and uniform

B. Holding cost per unit per time period is constant

C. Stock–outs (shortages) are not permitted.

D. Lead time is not zero

34. The value of $\iiint(\bar{\nabla}\cdot\bar{F})dV$ taken over the rectangular parallelopiped $0 \le x \le a$, $0 \le y \le b$, $0 \le z \le c$. where $\bar{F} = (x^2 - yz)\hat{i} + (y^2 - zx)\hat{j} + (z^2 - xy)\hat{k}$

A. abc B. $a + b + c$

C. $abc\,(a + b + c)$ D. $\frac{abc}{a+b+c}$

35. An unbiased die with faces marked 1, 2, 3, 4, 5 and 6 is rolled four times. Out of four faces values obtained, the probability that the minimum face value is not less than 2 and the maximum face value is not greater than 5 is then,

A. $\frac{16}{81}$ B. $\frac{1}{81}$

C. $\frac{80}{81}$ D. $\frac{65}{81}$

36. The residue of function $f(z) = \frac{z^3}{z^2 - 1}$ at $z = \infty$ is

A. 1 B. –1

C. ∞ D. None of these

37. Let, $x_1, x_2, \ldots\ldots x_n$ be n observations such that $\Sigma x_i^2 = 400$ and $\Sigma x_i = 80$. Then a possible value of n among the following is

A. 15 B. 18

C. 9 D. 12

38. Which ring of the following is not an integral domain.

A. (E, +, .) where E is the set of even integers inlcuding zero.

B. (C, +, .) where C is the set of complex numbers

C. $\left(\left\{a + b\sqrt{2}; a, b \in \text{I}\right\}, +, .\right)$: where I is the set of whole numbers

D. $(q, +, .)$ where q is the set of rational numbers.

39. Let, $X_1, X_2, \ldots\ldots X_{21}$ be a random sample form a distribution having the variance 5. Let,

$\bar{X} = \frac{1}{21}\sum_{i=1}^{21} x_i$ and $S = \sum_{i=1}^{21}(x_i - \bar{X})^2$. Then the value of $E(S)$ is

A. 5 B. 100

C. 0.25 D. 105

40. The function $f(x, y) = (e^x\cos y, e^x\sin y)$ from R^2 to R^2 is

A. one-one on all of IR

B. one-one on some neighbourhood of any point in R^2

C. an onto map

D. such that some neighbourhood of any neighourhood of any point subjects on to R^2.

41. Which equation represents the set of all curves in the xy plane which have slope at each point P equal to the reciprocal of the slope of the straight line through P and the origin?

A. $y^2 = x + c$ B. $x^2 + y^2 = c^2$

C. $x^2 - y^2 = c^2$ D. $xy = c^2$

42. A particular integral of the differential equation $\frac{d^2y}{dx^2} - \frac{dy}{dx} - 2y = \cos x + 3\sin x$ is

A. $\sin x$ B. $\cos x$

C. $-\sin x$ D. $-\cos x$

43. If a cyclic group has only 3 subgroups $\{e\}$, a subgroup of order 7 and the group itself. Then the order of group is

A. 7

B. 14

C. 49

D. cannot be determined

44. The Canonical form of one dimensional wave equation $\frac{\partial^2 z}{\partial x^2} - \frac{\partial^2 z}{\partial y^2} = 0$

A. $\frac{\partial^2 z}{\partial u^2} = 0$ B. $\frac{\partial^2 z}{\partial u \partial v} = 0$

C. $\frac{\partial^2 z}{\partial v^2} = 0$ D. None of these

45. Let $\vec{F} = xy\hat{i} + y\hat{j} - yz\hat{k}$ denote the force field on a particle traversing the path L from (0, 0, 0) to (1, 1, 1) along the curve of intersection of the cylinder $y = x^2$ and the plane $z = x$. The work done by $\vec{F}$ is

A. 0 B. $\frac{1}{4}$

C. $\frac{1}{2}$ D. 1

46. $f(z) = \sin\frac{1}{z}$, $z = 0$ is a

A. removable singularity
B. simple pole
C. branch point
D. essential singularity (Isolated)

47. Which of the following Banach spaces is not separable?

A. L^1 [0, 1] B. L^∞ [0, 1]
C. L^2 [0, 1] D. C [0, 1]

48. The L.P.P

$\max z = -3x_1 + x_2$
subject to $2x_1 + x_2 \leq 4$
$-x_1 + x_2 \leq 1$
$x_1 + x_2 \geq 1$
$-3x_1 + x_2 \geq -3$
$x_1, x_2 \geq 0$ has

A. Unique optimal solution
B. Alternative optimal solution
C. Constraints leading to an infeasible region
D. Constraints leading to an unbounded solution

49. Let T : $C^n \to C^n$ be a linear operator of rank $n - 2$. Then

A. 0 is not an eigenvalue of T.
B. 0 must be an eigenvalue of T.
C. 1 can never be an eigenvalue of T.
D. 1 must be an eigenvalue of T.

50. For the initial value problem (I.V.P.) : $y^1 = f(x, y)$ with $y(0) = 0$, which of the following statements is true.

A. $f(x,y) = \sqrt{xy}$ satisfy Lipschitz's condition and so I.V.P. unique solution
B. $f(x,y) = \sqrt{xy}$ does not satisfy Lipschitz's condition and so I.V.P. has no solution.
C. $f(x, y) = |y|$ satisfies Lipschitz's condition so I.V.P. has unique solution.
D. $f(x, y) = |y|$ does not satisfy Lipschitz's condition still I.V.P has unique solution.

51. Match the following primal their dual.

Primal

(*a*) max $z_x = cx$
s.t. $Ax \leq b, x \geq 0$
(*b*) min $z_x = cx$
s.t. $Ax \leq b, x \geq 0$
(*c*) max $z_x = cx$
s.t. $Ax = b$, x is unrestricted in sign

Dual

I. min $z_w = b^T W$
s.t. $A^T W = C^T$, W is unrestricted in sign
II. min $z_w = b^T W$
s.t. $A^T W \geq C^T, W \geq 0$
III. max $z_w = b^T W$
s.t. $A^T W \leq C^T, W \leq 0$
IV. max $z_w = b^T W$
s.t. $A^T W \geq C^T, W \geq 0$

	(*a*)	(*b*)	(*c*)
A.	II	III	I
B.	I	III	IV
C.	II	IV	I
D.	IV	II	III

52. Given L.P.P
Mas $(x_1 + 3x_2)$ S.t. $3x_1 + x_2 \leq 3, x_1 \geq 0, x_2 \geq 0$ the optimum value of the objective function will be :

A. 1 B. 3
C. 9 D. 10

53. If H and K are subgroups, then HK is a subgroup if and only if

A. HK$\subseteq$KH
B. KH$\subseteq$HK
C. HK=KH
D. HK$\neq$KH

54. Let $T : R^4 \to R^4$ be linear transformation satisfying $T^3 + 3T^2 = 4I$, where I is the identity transformation. Then the linear transformation $S = T^4 + 3T^3 - 4I$ is

A. one-one but not onto
B. onto but not one-one
C. invertible
D. non-invertible

55. Let **U** be a vector space over the field F of dimension n. Consider the following statements :

1. Every subset of **U** containing n elements is a basis of V.
2. No linearly independent subset of V contains more than n elements.

Which of the above statements is/are correct?

A. 1 only
B. 2 only
C. Both 1 and 2
D. Neither 1 nor 2

56. $\oint_c \frac{(x+1)dy - ydx}{(x+1)^2 + y^2}$ be

A. 0
B. π
C. 2π
D. 3π

57. If k is a parameter, then the orthogonal trajectories of the cardioid $r = k(1 - \cos\theta)$ is

A. $r = c(1 + \cos\theta)$
B. $r = c(1 - \sin\theta)$
C. $r(1 + \cos\theta) = c$
D. $r(1 - \sin\theta) = c$

58. Let f be an entire function. If f satisfies the following two equations

$f(z+1) = f(z)$

$f(z+i) = f(z)$ for every z in C, then

A. $f'(z) = f(z)$
B. $f(z) \in \to R\ \forall z$
C. f = constant
D. f is a non-constant polynomial.

59. The work done by the force $\vec{F} = 4y\hat{i} - 3xy\hat{j} + z^2\hat{k}$ in moving a particle over the circular path $x^2 + y^2 = 1$, $z = 0$ from (1, 0, 0) to (0, 1, 0) is

A. $\pi + 1$
B. $\pi - 1$
C. $-\pi + 1$
D. $-\pi - 1$

60. 1. Let $(R, +, .)$ be a ring. If $(R, +)$ is a cyclic group, then R is commutative ring.

2. If an integral domain is infinite, then it cannot be a field.

Which of the above statements is/are correct?

A. 1 only
B. 2 only
C. Both 1 and 2
D. Neither 1 nor 2

ANSWERS

1	2	3	4	5	6	7	8	9	10
C	C	B	C	C	C	C	A	A	D
11	**12**	**13**	**14**	**15**	**16**	**17**	**18**	**19**	**20**
B	A	A	B	C	B	C	B	A	B
21	**22**	**23**	**24**	**25**	**26**	**27**	**28**	**29**	**30**
D	B	D	B	A	A	A	B	C	D
31	**32**	**33**	**34**	**35**	**36**	**37**	**38**	**39**	**40**
A	A	D	C	A	B	B	A	B	C
41	**42**	**43**	**44**	**45**	**46**	**47**	**48**	**49**	**50**
B	C	B	B	C	C	C	A	B	C
51	**52**	**53**	**54**	**55**	**56**	**57**	**58**	**59**	**60**
C	C	C	D	B	A	C	C	D	A

SOME SELECTED EXPLANATORY ANSWERS

1. The given linear transformation is

$$T(x, y, z) = (x + y - z, x + y + z, y - z)$$

the given ordered basis are

$B = \{f_1 = (0, 1, 0), f_2 = (0, 0, 1), f_3 = (1, 0, 0)\}$

Now

$T(f_1) = T(0, 1, 0) = (1, 1, 1) = 1.f_1 + 1.f_2 + 1.f_3$

$T(f_2) = T(0, 0, 1) = (-1, 1, -1) = 1.f_1 - 1.f_2 - 1.f_3$

$T(f_3) = T(1, 0, 0) = (1, 1, 0) = 1.f_1 + 0.f_2 + 1.f_3$

i.e. matrix associated with $T = \begin{bmatrix} 1 & 1 & 1 \\ 1 & -1 & -1 \\ 1 & -1 & 1 \end{bmatrix}$.

3. From question, $\frac{dy}{dx} = 2x + 3y$

or, $\frac{dy}{dx} - 3y = 2x.$

I.F. $= e^{-3x}$

Now integrating, we get

$$ye^{-3x} = \int 2xe^{-3x}dx = 2\left[\frac{-xe^{-3x}}{3} - \frac{e^{-3x}}{9}\right] + C$$

or, $ye^{-3x} = C - \frac{2xe^{-3x}}{3} - \frac{2}{9}e^{-3x}$

or, $y = Ce^{3x} - \frac{2x}{3} - \frac{2}{9}.$

As the given curve is passing through (1, 2), hence

$$2 = Ce^3 - \frac{2}{9} - \frac{2}{3}$$

or, $C = \frac{26}{9}e^{-3}$

i.e. $y + \frac{2x}{3} + \frac{2}{9} = \frac{26}{9}e^{3(x-1)}$

or, $9y + 6x + 2 = 26\ e^{3(x-1)}.$

i.e. $2 + 6x + 9y = 26e^{3(x-1)}.$

4. Here Lagrange's auxiliary equations are

$$\frac{dx}{y^2} = \frac{dy}{-xy} = \frac{dz}{x(z-2y)} \quad ...(1)$$

taking the first two fractions of (1) and re-writing, we get

$2xdx + 2ydy = 0$ so that

$x^2 + y^2 = c_1.$

Now taking the last two fraction of (1) and rewriting, we get

$$\frac{dz}{dy} = -\frac{z-2y}{y}$$

or $\frac{dz}{dy} + \frac{1}{y}z = 2,$

which is linear in z and y.

Its I.F. $= e^{\int \frac{1}{y}dy} = e^{\log y} = y.$

Hence solution of (3) is $z.y = \int 2y\,dy + c_2$

$\Rightarrow \quad zy - y^2 = c_2$

i.e. $\phi(x^2 + y^2, zy - y^2) =$ 0 is desired general solution.

10. $\Delta^2 \cos 2x = (E - 1)^2 \cos 2x$ $[\because E = 1 + \Delta]$

$= (E^2 - 2E + 1) \cos 2x$

$= E^2(\cos 2x) - 2E(\cos 2x) + \cos 2x$

$= \cos 2(x + 2h) - 2 [\cos 2(x + h)] + \cos 2x$

$- \cos (2x + 4h) + \cos 2x - 2[\cos 2(x + h)]$

$= 2\cos\frac{x + 4h + 2x}{2}\cos\frac{2x + 4h - 2x}{2}$

$- 2 \cos 2 (x + h)$

$= 2 \cos 2 (x + h) \cos 2h - 2 \cos 2 (x + h)$

$= 2 \cos 2 (x + h) [\cos 2h - 1]$

$= 4 \sin^2 h \cos 2 (x + h).$

12. The characteristic equation is given by

$|P - \lambda I| = 0$

$\Rightarrow (\lambda - 1) (\lambda + 2) (\lambda - 3) = 0$

or $\lambda^3 - (1 + 3 - 2) \lambda^2 + (-2 - 6 + 3)\lambda + 6 = 0$

or $\lambda^3 - 2\lambda^2 - 5\lambda + 6 = 0.$

Hence by Cayley-Hamilton theorem,

$$P^3 - 2P^2 - 5P + 6I = 0$$

or $6I = 5P + 2P^2 - P^3$

or $\qquad 6P^{-1} = 5I + 2P - P^2$

or $\qquad P^{-1} = \frac{1}{6}(5I + 2P - P^2).$

16. Given, $\quad I = \int_c \bar{z}dz = \int_0^2 (t^2 - it)(2t + i)dt$

$$= \int_0^2 (2t^3 + t)dt - i\int_0^2 t^2 dt$$

$$= \left(2.\frac{2^4}{4} + \frac{2^2}{2}\right) - i.\frac{8}{3} = 10 - \frac{8i}{3}.$$

21. M is a Hermitian matrix, so it will have only real eigen values.

23. $\iiint_V ydxdydz = \int_{x=0}^{2}\int_{y=0}^{1}\int_{z=0}^{1-y} ydzdydx$

$$= \int_{x=0}^{2}\int_{y=0}^{1} y(1-y)dy\,dx = \int_{x=0}^{2} \left.\frac{y^2}{2} - \frac{y^3}{3}\right|_0^1 dx$$

$$= 2\left[\frac{1}{2} - \frac{1}{3}\right] = 2\left[\frac{3-2}{6}\right] = \frac{1}{3}.$$

25. The equation of the family of curves are

$$\frac{x^2}{a^2+\lambda} + \frac{y^2}{b^2+\lambda} = 1 \qquad ...(1)$$

(where λ is the parameter)

differentiating with respect to x, we get

$$\frac{x}{a^2+\lambda} + \frac{y}{b^2+\lambda}\frac{dy}{dx} = 0 \qquad ...(2)$$

or, $\qquad \frac{x}{a^2+\lambda} = -\frac{y}{b^2+\lambda}\frac{dy}{dx}$

or, $\qquad x(b^2+\lambda) = -y(a^2+\lambda)\frac{dy}{dx}$

or, $\qquad \lambda\left(x + y\frac{dy}{dx}\right) = -\left(b^2x + a^2y\frac{dy}{dx}\right)$

or, $\qquad \lambda = \dfrac{-\left(b^2x - a^2y\frac{dy}{dx}\right)}{x + y\frac{dy}{dx}}.$

Now, $\qquad a^2 + \lambda = a^2 - \dfrac{\left(b^2x + a^2y\frac{dy}{dx}\right)}{x + y\frac{dy}{dx}}$

$$= \frac{(a^2-b^2)x}{x + y\frac{dy}{dx}}$$

Also $\qquad b^2 + \lambda = \dfrac{b^2 - \left(b^2x + a^2y\frac{dy}{dx}\right)}{\left(x + y\frac{dy}{dx}\right)}$

$$= \frac{-(a^2-b^2)y\frac{dy}{dx}}{x + y\frac{dy}{dx}}.$$

Putting these values in equation (1) we get

or,

$$\frac{x^2}{(a^2-b^2)x}\left(x + y\frac{dy}{dx}\right) - \frac{y^2}{(a^2-b^2)y\frac{dy}{dx}}\left(x + y\frac{dy}{dx}\right) = 1$$

or, $\quad x\left(x + y\frac{dy}{dx}\right) - y\frac{dx}{dy}\left(x + y\frac{dy}{dx}\right) = a^2 - b^2$

or, $\quad \left(x + y\frac{dy}{dx}\right)\left(x - y\frac{dx}{dy}\right) = a^2 - b^2 \qquad ...(3)$

Replacing $\frac{dy}{dx}$ by $-\frac{dx}{dy}$ we get

$$\left(x - y\frac{dx}{dy}\right)\left(x + y\frac{dy}{dx}\right) = a^2 - b^2 \qquad ...(4)$$

which is same as (3)

hence the given family of curves (1) are self-orthogonal.

30. The given system of equations are

$Kx + y + z = 1$

$x + Ky + z = K$

$x + y + Kz = K^3.$

The system can't have unique solution if determinant of coefficient matrix is zero.

i.e. $\begin{vmatrix} K & 1 & 1 \\ 1 & K & 1 \\ 1 & 1 & K \end{vmatrix} = 0.$

i.e. $K(K^2 - 1) - 1(K - 1) + 1(1 - K) = 0$

or $K(K^2 - 1) - 2(K - 1)$ or $(K - 1)[K(K + 1) - 2] = 0$

or $(K - 1)[K^2 + 2K - K - 2] = 0$

$(K - 1)[K(K + 2) - 1(K + 2)] = 0$ or $(K - 1)^2 (K + 2) = 0$.

i.e. K = 1, 1, –2.

However for K = 1, the system will have infinitely many solution hence the system will not have solution for K = –2.

31. As if $\quad a_n = \sqrt{n}$

then $\quad |a_n - a_{n+1}| = |\sqrt{n} - \sqrt{n+1}|$

$$= \left|\frac{1}{\sqrt{n} + \sqrt{n+1}}\right| \to 0$$

However $a_n \to \infty$ as $n \to \infty$.

32. $N = \frac{1}{2}\int_0^{\pi} \sin x\, dx = \frac{1}{2}(-\cos x)_0^{\pi}$

$= \frac{1}{2}[-\cos \pi + \cos 0] = \frac{1}{2}(1+1) = 1$

Mean $= \frac{1}{2}\int_0^{\pi} x.\sin x\, dx = \frac{1}{2}(-x\cos x)_0^{\pi} + \frac{1}{2}\int_0^{\pi} \cos x\, dx = \frac{\pi}{2}$

Mode $y = \frac{1}{2}\sin x$, $y_1 = \frac{1}{2}\cos x = 0$ for max/min

$\Rightarrow x = \frac{\pi}{2}$

$y_2 = -\text{ve} < 0 \quad \therefore$ at $x = \frac{\pi}{2}$ (mode)

Median $Md = \frac{1}{2}\int_0^{Md} \sin x\, dx = \frac{1}{2}$

$\Rightarrow -(\cos x)_0^{Md} = 1$

$\Rightarrow \cos Md = 0$

$Md = \frac{\pi}{2}$.

34. The given integral is $\iiint(\bar{\nabla}\cdot\bar{F})\,dV$.

Now, the given vector function

$\bar{F} = (x^2 - yz)\hat{i} + (y^2 - zx)\hat{j} + (z^2 - xy)\hat{k}$.

Hence $\bar{\nabla}\cdot\bar{F} = \nabla\cdot[(x^2 - yz)\hat{i} + (y^2 - zx)\hat{j} + (z^2 - xy)\hat{k}]$

$= (2x + 2y + 2z) = 2(x + y + z)$.

Hence

$$\iiint(\bar{\nabla}\cdot\bar{F})\,dV = \int_{z=0}^{c}\int_{y=0}^{b}\int_{x=0}^{a} 2(x+y+z)\,dx\,dy\,dz$$

$$= 2\int_{z=0}^{c}\int_{y=0}^{b}\int_{x=0}^{a} (x+y+z)\,dx\,dy\,dz$$

$$= 2\int_0^c\int_0^b \left.\frac{x^2}{2} + xy + xz\right|_0^a dy\,dz$$

$$2\int_0^c\int_0^b \left(\frac{a^2}{2} + ay + az\right) dy\,dz$$

$$= 2\int_0^c \left.\frac{a^2}{2}\cdot y + \frac{ay^2}{2} + ayz\right|_0^b dz$$

$$= 2\int_{z=0}^{c}\left(\frac{a^2b}{2} + \frac{ab^2}{2} + abz\right) dz$$

$$= 2\left[\frac{a^2b}{2}\cdot z + \frac{ab^2}{2}\cdot z + \frac{abz^2}{2}\right]_0^c$$

$$= 2\left[\frac{a^2b\cdot c}{2} + \frac{ab^2c}{2} + \frac{abc^2}{2}\right]$$

$= abc\,(a + b + c)$.

42. The given differential equation is

$$\frac{d^2y}{dx^2} - \frac{dy}{dx} - 2y = \cos x + 3\sin x$$

for particular integral,

$$y = \frac{1}{(D^2 - D - 2)}(\cos x + 3\sin x)$$

$$\text{or, } y = \frac{1}{(D^2 - D - 2)}\cos x + \frac{1}{(D^2 - D - 2)}\cdot 3\sin x$$

$$= \frac{\cos x}{-1 - D - 2} + \frac{3\sin x}{(-1 - D - 2)}$$

$$= -\frac{\cos x}{(D+3)} - \frac{3\sin x}{(D+3)}$$

$$= -\frac{(D-3)\cos x}{(D^2-9)} - \frac{3(D-3)}{(D^2-9)}\sin x$$

$$= \frac{-(D-3)\cos x}{-1-9} - \frac{3(D-3)}{-1-9}\sin x$$

$$= \frac{(D-3)\cos x}{10} + \frac{3(D-3)\sin x}{10}$$

$$= \frac{-\sin x}{10} - \frac{3}{10}\cos x + \frac{3}{10}\cos x - \frac{9\sin x}{10}$$

$= -\sin x$.

44. Rewriting the given equation $r - t = 0$ ...(1)
The λ-equation is $\lambda^2 - 1 = 0$

$\Rightarrow \quad \lambda = \pm 1$. (Real and distinct roots)

Then the characteristic equations $\frac{dy}{dx} + 1 = 0$

and $\frac{dy}{dx} - 1 = 0$

integrating, these we get $y + x = c_1$

and $y - x = c_2$.

In order to reduce (1) to canonical form, we choose

$u = y + x$ and $v = y - x$.

$$\therefore \quad p = \frac{\partial z}{\partial x} = \frac{\partial z}{\partial u}.\frac{\partial u}{\partial x} + \frac{\partial z}{\partial v}.\frac{\partial v}{\partial x} = -\frac{\partial z}{\partial u} - \frac{\partial z}{\partial v}$$

$$\Rightarrow \quad \frac{\partial}{\partial x} \equiv \frac{\partial}{\partial u} - \frac{\partial}{\partial v}$$

Similarly $$q = \frac{\partial z}{\partial y} = \frac{\partial z}{\partial u} + \frac{\partial z}{\partial v}$$

$$\Rightarrow \quad \frac{\partial}{\partial y} \equiv \frac{\partial}{\partial u} + \frac{\partial}{\partial v}$$

$$\therefore \quad r = \frac{\partial^2 z}{\partial x^2} = \left(\frac{\partial}{\partial u} - \frac{\partial}{\partial v}\right)\left(\frac{\partial z}{\partial u} - \frac{\partial z}{\partial v}\right)$$

$$= \frac{\partial^2 z}{\partial u^2} - 2\frac{\partial^2 z}{\partial u \partial v} + \frac{\partial^2 z}{\partial v^2}$$

$$t = \frac{\partial^2 z}{\partial y^2} = \left(\frac{\partial}{\partial u} + \frac{\partial}{\partial v}\right)\left(\frac{\partial z}{\partial u} + \frac{\partial z}{\partial v}\right)$$

$$= \frac{\partial^2 z}{\partial u^2} + 2\frac{\partial^2 z}{\partial u \partial v} + \frac{\partial^2 z}{\partial v^2}$$

Hence $r - t = 0 \Rightarrow 4\frac{\partial^2 z}{\partial u \partial v} = 0$

$$\Rightarrow \quad \frac{\partial^2 z}{\partial u \partial v} = 0.$$

45. Work done

$$W = \int \vec{F}.d\vec{r} = \int xydx + ydy - yzdz$$

$$= \int_0^1 x.x^2dx + n^2.2x\,dx - x^2.x\,dx = \int_0^1 2x^3dx$$

$$= \left.\frac{2.x^4}{4}\right|_0^1 = \frac{1}{2}$$

48.

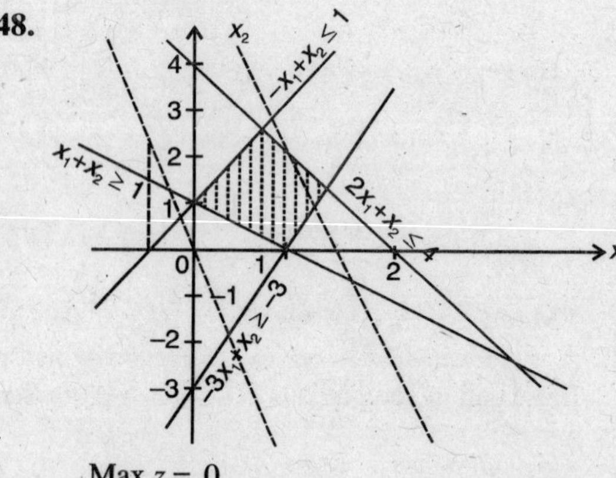

Max $z = 0$

$3x_1 = x_2$

$$\frac{x_1}{x_2} = \frac{1}{3}$$

49. As rank of T is less than the order of matrix. *i.e.* It must be a singular matrix and hence 0 must be an eigenvalue of T.

54.. As T satisfy $T^3 + 3T^2 = 4I$

i.e. it is satisfied by annihilating polynomial $\lambda^3 + 3\lambda^2 = 4$.

Which is satisfied by $\lambda = 1$

Now, $S = T^4 + 3T^3 - 4I = T(T^3 + 3T^2) - 4I$
$= 4(T - I) = 0$

i.e. $\lambda = 1$ satisfy $|T - \lambda I| = 0$

i.e. $S = 0$. i.e. $\lambda = 0$ satisfy $|S - \lambda I| = 0$

or $\lambda = 0$ is a root of eigen value of S.

Hence S is non-invertible.

57. The given trajectory is $r = k(1 - \cos\theta)$ taking logarithm, both the sides, we get

$$\log r = \log k + \log(1 - \cos\theta)$$

differentiating w.r.t. θ, we get

$$\frac{1}{r}\cdot\frac{dr}{d\theta} = \frac{\sin\theta}{1-\cos\theta}$$

for orthogonal trajectory, we replace $\frac{dr}{d\theta}$ by $-r^2\frac{d\theta}{dr}$

i.e. $$\frac{1}{r}\left(-r^2\frac{d\theta}{dr}\right) = \frac{2\frac{\sin\theta}{2}\cdot\frac{\cos\theta}{2}}{2\frac{\sin^2\theta}{2}}$$

or, $$\frac{\frac{\sin\theta}{2}}{\frac{\cos\theta}{2}}\cdot d\theta + \frac{dr}{r} = 0$$

integrating, we get

$$\log r + 2\log\frac{\sec\theta}{2} = \log c$$

or, $$r(1 + \cos\theta) = c.$$

58. A function which has no singularity in the finite part of the plane is called entire function.

59. Work done $\quad W = \int \overline{F}.d\overline{r}$

$$= \int\left(4y\overline{i} - 3xy\overline{j} + z^2\overline{k}\right).dx\overline{i} + dy\overline{j}$$

$$= \int_C 4ydx - 3xydy$$

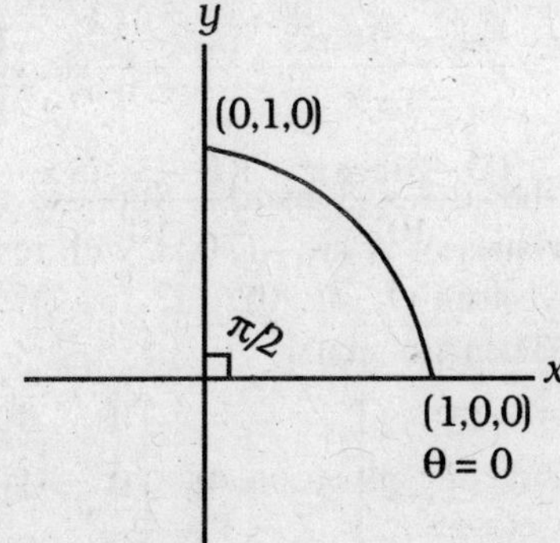

Change into polar co-ordinate by substitution $x = \cos\theta$, $y \sin\theta$

$$= \int_0^{\pi/2}\left(-4\sin^2\theta - 3\cos^2\theta\sin\theta\right)d\theta$$

$$= 4\int_0^{\pi/2}\sin^2\theta\, d\theta - \int_0^{\pi/2} 3\cos^2\theta\sin\theta\, d\theta$$

$$= -4.\frac{1}{2}.\frac{\pi}{2} + 3.\frac{\cos^3\theta}{3}\Bigg|_0^{\pi/2} = -\pi - 1$$

60. The ring of real numbers is an integral domain. Which is infinite. However it is also a field.

SET–10

CSIR–UGC (NET) MATHEMATICAL SCIENCES

PART-C

1. Let A be a 3 × 3 matrix. Suppose that the eigen-vlaues of A are –1, 0, 1 with respective eigen vectors $(1, -1, 0)^t$, $(1, 1, -2)^t$ and $(1, 1, 1)^t$. Then 6A equals

A. $\begin{bmatrix} -1 & 5 & 2 \\ 5 & -1 & 2 \\ 2 & 2 & 2 \end{bmatrix}$ B. $\begin{bmatrix} 1 & 0 & 0 \\ 0 & -1 & 0 \\ 0 & 0 & 0 \end{bmatrix}$

C. $\begin{bmatrix} 1 & 5 & 3 \\ 5 & 1 & 3 \\ 3 & 3 & 3 \end{bmatrix}$ D. $\begin{bmatrix} -3 & 9 & 0 \\ 9 & -3 & 0 \\ 0 & 0 & 6 \end{bmatrix}$

2. Let E be a measurable subset of (0, 1). Define two functions f_1 and f_2 on (0, 1) as follows:

$$f_1(x) = \begin{cases} \frac{1}{x} & \text{if } x \in E \\ 0 & \text{if } x \notin E \end{cases} \text{ and } f_2(x) = \begin{cases} 0 & \text{if } x \in E \\ \frac{1}{x} & \text{if } x \notin E \end{cases}.$$

Then

A. f_1 is measurable but not f_2

B. f_2 is measurable but not f_1

C. both f_1 and f_2 are measurable

D. neither f_1 nor f_2 is measurable

3. The eigenvalues of the linear operator T : $R^3 \to R^3$

where T(x, y, z) = (x + y + z, 2y + z, 2y + 3z) is equal to

A. 1, 2, 3 B. (1, 1, 4)

C. (0, 1, 5) D. (1, –1, 6)

4. Let $I = \oint_c f(z)dz$ where, $f(z) = \dfrac{e^{2z}}{(z+1)^4}$, and c is the circle $|z| = 3$. Then the value of I equals

A. $\dfrac{2\pi i e^{-1}}{3}$ B. $\dfrac{4\pi i e^{-2}}{3}$

C. $\dfrac{8\pi i e^{-2}}{3}$ D. $\dfrac{16\pi i e^{-2}}{3}$

5. Let $G = R \setminus \{0\}$ and $H = \{-1, 1\}$ be groups under multiplication. Then the map $\phi : G \to H$ defined by $\phi(x) = \dfrac{x}{|x|}$ is

A. not a homomorphism

B. a one-one homomorphism, which is not onto

C. an onto homomorphism, which is not one-one

D. an isomorphism

6. The solution of the differential equation $\dfrac{dy}{dx} = x + y$ using the Picard method after second approximation with the initial value $y(0) = 1$.

A. $1+x+\dfrac{x^2}{2}$ B. $1+x+\dfrac{x^2}{2}+\dfrac{x^3}{2}$

C. $1+x+x^2+\dfrac{x^3}{6}$ D. None of these

7. A differential equation.

$x(1 - x^2)dy + (2x^2y - y - ax^3)dx = 0$

has an integrating factor.

A. $e^{\int \frac{2x^2-1}{1-x}dx}$

B. $e^{\int \frac{2x^2-1}{x}dx}$

C. $e^{\int \frac{2x^2-1}{x(1-x^2)}dx}$

D. None of the above

8. A spring of mass M and spring constant K, hung vertically. Another mass m is suspended from it. Then the time period of the motion of the system is

A. $T = 2\pi\sqrt{\frac{(M+m)}{K}}$

B. $T = 2\pi\sqrt{\frac{M+3m}{K}}$

C. $T = 2\pi\sqrt{\frac{(M+3m)}{3K}}$

D. $T = 2\pi\sqrt{\frac{(3M+m)}{3K}}$

9. If $i^{i^i} = \cos\theta + i\sin\theta$, the value of θ is

A. $\left(2m+\frac{1}{2}\right)\pi e^{-\left(2n+\frac{1}{2}\right)\pi}$

B. $\left(2m-\frac{1}{2}\right)\pi e^{-\left(2n+\frac{1}{2}\right)\pi}$

C. $\left(2m+\frac{1}{2}\right)\pi e^{-\left(2n-\frac{1}{2}\right)\pi}$

D. $\left(2m+\frac{1}{2}\right)\pi e^{\left(2n-\frac{1}{2}\right)\pi}$

10. Maximum number of extreme points in a feasible region corresponding to an LPP having n equations and m decision variables ($n \le m$) can be

A. ${}^nC_m$ B. ${}^mC_n$
C. m D. n

11. What is the solution of the differential equation

$$\left(\frac{dy}{dx}\right) = (4x+y+1)^2 ?$$

A. $4x + y + 1 = 2\tan(2x + y + c)$
B. $4x + y = 1 = 2\tan(x + 2y + c)$
C. $4x + y + 1 = 2\tan(2y + c)$
D. $4x + y + 1 = 2\tan(2x + c)$

12. Consider the matrix $M = \begin{bmatrix} a^2 & ab & ac \\ ab & b^2 & bc \\ ac & bc & c^2 \end{bmatrix}$ where a, b and c are nonzero real numbers then the matrix has.

A. Three non-zero real eigen values
B. Complex eigen values
C. Two non-zero eigen value
D. Only one non-zero eigen value

13. If $D \equiv \frac{d}{dz}$ and $z = \log x$, then the differential equation $x\frac{d^2y}{dx^2} + 2\frac{dy}{dx} = 6x$ becomes.

A. $D(D - 1)y = 6e^z$ B. $D(D - 1)y = 6e^{2z}$
C. $D(D + 1)y = 6e^{2z}$ D. $D(D + 1)y = 6e^z$

14. Let $\sum_{n=-\infty}^{\infty} b_n z^n$ be the Laurent series expansion of $f(z) = \frac{z}{(z-1)(2-z)}$ valid for $1 < |z| < 2$, then which one of the following is correct?

A. $b_{-2} = 1, b_0 = 1, b_2 = 1$

B. $b_{-2} = -1, b_0 = 1, b_2 = \frac{1}{2}$

C. $b_{-2} = 1, b_0 = 1, b_2 = \frac{1}{4}$

D. $b_{-2} = 1, b_0 = 1, b_2 = \frac{1}{2}$

15. Extremals of the functional $\int_0^{\pi} (x^2 - y'^2)dx$; given that $y(0) = 0$, $y(1) = 0$ and $\int_0^{\pi} y^2 dx = 2\pi$ is

A. $\pm 2 \sin x$, $n \ne 0$ integer
B. $\pm 2 \cos nx$, $n \ne 0$ integer
C. $\pm 2 \sin nx$, n real number
D. $\pm 2 \cos nx$, n real number

16. Consider the real vector space $V = \mathbf{R}^3$ and following of its **subsets** :

1. $S = \{(x, y, z) \in V : x = y = 0\}$
2. $T = \{(x, y, z) \in V : x = 0\}$
3. $W = \{(x, y, z) \in V : z \ne 0\}$

Which one of the following statements is correct?

A. S, T and W are subspaces.

B. only S, W are subspaces.
C. only T, W are subspaces.
D. only S, T are subspaces.

17. Let the binary operation defined on Set of integer such that $a*b = a + (-1)^a b$ is
A. associative as well as commutative
B. associative but not commutative
C. commutative but not associative
D. Neither associative nor commutative

18. Which one is correct
A. A subgroup can be defined as a subset
B. Every subset of a group is subgroup
C. Every group is a subgroup of itself
D. Every group has two trivial subgroup

19. The singular integral of $x^2p^2 + y^2q^2 = z$
A. $z = 1$ B. $z = 0$
C. $z^2 + 1 = 0$ D. does not exist

20. Let $y_1(x)$ and $y_2(x)$ be linearly independent solutions of the differential equation $y'' + P(x)y' + Q(x)y = 0$, where $P(x)$ and $Q(x)$ are continuous functions on an interval I. Then $y_3(x) = ay_1(x) + by_2(x)$ and $y_4(x) = cy_1(x) + dy_2(x)$ are linearly independent solutions of the given differential equation if
A. $ad = bc$ B. $ac = bd$
C. $ad \neq bc$ D. $ac \neq bd$

21. The dimension of the vector space $\mathbf{U} = \{A = (a_{ij})_{n\times n} : a_{ij} \in \mathbf{C}, a_{ij} = -a_{ji}\}$ over the field R is
A. n^2 B. $n^2 - 1$
C. $n^2 - n$ D. $\frac{n^2}{2}$

22. Let $F : \mathrm{R} \to \mathrm{R}$ be a continuous function and $a > 0$. Then the integral $\int_0^a \left[\int_0^x F(y)\,dy\right] dx$ equals
A. $\int_0^a yF(y)dy$ B. $\int_0^a (a-y)F(y)dy$
C. D. $\int_a^0 yF(y)dy$

23. If y^a is an integrating factor of the differential equation $2xy\,dx - (3x^2 - y^2)\,dy = 0$, then the value of a is
A. -4 B. 4
C. -1 D. 1

24. For the chi-square distribution
$$f\left(\frac{1}{2}\chi^2\right)d\left(\chi^2\right)$$
$$= \frac{1}{\sqrt{\frac{n}{2}}}\, e^{-\frac{1}{2}\chi^2}\left(\frac{1}{2}\chi^2\right)^{\frac{1}{2}n-1} d\left(\chi^2\right), 0 \le \chi^0 < \infty$$
μ_r' (about origin) be.
A. $n(n + 1)(n + 2) \ldots. (n - 2r)$
B. $n(n + 2)(n + 4) \ldots. (n + 2r - 2)$
C. $n(n + 1)(n + 2) \ldots. (n + 2r - 1)$
D. $n(n + 2) + \ldots. + (n + 2r - 1)$

25. Which of the following is correct?
A. An assignment problem cannot be of maximization type
B. An assigment problem can be solved only if the number of rows and columns are equal.
C. The transportation method can be used to solve an assignment problem.
D. Unbalanced assignment problem cannot be solved

26. Under which one of the following conditions does the system of equations $\begin{bmatrix} 1 & 2 & 4 \\ 2 & 1 & 2 \\ 1 & 2 & a-4 \end{bmatrix}\begin{bmatrix} x \\ y \\ z \end{bmatrix} = \begin{bmatrix} 6 \\ 4 \\ a \end{bmatrix}$ have a unique solution?
A. For all $a \in \mathbf{R}$ B. $a = 8$
C. For all $a \in z$ D. $a \neq 8$

27. The value of $\oint_C (xy + y^2)dx + x^2dy$ where C is the closed curve of the region bounded by $y = x$ and $y = x^2$
A. $\frac{1}{20}$ B. $\frac{-1}{20}$
C. $\frac{19}{20}$ D. $\frac{-19}{20}$

28. $\frac{1}{2\pi i}\oint_c \frac{e^{zt}}{(z^2+1)^2}dz$ if $t > 0$ and C is the circle $|z| = 3$

A. $\frac{1}{2}(\sin t - t\cos t)$

B. $\frac{1}{2}(\sin t + t\cos t)$

C. $\frac{1}{2}(\sin t + \cos t)$

D. $\frac{1}{2}(t\sin t - \cos t)$

29. $f(xy) = xy^2$ on the rectangle $|x| \le 1$, $|y| \le 1$

1. Satisfies the Lipschitz condition.
2. Does not satisfy Lipschitz condition.

A. Only 1 B. Only 2
C. Both 1 and 2 D. None of these

30. The value of $\lim_{z\to 0}\left(\frac{\sin z}{z}\right)^{\frac{1}{z^2}}$ is equal to

A. $e^{\frac{1}{6}}$ B. $e^{\frac{1}{3}}$
C. $e^{-\frac{1}{6}}$ D. $e^{-\frac{1}{3}}$

31. What is the general solution of $2x\frac{dy}{dx} = 10x^3y^5 + y$?

A. $y^4 - cx^2 - 4x^3$ B. $y^{-4} = \frac{c}{x^2} + 4x^3$
C. $y^4 = \frac{c}{x^2} + 4x^3$ D. $y^{-4} = \frac{c}{x^2} - 4x^3$

32. If $A_1, A_2, A_3, \ldots A_{30}$ are thirty sets where each set having 5 elements and $B_1, B_2, \ldots B_n$ are n sets where each set having 3 elements. Also $\bigcup_{i=1}^{30} A_i = \bigcup_{j=1}^{n} B_j = S$ and each elements of S belong to exactly 10 of the A'_i S and exactly 9 of the B'_j S then n is equal to

A. 5 B. 15
C. 45 D. 135

33. All real solutions of the differential equation $y'' + 2ay' + by = \cos x$ (where a and b are real constants) are periodic if

A. $a = 1$ and $b = 0$
B. $a = 0$ and $b = 1$
C. $a = 1$ and $b \neq 0$
D. $a = 0$ and $b \neq 1$.

34. The set $S = \{(x, y) : xy \le 0\}$ is

A. Convex and unbounded
B. Convex and bounded
C. Non convex and unbounded
D. Non convex and bounded

35. The Newton-Raphson method was applied to solve the equation $e^x = x + 1$ with the initial guess $x_0 = 0$. What is the answer, correct upto 4 decimal places?

A. 1.3546 B. 0.8793
C. 3.8704 D. None of these

36. The characteristic curves of the PDE $yr + (x + y)s + xt = 0$ is

A. $x + y = u$, $x^2 + y^2 = v$

B. $y - x = u$, $v = \frac{y^2}{2} - \frac{x^2}{2}$

C. $x + y = u$, $\frac{x^3}{3} + \frac{y^3}{3} = v$

D. None of these

37. Let $f : C \to C$ be given by

$$f(z) = \begin{cases} (\bar{z})^2/z & \text{where } z \neq 0 \\ 0 & \text{when } z = 0 \end{cases} \text{ then } f$$

A. is not continuous at $z = 0$
B. is differentiable but not analytic at $z = 0$
C. is analytic at $z = 0$
D. satisfy the Cauchy-Riemann equation at $z = 0$

38. The *blocking probability* of M/M/1/N queueing system is

A. $\frac{(1-\rho)}{1-\rho^{N+1}}\rho^N$ B. $(1 - \rho)\rho^N$

C. $\frac{1-\rho}{1-\rho^{N+1}}$ D. $\frac{\rho}{1-\rho^N}$

39. The series $\sum_{n=1}^{\infty}\left(\frac{n}{n+1}\right)^{n^2} x^n$ is convergent for

A. $0 < x < e$ B. $x > e$
C. $2e < x < 3e$ D. $3e < x < 4e$

40. Let, A and B be two events such that $P(\overline{A \cup B}) = \frac{1}{6}$, $P(A \cap B) = \frac{1}{4}$ and $P(\bar{A}) = \frac{1}{4}$, where $\bar{A}$ stands for complement of event A. Then events A and B are

A. equally likely and mutually exclusive
B. equally likely but not independent
C. Independent but not equally likely
D. mutually exclusive and independent

41. Let S = $\{(x, y\} : x^2 + y^2 \leq 1\}$ then S has

A. No vertex
B. Finite number of vertices
C. Infinite number of vertices
D. None of the above

42. If $y = x$ is a solution of $x^2y'' + xy' - y = 0$, then the second linear independent solution of the above equation is

A. $1/x$ B. x^2
C. x^{-2} D. x^n

43. Let G be a finite abelian group of odd order. Let H = $\{x^2/\ x$ Î G$\}$, then

A. H is a subgroup of G only if G is cyclic
B. H is a proper subgroup of G
C. H = G
D. H may not be a subgroup of G

44. The value of $\iint_G \frac{\ln(x^2+y^2)}{x^2+y^2} dxdy$, where $G = \{(x,y) \in \mathrm{R}^2 : 1 \leq x^2 + y^2 \leq e^2\}$, is

A. π B. 2π
C. 3π D. 4π

45. Consider the following vector spaces over the reals :

1. The set of all complex numbers with usual operations.
2. The set of all polynomials with real coefficient of degree ≤ 3.
3. The set of point $x = 2t$, $y = -t$, $z = 4t$, $t \in$ R.
4. The set of all 3 × 3 matrices having real entries with usual operations.

The correct sequence of these vector spaces in decreasing order of their dimensions is

A. 1, 2, 3, 4 B. 2, 1, 4, 3
C. 4, 2, 1, 3 D. 4, 3, 2, 1

46. If three independent throws of a fair dice, let X denote the number of upper faces showing six. Then the value of $E(3 - X)^2$ is

A. $\frac{20}{3}$ B. $\frac{2}{3}$
C. $\frac{5}{2}$ D. $\frac{5}{12}$

47. Let $f : (1,4) \to$ R be a uniformly continuous function and let (a_n) be a Cauchy sequence in (1, 2). Let $x_n = a_n^2 f(a_n^2)$ and $y_n = \frac{1}{1+a_n^2} f(a_n^2)$, for all $n \in$ N. Which of the following statements is true?

A. Both (x_n) and (y_n) must be Cauchy sequences in R
B. (x_n) must be a Cauchy sequence in R but (y_n) need not be a Cauchy sequence in R
C. (y_n) must be a Cauchy sequence in R but (x_n) need not be a Cauchy sequence in R
D. Neither (x_n) nor (y_n) needs to be a Cauchy sequence in R

48. Let $S = \{a + bi : a, b$ is even integer$\}$ if $Z[i]$ is ring of Gaussian integer then S is

A. a subring of $Z[i]$ but not ideal.
B. an ideal of $Z[i]$ but not prime.
C. an ideal of $Z[i]$ but not maximal.
D. S is an ideal generated by $2 + 2i$.

49. Let G be the set of all 2 × 2 matrices $\begin{pmatrix} a & b \\ 0 & d \end{pmatrix}$ where $ad \neq 0$, under matrix multiplication and $N = \left\{\begin{pmatrix} 1 & b \\ 0 & 1 \end{pmatrix}\right\}$.

Where a, b, c, d are real number.

Consider the following statements:

1. N is not a subgroup of G.
2. N is a subgroup of G.
3. N is normal in G.
4. N is not normal in G.

Which of the statements give above is/are correct?

A. 1 only B. 2 only
C. 2 and 3 D. 2 and 4

50. Let $f, g : [-1, 1] \to R$, $f(x) = x^3$, $g(x) = x^2|x|$. Then

A. f and g are linearly independent on $[-1, 1]$

B. f and g are linearly dependent on $[-1, 1]$

C. $f(x)\,g'(x) - f'(x)g(x)$ is NOT identically zero on $[-1, 1]$

D. there exist continuous functions $p(x)$ and $q(x)$ such that f and g satisfy $y'' + py' + qy = 0$ on $[-1, 1]$

51. Sufficient condition for $f(z)$ to be analytic

A. u_x, u_y, v_x, v_y exist, continuous and satisfy C-R equation.

B. u_x, u_y, v_x, v_y exist

C. C-R satisfy

D. $f(z)$ is one-valued

52. A simple pendulum, consisting of a bob of mass m connected with a string of length a, is oscillating in a vertical plane. If the string is making an angle θ with the vertical, then the expression for the Lagrangian is given as

A. $ma^2\left[\dot{\theta}^2 - \frac{2g}{a}\sin^2\frac{\theta}{2}\right]$

B. $2mga\sin^2\frac{\theta}{2}$

C. $ma^2\left[\frac{\dot{\theta}^2}{2} - \frac{2g}{a}\sin^2\frac{\theta}{2}\right]$

D. $\frac{ma}{2}\left[\dot{\theta}^2 - \frac{2g}{a}\cos\theta\right]$

53. Let, E and F be two independent events. If the probability that both E and F happen is $\frac{1}{12}$ and the probability that neither E nor F happens is $\frac{1}{2}$, then $P(E)$ and $P(F)$ respectively are

A. $\frac{1}{3}, \frac{1}{4}$ B. $\frac{1}{2}, \frac{1}{6}$

C. $\frac{1}{6}, \frac{1}{2}$ D. $\frac{1}{4}, \frac{1}{3}$

54. A second degree polynomial passes through (0, 3), (1, 6), (2, 11), (3, 18) and (4, 27). The polynomial is

A. $x^2 + x + 1$

B. $x^2 + 2x + 3$

C. $x^2 + 2x + 1$

D. $x^2 + x + 2$

55. The set {4, 8, 12, 16} is a group under multiplication modulo 20 then the identity element is given by

A. 4 B. 8

C. 12 D. 16

56. Let $x = \{x \text{ in } Q \mid 0 < x < 1\}$ be the metric space with standard metric from R. The completion of x is

A. $\{x \text{ in } Q \mid 0 < x < 1\}$

B. $\{x \text{ in } R \mid 0 < x < 1\}$

C. $\{x \text{ in } Q \mid 0 \le x \le 1\}$

D. $\{x \text{ in } R \mid 0 \le x \le 1\}$

57. The space l_p is a Hibert space if and only if

A. $p > 1$ B. p = even

C. $p = \infty$ D. $p = 2$

58. If H and K are subgroups of a group G then

A. $H \cup K$ is a subgroup

B. $H \cap K$ is a subgroup

C. $H \cup K$ is a complex

D. $H \cap K = \phi$

59. The minimum cost for the transportation problem

1	2	5
3	2	10
8	7	

will be

A. 26 B. 28

C. 30 D. 32

60. The general solution of $(D^2 - 2DD' + D'^2)z = e^{x+2y} + x^3$ is given by

A. $z = \phi_1(y + x) + x\phi_2(y + x) + e^{x+2y} + 20x^5$

B. $z = \phi_1(y+x) + y\phi_2(x+y) + \frac{1}{3}e^{x+2y} + \frac{x^5}{20}$.

C. $z = \phi_1(y+x) + x\phi_2(y+x)e^{x+2y} + \frac{1}{20} - x^5$

D. None of these

ANSWERS

1	2	3	4	5	6	7	8	9	10
B	A	B	C	C	C	C	C	A	B
11	**12**	**13**	**14**	**15**	**16**	**17**	**18**	**19**	**20**
D	A	C	C	A	D	B	C, D	D	C
21	**22**	**23**	**24**	**25**	**26**	**27**	**28**	**29**	**30**
C	B	A	B	C	D	B	A	A	C
31	**32**	**33**	**34**	**35**	**36**	**37**	**38**	**39**	**40**
D	A	B	C	D	B	D	A	A	C
41	**42**	**43**	**44**	**45**	**46**	**47**	**48**	**49**	**50**
C	A	A	B	C	A	A	B	C	A
51	**52**	**53**	**54**	**55**	**56**	**57**	**58**	**59**	**60**
A	A	A	B	D	D	D	B, C	B	C

SOME SELECTED EXPLANATORY ANSWERS

3. Given linear operator T(x, y, z) = (x + y + z, 2y + z, 2y + 3z).

The standard eigen vectors of $\mathbf{R}^3$ are

$e_1 = (1, 0, 0)$, $e_2 = (0, 1, 0)$ and $e_3 = (0, 0, 1)$

then $T(1, 0, 0) = (1, 0, 0)$

$T(0, 1, 0) = (1, 2, 2)$

$T(0, 0, 1) = (1, 1, 3)$

i.e. $$[T] = \begin{bmatrix} 1 & 1 & 1 \\ 0 & 2 & 1 \\ 0 & 2 & 3 \end{bmatrix}$$

hence characteristic equation of T is given by

$$|T - \lambda I| = 0 \Rightarrow \begin{vmatrix} 1-\lambda & 1 & 1 \\ 0 & 2-\lambda & 1 \\ 0 & 2 & 3-\lambda \end{vmatrix} = 0$$

or, $(1 - \lambda)\{(2 - \lambda)(3 - \lambda) - 2\} = 0$

$\Rightarrow \quad (1 - \lambda)\{\lambda^2 - 5\lambda + 6 - 2\} = 0$

$(1 - \lambda)(\lambda - 1)(\lambda - 4) = 0$

$\Rightarrow \quad \lambda = 1, 1, 4.$

4. Given, $I = \int_c f(z)dz$, where $f(z) = \dfrac{e^{2z}}{(z+1)^4}$

Clearly $z = -1$ is a four order pole inside c then we know that Cauchy formula

$$I = \frac{2\pi i}{3!}\frac{d}{dz}\left(e^{2z}\right)\int_{z=-1} = \frac{8\pi i e^{-2}}{3}.$$

5. $\phi : G \to H$ by $\phi(x) = \dfrac{x}{|x|}$

Clearly $\phi(x) = 1 \quad \forall\, x > 0$

$= -1 \quad \forall\, x < 0$

Also $\phi(xy) = \dfrac{xy}{|xy|} = \dfrac{xy}{|x||y|}$

$= \dfrac{x}{|x|}\cdot\dfrac{y}{|y|} = \phi(x)\cdot\phi(y)$

It preserves composition

i.e., ϕ is homomorphism and onto but it is not one-one.

6. The given initial value problem is

$$\frac{dy}{dx} = x + y, \quad \text{with } y(0) = 1.$$

We have first approximation,

$$y^{(1)} = y_0 + \int_{x_0}^{x} f(x, y_0)dx$$

$$= 1 + \int_0^x (x+1)dx = 1 + x + \frac{x^2}{2}.$$

The second approximation

$$y^{(2)} = y_0 + \int_0^x f(x, y^{(1)})dx$$

$$= 1+\int_0^x \left[x+\left(1+x+\frac{x^2}{2}\right)\right]dx$$

$$= 1+\int_0^x \left(1+2x+\frac{x^2}{2}\right)dx$$

$$= 1+x+x^2+\frac{x^3}{6}.$$

8. Let at the lower end, where m is connected, velocity is given by y. It is maximum at lower end (S = l) and zero at fixed end (S = 0).

So velocity decreases as we move up. At any distance S, from the fixed end, the velocity will be given by $\left(\frac{S}{l}\right)\dot{y}$.

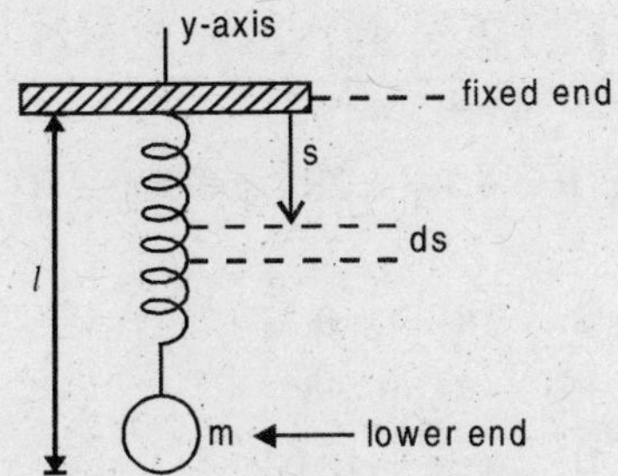

Fig.

Therefore K.E. associated with ds length of the spring is

$$dT = \frac{1}{2}\Delta m\cdot\left(\frac{S}{l}\dot{y}\right)^2$$

$$= \frac{1}{2}\rho ds\left(\frac{S}{l}\dot{y}\right)^2$$

whree ρ is the mass per unit length of the spiral.

For the whole spring, K.E. is

$$T = \frac{1}{2}\int_0^l \rho ds\left(\frac{S}{l}\dot{y}\right)^2$$

$$= \frac{1}{2}\rho\dot{y}^2\frac{1}{l^2}\left(\frac{S^3}{3}\right)_0^l = \frac{1}{6}\rho l\dot{y}^2$$

But total mass of the spring is $M = l\rho$. Therefore

$$T = \frac{1}{6}M\dot{y}^2$$

Further potential energy is $V = \frac{1}{2}Ky^2$

So that Lagrangian of the whose system (spring + mass, m) will be

$$L = \left(\frac{1}{2}m\dot{y}^2+\frac{1}{6}M\dot{y}^2\right)-\frac{1}{2}Ky^2$$

Putting for $\frac{\partial L}{\partial y}$ and $\frac{\partial L}{\partial y}$ in the Lagrange's equations, we get

$$\left(m+\frac{M}{3}\right)\ddot{y}+Ky = 0$$

which gives the period of oscillation equal to

$$T_p = 2\pi\sqrt{\frac{\left(\frac{M}{3}+m\right)}{k}}.$$

11. The given differential equation is

$$\frac{dy}{dx} = (4x + y + 1)^2$$

let $\qquad v = 4x + y + 1$

differentiating, we get

$$\frac{dv}{dx} = 4+\frac{dy}{dx}$$

or, $\qquad \frac{dy}{dx} = \frac{dv}{dx} - 4$

or, $\qquad \frac{dv}{dx} - 4 = v^2$

or, $\qquad \frac{dv}{dx} = 4 + v^2$

or, $\qquad \frac{dv}{4+v^2} = dx$

integrating, we get

$$\frac{1}{2}\tan^{-1}\frac{v}{2} = (x + c)$$

$\Rightarrow \qquad (4x + y + 1) = 2\tan(2x + c).$

14. $\because \quad f(z) = \frac{z}{(z-1)(2-z)} = \frac{2(z-1)+(2-z)}{(z-1)(2-z)}$

$$= \frac{2}{2-z}+\frac{1}{(z-1)}$$

$$= \frac{2}{2\left(1-\frac{z}{2}\right)} + \frac{1}{z\left(1-\frac{1}{z}\right)}$$

$$= \left(1-\frac{z}{2}\right)^{-1} + \frac{1}{z}\left(1-\frac{1}{z}\right)^{-1}$$

$$= \left(1+\frac{z}{2}+\frac{z^2}{4}+\frac{z^3}{8}+....\right) + \frac{1}{2}\left(1+\frac{1}{z}+\frac{1}{z^2}+....\right)$$

$$= \left(1+\frac{z}{2}+\frac{z^2}{4}+\frac{z^3}{8}+....\right) + \frac{1}{z}+\frac{1}{z^2}+\frac{1}{z^3}+....$$

$$\Rightarrow \quad b_{-2} = 1,\ b_0 = 1,\ b_2 = \frac{1}{4}.$$

20. $y_3(x) = ay_1(x) + by_2(x)$ &

$y_4(x) = cy_1(x) + dy_2(x)$

will be linearly independent if

$$\begin{vmatrix} a & b \\ c & d \end{vmatrix} \neq 0 \quad \Rightarrow \quad ad \neq bc.$$

22. The shaded area represent the integrand domain.

Hence $\int_0^a \left[\int_{y=0}^{a} F(y)\,dy \right] dx$

on changing the order of integral.

$$\int_{y=0}^{a} F(y) \int_{x=y}^{a} x\,dy = \int_{y=0}^{a} (a-y)F(y)dy$$

23. The given ODE is $2xydx - (3x^2 - y^2)dy = 0$. Comparing with standard equation

$$Mdx + Ndy = 0$$

we get $\qquad M = 2xy,\ N = y^2 - 3x^2$

$$\frac{\partial M}{\partial y} = 2x \quad \& \quad \frac{\partial N}{\partial x} = 6x.$$

As $\quad \frac{1}{M}\left(\frac{\partial N}{\partial x} - \frac{\partial N}{\partial y}\right) = \frac{-8x}{2xy} = \frac{-4}{y}$

Hence, I.F. $e^{-\int \frac{4}{y}dy} = \frac{1}{y^4} = y^{-4} = y^a \Rightarrow a = -4.$

24. $\mu_r' = \frac{1}{\gamma_{n/2}} \int_0^\infty 2^r e^{-t}\, t^{\frac{n}{2}+r-1}\, dt \qquad \because \frac{1}{2}\chi^2 = t$

$$= 2^r \cdot \frac{\gamma_{n/2+r}}{\gamma_{n/2}}$$

$$= 2^r\, \frac{n}{2}\cdot\left(\frac{n}{2}+1\right)\left(\frac{n}{2}+2\right)....\left(\frac{n}{2}+r-1\right)$$

$$= n\,(n+2)\,(n+4)\,....\,(n+2r-2)$$

$\mu_1' = n$

$\mu_2' = n\,(n+2)$

$\mu_2 = \mu_2' - (\mu_1')^2 = 2n.$

26. The augmented matrix is given by

$$\left[\begin{array}{ccc|c} 1 & 2 & 4 & 6 \\ 2 & 1 & 2 & 4 \\ 1 & 2 & a-4 & a \end{array}\right]$$

Apply $R_2 \to R_2 - 2R_1$ and $R_3 \to R_3 - R_1$ we get

$$\left[\begin{array}{ccc|c} 1 & 2 & 4 & 6 \\ 0 & -3 & -6 & -8 \\ 0 & 0 & a-8 & a-6 \end{array}\right]$$

for unique solution, determinant of co-efficient matrix should be non-zero

i.e. $\quad a - 8 \neq 0 \quad \Rightarrow \quad a \neq 8.$

27. The given line integral is $\int_C (xy + y^2)dx + x^2dy$.

Now by using Green's theorem, we can convert the given line integral into a surface integral as

$$\int_C Mdx + Ndy = \iint_S \left(\frac{\partial N}{\partial x} - \frac{\partial M}{\partial y}\right) dx\,dy$$

$$= \iint_S (2x - x - 2y)\,dx\,dy = \iint_S (x-2y)\,dx\,dy$$

$$= \int_{x=0}^{1} \int_{y=x^2}^{x} (x-2y)\,dy\,dx = \int_{x=0}^{1} \left[xy - y^2\right]_{x^2}^{x} dx$$

$$= \int_{x=0}^{1} (x\cdot x - x^2) - (x\cdot x^2 - x^4)\,dx$$

$$= \int_0^1 (x^4 - x^3)\,dx = \left.\frac{x^5}{5} - \frac{x^4}{4}\right|_0^1$$

$$= \frac{1}{5} - \frac{1}{4} = \frac{4-5}{20} = \frac{-1}{20}.$$

31. This is final the given differential equation is

$$\frac{2x\,dy}{dx} = 10x^3y^5 + y$$

or, $$\frac{2x\,dy}{dx} - y = 10x^3y^5$$

or, $$\frac{2x}{y^5}\frac{dy}{dx} - \frac{1}{y^4} = 10x^3 \qquad ...(1)$$

put $$v = -\frac{1}{y^4}$$

then $$\frac{dv}{dx} = \frac{4}{y^5}\frac{dy}{dx}$$

hence (1) reduces to

$$\frac{x}{2}\frac{dv}{dx} + v = 10x^3$$

or, $$\frac{dv}{dx} + \frac{2}{x}\cdot v = 20x^2$$

integrating, we get

$$v.x^2 + c = 4x^5$$

or $$v.x^2 = c - 4x^5$$

$$-\frac{1}{y^4} = \frac{-c}{x^2} + 4x^3$$

$$y^{-4} = \frac{c}{x^2} - 4x^3.$$

36. Given PDE is $yr + (x + y)s + xt = 0$ ...(1)
Comparing (1) with $Rr + Ss + Tt + f(x, y, z, p, q) = 0$.
Here $R = y$, $S = (x + y)$ and $T = x$ so that $S^2 - 4RT = (x + y)^2 - 4xy = (x - y)^2 > 0$ for $x \neq y$ and so (1) is hyperbolic.
Its λ-quadratic equation $R\lambda^2 + S\lambda + T = 0$ reduces to $y\lambda^2 + (x + y)\lambda + x = 0$
or $(y\lambda + x)(\lambda + 1) = 0$ so that $\lambda = -1, -x/y$.
Then the corresponding characteristic equations are given by

$$\frac{dy}{dx} - 1 = 0 \text{ and } \frac{dy}{dx} - \frac{x}{y} = 0$$

integrating these $y - x = c_1$ and $y^2/2 - x^2/2 = c_2$.
i.e. Characteristic curve is $y - x = u$,

$$\frac{y^2}{2} - \frac{x^2}{c} = v.$$

44. $$\iint_C \frac{(x^2 + y^2)}{x^2 + y^2}\,dxdy \qquad 1 \le x^2 + y^2 \le e^2$$

= Changing into polar co-ordinate by putting $x = r\cos\theta$, $y = r\sin\theta$, we get

$$= \int_{r=1}^{e}\int_{\theta=0}^{2\pi} \frac{\ln r^2}{r^2}.r\,d\theta\,dr = 2\int_{r=11}^{e}\frac{\ln r}{r}\,dr\int_{\theta=0}^{2\pi} d\theta$$

$$= 2\left.\frac{(\ln r)^2}{2}\right|_1^e 2\pi = \frac{8}{8}\left[(\ln e)^2 - \ln 1^2\right].2\pi$$

$$= 2\pi$$

49. Given $$G = \left\{\begin{pmatrix} a & b \\ 0 & d \end{pmatrix} : ad \neq 0\right\}$$

& $$N = \left\{\begin{pmatrix} 1 & b \\ 0 & 1 \end{pmatrix}\right\}.$$

Clearly $\begin{pmatrix} 1 & 0 \\ 0 & 1 \end{pmatrix}$ is identity of both N and G.

Also $\begin{pmatrix} 1 & -b \\ 0 & 1 \end{pmatrix}$ is the inverse of $\begin{pmatrix} 1 & b \\ 0 & 1 \end{pmatrix}$

Also N is closed under multiplication.
Hence N is a subgroup of G.

However let consider $\begin{pmatrix} a & b \\ 0 & d \end{pmatrix} \in G$ where $ad \neq 0$ then inverse of above matrix is

$\begin{pmatrix} \frac{1}{a} & -\frac{b}{ad} \\ 0 & \frac{1}{a} \end{pmatrix}$ if $\begin{pmatrix} 1 & b \\ 0 & 1 \end{pmatrix} \in N$, then $\begin{pmatrix} a & b \\ 0 & d \end{pmatrix}$

$$\begin{pmatrix} 1 & b \\ 0 & 1 \end{pmatrix}\begin{pmatrix} \frac{1}{a} & -\frac{b}{ad} \\ 0 & \frac{1}{d} \end{pmatrix} = \begin{pmatrix} 1 & \frac{ab}{d} \\ 0 & 1 \end{pmatrix} \in N.$$

i.e. N is a normal subgroup.

50. Given $f(x) = x^3 \quad -1 \le x \le 1$

$g(x) = -x^3 \quad -1 \le x \le 0$

$= x^3 \quad 0 \le x \le 1$

Consider $a\,f(x) + g(x) = 0$

$\Rightarrow \quad ax^3 + bx^3 = 0 \quad 0 \le x \le 1$

and $\quad ax^3 - bx^3 = 0 \quad -1 \le x \le 0$

which is true if $a = b = 0 \quad \forall x \in [-1, 1]$

i.e. $f(x)$ and $g(x)$ are linear independent.

54. The difference table is given below :

x	y	Δy	$\Delta^2 y$	$\Delta^3 y$
0	3			
		3		
1	6		2	
		5		0
2	11		2	
		7		0
3	18		2	
		9		
4	27			

In Newton's formula for interpolation
$a = 0,\ h = 1;\ f(a + hx) = f(x)$

$$\therefore\ y = f(x) = 3 + x(3) + \frac{x(x-1)}{2}(2) + \frac{x(x-1)(x-2)}{6}(0) + \ldots$$

or $y = 3 + 3x + x(x - 1) = x^2 + 2x + 3$.

55. $G = \{4, 8, 12, 16\}$ is a group under multiplication modulo 20, then $4 \odot 16 = 4$, $8 \odot 16 = 8$, $12 \odot 16 = 12$ and $16 \odot 16 = 16$.

60. The auxiliary equation is $(m - 1)^2 = 0$ so that $m = 1, 1$.

$\therefore$ C.F. $= \phi_1(y + x) + x\phi_2(y + x)$,

ϕ_1, ϕ_2 being arbitrary function.

Now P.I. corresponding to

$$e^{x+2y} = \frac{1}{(D - D')^2} e^{x+2y}$$

$$= \frac{1}{(1-2)^2} \iint e^v\, dv\, dv \text{ where } v = x + 2y$$

$$= e^{x+2y}.$$

Now P.I. corresponding to

$$x^3 = \frac{1}{(D - D')^2} x^3 = \frac{1}{D^2\left(1 - \frac{D'}{D}\right)^2} x^3$$

$$= \frac{1}{D^2}(1 + \ldots)x^3 = \frac{x^5}{20}.$$

i.e. General solution is $z = \phi_1(y + x) + x\phi_2(y + x) + e^{x+2y} + \frac{x^5}{20}$.

SET–11

CSIR–UGC (NET) MATHEMATICAL SCIENCES

PART-C

1. Let A be a 2 × 2 orthogonal matrix of trace and determinant 1. Then the angle between Au and u ($u = (1, 0)^t$) is

A. 15° B. 30°
C. 45° D. 60°

2. Let * be the binary operation defined by $x*y = ax + by \ \forall\ x, y \in R$ then the value of a, b for which * is commutative is

A. $a = 0, 1$ and $b = -1, 1$
B. $a = 0, 1$ and $b = 0, 1$
C. $a = -1, 1$ and $b = -1, 1$
D. $a = 0, -1$ and $b = 0, -1$

3. What is the solution of the equation

$$x\frac{dy}{dx}+\frac{y^2}{x}=y?$$

A. $\log\left(\frac{y}{x}\right)-\left(\frac{1}{x}\right)=c$ B. $\log x-\left(\frac{x}{y}\right)=c$

C. $\log(x/y)-\left(\frac{1}{x}\right)=c$ D. $\log x+\left(\frac{x}{y}\right)=c$

4. The functional $F[y(x)] = \int_0^1 (1-e^{-y'})\,dx;$

$y(0) = 0, y(1) = 4$ has

A. Weak minimum on the function $y = 4x$
B. Weak maximum on the function $y = 4x$
C. Strong maximum on the function $y = 4x$
D. Strong minimum

5. Define $f : c \to c$ by

$$f(z) = \begin{cases} 0, & \text{if } \operatorname{Re}(z)=0 \text{ or } \operatorname{Im}(z=0) \\ z, & \text{otherwise} \end{cases}$$

Then the set of points where f is analytic is

A. $\{z : \operatorname{Re}(z) \neq 0$ as $\operatorname{Im}(z) \neq 0\}$
B. $\{z : \operatorname{Re}(z) \neq 0\}$
C. $\{z : \operatorname{Re}(z) \neq 0$ or $\operatorname{Im}(z) \neq 0\}$
D. $\{z : \operatorname{Im}(z) \neq 0\}$

6. Which of the following is not necessarily subgroup?

A. The Kernel of a group homomorphism.
B. The centre of a group.
C. The subgroup consisting of all matrices with positive determinant in the group of all invertible matrices with real entries (under matrix multiplication).
D. None of these

7. The second order partial differential equation

$$\left(1-\sqrt{xy}\right)\frac{\partial^2 u}{\partial x^2}+\frac{\partial^2 u}{\partial x \partial y}+\left(1+\sqrt{xy}\right)\frac{\partial^2 u}{\partial y^2}=0 \text{ is}$$

A. Hyperbolic in second and the fourth quadrants.
B. Elliptic in the first and third quadrants.
C. Hyperbolic in second and elliptic in the fourth quadrant.
D. Hyperbolic in the first and the third quadrant.

8. If $G = \{1, \omega, \omega^2\}$, then there may be

A. 2 subgroups
B. 3 subgroups
C. 4 subgroups
D. No subgroup possible

9. The function $f(x) = \frac{1}{1-x}$. What is the number of points of discontinuity of the composite function $y = f^{3n}(x)$, where $f^n(x) = fofo.....(n$ times)?

A. 1 B. 2
C. n D. $3n$

10. What are the order and degree respectively of the differential equation of the family of curves $y^2 = 2c\left(x+\sqrt{c}\right)$, where c is an arbitrary constant?

A. 1, 1
B. 1, 2
C. 1, 3
D. 2, 1

11. The Lagrangian L of a dynamical system with two degress of freedom is given by $L = \alpha + \beta\dot{q}_1 + \gamma\dot{q}_2$ where α, β and γ are functions of the generalized co-ordinates q_1, q_2 only. If p_1, p_2 denote the generalized momenta, then Hamiltonian H.

A. depends on p_1, p_2 but not on q_1, q_2
B. depends on q_1, q_2 but not on p_1, p_2
C. depends on p_1, q_1 but not on p_2, q_2
D. is independent of p_1, p_2, q_1, q_2

12. Let $S = \left\{\begin{pmatrix} a & b \\ 0 & 0 \end{pmatrix} : a, b, 0 \in R\right\}$ be the ring under matrix addition and multiplication. Then the subset $\left\{\begin{pmatrix} 0 & b \\ 0 & 0 \end{pmatrix} : b \in R\right\}$ is

A. not an ideal of S.
B. an ideal but not a prime ideal of S.
C. is a prime ideal but not a maximal ideal of S.
D. is a maximal ideal of S.

13. For a subset A of a metric space, which of the following implies the other three?

A. A is closed
B. A is bounded
C. Closure of B is compact for every B $\subseteq$ A
D. A is compact

14. Every non-empty set of real numbes that has a lower bounded has

A. A supremum
B. An infimum
C. Neither infimum nor supremum
D. Both infimum and supremum.

15. If a power series is given by $\sum_{n=1}^{\infty} \frac{(z+2)^{n-1}}{(n+1)^3 4^n}$.

Then which one of the following is correct?

A. The series converges absolutely fog $|z + 2| > 4$.
B. The series converges absolutely for $|z + 2) < 4$.
C. The series converges absolute for $|z + 2| \leq 4$.
D. None of the above

16. The minimal polynomial associated with the matrix $\begin{bmatrix} 0 & 0 & 3 \\ 1 & 0 & 2 \\ 0 & 1 & 1 \end{bmatrix}$ is

A. $x^3 - x^2 - 2x - 3$
B. $x^3 - x^2 + 2x - 3$
C. $x^3 - x^2 - 3x - 3$
D. $x^3 - x^2 + 3x - 3$

17. Consider the differential equation

$$\frac{dx}{dt} = -ay, \quad \frac{dy}{dt} = ax.$$

Then

A. The point (x, y) will lie on a ellipse.
B. The point (x, y) will lie on a sphere.
C. The point (x, y) will lie on a circle.
D. The point (x, y) will lie on a parabola.

18. General sol of

$\frac{\partial^2 u}{\partial x^2} + \frac{\partial^2 u}{\partial y^2} = 0$ is of the form then

A. $u = f(x + iy) + g(x - iy)$
B. $u = f(x - iy) + g(x + iy)$
C. $u = f(x + iy) - g(x - iy)$
D. $u = f(x - iy) - g(x - iy)$

19. With reference to the simple deterministic inventory model which of the following is false? EOQ formula is sensitive to changes in:

A. The cost of holding
B. The cost of ordering
C. The cost of the item
D. None of the above three cost

20. India plays two matches each with West Indies and Australia in any tournament, the probabilities of India getting points 0, 1 and 2 are 0.45, 0.50 and 0.50 respectively. Assuming that the outcomes are independent, the probability of India getting at least 7 points is

A. 0.8750　　B. 0.0875
C. 0.0625　　D. 0.0250

21. The harmonic conjugate of $u(x, y) = x^2 - y^2 + xy$ is
A. $x^2 - y^2 + xy$
B. $x^2 - y^2 - xy$
C. $2xy+\frac{1}{2}\left(-x^2+y^2\right)$
D. $\frac{1}{2}xy+2\left(y^2-x^2\right)$

22. A random variable X has Poisson distribution with mean 2. Then $P(X > 1.5)$ equals
A. $\frac{2}{e^2}$　　B. 0
C. $1-\frac{3}{e^2}$　　D. $\frac{3}{e^2}$

23. Let $T : C^n \to C^n$ be a linear operator having n distinct eigenvalues. Then
A. T is invertible
B. T is invertible as well as diagonalizable
C. T is not diagonalizable
D. T is diagonalizable

24. The root of the equation $x^4 - x - 10 = 0$ near to $x = 2$ correct to three places using Newton-Raphson's method after second iteration is
A. 1.932　　B. 1.871
C. 1.856　　D. 2.152

25. Before moving towards optimality it should be confirmed in an $m \times n$ transportation table that there are exactly .... non-basic cells
A. $m + n - 1$　　B. $mn - m - 1$
C. $(m - 1)(n - 1)$　　D. None of these

26. The application of Gram-Schmidt process of orthonormalization to

$u_1 = (1, 1, 0)$, $u_2 = (1, 0, 0)$, $u_3 = (1, 1, 1)$ yields.

A. $\frac{1}{\sqrt{2}}(1, 1, 0), (1, 0, 0), (0, 0, 1)$
B. $\frac{1}{\sqrt{2}}(1, 1, 0), \frac{1}{\sqrt{2}}(1, -1, 0), \frac{1}{\sqrt{2}}(1, 1, 1)$
C. $(0, 1, 0), (1, 0, 0), (0, 0, 1)$
D. $\frac{1}{\sqrt{2}}(1, 1, 0), \frac{1}{\sqrt{2}}(1, -1, 0), (0, 0, 1)$

27. All the differential equation
A. May be sloved
B. May not be solved
C. Have been solved
D. None of the above

28. Consider the following improper integrals:

$$I_1 = \int_1^\infty \frac{dx}{(1+x^2)^{1/2}} \text{ and } I_2 = \int_1^\infty \frac{dx}{(1+x^2)^{3/2}}$$

Then
A. I_1 converges but not I_2
B. I_2 converges but not I_1
C. both I_1 and I_2 converges
D. neither I_1 nor I_2 converges

29. Choose the correct answers : If H is a normal sub-group of G and K is a normal subgroup of H then
A. K is a normal subgroup of G
B. K is not a normal subgroup of G
C. K is a subgroup of G
D. K is not a subgroup of G

30. Let, E, F and G be the three events such that the events E and F are mutually exclusive, $P(E \cup F) = 1$, $P(E \cap F) = \frac{1}{4}$ and $P(G) = \frac{7}{12}$.

Then $P(F \cap G)$ equals
A. $\frac{1}{12}$　　B. $\frac{1}{4}$
C. $\frac{5}{12}$　　D. $\frac{1}{3}$

31. The cross ratio of the four points (z_1, z_2, z_3, z_4) is real if and only if the four points lie on a
A. circle
B. straight line
C. circle and on a straight line
D. circle or a straight line

32. The general solution of the differential equation

$(x + a)p^2 + (x - y)p - y = 0$ is

A. $y = cx + \frac{ac^2}{c+1}$　　B. $y = cx - \frac{ac^2}{c+1}$
C. $y = -cx + \frac{ac^2}{c+1}$　　D. $y = -cx - \frac{ac^2}{c+1}$

33. Let $f(x) = (x-2)^{17}(x+5)^{24}$. Then
A. f does not have a critical point at 2
B. f has a minimum at 2
C. f has a maximum at 2
D. f has neither a minimum nor a maximum at 2

34. The number of maximal ideals in Z_{27} is
A. 0 B. 1
C. 2 D. 3

35. $\int x^3 J_0(x)$ is equal to (up to a constant)
A. $xJ_0(x) - x^3J_1(x)$ B. $x^2J_0(x) + J_1(x)$
C. $x^3J_1(x) - 2x^2J_2(x)$ D. $2x^2J_1(x) + xJ_2(x)$

36. The differential equation representing the family of circles touching y-axis at the origin is
A. linear and of first order
B. linear and of second order
C. nonlinear and of first order
D. nonlinear and of second order

37. Let T: $C^n \to C^n$ be a linear operator having n distinct eigen values. Then
A. T is invertible
B. T is invertible as well as diagonalizable
C. T is not diagonalizable
D. T is diagonaliable

38. The value $\int_C (e^{-x}\sin y\,dx + e^{-x}\cos y)dy$ where C is the rectangle with vertices $(0, 0), (\pi, 0), \left(\pi, \frac{1}{2}\pi\right), \left(0, \frac{1}{2}\pi\right)$ is
A. $(e^{-\pi} - 1)$ B. $(1 - e^{-\pi})$
C. $2(e^{-\pi} - 1)$ D. none of these

39. A mobius transformation which transform the upper half plane into the lower half plane is
A. $w = \bar{z}$ B. $w = \frac{z-i}{z+i}$
C. $w = \frac{1}{z}$ D. $w = \frac{z+i}{z-i}$

40. The joint probability density function of the random variables x, y and z is $F(x, y, z) = 8xyz$, $0 < x, y, z < 1$, then $P(x < y < z)$ is
A. $\frac{1}{8}$ B. $\frac{1}{3}$
C. $\frac{1}{6}$ D. $\frac{3}{8}$

41. $\tan z = \frac{a}{z}$, $a > 0$ has roots
A. infinitely many real roots but only one imaginary roots
B. finitely many real roots but no imaginary roots
C. finitely many real roots but one imaginary roots
D. infinitely many real roots but no imaginary roots.

42. The general solution of PDE $(2D^2 - 5DD' + 2D'^2)z = 5\sin(2x + y)$ is given by
A. $z = \phi_1(y + 2x) + \phi_2(2y + x) + 5\cos(2x + y)$
B. $\phi_1(y-2x)+\phi_2(2x-y)-\frac{5}{3}x\cos(2x+y)$
C. $\phi_1(y+2x)+\phi_2(2x+y)-\frac{5}{3}x\cos(2x+y)$
D. None of these

43. If $S = \{(1, 1, 0), (2, 1, 3)\} \subseteq R^3$, then which one of the following vectors of $\mathbf{R}^3$ is **not** in the span [S]?
A. (0, 0, 0) B. (3, 2, 3)
C. (1, 2, 3) D. (4/3, 1, 1)

44. For every function $f : [0, 1] \to R$ which is twice differentiable and satisfies $f'(x) \geq 1$ for all $x \in [0, 1]$, we must have
A. $f''(x) \geq 0$ for all $x \in [0, 1]$
B. $f(x) \geq x$ for all $x \in [0, 1]$
C. $f(x_2) - x_2 \leq f(x_1) - x_1$ for all $x_1, x_2 \in [0, 1]$ with $x_2 \geq x_1$
D. $f(x_2) - x_2 \geq f(x_1) - x_1$ for all $x_1, x_2 \in [0, 1]$ with $x_2 \geq x_1$

45. If $a_n > 0$ for all n then $\lim_{n\to\infty}(a_n)^{1/n}$ is equal to
A. $\lim_{n\to\infty}\frac{a_n}{a_{n+1}}$ B. $\lim_{n\to\infty}\frac{a_n}{a_{n+1}}$
C. $\lim_{n\to\infty}\frac{a_n}{a_{n+1}}$ D. $\lim_{n\to\infty}\frac{a_n}{a_{n+1}}$
provided the latter limit exists

46. Which is true.

A. With increases in the carrying cost, the optimum order quantity also increases

B. Total ordering cost equals total holding cost

C. An increase in the set up cost per production run leads to decrease in the economic lot size.

D. For ecomomic lot size, the total setup cost need not be equal to the total holding cost

Directions (Qs. 47 and 48): Study the given information and answer the next questions:

x	y	Δ	Δ^2	Δ^3	Δ^4
0	–3				
		6			
1	3		2		
		8		6	
2	11		8		0
		16		6	
3	27		14		
		30			
4	57				

47. What is the polynomial that can be fitted into these data by Newton's forward difference formula?

A. $x^3 - 2x^2 - 7x - 3$

B. $x^3 - 3x^2 - 5x + 2$

C. $x^3 - 7x^2 - 4x - 4$

D. $3x^3 - 2x^2 - 5x - 3$

48. What is the approximate value of y for $x = 3.5$ given by Newton's interpolation?

A. –8 B. 48

C. 53 D. 40

49. Consider the function $f : R \to R$ defined by

$$f(x) = \begin{cases} x^4, & \text{if } x \text{ is rational} \\ 2x^2 - 1, & \text{if } x \text{ is irrational} \end{cases}$$

Let S be the set of points where F is continuous. Then

A. $S = \{1\}$ B. $S = \{-1\}$

C. $S = \{-1, 1\}$ D. $S = \phi$

50. Let $\left\{0, \frac{1}{2}, 1\right\}$ be three distinct points on [0, 1].

Let p be the unique interpolating polynomial of suitable degree on [0, 1] such that $p(0) = 0$, $p\left(\frac{1}{2}\right) = 0$, $p(1) = 1$, then $p\left(\frac{1}{4}\right)$ is equal to

A. $-\frac{1}{8}$ B. $-\frac{1}{2}$

C. $\frac{2}{5}$ D. None of these

51. Which is not correct

A. Ring without zero divisors means $\exists\, a, b \in$ Ring such that $ab = 0 \Rightarrow$ either $a = 0$ or $b = 0$

B. The ring of whole numbers modulo p is an integral domain if and only if P is a prime

C. The characteristic of every finite integral domain is finite

D. The characteristic of every integral domain D is zero or prime

E. Every isomorphic image of an integral domain is not an integral domain

F. A commulative ring with unity is an integral domain if it has zero divisors.

52. The set $U = \left\{x \in R \middle| \sin x = \frac{1}{2}\right\}$

A. open

B. closed

C. both open and closed

D. neither open nor closed

53. Consider the field **R** of real numbers and following spaces :

1. Set of real valued functions on [0, 1] having discontinuity at $x = \frac{1}{2}$.

2. $\{(x, y) \in R^2 : x > 0\}$.

Which of the above is/are vector space(s)?

A. 1 only

B. 2 only

C. Both 1 and 2

D. Neither 1 nor 2

54. Let $T(x, y, z) = xy^2 + 2z - x^2 z^2$ be the temperature at the point (x, y, z). The unit vector in the direction in which the temperature decreases most rapidly at (1, 0, –1) is

A. $-\frac{1}{\sqrt{5}}\hat{i}+\frac{2}{\sqrt{5}}\hat{k}$

B. $\frac{1}{\sqrt{5}}\hat{i}-\frac{2}{\sqrt{5}}\hat{k}$

C. $\frac{2}{\sqrt{14}}\hat{i}+\frac{3}{\sqrt{14}}\hat{j}+\frac{1}{\sqrt{14}}\hat{k}$

D. $-\left(\frac{2}{\sqrt{14}}\hat{i}+\frac{3}{\sqrt{14}}\hat{j}+\frac{1}{\sqrt{14}}\hat{k}\right)$

55. Let $\{a_n\}$, $\{b_n\}$ and $\{c_n\}$ be sequences of real numbers such that $b_n = a_{2n}$ and $c_n = a_{2n+1}$. Then $\{a_n\}$ is convergent

A. implies $\{b_n\}$ is convergent but $\{c_n\}$ need not be convergent

B. implies $\{c_n\}$ is convergent but $\{b_n\}$ need not be convergent

C. implies both $\{b_n\}$ and $\{c_n\}$ are convergent

D. if both $\{b_n\}$ and $\{c_n\}$ are convergent

56. If U b is the real vector space of all mappings from R to R, $V_1 = \{f \in V \mid f(-x) = f(x)\}$ and $V_2 = \{f \in V \mid f(-x) = -f(x)\}$, then which one of the following is correct?

A. Neither V_1 nor V_2 is a subspace of V.

B. V_1 is a subspace of V, but V_2 is not a subspace of V.

C. V_1 is not a subspace of V, but V_2 is a subspace of V.

D. Both V_1 and V_2 are subspaces of V.

57. The general solution of $x^2\left(\frac{\partial^2 z}{\partial x^2}\right)-y^2\left(\frac{\partial^2 z}{\partial y^2}\right)=0$ can be written as

A. $f(x/y) + g(xy)$

B. $xf(x/y) + g(x/y^2)$

C. $xf(x/y) + g(xy)$

D. $f(x/y) + yg(xy)$

58. The number of elements of S_5 (the symmetric group on 5 letters) which are their own inverses equals

A. 10 B. 11

C. 25 D. 26

59. What is the solution of the differential equation

$$\frac{dy}{dx}=e^{x-y}\left\{e^x-e^y\right\}?$$

A. $e^{e^y}\left(e^x-e^y+1\right)=c$

B. $e^{e^y}\left(e^y-e^x+1\right)=c$

C. $e^{e^x}\left(e^x-e^y+1\right)=c$

D. $e^{e^x}\left(e^y-e^x+1\right)=c$

60. Let $T:\mathbb{R}^n \to \mathbb{R}^n$ be a linear transformation, where $n \geq 2$. For $k \leq n$, let $E=\{v_1, v_2, ..., v_k\} \subseteq \mathbb{R}^n$ and $F=\{Tv_1, Tv_2,..,Tv_k\}$. Then

A. If E is linearly independent, then F is linearly independent

B. If F is linearly independent, then E is linearly independent

C. If E is linearly independent, then F is linearly dependent

D. If F is linearly independent, then E is linearly dependent

ANSWERS

1	2	3	4	5	6	7	8	9	10
C	C	B	B	A	D	C	A	B	C
11	**12**	**13**	**14**	**15**	**16**	**17**	**18**	**19**	**20**
A	D	D	B	C	A	A	A	A	B
21	**22**	**23**	**24**	**25**	**26**	**27**	**28**	**29**	**30**
C	C	D	C	A	D	B	C	B, C	D
31	**32**	**33**	**34**	**35**	**36**	**37**	**38**	**39**	**40**
D	A	D	B	C	C	B	C	A	A
41	**42**	**43**	**44**	**45**	**46**	**47**	**48**	**49**	**50**
D	C	C	D	D	B	A	D	C	A
51	**52**	**53**	**54**	**55**	**56**	**57**	**58**	**59**	**60**
E, F	B	D	B	C	D	C	B	D	D

SOME SELECTED EXPLANATORY ANSWERS

1. The general form of a 2 × 2 orthogonal matrix is given by

$$A = \begin{bmatrix} \cos\theta & \sin\theta \\ -\sin\theta & \cos\theta \end{bmatrix}$$

from question Trace (A) = 1

$\Rightarrow 2\cos\theta = 1 \Rightarrow \theta = 60°$

i.e.
$$A = \begin{bmatrix} \frac{1}{2} & \frac{\sqrt{3}}{2} \\ \frac{-\sqrt{3}}{2} & \frac{1}{2} \end{bmatrix}$$

also
$$Au = \begin{bmatrix} \frac{1}{2} & \frac{\sqrt{3}}{2} \\ \frac{-\sqrt{3}}{2} & \frac{1}{2} \end{bmatrix}\begin{bmatrix} 1 \\ 0 \end{bmatrix} = \begin{bmatrix} \frac{1}{2} \\ \frac{-\sqrt{3}}{2} \end{bmatrix}$$

Hence if ϕ be the angle between Au and u then from the dot product of Au and u.

$$\cos\phi = \frac{\frac{1}{\sqrt{2}}}{1.1} \Rightarrow \phi = 45°.$$

9. The given function $f(x) = \dfrac{1}{1-x}$

clearly at $x = 1$, $f(x)$ has a point of discontinuity.

Now for $fof(x) = \dfrac{1}{1-\frac{1}{1-x}} = \dfrac{1-x}{-x} = \dfrac{x-1}{x}$

clearly at $x = 0$, $fof(x)$ has a point of discontinuity.

Now for $fofof(x) = \dfrac{1}{1-\frac{x-1}{x}} = x.$

which is continuous everywhere the cycle of $f(x)$ will be repeated for $fofofof(x)$.

Hence for function $y = f^{3n}(x)$, the points of discontinuity are $x = 0$ & $x = 1$.

10. The given family of curves are

$$y^2 = 2c\,(x + \sqrt{c}) \qquad ...(1)$$

differentiating both sides w.r.t. x, we get

$$2yy_1 = 2c \quad \text{or} \quad c = yy_1.$$

Putting the value of c in equation (1), we get

$$y^2 = 2yy_1\left(x+\sqrt{yy_1}\right)$$

or, $$\frac{y}{2y_1} - x = \sqrt{yy_1}$$

or, $$\left(\frac{y}{2y_1} - x\right)^2 = yy_1$$

or, $$(y - 2xy_1)^2 = 4yy_1^3.$$

Clearly the order & degree of above O.D.E. are 1 and 3 respectively.

12. Given $S = \left\{\begin{pmatrix} a & b \\ 0 & 0 \end{pmatrix} : a, b \in R\right\}$ and the subset

S' (say) $= \left\{\begin{pmatrix} 0 & b \\ 0 & 0 \end{pmatrix} : b \in R\right\}$ clearly S' is an ideal of S.

Now it is clearly to see that $M = \left[\begin{pmatrix} a & 0 \\ 0 & 0 \end{pmatrix} : a \in Q\right]$ is a subfield of R in which $\begin{pmatrix} 1 & 0 \\ 0 & 0 \end{pmatrix}$ is the unity and the multiplicative inverse of $\begin{pmatrix} a & 0 \\ 0 & 0 \end{pmatrix}$ is $\begin{pmatrix} a^{-1} & 0 \\ 0 & 0 \end{pmatrix}$, for each $a \neq 0$.

The mapping $\theta : S \to M$ defined as

$$\theta\left\{\begin{pmatrix} a & b \\ 0 & 0 \end{pmatrix}\right\} = \begin{pmatrix} a & 0 \\ 0 & 0 \end{pmatrix}$$

Clearly θ is an onto homomorphism and

$$\text{Ker}\ \theta = \left\{\begin{pmatrix} a & b \\ 0 & 0 \end{pmatrix} \in S : \theta\begin{pmatrix} a & b \\ 0 & 0 \end{pmatrix} = \begin{pmatrix} 0 & 0 \\ 0 & 0 \end{pmatrix}\right\}$$

$$= \left\{\begin{pmatrix} a & b \\ 0 & 0 \end{pmatrix} : \theta\begin{pmatrix} a & 0 \\ 0 & 0 \end{pmatrix} = \begin{pmatrix} 0 & 0 \\ 0 & 0 \end{pmatrix} i.e., a = 0\right\}$$

$$= \left\{\begin{pmatrix} 0 & b \\ 0 & 0 \end{pmatrix}, b \in Q\right\} = S_1.$$

$\therefore$ By Fundamental Theorem of ring $\frac{S}{S_1} \approx M$ or $\frac{S}{S_1} \approx M$. Since M_0 is a field, so $\frac{S}{S_1}$ is also a field.

Hence, S_1 is a maximal ideal.

15. The given power series is $\sum_{n=1}^{\infty} \frac{(z+2)^{n-1}}{(n+1)^3 4^n}$

Now, if $u_n = \frac{(z+2)^{n-1}}{(n+1)^3 4^n}$,

then, $u_{n+1} = \frac{(z+2)^{n-1+1}}{(n+2)^3 . 4^{n+1}}$

Hence, excluding $z = -2$ for which the given series converges, we've

$$\lim_{n\to\infty}\left|\frac{u_{n+1}}{u_n}\right| = \lim_{n\to\infty}\left|\frac{z+2}{4} . \frac{(n+1)^3}{(n+2)^3}\right| = \frac{|z+2|}{4}$$

Then the series converges absolutely for $\frac{|z+2|}{4} < 1$ *i.e.* $|z + 2| < 4$. The point $z = -2$ is included in $|z + 2| < 4$. If $\frac{|z+2|}{4} = 1$ then $|z + 2| = 4$, the ratio test fails in this case

$$\left|\frac{(z+2)^{n-1}}{(n+1)4^n}\right| = \frac{1}{4(n+1)^3} \le \frac{1}{n^3}.$$

As $\sum \frac{1}{n^3}$ converges [p series with $p = 3$], the given series converges (absolutely).

i.e. The given series converges (absolutely) for $|z + 2| \le 4$.

16. The characteristic equation of the given polynomial is

$$|M - xI| = 0 \text{ where } M = \begin{bmatrix} 0 & 0 & 3 \\ 1 & 0 & 2 \\ 0 & 1 & 1 \end{bmatrix}$$

$$\text{Now} \begin{vmatrix} -x & 0 & 3 \\ 1 & -x & 2 \\ 0 & 1 & 1-x \end{vmatrix} = 0$$

or, $-x\{x(x-1) - 2\} + 3(1 - 0) = 0$

or $x(2 - x(x - 1) + 3) = 0$

or, $2x - x^3 + x^2 + 3 = 0$

or, $x^3 - x^2 - 2x - 3 = 0.$

In this case, characteristic polynomial is also the minimum polynomial.

18. $D^2 + D'^2 = 0$

A.E is $D^2 + 1 = 0 \Rightarrow D = \pm i$

$\therefore \quad u = f(x + iy) + g(x - iy)$

or, Alternative Method

$$u = f(x + iy) + g(x - iy)$$

$$\frac{\partial u}{\partial x} = f'(x + iy) + g'(x - iy)$$

$$\frac{\partial^2 u}{\partial x^2} = f''(x + iy) + g''(x - iy) \quad \text{... (i)}$$

$$\frac{\partial u}{\partial y} = i f'(x + iy) + (-i)\, g'(x - iy)$$

$$\frac{\partial^2 u}{\partial y^2} = i^2 f''(x + iy) + (-i)^2 g(x - iy)$$

$$\frac{\partial^2 u}{\partial y^2} = -f(x + iy) - g(x - iy) \quad \text{... (ii)}$$

$$\therefore \frac{\partial^2 u}{\partial x^2} + \frac{\partial^2 u}{\partial y^2} = 0$$

21. $u_x = 2x + y$, $u_y = -2y + x$

$$f(z) = \int [u_x(z,0) + iv_x(z,0)]dz$$

$$= \int [u_x(z,0) - iv_y(z,0)]dz$$

$$= \int (2z - iz)dz = z^2 - \frac{iz^2}{2}$$

$$\Rightarrow \quad v = \frac{y^2 - x^2}{2} + 2xy$$

24. Here, $f(x) = x^4 - x - 10$

$\therefore \quad f'(x) = 4x^3 - 1$

$$\therefore \quad x_{n+1} = x_n - \frac{f(x_n)}{f'(x_n)} = x_n - \frac{x_n^4 - x_n - 10}{4x_n^3 - 1}$$

$$= \frac{3x_n^4 + 10}{4x_n^3 - 1}$$

The approximate value of the root is given to be 2. Taking $x_0 = 2$, we get

$$x_1 = \frac{3\cdot x_0^4+10}{4x_0^3-1} = \frac{3\cdot 2^4+10}{4\cdot 2^3-1} = 1.871$$

$$x_2 = \frac{3x_1^4+10}{4x_1^3-1} = \frac{3(1.871)^4+10}{4(1.871)^3-1} = 1.856$$

i.e., choice (*c*) is correct.

26. First we normalize u_1, *i.e.* we get

$$v_1 = \frac{u_1}{\|u_1\|} = \frac{(1,1,0)}{\sqrt{1+1}} = \frac{1}{\sqrt{2}}(1,1,0).$$

Next we set,

$$w_2 = u_2 - \langle u_2, v_1\rangle v_1$$

$$= (1,0,0)-\frac{1}{\sqrt{2}}\cdot\frac{1}{\sqrt{2}}(1,1,0)$$

$$= (1,0,0)-\frac{1}{2}(1,1,0)=\left(\frac{1}{2},\frac{-1}{2},0\right)$$

Now we normalize w_2, *i.e.* we set

$$v_2 = \frac{w_2}{\|w_2\|} = \frac{\left(\frac{1}{2},\frac{-1}{2},0\right)}{\frac{1}{\sqrt{2}}} = \frac{1}{2}(1,-1,0).$$

Finally, we get

$$w_3 = u_3 - (u_3, v_1)v_1 - (u_3, v_2)v_2$$

$$\Rightarrow \quad w_3 = (1, 1, 1) - \sqrt{2}\cdot\frac{1}{\sqrt{2}}(1, 1, 0) - 0$$

$$= (0, 0, 1).$$

Now we normalize $w_3 = (0, 0, 1)$

i.e. the required orthonormal set are

$$\left\{\frac{1}{\sqrt{2}}(1,1,0), \frac{1}{\sqrt{2}}(1,-1,0), (0,0,1)\right\}.$$

28. The given improper integrals is

$$I_1 = \int_1^\infty \frac{dx}{(1+x^2)^{1/2}}$$

and $$I_2 = \int_1^\infty \frac{dx}{(1+x^2)^{3/2}}$$

Consider $$I_1 = \int_1^\infty \frac{dx}{(1+x^2)^{1/2}}$$

let $x = \tan\theta$

then $dx = \sec^2\theta\, d\theta$

$$= \int_{\pi/4}^{\pi/2} \frac{\sec^2\theta\, d\theta}{\sec\theta} = \int_{\pi/4}^{\pi/2} \sec\theta\, d\theta$$

$$= \ln(\sec\theta+\tan\theta)\Big|_{\pi/4}^{\pi/2}$$

$\Rightarrow I_1 \to \infty$ (*i.e.* I_1 is divergent).

Now consider

$$I_2 = \int_1^\infty \frac{dx}{(1+x^2)^{3/2}}$$

let $x = \tan\theta$

then $dx = \sec^2\theta\, d\theta$

then $$I_2 = \int_{\pi/4}^{\pi/2} \frac{\sec^2\theta\, d\theta}{\sec^3\theta} = \int_{\pi/4}^{\pi/2} \cos\theta\, d\theta$$

$$= \sin\theta\Big|_{\pi/4}^{\pi/2} = \left(1-\frac{1}{\sqrt{2}}\right)$$

$$= \frac{\sqrt{2}-1}{\sqrt{2}}.$$

33. $f(x) = (x - 2)^{17}\ (x + 5)^{24}$

$\Rightarrow$ for $x < 2, f(x) < 0$ and for $x > 2$

$f(x) > 0$

so, $x = 2$ is neither maxima nor minima point.

36.

Y

X

$(a,0)$

The equation of circle will be

$$(x - a)^2 + y^2 = a^2$$

$$\Rightarrow x^2 + y^2 - 2ax = 0$$

$$\Rightarrow 2x+2y\frac{dy}{dx}-2a=0$$

$$\Rightarrow a = x+y\frac{dy}{dx}$$

$$\Rightarrow x^2+y^2-2x\left[x+y\frac{dy}{dx}\right]=0$$

$$\Rightarrow 2xy\frac{dy}{dx} = y^2-x^2$$

$$\Rightarrow \frac{dy}{dx} = \frac{y}{2x}-\frac{x}{2y}$$

which is non linear of order one.

38. The given line integral is

$$\oint_C (e^{-x} \sin y_{dx} + e^{-x} \cos y)\, dy.$$

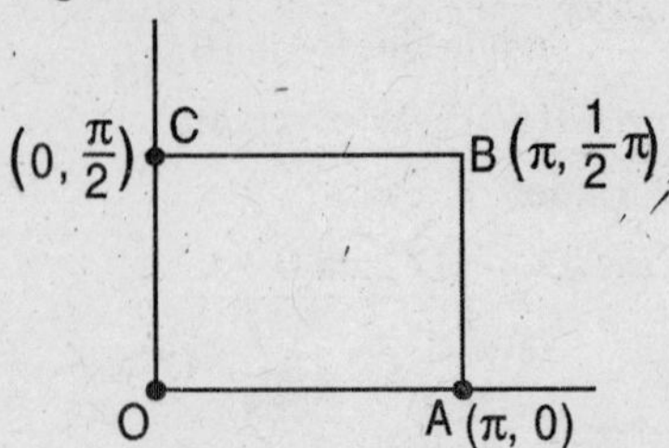

Now by using the Green's theorem, we can convert the given line integral into a surface integral.

i.e. $\int_C e^{-x} \sin y dx + e^{-x} \cos y dy$

$$= \int_{y=0}^{\pi/2} \int_{x=0}^{\pi} \left\{ \frac{\partial}{\partial x}(e^{-x} \cos y) - \frac{\partial}{\partial y}(e^{-x} \sin y) \right\} dx\, dy$$

$$= -\int_{x=0}^{\pi} \int_{y=0}^{\pi/2} (e^{-x} \cos y + e^{-x} \cos y)\, dx\, dy$$

$$= -2\int e^{-x} dx \int_0^{\pi/2} \cos y\, dy$$

$$= -2\left[-e^{-x}\right]_0^{\pi} \cdot \left[\sin y\right]_0^{\pi/2}$$

$$= -2(-e^{-\pi} + 1)\cdot 1 = 2(e^{-\pi} - 1).$$

42. Here auxiliary equation is $2m^2 - 5m + 2 = 0$ so that $m = 2, 1/2$

$\therefore$ C.F. $= \phi_1(y + 2x) + \phi_2(2y + x)$,

ϕ_1, ϕ_2 is arbitrary function.

Now P.I. $= \dfrac{1}{2D^2 - 5DD' + 2D'^2} 5\sin(2x + y)$

$$= \frac{5.1}{(D - 2D')}\left[\frac{1}{(2D - D')}\sin(2x + y)\right]$$

$$= \frac{5.1}{(D - 2D')} \frac{1}{2.2 - 1} \int \sin v dv,$$

where $v = 2x + y$.

$$= \frac{5}{3} \cdot \frac{1}{D - 2D'}(-\cos v)$$

$$= -\frac{5}{3} \cdot \frac{1}{(D - 2D')}\cos(2x + y)$$

$$= -\frac{5}{3} \frac{x}{1!}\cos(2x + y)$$

$$= -\frac{5}{3} x \cos(2x + y)$$

hence general solution is given by

$$z = \text{C.F.} + \text{P.I.} = \phi_1(y + 2x) + \phi_2(2y + x) - \left(\frac{5}{3}\right) x \cos(2x + y).$$

43. As $(0, 0, 0) = 0.(1, 1, 0) + 0.(2, 1, 3)$

$(3, 2, 3) = 1.(1, 1, 0) + 1.(2, 1, 3)$

$\left(\frac{4}{3}, 1, 1\right) = \frac{2}{3}(1, 1, 0) + \frac{1}{3}(2, 1, 3).$

44. $f'(x) \geq 1 \Rightarrow f(x)$ is an increasing function.

$\Rightarrow f'(x) - 1 \geq 0$

$\Rightarrow f(x) - x \geq c$

$\Rightarrow f(x_2) - x_2 \geq f(x_1) - x_1$ for all $x_1, x_2 \in [0, 1]$ with $x_2 \geq x_1$.

50. The difference table is under

x	y	Δy	$\Delta^2 y$
0	0	0	
$\frac{1}{2}$	0	1	1
1	1		

Here $a = 0$, $h = \frac{1}{2}$.

Also for $x = \frac{1}{4}$, $n = \dfrac{x - a}{h} = \dfrac{\frac{1}{4} - 0}{1/2} = \dfrac{1}{2}$.

$\therefore$ Using formula we get

$$f(a + nh) = f(a) + n\Delta f(a) + \frac{n(n-1)}{2}\Delta^2 f(a) + \ldots,$$

Here $a = 0$ and $nh = \frac{1}{4}$ where $n = \frac{1}{2}$.

$$\therefore f\left(\frac{1}{4}\right) = 0 + \frac{1}{2}(0) + \frac{\frac{1}{2}\left(\frac{1}{2} - 1\right)}{2}(1)$$

$$= -\frac{1}{8}.$$

52. Clearly, $U = \left\{ \ldots, \frac{-11\pi}{6}, \frac{-7\pi}{6}, \frac{\pi}{6}, \frac{5\pi}{6}, \frac{13\pi}{6}, \frac{17\pi}{6}, \ldots \right\}$

$\therefore$ Derived set of U i.e. $U' = \phi$

As $U' \subseteq U$, so U is closed.

No point of U is interior point, so U is not open.

54. $\nabla T = (y^2 - 2xz^2)\hat{i}\,(2xy)\,\hat{j} + (2 - 2x^2 z)\hat{k}$

$\nabla T|_{(1,0-1)} = -2\hat{i} + 4\hat{k}$

If ∇T changes rapidly along the unit vector $\perp_r$ to T at that point (*i.e.* along ∇T).

Hence if decreases rapidly along $(-\nabla T)$ direction Hence, unit vector along it $\frac{1}{\sqrt{5}}\hat{i} - \frac{2}{\sqrt{5}}\hat{k}$.

55. $\{a_n\}$ is convergent implies both it's odd numbered term (subsequence) and even numbered term (subsequence) converges individually.

57. The λ-quadratic equation is $\lambda^2 x^2 - y^2 = 0$

$$\Rightarrow \quad \lambda = \frac{y}{x}, -\frac{y}{x}$$

and hence the corresponding characteristic equations becomes.

$$\frac{dy}{dx} + \frac{y}{x} = 0 \text{ and } \frac{dy}{dx} - \frac{y}{x} = 0$$

integrating these, we get $u = xy$ and $v = x/y$.

$$\Rightarrow \quad p = \frac{\partial z}{\partial x} = \frac{\partial z}{\partial u}\cdot\frac{\partial u}{\partial x} + \frac{\partial z}{\partial v}\cdot\frac{\partial v}{\partial x}$$

$$= y\cdot\frac{\partial z}{\partial u} + \frac{1}{y}\cdot\frac{\partial z}{\partial v}$$

$$\text{and } q = \frac{\partial z}{\partial y} = \frac{\partial z}{\partial u}\cdot\frac{\partial u}{\partial y} + \frac{\partial z}{\partial v}\cdot\frac{\partial v}{\partial y}$$

$$= x\frac{\partial z}{\partial u} - \frac{x}{y^2}\cdot\frac{\partial z}{\partial v}$$

$$\text{and} \quad r = y^2\frac{\partial^2 z}{\partial u^2} + 2\frac{\partial^2 z}{\partial u \partial v} + \frac{1}{y^2}\frac{\partial^2 z}{\partial y^2}$$

$$\text{and} \quad t = x^2\frac{\partial^2 z}{\partial u^2} - 2\frac{x^2}{y^2}\frac{\partial^2 z}{\partial u \partial v} + \frac{2x}{y^3}\frac{\partial z}{\partial v} + \frac{x^2}{y^4}\frac{\partial^2 z}{\partial v^2}$$

hence $x^2 r - y^2 t = 0$

$$\Rightarrow \quad 4x^2\frac{\partial^2 z}{\partial u \partial v} - \frac{2x}{y}\frac{\partial z}{\partial v} = 0$$

$$\Rightarrow \quad 2xy\frac{\partial^2 z}{\partial u \partial v} - \frac{\partial z}{\partial v} = 0$$

$$\text{or} \quad 2u\left(\frac{\partial^2 z}{\partial u \partial v}\right) - \frac{\partial z}{\partial v} = 0$$

or $\quad (2uvDD' - vD')z = 0$

where $\quad D \equiv \frac{\partial}{\partial u} \quad D' \equiv \frac{\partial}{\partial v}$.

put $u = e^X$, $v = e^Y \Rightarrow X = \log u$, $Y = \log v$

$\Rightarrow (2uv\, DD' - vD')z = 0$,

reduces to $(2D_1 D_1' - D_1')z = 0$

where $D_1 \equiv \frac{\partial}{\partial X}$, $D_1' = \frac{\partial}{\partial Y}$,

or $\quad D_1'(2D_1 - 1)z = 0$

$\Rightarrow z = e^{X/2}\,\phi_1(Y) + \phi_2(X) = u^{1/2}\phi_1(\log v) + \phi_2(\log u)$

$= u^{1/2}\psi_1(v) + \psi_2(u) = (xy)^{1/2}\,\psi_1(x/y) + \psi_2(xy)$

$= x(y/x)^{1/2}\,\psi_1(x/y) + \psi_2(xy) = xf(x/y) + \psi_2(xy)$.

58. Total no. of such elements $= 5c_2 + 1 = 11$.

As such elements satisfy $S^2 = I$ which will be possible if cycle length is equal to 2.

59. The given differential equation is

$$\frac{dy}{dx} = e^{x-y}\left(e^x - e^y\right)$$

$$\text{or,} \quad \frac{e^y dy}{e^x dx} = e^x - e^y$$

let $\quad v = e^y$ and $u = e^x$

$$\text{then} \quad \frac{dv}{du} = \frac{e^y dy}{e^x dx}$$

$$\text{or,} \quad \frac{dv}{du} = u - v \quad \text{or,} \quad \frac{dv}{du} + v = u$$

i.e. $\quad$ I.F. $= e^{\int du} = e^u$

integrating after multiplying integrating factor both sides, we get

$$v.e^u = \int ue^u du = ue^u - e^u + c$$

or, $\quad e^u\{v - u + 1\} = c$

i.e. $\quad e^{e^x}\{e^y - e^x + 1\} = c$

or, $\quad e^{e^x}\{e^y - e^x + 1\} = c$.

SET–12

CSIR–UGC (NET) MATHEMATICAL SCIENCES

PART-C

1. Let $f(z)=(z-3)\sin\left(\frac{1}{z+2}\right)$. If Laurent series of $f(z)$ about $z = -2$ is given by $\sum_{n=-\infty}^{\infty} a_n (z+2)^n$ then

A. $a_0 = 1,\ a_{-1} = 5,\ a_{-2} = \frac{1}{6}$

B. $a_0 = 1,\ a_{-1} = \frac{1}{5},\ a_{-2} = \frac{1}{6}$

C. $a_0 = 1,\ a_{-1} = -5,\ a_{-2} = -\frac{1}{6}$

D. $a_0 = 1,\ a_{-1} = 5,\ a_{-2} = 6$

2. Consider the following statements in respect of the differential equation $2xy\frac{dy}{dx} = y^2 - x^2$.

1. The differential equation is a homogeneous equation.
2. The curve represented by the differential equation is a family of circles.
3. The differential equation of its orthogonal trajectories is $\frac{dy}{dx} = \frac{2xy}{x^2 - y^2}$.

Which of the statements given above are correct?

A. 1 and 2 only B. 1 and 3 only

C. 2 and 3 only D. All of these

3. If $\sum_{n=1}^{\infty} a_n$ converges, then $\lim_{n\to\infty} \frac{a_n - 1}{n\sqrt{n}}$ is equal to

A. 0 B. 1

C. –1 D. $\frac{-1}{n\sqrt{n}}$

4. Consider the matrix $M = \begin{bmatrix} 1 & 0 & -1 \\ 0 & 1 & 0 \\ 1 & 1 & -1 \end{bmatrix}$ and let S_M be the set of 3 × 3 matrices N such that MN = 0. Then the dimension of the real vector space S_M is equal to

A. 0 B. 1

C. 2 D. 3

5. Joint distribution of two random variable is

$$f_{XY}(x, y) = \begin{cases} K, & 0 < y < x \\ 0 & \text{otherwise} \end{cases} \quad 0 < x, y < 1$$

then $E(X)$ is equal to

A. 1 B. $\frac{1}{2}$

C. $\frac{1}{3}$ D. Not exist

6. Let $f(z)$ be an analytic function. Then the value of $\int_0^{2\pi} f(e^{it})\cos t\, dt$ equals

A. 0 B. $2\pi f(0)$

C. $2\pi f'(0)$ D. $\pi f'(0)$

7. If H and K are two subgroups of G of orders 6 and 8 then order of HK is 16 if

A. Order of $H \cap K$ is 3

B. Order of $H \cap K$ is 4

C. Order of $H \cap K$ is 5

D. None of these

8. Let $y_1(x)$ and $y_2(x)$ be two linearly independent solutions of $xy'' + y' + x^2y = 0$, in the neighbourhood of $x = 0$. If $y_1(x)$ is a power series around $x = 0$, then

A. $y_2(x)$ is bounded around $x = 0$

B. $y_2(x)$ is unbounded around $x = 0$

C. $y_2(x)$ has power series solution

D. $y_2(x)$ has solution of the form $\Sigma b_n x^{n+r}$, where $r \neq 0$ and $b_0 \neq 0$.

9. The complete integral of PDE $(D^2 - 2DD' + D'^2)z = \tan(y + x)$ is given by

A. $z = \phi_1(y + x) + y\phi_2(y + x) + x^2\tan(y + x)$

B. $z = \phi_1(y + x) + xy\phi_2(y + x) + x^2\cot(y + x)$

C. $z = \phi_1(y+x) + x\phi_2 y(y+x) + \frac{x^2}{2}\tan(y+x)$

D. None of these

10. The set $\{(x, y) : y < x^2 + 2x + 1\}$ is

A. Convex set

B. Non convex set

C. Convex polyhedron

D. None of the above

11. Let G be a group and $f : G \to G$ such that $f(x) = x^{-1}$ be a homomorphism then

A. G is abelian
B. G is cyclic
C. G is non-abelian
D. None of these

12. A bag contains 4 red and 3 black balls. A second bag contains 2 red and 4 black balls. One bag is selected at random. It from the select bag one ball is drawn, then the probability that the ball drawn is red is

A. $\frac{1}{42}$
B. $\frac{3}{41}$
C. $\frac{9}{42}$
D. $\frac{19}{42}$

13. $\lim_{n\to\infty}\left[\frac{1}{n}\left\{1+2^{1/2}+3^{1/3}+...+n^{1/n}\right\}\right]$ is equal to

A. -1
B. 0
C. 1
D. $\frac{13}{3}$

14. The homogeneous differential equation $M(x, y)\,dx + N(x, y)dy = 0$ can be reduced to a differential equation, in which the variables are separated, by the substitution.

A. $y = vx$
B. $xy = v$
C. $x + y = v$
D. $x - y = v$

15. Let $(Z, +)$ denote the group of all integers under addition. Then the number of all automorphism of $(Z, +)$ is

A. 1
B. 2
C. 3
D. 4

16. If the nullity of the matrix $\begin{bmatrix} k & 1 & 2 \\ 1 & -1 & -2 \\ 1 & 1 & 4 \end{bmatrix}$ is 1, then the value of k is

A. -1
B. 0
C. 1
D. 2

17. What is the degree of the differential equation for a given curve in which $(\text{subtangent})^m = (\text{subnormal})^n$ in cartesian form, where $0 < n < m$, m, n are integers?

A. $m + n$
B. $m - n$
C. mn
D. m/n

18. For any two events A and B in a sample space

A. $P\left(\frac{A}{B}\right) \geq \frac{P(A)+P(B)-1}{P(B)}$, $P(B) \neq 0$ is always true.

B. $P(\bar{A}) = P(A) - P(\bar{A})\,P(\bar{B})$ does not hold.

C. $P(A \cap B) = 1 - P(\bar{A})\,P(\bar{B})$, if A and B are independent.

D. $P(A \cup B) = 1 - P(\bar{A})\,P(\bar{B})$, if A and B are disjoint.

19. The differential equation $(3a^2x^2 + by\cos x)dx + (2\sin x - 4ay^3)\,dy = 0$ is exact for

A. a be any value, but $b \neq 2$

B. a be any value, but $b = 2$

C. b be any value, but $a = 2$

D. a and b may be any value.

20. Let $a > 1$ and $f, g, h : [-a, a] \to R$ be twice differentiable functions such that for some c with $0 < c < 1 < a$,

$f(x) = 0$ only for $x = -a, 0, a$;

$f'(x) = 0 = g(x)$ only $x = -1, 0, 1$;

$g'(x) = 0 = h(x)$ only for $x = -c, c$.

The possible relations between f, g, h are

A. $f = g'$ and $h = f'$
B. $f' = g$ and $g' = h$
C. $f = -g'$ and $h' = g$
D. $f = -g'$ and $h' = f$

21. Let G be the group of order 30. Let A and B are normal subgroup of order 2 and 5 respectively. Then $O\left(\frac{G}{AB}\right)$ is

A. 10
B. 3
C. 2
D. 5

22. If a PDE is given by $\frac{\partial u}{\partial x} = u + 2\left(\frac{\partial u}{\partial t}\right)$ where $u(x, 0) = 6e^{-3x}$ then $u(1, 2)$ is given by

A. $u = 6e^{-3}$
B. $u = 6e^{-4}$
C. $u = 6e^{-5}$
D. $u = 6e^{-6}$

23. If A, B are two square matrices such that AB = A and BA = B, then

A. both A and B are idempotent.
B. only A is idempotent.
C. only B is idempotent.
D. both A and B are not idempotent.

24. Let $V = \left\{(x, y, z) \in R^3 : \frac{1}{4} \le x^2 + y^2 + z^2 \le 1\right\}$

and $\vec{F} = \frac{x\hat{i} + y\hat{j} + z\hat{k}}{(x^2 + y^2 + z^2)^2}$ for $(x, y, z) \in V$.

Let $\hat{n}$ denote the outward unit normal vector to the boundary of V and S denote the part $\left\{(x, y, z) \in R^3 : x^2 + y^2 + z^2 = \frac{1}{4}\right\}$ of the boundary of V. Then $\iint_S \vec{F}.\hat{n}dS$ is equal to

A. -8π
B. -4π
C. 4π
D. 8π

25. Let G be a cyclic group of order 8, then its group of automorphism has order

A. 2
B. 4
C. 6
D. 8

26. Let T: $C^n \to C^n$ be a linear operator of rank $n - 2$. Then

A. 0 in not an eigen value of T
B. 0 must be an eigen value of T
C. 1 can never be an eigen value of T
D. 1 must be an eigen value of T.

27. The maximum value of $f(x)$, where $f(x) = \int_0^x \sin\{x(1-x)\}dx$ occurs at which one of the following points?

A. $x = 0$
B. $x = 1$
C. $x = -1$
D. None of the above

28. Consider the differential equation $2\cos(y^2)\, dx - xy \sin(y^2)\, dy = 0$. Then

A. e^x is an integrating factor
B. e^{-x} is an integrating factor
C. $3x$ is an integrating factor
D. x^3 is an integrating factor

29. A degenerate basic feasible solution of the convex region formed by the following closed half spaces in R^2

$x_1 + 2x_2 \le 12$
$x_1 + x_2 \le 6$
$2x_1 - x_2 \le 6$
$0 \le x_1 \le 4$
$x_2 \ge 0$ is

A. (3, 0)
B. (0, 4)
C. (4, 2)
D. (3, 3)

30. Let x^2 and xe^x are two solution of the differential of $Ay'' + By' + y = e^{3x}$ then, $x(3x - 2e^x)$ is solution of differential equation only if

A. A > 0, B > 0
B. A > 0, B < 0
C. A < 0, B < 0
D. For any value of A and B

31. Consider the motion of a three-particle system in the 3-dimensional space. Suppose that all pairs of particles are at invariant distance apart, so that the system constitute a rigid body, for such a system, the number of degrees of freedom is

A. 6
B. 3
C. 1
D. 9

32. If $z = \lambda + 3 + i\sqrt{5 - \lambda^2}$ then the locus of z is given by

A. a straight line
B. a circle
C. an ellipse
D. a parabola.

33. The function sin$z$ has simple zeros at

A. $z = 0$
B. $z = 0, \pm 2\pi, \pm 4\pi, ...$
C. $z = 0, \pm \pi, \pm 2\pi, \pm 3\pi, ...$
D. None of these

34. The value of $\iint(\bar{\nabla}\times\bar{F})\hat{n}ds$ where $\bar{F} = -y^3\hat{i}+x^3\hat{j}$ where S is the circular disc $x^2 + y^2 \leq 1, z = 0$

A. $\frac{\pi}{2}$ B. π

C. $\frac{3\pi}{2}$ D. 2π

35. Let T : $\mathbf{R}^2 \to \mathbf{R}^2$ be a map defined by T(x, y) = (x + y, x − y). Which one of the following statements is correct?

A. T is linear and its kernel has infinite number of elements of $\mathbf{R}^2$

B. T is not linear

C. The kernel of T consists of only two elements of $\mathbf{R}^2$

D. Nullity of T is zero

36. The topology on the real line R generated by left-open right-closed intervals [a, b] is

A. strictly coarser than the usual topology.

B. strictly finer than the usual topology.

C. not comparable with the usual topology.

D. same as the usual topology.

37. If F is a homomorphism of a group G into a group G′ with kernal K then.

A. K is a complex of G

B. K is a subroup of G but not a normal subgroup of G

C. K is a normal subgroup of G

D. None of theswe

38. The probability that it will rain today if it rained yesterday is 0.7 and it will rain today if it did not rained yesterday is 0.4, then calculate the probability that it will rain 3 days from today if it rained yesterday

A. 0.5749 B. 0.4251

C. 0.5668 D. 0.4332

39. Let F be a field and f be a homomorphism from F onto itself defined as $f(x) = x^5$ then

A. F is isomorphism to Z_2

B. F is isomorphism to Z_5

C. F has characteristic 2 or 5

D. F has characteristic 5

40. If k is a constant such that $xy+k=e^{(x-1)^2/2}$ satisfies the differential equation $x\frac{dy}{dx} = (x^2- x-1)y\ (x-1)$, then k is equal to

A. 1 B. 0

C. −1 D. −2

41. The differential equation

$$f(x,y)\left(\frac{d^m y}{dx^m}\right)^p + \phi(x,y)\left(\frac{d^{m-1}y}{dx^{m-1}}\right)^q + \ldots = 0 \text{ in of}$$

order

A. p B. q

C. m D. None

42. The rank of the matrix :

$$\begin{bmatrix} 1 & 1 & 1 \\ a & b & c \\ a^3 & b^3 & c^3 \end{bmatrix}$$

a, b, c being all real, is 3 if

A. a, b, c are all different and $a + b + c \neq 0$

B. $a = b = c$

C. a, b, c are all different but $a + b + c = 0$

D. Two of the numbers a, b, c are equal but are different from the third.

43. The integral $\int_{|z|=2} \frac{\cos z}{z^3} dz$ equals

A. πi B. $-\pi i$

C. $2\pi i$ D. $-2\pi i$

44. Let, X and Y have the joint probability mass function $P(X = x, Y = y) = \frac{1}{3x}$, $y = 1, 2, \ldots\ldots x$; $x = 1, 2, 3$. Then the value of the conditional expectation $E\ (Y/X = 3)$ is

A. 1 B. 2

C. 1.5 D. 2.5

45. For the function $f(z) = \frac{1-e^z}{z}$, the point $z = 0$ is

A. an essential singularity

B. a pole of order zero

C. a pole of order one

D. a removable singularity

46. The value of the objective function at an optimal solution of the L.P

$\min x_1 + x_2$ s.t. $x_1 - x_2 = -5, x_1 \geq 0, x_2 \geq 0$

will be

A. 10 B. –5
C. 0 D. 5

47. Assertion (*P*) : sin | *x* | is differentiable at *x* = 0.

Reason (*Q*) : sin *x* is continuous at *x* = 0.

Which of the following is true ?

A. Both *P* and *Q* are true and *Q* is the correct explanation for *P*.
B. Both *P* and *Q* are true but Q is not the correct explanation
C. *P* is true but *Q* is false.
D. *P* is false but *Q* is true.

48. Let *R* be a Principal Ideal Domain and *a, b* any two non-unit elements of *R*. Then the ideal generated by *a* and *b* is also generated by

A. *a* + *b* B. *ab*
C. *gcd* (*a, b*) D. *lcm* (*a, b*)

49. For deleting a disease, a test given correct diagnosis with probability 0.99. It is known that 1% of a population suffers from this disease. If a randomly selected individual form this population test positive, then the probability that the selected individual actually has the disease.

A. 0.01 B. 0.05
C. 0.5 D. 0.09

50. A basis of V = $\{(x, y, z, w) \subset R^4 : x + y - z = 0, y + z + w = 0, 2x + y - 3z - w = 0\}$ is

A. {(1, 1, –1, 0), (0, 1, 1, 1), (2, 1, –3, 1)}
B. {(1, –1, 0, 1)}
C. {(1, 0, 1, –1)}
D. {(1, –1, 0, 1), (1, 0, 1, –1)}

51. Consider the differential equation

$y''' + xy'' + (x^2 - x)\, y = xe^x + 1$

with $y(0) = 1, y'(0) = 1, y''(0) = 0$.

Then the corresponding integral equation is

A. Homogeneous Volterra's Integral Equation of 2nd Kind.
B. Non-homogeneous Volterra's Integral Equation of 2nd Kind.
C. Homogeneous Fredholm's Integral Equation of 2nd Kind
D. Non-homogeneous Fredholm's Integral Equation of 2nd Kind.

52. Which one of the following statements is correct? The differential equation

$\left(\dfrac{dx}{dy}\right)^2 + 5y^{1/3} = x$ is

A. linear equation of order 2 and degree 1.
B. non-linear equation of order 1 and degree 2.
C. non-linear equation of order 1 and degree 6.
D. linear equation of order 1 and degree 6.

53. Let $f : (0, 2) \to R$ be defined by

$f(x) = x^2$ if *x* is rational
$= 2x - 1$ if *x* is irrational

Then

A. *f* is differentiable exactly at one point
B. *f* is differentiable exactly at two points
C. *f* is not differentiable at any point in (0, 2)
D. *f* is differentiable at every point in (0, 2)

54. An iterative method to find the *n*th root ($n \in N$) of a positive number *a* is given by

$x_{K+1} = \dfrac{1}{2}\left[x_K + \dfrac{a}{x_K^{n-1}}\right]$. A value of *n* for which this iterative method fails to converge is

A. 1 B. 2
C. 3 D. 8

55. If $f(x) = \tan^{-1}\left\{\log\left(e/x^2\right)/\log\left(ex^2\right)\right\} + \tan^{-1}\left\{\dfrac{3+2\log_e x}{1-6\log_e x}\right\}$ then $\dfrac{d^2}{dx^2}\{f(x)\}$ is equal to

A. – 1 B. 0
C. 1 D. 5

56. The minimum number of lines covering all zeros in a reduced cost matrix of order *n* can be.

A. At the most *n* B. At the least *n*
C. *n* – 1 D. *n* + 1

57. The set S = {$a + ib$, $c + id$} is a basis for the vector space **C** over **R** iff

A. $ad - bc = 0$ B. $ad + bc = 0$

C. $ad + bc \neq 0$ D. $ad - bc \neq 0$

58. Let **U** be a 3 × 3 complex Hermitian matrix which is unitary. Then the distinct eigenvalues of **U** are :

A. $\pm i$ B. $1 \pm i$

C. ± 1 D. $\frac{1}{2}(1+i)$

59. The characteristic equation of

$$\frac{\partial^2 u}{\partial x^2}+2\cos x\frac{\partial^2 u}{\partial x\partial y}-\sin^2 x\frac{\partial^2 u}{\partial y^2}-\sin x\frac{\partial u}{\partial x}=0$$

are

A. $\frac{dy}{dx}=\cos x\pm 1$

B. $\frac{dy}{dx}=\sin x\pm 1$

C. $\frac{dy}{dx}=\frac{1}{2}(\cos x\pm 1)$

D. $\frac{dy}{dx}=\frac{1}{2}(\sin x\pm 1)$

60. Let S be an infinite subset of R such that $S \cap Q = \phi$. Which of the following statements is true?

A. S must have a limit point which belongs to Q

B. S must have a limit point which belongs to R/Q

C. S cannot be a closed set in R

D. R/S must have a limit point which belongs to S

ANSWERS

1	2	3	4	5	6	7	8	9	10
C	D	A	B	B	D	A	A	C	B
11	**12**	**13**	**14**	**15**	**16**	**17**	**18**	**19**	**20**
A	D	C	A	B	A	A	A	B	B
21	**22**	**23**	**24**	**25**	**26**	**27**	**28**	**29**	**30**
D	C	A	A	D	B	B	D	A	D
31	**32**	**33**	**34**	**35**	**36**	**37**	**38**	**39**	**40**
A	B	C	C	D	D	C	B	B	A
41	**42**	**43**	**44**	**45**	**46**	**47**	**48**	**49**	**50**
C	A	B	B	D	D	D	C	C	D
51	**52**	**53**	**54**	**55**	**56**	**57**	**58**	**59**	**60**
	C	A	B	B	A	D	C	A	C

SOME SELECTED EXPLANATORY ANSWERS

1. Given, $f(z) = (z-3)\sin\left(\frac{1}{z+2}\right)$

Let, $z + 2 = u$ or $z = u - 2$.

Then, $(z-3)\sin\frac{1}{z+2} = (u-5)\sin\frac{1}{u}$

$$= (u-5)\left[\frac{1}{u}-\frac{1}{3!}\frac{1}{u^3}+\frac{1}{5!}\frac{1}{u^5}-...\right]$$

$$= 1-\frac{5}{u}-\frac{1}{3!u^2}+\frac{5}{3!u^3}+\frac{1}{5!u^4}-...$$

$$= 1-\frac{5}{z+2}-\frac{1}{6(z+2)^2}+\frac{5}{6(z+2)^3}+\frac{1}{120(z+2)^4}-....$$

6. Given $I = \int_0^{2\pi} f\left(e^{it}\right)\cos t\, dt$

put $z = e^{it}$ $dz = ie^{it}dt \Rightarrow dt = \frac{dz}{iz}$

$$\Rightarrow \quad I = \oint_{|z|=1} \frac{f(z)}{2}\left(z+\frac{1}{2}\right).\frac{dz}{iz}$$

$$= \frac{1}{2i}\oint \frac{f(z)(z^2+1)}{z^2}dz$$

$$= \frac{1}{2i}\oint \frac{F(z)}{z^2}dz$$

where $F(z) = f(z)\,(z^2 + 1)$
using Cauchy integral formula, the value of above integral.

$$I = 2\pi i \frac{1}{2i} F'(0) = \pi F'(0)$$

Also, $F(z) = f(z)\,(z^2 + 1)$

$\Rightarrow \quad F'(z) = 2z\,f(z) + (z^2 + 1)\,f'(z)$

$\therefore \quad F'(0) = f'(0) \quad \therefore \quad I = \pi f'(0).$

9. Here the auxiliary equation is $(m - 1)^2 = 0$ so that $m = 1, 1$.

$\therefore$ C.F. $= \phi_1(y + x) + x\phi_2(y + x)$, where ϕ_1, ϕ_2 are arbitrary function.

Now P.I. $= \dfrac{1}{(D-D')^2}\tan(y+x)$

$$= \frac{x^2}{1^2.2!}\tan(y+x) = \frac{x^2}{2}\tan(y+x)$$

hence complete integral is

$$z = \phi_1(y+x) + y\phi_2(y+x) + \frac{x^2}{2}\tan(y+x).$$

10. $y < x^2 + 2x + 1$

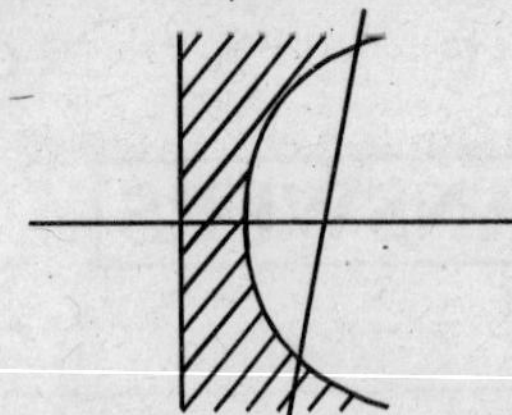

Hence given set is non convex set.

11. Given $f: G \to G$ such that $f(x) = x^{-1}$ be a homomorphism.
We shall prove that G is abelian.
Let x, y be arbitrary we have

$f(x, y) = f(x)\,f(y)$

or $\quad (xy)^{-1} = x^{-1}y^{-1}$

$\Rightarrow \quad e = (xy)\,(x^{-1}y^{-1})$

$\Rightarrow \quad ey = xyx^{-1}$

$\Rightarrow \quad yx = xy \;\forall\; x, y \in G$

Hence, G is abelian.

16. As the nullity of matrix $\begin{bmatrix} K & 1 & 2 \\ 1 & -1 & -2 \\ 1 & 1 & 4 \end{bmatrix}$ is 1,

and hence it must have rank = 2.

i.e. $\det\begin{vmatrix} K & 1 & 2 \\ 1 & -1 & -2 \\ 1 & 1 & 4 \end{vmatrix} = 0$

or $K(2 - 4) - 1(4 + 2) + 2(1 + 1) = 0$

or $\quad -2K - 6 + 4 = 0$

or $\quad 2K = -2$ or $K = -1$.

19. $\quad M = 3a^2x^2 + by\cos x$
$\quad N = 2\sin x - 4ay^3$

To be exact

$$\frac{\partial M}{\partial y} = \frac{\partial N}{\partial x}$$

$$b\cos x = 2\cos x \Rightarrow b = 2$$

20. From the given relation
$f' = g$ and $g' = h$.

21. As $\quad 0(A) = 2, \quad 0(B) = 5$
Also $\quad (2, 5) = 1$

$$\Rightarrow \quad 0(AB) = \frac{0(A)\cdot 0(B)}{0(A\cap B)} = \frac{2.3}{1} = 6.$$

$$\therefore \quad 0\left(\frac{G}{AB}\right) = \frac{0(G)}{0(A)\cdot 0(B)} = \frac{30}{6} = 5.$$

24. $\vec{F} = \dfrac{x\hat{i} + y\hat{j} + z\hat{k}}{(x^2 + y^2 + z^2)^2}$

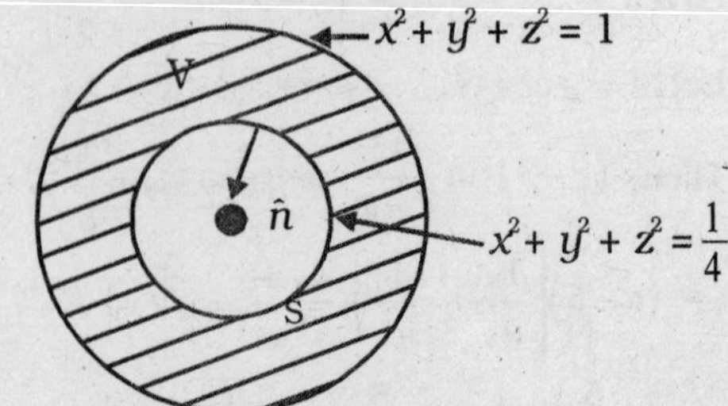

Now $\hat{n}$ on S is given by

$$= -\nabla f.$$

where $f = x^2 + y^2 + z^2 - 1/4.$

$$\Rightarrow \quad \hat{n} = \frac{(x\hat{i} + y\hat{j} + z\hat{k})}{\sqrt{x^2 + y^2 + z^2}}$$

$$\Rightarrow \quad \bar{F}.\hat{n} = -\frac{(x^2 + y^2 + z^2)}{(x^2 + y^2 + z^2)^{5/2}}$$

$$\text{Now} \quad \iint \bar{F}.\hat{n}\, dS = -\iint_S \frac{1}{(x^2 + y^2 + z^2)^{3/2}} dS$$

$$= -4\iint_S dS$$

$$= -8.4\pi\left(\frac{1}{2}\right)^2 = -8\pi$$

27. The given function is $f(x) = \int_0^x \sin\{x(1-x)dx$

for extremum value $f'(x) = \sin x(1 - x) = 0$

i.e. $\sin x(1 - x) = 0$

$\Rightarrow \quad x = 0, 1.$

Now $\quad f''(x) = \cos x\,(1 - x)\,[1 - 2x]$

Now for $x = 0$

$$f''(0) = \cos 0(1 - 0) = 1$$

at $x = 1$.

$$f''(1) = \cos 1.0(1 - 2)$$

$$= -1 < 0$$

i.e. $f(x)$ is maximum at $x = 1$.

28. The differential equation is

$2\cos y^2 dx - xy \sin y^2 dy = 0$

$M = 2\cos y^2, \quad N = -xy \sin y^2$

$$\Rightarrow \quad \frac{\partial M}{\partial y} = 4y \sin y^2, \ \frac{\partial N}{\partial y} = -y\sin y^2$$

$$\frac{1}{N}\left\{\frac{\partial M}{\partial y} - \frac{\partial N}{\partial x}\right\} = \frac{-5}{x} = f(x)$$

i.e $\quad$ I.F. $= -e^{\int \frac{5}{x}dx} = \frac{1}{x^5}$

29.

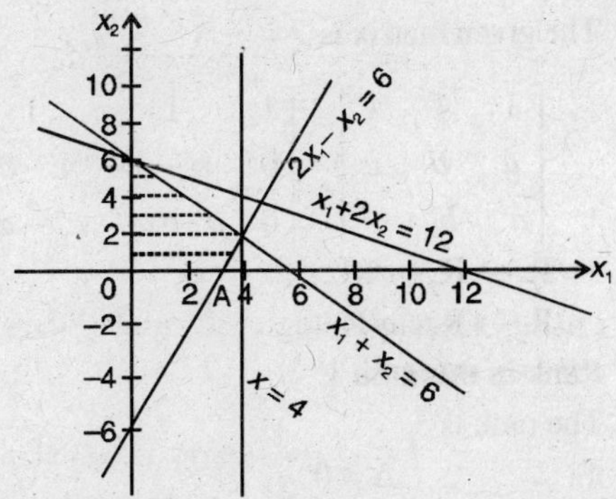

34. The given surface integral is $\iint_{x^2+y^2\le 1} (\bar{\nabla} \cdot \bar{F}) \cdot \hat{n}\, ds$

$z = 0$ with the help of Stoke's theorem, the above surface integral can be converted into line integral.

$$\text{i.e.} \quad \iint(\bar{\nabla} \times \bar{F}) \cdot \hat{n}\, ds = \int_C \bar{F} \cdot d\bar{r}$$

$$\int(-y^3\hat{i} + x^3\hat{j}) \cdot (dx\hat{i} + dy\hat{j})$$

$$= \int_{x^2+y^2=1} (x^3 dy - y^3 dx)$$

let $x = \cos\theta$ and $y = \sin\theta$

then $dy = \cos\theta\, d\theta$ & $dx = -\sin\theta\, d\theta$.

$$\int_{\theta=0}^{2\pi} (\cos^3\theta \cdot \cos\theta + \sin^3\theta \cdot \sin\theta)\, d\theta$$

$$= \int_{\theta=0}^{2\pi} (\cos^4\theta + \sin^4\theta)\, d\theta$$

$$= 2\int_{\theta=0}^{2\pi} \cos^4\theta\, d\theta = 2.4\int_{\theta=0}^{\pi/2} \cos^4\theta\, d\theta$$

$$= 8 \cdot \frac{3}{4} \cdot \frac{1}{2} \cdot \frac{\pi}{2} = \frac{3}{2}\pi.$$

40. $xy + k = e^{(x-1)^2/2}$

$$\Rightarrow \ y + x\frac{dy}{dx} = (x-1)e^{(x-1)^2/2}$$

$$\Rightarrow \ x\frac{dy}{dx} = -y + (x-1)e^{(x-1)^2/2}$$

$$= -y + (x-1)[xy + k]$$

$$= (x^2 - x - 1)y + k(x - 1)$$

$\Rightarrow k = 1$

42. The given matrix is

$$\begin{bmatrix} 1 & 1 & 1 \\ a & b & c \\ a^3 & b^3 & c^3 \end{bmatrix} \sim \begin{bmatrix} 1 & 1 & 1 \\ 0 & b-a & c-a \\ 0 & b^3-a^3 & c^3-a^3 \end{bmatrix}$$

$R_2 \to R_2 - aR_1$

$R_3 \to R_3 - a^3R_1$

Rank in this case 1.

The rank is 3.

if $\Delta \neq 0$

$\Rightarrow (b-a)(c-a)[c^2 + ca + a^2 - b^2 - ab - a^2]$

$(b-a)(c-a)(c-b)[c+b+a] \neq 0$

i.e. $a \neq b \neq c$ & $a+b+c \neq 0$.

50. The given subspace **U** is

$V = \{(x, y, z, w) \in R^4 : x + y - z = 0, y + z + w = 0, 2x + y - 3z - w = 0\}$

Writing the above information in matrix form we get

$$\begin{bmatrix} 1 & 1 & -1 & 0 \\ 0 & 1 & 1 & 1 \\ 2 & 1 & -3 & -1 \end{bmatrix} \begin{bmatrix} x \\ y \\ z \\ w \end{bmatrix} = \begin{bmatrix} 0 \\ 0 \\ 0 \\ 0 \end{bmatrix}$$

Apply $R_3 \to R_3 - 2R_1$, we get

$$\begin{bmatrix} 1 & 1 & -1 & 0 \\ 0 & 1 & 1 & 1 \\ 0 & -1 & -1 & -1 \end{bmatrix} \begin{bmatrix} x \\ y \\ z \\ w \end{bmatrix} = \begin{bmatrix} 0 \\ 0 \\ 0 \\ 0 \end{bmatrix}.$$

$$\begin{bmatrix} 1 & 1 & -1 & 0 \\ 0 & 1 & 1 & 1 \\ 0 & 0 & 0 & 0 \end{bmatrix} \begin{bmatrix} x \\ y \\ z \\ w \end{bmatrix} = \begin{bmatrix} 0 \\ 0 \\ 0 \\ 0 \end{bmatrix}$$

Apply $R_3 \to R_3 + R_2$, we get

i.e. $x + y - z = 0$

$y + z + w = 0$

Choose z, w as free variables, then

(*i*) $z = 1, w = 0 \Rightarrow y = -1 \Rightarrow x = 2.$

(*ii*) $z = 0, w = 1 \Rightarrow y = 0 - 1 \Rightarrow x = 1$

i.e. $\{(2, -1, 1, 0), (1, -1, 0, 1)\}$ are basis of V

or $\{(1, 0, 1, -1), (1, -1, 0, 1)\}$ are basis of V.

58. The eigenvalues of a unitary matrix have unit modulus. On the other hand, the eigenvalues of a Hermitian matrix have real.

As **U** is a complex Hermitian unitary matrix. Hence choice (C) is correct.

SET–13
CSIR–UGC (NET) MATHEMATICAL SCIENCES
PART-C

1. Let $T : C^3 \to C^3$ be defined by

$$T\begin{pmatrix} z_1 \\ z_2 \\ z_3 \end{pmatrix} = \begin{pmatrix} z_1 - iz_2 \\ iz_1 + z_2 \\ z_1 + z_2 + iz_3 \end{pmatrix}.$$ Then the adjoint T*

of T is given by $T^*\begin{pmatrix} z_1 \\ z_2 \\ z_3 \end{pmatrix} =$

A. $\begin{bmatrix} z_1 + iz_2 \\ -iz_1 + z_2 \\ z_1 + z_2 - iz_3 \end{bmatrix}$ B. $\begin{bmatrix} z_1 - iz_2 + z_3 \\ -iz_1 + z_2 + z_3 \\ iz_3 \end{bmatrix}$

C. $\begin{bmatrix} z_1 - iz_2 + z_3 \\ iz_1 + z_2 + z_3 \\ -iz_3 \end{bmatrix}$ D. $\begin{bmatrix} iz_1 + z_2 \\ z_1 - iz_2 \\ z_1 - z_2 - iz_3 \end{bmatrix}$

2. The series $\frac{x}{1.2} + \frac{x^2}{2.3} + \frac{x^3}{3.4} + \ldots\ldots$ is convergent if

A. $|x| \le 1$ B. $|x| \le 2$

C. $|x| > 2$ D. $|x| \ge 4$

3. Given the L.P.P

max $z = x_1 + 3x_2$

subject to $3x_1 + x_2 \le 3$

$x_1, x_2 \ge 0,$

the optimal value of the objective function will be

A. 1 B. 2

C. 9 D. 10

4. The analytic function of $w(z)$ whose imaginary part is $\frac{x+y}{x^2+y^2}$ is given by

A. $-\frac{1+i}{z} + c$ (c, a real constant)

B. $\frac{1+i}{z} + c$

C. $\frac{1-i}{z} + c$

D. $-\frac{1-i}{z} + c$

5. Let $\alpha \in (0, 1)$, then for the sequence (x_n) of real number satisfying the relation

$x_{n+1} = \alpha x_n + (1 - \alpha)x_{n-1}$, x_0, x_1 are given

Read the following statements:

1. bounded
2. converges to $\frac{(1-\alpha)x_0 + x_1}{2-\alpha}$
3. monotonic

Codes:

A. 1 and 2 are correct

B. 1 and 3 are correct

C. 1, 2 and 3 are correct

D. only 1 is correct

6. Let I be the set of irrational real numbers and let $G = I\ U\{0\}$. Then, under the usual addition of real numbers, G is

A. a group, since R and Q are groups under addition.

B. a group, since the additive identity is in G.

C. not a group, since addition on G is not a binary operation.

D. not a group, since not all elements in G have an inverse.

7. Let the characteristices equation of a matrix M be $\lambda^2 - \lambda - 1 = 0$, then

A. M^{-1} does not exist

B. M^{-1} exists but cannot be determined from the data.

C. $M^{-1} = M + 1$
D. $M^{-1} = M - 1$

8. If $P(B) = \frac{3}{4}$, $P(\bar{A} \cap B \cap \bar{C}) = \frac{1}{3}$ and $P(A \cap B \cap \bar{C}) = \frac{1}{3}$, then $P(B \cap C)$ is

A. $\frac{1}{12}$ B. $\frac{3}{4}$
C. $\frac{5}{12}$ D. $\frac{23}{36}$

9. The value of $\int_0^{2\pi} \exp(e^{i\theta} - i\theta)d\theta$ equals

A. $2\pi i$ B. 2π
C. π D. $i\pi$

10. Suppose that H and K are subgroups of a group G with $O(H) = 10$ and $O(K) = 12$. If $H \cap K$ is non-trivial, then what is the number of elements in the complex HK?

A. 120 B. 60
C. 30 D. 22

11. Choose the correct matching from A, B, C and D for the transformation T_1, T_2 and T_3 (mappings from R^2 to R^3) as defined in Group 1 with the statements given in Group 2.

Group 1

P. $T_1(x, y) = (x, x, 0)$
Q. $T_2(x, y) = (x, x + y, y)$
R. $T_3(x, y) = (x, x + 1, y)$

Group 2

1. Linear transformation of rank 2.
2. Not a Linear transformation.
3. Linear transformation of rank 1.

A. P–3, Q–1, R–2
B. P–1, Q–2, R–3
C. P–3, Q–2, R–1
D. P–1, Q–3, R–2.

12. The differential equation whose general solution is.

$y = K_1 + K_2x + K_3x^2$, is given by

A. $y^3 = x^2 + x$ B. $y^3 = 2x + x^2$
C. $y''' = 0$ D. $y^2 + x^2 = 4x$

13. Let H, T and V denote the Hamiltonian, the kinetic energy and the potential energy respectively of a mechanical system at time t.

If H contains t explicitly, then $\frac{\partial H}{\partial t}$ is equal to

A. $\frac{\partial T}{\partial t} + \frac{\partial V}{\partial t}$ B. $\frac{\partial T}{\partial t} - \frac{\partial V}{\partial t}$
C. $\frac{\partial V}{\partial t} - \frac{\partial T}{\partial t}$ D. $\frac{-\partial V}{\partial t} - \frac{\partial T}{\partial t}$

14. $\lim_{z \to n\pi i} (z - n\pi i)\left(\frac{e^z}{\sin z}\right) = ?$

A. $\frac{e^{n\pi i}}{\cos hn\pi}$ B. $\frac{e^{n\pi i}}{\sin hn\pi}$
C. $\frac{-e^{n\pi i}}{\sin hn\pi}$ D. $\frac{-e^{n\pi i}}{\cos hn\pi}$

15. Let $R = \left\{\begin{bmatrix} a & b \\ c & d \end{bmatrix} : a,b,c,d \in Z[i]\right\}$ and $A = [a_{ij}]$ and $B = [b_{ij}]$ defined as $A + B = [a_{ij} + b_{ij}]$ and $A \cdot B = [a_{ij}\, b_{ij}]$, then select the correct statement /statements:

1. R is commutative ring.
2. R is ring with unity.
3. R has 256 units.
4. The group of units G is isomorphic to Z_{256}.

Codes :

A. 2, 3, 4 B. 1, 2, 3
C. 1, 2 D. All of these

16. A non-empty subset S of a ring R is called ideal if

A. S is a subring of R under addition, and $\forall\, S \in S$ and $r \in R \Rightarrow sr \in S$ and $rs \in S$
B. S is closed under addition and $\forall s \in S$ and $r \in R \Rightarrow sr \in S$ and $rs \in S$
C. S is a subring only
D. None is true

17. Which one of the following curves is the orthogonal trajectory of straight lines passing through a fixed point (a, b)?

A. $(x - a) = k(y - b)$
B. $(x - a)(y - b) = k$
C. $(x - a)^2 = k(y - b)$
D. $(x - a)^2 + (y - b)^2 = k$

18. Let X, Y be topological spaces and $f : X \to Y$ be a continuous and bijective map. Then f is a homeomorphism, if
A. X and Y are compact
B. X is Hausdorff and Y is compact
C. X is compact and Y is Hausdorff
D. X and Y are Hausdorff

19. If a 3×3 real skew-symmetric matrix has an eigenvalue $2i$, then one of the remaining eigenvalues is

A. $\frac{1}{2i}$ B. $-\frac{1}{2i}$
C. 0 D. 1

20. Let, $x_1 = 3$, $x_2 = 4$, $x_3 = 3.5$, $x_4 = 2.5$ be the observed value of a random sample from the probability density function

$$f(x \mid \theta) = \frac{1}{3}\left[\frac{1}{\theta}e^{\frac{-x}{\theta}} + \frac{1}{\theta^2}e^{\frac{-x}{\theta^2}} + e^{-x}\right],$$

$x > 0, \theta > 0$.

Then the method of moments estimate (*MME*) of θ is
A. 3.5 B. 4
C. 2.5 D. 1

21. Under which one of the following conditions does the function $f(x) = \left\{(x^2)^m \cdot \sin(x^{-2})^n\right\}$ $x \neq 0$, $n > 0$ and $f(0) = 0$ have a derivative at $x = 0$?

A. $m \geq -\frac{1}{2}$ B. $m > 0$
C. $m > \frac{1}{2}$ D. $m \geq \frac{1}{2}$

22. If a function f is continuous in a closed interval $[a, b]$, then it attains
A. Supremum only
B. Infimum only
C. Both supremum and infimum
D. None of these

23. Let G be a group of order 15. Then the number of 3-Sylow subgroups of G is
A. 0 B. 1
C. 3 D. 5

24. In the above question, the moment generating function of X is
A. $\log(1 - t)$ B. $\log t$
C. $-\log(1 - t)$ D. Not exist

25. Given the vectors $\alpha = (1, 2, 3)$, $\beta = (3, 1, 0)$, $\gamma = (2, 1, 3)$ and $\delta = (-1, 3, 6)$ consider the following statements :
1. γ is a linear combination of α and β.
2. δ is a linear combination of α and β.

Which of the following statements given above is/are correct?
A. 1 only B. 2 only
C. Both 1 and 2 D. Neither 1 nor 2

26. Solution of partial differential equation

$$2x^2\frac{\partial^2 z}{\partial x^2} + 5xy\frac{\partial^2 z}{\partial x \partial y} + 2y^2\frac{\partial^2 z}{\partial y^2} + 2\left(x\frac{\partial z}{\partial x} + y\frac{\partial z}{\partial y}\right) = 0$$

is
A. $z = f_1(xy) + f_2(x^2y^2)$
B. $z = f_1(x^2y) + f_2(xy^2)$
C. $z = f_1(x/y) + f_2(x^2y)$
D. $z = f_1(xy^2) + f_2(x/y)$.

27. If $I = \int_0^\infty \sin x^2 dx$ then value of I equals

A. $\sqrt{\frac{\pi}{2}}$ B. $\frac{\pi}{2}$
C. $\frac{1}{2}\sqrt{\frac{\pi}{2}}$ D. $\frac{\pi^2}{4}$

28. An iterative scheme is given by

$x_{n+1} = \frac{1}{5}\left(16 - \frac{12}{x_n^K}\right)$, $n \in N \cup \{0\}$. Such a scheme with suitable x_0, will
A. not converge B. converge to 1.6
C. converge to 1.8 D. converge to 2

29. Let A be a non-zero upper triangular matrix all of whose eigenvalues are 0. Then I + A is
A. invertible

B. singular
C. idempotent
D. purely imaginary or zero

30. If a random variable X has cumulative distribution function

$$F(x) = \begin{cases} 0, & \text{if } x < 0 \\ \frac{1}{3} & \text{if } x = 0 \\ \frac{1+x}{3} & \text{if } \alpha\, x < 1 \\ 1, & x \geq 1 \end{cases}$$

then $E(X)$ equals

A. $\frac{1}{3}$ B. 1
C. $\frac{1}{6}$ D. $\frac{1}{2}$

31. Let G be the set of all irrational numbers. The interior and the closure of G are denoted by G^0 and $\overline{G}$, respectively (when ψ is the set of all real number). Then

A. $G^0 = \phi$, $\overline{G} = G$ B. $G^0 = \psi$, $\overline{G} = \psi$
C. $G^0 = \phi$, $\overline{G} = \psi$ D. $G^0 = G$, $\overline{G} = \psi$

32. If N is normal subgroup of G and H is any subgroup of G then which answer is correct.
A. NH is a subgroup of G
B. NH is normal subgroup of G
C. Either (A) or (B)
D. None of these

33. In *transhipment* problem with m sources and n destinations there are .... basic variables in basic feasible solution.
A. $2(m + n) - 1$ B. $2(m + n - 1)$
C. $m + n - 1$ D. $2(m + n - 1) - 1$

34. For the given functional, which of the following cannot be Euler's equation

$$J = \int_{\alpha}^{\beta} F(x, y, y')\, dx.$$

A. $\frac{\partial F}{\partial y} = \frac{d}{dx}\left(\frac{\partial F}{\partial y'}\right)$ B. $F = \frac{\partial F}{\partial y'} y'$
C. $\frac{\partial F}{\partial y'} = C$ D. None of these

35. Let $f : R^2 \to R$ be defined by

$$f(x, y) = \begin{cases} x^2 + y^2 & \text{if } x \text{ and } y \text{ are rational} \\ 0 & \text{otherwise} \end{cases}$$

Then
A. f is not continuous at (0, 0)
B. f is continuous at (0, 0) but not differentiable at (0, 0)
C. f is differentiable only at (0, 0)
D. f is differentiable everywhere

36. General solution of diff. equ.

$$\frac{dy}{dx} + \tan x \tan y = \cos x \sec y$$

A. $\sin y = (x + c) \cos x$
B. $\sin y = (x + c) \sin y$
C. $\sin x = (x + c) \sin y$
D. $\cos y = (x + c) \sin x$

37. In an assignment problem involving four workers and three jobs, total number of assignments possible are.
A. 4 B. 3
C. 7 D. 12

38. What are the orthogonal trajectories of the system of curves $\left(\frac{dy}{dx}\right)^2 = \frac{a}{x}$ is
A. $9a(y + c)^2 = \pm 2x^{3/2}$
B. $9a(y + c)^2 = \pm 2x^{2/3}$
C. $9a(y + c)^3 = 4x^2$
D. $9a(y + c)^2 = 4x^3$

39. True and False.
Continuity is a necessary but not a sufficient condition for the existence of a finite derivative.
$f(z) = |z|^2$ is continuous every where but nowhere differentiable
A. except at origin
B. except at infinity
C. Including origin
D. Including ∞

40. What is the rank of the linear transformation $T : \mathbf{R}^3 \to \mathbf{R}^3$ defined by $T(x, y, z) = (y, 0, z)$.
A. 3 B. 2
C. 1 D. 0

41. The line passing through two points x_1 and x_2 is the set

A. $\{x : x = (1-\lambda)\,x_1 + \lambda x_2, \lambda \in R\}$

B. $\{x : x = (1-\lambda)\,x_1 + \lambda x_2, 0 \le \lambda \le 1\}$

C. $\{x : x = (1-\lambda)\,x_1 + \lambda x_2, 0 \ge \lambda \ge 1\}$

D. $\{x : x = (1-\lambda)\,x_1 + \lambda x_2, 0 < \lambda < 1\}$

42. An iterative method to find the nth root ($n \in N$) of a positive number 'α' is given by $x_{K+1} = \frac{1}{2}\left[x_K + \frac{\alpha}{x_K^{n-1}}\right]$. Then value of '$n$' for which of this iterative method NOT converges is

A. 1 B. 2

C. 3 D. 4

43. Solution of ordinary differential equation is $(xy\sin xy + \cos xy)y\,dx + (xy\sin xy - \cos xy)x\,dy$ Z= 0

A. $\left(\frac{x}{y}\right)\cos xy = c$ B. $\left(\frac{y}{x}\right)\tan\frac{x}{y} = c$

C. $\left(\frac{x}{y}\right)\sec xy = c$ D. None of these.

44. The singularity of $e^{\sin z}$ at $z = \infty$ is

A. pole

B. a removable singularity

C. nonisolated essential singularity

D. isolated essential singularity

45. The convex hull of the set A = $\{(x_1, x_2)\}$ is

A. $< A > = \{\underline{x} \mid \underline{x} = \lambda\, x_1 + (1-\lambda)\, x_2\,; 0 < \lambda < 1\}$

B. $< A > = \{\underline{x} \mid \underline{x} = \lambda\, x_1 + (1-\lambda)\, x_2\,; 0 \le \lambda < 1\}$

C. $< A > = \{\underline{x} \mid \underline{x} = \lambda\, x_1 + (1-\lambda)\, x_2\,; 0 < \lambda \le 1\}$

D. $< A > = \{\underline{x} \mid \underline{x} = \lambda\, x_1 + (1-\lambda)\, x_2\,; 0 \le \lambda \le 1\}$

46. The equation $x(2p + 4q - 1) + y(3p - 1) = 8pq$ is

A. Linear B. Non-linear

C. Quasi-linear D. Semi-linear

47. Let G be a group of order 49. Then

A. G is abelian

B. G is cyclic

C. G is non-abelian

D. centre of G has order 7.

48. Let G be a finite group and H be a normal subgroup of G of order 2. Then the order of the center G is

A. 0

B. 1

C. an even integer ≥ 2

D. an odd integer ≥ 3

49. A necessary and sufficient condition for a monotonic sequence to be convergent is that it

A. is bounded

B. is unbounded

C. May be bounded or unbounded

D. None of these

50. Differential equation $xdy - ydx - 2x^3dx = 0$ has solution

A. $y + x^3 = cx$ B. $y - x^2 = cx$

C. $-y + x^3 = cx$ D. $y^3 - x^3 = cx$

51. The general solution of the differential equation $(D^2 + D - 2)\, y = e^x$ is given by

A. $y = c_1e^x + c_2e^{-2x} + \frac{1}{3}xe^x$

B. $y = c_1e^x + c_2e^{-2x}$

C. $y = c_1e^x + c_2e^{-2x} + \frac{1}{6}x^2e^x$

D. $y = \frac{1}{3}xe^x + (c_1 + c_2x)e^{-2x}$

52. If $Z(G)$ denotes the centre of a group G, then the order of the quotient group $\frac{G}{Z(G)}$ cannot be

A. 4 B. 6

C. 15 D. 25

53. The vectors

$\vec{i} + 2p\,\vec{j} + 4q\,\vec{k}$ and $\vec{i} + 4p\,\vec{j} + 2q\,\vec{k}$ are

A. Orthogonal if $p = q$

B. Orthogonal if $p = -q$

C. Orthogonal if $p^2 = q^2 = -1$

D. Never orthogonal

54. Let V be the vector space of all 6 × 6 real matrices over the field R. Then the dimension of the subspace of V consisting of all symmetric matrices is:

A. 15 B. 18
C. 21 D. 35

55. In the differential equation $(x - y^2)dx + 2xydy = 0$. Whih one of the following substitutions makes variable separable?

A. $y=\sqrt{vx}$ B. $y = vx$
C. $y^2 = v$ D. $y^2 = vx$
where v is a function of x.

56. In the simplex method, artificial variable technique is used
A. for starting a Basic feasible solution
B. to get an optimal solution
C. to restrict the infeasible solution
D. None of these

57. Which of the following changes the nature of the constraints in the given L.P.P.
A. Multiplying it by any positive number
B. Multiplying it by any negative number
C. Adding one variable on any side when it is in equation form
D. None of these

58. Which of the following sets is a basis for the subspace

$$W = \left\{\begin{bmatrix} x & y \\ 0 & t \end{bmatrix} : x+2y+t=0,\ y+t=0\right\}$$

of the vector space of all real 2 × 2 matrices?

A. $\left\{\begin{bmatrix} 1 & 0 \\ 0 & 0 \end{bmatrix}, \begin{bmatrix} 0 & 1 \\ 0 & 0 \end{bmatrix}, \begin{bmatrix} 0 & 0 \\ 0 & 1 \end{bmatrix}\right\}$

B. $\left\{\begin{bmatrix} 2 & 1 \\ 0 & -1 \end{bmatrix}, \begin{bmatrix} 1 & -1 \\ 0 & 1 \end{bmatrix}\right\}$

C. $\left\{\begin{bmatrix} -1 & 1 \\ 2 & -1 \end{bmatrix}\right\}$

D. $\left\{\begin{bmatrix} 1 & -1 \\ 0 & 1 \end{bmatrix}\right\}$

59. The differential equation

$\frac{d^2y}{dx^2} - y = 0$ has solution

A. $e^x + C$
B. e^x
C. e^{2x}
D. None of the above

60. If det A = 7, where $A = \begin{bmatrix} a & b & c \\ d & e & f \\ g & b & c \end{bmatrix}$, then det $(2A)^{-1}$ is equal to

A. $\frac{1}{14}$ B. $\frac{1}{49}$

C. $\frac{1}{56}$ D. $\frac{7}{2}$

ANSWERS

1	2	3	4	5	6	7	8	9	10
C	A	C	A	C	B	D	A	B	B
11	**12**	**13**	**14**	**15**	**16**	**17**	**18**	**19**	**20**
A	C	A	A	D	A	D	C	C	C
21	**22**	**23**	**24**	**25**	**26**	**27**	**28**	**29**	**30**
C	C	B	A	B	B	C	C	A	D
31	**32**	**33**	**34**	**35**	**36**	**37**	**38**	**39**	**40**
C	A	D	B	B	A	A	D	A	D
41	**42**	**43**	**44**	**45**	**46**	**47**	**48**	**49**	**50**
B	D	C	D	A	B	A	C	A	A
51	**52**	**53**	**54**	**55**	**56**	**57**	**58**	**59**	**60**
A	C	D	C	C	D	B	D	B	C

SOME SELECTED EXPLANATORY ANSWERS

1. The standard basis of C^3 are $e_1 = (1, 0, 0)$, $e_2 = (0, 1, 0)$, $e_3 = (0, 0, 1)$

hence $T\begin{pmatrix}1\\0\\0\end{pmatrix} = \begin{pmatrix}1\\i\\1\end{pmatrix}$, $T\begin{pmatrix}0\\1\\0\end{pmatrix} = \begin{pmatrix}-i\\1\\1\end{pmatrix}$,

$$T\begin{pmatrix}0\\0\\1\end{pmatrix} = \begin{pmatrix}0\\0\\i\end{pmatrix}$$

i.e. $T = \begin{bmatrix}1 & -i & 0\\ i & 1 & 0\\ 1 & 1 & i\end{bmatrix}$ hence $T^* = \begin{bmatrix}1 & -i & 1\\ i & 1 & 1\\ 0 & 0 & -i\end{bmatrix}$

Hence $T^*\begin{pmatrix}z_1\\z_2\\z_3\end{pmatrix} = \begin{bmatrix}1 & -i & 1\\ i & 1 & 1\\ 0 & 0 & -i\end{bmatrix}\begin{bmatrix}z_1\\z_2\\z_3\end{bmatrix}$

$$= \begin{bmatrix}z_1 - iz_2 + z_3\\ iz_1 + z_2 + z_3\\ -iz_3\end{bmatrix}.$$

2. The given series is

$$S = \frac{x}{1.2} + \frac{x^2}{2.3} + \frac{x^3}{3.4} + \ldots\ldots$$

The *n*th term of the series

$$u_n = \frac{x^n}{n(n+1)}$$

and $\quad u_{n+1} = \dfrac{x^{n+1}}{(n+1)(n+2)}.$

Now,

$$\lim_{n\to\infty}\frac{u_n}{u_{n+1}} = \lim_{n\to\infty}\frac{x^n}{n(n+1)}\cdot\frac{(n+1)(n+2)}{x^{n+1}}$$

$$= \lim_{n\to\infty}\frac{(n+2)}{n}\cdot\frac{1}{x} > 1$$

(for covergence)

i.e. $\quad x < 1.$

Further for $\quad x = 1.$

$$u_n = \frac{1}{n(n+1)} = \frac{1}{n} - \frac{1}{n+1}$$

$$\Rightarrow \quad \Sigma u_n = 1 - \frac{1}{2} + \frac{1}{2} - \frac{1}{3} + \frac{1}{3} - \frac{1}{4} + \ldots\ldots$$

$= 1$ (convergent)

i.e. S is convergent for $|x| \le 1$.

3. $\because$ optimal sol. is (0, 3)

$\therefore$ optimal value

max $z = 0 + 3 \times 3 = 9$.

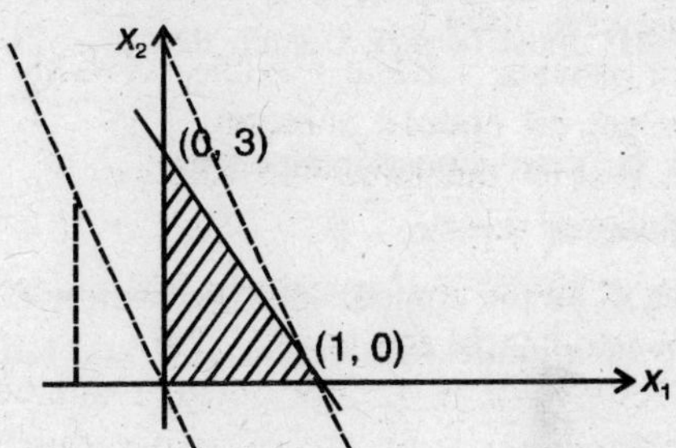

$z = 0$

$$\frac{x_1}{x_2} = -\frac{1}{3}$$

$\because |x| < 1$

7. $\lambda^2 - \lambda - 1 = 0 \Rightarrow \lambda^{-1} = \lambda - 1$

$\Rightarrow M^{-1} = M - 1$

9. The given integral is

$$I = \int_0^{2\pi} \exp\left(e^{i\theta} - i\theta\right)d\theta$$

putting $z = e^{i\theta}$ then $dz = ie^{i\theta}\,d\theta \Rightarrow d\theta = \dfrac{dz}{iz}$

$$\Rightarrow \quad I = \int \frac{e^z}{z}\cdot\frac{dz}{iz} = \frac{1}{i}\oint\frac{e^z}{z^2}dz$$

Hence, by Cauchy integral formula

$$I = 2\pi i.\frac{1}{i}f'(0) \quad \text{where } f(z) = e^z$$

$$= 2\pi i.\frac{1}{i}.e^0 = 2\pi.$$

10. $0(H) = 10$, $\quad 0(K) = 12$

as $H \cap K$ is non-trivial.

$\Rightarrow \quad 0(H \cap K) = \langle 10, 12 \rangle = 2$

$\therefore \quad 0(HK) = \dfrac{0(H) \cdot 0(K)}{0(H \cap K)} = \dfrac{10.12}{2} = 60$

19. As the diagonal element of a real skew-symmetric matrix is 0.

i.e. Trace of 3 × 3 skew-symmetric matrix = 0.

Also the eigenvalue of skew-symmetric matrix are either zero or purely imaginary.

i.e. The remaining two eigenvalues of the matrix must be $-2i$, 0 such that $2i - 2i + 0 = 0$.

25. α, β, γ are linear independent.

However $\gamma = 2\alpha - \beta$.

27. Let, C be the contour indicated where C is the arc of a circle with centre at 0 and radius R.

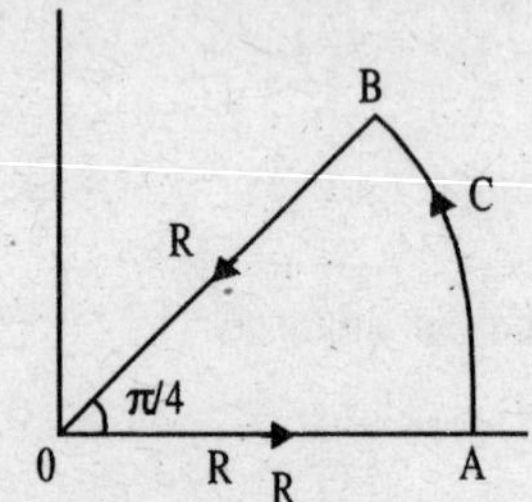

∴ By Cauchy's theorem

$$\oint e^{iz^2} dz = 0.$$

or, $\displaystyle\int_{OA} e^{iz^2} dz + \int_{AB} e^{iz^2} dz + \int_{BO} e^{iz^2} dz = 0$ ...(*i*)

Now, on 0A, $z = x$ on AB $z = \text{R}e^{i\theta}$ (θ from 0 to π/4) & on B0. $z = re^{i\pi/4}$ with $r = \text{R}$ to $r = 0$. Hence (*i*) becomes

$$\int_0^{\text{R}} e^{ix^2} dx + \int_0^{\pi/4} e^{i\text{R}^2 e^{2i\theta}} . i\text{R}e^{i\theta}\, d\theta + \int_{\text{R}}^{0} e^{ir^2 e^{\frac{\pi}{2} i}} e^{i\frac{\pi}{4}} dr = 0$$

$$\text{or, } \int_0^{\text{R}} \left(\cos x^2 + i \sin x^2\right) dx = e^{i\frac{\pi}{4}} \int_0^{\text{R}} e^{-r^2} dr$$

$$- \int_0^{\pi/4} e^{i\text{R}^2} \cos z\theta - \text{R}^2 \sin 2\theta . i\, \text{R}e^{i\theta}\, d\theta.$$

Now, consider the limit as R → ∞. The integral on the right side becomes.

$$e^{i\frac{\pi}{4}} \int_0^{\infty} e^{-r^2} dr = \sqrt{\frac{\pi}{2}} e^{i\frac{\pi}{4}} = \frac{1}{2}\sqrt{\frac{\pi}{2}} + \frac{i}{2}\sqrt{\frac{\pi}{2}}$$

and the absolute value of second integral on the right is

$$\left| \int_0^{\pi/4} e^{i\text{R}^2 \cos 2\theta - \text{R}^2 \sin 2\theta} . i\,\text{R}e^{i\theta} d\theta \right| \leq \int_0^{\pi/4} e^{-\text{R}^2 \sin 2\theta} - \text{R} d\theta$$

$$= \frac{\text{R}}{2} \int_0^{\pi/2} e^{-\text{R}^2 \sin\phi} d\phi$$

$$\leq \frac{\text{R}}{2} \int_0^{\pi/2} e^{-\text{R}^2 \phi/\pi} d\phi$$

$$= \frac{\pi}{4\text{R}}\left(1 - e^{-\text{R}^2}\right) \to 0 \text{ as R} \to \infty$$

$$\text{i.e. } \int_0^{\infty} \left(\cos x^2 + i \sin x^2\right) dx = \frac{1}{2}\sqrt{\frac{\pi}{2}} + \frac{i}{2}\sqrt{\frac{\pi}{2}}$$

$$\Rightarrow \int_0^{\infty} \sin x^2 dx = \frac{1}{2}\sqrt{\frac{\pi}{2}}.$$

31. No point is interior as every neighbourhood contains rational numbers.

So, $G^0 = \phi$

Also each real number is a limit point as nbd of real number contains infinite irrationals.

$\Rightarrow \bar{G} = R$

38. The equation of the given curve is $\left(\dfrac{dy}{dx}\right)^2 = \dfrac{a}{x}$ replacing $\dfrac{dy}{dx}$ by $-\dfrac{dx}{dy}$ for orthogonal trajectory, we get

$$\left(-\frac{dx}{dy}\right)^2 = \frac{a}{x}$$

$$\text{or, } \frac{dx}{dy} = \pm\sqrt{\frac{a}{x}}$$

$$\text{or, } \pm\sqrt{\frac{x}{a}}\, dx = dy$$

integrating, we get

$$\pm\frac{1}{\sqrt{a}} \cdot \frac{x^{3/2}}{3/2} = (y + c)$$

or, $\frac{4}{a}x^3 = 9(y + c)^2$

$\Rightarrow$ $4x^3 = 9a(y + c)^2$.

39. Continuous every where

$$f'A. = \lim_{\Delta z \to a} \frac{|a+\Delta z|^2 - |a|^2}{\Delta z}$$

$$= \lim_{\Delta z \to 0} \frac{(a+\Delta z)(\bar{a}+\Delta \bar{z}) - a\bar{a}}{\Delta z}$$

$$= \lim_{\Delta z \to 0}\left(\bar{a} + \Delta\bar{z} + a.\frac{\Delta \bar{z}}{\Delta z}\right)$$

$$= \lim_{\Delta z \to 0}\left(\bar{a} + a.\frac{\Delta \bar{z}}{\Delta z}\right)$$

($\because$ $\Delta\bar{z} \to 0$ as $\Delta z \to 0$)

$f'A. = 0$ at $a = 0$

when $a \neq 0$ $\Delta z = \rho(\cos\phi + i\sin\phi)$

$\Delta\bar{z} = \rho(\cos\phi - i\sin\phi)$

$\frac{\Delta\bar{z}}{\Delta z} = \cos 2\phi - i\sin\phi \Rightarrow \to$ unique limit

since limit depends upon arg Δz.

Function $f(z)$ is non-differentiable for any non-zero value of z.

43. The given differential equation is

$(xy\sin xy + \cos xy)\, y\, dx + (xy\sin xy - \cos xy)\, x\, dy = 0$ ...(1)

The integrating factor of the differential equation is given by,

$$\frac{1}{Mx - Ny} = \frac{1}{xy[xy\sin xy + \cos xy - xy\sin xy + \cos xy]}$$

$$= \frac{1}{2xy\cos xy}.$$

Hence (1) reduces to

$$\frac{(xy\sin xy + \cos xy)y\,dx}{xy\cos xy} + \frac{(xy\sin xy - \cos xy)x\,dy}{xy\cos xy} = 0$$

or, $y\tan xy\,dx + x\tan x\,y\,dy + \frac{1}{x}dx - \frac{1}{y}dy = 0$

or, $\tan xy\,[ydx + xdy] + \frac{1}{x}dx - \frac{1}{y}dy = 0$

integrating, we get

$\log\sec xy + \log x - \log y = \log c$

or, $\frac{x}{y}\sec xy = c.$

44. $e^{\sin z} = e^{\sin 1/w} = 1 + \sin\frac{1}{\omega} + \frac{\left(\sin\frac{1}{\omega}\right)^2}{2!} + \ldots$ at $\omega = 0$

$\therefore$ at $z = \infty$ the function $e^{\sin z}$ is isolated essential singularity.

47. If $0(G) = p^2$ where p is a prime then G must be an abelian group [standard result].

48. As centre of z is subgroup of G $\Rightarrow$ $0(z)|0(G)$

Also element of H belongs to $z \Rightarrow H \subseteq z$

i.e. $0(z) \geq 2$.

Also 0(H) is even

i.e. 0(G) is an even integer *i.e.* $0(G) \geq 2m$

51. The given differential equation is

$$(D^2 + D - 2)y = e^x.$$

The auxiliary equation is $m^2 + m - 2 = 0$

or, $m^2 + 2m - m - 2 = 0$

or, $m(m + 2) - 1(m + 2) = 0$

or, $(m - 1)(m + 2) = 0$

or, $m = 1, -2$

hence complementary function

$$y = c_1e^x + c_2e^{2x}$$

and Particular integral,

$$y = \frac{1}{D^2 + D - 2}\cdot e^x$$

$$= \frac{1}{(D-1)(D+2)}e^x = \frac{xe^x}{3}.$$

53. If $\vec{P}$ and $\vec{Q}$ are orthogonal then $\vec{P}.\vec{Q} = 0$

Now, $\left(\vec{i} + 2p\vec{j} + 4q\vec{k}\right).\left(\vec{i} + 4p\vec{j} + 2q\vec{k}\right) = 0$

$\Rightarrow 8p^2 + 8q^2 + 1 = 0$

Not possible for real p and q.

54. In symmetric matrix $a_{ij} = a_{ji}$

i.e., dimension of a 16×6 real matrix = No. of independent variable

= No. of diagonal elements + $\frac{\text{No. of non-diagonal elements}}{2}$

$$= 6 + \frac{30}{2} = 21.$$

58. $x + 2y + t = 0$ & $y + t = 0$

$\Rightarrow$ $y = -t$ & $x = t$

Thus a basis is $\left\{\begin{bmatrix} 1 & -1 \\ 0 & 1 \end{bmatrix}\right\}$

SET–14

CSIR–UGC (NET) MATHEMATICAL SCIENCES

PART-C

1. Consider the following functions:

1. $y = x \sin\frac{1}{x}$ if $x \neq 0$; and $y = 0$ if $x = 0$
2. $y = x^2 \sin\frac{1}{x}$ if $x \neq 0$; and $y = 0$ if $x = 0$
3. $y = x^2 \cos\frac{1}{x}$ if $x \neq 0$; and $y = 0$ if $x = 0$
4. $y = x \cos\frac{1}{x}$ if $x \neq 0$; and $y = 0$ if $x = 0$

The functions differentiable at $x = 0$ are

A. 1 and 2 B. 2 and 3
C. 3 and 4 D. 1 and 4

2. Which of the following statement is true?

A. Every quotient group of a group is abelian and its converse is also true.
B. Every quotient group of an abelian group is abelian and its converse is also true.
C. Every quotient group of a group is abelian but its converse is not true.
D. Every quotient group of an abelian group is abelian but converse is not true.

3. In dual simplex method which of the following is not correct.

A. Key column corresponds to most negative not evaluation $(z_j - c_j)$
B. Key row corresponds to the basic variable having most negative value.
C. Ratio of net evaluation numbers to the corresponding coefficients (which are negative) in the key row are computed.
D. Column corresponding to smallest of these ratio is selected as key column.

4. Let $T : R^4 \to R^4$ be the linear map satisfying.
$T(e_1) = e_2$, $T(e_2) = e_3$, $T(e_3) = 0$, $T(e_4) = e_3$,
where $\{e_1, e_2, e_3, e_4\}$ is the standard basis of $\mathbf{R}^4$. Then

A. T is idempotent B. T is invertible
C. Rank T = 3 D. T is nilpotent

5. For computing $\sqrt{a}$ by Newton's method, the $(n + 1)$th iterative is given by

A. $x_{n+1} = \frac{x_n}{2} + \frac{a}{2x_n}$
B. $x_{n+1} = \frac{a}{x_n}$
C. $x_{n+1} = x_n + x_n^2 - a$
D. None of these

6. Let u be a solution of the initial value problem
$\frac{\delta^2 u}{\delta t^2} - \frac{\delta^2 u}{\delta x^2} = 0$, $u(x, 0) = x^2$, $\frac{\delta u}{\delta t}(x,0) = 0$ then $u(0,1)$ equals

A. 1 B. 0
C. 2 D. 1/2

7. The number of points of inflexion which lie on a straight line of the curve $y = \frac{1-x}{1+x^2}$ is given by

A. 0 B. 1
C. 2 D. 3

8. The order of the differential equation
$y = c_1 \cos 2x + c_2 \cos^2 x + c_3 \sin^2 x + c_4$ is

A. Two B. Three
C. Four D. One

9. In **R** with the usual topology, the set $\mathbf{U} = \{x \in R : -1 \leq x \leq 1, x \neq 0\}$ is

A. neither Hausdorff nor first countable
B. Hausdorff but not first countable
C. first countable but not Hausdorff
D. both Hausdorff and first countable

10. A curve r in the xy-plane is such that the line joining the origin to any point P(x, y) on the curve and the line parallel to the y-axis through P are equally inclined to the tangent to the curve at P. Then, the differential equation of the curve r is

A. $x\left(\frac{dy}{dx}\right)^2 + 2y\left(\frac{dy}{dx}\right) = x$

B. $x\left(\frac{dy}{dx}\right)^2 + 2y\left(\frac{dy}{dx}\right) = 0$

C. $x\left(\frac{dy}{dx}\right)^2 + 2y\left(\frac{dx}{dy}\right) = 0$

D. $x\left(\frac{dx}{dy}\right)^2 + 2y\left(\frac{dx}{dy}\right) = x$

11. Let $f, g : R^2 \to R$ be defined by $f(x, y) = x^4 + y^2$; $g(x, y) = x^4 + y^2 - 10x^2y$.
Then at (0, 0)
A. f has a local minimum but not g.
B. g has a local minimu but not f.
C. both f and g have a local minimum.
D. Neither f nor g has a local minimum.

12. Two numbers are chosen from {1, 2, 3, 4, 5, 6} one after another without replacement. Find the probability that the smaller of the two is less than 4.

A. $\frac{4}{5}$ B. $\frac{1}{15}$

C. $\frac{1}{5}$ D. $\frac{14}{15}$

13. The distinct eigenvalues of the matrix

$$\begin{bmatrix} 1 & 1 & 0 \\ 1 & 1 & 0 \\ 0 & 0 & 0 \end{bmatrix}$$ are

A. 0 and 1 B. 1 and –1
C. 1 and 2 D. 0 and 2

14. A horizontal lever is in static equilibrium under the application of vertical forces F_1 at a distance l_1 from the fulcrum and F_2 at a distance l_2 from the fulcrum. The equilibrium for the above quantities can be obtained if

A. $F_1l_1 = 2F_2l_2$ B. $2F_1l = F_2l_2$
C. $F_1l_1 = F_2l_2$ D. $F_1l_1 < F_2l_2$

15. If H and K are normal subgroups of G then which one is true.
A. $H \cap K$ and HK are normal in G
B. HK and $H \cup K$ are normal in G
C. $H \cap K$ is normal but HK is not normal
D. $H \cup K$ is normal but HK is not normal

16. Limiting form of Binomial distribution when neither p nor q is very small is

A. Possion (1) B. Bernoulli $\left(\frac{1}{2}\right)$

C. Cauchy (0, 1) D. N (0, 1)

17. The radius of convergence of $\sum_{n=0}^{\infty} \frac{\left(1+\frac{1}{n}\right)^{n^2}}{n^3} z^n$ is

A. e B. $\frac{1}{e}$

C. 1 D. ∞

18. The L.P.P. max
$z = 2x_1 + 3x_2$
subject to $x_1 + x_2 \le 2$
$2x_1 + x_2 \le -2$
$x_1, x_2 \ge 0$ has
A. No feasible solution
B. A unique optimal solution
C. Unbounded solution
D. Multiple optimal solution

19. The extremal for the functional $I[y(x)] = \int_0^{\pi/2} (y^2 - y'^2 - 2y\sin x)\,dx$, $y(0) = 0$, $y(\pi/2) = 1$.

A. $y = \sin x - \frac{x}{2}(\cos x)$

B. $y = \sin x + \frac{x}{2}(\cos x)$

C. $y = \cos x - \frac{x}{2}(\cos x)$

D. $y = \cos x + \frac{x}{2}(\cos x)$

20. Let F be a field. Given below are six statements about F.

1. F is a skew field
2. F is a group with respect to multiplication
3. F is an integral domain
4. F has zero divisors
5. F has no zero divisors
6. Only ideals of F are $\{0\}$ and itself

In which of the following options all the statements are correct?

A. 1, 2, 3 B. 1, 3, 5, 6
C. 2, 4, 6 D. 4, 5, 6

21. A function of z is Holomorphic if

A. It is single valued and differentiable at every pt of a doman D.
B. It is differentiable
C. It hold C-R conditions.
D. u_x, v_x, u_y, v_y exist and continuous

22. What is the equation of orthogonal trajectories of the family of concentric circles $x^2 + y^2 = a^2$, where a is a parameter?

A. $y^2 = 4ax$ B. $x^2 - y^2 = c^2$
C. $y = cx$ D. $x + y = a$

23. In a determinant A of order 3, a_{ij} denotes the element in i^{th} row and jth column. $i = 1, 2, 3$, and $j = 1, 2, 3$. If $a_{ij} = a_{ji}$ for all i and j then the elements in principal diagonal are necessary

A. – 1 B. 0
C. 1 D. None of these

24. If the joint probability density function of (X, Y) is given by $f(x, y) = \frac{1}{y}e^{-\frac{x}{y}}$, $x > 0$, $0 < y < 1$, then

A. $E(X) = 0.5$ and $E(Y) = 0.5$
B. $E(X) = 1.0$ and $E(Y) = 0.5$
C. $E(X) = 0.5$ and $E(Y) = 1.0$
D. $E(X) = 1.0$ and $E(Y) = 1.0$

25. Let $A = \begin{bmatrix} 2 & 0 \\ 3 & 5 \end{bmatrix}$ be expressed as P + Q where P is symmetric matrix and Q is skew-symmetric matrix. Which one of the following is correct?

A. $Q = \begin{bmatrix} 1/2 & -3/2 \\ 3/2 & 0 \end{bmatrix}$

B. $Q = \begin{bmatrix} 0 & 3/2 \\ 3/2 & 0 \end{bmatrix}$

C. $Q = \frac{1}{2}\begin{bmatrix} 0 & -3 \\ 3 & 0 \end{bmatrix}$

D. $Q = \frac{1}{2}\begin{bmatrix} 2 & 3 \\ 0 & 5 \end{bmatrix}$

26. Which of the followning is true.

A. The cost difference in the Vogel's Approximation Method indicate the penalties for not using the respective least cost routes.
B. If some routes are prohibited, VAM cannot be used to find an initial solution to a transportation problem.
C. The initial solution obtained by the NW corner Rule would invariably be optimum.
D. The least cost method does not provide the least cost solution to a transportation problem.

27. Let $M = \begin{bmatrix} 1 & 1+i & 2i & 9 \\ 1-i & 3 & 4 & 7-i \\ -2i & 4 & 5 & i \\ 9 & 7+i & -i & 7 \end{bmatrix}$. Then

A. M has purely imaginary eigen values.
B. M is not diagonalizable.
C. M has eigen values which are neither real nor purely imaginary.
D. M has only real eigen values.

28. If H is a subgroup of a finite group G then

A. Order of H is a divisor of order of the group G.
B. Order of G is divisor of the order of the group H
C. Order of H is not a divisor of the order of the group.
D. None of these

29. Let $f : G \to H$ be a group homomorphism from a group G into a group H, with Kernel K. If the order of G, H and K are 75, 45 and 15 respectively, then the order of the image $f(G)$ is

A. 3 B. 5
C. 15 D. 45

30. Identify the false statement : A finite group G is abelian if

A. $(ab)^2 = a^2 b^2$ for all a, b in G
B. the order of G is less than or equal to 4
C. the order of G is 11
D. None of the above

31. Let $f(x) = x^n[x]$ for real x. $f(x)$ is differentiable at the origin if n is equal to which one of the following?
A. −1
B. 0
C. any real number
D. any positive integer

32. The fourth divided difference of the polynomial $3x^3 + 11x^2 + 5x + 11$ over the point $x = 0, 1, 4, 6$ and 7 is
A. 18 B. 11
C. 3 D. 0

33. Type of the following defferential equation.

$$\frac{d^2y}{dx^2} + \sin(x+y) = \sin x$$

A. linear
B. homogeneous
C. linear homogeneous
D. non-linear homogeneous

34. Which of the following is incorrect about f

where $f(z) = \dfrac{z\cos\left(\dfrac{\pi z}{2a}\right)}{(z-a)(z^2+b^2)\sin^5 z}$

A. f has removable singularities at $z = a$
B. f has pole of order 7 at $z = \pm bi$
C. pole of order 5 at $z = 0$
D. pole of order 5 at $z = kp$, $k = \pm 1, \pm 2, ...$

35. The eigenvalues of a skew-symmetric matrix are
A. negative
B. real
C. of absolute value 1
D. purely imaginary or zero

36. Let, $x_1 = -2$, $x_2 = 1$, $x_3 = 2$, $x_4 = -4$ be the observed valued of a random sample from the distribution having probability density function

$$f(x \mid \theta) = \frac{e^{-x}}{e^{\theta} - e^{-\theta}}, \quad -\theta \le x \le \theta,\ \theta > 0.$$

Then the maximum likelihood estimate of θ is
A. 3
B. 0.5
C. 4
D. Any value between 1 and 2

37. Consider the following statements:
⟨A⟩ Every infinite abelian group is either isomorphic to $(Z, +)$ or isomorphic to $(R, \cdot)$.
⟨B⟩ Every infinite cycle group is isomorphic to $(Z, +)$.
A. Both A and B are true
B. Both A and B are false
C. A is false but B is true
D. A is true but B is false

38. Choose the correct matching from A, B, C and D for the transformation T_1, T_2 and T_3 (mapping from R^2 to R^3) as defined in Group I with the statements given in Group II.

Group I	Group II
P. $T_1(x, y) = (x, x, 0)$	1. Linear tranasformation of rank 2
Q. $T_2(x, y) = (x, x+y, y)$	2. Not a linear trans formation
R. $T_3(x, y) = (x, x+1, y)$	3. Linear transformation of rank 1.

	P	Q	R
A.	3	1	2
B.	1	2	3
C.	3	2	1
D.	1	3	2

39. A travelling salesman problem always provide
A. More than one solution
B. Exactly one solution
C. One or more than one solution
D. None of these

40. The set of linearly independent solution of the differential equation $\dfrac{d^4y}{dx^2} - \dfrac{d^2y}{dx^2} = 0$ is
A. $\{1, x, e^x, e^{-x}\}$ B. $\{1, x, e^{-x}, xe^{-x}\}$
C. $\{1, x, e^x, xe^x\}$ D. $\{1, x, e^x, xe^{-x}\}$

41. If in a group G, $(ab)^3 = a^3b^3\ \forall\ a, b \in G$ and order of G is not a multiple of 3, then which is following is true

A. G is cyclic group
B. G must be an infinite
C. G is non-abelian
D. G is abelian

42. A function of z *i.e.* $f(z)$ is analytic if
A. It is single valued and differentiable at every point of a domain D.
B. It is differentiable.
C. It hold C-R conditions.
D. u_x, v_x, u_y, v_y exist and continuous.

43. For the function $f(z) = \dfrac{z - \sin z}{z^3}$, at the point $z = 0$ is
A. a pole of order 3
B. a pole of order 2
C. an essential singularity
D. a removable singularity

44. The least positive integer n, such that $\begin{pmatrix} \cos\frac{\pi}{4} & \sin\frac{\pi}{4} \\ -\sin\frac{\pi}{4} & \cos\frac{\pi}{4} \end{pmatrix}^n$ is the identity matrix of order 2, is
A. 4 B. 8
C. 12 D. 16

45. In the group (Z, +), the subgroup generated by 2 and 7 is
A. Z B. 5Z
C. 9Z D. 14Z

46. The value of c for which there exists a twice differentiable vector field $\vec{F}$ with curl $\vec{F} = 2x\hat{i} - 7y\hat{j} + cz\hat{k}$ is
A. 0 B. 2
C. 5 D. 7

47. If a differential equation has the general solution $(x + c^2) + y^2(3 - y)$, then the singular solution is
A. $y = 0$
B. $y = 1$
C. $y = 3$
D. None of the above

48. The hypotenuse of a right triangle is 10 inches but the lengths of the two legs are variable. The triangle is rotated about its hypotenuse, thus generating a top shaped solid consisting of two cones with a common base and with altitudes whose sum is 10 inches. The maximum possible volume of this solid is
A. $\dfrac{250}{3}\pi$ in^3 B. $\dfrac{160}{3}\pi$ in^3
C. $\dfrac{325}{3}\pi$ in^3 D. None of these

49. The number of real roots of the equation $x^3 + x - 1 = 0$ is
A. 0 B. 1
C. 2 D. 3

50. If A is an invertible matrix whose inverse is the matrix $\begin{bmatrix} 3 & 4 \\ 5 & 6 \end{bmatrix}$, then A is the matrix
A. $\begin{bmatrix} 6 & -4 \\ -5 & 3 \end{bmatrix}$ B. $\begin{bmatrix} 1/3 & 4 \\ 5 & 1/6 \end{bmatrix}$
C. $\begin{bmatrix} -3 & 2 \\ 5/2 & -3/2 \end{bmatrix}$ D. $\begin{bmatrix} 1/3 & 1/4 \\ 1/5 & 1/6 \end{bmatrix}$

51. Consider the Primal Linear Programming Problem
Maximize $z = c_1x_1 + c_2x_2 + ... + c_nx_n$
subject to

$$P\begin{cases} a_{11}x_1 + a_{12}x_2 + ... + a_{1n}x \le b_1 \\ a_{21}x_1 + a_{22}x_2 + ... + a_{2n}x \le b_2 \\ \vdots \\ a_{m1}x_1 + a_{m2}x_2 + ... + a_{mn}x_n \le b_m \end{cases}$$

$x_j \geq 0, j = 1, 2, ... n$

The dual of P is
Minimize $z' = b_1w_1 + b_2w_2 + ... b_mw_m$
subject to

$$D\begin{cases} a_{11}w_1 + a_{21}w_2 + ... + a_{m1}w_m \ge c_1 \\ a_{12}w_1 + a_{22}w_2 + ... + a_{m2}w_m \ge c_2 \\ \vdots \\ a_{1n}w_1 + a_{2n}w_2 + ... + a_{mn}w_m \ge c_n \end{cases}$$

$w_i \geq 0 \; i = 1, 2, ... m.$

Which of the following statement is False?

A. If P has an optimal solution, then D also has an optimal solution.

B. The dual of the dual problem is a primal problem.

C. If P has an unbounded solution, then D has no feasible solution.

D. If P has no feasible solution, then D has a feasible solution.

52. Let $\overrightarrow{F} = 2xyz\, e^{x^2}\hat{i} + ze^{x^2}\hat{j} + ye^{x^2}\hat{k}$ be the gradient of a scalar function. The value of $\int_L \overrightarrow{F}.\,dr$ along the oriented path L from (0, 0,0) to (1, 0, 2) and then to (1, 1, 2) is

A. 0 B. $2e$

C. e D. e^2

53. The supremum and infimum of the set $B = \left\{\frac{mn}{4m^2+n^2} : m \in z, n \in N\right\}$ are respectively

A. 4 and 0

B. 4 and –4

C. $\frac{1}{4}$ and $-\frac{1}{4}$

D. 4 and does not exist

54. A simplex is an n-dimensional convex Polyhedron having exactly

A. n vertices B. $(n + 1)$ vertices

C. $n\ (n + 1)$ vertices D. $(n + 1)^2$ vertices

55. If a and a^2 are both generators of a cyclic group of order n, then

A. n must be odd

B. n must be even

C. n must be prime

D. n must not be a prime

56. If $A = \begin{bmatrix} 3 & -4 \\ 1 & -1 \end{bmatrix}$, then what is A^n equal to?

A. $\begin{bmatrix} 1+2n & -4n \\ n & 1-2n \end{bmatrix}$ B. $\begin{bmatrix} 3^n & (-4)^n \\ 1 & (-1)^n \end{bmatrix}$

C. $\begin{bmatrix} 1+3n & 1-4n \\ 1+n & 1-n \end{bmatrix}$ D. $\begin{bmatrix} 1+2n & -4n \\ 1+n & 1-2n \end{bmatrix}$

57. If $\phi_1(x)$ is a particular integral of $Ly = \frac{d^2y}{dx^2} - a\frac{dy}{dx} + by = e^{ax} + f(x)$ and $\phi_2(x)$ is a particular integral of $Ly = x^{ax} - f(x)$; a, b being constants, then a particular integral, of $Ly = 2be^{ax}$ is

A. $b\phi_1(x) + \phi_2(x)$ B. $\phi_1(x) - b\phi_2(x)$

C. $a\phi_1(x) + b\phi_2(x)$ D. $b[\phi_1(x) + \phi_2(x)]$

58. At $z = 0$, the function $f(z) = z^{2-}z$

A. does not satisfy Cauchy-Riemann equations

B. satisfies Cauchy-Riemann equation but is not differentiable

C. is differentiable

D. analytic

59. The function $f(x) = x^{1/x}$ has a minimum value at

A. $x = e$ B. $x = e^{-1}$

C. $x = e^2$ D. $x = 0$

60. Which of the following changes the nature of the objective funciton in the given L.P.P.

A. Artificial variables B. Slack variables

C. Surplus variables D. None of these

ANSWERS

1	2	3	4	5	6	7	8	9	10
B	D	A	C	A	B	D	A	C	A
11	**12**	**13**	**14**	**15**	**16**	**17**	**18**	**19**	**20**
D	A	A	C	A	D	C	A	A	B
21	**22**	**23**	**24**	**25**	**26**	**27**	**28**	**29**	**30**
A	B	D	A	C	A	D	A	B	D

31	32	33	34	35	36	37	38	39	40
C	D	D	A	D	C	C	A	C	A
41	**42**	**43**	**44**	**45**	**46**	**47**	**48**	**49**	**50**
D	A	D	D	D	C	C	A	B	C
51	**52**	**53**	**54**	**55**	**56**	**57**	**58**	**59**	**60**
D	B	C	A	A	A	B	B	A	A

SOME SELECTED EXPLANATORY ANSWERS

13. The characteristic equation of the above equation is given by $\begin{vmatrix} 1-\lambda & 1 & 0 \\ 0 & 1-\lambda & 0 \\ 0 & 0 & 1-\lambda \end{vmatrix} = 0$

or $(1-\lambda)(1-\lambda)(-\lambda) = 0 \Rightarrow \lambda = 0, 1.$

17. As radius of convergence $= \lim_{n\to\infty} \frac{a_n}{a_{n+1}} = 1.$

21. Necessary condition of $f(z)$ to be analytic. u_x, v_x, u_y, v_y should exist, and $u_x = v_y$ and $u_y = -v_x$ sufficient condition for $f(z)$ to be analytic. u_x, u_y, v_n, v_y exist, continuous and satisfy CR at each point of D.

23. $a_{ij} = a_{ji} \Rightarrow a_{ii} = a_{ii}$

By putting $i = j$; so it is an identity, hence any value is possible.

25. Every matrix A can be written as

$$A = \frac{1}{2}(A+A')+\frac{1}{2}(A-A') = P + Q.$$

Hence $Q = \left[\frac{1}{2}(A-A')\right)$

$\because \quad A = \begin{bmatrix} 2 & 0 \\ 3 & 5 \end{bmatrix}$

$\therefore \quad A - A' = \begin{bmatrix} 2 & 0 \\ 3 & 5 \end{bmatrix} - \begin{bmatrix} 2 & 3 \\ 0 & 5 \end{bmatrix} = \begin{bmatrix} 0 & -3 \\ 3 & 0 \end{bmatrix}$

$\therefore \quad Q = \frac{1}{2}(A-A') = \frac{1}{2}\begin{bmatrix} 0 & -3 \\ 3 & 0 \end{bmatrix}.$

27. M is a Hermitian matrix. Hence it should have only real eigenvalues.

38. $p: T_1 = \begin{bmatrix} 1 & 0 \\ 1 & 0 \\ 0 & 0 \end{bmatrix} \Rightarrow \text{Rank} = 1$ [$\because$ take any basis]

$q: T_2 = \begin{bmatrix} 1 & 0 \\ 2 & 1 \\ 1 & 1 \end{bmatrix} \Rightarrow \text{Rank} = 2$[Better for S.D. Basis]

43. $f(z) = \frac{z - \sin z}{z^3}$

$$\Rightarrow \lim_{z\to 0} f(z) = \lim_{z\to 0} \frac{z - \left(z - \frac{z^3}{3!} + \frac{z^5}{5!} + \ldots\right)}{z^3}$$

$$= \lim_{z\to 0} \frac{\frac{z^3}{3!} - \frac{z^5}{5!} + \ldots}{z^3}$$

$$= \lim_{z\to 0} \frac{1}{6} - \frac{z^2}{5!} + \ldots = \frac{1}{6}$$

Hence $z = 0$ is a removable singularity of $f(z)$.

44. If $A = \begin{bmatrix} \cos\theta & \sin\theta \\ -\sin\theta & \cos\theta \end{bmatrix}$ then,

$$A^n = \begin{bmatrix} \cos n\theta & \sin n\theta \\ -\sin n\theta & \cos n\theta \end{bmatrix}$$

i.e. $A^n = \begin{bmatrix} 1 & 0 \\ 0 & 1 \end{bmatrix} \Rightarrow \cos n\theta = 1$

$\Rightarrow \quad n\theta = 2m\pi \quad m = 0, 1, 2, \ldots.$

$\Rightarrow \quad n\frac{\pi}{4} = 2m\pi \quad \Rightarrow n = 8m,$

i.e. $n = 8 <$ minimum positive $m >$.

45. (2) = {–14, –12, –10, –8, –6, –4, –2, 0, 2, 4, 6, 8, 10, 12, 14, ...}

(7) = {.......... –14, –7, 0, 7, 14, 21, ...}

hence (2) ∩ (7) = {–14, 0, 14, 28, 42, ...}

$\Rightarrow$ 14Z.

46. $$\bar{\nabla}\times \bar{F} = 2x\hat{i} - 7\hat{j} + cz\hat{k}$$

Also $\nabla.\left(\bar{\nabla}\times\bar{F}\right) = 0 \Rightarrow 2 - 7 + C = 0$

$\therefore$ $C = 5$

48.

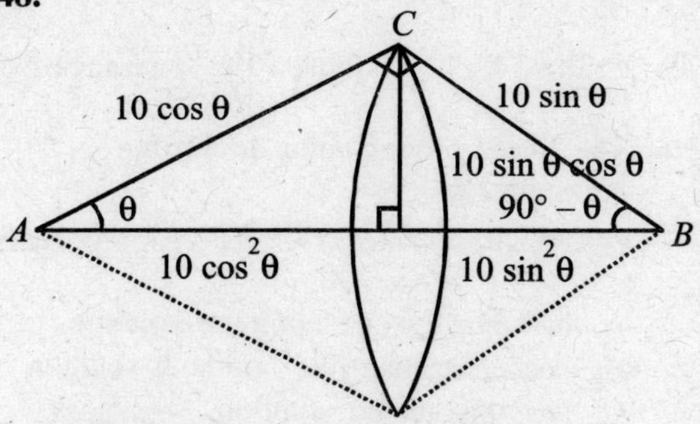

10 cos θ, 10 sin θ, 10 sin θ cos θ, θ, 90° – θ, $10\cos^2\theta$, $10\sin^2\theta$, A, B, C

Volume $V=$

$$\frac{1}{3}\pi.100\sin^2\theta\cos^2\theta[10\cos^2\theta + 10\sin^2\theta]$$

$$= \frac{1000\pi}{3}\sin^2\theta\cos^2\theta \qquad ...(i)$$

$$\frac{dV}{d\theta} = 0 \Rightarrow 2\sin\theta\cos^3\theta - 2\cos\theta\sin^3\theta = 0$$

$$\Rightarrow \sin\theta\cos\theta(\cos^2\theta - \sin^2\theta) = 0$$

$$\Rightarrow \theta = 0, \frac{\pi}{2}, \frac{\pi}{4}$$

V is max^m at $\theta = \frac{\pi}{4}$

$$\therefore V^{max} = \frac{1000\pi}{3}.\frac{1}{4} = \frac{250\pi}{3}$$

49. Given equation is

$x^3 + x - 1 = 0$ as $f(0) = -1$ and $f(1) = 1$

$\Rightarrow$ there exist a real root lying between 0 and 1.

Also $f'(x) = 3x^2 + 1 > 0\ \forall\ x > 0$

i.e. It is an increasing function for all x. Hence, it does not have any other real solution.

50. As $A = \begin{bmatrix} 3 & 4 \\ 5 & 6 \end{bmatrix}$

hence $|A| = 18 - 20 = -2.$

$$\text{Adj } A = \begin{bmatrix} 6 & -4 \\ -5 & 3 \end{bmatrix}$$

$$\therefore \quad A^{-1} = \frac{1}{|A|}\text{adj } A = \frac{1}{-2}\begin{bmatrix} 6 & -4 \\ -5 & 3 \end{bmatrix}$$

$$= \begin{bmatrix} -3 & 2 \\ 5/2 & -3/2 \end{bmatrix}.$$

56. Given $A = \begin{bmatrix} 3 & -4 \\ 1 & -1 \end{bmatrix}$

then $A^2 = \begin{bmatrix} 3 & -4 \\ 1 & -1 \end{bmatrix}\begin{bmatrix} 3 & -4 \\ 1 & -1 \end{bmatrix} = \begin{bmatrix} 5 & -8 \\ 2 & -3 \end{bmatrix}$

and $A^3 = \begin{bmatrix} 5 & -8 \\ 2 & -3 \end{bmatrix}\begin{bmatrix} 3 & -4 \\ 1 & -1 \end{bmatrix}$

$$= \begin{bmatrix} 7 & -12 \\ 3 & -5 \end{bmatrix}$$

Clearly A^3 can be written as $= \begin{bmatrix} 1+2.3 & -4.3 \\ 3 & 1-2.3 \end{bmatrix}$

i.e. $A^n = \begin{bmatrix} 1+2.n & -4.n \\ n & 1-2.n \end{bmatrix}$

i.e. choice A is correct.

59. $\because$ $f(x) = x^{1/x}$

$$\Rightarrow \quad \ln f(x) = \frac{1}{x}\ln x$$

$$\Rightarrow \quad \frac{1}{y}\frac{dy}{dx} = -\frac{1}{x^2}\ln x + \frac{1}{x^2}$$

$$\Rightarrow \quad \frac{dy}{dx} = x^{\frac{1}{x}}\left[\frac{(1-\ln x)}{x^2}\right] = 0$$

$\therefore$ $1 - \log x = 0$

$\Rightarrow$ $\ln x = 1$

$\therefore$ $x = e.$

SET–15

CSIR–UGC (NET) MATHEMATICAL SCIENCES

PART-C

1. The minimal polynomial of $\begin{bmatrix} 1 & 0 & 0 & 0 \\ 1 & 1 & 0 & 0 \\ 0 & 0 & 2 & 0 \\ 0 & 0 & 0 & 2 \end{bmatrix}$ is

A. $(x-1)^2 (x-2)$ B. $(x-1)(x-2)^2$
C. $(x-1)(x-2)$ D. $(x-1)^2 (x-2)^2$

2. Let R be the ring of all 2×2 matrices with integer entries which of the following subsets of R is an integral domain?

A. $\left\{\begin{pmatrix} 0 & a \\ b & 0 \end{pmatrix} : a,b \in Z\right\}$

B. $\left\{\begin{pmatrix} a & 0 \\ 0 & b \end{pmatrix} : a,b \in Z\right\}$

C. $\left\{\begin{pmatrix} a & 0 \\ 0 & a \end{pmatrix} : a \in Z\right\}$

D. $\left\{\begin{pmatrix} a & b \\ b & c \end{pmatrix} : a,b,c \in Z\right\}$

3. Let $T : \mathbf{R}^3 \to \mathbf{R}^3$ be a linear transformation given by $T(x, y, z) = (x, y, 0)$. Then the null space is generated by which one of the following?

A. (0, 0, 1) B. (0, 1, 0)
C. (1, 0, 0) D. None of these

4. In $\mathbf{R}^3$ with usual topology, let $V = \{(x, y, z) \in \mathbf{R}^3 : x^2 + y^2 + z^2 = l, y \neq 0\}$ and $W = \{(x, y, z) \in \mathbf{R}^3 : y = 0\}$. Then $V \cup W$ is

A. connected and compact
B. connected but not compact
C. compact but not connected
D. neither connected nor compact

5. For the positively oriented unit circle,

$$\int_{|z|=1} \frac{2\,\text{Re}(z)}{z+2}\, dz =$$

A. 0 B. πi
C. $2\pi i$ D. $4\pi i$

6. The linear programming problem
Maximize $Z = x_1 + x_2$
subject to $x_1 + 2x_2 \leq 20,\ x_1 + x_2 < 15,\ x_2 \leq 6$
$x_1, x_2 \geq 0$

A. has exactly one optimum solution
B. has more than one optimum solution
C. has unbounded solution
D. has no solution

7. If a is a whole number and p is a prime number then according to Fermat's theorem

A. $2^p - 2$ is divisible by p
B. $2^P - 2$ is not divisible by p
C. $2^p - 1$ is divisible by p
D. None of these

8. Consider the LPP : Maximize $Z = 3x + 5y$, subject to : $x + 2y \leq 4$, $2x + y \geq 6$ and $x \geq 0, y \geq 0$. This problem represents a :

A. Non L.P.P B. Mixed L.P.P
C. Pure L.P.P D. Zero-one L.P.P

9. Consider the following subsets of $\mathbb{R}$:

$$E = \left\{\frac{n}{n+1} : n \in \mathbb{N}\right\},\ F = \left\{\frac{1}{1-x} : 0 \leq x < 1\right\}.$$

Then

A. Both E and F are closed
B. E is closed and F is NOT closed
C. E is NOT closed and F is closed
D. Neither E nor F is closed

10. A function F is defined as follows:

$$f(x) = x^{1/3}, \quad \text{if } x < 1$$
$$= (2 - x)^{1/2}, \quad \text{if } 1 \le x \le 2$$
$$= (x - 2)^{1/4}, \quad \text{if } x \ge 2$$

What is the total number of points where derivative do not exist?

A. 1 B. 2
C. 3 D. None of these

11. The interpolating polynomial of highest degree which corresponds the functional values $f(-1) = 9$, $f(0) = 5$, $f(2) = 3$, $f(5) = 15$ is

A. $x^3 + x^2 + 2x + 5$
B. $x^2 - 3x + 5$
C. $x^4 + 4x^3 + 5x^2 + 5$
D. $x + 5$

12. The resolvent kernel of integral equations $\phi(x) = 1+\int_0^x (\xi - x)\phi(\xi)\,d\xi$.

A. $1 + \cos x$ B. $1 - \cos x$
C. $\cos x$ D. $\sin x$

13. $f(x) = x\sin\dfrac{\pi}{x}$ when $0 < x \le 1$
$= 0$ when $x = 0$

then in [0, 1]

A. $f(x)$ is continuous on [0, 1] and f bounded variation [0, 1]
B. $f(x)$ is continuous on [0, 1] and f is not bounded variation [0, 1]
C. $f(x)$ is not continuous on (0, 1] and f is bounded variation [0, 1]
D. $f(x)$ is not continuous on [0, 1] and f is not bounded variation [0, 1]

14. Let $P_n(x)$ denote the Legendre polynomial of degree n. If

$$f(x) = \begin{cases} x, \text{ if } -1 \le x \le 0 \\ 0, 0 \le x \le 1 \end{cases}$$

and $f(x) = a_0P_0(x) + a_1P_1(x) + a_2P_2(x) + \ldots$

then

A. $a_0 = -\frac{1}{4}, a_1 = -\frac{1}{2}$ B. $a_0 = -\frac{1}{4}, a_1 = \frac{1}{2}$

C. $a_0 = \frac{1}{2}, a_1 = -\frac{1}{4}$ D. $a_0 = -\frac{1}{2}, a_1 = -\frac{1}{4}$

15. For the function $f(z) = \dfrac{1-e^z}{z}$, then the point $z = 0$ is

A. an essential singularity
B. a pole of order zero
C. a pole of order 1
D. a removable singularity

16. Which one of the following is correct?

If $\alpha, \beta \in S_n$, then $\alpha^{-1}\beta^{-1}\alpha\beta$ is an even permutation.

A. for all $\alpha, \beta \in S_n$
B. only if α, β are odd
C. only if α, β are even
D. only if one of α, β is odd and other is even

17. The singular solution of the equation $y = px + f(p), p \equiv \dfrac{dy}{dx}$ is obtained of eliminating p between original equation and the equation

A. $x - f'(p) = 0$ B. $x + f'(p) = 0$
C. $y - f'(p) = 0$ D. $y + f'(p) = 0$

18. The general solution of the differential equation $y''(x) - 4y'(x) + 8y(x) = 10e^x \cos x$ is

A. $e^{2x}(k_1 \cos 2x + k_2 \sin 2x) + e^x(2\cos x + \sin x)$

B. $e^{2x}(k_1 \cos 2x + k_2 \sin 2x) + e^x(2\cos x - \sin x)$

C. $e^{-2x}(k_1 \cos 2x + k_2 \sin 2x) - e^x(2\cos x - \sin x)$

D. $e^{-2x}(k_1 \cos 2x + k_2 \sin 2x) + e^x(2\cos x + \sin x)$

19. Let W be the space spanned by $f = \sin x$ and $g = \cos x$. Then for any real value of θ, $f_1 = \sin(x + \theta)$ and $g_1 = \cos(x + \theta)$

A. are vectors in W.
B. are linearly independent.
C. do not form a basis for W.
D. form a basis for W.

20. Three distinct numbers are chosen randomly from first 100 natural numbers, then the probability that all are divisible by 2 and 3 both is

A. $\dfrac{4}{33}$ B. $\dfrac{4}{35}$

C. $\dfrac{4}{25}$ D. $\dfrac{4}{1155}$

21. Let T: $v \rightarrow v$ be a linear transformation on a vector space V over a field k satisfying the property $Tx = 0 \Rightarrow x = 0$. If $x_1, x_2, \ldots x_n$ are L.I elements in V then $Tx_1, Tx_2, \ldots Tx_n$ are

A. LI

B. LD

C. Data are insufficient

D. None of these

22. The number of arbitrary constants in the complete primitive of the differential equation

$$\phi\left(x, y, \frac{dy}{dx}, \frac{d^3y}{dx^3}\right) = 0 \text{ is}$$

A. 1 B. 2

C. 3 D. 4

23. Let G be a group of order 168 then which of the following may not be always true

A. G has a non-trivial centre

B. G has a subgroup of index 2

C. G has a subgroup of order 42

D. All of the above

24. The vector $-i + j - k$ bisects the angle between the vectors c and $3i + 4j$ the unit vector along c is

A. $\frac{1}{15}(11i + 10j + 2k)$

B. $\frac{15}{2}(-11i + 10j - 2k)$

C. $\frac{.1}{15}(-11i + 10j - jk)$

D. None of these

25. Let G be a cyclic group of order 6. Then the number of elements $g \in G$ such that $G = \langle g \rangle$ is

A. 5 B. 3

C. 4 D. 2

26. The value of $f(x)$ given only at $x = 0, \frac{1}{3}, \frac{2}{3}, 1$. Which of the following can be used to evaluate $\int_0^1 f(x)dx$ approximately.

A. Trapezoid rule

B. Simpson's rule

C. Trapezoidal as well as Simpson rule

D. None of these

27. For any $n \in$ N, let P_n denote the vector space of all polynomials with real co-efficients and of degree at most n. Define $T : P_n \rightarrow P_{n+1}$ by

$$T(p)(x) = p'(x) - \int_0^x p(t)\,dt$$

Then the dimension of the null space of T is

A. 0 B. 1

C. n D. $n + 1$

28. Given a system of m simultaneous linear equation in n unknowns ($m < n$), the number of basic variables will be

A. m B. n

C. $n - m$ D. $n + m$

29. There are two identical locks, with two identical keys, and the keys are among the six different ones which a person carries in his pocket. In a hurry he drops one key somewhere. Then the probability that the locks can still be opened by drawing one key at random is equal to

A. $\frac{1}{3}$ B. $\frac{5}{6}$

C. $\frac{1}{30}$ D. $\frac{1}{12}$

30. The radius of convergence of the power series $\sum_{n=1}^{\infty} \frac{n!}{n^n} x^n$ is

A. $1\ x\ 1 < 1$

B. $|x| < \log 2$

C. $|x| < e$

D. None of the above

31. Polar form of C.R equations.

A. $ru_r = v_\theta$; $u_\theta = -rv_r$

B. $u_r = rv_\theta$; $ru_\theta = -v_r$

C. $u_r = -rv_\theta$; $u_\theta = rv_r$

D. $u_\theta = v_\theta$; $u_r = rv_r$

32. If $u = \tan^{-1}\left(\frac{x^3+y^3}{x-y}\right)$ the value of

$$x^2\frac{\partial^2 u}{\partial x^2}+2xy\frac{\partial^2 u}{\partial x\,\partial y}+y^2\frac{\partial^2 u}{\partial y^2}$$ is

A. $\sin 3u \sin 2u \sin u$
B. $\cos 2u\ (2 - 3\cos^2 u)$
C. $\tan 2u\ (\cos 2u - \sin 2u)$
D. $\sin 2u\ (1 - 4\sin^2 u)$

33. Suppose C_1 is the boundary of $\{(x, y) \in \mathbb{R}^2 : 0 \le x \le 1, 0 \le y \le 1\}$ and C_2 is the boundary of $\{(x, y) \in \mathbb{R}^2 : -1 < x < 0, -1 \le y \le 0\}$.

Let $\alpha_i = \int_{C_i} xy^2dx+(x^2y+2x)dy,\ i = 1, 2$

be evaluated in the counterclock wise direction. Then
A. $\alpha_1 = 1, \alpha_2 = -1$
B. $\alpha_1 = \alpha_2 = 1$
C. $\alpha_1 = 2, \alpha_2 = -2$
D. $\alpha_1 = \alpha_2 = 2$

34. In any system of particles, suppose we do not assume that the internal forces come in pairs. Then the fact that the sum of internal forces is zero follows from
A. Newton's second law
B. Conservation of angular momentum
C. Conservation of energy
D. Principle of virtual displacement

35. Diff. equ.

$$\frac{d^2y}{dx^2}+4y = \sec^2 2x$$

Using the method of variation of parameters.

A. $y = c_1\cos 2x+c_2\sin 2x-\frac{1}{4}+\frac{1}{4}\sin 2x\ \log(\sec 2x+\tan 2x)$

B. $y = c_1\cos 2x-c_2\sin 2x+\frac{1}{4}\sin 2x.\ \log(\sec 2x+\tan 2x)$

C. $y = (c_1+c_2x)e^{2x}+\frac{1}{4}\log(\sec 2x+\tan 2x)$

D. $y = c_1\cos 2x+c_2\sin 2x+\frac{1}{4}-\frac{1}{4}\sin 2x$

36. Let T be an arbitrary linear transformation from $\mathbf{R}^n$ to $\mathbf{R}^n$, which is not one-one
A. Rank T > 0
B. Rank T = n
C. Rank T < n
D. Rank T = $n - 1$

37. Let T : $\mathbf{R}^2 \to \mathbf{R}^2$ be defined by T(x, y) = ($x + y$, $x - y$). Which one of the following is the matrix of T for (0, 1) and (1, 0) as a basis for both domain and range of T?

A. $\begin{bmatrix}1 & 1\\1 & -1\end{bmatrix}$
B. $\begin{bmatrix}-1 & 1\\1 & 1\end{bmatrix}$
C. $\begin{bmatrix}1 & -1\\1 & 1\end{bmatrix}$
D. $\begin{bmatrix}1 & 1\\-1 & 1\end{bmatrix}$

38 Every non-empty subset of the real line R is
A. ordered as well as complete
B. complete but not necessarily ordered
C. ordered but not necessarily complete
D. neither ordered nor complete

39. The residue of $f(z)=\frac{z^3}{(z-1)(z-2)(z-3)}$ at $z = \infty$ is
A. 0
B. –6
C. 6
D. None of these

40. The particular integral of the partial differential equation $(D - 3D^1 - 2)^2z = 2e^{2x}\tan(y + 3x)$ where $D=\frac{\partial}{\partial x}$, $D^1=\frac{\partial}{\partial y}$ is
A. $xe^{2x}\tan(y + 3x)$
B. $x^2e^{2x}\tan(y + 3x)$
C. $\frac{x^2}{2!}e^{2x}\tan(y+3x)$
D. $3xe^{2x}\tan(y + 3x)$.

41. If G is a group and H is a subgroup of index 2 in G, then choose the correct answer.
A. H is a normal subgroup of G
B. H is not a normal subgroup of G
C. He is a subgroup of G
D. None of these

42. The scientific method in OR consists of.
A. Formulation phase
B. Judgement phase
C. Research phase
D. Action phase

43. The set of all the accumulation points of the set

$\left\{(-1)^n + \frac{1}{m} : m, n \in N\right\}$ is

A. {0} B. N
C. {–1, 1} D. None of these

44. If $f(x)$ has an isolated zero of multiplicity 3 at $x = a$, and the iteration $x_{n+1} = x_n - \frac{3f(x_n)}{f'(x_n)}$, $n = 0, 1, 2, \ldots$ converges to a, then the rate of convergence is

A. linear
B. faster than linear but slower than quadratic
C. quadratic
D. cubic

45. For two events A and B, $P(A \cup B)$ is

A. not less than $P(A) + P(B) - 1$
B. not greater than $P(A) + P(B)$
C. equal to $P(A) + P(B) - P(A \cup B)$
D. equal to $P(A) + P(B) + P(A \cup B)$

46. If $f(x, y, z)$ is a harmonic function in a domain D containing the region T : $x^2 + y^2 + z^2 \leq 100$, then the surface integral

$\int_S \left(x\frac{\partial f}{\partial x} + \frac{\partial f}{\partial y} + \frac{\partial f}{\partial z}\right) ds$ where S : $x^2 + y^2 + z^2 = 100$, equals

A. 0 B. 1
C. 10 D. 100

47. In a minimization program penalty costs associated with artificial variables are

A. M ; M >> 0 B. –M ; M >> 0
C. M ; M < 0 D. None

48. In the sufficiently small neighbourhood around $x = 2$, the differential equation

$\frac{dy}{dx} = \frac{y}{\sqrt{x}}, \ y(2) = 4$ has

A. no solution
B. a unique solution
C. exactly two solutions
D. infinitely many solution

49. The system of equations

$$4x_1 + x_2 - 3x_3 - x_4 = 0$$
$$2x_1 + 3x_2 + x_3 - 5x_4 = 0$$
$$x_1 - 2x_2 - 2x_3 + 3x_4 = 0 \text{ has}$$

A. no solution
B. only one solution (0, 0, 0, 0)
C. infinite number of solutions
D. only two solutions (0, 0, 0, 0) and $\left(\frac{3}{5}, 1, \frac{4}{5}, 1\right)$

50. Which one of the following is not a group?

A. The set of rotations about a point 0 in the plane with binary operation as the resultant of two rotations.
B. The set of complex numbers whose modulus is 1 with respect to mutliplication of complex number.
C. The set of non-zero residue classes modulo a composite positive integer m with respect to multiplication of residue classes.
D. The power set of a non-empty set X with symmetric difference of sets as binary operation.

51. In the queueing system arrival process is

A. A Poisson process
B. An exponentially distributed random variable
C. Geometrically distributed
D. Arbitrarily distributed

52. The differential equation satisfied by family of curvcs $y = ae^{-x} + be^{-2x} + ce^{-3x}$ (where a, b, c are parameters) is

A. $y'' + 2y' = 5x$
B. $y''' + 5y'' + 7y' = 7$
C. $y''' + 6y'' + 11y' + 6y = 0$
D. None of the above

53. Which of the following transformation reduce the differential equation $\frac{dz}{dx} + \frac{z}{x}\log z = \frac{z}{x^2}(\log z)^2$ into the form

$\frac{du}{dx} + P(x)(u) = Q(x)$

A. $u = \log z$ B. $u = \frac{1}{\log z}$

C. $u = e^z$ D. $u = (\log z)^2$

54. Assuming that the petrol burnt (per hour) in driving a motor boat varies inversely as the cube of its velocity, the most economical speed when going against a current of 10 km/hr is

A. 15 km/hr B. 20 km/hr

C. 25 km/hr D. 30 km/hr

55. Let $T : R^3 \to R^3$ be a linear transformation and I be the identity transformation of R^3. If there is a scalar c and a non-zero vector $x \in R^3$ such that $T(x) = cx$, then rank $(T - cI)$

A. cannot be 0 B. cannot be 1

C. cannot be 2 D. cannot be 3

56. The number of roots of the equation $z^4 + 6z + 3 = 0$ have their moduli between 1 and 2.

A. 1 B. 2

C. 3 D. 4

57. Let G and G' are cyclic group of order 45 and 15 respectively then number of homomorphism from G into G' are

A. 15 B. 8

C. 7 D. None of these

58. The partial differential equation of the family of surfaces $z = (x + y) + A(xy)$ is

A. $xp - yq = 0$ B. $xp - yq = x - y$

C. $xp + yq = x + y$ D. $xp + yq = 0$

59. Let C be the circle $x^2 + y^2 = 1$ taken in the anti-clockwise sense. Then the value of the integral

$$\int_C \left[(2xy^3 + y)dx + (3x^2y^2 + 2x)dy\right] \text{ equals}$$

A. 1 B. $\pi/2$

C. π D. 0

60. If the derivative f' exists and is bounde on $[a, b]$, then

A. the function f is of bounded variation on $[a, b]$

B. the function f is not of bounded variation on $[a, b]$

C. the function f is necessarily continuous.

D. the function f is not continous.

ANSWERS

1	2	3	4	5	6	7	8	9	10
A	C	A	D	A	B	A	A	D	B
11	12	13	14	15	16	17	18	19	20
B	C	B	B	D	A	B	B	D	D
21	22	23	24	25	26	27	28	29	30
A	C	D	D	D	C	A	A	A	C
31	32	33	34	35	36	37	38	39	40
A	D	D	D	A	C	A	A	B	B
41	42	43	44	45	46	47	48	49	50
A	A	C	A	B	D	B	B	C	C
51	52	53	54	55	56	57	58	59	60
B	C	B	A	D	C	A	D	C	A

SOME SELECTED EXPLANATORY ANSWERS

1. Characteristic polynomial is given by

$$A(x) = (x - 1)^2 (x - 2)^2$$

Now we check for

$(x - 1)(x - 2)$ then $x = A$

$$i.e. \ (A - 1)(A - 2) = \begin{bmatrix} 0 & 0 & 0 & 0 \\ 1 & 0 & 0 & 0 \\ 0 & 0 & 1 & 0 \\ 0 & 0 & 0 & 1 \end{bmatrix}$$

$$\begin{bmatrix} -1 & 0 & 0 & 0 \\ 1 & -1 & 0 & 0 \\ 0 & 0 & 0 & 0 \\ 0 & 0 & 0 & 0 \end{bmatrix} = \begin{bmatrix} 0 & 0 & 0 & 0 \\ -1 & 0 & 0 & 0 \\ 0 & 0 & 0 & 0 \\ 0 & 0 & 0 & 0 \end{bmatrix}$$

i.e. $(x-1)(x-2)$ is not minimal polynomial.

$$\text{However } (x-1)^2(x-2) = \begin{bmatrix} 0 & 0 & 0 & 0 \\ 1 & 0 & 0 & 0 \\ 0 & 0 & 1 & 0 \\ 0 & 0 & 0 & 1 \end{bmatrix}$$

$$\begin{bmatrix} 0 & 0 & 0 & 0 \\ 1 & 0 & 0 & 0 \\ 0 & 0 & 1 & 0 \\ 0 & 0 & 0 & 1 \end{bmatrix}\begin{bmatrix} -1 & 0 & 0 & 0 \\ 1 & -1 & 0 & 0 \\ 0 & 0 & 0 & 0 \\ 0 & 0 & 0 & 0 \end{bmatrix}$$

$$= \begin{bmatrix} 0 & 0 & 0 & 0 \\ 0 & 0 & 0 & 0 \\ 0 & 0 & 0 & 0 \\ 0 & 0 & 0 & 0 \end{bmatrix}.$$

3. Given $T(x, y, z) = (x, y, 0)$

Standard basis of $\mathbf{R}^3$ are given by $\{(1, 0, 0), (0, 1, 0), (0, 0, 1)\}$

hence $T(1, 0, 0) = (1, 0, 0)$

$T(0, 1, 0) = (0, 1, 0)$

& $T(0, 0, 1) = (0, 0, 0)$

$\Rightarrow (0, 0, 1) \in \text{Ker } T.$

Or, null space is generated by (0, 0, 1).

6. The solution space of the given LPP is given by the shaded portion of the plotted graph.

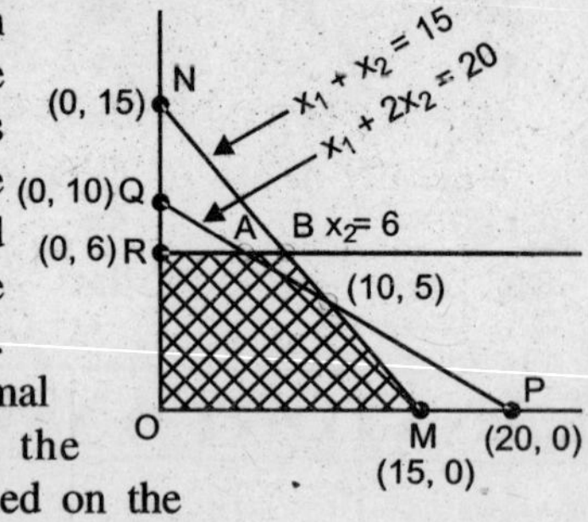

As the optimal solution of the LPP is obtained on the boundary of the set.

i.e. The optimality criteria will be checked at the point R, A, C and M, the

$Z(R) = x_1 + x_2 = 0 + 6 = 6$

$Z(A) = x_1 + x_2 = 8 + 6 = 14$

$Z(C) = x_1 + x_2 = 10 + 5 = 15$

$Z(M) = x_1 + x_2 = 15 + 0 = 15$

i.e. optimal value of Z is obtained both at and M.

i.e. So solution of Z also consist of a point lying on the line CM.

i.e. The Z has more than one (infinite) numb of solution.

9. The given subset of $\mathbb{R}$ are

$$E = \left\{\frac{n}{n+1} : n \in \mathbb{N}\right\},\ F = \left\{\frac{1}{1-x} : 0 \le x < 1\right\}$$

$$\text{Clearly } E = \left\{\frac{1}{2}, \frac{2}{3}, \frac{3}{4}, \ldots\ldots\right\}$$

i.e. E is bounded by upper bound $\frac{1}{2}$ a lower bound 0.

However $0 \notin E$ *i.e.* E is not closed as lin point do not belong to E.

$$\text{Also} \qquad F = \left\{\frac{1}{1-x} : 0 \le x < 1\right\}$$

Clearly, it is an unbounded set a

$$\lim_{x \to 1} \frac{1}{1-x} \to \infty.$$

Hence, it is also not closed.

13. Clearly f is continuous on [0, 1]

Let partition

$$P = \left\{0, \frac{2}{2n+1}, \frac{2}{2n-1}, \frac{2}{2n-3}, \ldots \frac{2}{5}, \frac{2}{3}, 1\right\}$$

$$\therefore \sum_i |f(x_i) - f(x_{i-1})|$$

$$= \left|f(1) - f\left(\frac{2}{3}\right)\right| + \left|f\left(\frac{2}{3}\right) - f\left(\frac{2}{5}\right)\right| + \ldots$$

$$+ \left|f\left(\frac{2}{2n+1}\right) - f(\right.$$

$$= \frac{2}{3} + \left(\frac{2}{3} + \frac{2}{5}\right) + \left(\frac{2}{5} + \frac{2}{7}\right) + \ldots + \left(\frac{2}{2n-1} + \frac{2}{2n+1}\right.$$

$$+ \frac{2}{2n+}$$

$$= 4\left[\frac{1}{3} + \frac{1}{5} + \frac{1}{7} + \ldots + \frac{1}{2n+1}\right]$$

Infinite series $\frac{1}{3}+\frac{1}{5}+\frac{1}{7}+...+...$ is dgt, its partial sums sequence $\{S_n\}$, where

$S_n = \frac{1}{3}+\frac{1}{5}+\frac{1}{7}+...+\frac{1}{2n+1}$ is not bounded above.

Thus $\sum_i |f(x_i)-f(x_{i-1})|$ can be made arbitrarily large by taking n sufficiently large. consequently. $V(f, 0, 1) \to \infty$
and so f is not of bounded variation on [0, 1]

8. $y''(x)-4y'(x)+8y(x)=10e^x \cos x$

$\Rightarrow (D^2-4D+8)\,y=10e^x \cos x$

$\Rightarrow [(D-2)^2+4]\,y=10e^x \cos x$

Auxiliary equation is

$(m-2)^2+4=0 \quad \Rightarrow \quad m=2\pm 2i$

So, complementary function is

$y=e^{2x}\,[k_1 \cos 2x+k_2 \sin 2x]$ ...(1)

Particular Integral is

$$\frac{1}{(D-2)^2+4}10e^x \cos x$$

$$= 10e^x \frac{1}{(D+1-2)^2+4}\cos x$$

$$= 10e^x \left[\frac{1}{D^2-2D+5}\cos x\right]$$

$$= 10e^x \left[\frac{1}{-1-2D+5}(\cos x)\right]$$

$$= 10e^x \frac{4+2D}{16-4D^2}\cos x$$

$$= \frac{e^x}{2}(4 \cos x-2 \sin x)$$

$$= e^x (2 \cos x-\sin x) \quad ...(2)$$

Solution is $y=$ C.F. + P.I.

$\Rightarrow \quad y=e^{2x}(k_1 \cos 2x+k_2 \sin 2x) + e^x (2 \cos x-\sin x)$

9. $f_1 = \sin(x+\theta) = \sin x\cdot\cos\theta + \sin\theta\cdot\cos x$

$f_2 = \cos(x+\theta) = \cos x\cdot\cos\theta - \sin x\cdot\sin\theta$

i.e. $\begin{bmatrix}\sin(x+\theta)\\ \cos(x+\theta)\end{bmatrix} = \begin{bmatrix}\cos\theta & \sin\theta\\ -\sin\theta & \cos\theta\end{bmatrix}\begin{bmatrix}\sin x\\ \cos x\end{bmatrix}$

i.e. Both are connected are by non-singular matrix.

i.e. $\sin(x+\theta)$ and $\cos(x+\theta)$ also span W.

i.e. It also form a basis for W.

21. $\because x_1, x_2 \ldots x_n$ are L.I.

so, $a_1x_1 + a_2x_2 + \ldots + a_nx_n = 0$

and $T(a_1x_1 + a_2x_2 + \ldots + a_nx_n) = T(0) = 0$

i.e., T is 1 – 1

$\therefore a_1T(x_1) + a_2T(x_2) + \ldots + a_nT(x_n) = 0$

$a_1Tx_1 + a_1Tx_2 + \ldots + a_nTx_n = 0$

for $\quad a_1 = a_2 = \ldots = a_n = 0$

Hence $Tx_1, Tx_2, \ldots Tx_n$ are also L.I.

24. Let C be $xi+yj+zk$

$\Rightarrow$ Bisector of C and $3i+4j$

$$= \frac{C+3i+4j}{2} = -i+j-k$$

$\Rightarrow (x+3)i+(y+4)j+zk=-2i+2j-2k$

$\Rightarrow x+3=-2\,;y+4=2\,;z=-2$

$\Rightarrow x=-5, y=-2, z=-2$

$\Rightarrow$ unit vector along $\vec{C}=\dfrac{-5\vec{i}-2\vec{j}-2\vec{k}}{\sqrt{33}}$

$\Rightarrow C=-5i-2j-2k.$

27. $T(p)(x) = p'(x)-\int_0^x p(t)\,dt$

Now for null space of T, $T(p)(x) = 0$.

or $p'(x)-\int_0^x p(t)\,dt = 0$ or $p'(x) = \int_0^x p(t)\,dt$

or $p''(x) = p(x) \Rightarrow p(x) = 0$.

i.e. null space of T has dimension = 0.

30. $\left|\lim_{n\to p}\frac{U_{n+1}}{U_n}\right| = \left|\lim_{n\to\infty}\frac{(n+1)\,(n)^n}{(n+1)^{n+1}}x\right|$

$$= \left|\lim_{n\to\infty}\frac{x}{\left(1+\frac{1}{n}\right)^n}\right| = \left|\frac{x}{e}\right| < 1$$

$\Rightarrow |x| < e \quad \Rightarrow \quad -e < x < e$

At $x = -e$ $\; e^n\Sigma(-1)^n\, n!/n^n$ is divergent

At $x = e$ $\; \Sigma n!/n^n\, e^n$ is divergent

So $|x| < e$

32. $z = \tan u = \dfrac{x^3+y^3}{x-y}$ homogeneous function of degree 2

$$\Rightarrow x\frac{\partial z}{\partial x} + y\frac{\partial z}{\partial y} = nz \quad \text{(Euler Theorem)}$$

$$\Rightarrow x\sec^2 u\frac{\partial u}{\partial x} + y\sec^2 u\frac{\partial u}{\partial y} = 2\tan u$$

$$\Rightarrow x\frac{\partial u}{\partial x} + y\frac{\partial u}{\partial y} = 2\sin u\cos u = \sin 2u \quad ...(i)$$

Taking p.d. of both sides w.r.t. x and y we get

$$x\frac{\partial^2 u}{\partial x^2} + \frac{\partial u}{\partial x} + \frac{\partial^2 u}{\partial x\partial y}y = 2\cos 2u\frac{\partial u}{\partial x} \quad ...(ii)$$

$$x\frac{\partial^2 u}{\partial x\partial y} + y\frac{\partial^2 u}{\partial y^2} + \frac{\partial u}{\partial y} = 2\cos 2u\frac{\partial u}{\partial y} \quad ...(iii)$$

$(2)\times(x)+(3)\times(y)$

$$\Rightarrow R + \left(x\frac{\partial u}{\partial x} + y\frac{\partial u}{\partial y}\right) = 2\cos 2u\left(x\frac{\partial u}{\partial x} + y\frac{\partial u}{\partial y}\right)$$

$$\Rightarrow R = (2\cos 2u - 1)\sin 2u$$

$$= \sin 2u\,(1 - 4\sin^2 u)$$

35. A.E. $m^2+4=0 \Rightarrow m = \pm 2i$

C.F. $= y = c_1\cos 2x + c_2\sin 2x$

$$\text{Wronskian } w = \begin{vmatrix} y_1 & y_2 \\ y_1^1 & y_2^1 \end{vmatrix}$$

$$= \begin{vmatrix} \cos 2x & \sin 2x \\ -2\sin 2x & 2\cos 2x \end{vmatrix} = 2$$

$$\text{when P.I} = -\cos 2x\int\frac{\sin 2x.\sec^2 2x}{2}dx + \sin 2x\int\frac{\cos 2x.\sec^2 2x}{2}dx$$

$$= -\frac{\cos 2x}{2}.\frac{\sec 2x}{2} + \frac{\sin 2x}{2}\frac{1}{2}\log(\sin 2x + \tan 2x)$$

$$= -\frac{1}{4} + \frac{1}{4}\sin 2x\log(\sec 2x + \tan 2x)$$

$\therefore$ Complete sol. = C.F + P.I.

49. Clearly the rank of the given system of equations at maximum is equal to 3. Which is less than the number of variables (4). Hence the system will have infinite number of solution.

54. If speed of motor boat = V

then actual velocity = (V – 10)

hence consumption of petrol (P) = $\dfrac{(V-10)}{V^3}$

Now $\quad P = \dfrac{1}{V^2} - \dfrac{10}{V^3}$

$$\therefore \quad \frac{dP}{dV} = \frac{-2}{V^3} = \frac{-2}{V^3} + \frac{30}{V^4} = 0$$

$$\Rightarrow \quad V = 15 \text{ km/hr.}$$

i.e. most economical speed = 15 km/hr.

55.
$$(T-CI)x = T(x) - CI(x)$$
$$= Cx - Cx = 0$$
$$\Rightarrow \quad |T-CI| = 0$$
$$\Rightarrow \quad r(T-CI) \neq 3$$

59. By Green's theorem

$$\int_C Pdx + Qdy = \iint_S\left(\frac{\partial Q}{\partial x} - \frac{\partial P}{\partial y}\right)dxdy$$

$$\Rightarrow \int\left[(2xy^3+y)dx + (3x^2y^2+2x)dy\right]$$

$$= 4\int_0^1\int_0^{\sqrt{1-x^2}}[(6xy^2+2)-(6xy^2+1)]dy\,dx$$

$$= 4\int_0^1\int_0^{\sqrt{1-x^2}}dy\,dx = 4\int_0^1\sqrt{1-x^2}\,dx$$

$$= 4\cdot\left[\frac{x\sqrt{1-x^2}}{2} + \frac{1}{2}\sin^{-1}x\right]_0^1$$

$$= 4\cdot\frac{1}{2}\cdot\frac{\pi}{2} = \pi$$

60. Since f' is bounded on $[a, b]$, therefore there exists K such that

$|f'[(x)| \leq K, \forall x \in [a, b]$

Let P $= \{a = x_0, x_1, x_2, \ldots x_n = b\}$ be any partition of $[a, b]$

$$\therefore \sum_i |f(x_i) - f(x_{i-1})| = \sum_i (x_i - x_{i-1})|f'(\xi)|$$

$\in\,]a, b[\leq K(b-a)$

$\Rightarrow V(f, a, b)$ is finite and therefore f is of bounded variation.

Note : Boundedness of f' is a sufficient condition. It is not necessary.

SET–16

CSIR–UGC (NET) MATHEMATICAL SCIENCES

PART-C

1. Let $\mathbf{U}$ be the subspace of $\mathbf{R}^3$ spanned by $u = (1, 1, 1)$ and $v = (1, 1, -1)$. The orthonormal basis of $\mathbf{U}$ obtained by the Gram-Schmidt process on the ordered basis (u, v) of $\mathbf{U}$ is

A. $\left\{\left(\frac{1}{\sqrt{3}}, \frac{1}{\sqrt{3}}, \frac{1}{\sqrt{3}}\right), \left(\frac{2}{3}, \frac{2}{3}, \frac{-4}{3}\right)\right\}$

B. $\{(1, 1, 0), (1, 0, 1)\}$

C. $\left\{\left(\frac{1}{\sqrt{3}}, \frac{1}{\sqrt{3}}, \frac{1}{\sqrt{3}}\right), \left(\frac{1}{\sqrt{6}}, \frac{1}{\sqrt{6}}, \frac{-2}{\sqrt{6}}\right)\right\}$

D. $\left\{\left(\frac{1}{\sqrt{3}}, \frac{1}{\sqrt{3}}, \frac{1}{\sqrt{3}}\right), \left(\frac{2}{\sqrt{6}}, \frac{-1}{\sqrt{6}}, \frac{-1}{\sqrt{6}}\right)\right\}$

2. The residue of $f(z) = \dfrac{z^3}{(z-1)^4(z-2)(z-3)}$ at $z = 1$ is

A. $\frac{51}{16}$ B. $\frac{101}{16}$

C. $\frac{151}{16}$ D. $\frac{201}{16}$

3. The singular solution of the differential equation

$$y = px + p^3, \left(p \equiv \frac{dy}{dx}\right) \text{ is}$$

A. $4y^3 + 27x^3 = 0$ B. $4x^2 + 27y^3 = 0$

C. $4y^2 + 27x^3 = 0$ D. $4x^3 + 27y^2 = 0$

4. A student appears for tests I, II and III. The student is successful if he passes either in tests I and II or I and III. The probabilities of the student passing in tests I, II and III are p, q and $\frac{1}{2}$ respectively. If the probability that the student is successful is $\frac{1}{2}$, then

A. $p = q = 1$ B. $p = q = \frac{1}{2}$

C. $p = 1, q = 0$ D. $p = 1, q = \frac{1}{2}$

5. For the fastest convergence of the method $x_{n+1} = \dfrac{ax_n - x_n^2 + 1}{a + n}$ the value of a is (given α is exact root)

A. $a = \frac{1}{\alpha}$ B. $a = \frac{2}{\alpha^2}$

C. $a = \frac{1}{\alpha^3}$ D. $a = \frac{2}{\alpha^3}$

6. A 6-faced fair dice is rolled repeatedly till 1 appears for the first time. The probability that the dice is rolled for even number of times is

A. $\frac{1}{6}$ B. $\frac{5}{36}$

C. $\frac{6}{11}$ D. $\frac{5}{11}$

7. Let $w = f(z)$ be the bilinear transformation that maps -1, 0 and 1 to $-i$, 1 and i respectively. Then $f(1 - i)$ equals

A. $-1 + 2i$ B. $2i$

C. $-2 + i$ D. $-1 + i$

8. Suppose G is a group of 53, then which of the following is true

A. G is not abelian.

B. G has no subgroup other than $\{e\}$ and G.

C. There is a group H of order 53 which is not isomorphic of G.

D. G is a subgroup of a group of order 54.

9. Consider the matrix $M = \begin{bmatrix} 1 & 0 & -1 \\ 0 & 1 & 0 \\ 1 & 1 & -1 \end{bmatrix}$ and let S_m be the set of 3×3 matrices N such that MN = 0, then the dimension of the real vector space S_m is equal to

A. 0
B. 1
C. 2
D. 3

10. The integrating factor of $\cos^2 x \dfrac{dy}{dx} + y = \tan x$ is

A. $e^{\sec x}$
B. $e^{\cos x}$
C. $e^{\cot x}$
D. $e^{\tan x}$

11. A ring $(R, +, \cdot)$ whose all elements are idempotent is

A. always abelian
B. an integral domain
C. a division ring
D. a field

12. The function $f(x) = \int_2^x \dfrac{(t-2)(t-3)}{t-1} dt$ is strictly decreasing on the set

A. $(-\infty, 1) \cup (2, 3)$
B. $(1, 2) \cup (3, \infty)$
C. $(1, 3)$
D. $R - (1, 2)$

13. The solution of the partial differential equation $2\dfrac{\partial z}{\partial x} + y\dfrac{\partial z}{\partial y} = z$ for initial data curve $(x_0, y_0, z_0) = (S, S^2, S)$; $1 \le S \le 2$ is

A. $z^2 = y\exp\left\{\dfrac{(xy - z)}{2z}\right\}$

B. $z^2 = x\exp\left\{\dfrac{(xz - y)}{2z}\right\}$

C. $z^2 = y\exp\left\{\dfrac{(xz - y)}{2z}\right\}$

D. $z^2 = x\exp\left\{\dfrac{(yz - x)}{2z}\right\}$.

14. In $\mathbf{R}^2$ with usual topology, the set $U = \{(x, -y) \in \mathbf{R}^2 : x = 0, 1, -1 \text{ and } y \in N\}$ is

A. neither closed nor bounded
B. closed but not bounded
C. bounded but not closed
D. closed and bounded

15 If H and K are subgroups of G then

A. HK is a subgroup but $H \cap K$ may not be a subgroup.
B. $H \cap K$ is a subgroup but HK may not be a subgroup
C. Either (A) or (B)
D. None of these

16. Which of the following is not correct?

A. Break–even models are the examples of stocastic models
B. OR replaces management by personality
C. OR is concerned with optimization.
D. OR is a bunch of mathematical techniques

17. Consider the mappings

1. $T : \mathbf{R}^2 \to \mathbf{R}^2 : T(x, y, z) = (x + 1, y + z)$
2. $T : \mathbf{R}^2 \to \mathbf{R} : T(x, y) = (xy)$
3. $T : \mathbf{R}^3 \to \mathbf{R}^2 : T(x, y, z) = (|x|, 0)$

Which of the above are linear transformations?

A. 1, 2 and 3
B. 1 and 2 only
C. 2 and 3 only
D. None of these

18. Let a primal linear programming problem admit an optimal solution. Then the corresponding dual problem

A. does not have a feasible solution
B. has a feasible solution but does not have any optimal solution
C. does not have a convex feasible region
D. has an optimal solution

19. The sum to infinity of the series $\dfrac{2}{1.2.3} + \dfrac{3}{3.4.5} + \dfrac{4}{5.6.7} + \ldots\ldots$ is equal to

A. $\sqrt{\pi}$
B. $\log 2 - \dfrac{1}{6}$
C. $e - \dfrac{1}{2}$
D. None of the above

20. The series $\sum \dfrac{1}{4}\left\{1 + (-1)^{n+1}(2n+1)\right\}$ is

A. Cgt
B. Dgt
C. Oscillating infinitely
D. Oscillating finitely

21. Let P be a matrix of order $m \times n$ and Q be a matrix of order $n \times p$. If rank (P) = n and rank (Q) = p, then rank (PQ) is

A. n B. p
C. np D. $n + p$

22. Let $\vec{u} = (ae^x \sin y - 4x)\hat{i} + (2y + e^x \cos y)\hat{j} + az\hat{k}$, where a is a constant. If the line integral $\oint_C \vec{u}.d\vec{r}$ over every closed curve C is zero, then a is equal to

A. −2 B. −1
C. 0 D. 1

23. If f be an entire function such that $|f'(z)| \le |z|$, then which one of the following statements(s) is/are correct?

(*i*) $f(z)$ is unbounded
(*ii*) f has pole of order 2 at $z = \infty$
(*iii*) $f(-z) = f(z)\ \forall\ z \in$ G

Select the correct statement:

A. (*i*) & (*ii*) are correct
B. (*ii*) & (*iii*) are correct
C. (*i*) & (*iii*) are correct
D. All are correct

24. Determine the types of the following differential equation $\frac{d^2y}{dx^2} + \sin(x + y) = \sin x$

A. Linear, homogeneous
B. Nonlinear, homogeneous
C. Linear, non-homogeneous
D. Nonlinear, non-homogeneous

25. The given integral equation $u(x) = x + \int_0^x e^{xt}\, u(t)\, dt$.

A. Linear, Fredholm, non-homogeneous, integral with degenerate kernel and of 1st kind.
B. Linear, non-homogeneous, Volterra integral equation with degenerate kernel and of 1st kind.
C. Linear, homogeneous, Volterra integral equation with non-degenerate kernel and of 2nd kind.
D. Linear non-homogeneous, Volterra integral equation with non-degenerate kernel and of 2nd kind.

26. Let G be the additive group Z_8 of the residue classes modulo 8. Then what is the order of the residue class $\overline{3}$ in G?

A. 8 B. 6
C. 4 D. 2

27. Let T : $\mathbf{R}^2 \to \mathbf{R}^2$ be a linear transformation such that $T\left(\begin{pmatrix}0\\1\end{pmatrix}\right) = \begin{pmatrix}1\\2\end{pmatrix}$ and $T\left(\begin{pmatrix}0\\1\end{pmatrix}\right) = \begin{pmatrix}2\\1\end{pmatrix}$ what is $T\left(\begin{pmatrix}1\\1\end{pmatrix}\right)$ equal to?

A. $\begin{pmatrix}1\\2\end{pmatrix}$ B. $\begin{pmatrix}2\\1\end{pmatrix}$
C. $\begin{pmatrix}3\\3\end{pmatrix}$ D. $\begin{pmatrix}2\\2\end{pmatrix}$

28. Let $y_1(x)$ and $y_2(x)$ be twice differentiable functions on an interval I satisfying the differential equations $\frac{dy_1}{dx} - y_1 - y_2 = e^x$ and $2\frac{dy_1}{dx} + \frac{dy_2}{dx} - 6y_1 = 0$. Then $y_1(x)$ is

A. $C_1e^{-2x} + C_2e^{3x} - \frac{1}{4}e^x$
B. $C_1e^{2x} + C_2e^{-3x} + \frac{1}{4}e^x$
C. $C_1e^{2x} + C_2e^{-3x} - \frac{1}{4}e^x$
D. $C_1e^{-2x} + C_2e^{3x} + \frac{1}{4}e^x$

29. Let G be a group of order 9 and $\phi(x) = x^{21}$, $x \in G$, then ϕ is

A. not one-one
B. not onto
C. not a homomorphism
D. one-one, onto and a homomorphism.

30. The conjugate (also called symmetric) point of $1 + i$ with respect to the circle $|z - 1| = 2$ is

A. $1 - i$ B. $1 + 4i$

C. $1 + 2i$ D. $-1 - i$

All other pt lie outside the circle

31. If α, β are the roots of the equations $ax^2 + bx + c = 0$, then

$$\lim_{x\to\alpha} \frac{1-\cos(ax^2+bx+c)}{(x-\alpha)^2} \text{ is equal to}$$

A. 0 B. $\frac{a}{2}(\alpha-\beta)^2$

C. $\frac{-a^2}{2}(\alpha-\beta)^2$ D. $\frac{a^2}{2}(\alpha-\beta)^2$

32. If Δ and ∇ are the forward and backward difference operator respectively, then $\Delta - \nabla$ is equal to

A. $-\Delta\nabla$ B. $\Delta\nabla$

C. $\Delta + \nabla$ D. $\frac{\Delta}{\nabla}$

33. A bead slides on a smooth rod which is rotating about one end in a vertical plane with uniform angular velocity w. If g denotes the acceleration due to gravity, then the Lagrange equation of motion is

A. $\ddot{r} = rw^2 - g\sin wt$

B. $\ddot{r} = rw^2 - g\cos wt$

C. $\ddot{r} = -g\sin wt$

D. $\ddot{r} = g\cos wt$

34. A second degree polynomial passes through (0, 1), (1, 3), (2, 7) and (3, 13). The polynomial is

A. $x^2 + 5x + 4$ B. $x^2 + 2x + 1$

C. $x^2 + x + 1$ D. None of these

35. If $J_n(x)$ and $Y_n(x)$ denote Bessel functions of order n of the first and the second kind, then the general solution of the differential equation $x\frac{d^2y}{dx^2} - \frac{dy}{dx} + xy = 0$ is given by

A. $y(x) = \alpha xJ_1(x) + \beta x\, Y_1(x)$

B. $y(x) = \alpha J_1(x) + \beta Y_1(x)$

C. $y(x) = \alpha J_0(x) + \beta Y_0(x)$

D. $y(x) = \alpha xJ_0(x) + \beta x\, Y_0(x)$

36. Independent trials consisting of rolling a fair dice are performed. The probability that 2 appears before 3 or 5 is

A. $\frac{1}{2}$ B. $\frac{1}{3}$

C. $\frac{1}{4}$ D. $\frac{1}{5}$

37. The supremum and infimum of the set $\left\{m+\frac{1}{n} : m, n \in N\right\}$ are respectively

A. 1, 0 B. does not exist, 2

C. does not exist, 1 D. none of these

38. Which one is true?

A. Every quotient group of a cyclic group is cyclic and the converse is also true

B. Every quotient group of a group is abelian and the converse is not true.

C. Every quotient group of a cyclic group is cyclic and the converse is not true

D. None of these

39. The number of basic solution to the system

$x_1 + 2x_2 + 10x_3 + 4x_4 = 5$

$x_1 + x_2 + 5x_3 + 4x_4 = -8$

is

A. 0 B. 4

C. 6 D. Infinite

40. The set of all limit points of the sequence $1, \frac{1}{2}, \frac{1}{4}, \frac{3}{4}, \frac{1}{8}, \frac{3}{8}, \frac{5}{8}, \frac{7}{8}, \frac{1}{16}, \frac{3}{16}, \frac{5}{16}, \frac{7}{16}, \frac{9}{16}, \ldots$ is

A. [0, 1]

B. (0, 1]

C. the set of all rational numbers in [0, 1]

D. the set of all rational numbers in [0, 1] of the form $\frac{m}{2^n}$ where m and n are integers

41. The series $\sum_{n=1}^{\infty} \frac{z^n}{n\sqrt{n+1}}$, $|z|$ £ 1 is

A. uniformly but not absolutely convergent.

B. uniformaly and absolutely convergent.

C. absolutely convergent but not uniformly convergent.

D. covergent but no uniformaly convergent.

42. For the differential equation

$$x^2(1-x)\frac{d^2y}{dx^2}+x\frac{dy}{dx}+y=0$$

A. $x = 1$ is an ordinary point
B. $x = 1$ is a regular singular point
C. $x = 0$ is an irregular singular point
D. $x = 0$ is an ordinary point

43. Complete integral for the PDE $z = px + qy - \sin pq$ is
A. $z = ax + qy - \sin aq$
B. $z = ax + by - \sin ab$
C. $z = ax - by + \sin ab$
D. $z = bx + ay + \sin ab$

44. Let H be a group of order 23. What is the number of subgroups of H?
A. 2^{23}
B. 23!
C. 2
D. 1

45. In case of normal distribution, the value of maximum probability and the point at where maximum probability occur are

A. $f(x) = \frac{1}{\sigma\sqrt{2\pi}}e^{-\frac{1}{2}}$; $x = \mu + \sigma$

B. $f(x) = \frac{1}{\sigma\sqrt{2\pi}}$; $x = \mu$

C. $f(x) = \frac{1}{\sigma\sqrt{2\pi}}e^{-\frac{1}{2}}$; $x = \mu$

D. $f(x) = \frac{1}{\sigma\sqrt{2\pi}}$; $x = \sigma$

46. The area common to the curves $y^2 = x$ and $x^2 = y$ is
A. 0
B. 1/3
C. 2/3
D. 1

47. Consider the differential equation $(x + y + 1)\,dx + (2x + 2y + 1)\,dy = 0$. Which of the following statements is true?
A. The differential equation is linear
B. The differential equation is exact
C. e^{x+y} is an integrating factor of the differential equation
D. A suitable substitution transforms the differentiable equation to the variables separable form

48. A coin is tossed $(m + n)$ times $(m > n)$ then the probability of at least m consecutive heads is

A. $\frac{n+2}{2^m}$
B. $\frac{n+2}{2^{m+1}}$
C. $\frac{n-2}{2^m}$
D. $\frac{n-2}{2^{m+1}}$

49. The system of equations

$$x - y + 3z = 4$$
$$x + z = 2$$
$$x + y - z = 0$$

has
A. a unique solution
B. finitely many solutions
C. infinitely many solution
D. no solution

50. Let R be a ring. Then the necessary condition for which an ideal I of R is Principle Ideal is
A. R is commutative ring with unity
B. R is commutative ring
C. R is ring with unity
D. R is without zero divisor

51. A necessary and sufficient condition for a basic feasible solution to a minimization L.P.P. to be an optimum is that (for all j).
A. $z_j - c_j \geq 0$
B. $z_j - c_j \leq 0$
C. $z_j - c_j = 0$
D. $z_j - c_j > 0$ or $z_j - c_j < 0$

52. $f(x) = x^2 \cos\frac{1}{x}$ if $x > 0$
$= 0$ if $x \leq 0$

Then is [0, 1]
A. $f(x)$ is of bounded variation and $f'(x)$ exists
B. $f(x)$ is of bounded variation and $f'\left(\frac{1}{2}\right)$ does not exists
C. $f(x)$ is not of bounded variation and $f(x)$ is continuous
D. $f(x)$ is discontinuous at $x = \frac{2}{\pi}$

53. Consider the vector field $\vec{F} = (ax + y + a)\hat{i} + \hat{j} - (x + y)\hat{k}$, where a is a constant. If $\vec{F}.\text{curl}\ \vec{F} = 0$, then the value of a is

A. –1 B. 0

C. 1 D. $\frac{3}{2}$

54. Given the sequence $\left(\frac{n}{n+1}\right)_{n=1}^{\infty}$ and an arbitrarily small positive number $\in$. Then the value of a positive integer N such that $\left|\frac{n}{n+1}-1\right| < \in$ when ever $n \geq N$ must satisfy the relation

A. $N \leq \left(\frac{1}{\in}-1\right)$ B. $N < \left(\frac{1}{\in}-1\right)$

C. $N > \left(\frac{1}{\in}-1\right)$ D. $N \geq \left(\frac{1}{\in}-1\right)$

55. The differential equation of the system of circles touching the x-axis at origin is

A. $(x^2 - y^2)\frac{dy}{dx} - 2xy = 0$

B. $(x^2 - y^2)\frac{dy}{dx} + 2xy = 0$

C. $(x^2 + y^2)\frac{dy}{dx} - 2xy = 0$

D. $(x^2 + y^2)\frac{dy}{dx} + 2xy = 0$

56. Integral surface of $x^2p + y^2q = -z^2$ which passes through hyperbola $xy = x + y$, $z = 1$ is given by

A. $xy - 2yz + xz = 3xyz$

B. $yz + 2xy + xz = 3xyz$

C. $xy + 2zx + zy = 3xyz$

D. None of these

57. The general solution of the differential equation $p(y - z) + (x - y)q = z - x$ is given by

A. $f(x^2 + 2yz, x + y + z) = 0$

B. $f(y^2 + 2xz, x + y + z) = 0$

C. $f(z^2 + 2xy, x + y + z) = 0$

D. None of the these

58. In M/M/1 queueing system service time is

A. Exponentially distributed *r.v.*

B. A Poisson process

C. Arbitrarily distributed

D. None of these

59. Let M = $\begin{bmatrix} 1 & 0 & 0 \\ 0 & \cos\theta & -\sin\theta \\ 0 & \sin\theta & \cos\theta \end{bmatrix}$ where $0 < \theta < \frac{\pi}{2}$. Let $\mathbf{U} = \{u \in R^3 : Mu^t = u^t\}$. Then the dimension of $\mathbf{U}$ is

A. 0 B. 1

C. 2 D. 3

60. Let T be a linear transformation from $\mathbf{R}^3 \to \mathbf{R}^2$ defined by $T(x, y, z) = (x + y, y - z)$. Then the matrix of T with respect to the ordered bases {(1, 1, 1), (1, –1, 0), (0, 1, 0)} and {(1, 1), (1, 0)} is

A. $\begin{bmatrix} -2 & 0 & 1 \\ 1 & 1 & -1 \end{bmatrix}$ B. $\begin{bmatrix} 0 & -1 & 1 \\ 2 & 1 & 0 \end{bmatrix}$

C. $\begin{bmatrix} 2 & 1 \\ 0 & -1 \\ 1 & 1 \end{bmatrix}$ D. $\begin{bmatrix} 0 & 2 \\ -1 & 1 \\ 1 & 0 \end{bmatrix}$

ANSWERS

1	2	3	4	5	6	7	8	9	10
C	B	C	C	D	D	A	B	D	D
11	**12**	**13**	**14**	**15**	**16**	**17**	**18**	**19**	**20**
A	A	C	C	B	A	D	D	D	C
21	**22**	**23**	**24**	**25**	**26**	**27**	**28**	**29**	**30**
B	B	D	D	D	A	C	C	D	C

31	32	33	34	35	36	37	38	39	40
D	D	B	C	A	B	C	C	C	A
41	**42**	**43**	**44**	**45**	**46**	**47**	**48**	**49**	**50**
B	B	B	C	B	B	D	B	C	C
51	**52**	**53**	**54**	**55**	**56**	**57**	**58**	**59**	**60**
D	A	C	C	A	B	A	A	D	B

SOME SELECTED EXPLANATORY ANSWERS

1. First we normalize u *i.e.* we get

$$u_1 = \frac{u}{\|u\|} = \frac{(1,1,1)}{\sqrt{3}} = \left(\frac{1}{\sqrt{3}}, \frac{1}{\sqrt{3}}, \frac{1}{\sqrt{3}}\right).$$

Next we set,

$$w_2 = v - < v, u_1 > u_1$$

$$= (1,1,-1) - \frac{1}{\sqrt{3}}\left(\frac{1}{\sqrt{3}}, \frac{1}{\sqrt{3}}, \frac{1}{\sqrt{3}}\right)(1, 1, -1)$$

$$- \left(\frac{1}{3}, \frac{1}{3}, \frac{1}{3}\right)$$

$$= \left(\frac{2}{3}, \frac{2}{3}, \frac{-4}{3}\right)$$

i.e. Now we normalize

$$w_2 = \frac{w_2}{\|w_2\|} = \frac{\left(\frac{2}{3}, \frac{2}{3}, \frac{-4}{3}\right)}{\frac{2\sqrt{6}}{3}} = \left(\frac{1}{\sqrt{6}}, \frac{1}{\sqrt{6}}, \frac{-2}{\sqrt{6}}\right)$$

i.e. required orthonormal basis of V are

$$\left\{\left(\frac{1}{\sqrt{3}}, \frac{1}{\sqrt{3}}, \frac{1}{\sqrt{3}}\right), \left(\frac{1}{\sqrt{6}}, \frac{1}{\sqrt{6}}, \frac{-2}{\sqrt{6}}\right)\right\}.$$

3. The given differential equation is

$$y = px + p^3 \qquad ...(1)$$

differentiating partially with respect to p, we get

$$0 = x + 3p^2$$

or, $p^2 = -\dfrac{x}{3}$

or, $y = p(x + p^2)$

or, $y^2 = p^2 (x + p^2)^2$

or, $y^2 = -\dfrac{x}{3}\left(x - \dfrac{x}{3}\right)^2$

or, $y^2 = -\dfrac{x}{3}\left(\dfrac{2x}{3}\right)^2$

or, $y^2 = -\dfrac{4x^3}{27}$

or, $4x^3 + 27y^2 = 0.$

7. Using cross ratio property, if $f(1 - i) = w$ then

$$\frac{(w+i)(1-i)}{(-i-1)(i-w)} = \frac{(1-i+1)(0-1)}{(-1-0)(1-1+i)}$$

$$\Rightarrow \quad \frac{w+i}{w-i} = \frac{(2-i)(1+i)}{i(1-i)} = \frac{3+i}{1+i}$$

or, $\dfrac{2w}{2i} = \dfrac{4+2i}{2} = 2+i$

$\Rightarrow \quad w = -1 + 2i.$

19. The given series is

$$\sum \frac{(n+1)}{(2n-1)\,2n\,(2n+1)}$$

$$= \sum \frac{2n+1-n}{(2n-1)\,2n\,(2n+1)}$$

$$= \sum \frac{1}{(2n-1)(2n)} - \frac{1}{2}\sum \frac{1}{(2n-1)(2n+1)}$$

$$= \sum \frac{1}{2n(2n-1)} - \frac{1}{2}\sum \frac{1}{(2n-1)(2n+1)}$$

$$= \sum\left(\frac{1}{(2n-1)} - \frac{1}{2n}\right) - \frac{1}{4}\left(\sum \frac{1}{2n-1} - \frac{1}{2n+1}\right)$$

$$= \left(1 - \frac{1}{2} + \frac{1}{3} - \frac{1}{4} + ...\right) - \frac{1}{4}\left(1 - \frac{1}{3} + \frac{1}{3} - \frac{1}{5} + ...\right)$$

$$= \left(\log 2 - \frac{1}{4}\right)$$

22. $\because \oint \vec{u}.d\vec{r} = 0$

$\Rightarrow \quad \vec{u} = \nabla \text{ grad (V)}$

$$\Rightarrow \qquad \frac{\partial V}{\partial x} = ae^x \sin y - 4x$$

$$\Rightarrow \qquad V = ae^x \sin y - 2x^2 + f_1(y, z)$$

$$\frac{\partial V}{\partial y} = 2y + e^x \cos y$$

$$\Rightarrow \qquad V = y^2 - e^x \sin y + f_2(x, z)$$

$$\frac{\partial V}{\partial z} = az \Rightarrow V = \frac{az^2}{2} + f_3(x, y)$$

all the above three represent same scalar function

hence $\qquad a = -1.$

28. As $\frac{dy_1}{dx} - y_1 - y_2 = e^x$

$$\Rightarrow \frac{d^2y_1}{dx^2} - \frac{dy_1}{dx} - \frac{dy_2}{dx} = e^x$$

$$\Rightarrow \frac{d^2y_1}{dx^2} - \frac{dy_1}{dx} - \left(6y_1 - 2\frac{dy_1}{dx}\right) = e^x$$

$$\Rightarrow \frac{d^2y_1}{dx^2} + \frac{dy_1}{dx} - 6y_1 = e^x$$

C.F. is $m^2 + m - 6 = 0$

$\Rightarrow (m+3)(m-2) = 0$

$\Rightarrow m = 2, -3$

So, $y = c_1e^{2x} + c_2e^{-3x}$

Also, P.I. is $\frac{1}{D^2 + D - 6}e^x = -\frac{1}{4}e^x$

$$\Rightarrow y_1 = c_1e^{2x} + c_2e^{-3x} - \frac{1}{4}e^x.$$

31. Since, α, β are the roots of the equation $ax^2 + bx + c = 0$.

Hence $\quad \alpha + \beta = \frac{-b}{a} \quad \& \quad \alpha\beta = \frac{c}{a}.$

Now, $\lim\limits_{x\to\alpha} \frac{1-\cos(ax^2+bx+c)}{(x-\alpha)^2}$

$$= \lim_{x\to\alpha} \frac{2\sin^2\left(\frac{ax^2+bx+c}{2}\right)}{(x-\alpha)^2}$$

$$= \lim_{x\to\alpha} \frac{2\sin^2\left\{\frac{a(x-\alpha)(x-\beta)}{2}\right\}}{(x-\alpha)^2}$$

$$= \lim_{x\to\alpha} \frac{2\cdot\left\{\frac{a^2(x-\alpha)^2(x-\beta)^2}{2^2}\right\}}{(x-\alpha)^2}$$

$$= \lim_{x\to\alpha} \frac{2\cdot a^2(x-\alpha)^2(x-\beta)^2}{4(x-\alpha)^2}$$

$$= \frac{a^2}{2}(\alpha-\beta)^2.$$

34. The difference table is given below :

x	y	Δy	$\Delta^2 y$	$\Delta^3 y$
0	1			
		2		
1	3		2	
		4		0
2	7		2	
		6		
3	13			

In Newton's formula for interpolation
$a = 0, h = 1; f(a + hx) = f(x)$

$$\therefore \; y = f(x) = 1 + x(2) + \frac{x(x-1)}{2}(2) + \frac{x(x-1)(x-2)}{6}(0) + \ldots$$

$$= 1 + 2x + x(x-1) = x^2 + x + 1$$

40. By definition of limit point, the given sequence contains all the points of the interval [0,1].

43. Clairants form so its complete equ. is obtained by merely replacing p and q by a and b respectively

$\therefore$ complete integral is

$$z = ax + by - \sin(ab)$$

44. As $O(H) = 23$ which is a prime number.

i.e. It cannot have proper subgroup.

i.e. only subgroup of H are $\{0\}$ and H itself.

i.e. No. of subgroup of H = 2.

46. $y^2 = x$ and $x^2 = y$ intersects at $x^4 = x$

$\Rightarrow \quad x(x^3 - 1) = 0 \Rightarrow x = 0, 1,$

so, common area $= \int_0^1 (y_1 - y_2)dx$

$$= \int_0^1 (\sqrt{x} - x^2)dx = 2\frac{x^{3/2}}{3} - \frac{x^3}{3}\Big|_0^1 = \frac{1}{3}.$$

47. $(x + y + 1) + (2x + 2y + 1)\dfrac{dy}{dx} = 0$

put $\quad x + y = z$

$$\Rightarrow \quad \frac{dz}{dx} = \frac{dy}{dx} + 1$$

$$\Rightarrow (z+1) + (2z+1)\left(\frac{dz}{dx} - 1\right) = 0$$

$$\Rightarrow \quad \frac{dz}{dx}(2z+1) = z$$

$$\Rightarrow \quad \frac{zdx}{dz} = (2z+1)$$

or, $$dx = \left(2 + \frac{1}{z}\right)dz$$

i.e. both variables reduced into separable form.

49. The augmented matrix of above system of equations are given by,

$$[A : B] = \left[\begin{array}{ccc|c} 1 & -1 & 3 & 4 \\ 1 & 0 & 1 & 2 \\ 1 & 1 & -1 & 0 \end{array}\right] \sim$$

$$\left[\begin{array}{ccc|c} 1 & -1 & 3 & 4 \\ 0 & 1 & -2 & -2 \\ 0 & 2 & -4 & -4 \end{array}\right] \sim \left[\begin{array}{ccc|c} 1 & -1 & 3 & 4 \\ 0 & 1 & -2 & 0 \\ 0 & 0 & 0 & 0 \end{array}\right]$$

i.e. rank of [A : B] = 2.

i.e. System can have infinitely many solutions.

53. Given $\quad \vec{F} = (ax + y + a)\hat{i} + \hat{j} - (x + y)\hat{k}$

Hence $\quad$ curl $\vec{F} = \begin{vmatrix} \hat{i} & \hat{j} & \hat{k} \\ \dfrac{\partial}{\partial x} & \dfrac{\partial}{\partial y} & \dfrac{\partial}{\partial z} \\ ax + y + a & 1 & -(x+y) \end{vmatrix}$

$$= -\hat{i} + \hat{j} - \hat{k}.$$

Hence $\quad \vec{F}.\text{curl}\vec{F} = -ax - y - a + 1 + x + y = 0$

$\Rightarrow \quad x(1 - a) = -(1 - a)$

As $\quad x \neq 0 \Rightarrow a = 1.$

60. The given linear transformation is

$$T(x, y, z) = (x + y, y - z)$$

Then $T(1, 1, 1) = (2, 0) = 0.(1, 1) + 2.(1, 0)$

$T(1, -1, 0) = (0, -1) = -1.(1, 1) + 1(1, 0)$

$T(0, 1, 0) = (1, 1) = 1(1, 1) + 0.(1, 0)$

Hence the matrix associated with T with respect to the given basis is $\begin{bmatrix} 0 & -1 & 1 \\ 2 & 1 & 0 \end{bmatrix}$.

SET–17

CSIR–UGC (NET) MATHEMATICAL SCIENCES

PART-C

1. The number of linearly independent eigenvectors of the matrix $\begin{bmatrix} 2 & 2 & 0 & 0 \\ 2 & 1 & 0 & 0 \\ 0 & 0 & 3 & 0 \\ 0 & 0 & 1 & 4 \end{bmatrix}$ is

A. 1 B. 2
C. 3 D. 4

2. The residue of $\dfrac{\phi(z)}{(z-a)^n}$ at $z = a$ is

A. $f^n(a)$ B. $\dfrac{\phi^n(a)}{n}$
C. $\dfrac{\phi^n(a)}{n!}$ D. $\dfrac{\phi^{n-11}(a)}{(n-1)!}$

3. If $u_n = \sqrt{n+1} - \sqrt{n}$; $v_n = \sqrt{n^4+1} - n^2$ then

A. $\sum_{n=1}^{\infty} u_n$ converges but $\sum_{n=1}^{\infty} v_n$ diverges

B. $\sum_{n=1}^{\infty} u_n$ diverges but $\sum_{n=1}^{\infty} v_n$ converges

C. $\sum_{n=1}^{\infty} u_n$ and $\sum_{n=1}^{\infty} v_n$ both converges

D. $\sum_{n=1}^{\infty} u_n$ and $\sum_{n=1}^{\infty} v_n$ both diverges

4. The equation of the envelope of the family of curves represented by the general solution of the differential equation is called

A. complementary solution
B. particular solution
C. singular solution
D. none of these

5. Let G be a set of real number and * be an operation defined on G such that

$$\forall\, x, y \in G$$

$$x*y = \begin{cases} xy & x > 0 \\ x/y & x < 0, y \neq 0 \\ 0 & x = 0 \end{cases}$$

Then

A. * is associative but not binary operation
B. * is binary operation but not associative
C. * is associative but identity element not exist
D. None of these

6. In the Laurent series expansion of $f(z) = \dfrac{1}{z-1} - \dfrac{1}{z-2}$ valid in the region $|z| > 2$, the coefficient of $\dfrac{1}{z^2}$ is

A. –1 B. 0
C. 1 D. 2

7. Consider the Linear Programming Problem

Max. $z = x_1 + 5x_2 + 3x_3$

subject to $2x_1 - 3x_2 + 5x_3 \leq 3$

$3x_1 + 2x_3 \leq 5$

$x_1, x_2, x_3 \geq 0$

Then the dual of this Linear Programming Problem

A. has a feasible solution, but does not have a basic feasible solution
B. has a basic feasible solution
C. has infinite number of feasible solution
D. has no feasible solution

8. Three identical dice are rolled. The probability that the same number will appear on each of them is

A. $\frac{1}{6}$ B. $\frac{1}{36}$

C. $\frac{1}{18}$ D. $\frac{3}{28}$

9. The Newton-Raphson method is to be used to find the root of the equation $f(x) = 0$, where x_0 is the initial approximation and $f'(x)$ is the derivative of f. The method converges for

A. Always
B. Only if f is polynomial
C. Only if $f(x_0) < 0$
D. None of these

10. Functional $J = \int_0^{\pi/2} (y^2 - y'^2)\,dx$ has

A. Unique extremal if $y(0) = 0$, $y\left(\frac{\pi}{2}\right) = 1$.
B. Infinite extremal if $y(0) = 0$, $y(\pi) = 1$.
C. No extremal if $y(0) = 0$, $y(\pi) = 0$.
D. Infinite extremal if $y(0) = 0$, $y\left(\frac{\pi}{2}\right) = 1$.

11. Let $f(x) = 1$ if x is rational in [0, 1]
$= -1$ if x is irrational in [0, 1]
then is [0, 1]

A. $f(x)$ is continuous every where
B. $f(x)$ is Riemann integrable
C. $f(x)$ is not Riemann integrable
D. $f(x)$ is continous only at the irrationals

12. It is required to find the solution of the differential equation

$$2x(2+x)\frac{d^2y}{dx^2} + 2(3+x)\frac{dy}{dx} - xy = 0$$

around the point $x = 0$. The roots of the indicial equation are

A. $0, \frac{1}{2}$ B. 0, 2

C. $\frac{1}{2}, \frac{1}{2}$ D. $0, -\frac{1}{2}$

13. One of the solution of $\frac{dx}{x(x+y)} = \frac{dy}{-y(x+y)}$

$= \frac{dz}{-(x-y)(2x+2y+z)}$ is

A. $(x + y + z)(x + y)^2 = c$
B. $(x + y + z)^2 (x + y) = c$
C. $(x + y + z)(x + y) = c$
D. $\frac{(x+y+z)}{(x+y)} = c$

14. Let, E and F be two events such that 0 $(P(E)$ < 1 and $P(E/F) + P(E + F^C) = 1$. Then

A. E and F are mutually exclusive
B. $P(E^C/F) + P(E^C + F^C) = 1$
C. E and F are independent
D. $P(E/F) + P(E^C + P^C) = 1$

15. In Simpson's one-third rule the curve $y = f(x)$ is assumed to be a

A. circle B. parabola
C. hyperbola D. none of these

16. Given $f(x) = \begin{cases} x, & \text{when } 0 \le x < \frac{1}{2} \\ \frac{1}{2}, & \text{when } x = \frac{1}{2} \\ 1-x, & \text{when } \frac{1}{2} < x \le 1 \end{cases}$

and $G(x) = \left(x - \frac{1}{2}\right)^2$, $x \in R$

What is the area of the portion bounded between $G(x)$ and $f(x)$ and in the interval $\left[\frac{1}{2}, \frac{\sqrt{3}}{2}\right]$?

A. $\frac{\sqrt{3}}{4} - \frac{1}{3}$ B. $\frac{\sqrt{3}}{4} + \frac{1}{3}$

C. 0 D. $\frac{\sqrt{3}}{12}$

17. If $\langle\sigma\rangle$ and $\langle\tau\rangle$ are the cyclic subgroups of S_4, the symmetric group on four letter generated by

$$\sigma = \begin{pmatrix} 1 & 2 & 3 & 4 \\ 2 & 3 & 4 & 1 \end{pmatrix} \text{ and } \tau = \begin{pmatrix} 1 & 2 & 3 & 4 \\ 3 & 4 & 2 & 1 \end{pmatrix}$$

respectively, then $\langle\sigma\rangle \cap \langle\tau\rangle$ is a subgroup of order.

A. 0 B. 1
C. 2 D. 4

18. Let G be a group and H is a subgroup of G then which statement is false :

A. $x\,h\,x^{-1} \in H \quad \forall\, x \in G,\, h \in H$
B. $x\,H\,x^{-1} = H \quad \forall\, x \in G,\, h \in H$
C. $x\,h\,x^{-1} \notin H \quad \forall\, x \in G,\, h \in H$
D. Every left coset of H in G is a right coset of H in G

19. Let G be a finite cyclic group of order n. Consider the following statement:

1. G is isomorphic to group $(Z_3, +)$ of residue modulo 3.
2. G is isomorphic to group $(C_n, \cdot)$ of nth roots of unity.

A. (1) is true and (2) is false
B. (1) is false (2) is true
C. (1) and (2) are false
D. (1) and (2) are true

20. In $\mathbf{R}^2$ $<(x_1, y_1), (x_2, y_2)> = x_1x_2 - \alpha(x_2y_1 + x_1y_2) + y_1y_2$ is an inner product

A. for all $\alpha \in \mathbf{R}$
B. if and only if $\alpha = 0$
C. if and only if $\alpha < 1$
D. if and only if $|\alpha| < 1$

21. A particle moves in the xy-plane under the influence of a central force which varies inversely to its distance from the centre of force. If t is the kinetic energy, V is the potential energy, L is the Lagrangian and H is Hamiltonian of the system, then

A. L = H – V B. H = T – V
C. H = T + V D. None of these

22. For a bounded function $f(x)$, the upper and lower bounds are M and m and $|f(x)|$ is R-integrable on the interval $[a, b]$. Given $\int_a^b f(x)dx = \mu(b - a)$ such that $m < \mu < M$. μ in $[a, b]$ can

A. always be determined
B. never be determined
C. only be conditionally determined
D. be determined only for $a < u < b$

23. A bag contains 5 brown and 4 white socks. A man pulls out two socks. The probability that both the socks are of the same colour is

A. $\dfrac{9}{108}$ B. $\dfrac{18}{108}$
C. $\dfrac{36}{108}$ D. $\dfrac{48}{108}$

24. The function $f(z) = |z|^2$ is

A. differentiable every where
B. differentiable only at the origin
C. not differentiable any where
D. differentiable on real x-axis

25. Let P and Q be square matrices such that PQ = I, the identity matrix. Then zero is an eigenvalue of

A. P but not of Q
B. Q but not of P
C. both P and Q
D. neither P nor Q

26. Mean and variance of poisson process are respectively

A. λt and $(\lambda t)^2$ B. $\lambda^2 t$ and λt^2
C. λt and λt D. λt and $\lambda^2 t$

27. The differential equation $f_1(x)\, g_2(y)dx + f_2(x)g_1(y)dy = 0$ has

A. only one integrating factor
B. only two integrating factor
C. infinitely many integrating factor
D. Not an integrable differentiable equation

28. The area included between the parabola $y^2 = 4ax$ and $x^2 = 4ay$ is equal to

A. $8a^2/3$
B. $16a^2/3$
C. $4a^2/3$
D. none of the above

29. In marketing assignments, which of the following should be preferred.

A. Only that row which have a single zero.
B. Only that column which has a single zero
C. Only a row/column having a single zero.
D. Only columns having more than one zero.

30. Let, $c : \{x + iy : x = 2\cos t, y = 3\sin t, t \in [0,2\pi]\}$

then $\dfrac{1}{2i}\int_c \bar{z}dz$ is

A. 0
B. 3π
C. 6π
D. 12π

31. $[x]$ denoting the greatest integer not greater than x, $\int_0^3 [x]\,dx$ has the value

A. $\frac{9}{4}$
B. 9
C. 3
D. non-existent

32. If A = $\begin{pmatrix} a & b+ic \\ b-ic & d \end{pmatrix}$ then $\bar{x}^T Ax$ for every choice of vector $x \in \mathbb{C}^2$, is :

A. Pure imaginary
B. Complex number
C. Zero
D. Real number

33. If one ball is drawn from each of the three boxes containing 3 white and 1 black, 2 white and 2 black, 1 white and 3 black balls, then the probability that 2 white and 1 black balls will be drawn is

A. $\frac{13}{12}$
B. $\frac{1}{4}$
C. $\frac{1}{32}$
D. $\frac{3}{36}$

34. Suppose ϕ (.) is a differentiable function. If $\phi(x + y) = \phi(x)\,\phi(y)$ for all x, y and $\phi(5) = 2$, $\phi'(0) = 3$ then $\phi'(5)$ is

A. 6
B. 3
C. 0
D. None of the above

35. In a maximization L.P.P., if at least one artificial variables is in the basic, but not at zero level and the cofficient of M in each of the net evolution $(z_j - c_j)$ is non–negative, then we have

A. A Feasible solution
B. No feasible solution
C. An unbounded solution
D. An optimum solution

36. The series $\sum_{n=1}^{\infty}\left(\frac{1}{n} - \sin\frac{1}{n}\right)^a$ converges if

A. $a > \frac{1}{3}$
B. $a < \frac{1}{3}$
C. $a > \frac{1}{2}$
D. $a < \frac{1}{2}$

37. Assertion A. : Let $G = N \cup \left\{\frac{1}{n} : n \in N\right\}$, where N is the set of all positive integers. Then G is a group with respect to the usual multiplication.

Reason (R) : Multiplication in both N and $\left\{\frac{1}{n} : n \in N\right\}$ is well-defined and associative $1 \in G$ and $a \in G \Rightarrow \frac{1}{a} \in G$.

A. Both (A) and (R) are individually true and (R) is the correct explanation of (A).
B. Both (A) and (R) are individually true but (R) is not the correct explanation of (A).
C. (A) is true but (R) is false.
D. (A) is false but (R) is true.

38. Let $s_n = \int_0^1 \frac{nx^{n-1}}{(1+x)}\,dx$ for $n \geq 1$. Then as $n \to \infty$, the sequence $\{s_n\}$ tends to

A. 0
B. 1/2
C. 1
D. $+\infty$

39. Value of r and θ (polar form) in expression of $(1 - \cos\alpha) + i\sin\alpha$.

A. $r = 2\sin\frac{1}{2}\alpha,\ \theta = \frac{\pi - \alpha}{2}$
B. $r = 2\cos\frac{\alpha}{2},\ \theta = \frac{\pi + \alpha}{2}$
C. $r = \tan\frac{\alpha}{2},\ \theta = \frac{\alpha}{2}$
D. $r = 2\sin\frac{\alpha}{2},\ \theta = \frac{\pi + \alpha}{2}$

40. Which of the following is not true?

A. Models are only an attempt in understanding operations and should never be considered as absolute in any sense
B. Iconic models are pictorial representation of real system

C. Heuristic models are particular cases of iconic models

D. Analogue models are most abstract than the iconic ones

41. Consider the real vector space $\mathbf{R}^3$. The subspace $\{(x, y, z) \in \mathbf{R}^3 : y = x\}$ of $\mathbf{R}^3$ is generated by which one of the following?

A. $\{(1, 1, 0), (0, 0, 1)\}$

B. $\{(1, 1, 0), (1, 0, 0)\}$

C. $\{(1, 0, 0), (0, 1, 0)\}$

D. $\{(1, 0, 1), (0, 0, 1)\}$

42. Consider the second order ordinary differential equation $y'' + by' + cy = 0$, where b, c are real constant. You are given that $y = e^{2x}$ is a solution. Then,

A. $b^2 + 4c < 0$ B. $b^2 + 4c \geq 0$

C. $b^2 - 4c < 0$ D. $b^2 - 4c \geq 0$

43. The solution of the partial differential equation, $z_x + z_y = z^2$, with the initial condition, $z(x, 0) = f(x)$ is

A. $z = \dfrac{f(x+y)}{1+yf(x-y)}$ B. $z = \dfrac{f(x-y)}{1-yf(x-y)}$

C. $z = \dfrac{f(x-y)}{1-yf(x+y)}$ D. $z = \dfrac{f(x+y)}{1+yf(x+y)}$

44. Integrating factor of $(x^7y^2 + 3y)dx + (3x^8y - x)dy = 0$ is x^my^n, then

A. $m = -7, n = 2$ B. $m = -1, n = 7$

C. $m = -7, n = 1$ D. $m = -7, n = -2$

45. Consider the following table:

x:	5	7	11	13	17
$f(x)$:	150	392	1452	2366	5202

Then the value of third divided difference in the Newton's divided difference formulae is

A. –1 B. 0

C. 1 D. 2

46. Six identical fair dice are thrown independently. Let, S denotes the number of dice showing even number on their upper faces. Then the variance of the random variable S is

A. $\frac{1}{2}$ B. 1

C. $\frac{3}{2}$ D. 3

47. Suppose G is a group and N is a normal subgroup of G.
Let F : G → G/N defined by
F(x) = Nx $\forall x \in$ G
Then,

A. F is a homomorphism of G into G/N with ker F ≠ N

B. F is a homomorphism of G onto G/N with ker F ≠ N

C. F is a homomorphism of G into G/N with ker F = N

D. F is a homomorphism of G onto G/N with ker F = N

48. The optimal value of the objective function of the problem

$$\text{Minimize } \left(\frac{1}{2}x_1 + 2x_2 + x_3 + 4x_4\right)$$

Subject to $x_1 + x_2 + x_3 + 3x_4 \leq 6$
$x_i \geq 0 ; i = 1, 2, 3, 4$

is

A. 6 B. 3

C. 0 D. 2

49. A generator for a group G is an element $g \in G$ such that every element of G is equal to some power of g. Let G be a cyclic group of order 20. Then the number of generators of G is

A. 1 B. 4

C. 8 D. 20

50. Let the characteristics equation of a matrix M be $\lambda^2 - \lambda - 1 = 0$, then

A. M^{-1} does not exist

B. M^{-1} exist but cannot be determined from the data

C. $M^{-1} = M + 1$

D. $M^{-1} = M - 1$

51. Let A = All numbers that are not integers B's
B = All integers are multiple of 3

A. there is 1 to 1 function A to B

B. there is 1 to 1 function B to A

C. there is 1 to 1 onto function A to B

D. there is 1 to 1 function neither A to B nor B to A.

52. The singular solution of the equation

$p^3 - 4xyp + 8p^2 = 0 \left(p \equiv \frac{dy}{dx}\right)$ is.

A. $27y = 4x$ B. $27y = 4x^2$
C. $27y = 4x^3$ D. $27y^3 = 4x$

53. The rank of the matrix $\begin{bmatrix} 1 & 4 & 8 \\ 2 & 10 & 22 \\ 0 & 4 & 12 \end{bmatrix}$ is

A. 3 B. 2
C. 1 D. 0

54. The function $f(z) = |z|^2$ is
A. differentiable every where
B. differentiable only origin
C. not differentiable any where
D. differentiable on real x-axis

55. For $n \in \mathbb{N}$, let $n\mathbb{Z} = \{nk : k \in \mathbb{Z}\}$. Then the number of units of $\mathbb{Z}/11\mathbb{Z}$ and $\mathbb{Z}/12\mathbb{Z}$, respectively, are
A. 11, 12 B. 10, 11
C. 10, 4 D. 10, 8

56. Let $f(x) = \int_{\sin x}^{\cos x} e^{-t^2} dt$. Then $f'(\pi/4)$ equals

A. $\sqrt{1/e}$ B. $-\sqrt{2/e}$
C. $\sqrt{2/e}$ D. $-\sqrt{1/e}$

57. The orthogonal trajectory to the family of circles $x^2 + y^2 = 2cx$ (c arbitrary) is described by the differential equation
A. $(x^2 + y^2)y' = 2xy$ B. $(x^2 - y^2)y' = 2xy$
C. $(y^2 - x^2)y' = xy$ D. $(y^2 - x^2)y' = 2xy$

58. The differential equation $ydx - 2xdy = 0$ represents
A. a family of straight lines
B. a family of parabolas
C. a family of circles
D. a family of catenaries

59. Let $f: R \to R$ be defined by $f(t) = t^2$ and let U be any non-empty open subset of R.
Then
A. $f(U)$ is open B. $f^{-1}(U)$ is open
C. $f(U)$ is closed D. $f^{-1}(U)$ is closed

60. If $A = \begin{bmatrix} 2 & 6 \\ 3 & 9 \end{bmatrix}$, $B = \begin{bmatrix} 3 & x \\ y & 2 \end{bmatrix}$, then in order that AB = 0, the values of x and y will be respectively.
A. –6 and –1 B. 6 and 1
C. –6 and –3 D. –5 and –14

ANSWERS

1	2	3	4	5	6	7	8	9	10
D	D	B	C	D	A	B	B	D	A
11	**12**	**13**	**14**	**15**	**16**	**17**	**18**	**19**	**20**
C	B	C	D	B	B	B	C	B	B
21	**22**	**23**	**24**	**25**	**26**	**27**	**28**	**29**	**30**
B	A	D	C	D	C	C	B	C	C
31	**32**	**33**	**34**	**35**	**36**	**37**	**38**	**39**	**40**
C	D	A	A	B	A	D	D	D	C
41	**42**	**43**	**44**	**45**	**46**	**47**	**48**	**49**	**50**
A	D	B	C	C	C	D	C	C	D
51	**52**	**53**	**54**	**55**	**56**	**57**	**58**	**59**	**60**
B	C	B	C	C	B	B	B	B	A

SOME SELECTED EXPLANATORY ANSWERS

3. Given $u_n = \sqrt{n+1} - \sqrt{n}$

$$= \frac{(\sqrt{n}+1-\sqrt{n})(\sqrt{n+1}+\sqrt{n})}{\sqrt{n+1}+\sqrt{n}}$$

$$= \frac{(n+1)-n}{\sqrt{n+1}+\sqrt{n}} = \frac{1}{\sqrt{n+1}+\sqrt{n}}$$

i.e. $u_n = \dfrac{1}{\sqrt{n+1}+\sqrt{n}} \sim \dfrac{1}{\sqrt{n}}$

i.e. $\dfrac{1}{2} < 1.$

Hence by *p*-ratio test.

Σu_n is divergent.

Also $v_n = \sqrt{n^4+1} - n^2$

$$= \frac{\left(\sqrt{n^4+1}-n^2\right)\left(\sqrt{n^4+1}+n^2\right)}{\left(\sqrt{n^4+1}+n^2\right)}$$

$$= \frac{n^4+1-n^4}{\left(\sqrt{n^4+1}+n^2\right)} = \frac{1}{\sqrt{n^4+1}+n^2}$$

i.e. $v_n = \dfrac{1}{\sqrt{n^4+1}+n^2} \sim \dfrac{1}{n^2}$ (as 2 > 1).

Hence the *p*-ratio test

Σv_n is convergent.

6. $\because f(z) = \dfrac{1}{z-1} - \dfrac{1}{z-2}$ for region $|z| > 2$

$\Rightarrow \dfrac{1}{|z|} < \dfrac{1}{2} < 1$

$$f(z) = \frac{1}{z\left(1-\frac{1}{z}\right)} - \frac{1}{z\left(1-\frac{2}{z}\right)}$$

$$= \frac{1}{z}\left(1-\frac{1}{z}\right)^{-1} - \frac{1}{z}\left(1-\frac{2}{z}\right)^{-1}$$

$$= \frac{1}{z}\left(1+\frac{1}{z}+\frac{1}{z^2}+....\right) - \frac{1}{z}\left(1+\frac{1}{z}+\frac{4}{z^2}+....\right)$$

$$= \frac{1}{z}+\frac{1}{z^2}+\frac{1}{z^3}+... - \frac{1}{z} - \frac{2}{z^2} - \frac{4}{z^3} - ....$$

$$= -\frac{1}{z^2} - \frac{3}{z^3} - \frac{7}{z^4} - ....$$

$\Rightarrow$ Coefficient of $\dfrac{1}{z^2} = -1.$

7. The given LPP is

Maximum $Z = x_1 + 5x_2 + 3x_3$

Subject to $2x_1 - 3x_2 + 5x_3 \le 3.$

$3x_1 + 2x_3 \le 5$

$x_1, x_2, x_3.$

As the number of variables are 3 and the number of constraints are 2.

Hence the basic solution can be obtained by making any one of the three variables equating to zero.

Case I: When $x_1 = 0$

then the constraints becomes

$-3x_2 + 5x_3 = 3$

$2x_3 = 5 \Rightarrow x_3 = \dfrac{5}{2}$

i.e. $-3x_2 + \dfrac{25}{2} = 3$

or $3x_2 = \dfrac{25}{2} - 3 = \dfrac{19}{2}$

$\Rightarrow x_2 = \dfrac{19}{6}$

i.e. the basic solution in this case is

$x_1 = 0, x_2 = \dfrac{19}{6}, x_3 = \dfrac{5}{2}.$

Case II: When $x_2 = 0$, then the constraints become

$2x_1 + 5x_3 = 3 \times 3$

$3x_1 + 2x_3 = 5 \times 2$

$\Rightarrow (15 - 4)x_3 = 9 - 10$

$\Rightarrow x_3 = \dfrac{-1}{11}$ (not a basic solution)

Case III: When $x_3 = 0$, then the constraint becomes

$2x_1 - 3x_2 = 3$

$3x_1 = 5 \Rightarrow x_1 = \dfrac{5}{3}$

$\Rightarrow \dfrac{10}{3} - 3x_2 = 3 \Rightarrow x_2 = \dfrac{1}{9}$

i.e. the basic solution in this case is

$$x_1 = \frac{5}{3},\ x_2 = \frac{1}{9},\ x_3 = 0$$

i.e. given LPP has basic feasible solution.

11. $\int_a^{\bar{b}} f dx = b - a$

$\int_{\underline{a}}^{b} f dx = -(b-a) \Rightarrow f$ is not integrable

Note : $|f(x)| = 1$, for all x, so that $\int_a^b |f| dx$ exists and is equal to $(b - a)$.
Thus $|f|$ is integrable while f is not.

25. As PQ = I.
It implies that both P and Q are invertible.
i.e. They must be non-singular matrix and hence they cannot have zero as an eigenvalue.

28. $y^2 = 4ax$ and $x^2 = 4ay$ have point of intersection as

$x^4 = 16a^2y^2 = 16a^2(4ax)$

$\Rightarrow x(x^3 - 64a^3) = 0$

$\Rightarrow x = 0, 4a$

So, area included between them will be.

$$\int_0^{4a} (y_1 - y_2)dx = \int_0^{4a} \left(\sqrt{4ax} - \frac{x^2}{4a}\right)dx$$

$$= 2\sqrt{a}\,\frac{x^{3/2}}{3/2} - \frac{x^3}{12a}\Bigg|_0^{4a}$$

$$= \frac{4\sqrt{a}}{3}(4a)^{3/2} - \frac{64a^3}{12a} = \frac{32}{3}a^2 - \frac{16}{3}a^2$$

$$= \frac{16a^2}{3}$$

30. Let, I $= \int \bar{z}dz$ then I $= \int (x - iy)(dxi + idy)$

$$= \int (xdx + ydy) - i\int_0^{2\pi} ydx - xdy\,.$$

Putting $x = 2\cos t$, $y = 3\sin t$

$$= \int_0^{2\pi} \left(6\cos^2 t - 6\sin^2 t\right)dt + i\int_0^{2\pi} 6\left(\sin^2 t + \cos^2 t\right)dt$$

$= 0 + i.12\pi$

$$\therefore \quad \frac{1}{2i}\int \bar{z}dz = \frac{1}{2i}.i12\pi = 6\pi\,.$$

31. $\int_0^3 [x]dx = \int_0^1 0dx + \int_1^2 1dx + \int_2^3 2dx$

$$= 0 + x\Big|_1^2 + 2x\Big|_2^3 = 0 + 1 + 2 = 3$$

34. $\phi(x + y) = \phi(x)\,\phi(y)$

$\Rightarrow \phi(5 + 0) = \phi(5)\,\phi(0)$

$\Rightarrow \phi(5)\,[\phi(0) - 1] = 0$

$\Rightarrow \phi(0) = 1 \qquad [\because \phi(5) \neq 0]$

Now, $\phi'(5) = \lim\limits_{h\to 0} \dfrac{\phi(5+h) - \phi(5)}{h}$

$$= \lim_{h\to 0} \frac{\phi(5)\phi(h) - \phi(0)}{h}$$

$= \phi(5)\,\phi'(0) = 2.3 = 6$

37. $\because\ G = NU\left\{\frac{1}{n} : n \in N\right\}$

Clearly $2 \in N$, $\frac{1}{3} \in \left\{\frac{1}{n} : n \in N\right\}$

Now $2\cdot\frac{1}{3} \notin G$.

i.e., it is not closed under multiplication.
i.e., *A* is false.

38. Important result

$\int_0^1 \frac{x^{a-1}}{1-x}dx$ is convergent if $0 < a < 1$ [Remember]

i.e. $\int \frac{x^{n-1}}{1+x}dx$ is divergent if $n \geq 1$.

Hence $\{S_n\}$ is divergent

or, $\qquad S_n = \int_0^1 \frac{nx^{n-1}}{1+x}dx$

put $x = \tan^2\theta \quad dx = 2\tan\theta\sec^2\theta\,d\theta$

$$S_n = \int_0^{\pi/4} 2n\tan^{2n-1}\theta d\theta$$

$$= \int_0^{\pi/4} 2n\tan^{2n-3}\theta\left(\sec^2\theta - 1\right)dx$$

$$= 2n\left[\frac{1}{2n-2} - \frac{1}{2n-4} + \frac{1}{2n-6} - \ldots \int_0^{\pi/4}\tan\theta d\theta\right]$$

$$= n\left[\frac{1}{n-1} - \frac{1}{n-2} + \frac{1}{n-3} - \ldots \text{ln sec}\sqrt{2}\right]$$

Clearly $S_n = nx$ some finite value $\Rightarrow S_n \to \infty$
i.e. S_n is divergent or $S_n \to \infty$

44. I.F. $= x^{\alpha}y^{\beta}$

then

$(x^{\alpha+7}y^{2+\beta} + 3x^{\alpha}y^{1+\beta})dx + (3x^{8+\alpha}y^{1+\beta} - x^{1+\alpha}y^{\beta})\, dy$

$$\frac{\partial M}{\partial y} = (2+\beta)x^{\alpha+7}y^{1+\beta} + 3\,(1+\beta)\,x^{\alpha}.\,y^{\beta}$$

$$\frac{\partial N}{\partial x} = (24+3\alpha)x^{7+\alpha}y^{1+\beta} - (1+\alpha)x^{\alpha}.y^{\beta}$$

$$\because \quad \frac{\partial M}{\partial y} = \frac{\partial N}{\partial x}$$

$2+\beta = 24+3\alpha \Rightarrow 3\alpha - \beta = -22$ ... *(i)*

$3+3\beta = -1-\alpha \Rightarrow 3(\alpha+3\beta) = -4\times 3$ ... *(ii)*

$\therefore \quad \alpha = -7, \beta = 1$

$\therefore \quad$ I.F $= x^{-7}y$

$m = -7, n = 1.$

45. The divided difference table is:

x	$f(x)$	1st divided difference	2nd divided difference	3rd divided difference
5	150			
		121		
7	392		24	
		265		1
11	1452		32	
		457		1
13	2366		42	
		709		
17	5202			

50. The characteristic equation of M is $\lambda^2 - \lambda - 1 = 0.$

Hence by Cayley-Hamilton Theorem, it should be satisfied by $\lambda = M$.

i.e. $M^2 - M - I = 0$ or $I = M^2 - M$.

Multiply both the sides by M^{-1} we get

$$M^{-1} = M - I.$$

53. $\begin{bmatrix} 1 & 4 & 8 \\ 2 & 10 & 22 \\ 0 & 4 & 12 \end{bmatrix} \sim \begin{bmatrix} 1 & 4 & 8 \\ 0 & 2 & 6 \\ 0 & 4 & 12 \end{bmatrix}$

By $R_2 \to R_2 - 2R_1$

$$\sim \begin{bmatrix} 1 & 4 & 8 \\ 0 & 2 & 6 \\ 0 & 0 & 0 \end{bmatrix}$$

By $R_3 \to R_3 - 2R_2$

Number of non-zero rows = 2 so rank = 2

55. As $\dfrac{Z}{11Z}$ is field as 11 is irreducible in z.

Hence, all non-zero element of $\dfrac{Z}{11Z}$ are invertible.

i.e. number of units of $\dfrac{Z}{11Z}$ are 10.

On the other hand, $\dfrac{Z}{10Z}$ is not a field, but a commutative ring whose units are given by the number of elements which are relatively prime to 12.

Which is given by Euler's formula.

i.e. $\quad \phi(n) =$ *i.e.* $\phi(12) = 12\left(1-\dfrac{1}{2}\right)\left(1-\dfrac{1}{3}\right)$

$$= 12.\frac{1}{2}.\frac{2}{3} = 4$$

i.e. No. of units in $\dfrac{Z}{12Z}$ are 4.

56. $$f(x) = \int_{\sin x}^{\cos x} e^{-t^2}\, dt$$

$$\Rightarrow f'(x) = -\sin x\, e^{-\cos^2 x} - \cos x\, e^{-\sin^2 x}$$

$$\Rightarrow f'(\pi/4) = -\frac{1}{\sqrt{2}}e^{-1/2} - \frac{1}{\sqrt{2}}e^{-1/2}$$

$$= -\sqrt{2}\,e^{-1/2} = -\sqrt{2/e}$$

59. $U \in\,]a, b[$

$\Rightarrow f(U) \in\,]a^2, b^2[$ is not necessarily true.

As $U \in\,]-5, 5[$

$\Rightarrow f(U) \in [0, 25[$

If $f(U)$ is invertible, $f^{-1}(U)$ is open.

60. $AB = \begin{bmatrix} 2 & 6 \\ 3 & 9 \end{bmatrix}\begin{bmatrix} 3 & x \\ y & 2 \end{bmatrix} = \begin{bmatrix} 6+6y & 2x+12 \\ 9+9y & 3x+18 \end{bmatrix}$

Now $AB = 0 \Rightarrow \begin{bmatrix} 6+6y & 2x+12 \\ 9+9y & 3x+18 \end{bmatrix} = \begin{bmatrix} 0 & 0 \\ 0 & 0 \end{bmatrix}$

$\Rightarrow \quad x = -6, \; y = -1.$

SET–18

CSIR–UGC (NET) MATHEMATICAL SCIENCES

PART-C

1. The series $\sum\left(\frac{z}{1+z}\right)^n$ converges if (where $z = x + iy$).

A. $x > -\frac{1}{2}, y \in (-\infty, \infty)$

B. $x < -\frac{1}{2}, y \in (-\infty, \infty)$

C. $y > -\frac{1}{2}, x \in (-\infty, \infty)$

D. $y < -\frac{1}{2}, x \in (-\infty, \infty)$

2. If $S_1 = \sum_{n=1}^{\infty} \frac{(n!)^n}{(n^n)^2}$ and $S_2 = \sum_{n=1}^{\infty} \frac{1}{(2n-1)(2n+1)}$ then which one of the following statements is correct?

A. Both S_1 and S_2 are convergent

B. S_1 is divergent and S_2 is convergent

C. S_1 is convergent and S_2 is divergent

D. Both S_1 and S_2 are divergent

3. Let $u(n)$ be the set of all positive integers less than n and relatively prime to n. Then $u(n)$ is a group under multiplication modulo n. For $n = 248$, the number of elements in $u(n)$ is

A. 60 B. 120

C. 180 D. 240

4. Which of the following is a valid solution of the partial differential equation $\frac{\partial^2 \psi}{\partial x^2} + \frac{\partial^2 \psi}{\partial y^2} = 0$?

A. $x^2 - y^2$ B. $ax^2 - by^2$

C. $x^2 + y^2$ D. $x^4 + y^4$

5. The formula $A_0 f\left(-\frac{1}{2}\right) + A_1 f(0) + A_2 f\left(\frac{1}{2}\right)$ which approximates the integral $\int_{-1}^{1} f(x)\,dx$ is exact for polynomials of degree less than or equal to 2 if

A. $A_0 = A_2 = \frac{4}{3}$, $A_1 = \frac{2}{3}$

B. $A_0 = A_1 = A_2 = 1$

C. $A_0 = A_2 = \frac{4}{3}$, $A_1 = -\frac{2}{3}$

D. None of the above

6. If $A = \begin{bmatrix} 1 & 0 & 0 \\ i & \frac{-1+i\sqrt{3}}{2} & 0 \\ 0 & 1+2i & \frac{-1-i\sqrt{3}}{2} \end{bmatrix}$, then the trace of A^{102} is

A. 0 B. 1

C. 2 D. 3

7. Consider the wave equation $\frac{\partial^2 u}{\partial t^2} = \frac{\partial^2 u}{\partial x^2}$, $0 < x < \pi$, $t > 0$.

$u(x, 0) = 2(\sin x + \sin 3x)$, $u_t(x, 0) = 0$

A. $u(x, t) = 4\cos x \,.\, \sin 4x \,.\, \cos 2t$

B. $u(x, t) = 4\cos x \cos 2t . \sin 2x$

C. $u(x, t) = 2\cos x . \cos 2t . \sin 4x$

D. $u(x, t) = 2\cos x . \sin 2x . \cos 2t$.

8. If $F(x) = \frac{1}{x^2}\left[\int_4^x \{4t^2 - 2F'(t)\}\,dt\right]$, then what is $F'(4)$ equal to?

A. $\frac{32}{9}$ B. $\frac{64}{3}$

C. $\frac{64}{9}$ D. $\frac{16}{3}$

9. The solutions of the differential equation $2y(y' + 2) - xy'^2 = 0$ are the functions.

1. $y = 0$ 2. $y = -4x$.

A. None of 1 and 2 is a singular solution.
B. Both 1 and 2 are singular solutions.
C. 1 is a singular solution but 2 is not.
D. 2 is a singular solution but 1 is not.

10. If M and N are two events, the probability that exactly one of them occurs is

A. $P(M) + P(N) - 2P(M \cap N)$
B. $P(M) + P(N) - P(M \cap N)$
C. $P(M^C) + P(N^C) - 2P(M^C \cap N^C)$
D. $P(M \cap N^C) + P(M^C \cap N)$

11. Let $f = u + iv$ and $g = v + iu$ be non-zero analytic functions on $|z| < 1$, then it follows that

A. $f' \equiv 0$
B. f is conformal on $|z| < 1$
C. $f \equiv kg$ for some real k
D. f is one to one.

12. For the differential equation

$$x^2(1-x)\frac{d^2y}{dx^2} + x\frac{dy}{dx} + y = 0.$$

A. $x = 1$ is an ordinary point
B. $x = 1$ is a regular singular point
C. $x = 0$ is an irregular singular point
D. $x = 0$ is an ordinary point

13. Let A and B be $n \times n$ matrices with the same minimial polynomial. Then

A. A is similar to B
B. A is diagonalizable if B is diagonalizable
C. A – B is singular
D. A and B commute

14. The Jacobi's iteration method for the set of equations $x_1 + ax_2 = 2$, $2ax_1 + x_2 = 7$, $\left(a \neq \frac{1}{\sqrt{2}}\right)$ converges for

A. all values of a B. $a = 1$

C. $|a| < \frac{1}{\sqrt{2}}$ D. $\frac{1}{\sqrt{2}} < a < \sqrt{\frac{3}{2}}$

15. A box contains 6 nails and 10 nuts. Half of the nails and half of the nuts are rusted. If one item is chosen at random, then the probability that it is rusted or a nail is

A. $\frac{3}{16}$ B. $\frac{5}{16}$

C. $\frac{11}{16}$ D. $\frac{14}{16}$

16. Which of the following sets of vectors is a basis for R^3.

1. {(1, 2, 3), (3, 5, 7), (5, 8, 11)}
2. {(1, 0, 1), (0, 1, 0), (1, 0, 1)}
3. {(1, 2, 3), (2, 3, 4), (2, 4, 6)}?

A. Only (1) and (2) B. Only (2)
C. Only (1) and (2) D. Only (1)

17. Let $\{v_1, v_2, v_3, v_4\}$ be a basis of $\mathbf{R}^4$ and $v = a_1v_1 + a_2v_2 + a_3v_3 + a_4v_4$, where $a_i \in R$, $i = 1, 2, 3, 4$. Then $\{v_1 - v, v_2 - v, v_3 - v, v_4 - v\}$ is a basis of $\mathbf{R}^4$ if and only if

A. $a_1 = a_2 = a_3 = a_4$
B. $a_1a_2\ a_3a_4 = -1$
C. $a_1 + a_2 + a_3 + a_4 \neq 1$
D. $a_1 + a_2 + a_3 + a_4 \neq 0$

18. For the differential equation $xy' - y = 0$. Which of the following is not an integrating factor?

A. $\frac{1}{x^2}$ B. $\frac{1}{y^2}$

C. $\frac{1}{xy}$ D. $\frac{1}{\text{ग} + \text{ज}}$

19. If $P_n(R)$ is the set of polynomials of order n over R. Then match list-I with list-II and select the correct answer using the codes given below the lists :

List-I

(Linear transformation)

(*a*) $T : R^3 \to R^2$
$T(x, y, z) = (x + y, y + z)$

(*b*) $T : R^3 \to P_2(R)$
$T(a, b, c) = (a + b) + (b + c)x + cx^2$

(*c*) $T : P_2(R) \to P_3(R)$
$T(p(x)) = xp(x)$

(*d*) $T : R^2 \to R^3$
$T(x, y) = (x, x + y, y)$

List-II
(*Matrices*)

1. $\begin{bmatrix} 1 & 0 \\ 1 & 1 \\ 0 & 1 \end{bmatrix}$ 2. $\begin{bmatrix} 0 & 0 & 0 \\ 1 & 0 & 0 \\ 0 & 1 & 0 \\ 0 & 0 & 1 \end{bmatrix}$

3. $\begin{bmatrix} 1 & 1 & 0 \\ 0 & 1 & 1 \end{bmatrix}$ 4. $\begin{bmatrix} 1 & 1 & 0 \\ 0 & 1 & 1 \\ 0 & 0 & 1 \end{bmatrix}$

Codes :

	(*a*)	(*b*)	(*c*)	(*d*)
A.	1	4	2	3
B.	2	3	4	1
C.	3	4	2	1
D.	3	1	4	2

20. If X is a Poisson random variable with $P(X = 1) = 2P(X = 3)$. What is expected value of X?

A. 3 B. $\sqrt{3}$
C. $\sqrt{6}$ D. 2

21. The solution of Volterra's type integral equation

$$f(x) = e^x - 1 + \int_0^1 t\,f(t)\,dt$$

A. e^x B. $e^x - 1$
C. $e^x + 1$ D. None of these

22. Choose the correct one. In sequencing algorithm.

A. The selection of an appropriate order for a senses of jobs is to be done on a finite service facilities.
B. All the jobs must be processed on a first come-first serviced bans.
C. A service facility can process more than one job at a time.
D. All the service facibilities are not of defferent type.

23. The area of the region enclosed by the curve $y(x^2 + 2) = 3x$ and $4y = x^2$ is given by

A. $\int_0^2 \int_{y=0}^{x^2/4} dx\,dy$ B. $\int_0^2 \int_{y=0}^{3x/(x^2+2)} dx\,dy$

C. $\int_0^1 \int_{y=x^2/4}^{3x/(x^2+2)} dx\,dy$ D. $\int_0^2 \int_{y=x^2/4}^{3x/(x^2+2)} dx\,dy$

24. Let G be finite group having unique proper subgroup H of order p. Then the quotient group $\frac{G}{H}$ is isomorphic to

A. $Z_p \times Z_p$
B. Z_p
C. Z_{p^n} for positive integer n
D. Z_q where $q \neq p$ (prime)

25. The function $u = 2x(1 - y)$ is harmonic. Find a function v such that $f(z) = u + iv$ is analytic [*i.e.*, find the conjugate function of u]

A. $v = 2x + x^2 - y^2$ B. $v = 2y + x^2 - y^2$
C. $v = 2x + x^2 + y^2$ D. $v = 2y - x^2 + y^2$

26. Which the following regarding a general L.P.P are valid.

1. The set of all possible solutions to an L.P.P is convex Hull of a set L.
2. Only a finite number of B.F.S exist to an L.P.P .
3. A bounded (finite) optimal solution to an L.P.P exists iff there exists a feasible solution to both primal and its dual.
4. The Dual of the L.P.P maximize $C'X$ such that $AX = b, X \geq 0$ is minimize $b'y$ such that $A'y \geq C, y \geq 0$

A. 1 B. 2
C. 3 D. 4

27. If $A = \begin{bmatrix} 0 & 1 & 0 & 0 \\ 0 & 2 & 0 & 1 \\ 0 & 3 & 2 & 0 \\ 1 & 4 & 1 & 0 \end{bmatrix}$ then what is $\det(A^{-1})$ equal to?

A. 2 B. −2
C. $\frac{1}{2}$ D. $\frac{-1}{2}$

28. The order of an element of a finite group is
A. Divisor of the order of the group
B. Not a divisor of the order of the group
C. Either (A) or (B)
D. None of these

29. Let $f(x) = \begin{cases} |x| & \text{if } x \text{ is irrational or } x = 0 \\ \dfrac{qx}{q+1} & \text{if } x = \dfrac{p}{q}, p \in z, q \in N \end{cases}$

where p, q are co-prime
then select the correct options
A. f is continuous only $x = 0$
B. f is continuous at all irrationals
C. f is Riemann integrable on [0, 1]
D. None of these

30. For initial value problem, $y^1 = 1 + y^2$, $y(0) = 0$, largest interval $|x| \le h$ on which the solution exist uniquely is given by

A. $h = \frac{1}{4}$ B. $h = \frac{1}{3}$
C. $h = \frac{1}{2}$ D. $h = 1$

31. When we solve a system of simultaneous linear equations by using *Two–Phase simplex method,* the value to *decision variables* may be
A. Positive
B. Negative
C. 0
D. Positive or negative

32. Let $f(x, y) = x - y$ and c be the boundary of the square $S = \{(x, y) : 0 \le x \le 1, 0 \le y \le 1\}$.

Then $\int_c f \frac{\partial f}{\partial n} ds$ equals

A. 0 B. 1
C. 2 D. None of these

33. $\int_0^{2\pi} \frac{d\theta}{13 - 5\sin\theta} =$

A. $-\frac{\pi}{6}$ B. $-\frac{\pi}{12}$
C. $\frac{\pi}{12}$ D. $\frac{\pi}{6}$

34. The unit cost c_{ij} of producing product i at plant j is given by the matrix:

$$\begin{bmatrix} 14 & 12 & 16 \\ 21 & 9 & 17 \\ 9 & 7 & 5 \end{bmatrix}$$

The total cost of optimal assignment is
A. 20 B. 22
C. 25 D. 28

35. $\lim_{x \to \infty} \left(\frac{x^2 + 5x + 3}{x^2 + x + 2} \right)^x$ is equal to
A. 1 B. e
C. e^2 D. e^4

36. A function $f(x)$ is differentiable in the closed and bounded interval $[p, q]$. The differential $f'(p)$ and $f'(q)$ are such that $f'(p) < 0$ and $f'(q) > 0$. Then $f(x)$ will assume on $[p, q]$
A. neither infimum nor supremum
B. supremum and not infimum
C. infimum and not supremum
D. supremum and infimum

37. The differential equation
$M(x, y)dx + N(x, y)dy = 0$ is an exact equation if

A. $\frac{\partial M}{\partial y} + \frac{\partial N}{\partial x} = 0$ B. $\frac{\partial M}{\partial y} - \frac{\partial N}{\partial x} = 0$
C. $\frac{\partial N}{\partial y} + \frac{\partial M}{\partial x} = 0$ D. $\frac{\partial N}{\partial y} - \frac{\partial M}{\partial x} = 0$

38. If probability density function of random variable X is $f(x) = 2axe^{-ax^2}$, $0 \le x < \infty$, then Var(X) is

$f(x) = 2axe^{-ax^2}$, $0 \le x < \infty$, then Var(X) is

A. $a\left(1 - \frac{\pi}{4}\right)$ B. $a\left(1 + \frac{\pi}{4}\right)$
C. $\frac{1}{2}\sqrt{\frac{\pi}{a}}$ D. $\frac{1}{a}\left(1 - \frac{\pi}{4}\right)$

39. In PDE, $p = \frac{\partial z}{\partial x}$, $q = \frac{\partial z}{\partial y}$, then

A. $r = \frac{\partial^2 z}{\partial x^2}$, $S = \frac{\partial^2 z}{\partial x \partial y}$

B. $r = \frac{\partial^2 z}{\partial y^2}$, S $= \frac{\partial^2 z}{\partial x \partial y}$

C. $r = \frac{\partial^2 z}{\partial y^2}$, S $= \frac{\partial^2 z}{\partial x^2}$

D. $r = \frac{\partial^2 z}{\partial x \partial y}$, S $= \frac{\partial^2 z}{\partial x^2}$

40. The differential equation $2ydx - (3y - 2x)\, dy = 0$ is

A. exact and homogeneous but not linear
B. homogeneous and linear but not exact
C. exact and linear but not homogeneous
D. exact, homogeneous and linear

41. Let S and T be two subspaces of $\mathbf{R}^{24}$ such that dim(S) = 19 and dim(T) = 17. Then, the

A. smallest possible value of dim(S ∩ T) is 2.
B. largest possible value of dim(S ∩ T) is 8.
C. smallest possible value of dim (S + T) is 19.
D. largest possible value of dim(S + T) is 22.

42. For the Sturm Liouville problems: $(1 + x^2)y'' + 2xy' + \lambda x^2 y = 0$ with $y'(1) = 0$ and $y'(10) = 0$ the eigen values, λ satisfy

A. $\lambda \geq 0$ B. $\lambda < 0$
C. $\lambda \neq 0$ D. $\lambda \leq 0$

43. The quadrature formulae

$$\int_{-1}^{1} f(x)dx = \frac{1}{9}\left[5f\left(-\sqrt{\frac{3}{5}}\right) + 8f(0) + 5f\left(\sqrt{\frac{3}{5}}\right)\right]$$

is exact for polynomials of degree less than are equal to

A. 3 B. 4
C. 5 D. 6

44. Let G be the set of 3 × 3 real matrices which are invertible consider G with the binary operation of matrix multiplication. Then

A. $(G, \bullet)$ is a finite group.
B. $(G, \bullet)$ is an infinite group.
C. $(G, \bullet)$ is an abelian group.
D. $(G, \bullet)$ is not a group.

45. The multiple points on the curve $x^4 - 2ay^3 - 3a^2y^2 - 2a^2x^2 + a^4 = 0$ are

A. (0, 0), (0, – a) and (a, 0)
B. (0, – a), (a, 0) and (a, – a)
C. (a, 0), (a, – a) and (– a, – a)
D. (a, 0), (– a, 0) and (0, – a)

46. Which one is true?

A. Every quotient group of a group is abelian and its converse is also true
B. Every quotient group of a group is abelian but its converse is not true
C. Every quotient group of an abelian group is abelian and its converse is also true
D. Every quotient group of an abelian group is abelian but the converse is not true

47. The statements (i), (ii) and (iii) marked below are associated with $f(x) = x^3 - 3x^2 - 9x - 2$

(i) $f(x)$ increase with x if $x > 3$
(ii) $f(x)$ decreases with x if $x < -1$
(iii) $f(x)$ decreases with x if $-1 < x < 3$

Which among the following is true?

A. Only (i) is true
B. Only (i) and (iii) are true
C. All of these
D. None of these

48. If $\log_{0.3}(x - 1) < \log_{.09}(x - 1)$ then x lies in the interval

A. $(2, \infty)$ B. (1, 2)
C. (– 2, – 1) D. (– 1, 1)

49. Let T be linear transformation on $\mathbf{R}^2$ into itself such that T(1, 0) = (1, 2) and T(1, 1) = (0, 2). Then T(a, b) is equal to

A. (a, 2b) B. (2a, b)
C. (a – b, 2a) D. (a – b, 2b)

50. Suppose (c_n) is a sequence of real numbers such that $\lim_n |c_n|^{1/n}$ exists and is non-zero. If the radius of convergence of the power series $\sum_{n=0}^{\infty} c_n x^n$ is equal to r, then the radius of convergence of the power series $\sum_{n=1}^{\infty} n^2 c_n x^n$ is

A. less than r B. greater than r
C. equal to r D. equal to 0

51. Complete solution of $p^2 - q^2 = 1$ is given by

A. $z = ax + (a^2 + 1)y + C$

B. $z = ax - (a^2 - 1)y + C$

C. $z = ax - (a^2 - 1)^{1/2}y + C$

D. None of the above

52. In phase-I of two phase simplex method we assign artificial variables coefficient equal to

A. –1 B. –M ; M >> 0

C. M ; M >> 0 D. Zero

53. Study the following assertions about a square matrix :

(*i*) The sum of the eigenvalues of A is equal to its trace

(*ii*) The product of the eigenvalues of A is equal to the determinant of A

(*iii*) All eigenvalues of A are non-zero if and only if A is non-singular.

(*iv*) If A^{-1} exists, then the eigenvalues of A^{-1} are equal to the reciprocal of the eigen values of A.

Which among the following is correct with respect to above assertions?

A. Only (*iii*) and (*iv*) are true

B. Only (*i*) and (*ii*) are true

C. Only (*ii*), (*iii*) and (*iv*) are true

D. (*i*), (*ii*), (*iii*) and (*iv*) are all true

54. Let $f : (-1, 1) \to R$ be defined as $f(x) = \dfrac{x^2}{1-\cos x}$ for $x \neq 0$ and $f(0) = 2$. If $f(x) = \sum_{n=0}^{\infty} a_n x^n$ is the Taylor expansion of f for all x in $(-1, 1)$, then $\sum_{n=0}^{\infty} a_{2n+1}$ is

A. 0 B. 1/2

C. 1 D. 2

55. If the set of integers with the operation defined by $m*n = m + n - 1$ forms a group, what is the inverse of m?

A. $-m$ B. $2m$

C. $2 - m$ D. $1 - m$

56. The value/values of k such that the following system

$kx + y + z = 1$

$x + ky + z = 1$

$x + y + kz = 1$, in unknowns x, y and z has a unique solution.

A. $k = 1$ B. $k = -1$

C. $k \neq 1$ and $k \neq -2$ D. Any value of k

57. The function $u = 2x(1 - y)$ is harmonic. Find a function v such that $f(z) = u + iv$ is analytic.

A. $v = 2x + x^2 - y^2$

B. $v = 2y + x^2 - y^2$

C. $v = 2x + x^2 + y^2$

D. $2y - x^2 + y^2$

58. Which of the following maps is not an automorphism.

A. G = cyclic group of order 6, $f : G \to G$ such that $f(x) = x^5$.

B. G = group of positive real numbers under multiplication $f : G \to G$ such that $f(x) = x^2$.

C. G = finite abelian group of order n, $f : G \to G$ such that $f(x) = x^m$, $1 \leq m < n$, g.c.d. $(m, n) = 1$.

D. None of these

59. Let PIQ, EU, UFD denote the set of all principal ideal domains Euclidean domains, unique factorization domains, respectively, then

A. UFD $\subset$ ED $\subset$ PID

B. PID $\subset$ ED $\subset$ UFD

C. ED $\subset$ PID $\subset$ UFD

D. PID $\subset$ UFD $\subset$ ED

[**Hint :** Euclidean domain is a PID but the converse is not true

$\therefore$ ED $\subseteq$ PID

PID and ED are unique factorization domains

$\therefore$ ED $\subseteq$ PID $\subseteq$ UFD

UFD need not be PID or ED]

60. Which of the following is not associated with an L.P.P?

A. Proportionality B. Uncertainty

C. Additivity D. Divisibility

ANSWERS

1	2	3	4	5	6	7	8	9	10
A	B	B	A	C	D	B	A	B	A
11	**12**	**13**	**14**	**15**	**16**	**17**	**18**	**19**	**20**
D	B	B	C	C	B	C	D	C	B
21	**22**	**23**	**24**	**25**	**26**	**27**	**28**	**29**	**30**
A	A	D	B	B	C	C	A	C	C
31	**32**	**33**	**34**	**35**	**36**	**37**	**38**	**39**	**40**
D	A	A	D	D	D	B	D	A	A
41	**42**	**43**	**44**	**45**	**46**	**47**	**48**	**49**	**50**
C	A	A	B	D	D	B	A	C	C
51	**52**	**53**	**54**	**55**	**56**	**57**	**58**	**59**	**60**
C	A	D	A	C	C	B	D	C	D

SOME SELECTED EXPLANATORY ANSWERS

3. Number of elements in $U(248)$ is given by $\phi(248)$ where ϕ is Euler function.

Now $248 = 2.2.2.31 = 2^3.31$

Hence $\phi(248) = 248\left(1-\frac{1}{2}\right)\left(1-\frac{1}{31}\right)$

$= 248\times\frac{1}{2}\times\frac{30}{31} = 120.$

5. $\int_{-1}^{1} f(x)dx = A_0\left(-\frac{1}{2}\right)+A_1 f(0)+A_2 f\left(\frac{1}{2}\right)$

when $f(x) = 1 \Rightarrow 2 = A_0 + A_1 + A_2$

$f(x) = x \Rightarrow 0 = -\frac{A_0}{2}+0+\frac{A_2}{2}$

$f(x) = x^2$

$\Rightarrow \frac{2}{3} = A_0\left(-\frac{1}{2}\right)^2 + A_1(0)^2 + A_2\left(\frac{1}{2}\right)$

$= \frac{A_0}{4}+\frac{A_2}{4} \Rightarrow A_0 = A_2 = \frac{4}{3}$

$A_1 = -\frac{2}{3}$

13. Since diagonalizability is characterized by the minimal polynomial, a matrix is diagonalizable if the minimal polynomial is written as a distinct linear factors.

17. Given $v = a_1v_1 + a_2v_2 + a_3v_3 + a_4v_4$

$v_1 - v = (1 - a_1)\, v_1 - a_2v_2 - a_3v_3 - a_4v_4$

$v_2 - v = -a_1v_1 + (1 - a_2)v_2 - a_3v_3 - a_4v_4$

$v_3 - v = -a_1v_1 - a_2v_2 + (1 - a_3)v_3 - a_4v_4$

$v_4 - v = -a_1v_1 - a_2v_2 - a_3v_3 + (1 - a_4)v_4.$

Now if $\{v_1 - v, v_2 - v, v_3 - v, v_4 - v\}$ is a basis of $\mathbf{R}^4$ then

$$\begin{vmatrix} 1-a_1 & -a_2 & -a_3 & -a_4 \\ -a_1 & 1-a_2 & -a_3 & -a_4 \\ -a_1 & -a_2 & 1-a_3 & -a_4 \\ -a_1 & -a_2 & -a_3 & 1-a_4 \end{vmatrix} \neq 0.$$

<*i.e.* They must have only trivial solution>

as v_1, v_2, v_3, v_4 are linear independent.

i.e. $a_1 + a_2 + a_3 + a_4 - 1 \neq 0$

or $a_1 + a_2 + a_3 + a_4 \neq 1.$

19. A. $T(x, y, z) = (x + y, y + z)$

hence $T(1, 0, 0) = (1, 0)$

$T(0, 1, 0) = (1, 1)$

$T(0, 0, 1) = (0, 1)$

i.e. $[T] = \begin{bmatrix} 1 & 1 & 0 \\ 0 & 1 & 1 \end{bmatrix}$

B. $T : R^3 \to P_2(R)$

$T(a, b, c) = (a + b) + (b + c)x + cx^2$

Hence, $T(1, 0, 0) = 1 + 0.x + 0.x^2$

$T(0, 1, 0) = 1 + 1.x + 0.x^2$

$T(0, 0, 1) = 0 + 1.x + 1.x^2$

i.e. $[T] = \begin{bmatrix} 1 & 1 & 0 \\ 0 & 1 & 1 \\ 0 & 0 & 1 \end{bmatrix}$

C. $T(p(x)) = xp(x)$

$T(1) = x.1 = 0.1 + 1.x + 0.x^2 + 0.x^3$

$T(x) = x.x = 0.1 + 0.x + 1.x^2 + 0.x^3$

$T(x^2) = x.x^2 = 0.1 + 0.x + 0.x^2 + 1.x^3$

i.e. $[T] = \begin{bmatrix} 0 & 0 & 0 \\ 1 & 0 & 0 \\ 0 & 1 & 0 \\ 0 & 0 & 1 \end{bmatrix}.$

D. $T(x, y) = (x, x + y, y)$

$T(1, 0) = (1, 1, 0)$, $T(0, 1) = (0, 1, 1)$

i.e. $[T] = \begin{bmatrix} 1 & 0 \\ 1 & 1 \\ 0 & 1 \end{bmatrix}.$

23. The point of intersection of the curve

$y(x^2 + 2) = 3x$ and $4y = x^2$ is equal to

$$\frac{3x}{x^2+2} = \frac{x^2}{4} \quad \text{or, } 12x = x^2(x^2+2)$$

$\Rightarrow x(x^3 + 2x - 12) = 0$

$\Rightarrow x(x-2)(x^2+2x+6) = 0 \quad \Rightarrow x = 0, 2$

Hence the area of region is given by

$$\int_0^2 \int_{y=x^2/4}^{3x/x^2+2} dxdy.$$

27. $|A| = \begin{vmatrix} 0 & 1 & 0 & 0 \\ 0 & 2 & 0 & 1 \\ 0 & 3 & 2 & 0 \\ 1 & 4 & 1 & 0 \end{vmatrix} \Rightarrow -1(1(0-2)) = 2.$

i.e. $\det(A^{-1}) = \frac{1}{2}.$

33. Given integral $\quad I = \int_0^{2\pi} \frac{d\theta}{13 - 5\sin\theta}$

putting $\quad z = e^{i\theta}$, $dz = iz d\theta$

or, $\quad d\theta = \frac{dz}{iz}$

or, $$\oint_{|z|=1} \frac{dz/iz}{13 - \frac{5}{2i}\left(z - \frac{1}{z}\right)} = -\frac{2}{5}\oint \frac{dz}{z^2 - \frac{26}{5}iz - 1}$$

If α, β be root of equation $z^2 - \frac{26}{5}iz - 1$

then as $|\alpha\beta| = 1$ also $\alpha + \beta = \frac{26}{5}i$

let $|\alpha| < 1$ lie inside $|z| = 1$

then residue at $z = \alpha = -\frac{2}{5}.\frac{1}{(\alpha - \beta)}$

$$= -\frac{2}{5}.\frac{1}{\sqrt{(\alpha-\beta)^2 - 4\alpha\beta}}$$

$$= -\frac{2}{\frac{5.24i}{5}} = \frac{-1}{12i}$$

$\therefore$ By residue theorem,

$$I = 2\pi i\left[-\frac{1}{12i}\right] = -\frac{\pi}{6}.$$

34. The given assignment cost matrix is

14	12	16
21	9	17
9	7	5

using the Hungarian method, (*i.e.* substracting the minimum cost of each row to the other clement of the same row).

Then

2	0	4
12	0	8
4	2	0

(as the first column does not have any zero, apply the Hungarian rule for the first column, we get).

[0]	~~0~~	4
10	[0]	8
2	2	[0]

Hence the optimal assignment cost

= 14 + 9 + 5 = 28.

35. $$y = \left(\frac{x^2+5x+3}{x^2+x+2}\right)^x$$

$$\log y = x\left[\log\left(1+\frac{5}{x}+\frac{3}{x^2}\right) - \log\left(1+\frac{1}{x}+\frac{2}{x^2}\right)\right]$$

$$= x\left[\left\{\left(\frac{5}{x}+\frac{3}{x^2}\right) - \frac{\left(\frac{5}{x}+\frac{3}{x}\right)^2}{2}+\ldots\right\}\right.$$

$$\left.-\left\{\left(\frac{1}{x}+\frac{2}{x^2}\right) - \frac{\left(\frac{1}{x}+\frac{2}{x^2}\right)^2}{2}+\ldots\right\}\right]$$

$$= \left(5+\frac{3}{x}\ldots\right) - \left(1+\frac{2}{x}\ldots\right)$$

$$\lim_{x\to\infty} y = e^4$$

40. $2ydx + (2x - 3y)\, dy = 0$ ...(1)

It is Homogeneous

$M = 2y$

$\Rightarrow \quad \dfrac{\partial M}{\partial y} = 2$

$N = 2x - 3y$

$\Rightarrow \quad \dfrac{\partial N}{\partial x} = 2$

As $\dfrac{\partial M}{\partial y} = \dfrac{\partial N}{\partial x}$ so it is exact

(1) can be written as

$$\frac{dy}{dx} = \frac{2y}{2x-3y}$$

$\Rightarrow$ it is not linear

41. dim (S + T) = dim(S) + dim(T) – dim(S ∩ T).

Clearly the maximum value of dim (S ∩ T) is min{dim(S), dim(T)}.

i.e. $\{\dim(S \cap T)\}_{max} = 17.$

i.e. $\{\dim(S \times T)\}_{min} = 19.$

45. At multiple points of $f(x, y) = 0$

$$\frac{\partial f}{\partial x} = 0 = \frac{\partial f}{\partial y}$$

$$\frac{\partial f}{\partial x} = 4x^3 - 4a^2x = 4x(x^2 - a^2) = 0$$

$\Rightarrow \quad x = 0,\ a, -a$

$$\frac{\partial f}{\partial y} = 0 \Rightarrow -6ay^2 - 6a^2y = 0$$

$\Rightarrow -6ay\,(y + a) = 0 \quad \Rightarrow \quad y = 0, -a$

$\therefore$ The combination of these which satisfy $f = 0$ are

$(a, 0)\ (-a, 0)\ \&\ (0, -a)$.

47. $\therefore$ $f(x) = x^3 - 3x^2 - 9x - 2$

$f'(x) = 3x^2 - 6x - 9$

$\Rightarrow x^2 - 2x - 3 = 0$

$\Rightarrow (x - 3)(x + 1) = 0$

$\Rightarrow x = -1, 3$

+ve | –1 | –ve | 3 | +ve

i.e. $f(x)$ is monotinic increasing

& $f(x)$ is monotonic decreasing for $x \in (-1, 3)$

48. $\log_{0.3}(x-1) < \log_{0.09}(x-1)$

$\Rightarrow \log_{0.09}(x-1)^2 < \log_{0.09}(x-1)$ ...(*i*)

(by squaring both base value and argument of logarithm)

$\Rightarrow (x-1)^2 > (x-1)$ (As base is less than 1 So inequallity changes)

$\Rightarrow (x-1)(x-2) > 0$

$\Rightarrow x > 2$ or $x < 1$; when $x < 1$ log is not defined so $x > 2$ i.e. $x \in (2, \infty)$

49. The basis of $\mathbf{R}^2$ are (1, 0) and (1, 1)

hence $(a, b) = (a - b)(1, 0) + b(1, 1)$

hence $T(a, b) = (a - b)\,T(1, 0) + b\,T(1, 1)$

$= (a - b)(1, 2) + b(0, 2)$

$= (a - b, 2a - 2b) + (0, 2b)$

$= (a - b, 2a)$.

50. $\lim\limits_{n\to\infty} (n^2 C_n x^n)^{1/n}$

$= \lim\limits_{n\to\infty} (n^{1/n})^2 \lim\limits_{n\to\infty} (C_n x^n)^{1/n}$

$= \lim\limits_{n\to\infty} (C_n x^n)^{1/n}$

so radius of convergence is same (r).

53. The sum of the eigenvalues of A is equal to its trace

The product of the eigenvalues of A is equal to its $|A|$

All eigen values of A are non-zero if $|A| \neq 0$

If A^{-1} exists, then the eigenvalues of A^{-1} are equal to reciprocal of the eigen values of A.

54. Given $f(x) = \dfrac{x^2}{1-\cos x} = \sum_{n=0}^{\infty} a_n x^n$

$$\Rightarrow \frac{x^2}{1-\cos x} = a_0 + a_1 x + a_2 x^2 + a_3 x^3 + \ldots$$

$$\Rightarrow \frac{1}{1-\cos 1} = a_0 + a_1 + a_2 + \ldots \qquad \ldots(i)$$

(put $x = 1$)

$$\Rightarrow \frac{(-1)^2}{1-\cos(-1)} = a_0 - a_1 + a_2 + \ldots \qquad \ldots(ii)$$

(put $x = -1$)

(i) and (ii)

$$\Rightarrow \quad 2\sum_{n=0}^{\infty} a_{2n+1} = 0 \quad \text{or,} \quad \sum_{n=0}^{\infty} a_{2n+1} = 0.$$

55. The given binary operation is

$$m * n = m + n - 1$$

if e is the identity of this operation

i.e., $\quad m * e = m$

$\Rightarrow \quad m + e - 1 = m$

or $\quad e = 1$

Now if n is inverse of m then

$$m * n = 1$$

$\Rightarrow \quad m + n - 1 = 1$

$\Rightarrow \quad n = 2 - m.$

56. $R_1 \to R_1 + R_2 + R_3$

$$\Rightarrow k+2 \begin{vmatrix} 1 & 1 & 1 \\ 1 & k & 1 \\ 1 & 1 & k \end{vmatrix} \neq 0$$

$R_1 \to R_1 - R_3$

$$\Rightarrow (k+2) \begin{vmatrix} 0 & 0 & 1-k \\ 1 & k & 1 \\ 1 & 1 & k \end{vmatrix} \neq 0$$

$\Rightarrow (k+2)(1-k)^2 \neq 0$

$\Rightarrow k \neq -2$ and $k \neq -1.$

SET–19

CSIR–UGC (NET) MATHEMATICAL SCIENCES

PART-C

1. What is the general solution of the equation $6y'' + 5y' - 6y = x$?

A. $y = c_1 e^{-x} + c_2 e^{x/6} - \left(\frac{x}{6}\right) - \left(\frac{5}{36}\right)$

B. $y = c_1 e^{2x/3} + c_2 e^{-3x/2} - \left(\frac{x}{6}\right) - \left(\frac{5}{36}\right)$

C. $y = c_1 e^{2x/3} - c_2 e^{-3x/2} - \left(\frac{x}{6}\right) - \left(\frac{5}{36}\right)$

D. $y = c_1 e^{2x/3} + c_2 e^{-3x/2} - \left(\frac{5x}{36}\right) - \left(\frac{1}{6}\right)$

2. Let $R[x]$ be the polynomial ring in x with real coefficients and let $I = \langle x^2 + 1 \rangle$ be the ideal generated by the polynomial $x^2 + 1$ in $R[x]$. Then

A. I is a maximal ideal
B. I is prime ideal but NOT a maximal ideal
C. I is NOT a prime ideal
D. $R[x]/I$ has zero divisors

3. The function $f(x, y) = (e^x \cos y, e^x \sin y)$ from R^2 to R^2 is

A. one-one on all of R^2
B. one-one on some neighbourhood of any points in R^2
C. an onto map.
D. such that some neighbourhood of any point surjects onto R^2.

4. $|z - 3i|^2 + |z + 3i|^2 = 10$ will represents

A. circle
B. ellipse
C. hyperbola
D. parabola

5. The value of y at $x = 1$ using Taylor's method for the differential equation $\frac{dy}{dx} = 2y + 3e^x$, given $y(0) = 0$.

A. 12.01
B. 13.01
C. 14.01
D. 15.01

6. The integral surface of the partial differential equation $p + q = 1$, passing through the curve $x = 0,\ y^2 = z$ is

A. $yz = (x + y)^2$
B. $x^3 - 3xy^2 = z^2 - 2yz$
C. $(y - x)^2 = z - x$
D. None of these

7. The value of $\int_{|z|=1} \frac{\cos(e^z)}{z} dz$ is

A. 0
B. $2\pi i$
C. $\pi i\ (e^i - e^{-i})$
D. $\pi i(e^i + e^{-i})$.

8. Three particles of masses 1, 2 and 4 move under a force field such that their position vectors at any time t are respectively given by

$\bar{r}_1 = 2\hat{i} + 4t^2\hat{k},\ \bar{r}_2 = 2t\hat{i} - \hat{k},$

$\bar{r}_3 = (\cos \pi t)\hat{i} + (\sin \pi t)\hat{j}$

For the above motion which of the following is true

A. the total momentum is zero
B. the total momentum has constant magnitude
C. the force acting on the system is constant
D. the force acting on the system has constant magnitude

9. The equation $\frac{d^2y}{dx^2} - \frac{2dy}{dx} + 10y = 0$ has characteristic roots.

A. $1 \pm 3i$
B. $1 \pm 2i$
C. $1 + \frac{3}{2}i$
D. $1 - \frac{3}{2}i$

10. Which of the following matrices is NOT diagonalizable?

A. $\begin{bmatrix} 1 & 1 \\ 1 & 2 \end{bmatrix}$ B. $\begin{bmatrix} 1 & 0 \\ 3 & 2 \end{bmatrix}$

C. $\begin{bmatrix} 0 & -1 \\ 1 & 0 \end{bmatrix}$ D. $\begin{bmatrix} 1 & 1 \\ 0 & 1 \end{bmatrix}$

11. The general solution of the Partial Differential Equation $z^2 = p^2 - q^2$ passing through the curve $x_0 = s$, $y_0 = 0$, $z_0 = s^2/4$

A. no solution exist
B. there is a unique solution
C. two solutions
D. more than two solutions

12. If E and F are events with $P(E) \leq P(F)$ and $P(E \cap F) > 0$, then

A. occurrence of $E \Rightarrow$ occurrence of F
B. occurrence of $F \Rightarrow$ occurrence of E
C. non occurrence of $E \Rightarrow$ non-occurrence of F
D. none of the above implication holds

13. Pick up the correct answer
If H be a subgroup of G then H is normal in G if

A. H is a subgroup of index 2 in G
B. H is a subgroup of index 3 in G
C. H is a subgroup of index 4 in G
D. None of these

14. Convex combination of three vectors in a space will be *locus* of

A. Triangle
B. Line segment
C. A straight line
D. A circle with constant radius

15. Which of the following statements associated with a first order non-linear differential equation $f\left(x, y, \frac{dy}{dx}\right) = 0$ are correct?

1. Its general solution must contain only one arbitrary constant.
2. Its singular solution can be obtained by substituting particular value of the arbitrary constant in its general solution.
3. Its singular solution is an envelope of its general solution which also satisfies the equation.

Select the correct answer using the codes below:

A. 1, 2 and 3 B. 1 and 2
C. 1 and 3 D. 2 and 3

16. If $f(z) = z^3$, then it

A. has an essential singularity at $z = \infty$
B. has a pole of order 3 at $z = \infty$
C. has a pole of order 3 at $z = 0$
D. is analytic at $z = \infty$

17. Let F be a finite field with n elements. What is the possible value of n?

A. 1 B. 36
C. 37 D. 125

18. Trapezoid rule for evaluation of $\int_a^b f(x)dx$ requires the interval (a, b) to be divided into

A. $2n$ sub-intervals of equal width.
B. $2n + 1$ sub-intervals of equal width.
C. any number of sub-intervals of equal width.
D. $3n$ sub-intervals of equal width.

19. Consider the following Linear Programming Problem (LPP).
Minimize $z = 2x_1 + 3x_2 + x_3$
subject to $x_1 + 2x_2 + 2x_3 - x_4 + x_5 = 3$
$2x_1 + 3x_2 + 4x_3 + ... + x_6 = 6$
$x_i \geq 0, \ i = 1, 2, ... 6$

A non degenerate basic feasible solution $(x_1, x_2, x_3, x_4, x_5, x_6)$ is

A. (1, 0, 1, 0, 0, 0) B. (1, 0, 0, 0, 0, 7)
C. (0, 0, 0, 0, 3, 6) D. (3, 0, 0, 0, 0, 0)

20. A two person game is said to be zero sum. if

A. gain of one player is exactly matched by a loss to the other so that their sum is equal to zero.
B. gain of one player does not match the loss to the other.
C. both the players must have an equal member of strategies.
D. diagonal entries of the pay off matrix are zero.

21. For the given functional

$$I[y(x)] = \int_0^2 (xy' + y^2)dx; \ y(0) = 1, \ y(2) = 0$$

A. Weak minima but not strong for $y = 1-\frac{x^2}{4}$

B. Strong minima for $y = 1-\frac{x^2}{4}$

C. Strong minima for $y = 1+\frac{x^2}{4}$

D. Strong maxima for $y = 1-\frac{x^2}{4}$

22. $\oint_c \frac{dz}{z-2}$ = ? around the circle ½z – 2½ = 4 and the square with the vertices at $2 + 2i$, $-2 \pm 2i$

A. $2\pi i$, 0 B. $2\pi i$, πi

C. $2\pi i$ in all cases D. 0, πi

23. The interval of convergence of

$1+x+\frac{x^2}{2!}+\frac{x^3}{3!}+...+\frac{x^4}{n!}+...$

A. Diverges for all values of x

B. Converges for all values of x

C. Oscillates for all values of x

D. Conditionally converges for all values of x

24. If a linear program has two optimal solution x_1, x_2 at the corner points of its feasible region then which of the following is true.

A. Only x_1 and x_2 are optimal solutions

B. Any $x = \lambda x_1 + (1 - \lambda)x_2$, for all λ is an optimal solution.

C. Any $x = \lambda x_1 + (1 - \lambda) x_2$, $0 \le \lambda \le 1$ is an optimal solution

D. None of the above.

25. Let $R^{2\times 2}$ be the real vector space of all 2 × 2 real matrices. For Q = $\begin{pmatrix} 1 & -2 \\ -2 & 4 \end{pmatrix}$ define a linear transformation T on $R^{2\times 2}$ as T(P) = QP. Then the rank of T is

A. 1 B. 2

C. 3 D. 4

26. The differential equation

$(x-y-2)dx+(x-2y-3)dy=0$

may (or may not) reduce.

A. To partial differential equation

B. To homogeneous equation

C. To non-homoeneous equation

D. None of the above

27. Which statements are true.

A. Every cyclic group is abelian

B. Every group of prime order is cyclic

C. Every group os composite order is cyclic

D. Every subgroup of a cyclic group is cyclic

28. Let **R** be the set of all real numbers and $\mathbf{R}^2 = \{(x_1, x_2) : x_1 \in \mathbf{R}, x_2 \in \mathbf{R}\}$. Then which one of the following is a subspace of $\mathbf{R}^2$ over **R**?

A. $\{(x_1, x_2) : x_1 > 0, x_2 > 0\}$

B. $\{(x_1, x_2) : x_1 \in \mathbf{R}, x_2 > 0\}$

C. $\{(x_1, x_2) : x_1 < 0, x_2 < 0\}$

D. $\{(x_1, 0) : x_1 \in \mathbf{R}\}$

29. Let T : $\mathbf{R}^3 \to \mathbf{R}^3$ be the linear transformation whose matrix with respect to the standard basis (e_1, e_2, e_3) of $\mathbf{R}^3$ is $\begin{pmatrix} 0 & 0 & 1 \\ 0 & 1 & 0 \\ 1 & 0 & 0 \end{pmatrix}$. Then T

A. maps the subspace spanned by e_1 and e_2 into itself

B. has distinct eigen values

C. has eigen vectors that span $\mathbf{R}^3$

D. has a non-zero null space

30. The least number of elements in a group having a proper non-abelian subgroup is

A. 8 B. 12

C. 24 D. 120

31. The singular solution(s) of the $y^2 - 2pxy + p^2(x^2 - 1) = m^2$ is/are.

A. $y^3 - m^2x^2 = m^2$ B. $y^3 + m^2x^2 = m^2$

C. $y^2 - m^2x^2 = m^2$ D. $y^2 + m^2x^2 = m^2$

32. The unit vector parallel to $a = 3i + 4j - 2k$ is

A. $\sqrt{29}\,(3i+4j-2k)$

B. $\frac{1}{\sqrt{29}}(3i+4j-2k)$

C. $29\,(3i + 4j - 2k)$

D. $\frac{1}{29}(3i+4j-2k)$

33. The number of roots of the equation $z^5 - 12z^2 + 14 = 0$ that lie in the region $\left\{z \in c : 2 \le |z| < \frac{5}{2}\right\}$ is

A. 2
B. 3
C. 4
D. 5

34. Let G be any group and $a \in G$ such that $o(a^5) = 12$, then which of the following is possible order of a.

A. 24
B. 36
C. 48
D. 60

35. If V be the vector space of polynomials in t over R of degree ≤ 3, and D : $v \to v$ be the differential operator defined by $D(p(t)) = \frac{d}{dt}(p(t))$. Compute the matrix of D in the basis $\{1, t, t^2, t^3\}$ be.

A. $\begin{bmatrix} 0 & 1 & 0 & 0 \\ 0 & 0 & 2 & 0 \\ 0 & 0 & 0 & 3 \\ 0 & 0 & 0 & 0 \end{bmatrix}$
B. $\begin{bmatrix} 0 & 0 & 0 & 0 \\ 0 & 0 & 0 & 0 \\ 1 & 0 & 0 & 0 \\ 0 & 2 & 0 & 3 \end{bmatrix}$

C. $\begin{bmatrix} 1 & 0 & 0 & 0 \\ 0 & 2 & 0 & 0 \\ 0 & 0 & 3 & 0 \\ 0 & 0 & 0 & 0 \end{bmatrix}$
D. $\begin{bmatrix} 1 & 2 & 3 & 0 \\ 0 & 1 & 2 & 3 \\ 0 & 0 & 1 & 2 \\ 0 & 0 & 0 & 3 \end{bmatrix}$

36. At the point $x = 1$, the function

$$f(x) = \begin{cases} x^2 - 1, & 1 < x < \infty \\ x - 1, & -\infty < x \leq 1 \end{cases} \text{ is}$$

A. continuous and differentiable
B. continuous and not differentiable
C. discontinuous and monotonically increasing
D. discontinuous and monotonically decreasing

37. Let f : [0, 1] → [0, 1] defined as

$$f(x) = \begin{cases} \frac{1}{2} & \text{if } x = 0 \\ \frac{x}{2x+1} & \text{if } x = \frac{1}{n}, \quad n \in N \\ x & \text{if } x \neq 0, \frac{1}{n} n \in N \end{cases}$$

then select the incorrect statement

A. f is 1–1 but not onto
B. the range of is uncountable
C. the map proves that (0, 1) is similar to [0, 1]
D. none of these

38. Let $S = \{(x, y) : x^2 + y^2 \leq 1\}$, then every interior point of S can be expressed as a convex co.nbination of

A. Exactly two vertices of S
B. Exactly three vertices of S
C. More then three vertices of S
D. None of the above

39. Let $f(x) = x^p \sin\left(\frac{1}{x}\right)$, when x ¹ 0

$= 0$ when $x = 0$

Then $f(x)$ can be differentiated at the origin provided p is

A. any real number
B. zero
C. one
D. an integer greater than 1

40. The value of α for which $G = \{\alpha, 1, 3, 9, 19, 27\}$ is a cyclic group under multiplication modulo 56 is

A. 5
B. 15
C. 25
D. 35

41. If $z = \frac{1+i}{2}$ then the expresson $2z^4 - 2z^2 + z + 3$ is equal to

A. $3 - \frac{i}{2}$
B. $3 + \frac{i}{2}$
C. $\frac{3+i}{2}$
D. $\frac{3-i}{2}$

42. The set of all $x \in$ R for which the vectors $(1, x, 0)$, $(0, x^2, 1)$ and $(0, 1, x)$ are linearly independent in $\mathbf{R}^3$ is

A. $\{x \in R : x = 0\}$
B. $\{x \in R : x \neq 0\}$
C. $\{x \in R : x \neq 1\}$
D. $\{x \in R : x \neq -1\}$

43. The equation $(4x + 3y + 1)dx + (3x + 2y + 1)dy = 0$ represents a family of

A. circles
B. parabolas
C. ellipses
D. hyperbolas

44. Let R be the ring of all functions from R to R under point-wise addition and multiplication. Let $I = \{f : R \to R \mid f$ is a bounded function$\}$, $J = \{f : R \to R \mid f(3) = 0$. Then

A. J is an ideal of R but I is not an ideal of R

B. I is an ideal of R but J is not an ideal of R

C. both I and J are ideals of R

D. neither I nor J is an ideal of R

45. If the set of all triples (x_1, x_2, x_3) of real numbers R form a vector space V_3, then a subspace denoted by a vertical plane $y = x$ can be obtained by a linear comibination of the sets

A. (1, 1, 0) and (0, 0, 1)

B. (1, 1, 0) and (1, 0, 0)

C. (1, 0, 0) and (0, 1, 0)

D. (1, 0, 1) and (0, 0, 1)

46. Fifteen coupon's are numbered 1, 2, ..., 15 respectively. Seven coupons are selected at random one at a time with replacement. The probability that the largest number appearing on a selected coupon is 9, is

A. $\left(\frac{9}{16}\right)^6$ B. $\left(\frac{8}{15}\right)^7$

C. $\left(\frac{3}{5}\right)^7$ D. None of these

47. Let $f(z) = u(x, y) + iv(x, y)$ be an entire function having Taylor's series expansion as $\sum_{n=0}^{\infty} a_n z^n$.

If $f(x) = u(x, 0)$ and $f(iy) = iv(0, y)$ then

A. $a_{2n} = 0$ for all n

B. $a_0 = a_1 = a_2 = a_3 = 0, a_n \neq 0$

C. $a_{2n+1} = 0$ for all n

D. $a_0 \neq 0$ but $a_2 = 0$

48. Let A be a 3 × 3 matrix with eigenvalues 1, –1 and 3. Then

A. $A^2 + A$ is non-singular

B. $A^2 - A$ is non-singular

C. $A^2 + 3A$ is non-singular

D. $A^2 - 3A$ is non-singular

49. If $X_1, X_2, \ldots\ldots X_n$ are independent $N(0, 1)$ variates. Then distribution of $\sum_{i=1}^{n} X_i^2$ subject to conditions $X_1 + X_2 - X_3 = 0$ and $X_1 + X_5 + X_9 + \ldots\ldots = 0$ is

A. χ_n^2 B. χ_{n-1}^2

C. χ_{n-2}^2 D. χ_{n-4}^2

50. Let $A \in C^{m \times n}$ and A′, A* denote respectively the transpose and conjugate transpose of A. Then

A. rank (AA*A) = rank (A)

B. rank (A) = rank (A^2)

C. rank (A) = rank (A′A)

D. rank (A^2) – rank(A) = rank(A^3) – rank(A^2)

51. The least possible number of positive roots of the equation $2x^7 - x^4 + 4x^3 - 5 = 0$ is

A. 2 B. 4

C. 6 D. none of the above

52. In Game theory, which is not true.

A. The value of game can be +ve, –ve, 0.

B. The value of game can be determined only if the game has a saddle point.

C. Saddle point in the pay off matrix is the point of equilibrium.

D. A game is strictly determinable and fair if saddle point value comes out to zero.

53. The number of homomorphism from Z_{20} onto Z_{10}.

A. 20 B. 10

C. 5 D. 4

54. Let A be a 3 × 3 matrix with trace $(A) = 3$ and det $(A) = 2$. If 1 is an eigenvalue of A, then the eigenvalues of the matrix $A^2 - 2I$ are

A. 1, $2(i - 1)$, $-2(i + 1)$

B. –1, $2(i - 1)$, $2(i + 1)$

C. 1, $2(i + 1)$, $-2(i + 1)$

D. –1, $2(i - 1)$, $-2(i + 1)$

55. If $\vec{u}(t) = u_1(t)\mathbf{i} + u_2(t)\, j + u_3(t)\mathbf{k}$ is a unit vector and $\frac{d\vec{u}}{dt} \neq 0$, then the angle between $\vec{u}(t)$ and $\frac{d\vec{u}}{dt}$ is

A. 0 B. $\frac{\pi}{4}$

C. $\frac{\pi}{3}$ D. $\frac{\pi}{2}$

56. The polynomial $f(x) = x^5 + 5$ is

A. Irreducible over C

B. Irreducible over R

C. Irreducible over q

D. Not irreducible over q

Where q. denotes the field of rational number.

57. For a given matrix A of order n, identify the false statement

A. Suppose there exists a polynomial $p(x)$ such that $p(0) \neq 0$ while $p(1)$ is the null matrix implies A must be non-singular

B. If f (.) is the characteristic polynomial then $f(1) = 0$

C. If A has n eigenvalues then A is diagonlizable

D. None of the above

58. The orthogonal trajectories of the family of parabolas $y = ax^2$ are given by the solution of the differential equation

A. $\frac{dy}{dx} = \frac{2y}{x}$ B. $\frac{dy}{dx} = -\frac{2y}{x}$

C. $\frac{dy}{dx} = \frac{x}{2y}$ D. $\frac{dy}{dx} = -\frac{x}{2y}$

59. If X has a Poisson distribution with $E(X) = \lambda$. The $E[(X + 1)^2]$ equals.

A. $(\lambda + 1)^2$ B. $\lambda^3 + 3\lambda + 1$

C. $\lambda^2 + 1$ D. $\lambda + 1$

60. If A is a 2×2 non-singular matrix, then what is adj(adj A) equal to?

A. A^2 B. A

C. A^{-1} D. –A

ANSWERS

1	2	3	4	5	6	7	8	9	10
B	A	A	B	C	B	D	D	A	D
11	12	13	14	15	16	17	18	19	20
B	D	A	D	A	B	C	C	C	A
21	22	23	24	25	26	27	28	29	30
B	C	B	C	B	C	A, B, D	D	C	A
31	32	33	34	35	36	37	38	39	40
B	B	B	D	A	B	A	A	D	C
41	42	43	44	45	46	47	48	49	50
A	C	D	A	A	C	B	C	B	C
51	52	53	54	55	56	57	58	59	60
D	B	D	A	D	A	C	D	B	B

SOME SELECTED EXPLANATORY ANSWERS

1. The given differential equation is $6y'' + 5y' - 6y = x$.

The auxiliary equation is $6m^2 + 5m - 6 = 0$.

Or, $m = \frac{-5 \pm \sqrt{25+144}}{12} = \frac{-5 \pm 13}{12}$

$\Rightarrow$ $m = \frac{2}{3}, \frac{-3}{2}$

i.e. C.F. $y = c_1 e^{2/3x} + c_2 e^{-3x/2}$.

Now for particular integral

$$y = \frac{1}{6D^2 + 5D - 6} x$$

$$= \frac{1}{-6\left[1 - \frac{(5D + 6D^2)}{6}\right]} x$$

$$= -\frac{1}{6}\left[1+\frac{(5D+6D^2)}{6}\right]x$$

$$= -\frac{1}{6}\left[x+\frac{5}{6}\right] = \frac{-x}{6}-\frac{5}{36}.$$

Hence, $y = c_1e^{2x/3}+c_2e^{-3x/2}-\frac{x}{6}-\frac{5}{36}.$

5. Given $\frac{dy}{dx} = 2y + 3e^x$ with $y(0) = 0$.

From Taylor's series expansion, we have

$$y(0 + h) = y(h) = y(0)+\frac{h}{1!}y'(0)+\frac{h^2}{2!}y''(0)$$

$$+\frac{h^3}{3!}y'''(0)+\frac{h^4}{4!}y^{iv}(0)+... \quad ...(1)$$

The value of the derivatives $y'(0)$, $y''(0)$, ... etc. are obtained as

$y(0) = 0$

$y'(x) = 2y + 3e^x$, $\quad y'(0) = 2y(0) + 3.e^0 = 3$

$y''(x) = 2y' + 3e^x$, $\quad y''(0) = 2y'(0) + 3 = 9$

$y'''(x) = 2y'' + 3e^x$, $\quad y'''(0) = 21$

$y^{iv}(x) = 2y''' + 3e^x$, $\quad y^{iv}(0) = 45$

$y^{v}(x) = 2y^{iv} + 3e^x$, $\quad y^{v}(0) = 93$

$y^{vi}(x) = 2y^{v} + 3e^x$, $\quad y^{vi}(0) = 189$

$y^{vii}(x) = 2y^{vI} + 3e^x$, $\quad y^{vii}(0) = 381$

$y^{viii}(x) = 2y^{vii} + 3e^x$, $\quad y^{viii}(0) = 765.$

Putting these values in (1), we get

$$y(h) = \frac{h}{1}\times 3+\frac{h^2}{2}\times 9+\frac{h^3}{6}\times 21+\frac{h^4}{24}\times 45$$

$$+\frac{h^5}{120}\times 93+\frac{h^6}{720}\times 189+\frac{h^7}{5040}\times 381$$

$$+\frac{h^8}{40320}\times 765+...$$

$$= 3h+\frac{9}{2}h^2+\frac{7}{2}h^3+\frac{15}{8}h^4+\frac{31}{40}h^5$$

$$+\frac{21}{80}h^6+\frac{127}{1680}h^7+\frac{17}{896}h^8+...$$

$$\Rightarrow y(1) = 3+\frac{9}{2}+\frac{7}{2}+\frac{15}{8}+\frac{31}{40}+\frac{21}{80}+\frac{127}{1680}$$

$$+\frac{17}{896}+... = 14.01.$$

25. Let $P = \begin{bmatrix} x & y \\ z & t \end{bmatrix} \in R^{2\times 2}$

then $T(P) = QP = \begin{bmatrix} 1 & -2 \\ -2 & 4 \end{bmatrix}\begin{bmatrix} x & y \\ z & t \end{bmatrix}$

$$= \begin{bmatrix} x-2z & y-2t \\ -2x+4z & -2y+4t \end{bmatrix}$$

$$= \begin{bmatrix} (x-2z) & (y-2t) \\ -2(x-2z) & -2(y-2t) \end{bmatrix}$$

$\Rightarrow$ Rank of T = 2.

29. $$T = \begin{bmatrix} 0 & 0 & 1 \\ 0 & 1 & 0 \\ 1 & 0 & 0 \end{bmatrix}$$

$$|T-\lambda I| = 0$$

$$\Rightarrow \begin{bmatrix} -\lambda & 0 & 1 \\ 0 & 1-\lambda & 0 \\ 1 & 0 & -\lambda \end{bmatrix}$$

$$\lambda^2(1-\lambda)+1(\lambda-1) = 0$$

$$\Rightarrow \quad (\lambda-1)(1-\lambda^2) = 0 \Rightarrow \lambda = 1, 1, -1$$

$\Rightarrow$ T has only zero null space.

$$|T-I| = 0 \begin{bmatrix} -1 & 0 & 1 \\ 0 & 0 & 0 \\ 1 & 0 & -1 \end{bmatrix}\begin{bmatrix} x \\ y \\ z \end{bmatrix} = \begin{bmatrix} 0 \\ 0 \\ 0 \end{bmatrix}$$

$$\Rightarrow \quad -x+z = 0$$

Then the eigen vector

$$[0, 1, 0] \ \& \ [1, 0, 1]$$

$$|T+I| = 0 \begin{bmatrix} 1 & 0 & 1 \\ 0 & 2 & 0 \\ 1 & 0 & 1 \end{bmatrix}\begin{bmatrix} x \\ y \\ z \end{bmatrix} = \begin{bmatrix} 0 \\ 0 \\ 0 \end{bmatrix}$$

$$x+z = 0 \quad y = 0$$

$\Rightarrow$ eigen vector $[1, 0, -1]$.

Clearly all are independent.

Hence, it span $\mathbf{R}^3$.

32. $a = 3i + 4j - 2k$

$\Rightarrow$ Unit vector parallel to $\vec{a}, \hat{a}$

$$= \frac{3i+4j-2k}{|3i+4j-2k|} = \frac{3i+4j-2k}{\sqrt{9+16+4}}$$

$$= \frac{1}{\sqrt{29}}(3i+4j-2k)$$

35. $D(1) = 0 = 0 + 0t + 0t^2 + 0t^3$

$D(t) = 1 = 1 + 0t + 0t^2 + 0t^3$

$D(t^2) = 2t = 0 + 2t + 0t^2 + 0t^3$

$D(t^3) = 3t^2 = 0 + 0t + 2t^2 + 0t^3$

40. If G is a cyclic group under multiplication modulo 56 and $G = \{\alpha, 1, 3, 9, 19, 27\}$

then every non-unity member of G is a generator of G. Hence 3.3 = 9, 3.3.3 = 27, 3.3.3.3 = 25 $\Rightarrow \alpha = 25$.

42. The given vectors are $(1, x, 0)$, $(0, x^2, 1)$, $(0, 1, x)$.

These vectors will be linear independent if

$a(1, x, 0) + b(0, x^2, 1) + c(0, 1, x) = (0, 0, 0)$

$\Rightarrow a = b = c = 0$

or, $(a, ax, 0) + (0, bx^2, b) + (0, c, cx) = (0, 0, 0)$

or, $(a, ax + bx^2 + c, b + cx) = (0, 0, 0)$

i.e. $a = 0$, $bx^2 + c = 0$ & $b + cx = 0$

$\Rightarrow b - bx^3 = 0$, $b(1 - x^3) = 0$

$b = 0 \Rightarrow x^3 - 1 \neq 0$

i.e. $x \neq 1$.

44. Give

$I = \{f : R \to R \mid f \text{ is a bounded function}\}$

$J = \{f : R \to R \mid f(3) = 0\}$ is a ring of $f : R \to R$

Infact product of a bounded function & an unbounded function not necessary a bounded function.

i.e., if $f \in I$ & $g \in R$ then fg not necessarily belong to I.

However $f : R \to R \mid f(3) = 0$ then

$\forall g \in R \qquad gf(3) = 0.$

[Hence J is ideal of R. Infact J is maximal ideal of IR]

48. Eigen values of A is 1, -1, 3

so, eigen values of A^2 is 1, 1, 9

$\Rightarrow$ eigen values of $A^2 + 3A$ is

$1 + 3 \cdot 1$, $1 + 3(-1)$, $9 + 3(3)$

i.e. 4, -2 and 18

As no eigen values is 0, so

$A^2 + 3A$ is non-singular.

51. The given equation is

$2x^7 - x^4 + 4x^3 - 5 = 0$

as the sign of maximum and minimum power are opposite.

Hence the above equation has at least one positive roots.

Further, By Descarte rule of sign change.

$f(x) = 0$ for $x > 0$ changes sign as $+ - + -$

i.e. thrice

i.e. $f(x) = 0$ has at most three positive roots.

Hence, $f(x) = 0$ has at most three positive roots.

54. Given A is 3×3 matrix such that trace $(A) = 3$ and det $(A) = 2 \Rightarrow$ A is non-singular and sum of eigenvalue of A are 3.

Also 1 is an eigenvalue of A

i.e. $(A - I)$ is singular.

i.e. $[A-I]\,[A-I] = A^2 - 2A + I = 0$

$\Rightarrow A^2 - 2I = 2A - 3I$

Now trace of $(A^2 - 2I)$ = trace of $(2A - 3I)$

$= 2.3 - 3.3 = -3.$

i.e. sum of eigenvalues of $A^2 - 2I$ are -3.

Hence, the correct choice is A.

55. As $\vec{u}.\vec{u} = |\vec{u}|^2$

So differentiating both sides with respect to 't'

$$2\left(\vec{u}\,.\,\frac{d\vec{u}}{dt}\right) = 0$$

$\Rightarrow$ $\vec{u}$ and $\dfrac{d\vec{u}}{dt}$ are perpendicular to each other.

SET–20

CSIR–UGC (NET) MATHEMATICAL SCIENCES

PART-C

1. Let **U** be the column space of the matrix A = $\begin{bmatrix} 1 & -1 \\ 1 & 2 \\ 1 & -1 \end{bmatrix}$. Then the orthogonal projection of $\begin{pmatrix} 0 \\ 1 \\ 0 \end{pmatrix}$ on V is

A. $\begin{pmatrix} 0 \\ 1 \\ 0 \end{pmatrix}$ B. $\begin{pmatrix} 0 \\ 0 \\ 1 \end{pmatrix}$

C. $\begin{pmatrix} 1 \\ 1 \\ 0 \end{pmatrix}$ D. $\begin{pmatrix} 1 \\ 0 \\ 1 \end{pmatrix}$

2. If $f(x) = x^2$ on [0, 1] and $P = \left\{0, \frac{1}{4}, \frac{1}{2}, \frac{3}{4}, 1\right\}$ be a partition of [0, 1] then $U(f, p)$ and $L(f, p)$ are respectively.

A. $\frac{1}{3}$ and $\frac{1}{3}$ B. $\frac{15}{32}$ and $\frac{7}{32}$

C. $\frac{1}{16}$ and $\frac{1}{32}$ D. $\frac{2}{3}$ and $\frac{1}{3}$

3. The function $f(x) = \int_0^{x^2} \left(\frac{t^2 - 5t + 4}{2 + e^t}\right) dt$ has

A. two maxima and two minima points
B. two maxima and three minima points
C. three maxima and two minima points
D. one maximum point and one minimum point

4. Let G be a finite abelian group of odd order and

$H = \{x^2 : x \in G\}$, then

A. H is a subgroup of G only if G is cyclic
B. H is a proper subgroup of G
C. $H = G$
D. H may not be a subgroup of G

5. Let V be an n-dimensional complex vector space. Let V_R denote the subset of V defined by $\{x \in V | x = \bar{x}\}$

Then V_R is not a

A. Real vector space
B. Real subspace of V
C. Subspace of V
D. Additive subgroup of V

6. If A is a 3 × 3 matrix with det A = 5 and if B = $4A^2$, then what is det B equal to?

A. 20 B. 100
C. 320 D. 1600

7. The solution of $(D + D' - 1)(D - D')z = 0$ is

A. $z = e^x\phi(x + y) + \psi(x - y)$
B. $z = e^y\phi(x - y) + \psi(x + y)$
C. $z = e^{-y}\phi(x - y) + \psi(x + y)$
D. $z = e^{-x}\phi(x + y) + \psi(x - y)$

8. The singular solution of the equation

$y = \frac{2}{3}x\frac{dy}{dx} - \frac{2}{3x}\left(\frac{dy}{dx}\right)^2, x > 0$ is

A. $y = x^3$ B. $y = x$
C. $y = x^3/6$ D. $y = x^3/2$

9. The number of zeroes, counting multiplicities, of the polynomial $z^5 + 3z^3 + z^2 + 1$ inside the circle $|z| = 2$ is

A. 0 B. 2
C. 3 D. 5

10. A particle of unit mass is moving under gravitational field, along the cycloid $x = \phi - \sin\phi$, $y = 1 + \cos\phi$. Then the Lagrangian for the motion is

A. $\dot{\phi}^2(1+\cos\phi)-g(1-\cos\phi)$

B. $\dot{\phi}^2(1-\cos\phi)+g(1+\cos\phi)$

C. $\dot{\phi}^2(1-\cos\phi)-g(1+\cos\phi)$

D. $2\dot{\phi}^2(1-\cos\phi)-g(1+\cos\phi)$

11. Consider Z_{24} as the additive group modulo 24. Then the number of elements of order 8 in the group Z_{24} is

A. 1 B. 2
C. 3 D. 4

12. Pick up the correct answer :

A. Group {1, –1} is a simple group.
B. Group {1, –1, *i*, *i*} is a simple group
C. {1, ω, ω²} is not a simple group
D. Any group of prime order is simple

13. L.P.P maximize $3x_1 - 4x_2$, subject to $x_1 - x_2 \geq 0$, $x_2 \leq 6$, $x_1, x_2 \geq 0$ has

A. No solution
B. Multiple optimum solutions
C. Unique optimum solutions
D. Unbounded solution

14. Let *F* be a field containing 11 elements. Which one of the following is correct?

A. If α is a non-zero element of *F*, then $5\alpha \neq 0$.
B. $\alpha^5 = 1$ for every non-zero $\alpha \in F$, where 1 is the multiplicative identity of *F*.
C. $\alpha^{10} = 1$ for all $\alpha \in F$.
D. Let α be a non-zero element of *F*. It is possible to find a proper subset *S* of *F* such that $\alpha \in S$ and $\beta S \in S$ for any $\beta \in F$, $S \in S$.

15. Consider the vector space $\mathbf{R}^3$ and the maps *f*, $g : \mathbf{R}^3 \to \mathbf{R}^3$ defined by $f(x, y, z) = (x, |y|, z)$ and $g(x, y, z) = (x + 1, y - 1, z)$. Then

A. both *f* and *g* are linear
B. neither *f* nor *g* is linear
C. *g* is linear but not *f*
D. *f* is linear but not *g*

16. Seven white balls and three black balls are randomly placed in a row. The probability that no two black balls are placed adjacently equals.

A. $\frac{1}{2}$ B. $\frac{7}{15}$
C. $\frac{2}{15}$ D. $\frac{1}{3}$

17. An urn contains ten marbles of which five are green, two are blue, three are red. Three marbles are to drawn from the urn, one at a time, without replacement. Then the probability that all three marbles drawn are green is

A. 0.0833 B. 0.0233
C. 0.0633 D. 0.0433

18. In the interval [–1, 1], the series

$$\sum_{n=1}^{\infty}(-1)^{n-1}\frac{x^2+n^2}{n^3} \text{ is}$$

A. uniformaly and absolutely convergent
B. absolutely convergent but not uniformly convrgent
C. neither uniformly nor absolutely convergent
D. uniformly convergent but not absolutely convergent.

19. For the integral equation, which of the following statement is NOT true?

A. IVP can be converted into Volterra integral equation.
B. BVP can be converted into Fredholm integral equation.
C. Eigen value of homogeneous Volterra integral equation does not exist.
D. Eigen values of homogeneous Fredholm integral equation does not exist.

20. If the cost matrix for an assignment problem is given by

$$\begin{bmatrix} a & b & c & d \\ b & c & d & a \\ c & d & a & b \\ d & a & b & c \end{bmatrix}$$

where $a, b, c, d > 0$ then the value of the assignment problem is

A. $a + b + c + d$
B. min {*a*, *b*, *c*, *d*}
C. max {*a*, *b*, *c*, *d*}
D. 4 min {*a*, *b*, *c*, *d*}

21. In some simple table of a minimization L.P.P., the column corresponding to a variable x_j is $(2, -1, 0, -3)^T$ and $z_j - c_j = 2$ is not most positive, then

A. The solution is unbounded

B. The solution may be bounded or unbounded

C. The solution is bounded

D. None of the above

22. The rate at which bacteria multiply is proportional to the instantaneous number present. If the original number doubles in 2 hours, then it will triple in

A. $2\dfrac{\log 3}{\log 2}$ B. $2\dfrac{\log 2}{\log 3}$

C. $\dfrac{\log 3}{\log 2}$ D. $\dfrac{\log 2}{\log 3}$

23. Which of the following sequences of functions is uniformly convergent on (0, 1)?

A. x^n B. $\dfrac{n}{nx+1}$

C. $\dfrac{x}{nx+1}$ D. $\dfrac{1}{nx+1}$

24. Let Q be the field of rational numbers and consider z_2 as a field modulo 2. Let $f(x) = x^3 - 9x^2 + 9x + 3$. Then $f(x)$ is

A. irreducible over Q but reducible over Z_2

B. irreducible over both Q and Z_2

C. reducible over Q but irreducible over Z_2

D. reducible over both Q and Z_2

25. A random variable Y has the following distribution:

Y	–1	0	1	2
$P(Y)$	$3C$	$2C$	0.4	0.1

The value of the constant C is:

A. 0.10 B. 0.15

C. 0.20 D. 0.25

26. The differential equation associated with the primitive

$y = Ax^2 + Bx + C$ is given by

A. $\dfrac{d^3y}{dx^3} = 0$ B. $\dfrac{d^2y}{dx^2} = 2A$

C. $\dfrac{dy}{dx} - 2Ax - B = 0$ D. None of these.

27. Solution of the differential equation $2xydy - (x^2 + y^2 + 1)dx = 0$ for $y(1) = 1$ is

A. $y^2 = x(x + 1) - 1$ B. $y = x(x + 1) - 1$

C. $y^2 = 2x(x + 1) - 3$ D. $y^2 = x(x + 2) - 2$

28. If $W_1 = \{0, a_2, a_3\}$ and $W_2 = \{b_1, 0, b_3\}$ are two subspaces of F^3, where F^n is a vector space of dimension n. Then the subspace $W_1 \cap W_2$ is isomorphic to the vector space

A. F^1 B. F^2

C. F^3 D. $2F^4$

29. The square root of 28 using the Newton-Raphson's method after second iteration is given by

A. 5.29545 B. 5.2915

C. 5.3915 D. 5.5

30. The general solution of the differential equation

$(\sin y - y\sin xy)dx + (x\cos y - x\sin xy)dy = 0$

is

A. $x\cos y + \sin xy = \lambda$

B. $x\cos y - \sin xy = \lambda$

C. $x\sin y + \cos xy = \lambda$

D. $x\sin y - \cos xy = \lambda$

31. The solution of $\dfrac{\partial^2 z}{\partial x^2} + \dfrac{\partial^2 z}{\partial x \partial y} - 6\dfrac{\partial^2 z}{\partial y^2} = y\cos x$ is

A. $\phi_1(y + 2x) + \phi_2(y + 3x) + x\sin x - y\cos y$

B. $\phi_1(y + 2x) + \phi_2(y + 3x) + \sin x - y\cos x$

C. $\phi_1(y + 2x) + \phi_2(y + 3x) + x\cos x + y\sin x$

D. $\phi_1(y + 2x) + \phi_2(y + 3x) + \sin x + \cos y$

32. Let, X and Y be the number of heads and number of tails in tossing a coin n times. Then the regression coefficient of Y on X is

A. 0 B. –1

C. 1 D. $\dfrac{1}{2}$

33. If G is a finite group and H is a normal subgroup of G, then O(G/H) is

A. $\dfrac{O(H)}{O(G)}$ B. $\dfrac{O(G)}{O(H)}$

C. O (G) . O (H) D. None of these

34. Let $f(x)$ be continuous and differentiable over $(a - h, a + h)$, $a \in R$

$$F(x) = \begin{cases} \dfrac{f'(x)}{f(x)-f(a)} - \dfrac{1}{x-a} & ; \text{ if } x \neq a \\ \alpha & ; \text{ if } x = a \end{cases}$$

What is $F(x)$ continuous at $x = a$?

A. $\alpha = 1$ B. $\alpha = \dfrac{f'(a)}{f(a)}$

C. $\alpha = a$ D. $\alpha = \dfrac{f''(a)}{2f'(a)}$

35. The maximum number of different possible non-zero entries in a skew symmetric matrix of order n is

A. $\dfrac{1}{2}(n^2 - n)$

B. $\dfrac{1}{2}(n^2 + n)$

C. n^2

D. none of the above

36.

Code I	Code II
(a) $f(z) = \dfrac{\sin z}{z}$ at $z = 0$	(i) Pole
(b) $f(z) = \dfrac{\cot \pi z}{(z-a)^2}$ at $z = a$	(ii) A removable singularities
(c) $f(z) = \dfrac{\cot \pi z}{(z-a)^2}$ at $z = \infty$	(iii) Isolated essential singularities
(d) $f(z) = \sin\left(\dfrac{1}{1-z}\right)$ at $z = 1$	(iv) Non-isolated essential singularities

Codes:

	(a)	(b)	(c)	(d)
A.	(ii)	(i)	(iv)	(iii)
B.	(ii)	(iii)	(iv)	(i)
C.	(ii)	(iv)	(iii)	(i)
D.	(iii)	(i)	(iv)	(ii)

37. Consider 2×2 matrix, $A = \begin{bmatrix} a & b \\ c & d \end{bmatrix}$. If $a + d = 1 = ad - bc$, then A^3 equals.

A. 0 B. -1

C. 31 D. None of these

38. A and B are two events such that $P(A) > 0$ and $P(B) \neq 1$, then $P(\bar{A}/\bar{B})$ is equal to

A. $1 - P(A/B)$ B. $1 - P(\bar{A}/B)$

C. $\dfrac{1 - P(A \cup B)}{P(\bar{B})}$ D. $\dfrac{P(\bar{A})}{P(\bar{B})}$

39. The general solution of the differential equation $(x^2 + y^2)dx - 2xydy = 0$ is

A. $x^2 - cx - y^2 = 0$, where c is an arbitrary constant

B. $(x - y)^2 = cx$, where c is an arbitrary constant

C. $x + y + 2xy = c$, where c is an arbitrary constant

D. $y = x^2 - 2x + c$, where c is an arbitrary constant

40. $f(z) = 2z + 6z^3$ has

A. a pole of second order at infinity

B. a pole of third order at infinity

C. a pole of 4th order at infinity

D. none.

41. Let P be a $n \times n$ matrix with integral entries and $Q = P + \dfrac{1}{2}I$, where I denotes the $n \times n$ identity matrix. Then Q is

A. idempotent, *i.e.* $Q^2 = Q$

B. invertible

C. nilpotent

D. unipotent, *i.e.* Q-I is nilpotent

42. Let $T : \mathbf{R}^3 \to \mathbf{R}^3$ be the linear transformation whose matrix with respect to the standard basis of $\mathbf{R}^3$ is $\begin{pmatrix} 0 & a & b \\ -a & 0 & c \\ -b & -c & 0 \end{pmatrix}$, where a, b, c are real numbers not all zero. Then T

A. is one-to-one

B. is onto

C. does not map any line through the origin onto itself

D. has rank 1

43. Let $f(x, y) = x^5 y^2 \tan^{-1}\left(\dfrac{y}{x}\right)$. Then $x\dfrac{\partial f}{\partial x} + y\dfrac{\partial f}{\partial y}$ equals

A. $2f$ B. $3f$
C. $5f$ D. $7f$

44. The residue of $\frac{\sin z}{z^8}$ at $z = 0$ is

A. 0 B. $-\frac{1}{7!}$

C. $\frac{1}{7!}$ D. None of these

45. Let T : $R^2 \to R^2$ be a linear transformation such that T((1, 2)) = (2, 3) and T((0, 1)) = (1, 4). Then T((5, 6)) is

A. (6, – 1) B. (– 6, 1)
C. (–1, 6) D. (1 – 6)

46. Let, $w(z)=\frac{az+b}{cz+d}$ and $f(z)=\frac{\alpha z+\beta}{rz+\delta}$ be bilinear transformations. Then the following is also a bilinear transformation.

A. $f(z).w(z)$ B. $f(w(z))$

C. $f(z) + w(z)$ D. $f(z)+\frac{1}{w(z)}$

47. The solution of the differential equation $(x-y)\frac{dy}{dx}=(x+y)$ is equal to

A. $\sin^{-1}\left(\frac{y}{x}\right)=\log_e\left(C\sqrt{x^2+y^2}\right)$

B. $\cos^{-1}\left(\frac{y}{x}\right)=\log_e\left(C\sqrt{x^2+y^2}\right)$

C. $\tan^{-1}\left(\frac{y}{x}\right)=\log_e\left(C\sqrt{x^2+y^2}\right)$

D. None of the above

where C is a constant.

48. Power series

$1+\frac{a.b}{1.c}x+\frac{a(a+1).b(b+1)}{1.2c(c+1)}x^2+\ldots$ has Radius of convergence

A. 1 B. $\frac{1}{2}$

C. e D. e^{-1}

49. Let $f(x) = x^2 + 1$, $g(x) = x^3 + x^2 + 1$ and $h(x) = x^4 + x^2 + 1$. Then

A. $f(x)$ and $g(x)$ are reducible over $\mathbf{Z}_2$

B. $g(x)$ and $h(x)$ are reducible over $\mathbf{Z}_2$

C. $f(x)$ and $h(x)$ are reducible over $\mathbf{Z}_2$

D. $f(x)$, $g(x)$ and $h(x)$ are reducible over $\mathbf{Z}_2$

50. Find the value of $\oint_c \bar{z}^2 dz$ around the circle $|z| = 1$ and $|z - 1| = 1$

A. 0, $4\pi i$ B. $2\pi i$, 0
C. $2\pi i$, $4\pi i$ D. 0, 0

51. A game is a fair game if

A. $\underline{v}=\bar{v}=v$ B. $\underline{v}=0$

C. $\bar{v}=0$ D. $\underline{v}=\bar{v}=0$

52. Equation which are not exact can often be made exact by multiplying them by some function of x and y. Such a function is called

A. A constant function
B. Dependent variable
C. An integrating factor
D. None of the above.

53. In the group {1, 2, ..., 16} under the operation of multiplication modulo 17, the order of the element 3 is

A. 4 B. 8
C. 12 D. 16

54. Define T on $\mathbf{R}^4$ into $\mathbf{R}^4$ by

$T(x_1, x_2, x_3, x_4) = (x_1 + x_2 + x_3, x_2 + x_3 + x_4, x_3 + x_4 + x_2)$

Then rank of T is equal to (**R** being the set of real numbers)

A. 1 B. 2
C. 3 D. 4

55. Which one of the following is correct?

A. Between any two rational numbers there is an integer.
B. Between any two irrational numbers, there is a rational number.
C. Between any two irrational numbers, there is an integer.
D. Sum of two irrational numbers is always irrational.

56. Let G be a group of order n and a is the only self inverse element in G then $O[N(a)]$ is

A. 1 B. $n - 1$

C. n D. 2

57. Which one of the following group is cyclic?

A. $Z_{12} \times Z_9$ B. $Z_{10} \times Z_{85}$

C. $Z_4 \times Z_{25} \times Z_6$ D. $Z_{22} \times Z_{21} \times Z_{65}$

58. If $y_1(x) = x^2$ and $y_2(x) = x^2 \log x$. Then

A. y_1 and y_2 are linear independent solution in $(-\infty, \infty)$.

B. y_1 and y_2 are linear independent solution in $(0, \infty)$.

C. y_1 and y_2 are linear independent solution in $[0, \infty]$.

D. All of the above.

59. Let σ and π be the permutations defined by

$$\sigma = \begin{pmatrix} 1 & 2 & 3 & 4 & 5 & 6 & 7 & 8 & 9 \\ 1 & 3 & 5 & 7 & 9 & 6 & 4 & 8 & 2 \end{pmatrix} \text{ and}$$

$$\tau = \begin{pmatrix} 1 & 2 & 3 & 4 & 5 & 6 & 7 & 8 & 9 \\ 7 & 8 & 3 & 4 & 9 & 6 & 5 & 2 & 1 \end{pmatrix}$$

Then

A. σ and τ generate the group of permutations on $\{1, 2, 3, 4, 5, 6, 7, 8, 9\}$

B. σ is contained in the group generated by τ

C. τ is contained in the group generated by σ

D. σ and τ are in the same conjugacy class

60. Poly type is intersection of

A. Finite number of open half spaces

B. Arbitrary number of open half spaces

C. Finite number of closed half spaces

D. Arbitrary number of closed half spaces

ANSWERS

1	2	3	4	5	6	7	8	9	10
D	A	A	C	C	D	B	C	D	B
11	**12**	**13**	**14**	**15**	**16**	**17**	**18**	**19**	**20**
B	A, D	D	A	B	B	A	A	D	A
21	**22**	**23**	**24**	**25**	**26**	**27**	**28**	**29**	**30**
D	B	A	A	A	A	A	A	B	C
31	**32**	**33**	**34**	**35**	**36**	**37**	**38**	**39**	**40**
B	B	B	D	A	B	D	C	A	B
41	**42**	**43**	**44**	**45**	**46**	**47**	**48**	**49**	**50**
B	C	D	B	A	B	C	A	C	A
51	**52**	**53**	**54**	**55**	**56**	**57**	**58**	**59**	**60**
A	C	D	C	B	A	D	B	D	C

SOME SELECTED EXPLANATORY ANSWERS

8. The given differential equation is

$$y = \frac{2}{3}x \cdot \frac{dy}{dx} - \frac{2}{3x}\left(\frac{dy}{dx}\right)^2$$

The p-discriminant of the above equation is given by

$$\left(\frac{2}{3}x\right)^2 - \frac{4.2}{3x} \cdot y = 0$$

or, $$\frac{4x^2}{9} - \frac{4.2}{3x} y = 0 \Rightarrow y = \frac{x^3}{6}.$$

20. The given cost matrix of the assignment problem is

$$\begin{bmatrix} a & b & c & d \\ b & c & d & a \\ c & d & a & b \\ d & a & b & c \end{bmatrix}$$

if let a is the minimum among the a, b, c, d, then apply the Hungarian method for the given cost matrix, we get

$$\begin{bmatrix} 0 & b-a & c-a & d-a \\ b-a & c-a & d-a & 0 \\ c-a & d-a & 0 & b-a \\ d-a & 0 & b-a & c-a \end{bmatrix}$$

clearly all the rows and column consist exactly one zero element. Hence it will be the minimum cost matrix.

i.e. The optimal cost in this case = $a + a + a + a = 4a$.

Similarly when b is the minimum among the $a, b, c, d,$

then by the Hungarian method, the optimal cost in this case = $b + b + b + b = 4b$.

i.e. The required optimal cost = 4.min $\{a, b, c, d\}$.

23. In the given option only $\{x^n\}$ converges uniformly to 0.

On the other hand $\left\{\frac{n}{n^x+1}\right\}$ is decreasing sequence with $f_n \to \infty$ at similarly. $\left\{\frac{x}{n^x+1}\right\}$ is an increasing sequence.

25. The given distribution is a discrete distribution.

Hence from the properties of such distribution.

$$3C + 2C + 0.4 + 0.1 = 1$$

$$\Rightarrow \quad 5C + 0.5 = 1$$

$$\Rightarrow \quad C = 0.1.$$

27. The given differential equation is $2xydy - (x^2 + y^2 + 1)dx = 0 \quad y(1) = 1.$

or, $\quad 2xy\frac{dy}{dx} = x^2 + y^2 + 1$

let $\quad v = y^2$ then $\frac{dv}{dx} = 2y\frac{dy}{dx}$

or, $\quad \frac{xdv}{dx} = x^2 + V + 1$

or, $\quad \frac{xdv}{dx} - v = (x^2 + 1)$

or, $\quad \frac{dv}{dx} - \frac{1}{x}\cdot v = \left(x + \frac{1}{x}\right)$

or, $\quad \frac{1}{x}\cdot\frac{dv}{dx} - \frac{v}{x^2} = \left(1 + \frac{1}{x^2}\right)$

integrating both the sides, we get

$$\frac{v}{x} = \left(x - \frac{1}{x}\right) + c$$

or, $\quad y^2 = x^2 - 1 + cx$

as $\quad y(1) = 1$

$\Rightarrow \quad 1 = 1 - 1 + c.1$

$\Rightarrow \quad c = 1$

i.e. $\quad y^2 = x(x + 1) - 1$

is the required answer.

29. Let $\quad x = \sqrt{28}$ so that $x^2 - 28 = 0$.

Taking $f(x) = x^2 - 28$, *N-R* method gives ...(*i*)

$$x_{n+1} = x_n - \frac{f(x_n)}{f'(x_n)} = x_n - \frac{(x_n^2 - 28)}{2x_n}$$

$$= \frac{1}{2}\left(x_n + \frac{28}{x_n}\right) \quad ...(ii)$$

Now $f(5) = -3$, $f(6) = 8$, a root of (*i*) lies between 5 and 6.

$\therefore$ Taking $x_0 = 5.5$, (*ii*) gives

$$x_1 = \frac{1}{2}\left[x_0 + \frac{28}{x_0}\right] = \frac{1}{2}\left[5.5 + \frac{28}{5.5}\right]$$

$$= 5.29545$$

$$x_2 = \frac{1}{2}\left[x_1 + \frac{28}{x_1}\right]$$

$$= \frac{1}{2}\left[5.29545 + \frac{28}{5.29545}\right] = 5.2915.$$

34. The given function F(*x*) is

$$F(x) = \frac{f'(x)}{f(x) - f(a)} - \frac{1}{x-a} \quad : \text{if } x \neq a$$

$$= \alpha \quad : \text{if } x = a.$$

Now $f(x)$ is continuous at $x = a$.

$\Rightarrow \quad \lim_{x\to a} F(x) = F(a) = \alpha.$

Now $\quad \lim_{x\to a} F(x) = \lim_{x\to a} \frac{f'(x)}{f(x) - f(a)} - \frac{1}{(x-a)}$

$$= \lim_{x\to a} \frac{f'(x)(x-a) - f(x) + f(a)}{(x-a)[f(x) - f(a)]}$$

$$= \lim_{x \to a} \frac{f'(x)(x-a) - f(x) + f(a)}{(x-a)[f(x) - f(a)]} = \left[\frac{0}{0}\right] \text{form}$$

By L'Hospital Rule

$$= \lim_{x \to a} \frac{f''(x)(x-a) - f'(x) - f'(x)}{f(x) - f(a) + (x-a)f'(x)}$$

$$= \lim_{x \to a} \frac{f''(x)(x-a)}{f(x) - f(a) + (x-a)f'(x)}$$

$$= \lim_{x \to a} \frac{f''(x)}{\frac{f(x) - f(a)}{x-a} + f'(x)}$$

$$= \lim_{x \to a} \frac{f''(x)}{f'(x) + f'(x)} = \frac{f''(a)}{2f'(a)}$$

i.e. $\alpha = \dfrac{f''(a)}{2f'(a)}.$

35. In skew symmetric matrix $a_{ij} = -a_{ji}$

$\Rightarrow \quad a_{ii} = -a_{ii} \quad \Rightarrow \quad a_{ii} = 0$

i.e. diagonal elements are always zero

Hence maximum number of non-zero elements

$$= \frac{1}{2}(n^2 - n).$$

39. The given differential equation is

$$(x^2 + y^2)dx - 2xydy = 0$$

or, $\dfrac{dy}{dx} = \dfrac{x^2 + y^2}{2xy}$

which is a homogenous equation,

put $y = vx$

then $\dfrac{dy}{dx} = v + \dfrac{xdv}{dx}$

or, $v + x\dfrac{dv}{dx} = \dfrac{1+v^2}{2v}$

or, $x\dfrac{dv}{dx} = \dfrac{1+v^2}{2v} - v = \dfrac{1-v^2}{2v}$

or, $\dfrac{dx}{x} = \dfrac{2v}{1-v^2}dv$

or, $\dfrac{dx}{x} + \dfrac{2v}{v^2-1}dv = 0$

integrating we get

$$\log x + \log(v^2 - 1) = \log c$$

or, $x\left(\dfrac{y^2}{x^2} - 1\right) = c$

or, $y^2 - x^2 = cx$

or, $x^2 + cx - y^2 = 0,$

where c is arbitrary constant.

42. $T = \begin{bmatrix} 0 & a & b \\ -a & 0 & c \\ -b & -c & 0 \end{bmatrix}$

Clearly T is a skew - symmetric matrix

$|T| = -a[bc] + b.ac = 0$

$\Rightarrow$ Rank(T) is less than 3.

Also it has a non-zero 2 × 2 co-factor

$\Rightarrow \quad$ Rank(T) = 2

$\Rightarrow$ T is not one-to-one.

Also from question

$T(1, 0, 0) = (0, -a, -b)$

$T(0, 1, 0) = (a, 0, -c)$

$T(0, 0, 1) = (b, c, 0)$

Now $T(x, y, z) = (x, y, z)$

$(0, -ax, -bx) + (ay, 0, -cy) + (bz, cz, 0) = (x, y, z)$

$$\begin{aligned} ay + bz - x &= 0 \\ -ax + cz - y &= 0 \\ -bx - cy - z &= 0 \end{aligned} \qquad \begin{bmatrix} -1 & a & b \\ -a & -1 & c \\ -b & -c & -1 \end{bmatrix}\begin{bmatrix} x \\ y \\ z \end{bmatrix} = \begin{bmatrix} 0 \\ 0 \\ 0 \end{bmatrix}$$

Now $\begin{vmatrix} -1 & a & b \\ -a & -1 & c \\ -b & -c & -1 \end{vmatrix}$

$= -1\,(1 + c^2) - a(a + bc) + b\,(ac - b^2)$

$= -(a^2 + b^2 + c^2 + 1) \neq 0$

i.e. $(x, y, z) = (0, 0, 0)$ only satisfy

$T(x, y, z) = (x, y, z).$

43. $f(x, y) = x^5 y^2 \tan^{-1}\left(\dfrac{y}{x}\right)$

$= x^7\left[\left(\dfrac{y}{x}\right)^2 \tan^{-1}\left(\dfrac{y}{x}\right)\right]$

$f(x, y) = x^7 F\left(\dfrac{y}{x}\right)$

Hence by Euler Theorem,

$$x\frac{\partial f}{\partial x}+y\frac{\partial f}{\partial y}=nf$$

[n = order of homogeneous equation]

$= 7f.$

45. $T((1, 2)) = (2, 3)$

$T((0, 1)) = (1, 4)$

$T((5, 6)) = 5T((1, 2)) - 4T((0, 1))$

$= 5(2, 3) - 4(1, (4)$

$= (10, 15) - (4, 16)$

$= (6, -1).$

47. $\because \quad \frac{dy}{dx} = \frac{x+y}{x-y}$ ...(*i*)

put $y = vx$

then (*i*) reduces to

$$\Rightarrow v + x\frac{dv}{dx} = \frac{1+v}{1-v}$$

$$\Rightarrow \frac{1-v}{1+v^2}\,dv = \frac{dx}{x}$$

$$\Rightarrow \tan^{-1} v - \frac{1}{2}\ln(1+v^2) = \ln x + \ln c$$

$$\Rightarrow \tan^{-1}\frac{y}{x} = \ln c\sqrt{x^2+y^2}\,.$$

48. $a_n = \frac{a(a+1)(a+2)...(a+n-1).b(b+1)...(b+n-1)}{1.2....n\,c(c+1)(c+2)...(c+n-1)}$

$$a_{n+1} = \frac{a(a+1)(a+2)...(a+n)b(b+1)...(b+n)}{1.2....(n+1)c(c+1)(c+2)...(c+n)}$$

$$\therefore \quad R = \lim_{n\to\infty}\left|\frac{a_n}{a_{n+1}}\right| = \lim_{n\to\infty}\frac{(n+1)(c+n)}{(a+n)(b+n)}$$

$$= \lim_{n\to\infty}\frac{\left(1+\frac{1}{n}\right)\left(1+\frac{c}{n}\right)}{\left(1+\frac{a}{n}\right)\left(1+\frac{b}{n}\right)} = 1$$

49. Let $f(x) = x^2 + 1 = (x + a)(x + b)$

$\Rightarrow \quad a + b = 0;\ ab = 1$ ...(1)

$a = [1]$ and $b = [1]$ is the solution of 1 in z_2

i.e., modulo 2 field.

so $f(x)$ is reducible.

$g(x) = x^3 + x^2 + 1 = (x + a)(x^2 + bx + c)$

$\Rightarrow \quad a + b = 1;\ ab + c = 0;\ ac = 1$ ...(2)

equation (2) is not satisfied by any choice so it is not reducible.

$h(x) = x^4 + x^2 + 1 = (x + 1)(x^3 + ax^2 + bx + 1)$

$\Rightarrow \quad a + 1 = 0;\ a + b = 1;\ b + 1 = 0$ ...(3)

$\Rightarrow$ (3) is not satisfied, but

$x^4 + x^2 + 1 = (x^2 + ax + 1)(x^2 + bx + 1)$

$\Rightarrow \quad a + b = 0;\ 1 + 1 + ab = 1$

$\Rightarrow \quad [a] = [b] = 1$ is satisfied

$\Rightarrow \quad h(x)$ is reducible

53. $[3]^4_{\times_{17}} = [13]_{\times_{17}}$

$[13]^2_{\times_{17}} = [16]_{\times_{17}}$

$[16]^2_{\times_{17}} = [1]_{\times_{17}}$

$\Rightarrow [3]^{16}_{\times_{17}} = [1]$

$\Rightarrow$ order of 3 is 16.

54. The given linear transformation is

$T(x_1, x_2, x_3, x_4) = (x_1 + x_2 + x_3 + x_4,\ x_3 + x_4,\ x_2)$

The standard basis of $\mathbf{R}^4$ are {(1, 0, 0, 0,), (0, 1, 0, 0), (0, 0, 1, 0), (0, 0, 0, 1)}.

Hence $T(1, 0, 0, 0) = (1, 0, 0, 0)$

$T(0, 1, 0, 0) = (1, 1, 0, 1)$

$T(0, 0, 1, 0) = (1, 1, 1, 0)$

$T(0, 0, 0, 1) = (0, 1, 1, 0)$

Now dimension of rank of T = Number of independent rows in

$$\begin{bmatrix}1&0&0&0\\0&1&0&1\\0&1&1&0\\0&1&1&0\end{bmatrix} \sim \begin{bmatrix}1&0&0&0\\0&1&0&1\\0&1&1&0\\0&1&1&0\end{bmatrix} \sim$$

$$\begin{bmatrix}1&0&0&0\\0&1&0&1\\0&1&1&0\\0&0&0&0\end{bmatrix} \sim \begin{bmatrix}1&0&0&0\\0&1&0&1\\0&0&1&-1\\0&0&0&0\end{bmatrix}$$

i.e. rank of T = 3.

SET–21

CSIR–UGC (NET) MATHEMATICAL SCIENCES

PART-C

1. Let M be a square matrix of order, 2 such that rank of M is 1. Then M is

A. diagonalizable and non-singular
B. diagonalizable and nilpotent
C. neither diagonalizable nor nilpotent
D. either diagonalizable or nilpotent but not both

2. Let $f : c \to c$ be given by

$$f(z)=\begin{cases}(\bar{z})^2/z & \text{where } z \neq 0\\ 0 & \text{when } z=0\end{cases}$$

then f

A. is not continuous at $z = 0$
B. is differentiable but not analytic at $z = 0$
C. is analytic at $z = 0$
D. satisfy the Cauchy-Riemann equation at $z=0$

3. The general solution of $px = qy = 3z$ is given by

A. $f\left(\frac{z}{x^3},\frac{y}{x}\right) = 0$ B. $f\left(\frac{y}{x^3},\frac{z}{x}\right) = 0$

C. $f\left(\frac{x}{y^3},\frac{z}{y}\right) = 0$ D. $f\left(\frac{x}{y},\frac{z}{x^3}\right) = 0$

4. The general solution of the differential equation $\frac{d^2y}{dx^2}+4y=\sin^2 x$ is given by

A. $y = c_1e^{2x} + c_2e^{-2x} + 2\sin x \cos x$

B. $y=c_1\cos 2x+c_2\sin 2x+\frac{1}{8}-\frac{x}{8}\sin 2x$

C. $y=(c_1+c_2\cos 2x)e^{-2x}-\frac{x}{8}\cos 2x$

D. $y=c_1\cos(2x+c_2)+\frac{1}{8}$

5. Let $f(x) = \frac{x}{(1+x^n)^{1/n}}$, $n \geq 2$ $g(x) = (fofof......\ n$ times) (x), then what is $\int x^{n-2}g(x)dx$ equal to?

A. $\frac{(1+nx^n)^{1-\frac{1}{n}}}{n-1}+C$ B. $(1+nx^n)^{1-\frac{1}{n}}+C$

C. $\frac{(1+nx^n)^{1+\frac{1}{n}}}{n+1}+C$ D. $\frac{(1+nx^n)^{1+\frac{1}{n}}}{n(n+1)}+C$

6. The integral surface of equation $(2xy-1)p + (z-2x^2)q = 2(x-yz)$ which passes through the line $x_0(s) = 1$, $y_0(s) = 0$ and $z_0(s)$ is

A. $x^2 + z^2 - xz - ytz = 1$
B. $x^2 + y^2 - zx - y + z = 1$
C. $y^2 + z^2 - yz - x + z = 1$
D. $x^2 + y^2 - xy - x + z = 1$

7. If the total kinetic energy of a system of particles about the origin is equal to its kinetic energy about the centre of mass, then the centre of mass is

A. at rest
B. moving along a circle
C. moving on a straight line
D. moving along an ellipse

8. A given complex function of a complex variable takes real values for real values of the variable, then

A. it may be analytic in a open disc of the complex plane but not differentiable on any interval as real function of a real variable.
B. its power series expansion, when available around a point on the real axis has only real coefficients.

C. its power series expansion, when available, around any points in the complex plane has real coefficients.

D. if may not posses a power series expansion around a point on the real axis as a real function but may be analytic in some open disc centred at the point.

9. Let F be a field of finite cardinality and $a \in F$ be non-unity, non-zero self inverse element under multiplication. Then possible cardinality of F is

A. 8 B. 27
C. 121 D. All of the above

10. Consider the transportation problem given below. The bracketted elements in the table indicate a feasible solution and the elements on the left hand corner are the costs c_{ij}.

				a_i
	2 (1)	5	1	1
	1	3 (1)	4 (1)	2
b_j	1	1	1	3

A. this solution is a basic feasible solution
B. this solution can be made basic feasible
C. this is an optimal solution
D. the problem does not have an optimal solution

11. Let T : $R^3 \to R^3$ be a linear transformation defined by $T(x, y, z) = (x + y, y + z, z - x)$. Then an orthonormal basis for the range of T is

A. $\left\{\left(\frac{1}{\sqrt{2}}, \frac{1}{\sqrt{2}}, 0\right), \left(\frac{1}{\sqrt{3}}, \frac{-1}{\sqrt{3}}, \frac{1}{\sqrt{3}}\right)\right\}$

B. $\left\{\left(\frac{1}{\sqrt{2}}, \frac{-1}{\sqrt{2}}, 0\right), \left(\frac{1}{\sqrt{6}}, \frac{1}{\sqrt{6}}, \frac{2}{\sqrt{6}}\right)\right\}$

C. $\left\{\left(\frac{1}{\sqrt{2}}, \frac{1}{\sqrt{2}}, 0\right), \left(\frac{1}{\sqrt{6}}, \frac{-1}{\sqrt{6}}, \frac{-2}{\sqrt{6}}\right)\right\}$

D. $\left\{\left(\frac{1}{\sqrt{2}}, \frac{1}{\sqrt{2}}, 0\right), \left(\frac{1}{\sqrt{3}}, \frac{-1}{\sqrt{3}}, \frac{-1}{\sqrt{3}}\right)\right\}$

12. For the diffusion problem $u_{xx} = u_t$ $(0 < x < \pi, t > 0)$. $u(0, t) = 0$, $u(\pi, t) = 0$ and $u(x, 0) = 3\sin 2x$ then solution is given by

A. $3e^{-t}\sin 2x$ B. $3e^{-4t}\sin 2x$
C. $3e^{4t}\sin 2x$ D. $3e^{t}\sin 2x$.

13. Let X = (0, 1) ∪ (2, 3) be an open set in R. Let f be a continuous function on X such that the derivative $f'(x) = 0$ for all x. Then the range of f has

A. Uncountable number of points
B. Countably infinite number of points
C. at most 2 points
D. at most 1 point

14. Let $A = N - \{1\} = \{k \in N : k > 1\}$, $X_2 = \{2k : k \in A\}$, $X_3 = \{3k : k \in A\}$, ... $X_j = \{jK : k \in A\}$ ...... then what is the complement of $\bigcup_{j=2}^{\infty} X_j$ in A equal to?

A. A finite non empty set
B. ϕ
C. The set of primes
D. The set of composite numbers

15. The number of zeros of $f(z) = z^5 + 5z + 1$ in $\frac{3}{2} < |z| < 2$ are

A. 2 B. 8
C. 4 D. 5

16. The residue of $\frac{\sin z}{z^{10}}$ at $z = 0$ is

A. 0 B. $\frac{1}{9!}$

C. $-\frac{1}{9!}$ D. None of these

17. $\int e^{-2z} dz$ will be

A. $-\frac{1}{2}e^{-2z} + C$ B. $e^{-2z} + C$
C. 0 D. πi

18. The equation of the curve satisfying the differential equation $(1 + x^2)\frac{dy}{dx} + 2xy - 4x^2 = 0$ and passing through the origin is

A. $4x^2 = 3y(1 + x)$ B. $4x^3 = 3y(1 + x^2)$
C. $4x = 3y^2(1 + x^2)$ D. $4x^3 = 3y^2(1 + x)$

19. Write false : If H is normal subgroup of a group G then

A. $xH = Hx \quad \forall x \in G$
B. $x^{-1}h\,x \in H \quad \forall x \in G$ and $\forall h \in H$
C. $x\,H\,x^{-1} = H \quad \forall x \in G$
D. The product of two right cosets of H in G under coset multiplication is not a right cosets of H.

20. Let $(R, +)$ be an abelian group. If multiplication '·' is defined on R by setting $a{\cdot}b = 0$ for all a, $b \in R$, then which one of the following statements is correct?

A. $(R, +, \cdot)$ is not a ring.
B. $(R, +, \cdot)$ is a ring, but not commutative.
C. $(R, +, \cdot)$ is a commutative ring, but has no unity.
D. $(R, +, \cdot)$ is a field.

21. Two fair dice are tossed. Let X be the event the first die shows an even number, and Y be the event that the second die shows an odd number. The two events X and Y are

A. mutually exclusive
B. independent and mutually exclusive
C. dependent
D. none of these

22. A warehouse contains ten printing machines, four of which are defective. A company select five of the machines at random, thinking all are in working condition. Then the probability that all five of the machines are non-defective is

A. 0.0238 B. 0.032
C. 0.32 D. 0.0032

23. The solution $y = A \sin x + B \cos (x + c)$ contains three arbitrary constants, they are really equivalent to

A. Only four constants
B. Only three constants
C. Two only
D. None of the above

24. Let $f(x) = px + 1 \quad x \geq 1$
$= x^2 + p \quad x < 1$

Read the following statements

1. f is continuous for all p at $x = 1$.
2. there is unique p for which f is differentiable at $x = 1$.

Code:

A. 1 is true but 2 is not
B. 2 is true but 1 is not
C. both are true
D. both are false

25. A random variable X has Poisson Distribution if 2P (X = 2) = P (X = 1) + 2P (X = 0) then the variance of X is

A. $\frac{3}{2}$ B. 2
C. 1 D. $\frac{1}{2}$

26. The complement of union of two half spaces of a hyper plane represents

A. A hyperplane parallel to the given hyper plane
B. The original hyper plane
C. The whole space
D. The whole space except the given hyper plane.

27. The solution of the equation $\frac{d^2y}{dx^2} - y = k$ ($k = a$ non-zero constant) which vanishes when $x = 0$ and which tends to a finite limit as x tends to infinity, is

A. $y = k(1 + e^{-x})$ B. $y = k(e^{-x} - 1)$
C. $y = k(e^x + e^{-x} - 2)$ D. $y = k(e^x - 1)$

28. The integral equation

$$y(x) = 1+\lambda\int_0^{2\pi} \sin x(x+t)\,y(t)\,dt \text{ has}$$

A. Unique solution for all values of λ
B. Infinite solution for finite values of λ
C. No solution for every value of λ
D. Infinite solution for every value of λ

29. Let r be the curve $r = 2 + 4\cos q$, $(0 \leq \theta \leq 2p)$.

If $I_1 = \int \frac{dz}{z-1}$ and $I_2 = \int \frac{dz}{z-3}$ then

A. $I_1 = 2I_2$ B. $I_1 = I_2$
C. $2I_1 = I_2$ D. $I_1 = 0;\ I_2 \neq 0$

30. A biased coin is tested 4 times or until a head turns up whichever occurs earlier. The distribution of the number of fails turning up is

A. Binomial B. Geometric

C. Negative Binomial D. None of these

31. $z_1 = -z$, $z_2 = iz$, $z_3 = z - iz$, Area of the triangle in the Gausian plane.

A. $|z|^2$ B. $\frac{3}{2}|z|^2$

C. $\frac{1}{2}|z|^2$ D. None

32. The general solution of the differential equation

$$y = x\left(\frac{dy}{dx}\right) + \left(\frac{dy}{dx}\right)^2 \text{ is}$$

A. $y = cx - c^2$, c is an arbitrary constant

B. $y = cx + c$, c is an arbitrary constant

C. $y = cx - c$, c is an arbitrary constant

D. $y = cx + c^2$, c is an arbitrary constant

33. If $W_1 = \{(0, x_2, x_3, x_4, x_5) : x_2, x_3, x_4, x_5 \in \mathbf{R}\}$ and $W_2 = \{(x_1, 0, x_3, x_4, x_5) : x_1, x_3, x_4, x_5 \in \mathbf{R}\}$ be subspaces of $\mathbf{R}^5$, then dim $(W_1 \cap W_2)$ is equal to

A. 5 B. 4

C. 3 D. 2

34. The entire length of the given curve $x^{2/3} + y^{2/3} = a^{2/3}$ is given by

A. $8a$ B. $6a$

C. $\sqrt{8ay}$ D. $4\sqrt{3a}$

35. The solution of the equation $\frac{dy}{dx} = \frac{2x - y + 1}{x + 2y - 3}$ is

A. $xy + y^2 + x^2 + 3y - x = c$

B. $xy + y^2 - x^2 - 3y - x = c$

C. $xy + y^2 + x^2 - 3y - x = c$

D. $xy + y^2 - x^2 - 3y + x = c$

36. The number of subgroups of a cyclic group with 100 elements is

A. 2 B. 5

C. 9 D. 10

37. A fair coin is tossed repeatedly. If tail appears on first four tosses, then the probability of head appearing on fifth toss equals

A. $\frac{1}{2}$ B. $\frac{1}{32}$

C. $\frac{31}{32}$ D. $\frac{1}{5}$

38. Let $\phi : R^2 \to R$ and $\sigma : R^2 \to R$ be the linear functionals defined by $\phi(x, y) = x + 2y$ $\sigma(x, y) = 3x - y$ then

Group I	Group II
(a) $\phi + \sigma$	1. $4x + 8y$
(b) 4ϕ	2. $-13x + 9y$
(c) $2\phi - 5\sigma$	3. $4x + y$

	(a)	(b)	(c)
A.	3	1	2
B.	1	2	3
C.	1	3	2
D.	2	1	3

39. Match List-I with List-II and select the correct answer:

List-I	List-II
(a) $\sum_{1}^{\infty}(-1)^{n-1}\frac{n^2}{(n+1)!}$	1. Diverges
(b) $\sum_{n=1}^{\infty}\frac{n^n}{n!}$	2. Converges
(c) $\sum_{n=1}^{\infty}(-1)^n\frac{\log n}{n^2}$	3. Converges conditionally
(d) $\sum_{n=1}^{\infty}\frac{(-1)^n}{\log n}$	4. Converges absolutely

	(a)	(b)	(c)	(d)
A.	2	4	1	3
B.	4	3	2	1
C.	4	1	2	3
D.	3	1	4	2

40. In Replacement, which is correct?

A. When the time value of money is considered, costs need to be discounted.

B. When there are two items to be replaced, the one with longer replacement interval is decidedly better.

C. The total cost of an item over a given period of n years would be equal to Purchase price + Maintenance cost of n years + Value of the item after n years.

D. An optimum replacement interval of five years indicates that the item in equation should be replaced at the beginning of every five years.

41. The order of convergence in the Newton-Raphson's method in case of multiple root is given by

A. Linear

B. Quadratic

C. Depends on the order of root

D. None of these

42. Let S be a closed surface for which $\iint_S \bar{r}.\hat{n}d\sigma = 1$. Then the volume enclosed by the surface is

A. 1 B. 1/3

C. 2/3 D. 3

43. Considering four sub-intervals, the value of $\int_0^1 \frac{1}{1+x}dx$ by Trapezoid rule is

A. 0.6870 B. 0.6677

C. 0.6970 D. 0.3597

44. The number of basic solution to the system

$$x_1 + 2x_2 + 10x_3 + 4x_4 = 5$$
$$x_1 + x_2 + 5x_3 + 4x_1 = -8$$

is

A. 0 B. 4

C. 6 D. infinite

45. If A = $\begin{bmatrix} a & b \\ b & -a \end{bmatrix}$ and MA = A^{2m}, $m \in N$ for some matrix M, then which one of the following is correct?

A. M = $\begin{bmatrix} a^{2m} & b^{2m} \\ b^{2m} & -a^{2m} \end{bmatrix}$

B. M = $(a^2+b^2)^m \begin{bmatrix} 1 & 0 \\ 0 & 1 \end{bmatrix}$

C. M = $(a^m+b^m)\begin{bmatrix} 1 & 0 \\ 0 & 1 \end{bmatrix}$

D. M = $(a^2+b^2)^{m-1}\begin{bmatrix} a & b \\ b & -a \end{bmatrix}$

46. The L.P.P. max $z = x_1 + x_2 + x_3 + x_4$

$x_1, x_2, x_3, x_4 \geq 0$

A. Has no solution

B. Has an unbounded solution

C. Can not be solved

D. None of the above

47. The area of an equilateral triangle with base lying on the line $px + qy + r = 0$ and vertex (0, 0) is

A. $\frac{r^2}{\sqrt{3}\sqrt{p^2+q^2}}$ B. $\sqrt{\frac{3r^2}{p^2+q^2}}$

C. $\frac{r^2}{\sqrt{3}(p^2+q^2)}$ D. $\frac{\sqrt{3}}{2}\frac{r^2}{(p^2+q^2)}$

48. Set of multiples of 4 forms an ideal in Z, the ring of integers under usual addition and multiplication. This ideal is

A. a prime ideal but not a maximal ideal

B. a maximal ideal but not a prime ideal

C. both a prime ideal and a maximal ideal

D. neither a prime ideal nor a maximal ideal

49. The singular solution of $p = \log(px - y)$ is

A. $y = x(\log x - 1)$ B. $y = x\log x - 1$

C. $y = \log x - 1$ D. $y = x\log x$

50. A random sample of 15 people is taken from a population in which 40% favour a particular political stand. What is the probability that exactly 6 individuals in the sample favour this political stand?

A. 0.4 B. 0.5

C. 0.4100 D. 0.2066

51. Consider z_5 as a field modulo 5 and let

$$f(x) = x^5 + 4x^4 + 4x^3 + 4x^2 + x + 1.$$

Then the zero of $f(x)$ over z_5 are 1 and 3 with respective multiplicity.

A. 1 and 4 B. 2 and 3

C. 2 and 2 D. 1 and 2

52. The number of 2×2 matrices over Z_3 (the field with three elements) with determinant 1 is

A. 24 B. 60
C. 20 D. 30

53. Let $A(t)$ denote the area bounded by the curve $y = e^{-|x|}$, the x-axis and the straight lines $x = -t$ and $x = t$. Then $\lim_{t \to \infty} A(t)$ is equal to

A. 2 B. 1
C. 1/2 D. 0

54. Let w_1 and w_2 be any two subspaces of a finite dimensional vector space V over a field F, then which of the following is *true*?

A. $\dim w_1 + \dim w_2 = \dim V$
B. $\dim (w_1 + w_2) = \dim V$
C. $\dim (w_1 + w_2) \le \dim (w_1) + \dim (w_2)$
D. $\dim (w_1 + w_2) \ge \dim (w_1) + \dim (w_2)$

55. The smallest odd order for non-abelian group is

A. 9 B. 15
C. 21 D. 23

56. Let a be a non-zero real number. Then $\lim_{x \to 0} \frac{1}{x^2 - a^2} \int_a^x \sin(t^2)\, dt$ equals

A. $\frac{1}{2a}\sin(a^2)$ B. $\frac{1}{2a}\cos(a^2)$
C. $-\frac{1}{2a}\sin(a^2)$ D. $-\frac{1}{2a}\cos(a^2)$

57. Let A be the 4×4 real matrix

$$A = \begin{bmatrix} 1 & 1 & 0 & 0 \\ -1 & -1 & 0 & 0 \\ -2 & -2 & 2 & 1 \\ 1 & 1 & -1 & 0 \end{bmatrix}$$

Then the characteristic polynomial for A is

A. $x^2 (x - 1)^2$
B. $(x - 1)^2 (x + 1)^2$
C. $x^2 (x + 1)^2$
D. None of the above

58. Let A be a $m \times n$ matrix with row rank $= r$ = column rank. The dimension of the space of solutions of the system of linear equations AX = 0 is

A. r B. $n - r$
C. $m - r$ D. $\min (m, n) - r$

59. The surface area of the solid generated by revolving the line segment $y = x + 2$ for $0 \le x \le 1$ about the line $y = 2$ is

A. $\sqrt{2}\pi$ B. 2π
C. $2\sqrt{2}\pi$ D. 4π

60. A linear constraint $\alpha x_1 + \beta x_2 \ge b$ is equivalent to

A. $\alpha x_1 - \beta x_2 \le b$
B. $-\alpha x_1 - \beta x_2 \le -b$
C. $-\alpha x_1 + \beta x_2 \ge b$
D. None of the above

ANSWERS

1	2	3	4	5	6	7	8	9	10
A	D	A	B	B	B	A	D	A	B
11	**12**	**13**	**14**	**15**	**16**	**17**	**18**	**19**	**20**
C	C	D	B	C	B	A	B	D	C
21	**22**	**23**	**24**	**25**	**26**	**27**	**28**	**29**	**30**
D	A	C	C	D	D	A	D	B	B
31	**32**	**33**	**34**	**35**	**36**	**37**	**38**	**39**	**40**
A	D	C	B	D	C	A	A	C	A
41	**42**	**43**	**44**	**45**	**46**	**47**	**48**	**49**	**50**
A	B	C	C	D	B	C	D	A	D
51	**52**	**53**	**54**	**55**	**56**	**57**	**58**	**59**	**60**
D	A	A	C	C	A	D	A	A	B

SOME SELECTED EXPLANATORY ANSWERS

4. The given differential equation is

$$\frac{d^2y}{dx^2}+4y = \sin^2 x$$

the auxiliary equation is $m^2 + 4 = 0$

$\Rightarrow \quad m = \pm 2i$

hence $\quad y = C_1\cos 2x + C_2\sin x.$

Now, for particular integral,

$$y = \frac{1}{(D^2+4)}\sin^2 x = \frac{1}{2}\frac{(1-\cos 2x)}{(D^2+4)}$$

$$= \frac{1}{2}\cdot\frac{1}{(D^2+4)}\cdot 1-\frac{1}{2}\cdot\frac{\cos 2x}{D^2+4}$$

$$= \frac{1}{8}-\frac{1}{2}\frac{x\sin 2x}{4}$$

$$= \frac{1}{8}-\frac{x\sin 2x}{8}.$$

5. From question,

$$f(x) = \frac{x}{(1+x^n)^{1/n}}.$$

$$\text{Now } fof(x) = fo\left(\frac{x}{(1+x^n)^{1/n}}\right)$$

$$= \frac{\dfrac{x}{(1+x^n)^{1/n}}}{\left(1+\dfrac{x^n}{1+x^n}\right)^{1/n}} = \frac{x}{(1+2x^n)^{1/n}}$$

$$fofof(x) = \frac{\dfrac{x}{(1+2x^n)^{1/n}}}{\left(1+\dfrac{x^n}{1+2x^n}\right)^{1/n}} = \frac{x}{(1+3x^n)^{1/n}}$$

$$\text{i.e.} \quad g(x) = \underbrace{fofofo......fo(x)}_{n \text{ times}} = \frac{x}{(1+nx^n)^{1/n}}.$$

$$\text{Now } \int x^{n-2}g(x)\,dx = \int x^{n-2}\cdot\frac{x}{(1+nx^n)^{1/n}}dx$$

$$= \int\frac{x^{n-1}}{(1+nx^n)^{1/n}}dx$$

let $y = 1 + nx^n$ then $dy = n.nx^{n-1}\,dx$

$$\Rightarrow \quad x^{n-1}dx = \frac{dy}{n^2}$$

$$= \int\frac{1}{y^{\frac{1}{n}}}\cdot\frac{dy}{n^2} = \frac{1}{n^2}\int y^{-\frac{1}{n}}dy$$

$$= \frac{1}{n^2}\cdot\frac{y^{-\frac{1}{n}+1}}{-\frac{1}{n}+1}+C = \frac{y^{1-\frac{1}{n}}}{n(n-1)}+C.$$

$$\text{i.e. } \int x^{n-2}g(x)\,dx = \frac{(1+nx^n)^{1-\frac{1}{n}}}{n(n-1)}+C.$$

7. Total KE of a system of particles about origin = K.E. of particles about centre of mass + K.E. of centre of mass

as $\Rightarrow$ Kinetic energy of centre of mass = 0.

So the centre of mass is at rest.

11. The given linear transformation is

$$T(x, y, z) = (x + y, y + z, z - x)$$

i.e. $\quad T(1, 0, 0) = (1, 0, -1)$

$\quad T(0, 1, 0) = (1, 1, 0)$

$\quad T(0, 0, 1) = (0, 1, 1)$

Clearly the range are linear dependent.

As $\quad (1, 0, 1) = (1, 1, 0) - (0, 1, 1)$

let $$u_1 = \frac{(1,1,0)}{\sqrt{2}} = \frac{1}{\sqrt{2}}(1,1,0).$$

Now define $w_1 = v_2 - \langle v_2, u_1\rangle u_1$

$$= (0,1,1)-\frac{1}{\sqrt{2}}\cdot\frac{1}{\sqrt{2}}(1,1,0)$$

$$= \left(\frac{-1}{2},\frac{1}{2},1\right)$$

$$\text{define } u_2 = \frac{\left\langle\frac{-1}{2},\frac{1}{2},1\right\rangle}{\left\|\left\langle\frac{-1}{2},\frac{1}{2},1\right\rangle\right\|} = \left(\frac{-1}{\sqrt{6}},\frac{1}{\sqrt{6}},\frac{2}{\sqrt{6}}\right)$$

Hence, from the given choice C is correct choice.

15. The given equation is $z^5 + 15z + 1 = 0$

let, $f(z) = z^5$ and $g(z) = 15z + 1$

Now on circle $|z| = 2$, we've

$$|f(z)| = |z|^5 = 2^5 = 32$$

and $|g(z)| = |152 + 1| \leq 15|z| + 1 = 31$

$\therefore$ $|g(z)| < |f(z)|$ on the circle $|z| = 2$.

Hence, by Rouche's theorem, the function $f(z) + g(z) = z^5 + 15z + 1$ has as many zeros in $|z| < 2$ as the function $f(z) = z^5$.

As the function $f(z)$ has a zero of order 5 at $z = 0$ therefore all the five roots of $z^5 + 15z + 1 = 0$ must lie inside the disc $|z| < 2$.

Again for $|z| = \frac{3}{2}$, we have

$$|z^5 + 1| \leq |z|^5 + 1$$

$$= \frac{243}{32} + 1 < \frac{45}{2} = |15z|.$$

i.e. The function $z^5 + 15z + 1$ has as many zeros in $|z| < \frac{3}{2}$ as the function $15z$. Since $15z$ has exactly one zero in this region, so does $z^5 + 15z + 1$. Hence four of zeros of $z^5 + 15z + 1$ must lie in the ring $\frac{3}{2} < |z| < 2$.

18. The given differential equation is

$$(1+x^2)\frac{dy}{dx} + 2xy - 4x^2 = 0$$

or, $$(1+x^2)\frac{dy}{dx} + 2xy = 4x^2$$

integrating both the sides, we get

$$(1 + x^2)y = \frac{4x^3}{3} + c.$$

As the curve is passing through the origin, hence

$$c = 0$$

i.e. $3y(1 + x^2) = 4x^3$ is the answer.

20. The multiplication is defined as

$a \cdot b = 0 \quad \forall\ a, b \in R.$

Clearly it is closed as well commutative. however it does not possesses an unity element which satisfy $a.e = a$.

As all the multiplication identically zero. Hence it is a ring which is commutative but has no unity.

Also this ring has zero divisor, hence, it is not an integral domain.

25. 2P (X = 2) = P (X = 1) + 2P (X = 0) when a random variable X is Poisson Distribution

$$P(X = n) = \frac{e^{-\lambda}\lambda^n}{n!}$$

$$\therefore\ 2.\frac{e^{-\lambda}\lambda^2}{2!} = \frac{e^{-\lambda}\lambda^1}{1!} + 2e^{-\lambda}$$

For a Poisson distribution with parameter λ.

$\lambda^2 - \lambda - 2 = 0$ mean = var. = $\frac{1}{\lambda}$

$\lambda = 2, -1$ var. = $\frac{1}{\lambda} = \frac{1}{2}$.

29. Both singularities are within the curve and are equal. So, by Cauchy Residue theorem,

$$I_1 = I_2.$$

34. The curve is symmetric about x and y axis

as $x^{2/3} + y^{2/3} = a^{2/3}$ ...(1)

any general point on curve (i) is given

$$x = a\cos^3\theta,\ y = a\sin^3\theta$$

$$4\int_{x=0}^{a}\sqrt{1+\left(\frac{dy}{dx}\right)^2}\,dx = 4\int_{\theta=\frac{\pi}{2}}^{0}\sec\theta\left(-3a\cos^2\theta\sin\theta\right)d\theta$$

$$= 12a\int_0^{\frac{\pi}{2}}\sin\theta\cos\theta\,d\theta$$

$$= 12a\left[\frac{\sin^2\theta}{2}\right]_0^{\frac{\pi}{2}} = 6a.$$

35. The given differential equation is

$$\frac{dy}{dx} = \frac{2x - y + 1}{x + 2y - 3}$$

or, $xdy + 2ydy - 3dy = 2xdx - ydx + dx$

or, $xdy + ydx + 2ydy - 2xdx - dx - 3dy = 0$

integrating both the sides, we get

$$xy + y^2 - x^2 - 3y - x = c.$$

38. $(\phi + \sigma)(x, y) = \phi(x, y)\,\sigma(x, y)$
$= x + 2y + 3x - y = 4x + y$
$(4\phi)(x, y) = 4\phi(x, y) = 4(x + 2y) = 4x + 8y$
$(2\phi - 5\sigma)(x, y) = 2\phi(x, y) - 5\sigma(x, y)$
$= 2(x + 2y) - 5(3x - 5)$
$= -13x + 9y.$

42. $\iint_S \vec{r} \cdot \vec{n}\, d\sigma = 1$

$\Rightarrow 3\iiint_V dx\, dy\, dz = 1$

$\Rightarrow \iiint_V dx\, dy\, dz = 1/3$

43. Here $n = 4$, $\Delta x = h = \dfrac{b-a}{n} = \dfrac{1-0}{4} = 0.25.$

The values of x and y are tabulated below, where $y = f(x) = \dfrac{1}{1+x}$.

x	0	0.25	0.50	0.75	1.00
y	1	0.8000	0.6667	0.5714	0.5
	(y_0)	(y_1)	(y_2)	(y_3)	(y_4)

Trapezoid rule gives

$$\int_0^1 \frac{1}{1+x}dx = \frac{h}{2}\{y_0 + 2(y_1 + y_2 + y_3) + y_4\}$$

$$= \frac{0.25}{2}\{1 + 2(0.8 + 0.6667 + 0.5714) + 0.5\}$$

$= 0.6977.$

45. As $\quad A = \begin{bmatrix} a & b \\ b & -a \end{bmatrix}$

hence $\quad A^2 = \begin{bmatrix} a & b \\ b & -a \end{bmatrix}\begin{bmatrix} a & b \\ b & -a \end{bmatrix}$

$= \begin{bmatrix} a^2+b^2 & 0 \\ 0 & a^2+b^2 \end{bmatrix}$

i.e. $\quad A^2 = (a^2+b^2)\begin{bmatrix} 1 & 0 \\ 0 & 1 \end{bmatrix}$

and $\quad A^3 = (a^2+b^2)\begin{bmatrix} a & b \\ b & -a \end{bmatrix}$

hence $\quad A^4 = \left(a^2+b^2\right)^2\begin{bmatrix} 1 & 0 \\ 0 & 1 \end{bmatrix}$

i.e. $\quad A^{2m} = \left(a^2+b^2\right)^m\begin{bmatrix} 1 & 0 \\ 0 & 1 \end{bmatrix}$

i.e. $\quad A^{2m} = MA$

$\Rightarrow \quad M = \left(a^2+b^2\right)^{m-1}\begin{bmatrix} a & b \\ b & -a \end{bmatrix}$

47.

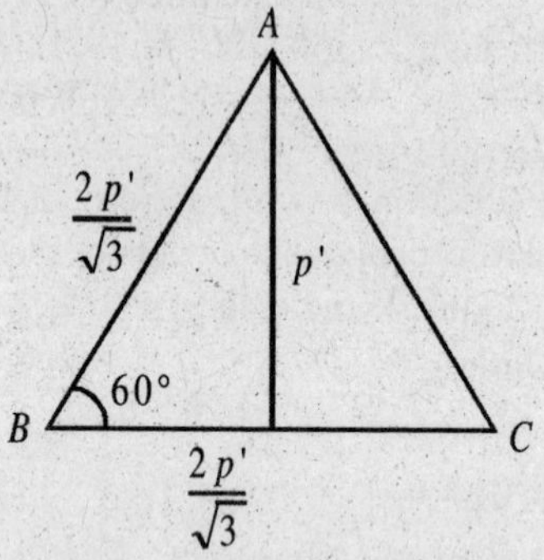

A, B, C; $60°$; $\frac{2p'}{\sqrt{3}}$; p'; $\frac{2p'}{\sqrt{3}}$

$\Rightarrow$ Area $= \dfrac{1}{2}.p'.\dfrac{2p'}{\sqrt{3}} = \dfrac{p'^2}{\sqrt{3}}$

Now, $p' = \dfrac{r}{\sqrt{p^2+q^2}}$

$\Rightarrow \Delta = \dfrac{r^2}{\sqrt{3}\left(p^2+q^2\right)}$

49. The given differential equation is

$p = \log(px - y)$ ...(1)

or, $\quad px - y = e^p$

or, $\quad y = px - e^p$

which is in clairaut form.

Hence the general solution is given by

$y = cx - e^c$ ...(2)

Now differentiating (2) partially, w.r.t. c, we get

$0 = x - e^c$

or, $\quad c = \log x$

$\Rightarrow \quad y = x \log x - x$

is the required singular solution.

51. Given $\quad f(x) = x^5 + 4x^4 + 4x^3 + 4x^2 + x + 1$

Clearly $f(1) = 1 + 4 + 4 + 4 + 1 + 1 = 0$

and $\quad f(3) = 3^5 + 4.3^4 + 4.3^3 + 4.3^2 + 3 + 1$

$= 3 + 4 + 3 + 2 + 1 + 1 = 0$

Now $f'(x) = 0.x^4 + x^3 + 2x^2 + 3x + 1$

$f'(1) = 1 + 2 + 3 + 1 \neq 0$

and $f'(3) = 2 + 3 + 4 + 1 = 0.$

52. 2×2 matrix can be written as

$$A = \begin{bmatrix} a & b \\ c & d \end{bmatrix}$$

where a, b, c, d can take three (0, 1, 2) values.

Now from question $| ad - bc | = 1$.

$ad = 1, bc = 0$. Now $bc = 0$, is possible as

or $ad = 0, bc = 1$ | $b = 0, \; c = 1$

$b = 0, \; c = 0$

$b = 1, \; c = 0$

$ad = 1$ | $b = 2, \; c = 0$

either through | $b = 0, \; c = 1$

$a = 1, \; b = 1$

$a = 2, \; b = 2$

$\Rightarrow$ Total no. of such matrix $= 2 \times 2 \times 5 = 20$

Also when $ad = 2, \; bc = 1$

or $ad = 1, \; bc = 2$

then $| ad - bc | = 1$

No. of such matrix $= 2 + 2 = 4$.

53. $A(t) = \int_{-t}^{t} y dx = \int_{-t}^{t} e^{-|x|} dx$

$= 2\int_0^t e^{-x} dx$; as $e^{-|x|}$ is even function.

$= 2(-e^{-x})\Big|_0^t = 2(1 - e^{-t})$

$\lim_{t \to \infty} A(t) = \lim_{t \to \infty} 2(1 - e^{-t}) = 2$

54. $\dim (w_1 + w_2) = \dim w_1 + \dim w_2 - dm (w_1 \cap w_2)$

$\Rightarrow \dim (w_1 + w_2) \leq \dim w_1 + \dim w_2$.

56. The given expression

$$\lim_{x \to a} \frac{1}{x^2 - a^2} \int_a^x \sin t^2 \, dt \quad \left[\frac{0^-}{0} \text{ form}\right]$$

By L'Hospital Rule $\lim_{x \to a} \frac{\sin 2^2.1 - 0}{2x} = \frac{1}{2a} \sin a^2$.

57. The characteristic polynomial is

$| A - xI | = 0$

$$\Rightarrow \quad = \begin{vmatrix} 1-x & 1 & 0 & 0 \\ -1 & -1-x & 0 & 0 \\ -2 & -2 & 2-x & 1 \\ 1 & 1 & -1 & -x \end{vmatrix} = 0$$

$(x - 1)^2 \, [x^2 - 1 + 1) = 0$

$\Rightarrow x^2 \, (x - 1)^2 = 0.$

59.

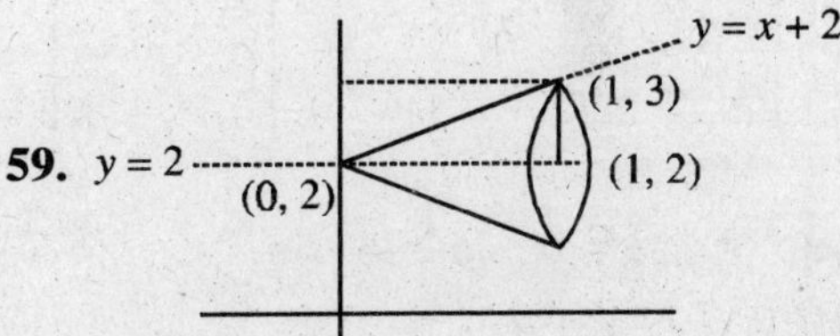

The required solid is a cone with $r = 1$ and height, $h = 1$

Slant height $l = \sqrt{1+1} = \sqrt{2}$

Surface Area $= \pi r l = \sqrt{2}\pi$

SET–22

CSIR–UGC (NET) MATHEMATICAL SCIENCES

PART-C

1. Let T : $P_3[0, 1] \to P_2[0, 1]$ be defined by $(Tp)(x) = p''(x) + p'(x)$. Then the matrix representation of T with respect to the bases $\{1, x, x^2, x^3\}$ and $\{1, x, x^2\}$ of $P_3[0, 1]$ and $P_2[0, 1]$ respectively is

A. $\begin{bmatrix} 0 & 0 & 0 \\ 1 & 0 & 0 \\ 2 & 2 & 0 \\ 0 & 6 & 3 \end{bmatrix}$ B. $\begin{bmatrix} 0 & 1 & 2 & 0 \\ 0 & 0 & 2 & 6 \\ 0 & 0 & 0 & 3 \end{bmatrix}$

C. $\begin{bmatrix} 0 & 2 & 1 & 0 \\ 6 & 2 & 0 & 0 \\ 3 & 0 & 0 & 0 \end{bmatrix}$ D. $\begin{bmatrix} 0 & 0 & 0 \\ 0 & 0 & 1 \\ 0 & 2 & 2 \\ 3 & 6 & 0 \end{bmatrix}$

2. Let, $f(x, y) = x^2 \sin\frac{1}{x} + y^2 \sin\frac{1}{y}$, when $(x, y) \neq (0, 0)$

$f(x, 0) = x^2 \sin\frac{1}{x}$ when $x \neq 0$

$f(0, y) = y^2 \sin\frac{1}{y}$ when $y \neq 0$

$f(0, 0) = 0$,

then at (0, 0)

A. f_x is continuous but not f_y.
B. f_y is continuous but not f_x.
C. f_x and f_y both are continuous.
D. neither f_x nor f_y is continuous.

3. The degree and order of the differential equation $\sin\left(\frac{d^2y}{dx^2}\right) + \frac{dy}{dx} = y^2$ are

A. 1 and 2
B. Not defined and 2
C. 3 and 4
D. 2 and not defined

4. Let $R = \left\{\begin{bmatrix} a & b \\ 0 & 0 \end{bmatrix}; a, b \in Q\right\}$

$S = \left\{\begin{bmatrix} 0 & x \\ 0 & 0 \end{bmatrix}; x \in Q\right\}$

then select the incorrect statements.

A. R is commutative ring
B. S is an ideal of R
C. R/S is field
D. None of these

5. If $X_1, X_2, \ldots\ldots, X_n$ is a random sample from the population having the density function,

$f(x, \mu) = \frac{1}{\sqrt{2\pi\mu}} e^{\frac{-x^2}{2\mu}}$, $-\infty < x < \infty$, then the maximum likelihood estimator for μ is

A. $\sqrt{\frac{\Sigma x_i^2}{n^2}}$ B. $\sqrt{\frac{\Sigma x_i^2}{n}}$

C. $\frac{\Sigma x_i^2}{n}$ D. $\frac{\Sigma x_i^2}{\sqrt{n}}$

6. If from each of the three boxes containing 3 white and 1 black, 2 white and 2 black, 1 white and 3 black balls, one ball is drawn at random, then the probability that 2 white and 1 black ball will be drawn is

A. $\frac{13}{32}$ B. $\frac{1}{4}$

C. $\frac{1}{32}$ D. $\frac{3}{16}$

7. An example of a function with a non-isolated essential singularity at $z = 2$ is

A. $\tan\frac{1}{z-2}$ B. $\sin\frac{1}{z-2}$

C. $e^{-(z-2)}$ D. $\tan\frac{z-2}{z}$

8. A jury of six people was selected from a group of twenty potential jurors, of whom eight were African-America and twelve were white. Then the probability that the jury contains one or fewer African-American is

A. 0.187 B. 0.0187
C. 0.813 D. 0.0813

9. Let $f: R \to R$ be a continuous function. If $f(q) \subseteq N$, then

A. $f(R) = N$
B. $f(R) \subseteq N$ but f need not be constant
C. f is unbounded
D. f is a constant function

10. The series $\sum \frac{1}{4}\{1+(-1)^{n+1}(2n+1)\}$ is

A. convergent
B. divergent
C. oscillating infinitely
D. oscillating finitely

11. A matrix M has eigenvalues 1 and 4 with corresponding eigenvectors $(1, -1)^T$ and $(2, 1)^T$ respectively. Then M is

A. $\begin{bmatrix} -4 & -8 \\ 5 & 9 \end{bmatrix}$ B. $\begin{bmatrix} 9 & -8 \\ 5 & -4 \end{bmatrix}$

C. $\begin{bmatrix} 2 & 2 \\ 1 & 3 \end{bmatrix}$ D. $\begin{bmatrix} 3 & 2 \\ 1 & 2 \end{bmatrix}$

12. The complete integral of the partial differential equation
$xp^3q^2 + yp^2q^3 + (p^3 + q^3) - zp^2q^2 = 0$ is z

A. $ax + by + (ab^{-2} + ba^{-2})$
B. $ax - by + (ab^{-2} - ba^{-2})$
C. $-ax + by + (ba^{-2} - ab^{-2})$
D. $ax + by - a(b^{-3} + ba^{-2})$

13. The particular integral of the differential equation $(D^2 + 4)y = x$ is

A. xe^{-2x} B. $x\cos 2x$
C. $x\sin 2x$ D. $x/4$

14. Which of the following statement is TRUE for $Rr + Ss + Tt + f(x, y, z, p, q)$

A. The canonical form of hyperbolic equation is $\frac{\partial^2 z}{\partial u \partial v} = \phi\left(u, v, z, \frac{\partial z}{\partial u}, \frac{\partial z}{\partial v}\right)$.

B. The canonical form of parabolic equation is $\frac{\partial^2 z}{\partial u \partial v} = \phi\left(u, v, z, \frac{\partial z}{\partial u}, \frac{\partial z}{\partial v}\right)$.

C. The canonical form of elliptic equation is $\frac{\partial^2 z}{\partial v^2} = \phi\left(u, v, z, \frac{\partial z}{\partial u}, \frac{\partial z}{\partial v}\right)$.

D. All are true

15. In general solution, the arbitrary constants are

A. Dependent
B. Independent
C. Dependent variables
D. None of the above

16. If M is a 7×5 matrix of rank 3 and N is a 5×7 matrix of rank 5, then rank (MN) is

A. 5 B. 3
C. 2 D. 1

17. For a given function

$J = \int_0^1 (y'^2 - 2\alpha yy' - 2\beta y')\, dx$ with $y(0) = 0$ the extremal is

A. $y = x$
B. $y = \frac{\beta x}{1-\alpha}; \alpha \neq 1$
C. $y = \frac{(1-\beta)x}{\alpha}$
D. Cannot be determined

18. "In the context of inventory management the following need to be addressed" is not true.

A. How much to order?
B. When to order?
C. How much safety stock to keep?
D. Maximum of the total inventory cost.

19. The radius of convergence of the power series $\sum_{n=0}^{\infty} a_n z^{n^2}$, where $a_0 = 1$, $a_n = 3^{-n} a_{n-1}$ for $n \in N$, is

A. 0 B. $\sqrt{3}$
C. 3 D. ∞

20. When we solve a system of simultaneous linear equations by using two-phase simplex method, the values of decision variables may be

A. Positive
B. Negative
C. Non-negative
D. Positive or Negative

21. If T be the linear operator of R^2 defined by $T(x, y) = (4x - 2y, 2x + y)$, then compute the matrix of T in the basis $\{f_1 = (1, 1), f_2 = (-1, 0)\}$.

A. $[T]_f = \begin{bmatrix} 3 & 2 \\ 1 & 2 \end{bmatrix}$ B. $[T]_f = \begin{bmatrix} 3 & -2 \\ 1 & -2 \end{bmatrix}$

C. $[T]_f = \begin{bmatrix} 3 & -2 \\ 1 & 2 \end{bmatrix}$ D. $[T]_f = \begin{bmatrix} 3 & 1 \\ -2 & 2 \end{bmatrix}$

22. The set of all boundary points Q in R is
A. R B. R/Q
C. Q D. $\varnothing$

23. $\int_c \frac{e^z}{\left(z^2+\pi^2\right)^2} dz$ where C is the circle $|z| = 4$

A. $\frac{i}{\pi}$ B. $\frac{2i}{\pi}$

C. $\frac{4i}{\pi}$ D. $8\pi i$

24. The dimension of the subspace $\{(x_1, x_2, x_3, x_4, x_5) : 3x_1 - x_2 + x_3 = 0\}$ of $\mathbf{R}^5$ is
A. 1 B. 2
C. 3 D. 4

25. The number of roots of the equation $x^6 + x^5 + x^4 + x^3 + x^2 + x + 1 = 0$ in Z_7 is
A. 1 B. 2
C. 3 D. 4

26. A box contains two coins, one of which is fair and the other two headed. One coin is chosen at random and tossed twice. If two heads appear, then the probability that the chosen coin was two headed is

A. $\frac{1}{2}$ B. $\frac{1}{4}$

C. $\frac{1}{3}$ D. $\frac{4}{5}$

27. Consider the following system of linear equation

$$83x + 11y - 4z = 95;$$
$$7x + 52y + 13z = 104;$$
$$3x + 8y + 29z = 71$$

then value of (x, y, z) after second iteration using Jacobi method is equal to
A. (1.14, 2, 2.45)
B. (1, 2, 3)
C. (0.993, 1.254, 1.999)
D. (1.07, 1.543, 1.913)

28. Let G be a group and let A, B be subgroups of G. Which one of the following statements is false?
A. If A and B are normal subgroups of G then $AB = BA$
B. If A and B are normal subgroups of G and $A \cap B = \{e\}$, where e is the identity of G then $ab = ba$ for all a in A and b in B
C. If A is normal subgroup of B and B is a normal subgroup of G then A is a normal subgroup of G
D. None of the above

29. If $A = \begin{pmatrix} 1 & 0 & -1 \\ -2 & -1 & 0 \\ -1 & 0 & 0 \end{pmatrix}$, then inverse of matrix A will be

A. $\begin{pmatrix} -1 & 0 & 1 \\ 2 & 1 & 0 \\ 1 & 0 & 0 \end{pmatrix}$ B. $\begin{pmatrix} 1 & -2 & -1 \\ 0 & -1 & 0 \\ -1 & 0 & 0 \end{pmatrix}$

C. $\begin{pmatrix} 0 & 0 & 1 \\ 2 & 2 & 0 \\ 1 & 0 & 1 \end{pmatrix}$ D. $\begin{pmatrix} 0 & 0 & -1 \\ 0 & -1 & 2 \\ -1 & 0 & -1 \end{pmatrix}$

30. Let G be an Abelian group of order 10. Let $S = \{g \in G : g^{-1} = g\}$. Then the number of non-identity elements in S is
A. 5 B. 2
C. 1 D. 0

31. Under the steriographic projection of points on the unit sphere $x^2 + y^2 + z^2 = 1$ in R^2 to the extended plane $z = x + iy$, the plane $z = x + iy$ corresponds to

A. $\left(\frac{x^2}{x^2+y^2+1}, \frac{y^2}{x^2+y^2+1}, \frac{x^2+y^2-1}{x^2+y^2+1}\right)$

B. $\left(\frac{x}{x^2+y^2+1}, \frac{y}{x^2+y^2+1}, \frac{x+y+1}{x^2+y^2+1}\right)$

C. $\left(\frac{2x}{x^2+y^2+1}, \frac{2y}{x^2+y^2+1}, \frac{2x+2y+1}{x^2+y^2+1}\right)$

D. $\left(\frac{2x}{x^2+y^2+1}, \frac{2y}{x^2+y^2+1}, \frac{x^2+y^2-1}{x^2+y^2+1}\right)$

32. For the system

$$x_1 + 2x_2 + x_3 + x_4 = 2$$

$$x_1 + 2x_2 + \frac{x_3}{2} + x_5 = 2$$

Which of the following is a basic feasible solution.

A. $x_1 = -1, x_2 = 1/2, x_3 = x_4 = x_5 = 0$
B. $x_1 = +1, x_2 = 1/2, x_3 = x_4 = x_5 = 0$
C. $x_1 = 1, x_2 = x_4 = x = 0, x_3 = 0.5$
D. None of these

33. For a group of order 91 which statement is false.

A. It has one subgroup of order 7
B. It has two subgroups of order 13
C. It has a subgroups of order 7 and 13
D. None of these

34. Define T on $\mathbf{R}^2$ into itself by $T(x_1, x_2) = (x_1 + x_2, x_1 - x_2)$. Then matrix of T^{-1} relative to the standard basis for $\mathbf{R}^2$ is

A. $\begin{bmatrix} 1 & 1 \\ 1 & 1 \end{bmatrix}$

B. $\begin{bmatrix} -1 & -1 \\ -1 & 1 \end{bmatrix}$

C. $\begin{bmatrix} 1/2 & 1/2 \\ 1/2 & -1/2 \end{bmatrix}$

D. $\begin{bmatrix} -1/2 & -1/2 \\ -1/2 & 1/2 \end{bmatrix}$

35. The number of generalized co-ordinates required to describe motion of a rigid body with one of its points fixed is

A. 9
B. 6
C. 3
D. 1

36. If in a culture of yeast, y_0 is the amount of yeast present initially, and the rate of growth $\frac{dy}{dt}$ is proportional to the amount y at time t and if y doubles in one day then the amount expected after 3 days equals.

A. $3y_0$
B. $8y_0$
C. $9y_0$
D. $27y_0$

37. In a metric space (x, d)

A. Every infinite set E has a limit point in E
B. Every closed subset of a compact set is compact.
C. Every closed and bounded set is compact.
D. Every subset of a compact set is closed.

38. The number of the basic feasible solution of an L.P.P. can not be

A. Exactly one
B. Exactly two
C. Infinite
D. Finite

39. If $f(z) = \frac{\sin z^2}{z^2}$, then $\int_{|z|=1} f(z)dz$ is equal to

A. $\frac{1}{2}$
B. 0
C. 2
D. 4

40. The expression $x^2 + x + 5$ in $F[x]$, where F is the field of integer modulo 11 can be written as

A. $(x + 2)(x + 3)$
B. $(x + 3)(x + 6)$
C. $(x + 3)(x + 9)$
D. $(x + 1)(x + 5)$

41. The values of a, b, c for which the function

$$f(x) = \begin{cases} \frac{\sin(a+1)x + \sin x}{x}, & x < 0 \\ c, & x = 0 \\ \frac{(x + bx^2)^{1/2} - x^{1/2}}{bx^{1/2}}, & x > 0 \end{cases}$$

is continuous at $x = 0$, are

A. $a = \frac{3}{2}, b = -\frac{3}{2}, c = \frac{1}{2}$

B. $a = -\frac{3}{2}, c = \frac{3}{2}$, b is arbitrary non-zero real

C. $a = -\frac{5}{2}, b = -\frac{3}{2}, c = \frac{3}{2}$

D. None of the above

42. Let F be a homomorphic mapping of a group G into a group G′. Let F(G) be the homomorphic image of G in G′. Then

A. F(G) is a complex of G′.
B. F(G) = G′
C. F(G) is a subgroup of G′.
D. F(G) is a normal subgroup of G.

43. Let, *X* be a normal random variable with mean zero and variance 9. If $a = P(X \geq 3)$, then $P(|X| \leq 3)$ equals

A. a B. $1 - a$
C. $2a$ D. $1 - 2a$

44. Which of the following transformations reduces the given differential equation $\frac{dy}{dx} = \frac{x - y + 1}{x + 2y - 3}$ into homogeneous one?

A. $x = X - 3, y = Y - 4$
B. $x = X + 1/3, y = Y + 3/4$
C. $x = X + 5, y = Y - 4$
D. None of these

45. Which one of the following functions is continuous at origin?

A. $f(x) = \cos\left(\frac{1}{x}\right)$; when $x \neq 0$, $f(0) = 0$

B. $f(x) = \sin x \cdot \sin\left(\frac{1}{x}\right)$; when $x \neq 0$ $f(0) = 0$

C. $f(x) = x + \sin\left(\frac{1}{x}\right)$; when $x \neq 0$, $f(0) = 1$

D. $f(x) = x\sin\left(\frac{1}{x}\right)$; when $x \neq 0$ $f(0) = 1$

46. Let $a_n = \begin{cases} \frac{1}{3^n} \text{ if } n \text{ is a prime,} \\ \frac{1}{4^n} \text{ if } n \text{ is not a prime.} \end{cases}$

Then the radius of convergence of the power series $\sum_{n=1}^{\infty} a_n x^n$ is

A. 4 B. 3
C. $\frac{1}{3}$ D. $\frac{1}{4}$

47. Let $s = \begin{pmatrix} 1 & 2 & 3 & 4 & 5 & 6 & 7 & 8 & 9 & 10 & 11 & 12 \\ 2 & 10 & 8 & 5 & 9 & 3 & 6 & 11 & 4 & 12 & 1 & 7 \end{pmatrix}$.

the cardinality of the orbit of 2 under σ is

A. 3 B. 6
C. 9 D. 12

48. Let p be the unique polynomial of suitable degree such that $p(1) = 2$, $p'(1) = 3$, $p(2) = 6$, $p'(2) = 7$, $p''(2) = 8$ then $p(0)$ is

A. − 8 B. 0
C. 16 D. None of these

49. If $e^{ax}u(x)$ is a particular integral of $\frac{d^2y}{dx^2} - 2a\frac{dy}{dx} + a^2y = f(x)$, where a is a constant, then $\frac{d^2y}{dx^2}$ is equal to

A. $f(x)$ B. $f(x)e^{ax}$
C. $f(x)e^{-ax}$ D. $f(x)[e^{ax} + e^{-ax}]$

50. Let C denote the boundary of the semi-circular disk $D = \{(x, y) \in R^2 : x^2 + y^2 \leq 1, y \geq 0\}$ and let $\varphi(x, y) = x^2 + y$ for $(x, y) \in D$. If $\hat{n}$ is the outward unit normal to C, then the integral $\oint_C (\vec{\nabla}\varphi).\hat{n}ds$, evaluated counter-clockwise over C, is equal to

A. 0 B. $\pi - 2$
C. π D. $\pi + 2$

51. The curve satisfying $\frac{dy}{dx} = \frac{y^2 - 2xy - x^2}{y^2 + 2x - x^2}$ and passing through $(1, -1)$ is given by

A. a straight line B. a circle
C. an ellipse D. parabola

52. A function F(X) is strictly concave if

A. F(X) – strictly convex
B. F(X) – concave
C. –F(X) – strictly convex
D. None

53. A function f is defined such that for all real x, y.

(*i*) $f(x + y) = f(x) f(y)$
(*ii*) $f(x) = 1 + xg(x)$, where $\lim_{x \to 0} g(x) = 1$

What is $\frac{d}{dx}f(x)$ equal to?

A. $g(x)$ B. $f(x)$
C. $g'(x)$ D. $g(x) + xg'(x)$

54. The singular solution of the differential equation
$(xp - y)^2 = p^2 - 1$ is
A. $x^2 + y^2 = 1$ B. $x^2 - y^2 = 1$
C. $x^2 + 2y^2 = 1$ D. $2x^2 + y^2 = 1$

55. A variable takes values 0, 1, 2, ..., n with frequencies proportional to the binomial coeffieients
$1, \binom{n}{1}, \binom{n}{2}, \binom{n}{3}, \ldots, \binom{n}{n}$
relation between mean and variance.
A. Var. = $\frac{1}{2}$ mean B. Var. = 2 mean
C. Var. = 3 mean D. Var. = $\frac{1}{3}$ mean

56. Let $f_n(x) = n \sin^{2n+1} x \cos x$. Then the value of
$$\lim_{n\to\infty} \int_0^{\pi/2} f_n(x)dx - \int_0^{\pi/2} \left(\lim_{n\to\infty} f_n(x)\right)dx$$ is
A. 1/2 B. 0
C. −1/2 D. $-\infty$

57. Let $f(z) = u + iv$ be an analytic function such that $v = e^x (y \cos y + x \sin y)$, then $f(z)$ is
A. ze^z B. ize^z
C. ze^{iz} D. e^z/z

58. If v_1, v_2, v_3 are linearly dependent vectors in $R^{(3)}$ over R, then
A. one of them must be zero
B. all of them must be scalar multiples of a fixed vector in $R^{(3)}$.
C. $\alpha v_1 + \beta v_2 + \gamma v_3 = 0$ for $\alpha, \beta, \gamma \in F \Rightarrow \alpha = \beta = \gamma = 0$
D. There exist scalars α_1, $\beta_1 \gamma$ not all 0 such that $\alpha v_1 + \beta v_2 + \gamma v_3 = 0$

59. A function $f(x)$ on S is said to be convex if for any two vectors x_1 and x_2 in S.
A. $f[\lambda x_1 + (1 - \lambda) x_2] < \lambda f(x_1) + (1 - \lambda) f(x_2)$
B. $f[\lambda x_1 + (1 - \lambda) x_2] \le \lambda f(x_1) + (1 - \lambda) f(x_2)$
C. $f[\lambda x_1 + (1 - \lambda) x_2] \ge \lambda f(x_1) + (1 - \lambda) f(x_2)$
D. $f[\lambda x_1 + (1 - \lambda) x_2] > \lambda f(x_1) + (1 - \lambda) f(x_2)$

60. The series whose nth term is
$$t_n = \sqrt{n^2 + 1} - n$$
A. converges to the sum 0
B. converges to the sum $\frac{1}{2}$
C. converges to the sum 1
D. diverges

ANSWERS

1	2	3	4	5	6	7	8	9	10
B	C	B	B	D	A	A	A	C	C
11	**12**	**13**	**14**	**15**	**16**	**17**	**18**	**19**	**20**
D	A	D	A	B	B	B	B	A	D
21	**22**	**23**	**24**	**25**	**26**	**27**	**28**	**29**	**30**
C	A	A	D	A	D	C	C	D	C
31	**32**	**33**	**34**	**35**	**36**	**37**	**38**	**39**	**40**
D	B	B	C	C	B	B	A	B	C
41	**42**	**43**	**44**	**45**	**46**	**47**	**48**	**49**	**50**
D	C	B	D	B	B	C	A	C	B
51	**52**	**53**	**54**	**55**	**56**	**57**	**58**	**59**	**60**
A	C	D	B	A	A	A	D	B	D

SOME SELECTED EXPLANATORY ANSWERS

1. $(Tp)(x) = p''(x) + p'(x)$

$(Tp)(1) = 0 + 0 = 0.1 + 0.x + 0.x^2$

$(Tp)(x) = 0 + 1 = 1.1 + 0.x + 0.x^2$

$(Tp)(x^2) = 2 + 2x = 2.1 + 2.x + 0.x^2$

$(Tp)(x^3) = 6x + 3x^2 = 0.1 + 6.x + 3.x^2$

hence matrix representation of

$$T = \begin{bmatrix} 0 & 1 & 2 & 0 \\ 0 & 0 & 2 & 6 \\ 0 & 0 & 0 & 3 \end{bmatrix}.$$

11. We know that from the diagonalization theorem

$$D = P^{-1}MP$$

or $$M = PDP^{-1}$$

where $$P = \begin{bmatrix} 1 & 2 \\ -1 & 1 \end{bmatrix}$$

$$D = \begin{bmatrix} 1 & 0 \\ 0 & 4 \end{bmatrix}$$

$$|P| = 1 + 2 = 3$$

$$P^{-1} = \frac{1}{3}\begin{bmatrix} 1 & -2 \\ 1 & 1 \end{bmatrix}$$

$$\therefore \quad M = \frac{1}{3}\begin{bmatrix} 1 & 2 \\ -1 & 1 \end{bmatrix}\begin{bmatrix} 1 & 0 \\ 0 & 4 \end{bmatrix}\begin{bmatrix} 1 & -2 \\ 1 & 1 \end{bmatrix}$$

$$= \frac{1}{3}\begin{bmatrix} 1 & 2 \\ -1 & 1 \end{bmatrix}\begin{bmatrix} 1 & -2 \\ 4 & 4 \end{bmatrix}$$

$$= \frac{1}{3}\begin{bmatrix} 9 & 6 \\ 3 & 6 \end{bmatrix} = \begin{bmatrix} 3 & 2 \\ 1 & 2 \end{bmatrix}.$$

19. If R be the radius of convergence of the power series.

Then $$\frac{1}{R} = \lim_{n\to\infty}\left|\frac{a_n}{a_{n+1}}\right|$$

$$= \lim_{n\to\infty}\left|\frac{a_n}{3^{-(n+1)}a_n}\right| = \lim_{n\to\infty}\frac{1}{3^{-(n+1)}}$$

$$\Rightarrow \frac{1}{R} \to \infty \quad \Rightarrow R \to 0.$$

21. $T(f_1) = T(1, 1) = (2, 3) = 3(1, 1) + (-1, 0)$

$= 3f_1 + f_2$

$T(f_2) = T(-1, 0) = (-4, -2)$

$= -2(1, 1) + (-1, 0)$

$= -2 f_1 + 2f_2$

$$\therefore [T]_F = \begin{bmatrix} 3 & -2 \\ 1 & 2 \end{bmatrix}$$

22. As neighbourhood of every real number contains some points of Q and some points of R – Q, so R is the set of boundary points of Q.

26. P (Getting a head in a fair coin) = $\frac{1}{2}$

P (Getting a head in two headed coin) = 1

Total probability

= *1st coin.* head. head + *2n coin.* head. head

$$= \frac{1}{2}.\frac{1}{2}.\frac{1}{2} + \frac{1}{2}.1.1 = \frac{5}{8}$$

$$\text{Pr.} = \frac{1/2}{5/8} = \frac{4}{5}.$$

27. As the requirement for iteration is satisfied by these equations, we solve each equation for the unknown having the largest coefficient and the new equations are

$$x = \frac{1}{83}(95 - 11y + 4z),$$

$$y = \frac{1}{52}(104 - 7x - 13z)$$

and $$z = \frac{1}{29}(71 - 3x - 8y)$$

Starting with $(x, y, z) = (0, 0, 0)$ we get,

$$x^{(1)} = \frac{95}{89} = 1.14;$$

$$y^{(1)} = \frac{104}{52} = 2,$$

and $$z^{(1)} = \frac{71}{29} = 2.45$$

$$x^{(2)} = \frac{1}{83}[(95-11y^{(1)}+4z^{(1)}]$$

$$= \frac{1}{83}[(95-11\times2+4\times2.45]$$

$$=0.993$$

$$y^{(2)} = \frac{1}{52}[104-7x^{(1)}-13z^{(1)}]$$

$$= \frac{1}{52}[104-7\times1.14-13\times2.45]$$

$$= 1.254$$

and $$z^{(2)} = \frac{1}{29}[71-3x^{(1)}-8y^{(1)}]$$

$$= \frac{1}{29}[71-3\times1.4-8\times2] = 1.999$$

i.e. $(x^{(2)}, y^{(2)}, z^{(2)}) = (0.993, 1.254, 1.999)$.

29. The given matrix A is

$$A = \begin{bmatrix} 1 & 0 & -1 \\ -2 & -1 & 0 \\ -1 & 0 & 0 \end{bmatrix} \text{ hence } |A| = 1.$$

$$\text{Adj } A = \begin{bmatrix} 0 & 0 & -1 \\ 0 & -1 & 0 \\ -1 & 2 & -1 \end{bmatrix}^T = \begin{bmatrix} 0 & 0 & -1 \\ 0 & -1 & 2 \\ -1 & 0 & -1 \end{bmatrix}$$

$$\therefore\ A^{-1} = \frac{\text{Adj } A}{|A|} = \begin{bmatrix} 0 & 0 & -1 \\ 0 & -1 & 2 \\ -1 & 0 & -1 \end{bmatrix}.$$

30. $\{[0], [1], [2], [3], [4], [5], [6], [7], [8], [9]\}_{+10}$ is an abelian group of order 10.
$[0]^{-1} = [0]$ & $[5]^{-1} = [5]$
[0] is identity and [5] is non-identity element.

33. If $0(G) = p.q$ where both p and q are prime and $q \nmid (p-1)$ then it is cyclic group.

Also, it possesses a unique subgroup of order p and order q.

i.e. $0(G) = 13.7$

$\Rightarrow$ It has only one subgroup of order 13 and order 7.

34. Matrix of T with respect to standard basis $e_1 = (1, 0)$ and e_2 (0, 1) are

T(1, 0) = (1, 1) and T(0, 1) = (1, –1).

$$\textit{i.e.} \quad [T] = \begin{bmatrix} 1 & 1 \\ 1 & -1 \end{bmatrix} = [T^{-1}] = \frac{-1}{2}\begin{bmatrix} -1 & -1 \\ -1 & 1 \end{bmatrix}$$

$$= \begin{bmatrix} 1/2 & 1/2 \\ 1/2 & -1/2 \end{bmatrix}.$$

40. We have $F = Z_{11} = \{0, 1, 2, 3, 4, 5, 6, 7, 8, 9, 10\}$.

Let $x^2 + x + 5 = (x + a)(x + b)$, $a, b \in F$.

Comparing with coefficients of x and constant terms on both the sides, we get

$a + b = 1$ & $5 = ab$.

$a + b = 1$ is satisfied by (1, 0), (2, 10), (3, 9), (4, 8), (5, 7), (6, 6) and ab for above combination are 0, 9, 5, 10, 2, 3 respectively.

Clearly $ab = 5$ & $a + b = 1$ is satisfied for (3, 9).

i.e., $(x^2 + x + 5) = (x + 3)(x + 9)$.

41.
$$\lim_{x\to0^-} f(x) = \lim_{x\to0^-} \frac{\sin(a+1)x+\sin x}{x}$$

$$= (a+1)+1=(a+2)$$

$$\lim_{x\to0^+} f(x) = \frac{(x+bx^2)^{\frac{1}{2}} - x^{\frac{1}{2}}}{bx^{\frac{1}{2}}}$$

$$= \frac{\sqrt{1+bx}-1}{b} = 0 \text{ if } b \neq 0$$

Also $\quad f(0) = c$

$f(x)$ is continuous at $x=0 \Rightarrow a+2=c=0$

$\Rightarrow a=-2, c=0 \quad \& \ b\neq0.$

44.
$$\frac{dy}{dx} = \frac{x-y+1}{x+2y-3}$$

If $x = X + h$ and $y = Y + k$ is taken, then $h - k + 1 = 0$ and $h + 2k - 3 = 0$

$$\Rightarrow \quad h = 1/3;\ k = \frac{4}{3} \Rightarrow x = X + 1/3;\ y = Y + \frac{4}{3}$$

46. If r_1 be radius of convergence when n is prime

then $$r_1 = \lim_{n\to\infty}\left[\frac{1}{an}\right]^{1/n} = 3$$

Similarly $$r_2 = \lim_{n\to\infty}\left[\frac{1}{an}\right]^{1/n} = 4$$

$\Rightarrow$ radius of convergence $\min(r_1, r_2) = 3$

47. Orbit of 2 is (2, 10, 12, 7, 6, 3, 8, 11, 1) whose cardinality is 9.

48. Let $p(x) = Ax^4 + Bx^3 + Cx^2 + Dx + E$

$p(1) = A + B + C + D + E = 2$ ...(i)

$p'(1) = 4A + 3B + 2C + D = 3$ ...(ii)

$p(2) = 16A + 8B + 4C + 2D + E = 6$ ...(iii)

$p'(2) = 32A + 12B + 4C + D = 7$ ...(iv)

$p''(2) = 48A + 12B + 2C = 8$ ...(v)

Solving all these equations we get

$A = -1, B = 8, C = -20, D = 23, E = -8$

$\therefore$ The polynomial is

$p(x) = -x^4 + 8x^3 - 20x^2 + 23x - 5$

$\therefore$ $p(0) = -8$.

50. $\phi = x^2 + y \Rightarrow \vec{\nabla}\phi = 2x\hat{i} + \hat{j}$

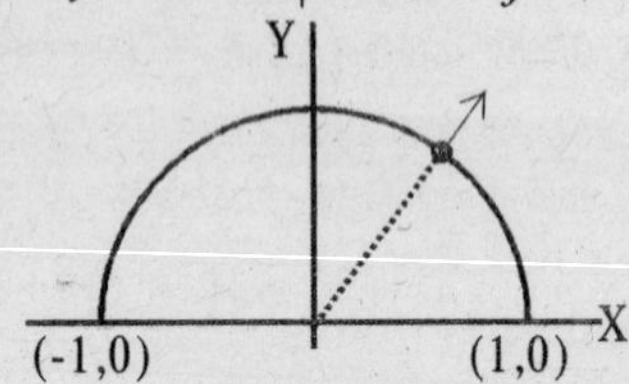

Outward unit normal $\hat{n}$ at $(x, y) = x\hat{i} + y\hat{j}$

$$\Rightarrow \int_C (\nabla\phi)\cdot\hat{n}dS = \int_C (2x^2 + y)dS$$

For $x^2 + y^2 = 1$, $\frac{dy}{dx} = \frac{-x}{y}$

$$\Rightarrow dS = \sqrt{1 + \frac{x^2}{y^2}}dx = \frac{1}{y}dx$$

Thus by putting these, we get the integral as $\pi - 2$.

54. The given differential equation is

$$(xp - y)^2 = (p^2 - 1)$$

or, $p^2x^2 + y^2 - 2xyp = p^2 - 1$

or, $p^2(x^2 - 1) - 2xyp + (y^2 + 1) = 0$.

The p-discriminant of the above equation is given by

$$4x^2y^2 - 4(x^2 - 1)(y^2 + 1) = 0$$

or, $x^2y^2 - (x^2 - 1)(y^2 + 1) = 0$

or, $x^2y^2 - (x^2y^2 + x^2 - y^2 - 1) = 0$

or, $x^2 - y^2 = 1$.

55. Total frequency

$1 + {}^nC_1 + {}^nC_2 + ... + {}^nC_n$

$= (1 + 1)^n = 2^n$

Probabilities for $\downarrow$ 0 $\downarrow$ 1 $\downarrow$ 2 $\downarrow$ n values of the variate are

$$\frac{1}{2^n}, \frac{{}^nC_1}{2^n}, \frac{{}^nC_2}{2^n} .... \frac{{}^nC_n}{2^n}$$ respectively

Binomial distribution $(q + p)^n$ in which

$$q = p = \frac{1}{2}$$

$$\text{mean} = np = \frac{n}{2}$$

$$\text{varinace} = npq = \frac{n}{4}$$

$$\text{var} = \frac{1}{2}\ \text{mean.}$$

56. $\lim_{n\to\infty} f_n(x) = \lim_{n\to\infty} n\sin^{2n+1} x\cos x$

$$= \lim_{n\to\infty} \frac{\sin^{2n+1} x\cos x}{1/n}$$

$$\left[\frac{0}{0} \text{ case for } x \in (0, \pi/2)\right]$$

$$= \lim_{n\to\infty} \frac{(2n+1)\sin^{2n} x\cos^2 x - \sin^{2n+2} x}{\frac{-1}{n^2}}$$

$$= \lim_{n\to\infty} \frac{-2(n+1)\sin^{2(n+1)} x + (2n+1)\sin^{2n} x}{\frac{-1}{n^2}} \to 0$$

$$\int_0^{\pi/2} f_n(x)dx = \int_0^{\pi/2} n\sin^{2n+1} x\cos x dx$$

$$= \frac{n\cdot 2n : (2n-2)(2n-4)...}{2(n+1)\cdot 2n\cdot(2n-4)...}$$ by Walli's theorem

$$= \frac{1}{2}\cdot\frac{n}{n+1}$$

$$\Rightarrow \lim_{n\to\infty} \int_0^{\pi/2} f_n(x)dx \lim_{n\to\infty} \frac{1}{2}\cdot\frac{n}{n+1} = \frac{1}{2}$$

$\Rightarrow$ Required integral = 1/2

SET—23

CSIR–UGC (NET) MATHEMATICAL SCIENCES

PART-C

1. Let $F = \{f : \mathbf{R} \to \mathbf{R} : |f(x) - f(y)| \le K\,|(x - y)|^{\alpha}\}$ For all $x, y \in \mathbf{R}$ and for some $\alpha > 0$ and some $K > 0$.

Which of the following is/are true?

A. Every $f \in F$ is continuous

B. Every $f \in F$ is uniformly continuous

C. Every differentiable function f is in F

D. Every $f \in F$ is differentiable

2. Let $a_{ij} = a_i a_j$, $1 \le i, j \le b$, where $a_1, \ldots\ldots, a_n$ are real numbers. Let $A = ((a_{ij}))$ be the $n \times n$ matrix $((a_{ij}))$. Then

A. It is possible to choose $a_1, \ldots., a_n$ so as to make the matrix A non singular

B. The matrix A is positive definite if $(a_1\ldots.,\ a_n)$ is a non zero vector

C. The matrix A is positive semi definite for all $(a_1, \ldots., a_n)$

D. For all $(a_1, \ldots., a_n)$, zero is an eigenvalue of A.

3. Suppose A, B are $n \times n$ positive definite matrices and I be the $n \times n$ identity matrix. Then which of the following are positive definite.

A. $A + B$ B. ABA^*

C. $A^2 + I$ D. AB

4. Let T be a linear transformation on the real vector space $\mathbf{R}^n$ over $\mathbf{R}$ such that $T^2 = \lambda T$ for same $\lambda \in \mathbf{R}$. Then

A. $\|Tx\| = |\lambda|\,\|x\|$ for all $x \in \mathbf{R}^n$

B. If $\|Tx\| = \|x\|$ for some non zero vector $x \in \mathbf{R}^n$, then $\lambda = \pm 1$

C. $T = \lambda I$ where I is the identity transformation or $\mathbf{R}^n$

D. If $\|Tx\| > \|x\|$ for a non zero vector $x \in \mathbf{R}^n$, then T is necessarily singular.

5. Let M be the vector space of all 3×3 real matrices and let

$$A = \begin{pmatrix} 2 & 1 & 0 \\ 0 & 2 & 0 \\ 0 & 0 & 3 \end{pmatrix}$$

Which of the following are subspaces of M?

A. $\{X \in M : XA = AX\}$

B. $\{X \in M : X + A = A + X\}$

C. $\{X \in M : \text{trace}\ (AX) = 0\}$

D. $\{X \in M : \det\ (AX) = 0\}$

6. The Green's function $G(x, \zeta)$, $0 \le x, \zeta \le 1$ of the boundary value problem

$y'' + \lambda y = 0,$

$y(0) = 0 = y(1)$

is

A. Symmetric in x and ζ

B. Continuous at $x = \zeta$

C. $\left.\dfrac{\partial G(x,\zeta)}{\partial x}\right|_{x=\zeta^-} - \left.\dfrac{\partial G(x,\zeta)}{\partial x}\right|_{x=\zeta^+} = -1$

D. $\left.\dfrac{\partial G(x,\zeta)}{\partial x}\right|_{x=\zeta^-} - \left.\dfrac{\partial G(x,\zeta)}{\partial x}\right|_{x=\zeta^+} = 1$

7. For the boundary value problem,

$y'' + \lambda y = 0,$

$y(-\pi) = y(\pi)$

$y'(-\pi) = y'(\pi)$

to each eigen value λ, there corresponds

A. Only one eigen function

B. Two eigen functions

C. Two linearly independent eigen functions

D. Two orthogonal eigen functions

8. Let $y_1(x)$ and $y_2(x)$ form a fundamental set of solutions to the differential equation

$$\frac{d^2y}{dx^2} + p(x)\frac{dy}{dx} + q(x)y = 0,\ \ 0 \le x \le b,$$

Where $p(x)$ and $q(x)$ are continuous in $[a, b]$, and x_0 is a point in (a, b). Then

A. Both $y_1(x)$ and $y_2(x)$ cannot have a local maximum at x_0.
B. Both $y_1(x)$ and $y_2(x)$ cannot have a local minimum at x_0.
C. $y_1(x)$ cannot have a local maximum at x_0 and $y_2(x)$ cannot have local minimum at x_0 simultaneously.
D. Both $y_1(x)$ and $y_2(x)$ cannot vanish at x_0 simultaneously.

9. A general solution of the PDE $uu_x + yu_y = x$ is of the form

A. $f\left(u^2 - x^2, \frac{y}{x+u}\right) = 0$, where $f : \mathbf{R}^2 \to \mathbf{R}$ is C^1 and $\nabla f \neq (0, 0)$ at every point
B. $u^2 = g\left(\frac{y}{x+u}\right) + x^2, g \in C^1(\mathbf{R})$
C. $f(u^2 + x^2) = 0, f \in C^1(\mathbf{R})$
D. $f(x + y) = 0, f \in C^1(\mathbf{R})$

10. The PDE

$$\left.\begin{array}{ll} u_{xx} + u_{yy} + \lambda u = 0, & 0 < x, y < 1 \\ u(x,0) = u(x,1) = 0, & 0 \le x \le 1 \\ u(0,y) = u(1,y) = 0, & 0 \le y \le 1 \end{array}\right\}$$

has

A. A unique solution u for any $\lambda \in \mathbf{R}$
B. Infinitely many solutions for some $\lambda \in \mathbf{R}$
C. A solution for countably many values of λ
D. Infinitely many solutions for all $\lambda \in \mathbf{R}$.

11. Consider the function

$f(x) = |\cos x| + |\sin(2 - x)|$

At which of the following points is f not differentiable?

A. $\left\{(2n+1)\frac{\pi}{2} : n \in Z\right\}$
B. $\{n\pi \; ; n \in Z\}$
C. $\{n\pi + 2 : n \in Z\}$
D. $\left\{\frac{n\pi}{2} : n \in Z\right\}$

12. Which of the following subsets of R^2 are convex?

A. $\{(x, y) : |x| \le 5 \; |y| \le 10\}$
B. $\{(x, y) : x^2 + y^2 = 1\}$
C. $\{(x, y) : y \ge x^2\}$
D. $\{(x, y) : y \le x^2\}$

13. Which of the following is/are matrix on R?

A. $d(x, y) = \min(x, y)$
B. $d(x, y) = |x - y|$
C. $d(x, y) = |x^2 - y^2|$
D. $d(x, y) = |x^3 - y^3|$

14. Let X denote the two-point set $\{0, 1\}$ and write $X_j = \{0, 1\}$ for every $j = 1, 2, 3, \ldots$ Let $Y = \prod_{j=1}^{\infty} X_j$. Which of the following is/are true?

A. Y is a countable set
B. Card Y = card, $[0, 1]$
C. $\bigcup_{n=1}^{\infty}\left(\prod_{j=1}^{\infty} X_j.\right)$ is uncountable
D. Y is uncountable

15. Which of the following is/are correct?

A. $n\log\left(1 + \frac{1}{n+1}\right) \to 1$ as $n \to \infty$
B. $(n+1)\log\left(1 + \frac{1}{n+1}\right) \to 1$ as $n \to \infty$
C. $n^2\log\left(1 + \frac{1}{n}\right) \to 1$ as $n \to \infty$
D. $n\log\left(1 + \frac{1}{n^2}\right) \to 1$ as $n \to \infty$

16. Let $f : \mathbf{D} \to \mathbf{D}$ be holomorphic with $f(x) = \frac{1}{2}$ and $f\left(\frac{1}{2}\right) = 0$, where $\mathbf{D}$ $\{z : |z| \le 1\}$.

Which of the following is correct?

A. $|f'(0)| \le \frac{3}{4}$
B. $\left|f'\left(\frac{1}{2}\right)\right| \le \frac{4}{3}$
C. $|f'(0)| \le \frac{3}{4}$ and $\left|f'\left(\frac{1}{2}\right)\right| \le \frac{4}{3}$
D. $f'(z) = z, z \in \mathbf{D}$

17. Define

$H^+ = \{z \in \mathbf{C} : y > 0\}$
$H^+ = \{z \in \mathbf{C} : y < 0\}$
$L^+ = \{z \in \mathbf{C} : x > 0\}$
$L^- = \{z \in \mathbf{C} : x < 0\}$

The function $f(z) = \dfrac{z}{3z+1}$

A. Maps H^+ onto H^+ and H^- onto H^-
B. Maps H^+ onto H^- and H^- onto H^+
C. Maps H^+ onto L^+ and H^- onto L^-
D. Maps H^+ onto L^- and H^- onto L^+

18. At $z = 0$ the function $f(z) = \dfrac{e^z+1}{e^z-1}$ has

A. A removable singularity
B. A pole
C. An essential singularity
D. The residue of $f(z)$ at $z = 0$ is 2.

19. Let $H = \{e, (1, 2)(3, 4)\}$ and $K = \{e, (1, 2)(3, 4), (1, 3)(2, 4), (1, 4)(2, 3)\}$ be subgroups of S_4, where e denotes the identify element of S_4. Then

A. H and K are normal subgroups of S_4
B. H is normal in K and K is normal in A_4
C. H is normal in A_4 but not normal in S_4
D. K is normal in S_4, but H is not.

20. Let $\langle p(x)\rangle$ denote the ideal generated by the polynomial $p(x)$ in $\mathbf{Q}[x]$. If $f(x) = x^3 + x^2 + x + 1$ and $g(x) = x^3 - x^2 + x - 1$, then

A. $\langle f(x)\rangle+\langle g(x)\rangle=\langle x^3+x\rangle$
B. $\langle f(x)\rangle+\langle g(x)\rangle=\langle f(x)\cdot g(x)\rangle$
C. $\langle f(x)\rangle+\langle g(x)\rangle=\langle x^2+1\rangle$
D. $\langle f(x)\rangle+\langle g(x)\rangle=\langle x^2-1\rangle$

21. Consider the force free motion of a rigid body about a fixed point 0. Suppose 3A, 5A and 6A are the principal moments of inertia at 0, and initially the angular velocity has components $\omega_1 = \sqrt{5}$, $\omega_2 = 0$, $\omega_3 = \sqrt{5}$ about the corresponding principal axes; if the body ultimately rotates about the mean axis, then

A. $\omega_1^2 + \omega_2^2 = 5$ B. $5\omega_2^2 + g\omega_1^2 = 45$
C. $\omega_3^2 = \omega_1^2$ D. $\omega_2^2 \neq \omega_1^2$

22. Using Euler's dynamical equation for force free motion of a rigid body, symmetrical about the Z-principal axis, with angular velocity $\overline{\omega} = (\omega_1, \omega_2, \omega_3)$, where ω_i, $i = 1, 2, 3$, are the components along the three principal axes, it follows that

A. ω_i = constant
B. $\omega_2 = a \sin(\lambda t + b)$ with a a, λ and b as constant
C. ω_3 = constant
D. $\omega_1^2 + \omega_2^2$ constant

23. Let $M_3(R)$ be the ring of all 3 × 3 real matrices. If $I, J \subseteq M_3(R)$ are defined as

$$I = \left\{\begin{pmatrix} a & b & c \\ 0 & 0 & 0 \\ 0 & 0 & 0 \end{pmatrix} \mid a,b,c \in R\right\},$$

$$J = \left\{\begin{pmatrix} a & 0 & 0 \\ b & 0 & 0 \\ c & 0 & 0 \end{pmatrix} \mid a,b,c \in R\right\}$$

then

A. I is a right ideal and J is a left ideal.
B. I and J are both left ideals.
C. I and J are both right ideals.
D. I is a left ideal and J is a right ideal.

24. If R is a finite integral domain with n elements, then what is the number of invertible elements under multiplication in R?

A. 1 B. n
C. $n - 1$ D. $\left[\dfrac{n}{2}\right]$

where [ ] is the bracket function.

25. Which one of the following is a group?

A. $(N, *)$, where $a*b = a$ for all $a, b \in N$.
B. $(Z, *)$, where $a*b = a - b$ for all $a, b \in Z$.
C. $(Q, *)$, where $a*b = \dfrac{ab}{2}$ for all $a, b \in Q$.
D. $(R, *)$, where $a*b = a + b + 1$ for all $a, b \in \mathbb{R}$.

26. The matrices $\begin{bmatrix}1 & 0\\0 & 0\end{bmatrix}, \begin{bmatrix}-1 & 0\\0 & 0\end{bmatrix}, \begin{bmatrix}i & 0\\0 & 0\end{bmatrix}$ and $\begin{bmatrix}-i & 0\\0 & 0\end{bmatrix}$ for a group with respect to matrix multiplication. Which one of the following statements about this group is correct?
A. The group has no element of order 4.
B. The group has an element of order 3.
C. The group is non-abelian.
D. $\begin{bmatrix}-1 & 0\\0 & 0\end{bmatrix}$ is its own inverse.

27. Which one of the following is correct?
A. Let $G = S_n$ be the permutation group on n symbols. Then for all $\sigma, \tau \in G\ (\sigma c)^2 = \sigma^2\tau^2$.
B. If in a group G, $(xy)^2 = x^2y^2$ for all $x, y \in G$, then G must be cyclic.
C. Let $G = S_3$. Let $A = \{\sigma \in G : \sigma^3 = \text{identity}\}$. Then A is a subgroup of S_3.
D. Let $G = S_4$. Let $B = \{\sigma \in S_4 : \sigma^4 = \text{identity}$ but $\sigma^2 \neq \text{identity}\}$. Then B contains exactly 7 elements.

28. Which of the following rings are integral domains?
1. $\mathbb{Z}_{60}$
2. $\mathbb{Z}_{71}$
3. $\mathbb{Z}_{82}$
4. $\mathbb{Z}_{97}$

Select the correct answer using the codes given below:
A. 1 and 2
B. 2 and 3
C. 2 and 4
D. 3 and 4

29. Let $C_{2\pi}$ denote the set of all 2π periodic continuous functions. Let S_f denote the Fourier series of f. That $S_f \notin C_{2\pi}$ for some $f \notin C_{2\pi}$, follows from
A. Principle of Uniform Boundedness
B. Hahn-Banach Theorem
C. Open Mapping Theorem
D. Closed Graph Theorem

30. In a metric space (X, d)
A. Every infinite set E has a limit point in E.
B. Every closed subset of a compact set is compact.
C. Every closed and bounded set is compact.
D. Every subset of a compact set is closed.

31. Let $W = \{p(B) : p$ is a polynomial with real coefficients$\}$, where $B = \begin{pmatrix}0 & 1 & 0\\0 & 0 & 1\\1 & 0 & 0\end{pmatrix}$

The dimension d of the vector space W satisfies
A. $4 \leq d \leq 6$
B. $6 \leq d \leq 9$
C. $3 \leq d \leq 8$
D. $3 \leq d \leq 4$

32. Let N be a 3 × 3 non zero matrix with the property $N^3 = 0$. Which of the following is/are true?
A. N is not similar to a diagonal matrix
B. N is similar to a diagonal matrix
C. N has one non-zero eigenvector
D. N has three linearly independent eigenvector.

33. Let $x, y \in \mathbf{C}^n$. Consider

$$f(x, y) = \sup_{\theta,\varphi}\left\|e^{i\theta}x - e^{i\varphi}y\right\|_2,\ \theta, \phi \in \mathbf{R}.$$

Which of the following is/are correct?
A. $f(x,y) \leq \|x\|^2 + \|y\|^2 - 2\operatorname{Re}|\langle x,y\rangle|$
B. $f(x,y) \leq \|x\|^2 + \|y\|^2 + 2\operatorname{Re}|\langle x,y\rangle|$
C. $f(x,y) = \|x\|^2 + \|y\|^2 + 2|\langle x,y\rangle|$
D. $f(x,y) \geq \|x\|^2 + \|y\|^2 - 2\operatorname{Re}|\langle x,y\rangle|$

34. Let $\mathbf{D} = \{z \in \mathbf{C} : |z| < 1\}$ be the unit disc. Let $f : \mathbf{D} \to \mathbf{C}$ be an analytic function satisfying $f\left(\frac{1}{n}\right) = \frac{2n}{3n+1}$ for $n \geq 1$. Then
A. $f(0) = \frac{2}{3}$
B. f has a simple pole at $z = -3$
C. $f(3) = \frac{1}{3}$
D. No such f exists

35. Let f be an entire function. If Re f is bounded then
A. $Im\ f$ is constant
B. f is constant
C. $f \equiv 0$
D. f' is a non zero constant

36. Let I_1 be the ideal generated by $x^2 + 1$ and I_2 be the ideal generated by $x^3 - x^2 + x - 1$ in $\mathbf{Q}[x]$.

If $R_1 = \frac{\mathbf{Q}[x]}{I_1}$ and $R_2 = \frac{\mathbf{Q}[x]}{I_2}$, then

A. R_1 and R_2 are fields
B. R_1 is a field and R_2 is not a field
C. R_1 is an integral domain, but R_2 is not an integral domain
D. $R_1$and R_2 are not integral domains.

37. Let $G = \mathbf{Z}_{10} \times \mathbf{Z}_{15}$. Then
A. G contains exactly 1 element of order 2
B. G contains exactly 5 elements of order 3
C. G contains exactly 24 elements of order 5
D. G contains exactly 24 elements of order 10

38. The space C [0, 1] of continuous functions on [0, 1] is complete with respect to which of the following
A. $\|f\|_\infty = \sup\{|f(x)| : x \in |0,1|\}$
B. $\|f\|_2 = \left(\int_0^1 |f(x)|^2 \, dx \right)$
C. $\|f\|_{\infty,1/2} = \|f\|_\infty + \left| f\left(\frac{1}{2}\right) \right|$
D. $\|f\|_\infty$ and $\|f\|_{\infty,1/2}$

39. Consider the set
$$X = [-\infty, 0] \cup \left\{ \frac{1}{n} : n \in \mathbf{N} \right\} \subseteq \mathbf{R}$$
with the subspace topology. Then
A. 0 is an isolated point
B. (–2, 0] is an open set
C. 0 is a limit point of the subset $\left\{ \frac{1}{n} : n \in \mathbf{N} \right\}$
D. (–2, 0) is an open set.

40. Consider three subsets of $\mathbf{R}^2$, namely
$$A_1 = \{(x, y) : x^2 + y^2 \le 1\}$$
$$A_2 = \{(1, y) : y \in \mathbf{R}\}$$
$$A_3 = \{(0,2)\}$$
Then there always exists a continuous real-valued function f on $\mathbf{R}^2$ such that $f(x) = a_j$ for $x \in A_j$, $j = 1, 2, 3$
A. If and only if at least two of the numbers a_1, a_2, a_3 are equal
B. If $a_1 = a_2 = a_3$
C. For all real values of a_1, a_2, a_3
D. If and only if $a_1 = a_2$

41. If $\{x_n\}$ and $\{y_n\}$ are sequences of real numbers, which of the following is/are true?
A. $\limsup_n (x_n + y_n) \le \limsup_n x_n + \limsup_n y_n$
B. $\limsup_n (x_n + y_n) \ge \limsup_n x_n + \limsup_n y_n$
C. $\liminf_n (x_n + y_n) \le \liminf_n x_n + \liminf_n y_n$
D. $\liminf_n (x_n + y_n) \ge \liminf_n x_n + \liminf_n y_n$

42. Let $\{f_n\}$ be a sequence of integrable functions defined on an interval $[a, b]$. Then
A. If $f_n(x) \to 0$ a.e., then $\int_a^b f_n(x)dx \to 0$
B. If $\int_a^b f_n(x)dx \to 0$, then $f_n(x) \to 0$ a.e.
C. If $f_n(x) \to 0$ a.e. and each f_n is a bounded function, then $\int_a^b f_n(x)dx \to 0$
D. If $f_n(x) \to 0$ a.e. and the f_n's are uniformly bounded, then $\int_a^b f_n(x)dx \to 0$

43. For $x = (x_1, x_2, ..., x_4) \in R^d$, and $p \ge 1$, define
$$\|x\|_p = \left(\sum_{j=1} |X_j|^p \right)^{1/p} \text{ and}$$
$$\|x\|_\infty = \max\{|x_j| : j = 1, 2, ...d\}$$
Which of the following inequalities holds for all $x \varepsilon R^d$?
A. $\|x\|_1 \ge \|x\|_2 \ge \|x\|_\infty$
B. $\|x\|_1 \ge d\|x\|_\infty$
C. $\|x\|_1 \le \sqrt{d}\,\|x\|_\infty$
D. $\|x\|_1 \le \sqrt{d}\,\|x\|_2$

44. Consider the map $f : \mathbf{R}^2 \to \mathbf{R}^2$ defined by $f(x, y) = (3x - 2y + x^2, 4x + 5y + y^2)$. Then

A. f is discontinuous at (0, 0)

B. f is continuous at (0, 0) and all directional derivatives exists at (0, 0)

C. f is differentiable at (0, 0) but the derivative $Df(0, 0)$ is not invertible

D. f is differentiable at (0, 0) and the derivative $Df(0, 0)$ is invertible.

45. Which of the following sets are dense in $\mathbf{R}$ with respect to the usual topology.

A. $\{(x, y) \in \mathbf{R}^2 : x \in \mathbf{N}\}$

B. $\{(x, y) \in \mathbf{R}^2 : x + y \text{ is a rational number}\}$

C. $\{(x, y) \in \mathbf{R}^2 : x^2 + y^2 = 5\}$

D. $\{(x, y) \in \mathbf{R}^2 : xy \neq 0\}$

46. The Cauchy problem

$$\left.\begin{array}{ll} u_x(x,y)+u_y(x,y)=0 & \text{for } (x,y)\in\mathbf{R}^2 \\ u(x,0)=0 & \text{for all } x\in\mathbf{R} \end{array}\right\}$$

has

A. A unique solution

B. A family of straight lines as characteristics

C. Solution which vanishes at (2, 1)

D. Infinitely many solutions.

47. Consider a linear system $Ax = b$ with a computed solution x_C; the error and the residue are defined, respectively by

$e = x - x_c$

$r = Ax - Ax_c$

Then

A. A small error necessarily implies a small residue

B. The error can be larger with relatively small residue

C. The error can be small with relatively large residue

D. The error and the residue are always equal.

48. Consider the iteration function for Newton's method

$$g(x) = x - \frac{f(x)}{f'(x)}$$

and its application to find (approximate) square root of 2, starting with $x_0 = 2$. Consider the first and the second iterates x_1 and x_2, respectively; then

A. $1.5 < x_1 \leq 2$

B. $1.5 \leq x_1 < 2$

C. $x_1 \leq 1.5$; $x_2 \leq 1.5$

D. $x_1 = 1.5$; $x_2 < 1$

49. In the Ritz method, seeking an extremum of the functional

$$I(y) = \int_{x_0}^{x_1} F\left(x, y, \frac{dy}{dx}\right) dx;\ y(x_0) = a, y(x_1) = b,$$

The coordinate function/or the admissible function $\phi_i(x)$, $i = 1, 2, \ldots$ defined on $[x_0, x_1]$ must be

A. Linearly independent

B. Continuous

C. Smooth

D. Linearly independent, smooth and the functional be considered not along admissible curves $y = y(x)$ but only along all possible linear combinations of admissible functions.

50. The integral equation, involving a parameter λ,

$$\phi(x) = \cos xz + \lambda \int_0^{\pi} \cos(x + \zeta)\, d\zeta \text{ has}$$

A. A unique solution if $\lambda = 1$, and an infinite number of solution if $\lambda = \frac{2}{\pi}$

B. A unique solution if $\lambda = -1$, and an infinite number of solution if $\lambda = -\frac{2}{\pi}$

C. A unique solution if $\lambda \neq \frac{2}{\pi}$

D. No solution if $\lambda = \pm\frac{2}{\pi}$

51. The Newton-Raphson method is used to find the root of the equation $x^2 - 2 = 0$. If iterations are started from –1, they

A. converge to –1

B. not converge

C. converge to $-\sqrt{2}$

D. converge to $\sqrt{2}$

52. Using the least square approximation of second degree. For the following discrete data is given by

x	−2	−1	0	1	2
$y = f(x)$	15	1	1	3	19

A. $\frac{1}{35}(-35+37x+155x^2)$

B. $\frac{1}{35}(-37+35x+155x^2)$

C. $\frac{1}{37}(-37+35x+155x^2)$

D. None of these

53. The bisection method was used to approximate a root of the equation $f(x) = 0$, starting from the interval [1, 2]. It was found that the 10th and 11th iterations are $x_{10} = 1.2435$, $x_{11} = 1.2436$ what can be concluded?

I. $10 > \ln 2 - \ln(0.001)$

II. $10 < \ln 2 - \ln(0.001)$

III. $x_{12} < 1.2436$

A. I only B. II only

C. III only D. I and III only

54. Suppose the function $u(x)$ interpolates $f(x)$ at $x_0, x_1, x_2, \ldots\ldots x_{n-1}$ and the function $v(x)$ interpolates $f(x)$ at $x_1, x_2, \ldots\ldots x_{n-1}, x_n$. Then a function $F(x)$ which interpolates $f(x)$ at all the points $x_0, x_1, x_2, \ldots\ldots x_{n-1}, x_n$ is given by

A. $F(x) = \dfrac{(x_n - x)u(x) - (x - x_0)v(x)}{(x_n - x_0)}$

B. $F(x) = \dfrac{(x_n - x)u(x) + (x - x_0)v(x)}{(x_n - x_0)}$

C. $F(x) = \dfrac{(x_n - x)v(x) + (x - x_0)u(x)}{(x_n - x_0)}$

D. $F(x) = \dfrac{(x_n - x)v(x) - (x - x_0)u(x)}{(x_n - x_0)}$

55. The partial differential equation

$$x\frac{\partial^2 u}{\partial x^2} + 2xy\frac{\partial^2 u}{\partial x \partial y} + y\frac{\partial^2 u}{\partial y^2} + x\frac{\partial u}{\partial y} + y\frac{\partial u}{\partial x} = 0 \text{ is}$$

A. elliptic in the region $x < 0, y < 0, xy > 1$.

B. elliptic in the region $x > 0, y > 0, xy > 1$.

C. parabolic in the region $x < 0, y < 0, xy > 1$.

D. hyperbolic in the region $x < 0, y < 0, xy > 1$.

56. If $u(x, y, z, t) = f(x + i\beta y - vt) + g(x - i\beta y - vt)$, where f and g are arbitrary and twice differential functions, is solution of the wave equation

$\frac{\partial^2 u}{\partial x^2} + \frac{\partial^2 u}{\partial y^2} = \frac{1}{c^2}\frac{\partial^2 u}{\partial t^2}$, then β is

A. $\left(1 - \frac{v}{c}\right)^{1/2}$ B. $\left(1 - \frac{v}{c}\right)$

C. $\left(1 - \frac{v^2}{c^2}\right)^{1/2}$ D. $\left(1 - \frac{v^2}{c^2}\right)$

57. An inverted pendulum consists of a particle of mass m supported by a rigid massless rod of length l. The pivot O has a vertical motion given by $z = A\sin wt$. Then the Lagrangian function (L) is given by

A. $L = \frac{1}{2}ml^2\dot{\theta}^2 - mgl\cos\theta + mlAw^2\sin wt\cos\theta$

B. $L = \frac{1}{2}ml^2\dot{\theta}^2 - mgl\sin\theta + mlAw^2\sin wt\sin\theta$

C. $L = \frac{1}{2}ml^2\dot{\theta}^2 + mgl\cos\theta + mlAw^2\cos wt\cos\theta$

D. None of these

58. Three newspapers A, B, C are published in a city and survey of readers indicates the following: 20% reads A, 16% read B, 14% read C, 8% read both A and B, 5% read both A and C, 4% read both B and C, 2% read all the three. For a person chosen at random, find the probability that he reads none of the paper

A. $\frac{7}{20}$ B. $\frac{9}{20}$

C. $\frac{13}{20}$ D. $\frac{11}{20}$

59. The expression $x^2 + x + 1$ in $F[x]$, where F is field of integers mod 2 can be written as

A. $(x + 1)(x + 1)$ B. $(x + 1)x$
C. $(x + 2)(x + 1)$ D. None of these

60. Suppose $X = \left\{\begin{bmatrix} a \\ b \\ c \\ d \end{bmatrix} : b - c = 4\right\}$, $Y = \left\{\begin{bmatrix} a \\ b \\ c \\ d \end{bmatrix} : a = b + c\right\}$ and $Z = \left\{\begin{bmatrix} a \\ b \\ c \\ d \end{bmatrix} : b = 0, c = d\right\}$

which of these subsets of the vector space $\mathbf{R}^4$ is/are subspace(s)?

A. X only B. Y and Z
C. X, Y and Z D. X and Z

ANSWERS

1	2	3	4	5	6	7	8	9	10
A,B	C,D	A,B,C	A,B	A,B,C	A,B,D	C,D	A,B,C,D	A,B	B,C
11	**12**	**13**	**14**	**15**	**16**	**17**	**18**	**19**	**20**
A,C	A,C	B,D	B,C,D	A,B	B	A	B,D	B,D	C
21	**22**	**23**	**24**	**25**	**26**	**27**	**28**	**29**	**30**
A,C,D	C,D	A	C	D	D	C	C	A	B
31	**32**	**33**	**34**	**35**	**36**	**37**	**38**	**39**	**40**
C,D	A,C	B,D	A,B,C	A,B	B,C	A,C,D	A	C,D	B,D
41	**42**	**43**	**44**	**45**	**46**	**47**	**48**	**49**	**50**
A,D	D	A,B	B,D	B,D	B,C,D	B,C	B,C	A,B,C,D	A,B
51	**52**	**53**	**54**	**55**	**56**	**57**	**58**	**59**	**60**
C	B	A	B	D	C	A	C	D	B

SOME SELECTED EXPLANATORY ANSWERS

23. Given $I = \begin{pmatrix} a & b & c \\ 0 & 0 & 0 \\ 0 & 0 & 0 \end{pmatrix} \mid a, b, c \in R.$

Then let $A \in M_3(R)$ such that $A = \begin{bmatrix} l & m & n \\ p & q & r \\ x & y & z \end{bmatrix}$

then

$$IA = \begin{bmatrix} al+bp+cx & am+bq+cy & an+br+cz \\ 0 & 0 & 0 \\ 0 & 0 & 0 \end{bmatrix}$$

i.e. I is a Right ideal.

Also $J = \begin{bmatrix} a & 0 & 0 \\ b & 0 & 0 \\ c & 0 & 0 \end{bmatrix}$.

then $AJ = \begin{bmatrix} l & m & n \\ p & q & r \\ x & y & z \end{bmatrix}\begin{bmatrix} a & 0 & 0 \\ b & 0 & 0 \\ c & 0 & 0 \end{bmatrix}$

$$= \begin{bmatrix} al+bp+cx & 0 & 0 \\ am+bq+cy & 0 & 0 \\ an+br+cz & 0 & 0 \end{bmatrix}$$

i.e., J is a left ideal.

24. As in an integral domain, all except the additive identity is invertible, hence, R will have $(n - 1)$ invertible element.

25. $(N, *)$ such that $a * b = a \ \forall\ a, b \in N$

then $a*(b * c) = a * b = a$

and $(a * b)*c = a * c = a$

It is associative. However it does not possible unique identity.

i.e., $a * e = a \neq e * a$.

Consider (Z, *) such that $a * b = a - b$

then $a*(b * c) = a*(b - c)$

$= a - (b - c) = a - b + c$

$(a *b)*c = (a - b)*c = a - b - c$

i.e., (Z, *) is not associative.

Consider $a * b = a + b + 1$

then $a * e = a + e + 1$

if e is identity then

$e + 1 = 0 \Rightarrow e = -1$.

Now if a' is inverse of a then

$a * a' = -1$

$\Rightarrow a + a' + 1 = -1$

$\Rightarrow a' = -2 - a$.

So this is a group.

But $(Q, *)$ fails to become a group for $0 \in Q$. Which do not possesses inverse in Q.

26. The member of the group

$$\begin{bmatrix}1 & 0\\0 & 0\end{bmatrix}, \begin{bmatrix}-1 & 0\\0 & 0\end{bmatrix}, \begin{bmatrix}i & 0\\0 & 0\end{bmatrix} \& \begin{bmatrix}-i & 0\\0 & 0\end{bmatrix}.$$

Clearly $\begin{bmatrix}1 & 0\\0 & 0\end{bmatrix}$ is unity of this group &

$$\begin{bmatrix}-1 & 0\\0 & 0\end{bmatrix}, \begin{bmatrix}-1 & 0\\0 & 0\end{bmatrix} = \begin{bmatrix}1 & 0\\0 & 0\end{bmatrix} \text{ i.e., } \begin{bmatrix}-1 & 0\\0 & 0\end{bmatrix}$$

has its own inverse.

Consider $\begin{bmatrix}i & 0\\0 & 0\end{bmatrix}\begin{bmatrix}i & 0\\0 & 0\end{bmatrix} = \begin{bmatrix}-1 & 0\\0 & 0\end{bmatrix}$

$$\begin{bmatrix}-1 & 0\\0 & 0\end{bmatrix}\begin{bmatrix}i & 0\\0 & 0\end{bmatrix} = \begin{bmatrix}-i & 0\\0 & 0\end{bmatrix}$$

& $\begin{bmatrix}-i & 0\\0 & 0\end{bmatrix}\begin{bmatrix}i & 0\\0 & 0\end{bmatrix} = \begin{bmatrix}1 & 0\\0 & 0\end{bmatrix}$

i.e., order of $\begin{bmatrix}i & 0\\0 & 0\end{bmatrix} = 4$.

$\Rightarrow G$ is abelian as $0(G) = 4$.

Hence, the correct choice is D.

28. Z_n is integral domain if and only if n is prime.

52. Let the least squares second degree polynomial to be fitted to give data be $y = P(x) = a + bx + cx^2$, where a, b, c are arbitrary constants to be determined.

Here, m = the number of given pairs of values of $(x, y) = 5$.

The normal equations are,

$$\left.\begin{aligned}\Sigma y &= ma + b\Sigma x + c\Sigma x^2, m = 5\\ \Sigma xy &= a\Sigma x + b\Sigma x^2 + c\Sigma x^3\\ \Sigma x^2 y &= a\Sigma x^2 + b\Sigma x^3 + c\Sigma x^4\end{aligned}\right\} \quad ...(1)$$

	x	y	x^2	x^3	x^4	xy	x^2y
	–2	15	4	–8	16	–30	60
	–1	1	1	–1	1	–1	1
	0	1	0	0	0	0	0
	1	3	1	1	1	3	3
	2	19	4	8	16	38	76
Total	0	39	10	0	34	10	140

Substituting the value of Σx, Σy, ... etc. in the normal equations (1),

we get, $5a + 10c = 39$, $10b = 10$,

$10a + 34c = 140$.

Solving these equations, we get

$$a = \frac{-37}{35}, \quad b = 1, \quad c = \frac{31}{7}$$

Hence, the required approximation is

$$P(x) = \frac{-37}{35} + x + \frac{31}{7}x^2$$

$$= \frac{1}{35}(-37 + 35x + 155x^2)$$

55. The given PDE is $xr + 2xys + yt + xq + yp = 0$.

Compare with $Rr + Ss + Tt + f(x, y, z, p, q) = 0$.

we get $R = x$, $S = 2xy$, $T = y$.

Now the λ quadratic is $R\lambda^2 + S\lambda + 7 = 0$

or $x\lambda^2 + 2xy\lambda + y = 0$

$$\Rightarrow \quad \lambda = \frac{-2xy \pm \sqrt{4x^2y^2 - 4xy}}{2x}$$

$$\Rightarrow \quad \lambda = \frac{-xy \pm \sqrt{x^2y^2 - xy}}{x}$$

But $x^2 y^2 - xy > 0 \Rightarrow xy(xy - 1) > 0$.

i.e., function is hyperbolic in the region $x < 0$, $y < 0$, $xy > 1$.

59. $x^2 + x + 1$ is irreducible over $Z_2[x]$.

SET–24

CSIR–UGC (NET) MATHEMATICAL SCIENCES

PART-C

1. If T be the linear operator of R^2 defined by $T(x, y) = (4x - 2y, 2x + y)$, then compute the matrix of T in the basis $\{f_1 = (1, 1), f_2 = (-1, 0)\}$.

A. $[T]_f = \begin{bmatrix} 3 & 2 \\ 1 & 2 \end{bmatrix}$ B. $[T]_f = \begin{bmatrix} 3 & -2 \\ 1 & -2 \end{bmatrix}$

C. $[T]_f = \begin{bmatrix} 3 & -2 \\ 1 & 2 \end{bmatrix}$ D. $[T]_f = \begin{bmatrix} 3 & 1 \\ -2 & 2 \end{bmatrix}$

2. Which one is not right statement.

A. Let $(G, \cdot)$ be group, $F : G \to G$ is such that $F(x) = e \ \forall \ x \in G$ is homomorphism.

B. Group $(R, +)$ and $(R_0, \cdot)$ are given, A mapping $F : R \to R_0$ is defined as $F(n) = 2^x$ is homomorphism.

C. Group $(I, +)$ is given $F : I \to I$ given by $F(x) = 2^x$, $\forall \ x \in I$, F is homomorphism.

D. $F : R \to R$ is given by $F(x) = 3x^2 \ \forall \ x \in R$ $(R, +)$ is a group, F is homomorphism.

3. Which statement is true

A. Let $(I, +)$ be addition group of integers and let $H = \{\delta n / n \in I\}$, then H is a subgroup of I.

B. A non empty subset H of a group G which is closed under binary operation is a subgroup of G.

C. If G is a group and H is a non-empty subset of G such that $H^2 = H$, then H is a subgroup of G.

D. None of these

4. Which statment is not true.

A. Two cyclic groups of same order are isomorphic

B. Isomorphic copy of a cyclic group is cyclic

C. Two groups of same dimension are isomorphic

D. None of these

5. Suppose G is a group and N is a normal subgroup of G.

Let $F : G \to G/N$ defined by
$F(x) = Nx \qquad \forall \ x \in G$
Then,

A. F is a homomorphism of G into G/N with ker $F \neq N$

B. F is a homomorphism of G onto G/N with ker $F \neq N$

C. F is a homomorphism of G into G/N with ker $F = N$

D. F is a homomorphism of G onto G/N with ker $F = N$

6. A second degree polynomial passes through (0, 3), (1, 6), (2, 11), (3, 18) and (4, 27). The polynomial is

A. $x^2 + x + 1$ B. $x^2 + 2x + 3$

C. $x^2 + 2x + 1$ D. $x^2 + x + 2$

7. The pressure P of wind corresponding to velocity V is given by the following data :

V	10	20	30	40
P	1.1	2.0	4.4	7.9

Value of P when V is equal to 25 is

A. 3 B. 3.0375

C. 3.3075 D. 3.5

8. Let $\left\{0, \frac{1}{2}, 1\right\}$ be three distinct points on [0, 1].

Let p be the unique interpolating polynomial of suitable degree on [0, 1] such that

$p(0) = 0$, $p\left(\frac{1}{2}\right)(1) = 1$, then $p\left(\frac{1}{4}\right)$ is equal to

A. $-\frac{1}{8}$ B. $-\frac{1}{2}$

C. $\frac{2}{5}$ D. None of these

9. From the following table, using Trapozoidal rule, the area bounded by the curve, the x-axis and the lines $x = 7.47$, $x = 7.52$ is

x :	7.47	7.48	7.49	7.50	7.51	7.52
$f(x)$:	1.93	1.95	1.98	2.01	2.03	2.06

A. 0.0996 B. 0.0896
C. 0.1096 D. 0.0776

10. In M/M/m system probability of n customers in the system ($n \geq m$) is

A. $\frac{1}{m!\,m^{n-m}}\left(\frac{\lambda}{\mu}\right)^n \rho_0$ B. $\frac{1}{m!}\left(\frac{\lambda}{\mu}\right)^n \rho_0$

C. $\left(\frac{\lambda}{\mu}\right)^n \rho_0$ D. $\left(\frac{\lambda}{\mu}\right)^n$

11. In dual simplex method which of the following is not correct.

A. Key column corresponds to most negative not evaluation $(z_j - c_j)$
B. Key row corresponds to the basic variable having most negative value.
C. Ratio of net evalution numbers to the corresponding coefficients (which are negative) in the key row are computed.
D. Column corresponding to smallest of these ratio is selected as key column.

12. In Replacement, which is/are not true.

A. The present value factors serve as the weights when time value of money is considered.
B. Expected cost of a replacement policy of individual replacements can be obtained—if expected cost per time period is equal to the number of units multiplied by replacement per units.
C. Staff replacement policies can be easily formulated because people retire at known times.
D. Mortality problems are like replacement policies for items whose values deteriorate gradually.

13. Consider the following statements S and R: S: both sin x and cos x are decreasing functions in the interval $(\pi/2, \pi)$ R:if a differentiable function decreases in an interval (a, b) then its derivative also decreases in(a, b)

Which of the following is true?

A. Both S and R are wrong.
B. Both S and R are correct,but R, is not the correct explanation for S
C. S is correct and R is the correct explanation for S.
D. S is correct and R is wrong

14. The function $f(x) = \frac{ln(\pi + x)}{ln(e + x)}$ is

A. increasing on $[0, \infty]$
B. decreasing on $[0, \infty]$
C. increasing on $\left[0, \frac{\pi}{e}\right)$ and decreasing on $\left[\frac{\pi}{e}, \infty\right)$
D. decreasing on $\left[0, \frac{\pi}{e}\right)$ and increasing on $\left[\frac{\pi}{e}, \infty\right)$

15. The straight lines whose direction cosines are given by $al + bm + cn = 0$, $fmn + gnl + hlm = 0$ are perpendicular if

A. $\frac{f}{a} + \frac{g}{b} + \frac{h}{c} = 0$
B. $\sqrt{\left(\frac{a}{f}\right)} + \sqrt{\left(\frac{b}{g}\right)} + \sqrt{\left(\frac{c}{h}\right)} = 0$
C. $\sqrt{(af)} = \sqrt{(bg)} = \sqrt{(ch)}$
D. $\sqrt{\left(\frac{a}{f}\right)} = \sqrt{\left(\frac{b}{g}\right)} = \sqrt{\left(\frac{c}{h}\right)}$

16. For positive integers the value of the expression

$(1+i)^{n_1} + (1+i^3)^{n_1} + (1+i^5)^{n_2} + (1+i^7)^{n_2}$

Where $i = \sqrt{-1}$ is a real number if and only if

A. $n_1 = n_2 + 1$ B. $n_1 = n_2 - 1$
C. $n_1 = n_2$ D. $n_1 > 0, n_2 > 0$

17. If ω is complex root of the equation $z^3 = 1$ then

$\omega + \omega^{\left(\frac{1}{2} + \frac{3}{8} + \frac{9}{23} + \frac{27}{128} + ...\right)}$ is

A. 0 B. 1
C. –2 D. –1

18. In a third order determinant,each element of the first column consists of sum of two terms each element of the second column consists of sum of three terms and each element of the third column consists of sum of four term. Then it can be decomposed in n determinants where n has the value

A. 24 B. 16
C. 9 D. 1

19. If $\Delta = \begin{vmatrix} -1 & 1 & 1 \\ 1 & -1 & 1 \\ 1 & 1 & -1 \end{vmatrix}$ then Δ is

A. – 4 B. 0
C. 2 D. 4

20. A root of the equation $\begin{vmatrix} 3-x & -6 & 3 \\ -6 & 3-x & 3 \\ 3 & 3 & -6-x \end{vmatrix} = 0$ is

A. 6 B. 2
C. 0 D. None of these

21. If x,y,z are in A.P., then $\frac{1}{\sqrt{x}+\sqrt{y}}, \frac{1}{\sqrt{z}+\sqrt{x}}, \frac{1}{\sqrt{y}+\sqrt{z}}$ are in

A. A.P B. G.P
C. H.P D. None of these

22. The next term of the geometric progresstion $x, x^2 + 2, x^3 + 10$ is

A. 0 B. 54
C. $\frac{792}{16}$ D. $\frac{16}{729}$

23. If a, b, c are in geometrical progression and l, m, n are also in geometrical progression then cl, bm, an, are in

A. arithmetical progression
B. geometrical progression
C. harmonical progression
D. none of these

24. On the interval [0,1] the function $x^{25}(1 - x)^{35}$ takes its maximum value at the point

A. 0 B. $\frac{1}{4}$
C. $\frac{1}{2}$ D. $\frac{1}{3}$

25. The function $f(x) = |px - q| + r|x|, x \in (-\infty, \infty)$ where $p > 0, q > 0, r > 0$ assumes its minimum value only at one point if

A. $p \neq q$ B. $r \neq q$
C. $r \neq p$ D. $p = q = r$

26. If $A_1, A_2, A_3, \ldots A_{30}$ are thirty sets where each set having 5 elements and $B_1, B_2, \ldots B_n$ are n sets where each set having 3 elements. Also $\bigcup_{i=1}^{30} A_i = \bigcup_{j=1}^{n} B_j = S$ and each elements of S belong to exactly 10 of the A'_i S and exactly 9 of the B'_j S then n is equal to

A. 5 B. 15
C. 45 D. 135

27. $f(x) = x \sin\frac{\pi}{x}$ when $0 < x \leq 1$
$= 0$ when $x = 0$
then in [0, 1]

A. $f(x)$ is continuous on [0, 1] and f bounded variation [0, 1]
B. $f(x)$ is continuous on [0, 1] and f is not bounded variation [0, 1]
C. $f(x)$ is not continuous on (0, 1] and f is bounded variation [0, 1]
D. $f(x)$ is not continuous on [0, 1] and f is not bounded variation [0, 1]

28. If the derivative f' exists and is bounded on $[a, b]$, then

A. the function f is of bounded variation on $[a, b]$
B. the function f is not of bounded variation on $[a, b]$
C. the function f is necessarily continuous.
D. the function f is not continous.

29. The formula $A_0 f\left(-\frac{1}{2}\right) + A_1 f(0) + A_2 f\left(\frac{1}{2}\right)$ which approximates the integral $\int_{-1}^{1} f(x)dx$ is exact for polynomials of degree less than or equal to 2 if

A. $A_0 = A_2 = \frac{4}{3}, A_1 = \frac{2}{3}$

B. $A_0 = A_1 = A_2 = 1$

C. $A_0 = A_2 = \frac{4}{3}, A_1 = -\frac{2}{3}$

D. None of the above.

30. Let $f_n(x) = \frac{\sin x}{\sqrt{n}}$, $n = 1, 2, \ldots$ and $x \in [-1, 1]$ then as $n \to \infty$

A. $\{f_n(x)\}_{n=1}^{\infty}$ does not converge uniformly in $[-1, 1]$

B. $\lim_{n\to\infty} \int_{-1}^{1} F_n(x)dx \neq 0$

C. $\{f_n^1(x)\}$ does not converge uniformly in $[-1, 1]$

D. $f_n(x)$, $n = 1, 2$, is not uniformly continuous in $[-1, 1]$

31. If $A = \begin{pmatrix} 1 & 2 & 3 & 4 & 5 \\ 1 & 3 & 4 & 5 & 2 \end{pmatrix}$ and $B = \begin{pmatrix} 1 & 2 & 3 & 4 & 5 \\ 5 & 4 & 3 & 2 & 1 \end{pmatrix}$, then which one is true.

A. $\begin{pmatrix} 1 & 2 & 3 & 4 & 5 \\ 5 & 4 & 3 & 2 & 1 \end{pmatrix}$

B. $\begin{pmatrix} 1 & 2 & 3 & 4 & 5 \\ 4 & 3 & 5 & 1 & 2 \end{pmatrix}$

C. $\begin{pmatrix} 1 & 2 & 3 & 4 & 5 \\ 5 & 3 & 2 & 1 & 4 \end{pmatrix}$

D. $\begin{pmatrix} 1 & 2 & 3 & 4 & 5 \\ 3 & 4 & 5 & 2 & 1 \end{pmatrix}$

32. Which one is correct definition of ring.

A. (R, +, .) is a ring if (R_1) (R, +) is an abelian ring (R_2) (R, .) is groupoid (R_3) ∵ distributive over '*t*'.

B. (R, +, .) is a ring if (R_1) (R, +) is an abelian ring (R_2) (R, .) is semi group (R_3) '.' is left distributive but not right distributive over '+'.

C. $(R_2$, +, .) is a ring if (R_1) (R, +) is an abelian ring (R_2) (R, .) is semi group (R_3) '.' is distributive (left and right both).

D. None of these

33. Which of the following are true?

(a) Every ring with unity has at least two elements (T)

(b) Every ring with unity has at most two elements (F)

(c) The distributive laws for a ring are not very important (F)

(d) Addition in every ring is commutative. (T)

(e) Every elements in a ring has no additive inverse (F)

(f) Every elements in a ring has multiplicative inverse (F)

(g) Every ring has unity (T)

(h) Every ring has zero divisors (F)

(i) Cancellation laws for multiplication hold in every ring (F)

(j) Every division ring is ring (T)

(k) Every ring is division ring (F)

A. *(a), (d), (f), (g), (j)* B. *(a), (b), (c), (d), (i)*

C. *(b), (d), (g), (h), (e)* D. *(k), (i), (e), (c), (b)*

34. Which is not correct?

A. Ring without zero divisors means $\exists$ *a*, *b* $\in$ Ring such that $ab = 0 \Rightarrow$ either $a = 0$ or $b = 0$

B. The ring of whole numbers modulo *p* is an integral domain if and only if P is a prime

C. The characteristic of every finite integral domain is finite

D. The characteristic of every integral domain D is zero or prime

E. Every isomorphic image of an integral domain is not an integral domain

F. A commulative ring with unity is an integral domain if it has zero divisors.

35. Which statement is exact about the polynomial P(z), if all zeros of P(z) lie in a half plane then

A. zeros of the derivative also lie in the same half plane.

B. at least one zero lies in the same half plane.

C. at the most one zero lies in the same half plane

D. no zero lies in the same half-plane.

36. $\frac{1}{2\pi i} \oint_c \frac{e^{zt}}{(z^2+1)^2} dz$ if $t > 0$ and C is the circle

½z½ = 3

A. $\frac{1}{2}(\sin t - t\cos t)$ B. $\frac{1}{2}(\sin t + t\cos t)$

C. $\frac{1}{2}(\sin t + \cos t)$ D. $\frac{1}{2}(t\sin t - \cos t)$

37. If $y_1(x)$ and $y_2(x)$ are solution of
$y'' + x^2y' + (1-x)y = 0$
such that
$y_1(0) = 0, y_1{}^1(0) = 1$
$y_2{}^1(0) = 1, y_2(0) = 1$
then the wronskian $W(y_1\, y_2)$ on R

A. 0 B. 1
C. – 1 D. 2

38. Diff. equ.

$$\frac{d^2y}{dx^2} + 4y = \sec^2 2x$$

Using the method of variation of parameters.

A. $y = c_1\cos 2x + c_2\sin 2x - \frac{1}{4} + \frac{1}{4}\sin 2x \log(\sec 2x + \tan 2x)$

B. $y = c_1\cos 2x - c_2\sin 2x + \frac{1}{4}\sin 2x. \log(\sec 2x + \tan 2x)$

C. $y = (c_1 + c_2x)e^{2x} + \frac{1}{4}\log(\sec 2x + \tan 2x)$

D. $y = c_1\cos 2x + c_2\sin 2x + \frac{1}{4} - \frac{1}{4}\sin 2x$

39. The general solution of $\frac{d^2y}{dx^2} - y = \sin x$ is $Ae^x + Be^x - \frac{1}{2}\sin x$, (A, B are constant). Which part of this solution is a particular integral

A. Ae^x B. Be^{-x}
C. $Ae^x + Be^{-x}$ D. $-\frac{1}{2}\sin x$

40. The solution of

$$\frac{dy}{dx} + \frac{\sqrt{1-y^2}}{1-x^2} = 0 \text{ is given by}$$

A. $x(y^2-1)/y = \log y + \frac{1}{2}x^2 + c$

B. $y(x^2-1)/x = \log x + \frac{1}{2}x^2 + c$

C. $2y(y^2 - 1) = \log x - \frac{1}{2}x^2 + C$

D. None of the above.

41. Match the following

Series (X)	*Domain of Convergence (Y)*
(a) $\sum \frac{x^n}{n^3}$	(i) $]-2-e, -2+e[$
(b) $\sum (-1)^n \frac{x^{2n+1}}{2n+1}$	(ii) $]0, 2[$
(c) $\sum \frac{(-1)^{n+1}}{n}(x-1)^n$	(iii) $[-1, 1]$
(d) $\sum \frac{n!(x+2)^n}{n^n}$	(iv) $]-1, 1[$

	(a)	(b)	(c)	(d)
A.	(iv)	(iii)	(ii)	(i)
B.	(iv)	(iii)	(i)	(ii)
C.	(iii)	(iv)	(i)	(ii)
D.	(i)	(ii)	(iv)	(iii)

42. Let A ∈ $R^{n \times n}$, B ← R^n, consider the two system of linear equations
(a) Ax = b
(b) A′Az = A′n
then

A. Both (a) and (b) have the same sol.
B. (a) has more solutions than (b)
C. Both (a) and (b) may not have any solution
D. (a) may not have any solution but (b) always has atleast one solution

43. Consider the basis S = $\{v_1, v_2, v_3\}$ for R^3 where $v_1 = (1, 1, 1)$, $v_2 = (1, 1, 0)$, $v_3 = (1, 0, 0)$ and let T: $R^3 \to R^2$ be a linear transformation such that
$Tv_1 = (1, 0)$
$Tv_2 = (2, -1)$
$Tv_3 = (4, 3)$
Then T (2, –3, 5) is

A. (–1, 5) B. (3, 4)
C. (0, 0) D. (9, 23)

44. Let T be a linear transformation from $R^3 \to R^2$ defined by T (x, y, z) = (x + y, y – z) then the matrix of T with respect to the ordered bases {(1, 1, 1), (1, –1, 0), (0, 1, 0)} and {(1, 1), (1, 0)}

A. $\begin{bmatrix} -2 & 0 & 1 \\ 1 & 1 & -1 \end{bmatrix}$ B. $\begin{bmatrix} 0 & -1 & 1 \\ 2 & 1 & 0 \end{bmatrix}$

C. $\begin{bmatrix} 2 & 1 \\ 0 & -1 \\ 1 & 1 \end{bmatrix}$ D. $\begin{bmatrix} 0 & 2 \\ -1 & 1 \\ 1 & 0 \end{bmatrix}$

45. Choose the correct matching from A, B, C and D for the transformation T_1, T_2 and T_3 (mapping from R^2 to R^3) as defined in Group I with the statements given in Group II.

Group I	**Group II**
P. $T_1(x, y) = (x, x, 0)$	1. Linear tranasformation of rank 2
Q. $T_2(x, y) = (x, x+y, y)$	2. Not a linear trans formation
R. $T_3(x, y) = (x, x+1, y)$	3. Linear transformation of rank 1.

	P	Q	R
A.	3	1	2
B.	1	2	3
C.	3	2	1
D.	1	3	2

46. Geometrical representation of $\frac{z_1}{z_2}$ ∵ OP show $\left(\frac{z_1}{z_2}\right)$

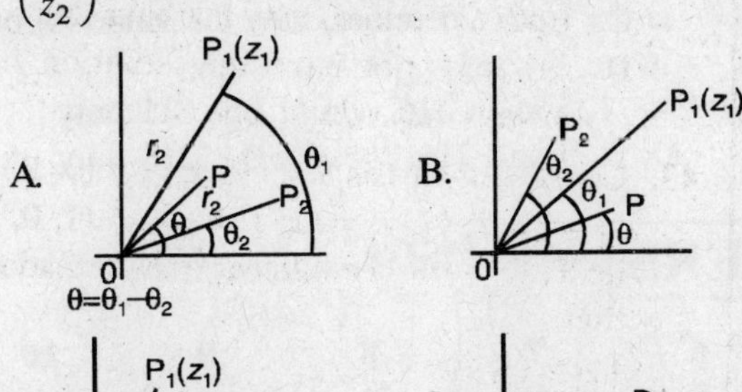

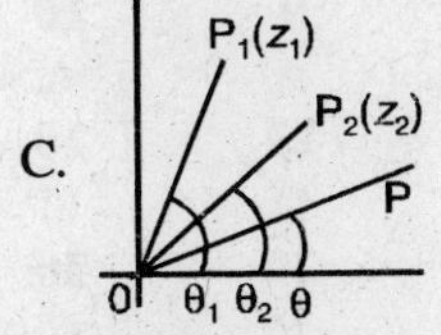

D. $P_2(z_2)$, P, $P_1(z_1)$, θ, θ_2, θ_1, O

Note : 1. $e^{2n\pi i} = \cos 2n\pi + i \sin 2n\pi = 1$

2. $\log_e(x + iy) = \log_e \sqrt{(x^2 + y^2)} + i.\tan^{-1}\frac{y}{x}$

47. If $z_1 = r_1(\cos\theta_1 + i\sin\theta_1)$ and $z_2 = r_2(\cos\theta_2 + i\sin\theta_2)$ then, which of the following is true.

A. $|z_1+z_2|^2 + |z_1-z_2|^2 = 2(|z_1|^2 + |z_2|^2)$

B. $|z_1+z_2|^2 + |z_1-z_2|^2 \geq 2(|z_1|^2 + |z_2|^2)$

C. $|z_1+z_2|^2 + |z_1-z_2|^2 \leq 2(|z_1|^2 + |z_2|^2)$

D. $|z_1+z_2|^2 - |z_1-z_2|^2 = 2(|z_1|^2 + |z_2|^2)$

48. Match the following, they represent the loci.

(a)	$\lvert z-4i\rvert^2 + \lvert z+4i\rvert^2 = 10$	1. Ellipse
(b)	$\lvert z-4i\rvert^2 + \lvert z+4i\rvert^2 = 10^2$	2. Straight line
(c)	$\lvert z-4i\rvert^2 - \lvert z+4i\rvert^2 = 10$	3. Circle
(d)	$\lvert z-4i\rvert + \lvert z+4i\rvert = 10$	4. None

	(a)	(b)	(c)	(d)
A.	4	3	2	1
B.	4	3	1	2
C.	1	2	3	4
D.	1	2	4	3

49 Let $f(z)$ be an analytic function with a simple pole at $z = 1$ and a double pole at $z = 2$ with residuces 1 and –2 respectively. Further if $f(0) = 0, f(z) = -\frac{3}{4}$ and f is bounded as $z \to \infty$, then $f(z)$ must be

A. $z(z-3) - \frac{1}{4} + \frac{1}{z-1} - \frac{2}{z-1} + \frac{1}{(z-2)^2}$

B. $-\frac{1}{4} + \frac{1}{z-1} - \frac{2}{z-2} + \frac{1}{(z-2)^2}$

C. $\frac{1}{z-1} - \frac{2}{z-2} + \frac{5}{(z-2)^2}$

D. $\frac{15}{4} + \frac{1}{z-1} + \frac{2}{z-2} - \frac{7}{(z-2)^2}$

50. A given complex function of a complex variable takes real values for real values of the variable, then

A. it may be analytic in a open disc of the complex plane but not differentiable on any interval as real function of a real variable.

B. its power series expansion, when available, around a point on the real axis has only real coefficients.

C. its power series expansion, when available, around any points in the complex plane has real coefficients.

D. if may not posses a power series expansion around a point on the real axis as a real function but may be analytic in some open disc centred at the point.

51. An n–digit number is a positive number with exactly n digits. Nine hundred distinct n digit numbers are to be formed using only the three digits 2,5 and 7. The smallest value of n for which this is possible is

A. 6 B. 7
C. 8 D. 9

52. A five digit number divisible by 3 is to be formed using the numerals 0,1, 2, 3, 4 and 5 without repetition. The total number of ways in which this can be done is

A. 216 B. 240
C. 600 D. 3125

53. The sum of the series

$$1+\frac{1}{5}+\frac{1.3}{5.10}+\frac{1.3.5}{5.10.15}+\text{.........} \text{ is}$$

A. $\sqrt{3}$ B. $\sqrt{5}$
C. $\sqrt{\frac{5}{3}}$ D. $\sqrt{\frac{3}{5}}$

54. If the numerical coefficent of the pth term in the expansion of $(2x + y)^6$ is 4869 then the value (s) of P is (are)

A. 2 B. 3
C. 4 D. 5

55. The product of n positive numbers is unity then their sum is

A. a positive integer B. divisible by n
C. equal to $n+\frac{1}{n}$ D. never less than n

56. Three linear equation will have consistent solution, if

A. $\begin{vmatrix} a_1 & b_1 & c_1 \\ a_2 & b_2 & c_2 \\ a_3 & b_3 & c_3 \end{vmatrix} \neq 0$ B. $\begin{vmatrix} a_1 & b_1 & c_1 \\ a_2 & b_2 & c_2 \\ a_3 & b_3 & c_3 \end{vmatrix} = 0$

C. $a_1b_1 + a_2b_2 + a_3b_3 = 0$ D. None of these

57. Let α, β be the roots of the equation $(x-a)(x-b)=c,\ c\neq 0$, then the roots of the equation $(x-\alpha)(x-\beta)+c=0$ are

A. a, c B. b, c
C. a, b D. $a+c, b+c$

58. The equation $(\cos p-1)x^2+(\cos p)x+\sin p=0$ in the variable x has real root. Then, p can take any value in the interval

A. $(0, 2\pi)$ B. $(-\pi, 0)$
C. $\left(\frac{\pi}{2}, \frac{\pi}{2}\right)$ D. $(0, \pi)$

59. The number of real solutions of the equation $\sin e^x = 5x + 5^{-x}$ is

A. 0 B. 1
C. 2 D. Infinitely

60. If one root of the equation $x^2 - 30x + \lambda = 0$ is the square of other, then the value (s) of λ is/are

A. 125 and –216 B. 125 only
C. 125 and 216 D. 216 only

ANSWERS

1	2	3	4	5	6	7	8	9	10
C	D	A	C	D	B	B	A	A	A
11	12	13	14	15	16	17	18	19	20
A	C	D	B	A	D	D	A	D	C
21	22	23	24	25	26	27	28	29	30
A	C	B	B	C	A	B	A	C	C
31	32	33	34	35	36	37	38	39	40
C	C	A	E, F	A	A	C	A	D	B
41	42	43	44	45	46	47	48	49	50
A	C	D	B	A	A	A	A	B	D
51	52	53	54	55	56	57	58	59	60
B	A	C	B	D	A	C	D	A	A

SOME SELECTED EXPLANATORY ANSWERS

6. The difference table is given below :

x	y	Δy	$\Delta^2 y$	$\Delta^3 y$
0	3	3		
1	6	5	2	0
2	11	7	2	0
3	18	9	2	
4	27			

In Newton's formula for interpolation
$a = 0, h = 1; f(a + hx) = f(x)$

$$y = f(x) = 3 + x(3) + \frac{x(x-1)}{2}(2) + \frac{x(x-1)(x-2)}{6}(0) + ...$$

or $y = 3 + 3x + x(x-1) = x^2 + 2x + 3.$

7. The difference table is as under

V	P	ΔP	Δ^2P	Δ^3P
10	1.1	0.9		
20	2.0	2.4	1.5	– 0.4
30	4.4	3.5	1.1	
40	7.9			

To calculate P when V = 25, we use forward interpolation formula for which

$$n = \frac{x-a}{h} = \frac{25-10}{10} = 1.5$$

$$P(25) = 1.1 + 1.5 \times 0.9 + \frac{1.5 \times 0.5}{2} \times 1.5 + \frac{1.5 \times 0.5 \times 0.5}{6} \times 0.4$$

$= 1.1 + 1.35 + 0.5625 + 0.0250 = 3.0375.$

8. The difference table is under

x	y	Δy	$\Delta^2 y$
0	0	0	
$\frac{1}{2}$	0	1	1
1	1		

Here $a = 0,\ h = \dfrac{1}{2}.$

Also for $x = \dfrac{1}{4}, n = \dfrac{x-a}{h} = \dfrac{\frac{1}{4}-0}{1/2} = \dfrac{1}{2}.$

Using formula we get

$$f(a+nh) = f(a) + n\Delta f(a) + \frac{n(n-1)}{2}\Delta^2 f(a) + ...$$

Here $a = 0$ $nh = \dfrac{1}{4}$ and where $n = \dfrac{1}{2}.$

$$\therefore\ f\left(\frac{1}{4}\right) = 0 + \frac{1}{2}(0) + \frac{\frac{1}{2}\left(\frac{1}{2}-1\right)}{2}(1)$$

$$= -\frac{1}{8}.$$

9. Since the area bounded by the x-axis is given by $\int_{x_1}^{x_2} f(x)\,dx$, according to the table

$$\int_{7.47}^{7.52} f(x)\,dx = \frac{h}{2}[y_0 + 2(y_1 + y_2 + y_3 + y_4) + y_5]$$

$$= \frac{(0.01)}{2}[1.93 + 2(1.95 + 1.98 + 2.01 + 2.03) + 2.06]$$

$$= \frac{(0.01)}{2}[1.93 + 15.94 + 2.06]$$

$= 0.0996.$

27. Clearly f is continuous on [0, 1]
Let partition

$$P = \left\{0, \frac{2}{2n+1}, \frac{2}{2n-1}, \frac{2}{2n-3}, ...\frac{2}{5}, \frac{2}{3}, 1\right\}$$

$$\therefore \sum_i |f(x_i) - f(x_{i-1})|$$

$$= \left|f(1) - f\left(\frac{2}{3}\right)\right| + \left|f\left(\frac{2}{3}\right) - f\left(\frac{2}{5}\right)\right| + ... + \left|f\left(\frac{2}{2n+1}\right) - f(0)\right|$$

$$= \frac{2}{3} + \left(\frac{2}{3} + \frac{2}{5}\right) + \left(\frac{2}{5} + \frac{2}{7}\right) + ... + \left(\frac{2}{2n-1} + \frac{2}{2n+1}\right) + \frac{2}{2n+1}$$

$$= 4\left[\frac{1}{3} + \frac{1}{5} + \frac{1}{7} + ... + \frac{1}{2n+1}\right]$$

Infinite series $\frac{1}{3}+\frac{1}{5}+\frac{1}{7}+...+...$ is dgt, its partial sums sequence $\{S_n\}$, where

$S_n = \frac{1}{3}+\frac{1}{5}+\frac{1}{7}+...+\frac{1}{2n+1}$ is not bounded above.

Thus $\sum_i |f(x_i)-f(x_{i-1})|$ can be made arbitrarily large by taking n sufficiently large. consequently. $V(f, 0, 1) \to \infty$ and so f is not of bounded variation on [0, 1]

28. Since f' is bounded on $[a, b]$, therefore there exists K such that

$|f'[(x)| \le K, \forall x \in [a, b]$

Let P $= \{a = x_0, x_1, x_2, ... x_n = b\}$ be any partition of $[a, b]$

$\therefore \sum_i |f(x_i)-f(x_{i-1})| = \sum_i (x_i - x_{i-1})|f'(\xi)|$, $\xi \in]a, b[\le K(b-a)$

$\Rightarrow V(f, a, b)$ is finite and therefore f is of bounded variation.

Note : Boundedness of f' is a sufficient condition. It is not necessary.

29. $\int_{-1}^{1} f(x)dx = A_0\left(-\frac{1}{2}\right)+A_1 f(0)+A_2 f\left(\frac{1}{2}\right)$

when $f(x) = 1 \Rightarrow 2 = A_0 + A_1 + A_2$

$f(x) = x \Rightarrow 0 = -\frac{A_0}{2}+0+\frac{A_2}{2}$

$f(x) = x^2$

$\Rightarrow \frac{2}{3} = A_0\left(-\frac{1}{2}\right)^2 + A_1(0)^2 + A_2\left(\frac{1}{2}\right)$

$= \frac{A_0}{4}+\frac{A_2}{4} \Rightarrow A_0 = A_2 = \frac{4}{3}$

$A_1 = -\frac{2}{3}$

41. *(i)* $\sum \frac{x^n}{n^3}$

$\because a_n = \frac{1}{n^3}; a_{n+1} = \frac{1}{(n+1)^3}$

$R = \lim_{n\to\infty}\left|\frac{a_n}{a_{n+1}}\right| = \lim_{n\to\infty}\left(1+\frac{1}{n}\right)^3 = 1$

so the domain of a_n is]– 1, 1[

For $x = 1$, the given power series is $\sum \frac{1}{n^2}$ which is convergent.

For $x = -1$ the given power series is

$-1+\frac{1}{2^3}-\frac{1}{3^3}+\frac{1}{4^3}...$

which is convergent, by leibnitz's test.

(ii) $\sum (-1)^n \frac{x^{2n+1}}{2n+1}$

$R = \lim_{n\to\infty}\left|\frac{a_n}{a_{n+1}}\right| = \lim_{n\to\infty}\frac{2n+3}{2n+1} = 1$

The interval of convergence]–1, 1[

for $x = 1$, the series becomes

$1-\frac{1}{3}+\frac{1}{5}$ .... which is convergent by Leibnetzs test

For $x = -1$ the series becomes $-1+\frac{1}{3}-\frac{1}{5}...$

which is again con.

Hence the exact interval of convergency is [– 1, 1]

(iii) $R = \lim_{n\to\infty}\left|\frac{a_n}{a_{n+1}}\right| = \lim_{n\to\infty}\left|\frac{n}{n-1}\right| = 1$

since the given power series is about the point $x = 1$ the interval of convergence is

$-1+1 < x < 1+1 = 0 < x < 2$

for $x = 2$, the given series $\sum \frac{(-1)^{n+1}}{n}$ which is convergent by leibnitz's test.

Hence the exact interval of convergence is]0, 2]

(iv) $\sum \frac{n!(x+2)^n}{n^n}$

The given power series is about the point $x = 2$

$R = \lim_{n\to\infty}\left|\frac{a_n}{a_{n+1}}\right| = \lim_{n\to\infty}\frac{n!}{n^n}\cdot\frac{(n+1)^{n+1}}{(n+1)!}$

$= \lim_{n\to\infty}\left(\frac{n+1}{n}\right)^n = \lim_{n\to\infty}\left(1+\frac{1}{n}\right)^n = e$

the interval of convergence is $[-2-e, -2+e]$.

SET–25

CSIR–UGC (NET) MATHEMATICAL SCIENCES

PART-C

1. Let $A=\begin{pmatrix}\lambda & a\\ 0 & \lambda\end{pmatrix}$ where $a\neq 0$. If $m(x)$ and $\xi(x)$ are the minimum and the characteristic polynomial respectively of A, then

A. $m(x)\neq\xi(x)$

B. the degree of the minimum polynomial is I

C. $m(x)=\xi(x)$

D. A has two distinct characteristic roots

2. For the following pair of groups which one is homomorphism

A. $F(x) = -x$, (R, +), (R, +)

B. $F(x) = \frac{x}{q}$ ($q \neq 0$ is a whole number) (I, +), (q, +)

C. $F(x) = 3^x$, (R, +), $(R_0, \cdot)$, where R_0 is the set of non zero real number

D. All of these

3. Mark true/false,

The non-empty set D together with + and '.' is division ring if

A. (a) (D, +) is abelian group
(b) (D, .) is group
(c) '.' is distributive over '+'. (Not True)

B. (a) (D, +) is abelian group
(b) (D – {0}, .) is group
(c) '.' is distributive over '+'. (True)

C. Either (A) or (B)

D. None of these

4. Which statement is true:

A. a finite ring is an integral domain.

B. a finite commutative ring is an integral domain.

C. a finite commutative ring with zero divisors is an integral domain.

D. a finite commutative ring without zero divisors is an integral domain.

5. If $V=\omega_1\oplus\omega_2\oplus\ ....\ \oplus\omega_n$ and the projection of V into its subspace ω_k is the mapping given by $G : V \to V$ defined by $G(v) = \omega_k$ where $v=\omega_1+\omega_2+ .....+\omega_n$ and $\omega_1\in\omega$; then

A. G is linear

B. G is non-linear

C. $G=G^3$

D. $G=G^4$

6. (*a*) If linear programming problem have feasible solution then it also has a basic feasible solution.

(*b*) There exist only finite number of feasible solutions.

A. (*a*) and (*b*) both false

B. (*a*) is true only

C. (*b*) is true only

D. (*a*) and (*b*) both true

7. Let R be a ring, $U\neq\phi\subset R$ is ideal of R then

(*a*) U is a sub–gorup of R under addition

(*b*) $\forall u\in U$ and $r\in R$; μr, $rU\in U$

A. (*a*) and (*b*) both are true

B. Only (*a*) is true

C. Only (*b*) is true

D. Both (*a*) and (*b*) are false

8. If (z_1, z_2, z_3) is an orientiation of Γ, then right side of Γ with respect to (z_1, z_2, z_3) is

A. $\{Z : \text{Im}(z, z_1, z_2, z_3) < 0\}$

B. $\{Z : \text{Im}(z, z_1, z_2, z_3) > 0\}$

C. $\{Z : \text{Re}(z, z_1, z_2, z_3) < 0\}$

D. None of these

9. If $y : [0, 1] \to C$ is closed rectifiable curve and $a\notin\{y\}$, then $\frac{1}{2\pi}\int_y \frac{dz}{z-a}$ is

A. An integer
B. Rational number
C. Real number
D. Complex number

10. Find the optimum integer solution to the following L.P.P.:

Maximise $Z = x_1 + 4x_2$ subject to the constraints:

$2x_1 + 4x_2 \leq 7, \quad 5x_1 + 3x_2 \leq 15; \quad x_1, x_2 \geq 0$ and are integers.

A. –1, 4 Max. $Z = 15$
B. 2, 3 Max. $Z = 14$
C. 1, 1, max. $Z = 5$
D. 0, –3, Max. $Z = -12$

11. Let σ and π be the permutations defined by

$$\sigma = \begin{pmatrix} 1 & 2 & 3 & 4 & 5 & 6 & 7 & 8 & 9 \\ 1 & 3 & 5 & 7 & 9 & 6 & 4 & 8 & 2 \end{pmatrix} \text{ and}$$

$$\tau = \begin{pmatrix} 1 & 2 & 3 & 4 & 5 & 6 & 7 & 8 & 9 \\ 7 & 8 & 3 & 4 & 9 & 6 & 5 & 2 & 1 \end{pmatrix}$$

Then

A. σ and τ generate the group of permutations on {1, 2, 3, 4, 5, 6, 7, 8, 9}
B. σ is contained in the group generated by τ
C. τ is contained in the group generated by σ
D. σ and τ are in the same conjugacy class

12. Let $H = Z_2 \times Z_6$ and $K = Z_2 \times Z_4$, then

A. H is isomorphic to K since both are cyclic
B. H is isomorphic to K since 2 divides 6 and *g.c.d* (3, 4) = 1
C. H is not isomorphic to K since K is cyclic whereas H is number.
D. H is not isomorphic to K since there is no homomorphism from H to K

13. If $f(x, y, z)$ is a harmonic function in a domain D containing the region $T : x^2 + y^2 + z^2 \leq 100$, then the surface integral

$$\int_S \left(x\frac{\partial f}{\partial x} + \frac{\partial f}{\partial y} + \frac{\partial f}{\partial z} \right) ds \text{ where } S : x^2 + y^2 + z^2 =$$

100, equals

A. 0 B. 1
C. 10 D. 100

14. Let $f(z)$ be defined on the domain $E = |z - 2i| < 3$ and on its boundary ∂E then which of the following statements is always true:

A. if $f(z)$ is analytic on E and $f(z) \neq 0$ for any z in E, then $|f|$ attains its maximum of ∂E
B. if $f(z)$ is analytic on E ∪ ∂E, then $|f|$ attains its minimum of ∂E
C. if $f(z)$ is analytic on E and continuous on E ∪∂E, then $|f|$ attains its maximum and minimum on ∂E
D. if $f(z)$ is analytic on E∪∂E and $f(z) \neq 0$ for any z in E∪∂E, then $|f|$ attains its minimum on ∂E.

15. If $f(x, y) = \begin{cases} x^3/x^2 + y^2; & (x,y) \neq (0,0) \\ 0 \quad ; & (x,y) = 0 \end{cases}$ then at (0, 0)

A. f_x, f_y do not exist
B. f_x, f_y exist and are equal
C. the directional derivative exists along any straight line
D. f is differentiable.

16. In a maximization *lpp*, if a variable corresponding to positive $Z_j - C_j$ is entered, the leaving variable rule is followed (and solutions space is not unbounded), then

A. The next basic solution will not be basic feasible solution
B. The value of the objective function will decrease
C. The value of the objective function will increase
D. The value of the objective function remains constant

17. The dual of maximize $3x_1 + 5x_2$ subject to

$2x_1 - 3x_2 = 8$
$4x_1 + x_2 \geq 3$
$x \leq 1$
and $x_1, x_2 \geq 0$

A. Min $8\mu_1 - 3\mu_2 + \mu_3$
Subject to
$2\mu_1 - 4\mu_2 \geq -3$
$-3\mu_1 - \mu_2 + \mu_3 \geq -5$
μ_1, unrestricted
$\mu_2, \mu_3 \geq 0$

B. Min $3x_1 + 5x_3$
Subject to
$2x_1 - 3x_2 \le 8$
$4x_1 + x_2 \le 3$
$x_2 \ge 1$
$x_1, x_2 \le 0$
C. (A) and (B) both true
D. None of these

18. The solution of
$3x + 7y + 8z = -13$
$2x + 9z = -5$
$-4x + y - 26z = 2$ is
A. $x = -7, y = 0, z = 2$
B. $x = 0, y = 0, z = 3$
C. $x = -7, y = 0, z = 1$
D. None of these

19. If F is a field then its only ideals are A : F a field itself, B : (0)
A. A and B are true
B. A is true, B is false
C. A is false, B is true
D. A and B false

20. The dual of the L.P.P
Minimize $z = 4x_1 + 6x_2 + 18x_3$
$s.t\ x_1+3x_2 \ge 3, x_2+ 2x_3 \ge 5, x_1 \ge 0$ is
A. Maximize $Z^* = 3w_1 + 5w_2$
$s.t\ w_1 \le 4, 3w_1 + w_2 \le 6, 2w_2 \le 18, w_1, w_2 \ge 0$
B. Maximize $Z^* = 3w_1 + 5w_2$
$s.t\ w_1 \ge 4, 3w_1+ w_2 \ge 6, 2w_2 \ge 18, w_1, w_2 \ge 0$
C. Minimize $Z^* = 3w_1 + 5w_2$
$s.t\ w_1 \ge 4, 3w_1+ w_2 \ge 6, 2w_2 \ge 18, w_1, w_2 \ge 0$
D. None of the above

21. A square of side a lies above the x – axis and has one vector at the origin. The side passing through the origin makes an angle $\alpha\left(0<\alpha<\frac{\pi}{4}\right)$ with the positive direction of x – axis. The equation of its diagonal not passing through the origin is
A. $y(\cos\alpha - \sin\alpha) - x(\sin\alpha - \cos\alpha) = a$
B. $y(\cos\alpha + \sin\alpha) + x(\sin\alpha - \cos\alpha) = a$
C. $y(\cos\alpha + \sin\alpha) + x(\sin\alpha + \cos\alpha) = a$
D. $y(\cos\alpha + \sin\alpha) + x(\cos\alpha - \sin\alpha) = a$

22. Events A, B, C are mutually exclusive events such that $P(A) = \frac{3x+1}{3}$, $P(B) = \frac{1-x}{4}$ and $P(C) = \frac{1-2x}{2}$. The set of possible value of x are in the interval
A. $\left[\frac{1}{3}, \frac{1}{2}\right]$
B. $\left[\frac{1}{3}, \frac{2}{3}\right]$
C. $\left[\frac{1}{3}, \frac{13}{3}\right]$
D. $[0, 1]$

23. P : Every bounded sequence is convergent
Q : Every convergent sequence is bounded
A. P and Q are true
B. P is true, Q is false
C. Q is true, P is false
D. P and Q are false

24. P : The intersection of any number of subspaces of a vector space V(f) is a subspace of V(f)
Q : The union of any number of subspaces of a vector space V(f) is a subspace of V(f)
A. P is false
B. P is true, Q is false
C. P and Q both true
D. P and Q both false

25. Suppose that E (x, y) is a function of two variables (vectors)$x \in E^n$ and $y \in E^m$ both max. min. E(x,y) and mini.max. E(x, y) exist. Then necessary and sufficient condition for E(x, y) to posses a saddle point (x^*, y^*) is that
A. $\max_x . \min_y E(x, y) = (x^*, y^*) = \min_y . \max_x E(x, y)$
B. $\max_x . \min_y E(x, y) \le \max_x . \min_y E(x, y)$
C. $\min_y E(x, y) \le \max_x E(x, y)$
D. None of these

26. A two person game is said to be zero sum, if:
A. gain of one player is exactly matched by a loss to the other so that their sum is equal to zero.

B. gain of one player does not match the loss to the other.
C. diagonal entries of the pay off matrix are zero.
D. both the players must have an equal member of strategies.

27. The value of θ lying between θ = 0 and $\theta = \pi/2$ satisfying the equation

$$\begin{vmatrix} 1+\sin^2\theta & \cos^2\theta & 4\sin 4\theta \\ \sin^2\theta & 1+\cos^2\theta & 4\sin 4\theta \\ \sin^2\theta & \cos^2\theta & 1+\sin 4\theta \end{vmatrix} = 0 \text{ are}$$

A. $7\pi/24$ B. $5\pi/24$
C. $10\pi/24$ D. $\pi/24$

28. Each of the four inequalities given below defines a region in the x y plane. One of these regions does not have the following property for any two points (x_1, y_1) and (x_2, y_2) in the region given below the points $\left\{\frac{x_1+x_1}{2}, \frac{y_1+y_2}{2}\right\}$ is also in the region. The inequality defining this region is

A. $x^2+2y^2 \le 1$ B. $Max\{|x|, |y|\} \le 1$
C. $x^2 - y^2 \le 1$ D. $y^2 \le x$

29. The solution of the differential equation $\sqrt{(1-x^2)}\,dy + \sqrt{(1-y^2)}dx = 0$ is

A. $\sin^{-1} y+\sin^{-1} x=c, \sin^{-1} y+\sin^{-1} x=\pi/3$
$x^2+2xy\cos c+y^2=\sin^2 c$
B. $\sin^{-1} y+\sin^{-1} x=\pi/3$ $\sin^{-1} x+\sin^{-1} y=\pi/2$, $\sin^{-1} y+\cos^{-1} x=1$
C. $\sin^{-1} y+\cos^{-1} x=\cos y$, $\sin^{-1} y+\sin^{-1} x=e$
D. $x^2+2xy\cos c+y^2=\sin^2 c, \sin^{-4} y+\sin^{-1} x=2\pi/3$

30. The values of *a, b, c* for, which the function

$$f(x) = \frac{\sin(a+3)x+\sin x}{x}, x<0$$

$$= c, x = 0$$

$$= \left((x+b_x^2)^{\frac{1}{2}} - x^{\frac{1}{2}}\right) \Big/ 2bx^{3/2}, x>0$$

is continuous at $x = 0$ are

A. $a = -3/2, b = 1, 2, c = 1/2$
B. $a = -3/2, b = 0, 1, c = 1/2$
C. $a = -3/2, b = 2, 2, c = -1/2$
D. $a = -3/2\ b = 2, 1, c = 1/2$

31. Singular solution of differential equation contains

1. Arbitrary constant
2. Can be obtained from general
3. Do not contains arbitrary constant
4. Cannot be obtained from general solution

A. 1, 2 are true
B. 3, 4 are true
C. 1, 4 are true
D. 2, 4 are true

32. If y_1 and y_2 are two solutions's of initial value, problem $y''+p(x)y'+q(x)y=0, y(x_0)=y_0$ $y'(x_0)=y_0$ and the Wornskion $w(y_1, y_2)=0$ then y_1 and y_2 are

A. Linearly dependent
B. Linearly independent
C. Proportional
D. None of these

33. The solution of $\frac{dy}{dx}+\frac{y\cos x+\sin y+y}{\sin x+x\cos y+x}=0$ is

A. $y\sin x + (\sin y + y)x = c$
B. $y\sin x + (\sin x + x) = c$
C. $y = \sin x + y\sin y + c$
D. None of these

34. Statement A : Every isomorphic image to a cyclic group is cyclic
Statement B: Every homomorphic image of a cyclic group is cyclic

A. Both A and B are true
B. Both A and B are false
C. A is true only
D. B is true only

35. Let *f* (*z*) be analytic in a simply connected domain D and let C be any closed continuous rectifiable curve in D. Then

$$\int_C f(z)dz = 0$$

This is the statement of:

A. Cauchy's Fundamental theorem
B. Cauchy Gourgat theorem
C. Cauchy's Integral Formula
D. Taylor's Theorem

36. Let primal LPP be
max $f(x) = c^T x$, $Ax \leq b$, $x \geq 0$ and dual be
min $g(y) = b^T y$, $A^T y \geq c$, $y \geq 0$. Let x^* and y^* be
feasible solution of primal and dual, then

A. $f(x^*) \leq g(y^*)$ B. $f(x^*) \geq g(y^*)$
C. $f(x^*) = g(y^*)$ D. None of these

37. The probability density function for the random variable whose probability distribution is given by $f(x) = \begin{Bmatrix} x & 0 \leq x \leq 1 \\ 0 & \text{otherwise} \end{Bmatrix}$

A. $f(x) = \begin{cases} 1 & 0 \leq x \leq 1 \\ 0 & \text{otherwise} \end{cases}$

B. $f(x) = \begin{cases} x & 0 \leq x \leq 1 \\ 0 & \text{otherwise} \end{cases}$

C. $f(x) = \begin{cases} 0 & 0 \leq x \leq 1 \\ 1 & \text{otherwise} \end{cases}$

D. $f(x) = \begin{cases} 0 & x \leq x \leq 1 \\ x & \text{otherwise} \end{cases}$

38. If $\begin{vmatrix} a & a^2 & 1+a^3 \\ b & b^2 & 1+b^3 \\ c & c^2 & 1+c^3 \end{vmatrix} = 0$ and vectors $(1, a, a^2)$, $(1, b, b^2)$ and $(1, c, c^2)$ are non-coplanar than the product abc equals

A. 2 B. – 1
C. 1 D. 0

39. If the system of linear equation
$x + 2ay + az = 0$
$x + 2by + bz = 0$
$x + 4cy + cz = 0$
has a non-zero solution, then a, b, c

A. are in A.P
B. are in G.P
C. are in H.P
D. satisfy $a + 2b + 3c = 0$

40. Let $f(x)$ be a function satisfying $f^1(x) = f(x)$ with $f(0) = 1$ and $g(x)$ be a function that satisfies $f(x) + g(x) = x^2$, then the value of the integral $\int_0^1 f(x)\, g(x)\, dx$, is

A. $e - \frac{e^2}{2} - \frac{5}{2}$ B. $e + \frac{e^2}{2} - \frac{3}{2}$
C. $e - \frac{e^2}{2} - \frac{3}{2}$ D. $e + \frac{e^2}{2} + \frac{5}{2}$

41. If x has the probability density $f(x)$ $\begin{cases} e^x & x > 0 \\ 0 & \text{otherewise} \end{cases}$ and $g(x) = e^{3x/4}$ what is the expected value of $g(x)$?

A. 4 B. 3
C. 2 D. 1

42. If x and w feasible solution to the primal and dual problems respectively then will be optimall iff

A. $w_1\left(b_1 - \sum_{t=1}^{n} a_n x_1^0\right) = 0$ and $x_1^0\left(\sum_{t=1}^{m} a_n w_1^0 - c_1\right) = 0$

B. $w_1\left(b_1 + \sum_{i=t}^{n} a_n x_t\right) = 0$ and $x_1\left(\sum_{i=1}^{m} a_n x_i - c_1\right) = 0$

C. $w_1\left(b_1 \pm \sum_{i=t}^{n} a_n x_t\right) = 0$ and $x_1\left(\sum_{i=t}^{n} a_{ij} + w_t + c_1\right) = 0$

D. None of these

43. If $f(x) = \tan^{-1}\left\{\log\left(\frac{e}{x^2}\right)/\log\left(ex^2\right)\right\} + \tan^{-1}\left\{\frac{3+2\log_e x}{1-6\log_e x}\right\}$ then $\frac{d^2}{dx^2}\{f(x)\}$ is equal to

A. – 1 B. 0
C. 1 D. 5

44. Let $f(x) = 1$ if x is rational in [0, 1]
$= -1$ if x is irrational in [0, 1]
then is [0, 1]
A. $f(x)$ is continuous every where
B. $f(x)$ is Riemann integrable
C. $f(x)$ is not Riemann integrable
D. $f(x)$ is continous only at the irrationals

45. Pick out the largest of the sets given below on which the sequence of functions $\left\{e^{-n\cos^2 x}\right\}_{n=1}^{\infty}$ converges uniformly

A. $\left[0, \frac{9\pi}{20}\right) \cup \left(\frac{11\pi}{20}, \pi\right]$

B. $\left[0, \frac{\pi}{2}\right) \cup \left(\frac{\pi}{2}, \pi\right]$

C. $\left[0, \frac{\pi}{2} - \delta\right) \cup \left(\frac{\pi}{2} + \delta, \pi\right], 0 < \delta < \frac{\pi}{100}$

D. $(0 \ \pi]$

46. The value of the game

	I	II	III
AI	6	8	6
II	4	12	2

A. 6 for A and – 6 for B
B. – 6 for A and 2 for B
C. 3 for A and 12 for B
D. None of these

47. A point D divides the line joining the point B to the point C in the ratio 1:3, A particle moves along BC with uniform speed of 10 *m/sec* from B to D, then moves with uniform speed of 20*m/sec* from D to C. If V is the avarage speed of the paricle from B to C, then the following is true
A. V = 8 *m/sec* B. V = 15 *m/sec*
C. V = 16 *m*/sec D. V = 17.5 *m/sec*

48. A particle moves towards from a point A to a point B at the rate of 4 k/h and then towards north from B to C at the rate of 5 km/h. If AB = 12 km and BC = 5 km, then its average speed for its journey from A to C and resultant average velocity direct from A to C are respectively.

A. $\frac{17}{4}$ k m/h and $\frac{13}{4}$ km/h
B. $\frac{13}{4}$ k m/h and $\frac{17}{4}$ km/h
C. $\frac{17}{9}$ km/h and $\frac{13}{9}$ km/h
D. $\frac{13}{9}$ km/h and $\frac{17}{9}$ km/h

49. The set of all values of a for which the function $f(x) = \left(\frac{\sqrt{a+y}}{1-a} - 1\right)x^5 - 3x + \log 5$ decrease for all real x is
A. $(-a, a)$
B. $(1, a)$
C. $\left(-3, \frac{5-\sqrt{27}}{2}\right), \cup(2, a)$
D. $\left(-4, \frac{3-\sqrt{21}}{2}\right) \cup(1, a)$

50. For a unbiased die, the probabilities for the different faces to form up are

Face	1	2	3	4	5	6
P	0.1	0.32	0.21	0.15	0.05	0.17

This die is tossed and you are told that either face 1or face 2 has turned up, then the probability that it is face1is
A. 16/21 B. 1/10
C. 5/16 D. 5/21

51. Find the optimum integer solution to the following L.P.P.:
Maximise $Z = x_1 + 4x_2$ subject to the constraints:
$2x_1 + 4x_2 \leq 7$, $5x_1 + 3x_2 \leq 15$; $x_1, x_2 \geq 0$ and are integers.
A. –1, 4 Max. $Z = 15$
B. 2, 3 Max. $Z = 14$
C. 1, 1, max. $Z = 5$
D. 0, –3, Max. $Z = -12$

52. Statement P : All cyclic groups are abelian
Statement Q : The order of cyclic group is same as the order of generator
A. P and Q are false B. P is true, Q is false
C. Q is true, P is false D. P and Q are true

53. Statement P : f is continuous
Statement Q : f is differentiable
A. If P is true, then Q is true
B. If P is false, then Q is false
C. If Q is true, then P is true
D. If Q is true, then P is false

54. If $(b_n)_{n=1}^{\infty}$ is an increasing bounded sequence then for the sequence $(b_n)_{n=1}^{\infty}$ which of the following statement is false
A. $(b_n)_{n=1}^{\infty}$ is a convergent sequence
B. $(b_n)_{n=1}^{\infty}$ is a divergent sequence
C. $(b_n)_{n=1}^{\infty}$ is a monotone sequence
D. $(b_n)_{n=1}^{\infty}$ is a Cauchy sequence

55. The drawback to use the transportation problem programming in solving an assignment problem is
A. The assignment problem can't be formulated as transportation problem
B. The assigment problem is an unbalanced transportation problem
C. Degeneracy results from every improvement in the total cost
D. None of these

56. Match the power series with the respective radius of convergence

(a) $\sum_{n=0}^{\infty}(3+4i)^n z^n$ 1. 0

(b) $\sum_{n=1}^{\infty}(-1)^n n^{-1}(z-2i)^n$ 2. 1

(c) $\sum_{n=1}^{\infty}\frac{1}{n^p}z^n$ 3. $\frac{1}{5}$

(d) $\sum_{n=1}^{\infty}(\log n)^n z^n$ 4. 1

	(a)	(b)	(c)	(d)
A.	1	2	3	4
B.	3	2	4	1
C.	3	2	1	4
D.	1	4	3	2

57. Under the steriographic projection of points on the unit sphere $x^2 + y^2 + z^2 = 1$ in R^2 to the extended plane $z = x + iy$, the plane $z = x + iy$ corresponds to

A. $\left(\frac{x^2}{x^2+y^2+1}, \frac{y^2}{x^2+y^2+1}, \frac{x^2+y^2-1}{x^2+y^2+1}\right)$

B. $\left(\frac{x}{x^2+y^2+1}, \frac{y}{x^2+y^2+1}, \frac{x+y+1}{x^2+y^2+1}\right)$

C. $\left(\frac{2x}{x^2+y^2+1}, \frac{2y}{x^2+y^2+1}, \frac{2x+2y+1}{x^2+y^2+1}\right)$

D. $\left(\frac{2x}{x^2+y^2+1}, \frac{2y}{x^2+y^2+1}, \frac{x^2+y^2-1}{x^2+y^2+1}\right)$

58. If $\bar{x}_B$ and x_B are two basic feasible solution to linear programming problem max, $z = \bar{c}\,\bar{x}$ subject to $\bar{A}\,\bar{x} = \bar{b}$, $\bar{x} \geq 0$, and $\bar{c}_B$ and c_B are respected cost associated vector to $\bar{x}_B$ and x_B. Then x_B is improved basic feasible solution, then $\bar{x}_B$ if

A. $x_B\ c_B \leq \bar{c}_B \bar{x}_B$ B. $c_B\ x_B \geq \bar{c}_B \bar{x}_B$

C. $\bar{c}_B\ \bar{x}_B < c_B\ x_B$ D. $\bar{c}_B\ \bar{x}_B > c_B\ x_B$

59. If polynomial is said to be integer monic if
A. Its coefficients are integers and highest coefficient is 1.
B. Its coefficients are real numbers.
C. Its coefficients are real numbers and highest coefficient is 0.
D. Its coefficients are integers and highest coefficient is 2.

60. If in using VAM or any other method to obtain a starting solution the allocation made in a cell is not maximum possible, then the resulting solution is
A. A basic feasible solution
B. A basic solution but not basic feasible solution
C. Not a basic feasible solution
D. None of these

ANSWERS

1	2	3	4	5	6	7	8	9	10
C	D	B	D	A	D	A	B	A	C
11	**12**	**13**	**14**	**15**	**16**	**17**	**18**	**19**	**20**
D	C	D	D	C	B	A	C	A	A
21	**22**	**23**	**24**	**25**	**26**	**27**	**28**	**29**	**30**
D	A	C	B	A	A	A	C	A	B
31	**32**	**33**	**34**	**35**	**36**	**37**	**38**	**39**	**40**
B	B	A	A	B	A	A	B	C	C
41	**42**	**43**	**44**	**45**	**46**	**47**	**48**	**49**	**50**
A	A	B	C	A	A	C	A	D	D
51	**52**	**53**	**54**	**55**	**56**	**57**	**58**	**59**	**60**
C	D	C	B	C	B	D	C	A	C

SOME SELECTED EXPLANATORY ANSWERS

17. Given maximize $3x_1 + 5x_2$

Subject to

$2x_1 - 3x_2 = 8$

$4x_1 + x_2 \geq 3$

$x_2 \leq 1$

Writing this in standard form leaving the equation in the constraints as it is, the primal is

maximize $-3x_1 - 5x_2$

Subject to

$2x_1 - 3x_2 = 8$

$4x_1 - x_2 \leq -3$

$x_2 \leq 1$

$x_1 \geq 0$

$x_2 \geq 0$

Now the dual is,

Minimize $8\mu_1 - 3\mu_2 + \mu_3$

Subject to

$2\mu_1 - 4\mu_2 \geq -3$

$3\mu_1 - \mu_2 + \mu_3 \geq -5$

$\mu_2 \geq 0$, $\mu_3 \geq 0$

and μ_1 is restricted in sign

18. $$\begin{bmatrix} 3 & 7 & 8 \\ 2 & 0 & 9 \\ -4 & 1 & -26 \end{bmatrix}\begin{bmatrix} x \\ y \\ z \end{bmatrix} = \begin{bmatrix} -13 \\ -5 \\ 2 \end{bmatrix}$$

By Cramer's rule

$$\frac{x}{\begin{vmatrix} -13 & -5 & 2 \\ 2 & 0 & 9 \\ -4 & 1 & -26 \end{vmatrix}} = \frac{y}{\begin{vmatrix} 3 & 7 & 8 \\ -13 & -5 & 2 \\ -4 & 1 & -26 \end{vmatrix}}$$

$$= \frac{z}{\begin{vmatrix} 3 & 7 & 8 \\ 2 & 0 & 9 \\ -13 & -5 & 2 \end{vmatrix}} = \frac{1}{\begin{vmatrix} 3 & 7 & 8 \\ 2 & 0 & 9 \\ -4 & 1 & -26 \end{vmatrix}}$$

$x = -7$, $y = 0$, $z = 1$

29. Equation is $\sqrt{(1-x^2)}dy + \sqrt{(1-y^2)}dx = 0$

Seperating the variables, we get

$\frac{dy}{c} + dx = 0 \Rightarrow \sin^{-1} y + \sin^{-1} x, \sqrt{(1-y^2)}\sqrt{(1-x^2)}$

$\sin^{-1} y + \sin^{-1} x = \pi/3$ (only a special case of C)

from $\sin^{-1} y + \sin^{-1} x = C$

$\cos\left[\sin^{-1} y + \sin^{-1} x\right] = \cos C$

$x^2 + 2xy \cos C + y^2 = \sin 2C$

52. If Q is true then P is true since every differential function is continuous.

53. $\{b_n\}_{n=1}^{\infty}$ is *a* increasing and bounded then $\{b_n\}_{n=1}^{\infty}$ is convergent sequence.